GO! with Microsoft® Windows 7 Comprehensive

Shelley Gaskin and Robert Ferrett

Prentice Hall
Boston Columbus Indianapolis New York San Francisco Upper Saddle River
Amsterdam Cape Town Dubai London Madrid Milan Munich Paris Montreal Toronto
Delhi Mexico City Sao Paulo Sydney Hong Kong Seoul Singapore Taipei Tokyo

Editor in Chief: Michael Payne
Executive Editor: Jenifer Niles
Editorial Project Manager: Laura Burgess
Product Development Manager: Eileen Bien Calabro
Development Editor: Ginny Munroe
Editorial Assistant: Carly Prakapas
Director of Marketing: Kate Valentine
Marketing Manager: Tori Olson Alves
Marketing Coordinator: Susan Osterlitz
Marketing Assistant: Darshika Vyas
Senior Managing Editor: Cynthia Zonneveld
Associate Managing Editor: Camille Trentacoste
Senior Production Project Manager: Rhonda Aversa
Senior Operations Specialist: Nick Sklitsis
Operations Specialist: Natacha Moore
Senior Art Director: Jonathan Boylan
Cover Photo: © Ben Durrant
Text and Cover Designer: Blair Brown
Director of Digital Development: Zara Wanlass
Editor, Digital Learning & Assessment: Paul Gentile
Media Development Manager: Cathi Profitko
Media Project Manager, Editorial: Alana Coles
Media Project Manager, Production: John Cassar
Full-Service Project Management: PreMediaGlobal
Composition: PreMediaGlobal
Printer/Binder: Quad/Graphics Leominster
Cover Printer: Lehigh-Phoenix Color/Hagerstown
Text Font: Bookman Light

Credits and acknowledgments borrowed from other sources and reproduced, with permission, in this textbook appear on appropriate page within text. Credits and acknowledgments borrowed from other sources and reproduced, with permission, in this textbook appear on appropriate page within text. Photos and video clips appearing in Chapter 6 supplied by Robert Ferrett and used with permission.

Library of Congress Cataloging-in-Publication Data

Gaskin, Shelley.
Go! with Microsoft Windows 7 : comprehensive / Shelley Gaskin and Robert Ferrett.
p. cm.
Includes index.
ISBN 978-0-13-237575-7 (alk. paper)
1. Microsoft Windows (Computer file) 2. Operating systems (Computers) I. Ferrett, Robert. II. Title.
QA76.76.O63G3865 2012
005.4'46—dc22

2011002778

10 9 8 7 6 5 4 3 2 1

Prentice Hall
is an imprint of

PEARSON

www.pearsonhighered.com

ISBN 10: 0-13-237575-3
ISBN 13: 978-0-13-237575-7

Brief Contents

Contents

GO! System Contributors

We thank the following people for their hard work and support in making the *GO!* System all that it is!

Instructor Resource Authors

Adickes, Erich	Parkland College
Baray, Carrie	Ivy Tech Community College
Behrens, Sharon	Mid-State Technical College
Bornstein, Abigail	City College of San Francisco
Bowman, Valeria	National College
Callahan, Michael	Lone Star College
Clausen, Jane	Western Iowa Tech Community College
Cleary, Kevin	University at Buffalo
Colucci, William	Montclair State University
Coyle, Diane	Montgomery County Community College
Crossley, Connie	Cincinnati State Technical and Community College
Damanti, Lori	
Edington, Barbara	St. Francis College
Emrich, Stefanie	Metropolitan Community College of Omaha, Nebraska
Faix, Dennis	Harrisburg Area Community College
Federico, Hilda	Jacksonville University
Hadden, Karen	Western Iowa Tech Community College
Hammerle, Patricia	Indiana University/Purdue University at Indianapolis
Hearn, Barbara	Community College of Philadelphia
Hicks, Janette	Binghamton University/State University of New York
Hines, James	Tidewater Community College
Hollingsworth, Mary Carole	Georgia Perimeter College
Holly, Terri	Indian River State College
Holland, Susan	Southeast Community College Nebraska
Jacob, Sherry	Kentucky Community and Technical College
Landenberger, Toni	Southeast Community College Nebraska
Leinbach, Andrea	Harrisburg Area Community College
Lutz, Mary	Southwestern Illinois College
McMahon, Richard	University of Houston—Downtown
Miller, Abigail	Gateway Community and Technical College
Miller, Sandra	Wenatchee Valley College
Monson, Shari	Black Hawk College
Neal, Ruth	Navarro College
Niebur, Katherine	Dakota County Technical College
Nowakowski, Anthony	Buffalo State
Pierce, Tonya	Ivy Tech Community College
Piziak, Dee	University of Wisconsin-Milwaukee
Pogue, Linda	NorthWest Arkansas Community College
Reynolds, Mark	Lone Star College
Roselli, Diane	Harrisburg Area Community College
Shing, Chen-Chi	Radford University
St. John, Steve	Tulsa Community College
Sterr, Jody	Blackhawk Technical College
Thompson, Joyce	Lehigh Carbon Community College
Tucker, William	Austin Community College
Volker, Bonita	Tidewater Community College
Walters, Kari	Louisiana State University

Technical Editors

Matthew Bisi
Mary Corcoran
Lori Damanti
Barbara Edington
Sarah Evans
Adam Layne
Joyce Nielsen
Janet Pickard
Sean Portnoy
Jan Snyder
Sam Stamport
Mara Zebest

Student Reviewers

Albinda, Sarah Evangeline	Phoenix College
Allen, John	Asheville-Buncombe Tech Community College
Alexander, Steven	St. Johns River Community College
Alexander, Melissa	Tulsa Community College
Bolz, Stephanie	Northern Michigan University
Berner, Ashley	Central Washington University
Boomer, Michelle	Northern Michigan University
Busse, Brennan	Northern Michigan University
Butkey, Maura	Central Washington University
Cates, Concita	Phoenix College
Charles, Marvin	Harrisburg Area Community College
Christensen, Kaylie	Northern Michigan University
Clark, Glen D. III	Harrisburg Area Community College
Cobble, Jan N.	Greenville Technical College
Connally, Brianna	Central Washington University
Davis, Brandon	Northern Michigan University
Davis, Christen	Central Washington University
De Jesus Garcia, Maria	Phoenix College
Den Boer, Lance	Central Washington University
Dix, Jessica	Central Washington University
Moeller, Jeffrey	Northern Michigan University
Downs, Elizabeth	Central Washington University
Elser, Julie	Harrisburg Area Community College
Erickson, Mike	Ball State University
Frye, Alicia	Phoenix College
Gadomski, Amanda	Northern Michigan University
Gassert, Jennifer	Harrisburg Area Community College
Gross, Mary Jo	Kirkwood Community College
Gyselinck, Craig	Central Washington University
Harrison, Margo	Central Washington University
Hatt, Patrick	Harrisburg Area Community College
Heacox, Kate	Central Washington University
Hedgman, Shaina	Tidewater College
Hill, Cheretta	Northwestern State University
Hochstedler, Bethany	Harrisburg Area Community College Lancaster
Homer, Jean	Greenville Technical College
Innis, Tim	Tulsa Community College
Jarboe, Aaron	Central Washington University
Key, Penny	Greenville Technical College
Klein, Colleen	Northern Michigan University
Lloyd, Kasey	Ivy Tech Bloomington
Moeller, Jeffrey	Northern Michigan University

Mullen, Sharita	Tidewater Community College
Nelson, Cody	Texas Tech University
Nicholson, Regina	Athens Tech College
Niehaus, Kristina	Northern Michigan University
Nisa, Zaibun	Santa Rosa Community College
Nunez, Nohelia	Santa Rosa Community College
Oak, Samantha	Central Washington University
Oberly, Sara	Harrisburg Area Community College Lancaster
Oertii, Monica	Central Washington University
Palenshus, Juliet	Central Washington University
Pohl, Amanda	Northern Michigan University
Presnell, Randy	Central Washington University
Reed, Kailee	Texas Tech University
Ritner, April	Northern Michigan University
Roberts, Corey	Tulsa Community College
Rodgers, Spencer	Texas Tech University
Rodriguez, Flavia	Northwestern State University
Rogers, A.	Tidewater Community College
Rossi, Jessica Ann	Central Washington University
Rothbauer, Taylor	Trident Technical College
Rozelle, Lauren	Texas Tech University
Schmadeke, Kimberly	Kirkwood Community College
Shafapay, Natasha	Central Washington University
Shanahan, Megan	Northern Michigan University
Sullivan, Alexandra Nicole	Greenville Technical College
Teska, Erika	Hawaii Pacific University
Torrenti, Natalie	Harrisburg Area Community College
Traub, Amy	Northern Michigan University
Underwood, Katie	Central Washington University
Walters, Kim	Central Washington University
Warren, Jennifer L.	Greenville Technical College
Wilson, Kelsie	Central Washington University
Wilson, Amanda	Green River Community College
Wylie, Jimmy	Texas Tech University

Series Reviewers

Abraham, Reni	Houston Community College
Addison, Paul	Ivy Tech Community College
Agatston, Ann	Agatston Consulting Technical College
Akuna, Valeria, Ph.D.	Estrella Mountain Community College
Alexander, Melody	Ball Sate University
Alejandro, Manuel	Southwest Texas Junior College
Alger, David	Tidewater Community College Chesapeake Campus
Allen, Jackie	Rowan-Cabarrus Community College
Ali, Farha	Lander University
Amici, Penny	Harrisburg Area Community College
Anderson, Patty A.	Lake City Community College
Andrews, Wilma	Virginia Commonwealth College, Nebraska University
Anik, Mazhar	Tiffin University
Armstrong, Gary	Shippensburg University
Arnold, Linda L.	Harrisburg Area Community College
Ashby, Tom	Oklahoma City Community College
Atkins, Bonnie	Delaware Technical Community College
Aukland, Cherie	Thomas Nelson Community College
Bachand, LaDonna	Santa Rosa Community College
Bagui, Sikha	University of West Florida
Beecroft, Anita	Kwantlen University College
Bell, Paula	Lock Haven College
Belton, Linda	Springfield Tech. Community College
Bennett, Judith	Sam Houston State University
Bhatia, Sai	Riverside Community College
Bishop, Frances	DeVry Institute—Alpharetta (ATL)
Blaszkiewicz, Holly	Ivy Tech Community College/Region 1
Boito, Nancy	HACC Central Pennsylvania's Community College
Borger-Boglin, Grietje L.	San Antonio College/Northeast Lakeview College
Branigan, Dave	DeVry University
Bray, Patricia	Allegany College of Maryland
Britt, Brenda K.	Fayetteville Technical Community College
Brotherton, Cathy	Riverside Community College
Brown, Judy	Western Illinois University
Buehler, Lesley	Ohlone College
Buell, C	Central Oregon Community College
Burns, Christine	Central New Mexico Community College
Byars, Pat	Brookhaven College
Byrd, Julie	Ivy Tech Community College
Byrd, Lynn	Delta State University, Cleveland, Mississippi
Cacace, Richard N.	Pensacola Junior College
Cadenhead, Charles	Brookhaven College
Calhoun, Ric	Gordon College
Cameron, Eric	Passaic Community College
Canine, Jill	Ivy Tech Community College of Indiana
Cannamore, Madie	Kennedy King
Cannon, Kim	Greenville Technical College
Carreon, Cleda	Indiana University—Purdue University, Indianapolis
Carriker, Sandra	North Shore Community College
Casey, Patricia	Trident Technical College
Cates, Wally	Central New Mexico Community College
Chaffin, Catherine	Shawnee State University
Chauvin, Marg	Palm Beach Community College, Boca Raton
Challa, Chandrashekar	Virginia State University
Chamlou, Afsaneh	NOVA Alexandria
Chapman, Pam	Wabaunsee Community College
Christensen, Dan	Iowa Western Community College
Clay, Betty	Southeastern Oklahoma State University
Collins, Linda D.	Mesa Community College
Cone, Bill	Northern Arizona University
Conroy-Link, Janet	Holy Family College
Conway, Ronald	Bowling Green State University
Cornforth, Carol G.	WVNCC
Cosgrove, Janet	Northwestern CT Community
Courtney, Kevin	Hillsborough Community College
Coverdale, John	Riverside Community College
Cox, Rollie	Madison Area Technical College
Crawford, Hiram	Olive Harvey College
Crawford, Sonia	Central New Mexico Community College

Crawford, Thomasina	Miami-Dade College, Kendall Campus
Credico, Grace	Lethbridge Community College
Crenshaw, Richard	Miami Dade Community College, North
Crespo, Beverly	Mt. San Antonio College
Crooks, Steven	Texas Tech University
Crossley, Connie	Cincinnati State Technical Community College
Curik, Mary	Central New Mexico Community College
De Arazoza, Ralph	Miami Dade Community College
Danno, John	DeVry University/Keller Graduate School
Davis, Phillip	Del Mar College
Davis, Richard	Trinity Valley Community College
Davis, Sandra	Baker College of Allen Park
Dees, Stephanie D.	Wharton County Junior College
DeHerrera, Laurie	Pikes Peak Community College
Delk, Dr. K. Kay	Seminole Community College
Denton, Bree	Texas Tech University
Dix, Jeanette	Ivy Tech Community College
Dooly, Veronica P.	Asheville-Buncombe Technical Community College
Doroshow, Mike	Eastfield College
Douglas, Gretchen	SUNYCortland
Dove, Carol	Community College of Allegheny
Dozier, Susan	Tidewater Community College, Virginia Beach Campus
Driskel, Loretta	Niagara Community College
Duckwiler, Carol	Wabaunsee Community College
Duhon, David	Baker College
Duncan, Mimi	University of Missouri-St. Louis
Duthie, Judy	Green River Community College
Duvall, Annette	
Ecklund, Paula	Duke University
Eilers, Albert	Cincinnati State Technical and Community College
Eng, Bernice	Brookdale Community College
Epperson, Arlin	Columbia College
Evans, Billie	Vance-Granville Community College
Evans, Jean	Brevard Community College
Feuerbach, Lisa	Ivy Tech East Chicago
Finley, Jean	ABTCC
Fisher, Fred	Florida State University
Foster, Nancy	Baker College
Foster-Shriver, Penny L.	Anne Arundel Community College
Foszcz, Russ	McHenry County College
Fry, Susan	Boise State University
Fustos, Janos	Metro State
Gallup, Jeanette	Blinn College
Gelb, Janet	Grossmont College
Gentry, Barb	Parkland College
Gerace, Karin	St. Angela Merici School
Gerace, Tom	Tulane University
Ghajar, Homa	Oklahoma State University
Gifford, Steve	Northwest Iowa Community College
Glazer, Ellen	Broward Community College
Gordon, Robert	Hofstra University
Gramlich, Steven	Pasco-Hernando Community College
Graviett, Nancy M.	St. Charles Community College, St. Peters, Missouri
Greene, Rich	Community College of Allegheny County
Gregoryk, Kerry	Virginia Commonwealth State
Griggs, Debra	Bellevue Community College
Grimm, Carol	Palm Beach Community College
Guthrie, Rose	Fox Valley Technical College
Hahn, Norm	Thomas Nelson Community College
Haley-Hunter, Deb	Bluefield State College
Hall, Linnea	Northwest Mississippi Community College
Hammerschlag, Dr. Bill	Brookhaven College
Hansen, Michelle	Davenport University
Hayden, Nancy	Indiana University—Purdue University, Indianapolis
Hayes, Theresa	Broward Community College
Headrick, Betsy	Chattanooga State
Helfand, Terri	Chaffey College
Helms, Liz	Columbus State Community College
Hernandez, Leticia	TCI College of Technology
Hibbert, Marilyn	Salt Lake Community College
Hinds, Cheryl	Norfolk State University
Hines, James	Tidewater Community College
Hoffman, Joan	Milwaukee Area Technical College
Hogan, Pat	Cape Fear Community College
Holland, Susan	Southeast Community College
Holliday, Mardi	Community College of Philadelphia
Hollingsworth, Mary Carole	Georgia Perimeter College
Hopson, Bonnie	Athens Technical College
Horvath, Carrie	Albertus Magnus College
Horwitz, Steve	Community College of Philadelphia
Hotta, Barbara	Leeward Community College
Howard, Bunny	St. Johns River Community
Howard, Chris	DeVry University
Huckabay, Jamie	Austin Community College
Hudgins, Susan	East Central University
Hulett, Michelle J.	Missouri State University
Humphrey, John	Asheville Buncombe Technical Community College
Hunt, Darla A.	Morehead State University, Morehead, Kentucky
Hunt, Laura	Tulsa Community College
Ivey, Joan M.	Lanier Technical College
Jacob, Sherry	Jefferson Community College
Jacobs, Duane	Salt Lake Community College
Jauken, Barb	Southeastern Community
Jerry, Gina	Santa Monica College
Johnson, Deborah S.	Edison State College
Johnson, Kathy	Wright College
Johnson, Mary	Kingwood College
Johnson, Mary	Mt. San Antonio College
Jones, Stacey	Benedict College
Jones, Warren	University of Alabama, Birmingham
Jordan, Cheryl	San Juan College
Kapoor, Bhushan	California State University, Fullerton
Kasai, Susumu	Salt Lake Community College
Kates, Hazel	Miami Dade Community College, Kendall
Keen, Debby	University of Kentucky

Keeter, Sandy	Seminole Community College
Kern-Blystone, Dorothy Jean	Bowling Green State
Kerwin, Annette	College of DuPage
Keskin, Ilknur	The University of South Dakota
Kinney, Mark B.	Baker College
Kirk, Colleen	Mercy College
Kisling, Eric	East Carolina University
Kleckner, Michelle	Elon University
Kliston, Linda	Broward Community College, North Campus
Knuth, Toni	Baker College of Auburn Hills
Kochis, Dennis	Suffolk County Community College
Kominek, Kurt	Northeast State Technical Community College
Kramer, Ed	Northern Virginia Community College
Kretz, Daniel	Fox Valley Technical College
Laird, Jeff	Northeast State Community College
Lamoureaux, Jackie	Central New Mexico Community College
Lange, David	Grand Valley State
LaPointe, Deb	
Larsen, Jacqueline Anne	A-B Tech
Larson, Donna	Louisville Technical Institute
Laspina, Kathy	Vance-Granville Community College
Le Grand, Dr. Kate	Broward Community College
Lenhart, Sheryl	Terra Community College
Leonard, Yvonne	Coastal Carolina Community College
Letavec, Chris	University of Cincinnati
Lewis, Daphne L, Ed.D.	Wayland Baptist University
Lewis, Julie	Baker College-Allen Park
Liefert, Jane	Everett Community College
Lindaman, Linda	Black Hawk Community College
Lindberg, Martha	Minnesota State University
Lightner, Renee	Broward Community College
Lindberg, Martha	Minnesota State University
Linge, Richard	Arizona Western College
Logan, Mary G.	Delgado Community College
Loizeaux, Barbara	Westchester Community College
Lombardi, John	South University
Lopez, Don	Clovis-State Center Community College District
Lopez, Lisa	Spartanburg Community College
Lord, Alexandria	Asheville Buncombe Tech
Lovering, LeAnne	Augusta Technical College
Lowe, Rita	Harold Washington College
Low, Willy Hui	Joliet Junior College
Lucas, Vickie	Broward Community College
Luna, Debbie	El Paso Community College
Luoma, Jean	Davenport University
Luse, Steven P.	Horry Georgetown Technical College
Lynam, Linda	Central Missouri State University
Lyon, Lynne	Durham College
Lyon, Pat Rajski	Tomball College
Macarty, Matthew	University of New Hampshire
MacKinnon, Ruth	Georgia Southern University
Macon, Lisa	Valencia Community College, West Campus
Machuca, Wayne	College of the Sequoias
Mack, Sherri	Butler County Community College
Madison, Dana	Clarion University
Maguire, Trish	Eastern New Mexico University
Malkan, Rajiv	Montgomery College
Manning, David	Northern Kentucky University
Marcus, Jacquie	Niagara Community College
Marghitu, Daniela	Auburn University
Marks, Suzanne	Bellevue Community College
Marquez, Juanita	El Centro College
Marquez, Juan	Mesa Community College
Martin, Carol	Harrisburg Area Community College
Martin, Paul C.	Harrisburg Area Community College
Martyn, Margie	Baldwin-Wallace College
Marucco, Toni	Lincoln Land Community College
Mason, Lynn	Lubbock Christian University
Matutis, Audrone	Houston Community College
Matkin, Marie	University of Lethbridge
Maurel, Trina	Odessa College
May, Karen	Blinn College
McCain, Evelynn	Boise State University
McCannon, Melinda	Gordon College
McCarthy, Marguerite	Northwestern Business College
McCaskill, Matt L.	Brevard Community College
McClellan, Carolyn	Tidewater Community College
McClure, Darlean	College of Sequoias
McCrory, Sue A.	Missouri State University
McCue, Stacy	Harrisburg Area Community College
McEntire-Orbach, Teresa	Middlesex County College
McKinley, Lee	Georgia Perimeter College
McLeod, Todd	Fresno City College
McManus, Illyana	Grossmont College
McPherson, Dori	Schoolcraft College
Meck, Kari	HACC
Meiklejohn, Nancy	Pikes Peak Community College
Menking, Rick	Hardin-Simmons University
Meredith, Mary	University of Louisiana at Lafayette
Mermelstein, Lisa	Baruch College
Metos, Linda	Salt Lake Community College
Meurer, Daniel	University of Cincinnati
Meyer, Colleen	Cincinnati State Technical and Community College
Meyer, Marian	Central New Mexico Community College
Miller, Cindy	Ivy Tech Community College, Lafayette, Indiana
Mills, Robert E.	Tidewater Community College, Portsmouth Campus
Mitchell, Susan	Davenport University
Mohle, Dennis	Fresno Community College
Molki, Saeed	South Texas College
Monk, Ellen	University of Delaware
Moore, Rodney	Holland College
Morris, Mike	Southeastern Oklahoma State University
Morris, Nancy	Hudson Valley Community College
Moseler, Dan	Harrisburg Area Community College
Nabors, Brent	Reedley College, Clovis Center
Nadas, Erika	Wright College
Nadelman, Cindi	New England College
Nademlynsky, Lisa	Johnson & Wales University
Nagengast, Joseph	Florida Career College
Nason, Scott	Rowan Cabarrus Community College

Ncube, Cathy	University of West Florida
Newsome, Eloise	Northern Virginia Community College Woodbridge
Nicholls, Doreen	Mohawk Valley Community College
Nicholson, John R.	Johnson County Community College
Nielson, Phil	Salt Lake Community College
Nunan, Karen L.	Northeast State Technical Community College
O'Neal, Lois Ann	Rogers State University
Odegard, Teri	Edmonds Community College
Ogle, Gregory	North Community College
Orr, Dr. Claudia	Northern Michigan University South
Orsburn, Glen	Fox Valley Technical College
Otieno, Derek	DeVry University
Otton, Diana Hill	Chesapeake College
Oxendale, Lucia	West Virginia Institute of Technology
Paiano, Frank	Southwestern College
Pannell, Dr. Elizabeth	Collin College
Patrick, Tanya	Clackamas Community College
Paul, Anindya	Daytona State College
Peairs, Deb	Clark State Community College
Perez, Kimberly	Tidewater Community College
Porter, Joyce	Weber State University
Prince, Lisa	Missouri State University-Springfield Campus
Proietti, Kathleen	Northern Essex Community College
Puopolo, Mike	Bunker Hill Community College
Pusins, Delores	HCCC
Putnam, Darlene	Thomas Nelson Community College
Raghuraman, Ram	Joliet Junior College
Rani, Chigurupati	BMCC/CUNY
Reasoner, Ted Allen	Indiana University—Purdue
Reeves, Karen	High Point University
Remillard, Debbie	New Hampshire Technical Institute
Rhue, Shelly	DeVry University
Richards, Karen	Maplewoods Community College
Richardson, Mary	Albany Technical College
Rodgers, Gwen	Southern Nazarene University
Rodie, Karla	Pikes Peak Community College
Roselli, Diane Maie	Harrisburg Area Community College
Ross, Dianne	University of Louisiana in Lafayette
Rousseau, Mary	Broward Community College, South
Rovetto, Ann	Horry-Georgetown Technical College
Rusin, Iwona	Baker College
Sahabi, Ahmad	Baker College of Clinton Township
Samson, Dolly	Hawaii Pacific University
Sams, Todd	University of Cincinnati
Sandoval, Everett	Reedley College
Santiago, Diana	Central New Mexico Community College
Sardone, Nancy	Seton Hall University
Scafide, Jean	Mississippi Gulf Coast Community College
Scheeren, Judy	Westmoreland County Community College
Scheiwe, Adolph	Joliet Junior College
Schneider, Sol	Sam Houston State University
Schweitzer, John	Central New Mexico Community College
Scroggins, Michael	Southwest Missouri State University
Sedlacek, Brenda	Tidewater Community College
Sell, Kelly	Anne Arundel Community College
Sever, Suzanne	Northwest Arkansas Community College
Sewell, John	Florida Career College
Sheridan, Rick	California State University-Chico
Silvers, Pamela	Asheville Buncombe Tech
Sindt, Robert G.	Johnson County Community College
Singer, Noah	Tulsa Community College
Singer, Steven A.	University of Hawai'i, Kapi'olani Community College
Sinha, Atin	Albany State University
Skolnick, Martin	Florida Atlantic University
Smith, Kristi	Allegany College of Maryland
Smith, Patrick	Marshall Community and Technical College
Smith, Stella A.	Georgia Gwinnett College
Smith, T. Michael	Austin Community College
Smith, Tammy	Tompkins Cortland Community Collge
Smolenski, Bob	Delaware County Community College
Smolenski, Robert	Delaware Community College
Southwell, Donald	Delta College
Spangler, Candice	Columbus State Community College
Stark, Diane	Phoenix College
Stedham, Vicki	St. Petersburg College, Clearwater
Stefanelli, Greg	Carroll Community College
Steiner, Ester	New Mexico State University
Stenlund, Neal	Northern Virginia Community College, Alexandria
St. John, Steve	Tulsa Community College
Sterling, Janet	Houston Community College
Stoughton, Catherine	Laramie County Community College
Sullivan, Angela	Joliet Junior College
Sullivan, Denise	Westchester Community College
Sullivan, Joseph	Joliet Junior College
Swart, John	Louisiana Tech University
Szurek, Joseph	University of Pittsburgh at Greensburg
Taff, Ann	Tulsa Community College
Taggart, James	Atlantic Cape Community College
Tarver, Mary Beth	Northwestern State University
Taylor, Michael	Seattle Central Community College
Terrell, Robert L.	Carson-Newman College
Terry, Dariel	Northern Virginia Community College
Thangiah, Sam	Slippery Rock University
Thayer, Paul	Austin Community College
Thompson, Joyce	Lehigh Carbon Community College
Thompson-Sellers, Ingrid	Georgia Perimeter College
Tomasi, Erik	Baruch College
Toreson, Karen	Shoreline Community College
Townsend, Cynthia	Baker College
Trifiletti, John J.	Florida Community College at Jacksonville
Trivedi, Charulata	Quinsigamond Community College, Woodbridge
Tucker, William	Austin Community College
Turgeon, Cheryl	Asnuntuck Community College
Upshaw, Susan	Del Mar College
Unruh, Angela	Central Washington University
Vanderhoof, Dr. Glenna	Missouri State University-Springfield Campus
Vargas, Tony	El Paso Community College

Vicars, Mitzi	Hampton University
Villarreal, Kathleen	Fresno
Vitrano, Mary Ellen	Palm Beach Community College
Vlaich-Lee, Michelle	Greenville Technical College
Volker, Bonita	Tidewater Community College
Waddell, Karen	Butler Community College
Wahila, Lori (Mindy)	Tompkins Cortland Community College
Wallace, Melissa	Lanier Technical College
Walters, Gary B.	Central New Mexico Community College
Waswick, Kim	Southeast Community College, Nebraska
Wavle, Sharon M.	Tompkins Cortland Community College
Webb, Nancy	City College of San Francisco
Webb, Rebecca	Northwest Arkansas Community College
Weber, Sandy	Gateway Technical College
Weissman, Jonathan	Finger Lakes Community College
Wells, Barbara E.	Central Carolina Technical College
Wells, Lorna	Salt Lake Community College
Welsh, Jean	Lansing Community College Nebraska
White, Bruce	Quinnipiac University
Willer, Ann	Solano Community College
Williams, Mark	Lane Community College
Williams, Ronald D.	Central Piedmont Community College
Wilms, Dr. G. Jan	Union University
Wilson, Kit	Red River College
Wilson, MaryLou	Piedmont Technical College
Wilson, Roger	Fairmont State University
Wimberly, Leanne	International Academy of Design and Technology
Winters, Floyd	Manatee Community College
Worthington, Paula	Northern Virginia Community College
Wright, Darrell	Shelton State Community College
Wright, Julie	Baker College
Yauney, Annette	Herkimer County Community College
Yip, Thomas	Passaic Community College
Zavala, Ben	Webster Tech
Zaboski, Maureen	University of Scranton
Zlotow, Mary Ann	College of DuPage
Zudeck, Steve	Broward Community College, North
Zullo, Matthew D.	Wake Technical Community College

About the Authors

Shelley Gaskin, Series Editor, is a professor in the Business and Computer Technology Division at Pasadena City College in Pasadena, California. She holds a bachelor's degree in Business Administration from Robert Morris College (Pennsylvania), a master's degree in Business from Northern Illinois University, and a doctorate in Adult and Community Education from Ball State University. Before joining Pasadena City College, she spent 12 years in the computer industry where she was a systems analyst, sales representative, and Director of Customer Education with Unisys Corporation. She also worked for Ernst & Young on the development of large systems applications for their clients. She has written and developed training materials for custom systems applications in both the public and private sector, and has written and edited numerous computer application textbooks.

This book is dedicated to my students, who inspire me every day.

Robert L. Ferrett recently retired as the Director of the Center for Instructional Computing at Eastern Michigan University, where he provided computer training and support to faculty. He has authored or co-authored more than 70 books on Access, PowerPoint, Excel, Publisher, WordPerfect, Windows, Word, OpenOffice, and Computer Fundamentals. He has been designing, developing, and delivering computer workshops for more than three decades. Before writing for the *GO! Series*, Bob was a series editor for the Learn Series. He has a bachelor's degree in Psychology, a master's degree in Geography, and a master's degree in Interdisciplinary Technology from Eastern Michigan University. His doctoral studies were in Instructional Technology at Wayne State University.

I'd like to dedicate this book to my wife Mary Jane, whose constant support has been so important all these years.

Teach the Course You Want in Less Time

A Microsoft® Office textbook designed for student success!

GO!

- **Project-Based –** Students learn by creating projects that they will use in the real world.
- **Microsoft Procedural Syntax –** Steps are written to put students in the right place at the right time.
- **Teachable Moment –** Expository text is woven into the steps—at the moment students need to know it—not chunked together in a block of text that will go unread.
- **Sequential Pagination –** Students have actual page numbers instead of confusing letters and abbreviations.

Student Outcomes and Learning Objectives – Objectives are clustered around projects that result in student outcomes.

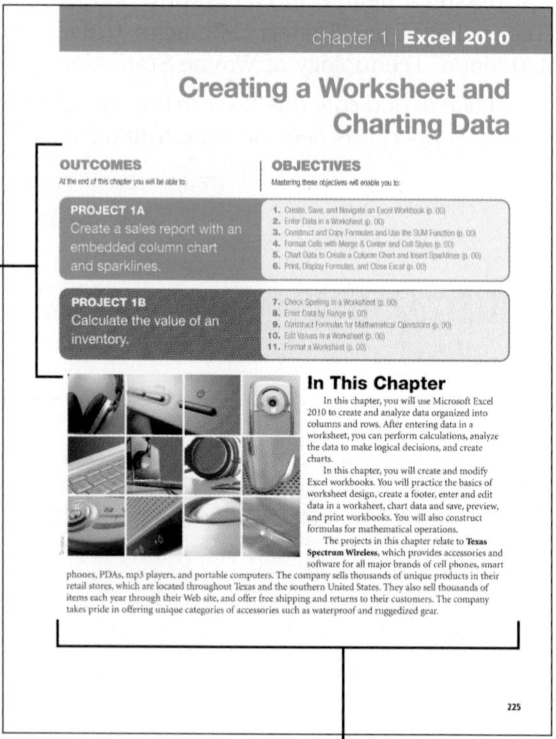

chapter 1 | **Excel 2010**

Creating a Worksheet and Charting Data

OUTCOMES
At the end of this chapter you will be able to:

OBJECTIVES
Mastering these objectives will enable you to:

PROJECT 1A
Create a sales report with an embedded column chart and sparklines.

1. Create, Save, and Navigate an Excel Workbook (p. 00)
2. Enter Data in a Worksheet (p. 00)
3. Construct and Copy Formulas and Use the SUM Function (p. 00)
4. Format Cells with Merge & Center and Cell Styles (p. 00)
5. Chart Data to Create a Column Chart and Insert Sparklines (p. 00)
6. Print, Display Formulas, and Close Excel (p. 00)

PROJECT 1B
Calculate the value of an inventory.

7. Check Spelling in a Worksheet (p. 00)
8. Enter Data by Range (p. 00)
9. Construct Formulas for Mathematical Operations (p. 00)
10. Edit Values in a Worksheet (p. 00)
11. Format a Worksheet (p. 00)

In This Chapter

In this chapter, you will use Microsoft Excel 2010 to create and analyze data organized into columns and rows. After entering data in a worksheet, you can perform calculations, analyze the data to make logical decisions, and create charts.

In this chapter, you will create and modify Excel workbooks. You will practice the basics of worksheet design, create a footer, enter and edit data in a worksheet, chart data and save, preview, and print workbooks. You will also construct formulas for mathematical operations.

The projects in this chapter relate to **Texas Spectrum Wireless**, which provides accessories and software for all major brands of cell phones, smart phones, PDAs, mp3 players, and portable computers. The company sells thousands of unique products in their retail stores, which are located throughout Texas and the southern United States. They also sell thousands of items each year through their Web site, and offer free shipping and returns to their customers. The company takes pride in offering unique categories of accessories such as waterproof and ruggedized gear.

225

Scenario – Each chapter opens with a story that sets the stage for the projects the student will create.

Project Activities – A project summary stated clearly and quickly.

Project Files – Clearly shows students which files are needed for the project and the names they will use to save their documents.

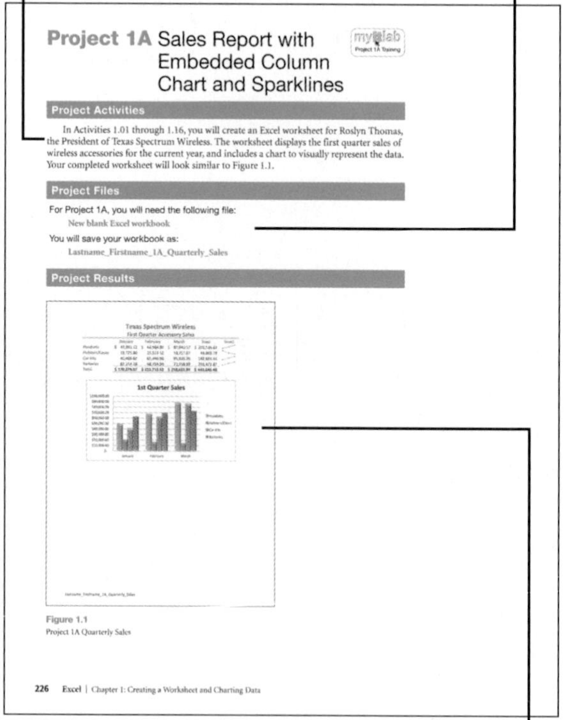

Project 1A Sales Report with Embedded Column Chart and Sparklines

myitlab Project 1A Training

Project Activities

In Activities 1.01 through 1.16, you will create an Excel worksheet for Roslyn Thomas, the President of Texas Spectrum Wireless. The worksheet displays the first quarter sales of wireless accessories for the current year, and includes a chart to visually represent the data. Your completed worksheet will look similar to Figure 1.1.

Project Files

For Project 1A, you will need the following file:
New blank Excel workbook

You will save your workbook as:
Lastname_Firstname_1A_Quarterly_Sales

Project Results

Figure 1.1
Project 1A Quarterly Sales

226 Excel | Chapter 1: Creating a Worksheet and Charting Data

Project Results – Shows students how their final outcome will appear.

Key Feature

Microsoft Procedural Syntax – Steps are written to put the student in the right place at the right time.

Color Coding – Color variations between the two projects in each chapter make it easy to identify which project students are working on.

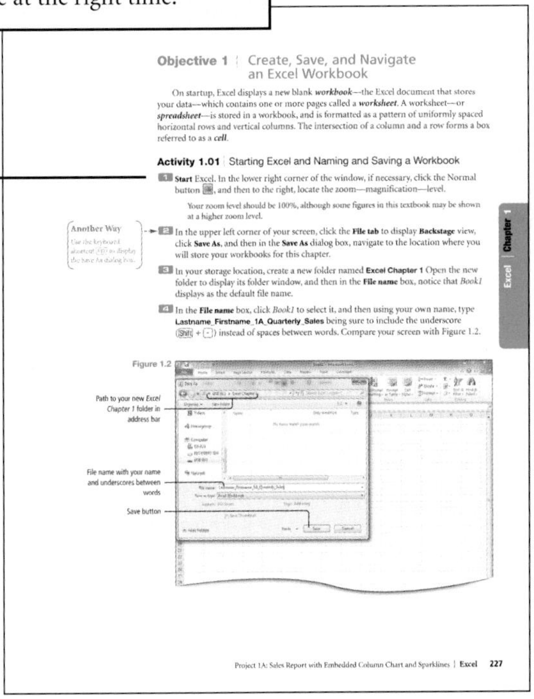

Objective 1 | Create, Save, and Navigate an Excel Workbook

On startup, Excel displays a new blank *workbook*—the Excel document that stores your data—which contains one or more pages called a *worksheet*. A worksheet—or *spreadsheet*—is stored in a workbook, and is formatted as a pattern of uniformly spaced horizontal rows and vertical columns. The intersection of a column and a row forms a box referred to as a *cell*.

Activity 1.01 | Starting Excel and Naming and Saving a Workbook

1. **Start** Excel. In the lower right corner of the window, if necessary, click the Normal button, and then to the right, locate the zoom—magnification—level.

   Your zoom level should be 100%, although some figures in this textbook may be shown at a higher zoom level.

2. In the upper left corner of your screen, click the **File tab** to display **Backstage** view, click **Save As**, and then in the **Save As** dialog box, navigate to the location where you will store your workbooks for this chapter.

3. In your storage location, create a new folder named **Excel Chapter 1** Open the new folder to display its folder window, and then in the **File name** box, notice that *Book1* displays as the default file name.

4. In the **File name** box, click *Book1* to select it, and then using your own name, type **Lastname_Firstname_1A_Quarterly_Sales** being sure to include the underscore (Shift + -) instead of spaces between words. Compare your screen with Figure 1.2.

Figure 1.2

Project 1A: Sales Report with Embedded Column Chart and Sparklines | Excel 227

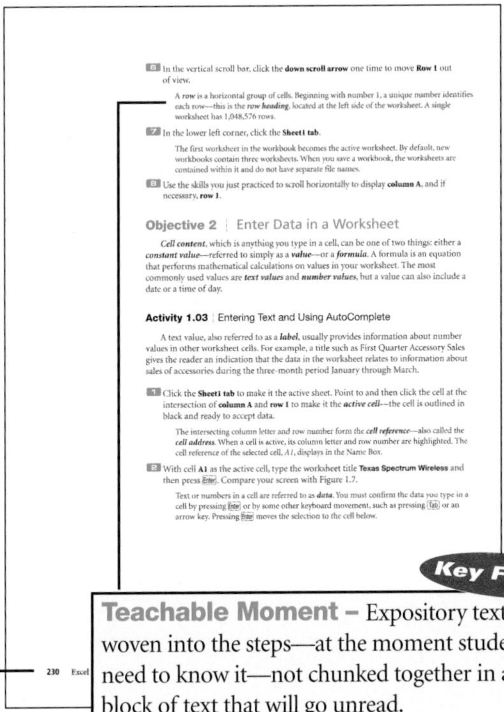

6. In the vertical scroll bar, click the **down scroll arrow** one time to move **Row 1** out of view.

   A *row* is a horizontal group of cells. Beginning with number 1, a unique number identifies each row—this is the *row heading*, located at the left side of the worksheet. A single worksheet has 1,048,576 rows.

7. In the lower left corner, click the **Sheet1 tab**.

   The first worksheet in the workbook becomes the active worksheet. By default, new workbooks contain three worksheets. When you save a workbook, the worksheets are contained within it and do not have separate file names.

8. Use the skills you just practiced to scroll horizontally to display **column A**, and if necessary, **row 1**.

Objective 2 | Enter Data in a Worksheet

Cell content, which is anything you type in a cell, can be one of two things: either a *constant value*—referred to simply as a *value*—or a *formula*. A formula is an equation that performs mathematical calculations on values in your worksheet. The most commonly used values are *text values* and *number values*, but a value can also include a date or a time of day.

Activity 1.03 | Entering Text and Using AutoComplete

A text value, also referred to as a *label*, usually provides information about number values in other worksheet cells. For example, a title such as First Quarter Accessory Sales gives the reader an indication that the data in the worksheet relates to information about sales of accessories during the three-month period January through March.

1. Click the **Sheet1 tab** to make it the active sheet. Point to and then click the cell at the intersection of **column A** and **row 1** to make it the *active cell*—the cell is outlined in black and ready to accept data.

   The intersecting column letter and row number form the *cell reference*—also called the *cell address*. When a cell is active, its column letter and row number are highlighted. The cell reference of the selected cell, *A1*, displays in the Name Box.

2. With cell **A1** as the active cell, type the worksheet title **Texas Spectrum Wireless** and then press Enter. Compare your screen with Figure 1.7.

   Text or numbers in a cell are referred to as *data*. You must confirm the data you type in a cell by pressing Enter or by some other keyboard movement, such as pressing Tab or an arrow key. Pressing Enter moves the selection to the cell below.

230 Excel

Key Feature

Sequential Pagination – Students are given actual page numbers to navigate through the textbook instead of confusing letters and abbreviations.

Key Feature

Teachable Moment – Expository text is woven into the steps—at the moment students need to know it—not chunked together in a block of text that will go unread.

End-of-Chapter

Content-Based Assessments – Assessments with defined solutions.

Objective List - Every project includes a listing of covered objectives from Projects A and B.

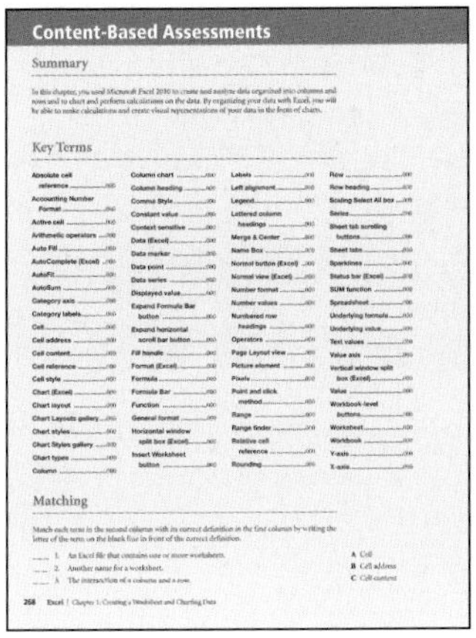

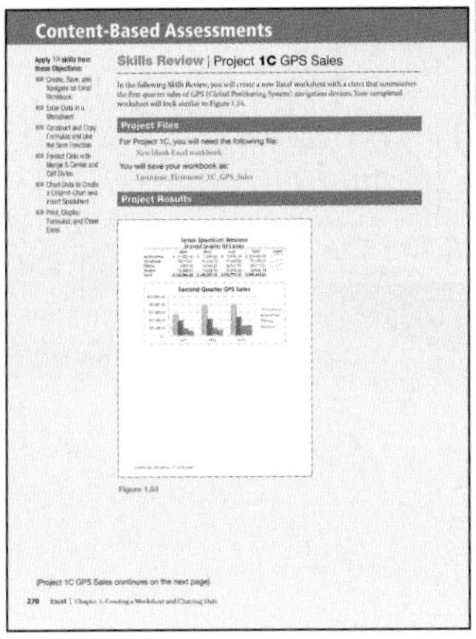

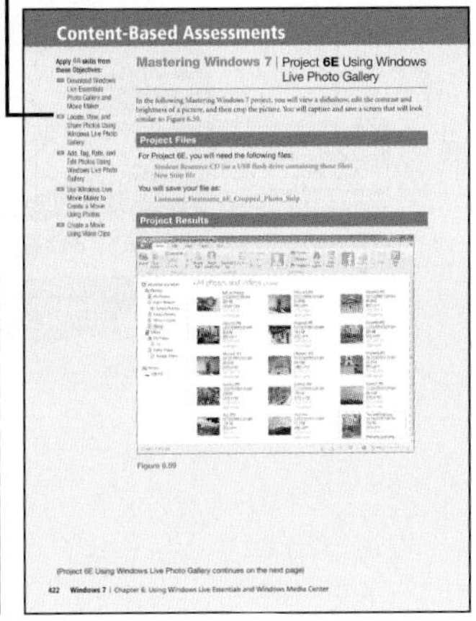

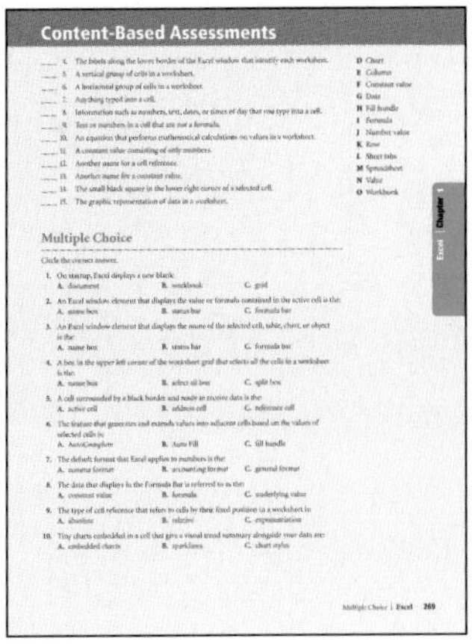

End-of-Chapter

Outcomes-Based Assessments – Assessments with open-ended solutions.

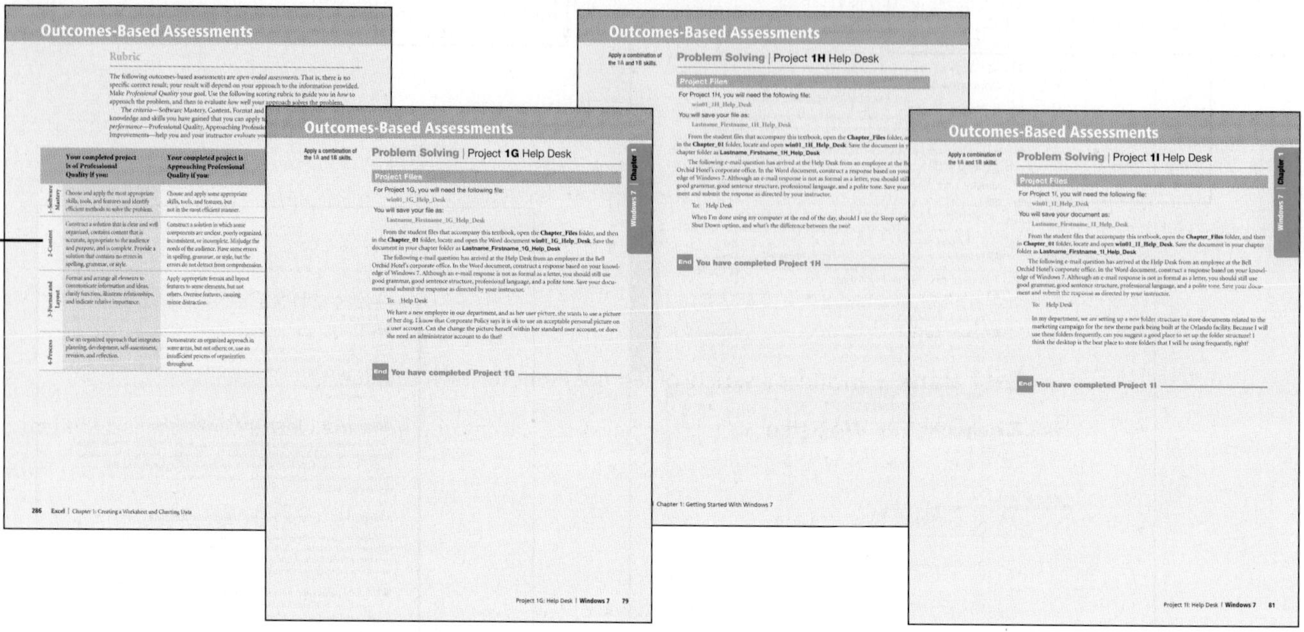

Outcomes Rubric – A matrix specific to the **GO! Think** projects that states the criteria and standards for grading these open-ended assessments.

Student CD – All student data files readily available on a CD that comes with the book.

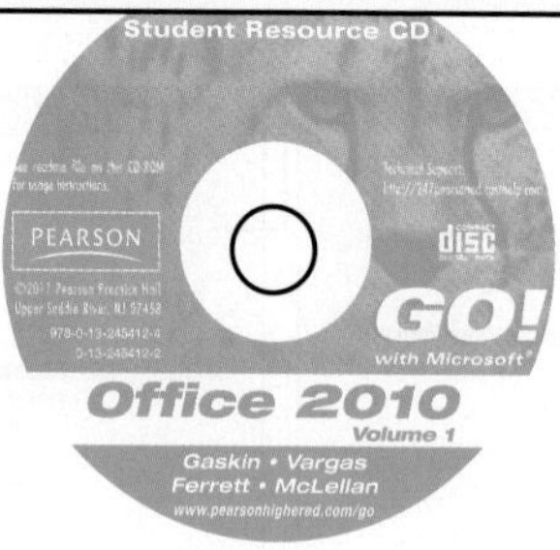

All Instructor materials available on the IRCD

Instructor Materials

Assignment Sheets – Lists all the assignments for the chapter. Just add in the course information, due dates, and points. Providing these to students ensures they will know what is due and when.

Scripted Lectures – Classroom lectures prepared for you.

Annotated Solution Files – Coupled with the assignment tags, these create a grading and scoring system that makes grading so much easier for you.

PowerPoint Lectures – PowerPoint presentations for each chapter.

Scorecards – Can be used either by students to check their work or by you as a quick check-off for the items that need to be corrected.

Test Bank – Includes a variety of test questions for each chapter.

Companion Website – Online content such as the Online Study Guide, Glossary, and Student Data Files are all at **www.pearsonhighered.com/go**.

Getting Started With Windows 7

OUTCOMES

At the end of this chapter you will be able to:

OBJECTIVES

Mastering these objectives will enable you to:

PROJECT 1A

Create a folder, save a file, and manage your user account.

1. Create a New Folder and Save a File on a Removable Storage Device (p. 3)
2. Identify the Functions of an Operating System (p. 18)
3. Use the Getting Started Information and Windows Help and Support (p. 19)
4. Log Off, Turn Off Your Computer, and View Power Options (p. 23)
5. Manage Your User Account (p. 25)

PROJECT 1B

Manage windows and open files and programs.

6. Display Libraries, Folders, and Files in a Window (p. 31)
7. Start Programs and Open Data Files (p. 45)
8. Manage the Display of Individual and Multiple Windows (p. 52)

Soundsnaps/Shutterstock

In This Chapter

In this chapter you will use Microsoft Windows 7, which is software that manages your computer's hardware, software, and data files. Compared to previous versions of Windows, you will find that Windows 7 is faster and less complex. In this chapter you will log on to your computer, explore the features of Windows 7, create folders and save files, manage multiple windows, log off of your computer, and examine user accounts.

The projects in this chapter relate to the **Bell Orchid Hotels**, headquartered in Boston, and which own and operate resorts and business-oriented hotels. Resort properties are located in popular destinations, including Honolulu, Orlando, San Diego, and Santa Barbara. The resorts offer deluxe accommodations and a wide array of dining options. Other Bell Orchid hotels are located in major business centers and offer the latest technology in their meeting facilities. The company plans to open new properties and update existing properties over the next ten years.

Project 1A Using Windows 7

Project Activities

In Activities 1.01 through 1.08, you will participate in training along with Steven Ramos and Barbara Hewitt, both of whom work for the Information Technology Department at the Boston headquarters office of the Bell Orchid Hotels. After completing this part of the training, you will be able to log on to and log off of your computer, create folders and save files on a removable storage device, and distinguish among types of users of the computer. You will capture two screens that will look similar to Figure 1.1.

Project Files

For Project 1A, you will need the following files:

Two new Snip files

You will save your files as:

Lastname_Firstname_1A_USB_Snip
Lastname_Firstname_1A_Modem_Snip

Project Results

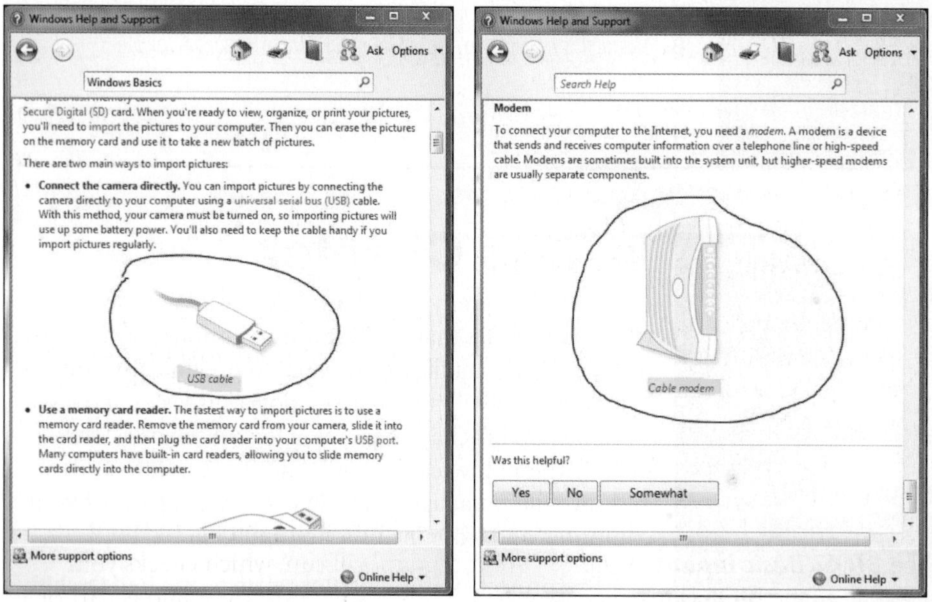

Figure 1.1
Project 1A Using Windows 7

Objective 1 | Create a New Folder and Save a File on a Removable Storage Device

A ***program*** is a set of instructions that a computer uses to accomplish a task, such as word processing, accounting, or data management. A program is also referred to as an ***application***.

Windows 7 is an ***operating system*** developed by Microsoft Corporation. An operating system is a computer program that manages all the other programs on your computer, stores files in an organized manner, allows you to use software programs, and coordinates the use of computer hardware such as the keyboard and mouse.

A ***file*** is a collection of information that is stored on a computer under a single name, for example a text document, a picture, or a program.

Every file is stored in a ***folder***—a container in which you store files—or a ***subfolder***, which is a folder within a folder. Windows 7 stores and organizes your files and folders, which is the primary task of an operating system.

Alert! | Variations in Screen Organization, Colors, and Functionality are Common in Windows 7

Individuals and organizations can determine how Windows 7 displays; thus, the colors and the organization of various elements on the screen can vary. Your college or organization may customize Windows 7 to display a college picture or logo, or restrict access to certain features. The basic functions and structure of Windows 7 are not changed by such variations. You can be confident that the skills you will practice in this textbook apply to Windows 7 regardless of available functionality or differences between the pictures in the book and your screen.

Activity 1.01 | Turning On Your Computer, Logging On to a Windows 7 User Account, and Exploring the Windows 7 Environment

Before you begin any computer activity, you must, if necessary, turn on your computer and its monitor. This process is commonly referred to as ***booting the computer***. Because Windows 7 does not require you to completely shut down your computer except to install or repair a hardware device, in most instances moving the mouse or pressing a key will wake your computer in a few seconds. Thus, most of the time you will skip the lengthier boot process.

In those instances where you must press the power button and initiate the boot process, the ***BIOS (Basic Input/Output System)*** program will run, which checks your hardware devices. The BIOS is installed by your computer's manufacturer and is part of the hardware of your system; it is *not* part of Windows 7. As its final process, the BIOS program loads Windows 7.

In this activity, you will turn on your computer and log on to Windows 7. If you are the only user of your own computer, you can disable the logon process if you want to do so. In most organizations, you will be required to log on in some manner.

Note | Comparing Your Screen with the Figures in This Textbook

Your screen will more closely match the figures shown in this textbook if you set your screen resolution to 1024 × 768. At other resolutions, your screen will closely resemble, but not match, the figures shown. To view your screen's resolution, on the desktop, right-click in a blank area, click Screen resolution, and then click the Resolution arrow. To adjust the resolution, move the slider to the desired setting, and then click OK.

1 If necessary, turn on your computer and monitor, and then compare your screen with Figure 1.2. If no password is required, move to Step 3.

The Windows 7 screen displays and indicates the names and pictures associated with all active user accounts. In this figure, only two users display. If you are able to set up your own user account, you can select a picture of your choice.

Your organization might have a custom logon screen with a logo or logon instructions, and thus will differ from the one shown.

There are several editions of Windows 7. The editions you might see commonly in the United States are Home Premium, Professional, Ultimate, and Enterprise. For the tasks you complete day to day, all of the functionality exists in all of these editions. Only larger organizations require the functions in Professional, Ultimate, and Enterprise.

Figure 1.2

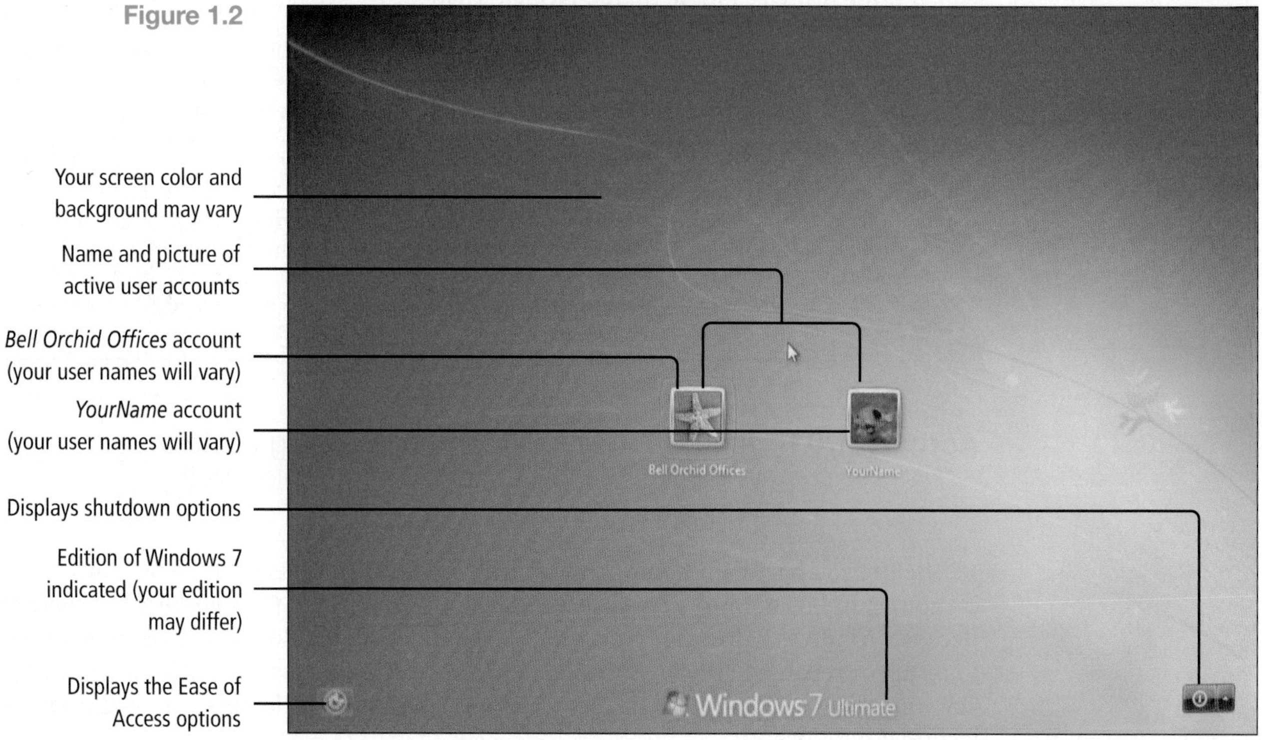

2 If there are two or more users on the computer you are using, point to your user account name to display a glow effect, and then click your user account name or its associated picture. If necessary, type your password in the Password box, and then click the circled arrow to the right of the Password box—or press Enter.

> **Note | Differing Logon Procedures and Passwords**
>
> Depending on whether you are working on your own computer, in a college lab, or in an organization, your logon process may differ. If you have a different logon screen, log on as directed and move to Step 3 of this activity. If you are working in a classroom or lab, ask your instructor or lab assistant about the user account name and password to use. On your own computer, use your own user account name and password. If no passwords are set on your computer and you do not need to log on, you are ready to begin Step 3.

3 Take a moment to compare your screen with Figure 1.3 and study the table in Figure 1.4.

Figure 1.3

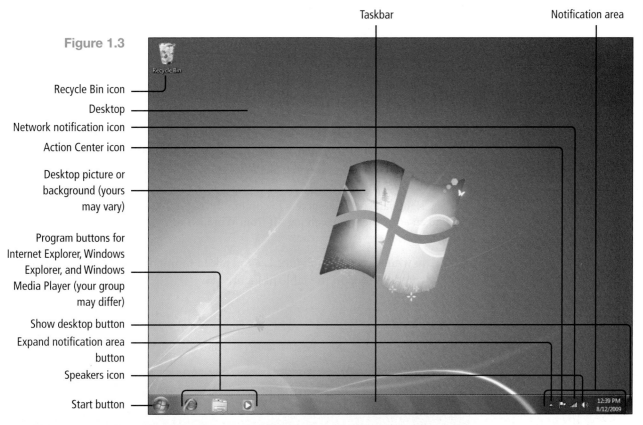

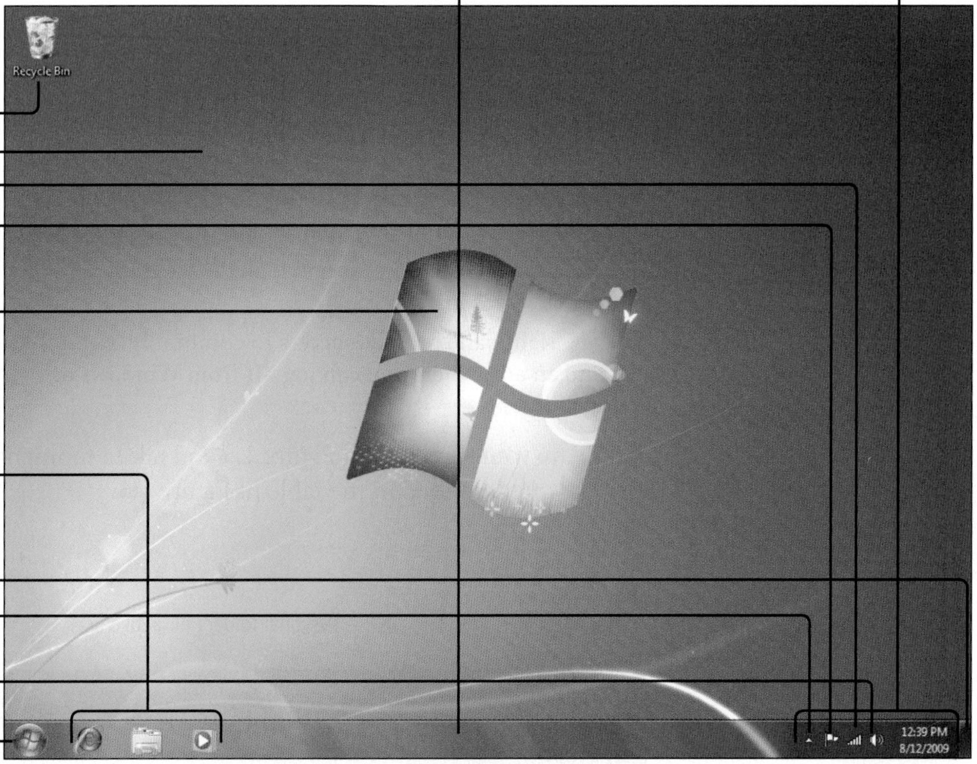

Parts of the Windows 7 Desktop

Action Center icon in the notification area	Displays the Action Center, which is a central place to view alerts and take actions related to things that need your attention.
Desktop	Serves as a surface for your work, like the top of an actual desk, and is the main screen area that you see after you turn on your computer; here you can arrange ***icons***—small pictures that represent a file, folder, program, or other object—on the desktop such as shortcuts to programs, files, folders, and various types of documents in the same manner you would arrange physical objects on top of a desk.
Desktop background	Displays the colors and graphics of your desktop; you can change the desktop background to look the way you want it such as using a picture or a solid color. Also called ***wallpaper***.
Network notification icon	Displays the status of your network.
Notification area	Displays notification icons and the system clock and calendar; sometimes referred to as the ***system tray***.
Program buttons	Launch Internet Explorer, the Web browser program developed by Microsoft that is included with Windows 7; Windows Explorer, the program that displays the files and folders on your computer; and Windows Media Player, the program that plays and organizes your digital media files.
Recycle Bin	Contains files and folders that you delete. When you delete a file or folder, it is not actually deleted; it stays in the Recycle Bin if you want it back, until you take action to empty the Recycle Bin.
Show desktop button	Displays the desktop by making any open windows transparent (when pointed to) or minimized (when clicked).
Speakers icon	Displays the status of your speakers (if any).
Start button	Displays the ***Start menu***—a list of choices that provides access to your computer's programs, folders, and settings.
Taskbar	Contains the Start button, optional program buttons, and buttons for all open programs; by default, it is located at the bottom of the desktop, but you can move it.

Figure 1.4

Another Way

Alternatively, press the Windows logo key located in the lower left corner of most keyboards.

4. In the lower left corner of your screen, move the mouse pointer over—***point*** to—the **Start** button, and then ***click***—press the left button on your mouse pointing device—to display the **Start** menu.

   The ***mouse pointer*** is any symbol that displays on your screen in response to moving your mouse.

   The Start menu has three parts: The left pane, the Search box at the bottom, and the right pane. The panes might be divided by menu separators into separate sections.

   The large left pane displays a list of some installed programs, which might be customized by your computer manufacturer, and the All Programs button.

   The Search box enables you to look for programs and files on your computer by typing search words in the box.

   The right pane provides access to commonly used folders, files, settings, and features, and an area where you can log off from Windows or shut down (turn off) your computer.

5. Compare your screen with Figure 1.5 and take a moment to study the parts of the **Start** menu described in the table in Figure 1.6.

Figure 1.5

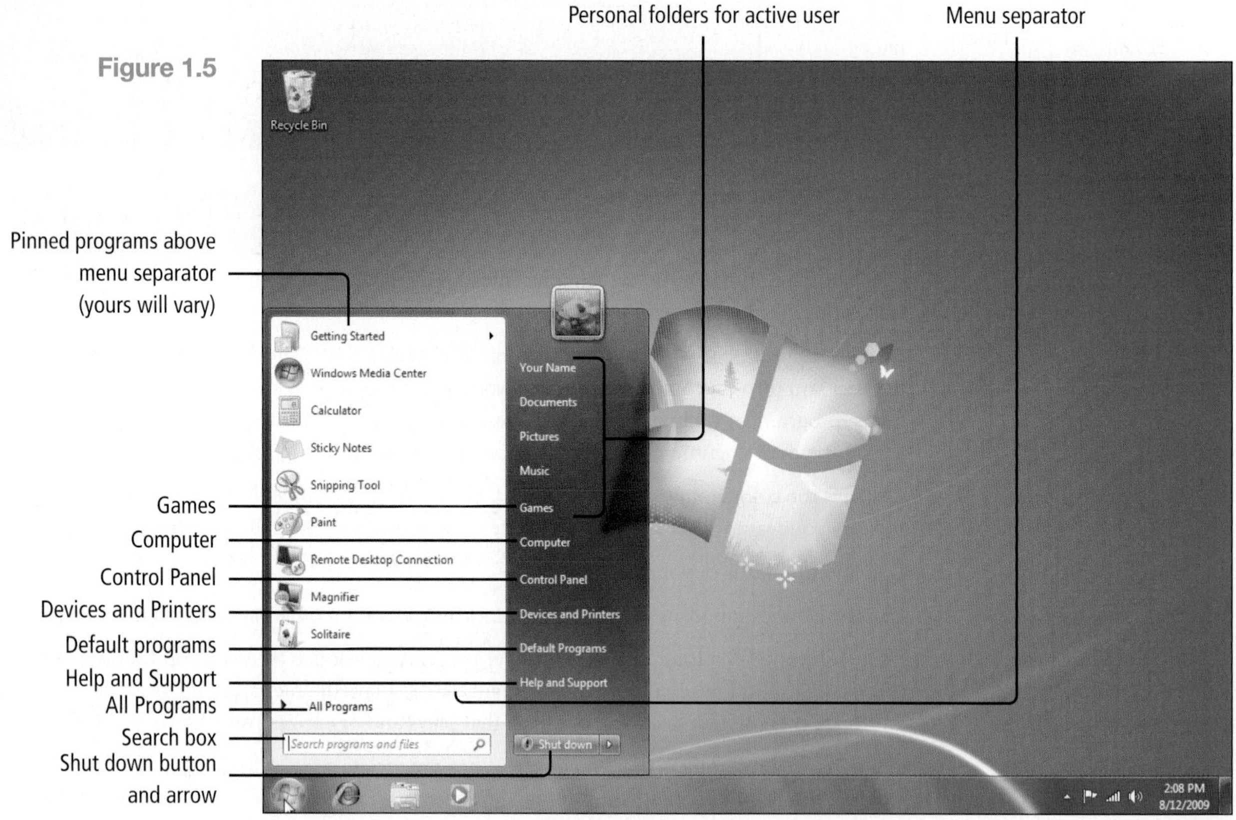

Parts of the Start Menu

All Programs	Displays all the programs on your computer system that are available to you; some groups of programs display in a folder.
Computer	Opens a window from which you can access disk drives, cameras, printers, scanners and other hardware connected to your computer.
Control Panel	Opens the Control Panel, where you can customize the appearance and functionality of your computer, install or uninstall programs, set up network connections, and manage user accounts.
Default Programs	Opens a window where you can choose which program you want Windows 7 to use for activities such as Web browsing or photo viewing.
Devices and Printers	Displays a window where you can view information about the printer, mouse, and other devices installed on your computer.
Games	Opens the Games folder, from which you can access all of the games on your computer.
Help and Support	Opens Windows Help and Support, where you can browse and search Help topics about how to use Windows and your computer.
Personal folders	Displays, for the user currently logged on, the user account picture, personal folder, and the user's Documents, Music, Pictures, and Videos folders, the locations in which the user logged on would most likely store files.
Pinned programs	Displays programs, at the top above the menu separator, that you have ***pinned***—placed in a manner that remains until you remove it—to the Start menu because they are programs you use frequently. Below the menu separator, Windows displays recently used programs or programs that Windows detects as those that you use frequently.
Search box	Searches your programs, personal folder, e-mail messages, saved instant messages, appointments, and contacts by typing search terms.
Shut down button and arrow	Turns off the computer; clicking the arrow displays a menu with additional options for switching users, logging off, restarting, or shutting down.

Figure 1.6

6 Be sure the Start menu is still displayed, and then compare your screen with Figure 1.7.

In Figure 1.7, portions of the Start menu are transparent; for example, you can see parts of the desktop design behind the right pane of the Start menu. If your version of Windows 7 has this capability and it is enabled, and if your computer system's graphics hardware supports transparency, you might also notice this transparent effect.

Figure 1.7

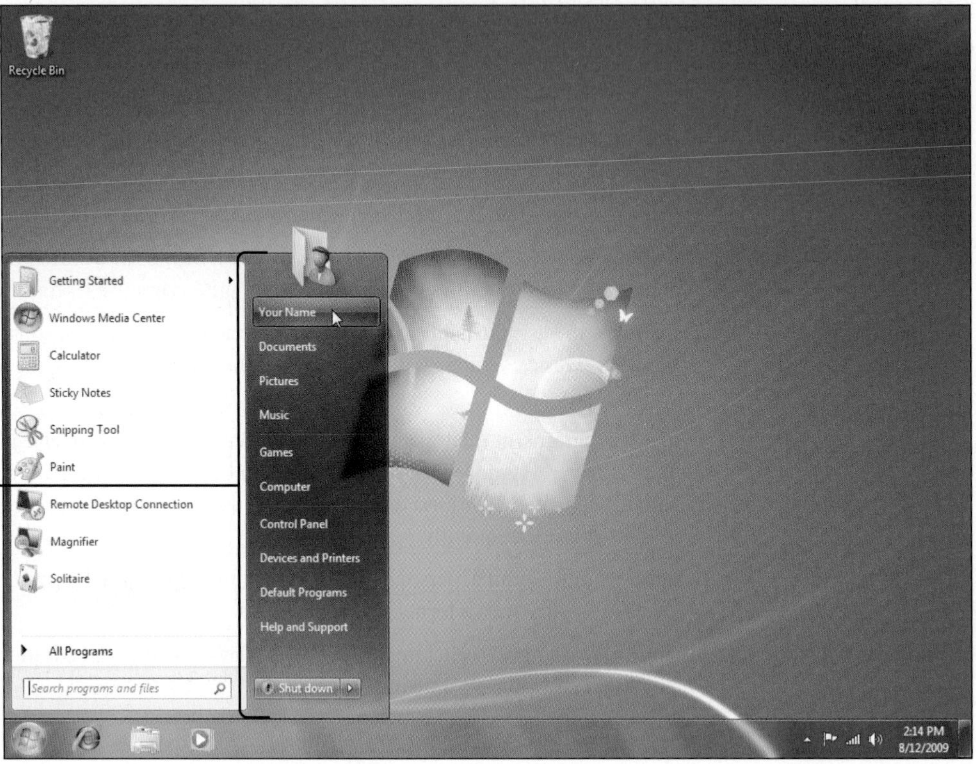

Right pane of Start menu transparent (yours may differ)

> **More Knowledge | Get Information About Your Computer's Ability to Display Transparency**
>
> In the Control Panel, click Appearance and Personalization, click Personalization, click Window Color, and then if necessary, click to put a checkmark in the box next to Enable transparency. Or, in Windows Help and Support, in the Search box type *transparency*. There you will find information about the system requirements for displaying transparency.

Activity 1.02 | Creating a New Folder on a Removable Storage Device

Recall that a file is a collection of information stored on a computer under a single name. Examples of a file include a Word document, an Excel workbook, a picture, a song, or a program. Recall also that a folder is a container in which you can store files. You probably store paper documents (files) in folders on your desk or in a file drawer. In the same manner, Windows 7 organizes and keeps track of your electronic files by letting you create and label electronic folders into which you can place your files.

In this activity, you will create a new folder on a ***removable storage device***. Removable storage devices, such as a USB flash drive or a flash memory card, are commonly used to transfer information from one computer to another. Such devices are also useful when you want to work with your files on different computers. For example, you probably have files that you work with at your college, at home, and possibly at your workplace.

A ***drive*** is an area of storage that is formatted with a file system compatible with your operating system and is identified by a drive letter. For example, your computer's ***hard disk drive***—the primary storage device located inside your computer where most of your files and programs are typically stored—is usually designated as drive C. Removable storage devices that you insert into your computer will be designated with a drive letter—the letter designation varies from one computer to another.

Alert! | Locate Your USB Flash Drive

You will need a USB flash drive to complete this activity.

1. Insert a USB flash drive into your computer. If this is the first time you have used this device in the computer, you may see one or more messages in your notification area indicating that device software is being installed and that your device is ready to use.

2. In the upper right corner of the **AutoPlay** window, **Close** the **AutoPlay** window, and click the small x in the upper right corner of any displayed message in the notification area.

   AutoPlay is a Windows 7 feature that lets you choose which program to use to start different kinds of media, such as music CDs, or CDs and DVDs containing photos. It displays when you plug in or insert media or storage devices.

   A ***window*** is a rectangular area on your screen that displays programs and content, and which can be moved, resized, minimized, or closed; the content of every window is different, but all windows display on the desktop.

3. Display the **Start** menu, and then on the right side, click **Computer**. Compare your screen with Figure 1.8.

   The ***folder window*** for *Computer* displays. A folder window displays the contents of the current folder, library, or device, and contains helpful parts so that you can ***navigate***—explore within the organizing structure of Windows.

Figure 1.8

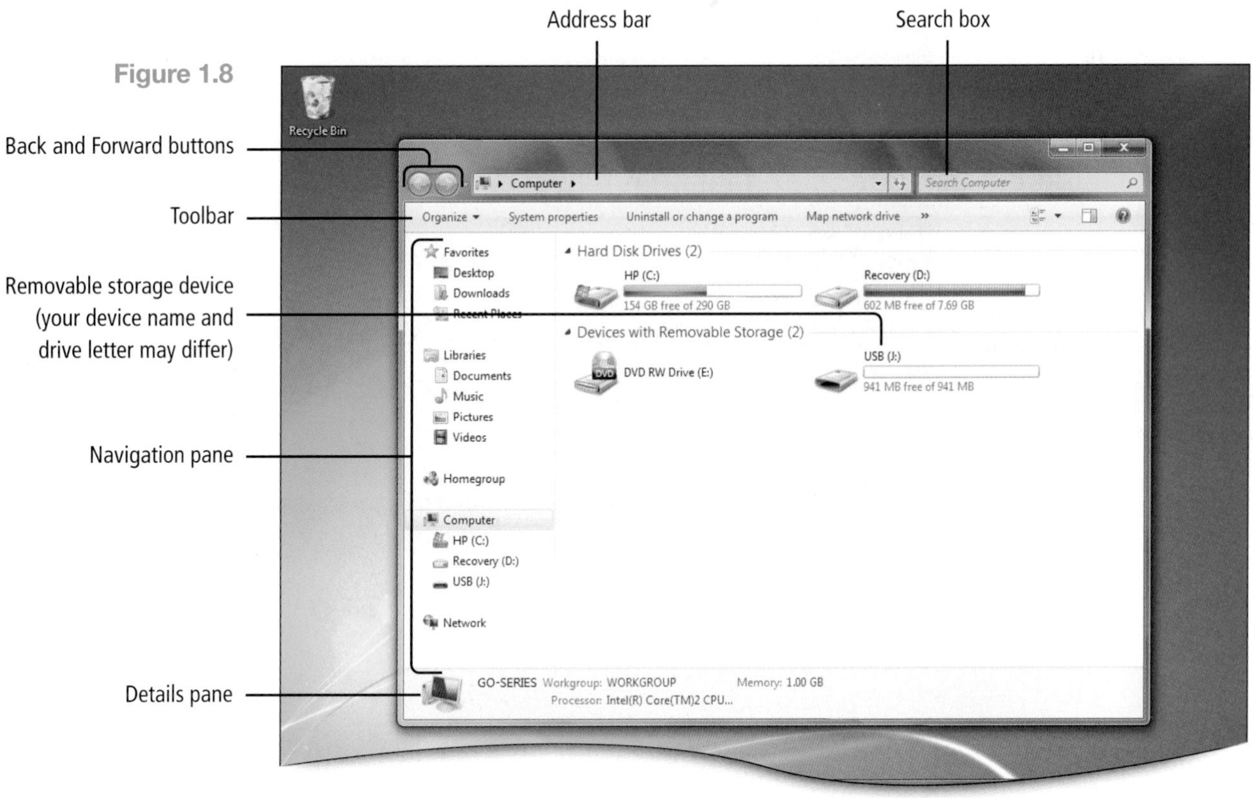

A ***library*** is a collection of items, such as files and folders, assembled from various locations. A ***location*** is any disk drive, folder, or other place in which you can store files and folders.

In the Computer window, you have access to all the storage areas inside and connected to your computer such as your hard disk drive, DVD or CD drives, removable storage devices, and network drive locations if you are connected to a network and have storage space there.

4 Under **Devices with Removable Storage**, locate the removable storage device you inserted in Step 1, move your mouse over—point to—the device name to display the pointer, and then click the *right* mouse button one time—referred to as ***right-click***—to display a ***shortcut menu***.

A shortcut menu is a context-sensitive menu that displays commands and options relevant to the selected object.

Another Way

Point to the device name and double-click to display the file list for the device.

5 On the displayed shortcut menu, click **Open** to display the file list for this device. Notice that in the **navigation pane**, *Computer* expands to display all of the drives that you can access, and the commands on the **toolbar** change. Compare your screen with Figure 1.9.

The ***navigation pane*** is the area on the left side of a folder window; it displays Favorites, Libraries, and an expandable list of drives and folders. If you are connected to a network, the name of the network, such as *Homegroup*, displays.

A ***toolbar*** is a row, column, or block of buttons or icons, usually displayed across the top of a window, which contains commands for tasks you can perform with a single click or buttons that display a menu of commands. The toolbar contains commands for common tasks that are relevant to the displayed folder window.

Figure 1.9

6 On the toolbar, click **New folder**, and notice in the file list, a folder icon displays with *New folder* highlighted in blue, as shown in Figure 1.10.

Figure 1.10

New folder command on toolbar

New folder on your device, the contents of your file list may vary

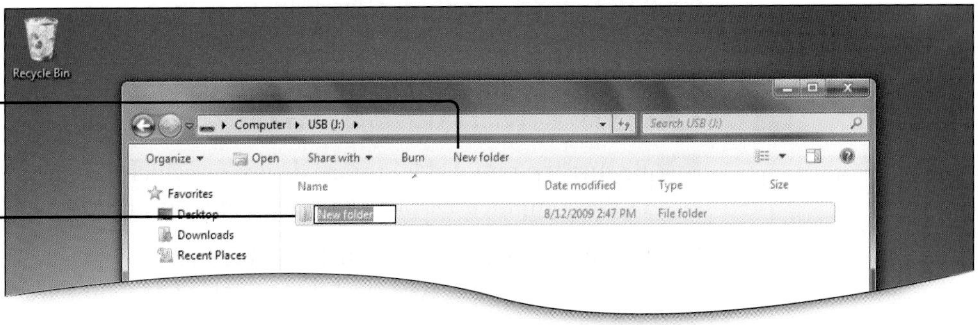

7 With the text *New folder* highlighted in blue, type **Windows 7 Chapter 1** and press Enter to confirm the folder name and select—highlight in blue—the new folder. With the folder selected, press Enter again to open the folder window. Compare your screen with Figure 1.11.

To ***select*** means to specify, by highlighting, a block of data or text on the screen with the intent of performing some action on the selection.

A new folder is created on your removable storage device. In the ***address bar***, the ***path*** from Computer to your device to your folder is indicated. The address bar displays your current location in the folder structure as a series of links separated by arrows. A path is a sequence of folders (directories) that leads to a specific file or folder.

Figure 1.11

Address bar indicates current location

New folder on your device

Navigation pane indicates selected location of folder

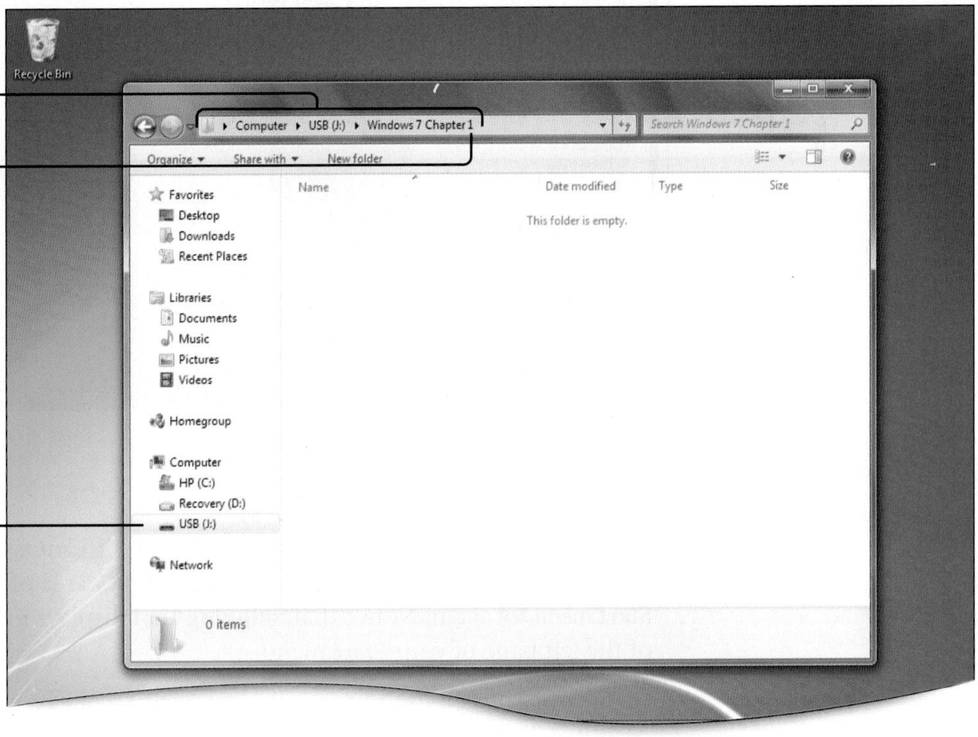

8 In the upper right corner of the window, click the Close button to close the window.

Activity 1.03 | Using Snipping Tool to Create a File

Snipping Tool is a program that captures an image of all or part of a computer screen. A ***snip***, as the captured image is called, can be annotated, saved, copied, or shared via e-mail. This is also referred to as a ***screen capture*** or a ***screenshot***.

1 Be sure the removable storage device on which you created your folder is still inserted in the computer. Display the **Start** menu, and then click **All Programs**.

2 On the list of programs, click the **Accessories** folder to display a list of Accessories. *Point* to Snipping Tool, and then right-click. Compare your screen with Figure 1.12.

Figure 1.12

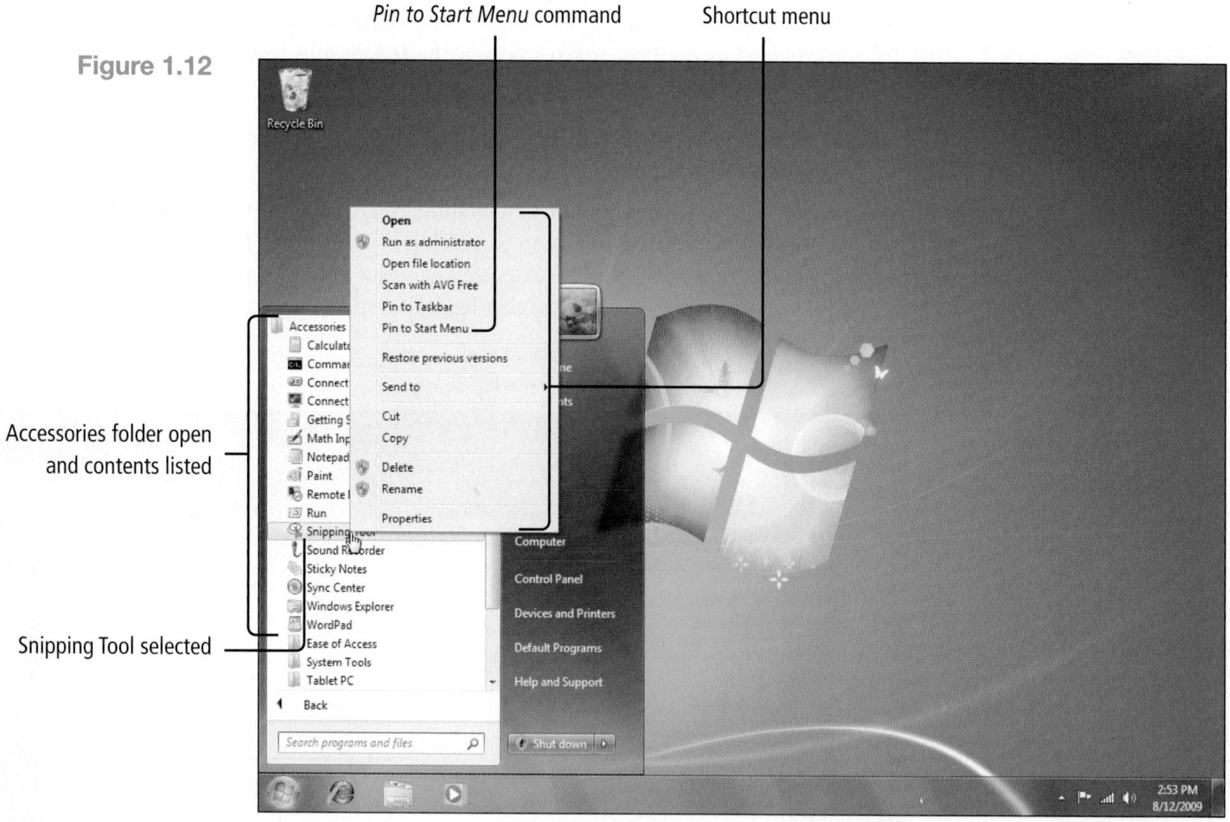

3 On the shortcut menu, click **Pin to Start Menu**, (if *Unpin from Start Menu* displays instead, skip this step) and then click in an empty area of your desktop. Display the **Start** menu again. Notice that **Snipping Tool** displays in the pinned (upper) portion of the left pane of your **Start** menu.

Because you will use Snipping Tool frequently while completing the projects in this textbook, it is recommended that you leave Snipping Tool pinned to your Start menu.

> **Another Way**
> If it displays, in the middle of the Windows Help and Support window, click Learn about Windows Basics.

4 From the displayed **Start** menu, at the bottom of the right pane, click **Help and Support**. In the **Windows Help and Support** window, in the **Search Help** box, type **Windows Basics** and then press Enter. On the displayed list, click **Windows Basics: all topics**. Compare your screen with Figure 1.13.

A vertical ***scroll bar*** displays on the right side of this window. A scroll bar displays when the contents of a window are not completely visible; you can use it to move the window up, down, left, or right to bring the contents into view. A scroll bar can be vertical as shown or horizontal and displayed at the bottom of a window.

Within the scroll bar, you can move the ***scroll box*** to move the window up, down, left, or right to bring the contents of the window into view. The position of the scroll box within the scroll bar indicates your relative position within the window's contents. You can click the ***scroll arrow*** at either end of the scroll bar to move within the window in small increments.

Each computer manufacturer has some control over the Help and Support opening screen. At the top of this screen, the manufacturer may place links to its own support and information about your computer's hardware.

Figure 1.13

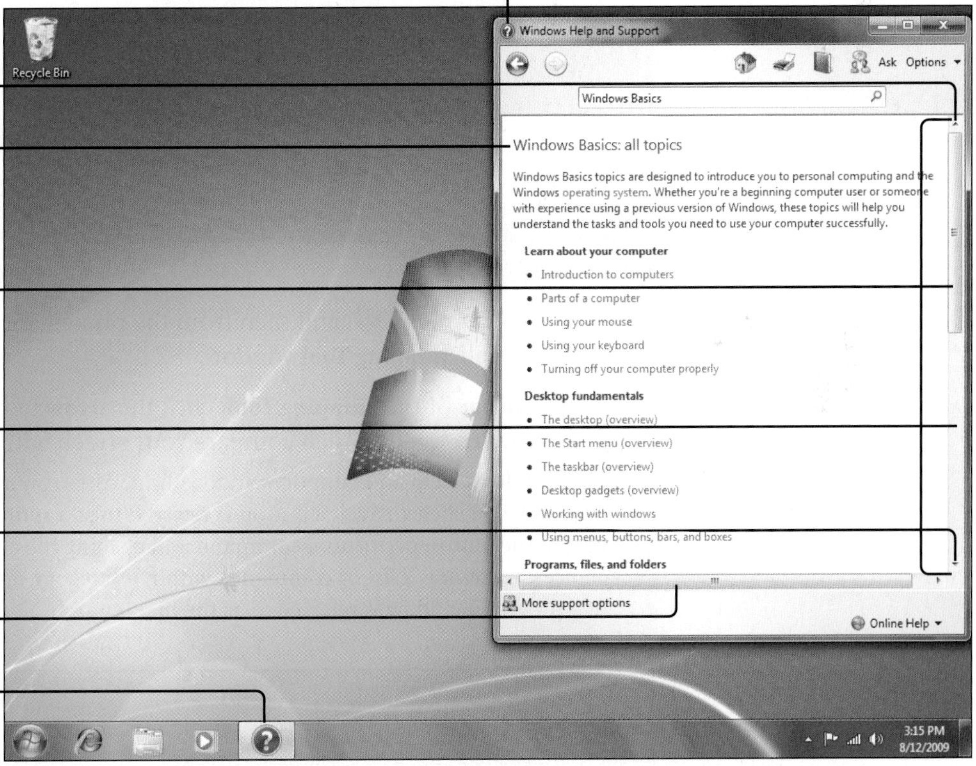

5 Click the down scroll arrow as necessary to bring the heading **Pictures and games** into view—or move the wheel on your mouse if you have one—and then click **Working with digital pictures**. Scroll down, if necessary, until you can see the illustration of a **USB cable**, as shown in Figure 1.14.

Figure 1.14

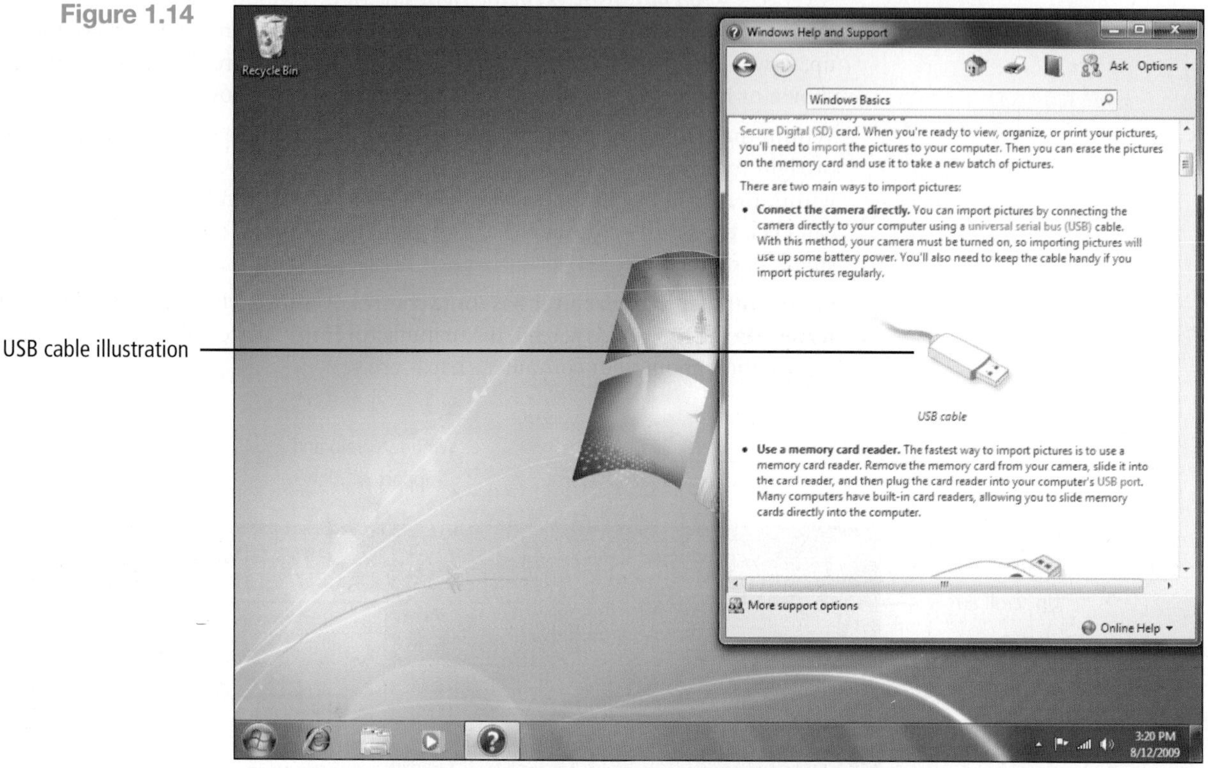

6 Display the **Start** menu, and then from the pinned area, click **Snipping Tool** to display the small **Snipping Tool** window.

7 On the **menu bar** of the **Snipping Tool**, click the **arrow** to the right of *New*—referred to as the **New arrow**—and then compare your screen with Figure 1.15.

The Windows Help and Support window dims. An arrow attached to a button will display a menu when clicked. Such a button is referred to as a ***split button***—clicking the main part of the button performs a command and clicking the arrow opens a menu with choices. A ***menu*** is a list of commands within a category, and a group of menus at the top of a program window is referred to as the ***menu bar***.

Figure 1.15

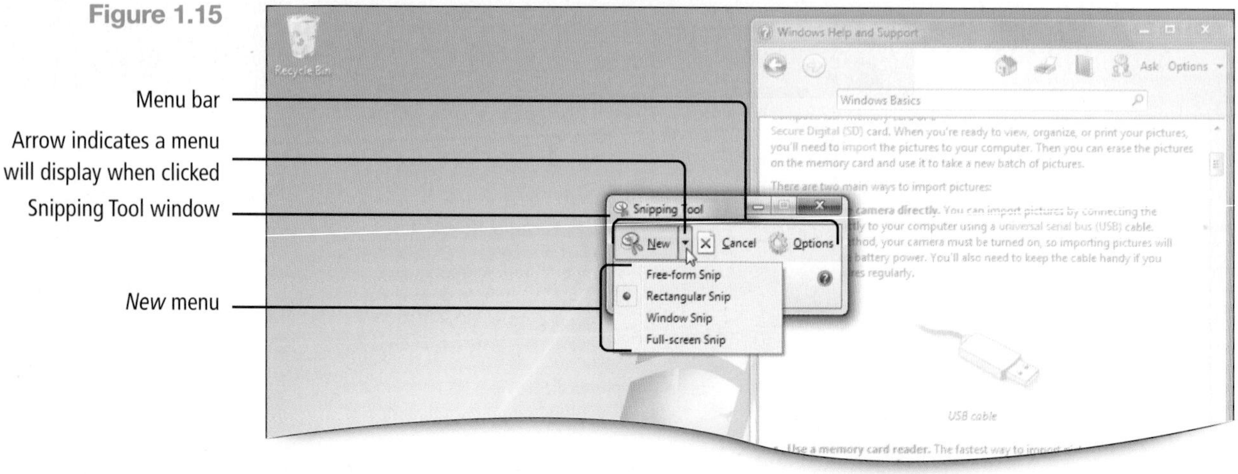

8 On the displayed menu, notice that there are four types of snips.

A ***free-form snip*** lets you draw an irregular line, such as a circle, around an area of the screen. A ***rectangular snip*** lets you draw a precise box by dragging the mouse pointer around an area of the screen to form a rectangle. A ***window snip*** captures the entire displayed window—such as the Help window. A ***full-screen snip*** captures the entire screen.

To ***drag*** is to move something from one location on the screen to another location while holding down the left mouse button; the action of dragging includes releasing the mouse button at the desired time or location.

9 From the displayed menu, click **Window Snip**. Then, move your mouse pointer over the open **Windows Help and Support** window, and notice that a red rectangle surrounds the window; the remainder of your screen dims.

10 With the pointer positioned anywhere over the surrounded window, click the left mouse button one time. Drag the scroll box to position the snip near the top of the window, and then compare your screen with Figure 1.16.

Your snip is copied to the Snipping Tool mark-up window. Here you can annotate—mark or make notes on—save, copy, or share the snip.

Snipping Tool mark-up window

Figure 1.16

Pen button arrow (arrow indicates a menu will display when clicked)

Scroll box

Your captured window snip

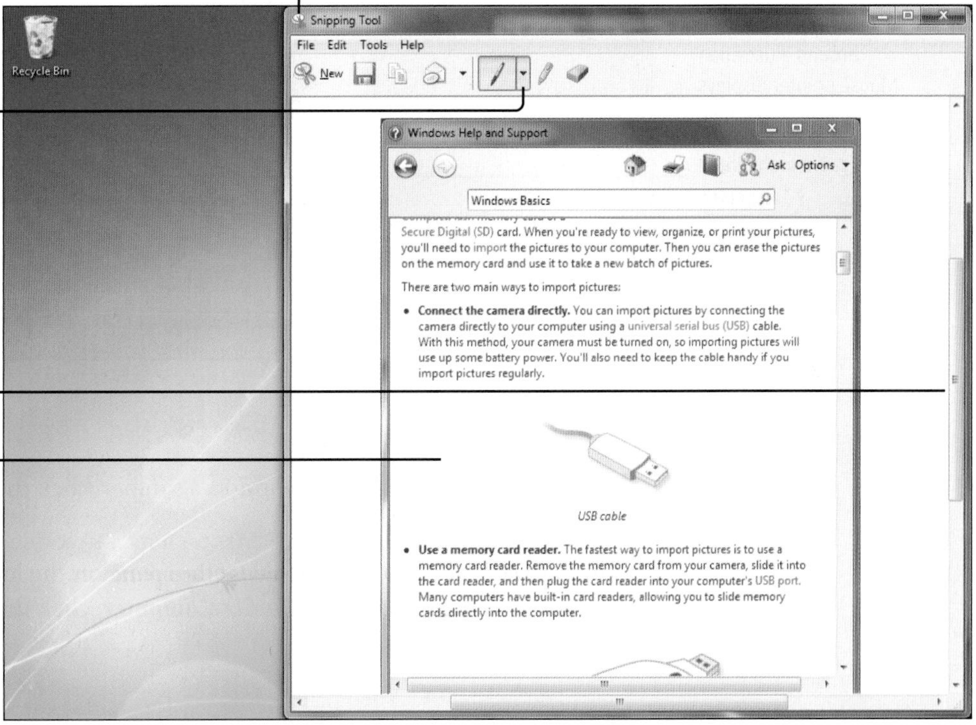

11 On the toolbar of the **Snipping Tool** mark-up window, click the **Pen button arrow**, and then click **Red Pen**. Notice that your mouse pointer displays as a red dot.

12 In the illustration of the USB cable, point to the end of the cable in the upper left portion of the picture, and then while holding down the left mouse button, draw a red free-form circle around the illustration of the USB cable as shown in Figure 1.17. If you are not satisfied with your circle, on the toolbar, click the Eraser button, point anywhere on the red circle, click to erase, and then begin again.

13 On the toolbar of the **Snipping Tool** mark-up window, click the **Highlighter** button. Notice that your mouse pointer displays as a small yellow rectangle.

14 Under the illustration of the USB cable, point to the caption text *USB cable*, hold down the left mouse button, and then drag over the text to highlight it in yellow. If you are not satisfied with your yellow highlight, on the toolbar, click the Eraser button, point anywhere on the yellow highlight, click to erase, and then begin again. Compare your screen with Figure 1.17.

Figure 1.17

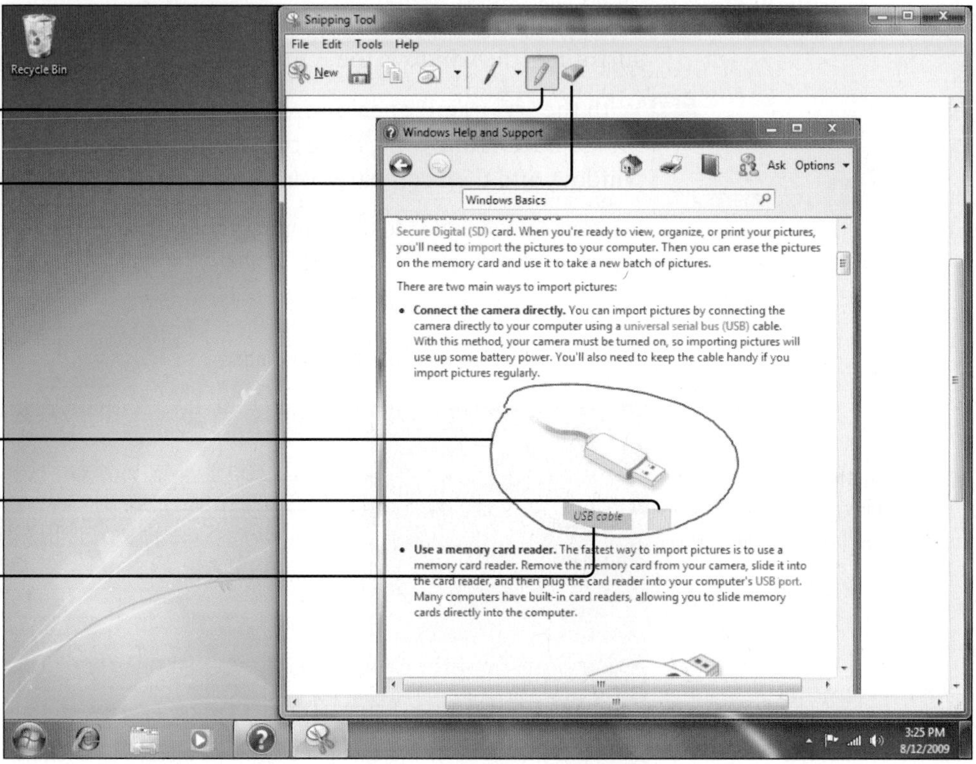

15 On the **Snipping Tool** mark-up window's toolbar, click the **Save Snip** button to display the **Save As** dialog box.

16 In the **Save As** dialog box, in the **navigation pane** on the left, drag the scroll box down as necessary to view **Computer**. Under **Computer**, click the name of your USB flash drive.

Another Way

Right-click the folder name and click Open.

17 In the **file list**, scroll as necessary, locate and ***double-click***—press the left mouse button two times in rapid succession while holding the mouse still—your **Windows 7 Chapter 1** folder. Compare your screen with Figure 1.18.

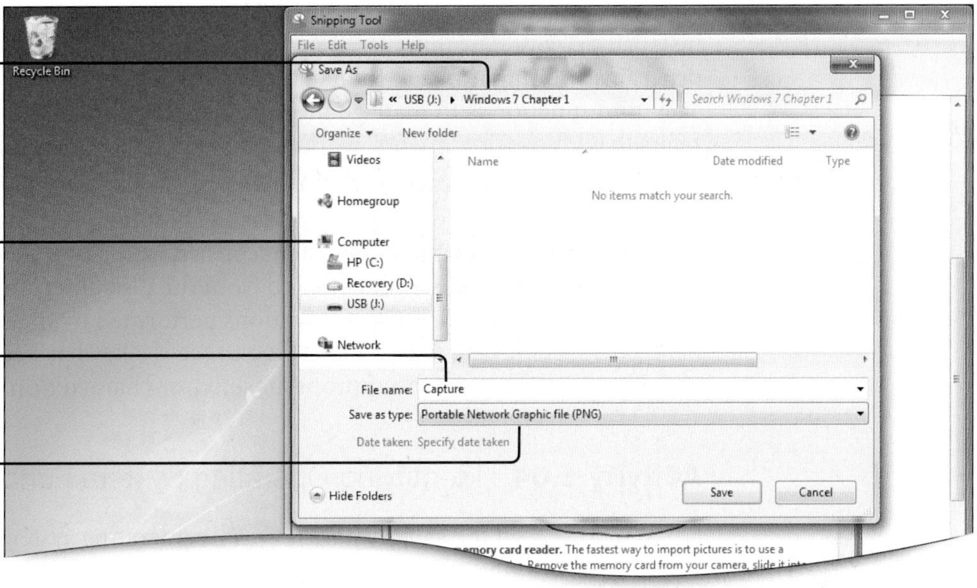

Figure 1.18

Note | Successful Double-Clicking Requires a Steady Hand

Double-clicking needs a steady hand. The speed of the two clicks is not so important as holding the mouse still between the two clicks. If you are not satisfied with your result, try again.

18 At the bottom of the **Save As** dialog box, locate the **Save as type** box, click anywhere in the box to display a list, and then from the displayed list click **JPEG file**.

JPEG, which is commonly pronounced *JAY-peg*, and stands for Joint Photographic Experts Group, is a common file type used by digital cameras and computers to store digital pictures. JPEG is popular because it can store a high-quality picture in a relatively small file.

19 At the bottom of the **Save As** dialog box, click in the **File name** box to select the text *Capture*, and then using your own name, type **Lastname_Firstname_1A_USB_Snip**

Within any Windows-based program, text highlighted in blue—selected—in this manner will be replaced by your typing.

Note | File Naming in This Textbook

Windows 7 recognizes file names with spaces. However, some older Internet file transfer programs do not. To facilitate sending your files over the Internet, in this textbook you will be instructed to save files using an underscore instead of a space. The underscore key is the shift of the - key—on most keyboards located two keys to the left of Bksp.

20 In the lower right corner of the window, click the **Save** button.

21 Close the **Snipping Tool** mark-up window and the **Windows Help and Support** window. Hold this file until you finish Project 1A, and then submit as directed by your instructor.

You have successfully created a folder on a removable storage device and saved a file within that folder.

Objective 2 | Identify the Functions of an Operating System

Operating system software has three major functions. The first function is to manage your computer's hardware—the printers, scanners, disk drives, monitors, and other hardware attached to it. The second function is to manage the application software installed on your computer—programs like those in Microsoft Office 2010 and other programs you might install to manage your money, edit photos, play games, and so on. The third function is to manage the ***data*** generated from your application software. Data refers to all those documents, worksheets, pictures, songs, and so on that you create and store during the day-to-day use of your computer.

In most instances, when you purchase a computer, the operating system software is already installed. The operating system consists of many smaller programs, stored as system files, which transfer data to and from the disk and transfer data in and out of your computer's memory. Other functions performed by the operating system include hardware-specific tasks such as checking to see if a key has been pressed on the keyboard and, if it has, displaying the appropriate letter or character on the screen.

Activity 1.04 | Identifying Operating System Functions

Windows 7, in the same manner as other operating systems and earlier versions of the Windows operating system, uses a ***graphical user interface***—abbreviated as ***GUI*** and pronounced GOO-ee. A graphical user interface uses graphics such as an image of a file folder or wastebasket that you click or double-click to activate the item represented. A GUI commonly incorporates the following:

A ***pointer***—any symbol that displays on your screen in response to moving your mouse and with which you can select objects and commands.

A ***pointing device***, such as a mouse or touchpad, to control the pointer.

Icons—small images that represent commands, files, or other windows. By selecting an icon and pressing a mouse button, you can start a program or move objects to different locations on your screen.

A ***desktop***—a simulation of a real desk that represents your work area; here you can arrange icons such as shortcuts to programs, files, folders, and various types of documents in the same manner you would arrange physical objects on top of a desk.

The parts of your computer such as the central processing unit (CPU), memory, and any attached devices such as a printer, are collectively known as ***resources***. The operating system keeps track of the status of each resource and decides when a resource needs attention and for how long. Fortunately, you need not be concerned about these operations; Windows 7 performs these tasks with no effort on your part.

There will be times when you want and need to interact with the functions of the operating system; for example, when you want to install a new hardware device like a color printer. Windows 7 provides tools such as Devices and Printers with which you can interact with the operating system about new hardware that you attach to your computer.

Software application programs are the programs that enable you to do work on, and be entertained by, your computer—programs such as Word and Excel found in the Microsoft Office suite of products, Adobe Photoshop, and computer games. An application program, however, cannot run on its own—it must run under the direction of the operating system.

For the everyday use of your computer, the most important and most often used function of the operating system is managing your files and folders—referred to as ***data management***. In the same manner that you strive to keep your paper documents and file folders organized so that you can find information when you need it, your goal when organizing your computer files and folders is to group your files so that you can find information easily. Managing your data files so that you can find your information when you need it is an important computing skill. Fortunately, the organization of Windows 7's filing system makes doing so a logical and straightforward process.

To check how well you can identify operating system functions, take a moment to answer the following questions:

1. Of the three major functions of the operating system, the first is to manage your computer's ___________ such as disk drives, monitors, and printers.
2. The second major function of the operating system is to manage the application ___________ such as Microsoft Word, Microsoft Excel, and video games.
3. The third major function of the operating system is to manage the ___________ generated from your applications—the files such as Word documents, Excel worksheets, pictures, and songs.
4. Windows 7 uses graphics such as images of a file folder or a wastebasket that you click to interact with the operating system; such a system is referred to as a ___________ ___________ ___________
5. One of the most important computing skills you can learn is how to manage your ___________ ___________ so that you can find your information quickly.

Objective 3 | Use the Getting Started Information and Windows Help and Support

The Windows 7 ***Getting Started*** feature is a task-centered grouping of links to tools that can help you get started with and add new features to your computer. Additionally, when you need information about the basic setup and operation of your computer or about how to do something, you can rely on ***Windows Help and Support***. Windows Help and Support is the built-in help system for Windows 7.

Activity 1.05 | Using the Getting Started Information and Windows Help and Support

Another Way

Getting Started may display on the Start menu; or, on the Start menu, click Help and Support, and then click the link *How to get started with your computer*. Then point to and click *Click to open Getting Started.*

1. On the taskbar, click the **Start** button, and then on the right, click **Control Panel**. Notice that in the upper right corner of the window, the insertion point is blinking in the search box. Type **get** and then compare your screen with Figure 1.19.

   Windows 7 searches using a lookup method known as ***word wheel***, in which each new character that you type into a search box further refines a search. In this instance, typing only *get* refines the search of Control Panel enough so that the Getting Started link displays at the top of the screen.

   The ***insertion point*** is a blinking vertical line that indicates where text or graphics will be inserted.

   The settings in the Control Panel control nearly everything about how Windows 7 looks and performs. For example, this is where you can change the color of your desktop. Some of the most common reasons to go to the Control Panel are to install new software programs, to uninstall software programs you no longer want, to connect to new networks, and to back up your computer.

Figure 1.19

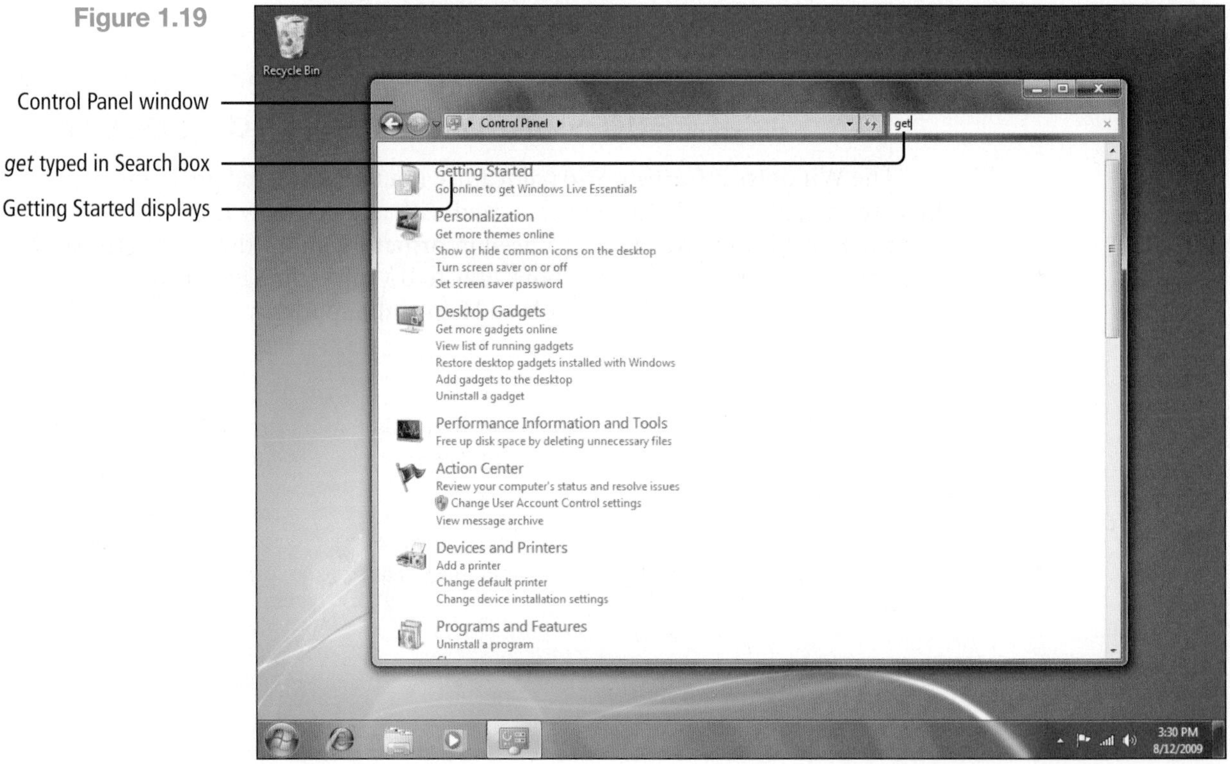

2 At the top of the **Control Panel** window, click **Getting Started**, and then compare your screen with Figure 1.20.

Here you can link to online resources or to information about basic tasks such as backing up your files or adding new users to your computer.

Figure 1.20

Getting Started window

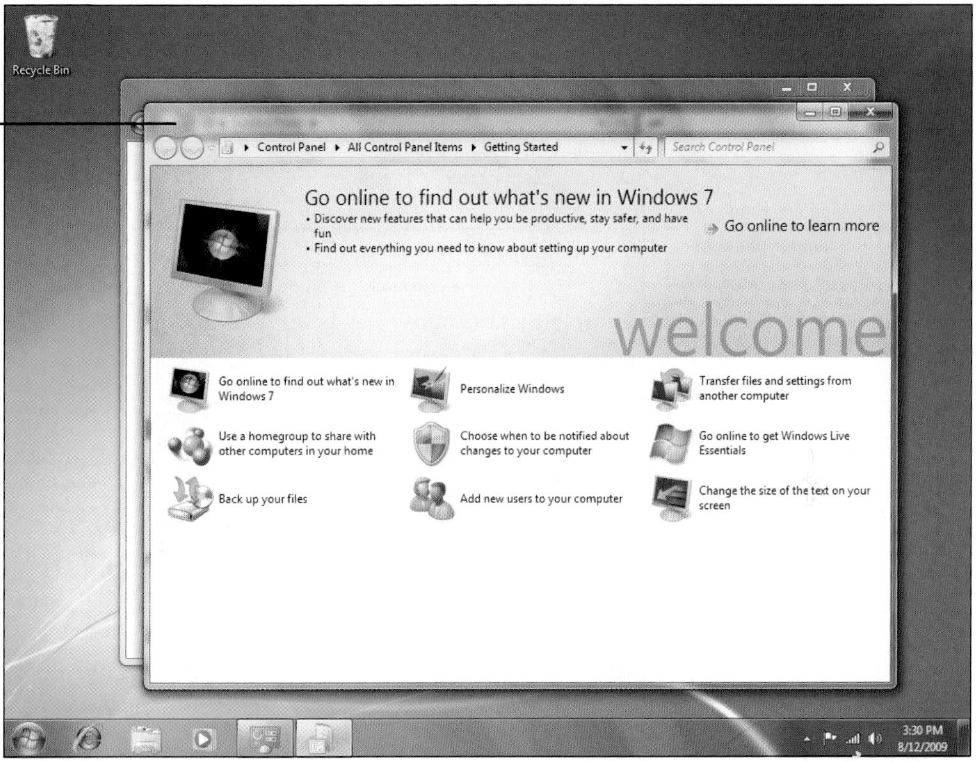

3 In the **Getting Started** window, click **Personalize Windows**, notice the description at the top of the window, and then in the center right of the window, click **Personalize Windows**.

The Personalization window displays. As you progress in your study of Windows 7, you will practice many distinctive ways to personalize your computer.

4 On the taskbar, click the **Start** button, and then on the right, click **Help and Support**. Locate and then display **Windows Basics: all topics**. Compare your screen with Figure 1.21.

The Windows Help and Support window displays a list of basic help topics. In this manner, you can have more than one window open on your desktop, and in fact it is common to have multiple windows open at one time.

Figure 1.21

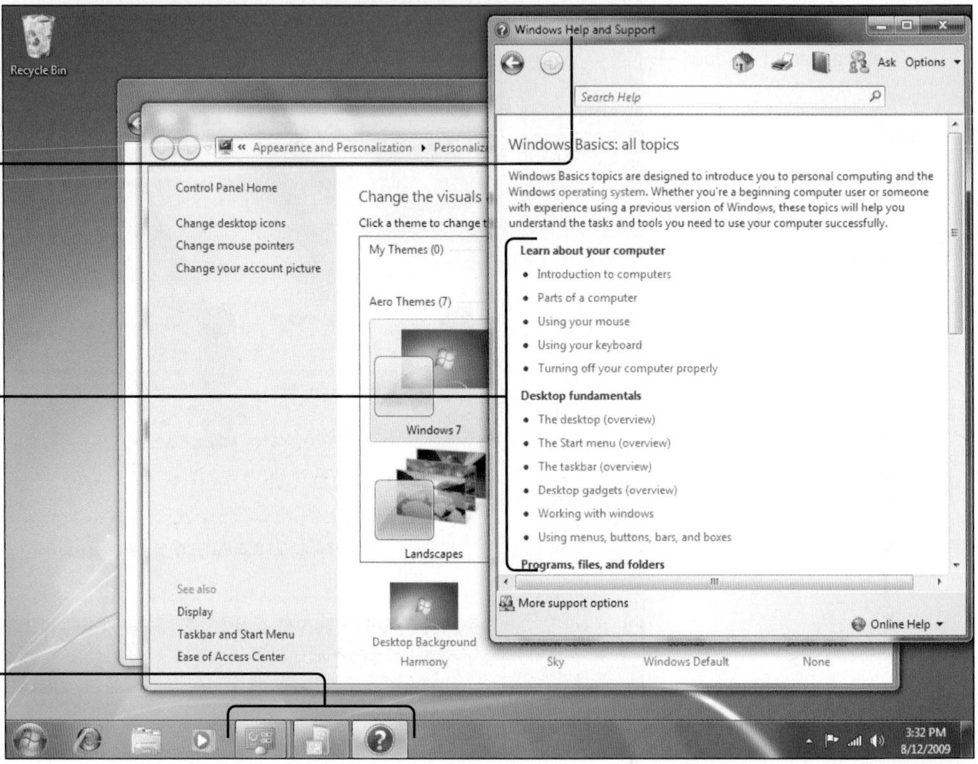

5 In the **Windows Help and Support** window, under **Learn about your computer**, click **Parts of a computer**. Under **In this article** click **Modem**, and then read the information about modems.

6 From the **Start** menu, click **Snipping Tool**, click the **New arrow**, click **Window Snip**, point to the modem picture, and then click one time. Using the red pen, draw a circle around the modem, and then highlight the text *Cable modem* in yellow.

7 Click the **Save Snip** button. Be sure the folder window for your chapter folder displays, be sure the type is **JPEG**, and then in the **File name** box, using your own name type **Lastname_Firstname_1A_Modem_Snip**

8 In the lower right corner, click the **Save** button or press Enter. Hold this file until the end of this project, and then submit as directed by your instructor.

9 **Close** the **Snipping Tool** window. In the upper left corner of the **Windows Help and Support** window, click the **Back** button. Under **Desktop fundamentals**, click **The desktop (overview)** and examine the available information.

You can see that Windows Help and Support offers useful information that is attractively presented and logically arranged.

10 At the top of the **Windows Help and Support** window, click in the box that indicates *Search Help*, type **security** and then press Enter.

You can also search the entire Windows Help and Support database by typing one or more words in the Search box.

11 In the displayed list, click **Security checklist for Windows 7**. At the top of the **Windows Help and Support** window, click the **Browse Help** button.

Contents is a list of information arranged by topic, similar to a table of contents in a book.

12 In the upper right corner of each open window, click the **Close** button until all windows are closed and only your desktop displays.

Objective 4 | Log Off, Turn Off Your Computer, and View Power Options

On your own computer, when you are done working, log off from Windows 7 if necessary, and then set your computer properly so that your data is saved, you save energy, and your computer remains secure.

When you turn off your computer by using the ***Sleep*** command, Windows 7 automatically saves your work, the screen goes dark, the computer's fan stops, and your computer goes to sleep. A light on your computer's case may blink or turn yellow to indicate the sleep mode. You need not close your programs or files because your work is saved. When you wake up your computer by pressing a key or moving the mouse, you need only to enter your password (if required); your screen will display exactly like it did when you turned off your computer. Your computer uses a small amount of power in sleep mode.

Activity 1.06 | Logging Off and Turning Off Your Computer

In an organization, there might be a specific process for logging off from Windows 7 and turning off the computer. The policy at Bell Orchid Hotels requires an employee to log off or lock the computer when away from his or her desk and to activate Sleep mode when leaving the building.

1 Display the **Start** menu, and then in the lower right corner, point to the **Shut down arrow** to display the submenu. Compare your screen with Figure 1.22, and then take a moment to study the table in Figure 1.23.

Figure 1.22

Shut down button submenu

Shut down button

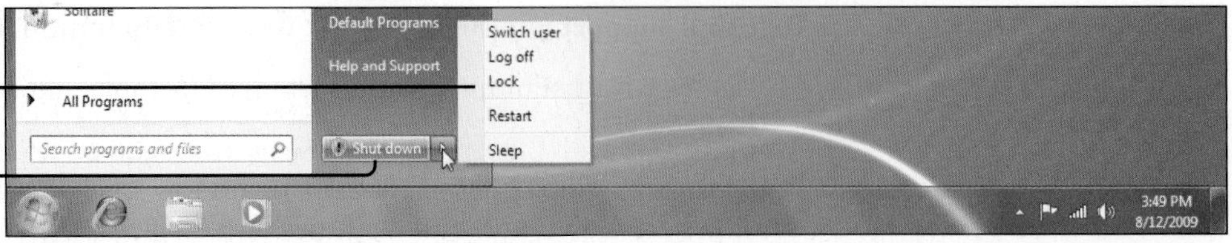

Options for Logging On To and Off From Windows 7 and Turning Off Your Computer Properly	
Switch user	Logs the active user account off of Windows, and then displays the Windows 7 welcome screen with all user accounts so that another user can log on to Windows.
Log off	Logs the active user account off of Windows, and then displays the Windows 7 welcome screen. From this point, you or another user can log on to Windows.
Lock	Locks the computer so that a password (if applicable) is required to log back on to your desktop. Others can log on to their own desktops while your desktop is locked by clicking the Switch User button. Use this feature if you are leaving your desk for a short time so that others cannot view your work and to prevent those who do not have a user account on your computer from using it.
Restart	Restarts the computer and clears the ***system cache***—an area of the computer's memory where Windows 7 stores information it needs to access quickly. Use this feature if your computer is operating slowly or having technical problems, or after installing new software or software updates.
Sleep	Saves your work, turns off the screen display, stops the computer's fan, and puts the computer to sleep; uses a small amount of power to keep your work in memory. After sleeping for several hours, everything in memory is saved on the hard disk.
Hibernate	Displays as an option on some laptop computers and is similar to Sleep.
Shut down	Closes all programs and network connections and stops the hard disk. No power is used. Shut down only to install or repair hardware inside the computer or attach hardware that does not connect with a USB cable.

Figure 1.23

2 On the right side of the **Start** menu, click **Control Panel**, and then click **Hardware and Sound**. Click **Power Options**.

Here you can change your power plan or make other changes to the manner in which your computer uses power. These options are set by your computer's manufacturer, and are usually optimized for the best use of power on your system. Consult the user manual for your computer before adjusting these settings.

3 On the left, click **Change when the computer sleeps**.

Here you can change the amount of time that elapses before your computer *automatically* turns off the display and puts the computer to sleep, which happens if you leave your computer unattended.

4 **Close** the **Edit Plan Settings** window.

Objective 5 | Manage Your User Account

On your own computer, you can elect to use no user accounts and disable the password on the first administrator account. If you do that, when you start or wake your computer, the desktop will display and no logon or password is required. The administrator will be the only user. Because Windows 7 supports multiple users, however, there is always at least one user—the initial administrator that was established when the system was purchased or when Windows 7 was installed.

As the administrator of your own computer, you can restrict access to your computer so that only people you authorize can use your computer or view its files. This access is managed through a user account, which is a collection of information that tells Windows 7 what files and folders the account holder can access, what changes the account holder can make to the computer system, and what the account holder's personal preferences are. Each person accesses his or her user account with a user name and password, and each user has his or her own desktop, files, and folders.

User accounts are useful because you can share a computer with other people in your family or organization while maintaining your own desktop and files that others cannot see and settings that others cannot change. For example, you may prefer that your screen displays with a light background, however another person using the same computer may prefer a screen with a dark background.

Windows 7 provides three types of user accounts—administrator, standard, and guest—and each one provides a different level of computer control. When upgrading a computer to Windows 7, you will be asked to create a user account. On a new computer with Windows 7 already installed, follow the steps provided by the computer manufacturer or those in the following activities to add a password to the administrator account if you want to do so.

An ***administrator account*** allows complete access to the computer. Administrators can make changes that affect other users, change security settings, install software and hardware, access all files on the computer, and make changes to other user accounts. It is the most powerful type of account, because it permits the most control over the computer.

Even if you are the only person using your computer, after you have finished setting up your computer, Microsoft recommends that you create and use a ***standard user account*** for your day-to-day computing. A standard user account enables you to use most of the capabilities of the computer, install some software, and change systems settings that do not affect other users or the security of the computer. While using a standard user account, you can do almost anything that you can do with an administrator account, but you might be prompted for the administrator password before you can perform certain tasks such as installing some software or changing security settings.

If you are the only person using your computer, you can use a single administrator account as your user account and even remove the password from the administrator account so that no logon or password is required. However, Windows 7 recommends that you set up a standard user account for most of your work and use the administrator account only when you need to perform tasks that affect the entire computer system. By doing so, you protect your computer by preventing anyone else from making changes to your computer.

A ***guest account*** allows people to have temporary access to your computer. People using the guest account cannot install software or hardware, change settings, or create a password. To use the guest account, you must turn it on. Because the guest account allows a user to log on to your network, if you have one, browse the Internet, and shut down the computer, it is a good idea to disable the guest account when it is not being used. A ***network*** refers to a group of computers or other devices, such as printers and scanners, which communicate either wirelessly or by using a physical connection. Small home networks of two or more computers and printers are becoming increasingly common.

Activity 1.07 | Managing Your Own User Account

If necessary, wake your computer by pressing any key or moving the mouse, and then if necessary, log on to Windows or use your organization's logon process.

1 Display the **Start** menu. On the right, click **Control Panel**, and then click **User Accounts and Family Safety** (or User Accounts)—this varies depending on your edition of Windows 7.

2 Under **User Accounts**, click **Change your account picture**. In the displayed **Change Your Picture** window, click the **soccer ball picture**, and then compare your screen with Figure 1.24.

You can use one of your own photos as the user picture by clicking *Browse for more pictures* and then navigating to a stored image.

Figure 1.24

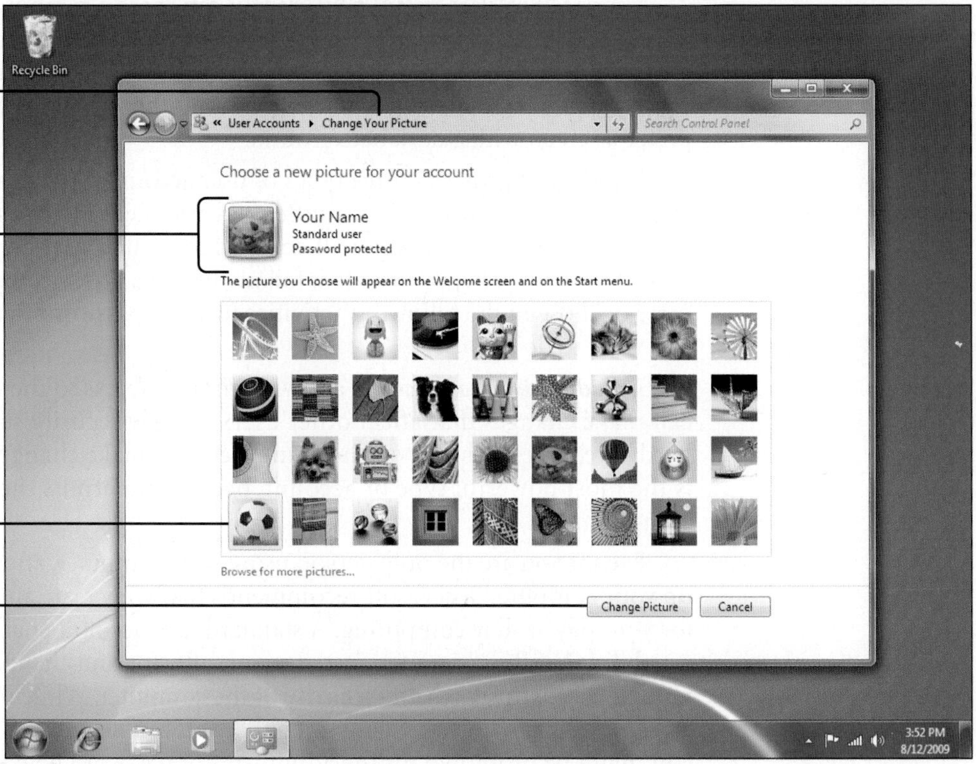

3 In the lower right corner, click the **Change Picture** button, and then at the top of the **Control Panel** window, click **Change your Windows password**. Notice that your new picture displays.

Here you can *change* your Windows 7 logon password, or, if you want to do so, you can *remove* your password completely so that no password is required to log on. If you do not want to have to enter a password each time you use your computer, and if you are confident that no one else will use your computer in an unauthorized manner, you can remove your password completely.

Here you can also change your account name. If you are logged on with an Administrator account, you can also manage the accounts of other users.

On this screen, you can also create a password reset disk, which you can insert if you forget your password. To do so, follow the instructions on the screen after starting the *Create a password reset disk* command.

4 **Close** [X] the **User Accounts** window.

> **More Knowledge** | **Using a Reset Disk if You Forget Your Password**
>
> If you use a password on your computer, it is a good idea to create a password reset disk. Then, if you forget your password when logging on, click OK in the displayed error message. Windows 7 will display the password hint you entered when you created the password, which might remind you of your password. If you still cannot remember your password, insert the flash drive on which you created your reset disk, click Reset password, and then follow the steps in the displayed Password Reset Wizard. Reserve a flash drive for this purpose and use it only if necessary to reset.

Activity 1.08 | Creating and Deleting User Accounts

> **Alert!** | **This is an Optional Activity**
>
> This activity is optional; you can complete this activity if you are logged on with an administrator account, or if you know the administrator password.

Some Windows 7 features are available only to users who are logged on with an administrator account; for example, only an administrator can add new user accounts or delete user accounts. If you are logged on with administrator rights, you can complete the steps in this activity. If you do not have an administrator account or do not know the administrator password, you can read through the steps for information.

1 From the **Start** menu, display **Control Panel**, and then under **User Accounts and Family Safety** (or User Accounts), click **Add or remove user accounts**—enter the password if prompted.

2 In the lower portion of the screen, click **Create a new account.**

The Create New Account window displays. Here you create the name for the new user account. The new user account name will display on the Windows 7 welcome screen. It will also display in the Start menu when this account holder is logged on. The default user account type is a standard user, as indicated by the selected option button.

When creating user names, consider developing a ***naming convention***—a plan that provides a consistent pattern for names.

3 In the **New account name** box, type **B Hewitt** and then in the lower right corner, click the **Create Account** button.

Windows 7 creates the new standard user account and applies one of the pictures. You may not see the user pictures if you are logged on as a standard user and accessed this screen by typing the administrator password.

4 In the **Manage Accounts** window, click **B Hewitt**. Then, in the **Change an Account** window, click **Create a password.**

Although not required, it is good practice to have a password for each user. Passwords prevent unauthorized access to that user's desktop and files. Effective passwords are at least eight characters in length and are not obvious to others. For example, using your pet's name is not a good password because it could be easily guessed by others. Passwords are also ***case sensitive***; that is, capitalization must match each time the characters are typed.

5 In the **New password** box, type **gowindows7** and press Tab. In the **Confirm new password** box, type **gowindows7** Notice that instead of your typing, a series of black circles displays to prevent others from seeing your password as you create it.

6 Point to and then click the link **How to create a strong password**, and then compare your screen with Figure 1.25.

The Windows Help and Support window displays. Here you can read valuable information about creating strong passwords. Use Windows 7's Help and Support system in this manner to enhance your learning and understanding of Windows 7.

Figure 1.25

Windows Help and Support window

Close button

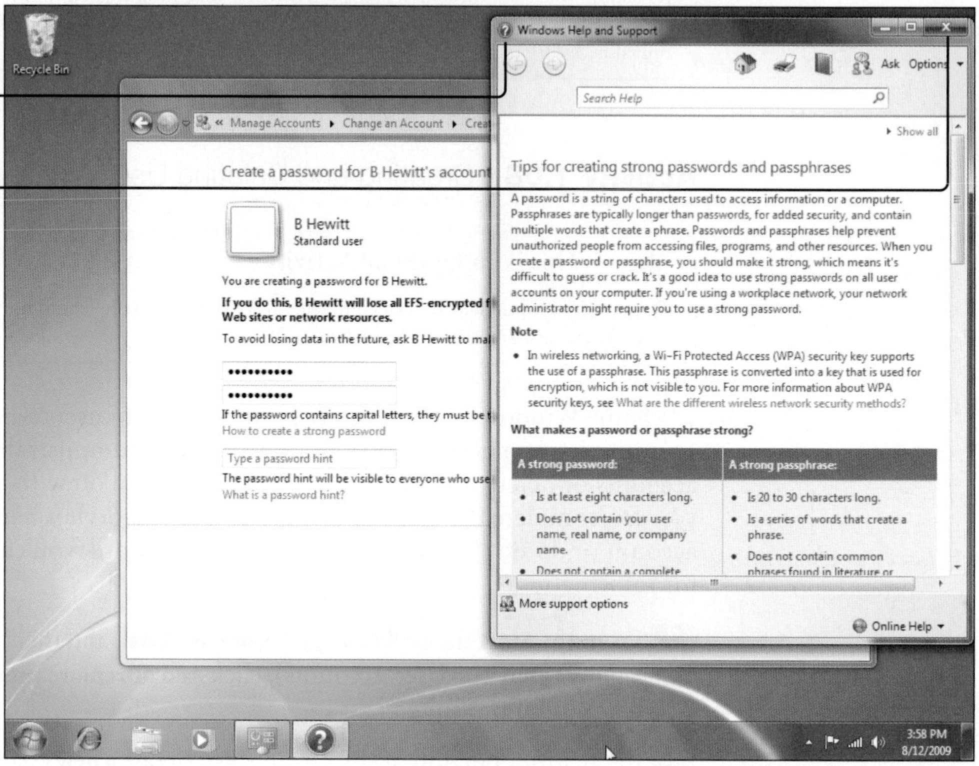

7 **Close** the **Windows Help and Support** window. Click in the **Type a password hint** box and type **textbook name**

8 In the lower right corner, click the **Create password** button, and then **Close** the **Change an Account** window.

9 On the **Start** menu, point to the **Shut down arrow**, and then click **Switch user.** Wait a moment for the Welcome screen to display, and then notice the new account for *B Hewitt*. Notice also that your name is indicated as *Logged on*.

10 Click your user name and type your password if necessary.

11 From the **Start** menu, display **Control Panel**, and then under **User Accounts and Family Safety** (or User Accounts), click **Add or remove user accounts.** Type your administrator password if necessary.

12 Click the **B Hewitt** account name to display the **Change an Account** window, and then under **Make changes to B Hewitt's account**, click **Delete the account.**

In the displayed Delete Account window, you have the option to keep the files and settings of the user you are about to delete. In those instances where you want to save these files, you can click Keep Files.

13 Click **Delete Files**, and then in the displayed **Confirm Deletion** window, click **Delete Account**.

14 **Close** [X] the **Manage Accounts** window.

15 Submit the two snip files that are the results of this project as directed by your instructor.

> More Knowledge | **Logging on the First Time with a New User Account**
>
> When a new account user logs on the first time, Windows indicates that a new desktop is being prepared. Recall that each user account has its own desktop and set of personal folders.

End **You have completed Project 1A**

Project 1B Working With Windows, Programs, and Files

Project Activities

In Activities 1.09 through 1.18, you will train with Steven Ramos and Barbara Hewitt, employees in the Information Technology Department at the Boston corporate office of the Bell Orchid Hotels, so that you will be able to open and use application programs, open data files, manage multiple windows on your desktop, and locate files and folders on your computer system. You will capture four screens that look similar to Figure 1.26.

Project Files

For Project 1B, you will need the following files:

Student Resource CD or a flash drive containing the student data files
New snip files

You will save your files as:

Lastname_Firstname_1B_Grouped_Snip
Lastname_Firstname_1B_WordPad_Snip
Lastname_Firstname_1B_SideBySide_Snip
Lastname_Firstname_1B_Snap_Snip

Project Results

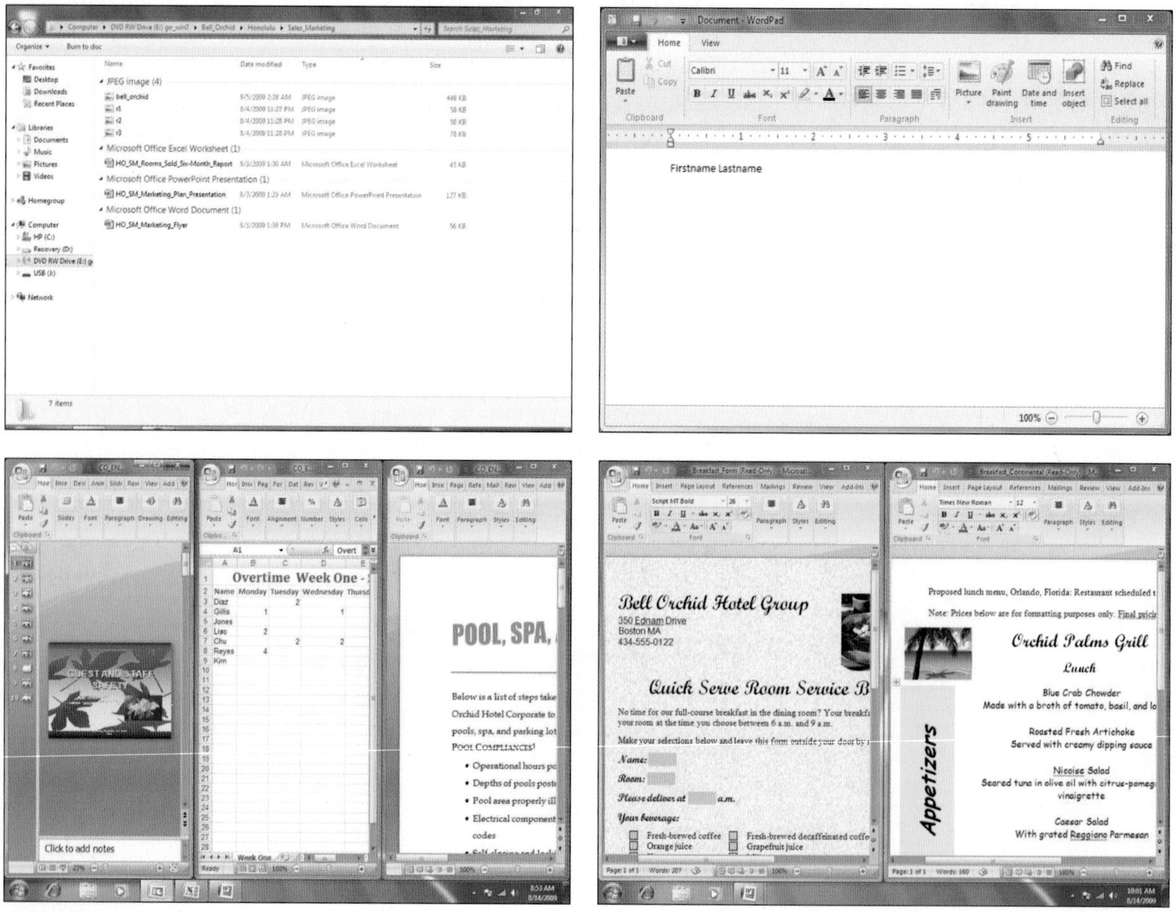

Figure 1.26
Project 1B Working With Windows, Programs, and Files

Objective 6 | Display Libraries, Folders, and Files in a Window

A file is the fundamental unit of storage that enables Windows 7 to distinguish one set of information from another. Recall that a file is a collection of information stored on a computer under a single name such as a Word document, an Excel workbook, a picture, a song, or a program.

A folder is the basic organizing tool for files. Recall that a folder is a container in which you store files. In a folder, you can store files that are related to one another. You can also put a folder inside of another folder, which is referred to as a subfolder. You can create any number of subfolders, and each can hold any number of files and additional subfolders.

Windows 7 arranges folders in a structure that resembles a ***hierarchy***—an arrangement where items are ranked and where each level is lower in rank than the item above it. In this manner, a hierarchy gives a visual representation of related files and folders. The hierarchy of folders is referred to as the ***folder structure***. A sequence of folders in the folder structure that leads to a specific file or folder is a path.

A library is a collection of items, such as files and folders, assembled from various locations; the locations might be on your computer, on an external hard drive connected to your computer, or on another computer in your network. A library does not actually store your items; rather, a library provides a single access point from which you can open folders and files from different locations.

Activity 1.09 | Displaying Libraries, Folders, and Files in a Folder Window

When you open a folder or library, a folder window displays. The folder window is the one feature you will use most often in Windows 7. A folder window shows you the contents of a folder or library. The design of the folder window helps you navigate—explore within the folder structure for the purpose of finding files and folders—Windows 7 so that you can save and locate your files and folders efficiently.

In this activity, you will open a folder window and examine its parts.

1 Log on to your computer to display your Windows 7 desktop, and then click the **Start** button. At the top of the right section, locate your user account name under the picture, point to the name to display the **ScreenTip** *Open your personal folder*, and then compare your screen with Figure 1.27.

A ***ScreenTip*** displays useful information when you perform various mouse actions, such as pointing to screen elements.

For each user account, Windows 7 creates a desktop and a ***personal folder***, and for the logged on user, the folder is always located at the top of the Start menu in this manner. Within the personal folder for each user account, Windows 7 creates a number of subfolders, some of which also display on the Start menu for your convenience; for example, *Documents*, *Pictures*, *Music*, and *Games*.

Figure 1.27

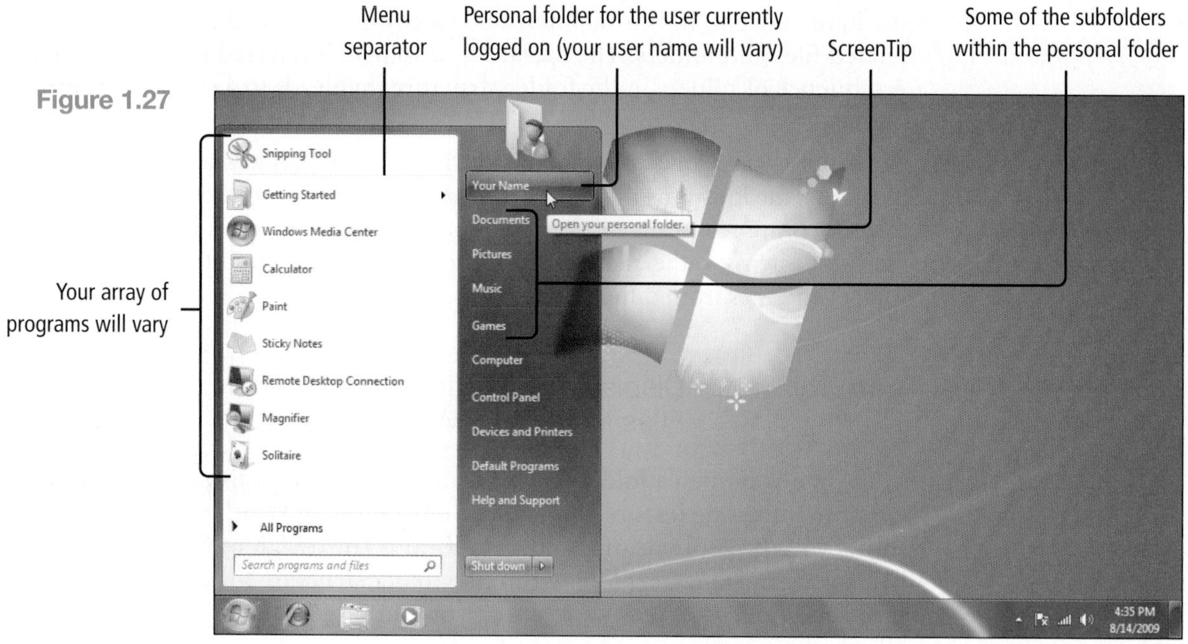

2 Click your user name, and then compare your screen with Figure 1.28.

For each user account, Windows 7 creates this group of folders. If you have set up other users on your system with passwords, they cannot access your set of folders when they are logged in.

Figure 1.28

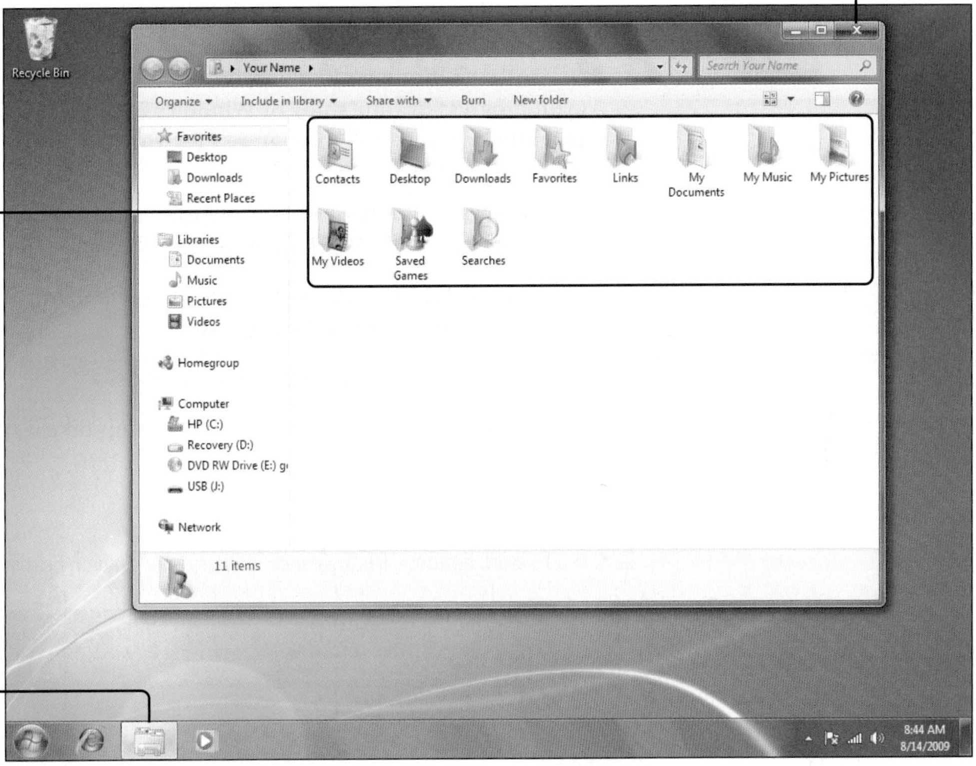

3 In the upper right corner of the window, click the **Close** button to close the window.

4 On the taskbar, click the **Windows Explorer** button to display the **Libraries** window.

Windows Explorer is the program within Windows 7 that displays the contents of libraries, folders, and files on your computer, and which also enables you to perform tasks related to your files and folders such as copying, moving, and renaming. Windows Explorer is at work any time you are viewing the contents of a library, a folder, or a file.

By default, the Windows Explorer button on the taskbar opens your Libraries. As you progress in your study of Windows 7, you will see that storing all of your files within a library will make it easy for you to find your files quickly when you need them.

The Windows Explorer icon shows a group of file folders to remind you that this program helps you find and organize your files and folders.

Another Way

Point to Documents, right-click to display a shortcut menu, and then click Open.

5 Under the text *Open a library to see your files and arrange them by folder, date, and other properties*, double-click **Documents**.

The window for the Documents library displays.

6 Compare your screen with Figure 1.29, and then take a moment to study the parts of the window as described in the table in Figure 1.30.

Figure 1.29

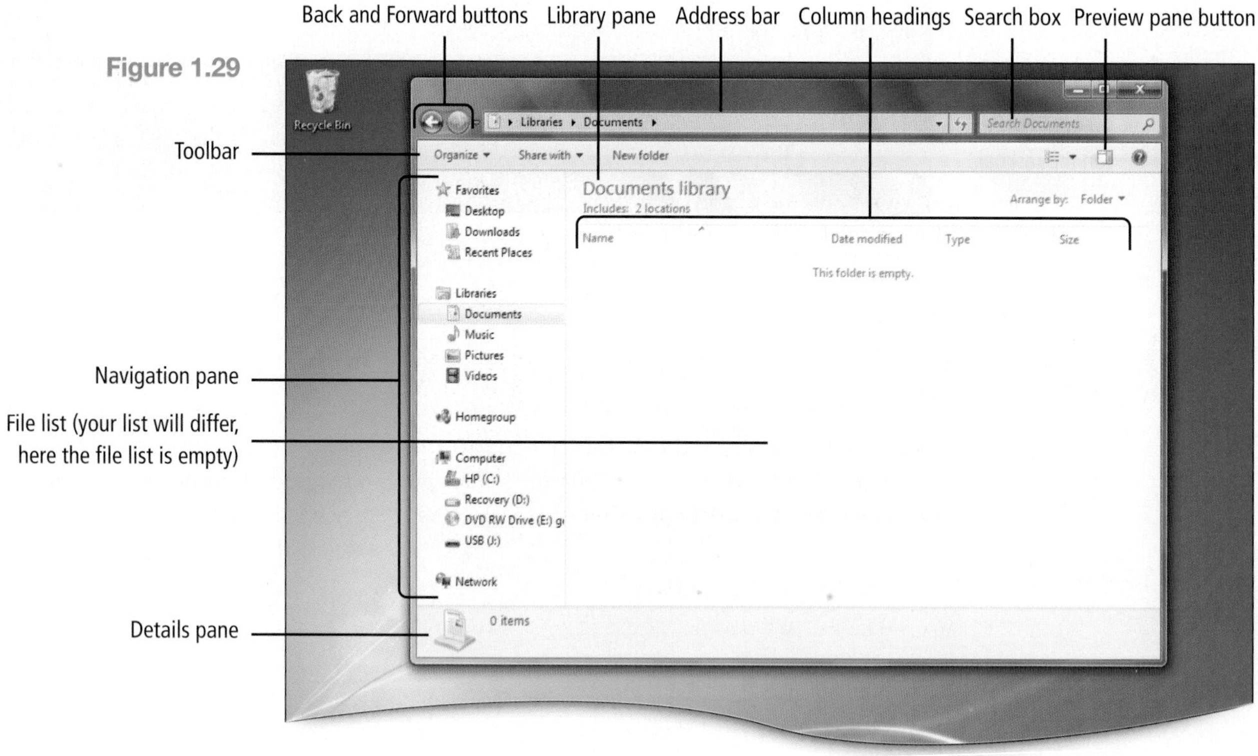

Parts of the Documents Library Window

Window Part	Function
Address bar	Displays your current location in the file structure as a series of links separated by arrows.
Back and Forward buttons	Provides the ability to navigate to other folders you have already opened without closing the current folder window. These buttons work with the address bar; that is, after you use the address bar to change folders, you can use the Back button to return to the previous folder.
Column headings	Identify the columns. By clicking on the column heading, you can change how the files in the file list are organized; by clicking on the arrow on the right, you can sort items in the file list.
Details pane	Displays the most common properties associated with the selected file.
File list	Displays the contents of the current folder or library. If you type text into the Search box, only the folders and files that match your search will display here—including files in subfolders.
Library pane	Enables you to customize the library or arrange files by different ***file properties***—information about the files, such as the author, the date the file was last changed, and any descriptive ***tags*** (a property that you create to help you find and organize your files) you might have added to the file. This pane displays only when you are in a library, such as the Documents library.
Navigation pane	Displays Favorites, Libraries, a Homegroup if you have one, and an expandable list of drives and folders in an area on the left side of a folder window. Use Favorites to open your most commonly used folders and searches; use Libraries to access your libraries. If you have a folder that you use frequently, you can drag it to the Favorites area so that it is always available.
Preview pane button	Opens an additional pane on the right side of the file list to display a preview of a file (not a folder) that you select in the file list.
Search box	Enables you to type a word or phrase and then searches for a file or subfolder stored in the current folder that contains matching text. The search begins as soon as you begin typing, so for example, if you type *G*, all the files that start with the letter *G* will display in the file list.
Toolbar	Provides buttons with which you can perform common tasks, such as changing the appearance of your files and folders, copying files to a CD, or starting a digital picture slide show. The buttons change in context with the type of file selected; for example, if a picture file is selected, different buttons display than if a music file is selected.

Figure 1.30

7 With the **Documents** folder window displayed, insert the **Student Resource CD** that came with this book—or a USB flash drive containing the files. Wait a few moments, and then **Close** the **AutoPlay** window that displays when removable media is inserted. In the **navigation pane**, under **Computer**, scroll down as necessary, and notice that your DVD or other inserted device displays.

Alert! | If you are not using the Student Resource CD

If your student data files are on a USB flash drive instead of a CD, insert the USB flash drive, and then in the following steps, select the appropriate USB flash drive instead of the CD.

8 Move your pointer anywhere into the **navigation pane**, and notice that a **black arrow** ◢ displays to the left of *Favorites*, *Libraries*, and *Computer*, to indicate that these items are expanded, and a **white arrow** ▷ displays to the right of items that are collapsed (hidden).

You can click these arrows to collapse and expand areas in the navigation pane.

9 In the **navigation pane**, under **Computer**, click your **CD/DVD** (or USB device) one time to display its contents in the **file list**. Compare your screen with Figure 1.31.

In the navigation pane, *Computer* displays all of the drive letter locations attached to your computer, including the internal hard drives, CD or DVD drives, and any connected devices such as USB flash drive.

Figure 1.31

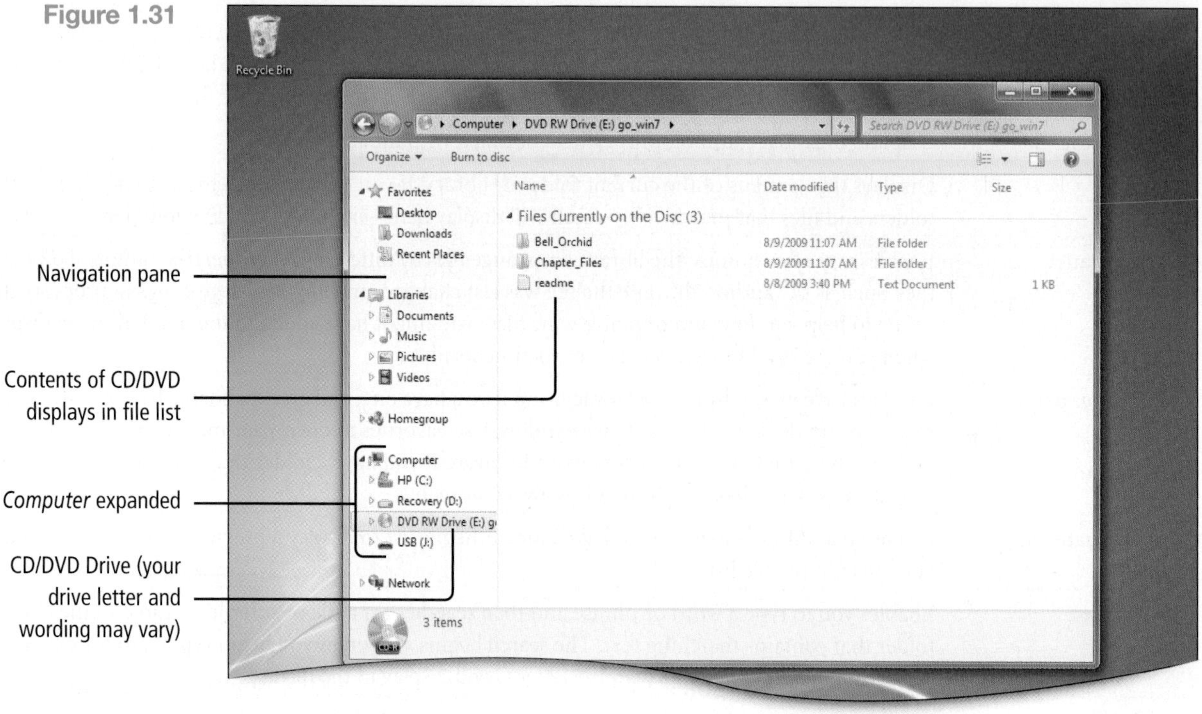

> **Another Way**
>
> Right-click the folder, and then click Open.

10 In the **file list**, double-click **Bell_Orchid** to display the subfolders.

Recall that the corporate office of the Bell Orchid Hotels is in Boston. The corporate office maintains subfolders labeled for each of its large hotels in Honolulu, Orlando, San Diego, and Santa Barbara.

11 In the **file list**, double-click **Orlando** to display the subfolders, and then look at the **address bar** to view the path. Compare your screen with Figure 1.32.

Within each city's subfolder, there is a structure of subfolders for the Accounting, Engineering, Food and Beverage, Human Resources, Operations, and Sales and Marketing departments.

Because folders can be placed inside of other folders, such an arrangement is common when organizing files on a computer.

In the address bar, the path from your CD/DVD (or flash drive) to the Bell_Orchid folder to the Orlando folder displays as a series of links.

Figure 1.32

Address bar displays path as links

Department subfolders in the Orlando folder

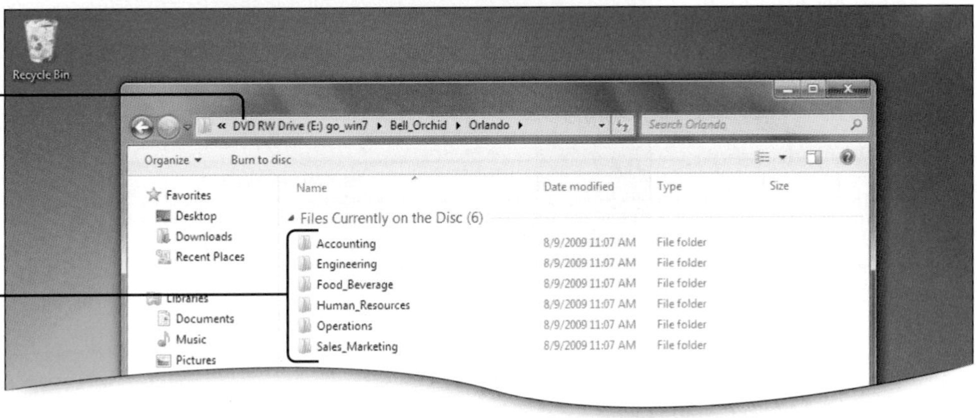

12 In the **address bar**, to the right of **Bell_Orchid**, click the ▶ arrow to display a list of the subfolders in the **Bell_Orchid** folder. On the list that displays, notice that **Orlando** displays in bold indicating it is open in the file list. Then, on the list, click **Honolulu**.

The subfolders within the Honolulu folder display.

13 In the **address bar**, to the right of **Bell_Orchid**, click the ▶ arrow again to display the subfolders in the **Bell_Orchid** folder. Then, on the **address bar** (not on the list), point to **Honolulu** and notice that the list of subfolders in the **Honolulu** folder displays.

After you display one set of subfolders in the address bar, all of the links are active and you need only point to them to display the list of subfolders.

Clicking an arrow to the right of a folder name in the address bar displays a list of the subfolders in that folder. You can click a subfolder name to display its contents. In this manner, the address bar is not only a path, but it is also an active control with which you can step from the current folder directly to any other folder above it in the folder structure just by clicking on a folder name.

> **Another Way**
> In the file list, double-click the Sales_Marketing folder.

14 On the list of subfolders for **Honolulu**, click **Sales_Marketing** to display its contents in the file list. Compare your screen with Figure 1.33.

The files in the Sales_Marketing folder for Honolulu display. To the left of each file name, an icon indicates the program used to create each file. Here, there is one PowerPoint file, one Excel file, one Word file, and four JPEG images.

Figure 1.33

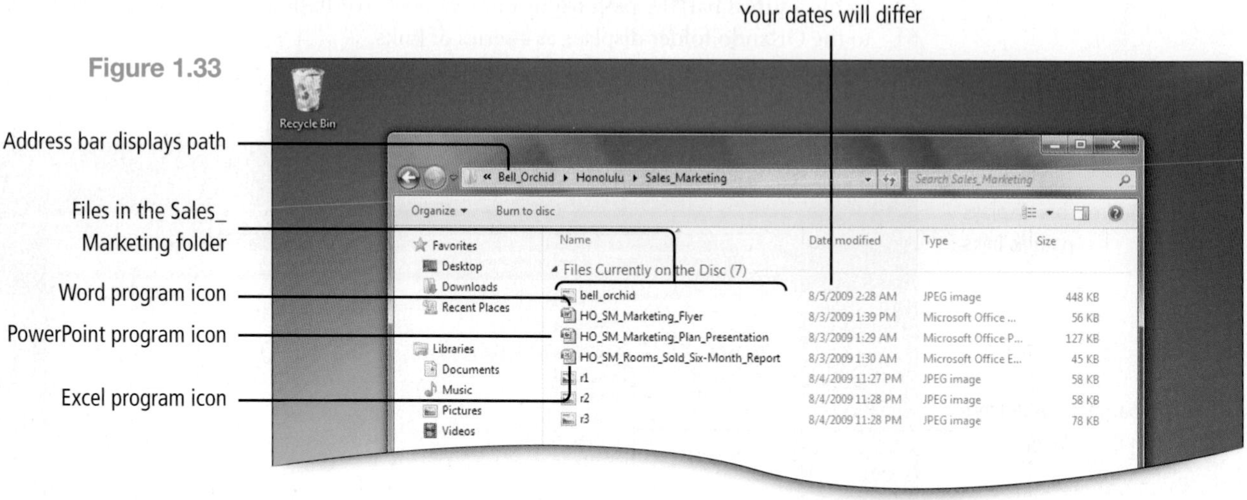

15 In the upper left corner of the folder window, click the **Back** button.

The Back button retraces each of your clicks in the same manner as clicking the Back button when you are browsing the Internet.

> **Another Way**
> Point to the folder, right-click, and then click Open.

16 In the **file list**, point to the **Human_Resources** folder, and double-click to open the folder.

17 In the **file list**, click one time to select the PowerPoint file **HO_HR_New_Employee_Presentation**. At the bottom of the window, notice the **details pane**, which displays information about the selected file.

18 In the upper right corner of the window, click the **Preview Pane** button [Preview Pane button] to display the first slide of the PowerPoint file in the **preview pane**. Compare your screen with Figure 1.34.

In the preview pane that displays on the right, you can use the scroll bar to scroll through the slides in the presentation; or, you can click the up or down scroll arrow to view the slides.

Figure 1.34

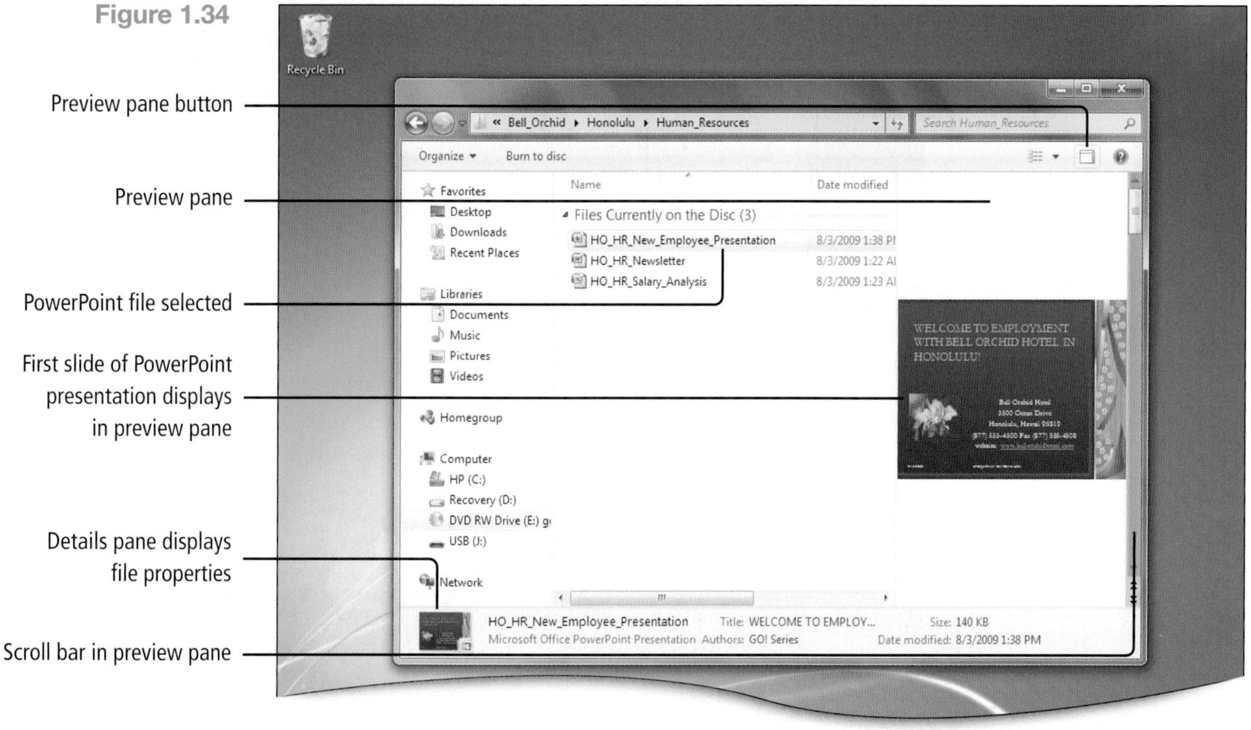

19 In the upper right corner, click the **Preview Pane** button again [Preview Pane button] to close the preview pane.

Use the preview pane when you want to look at a file quickly without actually opening it.

Activity 1.10 | Using the Navigation Pane to Display the Folder Structure

When it is useful to do so, you can use the navigation pane on the left side of a folder window to navigate files and folders and to display the folder structure.

1 On the left side of the window, in the lower portion of the **navigation pane**, point to your **CD/DVD** drive or USB device containing the student files, and then click the white expand arrow ▷ to display the two subfolders immediately below the name of your CD/DVD drive.

2 To the left of **Bell_Orchid**, click the expand arrow ▷ to display the subfolders. Scroll down if necessary, and then to the left of **San_Diego**, click the expand arrow ▷ to display the subfolders. Compare your screen with Figure 1.35.

In the navigation pane, the folder structure is shown in a visual hierarchy.

Figure 1.35

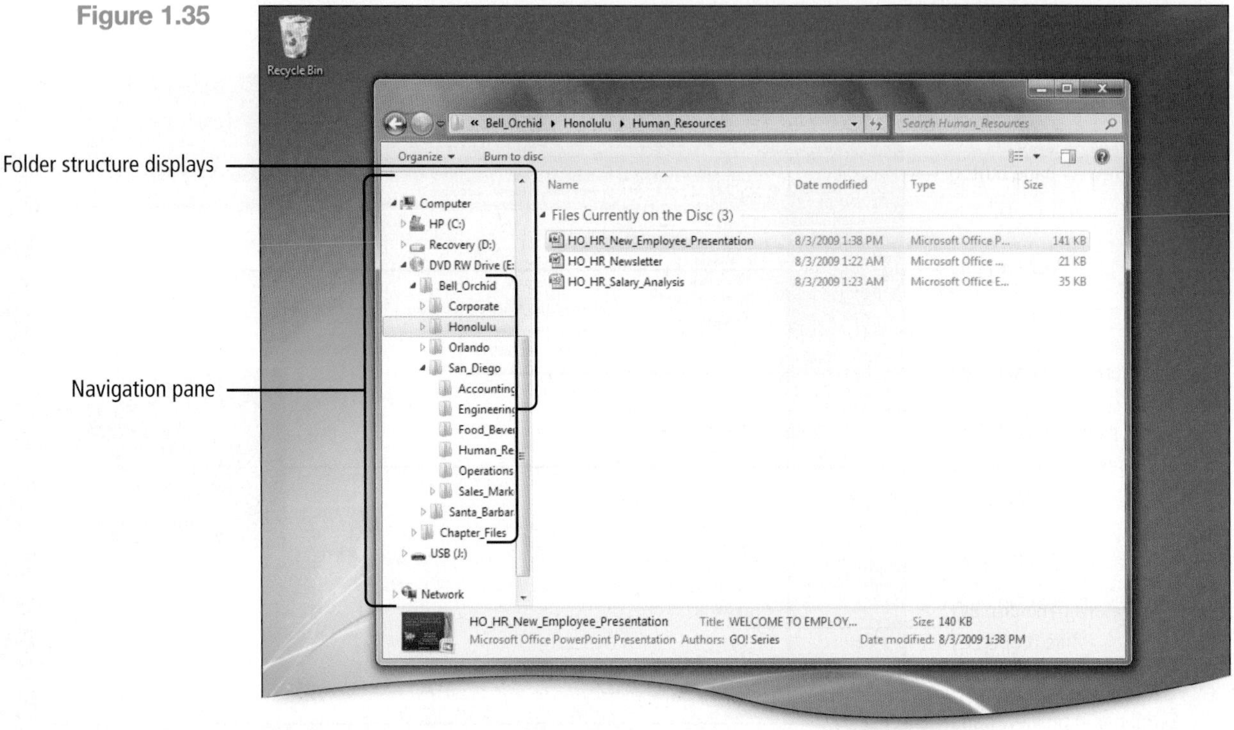

3 In the **navigation pane**, under **San_Diego**, click **Accounting** to display the files in the Accounting subfolder in the file list.

Optionally, you can hide the display of the navigation pane, but it is recommended that you leave the navigation pane displayed because of its usefulness in displaying the drives on your computer and the folder structure when you want to see the structure in a hierarchical view.

4 In the upper right corner of the window, click the **Close** button.

Activity 1.11 | Changing Views, Sorting, Grouping, and Filtering in a Folder Window

When looking at a list of files and folders in a folder window, there are a variety of useful arrangements in which you can view your data.

1 Be sure the device that contains the student files that accompany this textbook is inserted in your computer—either the Student Resource CD or a USB flash drive. Also, be sure that the removable storage device you are using to store files is inserted—this can be the same device on which the student files are located.

2 On the taskbar, click the **Windows Explorer** button. In the **navigation pane**, click **Computer** to display in the **file list** all the disk drives and removable devices attached to your computer.

3 In the upper right corner of the **Computer** window, on the toolbar, click the **View button arrow** . Compare your screen with Figure 1.36.

By default, the Computer window displays in Tiles view—small icons arranged in two columns. Seeing the icons helps you distinguish what type of devices are attached. For example, a CD or DVD displays a disc icon.

The Computer window is divided into the Hard Disk Drives section and the Devices with Removable Storage section.

Figure 1.36

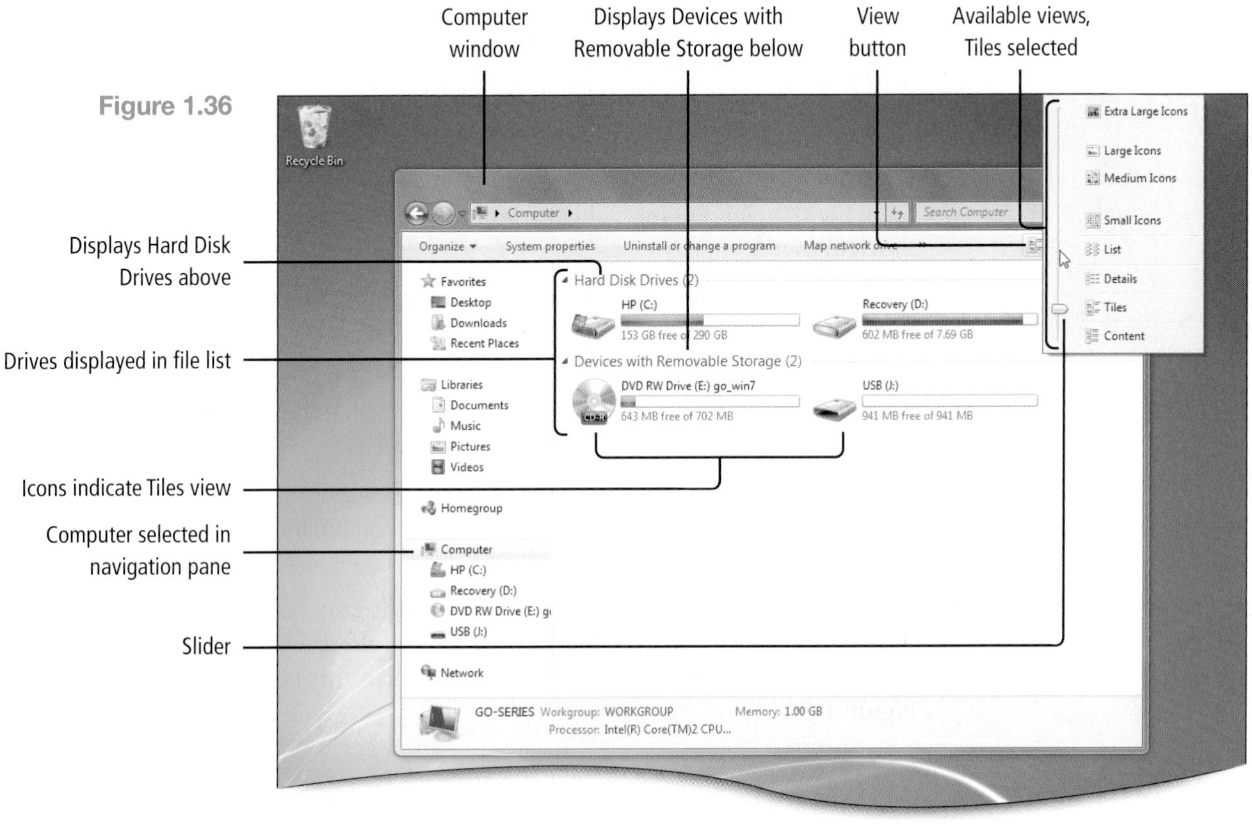

4 In the list of available views, drag the slider to the **Details** view, release the mouse button, and then notice the columnar arrangement in the **file list**. Click the **View button arrow** again, and this time, drag the slider up slowly, but do not release the left mouse button—instead, pause at each view and notice how the view in the **file list** changes as you move from one to the next.

5 Set the view to **Large Icons**, and then determine if you see the Windows logo on one of the hard disk drives.

On your own computer, you might see the Windows logo on the hard drive, which indicates the drive on which the Windows 7 operating system is installed. In a college lab, this may not display. In this manner, some views are convenient for different purposes.

6 Return the view to the Computer window's default **Tiles** view. In the **file list**, double-click the **CD/DVD drive** to display its contents. In the **file list**, double-click the **Bell_Orchid** folder to open it. Open the **Honolulu** folder to display its subfolders. In the list of **Honolulu** subfolders, open the **Sales_Marketing** folder.

7 Click the **View button arrow** [button], and notice that the default view for a list of files is the **Details** view. Slowly drag the slider up, pausing to examine each view in the file list, and then set the view to **Large Icons**.

The near-photographic quality of Windows 7 enables you to actually read the first slide in the PowerPoint file HO_SM_Marketing_Plan_Presentation. These are ***Live Icons***—for some applications, they display a small picture of the actual contents of each file or folder.

8 Click the **View button arrow** [button], and then set the view to **Content**.

Content view displays a vertical list that includes the program icon, the date the file was last modified, the file size, and other properties such as author names or tags. Information like this is referred to as ***metadata***, which is the data that describes other data; for example, the collective group of a file's properties, such as its title, subject, author, and file size.

9 Click the **View button arrow** [button], and then click **Details**. In the **file list**, point to the Excel file **HO_SM_Rooms_Sold_Six-Month_Report** and then right-click to display a shortcut menu.

From the shortcut menu, you can perform various tasks with the selected file. For example, you can open it—which will simultaneously start the program in which the file was created— print it, or copy it.

10 In the upper right corner of the folder window, click the **Maximize** button [button], and then notice that the folder window fills the screen.

When you are working with folder windows, enlarge or maximize windows as necessary to make it easier to view your work. The Maximize command optimizes your workspace for a single window.

11 In the column headings area, point to the light gray line on the right side of the **Type** column until the [pointer] pointer displays, hold down the left mouse button, and then drag to the right until all of the text in this column displays, as shown in Figure 1.37.

Figure 1.37

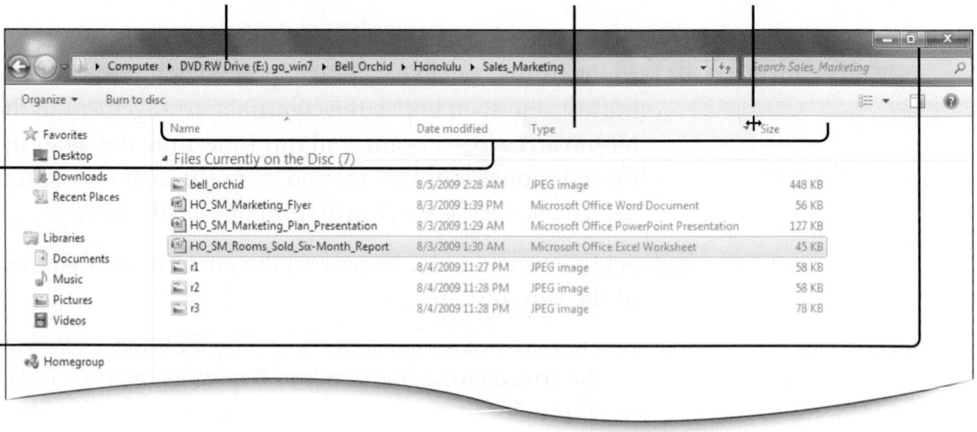

12 Point to the **Name** column heading and right-click. On the displayed shortcut menu, click **Size All Columns to Fit**.

The width of all columns adjusts to fit the contents.

13 Click the **Name** column heading to select it and notice the pale arrow near the upper edge. Click the column heading **Name** several times and notice how the alphabetical order of the file names changes each time you click, as indicated by the arrow.

When a column heading is selected, a small up or down arrow displays at the top of the heading. Each time you click the column heading, you will alternate between sorting that column in ascending or descending order.

For text, ascending order is from A to Z and descending order is from Z to A. For numbers, ascending order is from smallest to largest, and descending order is from largest to smallest.

14 Be sure the **Name** column is sorted in ascending order—the pale arrow at the top of the column points upward. Point to the **Type** column heading, and then at the right end of the heading, click the **black arrow ▼**. Click the check box to the left of **Microsoft Excel Worksheet**, click in a blank area of the **file list** to close the menu, and then compare your screen with Figure 1.38.

The list is ***filtered*** by Excel files—only files that meet the criteria of being an Excel file display. When you filter the contents of a folder by a file property such as *Type*, only the files with that property display. If you have a long list of files, this is a useful tool to narrow the list of files that you are looking at.

When you see a check mark at the right end of a column heading in this manner, you will know that the list is filtered.

Figure 1.38

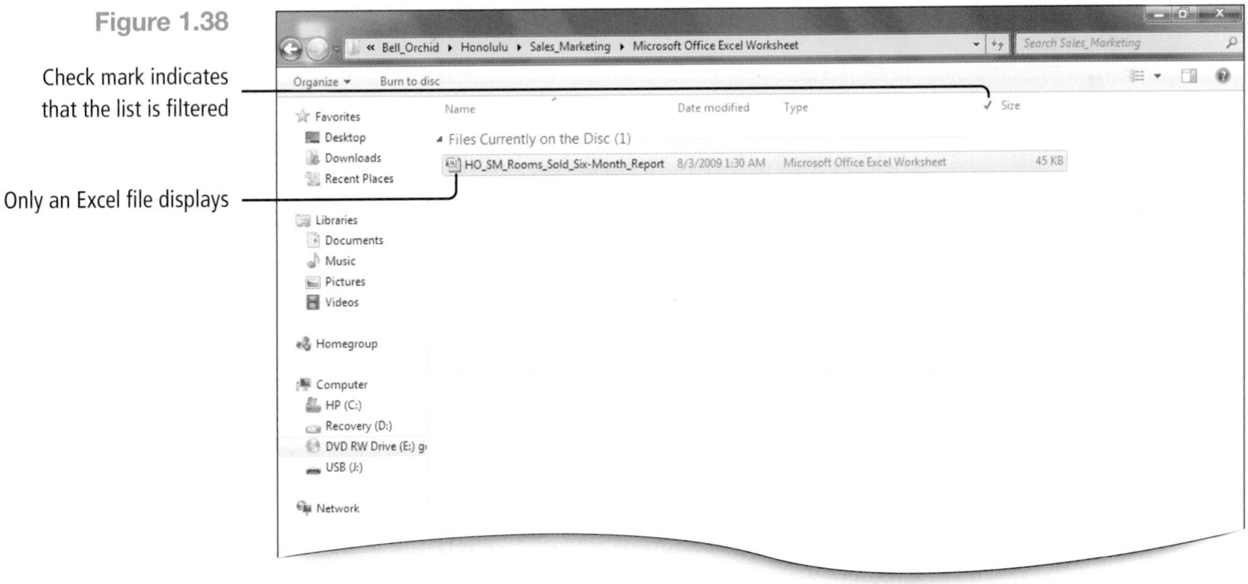

15 Point to the column heading **Type**, click the check mark that displays at the right, and then click to clear the check box to the left of **Microsoft Excel Worksheet** to redisplay all the files in the folder.

16 Click anywhere in a blank area of the file list, and then right-click. On the shortcut menu, point to **Group by**, and then on the submenu, click **Type**. If necessary, click the **Type** column heading to sort it in ascending order. Compare your screen with Figure 1.39.

The files are grouped by type, and the types are in alphabetical order. That is, JPEG is first, followed by Microsoft Excel, and so on. When you group files by a file property such as *Type*, a separate group will display for each file type, and a heading identifies each group and indicates the number of files in the group.

Figure 1.39

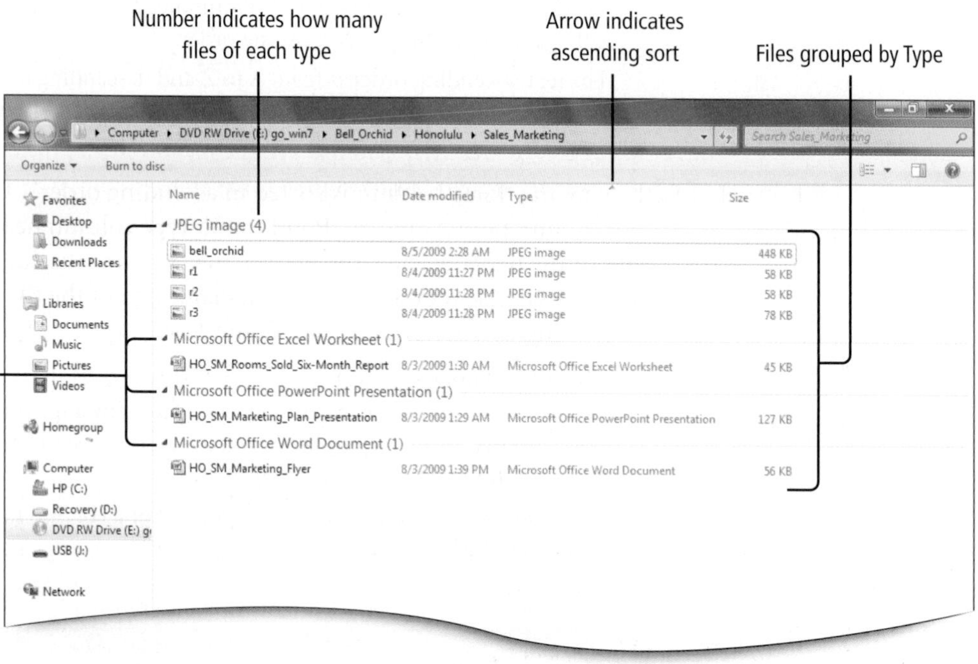

17 Display the **Start** menu, and then either from the pinned programs area, or by clicking All Programs, Accessories, and then Snipping Tool, display the **Snipping Tool window**.

18 Click the **New arrow**, click **Window Snip**, click anywhere in the **Sales_Marketing** folder window to select the window, and then on the **Snipping Tool** mark-up window's toolbar, click the **Save Snip** button.

19 In the **Save As** dialog box, in the **navigation pane** on the left, drag the scroll bar down as necessary to view **Computer**. Under **Computer**, click the name of your USB flash drive.

20 In the **file list**, scroll as necessary, locate and double-click your **Windows 7 Chapter 1** folder.

21 In the **File name** box and using your own name, type **Lastname_Firstname_1B_Grouped_Snip** Be sure the file type is **JPEG**. Click the **Save** button, and then **Close** the **Snipping Tool** window. Hold this file until you finish Project 1B, and then submit this file as directed by your instructor.

22 Right-click in a blank area of the **file list**, point to **Group by**, and then click **(None)** to ungroup the files.

23 In the upper right corner, click the **Restore Down** button, and then **Close** all open windows.

Restore Down returns the window to the size it was before you maximized it.

Objective 7 | Start Programs and Open Data Files

When you are using the software programs installed on your computer, you create and save data files—the documents, worksheets, databases, songs, pictures, and so on that you need for your job or personal use. Thus, most of your work with Windows 7 is concerned with locating and starting your programs and locating and opening your files.

You can start programs from the Start menu or from the desktop by creating a shortcut to the program there. You can open your data files from within the program in which they were created, or you can open a data file from a folder window, which will simultaneously start the program and open your file.

Activity 1.12 | Starting Programs and Opening Data Files

One way to start a program is from one of the three areas of the Start menu: the upper left, which displays the programs you have pinned there for easy access; the bottom left, which displays programs that you have recently used; or the All Programs list.

1 Be sure the Student Resource CD or flash drive containing the student data files is inserted in your computer. From the **Start** menu, point to **All Programs**, locate and click the **Accessories** folder, and then on the displayed list, click **Paint**. Compare your screen with Figure 1.40.

Paint is a program that comes with Windows 7 with which you can create and edit drawings and display and edit stored photos.

Recall that *All Programs* lists all of the programs available on your computer. If your list of programs is larger than the window, a scroll bar displays so that you can scroll the list. Names that display a file folder icon to the left will open to display the programs within the folder.

Figure 1.40

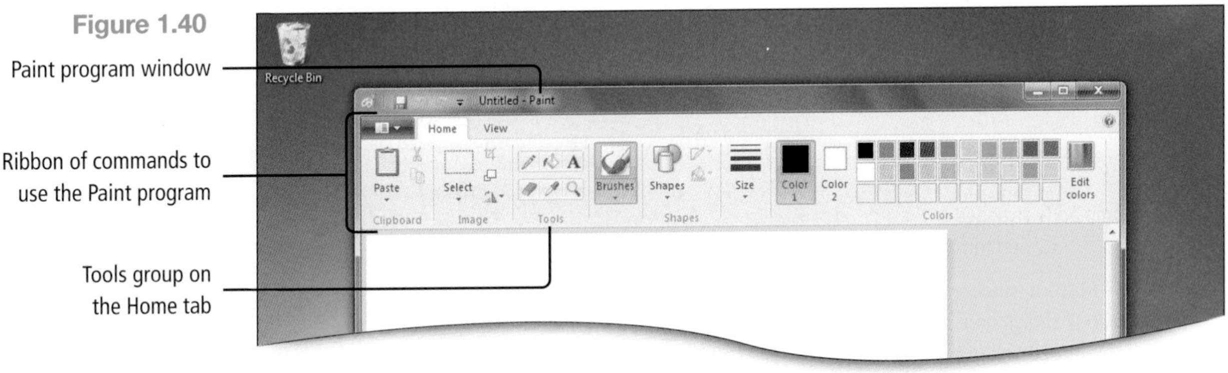

2 On the **Ribbon** across the top of the window, with the **Home tab** active, in the **Tools group**, click the **Pencil** icon. Move your mouse pointer into the white drawing area, hold down the left mouse button, and then try writing your first name in the white area of the window.

3 In the upper left corner, to the left of the **Home tab**, click the blue tab—the **Paint** tab— to display a menu of commands of things you can do with your picture.

4 On the **Paint** menu, click **Exit**. In the displayed message, click **Don't Save**.

Messages like this display in most programs to prevent you from forgetting to save your work. A file saved in the Paint program creates a graphic file in the JPEG format.

5 Display the **Start** menu 🪟, and then at the bottom of the menu, notice that your insertion point is blinking in the box labeled *Search programs and files*. Type **wordpad** When the program name displays in the list above, click the name to open the program. Notice that this program window has characteristics similar to the Paint program window; for example, it has a Ribbon of commands.

> If you do not immediately see a program on the All Programs list, type all or part of the name in the Search box in this manner. WordPad is another program included with Windows 7; it is a convenient program for simple word processing tasks.

6 With the insertion point blinking in the document window, type your first and last name.

7 From the **Start** menu 🪟, start **Snipping Tool** and create a **Window Snip**. Click anywhere in the WordPad window to display the **Snipping Tool** mark-up window. Save the snip in the chapter folder you created on your flash drive as **Lastname_Firstname_1B_WordPad_Snip** Hold this file until you finish Project 1B, and then submit this file as directed by your instructor.

8 **Close** ❌ the **Snipping Tool** window. In the upper right corner of the **WordPad** window, click the **Close** button ❌, and then click **Don't Save**.

9 From the **Start** menu 🪟, point to **All Programs**, click the **Microsoft Office** folder, and then from the displayed list, click **Microsoft Word**. Compare your screen with Figure 1.41.

Note | Version of Microsoft Office

You can use either Microsoft Word 2007 or Microsoft Word 2010.

The Word program window has features that are common to other programs you have opened; for example, commands are arranged on tabs. When you create and save data in Word, you create a Word document file.

Figure 1.41

Commands arranged on tabs

Word program window (Word 2007 shown here, Word 2010 has a similar arrangement)

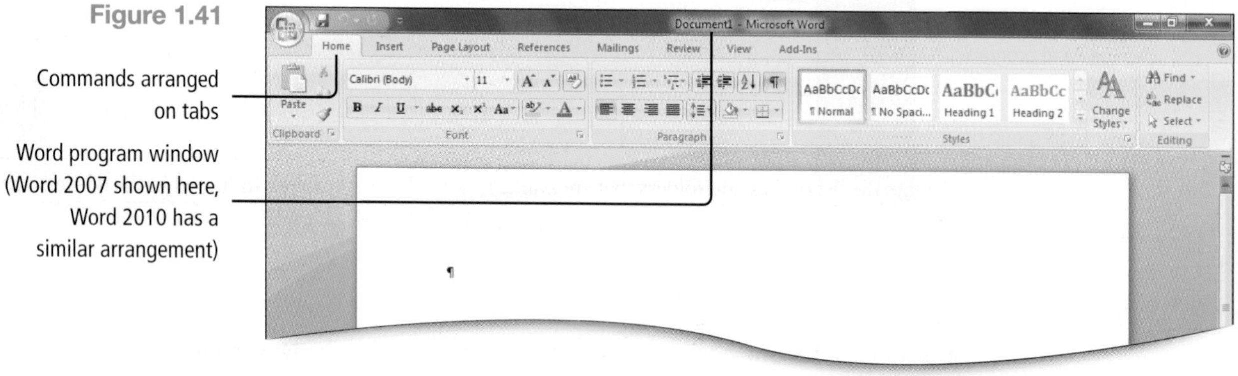

10 Press Ctrl + F12 to display the **Open** dialog box. Compare your screen with Figure 1.42, and then take a moment to study the table in Figure 1.43.

Recall that a dialog box is a window containing options for completing a task; its layout is similar to that of a folder window. When you are working in a program, use the Open dialog box to locate and open existing files that were created in the program.

By default, the Open dialog box displays the path to the *Documents* library of the user logged on. On your own computer, you can create a folder structure within the Documents library to store your documents. Alternatively, you can use the skills you have practiced to navigate to other locations on your computer, such as your removable USB flash drive.

Figure 1.42

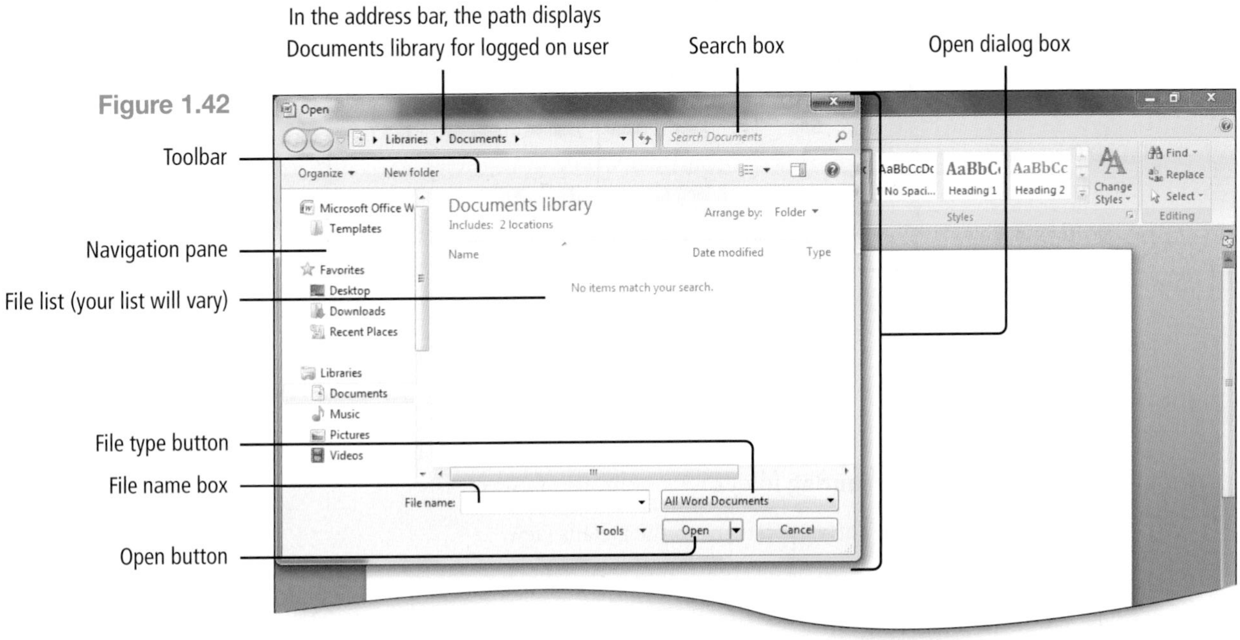

Dialog Box Element	Function
Address bar	Displays the path in the library or folder structure; by default, the path displays the Documents library for the active user.
File list	Displays the list of files and folders that are available in the library or folder indicated in the address bar.
File name box	Enables you to type the name of a specific file to locate it.
File type button	Enables you to restrict the type of files displayed in the file list, for example the default, All Word Documents, restricts the type of files displayed to only Word documents. You can click the arrow and adjust the restrictions to a narrower or wider group of files.
Navigation pane	Enables access to Favorites, Libraries, and Computer.
Search box	Filters the file list based on text that you type; the search is based on text in the file name and in the file itself, and on other properties that you can specify. The search takes place in the current folder or library, as displayed in the address bar, and in any subfolders within that folder.
Toolbar	Displays relevant tasks; for example, creating a new folder.

Figure 1.43

11 In the **navigation pane**, scroll down as necessary, and then under **Computer**, click your **CD/DVD Drive**. In the **file list**, double-click the **Bell_Orchid** folder to open it and display its contents in the file list. Click the **View button arrow**, and then set the view to **Large Icons**. Compare your screen with Figure 1.44.

Notice that the Live Icons feature indicates that each folder contains additional subfolders.

Figure 1.44

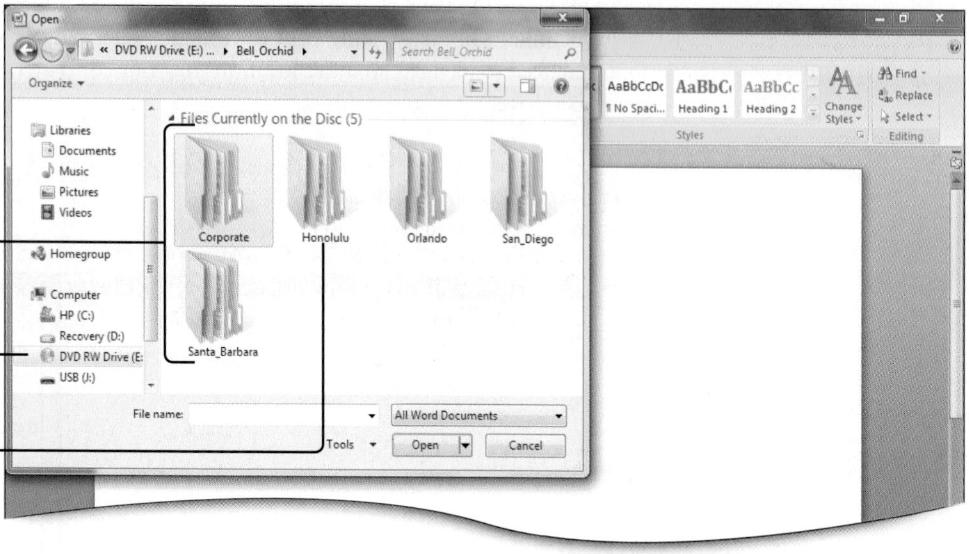

12 In the **file list**, double-click the **Corporate** folder, and then double-click the **Accounting** folder.

The view returns to the Details view.

13 In the **file list**, notice that only one document—a Word document—displays. In the lower right corner, locate the **File type** button, and notice that *All Word Documents* displays as the file type. Click the **File type arrow**, and then from the displayed list, click **All Files**. Compare your screen with Figure 1.45.

When you change the file type to *All Files*, you can see that the Word file is not the only file in this folder. By default, the Open dialog box displays only the files created in the active program; however, you can display variations of file types in this manner.

Figure 1.45

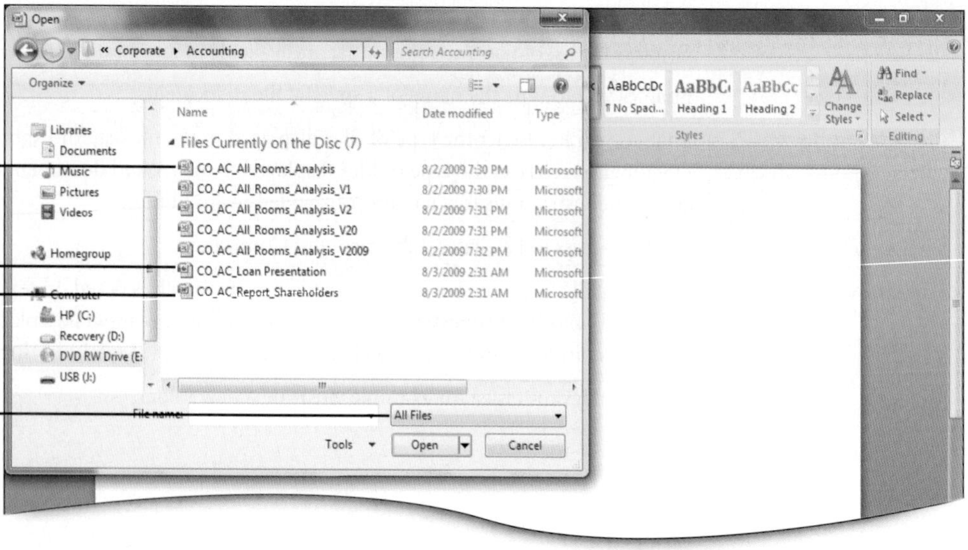

Microsoft Office file types are identified by small icons, which is a convenient way to differentiate one type of file from another. Although you can view all the files in the folder, you can open only the files that were created in the active program, which in this instance is Microsoft Word.

14 Change the file type back to **All Word Documents**. Then in the **file list**, double-click the **CO_AC_Report_Shareholders** Word file to open the document. Take a moment to scroll through the document.

15 **Close** the Word window. On the taskbar at the bottom of your screen, click the **Windows Explorer** button. In the **navigation pane**, under **Computer**, click your **CD/DVD Drive** to display its contents in the file list.

16 In the **file list**, open the **Bell_Orchid** folder, then open the **Corporate** folder, and then open the **Accounting** folder.

17 In the **file list**, double-click the **CO_AC_Loan_Presentation** file. When the **PowerPoint** window displays, if necessary **Maximize** the program window. Compare your screen with Figure 1.46.

Figure 1.46

PowerPoint program window

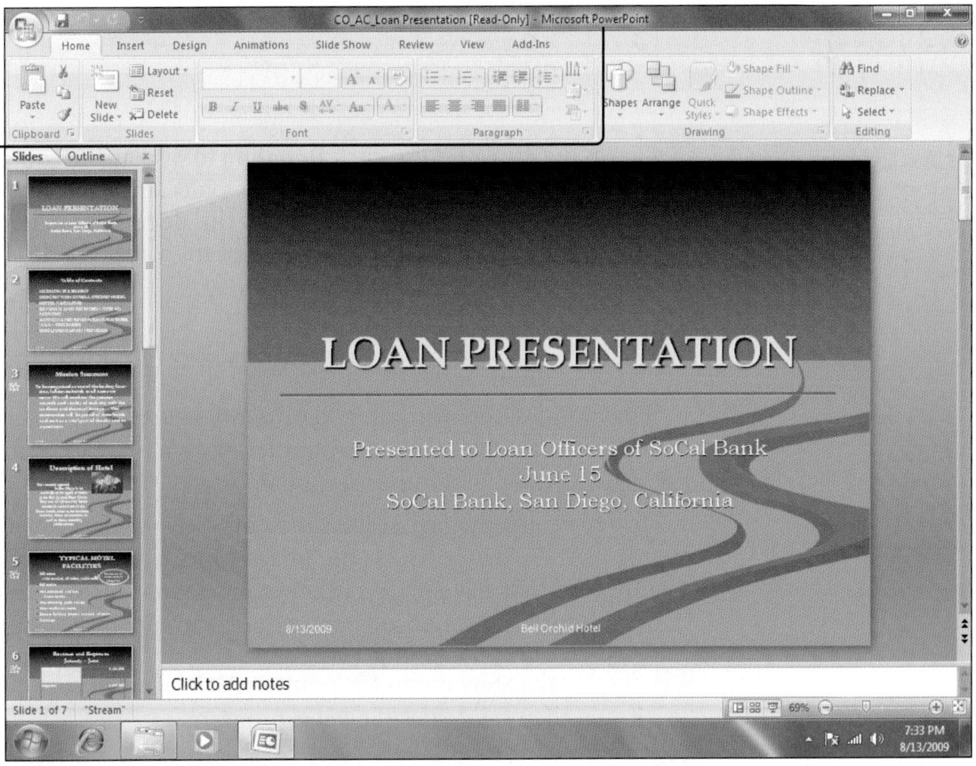

18 **Close** the PowerPoint program window.

Another Way

Expand each folder level in the navigation pane.

19 In the **address bar**, to the right of **Bell_Orchid**, click ▶, and then compare your screen with Figure 1.47.

Recall that the address bar is not just a path; rather, it contains active links from which you can click a folder name in the path, and then navigate directly to any displayed subfolders.

Figure 1.47

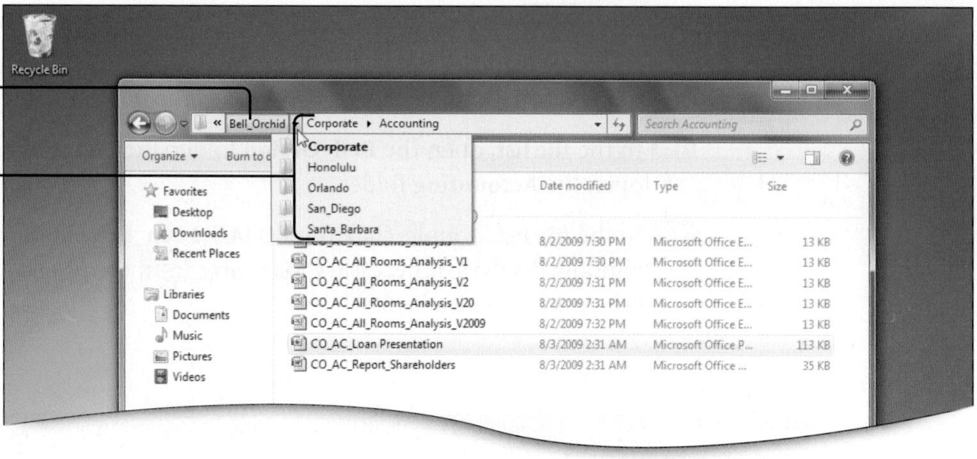

20 From the displayed list, click **Honolulu** to display the contents of the **Honolulu** folder in the **file list**. Open the **Food_Beverage** folder, and then open the **HO_FB_Banquet_Contract** file. Take a moment to view this document in the open Word program. **Close** [X] Word, and then **Close** [X] the folder window.

Activity 1.13 | Adding and Removing Desktop Icons

On your desktop, you can add or remove ***shortcuts***, which are desktop icons that link to any item accessible on your computer or on a network, such as a program, file, folder, disk drive, printer, or another computer.

You may already have some shortcuts on your desktop. By default, only one desktop icon displays in Windows 7—the Recycle Bin; however, your computer manufacturer or organization may have placed other icons, representing shortcuts, on your desktop. Many programs automatically create a desktop icon shortcut when they are installed.

1 Display the **Start** menu, point to **All Programs**, click the **Accessories** folder to open it, and then *right-click* the **Paint** program.

2 On the displayed shortcut menu, point to **Send to**, and then click **Desktop (create shortcut)**. Click anywhere on the desktop to close the Start menu, and then notice that an icon for the **Paint** program displays on the desktop.

If you want easy access from your desktop to a program, create a shortcut to the program by using this technique.

3 On the right side of the **Start** menu, *right-click* **Control Panel**. On the shortcut menu, click **Show on Desktop**. Click anywhere on the desktop to close the Start menu.

When creating desktop shortcuts, the command *Desktop (create shortcut)* creates an icon containing a small arrow like the Paint program shortcut. The command *Show on Desktop* displays an icon with no arrow like the Control Panel shortcut. Regardless, the icon will link you to the program, object, or location indicated.

4 On the taskbar, click the **Windows Explorer** button. In the **navigation pane**, click your **CD/DVD Drive**, and then in the **file list**, *right-click* the **Bell_Orchid** folder. On the shortcut menu, point to **Send to**, and then click **Desktop (create shortcut)**. **Close** the **Computer** window, and then compare your screen with Figure 1.48.

If you want easy access *from your desktop* to a folder or file that you use often, create shortcuts in this manner.

Figure 1.48

Desktop icon representing shortcut to Recycle Bin

Desktop icon representing shortcut to Control Panel

Desktop icon representing shortcut to Paint program

Desktop icon representing shortcut to Bell_Orchid folder on CD

5 Double-click the **Paint** desktop icon on your desktop, **Close** the **Paint** program, and then in a similar manner, test the other desktop icons that you created.

Because most of your work with Windows 7 is concerned with locating and opening your programs and files, you can see that using techniques like creating shortcuts on the desktop will speed your everyday computer work.

6 **Close** any open windows. On the desktop, point to the shortcut you created for the **Bell_Orchid** folder, right-click, and then on the shortcut menu, click **Delete**. Read the message that displays, and then click **Yes**.

When you delete shortcuts from the desktop, you are deleting only the shortcut icon; you are not deleting the actual programs or files associated with the icon. The shortcut icon serves only as a *pointer* to the actual location.

Note | If you *save* a file or folder directly to the desktop, deleting it from the desktop will delete the folder or file

If you *save* a file or create a folder directly on the desktop, it is stored there. The icon that displays is not a shortcut—it displays no arrow. If you delete that icon, you will delete the actual file or folder. The file or folder is still recoverable from the Recycle Bin until the Recycle Bin is emptied. The best organizing structure is to store all of your files in the appropriate library—Documents in the Documents library, and so on—and not clutter your desktop with individual files and folders. Likewise, avoid cluttering your desktop with too many program shortcut icons. As you progress in your study of Windows 7, you will see that the taskbar is a better place to create shortcuts to programs.

7 Point to the icon you created for the **Paint** program, hold down the left mouse button, drag the icon into the **Recycle Bin**, and then release the mouse button.

The ***Recycle Bin*** stores anything that you delete from your computer. Anything stored there can be retrieved, including the shortcuts that you just created, until the contents are permanently deleted by activating the Empty Recycle Bin command.

8 Using one of the techniques you have just practiced, remove the **Control Panel icon** from your desktop—do *not* remove the Recycle Bin icon.

More Knowledge | When is it a good idea to have desktop shortcuts for a program or a folder?

You have seen that removing shortcut icons from your desktop does not delete the actual files or programs associated with the icon. Rather, removing a shortcut deletes the pointer to the item. Thus, you can confidently remove from your desktop any shortcuts that are not useful to you.

For example, computer manufacturers commonly place shortcuts on the desktop for programs they hope you will purchase or use. Double-click each shortcut to see if it is of value to you, and if not, delete it from your desktop. Removing the shortcut does not remove the program or item, so if you decide you want this item later, it will still be available. If it is a program you will never use, also uninstall it from your computer by using the Uninstall a program command on the Control Panel.

Some computer manufacturers have started to reduce the number of shortcuts and offers to purchase programs on new computers because of complaints from consumers about the unnecessary confusion and clutter such shortcuts create. You should never feel obligated to use or purchase a program just because it appears on your computer. Remove those you do not want.

Placing desktop shortcuts for frequently used programs or folders directly on your desktop may seem convenient, but as you add more icons, your desktop becomes cluttered and the shortcuts are not as easy to find. A better organizing method is to use the taskbar for shortcuts to programs. For folders and files, the best organizing structure is to create a logical structure of folders within your Documents library.

You can also drag frequently-used folders to the Favorites area in the navigation pane so that they are available any time you open Windows Explorer. As you progress in your study of Windows 7 in this textbook, you will practice techniques for using the taskbar and the Favorites area of the navigation pane to streamline your work, instead of cluttering your desktop.

Objective 8 | Manage the Display of Individual and Multiple Windows

Activity 1.14 | Moving, Sizing, Hiding, Closing, and Switching Between Windows

When you start a program or open a folder, it displays in a window. A window is the screen element you work with most often in Windows 7. You can move, resize, maximize, minimize (hide from view), and close windows. You can also freely arrange and overlap multiple open windows on your screen, with the window currently in use on top.

1 From the **Start** menu, open the **WordPad** program—either from the recently used programs area on the left side, or by opening the Accessories folder from the All Programs menu.

2 Notice that in the taskbar, a button displays representing the open program, and the button displays a glass frame, indicating the program is open.

3 Point to the **WordPad** window's ***title bar***—the bar across the top of the window that displays the program name—to display the pointer, and then if necessary, drag the window until its position is approximately in the center of the desktop.

Use this technique to reposition any open window.

4 Point to the window's lower right corner until the pointer displays, and then drag up and to the left about 1 inch—the measurement need not be precise. Compare your screen with Figure 1.49.

When you drag the corner of a window in this manner, the window resizes both vertically and horizontally. You can resize a window by pointing to any of the window's borders or corners to display a two-headed arrow, and then drag the border or corner to shrink or enlarge the window.

Figure 1.49

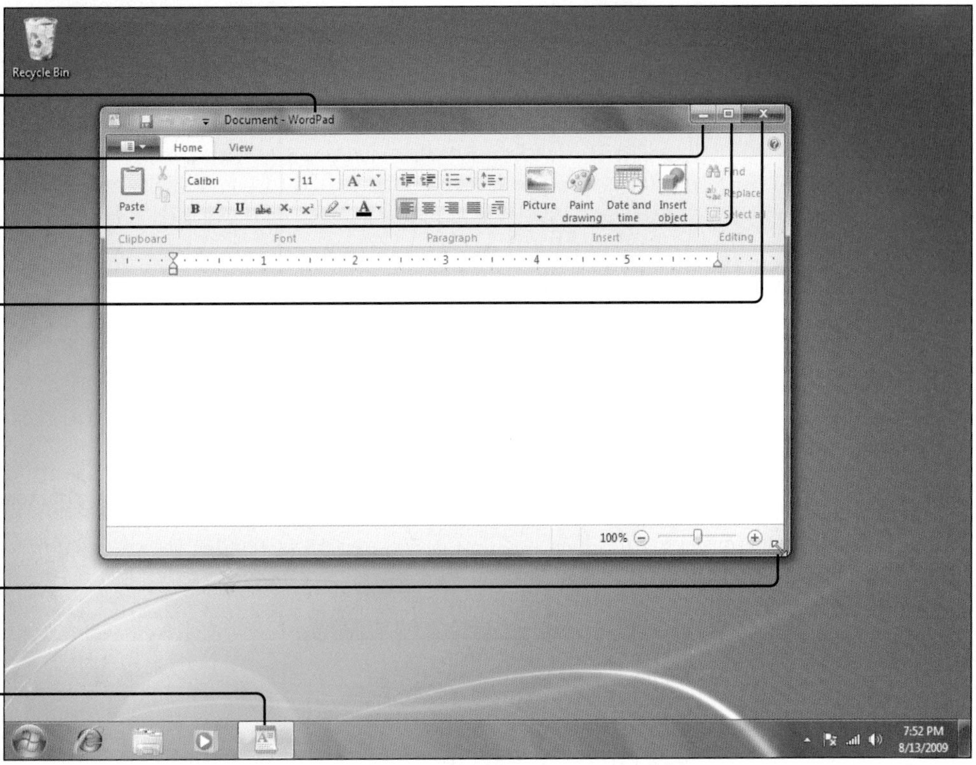

5 In the upper right corner, click the **Maximize** button so that the WordPad program fills the entire screen. Then, in the upper right corner, click the **Restore Down** button to return the window to its previous size.

The Restore Down button restores the window to the size it was before it was maximized.

6 From the **Start** menu, point to **All Programs**, click the **Accessories** folder, and then click **Calculator**. If necessary, drag the title bar of the **Calculator** window so that it overlaps an area of the **WordPad** window.

7 On the taskbar, notice that both programs—**WordPad** and **Calculator**—display a glass frame indicating the programs are both open; however, the **Calculator** program's button is slightly brighter, because it is the active window.

The most recently opened window is the active window.

8 Click anywhere in the **WordPad** window, and notice that it becomes the active window and moves in front of the **Calculator** window, as shown in Figure 1.50.

Additionally, the WordPad button on the taskbar becomes the brighter of the two open programs.

Figure 1.50

Calculator window behind WordPad window (yours may be blocked entirely from view)

WordPad window active

Taskbar buttons representing open programs, WordPad slightly brighter

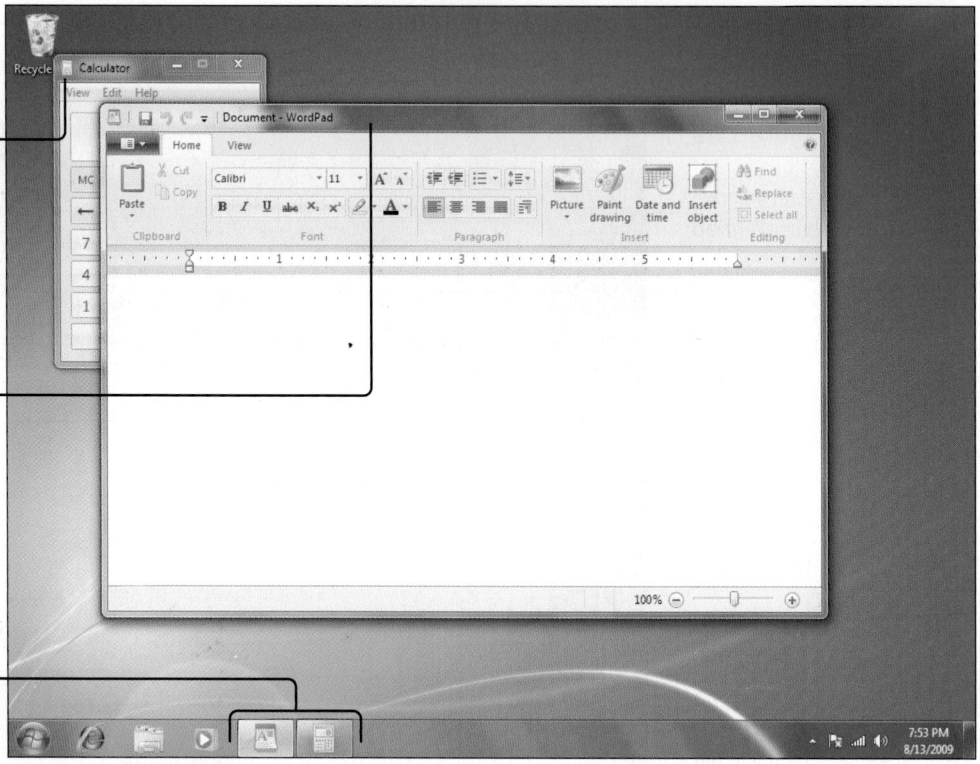

9 From the **Start** menu, open the **Paint** program—either from the recently used list on the Start menu or from the Accessories folder in the All Programs area. Notice that in the taskbar, three buttons, each representing an open program, display.

All open programs display an icon on the taskbar with a glass frame. The active program has the brightest frame.

10 In the upper right corner of the **Paint** window, click the **Minimize** button. Then, in the taskbar, click the **WordPad** button to minimize the window.

You can use either of these techniques to minimize a window without closing it.

11 Using either of the techniques you just practiced, minimize the **Calculator** window.

Minimizing a window hides the window and gets it out of the way, but it does not close the window. The window remains open—visible only as a button on the taskbar.

The taskbar is your tool to switch between open windows. To open or switch to another window, just click its taskbar button.

12 Move your mouse pointer into the desktop area, and then on the taskbar, point to the **Calculator** button to display a thumbnail representation of the program window. Then point to the **Paint** button to display its thumbnail.

A ***thumbnail*** is a reduced image of a graphic.

13 On the taskbar, click the **Paint** button, and notice that the window looks exactly as it did before you minimized it. **Close** the **Paint** window. Notice that the button is removed from the taskbar, because the window is closed.

> **Note | Buttons Pinned to the Taskbar**
>
> If the button remains on the taskbar but does not display a glass frame, it means the program has been pinned to the taskbar. As you progress in your study of Windows 7, you will practice pinning a program to the taskbar.

14 On the taskbar, point to the **WordPad** button, right-click, and then on the displayed **Jump List**, click **Close window**.

A ***Jump List*** displays destinations and tasks from a program's taskbar button.

15 Point to the **Calculator** button, and then move your mouse pointer into the thumbnail. Notice that the window opens and in the thumbnail, a **Close** button displays. In the thumbnail, click the small **Close** button.

Activity 1.15 | Using Aero Peek and Displaying Multiple Windows in the Cascade, Stack, and Side by Side Arrangements

You have seen that you can have multiple windows open and move among them by clicking the buttons on the taskbar. There are several different arrangements by which you can *display* multiple open windows on the desktop.

1 On the taskbar, click the **Windows Explorer** button, and then in the **navigation pane**, click your **CD/DVD Drive**. In the **file list**, open **Bell_Orchid**, then open **Corporate**, and then open **Engineering**.

2 With the files from the **Engineering** folder displayed in the **file list**, open the Word file **CO_EN_Pool_Report**, and notice that the **Word** program—the program in which the file was created—opens and displays the file. If necessary, **Maximize** the Word window so it fills the screen.

On the taskbar, both the Windows Explorer and Word program icons display with a glass frame.

3 On the taskbar, click the **Windows Explorer** button, and notice that the folder window for the **Engineering** folder displays.

4 From the **file list**, open the Excel file **CO_EN_Architect_Overtime**. If necessary, **Maximize** the Excel window.

5 On the taskbar, click the **Windows Explorer** button again to redisplay the **Engineering** folder window, and then open the PowerPoint file **CO_EN_April_Safety_Presentation**. If necessary, **Maximize** the PowerPoint window. Compare your screen with Figure 1.51.

Figure 1.51

PowerPoint file displays (PowerPoint 2007 displays here; you might have PowerPoint 2010)

Show desktop button

Buttons on taskbar indicate four windows open— Windows Explorer, Word, Excel, PowerPoint

6 In the taskbar, point to the **Word** icon, and then move your mouse pointer into the thumbnail that displays. Notice that the Word document fills the screen. Then, move your pointer back into the taskbar, and notice that the Word document no longer fills the screen.

This full-screen window preview is provided by ***Aero Peek***, a technology that assists you when you have multiple windows open by allowing you to *peek* at either the desktop that is behind open windows (***Preview Desktop***) or at a window that is hidden from view by other windows (***Full-Screen Window Preview***). Then, you can move the mouse pointer back into the taskbar to close the peek.

7 In the lower right corner of your screen, on the extreme right edge of the taskbar, point to the glass rectangle—the **Show desktop** button— to display the ScreenTip *Show desktop*, and then notice that you can peek at the desktop behind all the open windows—the open windows are hidden; windows that are not maximized display window outlines.

8 Click the **Show desktop** button to minimize, rather than hide, all of the open windows, and notice that no window outlines display.

9 Click the **Show desktop** button again to maximize all of the open windows. Notice that the PowerPoint window is still the active window.

By using Aero Peek, you can minimize all open windows, or just peek at the desktop. Aero Peek is useful if you need to locate a program shortcut or view other information items on your desktop.

10 On the taskbar, point to an open area—an area where no buttons display—and right-click. On the displayed shortcut menu, click **Cascade windows**. Compare your screen with Figure 1.52

In the ***cascade*** arrangement, the open windows display in a single stack, fanned out so that each title bar is visible. From the cascaded arrangement, you can click the title bar of any of the windows to make it the active window.

Figure 1.52

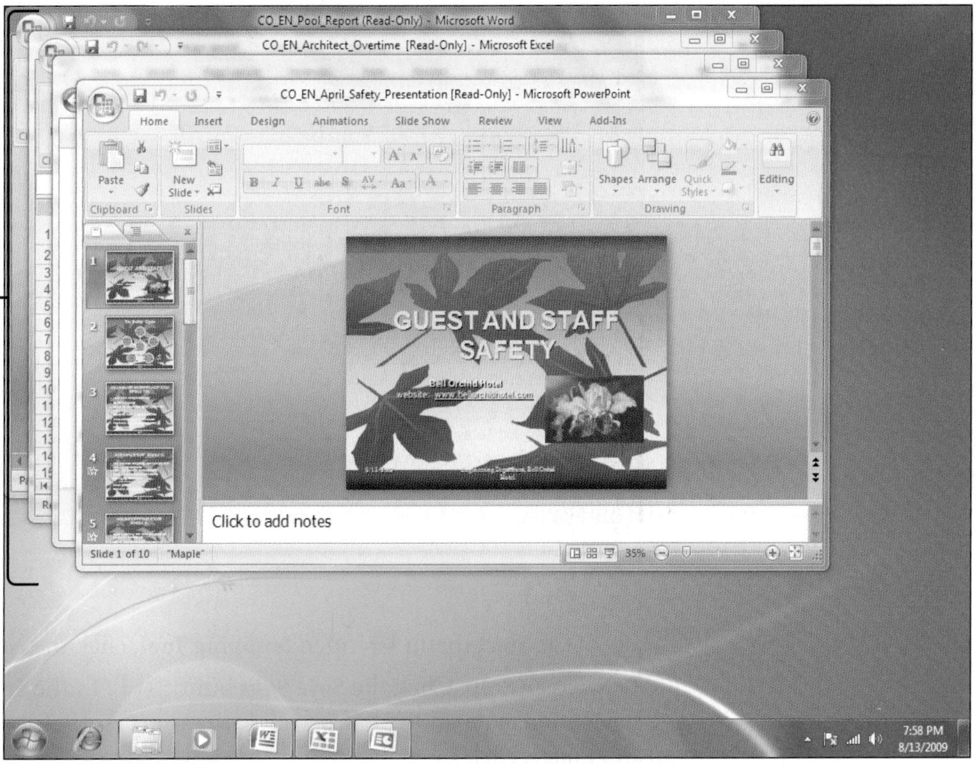

Four windows display in a cascaded arrangement (Office 2007 displays here; you might have Office 2010)

> **Another Way**
>
> Right-click the Windows Explorer button, and then on the Jump List, click Close window.

11 On the taskbar, point to the **Windows Explorer** button, move your mouse pointer into the thumbnail, and then click the small red **Close** button in the thumbnail.

12 Point to an open area of the taskbar, right-click, and then click **Show windows stacked.**

In the ***stacked*** arrangement, the three open windows display across the width of the screen in a vertical stack.

13 Display the taskbar menu again, and then click **Show windows side by side**. Compare your screen with Figure 1.53.

In the ***side by side*** arrangement, the open windows display side by side. You can work in any of the files. Clicking in a window makes it the active window until you click in another window.

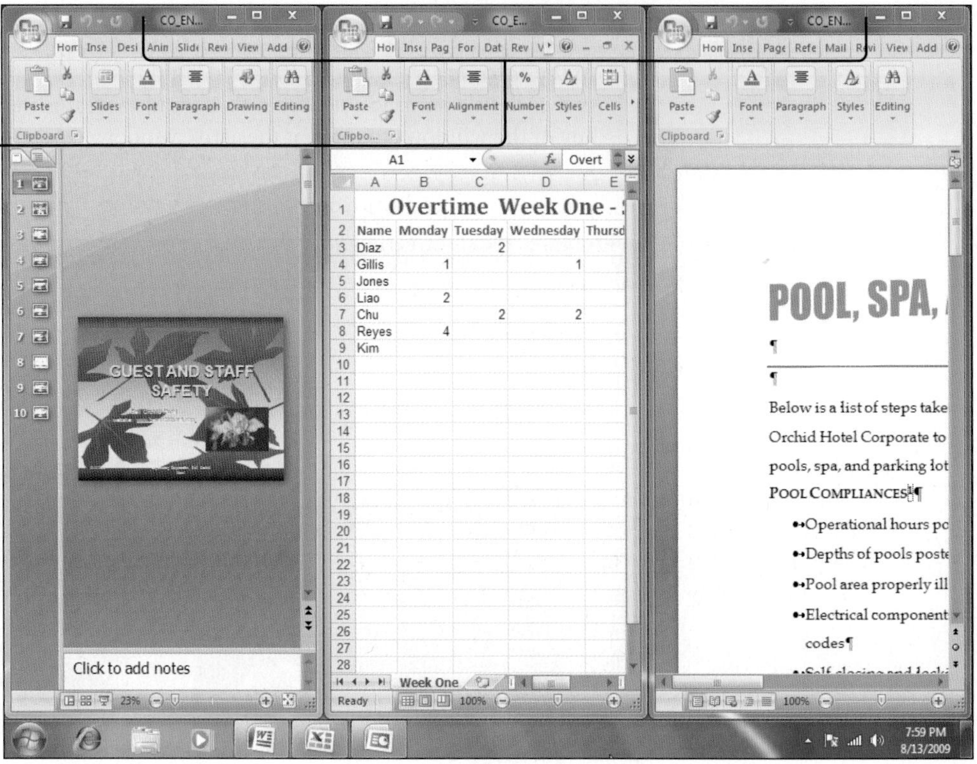

Figure 1.53

Three windows displayed side by side (your screens may display in a different order; Office 2007 shown here, you might have Office 2010)

14 From the **Start** menu, open **Snipping Tool**, click the **New arrow**, and then click **Full-screen Snip**. Click the **Save Snip** button. In the **Save As** dialog box in the **navigation pane** on the left, scroll down as necessary to view **Computer**. Under **Computer**, click the name of your USB flash drive.

15 In the **file list**, scroll as necessary, locate and double-click your **Windows 7 Chapter 1** folder.

16 In the **File name** box and using your own name, type **Lastname_Firstname_1B_SideBySide_Snip** Be sure the file type is **JPEG**. Click the **Save** button, and then **Close** the **Snipping Tool** window. Hold this file until you finish Project 1B, and then submit this file as directed by your instructor.

17 Right-click in an open area of the taskbar to display the taskbar menu again, and then click **Undo Show side by side**.

18 When the display returns to the stacked arrangement, in the upper right corner of *each* window, first click the **Maximize** button so that the program fills the entire screen, and then click the **Minimize** button to leave the window open but not displayed. Leave the three windows open on the taskbar for the next activity.

Maximizing the windows assures that the next time the program is opened, it will be maximized; otherwise, the program may display in its most recently used size.

Activity 1.16 | Switching Windows by Using Aero Flip 3D

Aero Flip 3D arranges your open windows in a three-dimensional stack that you can flip through quickly without having to click buttons on the taskbar.

> **Alert! | Versions of Windows 7 With Aero Flip 3D**
>
> Aero Flip 3D is available in Windows 7 Home Premium, Professional, Ultimate, and Enterprise editions.

1 Be sure the three files from the previous activity are open and minimized to display only as glass-framed buttons on the taskbar. On your keyboard, locate the ⊞ key, which is typically in the lower left corner of your keyboard between Ctrl and Alt.

2 Hold down ⊞ and then press the Tab key repeatedly to flip through the open windows as shown in Figure 1.54, and then release both keys to display the document at the top of the stack.

Your desktop is considered to be one of the open windows.

Figure 1.54

Open documents and the desktop display in a stack (your order may differ)

3 Repeat the technique you just practiced, and then flip through the stack until the PowerPoint presentation with the maple leaves is on top. Release the keys to maximize and make the PowerPoint document the active window.

4 **Close** ☒ the PowerPoint window.

5 In the taskbar, point to the **Excel** icon, right-click, and then on the displayed **Jump List**, click **Close window**.

6 In the taskbar, point to the **Word icon**, move your mouse pointer into the thumbnail, and then click the small red **Close** button.

You can use any of these techniques to close an open window.

Activity 1.17 | Using Snap to Display Windows

Snap is a Windows 7 feature that automatically resizes windows when you move—*snap*—them to the edge of the screen. You can use Snap to arrange windows side by side, expand windows vertically, or maximize a window.

You will find Snap useful to compare two documents, copy or move files between two windows, maximize a window by dragging instead of clicking the Maximize button, and to expand long documents to reduce the amount of scrolling.

1 Close any open windows, and then start the **Paint** program. If the window is maximized—fills the entire screen—click the **Restore Down** button.

2 Point to the **title bar**, and then drag to the left until your pointer reaches the edge of the screen and an outline of the window displays, as shown in Figure 1.55.

Figure 1.55

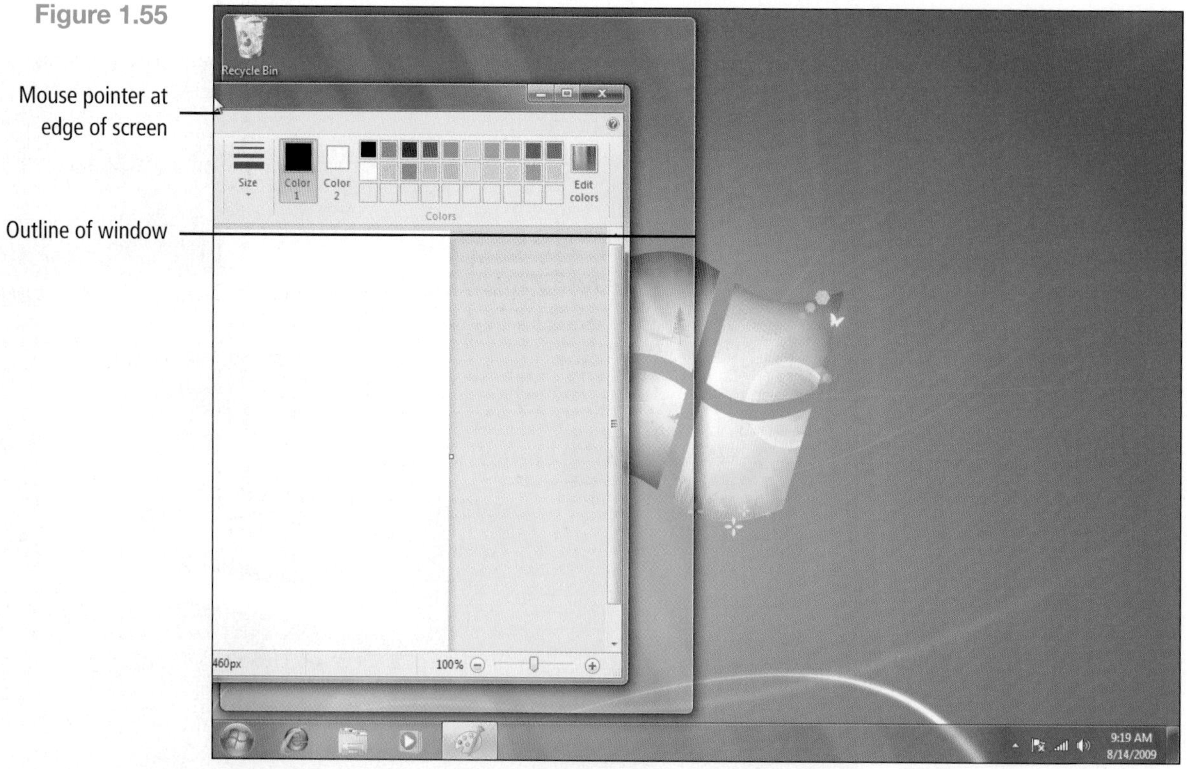

3 Release the mouse button, and notice that the window expands to half of the left side of the screen and extends fully from top to bottom.

4 Drag the title bar into the center of the screen, and notice that the window reverts to its former size.

5 To maximize vertically, but not horizontally, point to the bottom edge of the screen until the pointer displays, and then drag to the bottom of the screen.

The window maximizes vertically but not horizontally. You can also drag the upper edge of a window with the pointer for the same result.

6 Drag the title bar into the center of the screen so that the window reverts to its former size.

7 Drag the title bar upward until the pointer reaches the top of the screen and the window maximizes. Release the mouse button.

8 Drag the title bar into the center of the screen to restore the window to its former size, and then **Close** the **Paint** window.

> **More Knowledge | Aero Shake**
>
> If you have several unmaximized windows open, for example your Documents library window and your Music library window, you can point to the title bar of the active window, hold down the left mouse button, and then move your mouse back and forth vigorously in a shaking motion; all other windows will minimize. This feature is ***Aero Shake***. Shake the window again, and all the minimized windows will be visible again. Use Aero Shake when you want to focus on a single window without minimizing all your other open windows one by one.

Activity 1.18 | Using Snap to Display Two Windows Side by Side

1 From **Windows Explorer**, open your **CD/DVD** drive, open the **Bell_Orchid** folder, and then navigate to **Corporate ▶ Food_Beverage ▶ Restaurants**. Compare your screen with Figure 1.56.

Figure 1.56

Folder window; address bar displays path

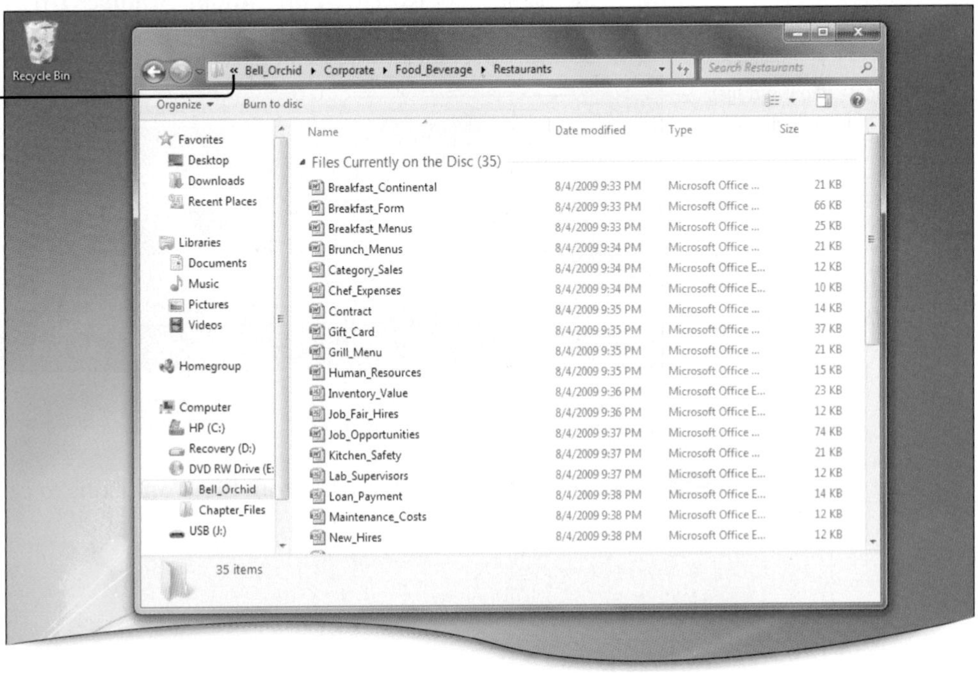

2 Open the Word file **Breakfast_Continental**. If necessary, **Maximize** the Word window. Click the **Windows Explorer** button again, and then open the Word file **Breakfast_Form**. In the taskbar, right-click the **Windows Explorer** button, and then click **Close window**.

3 In the taskbar, point to the **Word icon**, and notice that two stacked tiles display, indicating that two windows are open in Word. Notice also that the icon lights up in a color compatible with the Word icon. Compare your screen with Figure 1.57.

A program's taskbar icon will display stacked tiles in this manner for each open file, which provides a visual cue to indicate the number of open files. Additionally, when you point to an icon on the taskbar, the icon will light up in a color compatible with the icon color.

When you point to a program icon that has more than one file open, a thumbnail for each open file displays in a thumbnail grouping. To switch to a different file, simply click its thumbnail.

Figure 1.57

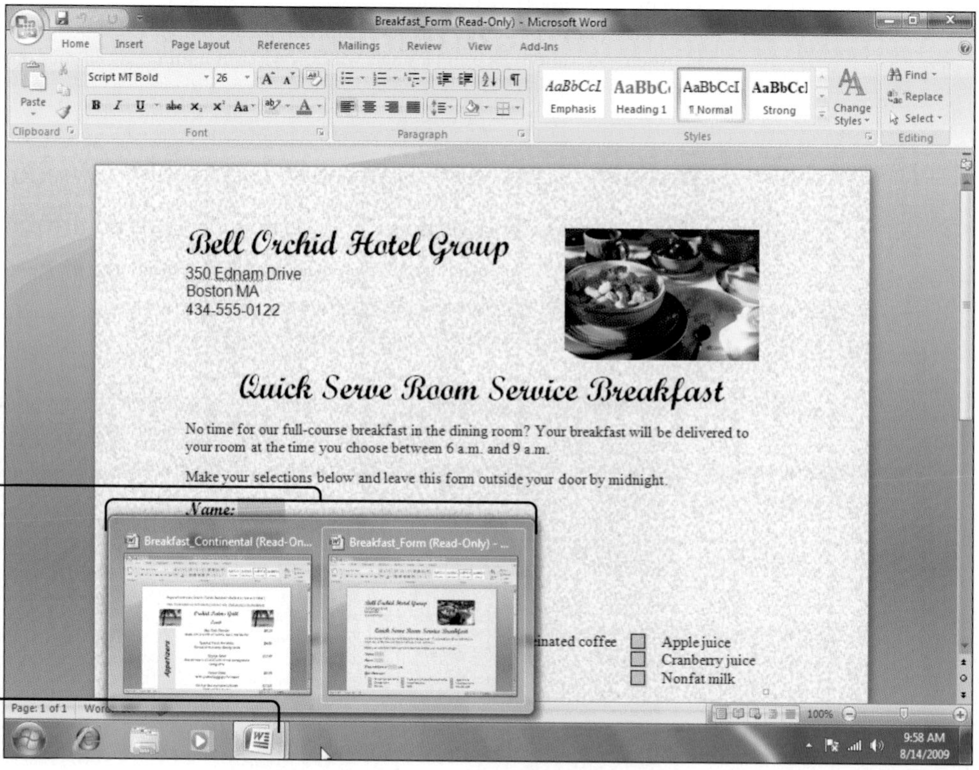

Grouped thumbnails indicate two Word files open in program

Icon lit up in compatible color when pointed to

4 Move your mouse pointer away from the Word icons to cancel the thumbnail display.

5 Point anywhere in the **title bar** of the displayed file, drag to the left until your pointer reaches the left edge of the screen, and then release the mouse button. Compare your screen with Figure 1.58.

The window for the Breakfast_Form file *snaps* to occupy the left half of the screen.

Figure 1.58

Breakfast_Form file occupies left half of screen

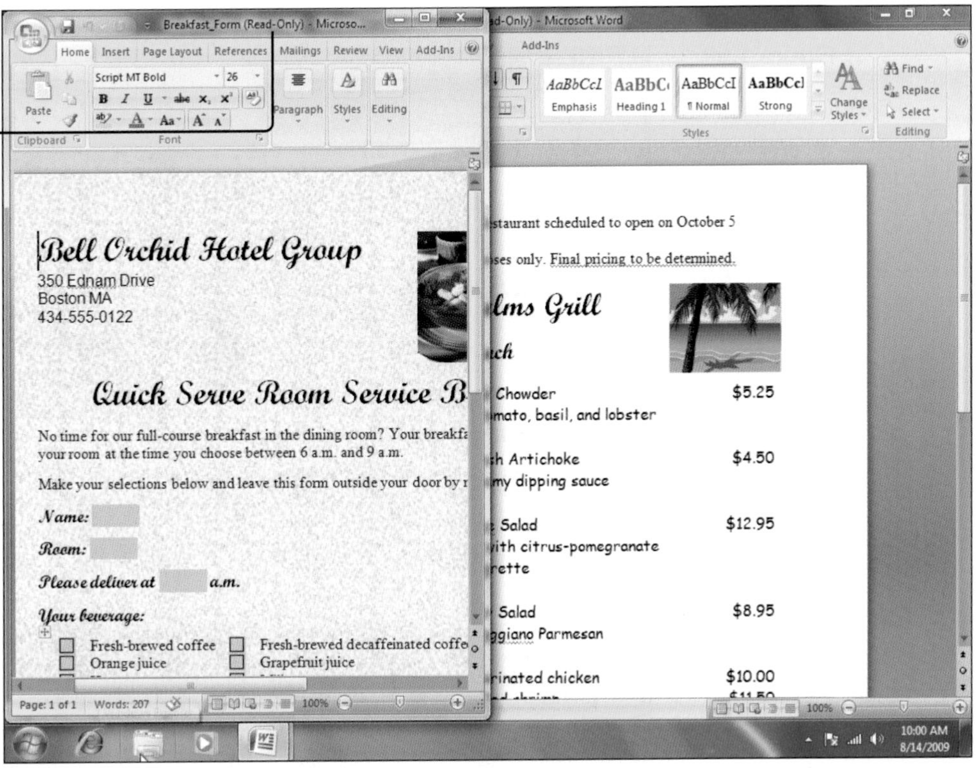

6 On the right side of the screen, point anywhere in the visible title bar of the **Breakfast_Continental** file, and then drag the pointer to the right side of the screen and release the mouse button. Notice that the window *snaps* to occupy the right half of the screen. Compare your screen with Figure 1.59.

Use this technique when you want to compare two files. As you progress in your study of Windows 7, you will also practice this technique for the purpose of copying files.

Figure 1.59

Breakfast_Continental file occupies left half of screen

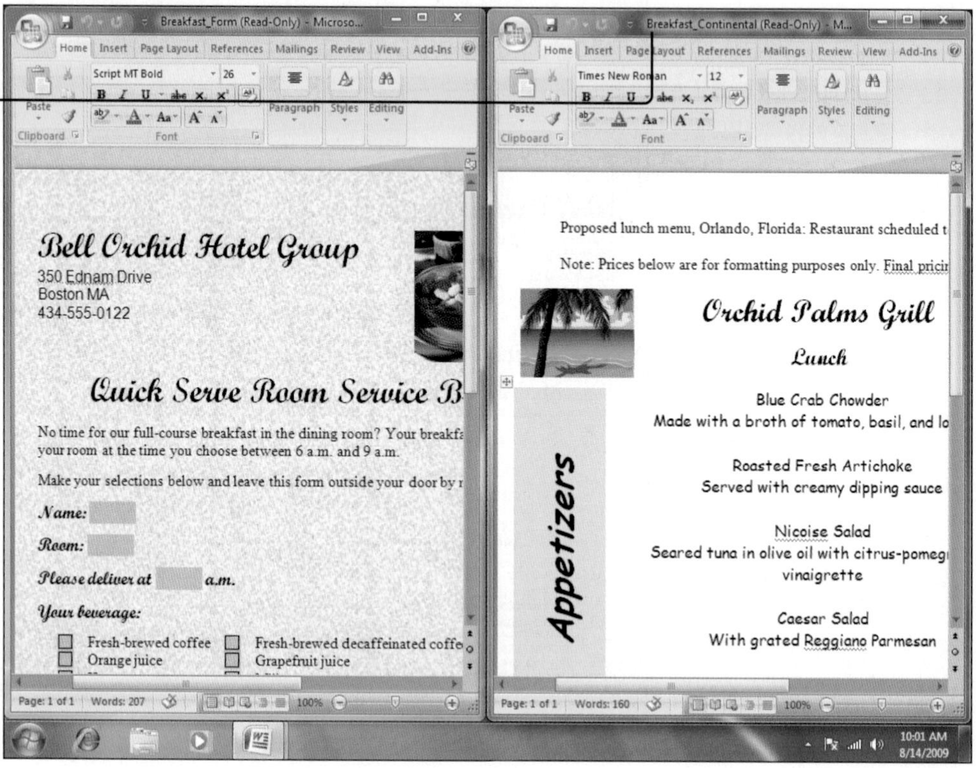

7 From the **Start** menu, open **Snipping Tool**, click the **New arrow**, and then click **Full-screen Snip**. Click the **Save Snip** button. In the **Save As** dialog box, in the **navigation pane** on the left, drag the scroll box down as necessary to view **Computer**. Under **Computer**, click the name of your USB flash drive.

8 In the **file list**, scroll as necessary, locate and double-click your **Windows 7 Chapter 1** folder.

9 In the **File name** box and using your own name, type **Lastname_Firstname_1B_Snap_Snip** Be sure the file type is **JPEG**. Click the **Save** button, and then **Close** the **Snipping Tool** window.

10 **Close** both Word files. Remove your Student Resource CD and any other removable storage devices. Submit the four snip files from this project to your instructor as directed.

End **You have completed Project 1B**

Content-Based Assessments

Summary

Windows 7 is an operating system program that manages your hardware, manages your software programs, and stores and manages your data. In this chapter, you used Snipping Tool to capture screen shots, created a folder on a removable device and saved files, and used Windows 7 Help and Support.

Key Terms

Content-Based Assessments

Matching

Match each term in the second column with its correct definition in the first column by writing the letter of the term on the blank line in front of the correct definition.

____ 1. A set of instructions that a computer uses to accomplish a task, such as word processing, accounting, or data management; also referred to as an *application*.

____ 2. A computer program that manages all the other programs on your computer, stores files in an organized manner, and coordinates the use of computer hardware such as the keyboard and mouse.

____ 3. An operating system developed by Microsoft Corporation.

____ 4. A collection of information that is stored on a computer under a single name, for example a text document, a picture, or a program.

____ 5. A container in which you store files.

____ 6. A folder within a folder.

____ 7. The area that serves as a surface for your work, like the top of an actual desk, and which is the main screen area that you see after you turn on your computer.

____ 8. The button that displays the Start menu.

____ 9. The screen area that contains the Start button, optional program buttons, and buttons for all open programs; by default, it is located at the bottom of the desktop, but you can move it.

____ 10. A window from which you can customize the look and functionality of your computer, add or remove programs, set up networks, and manage user accounts.

____ 11. A portable device on which you can store files, such as a USB flash drive, a flash memory card, or an external hard drive.

____ 12. An area of storage that is formatted with a file system compatible with your operating system and is identified by a drive letter.

____ 13. Displays the contents of the current folder, library, or device, and contains helpful parts so that you can navigate.

____ 14. A collection of items, such as files and folders, assembled from various locations.

____ 15. The area on the left side of a folder window, which displays favorites, libraries, and an expandable list of drives and folders.

A Control panel
B Desktop
C Drive
D File
E Folder
F Folder window
G Library
H Navigation pane
I Operating system
J Program
K Removable storage device
L Start button
M Subfolder
N Taskbar
O Windows 7

Content-Based Assessments

Multiple Choice

Circle the correct answer.

1. A row of buttons across the top of a window that contains commands for tasks is a:
   A. taskbar **B.** toolbar **C.** menu bar
2. The area that displays your current location in the folder structure as a series of links separated by arrows is the:
   A. file list **B.** taskbar **C.** address bar
3. A program included with Windows 7 with which you can capture an image of all or part of a computer screen, and then annotate, save, copy, or share the image via e-mail is:
   A. print screen **B.** capture **C.** Snipping Tool
4. The box in a scroll bar that you drag to reposition a document on the screen is the:
   A. scroll box **B.** text box **C.** search box
5. The system by which you interact with your computer and which uses graphics such as an image of a file folder or wastebasket that you click to activate the item represented is a graphical:
   A. user interface **B.** language **C.** program
6. Turning off your computer in a manner that closes all open programs and files, closes your network connections, stops the hard disk, and discontinues the use of electrical power is called:
   A. sleep **B.** shut down **C.** hibernate
7. The user account type that lets you make changes that will affect other users of the computer and permits the most control over the computer is the:
   A. administrator account **B.** guest account **C.** standard user account
8. A folder created for each user account labeled with the account holder's name, and which displays at the top of the Start menu and contains subfolders such as Documents, is the:
   A. Personal folder **B.** Contacts folder **C.** Videos folder
9. The program within Windows 7 that displays the contents of libraries, folders, and files on your computer, and which also enables you to perform tasks related to your files and folders such as copying, moving, and renaming is:
   A. Snipping Tool **B.** Windows Explorer **C.** Internet Explorer
10. The area that displays the contents of the current folder or library is the:
    A. details pane **B.** preview pane **C.** file list

Apply 1A skills from these Objectives:

1. Create a New Folder and Save a File on a Removable Storage Device
2. Identify the Functions of an Operating System
3. Use the Getting Started Information and Windows Help and Support
4. Log Off, Turn Off Your Computer, and View Power Options
5. Manage Your User Account

Skills Review | Project 1C Exploring Windows

Project Files

For Project 1C, you will need the following files:

Student Resource CD or a USB flash drive containing the student data files
win01_1C_Answer_Sheet (Word document)

You will save your file as:

Lastname_Firstname_1C_Answer_Sheet

1 **Close** all open windows. On the taskbar, click the **Windows Explorer** button. In the **navigation pane**, click the drive that contains the student files for this textbook, and then navigate to **Chapter_Files ▶ Chapter_01**. Double-click the Word file **win01_1C_Answer_Sheet** to open Word and display the document. Press F12 to display the **Save As** dialog box in Word, navigate to your **Windows 7 Chapter 1** folder, and then using your own name, save the document as **Lastname_Firstname_1C_Answer_Sheet** Click OK if you see a message regarding file formats.

On the taskbar, click the **Word** button to minimize the window and leave your Word document accessible from the taskbar. **Close** the **Chapter_01** folder window. As you complete each step in this project, click the Word button on the taskbar to open the document, type your one-letter answer in the appropriate cell of the Word table, and then on the taskbar, click the button again to minimize the window for the next step.

From the **Start menu**, display the **Control Panel**, and then with the insertion point blinking in the search box, type **get** In the list that displays, click **Getting Started**. Which of the following is true?

A. From this screen, you can create a new folder.

B. Several links on this screen will take you to online sources of information.

C. From this screen, you can shut down your computer.

2 Close the Getting Started window. What is your result?

A. All windows close and the desktop displays.

B. The Control Panel window remains open.

C. The Create Password window displays.

3 **Close** the **Control Panel** window. Display the **Start menu**, and then at the top of the right side of the menu, under the picture, click your user name. In the displayed window, where does your user name display?

A. In the address bar

B. In the details pane

C. In the file list

4 In the **navigation pane**, under **Libraries**, click **Documents**. What is your result?

A. The first document in the library opens in its application.

B. The contents of the Documents library displays in the file list.

C. The contents of the Documents library displays in the address bar.

(Project 1C Exploring Windows continues on the next page)

Skills Review | Project 1C Exploring Windows (continued)

5 In the **navigation pane**, click **Computer**. What is your result?

A. The storage devices attached to your computer display in the file list.

B. All of the files on the hard drive display in the file list.

C. Your computer restarts.

6 According to the toolbar in this window, which of the following is true?

A. From this window you can restart your computer.

B. From this window you can open the PowerPoint application.

C. From this window you can uninstall or change a program.

7 **Close** the **Computer** window. From the **Start** menu, display the **Control Panel**, and then click **User Accounts and Family Safety** (or User Accounts). Which of the following is true?

A. Both B. and C. are true.

B. From this screen, you can change your Windows password.

C. From this screen, you can change your account picture.

8 Click **Change your account picture**. According to this screen, where does your picture appear.

A. On the Start menu.

B. On the Welcome screen.

C. On both the Welcome screen and the Start menu.

9 **Close** the **Change Your Picture** window. From the **Start** menu, click **Help and Support**. In the **Search** box, type **shortcuts** and then press Enter. Click **Keyboard shortcuts**, scroll down as necessary, and then click **Windows logo key keyboard shortcuts**. Scroll as necessary to view the table. According to this information, to open the **Start** menu using the keyboard, you can press:

A. [Windows logo key]

B. [Windows logo key] + 1

C. Alt + F4

10 **Close** **Help and Support**. Display the **Start** menu, click **Control Panel**, click **Hardware and Sound**, and then click **Power Options**. In the introduction, click **Tell me more about power plans**. Based on the information in the Windows Help and Support window, which of the following is *not* true?

A. Power plans can reduce the amount of power your computer uses.

B. Power plans can maximize your system's performance.

C. A power plan is a collection of software settings.

Be sure you have typed all of your answers in your Word document. Save and close your Word document, and submit as directed by your instructor. **Close** all open windows.

End **You have completed Project 1C**

Apply 1B skills from these Objectives:

- 6 Display Libraries, Folders, and Files in a Window
- 7 Start Programs and Open Data Files
- 8 Manage the Display of Individual and Multiple Windows

Skills Review | Project 1D Working with Windows, Programs, and Files

Project Files

For Project 1D, you will need the following files:

Student Resource CD or a flash drive containing the student data files
win01_1D_Answer_Sheet (Word document)

You will save your file as:

Lastname_Firstname_1D_Answer_Sheet

1 Close [X] all open windows. On the taskbar, click the **Windows Explorer** button. In the **navigation pane**, click the drive that contains the student files for this textbook, and then navigate to **Chapter_Files ▶ Chapter_01**. Double-click the Word file **win01_1D_Answer_Sheet** to open Word and display the document. Press F12 to display the **Save As** dialog box in Word, navigate to your **Windows 7 Chapter 1** folder, and then using your own name, save the document as **Lastname_Firstname_1D_Answer_Sheet** If necessary, click OK regarding file formats.

On the taskbar, click the **Word** button to minimize the window and leave your Word document accessible from the taskbar. **Close** the **Chapter_01** folder window. As you complete each step in this project, click the Word button on the taskbar to open the document, type your one-letter answer in the appropriate cell of the Word table, and then on the taskbar, click the button again to minimize the window for the next step.

On the taskbar, click the **Windows Explorer** button. In the **navigation pane**, click the CD/DVD Drive or flash drive that contains the student files. In the file list on the right, how many *folders* display?

A. None
B. One
C. Two

2 In the file list on the right, double-click the **Bell_Orchid** folder to open it, and then double-click the **Corporate** folder to open it. Which of the following best describes the contents of the Corporate folder?

A. Only individual files display.
B. Only folders display.
C. Both individual files and folders display.

3 In the **address bar**, to the right of **Bell_Orchid**, click ▶. What is the result?

A. The file list no longer displays folders.
B. A small list drops down to display the names of the subfolders within the Bell_Orchid folder.
C. The navigation pane closes.

(Project 1D Working with Windows, Programs, and Files continues on the next page)

Skills Review | Project 1D Working with Windows, Programs, and Files (continued)

4 If necessary, click in an open area of the file list to close the list, and then in the **file list**, double-click the **Engineering** folder to open it. In an open area, right-click. On the displayed shortcut menu, point to **Group by**, and then on the displayed submenu, click **Type**. How many different groups of file types display?

A. Three

B. Four

C. Five

5 Be sure the **Engineering** folder is still grouped by type. How many Excel worksheets are in this folder?

A. One

B. Two

C. Three

6 Which file type group has the most number of files?

A. Microsoft Word Document

B. Microsoft PowerPoint Presentation

C. JPEG image

7 Right-click anywhere in the file list, point to **Group by**, and then click **(None)**. Click the **Name** column heading as necessary so that the files in the folder are sorted in alphabetical order—recall that clicking a column heading sorts the column alternately in ascending and descending order and that the pale arrow at the top of the column heading indicates how the column is sorted. Open the file **CO_EN_Meeting_Room_Construction**. What happens?

A. The file displays only as a button on the taskbar.

B. The file opens in the application program in which it was created—PowerPoint.

C. A message displays asking you what program to open for this file.

8 Close the **PowerPoint** window and the **Windows Explorer** window. Display the **Start** menu, click **All Programs**, click the **Accessories** folder, and then point to **Snipping Tool**. Right-click, point to **Send to**, and then click **Desktop (create shortcut)**. Click outside of the Start menu to close it. Which of the following is true?

A. A shortcut icon with an arrow, which when clicked will open the program, displays on the desktop.

B. The Snipping Tool program opens.

C. All of the snips that you created in Projects 1A and 1B display on the desktop.

9 Drag the **Snipping Tool** shortcut to the **Recycle Bin** to delete the shortcut from the desktop. Recall that deleting a shortcut deletes only the shortcut icon on the desktop. It does not delete the program. On the taskbar, click your Word Answer Sheet document to display it. From the **Start** menu, open **Microsoft Excel**. Point to an open area of the taskbar, right-click, and then click **Show windows side by side**. Which of the following is *not* true?

A. Two windows, one for Word and one for Excel, display—one on the left and one on the right.

B. The Excel window is larger than the Word window.

C. Both the Word and Excel buttons display on the taskbar.

(Project 1D Working with Windows, Programs, and Files continues on the next page)

Skills Review | Project 1D Working with Windows, Programs, and Files (continued)

10 In an empty area of the taskbar, right-click, and then click **Undo Show side by side**. Close the **Excel** window, and minimize the **Word** window. On the **Start** menu, click **All Programs**, click **Accessories**, and then click **Notepad** to start the program. Using the same technique, start the **Paint** program, and then the **Calculator** program. On the taskbar, which program button is shown as active—the glass frame is brighter and less translucent than the other two?

A. Notepad

B. Paint

C. Calculator

Be sure you have typed all of your answers in your Word document. Save and close your Word document, and submit as directed by your instructor. Close all open windows.

End You have completed Project 1D

Content-Based Assessments

Apply 1A skills from these Objectives:

1. Create a New Folder and Save a File on a Removable Storage Device
2. Identify the Functions of an Operating System
3. Use the Getting Started Information and Windows Help and Support
4. Log Off, Turn Off Your Computer, and View Power Options
5. Manage Your User Account

Mastering Windows 7 | Project 1E Windows Help and Support

In the following Mastering Windows 7 project, you will capture and save a snip that will look similar to Figure 1.60.

Project Files

For Project 1E, you will need the following file:

New Snip file

You will save your file as:

Lastname_Firstname_1E_Smartphone_Snip

Project Results

Figure 1.60

(Project 1E Windows Help and Support continues on the next page)

Mastering Windows 7 | Project 1E Windows Help and Support (continued)

1 Display the **Windows Help and Support** window, and then search for **smartphone** Click **Sync music, pictures, contacts, and calendars with a mobile device**. Maximize the window.

2 In the first paragraph, click the green word *sync* and read the definition. Then, scroll down as necessary to position the figure in the middle of your screen.

3 Start **Snipping Tool**, click the **New button arrow**, and then click **Window Snip**. Click anywhere in the **Windows Help and Support** window to capture it.

4 On the toolbar of the **Snipping Tool** mark-up window, click the **Pen button arrow** and then click **Red Pen**. Draw a circle around the picture of the phone, and then click the **Save Snip** button.

5 In the displayed **Save As** dialog box, in the **navigation pane**, scroll down, and then under **Computer**, click your USB flash drive. In the file list, open your **Windows 7 Chapter 1** folder so that its name displays in the address bar, and then as the **File name**, and using your own name, type **Lastname_Firstname_1E_Smartphone_Snip**

6 Be sure the file type is **JPEG**. **Save** the snip, **Close** **Snipping Tool**, and then **Close** the **Windows Help and Support** window.

Submit your snip file as directed by your instructor.

End **You have completed Project 1E**

Content-Based Assessments

Apply 1B skills from these Objectives:

- 6 Display Libraries, Folders, and Files in a Window
- 7 Start Programs and Open Data Files
- 8 Manage the Display of Individual and Multiple Windows

Mastering Windows 7 | Project 1F Cascade Screens

In the following Mastering Windows 7 project, you will navigate the Bell_Orchid folder structure, start a program by opening a file, open a file in a program, manage multiple windows, cascade multiple windows, and capture and save a screen that will look similar to Figure 1.61.

Project Files

For Project 1F, you will need the following file:

New Snip file

You will save your file as:

Lastname_Firstname_1F_Cascade_Snip

Project Results

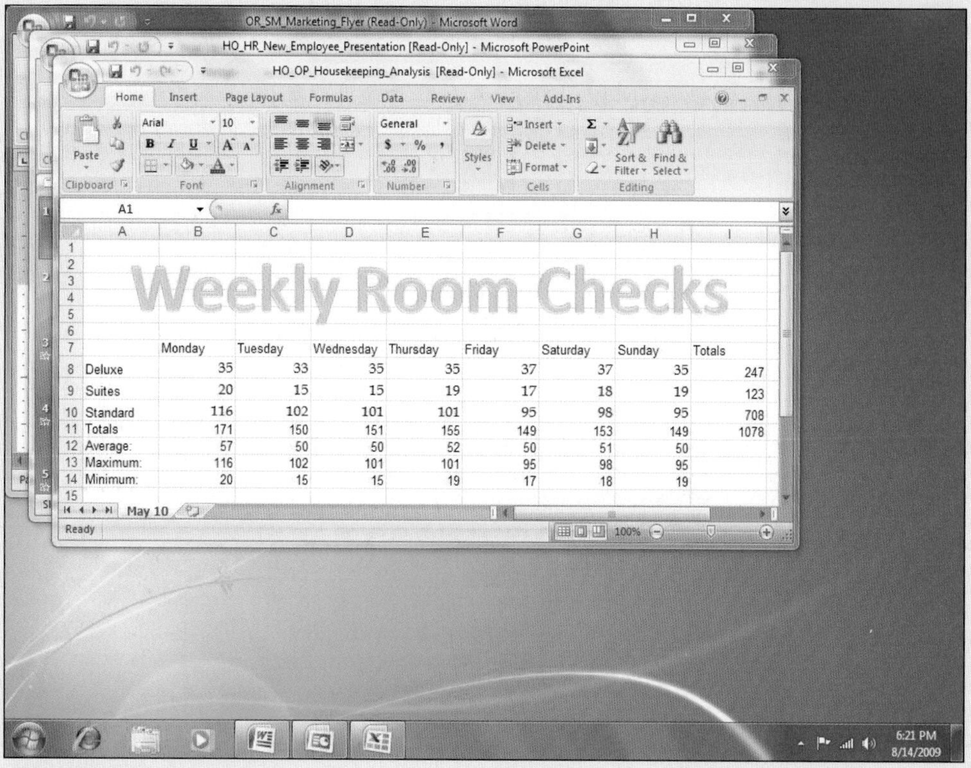

Figure 1.61

(Project 1F Cascade Screens continues on the next page)

Content-Based Assessments

Mastering Windows 7 | Project 1F Cascade Screens (continued)

1 From the **Start** menu, locate and open **Microsoft Word**. Press Ctrl + O to display the **Open** dialog box, in the **navigation pane** click the device that contains your student files, and then from the **Bell_Orchid** folder, locate and open the **Marketing Flyer** document for the **Orlando** hotel. If necessary, maximize the Word window.

2 With the **Word** document displayed on your screen, on the taskbar, click the **Windows Explorer** button, and then in the **navigation pane**, click the device that contains your student files. Open the **Bell_Orchid** folder, and then in the **Honolulu** folder, open the **HO_HR_New_Employee_Presentation** from the **Human_Resources** folder. If necessary, maximize the PowerPoint window.

3 On the taskbar, click the **Windows Explorer** button to redisplay the folder window. On the **address bar**, to the right of **Honolulu**, click ▶, and then click **Operations**. Open the Excel file **HO_OP_Housekeeping_Analysis**.

4 On the taskbar, right-click the **Windows Explorer** button, and then on the **Jump List**, click **Close window**. Display the three open windows in the **Cascade** arrangement.

5 Create a **Full-screen Snip** of your screen with the three cascaded windows, and then save it in your chapter folder as **Lastname_Firstname_1F_Cascade_Snip**

6 Close the **Snipping Tool** window.

Maximize and then **Close** each window. Submit your snip file as directed by your instructor.

End **You have completed Project 1F**

Outcomes-Based Assessments

Rubric

The following outcomes-based assessments are *open-ended assessments*. That is, there is no specific correct result; your result will depend on your approach to the information provided. Make *Professional Quality* your goal. Use the following scoring rubric to guide you in *how* to approach the problem, and then to evaluate *how well* your approach solves the problem.

The *criteria*—Software Mastery, Content, Format and Layout, and Process—represent the knowledge and skills you have gained that you can apply to solving the problem. The *levels of performance*—Professional Quality, Approaching Professional Quality, or Needs Quality Improvements—help you and your instructor evaluate your result.

	Your completed project is of Professional Quality if you:	**Your completed project is Approaching Professional Quality if you:**	**Your completed project Needs Quality Improvements if you:**
1-Software Mastery	Choose and apply the most appropriate skills, tools, and features and identify efficient methods to solve the problem.	Choose and apply some appropriate skills, tools, and features, but not in the most efficient manner.	Choose inappropriate skills, tools, or features, or are inefficient in solving the problem.
2-Content	Construct a solution that is clear and well organized, contains content that is accurate, appropriate to the audience and purpose, and is complete. Provide a solution that contains no errors in spelling, grammar, or style.	Construct a solution in which some components are unclear, poorly organized, inconsistent, or incomplete. Misjudge the needs of the audience. Have some errors in spelling, grammar, or style, but the errors do not detract from comprehension.	Construct a solution that is unclear, incomplete, or poorly organized; contains some inaccurate or inappropriate content; and contains many errors in spelling, grammar, or style. Do not solve the problem.
3-Format and Layout	Format and arrange all elements to communicate information and ideas, clarify function, illustrate relationships, and indicate relative importance.	Apply appropriate format and layout features to some elements, but not others. Overuse features, causing minor distraction.	Apply format and layout that does not communicate information or ideas clearly. Do not use format and layout features to clarify function, illustrate relationships, or indicate relative importance. Use available features excessively, causing distraction.
4-Process	Use an organized approach that integrates planning, development, self-assessment, revision, and reflection.	Demonstrate an organized approach in some areas, but not others; or, use an insufficient process of organization throughout.	Do not use an organized approach to solve the problem.

Outcomes-Based Assessments

Apply a combination of the 1A and 1B skills.

Problem Solving | Project 1G Help Desk

Project Files

For Project 1G, you will need the following file:

win01_1G_Help_Desk

You will save your file as:

Lastname_Firstname_1G_Help_Desk

From the student files that accompany this textbook, open the **Chapter_Files** folder, and then in the **Chapter_01** folder, locate and open the Word document **win01_1G_Help_Desk**. Save the document in your chapter folder as **Lastname_Firstname_1G_Help_Desk**

The following e-mail question has arrived at the Help Desk from an employee at the Bell Orchid Hotel's corporate office. In the Word document, construct a response based on your knowledge of Windows 7. Although an e-mail response is not as formal as a letter, you should still use good grammar, good sentence structure, professional language, and a polite tone. Save your document and submit the response as directed by your instructor.

To: Help Desk

We have a new employee in our department, and as her user picture, she wants to use a picture of her dog. I know that Corporate Policy says it is ok to use an acceptable personal picture on a user account. Can she change the picture herself within her standard user account, or does she need an administrator account to do that?

End **You have completed Project 1G**

Outcomes-Based Assessments

Apply a combination of the 1A and 1B skills.

Problem Solving | Project 1H Help Desk

Project Files

For Project 1H, you will need the following file:

win01_1H_Help_Desk

You will save your file as:

Lastname_Firstname_1H_Help_Desk

From the student files that accompany this textbook, open the **Chapter_Files** folder, and then in the **Chapter_01** folder, locate and open **win01_1H_Help_Desk**. Save the document in your chapter folder as **Lastname_Firstname_1H_Help_Desk**

The following e-mail question has arrived at the Help Desk from an employee at the Bell Orchid Hotel's corporate office. In the Word document, construct a response based on your knowledge of Windows 7. Although an e-mail response is not as formal as a letter, you should still use good grammar, good sentence structure, professional language, and a polite tone. Save your document and submit the response as directed by your instructor.

To: Help Desk

When I'm done using my computer at the end of the day, should I use the Sleep option or the Shut Down option, and what's the difference between the two?

End **You have completed Project 1H**

Outcomes-Based Assessments

Apply a combination of the 1A and 1B skills.

Problem Solving | Project 1I Help Desk

Project Files

For Project 1I, you will need the following file:

win01_1I_Help_Desk

You will save your document as:

Lastname_Firstname_1I_Help_Desk

From the student files that accompany this textbook, open the **Chapter_Files** folder, and then in **Chapter_01** folder, locate and open **win01_1I_Help_Desk**. Save the document in your chapter folder as **Lastname_Firstname_1I_Help_Desk**

The following e-mail question has arrived at the Help Desk from an employee at the Bell Orchid Hotel's corporate office. In the Word document, construct a response based on your knowledge of Windows 7. Although an e-mail response is not as formal as a letter, you should still use good grammar, good sentence structure, professional language, and a polite tone. Save your document and submit the response as directed by your instructor.

To: Help Desk

In my department, we are setting up a new folder structure to store documents related to the marketing campaign for the new theme park being built at the Orlando facility. Because I will use these folders frequently, can you suggest a good place to set up the folder structure? I think the desktop is the best place to store folders that I will be using frequently, right?

End **You have completed Project 1I**

Managing Libraries, Folders, Files, and Using Search

OUTCOMES

At the end of this chapter you will be able to:

OBJECTIVES

Mastering these objectives will enable you to:

PROJECT 2A

Navigate in Windows 7 using Windows Explorer; create, copy, move, and delete files and folders to create an organized computer file structure.

PROJECT 2B

Use Search to find programs, controls, files, and folders on a computer.

Laura Gangi Pond/Shutterstock

In This Chapter

In this chapter, you will practice the most useful computing skills you can acquire—managing your data so that you can find your files and folders easily. Many of the frustrations that computer users experience result from not being able to locate their desired information quickly and efficiently, or not understanding where a program saves new files. In this chapter, you will practice techniques that include creating and naming files and folders in a consistent format, organizing your files into folders, arranging folders into a logical folder structure, and searching for files when you are not certain where they are located. You will also practice navigating within a folder structure by using the navigational tools in the Windows Explorer program.

The projects in this chapter relate to the **Bell Orchid Hotels**, headquartered in Boston, and which own and operate resorts and business-oriented hotels. Resort properties are located in popular destinations, including Honolulu, Orlando, San Diego, and Santa Barbara. The resorts offer deluxe accommodations and a wide array of dining options. Other Bell Orchid hotels are located in major business centers and offer the latest technology in their meeting facilities. The company plans to open new properties and update existing properties over the next ten years.

Project 2A Managing Files and Folders

Project Activities

In Activities 2.01 through 2.13, you will assist Barbara Hewitt and Steven Ramos, who work for the Information Technology Department at the Boston headquarters office of the Bell Orchid Hotels. Barbara and Steven have been asked to organize some of the files and folders that comprise the corporation's computer data. You will capture screens that look similar to Figure 2.1.

Project Files

For Project 2A, you will need the following files:

Student Resource CD or a flash drive containing the student data files

You will save your files as:

Lastname_Firstname_2A_Europe_Folders_Snip
Lastname_Firstname_2A_HR_Snip
Lastname_Firstname_2A_Compressed_Snip

Project Results

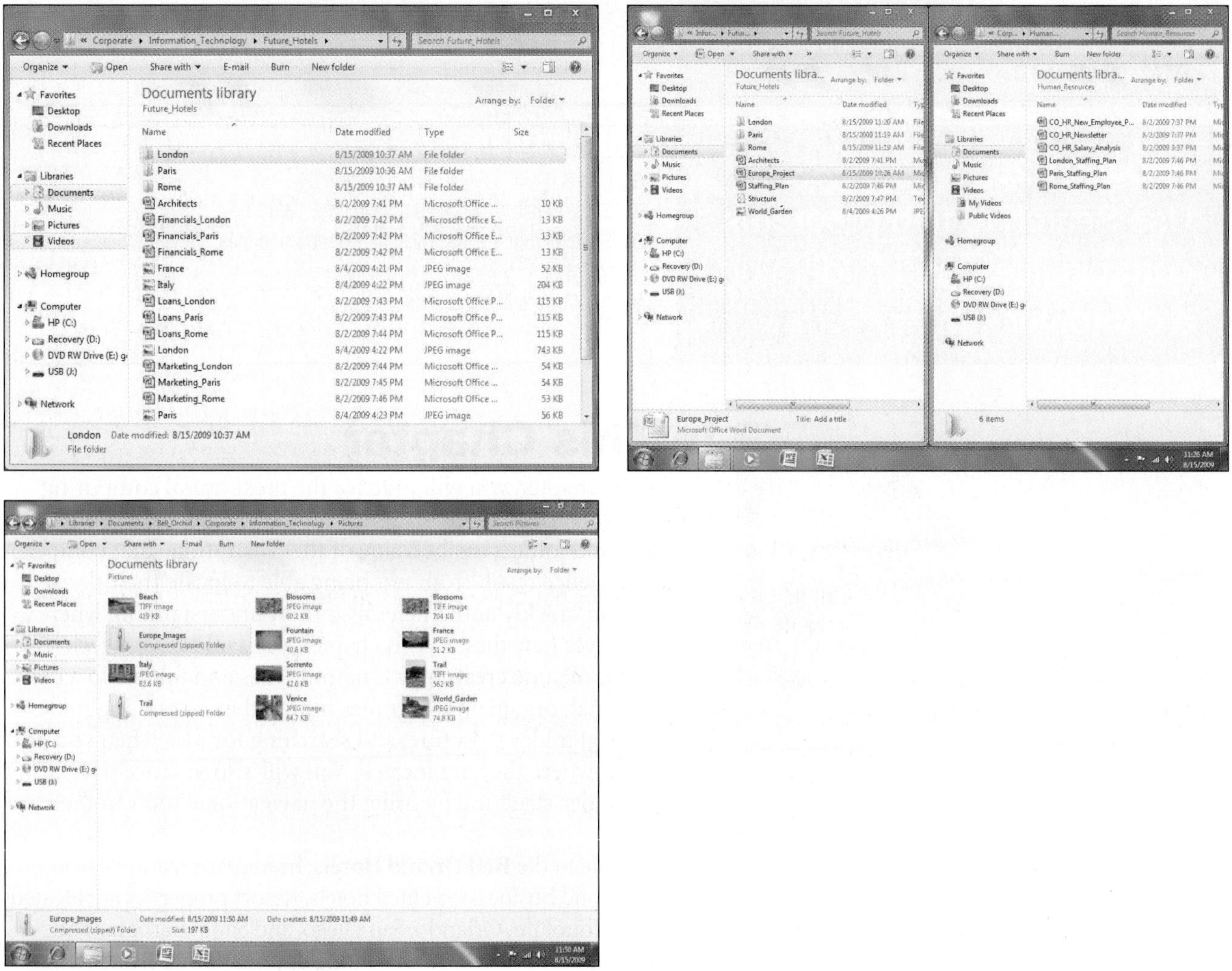

Figure 2.1
Project 2A Managing Files and Folders

Alert! | If you are working on a computer that is not your own, for example in a college lab, plan your time to complete Project 2A in one working session.

Because you will need to store and then delete files on the hard disk drive of the computer at which you are working, it is recommended that you complete this project in one working session—*unless you are working on your own computer or you know that the files will be retained.* In your college lab, it is possible that files you store will not be retained after you log off. Allow approximately 45 to 60 minutes to complete Project 2A.

Objective 1 | Copy Files From a Removable Storage Device to the Hard Disk Drive

A ***program*** is a set of instructions that a computer uses to accomplish a task, such as word processing, accounting, or data management. A program is also referred to as an ***application***.

Windows 7 is an ***operating system*** developed by Microsoft Corporation. An operating system is a computer program that manages all the other programs on your computer, stores files in an organized manner, allows you to use software programs, and coordinates the use of computer hardware such as the keyboard and mouse.

A ***file*** is a collection of information that is stored on a computer under a single name, for example a text document, a picture, or a program.

Every file is stored in a ***folder***—a container in which you store files—or a ***subfolder***, which is a folder within a folder. Windows 7 stores and organizes your files and folders, which is the primary task of an operating system.

Activity 2.01 | Copying Files From a Removable Storage Device to the Documents Library on the Hard Disk Drive

Barbara and Steven have the assignment to transfer and then organize some of the corporation's files to a computer that will be connected to the corporate network. Data on such a computer can be accessed by employees at any of the hotel locations through the use of sharing technologies. For example, ***SharePoint*** is a Microsoft technology that enables employees in an organization to access information across organizational and geographic boundaries.

1. Log on to your computer and display your Windows 7 desktop. Insert the Student Resource CD that accompanies this textbook into the **CD/DVD Drive**—or insert the USB flash drive that contains these files if you obtained them from a different source. Wait a moment for your computer to recognize the removable media, and then if necessary, **Close** the **AutoPlay** dialog box.

   Recall that the AutoPlay dialog box displays when you insert removable storage devices into your computer.

2. On the taskbar, click the **Windows Explorer** button to display the **Libraries** window.

   Recall that ***Windows Explorer*** is the program in Windows 7 that displays the contents of libraries, folders, and files on your computer, and which also enables you to perform tasks related to your files and folders such as copying, moving, and renaming. Windows Explorer is at work any time you are viewing the contents of a library, a folder, or a file.

3 In the **navigation pane**, under **Computer**, click your **CD/DVD** drive to display the contents in the **file list**. Compare your screen with Figure 2.2.

Recall that in the navigation pane, under Computer, you have access to all the storage areas inside your computer, such as your hard disk drives, and to any devices with removable storage, such as CDs or DVDs and USB flash drives.

Figure 2.2

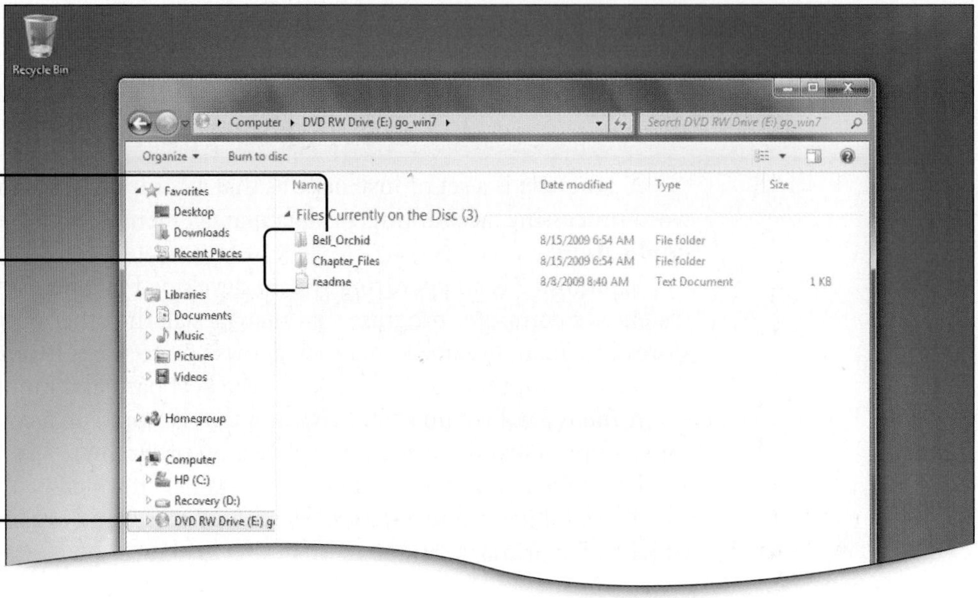

4 In the **file list**, point to the **Bell_Orchid** folder and right-click. On the displayed shortcut menu, point to **Send to**. Compare your screen with Figure 2.3.

From the Send to submenu, you can copy the selected file or folder to a variety of places. From this menu you can also create a desktop shortcut to the selected file or folder.

Figure 2.3

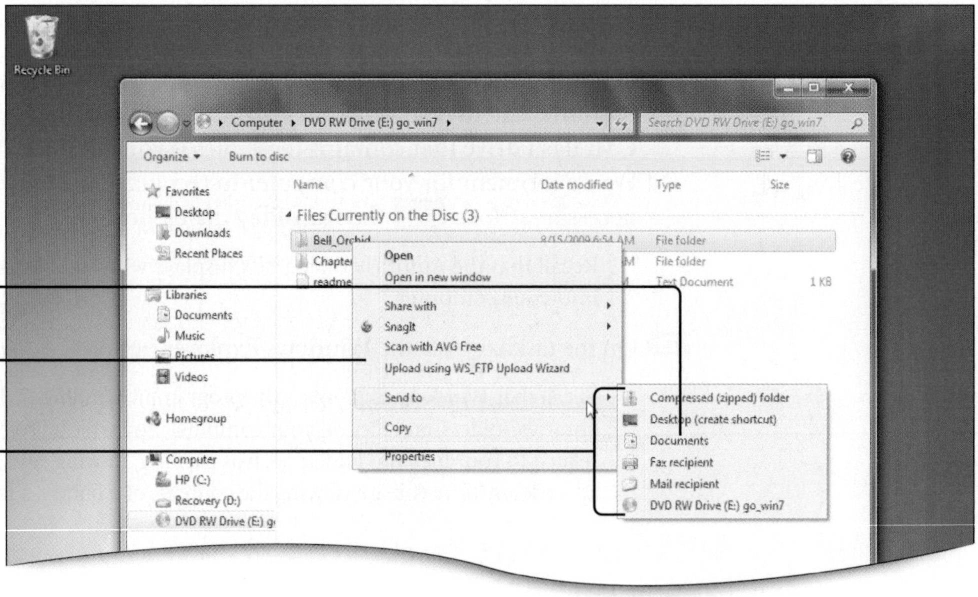

5 On the **Send to** submenu, click **Documents**, and then wait a few moments while Windows 7 copies the Bell_Orchid folder from your device to your Documents library on the hard disk drive.

A ***progress bar*** displays in a dialog box, and also displays on the Windows Explorer taskbar button with green shading. A progress bar indicates visually the progress of a task such as a download or file transfer.

Recall that the Documents library is one of several libraries within your personal folder stored on the hard disk drive. For each user account—even if there is only one user on the computer—Windows 7 creates a personal folder labeled with the account holder's name.

6 When the copy is complete, **Close** [X] the CD/DVD window.

More Knowledge | Deciding Where to Store Your Files

Where should you store your files? In the libraries created by Windows 7 (Documents, Pictures, and so on)? On a removable device like a flash drive or external hard drive?

The design of Windows 7 makes it easy to find your files, especially if you use the libraries. Regardless of where you save a file, Windows 7 will make it easy to find the file again, even if you are not certain where it might be.

The location in which you store your files and folders depends on how you use your computer and how you do your work. The knowledge you gain as you progress in your study of Windows 7 will enable you to decide the best folder structure and storage locations to meet your personal needs. This knowledge will also enable you to work easily with the folder structures in the organizations with which you might be employed.

In Windows 7, you will see that storing all of your files within a *library* will make it easy for you to find your files quickly when you need them. If you perform most of your work on your desktop system or your laptop that travels with you, you can store your files in the libraries created by Windows 7 for your user account—Documents, Pictures, Music, and so on. Within these libraries, you can create folders and subfolders to organize your data. There are several reasons why these libraries are a good choice for storing your files:

- From the Windows Explorer button on the taskbar, your libraries are always just one click away.
- The libraries are designed for their contents; for example, the Pictures folder displays small images of your digital photos.
- You can add new locations to a library; for example, an external hard drive, or a network drive on another computer or network. Locations added to a library behave just like they are on your hard drive.
- Other users of your computer cannot access your libraries.
- The libraries are the default location for opening and saving files within an application, so you will find that you can open and save files with fewer navigation clicks.

Although the libraries are named *Documents* and *Pictures* and so on, you are *not* restricted to storing only one type of file in a particular folder. You have already seen in the Bell_Orchid structure that folders can contain a combination of pictures and documents. However, if you like to store all of your photos together, for example all of the photos you have taken on various vacations, you might choose to store them in the Pictures library.

A storage device such as a USB flash drive is a good choice for storing files when you need to carry your files from one place to another; for example, between your own computer and computers in your campus labs. When you return to your computer, you can copy or move the files from your removable device to the appropriate folders within your user account.

An external hard drive, many of which are pocket sized, is a good choice because it can be included in a library, and thus is easily searchable when you need to find something.

In an organization or in your home, you might be connected to a network on which you have storage space on another computer or server. These can also be part of a library. And increasingly, storage is available on servers on which you can acquire space, such as Microsoft's Windows Live SkyDrive.

Objective 2 | Navigate by Using Windows Explorer

Managing your data—the files and the folders that contain your files—is the single most useful computing skill you can acquire. Become familiar with two important features in Windows 7 if you want to manage your data easily and efficiently—the Windows Explorer program and the ***folder window***.

Windows Explorer is the program within Windows 7 that displays windows such as Control Panel and displays the files and folders on your computer in a folder window. A folder window shows you the contents of a folder. Windows Explorer is at work whenever you are viewing the contents of files and folders in a folder window or viewing the features in a window such as Control Panel.

Activity 2.02 | Pinning a Location to a Jump List

There are numerous ways to ***navigate***—explore within the folder structure for the purpose of finding files and folders. ***Navigation*** refers to the actions you perform when you display a window to locate a command, or when you display the folder window for a folder whose contents you want to view.

In this activity, you will practice various ways in which you can navigate by using Windows Explorer. To do so, you will work with the Bell Orchid corporate data that you just copied to your hard disk drive.

1. On the taskbar, click the **Windows Explorer** button.

2. In the **file list**, double-click **Documents** to display the contents of the Documents library in the file list.

3. In the **file list**, locate and double-click the **Bell_Orchid** folder that you just copied to the Documents library to display its contents in the file list. Compare your screen with Figure 2.4.

Figure 2.4

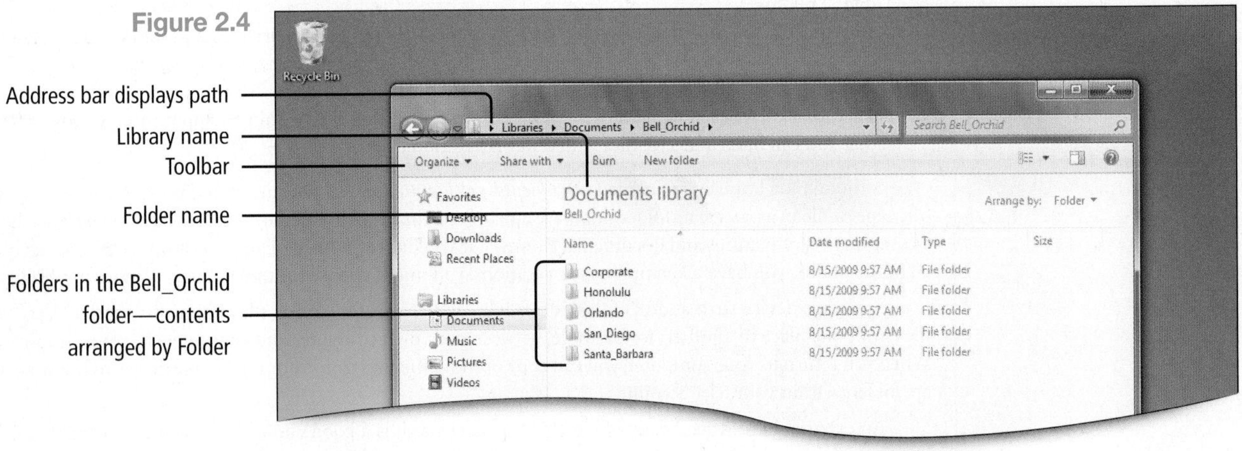

4. In the **file list**, double-click the **Corporate** folder to display its contents. *Point* to the **Accounting** folder, right-click, and then click **Open**.

   Use either technique to open a folder and display its contents. Most computer users use the double-click technique.

5 At the top of the window, in the **address bar**, click **Documents** to redisplay the contents of the Documents library in the file list. Compare your screen with Figure 2.5.

Recall that you can navigate by using the address bar.

Figure 2.5

Address bar displays path

Contents of Documents library displays in file list (your list may include other items)

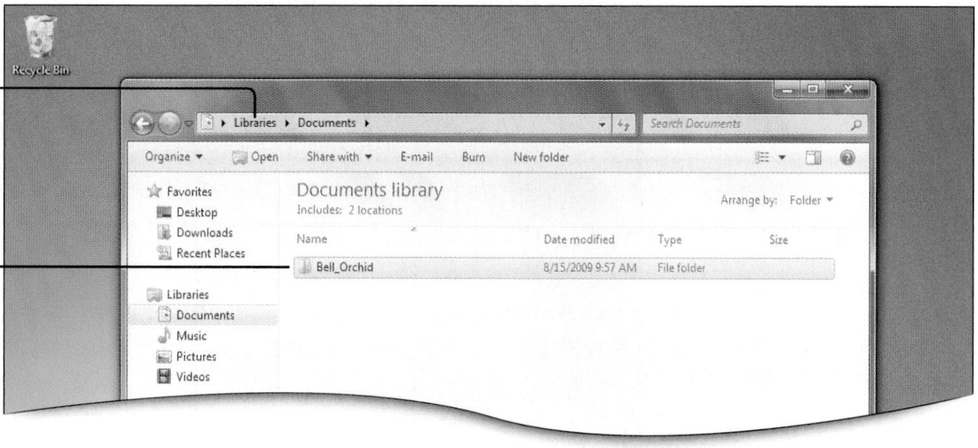

6 In the **file list**, *point* to the **Bell_Orchid** folder, hold down the left mouse button, and then as shown in Figure 2.6, drag the selected folder down to the **Windows Explorer** button until the ScreenTip *Pin to Windows Explorer* displays. Release the mouse button.

Figure 2.6

Bell_Orchid folder in file list

ScreenTip *Pin to Windows Explorer*

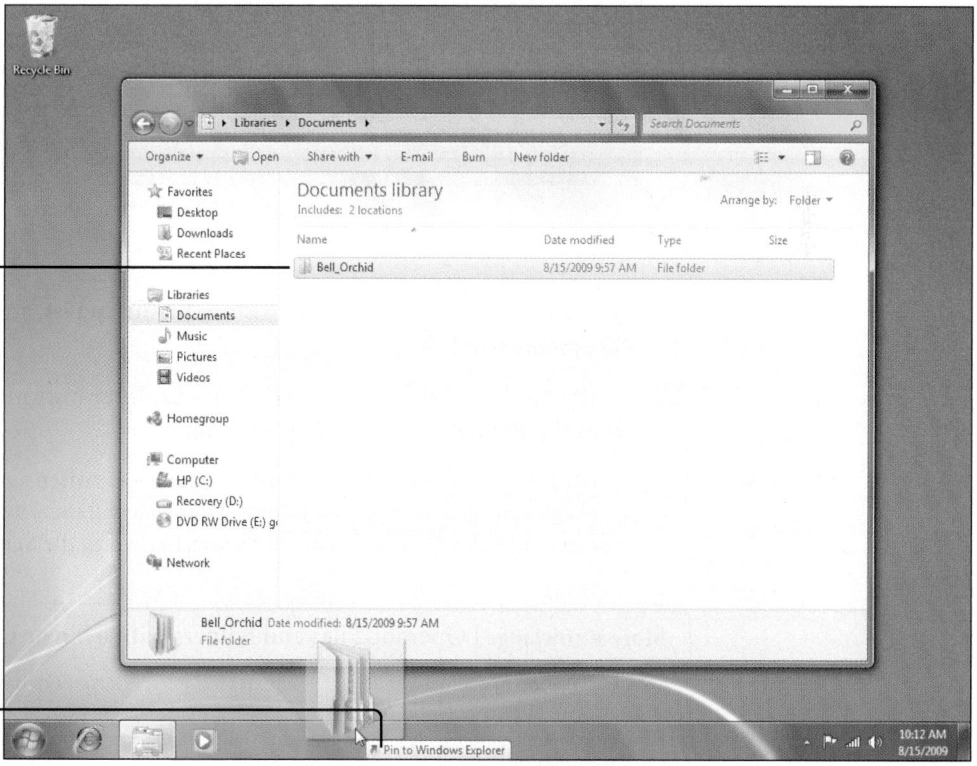

7 Notice the displayed **Jump List**, and then compare your screen with Figure 2.7.

Think of a ***Jump List*** as a mini start menu for a program; it displays locations in the upper portion and tasks in the lower portion.

Now that you have pinned Bell_Orchid to the Jump List, the locations portion of the list displays both Pinned and Frequent locations.

Figure 2.7

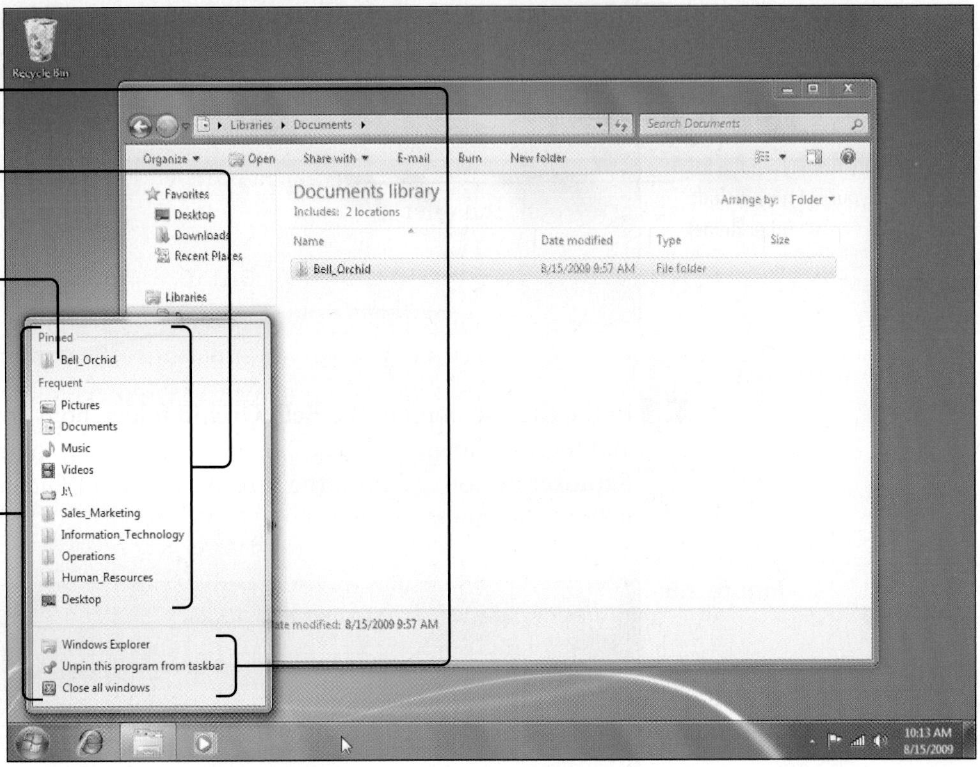

8 Click anywhere on the desktop to close the **Jump List**, and then **Close** the **Documents** window.

9 On the taskbar, right-click the **Windows Explorer** button to display the **Jump List**. From the **Pinned** area, click **Bell_Orchid**.

Use the taskbar—rather than the Start menu—as often as you can to start programs and navigate to specific files and folders. Doing so will increase your efficiency, because it eliminates extra clicks that are necessary to display the Start menu.

Another Way

Open a Jump List by dragging a taskbar button with your left mouse button slightly upward into the desktop.

More Knowledge | Opening Files and Folders with a Single Click in a Folder Window

When navigating in a folder window, if you prefer a single-click motion to open folders and files in the file list, you can set Windows Explorer to open items with a single click instead of a double click. To do so, on the toolbar of any folder window, click Organize, click Folder and search options, and then on the General tab, under Click items as follows, select the Single-click to open an item (point to select) option button. Alternatively, from the Start menu, display the Control Panel, click Appearance and Personalization, and then under Folder Options, click Specify single- or double-click to open; this will display the Folder Options dialog box.

Objective 3 | Create, Name, and Save Files

In many programs, for example in Paint and the programs in Microsoft Office, the program opens and displays a new unnamed and unsaved file. As you begin creating your file in the program, your work is temporarily stored in the computer's memory until you initiate a Save command, at which time you must choose a file name and a location that is reachable from your computer in which to save your file. Recall that a location is any disk drive, folder, or other place in which you can store files and folders.

For saving files or opening existing files, Windows-based programs use a set of ***common dialog boxes***. These are dialog boxes provided by the Windows programming interface that enable programs to have a consistent appearance and behavior. This means that in such dialog boxes, you will find navigation tools that are essentially the same as those in a Windows 7 folder window. For example, in a common dialog box, you will find a navigation pane, toolbar, address bar, Search box, and column headings in which you can sort, group, and filter.

Activity 2.03 | Pinning a Program to the Taskbar

For programs that you use frequently, it is useful to pin the program to the taskbar. The more you perform tasks from the taskbar, the more efficient you will become. Performing tasks from the taskbar reduces the number of times you must display the Start menu. Additionally, placing programs on the taskbar, instead of placing shortcuts to programs on your desktop, keeps your desktop free of clutter.

1. **Close** the **Bell_Orchid** folder window. From the **Start** menu, locate the **Microsoft Word** program on your system; the program might already be displayed on your Start menu, or you might need to locate it by displaying the All Programs menu and opening the Microsoft Office folder.

2. Point to the program name, and then as shown in Figure 2.8, drag the program to the taskbar. Release the mouse button when the ScreenTip *Pin to Taskbar* displays. (If the Word program is already pinned to the taskbar on your system, skip this step.)

   For programs you use frequently, pin them to the taskbar in this manner.

Figure 2.8

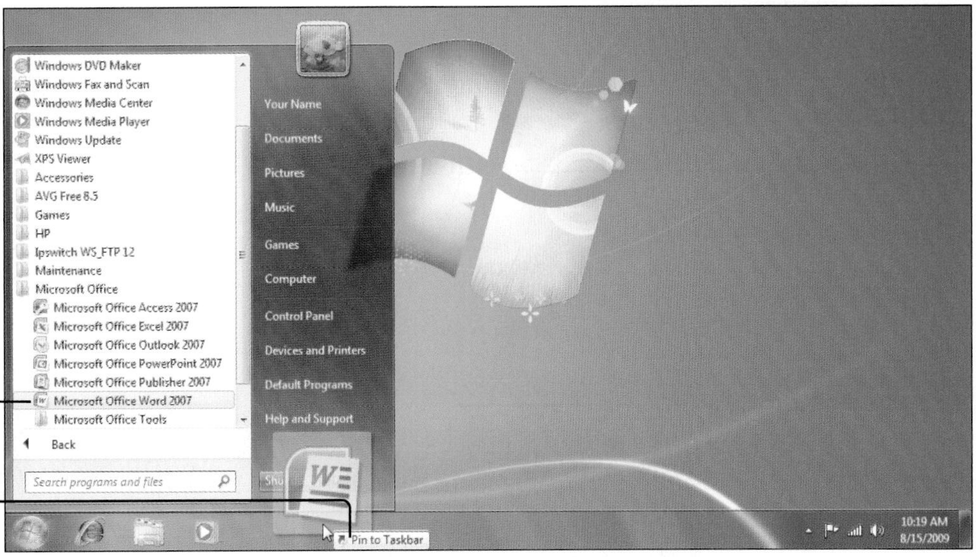

Word program on Start menu (you might have Word 2010)

ScreenTip indicates *Pin to Taskbar*

3 Using the technique you just practiced, pin the **Excel** program to the taskbar, and then click anywhere on the desktop to close the Start menu. Compare your screen with Figure 2.9.

Figure 2.9

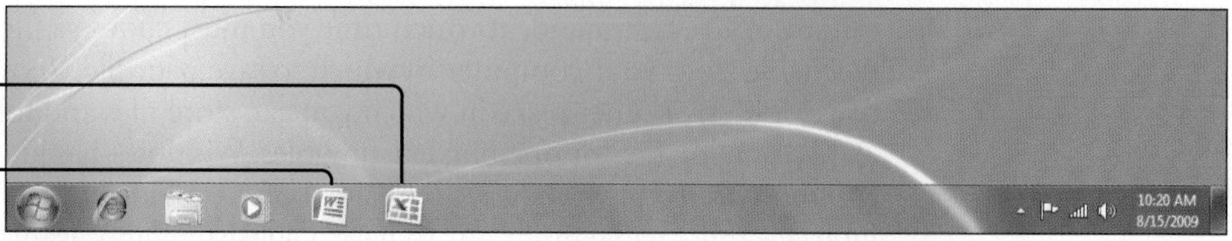

Excel program pinned to taskbar

Word program pinned to taskbar

Activity 2.04 | Naming and Saving Files in Word and Excel

Various managers at the Bell Orchid Hotels have been placing files related to the new European hotels in the Future_Hotels folder. Barbara and Steven have been asked to create some additional files in the Future_Hotels folder, and then managers will continue to add more information to the files as they gather more data about the new hotels.

1 On the taskbar, click the **Word** icon to start the program. If necessary, on the **Home tab**, in the **Paragraph group**, click the **Show/Hide** button ¶ to display formatting marks. Then, on the **View tab**, in the **Show group**, be sure the **Ruler** check box is selected. Compare your screen with Figure 2.10.

On the taskbar, the Word icon displays a glass frame to indicate that the program is open.

Figure 2.10

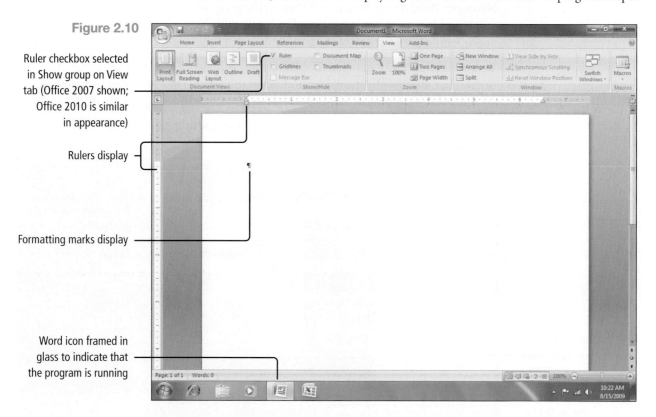

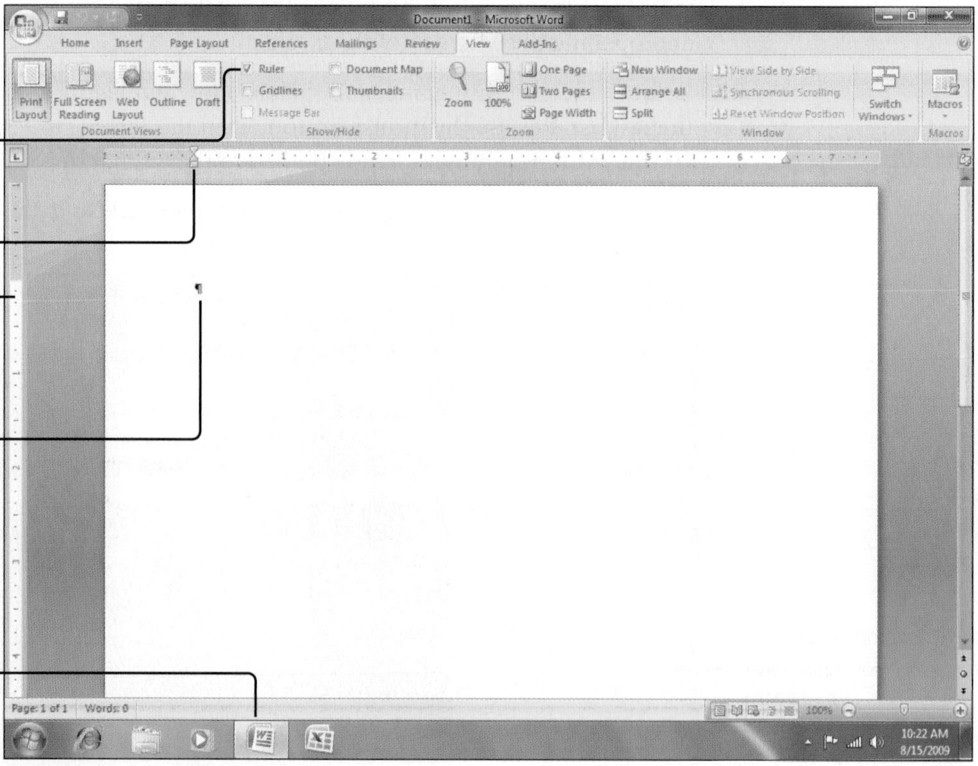

Ruler checkbox selected in Show group on View tab (Office 2007 shown; Office 2010 is similar in appearance)

Rulers display

Formatting marks display

Word icon framed in glass to indicate that the program is running

2 In the Word window, at the insertion point, type **The data for this overview of the Europe project will be provided at a later date by the Chief Operations Manager.**

3 Across the top of your keyboard, locate the function keys numbered F1 to F12, and then press F12 to display the **Save As** dialog box. Compare your screen with Figure 2.11.

In the Microsoft Office programs, F12 displays the Save As dialog box.

The Save As dialog box is an example of a common dialog box; that is, this dialog box looks the same in Excel and in PowerPoint and in most other Windows-based programs.

In the Save As dialog box, you must indicate the name you want for the file and the location where you want to save the file. Programs like Microsoft Word commonly ask you to choose a name and location when you save a file.

When working with your own data, it is good practice to pause at this point and determine the logical name and location for your file.

Figure 2.11

Save As dialog box

Address bar indicates path

Navigation pane

File name box, first characters typed become default file name

Save as type defaults to *Word Document*

Default save location is *Documents library* (yours may differ)

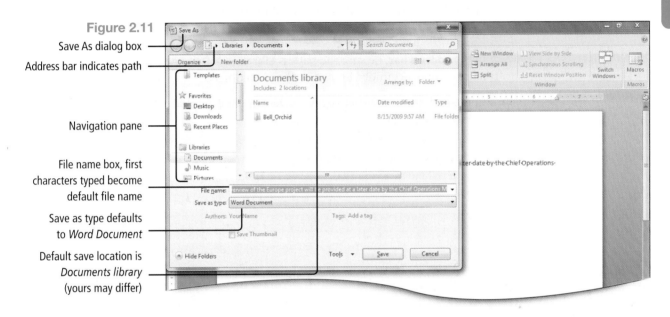

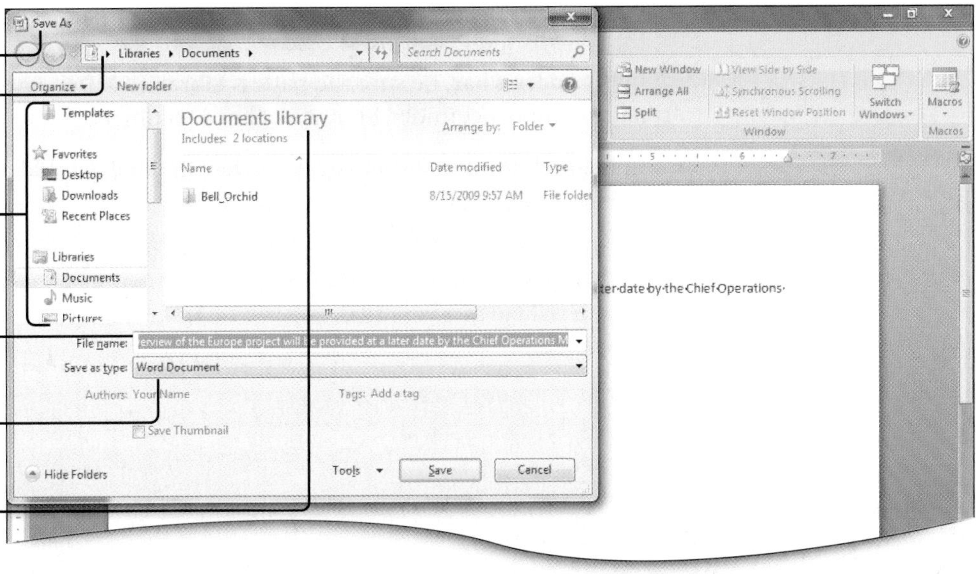

Alert! | **Do you have a different default location?**

If Documents is not your default storage location, in the navigation pane, under Libraries, click Documents. For most programs that you install on your computer, the default location for storing files will be one of the folders in your personal folder—based on the type of file. The default location for storing Word documents will be the Documents folder, the default location for storing pictures will be the Pictures folder, and so on.

Within a specific program, however, there is usually a method whereby you can change the default save location that displays in the Save As dialog box. You can change the default location to any storage area and folder accessible from your computer; to do so, refer to the documentation for the specific program.

4 In the **Save as type box**, notice that the default file type is a **Word Document**. In the **File name** box, notice that Word selects the first characters of the document as the default name.

Recall that many programs use the Documents library as the default storage location; however, you can navigate to other storage locations from this dialog box.

5. Be sure the text in the **File name** box is selected—highlighted in blue; if it is not, click one time with your mouse to select it. Type **Europe_Project** as the **File name**. Then in the lower right corner of the dialog box, click **Save** to save the file in the **Documents** folder.

   In any Windows-based application, such as Microsoft Word, text highlighted in blue will be replaced by your typing.

   The Word document is saved and the file name displays in the title bar of the Word window.

6. On the taskbar, click the **Excel** button to start the Excel program.

7. Be sure that cell **A1** is the active cell—it is outlined in black—and then type **An overview of the financial plan for the Europe project will be provided at a later date by the Chief Financial Officer.** and then press Enter.

8. Press F12 to display the **Save As** dialog box.

9. In the **address bar**, be sure the path is **Libraries ▶Documents ▶**; if necessary, in the navigation pane, under Libraries, click Documents.

10. In the **file list**, scroll if necessary to view the **Bell_Orchid** folder. Compare your screen to Figure 2.12.

    To save in a location other than the default location, which in this instance is your *Documents* folder, you must navigate to open the folder window for the folder in which you want to save your file.

Figure 2.12

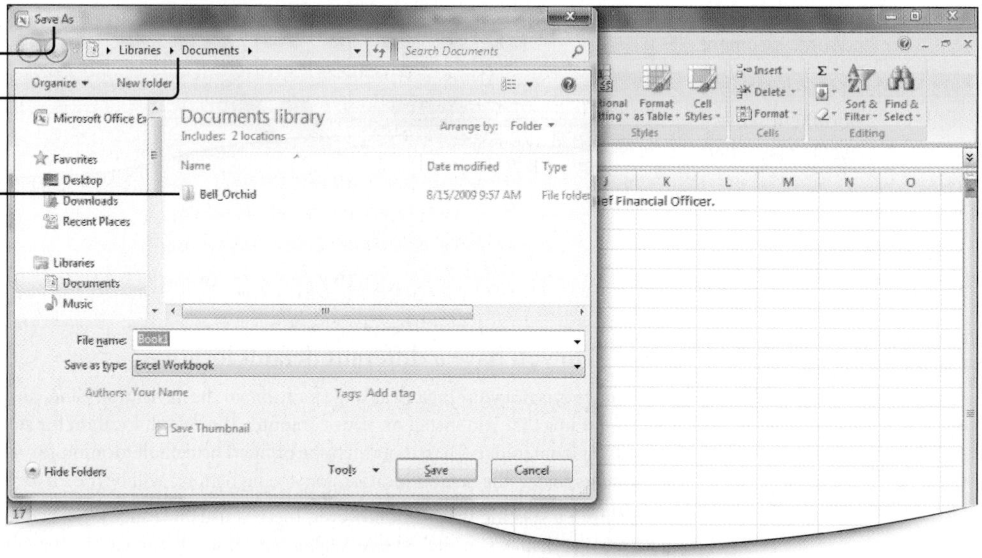

Save As dialog box

Address bar indicates *Libraries ▶ Documents ▶*

Bell_Orchid folder in file list (your list may vary)

11 In the **file list**, double-click the **Bell_Orchid** folder to open it. Double-click **Corporate**, and then double-click **Information_Technology**. Compare your screen with Figure 2.13.

Figure 2.13

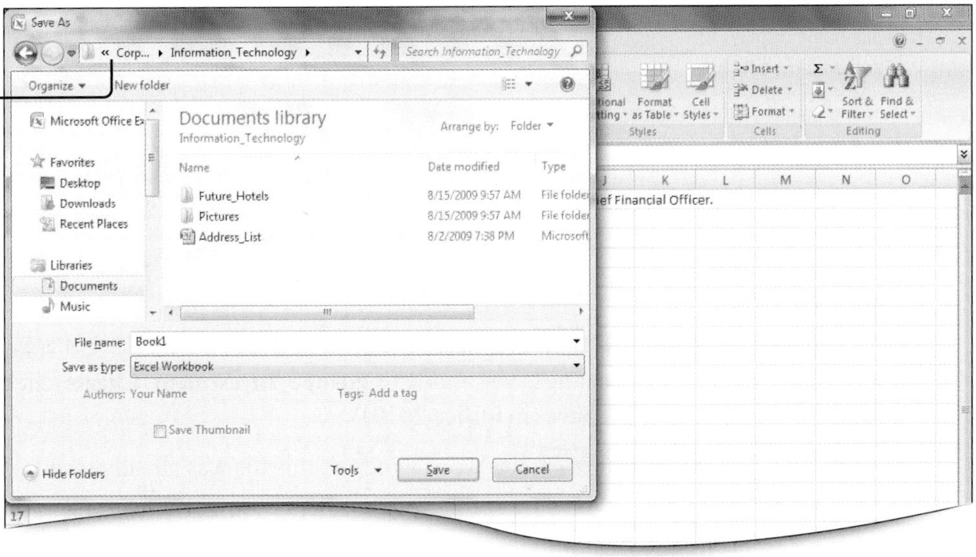

12 With the **Information_Technology** folder window displayed in the **Save As** dialog box, click in the **File name** box to select the default text *Book1*, type **Europe_Financials** and then in the lower right corner, click the **Save** button—or press Enter—to save the file and close the **Save As** dialog box.

The Excel workbook is saved and the file name displays in the title bar of the Excel window.

13 Press F12 to display the **Save As** dialog box again.

14 In the **address bar**, notice that the **Information_Technology** folder where you stored the previous Excel workbook displays—instead of the Documents folder.

Until you close Excel or change the storage location, Excel will continue to suggest the most recent location as the storage location. Most programs behave in this manner.

15 In the **File name** box, with the text *Europe_Financials* selected—highlighted in blue—type **Europe_Investment_Charts** and then press Enter or click **Save**.

Windows 7 saves and closes the Europe_Financials workbook, and then creates a new workbook, with the name you just typed, based on the old one. Use the Save As command in this manner when you want to create a new document that uses information from an existing document.

Note | The Difference Between Save and Save As

When you are saving something for the first time, for example a new unnamed Excel workbook, the Save and Save As commands are identical. That is, the Save As dialog box will display if you click Save or if you click Save As.

After you have named a file and stored it somewhere, the Save command saves any changes you make to the file without displaying any dialog box. The Save As command will display the Save As dialog box and let you name and save a new document based on the old one. After you name and save the new document, the original document closes, and the new document—based on the old one—displays.

16 In cell **A2**, type **A group of charts depicting the investment plan for the Europe project will be provided at a later date by the Chief Financial Officer.** Press Enter. Compare your screen with Figure 2.14.

Figure 2.14

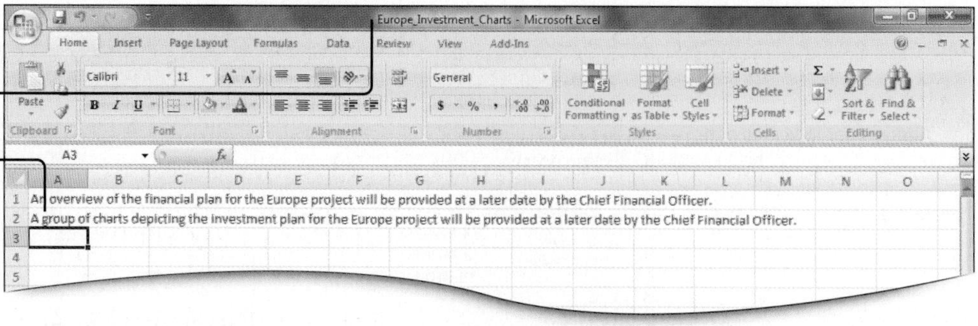

17 **Close** the Excel window, and when a message displays asking if you want to save the changes you made to **Europe_Investment_Charts**, click **Yes** (in Office 2007), or click **Save** (in Office 2010).

18 **Close** the Word window; this file was already saved, so no message displays.

More Knowledge | Rules for Naming Files

There are three rules to consider when naming files:

- File names usually cannot be longer than 255 characters.
- You cannot use any of the following characters in a file name:
  \ / ? : * " > < |
- File names must be unique in a folder; that is, two files of the same type—for example two Excel files—cannot have the exact same name. Likewise, two subfolders within a folder cannot have the exact same name.

You might also consider this guideline:

- You can use spaces in file names; however, some individuals and organizations prefer not to use spaces. There are some programs, especially when transferring files over the Internet, that may not work well with spaces in file names. In general, however, unless you encounter a problem, it is okay to use spaces. In this textbook, underscores are used instead of spaces in the names of files.

Objective 4 | Create Folders and Rename Folders and Files

As you create files, you will also want to create folders so that you can organize your files into a logical folder structure. It is common to rename files and folders so that the names reflect the content.

Activity 2.05 | Creating Folders and Renaming Folders and Files

Barbara and Steven can see that various managers have been placing files related to the new European hotels in the *Future_Hotels* folder. They can also see that the files have not been organized into a logical structure. For example, files that are related to each other are not in separate folders; instead, they are mixed in with other files that are not related to the topic.

In this activity, you will create, name, and rename folders to begin a logical structure of folders in which to organize the files related to the European hotels project.

1 If necessary, insert the USB flash drive on which you are storing your work for this chapter, and close the AutoPlay dialog box if it displays.

Another Way

If you were not able to pin the folder to the Jump List, click the Windows Explorer button, and then in the Documents library, navigate to the Bell_Orchid folder.

2 On the taskbar, right-click the **Windows Explorer** button to display the **Jump List**, and then under **Pinned**, click **Bell_Orchid**.

3 In the **address bar**, to the right of **Bell_Orchid**, click ▶, and then on the list click **Corporate**. To the right of **Corporate**, click ▶, and then click **Information_Technology**. To the right of **Information_Technology**, click ▶, and then click **Future_Hotels**.

Some computer users prefer to navigate a folder structure using the address bar in this manner. Use whichever method you prefer—double-clicking in the file list or clicking in the address bar. You can also expand folders in the navigation pane, although the viewing space there is smaller.

Another Way

Right-click in a blank area of the file list, point to View, and then click Details.

4 Be sure the items are in alphabetical order by **Name**. At the right end of the toolbar, click the **View button arrow**, and if necessary, set the view to **Details**. Compare your screen with Figure 2.15.

The ***Details view*** displays a list of files or folders and their most common ***properties***. Properties are descriptive pieces of information about a folder or file such as the name, the date modified, the type, and the size. These are the most common properties and the ones you see in the Details pane when a folder or file is selected.

This view is useful when you are organizing files and folders.

Figure 2.15

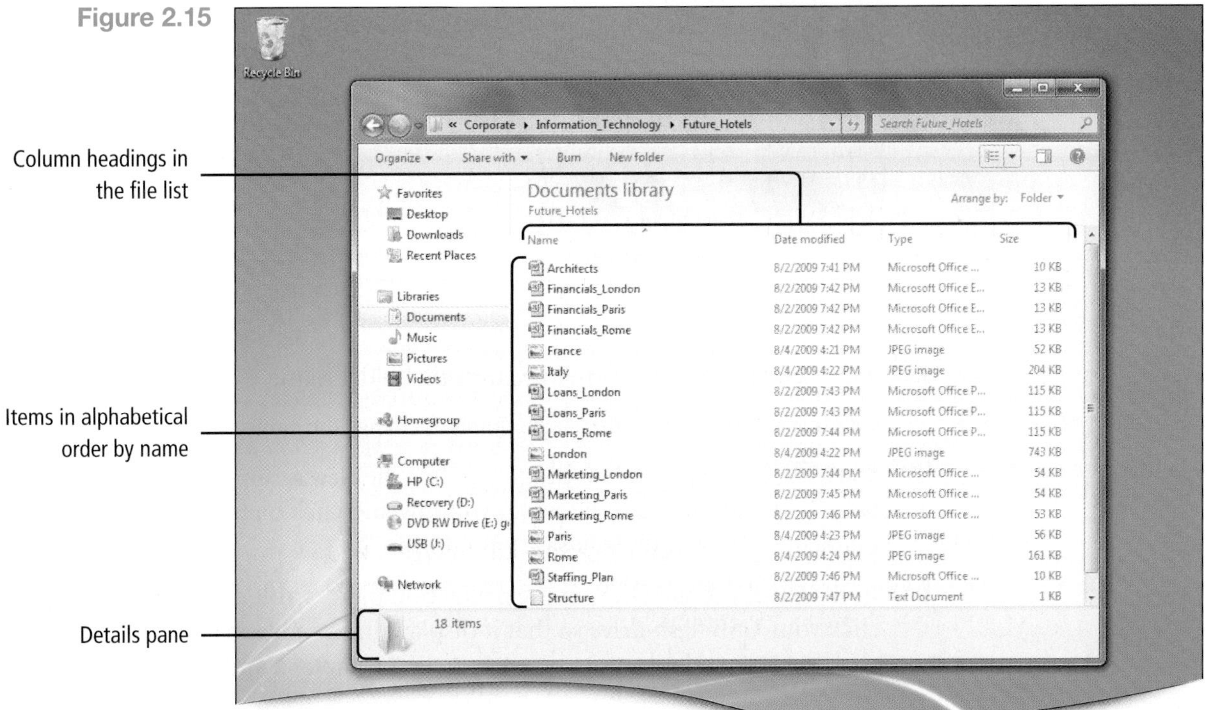

Note | Date Modified and Other Details May Vary

The Date modified and some other details shown in the Figures may differ from what displays on your screen.

5 On the toolbar, click the **New folder** button. With the text *New folder* selected, type **Paris** and press Enter. Click the **New folder** button again, and then type **Venice** and press Enter.

6 Notice how the folders automatically move into alphabetical order. Notice also that when you have both files and folders in a folder, the folders are listed first.

The default organization of a file list in Windows 7 is to list folders first, in alphabetical order, and then files in alphabetical order.

7 Create a new folder named **Essex** and press Enter. Point to the **Venice** folder and right-click. From the displayed menu, click **Rename**, and then notice that the text *Venice* is selected. Type **Rome** and press Enter.

8 Click the **Essex** folder one time to select it. Point to the selected **Essex** folder, and then click one time again. Compare your screen with Figure 2.16.

Recall that any time text like this is selected, your typing replaces the existing text.

Figure 2.16

Folder name
Essex selected

Subfolders display
before files

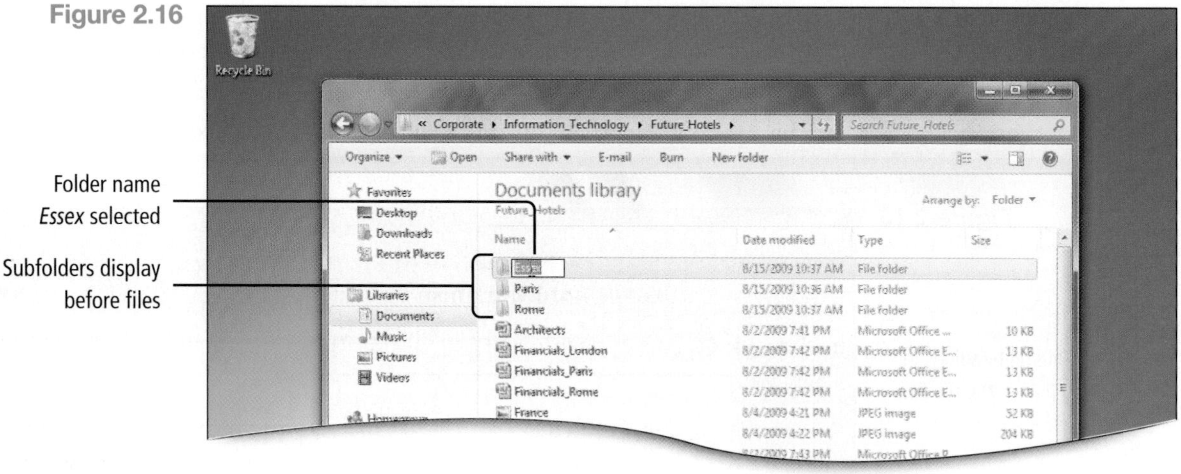

9 Type **London** and press Enter to change the folder name.

You can use either of these techniques to change the name of a folder.

10 Start ◉ the **Snipping Tool** program, click the **New arrow**, and then click **Window Snip**. Point anywhere in the folder window and click one time. In the **Snipping Tool** mark-up window, click the **Save Snip** button 🖫.

11 In the **Save As** dialog box, in the navigation pane, scroll down as necessary, and then click your USB flash drive so that it displays in the **address bar**. On the toolbar, click the **New folder** button, type **Windows 7 Chapter 2** and press Enter.

12 In the **file list**, double-click your **Windows 7 Chapter 2** folder to open it. Click in the **File name** box, and then replace the selected text by typing **Lastname_Firstname_2A_Europe_Folders_Snip** Compare your screen with Figure 2.17.

Figure 2.17

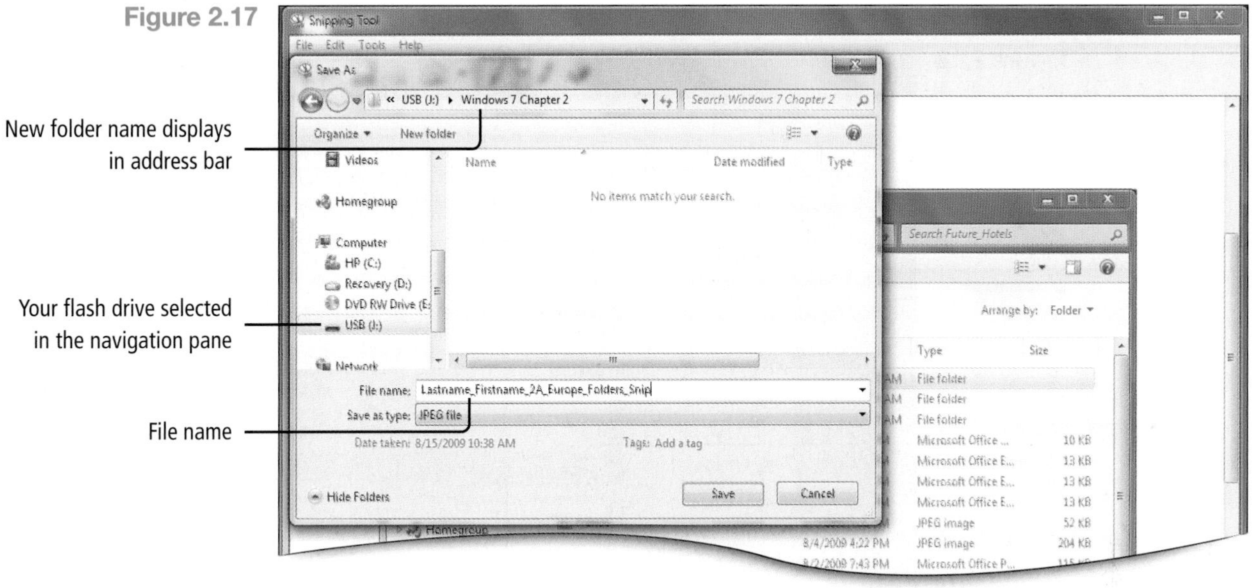

13 Be sure the file type is **JPEG**. Click **Save** or press Enter. **Close** the **Snipping Tool** window. Hold this file until you finish Project 2A.

14 In the **address bar**, click **Information_Technology** to move up one level in the folder structure.

Recall that you can move up by one or more levels by clicking the folder name on the address bar, and you can move to a subfolder in any folder on the address bar by clicking the ▶ arrow and displaying the list of subfolders.

15 In the **column headings area**, point to *Name*, right-click, and then click **Size Column to Fit**.

16 Point to the file **Europe_Investment_Charts** and click one time to select it. Click the file one time again to select the text. Position your mouse pointer anywhere over the selected text and notice that the I pointer displays. Compare your screen with Figure 2.18.

Figure 2.18

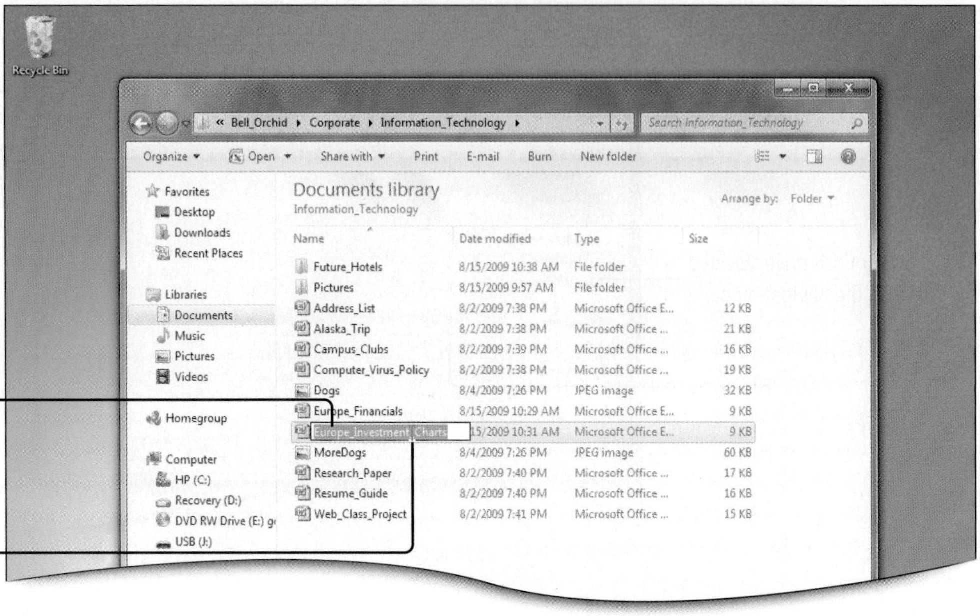

Text *Europe_Investment_ Charts* selected

I-beam pointer

17 Position the I pointer slightly to the left of the word *Investment* and click one time to position the insertion point within the file name. By using Del or the arrow keys or any other keys on your keyboard, edit the file name to **Europe_Charts** and press Enter.

You can use any of these techniques to change the name of a file or folder.

18 **Close** the window.

Objective 5 | Select, Copy, and Move Files and Folders

To ***select*** is to highlight, by clicking or dragging with the mouse, one or more file or folder names in the file list. Selecting in this manner is commonly done for the purpose of copying, moving, renaming, or deleting the selected files or folders.

Activity 2.06 | Selecting Groups of Files or Folders in the File List

There are several ways to select multiple items in a file list—use whatever method you prefer or that is convenient. The techniques you will practice in this activity apply not only to Windows 7, but also to lists of files that display in other applications.

1 On the taskbar, right-click the **Windows Explorer** button to display the **Jump List**, and then under **Pinned**, click **Bell_Orchid**. In the upper right corner of the window, click the **Maximize** button so that the window fills the entire screen.

Recall that starting from the taskbar is usually the fastest and most efficient way to navigate in Windows 7, so use the Jump Lists whenever it is practical to do so. Think of a Jump List as a mini start menu for a program.

2 With the **Bell_Orchid** folder window displayed, by double-clicking in the file list—or by clicking the links in the address bar—navigate to **Corporate ▶ Information_ Technology ▶ Future_Hotels.** Compare your screen with Figure 2.19.

Figure 2.19

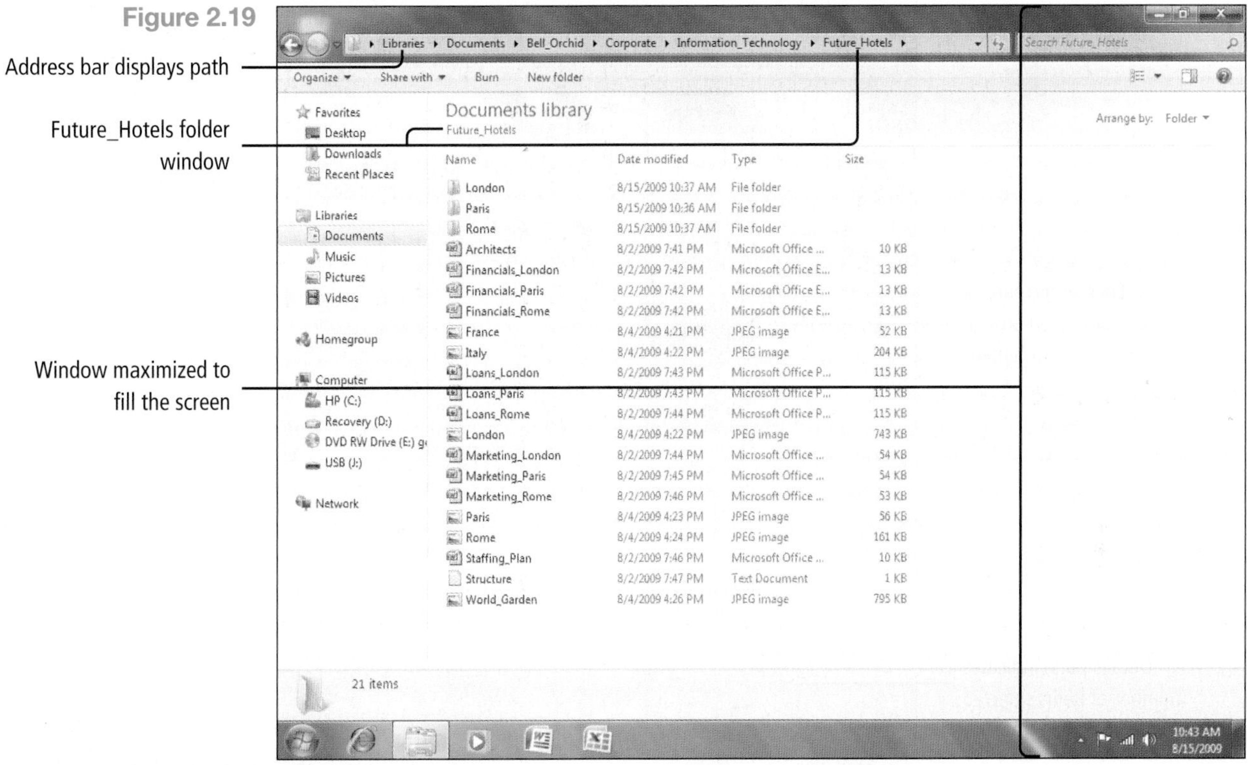

3 In the **file list**, click the Excel file **Financials_London** one time to select it. With the file name selected, hold down Shift, and then click the Word file **Staffing_Plan.**

This technique, commonly referred to as ***Shift Click***, selects a consecutive group of files or folders. To select all the items in a consecutive group, you need only to click the first item, hold down Shift, and then click the last item in the group.

4 Click in a blank area of the **file list** to cancel the selection—also referred to as ***deselect***. Point to, but do *not* click in, the empty space immediately to the right of the file name **Financials_London**, hold down the left mouse button, and then drag to the left side of the column and down to the **Financials_Rome** folder, creating a small square as you drag, as shown in Figure 2.20.

Figure 2.20

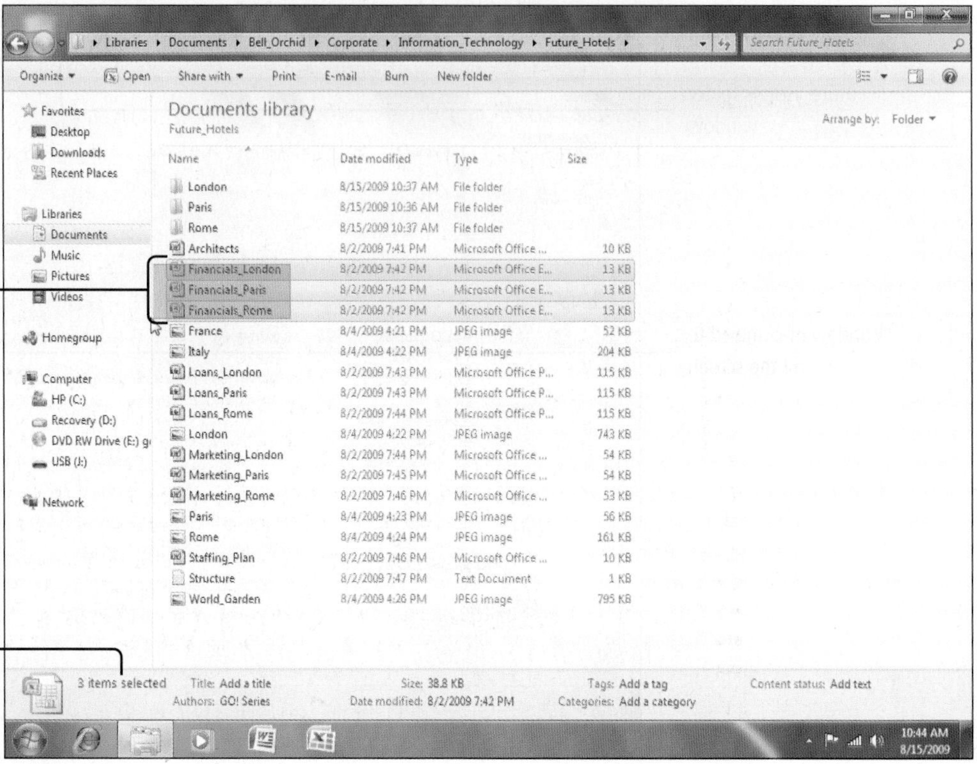

Dragging creates a selection area around the items

Details pane indicates number of items selected

5 Release the left mouse button, and notice that the three files are selected. If you are not satisfied with your result, click in a blank area of the file list to deselect, and then begin again.

In this manner, you can use only the mouse to create a selection around the outside of all the items you want to include in the selection.

6 Deselect by clicking in a blank area of the **file list**. Select the file **Financials_London**, hold down Ctrl, and then click **Marketing_London**. Notice that only the two files are selected. With the two files selected, hold down Ctrl, and then click **Financials_Rome** and **Marketing_Rome**. Release Ctrl.

Four files are selected. Use this Ctrl key technique when you want to select a group of *nonconsecutive* items.

7 With the four files still selected, hold down Ctrl, and then click the selected files **Marketing_Rome** and **Financials_Rome**. Release the key.

To cancel the selection of individual items within a selected group, hold down Ctrl, and then click the items you do *not* want to include.

Another Way

On the toolbar, click Organize, and then on the menu, click Select All.

8 Deselect by clicking in a blank area of the file list. Click any single file or folder in the list, and then hold down Ctrl and press A. Release the two keys.

Use this technique to select all of the files or folders in the file list.

9 Click anywhere in the file list to deselect. In the upper right corner, click the **Restore Down** button to restore the window to its previous size, and then **Close** the **Future_Hotels** folder window.

Activity 2.07 | Copying Files

When you *copy* a file or a folder, you make a duplicate of the original item and then store the duplicate in another location. In this activity, you will assist Barbara and Steven in making copies of the Staffing_Plan file, and then placing a copy in each of the three folders you created—London, Paris, and Rome.

1 In the taskbar, point to the **Windows Explorer** button, hold down the left mouse button, and then drag upward slightly into the desktop to display the **Jump List**. Then, on the **Jump List**, under **Pinned**, click **Bell_Orchid**.

You will increase your efficiency if you make it a habit to work mostly from the taskbar and to display Jump Lists using this technique. After the Jump List displays, you need only move your mouse pointer upward a little more to select the action that you want.

2 With the **Bell_Orchid** folder window displayed, by double-clicking in the file list or following the links in the address bar, navigate to **Corporate ▶ Information_Technology ▶ Future_Hotels**.

3 **Maximize** the folder window and if necessary, set the **View button arrow** to **Details**.

Another Way

To perform the Copy command and the Paste command, you can use the keyboard shortcut Ctrl + C to activate the Copy command and the keyboard shortcut Ctrl + V to activate the Paste command. Also, the Copy and Paste commands are available on the Organize menu on the toolbar.

4 In the **file list**, point to the file **Staffing_Plan** and right-click. On the displayed menu, click **Copy**.

The Copy command places a copy of your selected file or folder on the ***Clipboard*** where it will be stored until you replace it with another Copy command. The Clipboard is a temporary storage area for information that you have copied or moved from one place and plan to use somewhere else.

In Windows 7, the Clipboard can hold only one piece of information at a time. Whenever something is copied to the Clipboard, it replaces whatever was there before. In Windows 7, you cannot view the contents of the Clipboard nor place multiple items there in the manner that you can in Microsoft Word.

5 At the top of the **file list**, point to the **London folder**, right-click, and then click **Paste**. Then double-click the **London** folder to open it. Notice that the copy of the **Staffing_Plan** file displays. Compare your screen with Figure 2.21.

Figure 2.21

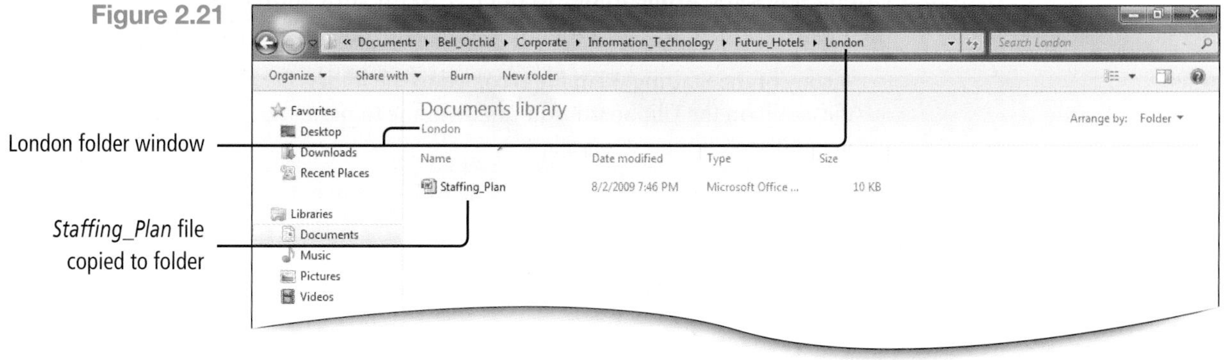

> **Another Way**
>
> On the left end of the address bar, you can press the Back button to retrace your clicks as necessary to display the window you want. Or, click in a blank area of the file list to deselect anything that is selected, and then press Bksp to move up one level in the folder structure.

6 With the **London** folder open, by using any of the techniques you have practiced, rename this copy of the **Staffing_Plan** file to **London_Staffing_Plan** (Hint: The most efficient way to rename this file is to click the file name three times—but not so rapidly that you actually open the file—to display the insertion point in the file name, and then edit the name as necessary.)

7 In the **address bar**, click **Future_Hotels** to redisplay this folder window and move up one level in the folder structure.

8 Select and then point to the **Staffing_Plan** file, hold down Ctrl, drag upward over the **Paris** folder until the ScreenTip + *Copy to Paris* displays as shown in Figure 2.22, and then release the mouse button and release Ctrl.

When dragging a file into a folder, holding down Ctrl engages the Copy command and places a copy of the file at the location where you release the mouse button. This is another way to copy a file or copy a folder.

Figure 2.22

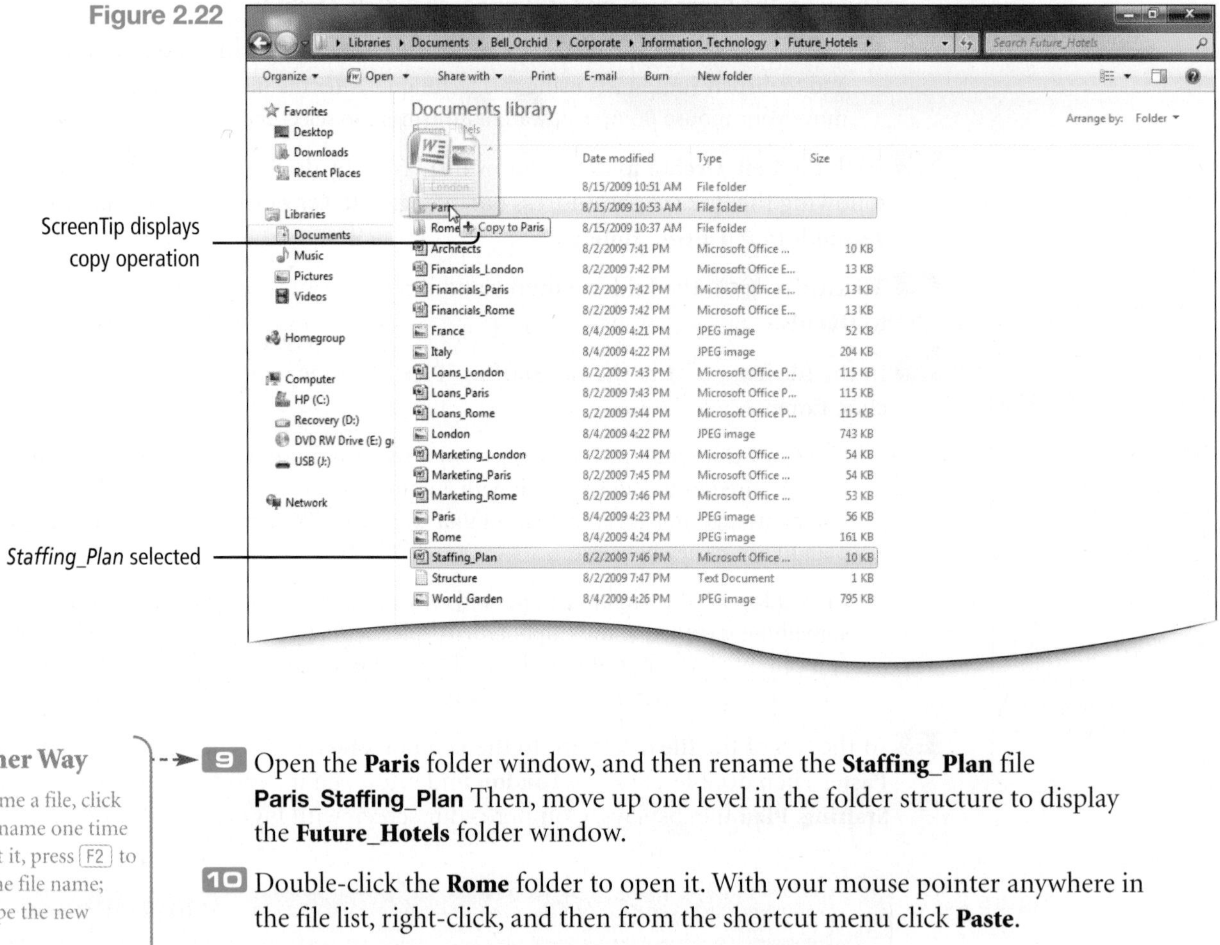

> **Another Way**
>
> To rename a file, click the file name one time to select it, press F2 to select the file name; then type the new name.

9 Open the **Paris** folder window, and then rename the **Staffing_Plan** file **Paris_Staffing_Plan** Then, move up one level in the folder structure to display the **Future_Hotels** folder window.

10 Double-click the **Rome** folder to open it. With your mouse pointer anywhere in the file list, right-click, and then from the shortcut menu click **Paste**.

A copy of the Staffing_Plan file is copied to the folder. Because a copy of the Staffing_Plan file is still on the Clipboard, you can continue to paste the item until you copy another item on the Clipboard to replace it.

11 Rename the file **Rome_Staffing_Plan** and then compare your screen with Figure 2.23.

Figure 2.23

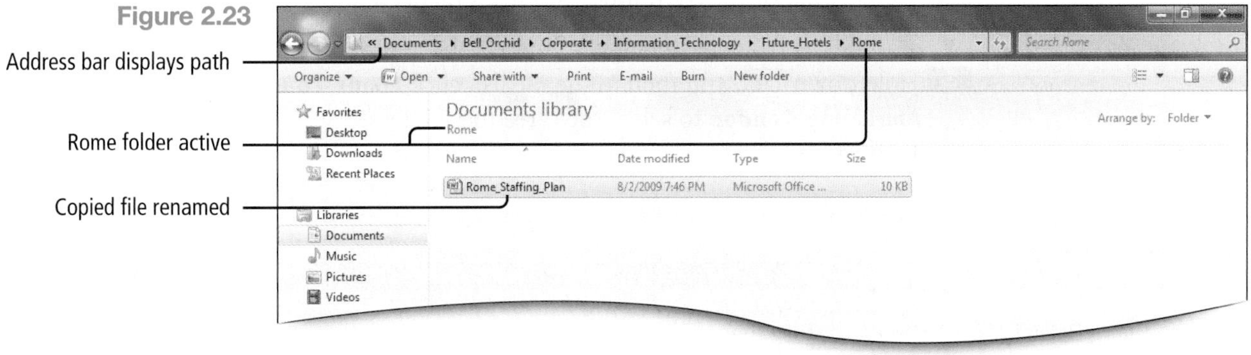

12 On the **address bar**, click **Future_Hotels** to move up one level and open the **Future_Hotels** folder window. Leave this folder open for the next activity.

Activity 2.08 | Moving Files

When you *move* a file or folder, you remove it from the original location and store it in a new location. In this activity, you will move items from the Future_Hotels folder into their appropriate folders.

Another Way

To initiate the Cut command, press Ctrl + X.

1 With the **Future_Hotels** folder open, in the **file list**, point to the Excel file **Financials_London** and right-click. On the displayed shortcut menu, click **Cut**.

The file's Excel icon is dimmed on the screen. This action places the item on the Clipboard.

Another Way

To initiate the Paste command, press Ctrl + V.

2 Point to the **London** folder, right-click, and then click **Paste**. Notice that the file is removed from the file list. Then open the **London** folder, and notice that the file was pasted into the folder.

3 On the **address bar**, click **Future_Hotels** to move up a level. In the **file list**, point to **Financials_Paris**, hold down the left mouse button, and then drag the file upward over the **Paris** folder until the ScreenTip →*Move to Paris* displays, as shown in Figure 2.24. Release the mouse button.

Figure 2.24

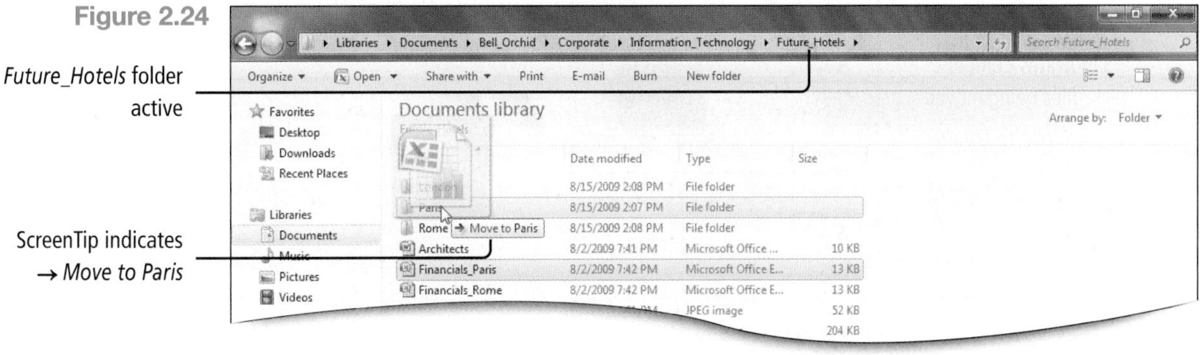

4 Open the **Paris** folder, and notice that the file was moved to this folder. On the **address bar**, click **Future_Hotels** to return to that folder.

5 Using either of the techniques you just practiced, move the **Financials_Rome** file into the **Rome** folder.

6 Hold down Ctrl, and then in the file list, click **Loans_London**, **London**, and **Marketing_London** to select the three files. Release the Ctrl key. Compare your screen with Figure 2.25.

Figure 2.25

Future_Hotels folder active

Three files selected

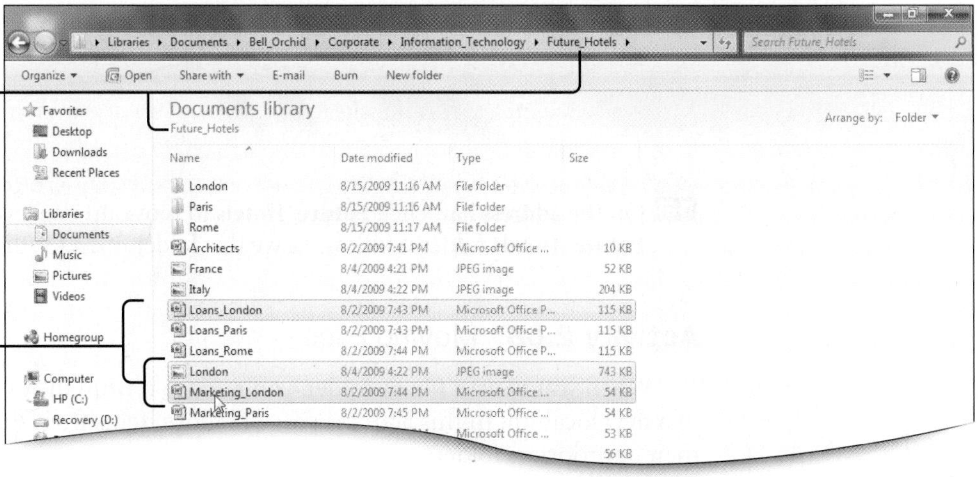

> **Another Way**
>
> Right-click over any of the selected files, click Cut, right-click over the London folder, and then click Paste.

7 Point to any of the selected files, hold down the left mouse button, and then drag upward over the **London** folder until the ScreenTip →*Move to London* displays and *3* displays over the files being moved, as shown in Figure 2.26. Release the mouse button.

The three files are moved to the London folder.

Figure 2.26

Future_Hotels folder active

3 indicates number of files being moved

→ *Move to London* indicates files being moved to London folder

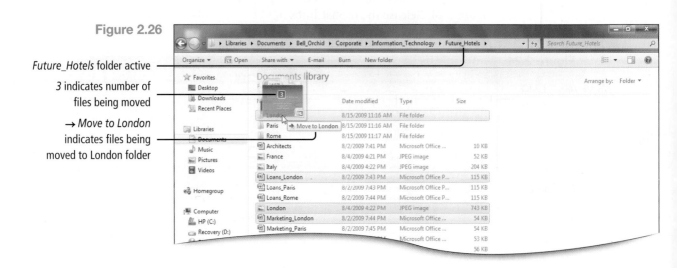

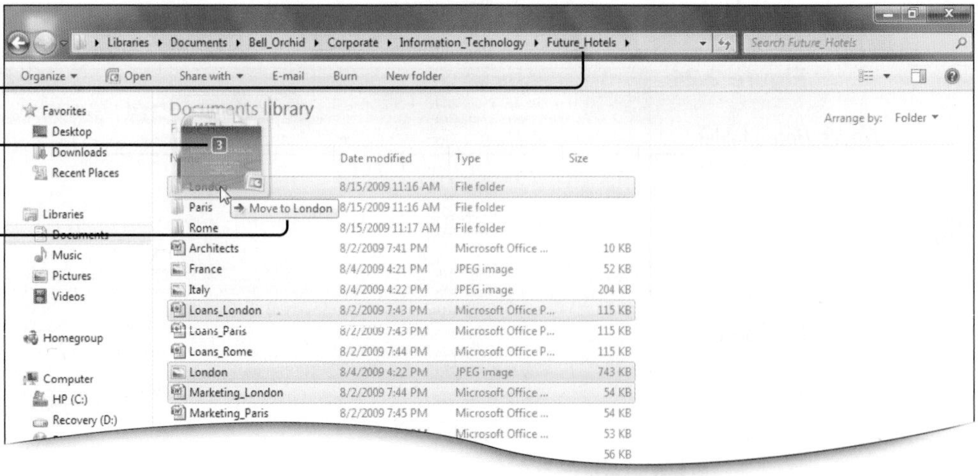

8 Using either the select and drag method, or the select and then Cut and Paste method, select the files **France**, **Loans_Paris**, **Marketing_Paris**, and **Paris**, and move these four files into the **Paris** folder.

9 Select the four files **Italy**, **Loans_Rome**, **Marketing_Rome**, and **Rome**, and move them into the **Rome** folder.

You can see that by keeping related files together, for example, all the files that relate to the Rome hotel, in folders that have an appropriately descriptive name, it will be easier to locate information later.

10 Move the **Architects** file into the **London** folder.

> **Another Way**
> Press Ctrl + Z to undo an action in the file list.

11 In an empty area of the file list, right-click, and then click **Undo Move**. Leave the window open for the next activity.

Any action that you make in a file list can be undone in this manner.

Activity 2.09 | Copying and Moving Files by Using Two Windows

Sometimes you will want to open, in a second window, another instance of a program that you are using; that is, two copies of the program will be running simultaneously. This capability is especially useful in the Windows Explorer program, because you are frequently moving or copying files from one location to another.

In this activity, you will open two instances of Windows Explorer, and then use the Snap feature to display both instances on your screen.

To copy or move files or folders into a different level of a folder structure, or to a different drive location, the most efficient method is to display two windows side by side and then use drag and drop; or use copy (or cut) and paste commands.

In this activity, you will assist Barbara and Steven in making copies of the Staffing_Plan files for the corporate office. You will also place the Europe_Project file, which is still in the Documents folder, in its proper location.

1 In the upper right corner, click the **Restore Down** button to restore the **Future_Hotels** folder window to its previous size and not maximized on the screen.

2 Point to the upper edge of the **Future_Hotels** folder window to display the pointer, and then drag the window to the left until the pointer reaches the left edge of the screen and the window snaps into place and occupies the left half of the screen.

> **Another Way**
> On the Jump List, click Windows Explorer to open a second copy of the program.

3 On the taskbar, point to the **Windows Explorer** button, drag upward slightly into the desktop to display the **Jump List**, and then click **Bell_Orchid** to open a new folder window. Snap this window to the right side of the screen.

4 In the folder window on the right, navigate to **Corporate ▶ Human_Resources.** Compare your screen with Figure 2.27.

Figure 2.27

Future_Hotels folder window snapped to left side of screen

Corporate ▶ Human_Resources folder window snapped to right side of screen

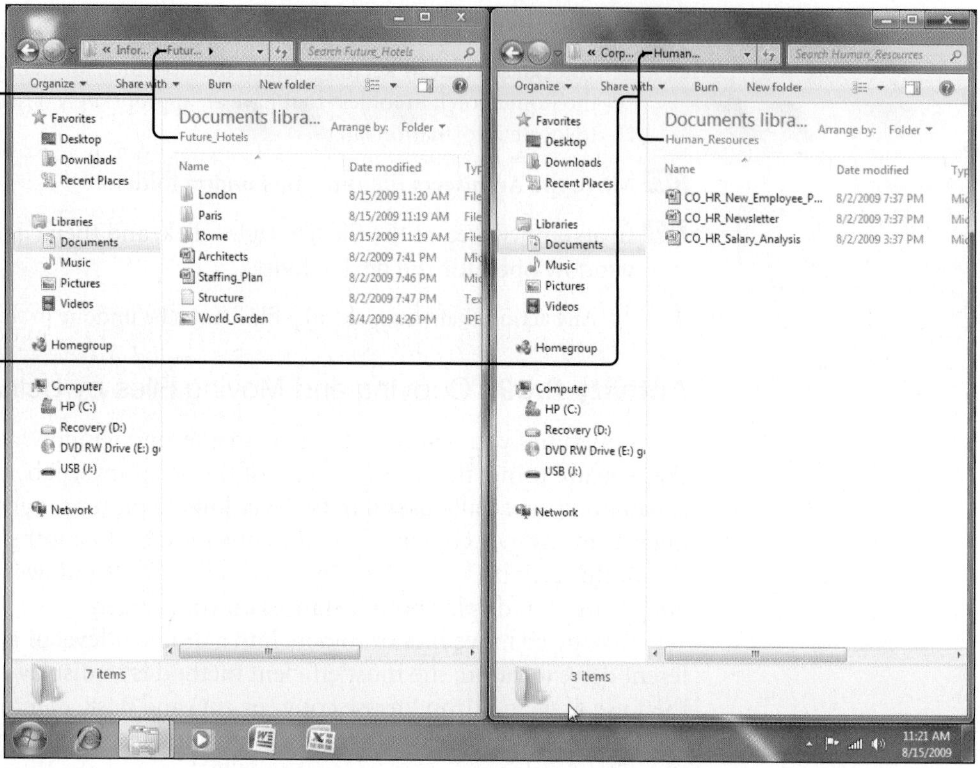

5 In the left window, open the **Rome** folder, and then select the file **Rome_Staffing_Plan.**

6 Hold down Ctrl, and then drag the file into the right window, into an empty area of the **Human_Resources file list**, until the ScreenTip + *Copy to Human Resources* displays, as shown in Figure 2.28, and then release the mouse button and the Ctrl key.

Figure 2.28

ScreenTip + *Copy to Human Resources*

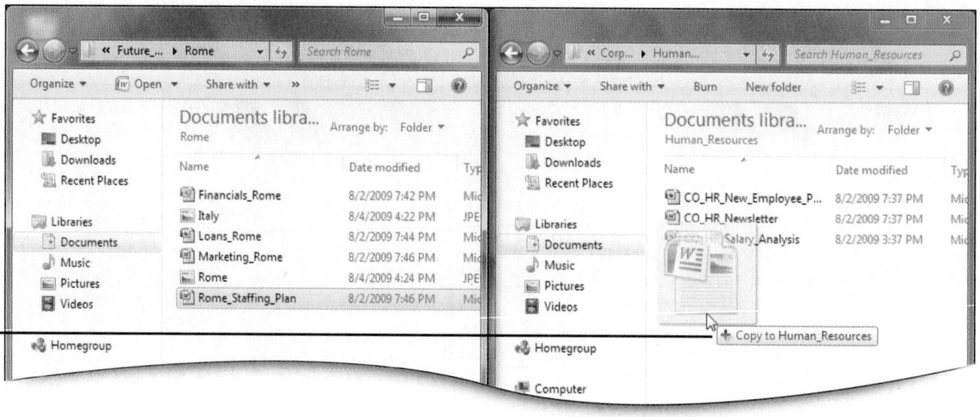

7 In the left window, on the **address bar**, click **Future_Hotels** to redisplay that folder window. Open the **Paris** folder, point to **Paris_Staffing_Plan** and right-click, and then click **Copy**.

8 In the right window, point anywhere in the **file list**, right-click, and then click **Paste**.

You can use either the Copy and Paste commands, or the Ctrl + drag technique, to copy files across two windows.

9 Using either of the techniques you have practiced, in the left window, navigate to the **London** folder, and then copy the **London_Staffing_Plan** file to the **Human_Resources** folder on the right. Compare your screen with Figure 2.29.

Copies of the three files regarding staffing plans for the three European locations display.

Figure 2.29

Three copied files

Navigation pane in right window

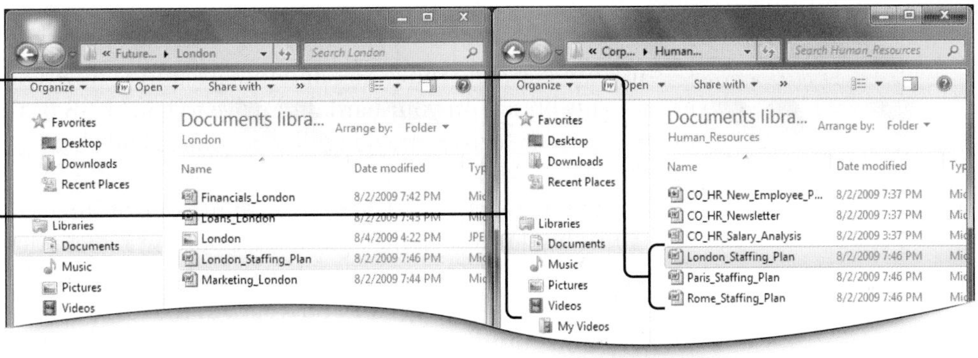

10 In the right window, in the **navigation pane**, click **Documents**. If necessary, scroll to view the file **Europe_Project** that was placed in the Documents folder.

11 In the left window, in the **address bar**, click **Future_Hotels** to redisplay that folder window. In the right window, in the **file list**, point to the **Europe_Project** file, and then drag it into the left window until the ScreenTip →*Move to Future_Hotels* displays, as shown in Figure 2.30, and then release the mouse button.

When dragging and dropping across two locations, to move an item, drag it. To copy an item, hold down Ctrl and then drag it.

This technique works in most Windows-based programs. For example, to copy a selection of text in Word, select it, hold down Ctrl, drag to another location in the document, and release the mouse button. To move a selection of text, simply drag it to the new location.

Figure 2.30

File list shows contents of Documents (your list will vary)

ScreenTip indicates → *Move to Future_Hotels*

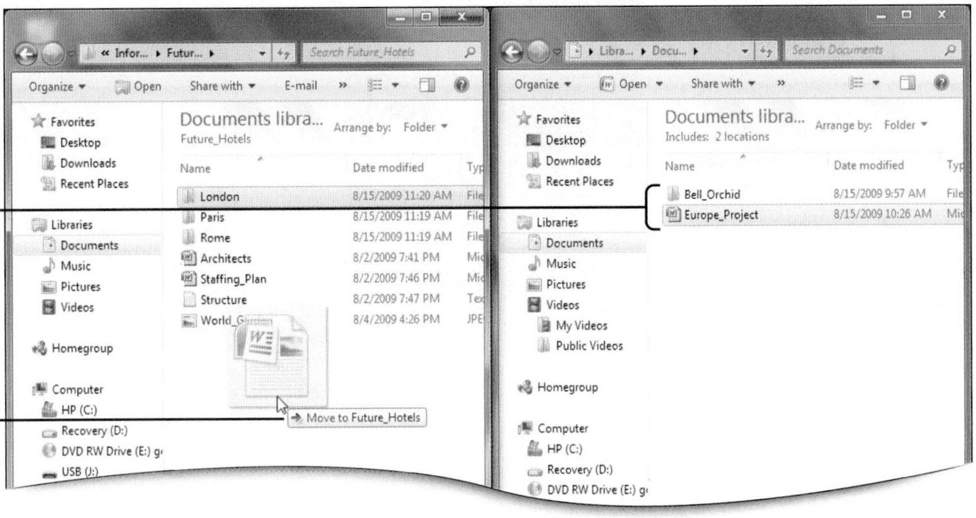

12 In the right window, navigate to **Bell_Orchid ▶ Corporate ▶ Human_Resources**. In the left window, be sure the **Future_Hotels** folder window displays.

13 **Start** the **Snipping Tool** program, click the **New arrow**, and then click **Full-screen Snip**. In the **Snipping Tool** mark-up window, click the **Save Snip** button.

14 In the displayed **Save As** dialog box, notice the path in the **address bar**. If necessary, in the navigation pane, under **Computer**, click your USB flash drive, and then display the folder window for your **Windows 7 Chapter 2** folder.

15 Be sure the file type is **JPEG**. Using your own name, name the file **Lastname_Firstname_2A_HR_Snip** and press Enter. Hold this file until you finish Project 2A.

16 **Close** all open windows.

Activity 2.10 | Copying and Moving Files Among Different Drives

You can copy and move files and folders among different drives; for example from the Documents library on your hard disk drive to your USB flash drive. When copying and moving between drives, dragging files or folders will always result in a copy, regardless of whether you hold down Ctrl.

To *move* files between drives, you can use one of three techniques: 1) right-drag—drag while holding down the *right* mouse button; 2) hold down the Shift key while dragging; 3) use the Cut and Copy commands.

In this activity, you will assist Barbara in moving some of her personal files from the corporate Information_Technology folder to a new folder on a USB flash drive. Additionally, Barbara has a Resume Guide in her personal files, which her colleagues in the Human Resources department would like to have a copy of to share with employees.

1 Be sure your USB flash drive is inserted in your computer. On the taskbar, click the **Windows Explorer** button, and then in the **navigation pane**, under **Computer**, click your USB flash drive to open its folder window. Compare your screen with Figure 2.31.

Figure 2.31

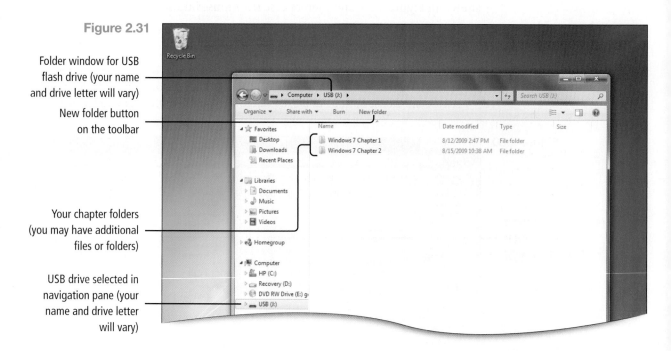

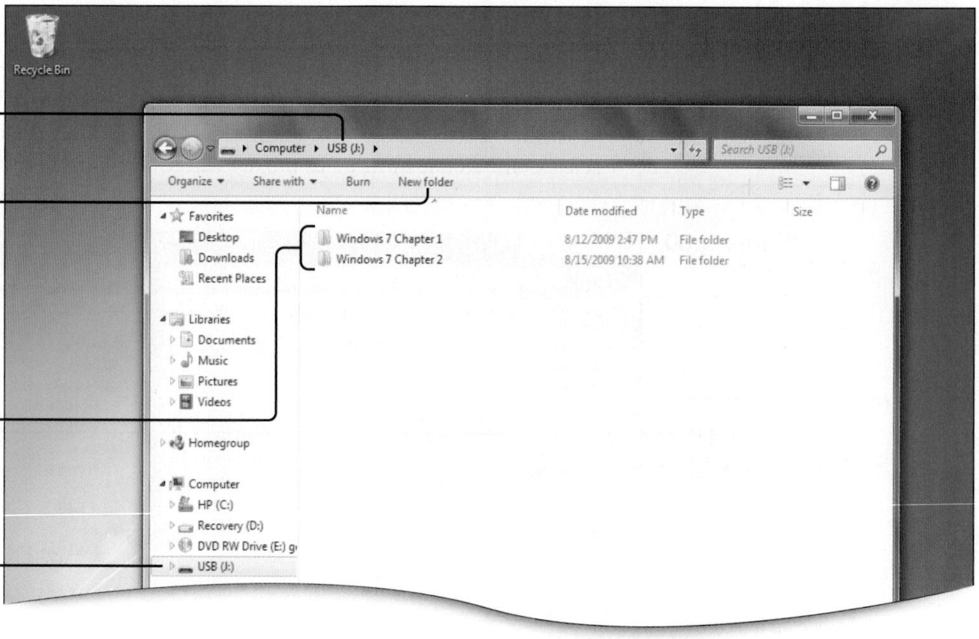

Folder window for USB flash drive (your name and drive letter will vary)

New folder button on the toolbar

Your chapter folders (you may have additional files or folders)

USB drive selected in navigation pane (your name and drive letter will vary)

2 On the toolbar, click the **New folder** button, and then with the text *New folder* selected, type **BHewitt_Files** and press Enter to name the folder.

3 Snap the folder window to the *right* side of the screen.

4 On the taskbar, right-click the **Windows Explorer** button, click **Bell_Orchid**, and then snap the window to the left side of the screen.

Note | Snap to the Left or to the Right?

When using two windows to copy and move files, it does not matter to which side of the screen you snap the window. You can move and copy files in either direction.

5 In the left window, navigate to **Bell_Orchid ▶ Corporate ▶ Information Technology**. Compare your screen with Figure 2.32.

In the taskbar, two overlapping glass-framed Windows Explorer icons display to indicate that two windows are open.

Figure 2.32

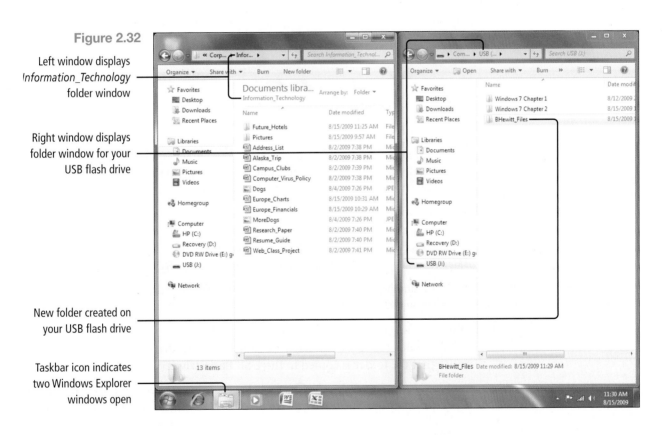

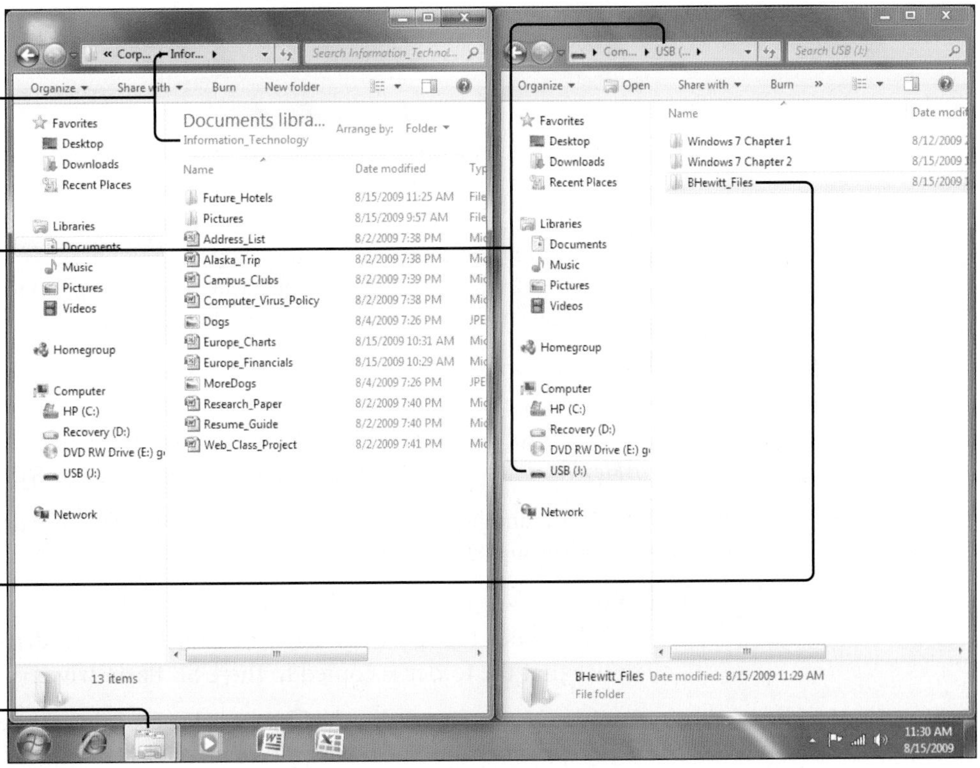
Left window displays *Information_Technology* folder window
Right window displays folder window for your USB flash drive
New folder created on your USB flash drive
Taskbar icon indicates two Windows Explorer windows open

6 Hold down Ctrl, and then in the left window, select the files **Alaska_Trip**, **Campus_Clubs**, **Dogs**, **MoreDogs**, **Research_Paper**, and **Resume_Guide**.

7 Release Ctrl, point to any of the selected files, hold down the *right* mouse button, drag across into the right window until the mouse pointer is over the **BHewitt_Files** folder, and then when you see the ScreenTip *+ Copy to BHewitt_Files*, release the right mouse button to display a shortcut menu. Compare your screen with Figure 2.33.

Figure 2.33

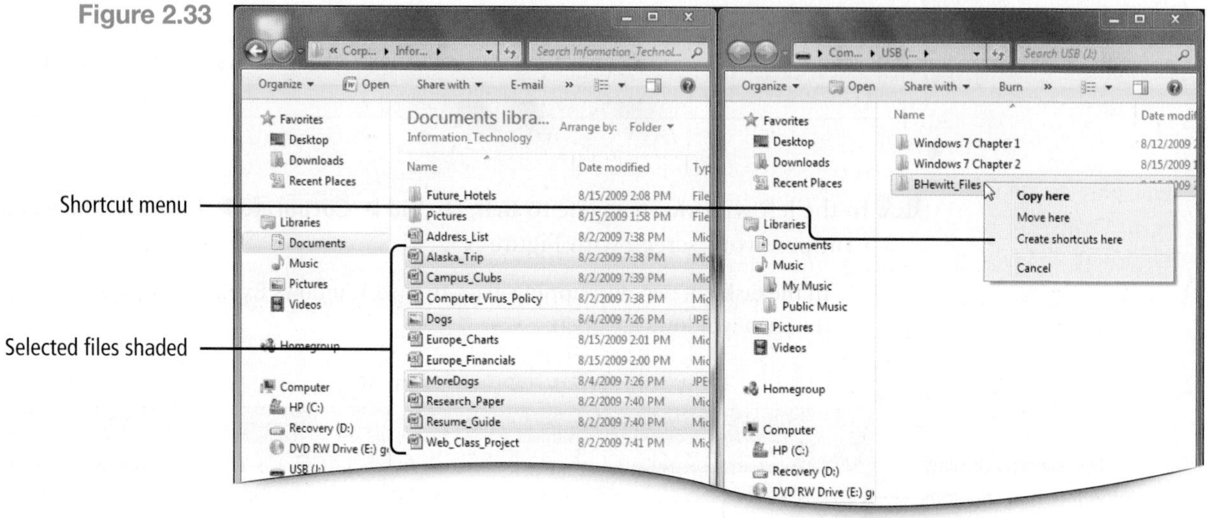

8 On the displayed menu, click **Move here**.

When *moving* among drives, this right-drag technique is useful, because when you release the right mouse button, you will always have the option to move *or* copy the files or folder. Use this technique to move a group of files or folders among different drives.

9 In the left window, select the file **Web_Class_Project**, which is another of Barbara's personal files that should move to the USB flash drive. Hold down Shift and then drag the file into the **BHewitt_Files** folder until you see the ScreenTip → *Move to BHewitt_Files*. Release the mouse button and release Shift.

This is another technique to move files among different drives; use it to move a single file or a group of consecutive files.

10 In the window on the left, point to the folder **Pictures**, right-click, point to **Send to**, and then click the drive and letter of your USB flash drive. In the right window, notice that the folder is copied to the USB flash drive.

A message indicates that the files are being copied to the destination. Recall that Send to is a *copy* command. You can copy files and folders directly to another drive by using the Send to command. You cannot, however, use this command to send the files to a specific folder on the drive; rather, the files are copied directly to the drive.

11 In the right window, double-click the **BHewitt_Files** folder to open it. Point to the **Resume_Guide** file and right-click, and then click **Copy** to place a copy of the file on the Clipboard.

12 In the left window, on the **address bar**, to the right of **Corporate**, click the ▶, and then compare your screen with Figure 2.34.

Figure 2.34

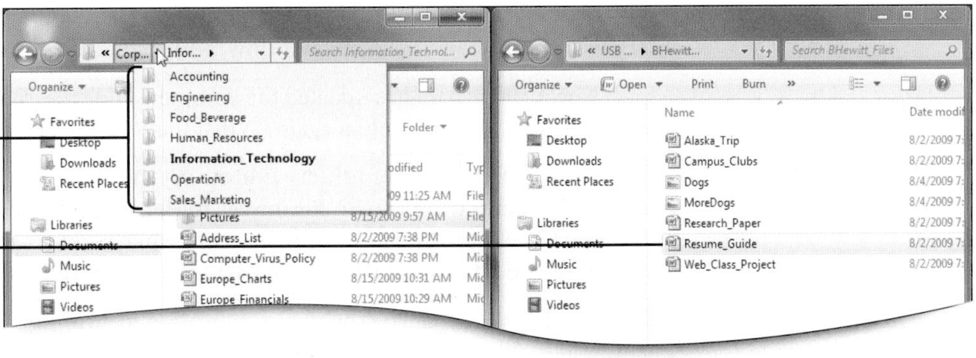

13 On the displayed list of subfolders, click **Human_Resources** to display this folder window.

Recall that the address bar is a convenient way to navigate up or down one or more levels in the folder structure.

Another method is to click the Back arrow as necessary to display the folder that you want. Recall that you can click the Back button to the left of the address bar to navigate through locations you have already visited, in the same manner you use your browser software when displaying sites and pages on the Internet.

14 In the **Human_Resources file list**, right-click in a blank area, and then click **Paste**. Notice that the copy of the file displays in the file list.

15 In the *right* window, in the **BHewitt_Files** folder window, point to the **Resume_Guide** file, and right-click. Compare your screen with Figure 2.35.

Figure 2.35

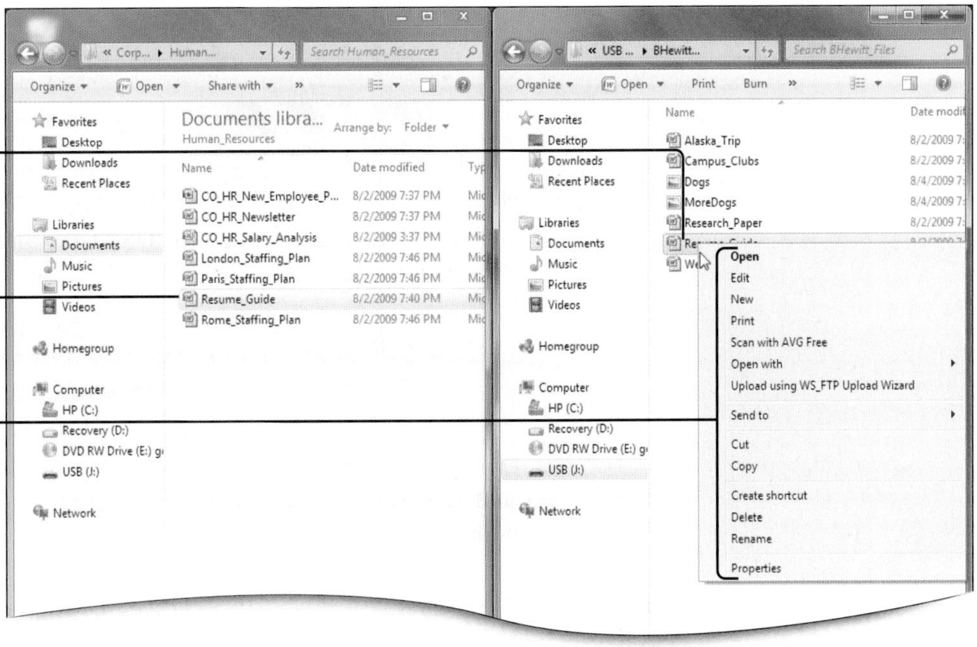

> **Another Way**
>
> Double-click the file to open it in the Word program.

16 On the displayed shortcut menu, click **Open** to open the file in the Word program.

17 At the top to the Word window, click the **Insert tab**, and then on the **Ribbon**, in the **Header & Footer group**, click the **Header** button. At the top of the displayed list, click **Blank**, and then type **Provided to the Human Resources Department by Barbara Hewitt** **Close** the Word window, and then click **Yes** or **Save** to save the changes.

Now that Barbara has updated the Resume_Guide file, she wants to copy it to the Human_Resources folder again, so that the copy they have is this updated copy.

18 From the **BHewitt_Files** folder window on the right, drag the **Resume_Guide** file to the left, into the **Human_Resources** folder window, and then when the ScreenTip + *Copy to Human_Resources* displays, release the mouse button to display the **Copy File** dialog box. Compare your screen with Figure 2.36.

Windows 7 recognizes that there is already a file with this name in the Human_Resources folder, although it is not the *most recent* copy now that Barbara has updated the original by adding a header. Within a folder, two files of the same type—a Word document in this instance—cannot have the same name. Likewise, within a folder, two subfolders cannot have the same name.

There are three actions you can take from this dialog box. You can click Copy and Replace, which will replace the old copy with your new copy. Or, you can abandon the copy operation by clicking *Don't copy*. Or, you can complete the copy operation by keeping both files, but Windows 7 will add *(2)* to the name of the new copy so that it will not have the same name.

Figure 2.36

Copy File dialog box

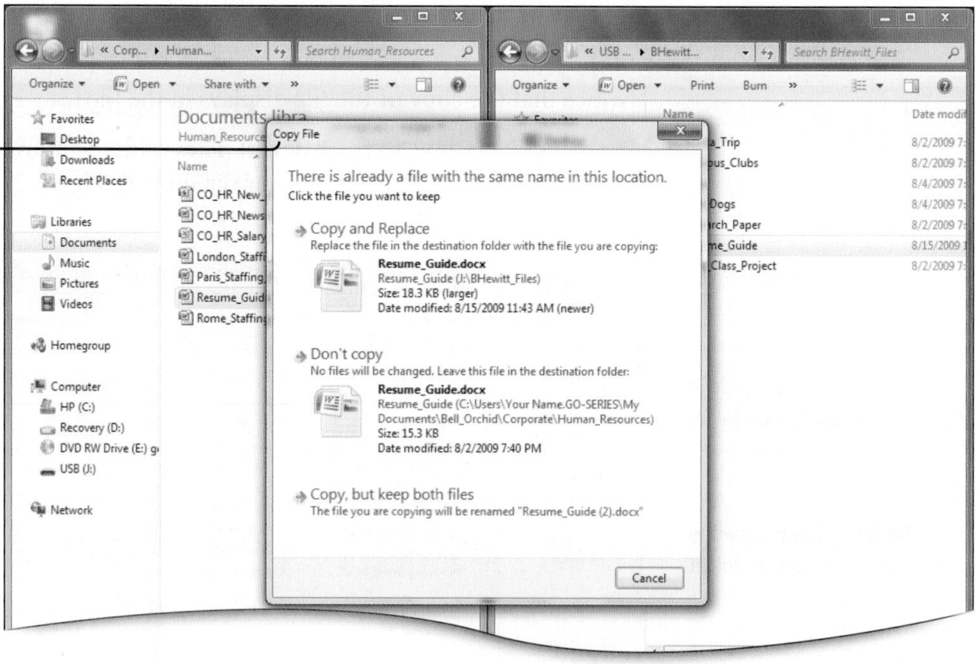

19 Click **Copy and Replace** to replace the old copy with the new updated copy. **Close** all open windows.

Activity 2.11 | Copying Files and Folders to a Compressed Folder

To ***compress*** is to reduce the size of a file. Compressed files take up less storage space and can be transferred to other computers, for example in an e-mail message, more quickly than uncompressed files. Because pictures are typically large files, it is common to compress graphic files like pictures. When the picture is expanded, there will be no loss of visual quality.

1 In the taskbar, drag the **Windows Explorer** button upward slightly into the desktop to display the **Jump List**. Then, on the **Jump List**, under **Pinned**, click **Bell_Orchid**. Navigate to **Bell_Orchid ▶ Corporate ▶ Information_Technology ▶ Pictures**.

2 In the upper right corner, click the **Maximize** button so that the folder window fills the screen. On the toolbar, click the **View button arrow**, and then set the view to **Tiles**. Compare your screen with Figure 2.37.

Figure 2.37

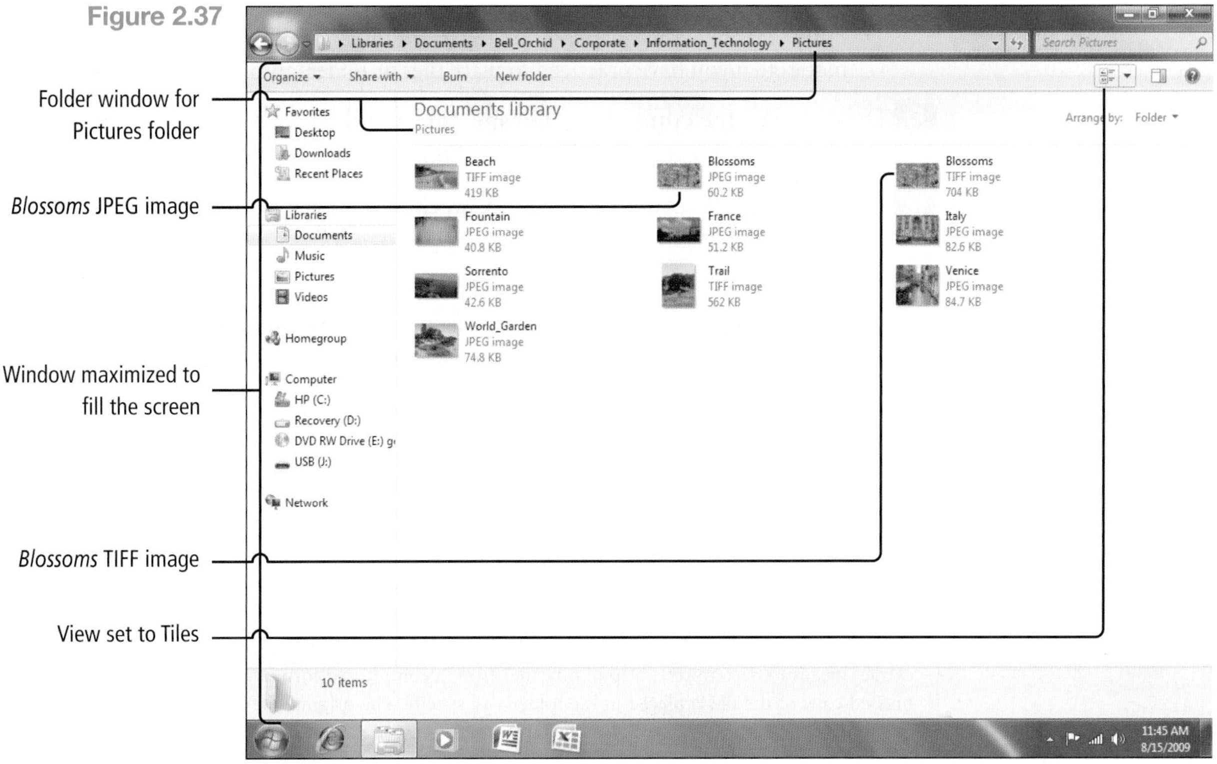

3 Locate the picture **Blossoms** that is a **JPEG** image and notice that its size is **60.2 KB**. Then locate the picture **Blossoms** that is a **TIFF** image and notice that its size is **704 KB**.

Within a folder, two files can have the same name so long as they are of different file types—in this instance a ***JPEG*** file type and a ***TIFF*** file type.

JPEG, which stands for *Joint Photographic Experts Group*, is a common file type used by digital cameras and computers to store digital pictures—it is a popular file type because it can store a high-quality picture in a relatively small file.

TIFF, which stands for *Tagged Image File Format*, is a file type used when a very high level of visual quality is needed; for example, if the file will be used to print 8-by-10-inch enlargements.

4 Hold down Ctrl, and then select the files **Beach**, **Fountain**, and **Trail**. Release Ctrl, point to *any* of the selected files, right-click, point to **Send to**, and then click **Compressed (zipped) folder.**

A compressed folder is created containing the three files and is stored in the existing folder—the Pictures folder. The new compressed folder will display the name of the file to which you were pointing when you right-clicked. You can change the name if you want to do so by using any renaming technique.

5 Point to a white area of the **file list** (do not be concerned if another file is framed), right-click, point to **New**, and then click **Compressed (zipped) Folder**. Type **Europe_Images** as the name of the compressed folder, and then press Enter.

6 Point to the **France** picture, and then drag it into the **Europe_Images** compressed folder, releasing the mouse button when you see the ScreenTip + *Copy*.

7 Click the **Italy** picture to select it, hold down Ctrl, and then select the **Venice** picture. Release Ctrl. Right-click over either of the selected files, and then click **Copy**. Point to the **Europe_Images** folder, right-click, and then click **Paste**.

In this manner you can create a compressed folder, and then use any of the copy techniques that you have practiced to place files or folders into the compressed folder.

8 Double-click the compressed **Europe_Images** folder to view its contents, and notice the three pictures you copied there—*France*, *Italy*, and *Venice*.

9 In the upper left corner of the window, click the **Back** button to move up one level in the folder structure.

10 Start the **Snipping Tool** program, create a **Full-screen Snip**, and then save the file in the JPEG format on your USB flash drive in your **Windows 7 Chapter 2** folder with the name **Lastname_Firstname_2A_Compressed_Snip**

11 **Close** the **Snipping Tool** window.

12 In the upper right corner of the folder window, click the **Restore Down** button to restore the window to its smaller size, and then **Close** the folder window.

More Knowledge | To Extract Files or Folders From a Compressed Folder

To extract files or folders from a compressed folder, locate the compressed folder that you want to extract. To extract means to decompress, or pull out, files from a compressed form. When you extract a file, an uncompressed copy of the file is placed in the folder you specify. The original file remains in the compressed folder. Compressed files typically have a .zip file name extension.

To extract a single file or folder, double-click the compressed folder to open it. Then, drag the file or folder from the compressed folder to a new location. To extract the entire contents of the compressed folder, right-click the folder, click Extract All, and then follow the instructions.

Activity 2.12 | Copying Files and Folders to a CD/DVD

If your computer includes a CD or DVD recorder, you can copy files to a ***writable disc***, which is a CD or DVD disc onto which files can be copied. This process is called ***burning a disc***.

Alert! | This is an Optional Activity

This activity is optional. You can complete this activity if the computer at which you are working has a writable CD or DVD drive and you have a blank CD or DVD.

For this activity, you will need a writable CD or DVD drive in your computer and a blank CD or DVD. If you do not have this equipment, you can read through this activity, and then move to Activity 2.13.

1 **Close** all open windows. On your computer's case, open your **CD/DVD Drive**, remove the Student Resource CD if it is in the drive, and then depending on your particular computer hardware, place a blank recordable or writable CD or DVD in the drive and close the drive. When the **AutoPlay** dialog box displays, click **Burn files to disc using Windows Explorer**.

2 In the **Disc title** box, replace the highlighted text by typing **Restaurant_Files** and then compare your screen with Figure 2.38.

The first option, *Like a USB flash drive*, will use the ***Live File System***. Discs formatted with Live File System enable you to copy files to the disc at any time, instead of copying (burning) them all at once.

The second option, *With a CD/DVD player*, will use the ***Mastered*** system. Discs created using the Mastered format are more likely to be compatible with older computers, but an additional step is required to burn the collection of files to the disc.

You can use the Live File System or choose to burn discs in the Mastered format, especially if you think the disc will be read on an older computer that does not use the Windows XP, Windows Vista, or the Windows 7 operating system.

Figure 2.38

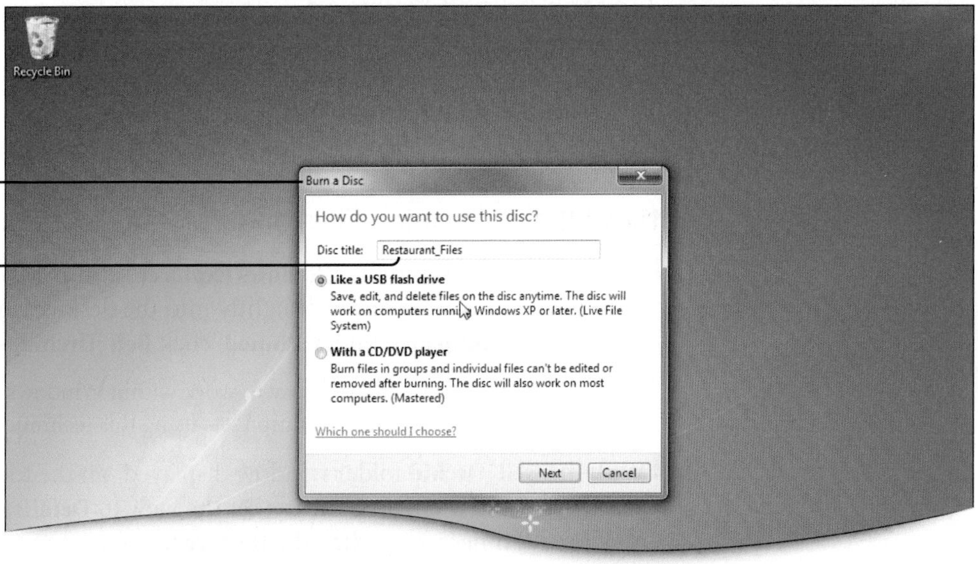

> **Note | Which CD or DVD Format?**
>
> For complete information on the formats for burning music and video discs, in the Windows Help and Support window type *Which CD or DVD format should I use?*

3 Click **Like a USB flash drive**, and then in the lower right corner, click **Next**; wait a few moments until the disc is formatted. Then, click **Open folder to view files**.

4 Snap this empty disc folder window to the right side of the screen.

5 On the taskbar, drag the **Windows Explorer** button slightly into the desktop, and then at the top of the **Jump List**, click **Bell_Orchid**. Snap this window to the left side of the screen, on the toolbar, click the **View button arrow**, and then set the view back to **Details**.

6 In the left window, navigate to **Bell_Orchid ▶ Corporate ▶ Food_Beverage**. Hold down Ctrl, and then in the **file list**, select the three files **CO_FB_Banquet_Contract**, **CO_FB_Menu_Analysis**, **CO_FB_Menu_Presentation**.

7 Drag the selected files into the right window. Release the mouse button when the ScreenTip + *Copy to Drive Restaurant_Files* (your exact text will vary). Wait a few moments for the copy to complete.

The files are copied to the CD.

8 **Close** both windows.

Later, you can continue to open files from and copy other files to this CD as needed.

9 Open your **CD/DVD Drive**, if necessary wait for it to eject, and then remove the disc and close your **CD/DVD Drive**.

Objective 6 | Delete Files and Folders and Use the Recycle Bin

It is good practice to delete files and folders that you no longer need from your hard disk drive and removable storage devices. Doing so frees up storage space on your devices and makes it easier to keep your data organized.

When you delete a file or folder from any area of your computer's hard disk drive, the file or folder is not immediately deleted. Instead, the deleted item is stored in the Recycle Bin and remains there until the Recycle Bin is emptied. Thus, you can recover an item deleted from your computer's hard disk drive so long as the Recycle Bin has not been emptied. Items deleted from removable storage devices like a USB flash drive and from some network drives are immediately deleted and cannot be recovered from the Recycle Bin.

Activity 2.13 | Deleting Files and Folders Using the Recycle Bin

1 In the taskbar, point to the **Windows Explorer** button, hold down the left mouse button, and then drag upward slightly into the desktop to display the **Jump List**. Then, on the **Jump List**, under **Pinned**, click **Bell_Orchid**.

Recall that the most efficient way to work within Windows is to use the taskbar program buttons and their associated Jump Lists using this technique.

2 With the **Bell_Orchid** folder window displayed, on the toolbar, click the **View button arrow**, and then, if necessary, set the view to **Details**. Be sure your window is not maximized. If necessary, click the **Restore Down** button.

3 Navigate to **Bell_Orchid ▶ Corporate ▶ Information_Technology**.

4 Point to the **Computer_Virus_Policy** file, right-click, and then from the shortcut menu, click **Delete**. In the displayed **Delete File** dialog box, notice that the message asks if you want to *move this file to the Recycle Bin*. Click **Yes**.

5 In the **file list**, hold down Ctrl, and then select the Excel files **Europe_Charts** and **Europe_Financials**. Release Ctrl, and then press Del. In the displayed **Delete Multiple Items** dialog box, click **Yes** to move the selected items to the **Recycle Bin**. Compare your screen with Figure 2.39.

You can delete a group of items in this manner.

Figure 2.39

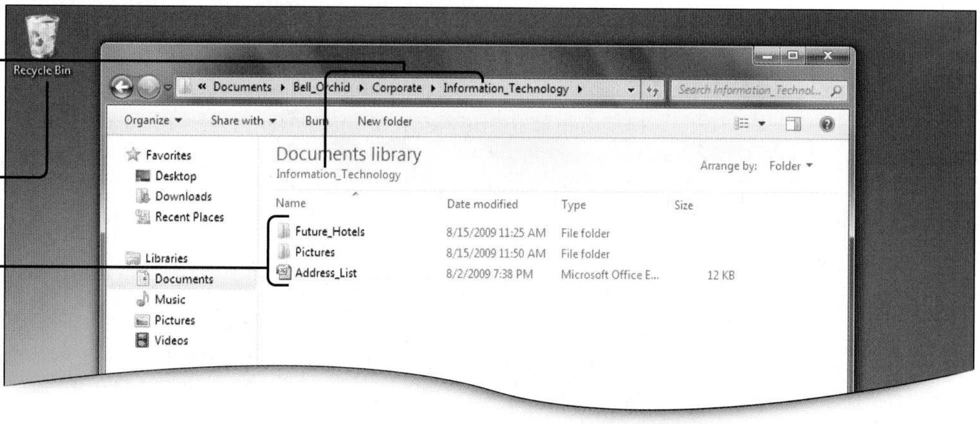

6 Snap the **Information_Technology** window to the right side of your screen. On the **Desktop**, double-click the **Recycle Bin** icon to open its folder window. Set the **View** to **Details**, and then snap the **Recycle Bin** folder to the left side of the screen. Notice that the items in the Recycle Bin are in alphabetic order.

7 In the upper right corner of the **Recycle Bin** window, click in the **Search** box, and then type **virus** Compare your screen with Figure 2.40.

You can scroll the list to try to find the deleted file you are looking for instead of using the Search box. Commonly, however, you might not remember the exact name of the file. In this instance, Barbara and Steven remembered that the deleted file contained something about *virus* policy, and thus using the Search box was a quick way to find the file.

Figure 2.40

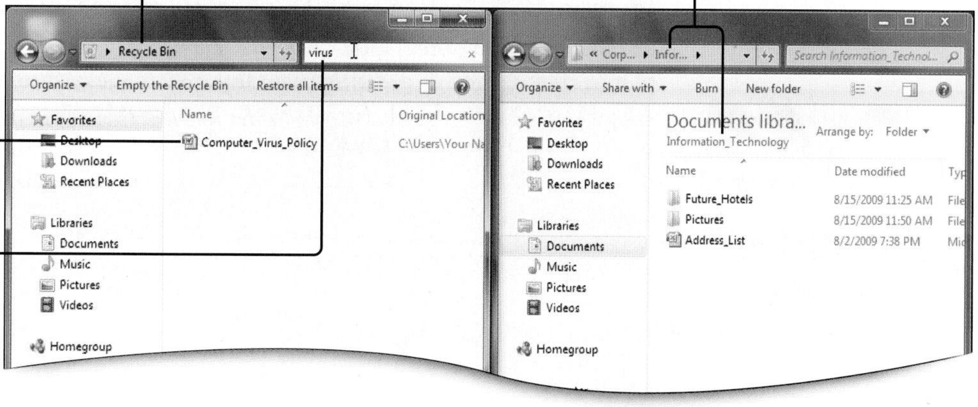

Another Way

Right-click over an item, and then click Restore.

8 In the **Recycle Bin** window, click the **Computer_Virus_Policy** file to select it, and then on the toolbar, click **Restore this item**. In the **Information_Technology** folder window, notice that the file is restored.

9 On the left, in the **Search** box of the **Recycle Bin** window, click ☒ to cancel the search.

10 In the **Recycle Bin file list**, scroll down to locate and then select the **Europe_Charts** file and the **Europe_Financials** file. With the two files selected, on the toolbar, if necessary click >> to display additional commands, and then click **Restore the selected items**.

11 **Close** ☒ the **Recycle Bin** window. In the **Information_Technology** folder window, notice the restored files.

12 Using one of the techniques you just practiced, delete the **Address_List** file—click **Yes** to move it to the Recycle Bin. Then, right-click in the **file list** and click **Undo Delete**.

You can undo a delete in this manner.

More Knowledge | Using the Recycle Bin Icon, Permanently Deleting an Item, and Restoring by Dragging

You can delete items by dragging them from the file list directly into the Recycle Bin icon on the Desktop. If you drag items into the Recycle Bin, you will see the ScreenTip →*Move to Recycle Bin*, but no confirmation message will display.

To permanently delete a file without first moving it to the Recycle Bin, click the item, hold down Shift, and then press Del.

You can restore items by dragging them from the file list of the Recycle Bin window to the file list of the folder window in which you want to restore.

13 In the **navigation pane**, under **Computer**, click your USB flash drive. Right-click the folder **BHewitt_Files**, click **Delete**, and then compare your screen with Figure 2.41.

A message indicates *Are you sure you want to permanently delete this folder?* and a red X displays on the folder icon.

The Recycle Bin only saves items deleted from your computer's hard disk drive. Anything that you delete from a removable storage device, for example a USB flash drive, a floppy disk, a memory card, an MP3 player, or a digital camera, will be permanently deleted.

Figure 2.41

Message indicates that the folder will be *permanently* deleted

Red X on folder icon

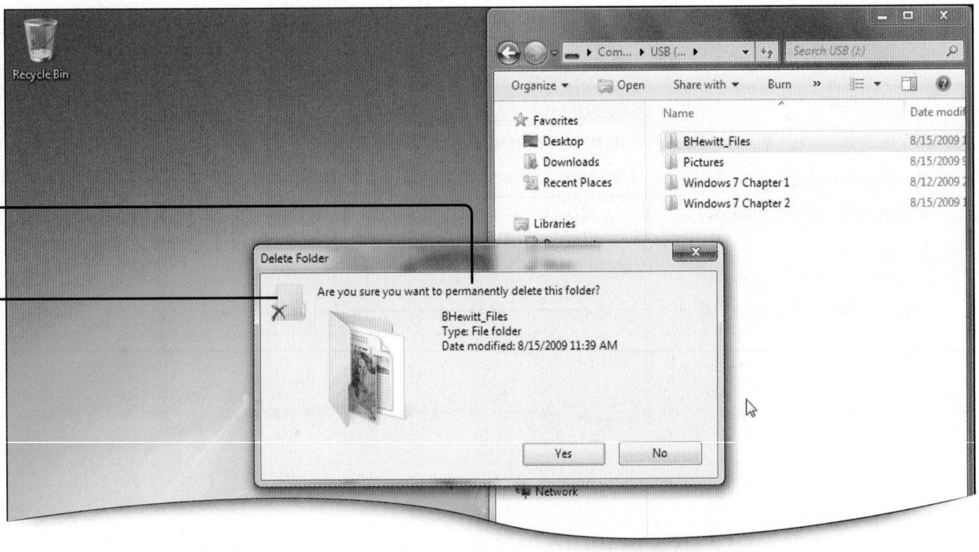

14 Click **Yes** to delete this folder from your USB flash drive. Delete the **Pictures** folder from your USB flash drive.

15 In the **navigation pane** under **Libraries**, click **Documents**. **Delete** the **Bell_Orchid** folder from your **Documents** folder.

For some of the projects in this textbook, like this one, you will copy files to the Documents folder of the computer at which you are working. At the end of the project, you can remove the files in this manner so that your own computer is not cluttered with extra files. In a college lab, it is possible that logging off automatically deletes files from the Documents folder.

16 On the taskbar, drag the **Windows Explorer** button slightly up into the desktop, and then on the **Jump List**, notice that the **Bell_Orchid** folder is still pinned there. Click **Bell_Orchid**, and then compare your screen with Figure 2.42.

Because the folder is now deleted from your hard disk drive, the Problem with Shortcut dialog box displays. Here you can restore the item to your Documents library or delete the shortcut from the Pinned area of the Jump List.

Figure 2.42

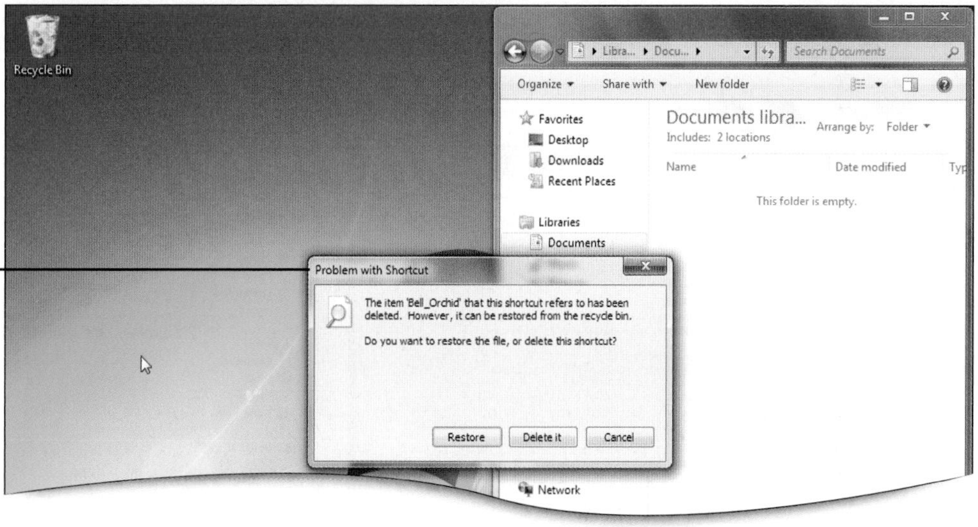

Problem with Shortcut dialog box

> **Another Way**
>
> On the Jump List, point to the pinned item, and then click the pin button on the right; or, right-click, and click Unpin from this list.

17 Click **Delete it**, and then **Close** all open windows. If you want to do so on your own computer and are permitted to do so on a college lab computer, empty the Recycle Bin as follows: Point to the **Recycle Bin** icon, right-click, click **Empty Recycle Bin**, and then click **Yes**.

18 Submit your three snip files from this project as directed by your instructor.

End **You have completed Project 2A**

Project 2B Searching Your Computer

Project Activities

In Activities 2.14 through 2.18, you will practice with Steven Ramos and Barbara Hewitt, employees in the Information Technology Department at the corporate office of the Bell Orchid Hotels, searching the hotel's files to find data quickly and efficiently. You will capture screens that look similar to Figure 2.43.

Project Files

For Project 2B, you will need the following files:

New Snip files

You will save your files as:

Lastname_Firstname_2B_Orlando_Snip
Lastname_Firstname_2B_Europe_Menus_Snip
Lastname_Firstname_2B_Tag_Snip

Project Results

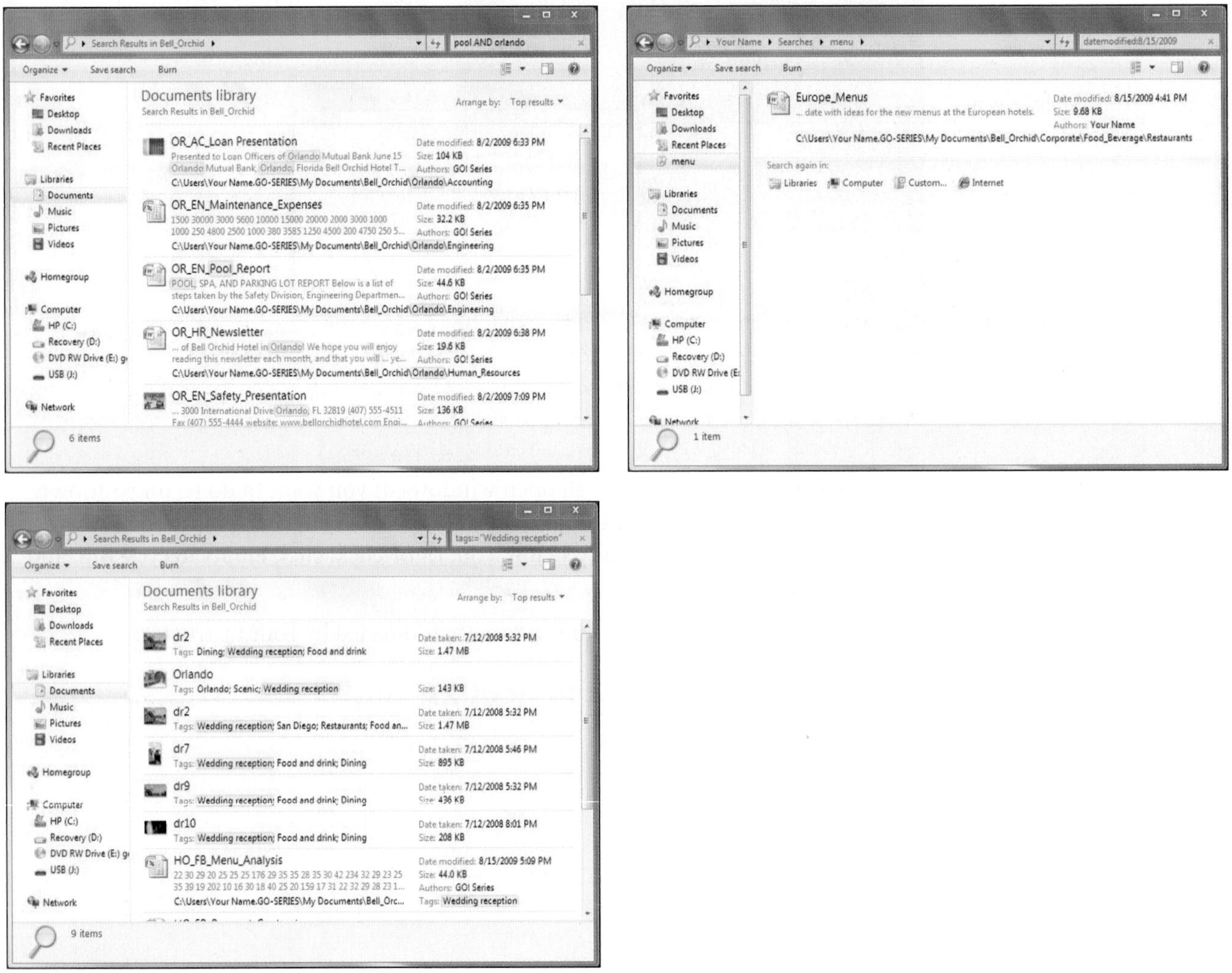

Figure 2.43
Project 2B Searching Your Computer

Objective 7 | Search From the Start Menu

Even if you have arranged your folders and files in a logical way, it is still sometimes challenging and time consuming to locate a specific file when you need it. The hierarchical nature of any filing system means that you often have to navigate downward through multiple levels of your folder structure to find what you are looking for. This navigation task is commonly referred to as ***drilling down***.

In Windows 7, you can search your PC in the same easy way that you search on the Internet. Instead of navigating within a folder window, rely on the capability of Windows 7 to conduct a search of your data. Searching for a file—rather than navigating a file structure—is the quick and modern way to locate files.

By using the Windows 7 search capabilities, you will eliminate the tedium of drilling down into your folders. Windows 7 can search for programs and files by using a name, a property, or even text contained within a file.

Activity 2.14 | Searching From the Start Menu

By typing in the search box located at the bottom of the Start menu, you can find installed programs, Web sites in your History or Favorites area, messages in your e-mail, contacts in your Contacts folder, as well as files and folders on your system.

In this activity, you will work with Barbara and Steven to search for information from the search box on the Start menu.

> **Alert! | For Convenience, Plan Your Time to Complete Project 2B in One Working Session**
>
> Because you will need to store and then delete files on the hard disk drive of the computer at which you are working, it is recommended that you complete this project in one working session—*unless you are working on your own computer or you know that the files will be retained.* In your college lab, it is possible that files you store will not be retained after you log off. Allow approximately 30 to 45 minutes to complete Project 2B.

1 If necessary, delete the **Bell_Orchid** folder from your **Documents** folder—for this project you will need a new copy of the files. Insert the Student Resource CD or other device that contains the student files that accompany this textbook. Using the **Send to** command that you practiced in Activity 2.1 of this chapter, copy the **Bell_Orchid** folder from the Student Resource CD to your **Documents** folder.

2 **Close** any open windows, and then display the **Start menu**. At the bottom of the Start menu, with your insertion point blinking in the search box, type **win** Compare your screen with Figure 2.44.

You need not *click* in the search box; as soon as you display the Start menu and begin to type, your typing displays there.

Your screen will not match the figure exactly, but you can see that Windows 7 instantly begins searching your computer for various categories of items that begin with *win*. Categories that might display include *Programs*, *Control Panel*, *Documents*, *Videos*, *Files*, and *Communications* (for e-mail messages, contacts, and items from Outlook such as events and tasks).

Figure 2.44

Names of items that contain *win* (yours will vary)

Search box with your typing

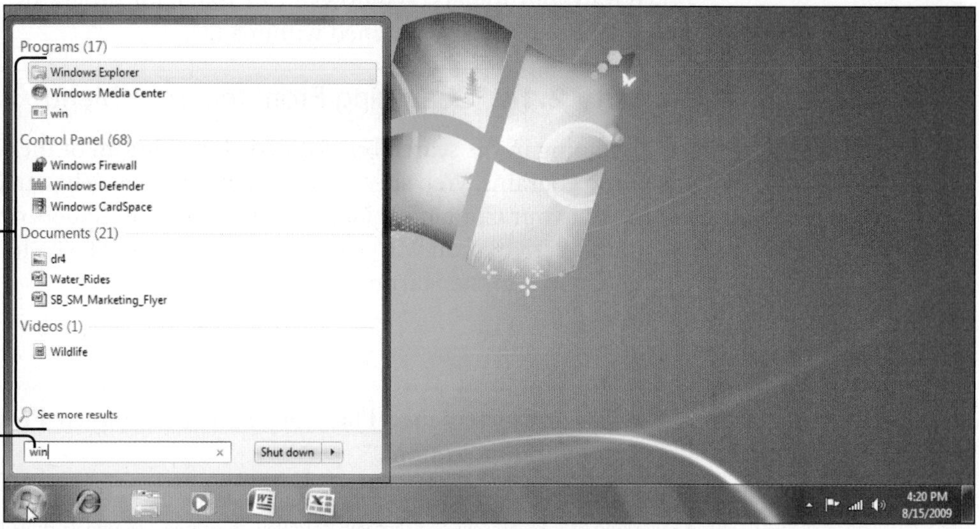

Another Way

Press Esc to clear the search box.

3 At the right end of the search box, click × to clear the search box and cancel the list. With the insertion point blinking in the search box, type **word** In the results listed above the search box, under **Programs**, click **Microsoft Word**. When the program displays, **Close** the Word window.

You can start a program directly from the search results list. If you have numerous programs on your computer, this is a fast way to find and start a program instead of navigating the All Programs menu.

4 Display the **Start** menu, and then type **b** Notice the results listed, and then type **e**

After typing *e*, your list of results changes to reflect items that begin with *be*. The search box is a ***word wheel***, which is a lookup method in which each new character that you type into the search box further refines the search.

5 Type **ll orchid**

Any item containing *bell orchid* is found. Because the list of results is too long for the display area, *See more results* displays just above the search box. In the displayed list under *Documents*, both file names and folder names are listed.

Search is not case sensitive; you can type all lowercase letters as a search term.

6 Click **See more results**, and then compare your screen with Figure 2.45.

A folder window displays the results of the search in the indexed locations, and applies yellow highlight to the search term in each folder or file found.

Windows 7 produces search results almost instantly because it employs an ***index***, which is a collection of detailed information about the files on your computer. As you work, Windows 7 constantly keeps track of information about your files—for example, words in titles and in the file itself, dates, file types, and so on—and stores that information in the index. When you search for something, Windows searches this summary information in the index instead of searching your entire hard disk drive each time you start a search.

It is this index feature that provides almost instant search results. The Windows 7 libraries—Documents, Pictures, Music, and so on—are always indexed on your system. This is why you should always begin with a library when you plan to save a file.

Figure 2.45

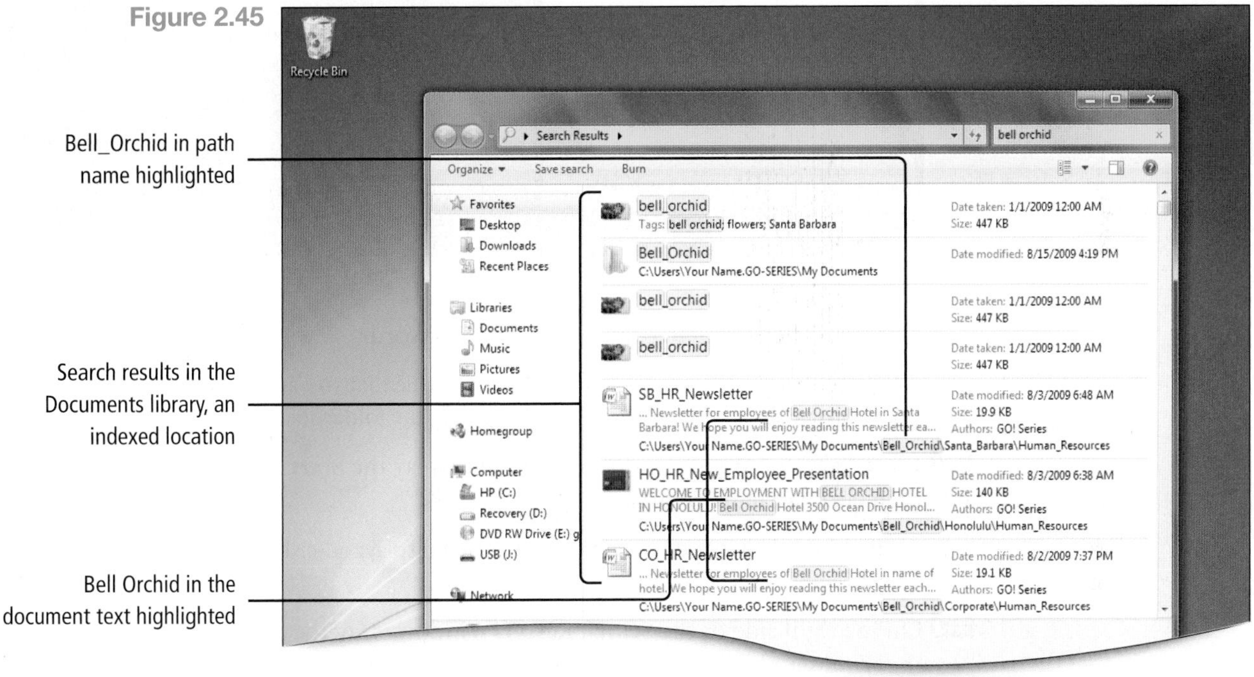

7 **Close** the window, and then display the **Start** menu. Type **newsletter** and then in the list of results, point to the file **SD_HR_Newsletter**. Compare your screen with Figure 2.46.

The ScreenTip displays information about the file.

Figure 2.46

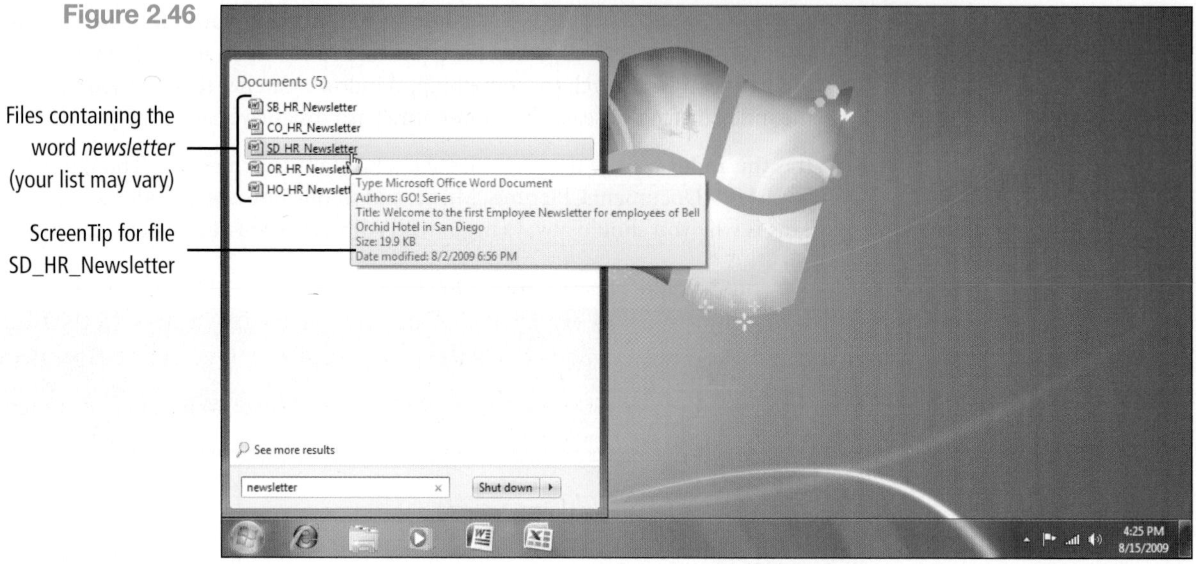

8 Click **SD_HR_Newsletter** to open the file in Word.

If you know one or two words related to the file that you are looking for, searching for it in this manner will be faster than navigating the folder structure.

9 **Close** the Word window, and then display the **Start menu**. Type **pool** and then click **See more results**.

Bell Orchid files that contain the word *pool* display; other files from your own hard disk drive might also display.

10 On the right side of the **Search Results** window, drag the scroll box to the bottom of the window, and then under **Search again in**, click **Internet**.

The default search engine displays information about pools. In this manner, you can begin an Internet search without first opening your Internet browser. In Windows 7, the default search engine is ***Bing***, unless you have changed the default. Bing is Microsoft's search engine.

11 **Close** all open windows.

More Knowledge | What Files Are In the Windows 7 Index?

You cannot view the index, but it is used by Windows 7 to perform very fast searches on the most common files on your computer.

Indexed locations include all of the files in your libraries—Documents, Pictures, Music, and so on—e-mail, and ***offline files***. Offline files are files from a network that have been copied to your hard disk drive for easy access when you are not connected to the network.

By default, program and system files are not indexed. You rarely need to search for those files, so not including them in the index makes your searches run faster.

Files stored directly on the C drive are not indexed, nor are files on a removable storage device such as a flash drive or CD. You can still search for files and folders stored in these locations. However, the search might not be quite as fast because the search is conducted on the device itself, not on the index.

Objective 8 | Search From a Folder Window

A search box displays in all windows. If you know approximately where a file or folder is, search from the folder window instead of the Start menu. Starting a search from a folder window searches only the files and subfolders in that folder, so your list of results will *not* include items that you know you are *not* looking for, such as an e-mail message or a Web site or a program.

Activity 2.15 | Searching From a Folder Window and Applying a Filter to Search Results

The results of a search in a folder window can be arranged by using any of the sorting, grouping, and filtering techniques that you have practiced. Similarly, you can also change the view of the search results.

1. On the taskbar, click the **Windows Explorer** button, and then in the **file list**, double-click **Documents** to display your Documents library window. In the **file list**, right-click the **Bell_Orchid** folder, and then on the shortcut menu, click **Properties**.

2. In the **Bell_Orchid Properties** dialog box, click the **General tab**. In the center of the tab, to the right of *Contains*, notice the number of files and folders contained in the Bell_Orchid folder.

   A search that you conduct in this folder window will be limited to searching the files and folders in this folder. Recall that the search is conducted on the index, not by searching file by file on the hard disk drive.

3. Close the **Bell_Orchid Properties** dialog box. In the **file list**, double-click the **Bell_Orchid** folder to display its folder window. In the upper right corner of the folder window, click in the **search** box, type **em** and then at the bottom of the window, in the **Details pane**, notice the number of items that are indicated.

4. Continue typing **ployee** Compare your screen with Figure 2.47.

   Recall that the word wheel technology filters the results of your search with each letter you type, eliminating any results that do not exactly match what you are typing. Within your documents folder, 37 items contain *employee* in the title, in the text, or in a property associated with the file. (Your number could vary if there are undeleted files from previous projects.)

Figure 2.47

Address bar indicates *Search Results* in *Bell_Orchid*

Small box displays and then fades

Details pane, items in *Bell_Orchid* that match search (yours could vary)

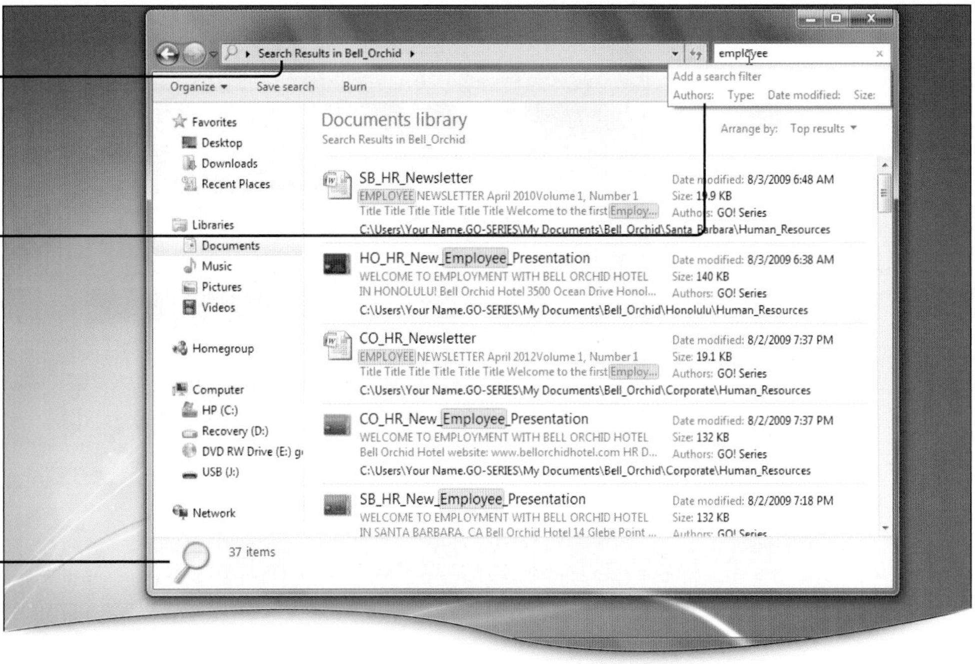

5 Click in the **search** box to display suggested filters. Under **Add a search filter**, click **Type:**, and notice that you can filter on either the file extensions for Excel, PowerPoint, and Word, or on the program name itself.

Based on the search results, Windows 7 will suggest some search filters (in blue text), or you can create your own filter.

Only the file types that are present in the search results will display. In this instance, the results include only Excel, PowerPoint, and Word files.

6 Click **Microsoft PowerPoint Presentation**, and then in the **Details pane** at the bottom of the window, notice that 11 items (your number could vary) are PowerPoint presentations that contain the word *employee* as a property.

7 On the toolbar, click the **View button arrow**, notice that the search results are arranged by **Content**, and then click **Extra Large Icons**.

By default, search results display in the Content view, because this view contains the most information about the file. You can change the view, however, to whatever is convenient for you. For example, here, seeing the first slide of all the presentations, might assist you in finding the exact file that you want.

8 Point in the white area between the two columns of icons, right-click to display a shortcut menu, point to **Sort by**, and then click **Name**. Display this menu again, point to **Sort by**, and then at the bottom, if necessary, click **Ascending** to sort the list alphabetically. Compare your screen with Figure 2.48.

The 11 items are alphabetized by name. You can arrange the results of a search by using any of the sorting, grouping, and filtering techniques that you have practiced.

Figure 2.48

9 On the toolbar, click the **View button arrow** [View button], and then return the view to **Content**. At the right end of the search box, click [×] to clear the search. Notice that recent filters you applied remain available for reuse.

10 With the **Bell_Orchid** folder window redisplayed, in the **search** box, type **seminar**

The Details pane indicates that 6 items in the Bell_Orchid folder have the word *seminar* in the text or as one of the properties associated with the item. (Your number could vary.)

Text that you type in the search box to conduct a search specifies the conditions that identify the specific files you are looking for. Such text is commonly referred to as ***criteria***. In this search, the criteria is *seminar*; that is, only files that contain the word *seminar* meet the condition.

11 With the insertion point blinking in the **search** box, press Spacebar, and then type **sales**

The number of items that meet the search criteria is reduced to 5 and the word *sales* is highlighted in yellow in the list of files that meet the criteria. (Your number could vary.)

12 **Clear** [×] the **search** box, and then type **honolulu**

Both files and folders contain the search term *Honolulu*—34 items in all. (Your number could vary.)

13 **Clear** [×] the **search** box, and then type **pool** In the **Details pane**, notice the number of items that meet the search term. Then, with the insertion point blinking in the **search** box, press Spacebar. Using all uppercase letters by holding down Shift, type **AND** release Shift, press the Spacebar, and then type **orlando** Compare your screen with Figure 2.49.

When you include the word *AND* in this manner—in all uppercase letters—Windows 7 searches for files or folders that contain *pool* and *Orlando*. Only items containing both words display in the search results. As you progress in your study of Windows 7, you will practice using more search techniques of this type.

Figure 2.49

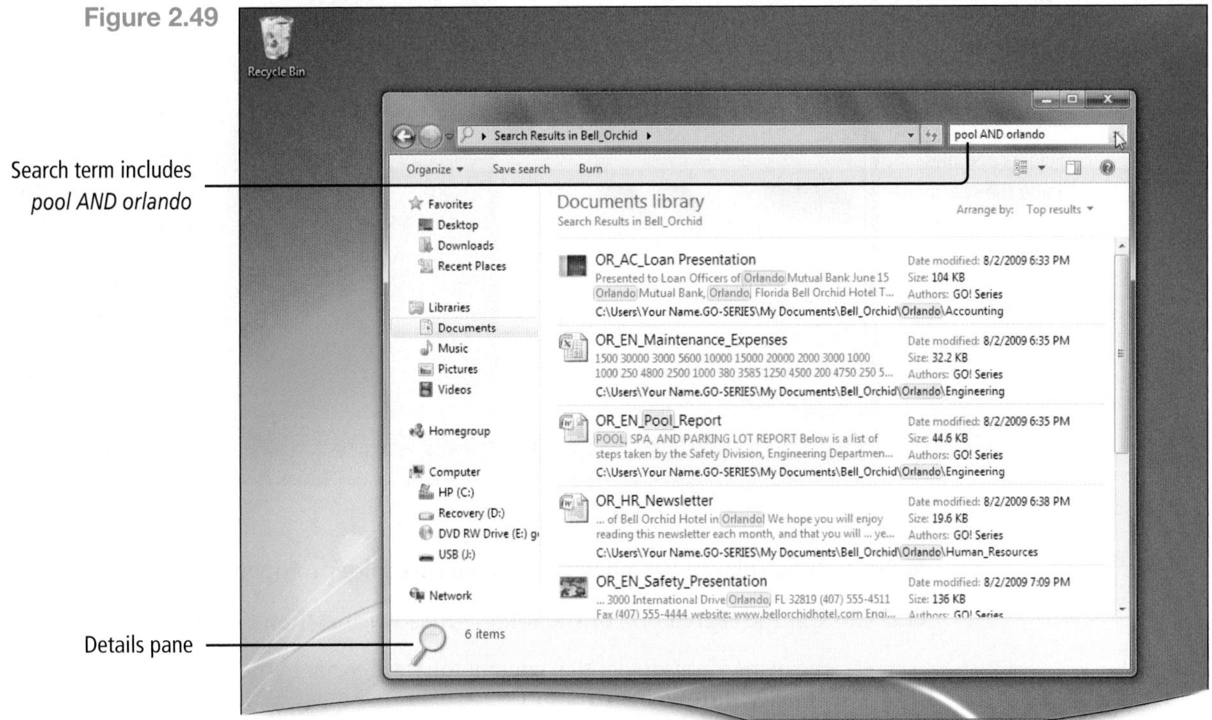

14 Create a **Window Snip**, click in the folder window to capture the window, and then on your USB flash drive, save the snip file in **JPEG** format in your **Windows 7 Chapter 2** folder as **Lastname_Firstname_2B_Orlando_Snip**

15 **Close** all open windows.

Objective 9 | Save, Reuse, and Delete a Search

If you find yourself searching for the same information repeatedly, you can save time by saving your search. After a search is saved, Windows 7 keeps the search current by automatically adding any newly created items that match the search criteria.

Activity 2.16 | Saving, Reusing, and Deleting a Search

At the Corporate office, the Food and Beverage Director tracks the menus for all of the hotel restaurants. In this activity, you will conduct a search that this Director uses frequently, and then save it for future use.

1 Display the **Start** menu. In the upper right corner, click your user name to open your personal folder. Notice that one of the folders that Windows 7 creates for each user is a **Searches** folder.

Any searches that you save will be saved in your Searches folder.

2 **Close** the window for your personal folder.

3 Redisplay the **Start** menu, in the **search** box, type **restaurants** and then compare your screen with Figure 2.50.

If you know the name, or even part of the name, of a folder on your system, this is a quick way to find a folder.

Figure 2.50

Restaurants folder displays (yours may vary)

Folders and files containing the search term (yours may vary)

restaurants typed in search box

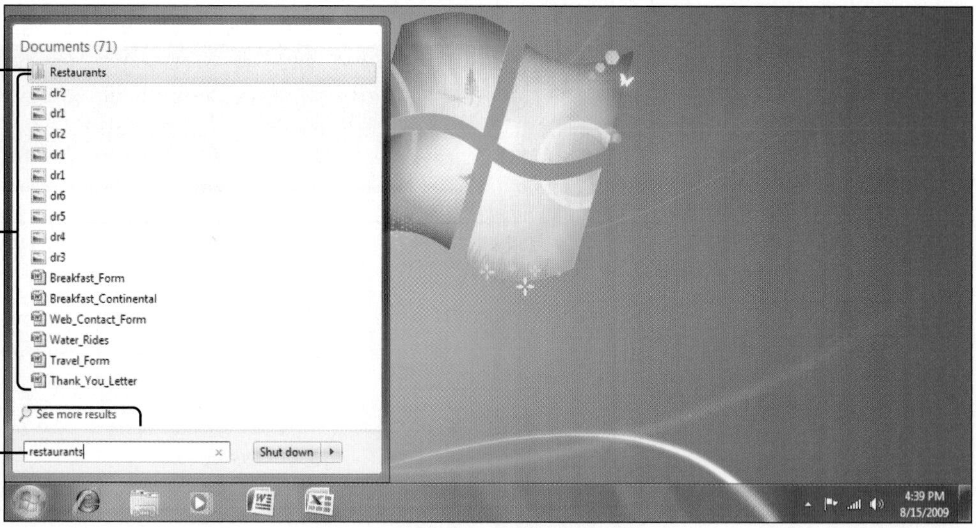

4 On the displayed list, click the **Restaurants** folder to open the folder window.

5 Click in the **search** box of the folder window, and then type **menu**

The items in this folder that contain the word *menu* in the title, in the content, or as a property, display.

6 On the toolbar, click the **Save search** button, and then compare your screen with Figure 2.51.

The Save As dialog box displays, in which you can save your search. The default save location is in the Searches folder and the default file name is the search term *menu*.

Figure 2.51

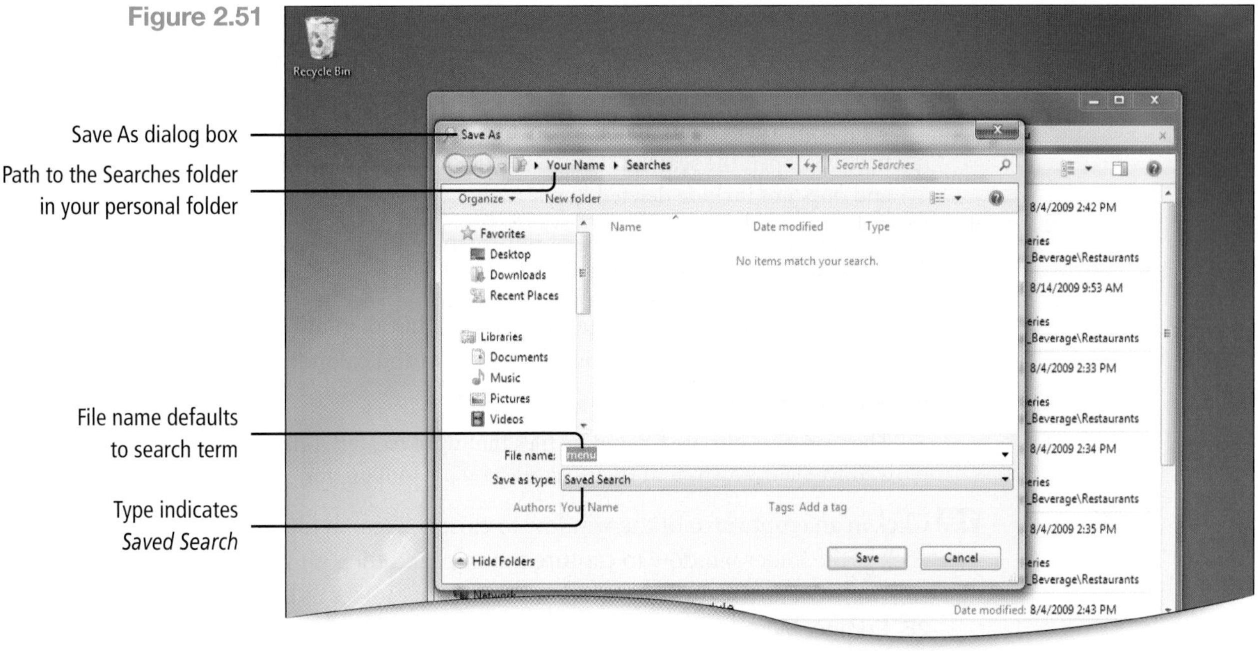

7 Click the **Save** button to save the *menu* search for future use.

8 **Close** the **menu** search window. Start **Word**, and then in the new blank document type **The research staff will complete this document at a later date with ideas for the new menus at the European hotels.** Press F12 to display the **Save As** dialog box. Navigate to **Bell_Orchid ▶ Corporate ▶ Food_Beverage ▶ Restaurants**. Compare your screen with Figure 2.52.

Figure 2.52

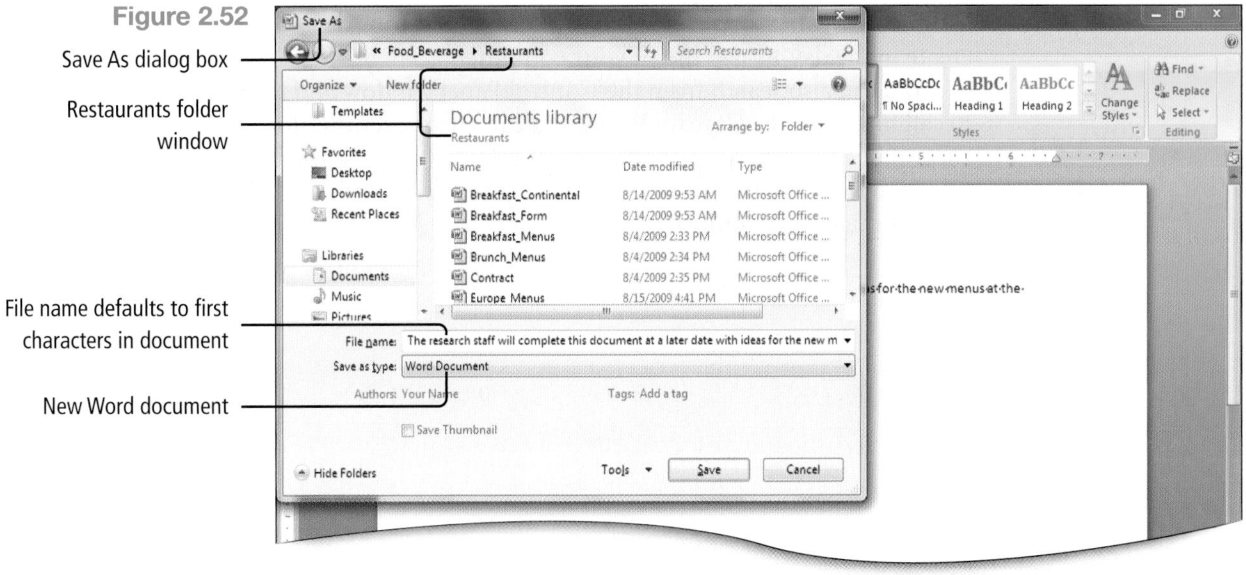

9. Click one time in the **File name** box to select the default text, and then type **Europe_Menus** Click **Save**, and then **Close** the Word window.

10. Display your **Documents** folder window. On the left, in the **navigation pane**, under **Favorites**, locate and then click your saved search **menu**. In the displayed results, scroll if necessary to locate the new file you just created—**Europe_Menus.**

    Windows 7 executes the search; the new search results display and include the file you just created.

    When you save a search, you are saving its specifications—in what folder to search and what search criteria to match—you are *not* saving the actual search results. Thus, each time you open the search folder, Windows 7 re-executes the search and includes new items and does not include deleted items.

    If you search for the same type of information frequently, consider saving your searches in this manner.

11. Click in the **search** box, and then in the box that displays, click **Date modified**. When the **Select a date or date range** box displays, on the calendar, click today's date, which is highlighted in blue.

    The search results are filtered by files that were created today. You can see that searching is a convenient way to find the exact file you are looking for.

12. Click in an empty area of the window to close the search filter box. Create a **Window Snip**, click in the folder window to capture the snip, and then on your USB flash drive, save the snip in JPEG format in your **Windows 7 Chapter 2** folder as **Lastname_Firstname_2B_Europe_Menus_Snip** **Close** the **Snipping Tool** mark-up window.

13. In the **navigation pane**, under **Favorites**, point to **menu**, right-click, and then click **Remove**.

    The saved search is removed from the navigation pane, but the search is still saved in your Searches folder, and will display in the search filter box for this window.

14. **Close** all open windows.

Objective 10 | Search From the Control Panel Window and the Computer Window

Most of your searching will involve searching your data—the files and folders that you create in the day-to-day use of your computer.

You can also search from the Control Panel window and the Computer window. Recall that from the Control Panel, you can change settings for Windows 7. These settings control nearly everything about how Windows 7 looks and works, so it is useful to be able to search for a command instead of trying to decide under which area of the Control Panel it might be found.

Activity 2.17 | Searching From the Control Panel and Computer Windows

1 From the **Start** menu, display the **Control Panel**. Notice that the insertion point is blinking in the **search** box, and thus you can begin to type immediately. Type **mouse** and notice that mouse commands display. Press Spacebar, type **pointer** and notice that different commands display. Press Spacebar, type **speed** and then compare your screen with Figure 2.53.

The Control Panel displays the commands related to the speed of the mouse pointer. Recall that the word wheel technology narrows down your search with each character and word that you type.

Figure 2.53

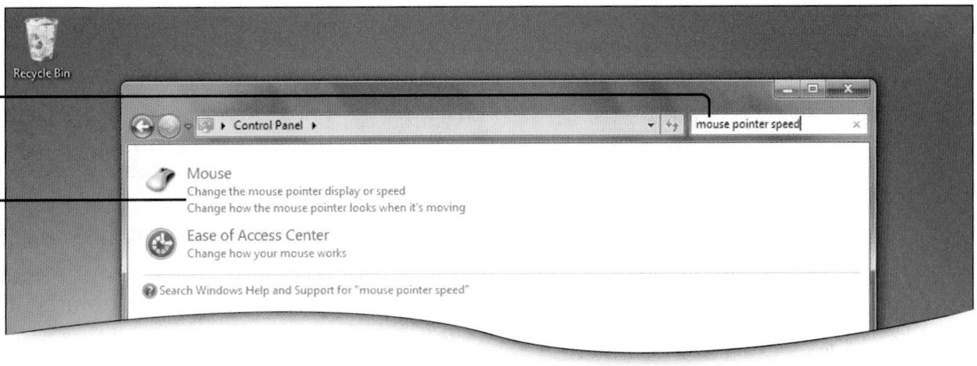

2 Under **Mouse**, click **Change the mouse pointer display or speed**.

In the Mouse Properties dialog box, you can change the speed of your mouse.

3 **Close** the **Mouse Properties** dialog box. In the **search** box, click to clear the search, and then search for **printer**

Various commands related to printers display.

4 **Close** the **Control Panel** window. Be sure your USB flash drive with your chapter folder is inserted. On the taskbar, click the **Windows Explorer** button, and then in the **navigation pane**, under **Computer**, click your USB flash drive.

5 Click in the **search** box and type **compressed** and wait for the search to complete; notice that a green progress bar displays in the **address bar**.

When the search is complete, the file you created in Project A, *Lastname_Firstname_2A_Compressed_Snip* displays in the search results. Other files on your flash drive might also display.

A search conducted from the Computer window searches the devices that you select. Recall that only the libraries associated with your personal folder are indexed, and no removable devices are indexed. Thus, searching outside of the personal folders may take a little longer.

6 **Close** the Search Results window.

Objective 11 | Add Tags to Improve a Search

When you type in the search box, Windows 7 *filters* the items in the folder that you are searching. By filtering, the search displays only those files and folders that meet the criteria specified in the search box. If the search criteria matches text in the item's name, in the item's content, or in one of the item's properties, then the item will display in the search results.

Recall that *properties* are descriptive pieces of information about a folder or file such as the title, the date modified, the size, the author, or the type of file. These are the most common properties and the ones you see in the Details pane when a folder or file is selected. You can search for specific properties in the search box. Recall that the *group* of properties associated with a file or folder is referred to as ***metadata***—the data that describes other data; for example, the collective group of a file's properties, such as its title, subject, author, and file size.

Activity 2.18 | Adding and Searching for a Tag

By default, Microsoft Office documents contain standard properties such as Author and Title for which you can specify your own text. Other programs have similar file properties. You can also create a ***tag***, which is a property that *you* create and add to a file to help you find and organize your files. In this activity, you will assist Barbara and Steven in adding the tag *Wedding reception* to some of the corporate files so that hotel managers can locate information that will help them promote wedding receptions in the hotels.

1 On the taskbar, click the **Windows Explorer** button, display your **Documents** library, and then navigate to **Bell_Orchid ▶ Honolulu ▶ Food_Beverage**. Compare your screen with Figure 2.54.

Figure 2.54

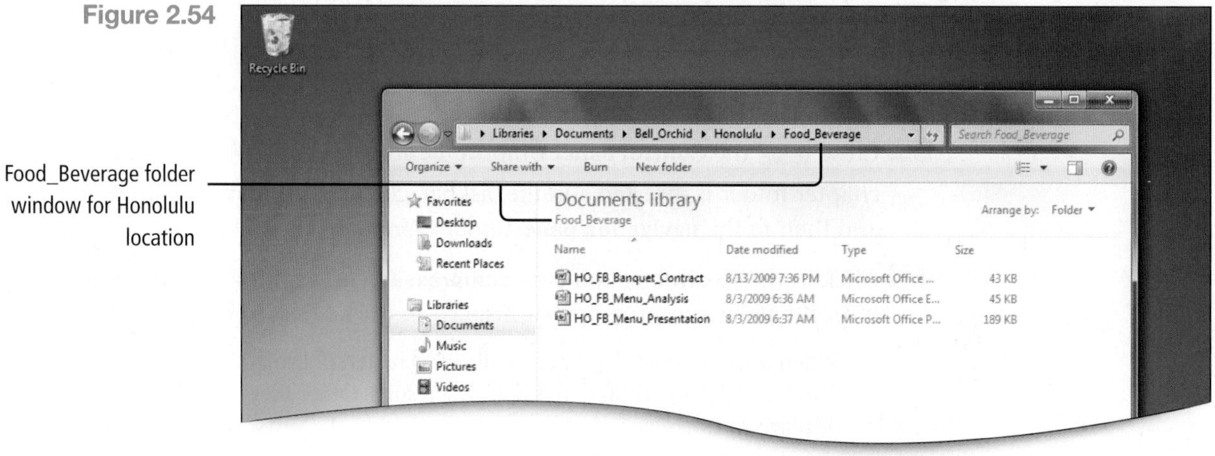

2 Point to one of the column headings, for example *Name* or *Size*, and right-click. Notice that there are numerous properties listed that you can display in the folder window if you want to do so. On the shortcut menu, click **Tags**.

3 Point to the Excel file **HO_FB_Menu_Analysis**, right-click, and then on the shortcut menu, click **Properties**. In the displayed dialog box, click the **Details tab**, under **Description**, click **Tags**, and then type **W** Compare your screen with Figure 2.55.

A list of existing tags that begin with *W* in the Bell_Orchid folder displays. Some files in this folder already have the tag *Wedding reception* and thus, it displays on the list of tags. This tag is helpful to hotel managers when they want to find files that contain information about promoting the sale of wedding receptions.

After a tag is created, it is easily added to other files without having to type the entire tag. The other tags on the list were created for other files within the Bell_Orchid folder structure.

For some file types, for example picture and music files, you can add a tag directly in the Details pane of the folder window.

Figure 2.55

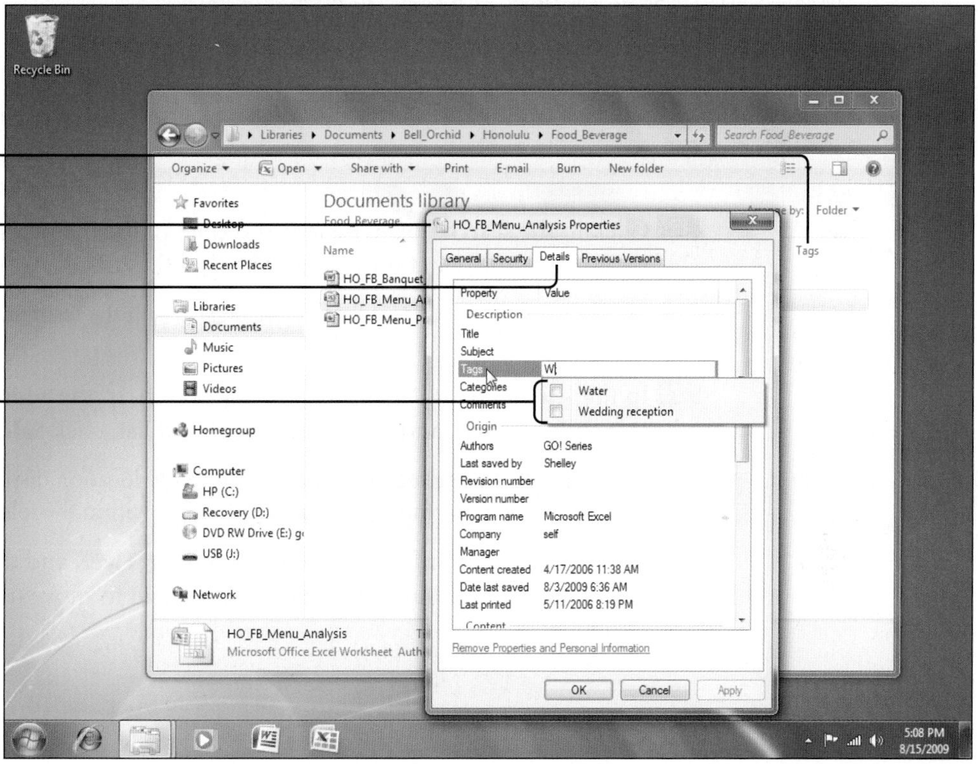

Tags column added to file list window

Properties dialog box for HO_FB_Menu_Analysis

Details tab

Existing tags that begin with W (your list may vary)

4 In the displayed list, scroll down if necessary, click the **Wedding reception** checkbox, and then at the bottom of the dialog box, click **OK**. In the **Tags column**, notice that *Wedding reception* displays.

5 In the **file list**, right-click the Word file **HO_FB_Banquet_Contract**. Display the **Properties** dialog box, click the **Details tab**, and then click **Tags**. Type **W** and then add the *Wedding reception* tag. Click **OK**, and then compare your screen with Figure 2.56.

In the Tags column, two files indicate Wedding reception.

Figure 2.56

Tags column

Two files in this folder indicate *Wedding reception* as a tag

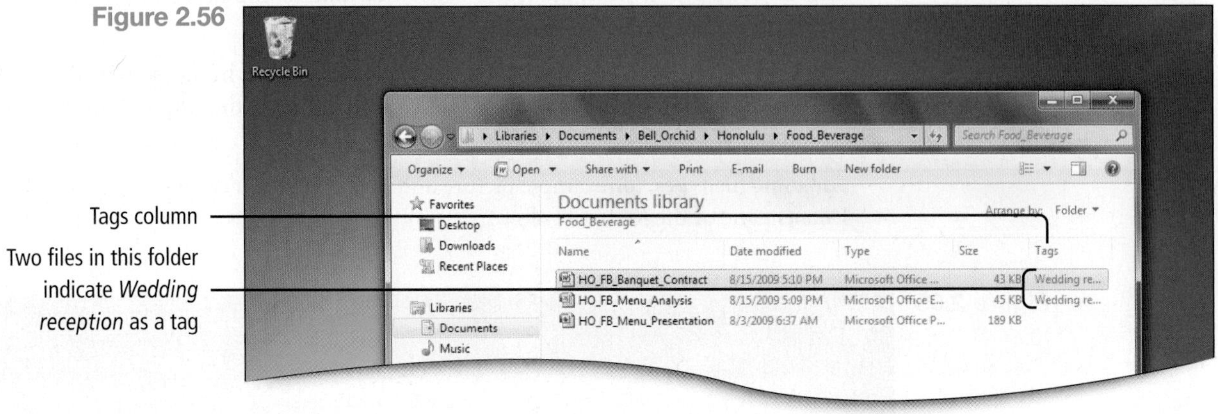

6 Click in the **search** box, type **tag:** and then in the displayed list of filters, click **Wedding reception**. Notice that only the two tagged files display.

Only the files in this folder that are tagged with the term *Wedding reception* display in the search results.

7 In the **search** box, click ☒ to clear the search. In the **address bar**, to the right of **Honolulu**, click ▶, and then in the displayed list, click **Sales_Marketing**.

The Sales_Marketing folder for the Honolulu location displays. Recall that the address bar is convenient for moving to different folders within the folder structure.

8 Right-click the Word file **HO_SM_Marketing_Flyer**, and then add the tag **Wedding reception**. In the **address bar**, click **Bell_Orchid** to move up to this level in the folder structure.

> **Another Way**
> Click tags:= "Wedding reception" if it displays.

9 In the **search box**, type **tag**: In the displayed list of search filters, scroll to the bottom of the list, and then locate and click **Wedding reception**. Compare your screen with Figure 2.57.

The three files in the Bell_Orchid folder structure that you tagged with *Wedding reception* display, in addition to some photos that already contained the tag *Wedding reception*.

Figure 2.57

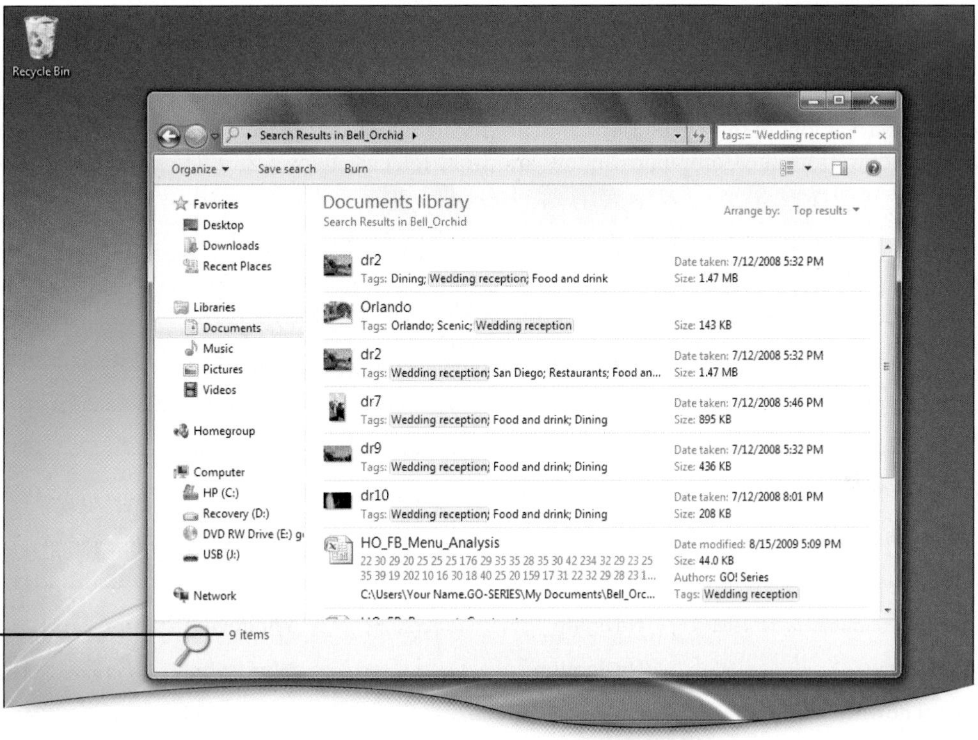

9 files have the tag *Wedding Reception*

10 Create a **Window Snip**, click anywhere in the window to capture, and then on your USB flash drive, save the snip in JPEG format in your **Windows 7 Chapter 2** folder as **Lastname_Firstname_2B_Tag_Snip Close** the **Snipping Tool** markup window.

11 In the **file list**, select the first file, and then in the **Details pane**, click the **Tags** box. Point to the text *Wedding reception* and click to select the text. Press Bksp to delete this tag, and then click the **Save** button.

You can add and delete tags as you need them.

12 In the **search** box, click × to clear the search and redisplay the **file list** for the **Bell_Orchid** folder.

13 Point to the **Tags** column heading, right-click, and then click to deselect **Tags** and remove the column from display. **Close** all open windows.

14 Display your **Documents** folder window, and then delete the **Bell_Orchid** folder from your **Documents** folder. Submit your three snip files from this project as directed by your instructor.

For some of the projects in this textbook, like this one, you will copy files to the Documents folder of the computer at which you are working. At the end of the project, delete the files in this manner.

End **You have completed Project 2B**

Content-Based Assessments

Summary

In this chapter, you used the Windows Explorer program and folder windows to increase your navigation skills to find your files and folders. Organizing your files and folders in a logical manner that suits your needs will help you to find your data quickly. In this chapter, you practiced naming, renaming, copying, and moving files and folders to create an organized folder structure. Another way to maintain good organization of your data is to delete the files and folders you no longer need. In this chapter, you deleted files and folders, and also restored deleted items from the Recycle Bin.

All of the search features in Windows 7 help you to find files quickly without having to perform extensive navigation. In this chapter, you practiced searching from the Start menu, from the Control Panel window, from the Computer window, and from folder windows. You also saved a search and added tags to files.

Key Terms

Content-Based Assessments

Matching

Match each term in the second column with its correct definition in the first column. Write the letter of the term on the blank line in front of the correct definition.

A Clipboard
B Common dialog boxes
C Deselect
D Details view
E Folder window
F Jump List
G Navigate
H Navigation
I Personal folder
J Progress bar
K Properties
L Select
M SharePoint
N Shift Click
O Windows Explorer

_____ 1. The program within Windows 7 that displays the contents of libraries, folders, and files on your computer, and which also enables you to perform tasks related to your files and folders such as copying, moving, and renaming.

_____ 2. A Microsoft technology that enables employees in an organization to access information across organizational and geographic boundaries.

_____ 3. In a dialog box or taskbar button, a bar that indicates visually the progress of a task such as a download or file transfer.

_____ 4. A folder created for each user account, labeled with the account holder's name, and which contains the subfolders Documents, Pictures, and Music, among others; always located at the top of the Start menu.

_____ 5. A window that displays the contents of the current folder, library, or device, and contains helpful parts so that you can navigate—explore within the organizing structure of Windows.

_____ 6. To explore within the folder structure of Windows 7 for the purpose of finding files and folders.

_____ 7. The actions you perform to display a window to locate a command or display the folder window for a folder whose contents you want to view.

_____ 8. A list that displays when you right-click a button on the taskbar, and which displays locations (in the upper portion) and tasks (in the lower portion) from a program's taskbar button; functions as a mini start menu for a program.

_____ 9. The dialog boxes, such as Save and Save As, provided by the Windows programming interface that enable programs to have a consistent appearance and behavior.

_____ 10. A file list view that displays a list of files or folders and their most common properties.

_____ 11. Descriptive pieces of information about a folder or file such as the name, the date modified, the author, the type, and the size.

_____ 12. To specify, by highlighting, a block of data or text on the screen with the intent of performing some action on the selection.

_____ 13. A technique in which the SHIFT key is held down to select all the items in a consecutive group; you need only click the first item, hold down SHIFT, and then click the last item in the group.

_____ 14. The term that refers to canceling the selection of one or more selected items.

_____ 15. A temporary storage area for information that you have copied or moved from one place and plan to use somewhere else.

Content-Based Assessments

Multiple Choice

Circle the correct answer.

1. The action that reduces the size of a file, and which is especially useful for pictures, is:
   A. compress B. compact C. copy
2. A common file type used by digital cameras and computers to store digital pictures is a:
   A. TIFF B. JPEG C. snip
3. A graphic image file type used when a very high level of visual quality is needed is a:
   A. TIFF B. JPEG C. snip
4. The action of decompressing (pulling out) files from a compressed form is:
   A. copying B. deselecting C. extracting
5. A CD or DVD disc onto which files can be copied is referred to as being:
   A. writable B. readable C. selected
6. The process of writing files on a CD or DVD is:
   A. drilling B. burning C. writing
7. A file storage system for creating CDs and DVDs that allows you to copy files to the disc at any time, instead of copying them all at once, is:
   A. Live File System B. Mastered C. Compressed
8. A file system for creating CDs and DVDs that is useful if the files will be read on an older computer is:
   A. Live File System B. Mastered C. Compressed
9. The process of navigating downward through multiple levels of your folder structure to find what you are looking for is called:
   A. deselecting B. selecting C. drilling down
10. A lookup method in which each new character that you type into the search box further refines the search is the:
    A. tag B. word wheel C. progress bar

Apply 2A skills from these Objectives:

1 Copy Files From a Removable Storage Device to the Hard Disk Drive
2 Navigate by Using Windows Explorer
3 Create, Name, and Save Files
4 Create Folders and Rename Folders and Files
5 Select, Copy, and Move Files and Folders
6 Delete Files and Folders and Use the Recycle Bin

Skills Review | Project 2C Managing Files and Folders

Project Files

For Project 2C, you will need the following files:

Student Resource CD or a flash drive containing the student data files
win02_2C_Answer_Sheet (Word document)

You will save your file as:

Lastname_Firstname_2C_Answer_Sheet

1 **Close** all open windows. On the taskbar, click the **Windows Explorer** button. In the **navigation pane**, click the drive that contains the student files for this textbook, and then navigate to **Chapter_Files ▶ Chapter_02**. Double-click the Word file **win02_2C_Answer_Sheet** to open Word and display the document. Press F12 to display the **Save As** dialog box in Word, navigate to your **Windows 7 Chapter 2** folder, and then using your own name, save the document as **Lastname_Firstname_2C_Answer_Sheet** If necessary, click OK regarding new formats.

On the taskbar, click the **Word** button to minimize the window and leave your Word document accessible from the taskbar. **Close** the **Chapter_02** folder window. As you complete each step in this project, click the Word button on the taskbar to open the document, type your one-letter answer in the appropriate cell of the Word table, and then on the taskbar, click the button again to minimize the window for the next step.

If necessary, insert the Student Resource CD in the appropriate drive, and then by using the **Send to** command, copy the **Bell_Orchid** folder to your **Documents** library—you will need a new copy of the files for this project. On your USB flash drive, create a folder named **Europe** By which of the following methods can you create a new folder:

A. In the file list, right-click, point to New, and then click Folder.

B. On the toolbar, click the New folder button.

C. Either A. or B.

2 Display the **Documents** file list, and then navigate to **Bell_Orchid ▶ Corporate ▶ Food_Beverage ▶ Restaurants**. The *quickest* way to select the **Breakfast_Continental**, **Breakfast_Form**, **Breakfast_Menus**, and **Brunch_Menus** files is:

A. Hold down Ctrl and click each file.

B. Hold down Ctrl and press A.

C. Draw a selection area around the four contiguous files.

3 **Maximize** the **Restaurants** window. Select the files **Breakfast_Continental**, **Breakfast_Form**, **Breakfast_Menus**, and **Brunch_Menus**, and then copy these files to your USB flash drive. Which of the following are methods you could use to perform this copy:

A. Create a compressed folder.

B. Use the Send to command.

C. Drag the selected files to the Desktop.

(Project 2C Managing Files and Folders continues on the next page)

Skills Review | Project 2C Managing Files and Folders (continued)

4 Be sure the **Restaurants** window displays. In the **file list**, the quickest way to select the noncontiguous files **Grill_Menu** and **Refreshments** is to:

A. Hold down Ctrl and then click each file name.

B. Hold down Tab and then click each file name.

C. Hold down Shift and then click each file name.

5 Select **Grill_Menu** and **Refreshments** and send them to your USB flash drive. Then display your USB flash drive window. Rename the folder **Europe** to **Menus** Rename the file **Refreshments** to **Pool_Menu** Which of the following is true:

A. Your USB flash drive now contains a folder named Europe and a folder named Menus.

B. You can use the same technique to rename a file and to rename a folder.

C. You must have permission to rename a folder or a file.

6 In your USB flash drive folder window, in the **file list**, select the files **Breakfast_Continental**, **Breakfast_Form**, **Breakfast_Menus**, **Brunch_Menus**, **Grill_Menu** and **Pool_Menu** and then drag them into the **Menus** folder. The result of this action is:

A. The files were copied to the Menus folder.

B. The files were moved to the Menus folder.

C. The files were deleted.

7 Open the **Menus** folder on your USB flash drive. Right-click the **Pool_Menu** file, and then from the displayed menu, click **Copy**. Right-click in an empty area of the **file list**, and then click **Paste**. Your result is:

A. A file named *Pool_Menu – Copy* displays in the file list.

B. A file named *Second_Pool_Menu* displays in the file list.

C. An error message indicates *Duplicate File Name, Cannot Copy*.

8 In the **Menus** folder, create a compressed folder and name it **Breakfast** Drag the files **Breakfast_Continental**, **Breakfast_Form**, and **Breakfast_Menus** into the compressed folder. The result of this action is:

A. The three files no longer display in the file list.

B. The three files remain displayed in the file list.

C. The three files display but are renamed as *Compressed_Breakfast_Continental*, *Compressed_Breakfast_Form*, and *Compressed_Breakfast_Menus*.

9 In the **navigation pane**, click to select your USB flash drive. Delete the **Menus** folder. In the **Delete Folder** dialog box, the following message displays:

A. Are you sure you want to permanently delete this folder?

B. Are you sure you want to copy this folder to the Recycle Bin?

C. Are you sure you want to move this folder to the Recycle Bin?

(Project 2C Managing Files and Folders continues on the next page)

Skills Review | Project 2C Managing Files and Folders (continued)

10 In the **Delete Folder** dialog box, click **Yes**. In the navigation pane, click **Documents**, and then delete the **Bell_Orchid** folder. In the **Delete Folder** dialog box, the following message displays:

A. Are you sure you want to permanently delete this folder?

B. Are you sure you want to copy this folder to the Recycle Bin?

C. Are you sure you want to move this folder to the Recycle Bin?

Click **Yes**. In the upper right corner of the folder window, click the **Restore Down** button. Be sure you have typed all of your answers in your Word document. **Save** and **Close** your Word document, and submit as directed by your instructor. **Close** all open windows.

End **You have completed Project 2C**

Content-Based Assessments

Apply **2B** skills from these Objectives:

- 7 Search From the Start Menu
- 8 Search From a Folder Window
- 9 Save, Reuse, and Delete a Search
- 10 Search From the Control Panel Window and the Computer Window
- 11 Add Tags to Improve a Search

Skills Review | Project 2D Searching Your Computer

Project Files

For Project 2D, you will need the following files:

Student Resource CD or a flash drive containing the student data files
win02_2D_Answer_Sheet (Word document)

You will save your file as:

Lastname_Firstname_2D_Answer_Sheet

1 **Close** all open windows, and then open Windows Explorer. From the student files that accompany this textbook, locate and open the **Chapter_Files** folder. In the **Chapter_02** folder, locate and open the Word document **win02_2D_Answer_Sheet**. Display the **Save As** dialog box, and then using your own name, save the document in your **Windows 7 Chapter 2** folder that you created on your removable storage device—or another location of your choice—as **Lastname_Firstname_2D_Answer_Sheet** If necessary, click OK regarding new formats.

On the taskbar, click the **Word** button to minimize the window and leave your Word document accessible from the taskbar. As you complete each step in this project, click the Word button on the taskbar to open the document, type your one-letter answer in the appropriate cell of the Word table, and then on the taskbar, click the button again to minimize the window for the next step. **Close** the **Chapter_02** folder window.

Insert the Student Resource CD, and then by using the **Send to** command, copy the **Bell_Orchid** folder to your **Documents** folder. Display your **Documents** folder, and then display the **Bell_Orchid** folder window. In the **search** box, type **beverage** What is your result?

A. Only folders containing the word *beverage* display.

B. Only files containing the word *beverage* display.

C. Both files and folders containing the word *beverage* display.

2 In the Details pane, notice the number of files that display, and then with *beverage* displayed in the **search** box, type **s** to form the word *beverages*. What is your result?

A. Both B and C are correct.

B. The number of items displayed decreases.

C. Only files display—no folder names contain the word *beverages*.

3 **Clear** the **search** box, and then search for **shareholders** What is your result?

A. Five Excel files display.

B. Three Word files display.

C. Five Word files display.

4 Open the **SD_AC_Report_Shareholders** file. In what year was the Bell Orchid Hotel in San Diego acquired?

A. 2005

B. 2006

C. 2007

(Project 2D Searching Your Computer continues on the next page)

Skills Review | Project 2D Searching Your Computer (continued)

5 **Close** the Word document that you just opened. **Clear** the **search** box, and then search for **guests** Be sure the View is set to Details, and then filter the **Type** column by **Microsoft PowerPoint Presentation**. How many presentations display in the file list?

A. 2

B. 10

C. 1

6 In the **Type** column, remove the **PowerPoint** filter, and then apply the **Word** filter. How many Word documents display?

A. 26

B. 15

C. 10

7 **Clear** the **search** box, and then begin a new search using the criteria **clerk AND newsletter** How many files display that contain both *clerk* and *newsletter*?

A. 3

B. 5

C. 7

8 Begin a new search using the criteria **housekeeping** and then filter the results in the **Type** column by **Microsoft Excel**. How many files display?

A. 2

B. 5

C. 10

9 **Close** the search window. From the **Start** menu, open **Control Panel**. In the **search** box, type **autoplay** Which of the following topics are listed?

A. Remove the Autoplay feature

B. Change default settings for media or devices

C. Both A and B

10 **Close** the **Control Panel** window. Display the **Start** menu, and then type **tag:flower** Which of the following is included in the displayed list?

A. Blossoms

B. bell_orchid

C. Both A and B

Delete the **Bell_Orchid** folder in the **Documents** window. Be sure you have typed all of your answers in your Word document. **Save** and **Close** your Word document, and submit as directed by your instructor. **Close** all open windows.

End **You have completed Project 2D**

Apply 2A skills from these Objectives:

1. Copy Files From a Removable Storage Device to the Hard Disk Drive
2. Navigate by Using Windows Explorer
3. Create, Name, and Save Files
4. Create Folders and Rename Folders and Files
5. Select, Copy, and Move Files and Folders
6. Delete Files and Folders and Use the Recycle Bin

Mastering Windows 7 | Project 2E Managing Files and Folders

In the following Mastering Windows 7 project, you will move, copy, rename, and organize files and folders. You will capture and save a screen that will look similar to Figure 2.58.

Project Files

For Project 2E, you will need the following file:

New Snip file

You will save your file as:

Lastname_Firstname_2E_Rooms_Snip

Project Results

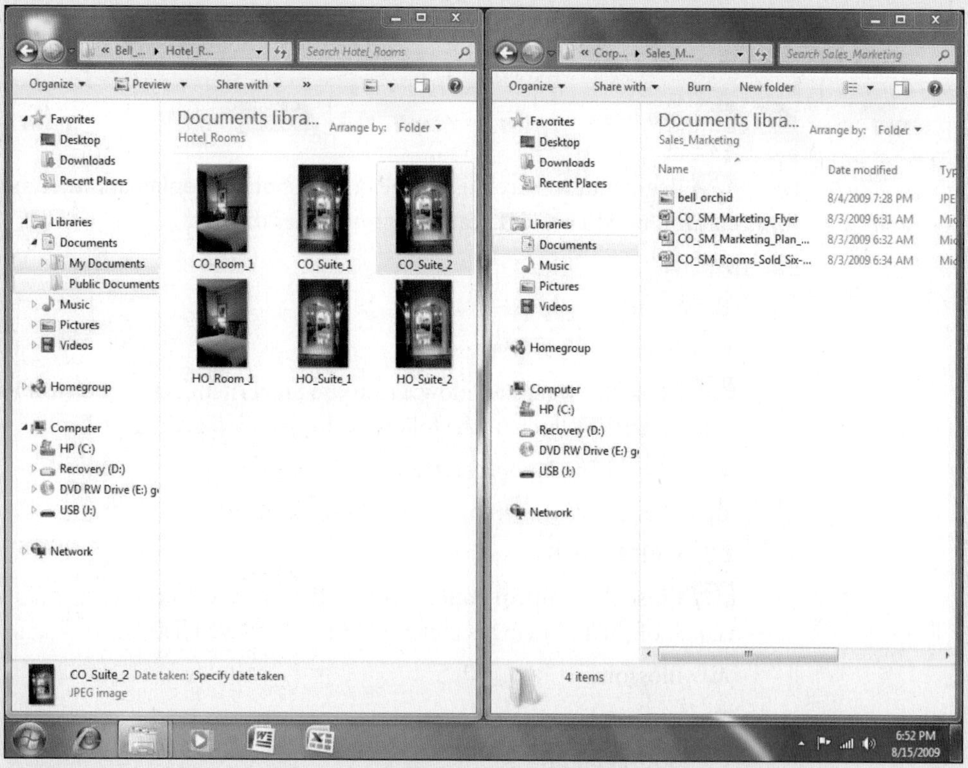

Figure 2.58

(Project 2E Managing Files and Folders continues on the next page)

Content-Based Assessments

Mastering Windows 7 | Project 2E Managing Files and Folders (continued)

1. Insert the Student Resource CD in the appropriate drive, and then by using the **Send to** command, copy the **Bell_Orchid** folder from the CD to your **Documents** library. Then, display the **Documents** folder window and open the **Bell_Orchid** folder window. In the **Bell_Orchid** folder, create a new folder named **Hotel_Rooms** and then open the **Hotel_Rooms** folder window. Snap this window to the left side of your screen.
2. On the taskbar, right-click the **Windows Explorer** button, and then on the **Jump List**, click **Windows Explorer** to open a second window. In the new window, navigate to **Documents ▶ Bell_Orchid ▶ Honolulu ▶ Sales_Marketing** to display this folder window, and then snap the window to the right side of your screen. Select the files **r1**, **r2**, and **r3**, and then *copy* them to the **Hotel_Rooms** folder. In the **Hotel_Rooms** folder, rename **r1** as **HO_Suite_1** Rename **r2** as **HO_Room_1** and rename **r3** to **HO_Suite_2**
3. In the right window, click the **Back arrow** as necessary, and then navigate to **Corporate ▶ Sales_Marketing** to display its folder window. Select the files **r1**, **r2**, and **r3**, and *move* them to the **Hotel_Rooms** folder. In the **Hotel_Rooms** folder, rename **r1** as **CO_Suite_1** Then rename **r2** as **CO_Room_1** and rename **r3** as **CO_Suite_2** In the left window, change the **View** to **Large Icons**.
4. Insert the USB flash drive on which you created your chapter folder. Create a **Full-screen Snip**, and then **Save** the snip in your **Windows 7 Chapter 2** folder as **Lastname_Firstname_2E_Rooms_Snip** and submit it as directed by your instructor.
5. **Close** the mark-up window. **Close** the **Hotel_Rooms** window. In the remaining window, display your **Documents** library, and then delete the **Bell_Orchid** folder. **Close** the window.

End **You have completed Project 2E**

Apply 2B skills from these Objectives:

- 7 Search From the Start Menu
- 8 Search From a Folder Window
- 9 Save, Reuse, and Delete a Search
- 10 Search From the Control Panel Window and the Computer Window
- 11 Add Tags to Improve a Search

Mastering Windows 7 | Project **2F** Searching Your Computer

In the following Mastering Windows 7 project, you will conduct a search, add tags, and then search for tagged files. You will capture and save a screen that will look similar to Figure 2.59.

Project Files

For Project 2F, you will need the following file:

New Snip file

You will save your file as:

Lastname_Firstname_2F_Umbrella_Tables

Project Results

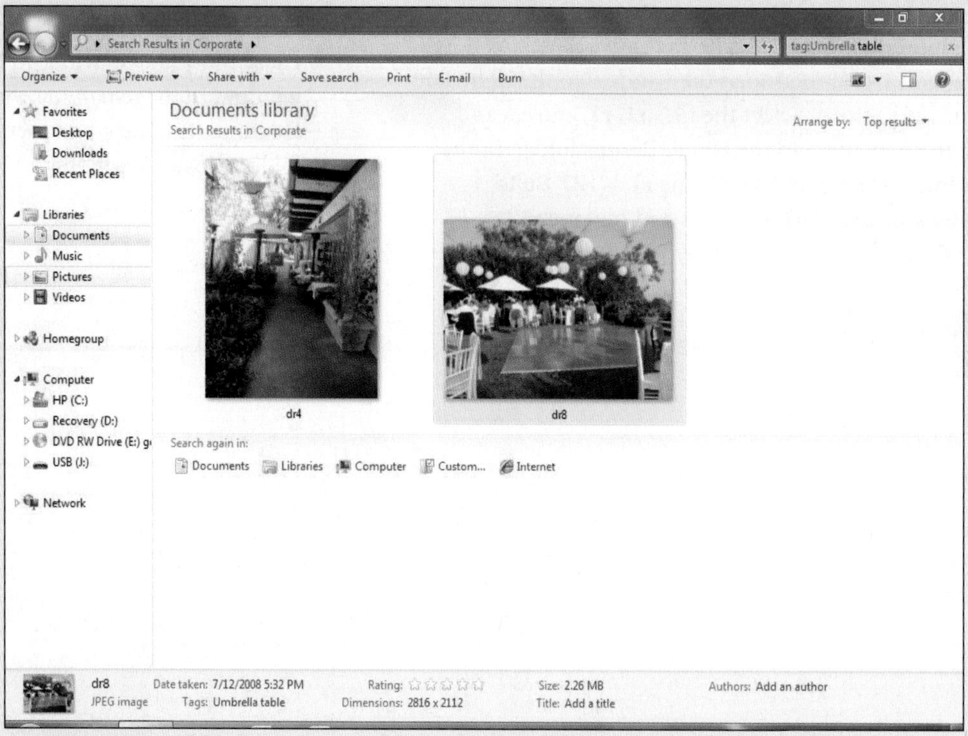

Figure 2.59

(Project 2F Searching Your Computer continues on the next page)

Mastering Windows 7 | Project 2F Searching Your Computer (continued)

1 Insert the Student Resource CD in the appropriate drive, and then by using the **Send to** command, copy the **Bell_Orchid** folder from the CD to your **Documents** folder. Then, open your **Documents** folder and navigate to **Bell_Orchid ▶ Corporate** to display this folder window. **Maximize** the window.

2 Search the folder using the criteria **dr** If necessary, set the view to **Details**. Point to the **Type** column heading, click the **arrow** that displays, and then filter the results by **JPEG Image**.

3 Select the file named **dr4**. At the bottom of the window, in the **Details pane**, click the **Tags** box, and then type **Umbrella table** to add this tag. At the right end of the **Details pane**, click **Save**. Add the same tag to the file **dr8** and click **Save**. Then, in the **Type** column, clear the filter from the search results.

4 Clear ✕ the **search** box, and then search for files using the criteria **tag:Umbrella table** Change the view to **Extra Large Icons**. Select the **dr8** file so that it displays in the **Details pane**.

5 Insert the USB flash drive on which you created your chapter folder. Create a **Window Snip**, and then click in the window to capture. **Save** the snip in your **Windows 7 Chapter 2** folder as **Lastname_Firstname_2F_Umbrella_Tables_Snip** and submit it as directed by your instructor.

6 **Close** all open windows. Then, display your **Documents** folder, delete the **Bell_Orchid** folder, in the upper right corner, click the **Restore Down** button, and then close the window.

End You have completed Project 2F

Outcomes-Based Assessments

Rubric

The following outcomes-based assessments are open-ended assessments. That is, there is no specific correct result; your result will depend on your approach to the information provided. Make Professional Quality your goal. Use the following scoring rubric to guide you in how to approach the problem, and then to evaluate how well your approach solves the problem.

The criteria—Software Mastery, Content, Format and Layout, and Process—represent the knowledge and skills you have gained that you can apply to solving the problem. The levels of performance—Professional Quality, Approaching Professional Quality, or Needs Quality Improvements—help you and your instructor evaluate your result.

	Your completed project is of Professional Quality if you:	**Your completed project is Approaching Professional Quality if you:**	**Your completed project Needs Quality Improvements if you:**
1-Software Mastery	Choose and apply the most appropriate skills, tools, and features and identify efficient methods to solve the problem.	Choose and apply some appropriate skills, tools, and features, but not in the most efficient manner.	Choose inappropriate skills, tools, or features, or are inefficient in solving the problem.
2-Content	Construct a solution that is clear and well organized, contains content that is accurate, appropriate to the audience and purpose, and is complete. Provide a solution that contains no errors in spelling, grammar, or style.	Construct a solution in which some components are unclear, poorly organized, inconsistent, or incomplete. Misjudge the needs of the audience. Have some errors in spelling, grammar, or style, but the errors do not detract from comprehension.	Construct a solution that is unclear, incomplete, or poorly organized; contains some inaccurate or inappropriate content; and contains many errors in spelling, grammar, or style. Do not solve the problem.
3-Format and Layout	Format and arrange all elements to communicate information and ideas, clarify function, illustrate relationships, and indicate relative importance.	Apply appropriate format and layout features to some elements, but not others. Overuse features, causing minor distraction.	Apply format and layout that does not communicate information or ideas clearly. Do not use format and layout features to clarify function, illustrate relationships, or indicate relative importance. Use available features excessively, causing distraction.
4-Process	Use an organized approach that integrates planning, development, self-assessment, revision, and reflection.	Demonstrate an organized approach in some areas, but not others; or, use an insufficient process of organization throughout.	Do not use an organized approach to solve the problem.

Apply a combination of the 2A and 2B skills.

Problem Solving | Project 2G Help Desk

Project Files

For Project 2G, you will need the following files:

win02_2G_Help_Desk

You will save your file as:

Lastname_Firstname_2G_Help_Desk

From the student files that accompany this textbook, open the **Chapter_Files** folder, and then in **Chapter_02** folder, locate and open the Word document **win02_2G_Help_Desk**. Save the document in your chapter folder as **Lastname_Firstname_2G_Help_Desk**

The following e-mail question has arrived at the Help Desk from an employee at the Bell Orchid Hotel's corporate office. In the Word form, construct a response based on your knowledge of Windows 7. Although an e-mail response is not as formal as a letter, you should still use good grammar, good sentence structure, professional language, and a polite tone. Save your document and submit the response as directed by your instructor.

To: Help Desk

I am not sure about the differences between copying and moving files and folders. When is it best to copy a file or a folder and when is it best to move a file or folder? Can you also describe some techniques that I can use for copying or moving files and folders? Which do you think is the easiest way to copy or move files and folders?

End **You have completed Project 2G**

Apply a combination of the 2A and 2B skills.

Problem Solving | Project 2H Help Desk

Project Files

For Project 2H, you will need the following files:

win02_2H_Help_Desk

You will save your file as:

Lastname_Firstname_2H_Help_Desk

From the student files that accompany this textbook, open the **Chapter_Files** folder, and then in **Chapter_02** folder, locate and open **win02_2H_Help_Desk**. Save the document in your chapter folder as **Lastname_Firstname_2H_Help_Desk**

The following e-mail question has arrived at the Help Desk from an employee at the Bell Orchid Hotel's corporate office. In the Word form, construct a response based on your knowledge of Windows 7. Although an e-mail response is not as formal as a letter, you should still use good grammar, good sentence structure, professional language, and a polite tone. Save your document and submit the response as directed by your instructor.

To: Help Desk

My colleague told me that there is a difference between deleting files and folders from my hard disk drive and from my removable media devices like my USB flash drive. What is the difference, if any?

End You have completed Project 2H

Apply a combination of the 2A and 2B skills.

Problem Solving | Project 2I Help Desk

Project Files

For Project 2I, you will need the following file:

win02_2I_Help_Desk

You will save your document as:

Lastname_Firstname_2I_Help_Desk

From the student files that accompany this textbook, open the **Chapter_Files** folder, and then in **Chapter_02** folder, locate and open **win02_2I_Help_Desk**. Save the document in your chapter folder as **Lastname_Firstname_2I_Help_Desk**

The following e-mail question has arrived at the Help Desk from an employee at the Bell Orchid Hotel's corporate office. In the Word document, construct a response based on your knowledge of Windows 7. Although an e-mail response is not as formal as a letter, you should still use good grammar, good sentence structure, professional language, and a polite tone. Save your document and submit the response as directed by your instructor.

To: Help Desk

I am the Banquet Manager at the Orlando hotel. I need to locate all the files that have to do with Banquets. When I search on the term *banquets*, I get all the files specifically relating to Banquets, but other files that are not banquet-related display in the results; for example, marketing materials that mention our banquet facilities. Do you have any suggestions on how I might locate only the files that I am interested in? In addition, I am constantly adding banquet-related files, so I would like to be able to reuse my search. Do you have any suggestions on how I could do that?

End **You have completed Project 2I**

Advanced File Management and Advanced Searching

OUTCOMES

At the end of this chapter you will be able to:

OBJECTIVES

Mastering these objectives will enable you to:

PROJECT 3A

Navigate and display your files and folders for maximum ease of use and efficiency in completing tasks.

PROJECT 3B

Conduct a search of your computer that includes multiple criteria and administer the search engine and index.

Shutterstock

In This Chapter

In this chapter, you will see that although most of the work with your data occurs inside the program in which the file was created, for example when working on an Excel worksheet, there are still many times when you are outside of the program and using Windows Explorer to find or organize your files and folders.

The address bar is a good way to navigate, and in this chapter, you will use more techniques to take advantage of everything it has to offer. You will also use Favorites to increase your efficiency. The Search feature in Windows 7 is powerful; using it properly can reduce frustration when you are trying to find your data. In this chapter, you will practice additional search techniques so that you will always be able to find your files quickly.

The projects in this chapter relate to the **Bell Orchid Hotels**, headquartered in Boston, and which own and operate resorts and business-oriented hotels. Resort properties are located in popular destinations, including Honolulu, Orlando, San Diego, and Santa Barbara. The resorts offer deluxe accommodations and a wide array of dining options. Other Bell Orchid hotels are located in major business centers and offer the latest technology in their meeting facilities. The company plans to open new properties and update existing properties over the next ten years.

Project 3A Using Advanced File Management Techniques

Project Activities

In Activities 3.01 through 3.07, you will work with Barbara Hewitt and Steven Ramos, employees in the Information Technology department at the headquarters office of Bell Orchid Hotels, as they explore how to navigate and display the files and folders on a computer for maximum efficiency and ease of use. You will capture screens that will look similar to Figure 3.1.

Project Files

For Project 3A, you will need the following files:

Student Resource CD (or a USB flash drive containing these files)
New Snip files

You will save your files as:

Lastname_Firstname_3A_Bella_Snip
Lastname_Firstname_3A_Checkbox_Snip
Lastname_Firstname_3A_Tag_Arrange_Snip
Lastname_Firstname_3A_Wordcount_Snip
Lastname_Firstname_3A_Extensions_Snip

Project Results

Figure 3.1
Project 3A Using Advanced File Management Techniques

Objective 1 | Navigate by Using the Address Bar

Recall that the address bar displays your current *location* as a series of links separated by arrows. The term *location* is used, rather than the term *folder*, because you can navigate to both folders and to other resources. For example, you can navigate to the Control Panel from the address bar.

Every element of the address bar—the folder names and each arrow—is an active control. That is, you can move from the currently displayed folder directly to any folder above it in the path just by clicking on a folder name. Additionally, you can click the Forward and Back buttons to the left of the address bar to navigate through folders you have already visited, just as if you were surfing the Internet. You can actually surf the Internet by typing a Web address into the address bar, which opens a new Internet Explorer window.

Activity 3.01 | Navigating by Using the Address Bar

A primary function of your operating system is to store and keep track of your files. A file folder on a disk in which you store files is referred to as a ***directory***. The location of any file can be described by its ***path***. A path is a sequence of folders—*directories*—that leads to a specific file or folder.

1. If necessary, *delete* the Bell_Orchid folder from your **Documents** folder—for this project you will need a new copy of the files. Insert the Student Resource CD or other device that contains the student files that accompany this textbook. By using the **Send to** command, copy the **Bell_Orchid** folder from the Student Resource CD to your **Documents** folder.

2. Insert your USB flash drive, and then **Close** all open windows. On the taskbar, click the **Windows Explorer** button, and then navigate to **Documents ▶ Bell_Orchid ▶ Corporate**. Be sure the **View** is set to **Details**. In the **address bar**, locate the **location icon**, as shown in Figure 3.2.

   The ***location icon*** depicts the location—library, disk drive, folder, and so on—you are currently accessing. Here, a buff-colored folder displays.

Figure 3.2

Address bar

Location icon for a folder

Folder window for *Corporate* folder

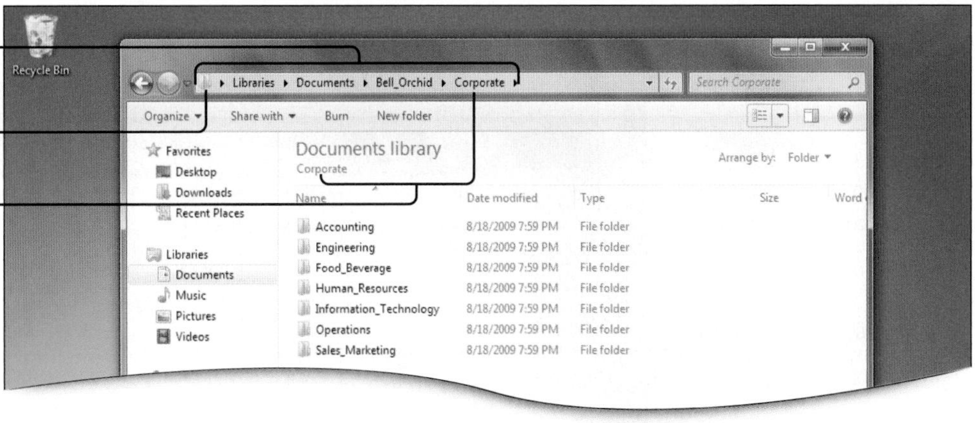

3 In the **address bar**, click the **location icon** one time, and then compare your screen with Figure 3.3.

The path that describes the folder's location displays and is highlighted. The path begins with the disk, which is indicated by *C:*—the main hard disk drive of your computer.

Following the disk is the sequence of subfolders, each separated by a backslash (\). On the *C:* hard disk drive, the folder *Users* contains your personal folder with your name and the name of your computer. Your personal folder contains the *Documents* library, which contains the *Bell_Orchid* folder that you copied there. The *Bell_Orchid* folder contains the *Corporate* folder.

Figure 3.3

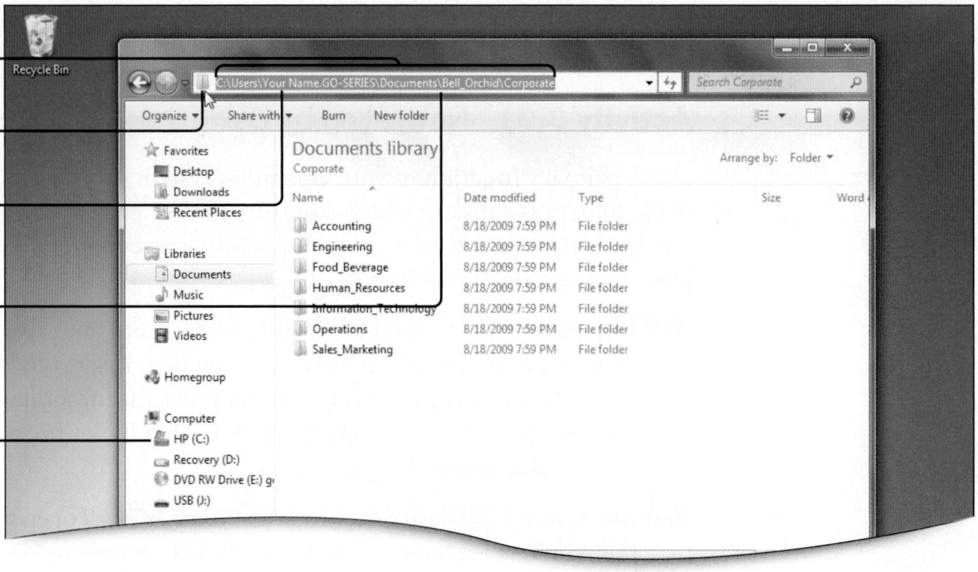

Another Way

Press Esc to cancel the path display.

4 Click in a blank area of the **file list** to cancel the display of the path.

5 In the **navigation pane**, under **Libraries**, click **Documents**, and then compare your screen with Figure 3.4.

The location icon changes to depict the location being accessed—the Documents library.

Figure 3.4

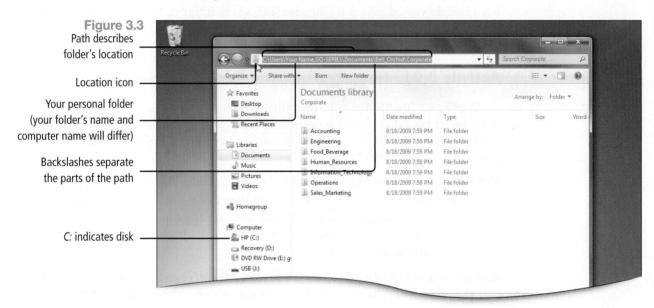

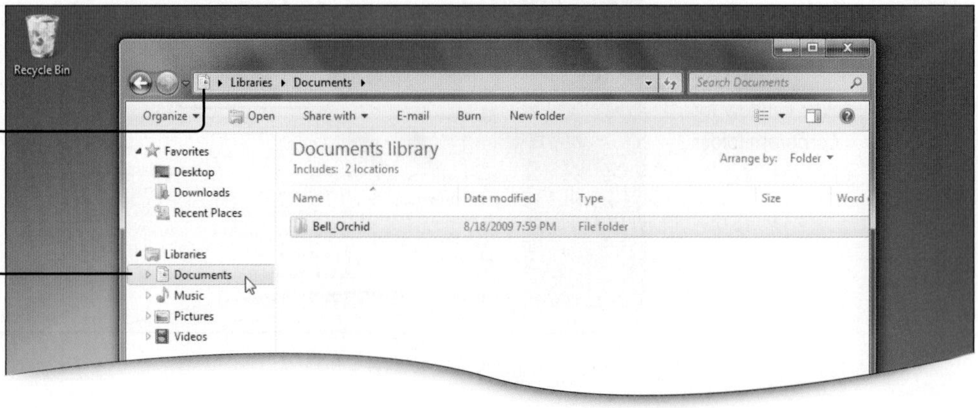

6 In the **navigation pane**, under **Computer**, click your **C:** hard disk drive. In the **address bar**, notice the hard disk drive icon that displays as the **location icon**—a small Windows logo may display there. In the **navigation pane**, click your **USB flash drive**, and notice the **location icon**.

7 If your Student Resource CD is still in the drive, in the **navigation pane**, click it one time. Notice that the **location icon** displays as a CD. Then, under **Libraries**, click **Music.** Compare your screen with Figure 3.5.

Figure 3.5

8 On the **address bar**, click the **Back** button five times or as many times as necessary to redisplay the **Corporate** folder window.

Recall that the Forward and Back buttons enable you to navigate to locations you have already visited. In a manner similar to when you are browsing the Web, the locations you have visited are stored in a location history, and you can browse that location history by clicking the Back and Forward buttons.

9 To the immediate right of the **Forward** button, locate and click the **Recent Pages** button. Compare your screen with Figure 3.6.

The ***Recent Pages*** button displays a list of recently accessed locations, and the current location is indicated by a check mark. By clicking an item on this list, you can move to a recently accessed location quickly. The list is limited to the current session; thus, only locations you have accessed since starting Windows Explorer display on the list.

Figure 3.6

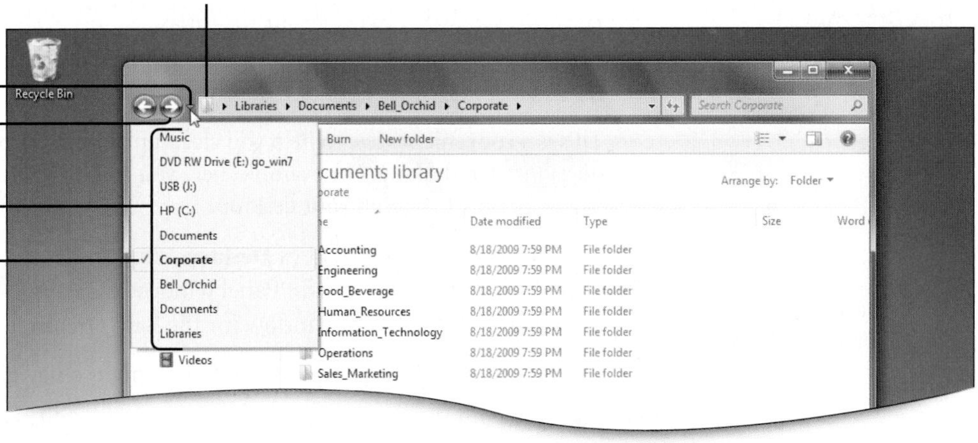

10 On the displayed list, click **Bell_Orchid**. If you do not see Bell_Orchid on the list, click Bell_Orchid in the address bar. To the right of the **location icon**, click ▶ and then compare your screen with Figure 3.7.

The ▶ to the immediate right of the location icon always displays, *below* the separator line, a list of available ***base locations***—locations that you frequently need to access to manage your computer. These include Libraries, your Homegroup if you have one, your personal folder, Computer, Network, Control Panel, and Recycle Bin.

Above the separator line, any folders in the path that cannot fit on the address bar will display, along with Desktop.

Figure 3.7

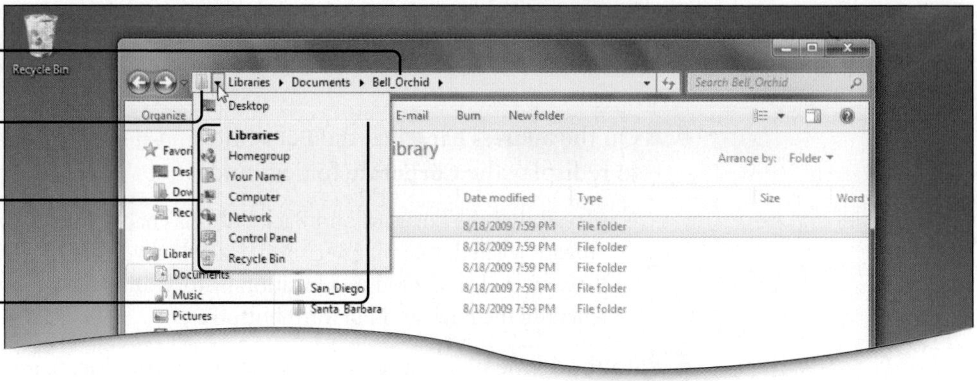

11 On the displayed list, notice the **separator line** below **Desktop**.

Locations above the separator line are part of the current path. Recall that your desktop is considered the top of your hierarchy; it is created for each user account name and contains your personal folder.

12 On the displayed list, click **Desktop**.

Here you can view and work with any shortcuts, files, or folders that you have stored on the desktop. In the file list, you can open items in the same manner you do in any other file list.

This is a convenient view to help you clean up any clutter on your desktop or to *find* items on a cluttered desktop. For example, here you could right-click a shortcut name and delete the shortcut from your desktop.

13 On the **address bar**, to the right of **Desktop**, click ▶. On the displayed list, click **Control Panel**, and then after the Control Panel window displays, click the **Back** button two times to return to the folder window for the **Bell_Orchid** folder.

Use the features of the address bar in this manner to navigate your computer efficiently.

14 In the **file list**, double-click **Honolulu** to display its folder window. In the **address bar**, to the right of **Bell_Orchid**, click ▶ and then on the displayed list, click **Orlando**.

You can access a subfolder of any folder displayed in the address bar by clicking the arrow to the right of the folder and displaying its list of subfolders.

15 In the **address bar**, to the right of **Bell_Orchid**, click ▶ and then on the displayed list, click **Corporate**. In the **file list**, double-click the **Information_Technology** folder to display its folder window, and then compare your screen with Figure 3.8.

On the address bar, to the right of the location icon, double chevrons << replace ▶. Double chevrons indicate that the current path is too long to fit in the address bar. If your window is larger than the one shown in Figure 3.8, you might not see the double chevrons.

Figure 3.8

Double chevrons indicate available space cannot display entire path (yours may differ)

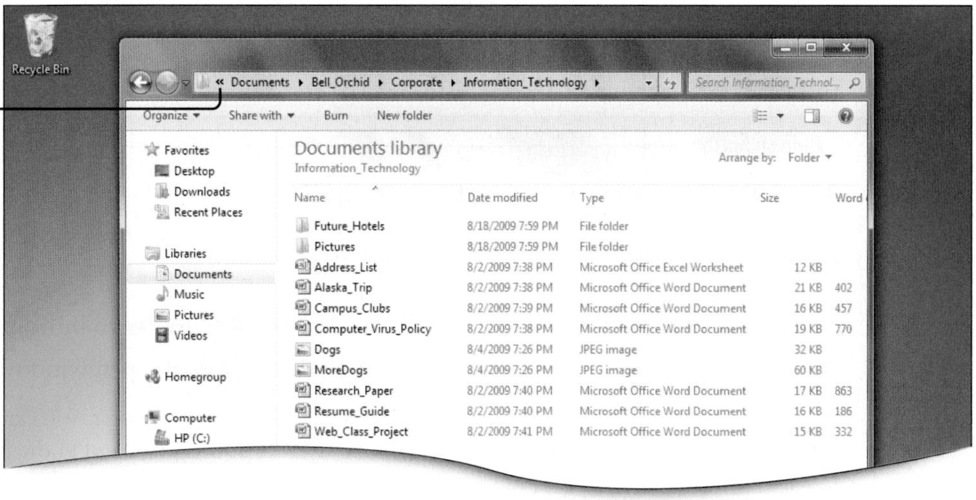

16 If the double chevrons << display in your folder window, click them, and then compare your screen with Figure 3.9. If they do not display, just examine Figure 3.9.

The part of the path that cannot display is shown above the separator line. Below the separator line, the base locations display.

Figure 3.9

Separator line

Parts of the path that cannot display in the available space

Base locations

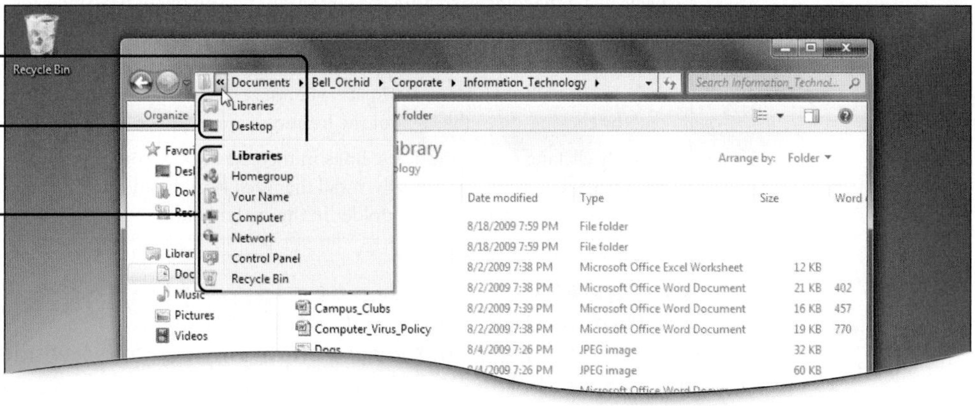

17 Press Esc to close the menu, and then **Maximize** the folder window. Notice that the entire path displays, and the double chevrons no longer display.

Even with the folder window maximized, a path that contains numerous subfolders will be forced to display the double chevrons. When you see the double chevrons in this manner, you will know that the entire path is not visible.

18 If your computer is connected to the Internet, in the **address bar**, click the **location icon** to display the path description. With the path selected (highlighted in blue), type **www.bls.gov** and press Enter.

The Web site for the U.S. Department of Labor's Bureau of Labor Statistics displays. In this manner, you can type a Web address directly in the address bar without opening Internet Explorer.

19 **Close** ☒ the Web page to redisplay your folder window. Compare your screen with Figure 3.10.

> Two additional buttons display at the end of the address bar. The Previous Locations button provides a drop-down list of locations you have accessed.
>
> The Refresh button updates the view and displays any updates to contents in the selected location, which is more likely to occur if you are viewing a network location.

Figure 3.10

Previous Locations button ————

Refresh button ————

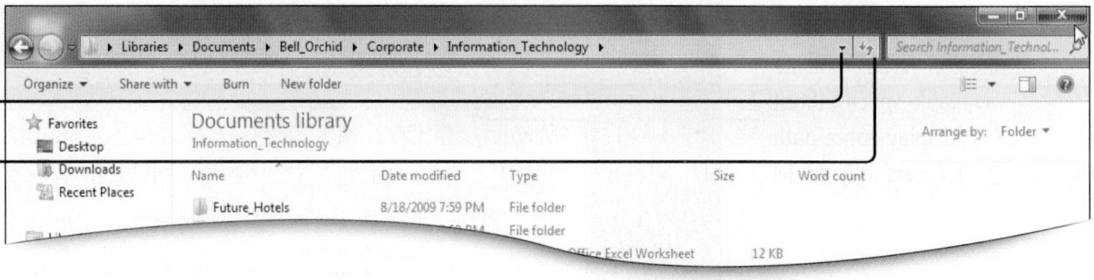

20 In the upper right corner, click the **Restore Down** button 🗗 to return the window to its previous size, and then **Close** ☒ all open windows.

> There is no *correct* way to navigate your computer. You can use any combination of techniques in the navigation pane, the address bar, and in the file list of a folder window to display the location you want.
>
> By using the various active controls in the address bar, you can significantly reduce the number of clicks that you perform when navigating your computer.

More Knowledge | **Are You Looking for the Up Button That Displays in Windows XP?**

If you are used to navigating in Windows XP, you might have developed the habit of clicking the Up button to navigate up the folder structure level by level. And you might be wondering where that button is in Windows 7.

With Windows 7, you have no need for the Up button, because the address bar enables you to navigate your folder structure in a more efficient manner. The entire path of your current location either displays in the address bar or, if the address bar space will not accommodate the entire path, you can view the remainder of the path by clicking << to the right of the location icon as shown in Figure 3.9.

By clicking one of the active links in the address bar, you can jump to any folder in the path without the need to drill upward. Additionally, recall that each ▶ in the address bar is an active link with which you can navigate directly to a subfolder of a folder in the current path.

Objective 2 | Create and Navigate Favorites

Favorites display in the navigation pane of a folder window and in the two common dialog boxes within applications—the Save As dialog box and the Open dialog box. Favorites are folders or locations that Windows 7 has determined as those you are likely to need to reach easily.

You can change the Favorites list any way you want. If you have a folder for a project that you are working on, you can add it to the Favorites area, and then delete it when you no longer need it. For each user account, all Windows Explorer libraries share the same list of Favorites.

Activity 3.02 | Creating and Navigating Favorites

Three items display in the Favorites area by default—Desktop, Downloads, and Recent Places. Recall that searches you save display under Favorites. Saved searches are an example of a *virtual folder*—a folder that does not represent a physical location but rather contains the results of a search.

1. **Close** [Close button] any open windows. On the taskbar, click the **Windows Explorer** button [button], double-click **Documents**, and then drag the **Bell_Orchid** folder to the **Windows Explorer** button [button] on the taskbar to pin it to the **Jump List**. Click on the desktop to close the **Jump List**.

   Recall that it is efficient to pin frequently used folders to the Jump List in this manner.

2. If you want to do so, pin Word and Excel to the taskbar—or leave them on the taskbar if they are still pinned there from your work on the previous chapter.

3. Double-click **Bell_Orchid** to display its folder window, and then on the toolbar, click **New folder**. Type **Bella Beach** and then press Enter to name the new folder.

4. Point to the **Bella Beach** folder, drag it to the left under **Favorites** until a line displays under the text *Favorites* and you see the ScreenTip *Create link in Favorites* as shown in Figure 3.11, and then release the mouse button.

   A link to the *Bella Beach* folder is created in the Favorites area of the navigation pane. The position is determined by where the black line displays as you drag into the Favorites area.

Figure 3.11

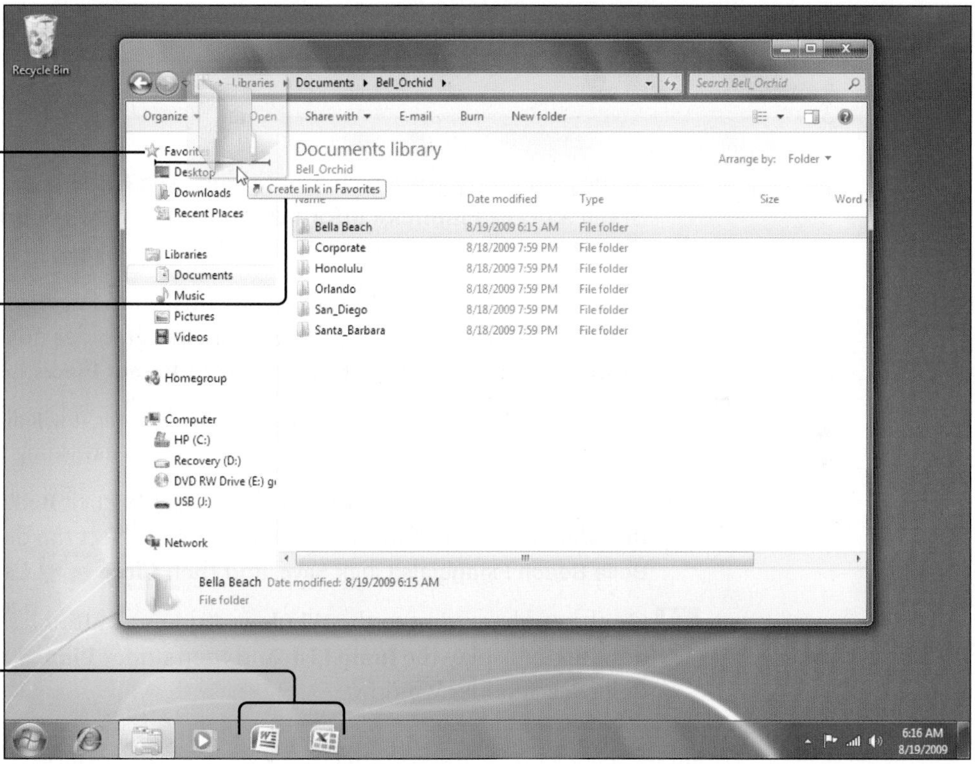

5. **Close** [Close button] the **Bell_Orchid** folder window, and then start the **Microsoft Word** program. Notice that the program might still be pinned to your taskbar from the activities in the previous chapter, or you might have to locate and start the program from the Start menu or the All Programs menu.

6. In the new blank document, type **Information regarding this new resort near Bella Beach will be added to this document at a later date.**

7 Press F12 to display the **Save As** dialog box. In the **navigation pane**, under **Favorites**, click the link to the **Bella Beach** folder to display its path in the **address bar**. As the **File name** type **Bella Beach Resort Overview** and then compare your screen with Figure 3.12.

Figure 3.12

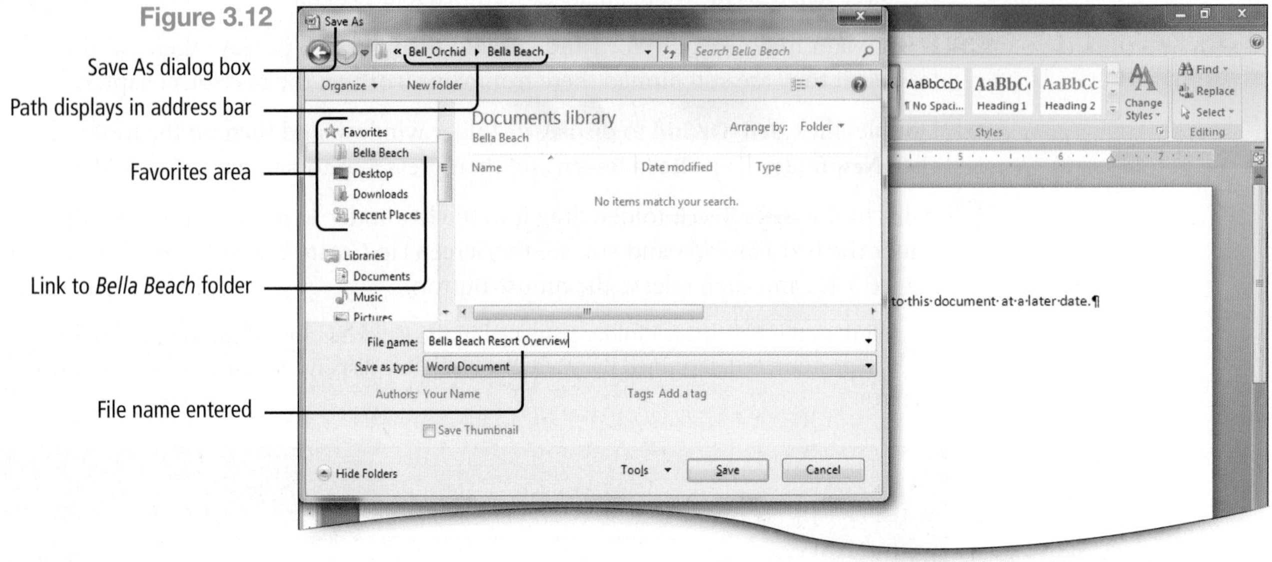

8 In the lower right corner, click **Save**, and then **Close** Word. Start **Microsoft Excel**. In cell **A1** type **Financial information for the new resort in Bella Beach will be added to this document at a later date.** Press Enter.

9 Press F12 to display the **Save As** dialog box. In the **navigation pane**, under **Favorites**, click **Recent Places.** Notice that the **Bella Beach** folder not only displays under **Favorites**, but it also displays in the list of **Recent Places**.

Because you recently accessed the Bella Beach folder, it will display in the list of Recent Places. Finding a recent location here is often easier than navigating within your folder structure.

10 In the list of **Recent Places** on the right, double-click **Bella Beach** to display its path in the **address bar**. Click in the **File name** box to select the default text, and then type **Bella Beach Financials** Click **Save**, and then **Close** Excel.

11 On the taskbar, point to the **Windows Explorer** button, drag it up slightly into the desktop to display the **Jump List**, and then under **Pinned**, click **Bell_Orchid**. Open the **Bella Beach** folder window.

Remember to practice using efficient methods like opening locations from the Jump List and displaying the Jump List by dragging instead of right-clicking.

12 **Start** the **Snipping Tool** program, click the **New arrow**, and then click **Window Snip**. Point anywhere in the folder window and click one time. In the **Snipping Tool** mark-up window, click the **Save Snip** button.

13 In the **Save As** dialog box, in the **navigation pane**, scroll down as necessary, and then click your USB flash drive so that it displays in the **address bar**. On the toolbar, click the **New folder** button, type **Windows 7 Chapter 3** and press Enter.

14 In the **file list**, double-click your **Windows 7 Chapter 3** folder to open it. Click in the **File name** box, and then replace the selected text by typing **Lastname_Firstname_3A_Bella_Snip** Be sure the file type is **JPEG**, and press Enter. **Close** the **Snipping Tool** mark-up window. Hold this file until you finish Project 3A, and then submit this file as directed by your instructor.

15 Under **Favorites**, point to **Bella Beach** and right-click. On the displayed shortcut menu, click **Remove**.

This action removes only the *link* to the folder; the folder itself is still contained in the Bell_Orchid folder.

Place folders under Favorites as you need them, and then remove them when you are no longer accessing them frequently.

16 **Close** the folder window and any other open windows.

By using the Favorites area, you have many ways to navigate quickly.

Objective 3 | Personalize the Display of Folders and Files

Windows 7 includes the word *personalize* prominently in various commands and in the Control Panel. For example, when you right-click on the desktop, the *Personalize* command displays on the shortcut menu. By using the tools available in Windows 7, you can change the way your files and folders function, as well as how the content in your folders displays.

Activity 3.03 | Locating and Identifying Subfolders in the Personal Folders

Recall that when you create a new user account and then log on as that user, Windows 7 creates a desktop and a personal folder. In this activity, you will locate and identify the subfolders in your Personal folder.

1 **Close** any open windows. On the taskbar, click the **Windows Explorer** button, and then in the **navigation pane**, under **Computer**, click your **C: drive**. Then in the **file list**, locate the **Users** folder and double-click it to display its folder window.

Each user of the system for which a user account has been created has a folder in the Users folder with his or her name.

2 In the **address bar**, to the right of the **location icon**, click ▶. On the displayed list, click your personal folder—the folder with your user name. Compare your screen with Figure 3.13.

Figure 3.13

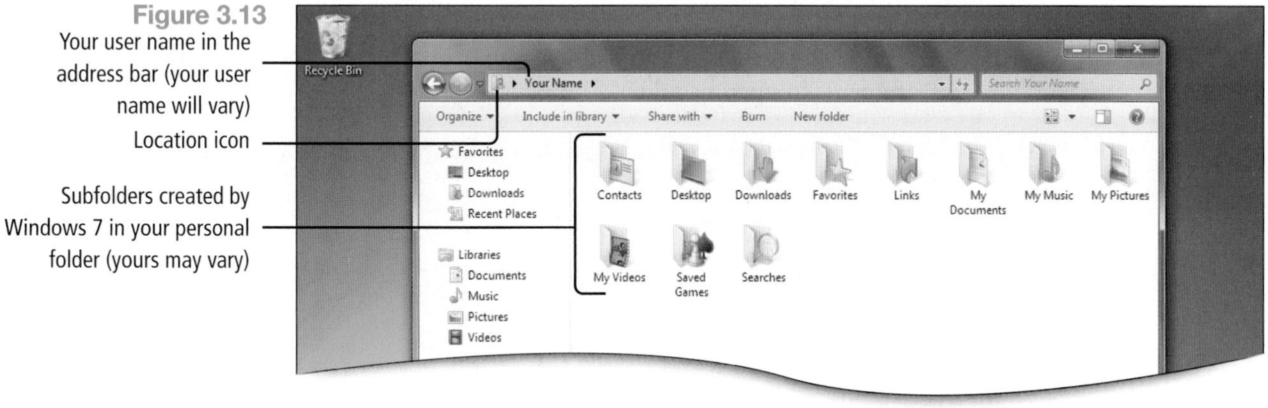

3 Take a moment to study what each folder in your personal folder stores as shown in the table in Figure 3.14.

Subfolders Created by Windows 7 in each User Account's Personal Folder	
Contacts	Contains information about contacts that you create—a ***contact*** is a collection of information about a person or organization, such as the contact's name, e-mail address, phone number, and street address.
Desktop	Contains the icons you place on your desktop; the desktop you see when you start Windows 7 is associated with this folder.
Downloads	Acts as the default location for files downloaded from the Web when using Internet Explorer; anything you download will be stored here unless you navigate to a different location during the download process.
Favorites	Contain folders for your Internet Explorer Favorites.
Links	Stores the shortcuts that appear in the Favorites area of the navigation pane; you can drag folders to which you need quick access into this folder and they will display in the Favorites area.
My Documents	Stores the files in your Documents library such as Word documents and text files, but can contain any type of file; this folder is the default location for the Save As dialog box in many applications.
My Music	Works with and stores digital music and other audio files; if you rip music from an audio CD or purchase music from an online music service such as Apple iTunes Music Store or Zune Store, those files will typically be saved to this folder by default.
My Pictures	Stores digital photographs and other picture files, although picture files can be stored anywhere.
My Videos	Stores digital videos of any kind, including home movies.
Saved Games	Stores game information for Windows 7-compatible game titles.
Searches	Stores search criteria that you have saved and named.

Figure 3.14

4 **Close** the folder window for your personal folder.

Activity 3.04 | Using the Folder Options Dialog Box to Change How Folders Function and Display

You can personalize the way your folders look and behave to suit your needs. For example, if you have difficulty performing a double-click, you can set all your files and folders to open with a single click. Many computer users make this change to their computers.

1 On the taskbar, click the **Windows Explorer** button, and then double-click **Documents** to open its folder window.

2 In the **file list**, point to the **Bell_Orchid** folder and right-click, and then on the displayed shortcut menu, click **Open in new window.** Compare your screen with Figure 3.15.

The Bell_Orchid folder opens in a new window. Open a folder in a new window if you want to keep open all the folders you are working with on the screen at the same time; for example, as another method to drag files from one folder to another.

Figure 3.15

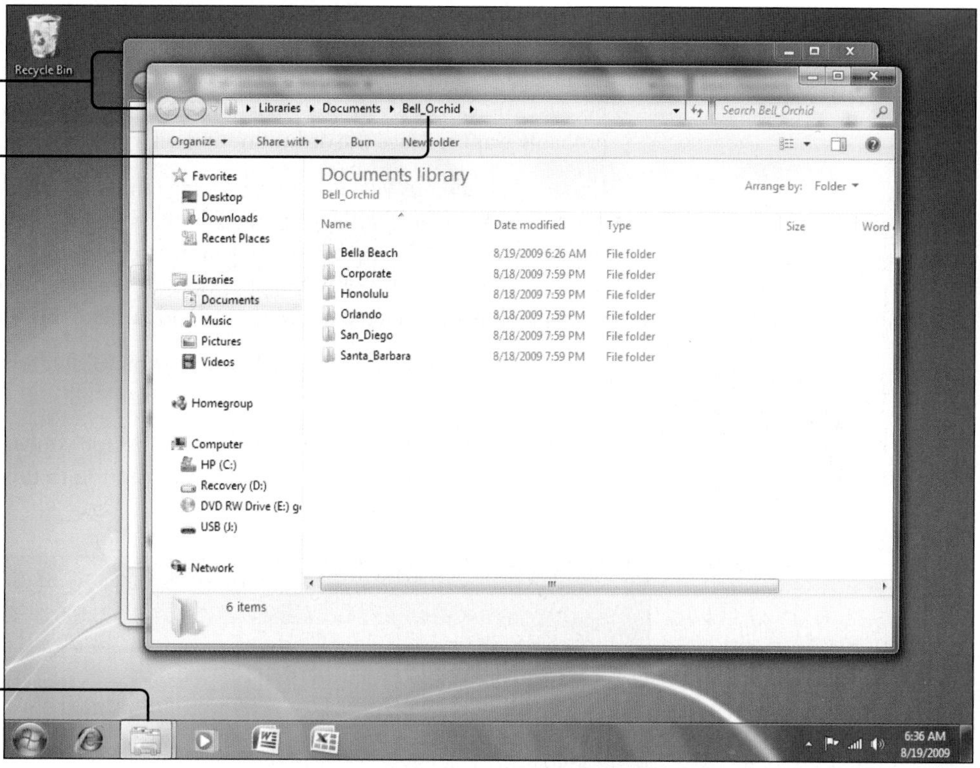

Another Way

Display the Control Panel, click Appearance and Personalization, and then click Folder Options.

3 **Close** the **Bell_Orchid** folder window. On the toolbar of the **Documents** window, click the **Organize** button. On the displayed menu, click **Folder and search options**, and then if necessary, click the **General tab**. Compare your screen with Figure 3.16.

Changes that you make in the Folder Options dialog box affect *all* of your folder windows, regardless of what disk drive or folder's content displays. On the General tab, there are three significant changes you can make to the behavior of *all* of your folder windows.

Under *Browse folders*, you can choose to open *every* new folder in its own folder window, in the manner that you did in Step 1 of this activity. Recall that this keeps *all* the folder windows you are working with on the screen at the same time. If you change this default setting, keep in mind that this behavior will apply to *all* folder windows *all* the time. Because you can easily do this on a folder-by-folder basis, as you did in Step 1, you will probably want to leave the default option selected.

Under *Click items as follows*, you can change the behavior of clicking items to open them. Changing the default setting by choosing the first option will change the behavior of your mouse as follows: To select an item, you need only point to it and it will be selected; to open an item, you need only single-click. This is similar to the manner in which you select and open links in a Web page. Many individuals like this option and make this change.

Under *Navigation pane*, you can choose to show all folders and automatically expand to the current folder.

If you select some of these changes and then decide you want to restore all of the original behaviors, you can click the Restore Defaults button in this dialog box.

Figure 3.16

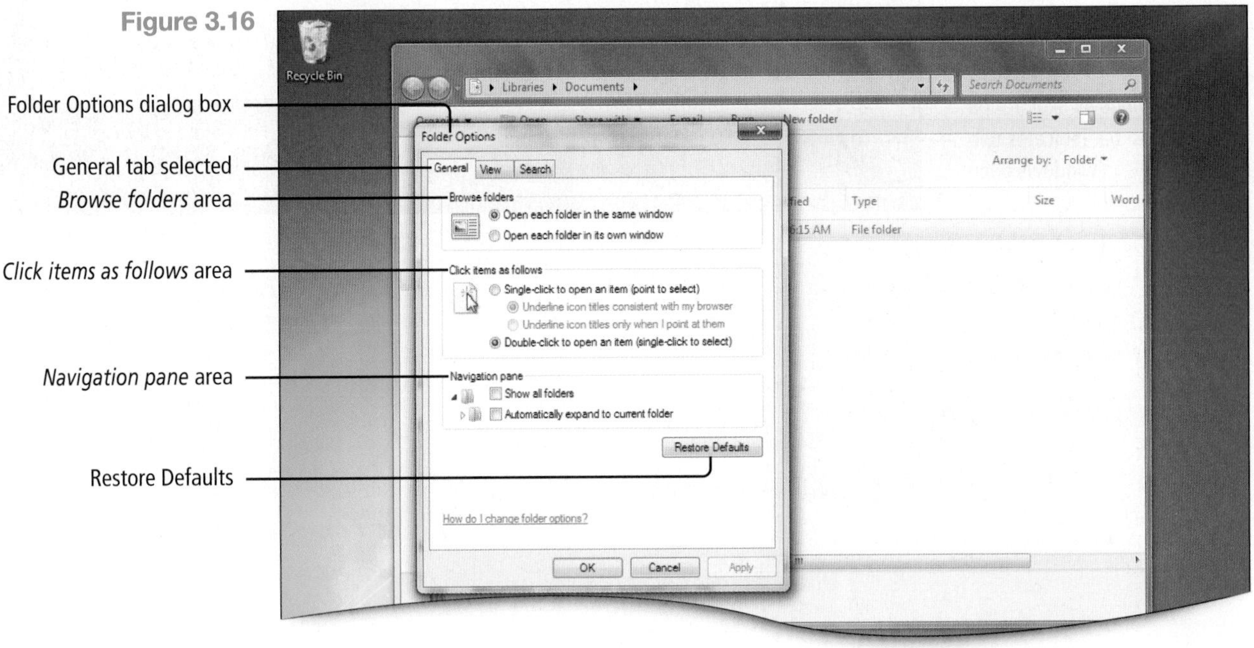

More Knowledge | Double-click or Single-click?

In earlier versions of Windows, testing was conducted with computer users on making the *single-click to open behavior* the default. However, the majority of computer users were accustomed to the double-click method, so double-click remains the default. Many computer users opt to change from the *double-click to open behavior* to the *single-click to open behavior*.

If you prefer to have Windows 7 behave more like a Web page, that is, you perform a single-click to activate something and you point to something to select it, you might want to consider making this change on your computer.

4 In the **Folder Options** dialog box, click the **View tab**, and then notice the two buttons under **Folder views**.

Here you can select one of the Windows 7 views, for example *Details* or *Content* or *Small Icons*, to apply to every folder window you open. To accomplish this, open any folder window and change it to the view you want for all folder windows. Then display this dialog box and click the Apply to Folders button.

Because Windows 7 selects a view that is appropriate for the type of data, and because you can change the view easily on a folder-by-folder basis, you will probably not want to adjust this setting. If you make the adjustment and do not like it, display the dialog box and click the Reset Folders button.

5 Under **Advanced settings**, scroll down to view the lower portion of the list, and then click to select the check box to the left of **Use check boxes to select items**. At the bottom of the dialog box, click **OK**. Notice that a check box displays next to Bell_Orchid in the file list and the check box is selected.

6 In your **Documents** folder window, navigate to **Bell_Orchid ▶ Corporate ▶ Information_Technology**. Point to the Excel file **Address_List**, and then compare your screen with Figure 3.17.

A check box displays in the *Name* column heading and in the upper left corner of the file to which you are pointing. By enabling the ***check box feature***, when you point to a file or folder, a check box displays in the upper left corner.

Figure 3.17

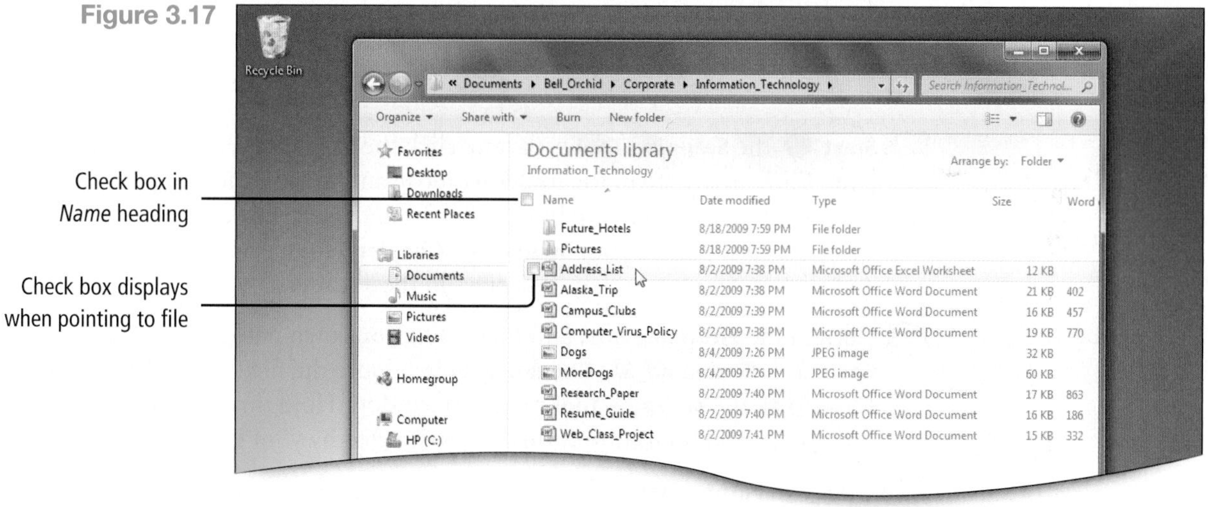

7 Click the **check box** for the **Address_List** file, and notice that a check mark displays in the check box. Point to the left of the file **Research_Paper** and click its check box. Point to the left of the file **Web_Class_Project** and click its check box. Compare your screen with Figure 3.18.

The files you select by clicking directly in the check box remain selected. Thus, you need not remember to hold down Ctrl to select a noncontiguous group of files. This setting also makes it easier to see which files are selected and which files are not selected.

Many individuals enable this feature to make selecting multiple files easier and visually distinctive. If you like this feature, you might consider enabling it on your own system.

Figure 3.18

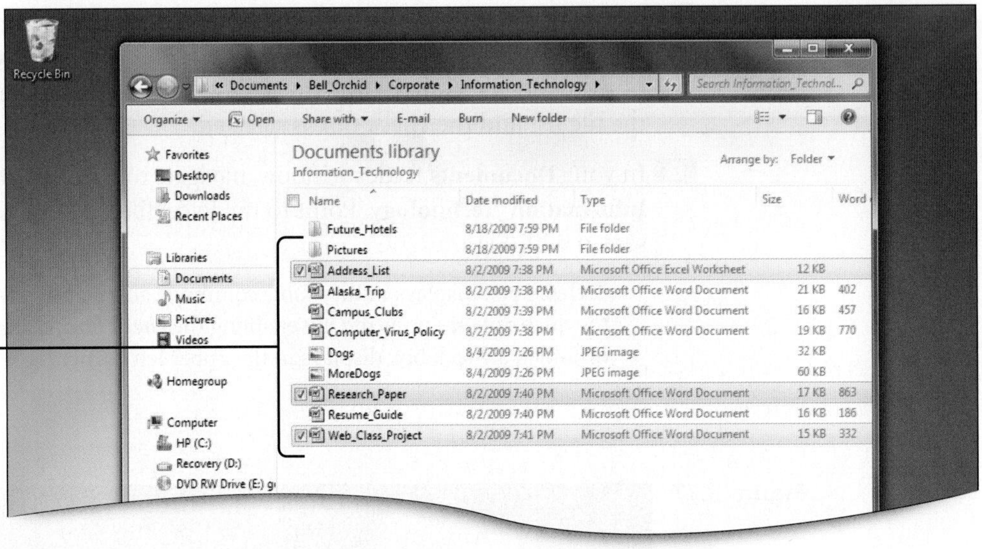

Three non-contiguous files selected

8 **Start** the **Snipping Tool** program, click the **New arrow**, and then click **Window Snip**. Click anywhere in the folder window, and then in the **Snipping Tool** mark-up window, click the **Save Snip** button. In the displayed **Save As** dialog box, if necessary, navigate to your **Windows 7 Chapter 3** folder on your USB flash drive and click to select it so that it displays in the address bar.

9 Click in the **File name** box, and then using your own name, name the file **Lastname_Firstname_3A_Checkbox_Snip** be sure the file type is **JPEG**, and press Enter. **Close** the **Snipping Tool** mark-up window. Hold this file until you finish Project 3A, and then submit this file as directed by your instructor.

10 Open the **Future_Hotels** folder window, set the view to **Large Icons**, and then point to various files in this folder. Notice that the check box feature continues to display.

Recall that any setting you change in the Folder Options dialog box will be applied to *all* files and folders on your computer.

11 On the toolbar, click **Organize**, click **Folder and search options**, click the **View tab**, and then under **Advanced settings**, select the first checkbox—**Always show icons, never thumbnails**. Click **OK**, and then compare your screen with Figure 3.19.

Changing this setting results in the display of a static (unchanging) icon instead of the Live Icon preview of the actual file. Some individuals select this setting to speed the performance of their computer, because it takes a little longer to display the Live Icons.

Unless you have an extremely large number of image files, however, you will probably *not* want to change this setting. Retaining the Live Icon preview is helpful to identify quickly the files for which you are looking.

Figure 3.19

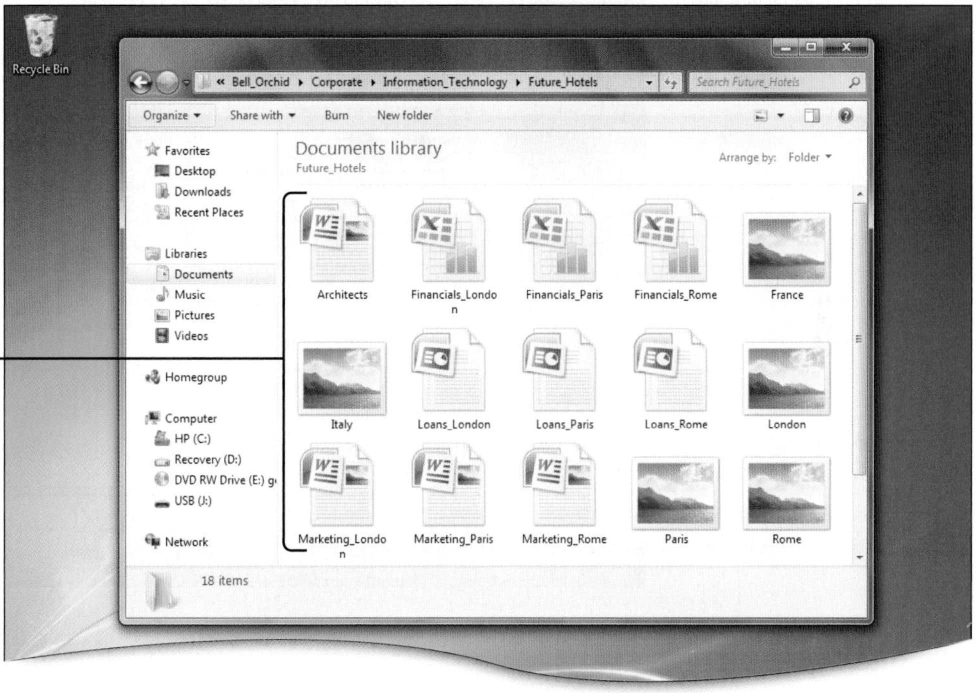

12 Return the **View** to **Details**, and then **Close** the folder window and any other open windows. From the **Start menu**, display the **Control Panel**. Click **Appearance and Personalization**, and then click **Folder Options**.

This is another method to display the Folder Options dialog box.

13 In the **Folder Options** dialog box, click the **View tab**. Compare your screen with Figure 3.20. Take a moment to scroll down the list under **Advanced settings** and study the table in Figure 3.21.

Becoming familiar with these settings will enable you to further personalize the manner in which your folders display to suit your own comfort and ease of use.

Figure 3.20

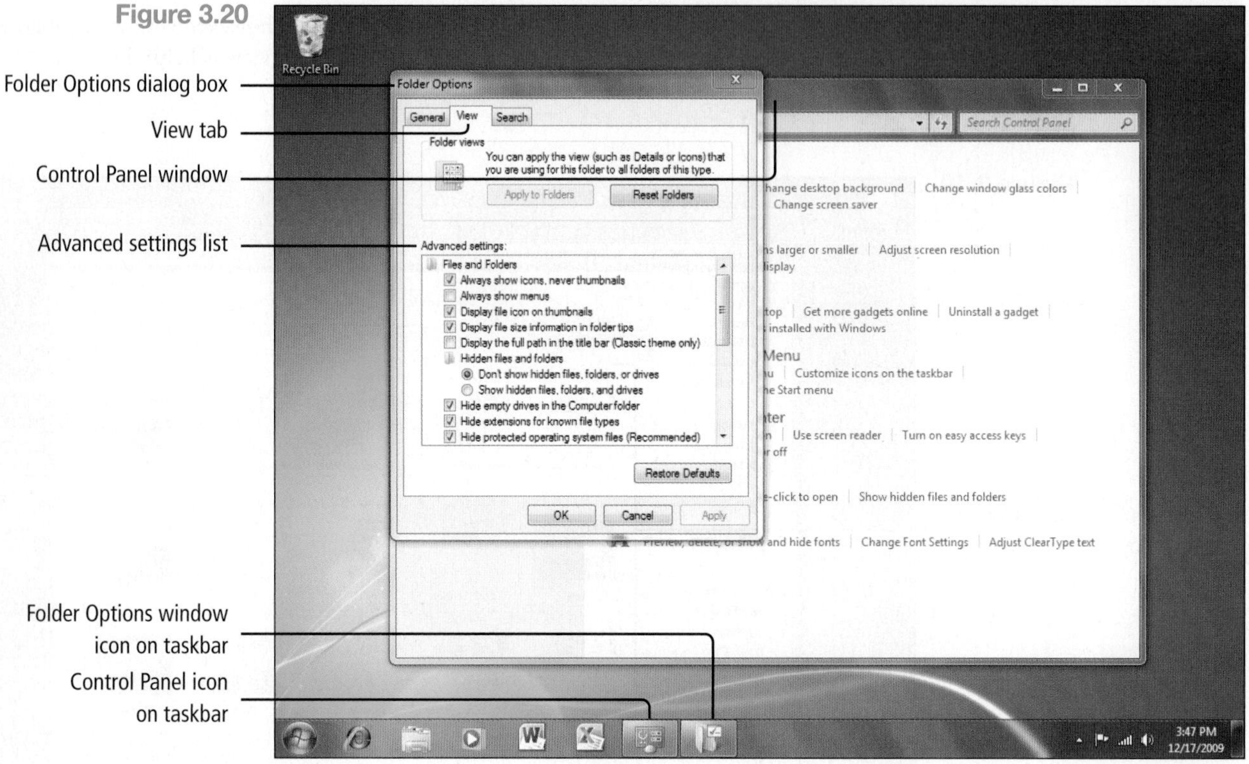

Advanced Settings in the View Tab of the Folder Options Dialog Box

Setting	Description and Default Setting
Always show icons, never thumbnails	Replaces Live Icons with a standard image. Off by default.
Always show menus	Displays a menu bar above the toolbar, which contains a few commands that are not available from the toolbar. Off by default.
Display file icon on thumbnails	Displays a small version of the application icon, for example the green Excel icon, on the file name, which makes it easier to determine which application opens the file. On by default.
Display file size information in folder tips	Displays the size of the file in a ScreenTip when you point to the file. On by default.
Display the full path in the title bar (Classic theme only)	Displays the full path of the file in the title bar of the folder window; however, this applies only to the Classic view of folders. Off by default.
Hidden files and folders	Displays hidden files and displays them as a paler ghost image. Off by default.
Hide empty drives in the Computer folder	Hides the display of drive letters in which there is no device attached. On by default.
Hide extensions for known file types	Hides the display of the file extensions for files, for example *.docx* for a Word 2007 file. On by default (by default, extensions are hidden from view).
Hide protected operating system files (Recommended)	Hides files with the *System* attribute from file listings. On by default.
Launch folder windows in a separate process	Launches each folder window in a separate memory space, increasing stability but decreasing performance. You might try this setting if your computer frequently fails, and you are trying to minimize problems or troubleshoot. Off by default.
Restore previous folder windows at logon	Redisplays, upon restart, any windows that you had open when Windows 7 was shut down. Off by default.
Show drive letters	Displays both the drive letter and the friendly name for a drive. If you clear this setting, only the friendly name will display. On by default.
Show encrypted or compressed NTFS files in color	Changes the text color for any files that use NTFS (New Technology File System) compression or NTFS encryption. On by default.
Show pop-up description for folder and desktop items	Displays a ScreenTip when you point to an item. On by default.
Show preview handlers in preview pane	Displays the contents of a file in the Preview pane when the Preview pane is enabled. On by default. Clearing this option could improve your computer's performance speed.
Use check boxes to select items	Displays a selection check box when you point to an item. Off by default.
Use Sharing Wizard (Recommended)	Limits the capability to assign complex permissions to files, which simplifies the process. On by default.
When typing into list view	Lets you choose between typing the value into the Search field automatically or displaying the results in the view. By default, set to *Select the typed item in the view.*

Figure 3.21

14 In the lower right corner of the **Folder Options** dialog box, click the **Restore Defaults** button to restore any settings that you have changed to the default settings. Click **OK**. **Close** the **Control Panel** window.

Activity 3.05 | Personalizing Views and Using the Arrange By Feature

In the file list of a folder window, in addition to setting the *view*—for example Details view, Large Icons view, and so on—you can also change the *arrangement* of items by using the ***Arrange by*** feature. In a folder window, the Arrange by feature enables you to arrange the items by Author, Date modified, Tag, Type, or Name. The default arrangement is Folder.

1 **Close** any open windows. On the taskbar, click the **Windows Explorer** button. In the **navigation pane**, click **Computer**. Be sure the **View** is set to **Tiles**.

The default view for the Computer window is Tiles; for most other windows the default view is Details. Recall, however, that Windows 7 remembers the most recently used view for a folder window, and continues to display that view each time that particular folder window is opened.

To change this view behavior, you could change the view for *all* of your folders on the General tab in the Folder Options dialog box.

Because you can change the view easily—recall that you can click the View button repeatedly to cycle through some of the views without actually displaying the View menu—you will probably *not* want to make any permanent changes.

2 In the **navigation pane**, under **Libraries**, click **Documents**, and then navigate to **Bell_Orchid ▶ Corporate ▶ Food_Beverage**. Be sure the **View** is **Details**. Click to select the Word file **CO_FB_Banquet_Contract**. Compare your screen with Figure 3.22.

Details view is the default view for most folder windows, but of course any window will display in its most recently displayed view. The Details view presents substantial information about each file. When a folder or file in the file list is selected, the Details pane at the bottom of the window displays information about the selected item.

Figure 3.22

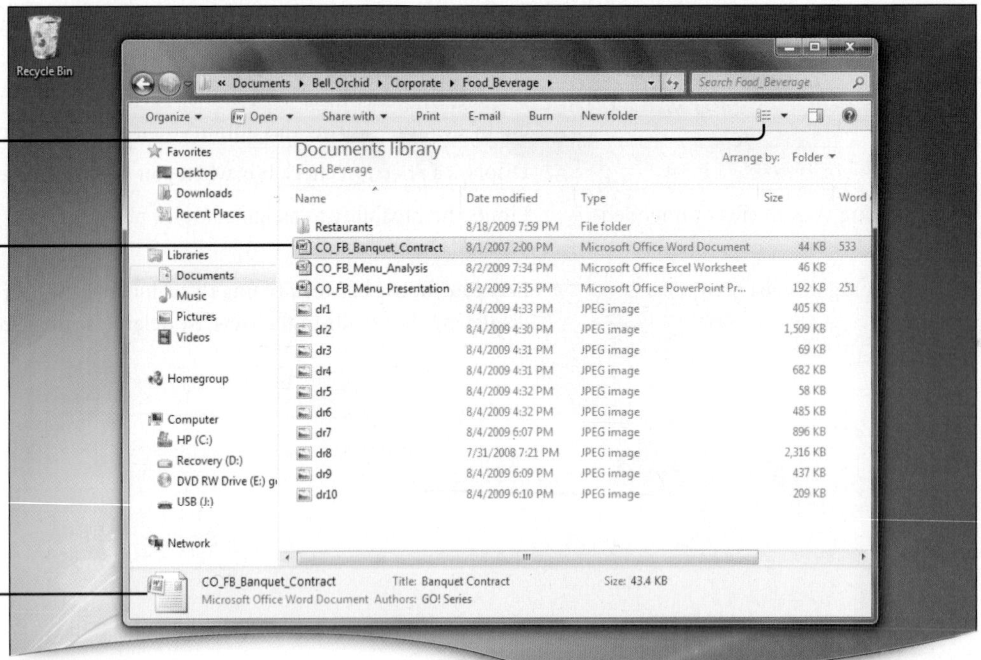

3 On the toolbar, click the **View** button one time to cycle to the **Tiles** view.

The Tiles view combines medium-sized icons with some information—file name, file type, and file size.

4 Click the **View** button two times to cycle to **Large Icons**.

The Large Icons view provides large icons, which make it easy to see the content of files that include the Live Icon preview. For example, here you can see the actual picture files and the first slide of the PowerPoint presentation when a file is selected.

5 Click the **View** button one time to cycle to the **List** view.

The List view displays only the file icon and the file name. The advantage of the List view is that you can see the full file name without widening the Name column.

6 Click the **View** button one time to cycle to the default **Details** view.

Repeatedly clicking the View button cycles the view through five of the seven available views—Tiles, Content, Large Icons, List, and Details.

7 At the right side of the **Documents library pane**, locate **Arrange by**, and notice that *Folder* is the current arrangement. Notice also that this **file list** includes the **Restaurants** subfolder and a list of files.

8 To the right of *Folder*, click the **Arrange by arrow**, and then click **Name**.

When you arrange the folder window by Name, all of the files in the folder *and* in any subfolders display. The subfolders themselves do not display.

This arrangement is useful when you want to see all the files in a folder without opening each subfolder.

9 Click the **Arrange by** arrow again, and then return the arrangement to **Folder**. In the **file list**, notice that the **Restaurants** subfolder once again displays. Notice also that the **Food_Beverage** folder contains only one PowerPoint file and one Excel file.

10 Set **Arrange by** to **Type**, point to the **Excel** stack, and then on the ScreenTip, notice that **16** Excel files display.

The Arrange by feature includes all items in the folder, plus any items in any subfolders. This is a useful way to see the number of files of a specific *type* in a folder without opening each subfolder.

11 Set **Arrange by** back to **Folder**, which is the default. Navigate to **Bell_Orchid ▶ Santa_Barbara ▶ Sales_Marketing ▶ Media**. Click the **Arrange by** arrow, and then click **Tag**. Click the stack **Gardens**, and then compare your screen with Figure 3.23.

Windows 7 sorts the group of files into stacks by tag, and when you select a stack, in the Details pane, the number of files with the tag *Gardens* is indicated.

Figure 3.23

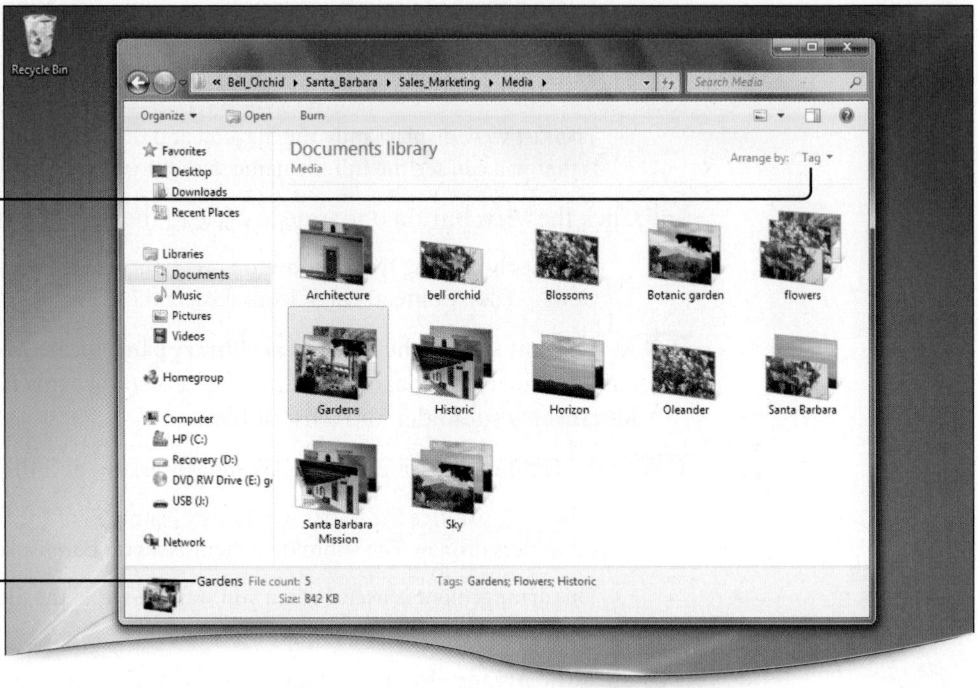

12 **Start** the **Snipping Tool** program, click the **New arrow**, and then click **Window Snip**. Click anywhere in the folder window, and then in the **Snipping Tool** mark-up window, click the **Save Snip** button. In the displayed **Save As** dialog box, if necessary navigate to your **Windows 7 Chapter 3** folder on your USB flash drive and click to select it so that it displays in the address bar.

13 Click in the **File name** box, and then using your own name, name the file **Lastname_Firstname_3A_Tag_Arrange_Snip** be sure the file type is **JPEG**, and press Enter. **Close** the **Snipping Tool** mark-up window, but leave the **Media** window open. Hold this file until you finish Project 3A, and then submit this file as directed by your instructor.

Activity 3.06 | Sorting Files by Properties

You can select any property that the file supports, and use it to sort files.

1 Set **Arrange by** back to **Folder**. Navigate to **Bell_Orchid ▶ Corporate ▶ Food_Beverage ▶ Restaurants. Maximize** the window.

2 In the **file list**, point to any of the column headings, right-click, and then at the bottom of the displayed menu, click **More**.

The Choose Details dialog box displays. From this dialog box, you can select any property that the file supports, and use it to sort files.

3 In the **Choose Details** dialog box, scroll down to the end of the list, and then select the **Word count** check box. Click **OK**.

4 Point to the **Word count column heading**, and then click two times so that the small arrow at the upper edge of the column heading points downward. Compare your screen with Figure 3.24.

A Word count column is added to the folder window, and the files that support Word count—Microsoft Word documents—are sorted in descending order. Microsoft Excel files do not contain a word count.

Properties such as those you can see in the Choose Details dialog box offer many ways to sort and find files.

Figure 3.24

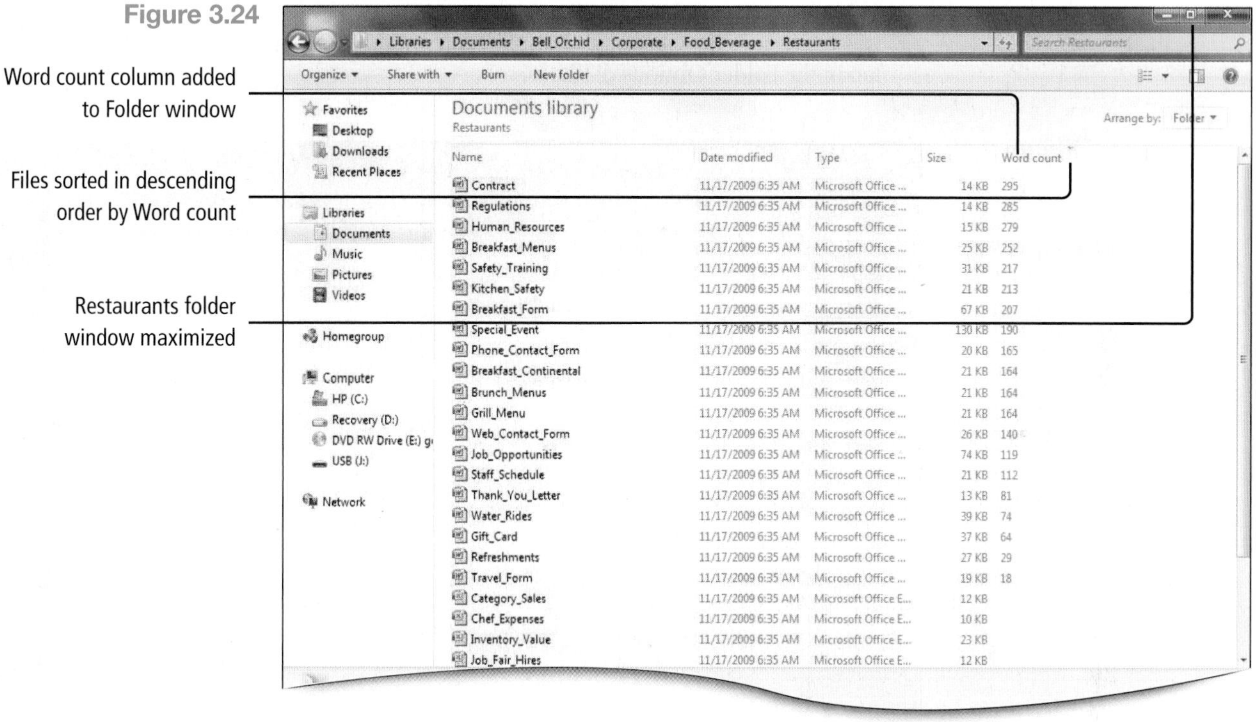

5 **Start** the **Snipping Tool** program, click the **New arrow**, and then click **Window Snip**. Point anywhere in the folder window and click one time. In the **Snipping Tool** mark-up window, click the **Save Snip** button.

6 Navigate to your chapter folder if necessary. Using your own name, name the file **Lastname_Firstname_3A_Wordcount_Snip** be sure the file type is **JPEG**, and press Enter. **Close** the **Snipping Tool** mark-up window; leave your **Restaurants** folder window displayed. Hold this file until you finish Project 3A, and then submit this file as directed by your instructor.

7 Point to any of the column headings, right-click, click **More**, and then notice that Word count moved to the upper portion of the list, in the group of Details that currently display in this folder window. Click to *clear* the **Word count** check box, and then click **OK**.

The Word count column no longer displays in the Folder window.

8 In the upper right corner, click the **Restore Down** button. Click *Name* in the **Name column** to resort the items alphabetically.

9 **Close** all open windows. On the taskbar, click the **Windows Explorer** button, double-click **Documents**, and then navigate to **Bell_Orchid ▶ Corporate ▶ Food_Beverage ▶ Restaurants**. If necessary, click the Name column to sort the files in alphabetic order.

10 Click to select the Word file **Breakfast_Menus**, and then press and release Alt. Compare your screen with Figure 3.25.

A menu bar displays above the toolbar. By default, Windows 7 does not show menu bars in Windows Explorer. This menu bar displayed in Windows XP, but is not so commonly used, because most of its offerings are now available from the Organize command on the toolbar.

If you prefer to have this menu display, you can do so by changing the setting on the View tab in the Folder Options dialog box.

Figure 3.25

Menu bar displays

Breakfast_Menus file selected

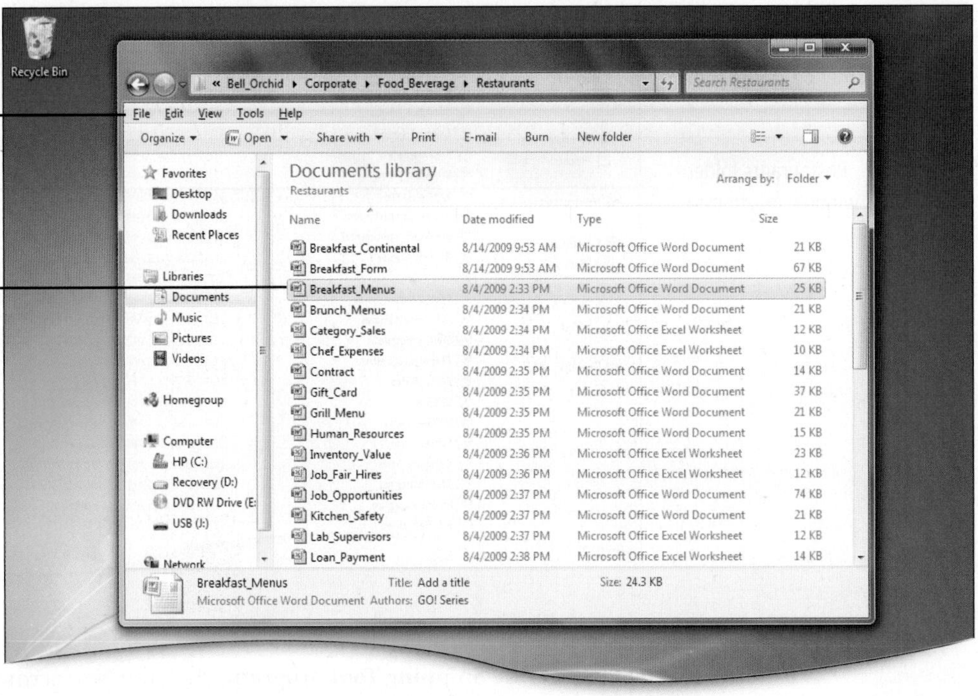

11 On the displayed menu bar, click **Edit**, and then at the bottom of the displayed menu, click **Invert Selection**.

In the file list, all of the files *except* the Breakfast_Menus file are selected. This command is not available from the toolbar, although you could, of course, simply select all the files, hold down Ctrl, and click those that you do not want to include in the selection.

As soon as you perform an action, the menu bar is hidden again and no longer displays.

12 **Close** all open windows.

Objective 4 | Recognize File Types and Associate Files with Programs

A ***file name extension*** is a set of characters that helps Windows 7 understand what kind of information is in a file and what program should open it. A ***program*** is a set of instructions that a computer uses to perform a specific task, such as word processing, accounting, or data management. A program is also commonly referred to as an ***application***.

A file name extension appears at the end of the file name, following a period. In the file name *Address_List.xlsx*, the extension is *xlsx*, which indicates to Windows 7 that this is an Excel 2007 or Excel 2010 file.

Activity 3.07 | Recognizing File Types and Associating Files with Programs

1. From the **Windows Explorer Jump List**, display the **Bell_Orchid** folder, and then navigate to **Bell_Orchid ▶ Corporate ▶ Food_Beverage**.

2. In the file list, click to select the Word file **CO_FB_Banquet_Contract**, and then on the toolbar, notice that the **Open** button displays the Word icon. Compare your screen with Figure 3.26.

Figure 3.26

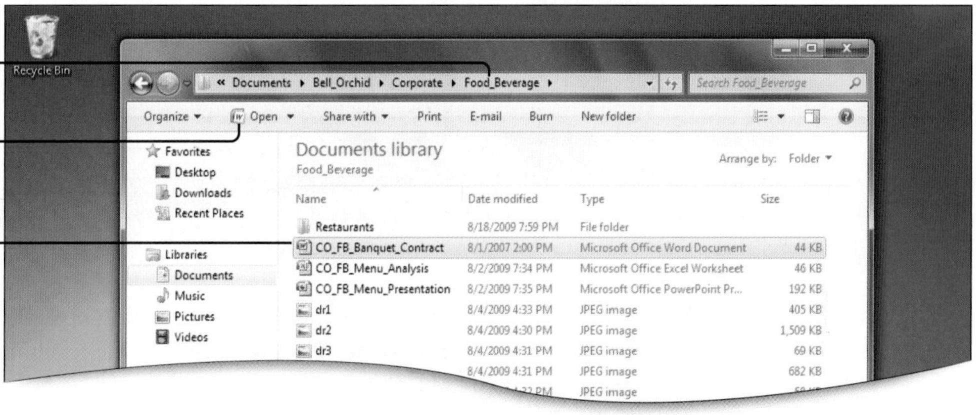

Path displays in address bar

Open button on toolbar displays Word icon

Word file selected in file list

3. On the toolbar, point to the **Open button arrow** to display the ScreenTip *More options*, and then click the arrow.

   The Open button is an example of a ***split button***; that is, when you point to the button, there are two parts—the arrow that displays a menu, and the part of the button with the command name, which will perform the command.

   When you open a file from the file list, Windows 7 uses the file extension of the file to determine which program to use to open the file. For most files, such as a Word document, Windows 7 not only determines which program to use to open the file, but also displays the icon representing the program on the toolbar.

   You can see by the icon which program will be used to open the file. If you are unfamiliar with the icon, click the Open button *arrow* to display the name of the program that will open the file.

4. On the displayed menu, click **Choose default program**, and then compare your screen with Figure 3.27.

   The Open with dialog box displays. Here you can view the file extension for a file. For a file created in Microsoft Word 2007 or Word 2010, the file extension is *.docx*. In this dialog box, Windows 7 indicates and selects the recommended program to use.

   For most files, you will probably open the file in the program in which it was created.

Figure 3.27

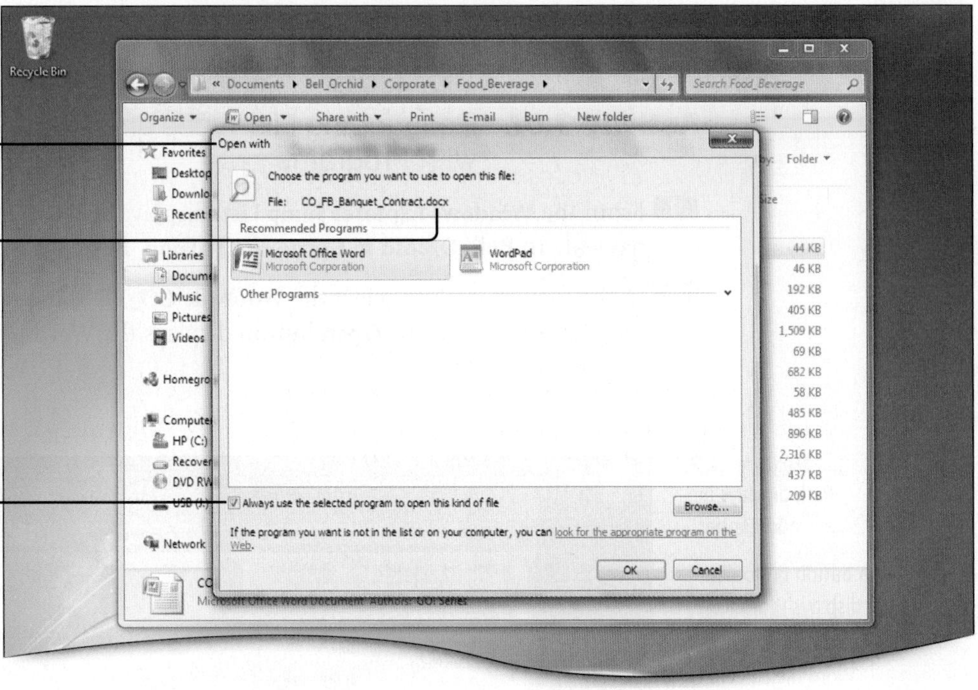

5. In the lower right corner of the **Open with** dialog box, click **Cancel**. In the **file list**, select the file **CO_FB_Menu_Presentation**. On the toolbar, click the **Open button arrow**, and then click **Choose default program**.

   Here you can see that the file extension for a file created with Microsoft PowerPoint 2007 or PowerPoint 2010 is *.pptx*.

6. Click **Cancel** to close the dialog box. On the toolbar, click **Organize**, and then click **Folder and search options**. In the displayed **Folder Options** dialog box, click the **View tab**.

7 Under **Advanced settings**, locate the **Hide extensions for known file types** setting, and then click to clear—remove the check mark from—the check box. Click **OK**. In the **Food_Beverage** folder window, in the **file list**, point to the **Name** column heading, right-click, and then click **Size Column to Fit**. Compare your screen with Figure 3.28.

By default, Windows 7 hides file name extensions to make file names easier to read. If for any reason you need to do so, you can choose to make extensions visible by changing the default setting in the Folder Options dialog box.

On your screen, you can see that displaying the file extensions results in a list of file names that includes the file extensions.

Figure 3.28

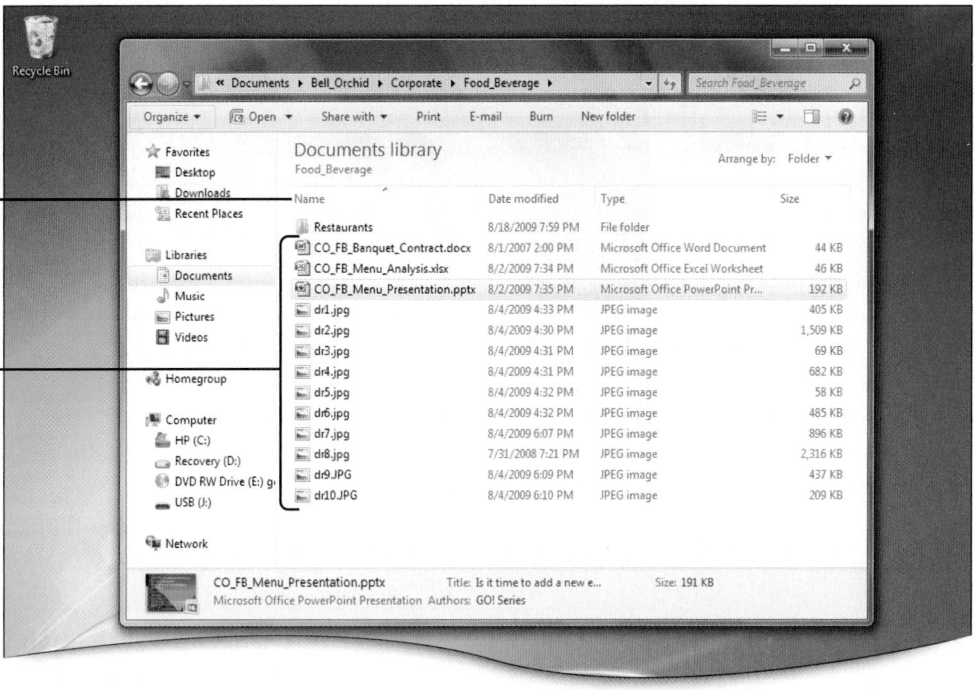

Name column widened

File extensions display for each file name

8 **Start** the **Snipping Tool** program, click the **New arrow**, and then click **Window Snip**. Point anywhere in the folder window and click one time. In the **Snipping Tool** mark-up window, click the **Save Snip** button.

9 Navigate to your chapter folder if necessary. Using your own name, name the file **Lastname_Firstname_3A_Extensions_Snip** be sure the file type is **JPEG**, and press Enter. **Close** the **Snipping Tool** mark-up window; leave your **Food_Beverage** folder window displayed. Hold this file until you finish Project 3A, and then submit this file as directed by your instructor.

10 Open the **Restaurants** folder window. Be sure the **View** is set to **Details** and that the **Name** column is sorted alphabetically. Right-click the **Name** column heading, and then click **Size Column to Fit**. Right-click the **Type** column heading, and then click **Size Column to Fit**.

Because the Type column displays in a folder window in Details view, and because file names commonly display an identifying icon, for most individuals, there is probably no need to display the file extensions.

11 Click to select the Word file **Brunch_Menus.docx**, and then click the file again to select the file name. Notice that only the file name, and not the file extension is selected. Compare your screen with Figure 3.29.

Usually, file extensions should *not* be changed, because you might not be able to open or edit the file after doing so. Because Windows 7 keeps track of which file is associated with which program—referred to as the *file association*—you do not have to be concerned about typing a file extension when you name a new file.

Here you can see that even if you choose to display file extensions, Windows 7 will help you avoid changing the file extension by only highlighting the portion of the name that you would normally rename.

Figure 3.29

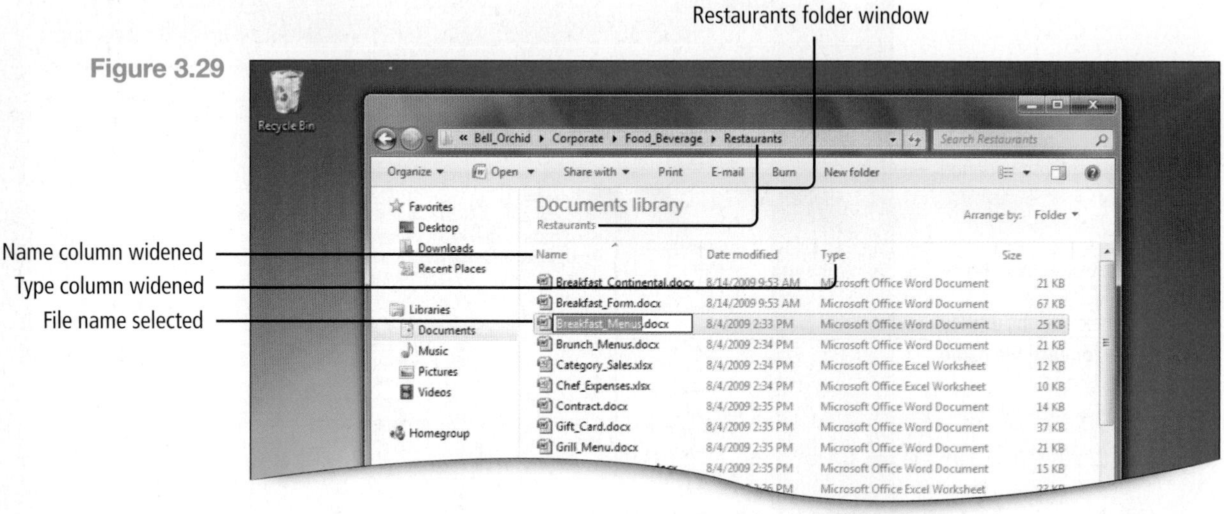

> **Note** | **Sometimes It Is Useful to Change a File Extension**
>
> There are times when it is useful to change a file extension; for example, when you want to change a text file (.txt) to an HTML file (.htm) so that you can view it in a Web browser. Delete the file extension and type the new one. Windows 7 will warn you that changing the file name extension might cause the file to stop working properly. Click Yes if you are certain that the extension you typed is appropriate for your file.

12 On the toolbar, click the **Organize** button, and then click **Folder and search options.** In the displayed **Folder Options** dialog box, click the **View tab**, and then in the lower right, click **Restore Defaults** to reselect the **Hide extensions for known file types** check box. Click **OK**.

In the file list of the Restaurants folder window, the file extensions no longer display; they are hidden.

13 In the **address bar**, to the right of **Corporate**, click ▶, and then from the displayed list, click **Information_Technology**. Display the **Future_Hotels** folder window.

14 Select the JPEG file **Italy**. On the toolbar, click the **Preview button arrow**, and then click **Choose default program**. Compare your screen with Figure 3.30.

When you select an image file, the Open button might display the word *Open* or *Preview* or *Edit*, depending on the default program.

Photographs differ from other files because there may be two or more programs on your computer that can display them.

The default program to view a photo in Windows 7 is Windows Photo Viewer. On the computer at which you are working, this default may have been changed.

Figure 3.30

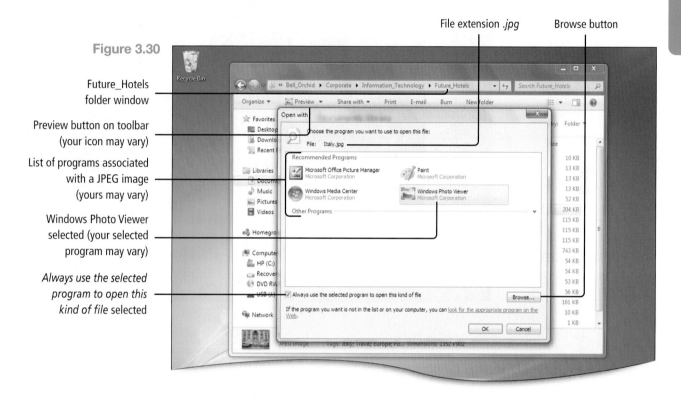

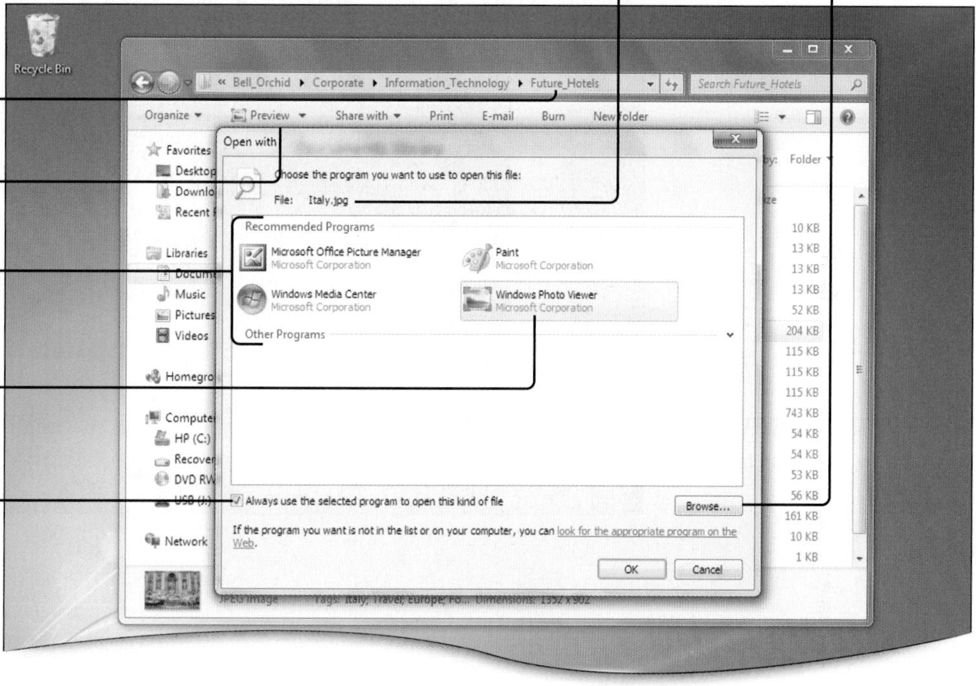

15 Under **Recommended Programs**, click **Paint** (or some other program if Paint is not available) and then click **OK**. Wait for the picture to display. If necessary, on the taskbar, click the **Paint** button to make the window active. **Close** the **Italy - Paint** window.

16 In the **file list**, be sure the **Italy** JPG file is still selected, and then notice on the **toolbar**, that the **Edit** button displays with the **Paint** program icon.

17 On the toolbar, click the **Edit button arrow**, click **Choose default program**, and then at the bottom of the **Open with** dialog box, notice that the check box **Always use the selected program to open this kind of file** is selected. Notice also that a **Browse** button displays in the lower right.

If this check box is selected, then a program that you select in this dialog box will become the default program to open this file. If you need to select a program that is not listed, you can click the Browse button to open the Program Files folder on your computer and select an appropriate program.

18 Under **Recommended Programs**, click **Windows Photo Viewer** and then click **OK**. Compare your screen with Figure 3.31.

The picture displays in Windows Photo Viewer.

Figure 3.31

Italy picture displays in Windows Photo Viewer

Windows Photo Viewer icon on taskbar

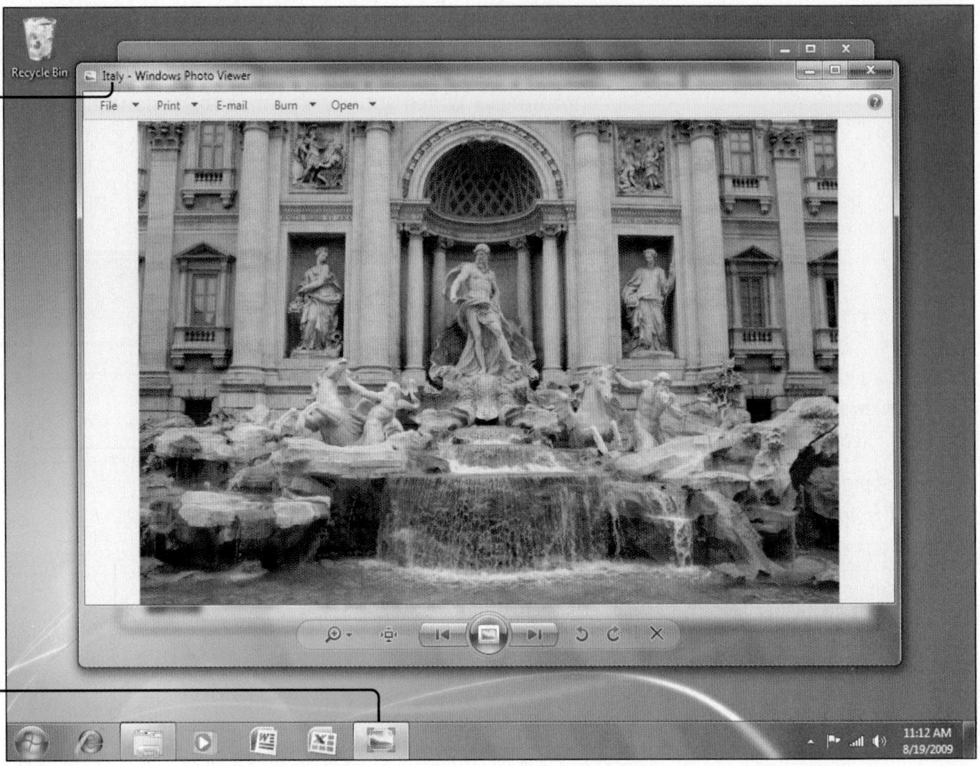

19 **Close** [Close button] all open windows. Display the **Start** menu [Start button], and then on the right, click **Default Programs**. Click **Associate a file type or protocol with a program**, and then compare your screen with Figure 3.32.

The Set Associations window displays. From the Start menu, the Default Programs command opens the Default Programs window of the Control Panel. In the Set Associations window, you can scroll to view a list of the many types of files that you might work with on your computer, and you can also change the program associated with a specific type of file.

Figure 3.32

Set Associations window (your list may vary)

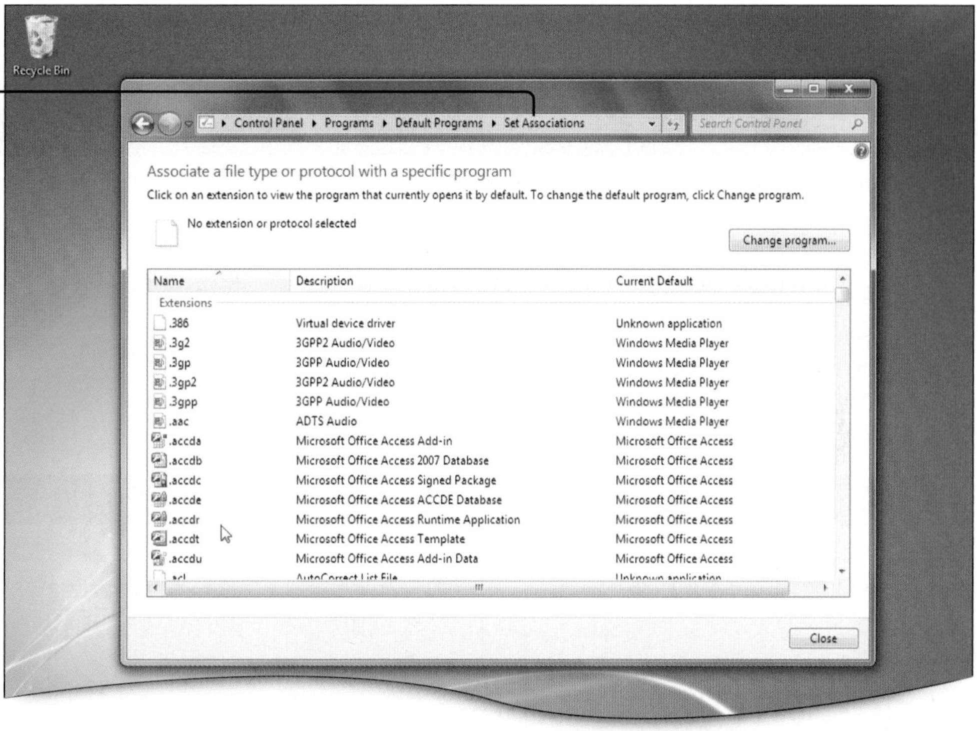

20 Display the **Documents** folder window, and then delete the **Bell_Orchid** folder. Unpin **Bell_Orchid** from the **Windows Explorer Jump List**. **Close** [Close button] all open windows.

More Knowledge | What if the wrong program loads a file or if no program will open a file?

In most instances, when you open a file from a folder window, Windows 7 automatically knows which program should open the file because of the file extension. If a program other than the one you intended opens your file, close the program, display the folder window, right-click the file, click Open with, and then in the displayed dialog box, use the techniques you have practiced to set a default program for this type of file. Alternatively, change the default in the Set Associations window of the Control Panel.

For example, different brands of media players are sometimes installed on new computers, and when you open a music file, a program that is not your program of choice might be set as the default. If no program will open your file, Windows 7 provides a dialog box from which you can search the Web to find an appropriate program if one is available. If you cannot find a program to open your file, you will have to check with whoever gave you the file and possibly purchase the program with which it is associated. It is not recommended that you try to open any file unless it came from a trusted source or was created on your own computer.

End **You have completed Project 3A**

Project 3B Using Advanced Search Techniques

Project Activities

In Activities 3.08 through 3.13 you will train with Steven Ramos and Barbara Hewitt, employees in the Information Technology department at the Bell Orchid Hotel, so that you will be able to use advanced search techniques. You will capture screens that look similar to Figure 3.33.

Project Files

For Project 3B, you will need the following files:

Student Resource CD (or a flash drive containing these files)
New Snip files

You will save your files as:

Lastname_Firstname_3B_Garden_Snip
Lastname_Firstname_3B_Natural_Snip
Lastname_Firstname_3B_Custom_Snip
Lastname_Firstname_3B_Saved_Search_Snip

Project Results

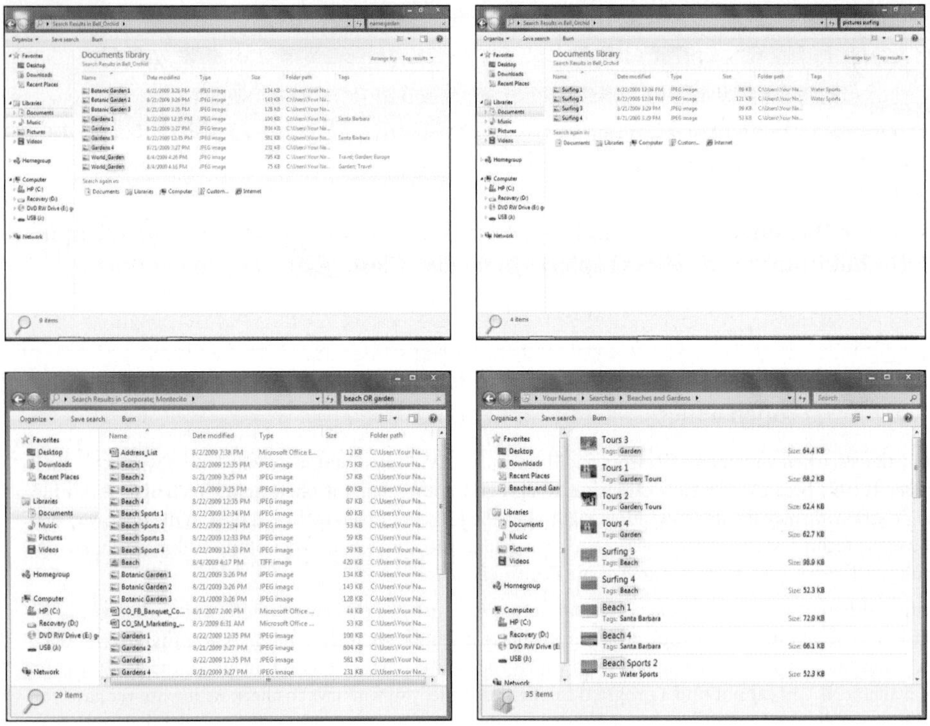

Figure 3.33
Project 3B Advanced Search Techniques

Objective 5 | Filter Searches in the Search Box

Your documents, music, video, photos, and e-mail messages are created, stored, and accessed in electronic form on your computer, resulting in an ever-increasing number of files. Additionally, each year the storage capacity of computer hard drives increases substantially. Thus, it becomes harder to keep track of your computer files, regardless of how careful you are when organizing your files in a folder structure.

Rely on Windows 7's Search features to help you find what you are looking for. If you can remember any detail about a file or a saved e-mail message that you need to access—for example, when it was created or some of its content—Windows 7 can find it for you quickly. Additionally, Windows 7 can help you visualize your files by arranging them in various ways; for example, by date or by author name.

Recall that every Windows Explorer window—folder windows, Control Panel, and so on—contains a search box in which you can enter part of a word, a complete word, or a phrase. The search feature immediately searches file names, ***file properties***—also called ***metadata***—and text within each file and then returns results instantly. File properties display information about your files, such as the name of the author and the date that the file was last modified. Metadata is the data that describes other data. For example, the collective group of a file's properties, such as its title, subject, author, and file size, comprise that file's metadata.

Three features define the search capabilities in Windows 7:

- *Search is everywhere.* You are never more than a few keystrokes away from what you are looking for, because a search box displays in every window and in the Start menu.
- *Search is fast.* Recall that Windows 7 produces search results almost instantly because it employs an ***index***, which is a collection of detailed information about the files on your computer. When you start a search, Windows 7 searches this summary information in the index rather than searching file by file on your hard disk drive.
- *Any search can be saved.* You can save any search that you conduct and then rerun that search. The results will include any new files that meet the search criteria since the last time the search was conducted. In this manner, the search that you rerun is said to be *live.*

Activity 3.08 | Creating and Adding Tags

Recall that a ***tag*** is a property that you create and add to a file. Tags help you to find and organize your files, because you can include a tag in a search of your files.

1. Copy *two* folders to your **Documents** folder as follows: First, if necessary, *delete* the Bell_Orchid folder from your Documents folder—for this project you will need a new copy of the files. Insert the Student Resource CD or other device that contains the student files that accompany this textbook. By using the **Send to** command that you practiced in Activity 2.1 of Chapter 2, copy the **Bell_Orchid** folder from the Student Resource CD (or other device) to your **Documents** folder. Leave the window open.

2. On your Student Resource CD (or other device) navigate to **Chapter_Files ▶ Chapter_03**. Right-click the **Montecito** folder, point to **Send to**, and then click **Documents**.

3. When the copy operation is complete, in the **navigation pane**, under **Libraries**, click **Documents** to display your **Documents** folder window.

4 Point to the **Montecito** folder and drag it into the **Bell_Orchid** folder; release the mouse button when the ScreenTip *Move to Bell_Orchid* displays, as shown in Figure 3.34.

Alternatively, you could use any other method you have practiced to move this folder into the Bell_Orchid folder.

Figure 3.34

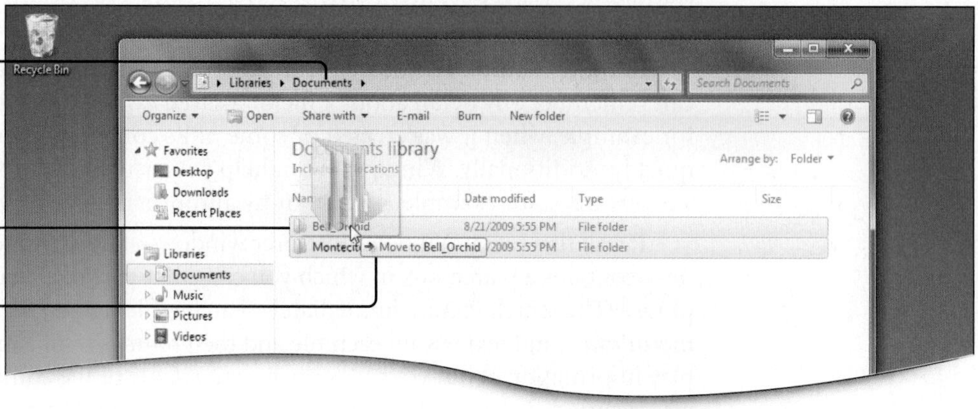

5 Drag the **Bell_Orchid** folder onto the **Windows Explorer** icon on the taskbar to pin it to the **Jump List**. Compare your screen with Figure 3.35.

Because you will be displaying the Bell_Orchid folder window numerous times in this project, pinning the Bell_Orchid folder to the Jump List will increase your efficiency by reducing the number of clicks necessary to display the folder window.

Recall that pinning locations like this one to the Jump List, and then deleting them when they are no longer useful to you, is one of the methods by which you can personalize your computing environment.

Figure 3.35

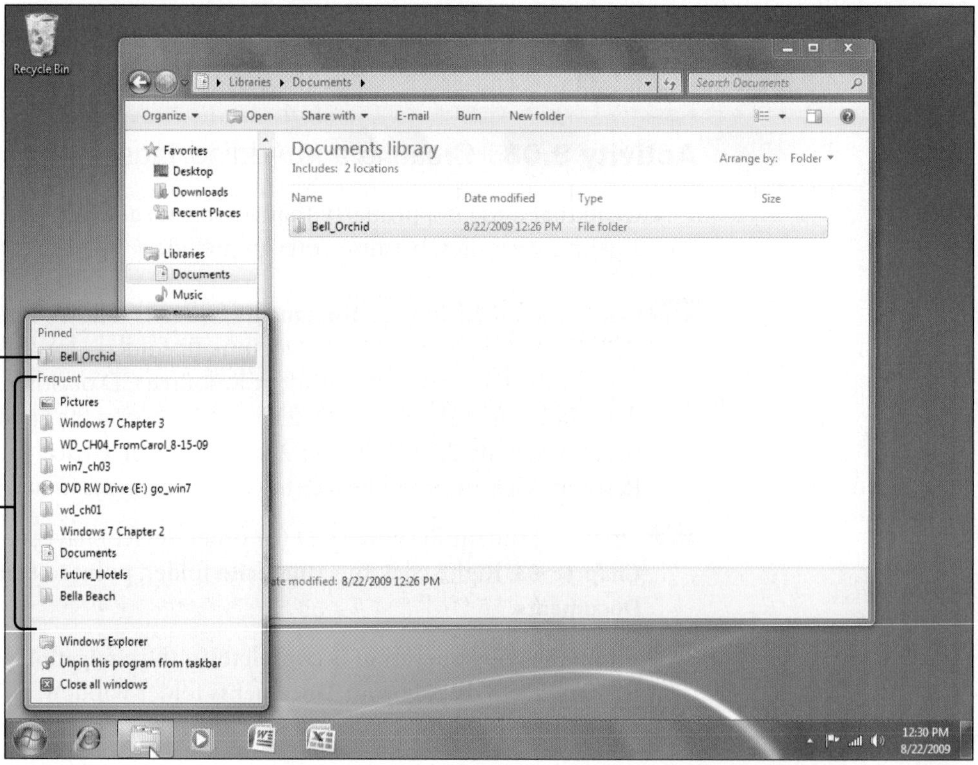

6 Navigate to **Bell_Orchid ▶ Montecito ▶ Activities** and then in the **file list**, right-click the Word file **Fishing**. At the bottom of the shortcut menu, click **Properties**

7 In the **Fishing Properties** dialog box, click the **Details tab**, under **Description**, click **Tags**, and then type **Fishing** Compare your screen with Figure 3.36.

Figure 3.36

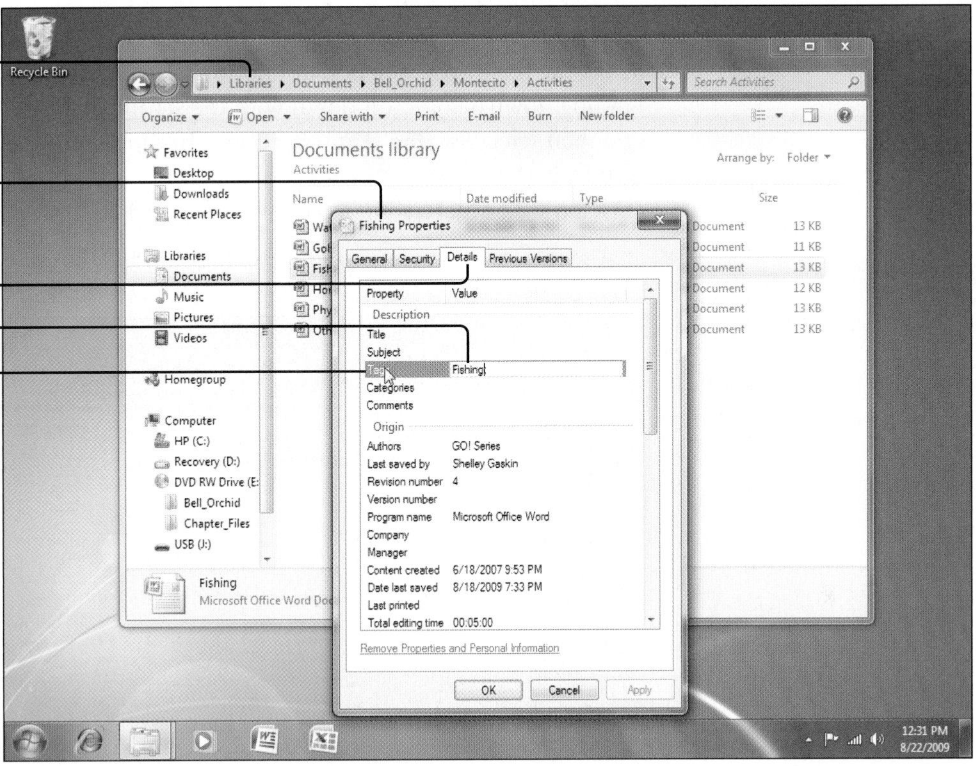

8 Click **OK** to add the tag and close the dialog box. In the **file list**, right-click the Word file **Golf**, and then use the technique you just practiced to add the tag **Golf**

9 Right-click the file **Other_Sports** and add the tag **Volleyball** Right-click the file **Water_Sports** and add the tag **Water Sports**

> **Note | Adding Tags to Multiple Word Files**
>
> You can select a group of Word documents, right-click any of the selected files, click Properties, click the Details tab, and then add the same tag to the selected group.

10 On the **address bar**, to the right of **Montecito**, click ▶, and then from the list click **Photos** to display this folder window. Select the file **Fly Fishing 1**, and then at the bottom of the window, in the **Details pane**, click in the **Tags** box. Begin typing **Fi** and then when the list of possible tags displays, click the **Fishing** check box. On the right end of the **Details pane**, click the **Save** button.

After a tag is created, you can select it from a list in this manner. Recall that for picture files, you can modify tags directly in the Details pane.

> **Alert! | Tags Can Vary Depending on Recent Use of Your Computer**
>
> The list of possible tags that displays can vary depending on previous usage of the computer at which you are working. Pictures on the computer that have been downloaded from other sources might have tags that will display on the list.

11 Using the technique you just practiced, locate the files **Golf 1** and **Golf 2** and add the **Golf** tag to both files—as soon as you begin typing you will be able to select the tag from a list and then click the **Save** button.

12 Scroll up as necessary, select the file **Beach Sports 3**, hold down Ctrl, and then select **Beach Sports 4**. In the **Details pane**, notice that *2 items* are selected. Click in the **Tags** box and type **Vo** and then from the displayed list of existing tags, click **Volleyball** to add this tag to both files—click **Save**.

13 Select the file **Beach Sports 1**, hold down Ctrl and select the file **Beach Sports 2**. While holding down Ctrl, scroll down with the scroll bar so the two files remain selected, and then select **Surfing 1**, and **Surfing 2**. In the **Details pane**, notice that *4 items selected* is indicated. Release Ctrl, click in the **Tags** box, add the **Water Sports** tag, and then click **Save**. Compare your screen with Figure 3.37.

Use the Ctrl key to select a group of files and add the same tag to each.

Figure 3.37

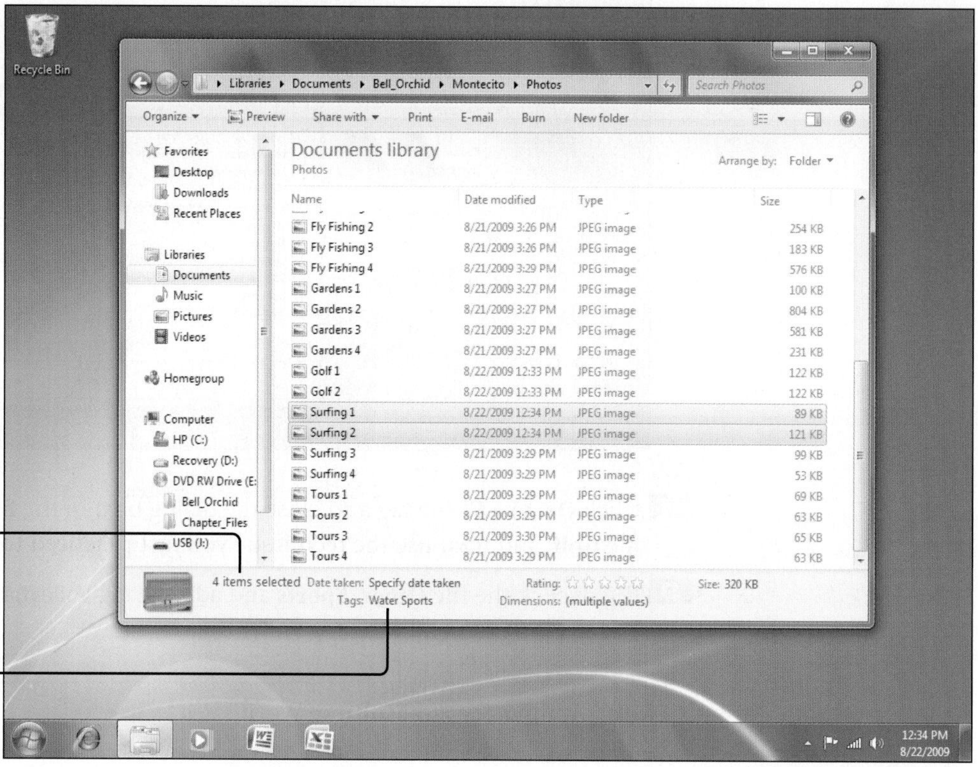

Details pane indicates *4 items selected*

Water Sports tag added

14 Select the files **Tours 1** and **Tours 2**. Add the tag **Tours** to these two files—the tag might already exist on other files; if so you will be able to select it from the displayed list. Click **Save**.

15 By using the techniques you have just practiced, add the tag **Santa Barbara** to the following four files: **Beach 1**, **Beach 4**, **Gardens 1** and **Gardens 3** and then click **Save**.

16 Navigate to **Montecito ▶ Tours**. Point to the Word file **Tours** and right-click. From the shortcut menu, click **Properties**, and then on the **Details tab**, add the tag **Tours**

Recall that the list of possible tags that displays will vary depending on previous usage of your computer.

17 **Close** [X] all open windows.

Activity 3.09 | Filtering a Search by Using Properties

Windows 7 will search all of the files in the current folder window for whatever you type in the search box. In the indexed locations, it will search by looking in the file name, file contents, and file properties—including tags. For example, if you type *April*, Windows 7 will find any file that contains *April* in the file name, in the file contents, in the tag, or authored by someone named *April*.

If you want to search more selectively, you can filter your search in the search box by specifying which file property to search. To filter by a file property, separate the name of the property and the search term with a colon.

1 On the taskbar, drag the **Windows Explorer** button up slightly into the desktop to display the **Jump List**, and then under **Pinned**, click **Bell_Orchid**. In the upper right corner, click in the **search** box, and then type **water**

Recall that Windows 7 can perform fast searches because the search is conducted on the *index*, not on each file on the hard disk drive. The index is a collection of detailed information about the files on your computer, which Windows 7 keeps track of and stores.

In the displayed Search Results window, a large number of files have one or more properties that match the criteria *water*. Your Documents folder is included in the ***Indexed locations***, which includes *all* of the folders in your personal folder (Documents, Pictures, and so on), e-mail, and offline files if any.

In indexed locations, Windows 7 searches file names and contents; that is, it will look for matches to your search term in file names, folder names, file properties including tags, folder properties, and in the actual text content of files.

In non-indexed locations, Windows 7 searches only file names and folder names.

2 Be sure the **View** is **Details** and the **Name** column is sorted alphabetically.

3 In the **search** box, click to clear the search. **Maximize** the window.

4 In the **search** box, type **tag:water**

5 In the **file list**, point to any of the column headings, right-click, and then click **Tags** to add this column to the **file list**. Right-click the **Tags** column heading, and then click **Size Column to Fit**. Compare your screen with Figure 3.38.

You can filter a search by searching only on the tags attached to files by typing *tag:* in the search box followed by your search criteria. Within all the subfolders in the Bell_Orchid folder, eight items have *water* as part of their tag, and in the Tags column, *water* is highlighted.

Figure 3.38

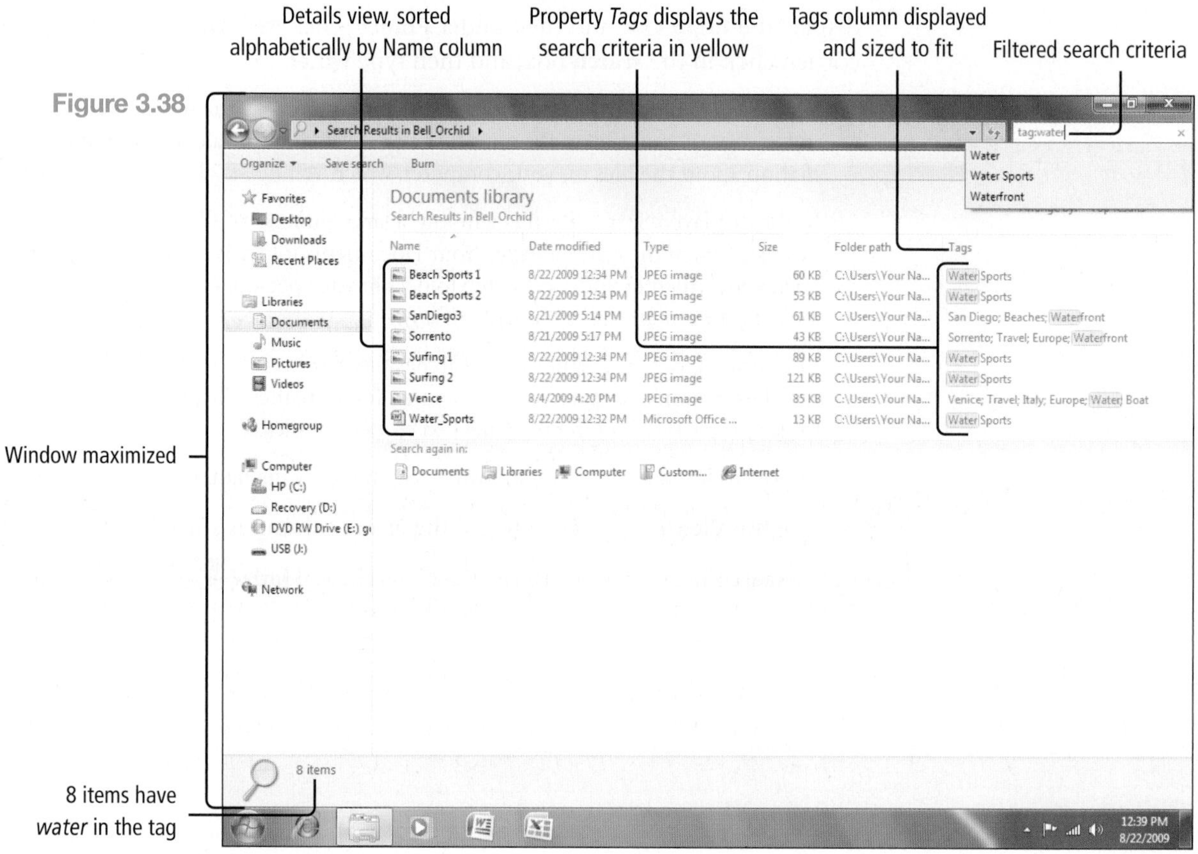

6 In the list of files that matched the search criteria, look at the tag for the files **SanDiego3** and **Sorrento**. Notice that *Waterfront* is among the tags attached to these two files, and thus this file is considered a match.

By default, Windows 7 uses ***partial matching***—matching to part of a word or phrase rather than to whole words. Thus, *waterfront* is a match for the criteria *water*. If you prefer to search by whole words only, you can change this option.

7 In the **search** box, click [×] to clear the search, and then type **tag:water sports**

Five items display in the Search Results folder window. The files that match the criteria are narrowed to those in the Bell_Orchid folder that have the exact tag *water sports*. Additionally, the word *Sports* is highlighted in yellow in the file names where it occurs.

8 **Clear** [×] the **search** box, and then type **tag:golf** Compare your screen with Figure 3.39.

Three files display.

Figure 3.39

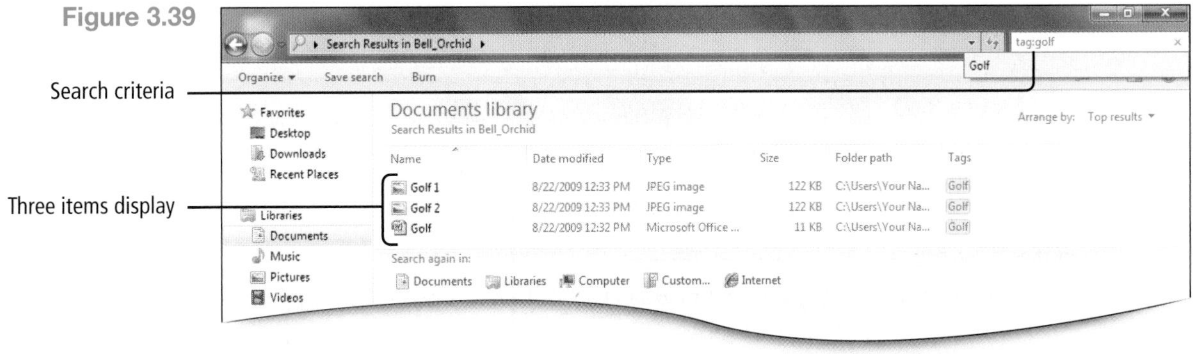

9 **Clear** [×] the **search** box, type **name:surfing**

Four files that contain *surfing* in the file name display. *Name* is a property that you can use as criteria in a filtered search. The Name filter searches only the file names.

10 **Clear** [×] the **search** box, type **name:garden**

Nine files contain *garden* somewhere in the file name.

11 **Start** the **Snipping Tool** program, click the **New arrow**, and then click **Window Snip**. Click anywhere in the folder window, and then in the **Snipping Tool** mark-up window, click the **Save Snip** button. In the displayed **Save As** dialog box, if necessary navigate to your **Windows 7 Chapter 3** folder on your USB flash drive and click to select it so that it displays in the address bar.

12 Using your own name, name the file **Lastname_Firstname_3B_Garden_Snip** be sure the file type is **JPEG**, and press Enter. **Close** the **Snipping Tool** mark-up window. Hold this file until you finish Project 3B, and then submit this file as directed by your instructor.

13 **Clear** [×] the **search** box, and then type **beach** Notice the number of files that display (27), and then **Clear** [×] the **search** box. Type **name:beach** and notice that only *9 items* contain the word *beach* in the file name.

When searching for files, keep in mind that when searching in indexed locations, typing a search term will search file names, folder names, file properties, folder properties, and in the actual text content of files.

To narrow the search for a tag, a file name, or some other property, type the name of the property followed by a colon and then type the search term.

14 Clear ☒ the **search** box, and then type **camera:canon** In the list of files that match the search criteria, right-click the file **Gardens 3**, and then on the shortcut menu, click **Properties**. Click the **Details tab**, drag the scroll box down about half way, and then compare your screen with Figure 3.40.

> There are numerous properties for picture files, many of which are applied to the file by the camera's software.

Figure 3.40

Details tab

Properties dialog box

Scroll box

Camera maker indicates *Canon*

Camera properties

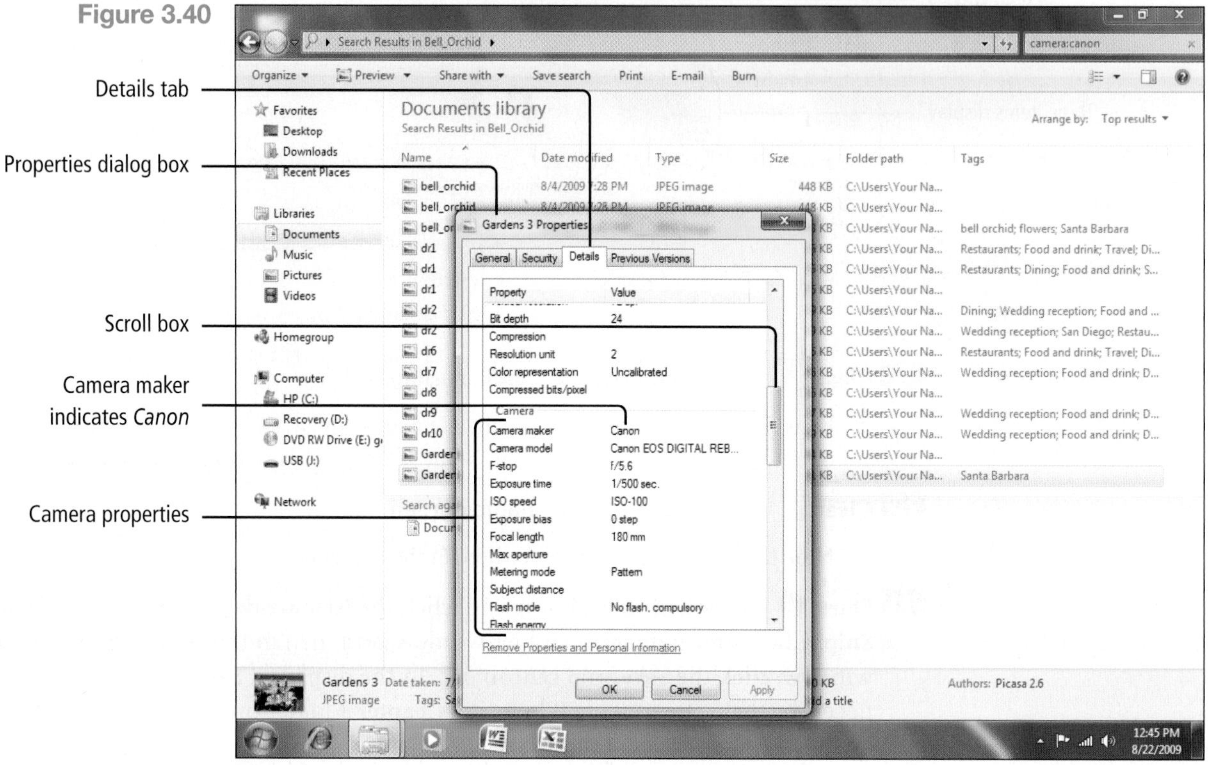

15 At the bottom of the **Gardens 3 Properties** dialog box, click **Cancel**. In the **file list**, point to the column heading **Name**, and then right-click. At the bottom of the shortcut menu, click **More**. Take a moment to scroll down the list and examine the properties that might be assigned to a file by one or more software programs.

> CDs and DVDs usually have various tags so that you can search by Artist or Genre (for example Jazz or Classical). Software programs such as those from a digital camera or a video camera commonly attach numerous properties to a file to make it easy to find the files based on specific technical details such as *F-stop*.

> Likewise, properties such as *Cell phone* and *Business phone* are assigned by contact management programs such as Microsoft Outlook.

16 Close ☒ the **Choose Details** dialog box, and then **Clear** ☒ the **search** box. Leave the window open.

More Knowledge | What's the Difference Between a Tag and a Property?

A tag is simply another type of property, but one that *you* create and add to a file. Whereas most file properties are added by either Windows 7 or the software that creates the file, a tag is probably the most useful property, because you can add tags that contain words or phrases that are meaningful to you.

In the future, more software programs will enable you to add tags at the time you create and save your file, which will enable you to rely more on tag searches to find what you are looking for.

Activity 3.10 | Filtering a Search by Using Boolean Operators, Quotes, and Natural Language

In addition to filtering by various properties, you can also filter a search by using the ***Boolean operators*** AND, OR, and NOT. The term Boolean is taken from the name George Boole, who was a 19th century mathematician. Boole developed the mathematics of logic that govern the logical functions—true and false. A statement using Boolean operators expresses a condition that is either true or false.

You can also use quotes to find an exact phrase in a search or enable the ***natural language*** feature of Windows 7. If you enable a natural language search, you can perform searches in a simpler way, without using colons and without the need to enter any Boolean operators.

1 If necessary **Clear** [×] the **search** box, and then type **shareholders AND orlando**

Boolean filters such as AND must be typed in all uppercase letters. The ***AND filter*** finds files that contain both the word *shareholders* and the word *orlando*—even if those words are not next to each other.

As you type *shareholders*, Windows 7 begins filtering based on the search term found in file names, folder names, file properties, folder properties, and in the actual text content of files. After you narrow the search by typing *AND orlando*, the search is narrowed down to one file.

You can see that if you know something about the contents or name of the file you are looking for, it might be easier to search for the file than to navigate your folder structure.

> **Note** | **Windows 7 Search Ignores Capitalization**
>
> You need not capitalize to have Windows 7 find your search term. For example, you can type *orlando* instead of *Orlando*. However, you must use uppercase letters for the Boolean operators.

2 **Clear** [×] the **search** box, and then type **shareholders NOT orlando** Be sure the view is **Details** and be sure the list is in alphabetical order by **Name**. Compare your screen with Figure 3.41.

The ***NOT filter*** finds files that contain the word *shareholders* but that do not contain the word *orlando*.

Figure 3.41

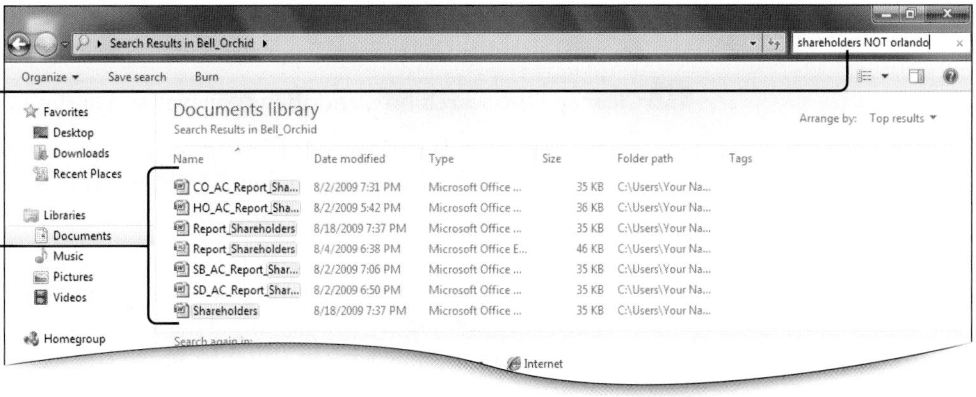

3 **Clear** [×] the **search** box, and then type **shareholders OR orlando**

The ***OR filter*** finds files that contain either the word *shareholders* or the word *orlando*. Because either of the conditions can be present, OR will result in a larger number of results, but will assist you in narrowing your search nonetheless.

4 **Clear** ☒ the **search** box, and then including the quote marks, type **"teenage restaurant workers"**

One file—*Kitchen_Safety*— displays. The exact phrase *teenage restaurant workers* is contained within the text of this document.

The ***quotes filter*** finds files that contain the exact phrase placed within the quotes. You can see that if you know just a little about what you are looking for, filtered searches can help you find files quickly without navigating a folder structure.

5 **Clear** ☒ the **search** box, type **type:pptx** and notice that only PowerPoint files display.

File type is one of the properties on which you can search. You can use the file extension associated with a program as the search criteria, or you can type the program name, for example *PowerPoint*.

6 Press [Spacebar] one time, and then continue typing so that the **search** box criteria indicates **type:pptx AND name:safety** Compare your screen with Figure 3.42.

In this manner, you can combine different property filters with Boolean filters to locate a file. Five files meet this criteria; that is, each file is a PowerPoint file and contains the word *safety* in the file name.

Figure 3.42

Search criteria

PowerPoint presentations containing *safety* in the file name

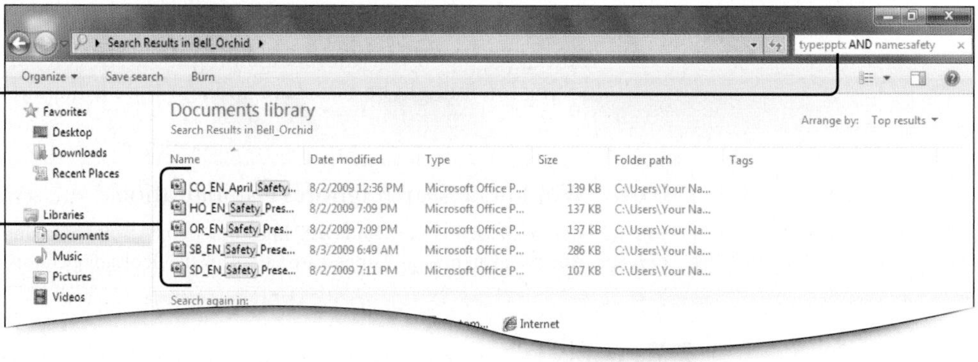

7 **Clear** ☒ the **search** box, and then type **pictures surfing** Notice that no files matching the search criteria display.

8 On the toolbar, click the **Organize** button, and then on the list, click **Folder and search options**. In the displayed **Folder Options** dialog box, click the **Search tab**. Under **How to search**, select the **Use natural language search** check box, and then click **OK**.

9 **Clear** ☒ the **search** box, and then type **pictures surfing**

Four files that contain the word *surfing* as a property and that are *pictures* display. If you enable natural language search, you can perform searches in a simpler way, without using colons and without the need to enter AND or OR in uppercase letters.

Even with natural language search turned on, you can continue to use the search box in *exactly* the same way. If you want to use Boolean filters or introduce filters with colons you can do so. Additionally, you can use all the same properties to refine your searches. The only difference is that you can also enter search criteria in a more informal manner.

10 **Start** the **Snipping Tool** program, click the **New arrow**, and then click **Window Snip**. Click anywhere in the folder window. In the **Snipping Tool** mark-up window, click the **Save Snip** button. In the displayed **Save As** dialog box, if necessary navigate to your **Windows 7 Chapter 3** folder on your USB flash drive and click to select it so that it displays in the address bar.

11 Using your own name, name the file **Lastname_Firstname_3B_Natural_Snip** be sure the file type is **JPEG**, and press Enter. **Close** ☒ the **Snipping Tool** mark-up window. Hold this file until you finish Project 3B, and then submit this file as directed by your instructor.

12 On the toolbar, click the **Organize** button, click **Folder and search options**, click the **Search tab**, and then in the lower right corner, click **Restore Defaults**. Click **OK** to close the dialog box.

> On your own computer, you might want to leave the natural language feature enabled.

13 In the **file list**, point to any column heading, right-click, and then click to deselect the **Tags** checkbox.

14 In the upper right corner of the window, click the **Restore Down** button ☐ to redisplay the window in its previous size, and then **Close** ☒ all open windows.

Objective 6 | Search by Using the Search Folder

The search box searches only the current view—the files that are in the current folder, including all the subfolders in that folder. If you search and do not find what you are looking for, it is possible that you began your search in the wrong folder.

For example, if you are looking for a video with the tag *Grand Canyon* that is stored in your Videos library, you will not find it by looking in your Documents library. Instead use the **Search folder**. The Search folder conducts a search in the entire set of indexed locations, which includes your personal folder with all of its libraries and any offline files. The Search folder is a good choice for searches whenever you:

- Do not know where a file or folder is located and you want to look in many locations at once; for example, in Documents and in Pictures.

- Want to search in two or more folders, but not *all* folders, at the same level within a hierarchy; for example, in Orlando and Honolulu but not in the other Bell_Orchid locations.

Activity 3.11 | Searching from the Search Folder

1 Hold down [Windows key] and press [F]. Compare your screen with Figure 3.43.

The Search folder displays and the insertion point is blinking in the search box. Here you can apply a filter based on *Kind*—for example a game or an instant message or a music file.

When the Search folder is displayed in this manner—by pressing [Windows key] + [F]—the search will be conducted on the set of locations called *indexed locations*, which includes *all* of the folders in your personal folder (Documents, Pictures, and so on) and offline files if any.

Recall that offline files refer to files from a network that have been copied to your hard disk drive for easy access when you are not connected to that network. This happens more typically in large organizations where you have access to files stored on a network.

Recall that in indexed locations, Windows 7 searches file names and contents; that is, it will look for matches to your search term in file names, folder names, file properties, folder properties, and in the actual text content of files. In non-indexed locations, Windows 7 searches only file names and folder names.

Figure 3.43

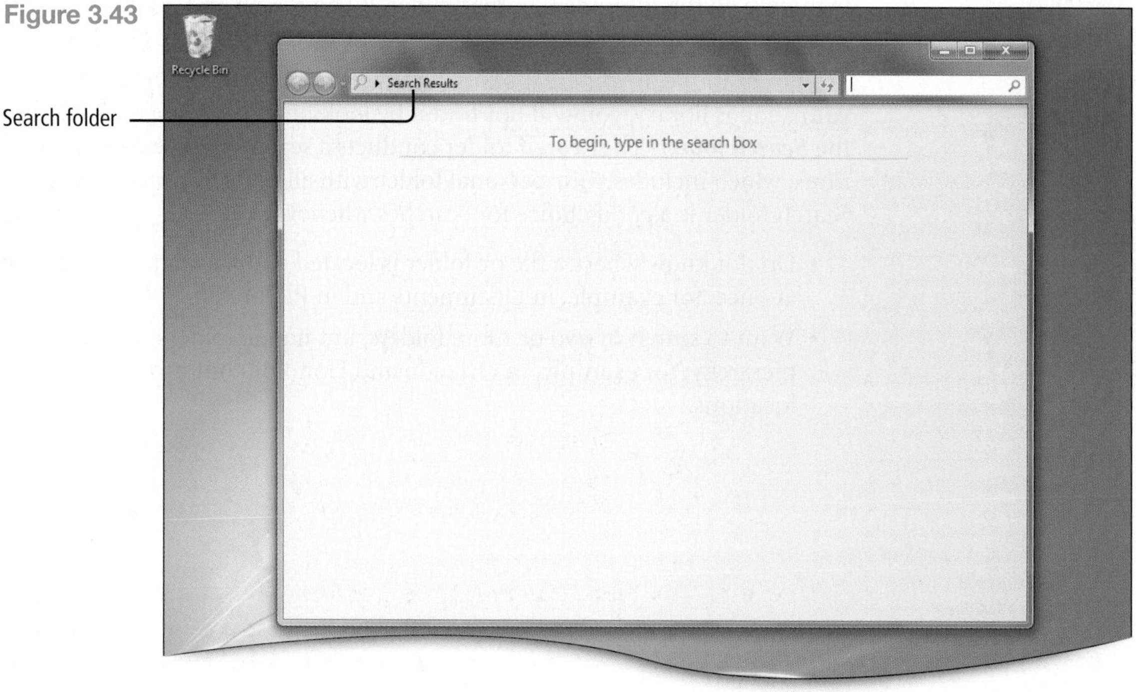

2 With the insertion point blinking in the **search** box, type **water** click in the Search box to display the filter box, and then under **Add a search filter**, click **Kind**. Compare your screen with Figure 3.44.

A list of various kinds of items by which you can filter the search displays.

Figure 3.44

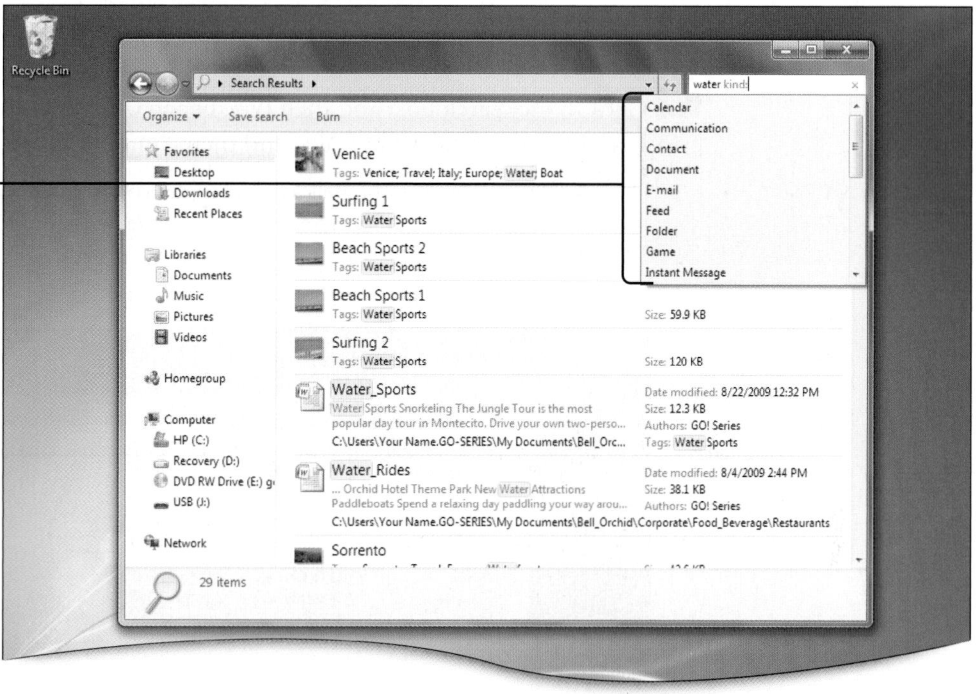

Alert! | Your Search Results May Differ From Those Shown

A search conducted in the *indexed locations* may display different results than the figures in this textbook, because you have additional files in your personal folder.

3 On the displayed list, scroll down and click **Picture**. Compare your screen with Figure 3.45.

By clicking one of the Kind filters, you can narrow the search results by certain kinds of files, for example pictures or e-mail. Filtering results in this manner makes it easier to find specific files.

Figure 3.45

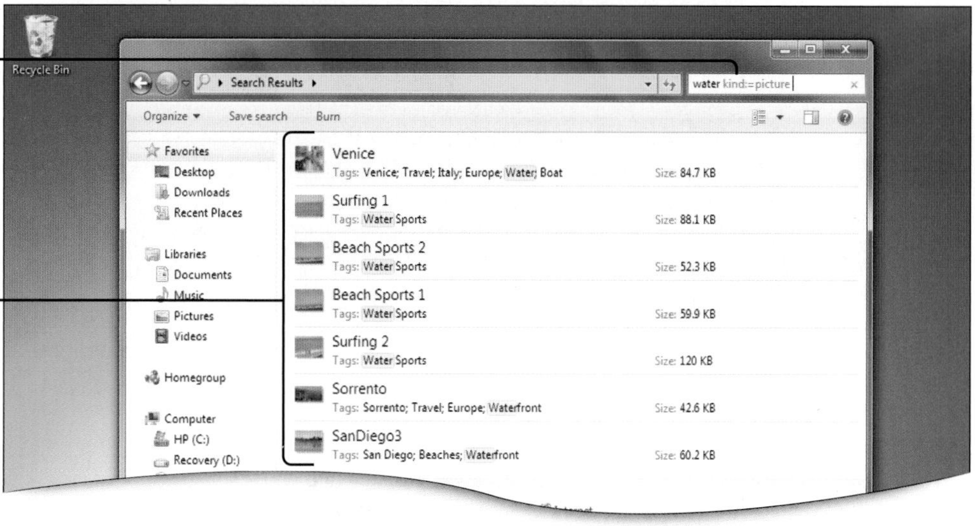

4 **Close** the **Search Results** window and any other open windows.

Activity 3.12 | Using Custom Search

To customize a search, use the Custom button in any Search Results folder.

1 On the taskbar, drag the **Windows Explorer** icon into the desktop, and then on the **Jump List**, under **Pinned**, click **Bell_Orchid**.

2 Click in the **search** box, and then type **beach OR garden** Drag the scroll box to the bottom of the displayed results, and then compare your screen with Figure 3.46.

A total of 48 items in the Bell_Orchid folder contain the word *beach* or the word *garden* as a property. Recall that in indexed locations, the word might be part of the text of the file.

Figure 3.46

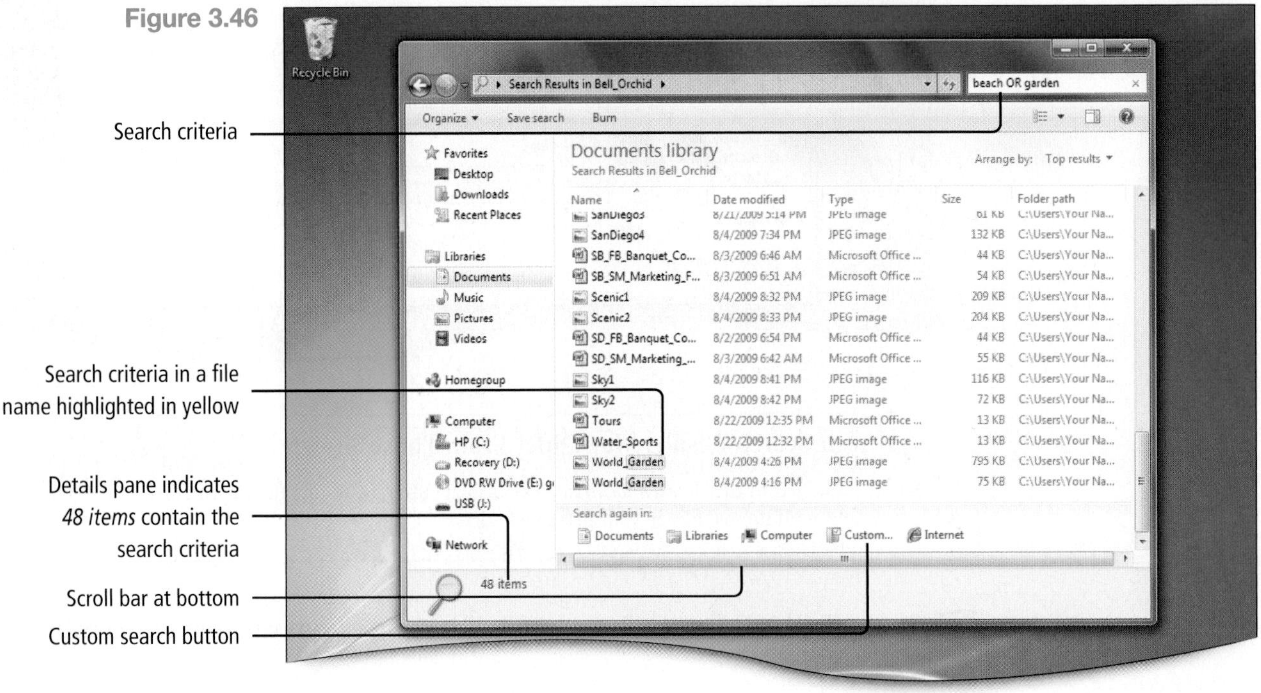

3 At the bottom of the search results, under **Search again in**, click **Custom**. In the **Choose Search Location** dialog box, under **Change selected locations**, to the left of **Libraries**, click ▷ to expand the folder structure.

Use the ***Custom search*** to define a specific scope—range of locations—for your search.

4 To the left of **Documents**, click ▷. Expand ▷ **My Documents**, and then expand ▷ **Bell_Orchid**. Compare your screen with Figure 3.47.

Figure 3.47

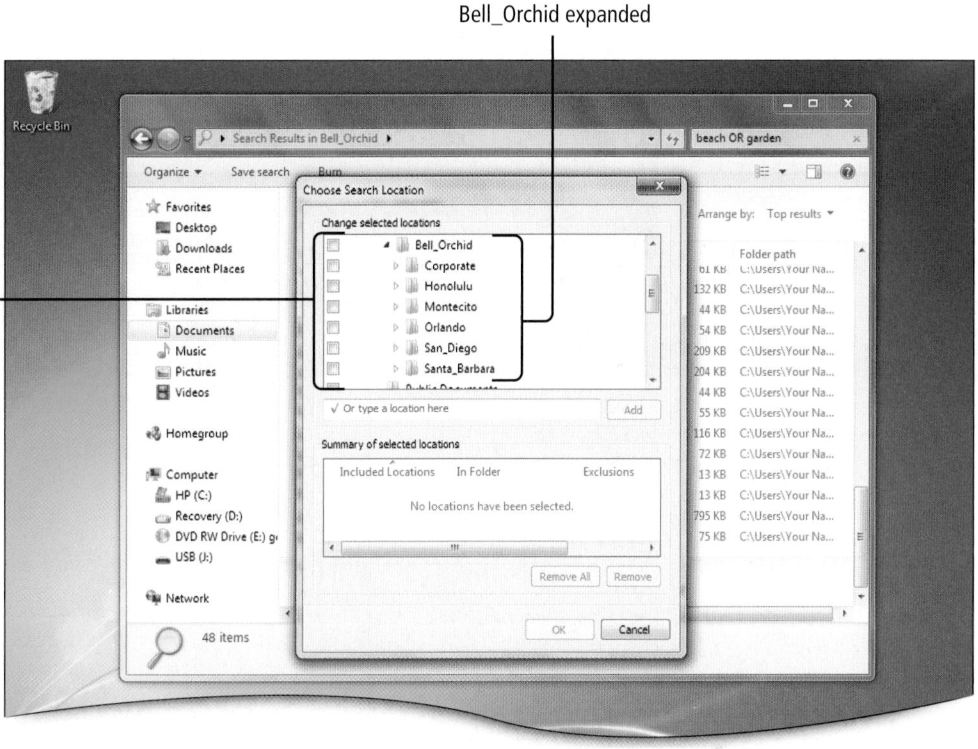

5 Under **Change selected locations**, in the column of check boxes along the left edge, click the **check box** for **Corporate**, and then notice that in the lower portion of the dialog box, under **Summary of selected locations**, the Corporate folder displays.

6 Click the **check box** for **Montecito**, and then compare your screen with Figure 3.48.

Under Summary of selected locations, the two folders that you selected display. Here you can select as many locations as you need. This is especially useful if you want to search in two folders at the same level of a hierarchy, for example in Corporate and Montecito but not in the other folders at this level. Or, you can select a number of different folders at various levels.

Figure 3.48

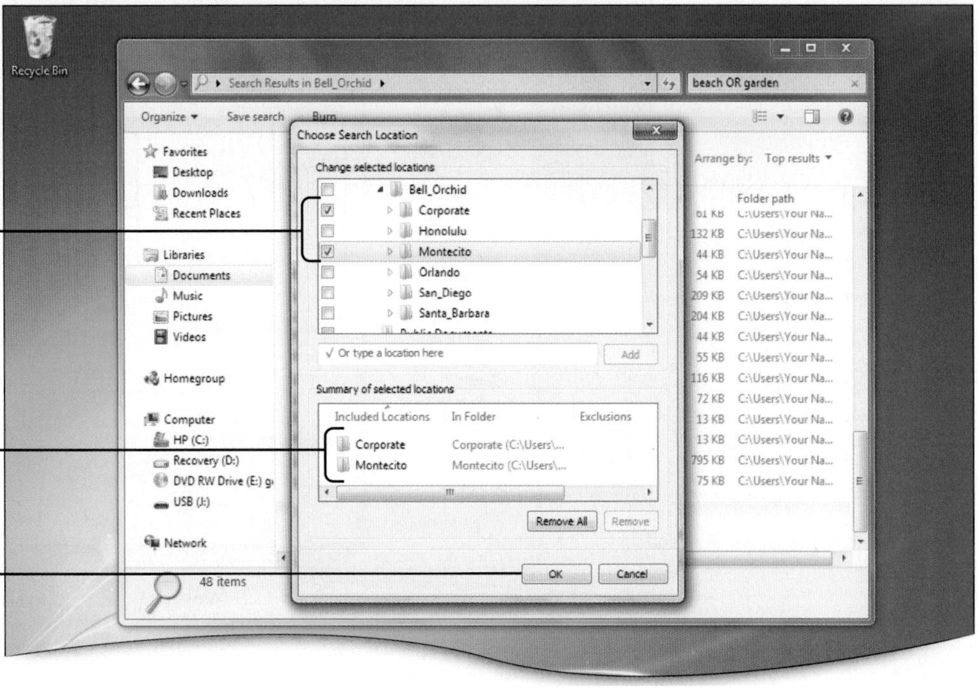

7 Click **OK** to apply the search criteria to only the two selected folders. In the **Details pane**, notice that *29 items* in the Corporate and Montecito folders have the word *beach* or *garden* as a property. Compare your screen with Figure 3.49.

Figure 3.49

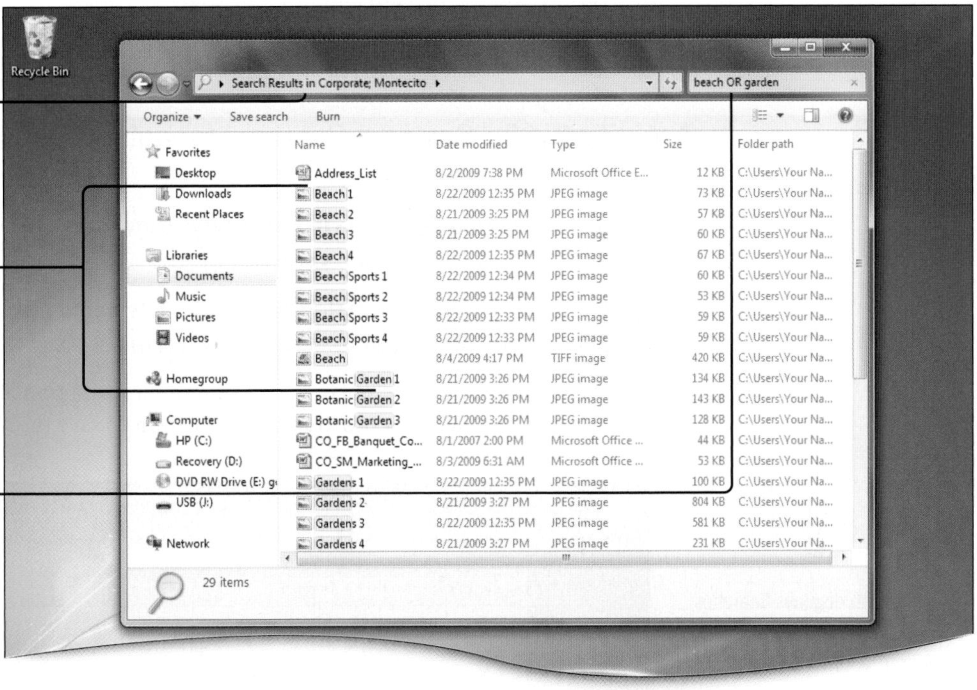

Scope of search results (Corporate and Montecito) indicated in address bar

Search criteria in a file name highlighted

Search criteria

8 **Start** the **Snipping Tool** program, click the **New arrow**, and then click **Window Snip**. Click anywhere in the **Search Results** window. In the **Snipping Tool** mark-up window, click the **Save Snip** button. In the displayed **Save As** dialog box, if necessary navigate to your **Windows 7 Chapter 3** folder on your USB flash drive and click to select it so that it displays in the address bar.

9 Using your own name, name the file **Lastname_Firstname_3B_Custom_Snip** be sure the file type is **JPEG**, and press Enter. **Close** the **Snipping Tool** mark-up window. Hold this file until you finish Project 3B, and then submit this file as directed by your instructor.

10 *Do not close the Search Results window*; leave the **Search Results in Corporate; Montecito** search folder window open for the next activity.

More Knowledge | Indexing an External Hard Drive Attached to Your Computer

You have seen that searching locations that are *indexed* results in a fast search result. You can include folders from an external hard drive in a library, which means they will become one of the indexed locations. Connect the external hard drive to your computer, and be sure that it is recognized in the Computer window under Hard Disk Drives. If the device displays there, folders on the drive can be included in a library and indexed. Some USB flash drives also have this capability. Just plug the device in, and if it displays in the Computer window under Hard Disk Drives, its data can be included in a library. Navigate to and select the folder or folders on the external drive that you want to include in the library. On the toolbar, click Include in library, and then click the library name, for example Documents.

Objective 7 | Save a Search, Manage Search Behavior, and Manage the Index

After you have built a search, you can save it. When you save a search, you are saving its criteria, not its current results. After the search is saved, it becomes a virtual subfolder in the Searches folder in your personal folder.

You can configure options to control the behavior of the search engine itself and also to manage the index.

Activity 3.13 | Saving a Search, Managing Search Behavior, and Managing the Index

1 Be sure your **Search Results in Corporate; Montecito** custom search displays, and then on the toolbar, click the **Save search** button.

2 In the displayed **Save As** dialog box, in the **File name** box, name the search **Beaches and Gardens** Compare your screen with Figure 3.50.

> The Bell Orchid Hotels plan to collect more information about beaches and gardens to use in new marketing brochures, so they want to save the search.

Figure 3.50

Save As dialog box

Path displays Searches folder in your personal folder (your name will vary)

Previous saved searches display (your list will vary)

File name

Save button

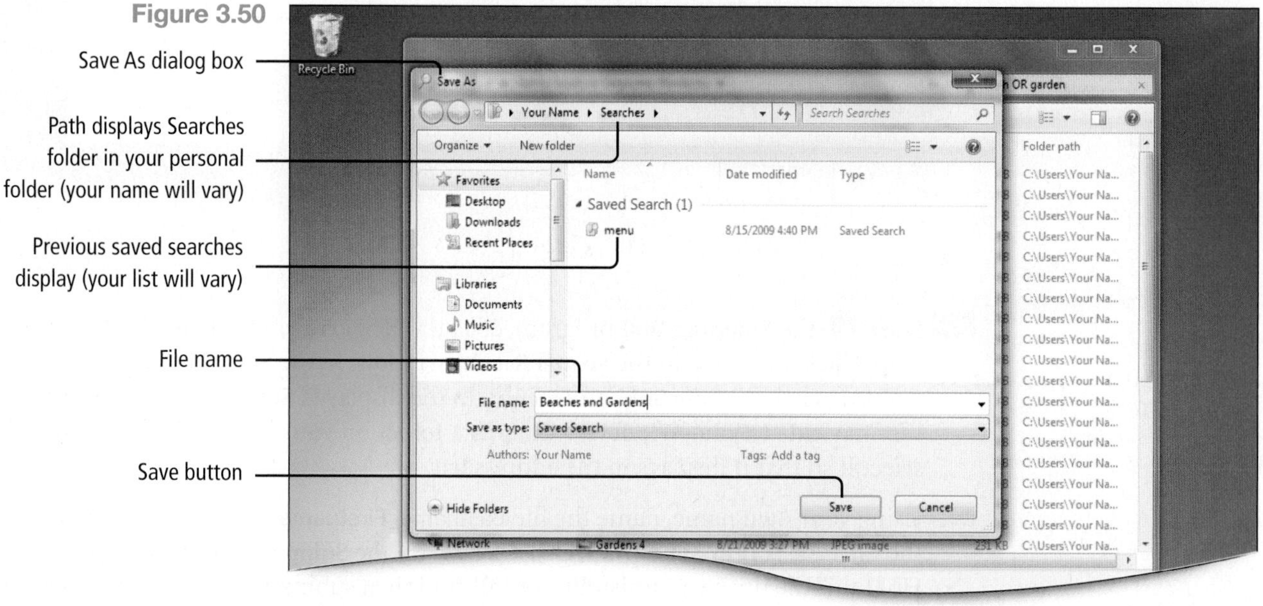

3 Click the **Save** button. If a message displays that the file exists, click Yes to replace it.

4 **Close** ![X] all open windows. Open the **Bell_Orchid** folder window again, and then navigate to **Montecito ▶ Photos**.

5 By selecting the files and typing in the **Tags** box in the **Details pane**, add the tag **Beach** to the following files: **Surfing 3** and **Surfing 4**. Be sure to click the **Save** button at the right end of the **Details pane**.

6 Using the same technique, add the tag **Garden** to **Tours 1**, **Tours 2**, **Tours 3**, and **Tours 4**. **Close** ![X] the folder window.

7 On the taskbar, click the **Windows Explorer** button, and then in the **navigation pane**, under **Favorites**, click your **Beaches and Gardens** saved search. In the **Details pane**, notice that 35 items display. Compare your results with Figure 3.51.

Recall that when you save a search, you are saving its criteria, not its current results. Thus, each time you reopen the Search folder, Windows 7 reruns the search with the most current results.

Figure 3.51

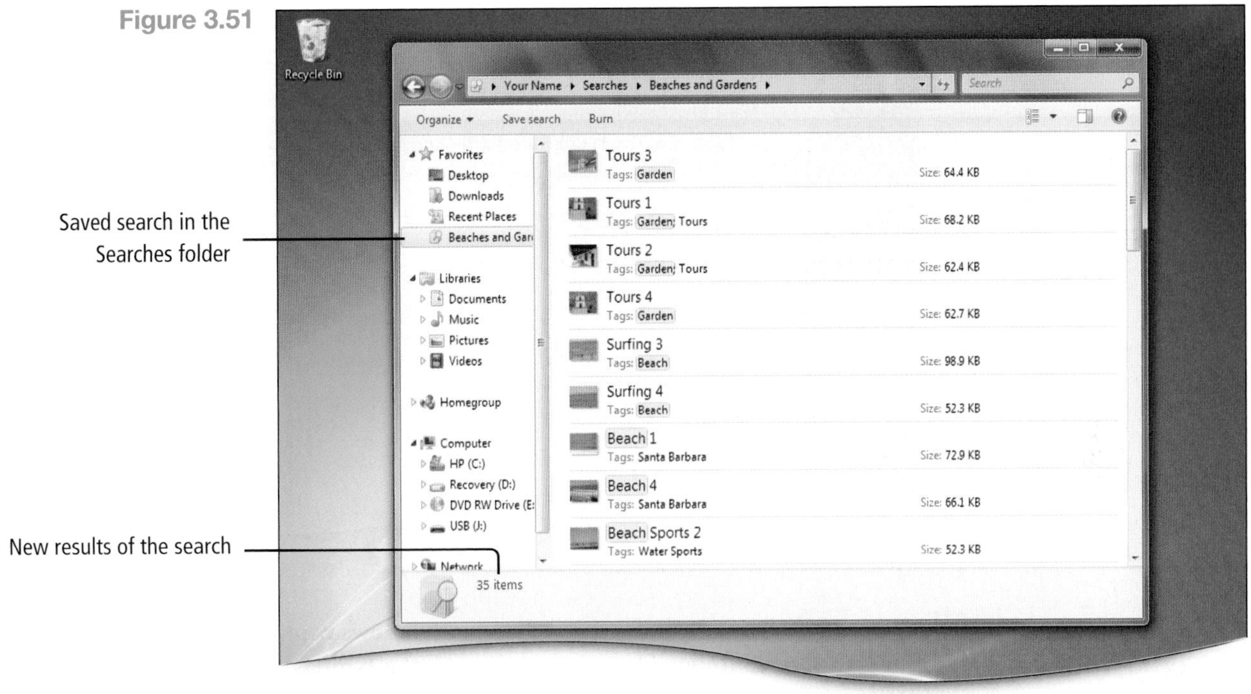

8 **Start** the **Snipping Tool** program, click the **New arrow**, and then click **Window Snip**. Click anywhere in the window. In the **Snipping Tool** mark-up window, click the **Save Snip** button. In the displayed **Save As** dialog box, if necessary navigate to your **Windows 7 Chapter 3** folder on your USB flash drive and click to select it so that it displays in the address bar.

9 Using your own name, name the file **Lastname_Firstname_3B_Saved_Search_Snip** be sure the file type is **JPEG**, and press Enter. **Close** the **Snipping Tool** mark-up window. Hold this file until you finish Project 3B, and then submit this file as directed by your instructor.

10 On the toolbar, click the **Organize** button, and then click **Folder and search options**. In the **Folder Options** dialog box, click the **Search tab**.

Here you can manage how the Search feature behaves. You can make changes to what is searched, how the search is conducted, and include additional files and directories when searching non-indexed locations.

You will probably want to maintain the default settings, although you might decide to include the natural language search that you have already practiced.

11 At the bottom of the **Folder Options** dialog box, click **Cancel**.

12 **Close** all open windows. Click **Start**, and then on the right, click **Control Panel**. In the **search** box, type **indexing options**, and then in the results, click **Indexing Options**. Compare your screen with Figure 3.52.

At the top of this dialog box, you can see if your index is up to date. For example, if you just added a number of new folders and files—perhaps by copying them into your Documents folder from another source—you might have to wait a short time for the index to be complete.

Figure 3.52

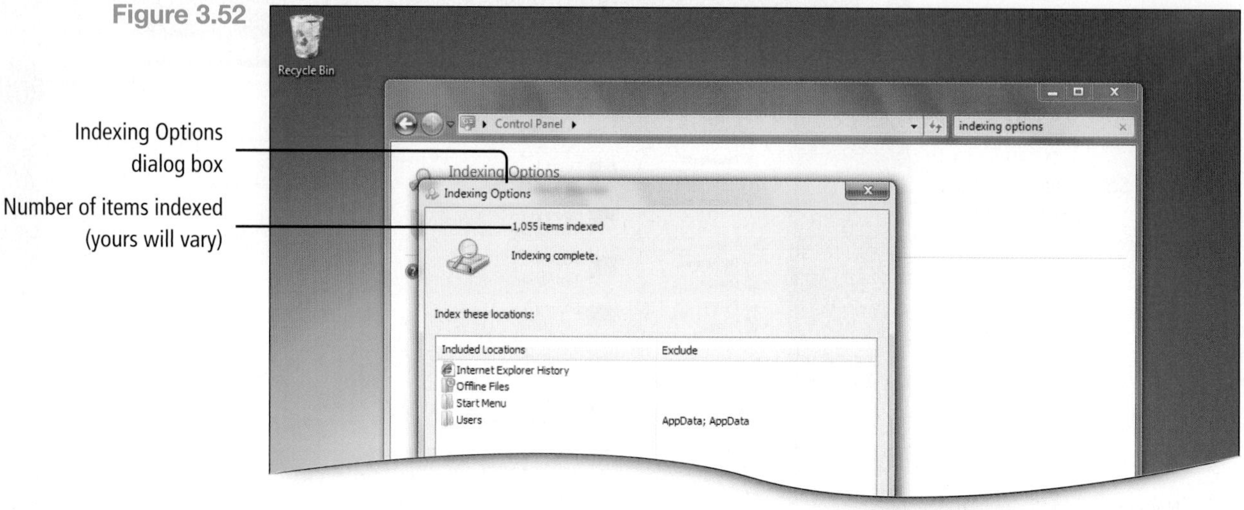

13 **Close** all open windows. Display the **Windows Explorer Jump List**, and unpin the **Bell_Orchid** folder. On the taskbar, click the **Windows Explorer** button, open the **Documents** library, and then delete the **Bell_Orchid** folder from the **Documents** library. In the **navigation pane**, delete the saved Search *Beaches and Gardens* from Favorites. Submit the four snip files from the project to your instructor as directed.

More Knowledge | Federated Search

In large organizations, files are commonly stored on large servers and managed by systems such as Microsoft SharePoint. If you have access to such files from your own computer, a technology called ***Federated Search*** enables you to search a remote server or Web service from Windows Explorer using the same techniques that you use to search for files that are stored on your own computer or in the libraries you have set up on your own computer.

End **You have completed Project 3B**

Content-Based Assessments

Summary

In this chapter you practiced using the address bar and other navigation techniques to locate files when you are working outside of an application program. The Favorites area is another area from which you can easily navigate to your folders and files. You also practiced techniques to personalize how folders display on your computer and to personalize the view of a folder window by changing the arrangement. You set folder properties and associated files with programs.

Search is one of the most powerful features in Windows 7. By using the search feature efficiently, you are relieved from tediously drilling down into your folder structure to find files that you are looking for. In this chapter, you practiced advanced search techniques and observed how to manage the behavior of the search feature and the index.

Key Terms

AND filter 195
Application 179
Arrange by 174
Base locations 160
Boolean operators 195
Check box feature 169
Contact 166
Custom search 201
Directory 157
Federated Search 206
File association 182
File name extension 179
File properties 187
Index 187
Indexed Locations 191
Location icon 157
Metadata 187
Natural language 195
NOT filter 195
OR filter 195
Partial matching 192
Path 157
Program 179
Quotes filter 196
Recent Pages 159
Search folder 197
Split button 179
Tag 187
Virtual folder 162

Matching

Match each term in the second column with its correct definition in the first column. Write the letter of the term on the blank line in front of the correct definition.

____ 1. A sequence or path of folders that leads to a specific file or folder.

____ 2. Another term for a path.

____ 3. A button on the address bar that depicts the location—library, disk drive, folder, and so on—that you are currently accessing.

____ 4. A button on the address bar that displays a list of recently accessed locations; the current location is indicated by a check mark.

____ 5. Locations that you frequently need to access to manage your computer including Libraries, Homegroup, your personal folder, Computer, Network, Control Panel, and Recycle Bin.

____ 6. A folder that does not represent a physical location but rather contains the results of a search.

____ 7. A folder option which, when applied, displays a small square box to the left of folders and files.

A Application
B Arrange by
C Base locations
D Check box feature
E Directory
F File association
G File name extension
H File properties
I Location icon
J Metadata
K Path
L Program
M Recent Pages
N Split button
O Virtual folder

_____ 8. In a folder window, a feature that enables you to arrange the items by Author, Date modified, Tag, Type, or Name; the default arrangement is Folder.

_____ 9. A set of characters at the end of a file name that helps Windows 7 understand what kind of information is in the file and what program should open the file.

_____ 10. A set of instructions that a computer uses to perform a specific task, such as word processing, accounting, or data management.

_____ 11. Another term for a program.

_____ 12. A button, for example on the toolbar, that when pointed to, displays in two parts—an arrow that displays a list and a button that starts the command.

_____ 13. The association between a file and the program that created the file.

_____ 14. Information about your files, such as the name of the author and the date that the file was last modified.

_____ 15. The data that describes other data; for example, the collective group of a file's properties, such as its title, subject, author, and file size.

Multiple Choice

Circle the correct answer.

1. A button with two parts—an arrow that displays a list and a button that starts the command—is a:
A. dual button **B.** split button **C.** partial button

2. The relationship between a file and the program that created the file is referred to as the file:
A. association **B.** application **C.** directory

3. Information about your files, such as the name of the author and the date that the file was last modified, is referred to as the file's:
A. path **B.** metadata **C.** properties

4. The data that describes other data—tags, title, subject, author, and file size—is referred to as:
A. properties **B.** extensions **C.** metadata

5. A collection of detailed information about the files on your computer that Windows 7 maintains for the purpose of conducting fast searches is the:
A. directory **B.** index **C.** path

6. All of the locations in your personal folder (Documents, Pictures, and so on) and offline files, if any, that Windows 7 includes in a search are referred to as the indexed:
A. locations **B.** folders **C.** filters

7. The terms AND, OR, and NOT that govern the logical functions and express a condition that is either true or false are referred to as Boolean:
A. programs **B.** operators **C.** properties

8. When used in a search, the Boolean filter that finds files that contain both search terms, even if those terms are not next to each other, is the:
A. AND filter **B.** NOT filter **C.** OR filter

9. When used in a search, the Boolean filter that finds files that contain the first word but that do not contain the second word is the:
A. AND filter **B.** NOT filter **C.** OR filter

10. When used in a search, the Boolean filter that finds files that contain either search term is the:
A. AND filter **B.** NOT filter **C.** OR filter

Content-Based Assessments

Apply 3A skills from these Objectives:

1. Navigate by Using the Address Bar
2. Create and Navigate Favorites
3. Personalize the Display of Folders and Files
4. Recognize File Types and Associate Files with Programs

Skills Review | Project 3C Using Advanced File Management Techniques

Project Files

For Project 3C, you will need the following files:

Student Resource CD (or a USB flash drive containing these files)
win03_3C_Answer_Sheet (Word document)

You will save your file as:

Lastname_Firstname_3C_Answer_Sheet

Project Results

1 **Close** [X] all open windows. On the taskbar, click the **Windows Explorer** button. In the **navigation pane**, click the drive that contains the student files for this textbook, and then navigate to **Chapter_Files** ▶ **Chapter_03**. Double-click the Word file **win03_3C_Answer_Sheet** to open Word and display the document. Press F12 to display the **Save As** dialog box in Word, navigate to your **Windows 7 Chapter 3** folder, and then using your own name, save the document as **Lastname_Firstname_3C_Answer_Sheet** If necessary, click OK if a message regarding formats displays.

On the taskbar, click the **Word** button to minimize the window and leave your Word document accessible from the taskbar. **Close** the **Chapter_03** folder window. As you complete each step in this project, click the Word button on the taskbar to open the document, type your one-letter answer in the appropriate cell of the Word table, and then on the taskbar, click the **Word** button again to minimize the window for the next step.

Insert the Student Resource CD in the appropriate drive, and then copy the **Bell_Orchid** folder to your **Documents** folder—you will need a *new* copy for this project. Display your **Documents** folder, and then navigate to **Bell_Orchid** ▶ **Corporate** ▶ **Information_Technology** ▶ **Future_Hotels**. At the left end of the **address bar**, click the **location icon**. What is your result?

A. All of the files in the Future_Hotels folder are selected.

B. In the address bar, the path that describes the folder's location displays separated by backslashes and is highlighted.

C. The Documents folder window displays.

2 Press Esc. In the **address bar**, click **Corporate** to display this folder window. In the **address bar**, to the immediate right of the **location icon**, click ▶. What is your result?

A. A list of available base locations displays below the separator line.

B. A list of the subfolders within the Corporate folder displays.

C. The path that describes the folder's location displays and is highlighted.

3 Display the **Bell_Orchid** folder window. On the toolbar, click **New folder**, and then create a new folder named **Florida_Keys** Drag the **Florida_Keys** folder to become the first item under **Favorites**. Which of the following is true?

A. The Florida_Keys folder no longer displays in the file list.

B. The Florida_Keys folder window opens.

C. The Florida_Keys folder displays in the Favorites area with a buff-colored folder.

4 On the **toolbar**, click the **Organize** button, and then click **Folder and search options**. Click the **General tab**. Which of the following is true?

(Project 3C Using Advanced File Management Techniques continues on the next page)

Skills Review | Project 3C Using Advanced File Management Techniques (continued)

A. On this tab, you can change folder behavior so that every folder opens in a new window.

B. On this tab, you can set programs to open with a single click.

C. On this tab, you can change folder behavior so that no folders display in the file list.

5 In the **Folder Options** dialog box, click the **View tab**. Which of the following settings can be adjusted on your computer?

A. Hiding or showing file extensions.

B. Displaying a folder in the view used when the folder was last displayed.

C. Both A and B.

6 **Close** the **Folder Options** dialog box. Navigate to **Corporate ▶ Information_Technology ▶ Future_Hotels**. Be sure the view is **Details**, and then **Arrange** the files by **Type**. How many different stacks display?

A. Four

B. Five

C. Six

7 How many files are in the **PowerPoint** stack?

A. Three

B. Four

C. Five

8 **Arrange** the files by **Tag**. How many files are in the **Garden** stack?

A. Two

B. Three

C. Four

9 **Arrange** the files by **Folder**, and then navigate to **Corporate ▶ Food_Beverage**. In the **file list**, right-click the **Restaurants** folder, and then click **Properties**. How many *folders* are in the **Restaurants** folder?

A. 35

B. 0

C. 2

10 Click the **Cancel** button. In the **file list**, select the file **CO_FB_Menu_Presentation**. On the **toolbar**, click the **Open button arrow**, and then click **Choose default program**. What is the file extension for this file?

A. .docx

B. .ppt

C. .pptx

Click the **Cancel** button, under **Favorites**, right-click **Florida_Keys** and click **Remove**. Delete the **Bell_Orchid** folder in the **Documents** window. Be sure you have typed all of your answers in your Word document. **Save** and **Close** your Word document, and submit as directed by your instructor. **Close** [X] all open windows.

End You have completed Project 3C

Apply 3B skills from these Objectives:

5 Filter Searches in the Search Box

6 Search by Using the Search Folder

7 Save a Search, Manage Search Behavior, and Manage the Index

Skills Review | Project 3D Using Advanced Search Techniques

Project Files

For Project 3D, you will need the following files:

Student Resource CD (or a USB flash drive containing these files)
win03_3D_Answer_Sheet (Word document)

You will save your file as:

Lastname_Firstname_3D_Answer_Sheet

Project Results

1 **Close** [X] all open windows. On the taskbar, click the **Windows Explorer** button. In the **navigation pane**, click the drive that contains the student files for this textbook, and then navigate to **Chapter_Files ▶ Chapter_03**. Double-click the Word file **win03_3D_Answer_Sheet** to open Word and display the document. Press F12 to display the **Save As** dialog box in Word, navigate to your **Windows 7 Chapter 3** folder, and then using your own name, save the document as **Lastname_Firstname_3D_Answer_Sheet** If necessary, click OK if a message regarding formats displays.

On the taskbar, click the **Word** button to minimize the window and leave your Word document accessible from the taskbar. **Close** the **Chapter_03** folder window. As you complete each step in this project, click the Word button on the taskbar to open the document, type your one-letter answer in the appropriate cell of the Word table, and then on the taskbar, click the button again to minimize the window for the next step.

From the Student Resource CD or other device that contains the Student Resource files, copy the **Bell_Orchid** folder to your **Documents** folder—you will need a *new* copy for this project. Display your **Documents** folder, and then navigate to **Bell_Orchid ▶ Corporate ▶ Food_Beverage ▶ Restaurants**. Hold down Ctrl, and then select the following group of files: **Breakfast_Continental**, **Breakfast_Menus**, **Brunch_Menus**, **Grill_Menu**, and **Refreshments**. Right-click any of the selected files, click **Properties**, and then as a group, apply the tag **Menu** Click **OK**, and then in the **search** box, type **menu** How many files display?

A. 5

B. 6

C. 7

2 **Clear** the **search** box, and then type **tag:menu** How many files display?

A. 4

B. 5

C. 6

3 **Clear** the **search** box, and then type **costs** How many files display?

A. 4

B. 5

C. 6

(Project 3D Using Advanced Search Techniques continues on the next page)

Skills Review | Project 3D Using Advanced Search Techniques (continued)

4 **Clear** the **search** box, and then type **type:xlsx** How many files display?

A. 5

B. 15

C. 16

5 **Clear** the **search** box, and then type **costs NOT overtime** How many files display?

A. 3

B. 4

C. 7

6 **Clear** the **search** box, and then type **menu AND breakfast** How many files display?

A. 4

B. 3

C. 2

7 **Clear** the **search** box, and then type **menu OR breakfast** How many files display?

A. 4

B. 6

C. 8

8 **Clear** the **search** box, and then type **costs type:Excel** How many files display?

A. 4

B. 3

C. 2

9 On the toolbar, click **Organize**, and then click **Folder and search options**. Click the **Search tab**. Which of the following is *not* true?

A. In terms of how the Search feature performs a search, you have the option to find or not find partial matches.

B. In terms of how the Search feature performs, you must always use Boolean operators instead of natural language.

C. When searching non-indexed locations, you have the option to include system directories.

10 **Close** the **Folder Options** dialog box. On the toolbar, click the **Save search** button. Which of the following is true?

A. By default, a saved search is saved in your Documents folder.

B. By default, a saved search is saved in your Searches folder.

C. By default, a saved search is saved in your Desktop folder.

In the **Save As** dialog box, click **Cancel**. Clear the **search** box, display the **Documents** folder, and then delete the **Bell_Orchid** folder in the **Documents** window. Be sure you have typed all of your answers in your Word document. **Save** and **Close** your Word document, and submit as directed by your instructor. **Close** [X] all open windows.

End **You have completed Project 3D**

Content-Based Assessments

Apply 3A skills from these Objectives:

1. Navigate by Using the Address Bar
2. Create and Navigate Favorites
3. Personalize the Display of Folders and Files
4. Recognize File Types and Associate Files with Programs

Mastering Windows 7 | Project 3E Using Advanced File Management Techniques

In the following Mastering Windows 7 project, you will change the way a folder displays. You will capture and save a screen that will look similar to Figure 3.53.

Project Files

For Project 3E, you will need the following files:

Student Resource CD (or a USB flash drive containing these files)
New Snip file

You will save your file as:

Lastname_Firstname_3E__HR_Snip

Project Results

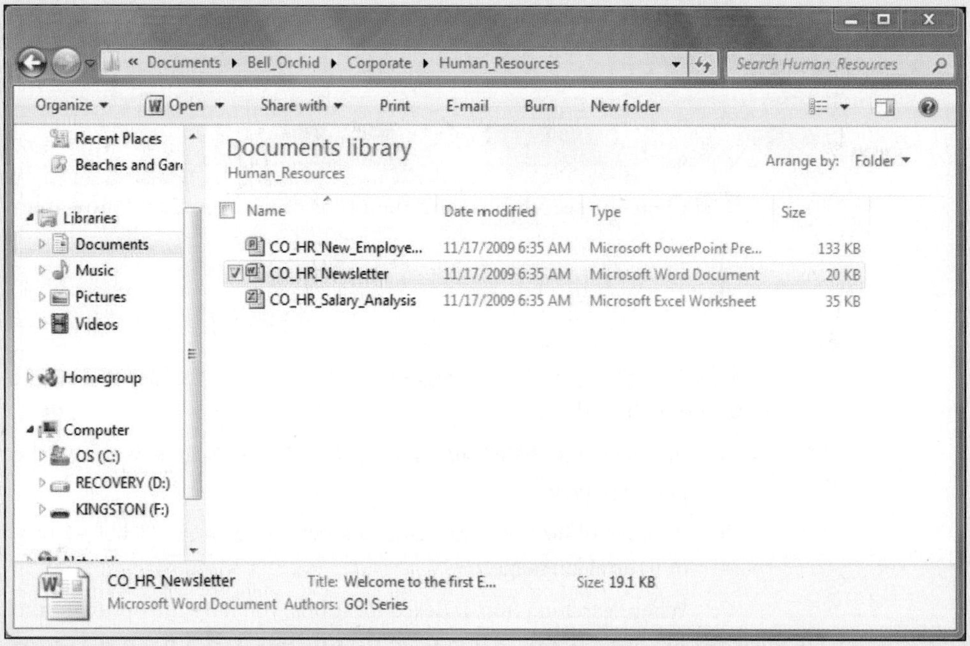

Figure 3.53

(Project 3E Using Advanced File Management Techniques continues on the next page)

Mastering Windows 7 | Project 3E Using Advanced File Management Techniques (continued)

1 Copy the **Bell_Orchid** folder from your Student Resource CD to your **Documents** folder. Navigate to **Documents ▶ Bell_Orchid**. Change the folder options so that check boxes display.

2 Navigate to **Bell_Orchid ▶ Corporate ▶ Human_Resources**, and then select the check box for the **CO_HR_Newsletter** file.

3 Create a **Window Snip** in your chapter folder and save it as **Lastname_Firstname_3E_HR_Snip**

4 Change the folder options so that check boxes do ***not*** display. **Close** all open windows, and delete the **Bell_Orchid** folder from your **Documents** folder. Submit this file as directed by your instructor.

End **You have completed Project 3E**

Apply **3B** skills from these Objectives:

- **5** Filter Searches in the Search Box
- **6** Search by Using the Search Folder
- **7** Save a Search, Manage Search Behavior, and Manage the Index

Mastering Windows 7 | Project **3F** Using Advanced Search Techniques

In the following Mastering Windows 7 project, you will create a search. You will capture and save a screen that will look similar to Figure 3.54.

Project Files

For Project 3F, you will need the following files:

Student Resource CD (or a USB flash drive containing these files)
New Snip file

You will save your file as:

Lastname_Firstname_3F_OR_Snip

Project Results

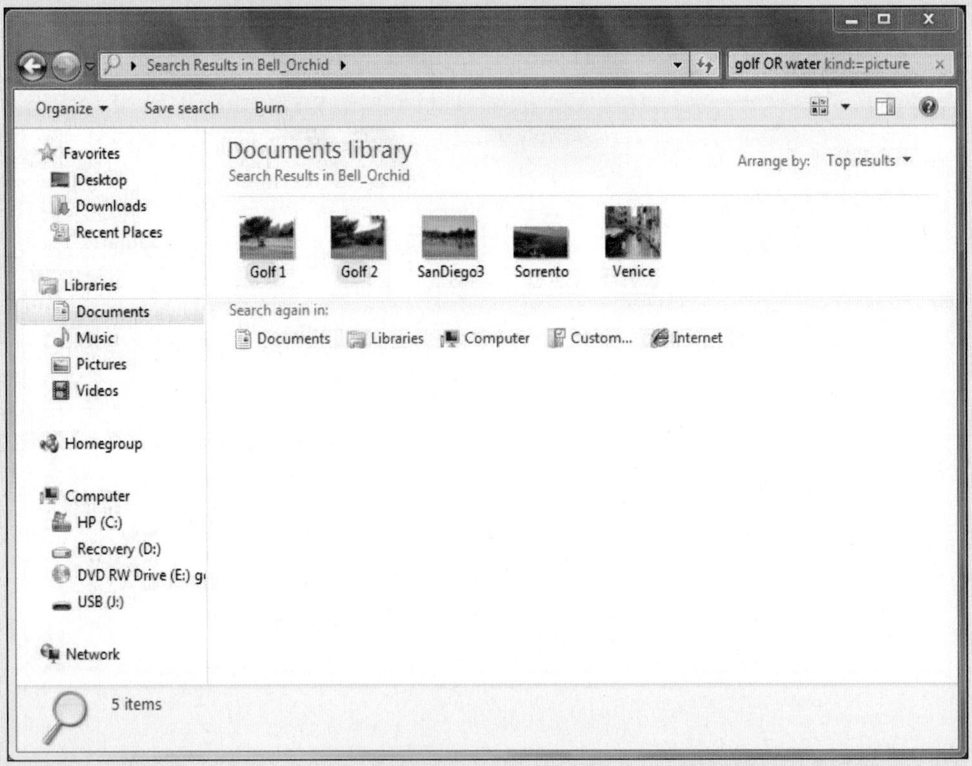

Figure 3.54

(Project 3F Using Advanced Search Techniques continues on the next page)

Mastering Windows 7 | Project 3F Using Advanced Search Techniques (continued)

1 Copy *two* folders to your **Documents** folder as follows: First, if necessary, *delete* the Bell_Orchid folder from your Documents folder—for this project you will need a new copy of the files. Insert the Student Resource CD or other device that contains the student files that accompany this textbook. By using the **Send to** command, copy the **Bell_Orchid** folder from the Student Resource CD (or other device) to your **Documents** folder. Leave the window open.

2 On your Student Resource CD (or other device) navigate to **Chapter_Files ▶ Chapter_03**. Right-click the **Montecito** folder, point to **Send to**, and then click **Documents**.

3 When the copy operation is complete, in the **navigation pane**, under **Libraries**, click **Documents** to display your **Documents** folder window. Move the **Montecito** folder into the **Bell_Orchid** folder.

4 Display the **Bell_Orchid** folder window. Conduct a search to find all the files that contain the word **golf** *OR* the word **water** After the search displays a list of results, with your insertion point still in the **search** box, press Spacebar and then type **kind:** Select **Picture** as the kind of file to search by. Change the view to **Medium Icons**.

5 Create a **Window Snip** and save it as **Lastname_Firstname_3F_OR_Snip**

6 Change the view back to **Details**. Delete the **Bell_Orchid** folder from your **Documents** folder, and then **Close** all open windows. Submit your file to your instructor as directed.

End **You have completed Project 3F**

Outcomes-Based Assessments

Rubric

The following outcomes-based assessments are *open-ended assessments*. That is, there is no specific correct result; your result will depend on your approach to the information provided. Make *Professional Quality* your goal. Use the following scoring rubric to guide you in *how* to approach the problem, and then to evaluate *how well* your approach solves the problem.

The *criteria*—Software Mastery, Content, Format and Layout, and Process—represent the knowledge and skills you have gained that you can apply to solving the problem. The *levels of performance*—Professional Quality, Approaching Professional Quality, or Needs Quality Improvements—help you and your instructor evaluate your result.

	Your completed project is of Professional Quality if you:	**Your completed project is Approaching Professional Quality if you:**	**Your completed project Needs Quality Improvements if you:**
1-Software Mastery	Choose and apply the most appropriate skills, tools, and features and identify efficient methods to solve the problem.	Choose and apply some appropriate skills, tools, and features, but not in the most efficient manner.	Choose inappropriate skills, tools, or features, or are inefficient in solving the problem.
2-Content	Construct a solution that is clear and well organized, contains content that is accurate, appropriate to the audience and purpose, and is complete. Provide a solution that contains no errors in spelling, grammar, or style.	Construct a solution in which some components are unclear, poorly organized, inconsistent, or incomplete. Misjudge the needs of the audience. Have some errors in spelling, grammar, or style, but the errors do not detract from comprehension.	Construct a solution that is unclear, incomplete, or poorly organized; contains some inaccurate or inappropriate content; and contains many errors in spelling, grammar, or style. Do not solve the problem.
3-Format and Layout	Format and arrange all elements to communicate information and ideas, clarify function, illustrate relationships, and indicate relative importance.	Apply appropriate format and layout features to some elements, but not others. Overuse features, causing minor distraction.	Apply format and layout that does not communicate information or ideas clearly. Do not use format and layout features to clarify function, illustrate relationships, or indicate relative importance. Use available features excessively, causing distraction.
4-Process	Use an organized approach that integrates planning, development, self-assessment, revision, and reflection.	Demonstrate an organized approach in some areas, but not others; or, use an insufficient process of organization throughout.	Do not use an organized approach to solve the problem.

Apply a combination of the 3A and 3B skills.

Problem Solving | Project 3G Help Desk

Project Files

For Project 3G, you will need the following file from the Student Resource CD:

win03_3G_Help_Desk

You will save your file as:

Lastname_Firstname_3G_Help_Desk

From the student files that accompany this textbook, open the **Chapter_Files** folder, and then in **Chapter_03** folder, locate and open the Word document **win03_3G_Help_Desk**. Save the document in your chapter folder as **Lastname_Firstname_3G_Help_Desk**

The following e-mail question has arrived at the Help Desk from an employee at the Bell Orchid Hotel's corporate office. In the Word document, construct a response based on your knowledge of Windows 7. Although an e-mail response is not as formal as a letter, you should still use good grammar, good sentence structure, professional language, and a polite tone. Save your document and submit the response as directed by your instructor.

To: Help Desk

I can navigate all over the Internet without having to double-click to display what I want to look at. Is there a way to avoid double-clicking so often when I am navigating in Windows 7?

End **You have completed Project 3G**

Outcomes-Based Assessments

Apply a combination of the 3A and 3B skills.

Problem Solving | Project 3H Help Desk

Project Files

For Project 3H, you will need the following file from the Student Resource CD:

win03_3H_Help_Desk

You will save your file as:

Lastname_Firstname_3H_Help_Desk

From the student files that accompany this textbook, open the **Chapter_Files** folder, and then in the **Chapter_03** folder, locate and open **win03_3H_Help_Desk**. Save the document in your chapter folder as **Lastname_Firstname_3H_Help_Desk**

The following e-mail question has arrived at the Help Desk from an employee at the Bell Orchid Hotel's corporate office. In the Word document, construct a response based on your knowledge of Windows 7. Although an e-mail response is not as formal as a letter, you should still use good grammar, good sentence structure, professional language, and a polite tone. Save your document and submit the response as directed by your instructor.

To: Help Desk

I just received over one hundred new photo files of golf courses, restaurants, and scenic mountain views of Palm Springs, California, where we are considering opening a new resort hotel. First, I want the photos to open in the Microsoft Picture Manager program, but every time I open a photo, it opens with the Windows Photo Viewer program. How can I change my system so that photos open in Microsoft Picture Manager? Second, I don't want to rename all the photos. Is there a way I could add identifying information so I could search for them by *golf* or by *restaurants*, and so on?

End **You have completed Project 3H**

Apply a combination of the 3A and 3B skills.

Problem Solving | Project 3I Help Desk

Project Files

For Project 3I, you will need the following file from the Student Resource CD:

win03_3I_Help_Desk

You will save your document as

Lastname_Firstname_3I_Help_Desk

From the student files that accompany this textbook, open the **Chapter_Files** folder, and then open the Word document **win03_3I_Help_Desk**. Save the document in your chapter folder as **Lastname_Firstname_3I_Help_Desk**

The following e-mail question has arrived at the Help Desk from an employee at the Bell Orchid Hotel's corporate office. In the Word document, construct a response based on your knowledge of Windows 7. Although an e-mail response is not as formal as a letter, you should still use good grammar, good sentence structure, professional language, and a polite tone. Save your document and submit the response as directed by your instructor.

To: Help Desk

I am the Corporate Director of Food and Beverage. I have hundreds of files from all of our different facilities that deal with various aspects of the Food and Beverage operation. I need to find files by location and also by type of menu. Is there a way I could find, for example, only files that pertain to brunch menus at our Orlando facility or only files that pertain to dinner menus at both the Honolulu and Montecito locations?

End **You have completed Project 3I**

Personalizing Your Windows 7 Environment and Using Windows Media Player

OUTCOMES

At the end of this chapter you will be able to:

OBJECTIVES

Mastering these objectives will enable you to:

PROJECT 4A

Create an environment on your computer that reflects your personal preferences and that makes it easier to manage your computer tasks.

1. Personalize the Desktop and Screen Saver (p. 225)
2. Personalize the Start Menu (p. 231)
3. Personalize the Taskbar (p. 240)
4. Personalize the Desktop by Adding Gadgets (p. 245)
5. Personalize the Ease of Access Center and Use the Problem Steps Recorder (p. 250)

PROJECT 4B

Use Windows Media Player to play, rip, and burn music and to watch videos.

6. Explore Windows Media Player (p. 256)
7. Play Music Using Media Player (p. 257)
8. Rip a CD (p. 265)
9. Burn a CD (p. 267)
10. Watch Videos Using Windows Media Player (p. 270)

Holger Mette/Shutterstock

In This Chapter

In this chapter, you will personalize your computer environment. Your physical desk—at home or at your office where you do your work—is as personal as you are. You probably have your own personal coffee mug, pens and pencils, reference books, and photos of family members or friends or pets. You can personalize your Windows 7 desktop too, by adding your own colors, backgrounds, photos, and tools that you work with most often.

In this chapter, you will also use Windows Media Player, which enables you to play music, look at pictures, watch videos, and watch recorded television shows. It also enables you to organize your digital media, rip CDs, burn CDs from your own playlists, synchronize with your portable media player, and purchase media content from online sources.

The projects in this chapter relate to the **Bell Orchid Hotels**, headquartered in Boston, and which own and operate resorts and business-oriented hotels. Resort properties are located in popular destinations, including Honolulu, Orlando, San Diego, and Santa Barbara. The resorts offer deluxe accommodations and a wide array of dining options. Other Bell Orchid hotels are located in major business centers and offer the latest technology in their meeting facilities. The company plans to open new properties and update existing properties over the next ten years.

Project 4A Personalizing Your Windows 7 Environment

Project Activities

In Activities 4.01 through 4.09, you will work with Barbara and Steven, employees in the Information Technology department at the headquarters office of Bell Orchid Hotels, as they explore how to personalize the desktop and arrange Windows 7 tools for a productive computer environment. Your completed screens will look similar to Figure 4.1.

Project Files

For Project 4A, you will need the following files:

Student Resource CD (or a USB flash drive containing these files)
New Snip files

You will save your files as:

Lastname_Firstname_4A_Desktop_Snip
Lastname_Firstname_4A_Customize_Snip
Lastname_Firstname_4A_Links_Snip
Lastname_Firstname_4A_Gadgets_Snip
Lastname_Firstname_4A_Steps_Snip

Project Results

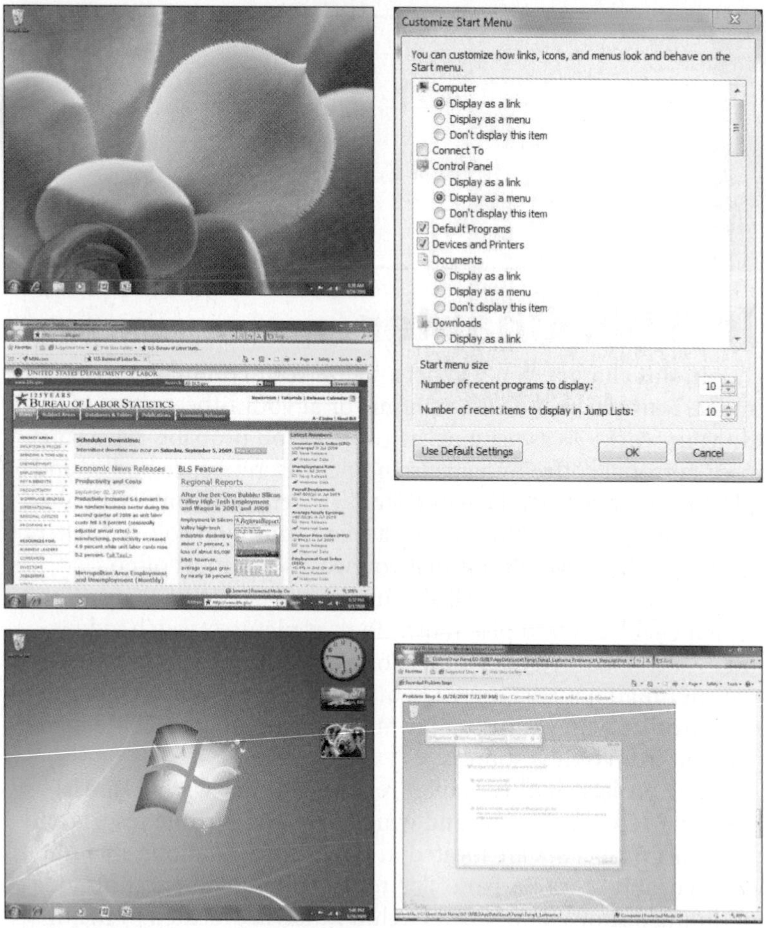

Figure 4.1
Project 4A Personalizing Your Windows 7 Environment

Objective 1 | Personalize the Desktop and Screen Saver

Recall that the ***desktop*** simulates the top of an actual desk and acts as your work area in Windows 7. The desktop is the main screen area that you see after you turn on your computer and log on. The desktop includes the taskbar at the bottom and the Start button in the lower left corner.

A ***screen saver*** is a moving picture or pattern that displays on your screen after a specified period of inactivity—that is, when the mouse or keyboard has not been used.

Activity 4.01 | Personalizing the Desktop Background

Selecting a desktop background—sometimes referred to as the ***wallpaper***—is one of the easiest ways to personalize your computer environment. Many attractive backgrounds are included with Windows 7, including photos, graphic designs, and solid colors. Creating a background from one of your own photos is a nice way to personalize to your desktop background.

A ***theme*** is a combination of pictures, colors, and sounds on your computer. A theme includes a desktop background, a screen saver, a window border color, and a sound scheme. Some themes include specific types of desktop icons and mouse pointers. Windows comes with several themes that you can use, or you can create your own customized themes. Additionally, you can download themes created by others from various Internet sites.

Another Way

From the Start menu, display the Control Panel, and then under Appearance and Personalization, click Change desktop background.

1 If necessary, *delete* the Bell_Orchid folder from your Documents folder—for this project, you will need a new copy of the files. Insert the Student Resource CD or other device that contains the student files that accompany this textbook. By using the **Send to** command that you have practiced, copy the **Bell_Orchid** folder to your **Documents** folder.

2 **Close** all open windows to display your desktop. Point anywhere on your desktop, right-click, and then on the shortcut menu, click **Personalize**.

3 At the bottom of the displayed **Personalization** window, click **Desktop Background**, and then compare your screen with Figure 4.2.

Figure 4.2

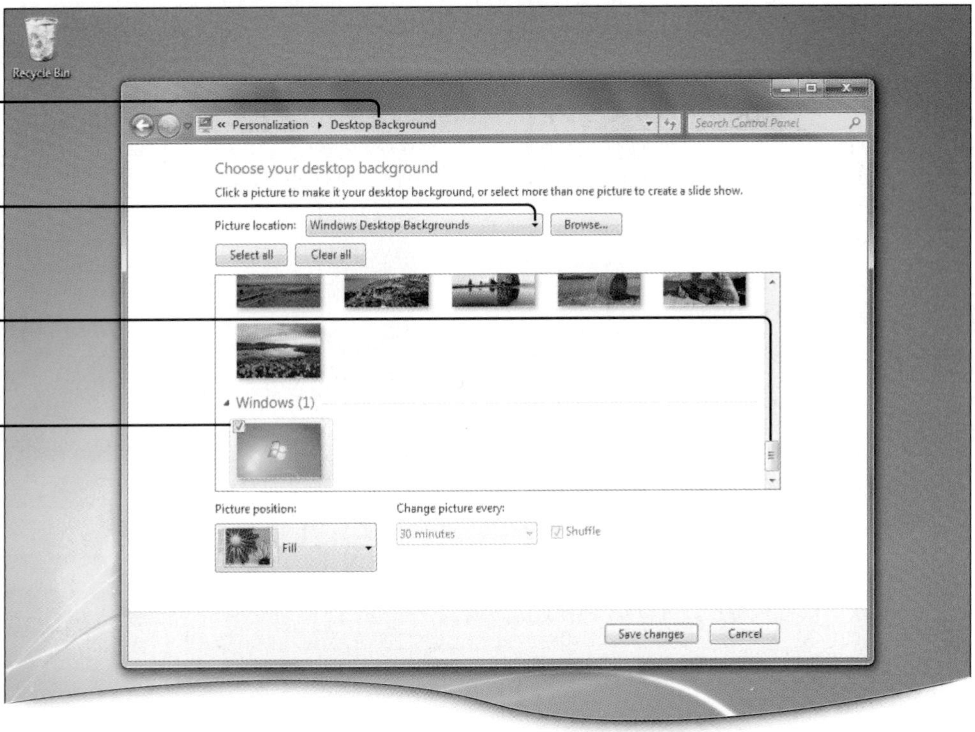

4 Move the scroll box up or down as necessary, and take a moment to view the various photos, designs, and graphics that are provided as **Windows Desktop Backgrounds**—some may be provided by your computer's manufacturer and display a stylized version of a logo.

Any theme that is included with Windows 7, for example the *Architecture* theme, will provide a changing background of the six pictures that will cycle on the desktop background, a complementary window color, and the Cityscape sound scheme.

5 Click the **Picture location arrow**, click **Solid Colors**, and then in the lower left corner, click **More**.

By using the tools provided, you can create any custom color. This is useful if you are trying to match your desktop background to a set of organization colors, for example the school colors of your college or university or the colors of your favorite sports team.

6 **Close** [X] the **Color** dialog box, click the **Picture location arrow**, and then click **Pictures Library**. At the bottom of the window, click the **Picture position arrow**, and notice that there are five arrangements by which Windows 7 can display a selected picture as a desktop background.

Behind this window, your desktop might display various pictures that accompany Windows 7.

Here, you can also select how often to change the background picture if you have selected multiple pictures.

7 Click in a white area of the dialog box to close the **Picture position** menu. To the right of the **Picture location** box, click the **Browse** button, and then compare your screen with Figure 4.3.

Browsing is a term used to describe the process of navigating within Windows 7 to look for a specific program, file, e-mail, Control Panel feature, or Internet favorite.

Your desktop might display one of the sample pictures.

Figure 4.3

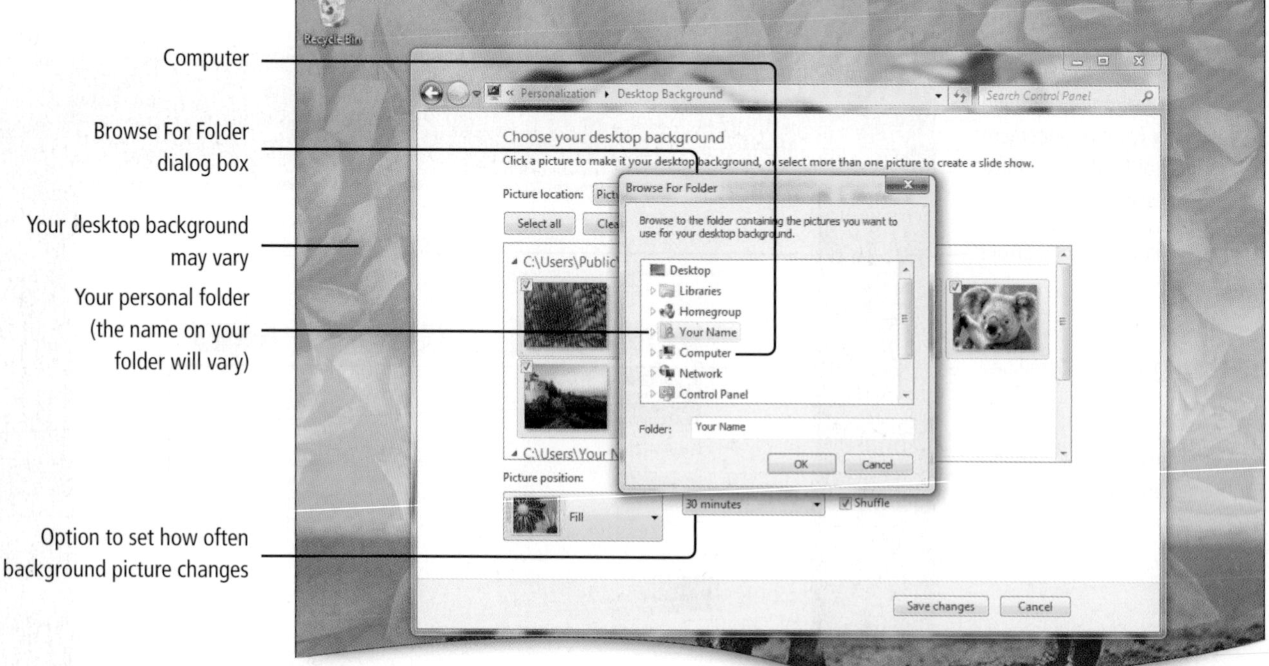

8 In the **Browse For Folder** dialog box, click **Computer** to expand it. Scroll down as necessary, and then click the location that contains your student files, either the CD/DVD drive or a USB flash drive.

9 Scroll down as necessary, click the **Chapter_Files** folder, scroll down again, and then click **Chapter_04**. Compare your screen with Figure 4.4.

Figure 4.4

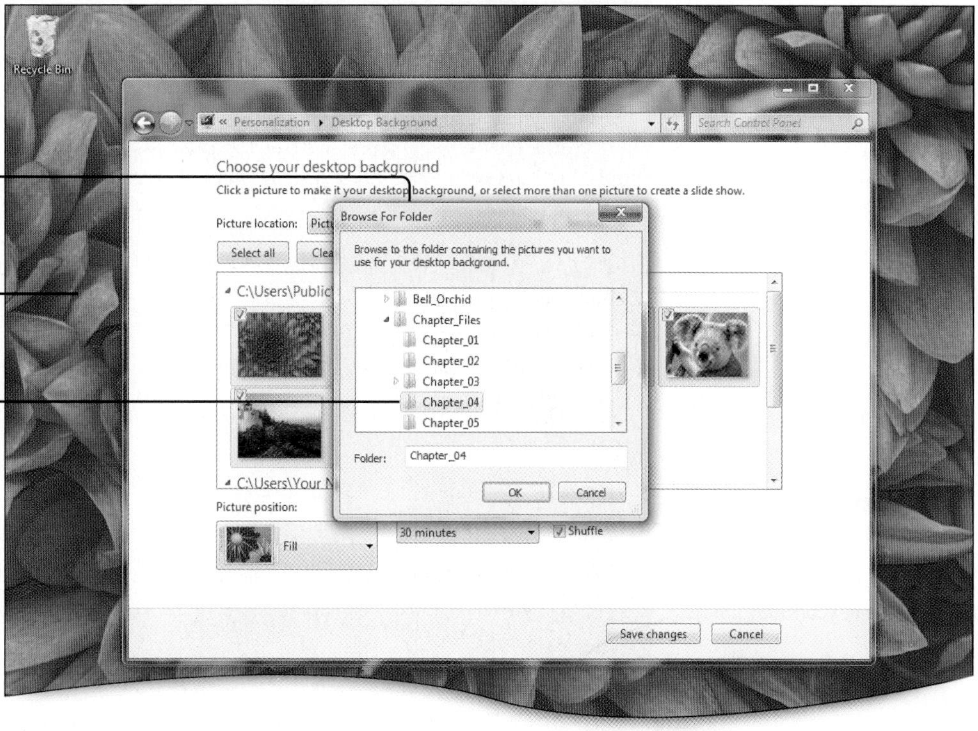

10 Click **OK**, and then compare your screen with Figure 4.5. Notice that one of the two displayed pictures might display on your desktop.

Figure 4.5

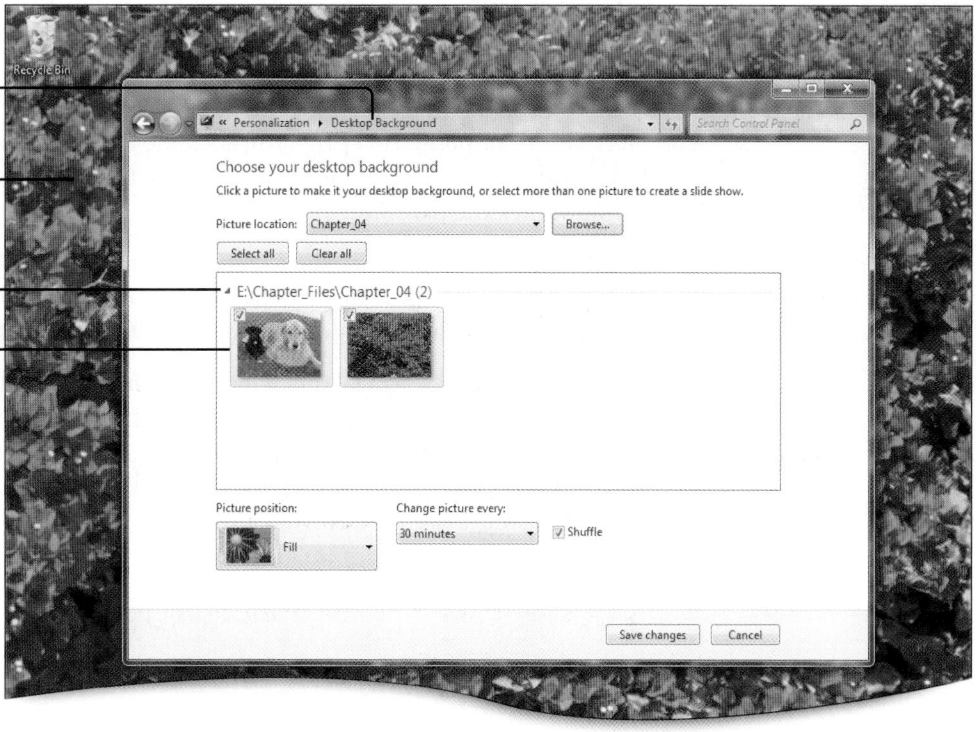

11 Click the picture of the two dogs, and then in the upper right corner of the **Desktop Background** dialog box, click the **Minimize** button [minimize] to minimize the window. Compare your screen with Figure 4.6.

Figure 4.6

Selected picture displays as background (your picture placement could vary depending on screen resolution)

Control Panel window minimized to taskbar

Word and Excel pinned to taskbar; yours may differ

12 On the taskbar, click the **Control Panel** button to redisplay the **Desktop Background** window.

13 Click the **Picture location arrow**, click **Windows Desktop Backgrounds**, scroll down to the **Nature** category, and then click **img2**—the second image that is a bright green plant. In the lower right corner, click **Save changes**, and then **Close** [close] the **Desktop Background** window.

This would be an appropriate image for computers at the Bell Orchid Hotels.

14 **Start** [start] the **Snipping Tool** program, click the **New arrow**, and then click **Window Snip**. Point anywhere on the desktop and click one time. In the **Snipping Tool** mark-up window, click the **Save Snip** button [save].

15 In the **Save As** dialog box, in the **navigation pane**, scroll down as necessary, and then under **Computer**, click your USB flash drive so that it displays in the **address bar**. On the toolbar, click the **New folder** button, type **Windows 7 Chapter 4** and press Enter.

16 In the **file list**, double-click your **Windows 7 Chapter 4** folder to open it. Click in the **File name** box, and then replace the selected text by typing **Lastname_Firstname_4A_Desktop_Snip** Be sure the file type is **JPEG file**, and then press Enter. **Close** [close] the **Snipping Tool** mark-up window. Hold this file until you finish Project 4A, and then submit this file as directed by your instructor.

17 Point anywhere on the desktop, right-click, and then click **Personalize**. Under **Aero Themes**, click **Windows 7**, and then compare your screen with Figure 4.7.

Aero refers to the desktop experience that features a translucent glass design for windows, attractive graphics, taskbar previews of open windows, and the Aero features you practiced in Chapter 1 such as Snap and Aero Peek.

Figure 4.7

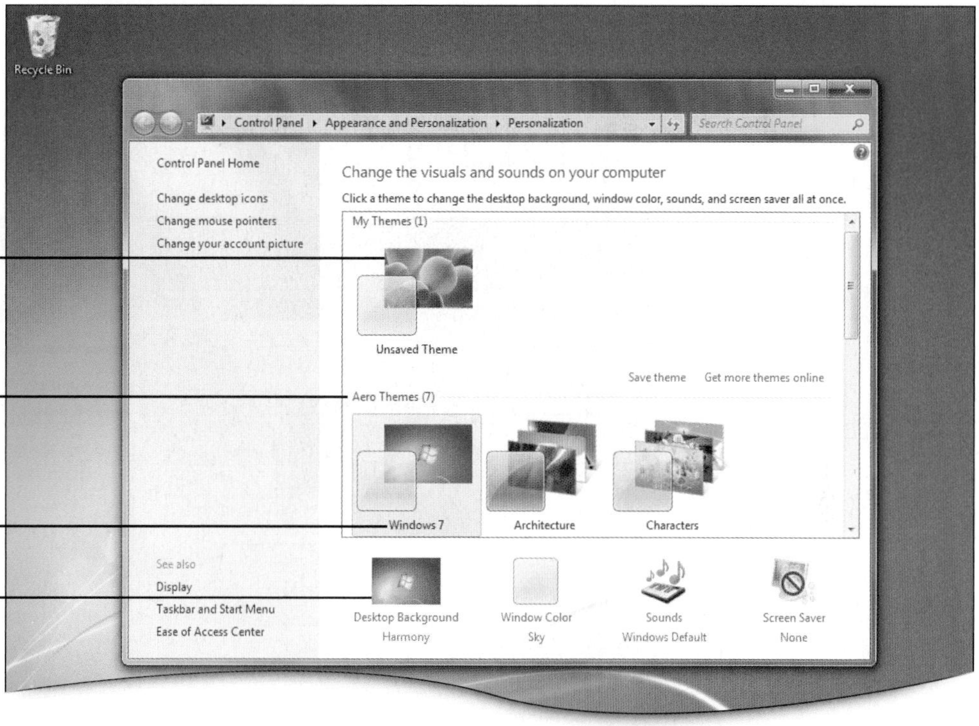

18 Under **My Themes**, point to the **Unsaved Theme** and right-click, and then click **Delete theme**. Click **Yes**.

On your own computer, experiment and create as many themes as you want.

19 **Close** the **Personalization** window.

> **More Knowledge | Storing Personal Photos to the Picture Location**
>
> In the manner that you practiced in this activity, you can click Browse and navigate to any personal photo you have stored in your personal folders or on a removable device, and then use it as your desktop background. If you would like to have your personal photos available immediately when you click Pictures from the Picture location arrow, store them in the Pictures subfolder of your personal folder. Recall that your personal folder is the folder created for your user account name, and contains subfolders for Documents, Pictures, Music, and so on.

Activity 4.02 | Personalizing the Screen Saver

Using a screen saver is a way to personalize your computer, keep others from viewing your screen when it is inactive, and enhance security by offering password protection.

1 Right-click on the desktop, and then click **Personalize**. In the displayed **Personalization** window, in the lower right corner, click **Screen Saver**.

The Screen Saver Settings dialog box displays. In the default Windows Aero theme, no screen saver is selected.

2 Click the **Screen saver arrow**, in the displayed list, click **Ribbons**, and then compare your screen with Figure 4.8.

Alert! | If the small screen displays a message

If the small screen indicates *This screen saver can't run because it requires a newer video card*, skip this step and move to Step 3.

You can view the screen savers that come with Windows 7 in this manner, and if you want to use one, select it by clicking OK. Or, click the Preview button to preview the full-screen view of the screen saver; move the mouse to cancel the full-screen preview and redisplay the dialog box.

Figure 4.8

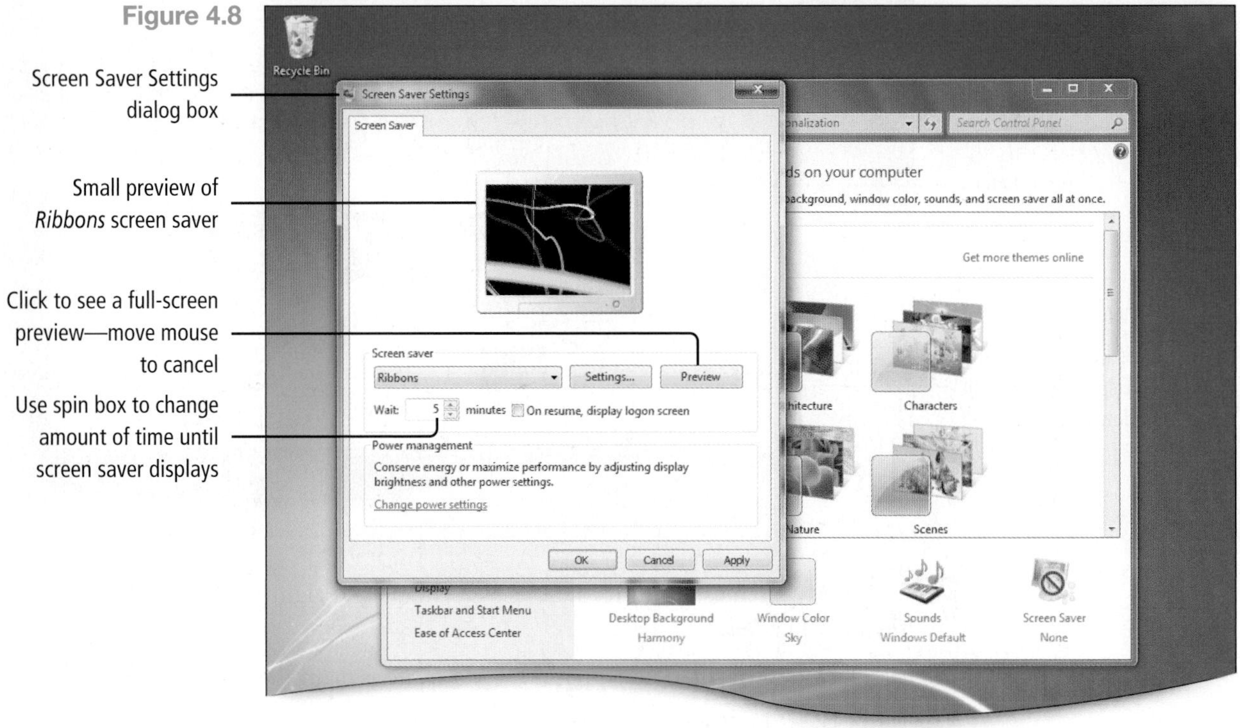

Note | A screen saver is not required

If you do not want a screen saver, but instead prefer that your screen is always displayed, in the Screen Saver Settings dialog box, click the Screen saver arrow, and then in the displayed list, click (None).

3 Click the **Screen saver arrow** again, and then in the displayed list, click **Photos.**

Use this screen saver to personalize your computer with one or more of your own photos. If no other pictures have been selected on the computer at which you are working, the default photos are those that come with Windows 7 in the Sample Pictures folder in the Pictures library.

4 In the center of the dialog box, click the **Settings** button.

The Photos Screen Saver Settings dialog box displays. Here you can select photos to use as your screen saver. Place the photos you want to use in a folder, and then browse for the folder by clicking the Browse button.

For more information about customizing your screen saver, you can click the **How do I customize my screen saver?** link in the lower left corner.

5 In the lower right corner, click **Cancel** to redisplay the **Screen Saver Settings** dialog box. Locate, but do *not* select, the check box next to **On resume, display logon screen**.

On your own computer, you might decide to select this check box to add additional security to your computer. By enabling this feature, you will be required to type your user password to cancel the screen saver display and continue using your computer. As soon as you move the mouse or press a key, the screen saver will close, and the log on screen will display requesting your password.

6 At the bottom of the **Screen Saver Settings** dialog box, click **Cancel** to close the dialog box without making any changes to the existing screen saver. **Close** the **Personalization** window.

> **More Knowledge | Downloading Screen Savers**
>
> Screen savers are available on the Internet for download. When you search for the term *screen savers*, you will find many to choose from. For example, you can search for *golf screen saver* to find screen savers with a golf theme. Only download screen savers from a trusted source. Screen savers have the potential to contain malicious software or ***spyware***. Spyware is software that sends information about your Web surfing habits to a Web site without your knowledge.

Objective 2 | Personalize the Start Menu

The ***Start menu*** is a list of choices that provides access to your computer's programs, folders, and settings. In Windows 7, you have control over the programs and files that appear there. Organize and customize the Start menu so that it is easy to find the programs, folders, and features that you use frequently.

You have already practiced many of the common tasks for which the Start menu is useful, for example to:

- Start programs
- Open commonly used folders
- Search in the search box for files, folders, and programs
- Adjust computer settings from the Control Panel
- Access the Windows 7 Help system
- Turn off your computer
- Log off from Windows or switch to a different user account

Activity 4.03 | Personalizing the Start Menu

1 In the lower left of your keyboard, press [Windows key]—this is the keyboard method to display the Start menu. Take a moment to review the main parts of the default Start menu by comparing your screen with Figure 4.9.

On the left, the ***programs list*** displays recently used programs on the bottom, programs that you have pinned to the Start menu at the top, and a button to display all the programs on your computer. On the right, ***common folders and features*** provide quick access to the folders and features you use most often.

At the lower left, you can type in the ***search box*** to search your entire computer for files, folders, e-mail messages, or programs. At the lower right, the ***Shut down button*** displays a menu for switching users, logging off, restarting, or shutting down.

Figure 4.9

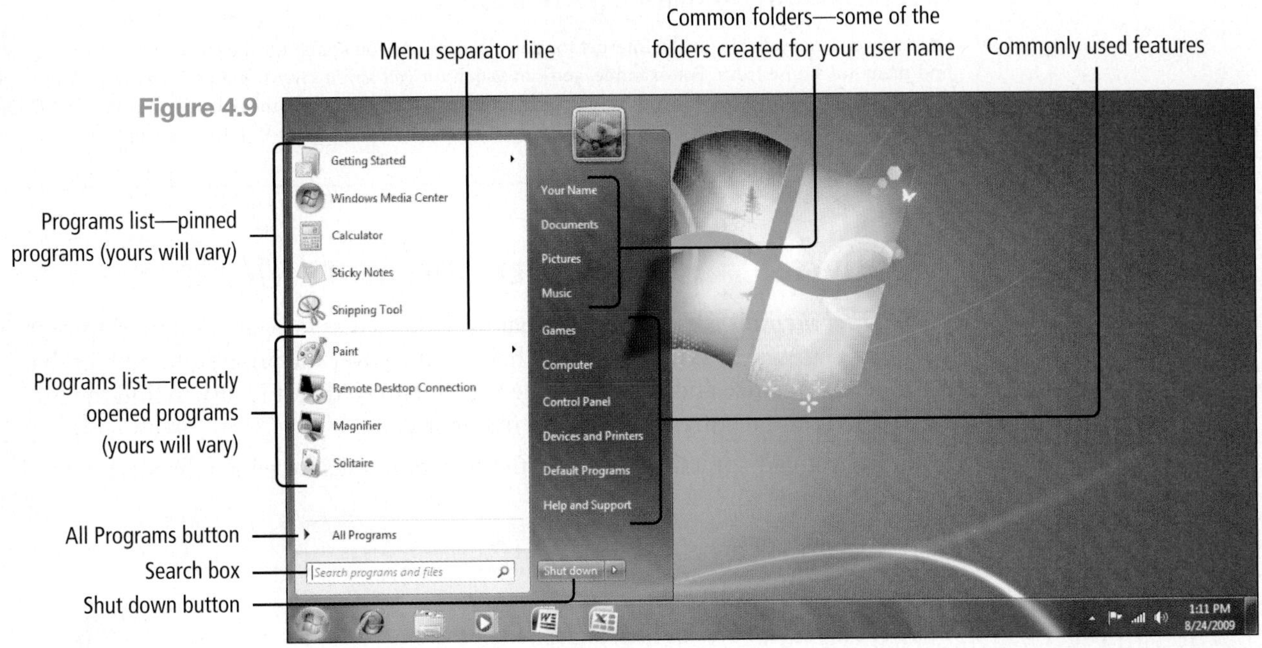

> **Note | The Recently Used Programs Area on a New Computer**
>
> On a new computer, the lower left portion of the Start menu might display programs that your computer manufacturer wants you to see and possibly purchase. As you begin to use your own programs, the list will display your recently opened programs.

2 On the displayed **Start menu**, click **All Programs**, and then click **Accessories**. Point to the **Notepad** program, right-click, and then click **Pin to Start Menu**. Click on the desktop to close the Start menu, and then display the **Start menu** again. Compare your screen with Figure 4.10.

The Notepad program is pinned to the Start menu and will remain there until you unpin it. All programs above the menu separator line are pinned programs. Recall that you practiced this technique previously by pinning Snipping Tool to the Start menu. If you use a program frequently, pin it to the Start menu so it is always readily available. For programs that you use every day, pin them to the taskbar.

Figure 4.10

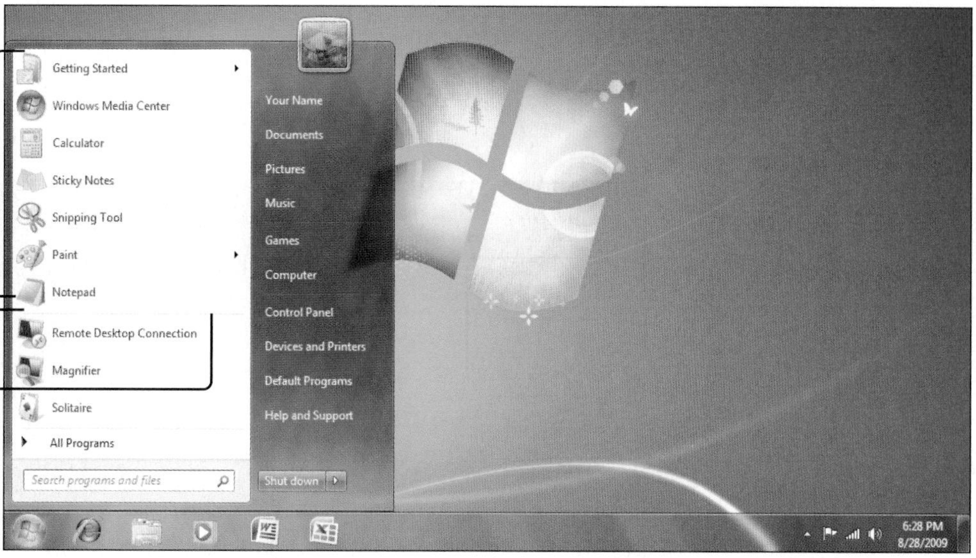

3 In the **Pinned programs area**, right-click **Notepad**, and then click **Unpin from Start Menu**.

4 Point to the **Start** button, and then right-click. On the displayed shortcut menu, click **Properties**. Compare your screen with Figure 4.11.

The Taskbar and Start Menu Properties dialog box displays. Here you can customize the appearance of your Start menu.

Figure 4.11

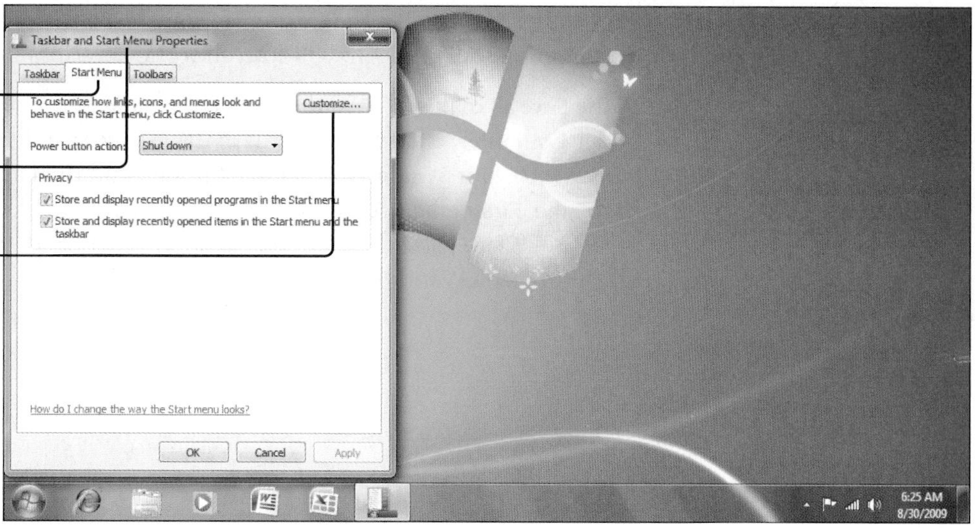

Another Way

To display this dialog box, on the desktop, right-click, click Personalize, and then in the lower left corner of the Personalization window, under See also, click Taskbar and Start Menu. Or, display the Control Panel, click Appearance and Personalization, and then click Taskbar and Start Menu.

5 On the **Start Menu tab**, click the **Customize** button. In this alphabetical list, under **Control Panel**, click the **Display as a menu** option button. Compare your screen with Figure 4.12.

On this list, you can customize how links, icons, and menus look and behave on your Start menu.

For items that have only a check box, for example *Devices and Printers*, removing the check mark—referred to as *clearing the check box*—removes the command from your Start menu. Other items have option buttons, for example *Computer*, which you can choose to determine if the item displays as a link that opens in a window, displays as a menu listing, or does not display on the Start menu at all.

Figure 4.12

6 **Start** the **Snipping Tool** program, click the **New arrow**, and then click **Window Snip**. Point anywhere in the **Customize Start Menu** dialog box, and click one time. In the **Snipping Tool** mark-up window, click the **Save Snip** button.

7 In the **Save As** dialog box, in the **navigation pane**, scroll down as necessary, and then under **Computer**, click your USB flash drive so that it displays in the **address bar**. Navigate to your **Windows 7 Chapter 4** folder, and then as the file name, type **Lastname_Firstname_4A_Customize_Snip** Be sure the file type is **JPEG file**, and then press Enter. **Close** the **Snipping Tool** mark-up window. Hold this file until you finish Project 4A, and then submit this file as directed by your instructor.

8 Click **OK** two times. Display the **Start menu**, and then notice that to the right of **Control Panel**, an arrow indicating a submenu displays. Point to **Control Panel**, and then compare your screen with Figure 4.13.

A menu of Control Panel features and commands displays.

From this submenu, you can click a menu item to move directly to the Control Panel area instead of displaying the Control Panel window and locating the item by clicking through various levels of commands.

Figure 4.13

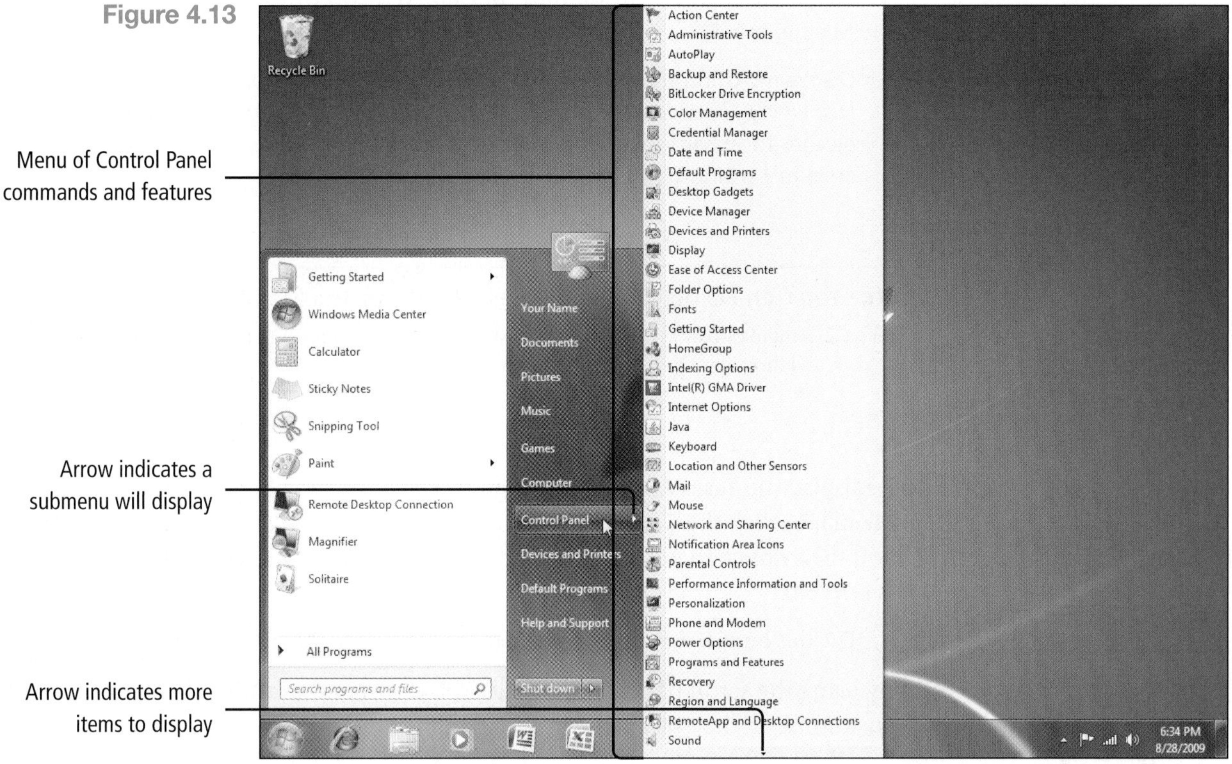

9 At the bottom of the menu, point to the **arrow** and notice that the menu scrolls to display more items. At the top of the menu, point to the **arrow** to scroll in the opposite direction. In the displayed list, click **Power Options**.

If you use the commands on the Control Panel frequently, for example if you manage a small network, you may find it easier to change the Start menu in this manner.

10 **Close** the **Power Options** window. Right-click the **Start** button, and then display the **Taskbar and Start Menu Properties** dialog box again. On the **Start Menu tab**, click the **Customize** button. Under **Control Panel**, click the **Display as a link** option button to return your Start menu to the default setting.

To remove an item from the Start menu completely, you can click the *Don't display this item* option button.

11 In the **Customize Start Menu** dialog box, at the top of the list under **Computer**, click the **Display as a menu** option button. Click **OK** two times to apply this change, display the **Start menu**, and then point to **Computer**.

Displaying Computer as a menu is probably not as useful as displaying it as a link. Displaying an item as a link opens the item in Windows Explorer, where you have more options for navigating. Thus, most of the defaults are set as links, which means the items open in a window, rather than display as a menu.

Note | You Can Display Items Both as a Link and as a Menu

If you set an item to display as a menu, you can still open it in a window. On the Start menu, point to the item, right-click, and then click Open.

12 Redisplay the **Taskbar and Start Menu Properties** dialog box, and then on the **Start Menu tab**, click the **Customize** button. In the lower left, click **Use Default Settings**, and then notice that under **Computer**, the default **Display as a link** option button is selected.

Use this button to return the Start menu settings to the default settings.

13 By using the scroll bar on the right, scroll down and examine the items that you can customize on the **Start menu.**

14 Position the scroll box approximately in the middle of the scroll bar, and then locate the check box for **Highlight newly installed programs.**

You can control some Start menu *behaviors* in this dialog box. For example, the first time you display the Start menu after installing a new program on your computer, the All Programs button on the Start menu is highlighted, and the program name is highlighted on the list of programs. This feature is controlled here. Because it is a helpful feature, you probably will choose to leave this feature enabled.

15 In the lower portion of the dialog box, locate the **spin box** under **Start menu size**, and then compare your screen with Figure 4.14.

By clicking the arrows in this spin box, you can increase or decrease the number of recently used programs on your Start menu.

If you like to have a large number of *pinned* programs, you might consider decreasing this number to enlarge the space available for pinned programs.

Here you can also control the number of recent items to display in Jump Lists, which are also available on the Start Menu.

Figure 4.14

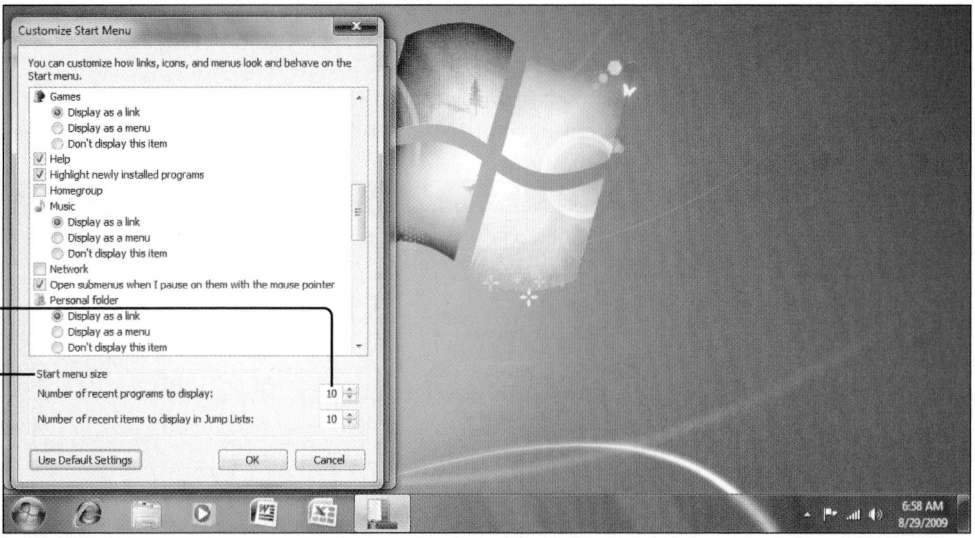

16 In the list of Start menu items that you can change, scroll to the end of the list and notice the **Use large icons** check box.

Windows 7 uses large icons on the Start menu by default, but if you have a large number of programs and want more programs to display on your Start menu, clear this check box to display smaller icons.

17 Click the **Use Default Settings** button to return any settings you may have changed on the Start menu to the default settings. Click **OK** two times to close both dialog boxes.

Activity 4.04 | Displaying Jump Lists from the Start Menu

The Jump Lists that you have displayed from programs open on the taskbar and pinned to the taskbar can also be displayed from programs you have pinned to the Start Menu. You can pin a program to both the Start Menu and the taskbar, and you will always see the same items in your Jump List for a program, regardless of whether you are viewing it on the Start menu or on the taskbar. For example, if you pin a file to a program's Jump List on the taskbar, the item also displays in that program's Jump List on the Start menu.

Another Way

On the Start menu, click All Programs, click the Microsoft Office folder, and then point to Microsoft PowerPoint and right-click.

1 Click the **Start** button, and then in the **Search** box, type **PowerPoint** On the displayed list, point to the **PowerPoint** program and right-click. Compare your screen with Figure 4.15.

Figure 4.15

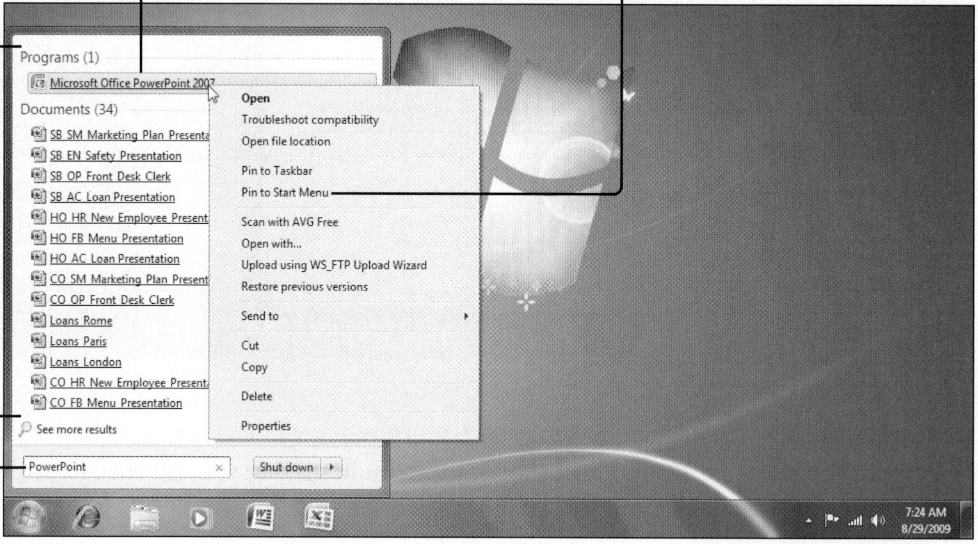

2 On the displayed shortcut menu, click **Pin to Start Menu.** Click anywhere on the desktop to close the **Start** menu.

3 On the taskbar, click the **Windows Explorer** button, and then navigate to **Documents ▶ Bell_Orchid ▶ Corporate ▶ Operations.** Double-click the PowerPoint file **CO_OP_Front_Desk_Clerk** to open the file in PowerPoint.

The Front Desk Staff Training Presentation displays in the PowerPoint program.

4 In the upper right corner, click the **Close** button to close the PowerPoint file. **Close** the **Operations** folder window.

5 Click the **Start** button, point to your pinned **PowerPoint** program, and then compare your screen with Figure 4.16.

The arrow to the right of a program pinned to the Start menu indicates that a Jump List of recently opened files will display.

Figure 4.16

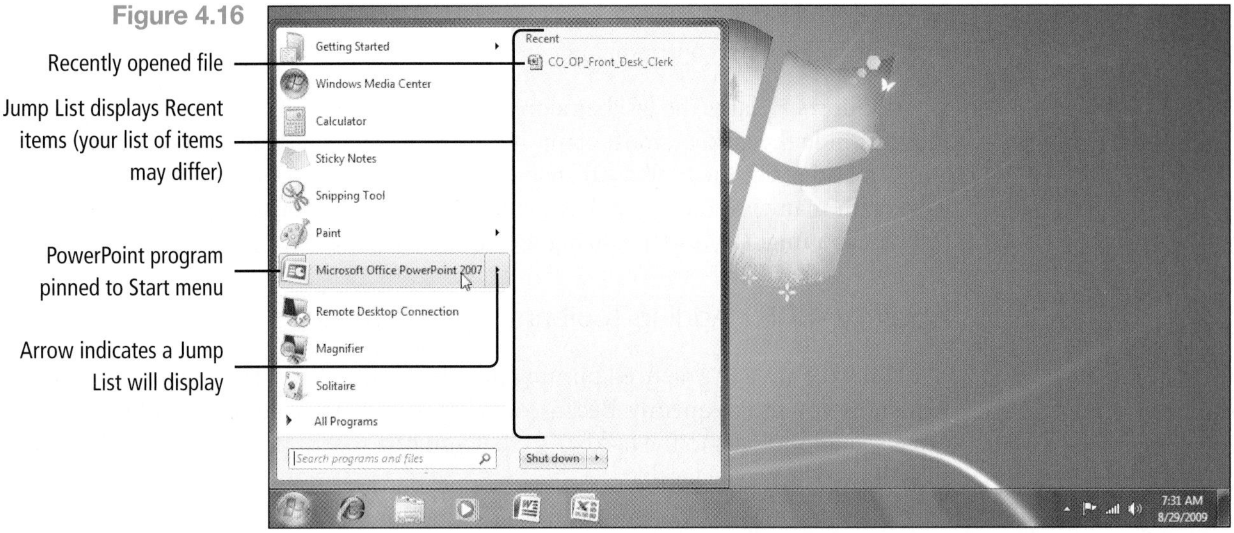

6 From the **Start** menu, drag the **PowerPoint icon** to an empty area on the taskbar, and then when the ScreenTip *Pin to Taskbar* displays, release the mouse button.

7 On the taskbar, point to the **PowerPoint** icon you just pinned, right-click to display the **Jump List**, and then compare your screen with Figure 4.17.

The file you just opened, CO_OP_Front_Desk_Clerk, displays under **Recent**. Recall that recent and pinned items on a Jump List will display regardless of whether you are viewing the Jump List from the program pinned to the Start menu or to the taskbar.

Figure 4.17

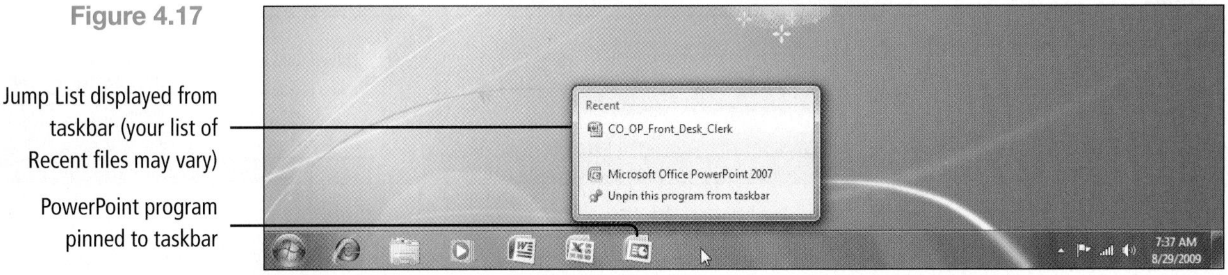

8 On the **Jump List**, click **Unpin this program from taskbar.**

9 Display the **Start** menu, right-click the **PowerPoint** icon, and then click **Unpin from Start Menu**. Click anywhere on the desktop to close the Start menu.

Objective 3 | Personalize the Taskbar

Recall that the ***taskbar*** contains the Start button and a button for all open programs. A program that has multiple windows open will display multiple overlapping program buttons on the taskbar. The important uses of the taskbar are to:

- Keep track of your windows
- Minimize and restore windows
- See previews of your open windows

Windows 7 places the taskbar along the lower edge of the desktop. Although you can move or hide the taskbar, most computer users leave the taskbar in its default location. You can also resize the toolbar to create additional space for buttons and toolbars. If you work with many programs regularly, and also like to add convenient toolbars to your taskbar, you might consider resizing the taskbar to view more items.

Activity 4.05 | Adding Toolbars to the Taskbar

You have already practiced pinning program buttons to the taskbar for the programs you know you use frequently. Because driving your work from the taskbar is efficient, you can also add toolbars to the taskbar so that you can access specific folders, files, or Internet sites directly from the taskbar.

Take advantage of toolbars to further reduce the time it takes to find files and folders and sites that you use frequently.

1 **Close** any open windows to display your desktop. Point to an empty area of your taskbar and right-click, point to **Toolbars**, and then compare your screen with Figure 4.18.

The toolbars shown in Figure 4.18 are included with Windows 7—others might display on your list.

Figure 4.18

2 In the displayed list of available toolbars, click **Address**. Compare your screen with Figure 4.19.

The Address toolbar provides a space to enter an Internet address or the name and path of a program, document, or folder.

Figure 4.19

3 Be sure your system is connected to the Internet, click in the **Address** box on the taskbar, type **www.bls.gov** and press Enter to display the Web site for the **U.S. Bureau of Labor Statistics**.

4 Point to an empty area of the taskbar, right-click, point to **Toolbars**, and then click **Links**. At the top of your screen, in the Web site's address in your Internet browser software, locate the Web page's icon—a blue and red star. Drag the Web page icon onto the **Links** toolbar, as shown in Figure 4.20, and release the mouse button when you see the text *Create link in Favorites bar.*

This action not only places the link on the Links toolbar on your taskbar, but also places the link on the Favorites bar in Internet Explorer. Thus, if you choose to have the Links toolbar on your taskbar, any links you add to the Favorites toolbar in Internet Explorer will also be accessible directly from your taskbar.

Figure 4.20

5 At the top of the **Internet Explorer** window, under the **address bar**, notice that the link to the U.S. Bureau of Labor Statistics displays on the **Favorites bar**. On the taskbar, to the right of **Links**, click the **double chevrons** >> to display a shortcut menu containing the link to U.S. Bureau of Labor Statistics. Compare your screen with Figure 4.21.

Figure 4.21

6 **Start** the **Snipping Tool** program, click the **New arrow**, and then click **Full-screen Snip**. In the **Snipping Tool** mark-up window, click the **Save Snip** button. In the displayed **Save As** dialog box, if necessary navigate to your **Windows 7 Chapter 4** folder on your USB flash drive and click to select it so that it displays in the address bar.

7 Click in the **File name** box, and then using your own name, type **Lastname_Firstname_4A_Links_Snip** Be sure the file type is **JPEG file**, and then press Enter. **Close** the **Snipping Tool** mark-up window. Hold this file until you finish Project 4A, and then submit this file as directed by your instructor.

8 On the taskbar, to the right of the word *Links*, click the **double chevrons** >>. In the displayed list, right-click **U.S. Bureau of Labor Statistics**, and then click **Delete** to remove the link from the list. Click **Yes** in the displayed dialog box.

The link is removed from both your Links toolbar and the Favorites bar in Internet Explorer.

9 **Close** the **U.S. Bureau of Labor Statistics** Web site and close Internet Explorer. Click in an open area of the taskbar, right-click, point to **Toolbars**, and then click the **Address** toolbar to remove it from the taskbar. Use the same technique to remove the **Links** toolbar from the taskbar.

You can see that it is easy to add and remove toolbars to the taskbar. Consider using such toolbars either permanently or on a short-term basis, for example when you are working on a project that requires visiting specific Web sites repeatedly.

10 Right-click the taskbar, point to **Toolbars** to display the list of available toolbars, and then notice the **Desktop** and **Tablet PC Input Panel** toolbars.

The Desktop toolbar provides copies of all the icons currently on your desktop and access to your computer's resources. Some computer users add this toolbar. However, recall that it is better not to clutter your desktop with icons and files, but rather to pin frequently used programs to your taskbar and use the toolbars to access frequently used folders.

If you have a tablet PC, you can use the Tablet PC Input Panel to enter text by using a tablet pen. It includes a writing pad and a character pad to convert handwriting into typed text, and an on-screen keyboard to enter individual characters.

11 On the list of available toolbars, click **New toolbar**. In the **New Toolbar – Choose a folder** dialog box, navigate to **Libraries ▶ Documents ▶ Bell_Orchid.** In the lower right corner, click the **Select Folder** button. Compare your screen with Figure 4.22.

Any folder on your system can become a toolbar, including a Windows system folder such as Control Panel. The folder's name displays on the taskbar, and by clicking the double chevrons, each item in the folder becomes accessible. Then by pointing to submenus, you can navigate within each folder.

Figure 4.22

Toolbar created from Bell_Orchid folder

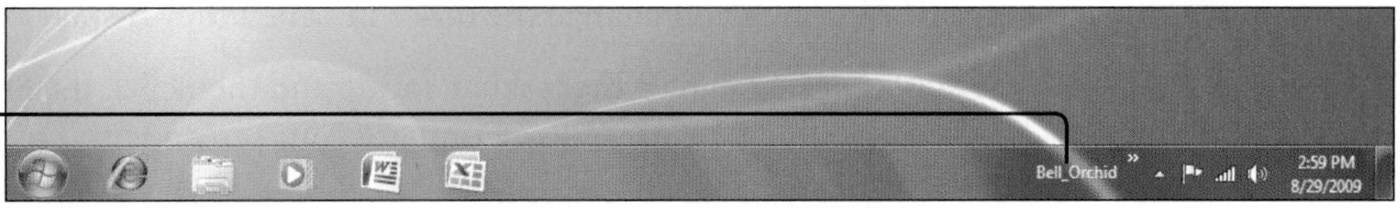

12 On the taskbar, to the right of **Bell_Orchid**, click the **double chevrons** >>. On the displayed menu, *point* to **Corporate**, and then *point* to **Information_Technology**. Compare your screen with Figure 4.23.

Consider using a toolbar like this for quick browsable access to the contents of a folder, especially if it is a folder that you access frequently.

Figure 4.23

Bell_Orchid folder and subfolders displayed for quick browsable access

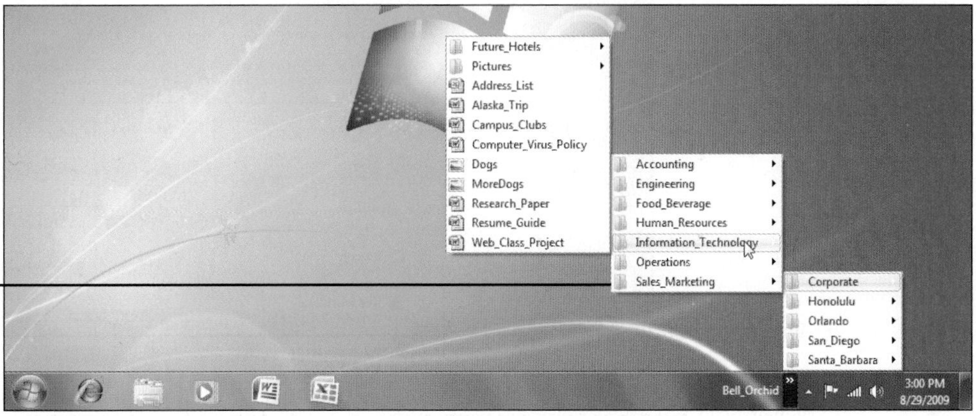

13 Right-click in an empty area of the taskbar, point to **Toolbars**, and then click the **Bell_Orchid** toolbar to remove it from the taskbar.

Enable the toolbars that are convenient for you when it makes sense to do so, and remove them when they are no longer useful. With your new knowledge about these convenient features, you can personalize your computer whenever it suits your needs.

Activity 4.06 | Controlling the Display of Icons in the Notification Area

Recall that the *notification area*—also referred to as the *system tray* or the *status area*—at the right end of your taskbar contains program icons and notifications. A *notification*, which is a small pop-up window providing information about status, progress, and the detection of new devices, might display from time to time. For example, notifications about things like incoming e-mail, updates, and network connectivity display here.

The *Action Center* lists important messages about security and maintenance settings on your computer that need your attention. It is a central place to view alerts and take actions, for example to view and install updates.

Some programs, upon installation, have an icon that you can add to the notification area if you want to do so. You can choose which icons and notifications display in the notification area and change the order in which they display.

1 At the right end of the taskbar, locate and then click the **Show hidden icons** arrow ▲, and then click **Customize**. Compare your screen with Figure 4.24.

Here you can select which icons and notifications display on the taskbar. By default, both icons and notifications display for Action Center, Network, and Volume.

For other installed programs that include a system tray icon, for example security software such as AVG as shown in this Figure, you can decide how you want the program to behave in the notification area.

Figure 4.24

List of Icons and Behaviors
(yours may vary)

Volume icon

Network icon

Action Center icon

Show hidden icons arrow

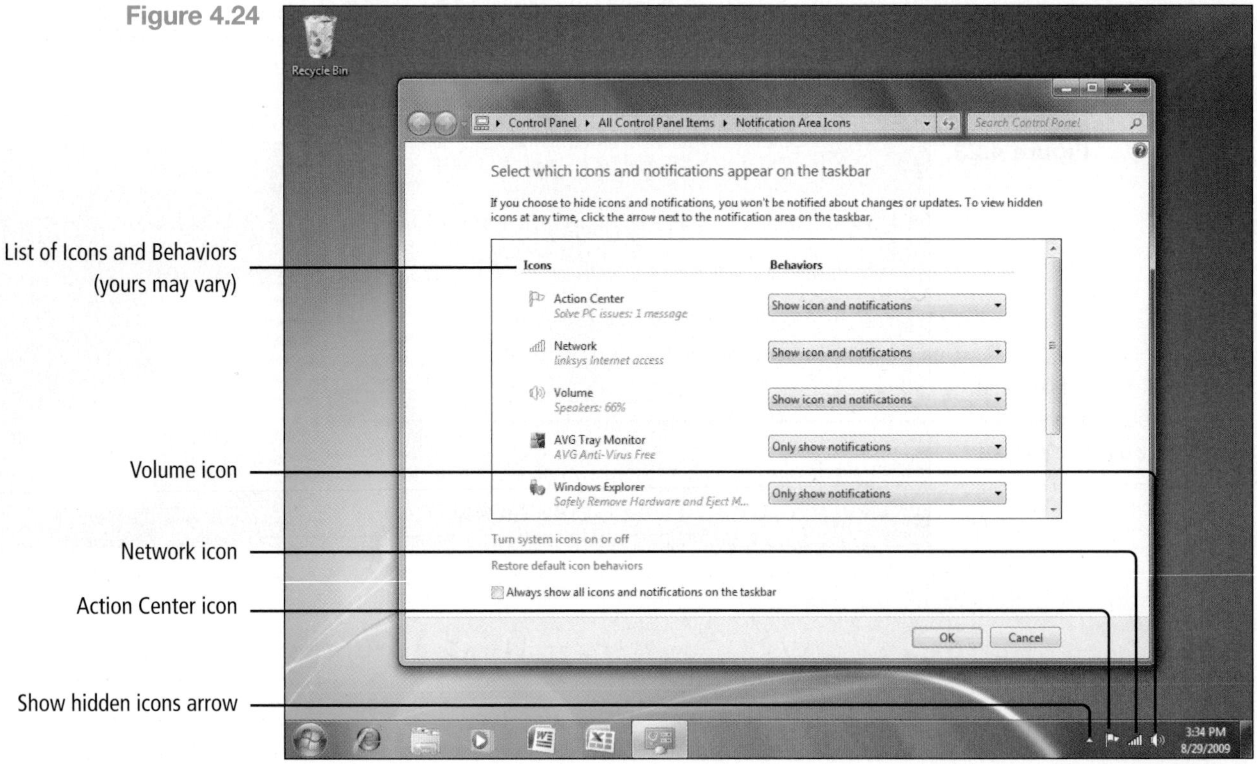

2 In the **Notification Area Icons** window, to the right of **Action Center**, click the arrow, and then compare your screen with Figure 4.25.

Here, for each available icon, you can choose to see both the icon and notifications, to see only the notifications, or to hide both the icon and the notifications.

Figure 4.25

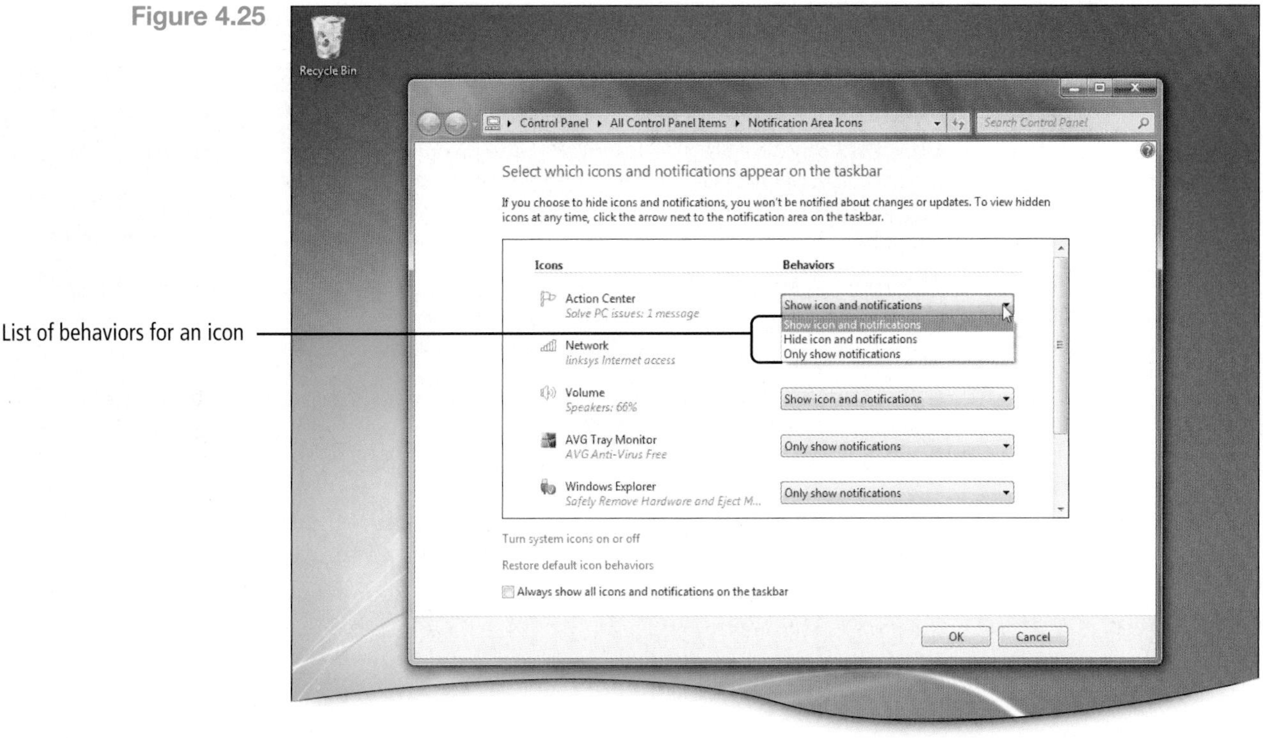

3 Click the arrow again to close the list, and then at the bottom of the **Notification Area Icons** window, click **Turn system icons on or off**.

Here you can control the behavior of the system icons if you want to make any changes.

4 **Close** the **System Icons** window.

5 On the taskbar, click the **Action Center** icon, and then click **Open Action Center**.

Here you can attend to any messages or notifications that display.

6 **Close** the **Action Center** window.

Objective 4 | Personalize the Desktop by Adding Gadgets

A ***gadget***, also referred to as a ***desktop gadget***, is a mini-program that offers information and provides easy access to tools that you use frequently. A gadget can display continuously updated information and enable you to perform common tasks without opening a window.

For example, you can install gadgets that display regularly updated weather forecasts, news headlines, traffic maps, Internet radio streams, or a picture slide show of your favorite photos. Gadgets can also integrate with your programs. For example, you can display a list of all your online instant messaging contacts and view who is online, or display the Day view from your Outlook calendar.

Activity 4.07 | Adding Gadgets to Your Desktop

1 **Close** any open windows. Right-click anywhere on the desktop, and then click **Gadgets**. Point to the **Clock** gadget, right-click, and then compare your screen with Figure 4.26.

Figure 4.26

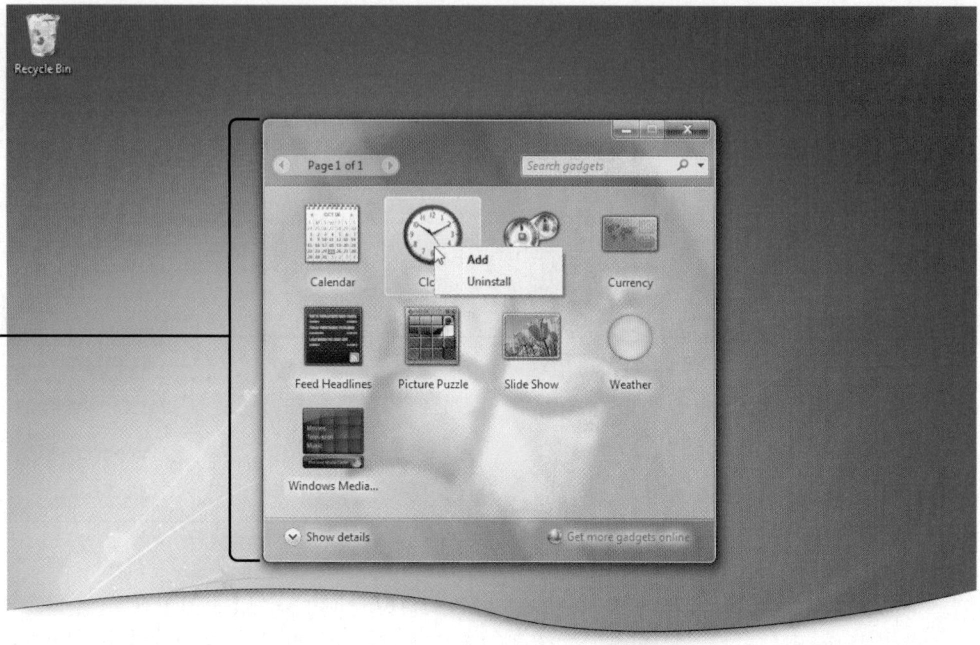

Default gadgets (your list may vary)

Another Way
Double-click a gadget to add it to the desktop.

2 On the shortcut menu, click **Add**, and notice that the clock displays in the upper right corner of your desktop. Using the same technique, add the **Weather** gadget and the **Slide Show** gadget. Compare your screen with Figure 4.27.

Figure 4.27

Three gadgets display (your desktop may differ if you have already added gadgets)

Clock gadget

Weather gadget

Slide Show gadget (your pictures will vary)

3 **Close** [icon] the **Gadgets** window. Point to the **Weather** gadget to display a small toolbar to the right, and then right-click to display a shortcut menu. Click **Options**.

4 In the **Search** box, type **Boston** and then click the **Search** button [icon]. On the displayed list, click **Boston, Massachusetts**, and notice that at the top of the window, your new locations displays. Compare your screen with Figure 4.28.

Figure 4.28

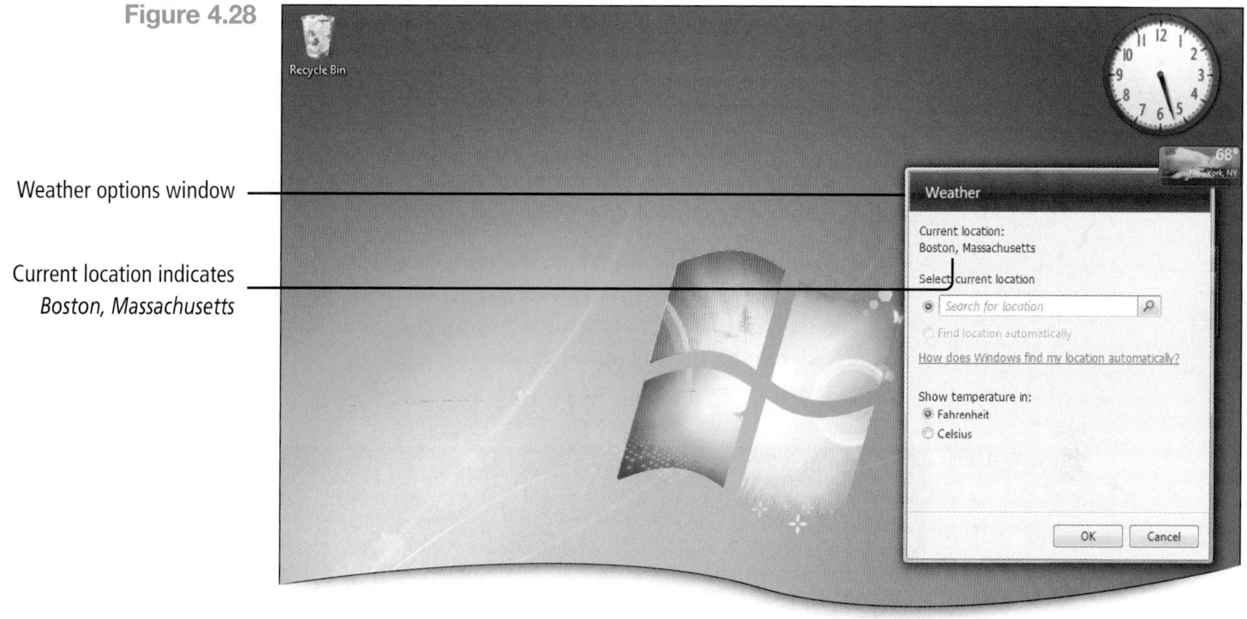

5 Click **OK** and notice the information in the **Weather** gadget, which displays the current temperature in Boston.

> **Note** | You Can Have More Than One Gadget of the Same Type
>
> You can have duplicates of the same gadget. For example, if you want to monitor weather in multiple locations, you can add multiple weather gadgets.

6 Point to the **Clock** gadget and right-click.

Here you can choose to always display the gadget on top of open windows, engage the Move pointer to move the gadget to another location, close (remove) the gadget, and set the Opacity.

7 Point to **Opacity**, and then click **60%**. Notice that the gadget dims. Point to the **Clock** gadget and notice that it displays with no transparency.

In this manner, you can make a gadget less prominent.

8 **Start** [icon] the **Snipping Tool** program, click the **New arrow**, and then click **Full-screen Snip**. In the **Snipping Tool** mark-up window, click the **Save Snip** button [icon]. In the displayed **Save As** dialog box, if necessary navigate to your **Windows 7 Chapter 4** folder on your USB flash drive and click to select it so that it displays in the address bar.

9 Click in the **File name** box, and then using your own name, type **Lastname_Firstname_4A_Gadgets_Snip** Be sure the file type is **JPEG file**, and then press Enter. **Close** [Close button] the **Snipping Tool** mark-up window. Hold this file until you finish Project 4A, and then submit this file as directed by your instructor.

10 Click on the **Slide Show** gadget, and notice that in addition to the toolbar, some controls display directly on the gadget. Point to each control to view its ScreenTip.

The controls on the Slide Show enable you to view the *Previous* picture, *Pause* on the current picture, move to the *Next* picture, or to *View* an enlargement of the picture on your screen.

11 Try out the controls, and when you are finished, on the small toolbar, click the **Options** button [Options button] for the **Slide Show** gadget. In the displayed **Slide Show** dialog box, to the right of the **Folder arrow**, click the **Browse** button [Browse button], and then compare your screen with Figure 4.29.

By default, Slide Show displays items in the Sample Pictures folder that comes with Windows 7. You may want to create a selection of pictures of your own to display here. To do so, create a folder of pictures on your computer, and then browse for and select the folder in this dialog box.

Figure 4.29

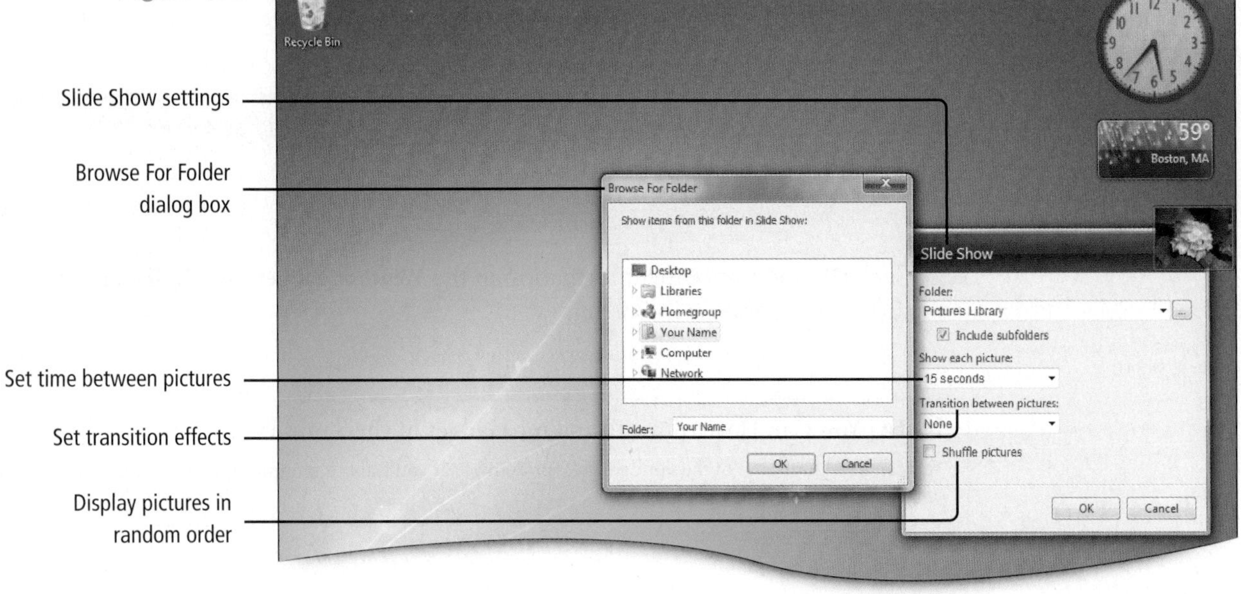

12 In the **Browse For Folder** window, click **Cancel**. Notice the **Show each picture** arrow and the **Transition between pictures** arrow.

If you have browsed and selected your folder of personal photos, you can use these options to set the time between the display of each picture and the transition effect to use when a new picture displays. The transition effects are similar to the slide transition effects in PowerPoint.

Here you can also choose to shuffle the pictures so that they display in random order.

13 Click **Cancel** to close the **Slide Show** dialog box. Right-click on the desktop, click **Gadgets**, and then in the lower right corner of the window, click **Get more gadgets online**. Scroll down as necessary to display the section for **Desktop gadgets**.

If you are connected to the Internet, the Microsoft site *Personalization Gallery* displays. Explore this site to find many other useful and entertaining gadgets to display on your desktop. Be aware that the arrangement of this site changes periodically.

14 **Close** [X] the Microsoft Web site. Point to the **Weather** gadget, and in the upper right corner, click the white **X** to close and remove the gadget from the desktop. Right-click the **Clock** gadget, and then click **Close gadget**. Use either technique to close the **Slide Show** gadget.

If you install a new gadget, for example from the Microsoft site, it will display in the Gadgets window. Removing a gadget from the desktop does not uninstall it—it will remain available in the Gadgets window.

15 **Close** [X] the Gadgets window.

More Knowledge | How does the Feed Headlines gadget work?

Feeds, also known as ***RSS*** feeds, XML feeds, syndicated content, or Web feeds, contain frequently updated content published by a Web site. RSS is an acronym for ***Really Simple Syndication***, and is a syndication format popular for collecting updates to blogs and news sites. A syndication format is a publishing format that lets you view headlines of the latest updates from your favorite blogs and Web sites all from within a single newsreader program.

By default, the Feed Headlines gadget will not display any headlines, but you can get started by clicking *View headlines* on the gadget.

To choose a feed from the Web, first display a Web page that has feeds, for example *www.microsoft.com/rss* and then click the square orange Feeds button. On the displayed Web page, click Subscribe to this feed, and then depending on the site, click Subscribe (or Subscribe to this feed, which might display a second time). If an Internet Explorer dialog box displays, click Subscribe. The feed should now be available to the Feed Headlines gadget.

On the gadget, display Options. In the Display this feed list, click the feed to which you subscribed, and then close the dialog box.

Objective 5 | Personalize the Ease of Access Center and Use the Problem Steps Recorder

The ***Ease of Access Center*** is a centralized location for accessibility settings and programs that can make your computer easier and more comfortable for you to use.

Activity 4.08 | Personalizing Settings in the Ease of Access Center

1 **Close** any open windows. From the **Start menu**, display **Control Panel**, at the lower right click **Ease of Access**, and then click **Ease of Access Center**. **Maximize** the window, and then compare your screen with Figure 4.30.

> **Alert! | Voice Commands Might be Audible**
>
> You might hear some voice commands if your speakers are enabled.

Figure 4.30

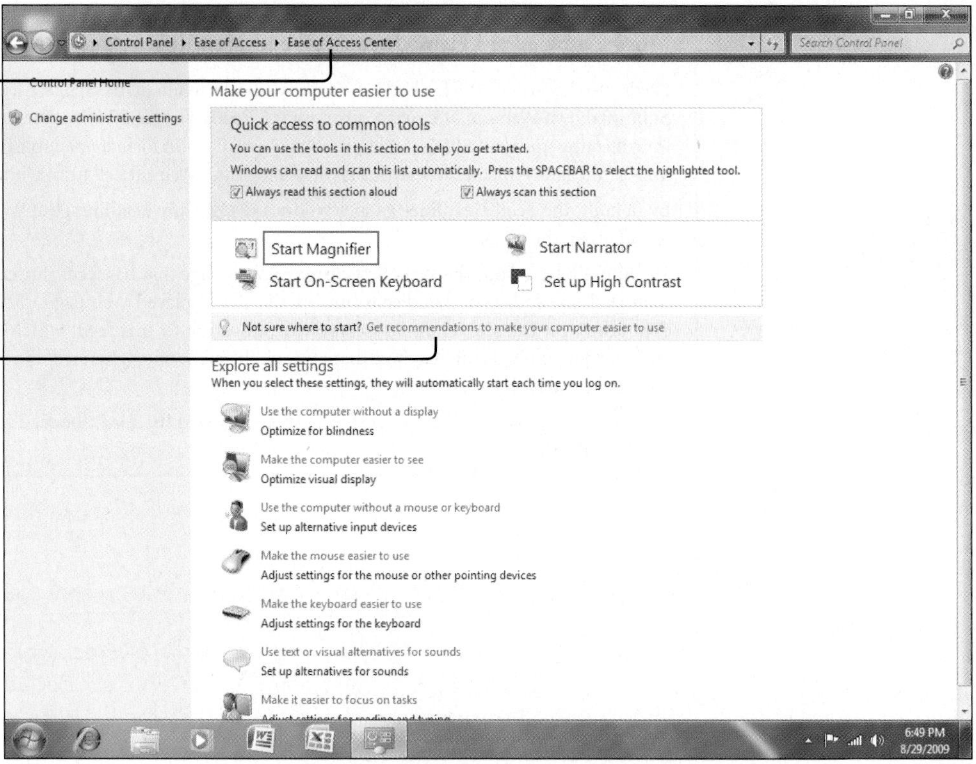

2 In the center of the screen, locate the yellow bar, and then click **Get recommendations to make your computer easier to use**.

If you are unsure what features might be useful to you, begin with this questionnaire to answer questions about how you interact with your computer in terms of your sight, dexterity, hearing, speech, and reasoning.

3 In the lower right corner, click **Cancel**. In the upper portion of the screen, click the **Start Magnifier** command.

Magnifier is a screen enlarger that magnifies a portion of the screen. This feature is helpful for computer users with impaired vision and for those who require occasional screen magnification for such tasks as editing art.

4 Move your mouse into each corner of your screen, and notice that the window is magnified. Then, point to the magnifying glass and click >>. Compare your screen with Figure 4.31.

Figure 4.31

Magnifier dialog box—screen magnified (your screen portion may differ)

Close button

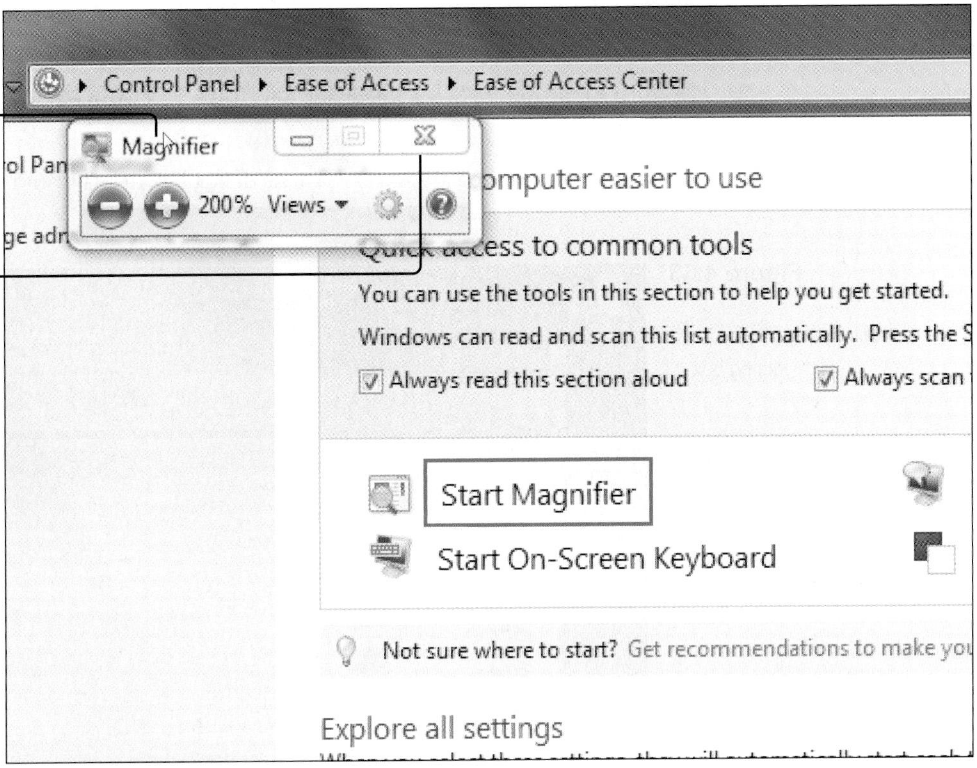

5 **Close** the **Magnifier** dialog box to turn off the **Magnifier**. In the upper right corner of the window, click the **Restore Down** button, and then **Close** the **Ease of Access Center**.

Use the Ease of Access Center as necessary to make your computer comfortable to use.

Activity 4.09 | Using the Problem Steps Recorder

The ***Problem Steps Recorder*** captures the steps you perform on your computer, including a text description of where you clicked and a picture of the screen during each click—referred to as a ***screenshot***. After you capture the steps, you can save them to a file, and then send them in an e-mail to your Help Desk or someone else who can help you with a computer problem. Conversely, if you are helping a friend, colleague, or family member with a computer problem, they can send a file to you so that you can view the steps they performed.

1 **Close** any open windows. Display the **Start menu**, and then type **problem steps** On the list of search results, click **Record steps to reproduce a problem**. Compare your screen with Figure 4.32.

Figure 4.32

Problem Steps Recorder window

2 Click **Start Record**. Click the **Start** button, in the **Search** box type **printer** and then on the list click **Add a printer**.

The steps you are performing are being recorded.

3 In the **Problem Steps Recorder** window, click **Add Comment**, and then in the **Highlight Problem and Comment** box, type **I'm not sure which one to choose.** Then click **OK**.

4 In the **Problem Steps Recorder** window, click **Stop Record**. Compare your screen with Figure 4.33.

The recording stops. The Save As dialog box displays, and the file type is set to ZIP Files.

Figure 4.33

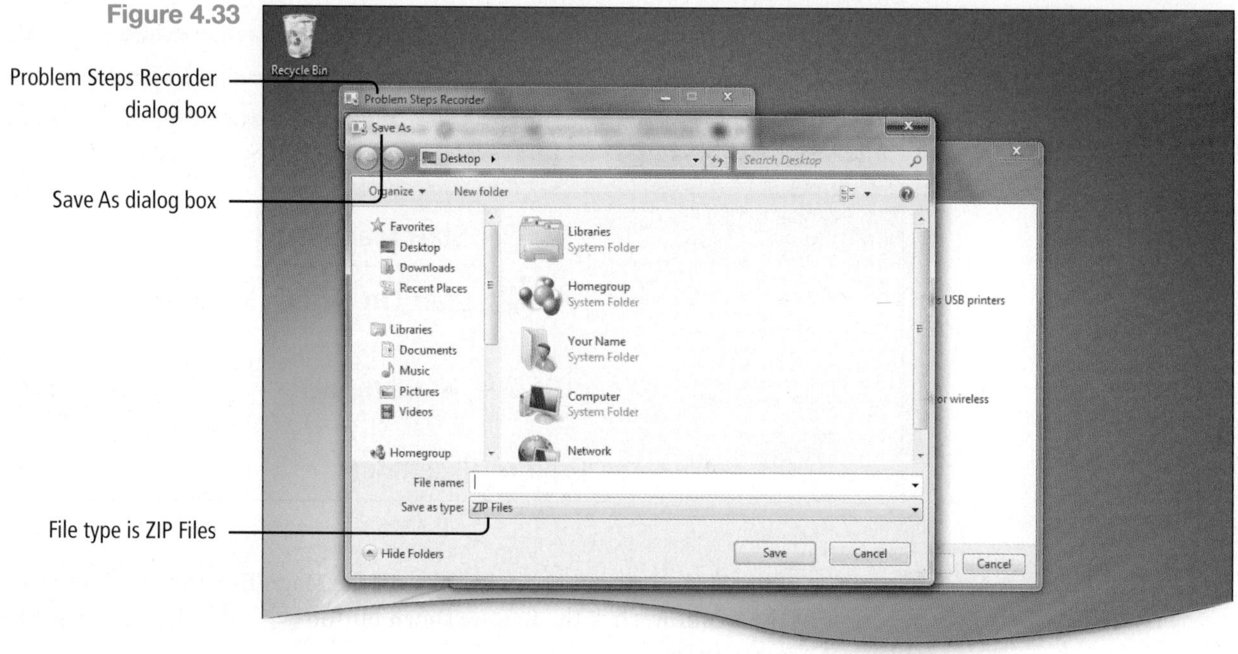

5 In the **Save As** dialog box, in the **navigation pane**, navigate to your **Windows 7 Chapter 4** folder on your USB flash drive. Then, as the **File name**, type **Lastname_Firstname_4A_Steps** and click **Save**.

6 **Close** [Close button] the **Problem Steps Recorder** window and the **Add Printer** dialog box. On the taskbar, click the **Windows Explorer** button [Windows Explorer button], navigate to your chapter folder, and then compare your screen with Figure 4.34.

Figure 4.34

Address bar displays path

ZIP file displays

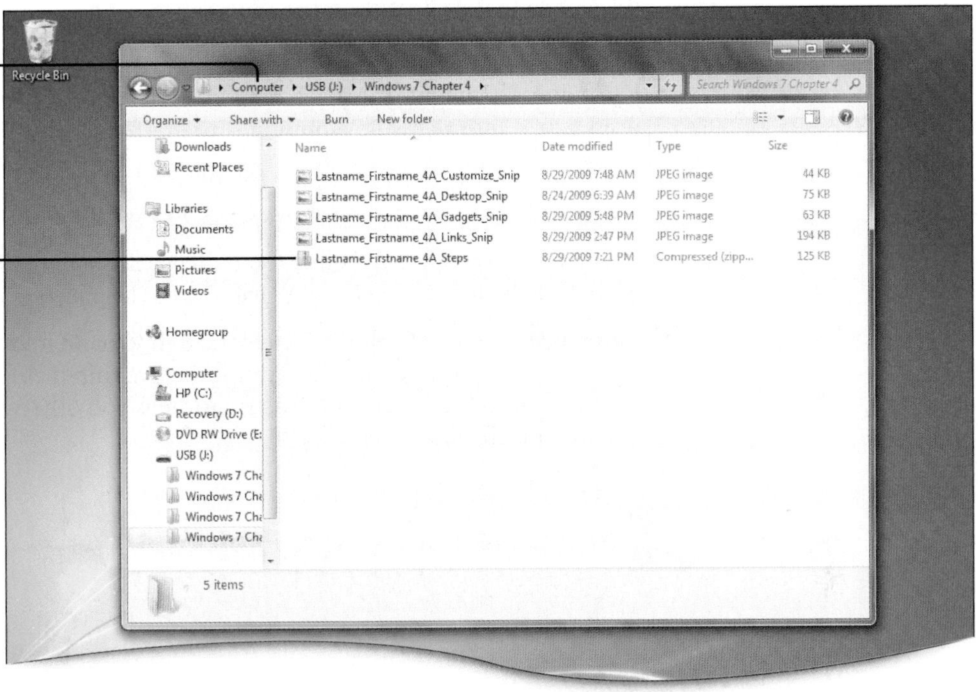

7 Point to your ZIP file, double-click, and then double-click to open the **Problem** file in Internet Explorer. Then, scroll down to display **Problem Step 4** on your screen, and notice that your comment displays, as shown in Figure 4.35.

Figure 4.35

Recorded Problem Steps displays in Internet Explorer

Problem Step 4 with your comment (your display may differ but you can see your comment)

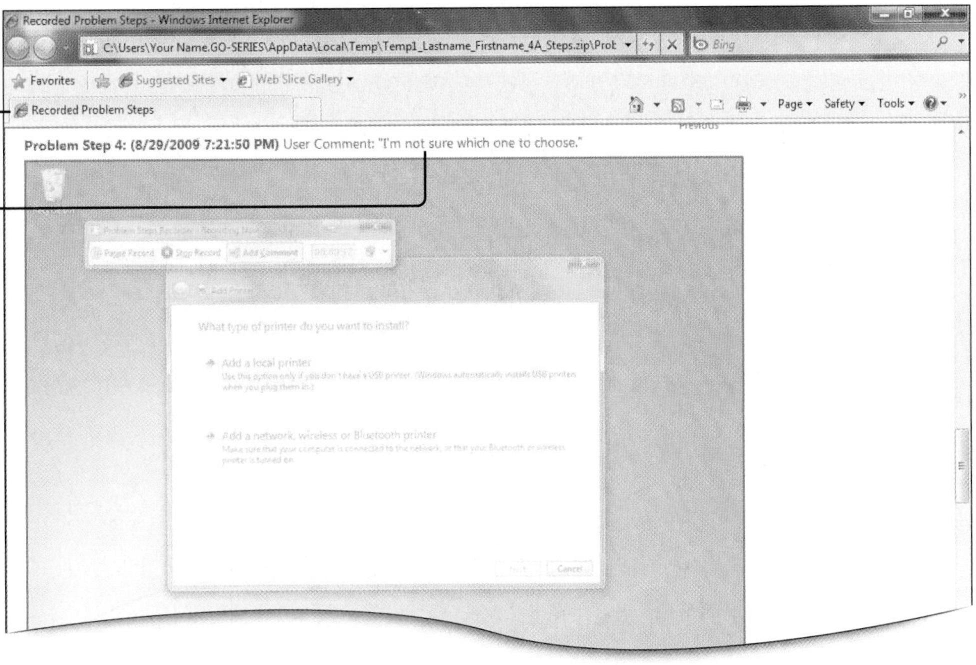

8 **Start** the **Snipping Tool** program, click the **New arrow**, and then click **Window Snip**. Click anywhere in the window, and then in the **Snipping Tool** mark-up window, click the **Save Snip** button. In the displayed **Save As** dialog box, if necessary navigate to your **Windows 7 Chapter 4** folder on your USB flash drive and click to select it so that it displays in the **address bar**.

9 Click in the **File name** box, and then using your own name, type **Lastname_Firstname_4A_Steps_Snip** Be sure the file type is **JPEG file**, and then press Enter. **Close** the **Snipping Tool** mark-up window.

10 Press Ctrl + Home to move to the top of the displayed file. Notice that you can view the recorded steps as a slide show. Click **Review the additional details.**

Here error messages and other technical details about the steps you performed are recorded, which can assist your Help Desk in helping you solve problems.

11 **Close** Internet Explorer. Delete the **Bell_Orchid** folder from your **Documents** folder. Close all open windows. Submit the five snip files from this project as directed by your instructor. Unless your instructor tells you otherwise, you need not submit the ZIP file you created.

End **You have completed Project 4A**

Project 4B Using Windows Media Player

Project Activities

In Activities 4.10 through 4.16, you will familiarize yourself with the Windows Media Player interface. You will view and play a music CD, rip a CD, create a playlist, and burn a CD. Your captured screens will look similar to Figure 4.36.

Project Files

For Project 4B, you will need the following files:

Student Resource CD or a USB flash drive containing the student files
One of your own music CDs (for one Optional activity if assigned)
One blank recordable CD (for one Optional activity if assigned)
New Snip files

You will save your files as:

Lastname_Firstname_4B_Playlist_Snip
Lastname_Firstname_4B_Rip_Snip (Optional)
Lastname_Firstname_4B_Burn_Snip (Optional)
Lastname_Firstname_4B_Video_Snip

Project Results

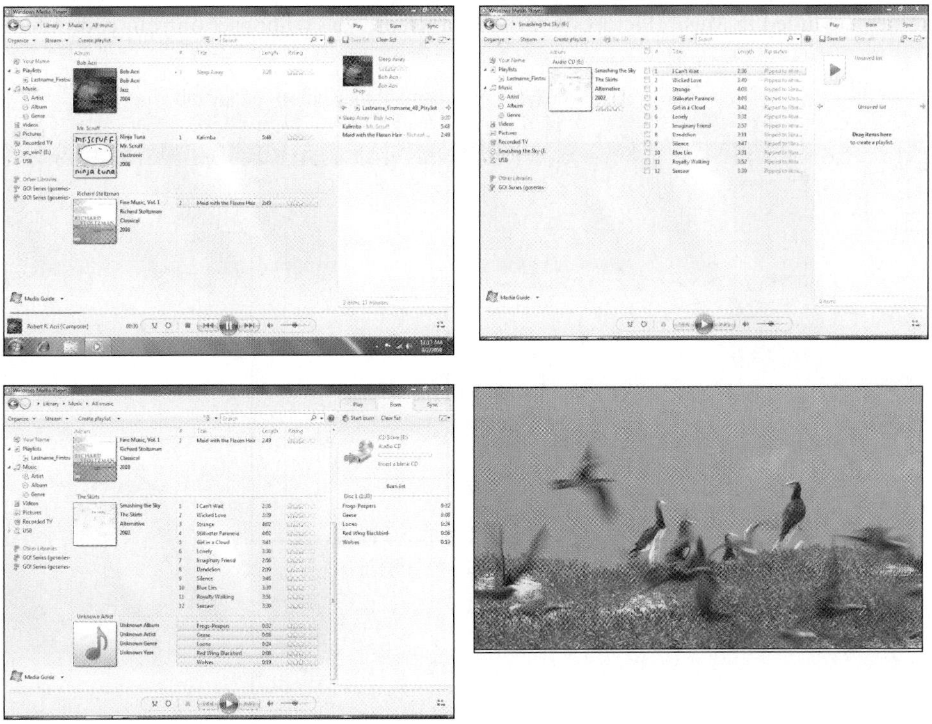

Figure 4.36
Project 4B Using Windows Media Player

Objective 6 | Explore Windows Media Player

Windows Media Player is an application in Windows 7 that provides an easy-to-use way for you to play digital media files, organize your digital media collection, ***burn*** CDs of your favorite music, ***rip*** music from CDs, ***sync*** digital media files to a ***portable device***, and shop for digital media content from online stores.

To burn a CD means to copy files to a recordable CD or DVD. To rip means to copy digital media content from an audio CD. Sync, in Windows Media Player, is the process of maintaining digital media files on your portable device based on specific rules. A portable device is any mobile electronic device that can exchange files or other data with a computer or device; for example, a smartphone or a portable music player.

Activity 4.10 | Getting Started with Windows Media Player

The Windows Media Player window looks similar to a window in Windows Explorer. The category of multimedia that you choose—music, pictures, or video—determines the appearance of the Windows Media Player window.

> **Another Way**
> Display the Start menu, in the Search box type *Windows Media Player*, and then click the program name on the list of search results.

1 On the taskbar, click the **Windows Media Player** icon. If a Welcome screen displays, click the Recommended settings option button, and then click Finish.

2 **Maximize** the window. In the upper right corner, click the **Play tab** to display the **list pane** on the right side of your screen, on the left, if necessary click Music, and then compare your screen with Figure 4.37.

When you start the Player for the first time, it automatically searches certain default folders included in Music, Pictures, Videos, and Recorded TV libraries on your computer.

Figure 4.37

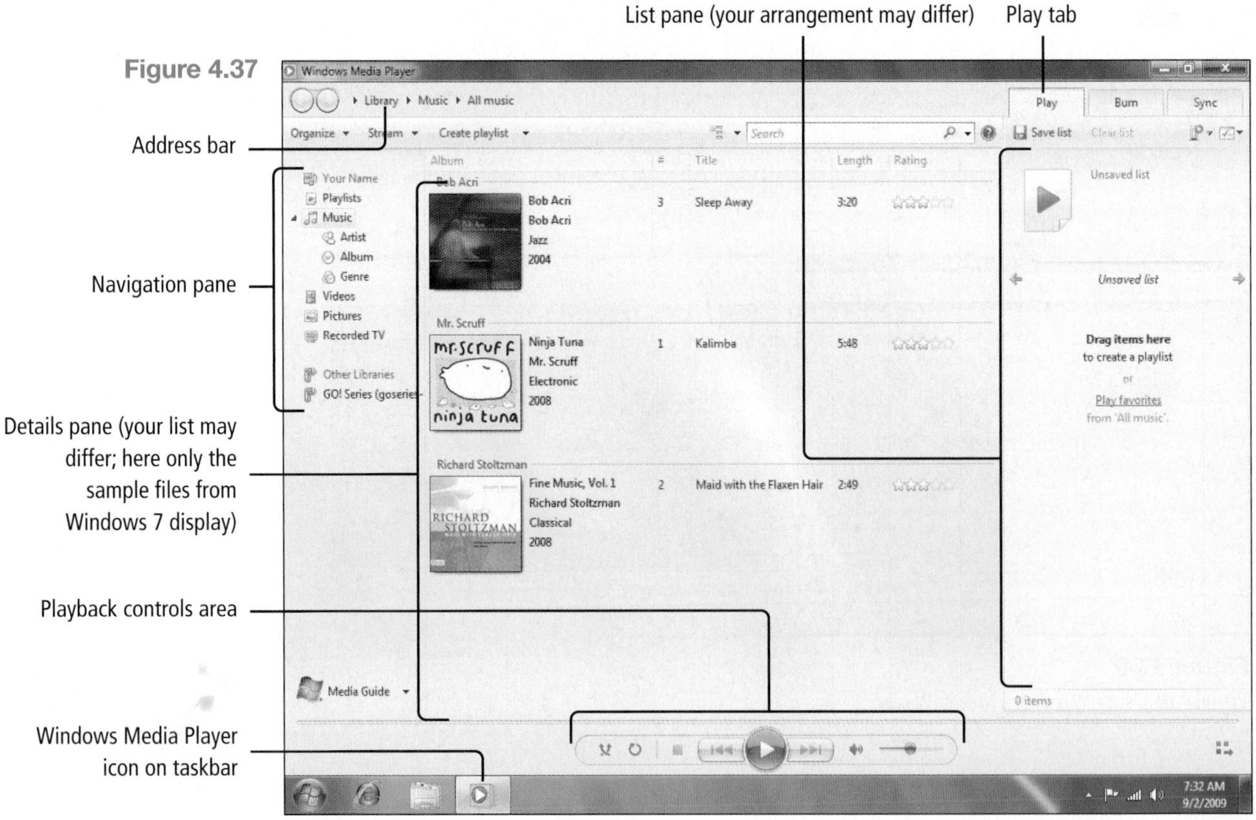

Alert! | Your screen will differ in content and arrangement

Most of the figures in this project use the files included in the Sample Music folder that comes with Windows 7. Your figures may differ. For example, iTunes selections might display, or podcasts that you have downloaded might display.

3 In the **navigation pane**, click **Videos.** If no videos have been added to your computer, the sample video included with Windows 7 will display.

4 Leave **Windows Media Player** open for the next activity.

Objective 7 | Play Music Using Media Player

You can use Windows Media Player to play music that you have stored on your computer or to play music directly from a CD. You can also set the Player window to display splashes of color and geometric shapes that change with the music, or you can minimize the Player window and let it play in the background while you are performing other tasks on your computer. This is referred to as the ***Now Playing mode***.

Activity 4.11 | Playing Music

Windows Media Player can play pre-recorded CDs. For this activity, you will need a music CD of your choice.

Alert! | This activity is optional

If you do not have a music CD of your own for this activity, you can either read through the steps without actually performing them, or try this activity on your own at a later time.

1 In the **navigation pane**, click **Music** to return to the Music library. In the **details pane**, notice that items are referred to as *Albums*.

The default sort order is by Album name and the default view is Expanded tile.

2 Turn on your speakers or plug headphones into your computer. Place an audio CD in your computer's CD/DVD drive. If the CD cover does not display, click the View options button, and then click Expanded tile. Compare your screen with Figure 4.38.

The details pane displays the cover, the name of the CD, the name of the artist, the type of music, a list of titles, and the length of each title.

Figure 4.38

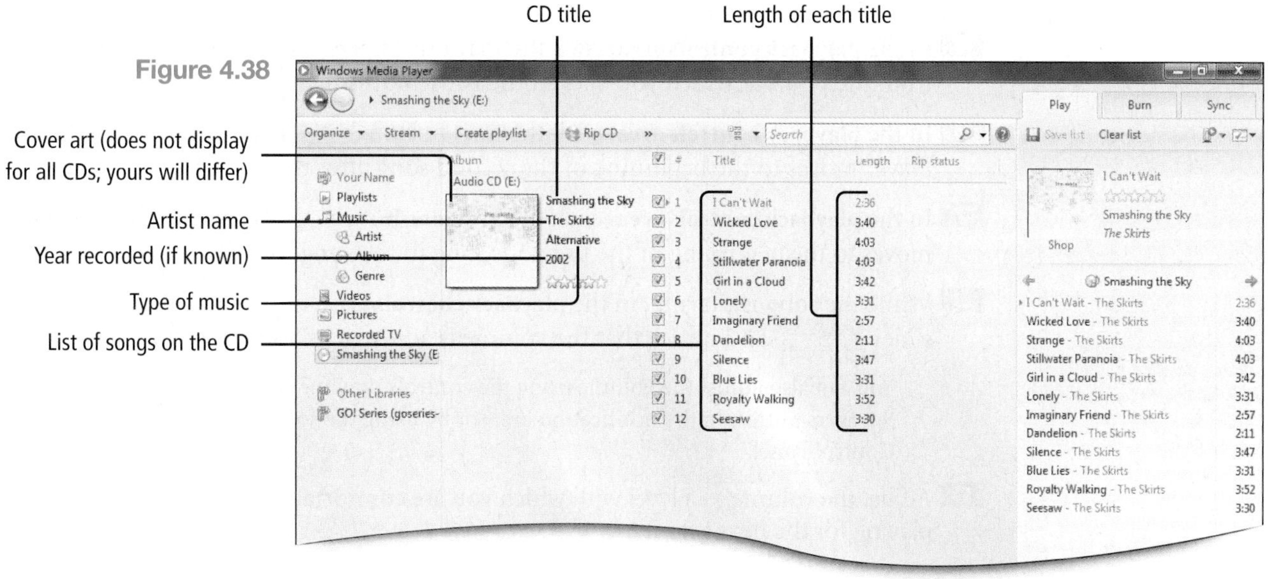

Alert! | If the CD information does not display

If you chose to play a commercial CD that was produced locally, or a CD that someone has created for you, the CD cover picture may be blank, and the CD information may be listed as *Unknown*. Also, instead of song titles, each song will be listed as Track 1, Track 2, and so on. This is not a concern; you can still complete the activity.

3 If the CD is not already playing, in the **playback controls area**, click the **Play** button.

Unless you clicked a song title other than the first one, the CD begins playing the first title, and will continue to play until the last title is finished. Information about the CD name, the artist, the composer, and the title name display on the left side of the playback controls area. The number of minutes and seconds the song has been playing displays, and a slider at the top of the playback controls area displays the progress of the song.

Alert! | If you cannot hear sound from your speakers

If you cannot hear the sound, be sure you have speakers or headphones plugged into your computer and turned on. If you still cannot hear the audio, open Control Panel, click Hardware and Sound, and then under Sound, click Adjust system volume. Adjust the sound bars for your Speakers and your Windows Sounds.

4 In the **playback controls area**, click the **Pause** button, and then compare your screen with Figure 4.39.

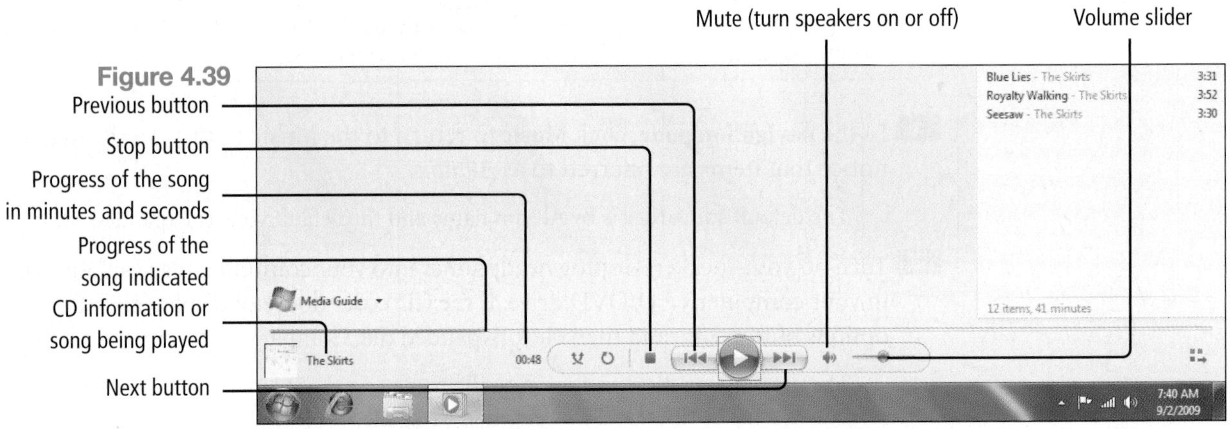

Figure 4.39

5 In the **playback controls area**, click the **Play** button. Notice that the song continues from the point at which you clicked the Pause button.

6 In the **playback controls area**, click the **Next** button two times. Notice that the Player moves to the beginning of the second song after the one that was playing.

7 In the **playback controls area**, click the **Previous** button. Notice that the Player moves to the beginning of the previous song in the song list.

8 While the song is playing, in the **playback controls area**, move the **Volume** button slider, and notice that the volume is adjusted as you move the slider.

You can also adjust the volume using the controls on your speakers, by clicking the Speakers button in the notification area, or by using the software found in the Windows Control Panel.

9 Adjust the volume to a level with which you are comfortable, and then leave the CD playing for the next activity.

Activity 4.12 | Using Now Playing Modes

The ***Player Library mode***, which is currently displayed, gives you comprehensive control over the numerous features of the Player. If you do not plan to use your computer for any other activities while the CD is playing, you can alter the window to display interesting visuals that are integrated with the music. If you are going to use your computer for other tasks while the CD is playing, you can switch to Now Playing mode, which gives you a simplified view.

1 With your CD still playing, in the lower right corner, click the **Switch to Now Playing** button. Move your pointer into the small window to display the **playback controls area**, and then *point* to but do not click the **Stop** button. Compare your screen with Figure 4.40.

The Player switches to and displays in the Now Playing mode.

Figure 4.40

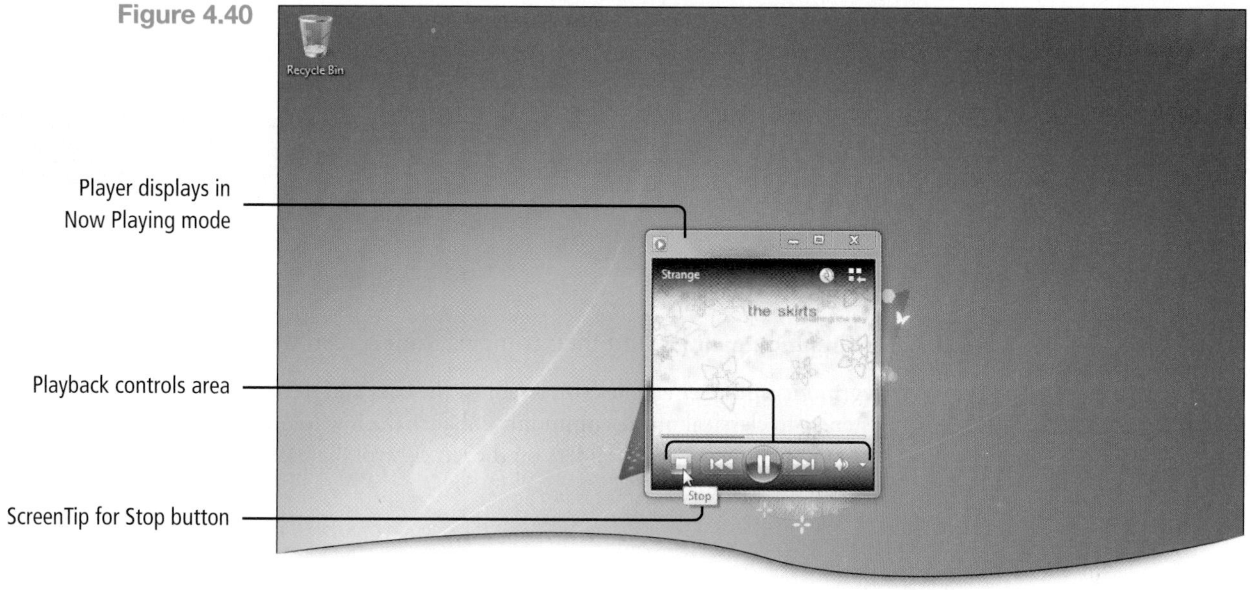

2 Point slightly to the left of the **Stop** button in an empty area of the **playback controls area**, right-click, and then point to **Enhancements**. Compare your screen with Figure 4.41.

Figure 4.41

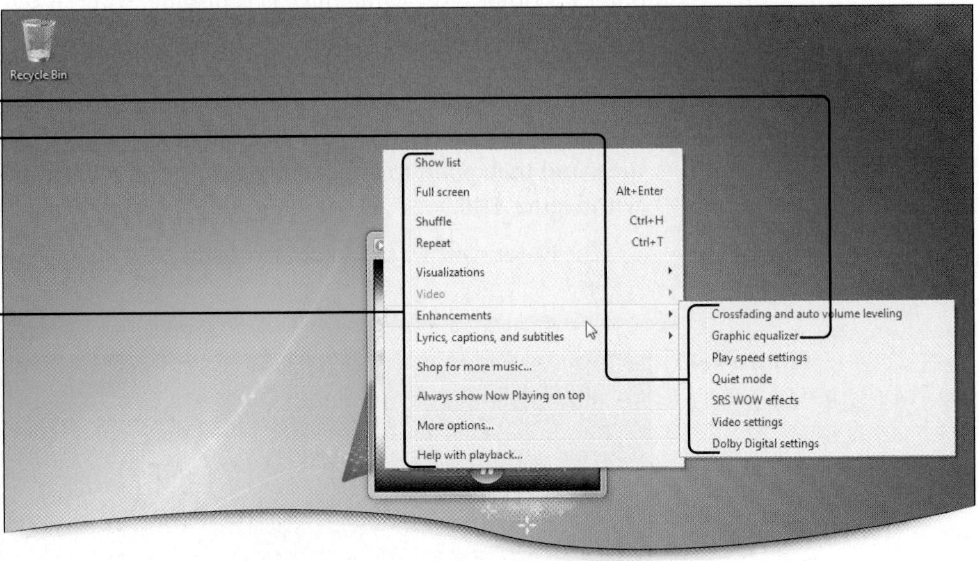

3 Click **Graphic equalizer**, and then compare your screen with Figure 4.42.

A ***graphic equalizer*** enables you to adjust the bass and treble that you hear. For example, listeners to classical music commonly enhance the low frequency ranges on the left side of the graphic equalizer. The sliders on the left control the bass; the sliders on the right control the treble.

Figure 4.42

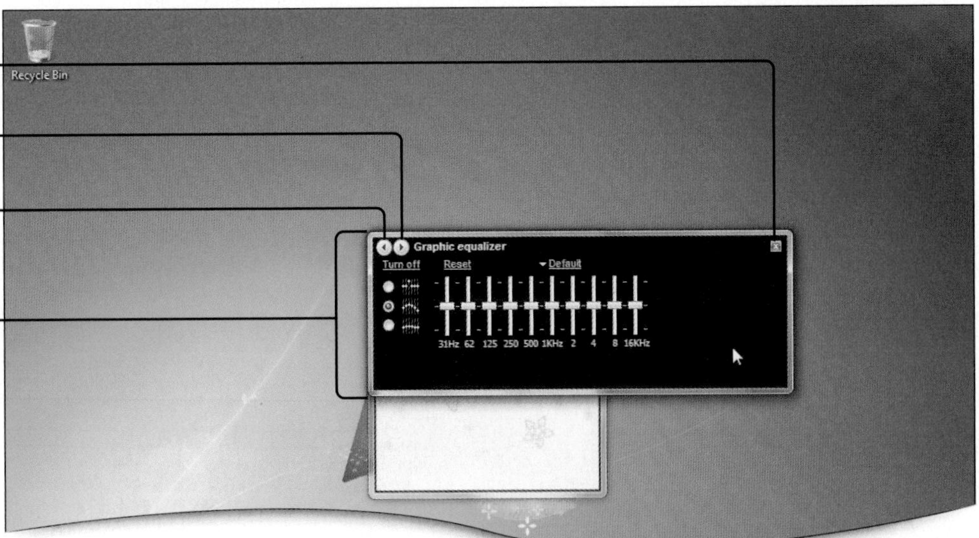

4 **Close** ![X] the **graphic equalizer**. Display the shortcut menu again, point to **Visualizations**, point to **Battery**, and then click **kaleidovision**. Then, **Maximize** ![□] the window, and compare your screen with Figure 4.43.

The active *visualizations*—splashes of color and geometric shapes—are available from three categories—*Alchemy*, *Bars and Waves*, and *Battery*—or from the Web.

The patterns change along with the rhythm and intensity of the music; this is more obvious in some visualizations than in others.

Figure 4.43

Restore down button

Kaleidovision visualization (yours may differ in color and pattern)

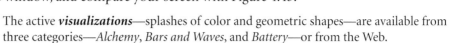

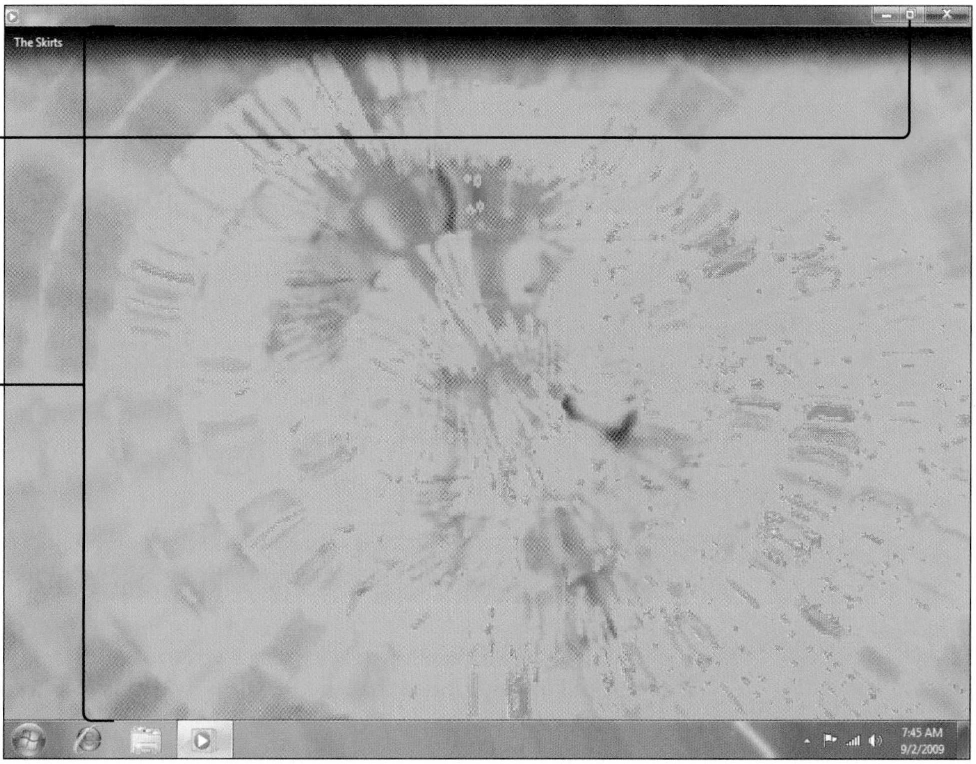

5 In the upper right corner, click the **Restore Down** button ![□]. Redisplay the shortcut menu, point to **Visualizations**, and then click **Album art** to return to the default view.

6 Point in the upper right corner of the album art; click the **Switch to Library** button to return to the Player Library mode. In the **playback controls area**, point slightly above the counter, right-click, and then point to **View**. Compare your screen with Figure 4.44.

Figure 4.44

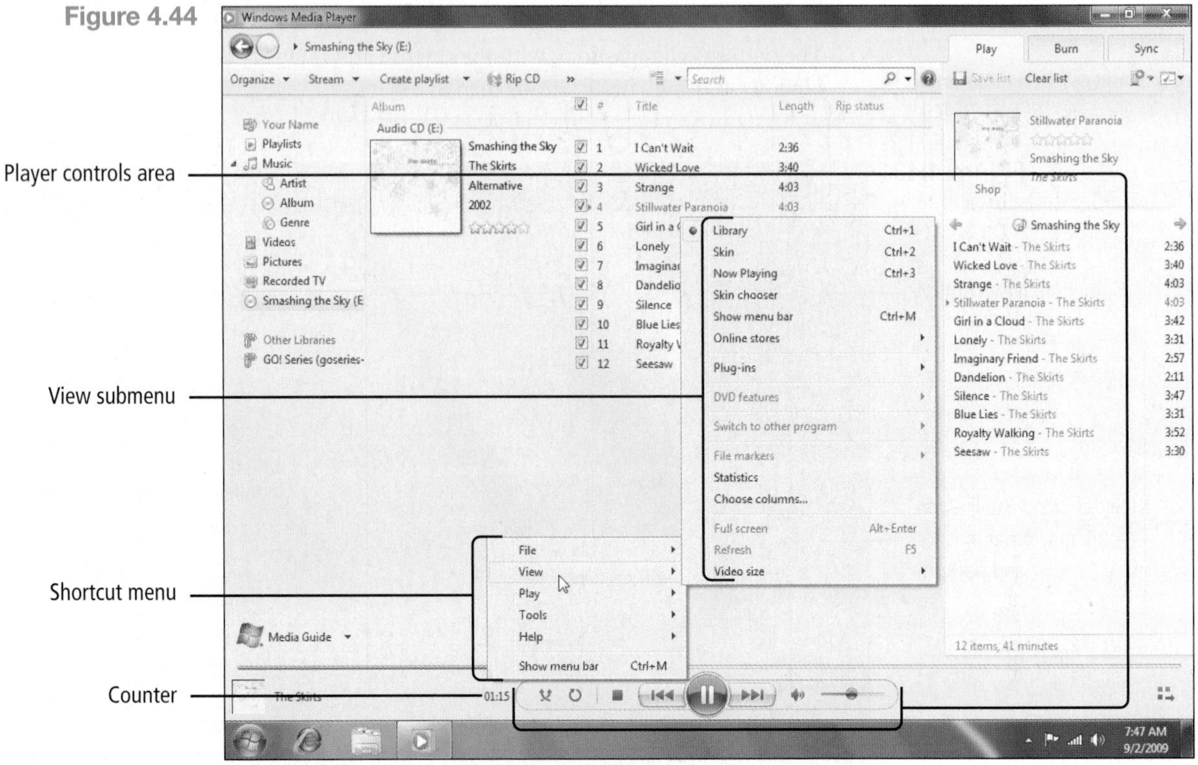

7 Click **Skin**, and notice that the Player now displays in a small window, as shown in Figure 4.45.

A ***skin*** is a user interface that displays an alternative appearance and customized functionality for software such as Windows Media Player. The ***skin mode***—a display mode in which the user interface is displayed as a skin—displays a small Media Player window that includes a menu, a video area, and playback controls.

Figure 4.45

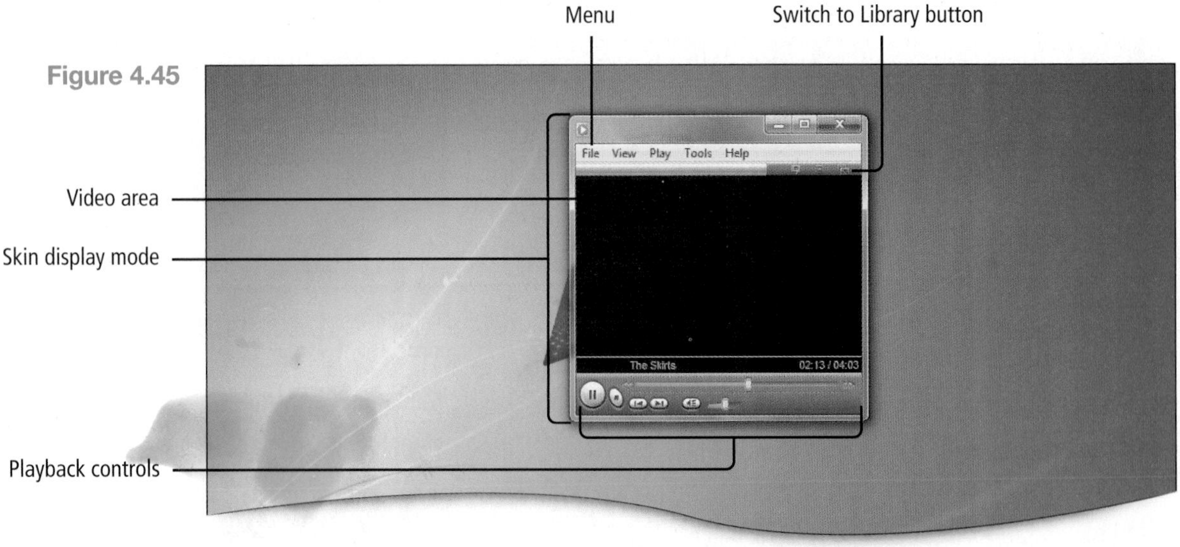

8 On the menu bar, click **View**, and then on the menu click **Now Playing** to return to this mode. In the upper right corner, click the **Switch to Library** button to return to the Player Library mode.

> **Note | To Keep the Windows Media Player in Front of Other Windows**
>
> When you are listening to music while performing other tasks on your computer, you might want to keep the small window for the Now Playing mode in front of other windows. To do this from Player Library mode, right-click an open area of the player controls area. From the displayed menu, point to Tools, and then click Options. In the Options dialog box, click the Player tab, and then under Player settings, select the *Keep Now Playing on top of other windows* check box.

9 In the **playback controls area**, click the **Stop** button. Leave Windows Media Player open for the next activity.

> **More Knowledge | Minimizing the Media Player to the Taskbar**
>
> If you want to keep control of the Windows Media Player, but do not want the window in your desktop work area, start playing your music, and then click the Minimize button. The Windows Media Player icon on the taskbar will display with a glass frame indicating an open program. If you point to the button, the thumbnail displays a small set of player controls that you can use from the thumbnail image.

Activity 4.13 | Creating and Saving a Playlist

A ***playlist*** is a list of digital media items that you create and save. A playlist is useful when you want to group items that you like to listen to or view frequently. An auto playlist continuously updates automatically based on the music in the Player Library. A regular playlist is a list you save that contains one or more digital files—any combination of songs, videos, or pictures in the Player Library.

1 Be sure you have stopped the CD that was playing. In the **navigation pane**, click **Music** to return to your Music library.

2 If the **list pane** does not display on the right side of your window, in the upper left corner, click **Organize**, point to **Layout**, and then click **Show list**.

3 In the **list pane** on the right side of your screen, at the top of the pane click **Clear list**. Notice that you can drag items to the list pane area to create a playlist.

> **Note | Using Windows Media Library Sample Files**
>
> When you install Windows 7, a group of sample files is installed in the Player Library. These include sample cuts from three CDs, but not the entire CDs. If your computer does not display the sample files shown, use other audio files in their place.

4 In the **details pane**, under **Bob Acri**, drag the **Sleep Away** title into the **list pane**, and then when the ScreenTip + *Add to list* displays, as shown in Figure 4.46, release the mouse button. If the song begins to play, in the playback controls area, click Stop.

The song displays in the **list pane** area, but still displays in the **details pane**.

Figure 4.46

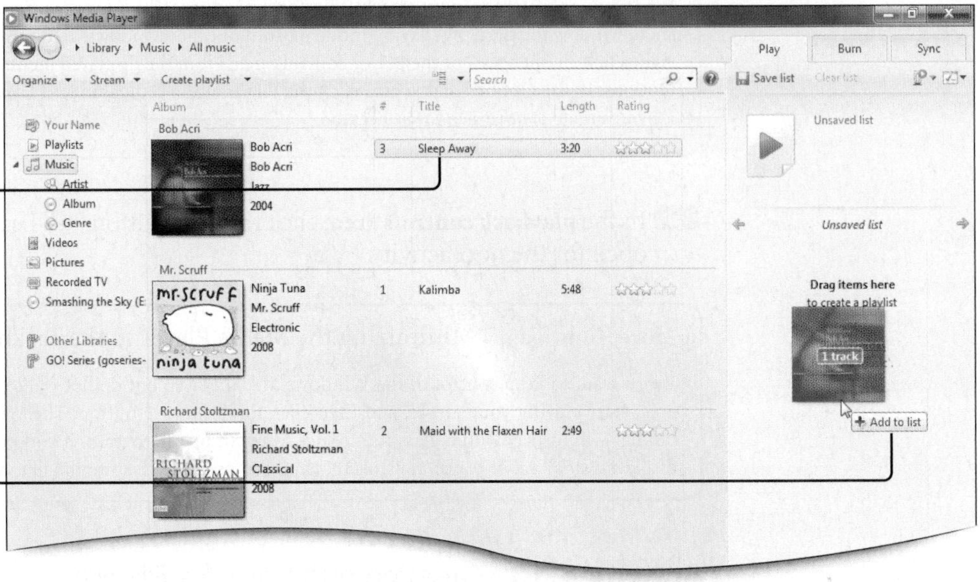

5 Use the same technique to drag two more songs to the playlist. Use songs of your choice, or, from the **Mr. Scruff album**, drag *Kalimba* and from the **Richard Stoltzman album**, drag *Maid with the Flaxen Hair*.

6 At the top of the **list pane**, click **Save list**, and then using your own name type **Lastname_Firstname_4B_Playlist** and press Enter. Compare your screen with Figure 4.47.

Figure 4.47

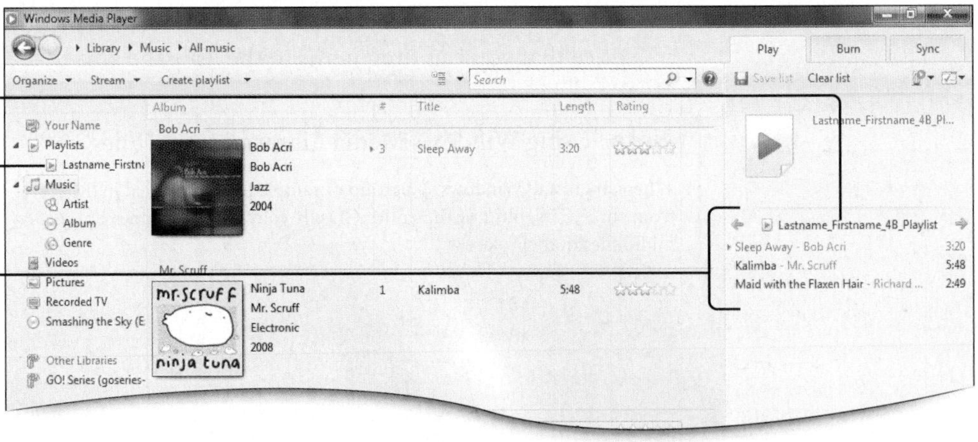

7 Start 🪟 the **Snipping Tool** program, click the **New arrow**, and then click **Full-screen Snip**. In the **Snipping Tool** mark-up window, click the **Save Snip** button 💾. In the displayed **Save As** dialog box, if necessary navigate to your **Windows 7 Chapter 4** folder on your USB flash drive and click to select it so that it displays in the **address bar**.

8 Click in the **File name** box, and then using your own name, type **Lastname_ Firstname_4B_Playlist_Snip** and press Enter. **Close** ❌ the **Snipping Tool** mark-up window. Hold this file until you finish Project 4B, and then submit this file as directed by your instructor.

9 At the top of the **list pane**, click the **Clear list** button to clear the list pane—this does not delete your playlist, but rather, clears it from the list pane. Leave the Player open for the next activity.

Objective 8 | Rip a CD

If you want to add songs to your computer from CDs, you can rip the CD—copy digital media tracks from a music CD to a format that can be played on your computer. You can rip an entire CD, or you can select only the tracks that you want.

Activity 4.14 | Ripping a CD

In this activity, you will rip tracks from a CD to your computer. You will need a CD of your own to complete this activity, and the songs and CD title displayed on your screens will not match the figures shown below.

> **Alert! | This activity is optional**
>
> If you do not have a music CD of your own for this activity, you can either read through the steps without actually performing them, or try this activity on your own at a later time.

1 With **Windows Media Player** still active, put an audio CD in your CD drive. If you already have a CD in the drive from the previous activities, find its name in the lower portion of the navigation pane, under Recorded TV and click the name.

2 At the top of the window, click **Rip CD**. Compare your screen with Figure 4.48.

During the process, each title will indicate *Pending*, or when complete, *Ripped to library*. When complete, the song's checkbox is also cleared.

To rip only specific titles, clear the checkbox before beginning the rip process.

Figure 4.48

Checkmark cleared after each song is ripped

Rip status

Name of CD in navigation pane (yours will differ)

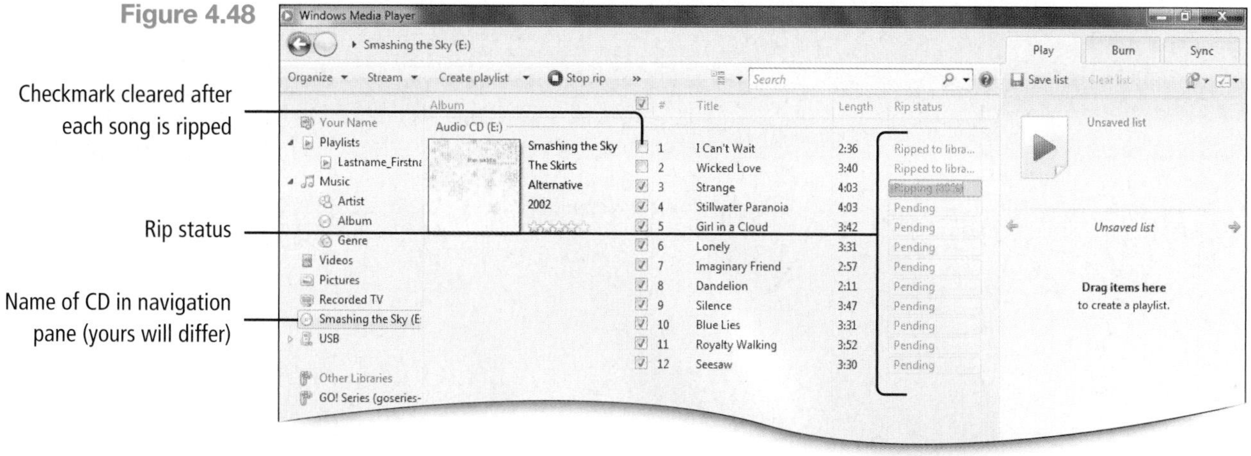

3 When your rip process is complete, to the right of **Rip CD**, click **Rip settings**, or click the **double chevrons** >>, point to **Rip settings**, and then point to **Format**. Compare your screen with Figure 4.49, and then take a moment to review the audio formats described in the table in Figure 4.50.

Figure 4.49

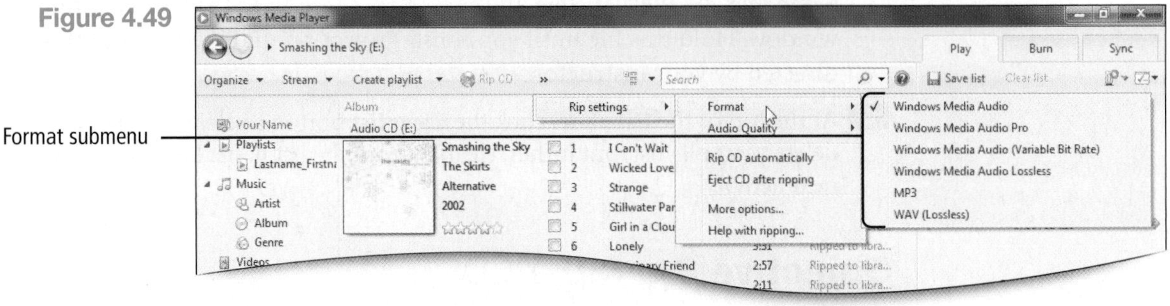

Audio Formats

Type	Description
Windows Media Audio	Balances sound quality and file size. This is the default Windows audio format, and will be used if you do not change the settings.
Windows Media Audio Pro	Saves the audio files in smaller files; often used for portable devices with limited storage capacities.
Windows Media Audio (Variable Bit Rate)	Varies the amount of information stored depending on the music being played. This format is used infrequently.
Windows Media Audio Lossless	Results in the best sound quality, but also creates the largest files.
MP3	Compresses the data used to record songs while keeping the sound quality relatively high.
WAV (Lossless)	Results in an uncompressed song format used for high-quality audio; this format can be read by both Windows and Apple computers. File sizes are relatively large.

Figure 4.50

> **Note** | Choosing a Bit Rate
>
> From the Rip settings submenu, if you point to Audio Quality, you can also choose a bit rate for your ripped audio files. The ***bit rate*** is the amount of information saved per second. The higher the bit rate, the better the sound, and the larger the files.

4 Click in an empty area of the window to close the menu.

5 **Start** the **Snipping Tool** program, click the **New arrow**, and then click **Window Snip**. Click anywhere in the window, and then in the **Snipping Tool** mark-up window, click the **Save Snip** button. In the displayed **Save As** dialog box, if necessary navigate to your **Windows 7 Chapter 4** folder on your USB flash drive and click to select it so that it displays in the address bar.

6 Click in the **File name** box, and then using your own name, type **Lastname_Firstname_4B_Rip_Snip** Be sure the file type is **JPEG**, and press Enter. **Close** the **Snipping Tool** mark-up window. Hold this file until you finish Project 4B, and then submit this file as directed by your instructor.

7 Leave the Player open for the next activity.

> Alert! | Copyright issues
>
> Commercial CDs are almost always protected by copyright laws. If you are ripping CDs that you own, and are making these copies for your own personal use, most people agree that this is legal. If, however, you use these files to create a CD for someone else, or if you trade or make the files available on the Internet, you are violating copyright laws. When ripping music from a CD to your own computer, be sure the CD you use is one that you own. If you are ripping the CD in a lab or on someone else's computer, in Windows Explorer, open the Music library folder and delete the files.

Objective 9 | Burn a CD

Windows Media Player can burn—write files to—CDs and DVDs. You can burn data CDs or music CDs. There are two types of CDs you can use. CD-Rs are CDs that can be written to one time. CD-RWs are rewritable discs that can be used over and over again.

Activity 4.15 | Burning a Music Disc by Using Windows Media Player

In this activity, you will burn a CD using the sample files included with Windows 7. If you prefer to use other audio files, substitute those for the ones indicated in the steps below. Your screens will differ from the ones shown.

> Alert! | This activity is optional
>
> If you do not have a blank CD of your own for this activity, you can either read through the steps without actually performing them, or try this activity on your own at a later time.

1 Remove the audio CD from your CD/DVD drive. Insert your Student Resource CD, or the device that contains the student files that accompany this textbook. Wait a few moments, and then **Close** the **AutoPlay** dialog box.

2 From the taskbar, open **Windows Explorer** . Display the student files, navigate to **Chapter_Files ▶ Chapter_04**. Select the folder **USFWS Sounds**, right-click, and then by using the **Send to** command, copy the files to your **Documents** folder, as shown in Figure 4.51.

Figure 4.51

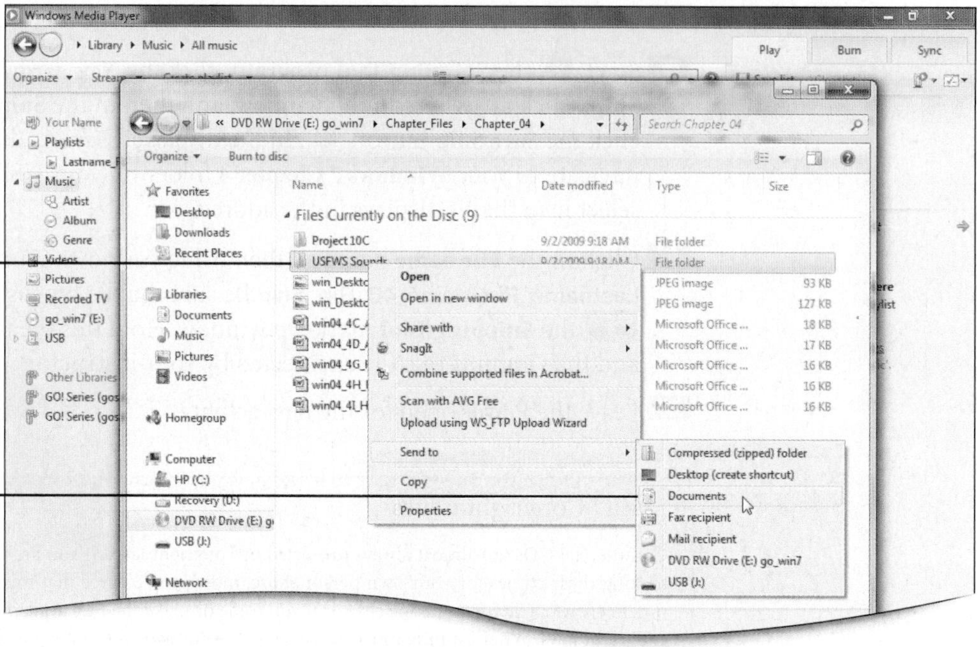

3 In the **navigation pane**, click **Documents**. Select the **USFWS Sounds** folder, hold down Ctrl, and then as shown in Figure 4.52, drag the folder into your **Music** folder in the **navigation pane** until the ScreenTip + *Copy to My Music* displays, and then release the mouse button and release Ctrl. **Close** the Documents window.

Figure 4.52

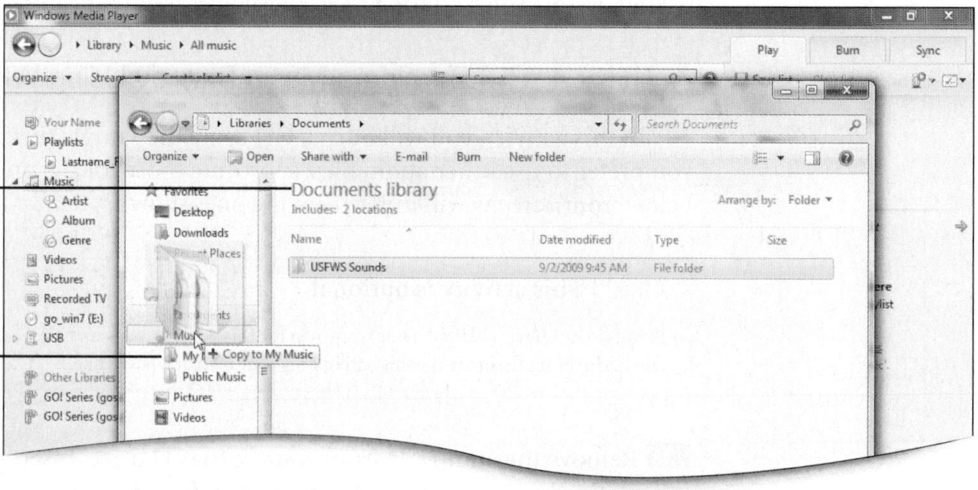

4 In the Player window, in the **navigation pane**, click **Music**, and then scroll down to view the new titles, which may be near the end of the list. Compare your screen with Figure 4.53.

No cover art or artist will display. These are sounds from the U.S. Fish and Wildlife Service.

Use this technique to get music into the Music library so that you can burn a music CD.

Figure 4.53

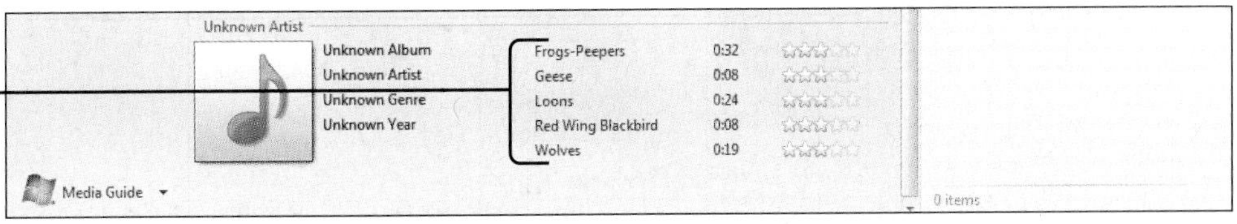

5 Remove the Student CD from your CD/DVD drive, and insert a blank recordable CD.

6 In the upper right corner, click the **Burn tab**, and notice that *Burn list* displays in the **list pane**.

7 In the **Title** column, click **Frogs-Peepers**, hold down Shift, click **Wolves**, release Shift, and then drag the entire selection into the **Burn list** until the ScreenTip *+ Add to Burn List* displays, as shown in Figure 4.54.

A burn list area displays in the list pane. At the top of the list pane, the drive with the blank CD displays, along with the amount of time used by the files and the amount of time left on the CD.

Figure 4.54

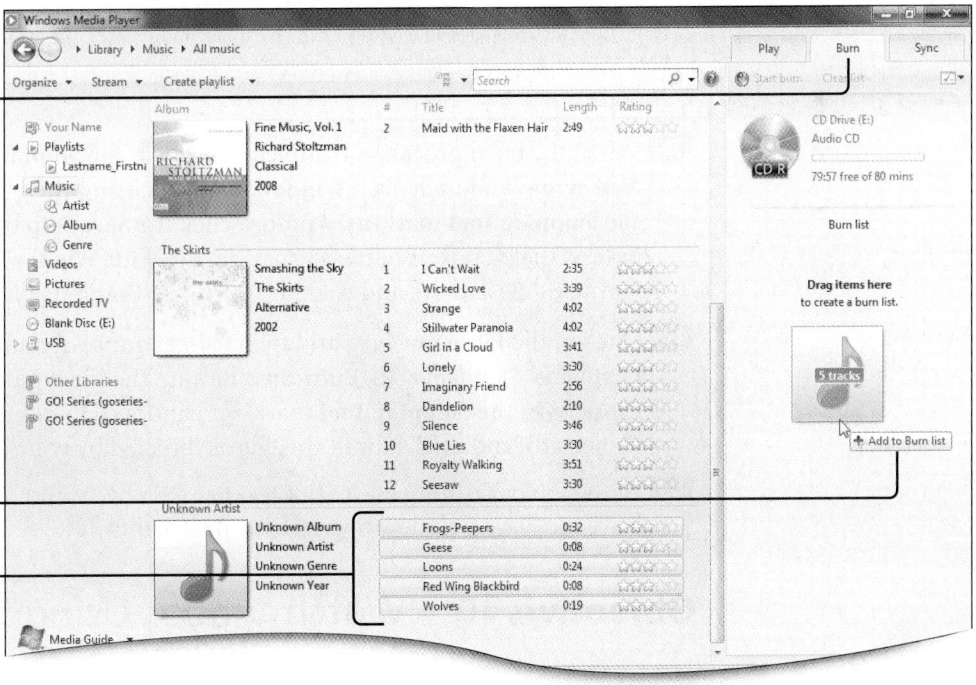

8 At the top of the **list pane**, click the **Start burn** button. Compare your screen with Figure 4.55.

A progress bar displays the burn process. When the burning process is complete, the CD will eject.

Figure 4.55

Alert! | If your list of titles is longer than the time available on the CD

If the titles that you have added to your Burn list take more time than the time available on your CD, you will need to delete titles until you have enough space to burn all of your titles on the CD.

9 When the burn process is complete, **Start** the **Snipping Tool** program, click the **New arrow**, and then click **Window Snip**. Click anywhere in the window, and then in the **Snipping Tool** mark-up window, click the **Save Snip** button. In the displayed **Save As** dialog box, if necessary navigate to your **Windows 7 Chapter 4** folder on your USB flash drive and click to select it so that it displays in the **address bar**.

10 Click in the **File name** box, and then using your own name, type **Lastname_Firstname_4B_Burn_Snip** Be sure the file type is **JPEG**, and press Enter. **Close** the **Snipping Tool** mark-up window. Hold this file until you finish Project 4B, and then submit this file as directed by your instructor.

11 At the top of the **list pane**, click **Clear list**. Remove your CD, close your CD drive, and leave the Player window open for the next activity.

Objective 10 | Watch Videos Using Windows Media Player

Windows Media Player provides a basic method for viewing pictures and videos. You can build playlists that include a combination of videos and pictures, and play them in the same manner in which you played audio files.

Activity 4.16 | Watching Videos

1 In the **navigation pane**, click **Videos**. In the **details pane**, scroll as necessary to see the title **Wildlife in HD**, which is a sample video that comes with Windows 7. Or, insert a DVD of your own and click its name in the navigation pane.

2 Click the video to select it, and then in the **playback controls area**, click the **Play** button. If necessary, **Maximize** the window, and then compare your screen with Figure 4.56.

Figure 4.56

Video playing in Media Player window (your scene may differ)

3 With the video playing (if necessary click Play again), **Start** the **Snipping Tool** program, click the **New arrow**, click **Window Snip**, click in the window, and then in the **Snipping Tool** mark-up window, click the **Save Snip** button. In the displayed **Save As** dialog box, if necessary navigate to your **Windows 7 Chapter 4** folder on your USB flash drive and click to select it so that it displays in the **address bar**.

4 Click in the **File name** box, and then using your own name, type **Lastname_Firstname_4B_Video_Snip** Be sure the file type is **JPEG**, and press Enter. **Close** the **Snipping Tool** mark-up window.

5 After the video completes, in the dark screen that displays, click **Go to Library**.

6 **Close** Windows Media Player. Delete the **USFWS Sounds** folder from your **Documents** folder and also from your **Music** folder, and then submit the four snip files that you created in this project as directed by your instructor.

End **You have completed Project 4B**

Content-Based Assessments

Summary

Windows 7 is your personal environment for computing. From the Control Panel, you can click Appearance and Personalization and see many different areas of your computer that you can customize to fit your computing needs.

Your computer can reflect your personality by customizing the desktop and screen saver, and by adding gadgets. You gain productivity, however, when you customize your computing environment to make your computer easier and faster to use. For example, in this chapter, you practiced techniques to customize the Start menu and the taskbar in various ways to place your programs, files, and folders within easy reach. You also explored ways to make your computing environment physically more comfortable.

In this chapter, you also used Windows Media Player to play music, rip and burn CDs, and watch videos.

Key Terms

Action Center 244
Aero 229
Browsing 226
Burn 256
Common folders and features 232
Desktop 225
Desktop gadget 245
Ease of Access Center..250
Feeds 249
Gadget...........................245
Magnifier 250
Notification 244
Notification area 244
Now Playing mode 257
Portable device.............256
Problem Steps Recorder 251
Programs list.................232
Really Simple Syndication 249
Rip 256
RSS 249
Screen saver 225
Screenshot 251
Search box 232
Shut down button..........232
Spyware.........................231
Start menu.....................231
Status area 244
Sync 256
System tray....................244
Taskbar 240
Theme 225
Wallpaper 225
Windows Media Player ..256

Matching

Match each term in the second column with its correct definition in the first column. Write the letter of the term on the blank line in front of the correct definition.

____ 1. The main screen area that you see after you turn on your computer and log on, and which acts as your work area in Windows 7.

____ 2. A moving picture or pattern that displays on your screen after a specified period of inactivity—that is, when the mouse or keyboard has not been used.

____ 3. The background of the desktop.

____ 4. A combination of pictures, colors, and sounds on your computer; includes a desktop background, a screen saver, a window border color, and a sound scheme.

____ 5. A term used to describe the process of navigating within Windows 7 to look for a specific program, file, e-mail, Control Panel feature, or Internet favorite.

____ 6. The term that refers to the desktop experience that features a translucent glass design for windows, attractive graphics, taskbar previews of open windows, and features such as Snap and Peek.

A Aero
B Browsing
C Common folders and features
D Desktop
E Desktop background
F Notification area
G Programs list
H Screen saver
I Search box
J Shut down button

____ 7.	Software that sends information about your Web surfing habits to a Web site without your knowledge.	**K** Spyware
____ 8.	A list of choices that provides access to your computer's programs, folders, and settings.	**L** Start menu
____ 9.	The left side of the Start menu that displays recently used programs on the bottom, programs that you have pinned to the Start menu at the top, and a button to display all the programs on your computer.	**M** System tray
____ 10.	The right side of the Start menu that provides quick access to the folders and features you use most often.	**N** Taskbar
____ 11.	An area on the Start menu from which you can search for programs, files, folders, and e-mail messages.	**O** Theme
____ 12.	On the Start menu, a button that displays a menu for switching users, logging off, restarting, or shutting down.	
____ 13.	The area along the lower edge of the desktop that contains the Start button, a button for all open programs, and the notification area.	
____ 14.	The area at the right end of the taskbar that contains some program icons and notifications.	
____ 15.	Another term for the notification area.	

Multiple Choice

Circle the correct answer.

1. A small pop-up window with information about the status of your computer or the detection of new devices is:
A. a warning **B.** a notification **C.** an action

2. A central place to view alerts and take actions related to your computer is the:
A. Ease of Access Center **B.** taskbar **C.** Action Center

3. A mini-program that offers information and provides easy access to tools that you use frequently is a:
A. gadget **B.** magnifier **C.** toolbar

4. Frequently updated content published by a Web site is referred to as:
A. comments **B.** feeds **C.** blogs

5. A central location for accessibility settings and programs that can make your computer easier to use is the:
A. Action Center **B.** Ease of Access Center **C.** Accessibility Center

6. The process of copying files *to* a recordable CD or DVD is called:
A. burning **B.** ripping **C.** syncing

7. The process of copying digital media content *from* a CD is called:
A. burning **B.** ripping **C.** syncing

8. A simplified Windows Media Player view that enables you to play music in the background while you are performing other tasks is:
A. Player Library mode **B.** Skin mode **C.** Now Playing mode

9. A list of digital media items that you create and save is a:
A. library **B.** playlist **C.** visualization

10. The default format for audio in Windows Media Player is:
A. Windows Media Audio **B.** MP3 **C.** WAV

Content-Based Assessments

Apply 4A skills from these Objectives:

1. Personalize the Desktop and Screen Saver
2. Personalize the Start Menu
3. Personalize the Taskbar
4. Personalize the Desktop by Adding Gadgets
5. Personalize the Ease of Access Center and Use Problem Steps Recorder

Skills Review | Project 4C Personalizing Your Windows 7 Environment

Project Files

Student Resource CD or a flash drive containing the student data files:

win04_4C_Answer_Sheet (Word document)

You will save your file as:

Lastname_Firstname_4C_Answer_Sheet

1 **Close** [X] all open windows. On the taskbar, click the **Windows Explorer** button. In the **navigation pane**, click the drive that contains the student files for this textbook, and then navigate to **Chapter_Files ▶ Chapter_04**. Double-click the Word file **win04_4C_Answer_Sheet** to open Word and display the document. Press F12 to display the **Save As** dialog box in Word, navigate to your **Windows 7 Chapter 4** folder, and then using your own name, save the document as **Lastname_Firstname_4C_Answer_Sheet** If necessary, click OK if a message regarding formats displays.

On the taskbar, click the **Word** button to minimize the window and leave your Word document accessible from the taskbar. **Close** the **Chapter_04** folder window. As you complete each step in this project, click the Word button on the taskbar to open the document, type your one-letter answer in the appropriate cell of the Word table, and then on the taskbar, click the button again to minimize the window for the next step.

Insert the Student Resource CD in the appropriate drive, and then copy the **Bell_Orchid** folder to your **Documents** folder—you will need a new copy for this project. On your desktop, right-click, and then click **Personalize**. Which window displays?

A. Desktop Background window

B. Personalize Appearance and Sounds window

C. Personalization window

2 From the displayed window, what would you click to display a solid blue color as your desktop background?

A. Desktop Background, Picture location arrow, Windows Wallpapers

B. Desktop Background, Picture location arrow, Solid Colors

C. Screen Saver, Solid Colors

3 Display the **Screen Saver Settings** dialog box, and then select the **Bubbles** screen saver in the dialog box. Click the **Preview** button, and then press Esc to return to the dialog box. Which of the following best describes the behavior of this screen saver?

A. The background is black and a large bubble fills the screen.

B. The background is black and small bubbles float on the screen.

C. The screen continues to display and transparent bubbles float on top.

4 **Cancel** the **Screen Saver Settings** dialog box so that no changes are made and close all open windows. Display the **Taskbar and Start Menu Properties** dialog box, click the **Start Menu** tab, and then click the **Customize** button. What action would be necessary to remove the Pictures folder from the Start menu?

A. Under Personal folder, click *Don't display this item.*

(Project 4C Personalizing Your Windows 7 Environment continues on the next page)

Skills Review | Project 4C Personalizing Your Windows 7 Environment (continued)

B. Clear the Pictures check box.

C. Under Pictures, click *Don't display this item.*

5 From this dialog box, how could you prevent *Devices and Printers* from displaying on the Start menu?

A. It is not possible to remove Devices and Printers from the Start menu.

B. Clear the Devices and Printers check box.

C. Change Devices and Printers to Control Panel.

6 Click the **Use Default Settings** button to undo any changes you have made, and then close all open windows. Display the **Taskbar tab** of the **Taskbar and Start Menu Properties** dialog box. How many screen locations can you choose from to display the taskbar?

A. Four

B. Three

C. Two

7 **Close** the dialog box and then display the **Problem Steps Recorder** window. Which of the following is *not* true?

A. There is a button to add voice recording.

B. There is a timer display.

C. There is a Help button.

8 **Close** the **Problem Steps Recorder**. Right-click the taskbar, and then add a **New toolbar**. From your **Bell_Orchid** folder, select the **Honolulu** folder, and then click **Select Folder**. On the taskbar, click the double chevrons >> to the right of *Honolulu*. Your result is:

A. A Jump List displays.

B. The Bell_Orchid folder window displays.

C. The subfolders in the Honolulu folder display.

9 Close all open windows. Delete the **Honolulu** toolbar from the taskbar. Add the **Calendar gadget** to your desktop. Right-click the **Calendar**, point to **Size**, and then click **Large size**. Your result is:

A. The calendar displays only the month.

B. The calendar displays both the month and the day.

C. The calendar displays only the day.

10 Remove the **Calendar** from the desktop; close all open windows. From the **Control Panel**, open the **Ease of Access Center**. Regarding how to make the mouse easier to use, which of the following is true?

A. You can change the color of the mouse pointer to red.

B. You can change the shape of the mouse to a star.

C. You can use the numeric keypad to move the mouse pointer around the screen.

Leave the **Bell_Orchid** folder in your **Documents** folder *only if* you plan to complete Project 4E; otherwise delete it. Be sure you have typed all of your answers in your Word document. **Save** and **Close** your Word document, and submit as directed by your instructor. **Close** [X] all open windows.

End **You have completed Project 4C**

Apply **4B** skills from these Objectives:

- **6** Explore Windows Media Player
- **7** Play Music Using Media Player
- **8** Rip a CD
- **9** Burn a CD
- **10** Watch Videos Using Windows Media Player

Skills Review | Project 4D Using Windows Media Player

Project Files

Student Resource CD or a flash drive containing the student data files:

win04_04D_Answer_Sheet (Word document)

You will save your file as:

Lastname_Firstname_4D_Answer_Sheet

1 **Close** [X] all open windows. On the taskbar, click the **Windows Explorer** button. In the **navigation pane**, click the drive that contains the student files for this textbook, and then navigate to **Chapter_Files ▶ Chapter_04**. Double-click the Word file **win04_4D_Answer_Sheet** to open Word and display the document. Press F12 to display the **Save As** dialog box in Word, navigate to your **Windows 7 Chapter 4** folder, and then using your own name, save the document as **Lastname_Firstname_4D_Answer_Sheet** If necessary, click OK if a message regarding formats displays.

On the taskbar, click the **Word** button to minimize the window; redisplay the document as necessary to type your answers. By using the **Send to** command, from the **Chapter_04** folder, copy the **Project 4D** folder to your **Documents** library. Navigate to **Documents ▶ Project 4D**. Hold down Ctrl, and then drag the **Pr04D Audio** folder into your **Music** library. Hold down Ctrl, and then drag the **Pr04D Video** folder into your **Videos** library. **Close** the window and start **Windows Media Player**. **Maximize** the window if necessary.

Be sure the **Play tab** is active. In the **navigation pane**, click **Videos**, and then in the **details pane**, locate **Flight into Grand Canyon**. What is the length, in minutes, of this video?

A. 7 minutes

B. 8 minutes

C. 9 minutes

2 Double-click the video **Flight into Grand Canyon** to being playing it. **Maximize** the window, and then move the mouse pointer into the lower portion of the screen to display the playback controls area. What displays to indicate how much of the video has played?

A. A thin blue bar moves from left to right.

B. A counter displays in minutes and seconds.

C. Both A. and B.

3 Point to the upper left corner of the screen. What displays?

A. The title of the video

B. A counter

C. Both A. and B.

4 In the **player controls area**, click the **Stop** button. What is your result?

A. The viewing area displays a thumbnail image of the video.

B. The viewing area displays the name of the video you just played.

C. A dark screen displays with options to *Play again* and *Go to Library*.

(Project 4D Using Windows Media Player continues on the next page)

Skills Review | Project 4D Using Windows Media Player (continued)

5 Click **Go to Library**. In the **navigation pane**, click **Music**. Scroll down to **Unknown Artist**, and then in the **Title list**, locate **WolfHowl**. What is the length of this audio file?

A. 18 seconds

B. 28 seconds

C. 19 seconds

6 On the menu bar, click **Organize**. Which of the following is *not* listed on the menu?

A. Manage libraries

B. Sort by

C. Create Auto Playlist

7 On the **Organize** menu, click **Options**, and then click the **Rip Music tab**. Under **Rip settings**, click the **Format** arrow. Which of the following is *not* a format you can use to rip a CD?

A. MP3

B. Window Media Audio

C. Windows Music Player

8 **Close** the **Options** dialog box. Click the **Start** button, click **Help and Support**, type **burn a cd** and press Enter. Click **Burn a CD or DVD in Windows Media Player**. Scroll down and click **Types of discs you can burn**. According to this information, which type of disc has the largest capacity?

A. Data CD

B. Data DVD

C. Audio CD

9 **Close** the **Windows Help and Support** window. In the search box at the top of the Player window, type **elk** What is your result?

A. The ElkBellow audio file begins to play.

B. *ElkBellow* displays in the list pane.

C. Only the title *ElkBellow* displays in the Title list.

10 In the lower left corner, click **Media Guide**. In the navigation bar across the top, click **Internet Radio**, under **Genres**, click **Jazz**, and then click **SKY.fm** or some other station. What is your result?

A. The station plays on your computer's speakers.

B. The station plays with accompanying visualizations.

C. Both A. and B.

Leave the **Pr04D Audio** folder in your **Music** library and the **Pr04 Video** folder in your **Videos** library *only if* you plan to complete Project 4F; otherwise delete the two folders from their respective libraries. Be sure you have typed all of your answers in your Word document. **Save** and **Close** your Word document, and submit as directed by your instructor. **Close** Windows Media Player and all open windows.

End **You have completed Project 4D**

Content-Based Assessments

Apply 4A skills from these Objectives:

1. Personalize the Desktop and Screen Saver
2. Personalize the Start Menu
3. Personalize the Taskbar
4. Personalize the Desktop by Adding Gadgets
5. Personalize the Ease of Access Center and Use Problem Steps Recorder

Mastering Windows 7 | Project 4E Personalizing Your Windows 7 Environment

In the following Mastering Windows 7 project, you will create two toolbars for your taskbar and add a gadget to your desktop. You will capture and save a screen that will look similar to Figure 4.57.

Project Files

For Project 4E, you will need the following file:

New Snip file

You will save your file as:

Lastname_Firstname_4E_Orlando_Snip

Project Results

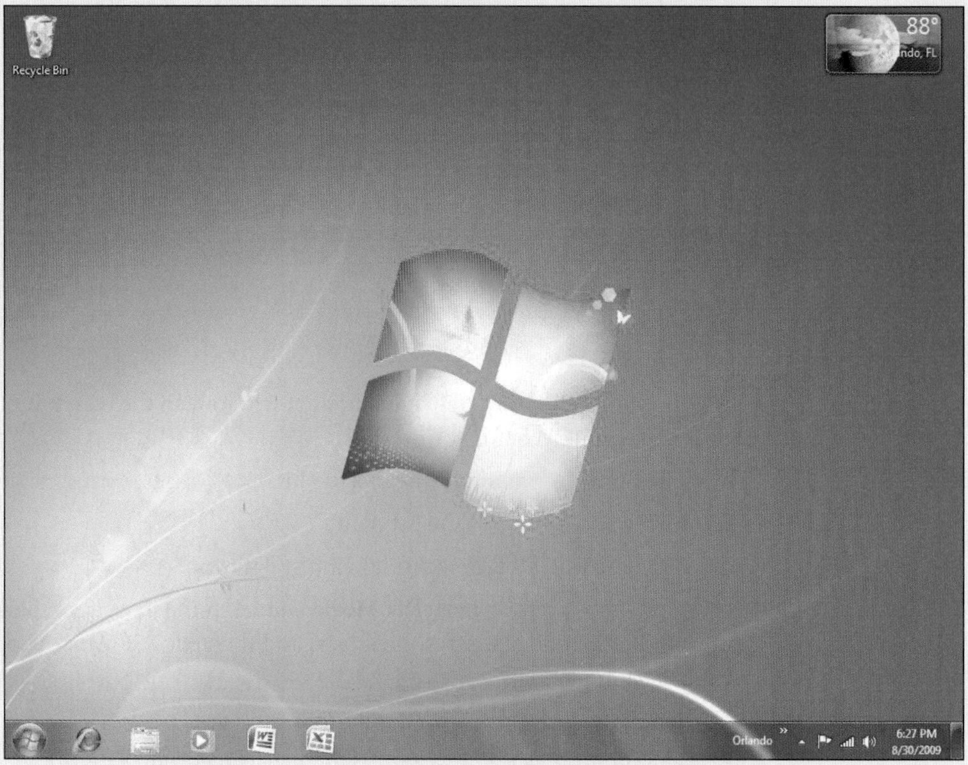

Figure 4.57

(Project 4E Personalizing Your Windows 7 Environment continues on the next page)

Mastering Windows 7 | Project 4E Personalizing Your Windows 7 Environment (continued)

1 If necessary, copy the **Bell_Orchid** folder to your **Documents** library. Create a **New toolbar** on your taskbar to display the **Orlando** folder from your Bell_Orchid folder.

2 Add the **Weather** gadget to your desktop, close the **Gadget** window, and then set the Weather location to Orlando, Florida. Close the Gadgets window.

3 Create a **Full-screen snip** and save it as **Lastname_Firstname_4E_Orlando_Snip**

4 Delete the toolbar that you created, and then remove the **Weather** gadget from your desktop. Delete the **Bell_Orchid** folder from the **Documents** library. Submit your snip file as directed by your instructor.

End **You have completed Project 4E**

Apply **4B** skills from these Objectives:

- **6** Explore Windows Media Player
- **7** Play Music Using Media Player
- **8** Rip a CD
- **9** Burn a CD
- **10** Watch Videos Using Windows Media Player

Mastering Windows 7 | Project 4F Using Windows Media Player

In the following Mastering Windows 7 project, you will create a playlist that includes both audio and video files. You will capture and save a screen that will look similar to Figure 4.58.

Project Files

For Project 4F, you will need the following file:

New Snip file

You will save your file as:

Lastname_Firstname_4F_Media_Snip

Project Results

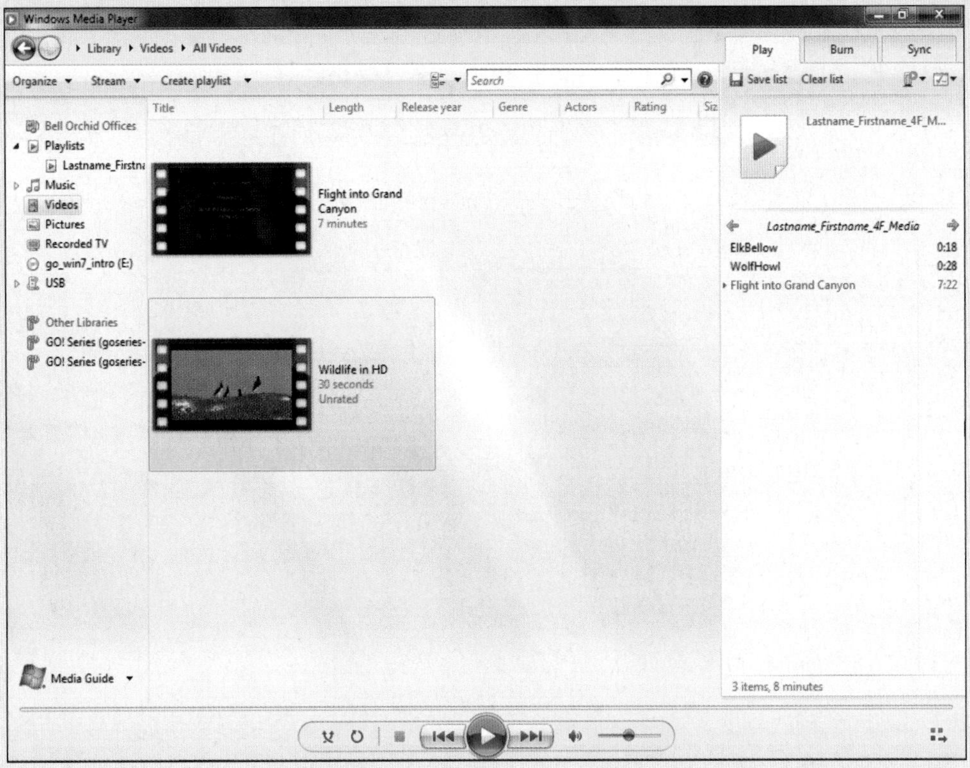

Figure 4.58

(Project 4F Using Windows Media Player continues on the next page)

Mastering Windows 7 | Project 4F Using Windows Media Player (continued)

1 If necessary, by using the **Send to** command, copy the **Project 4D** folder to your **Documents** library. Navigate to **Documents** ▶ **Project 4D**. Hold down Ctrl, and then drag the **Pr04D Audio** folder into your **Music** library. Hold down Ctrl, and then drag the **Pr04D Video** folder in your **Videos** library. **Close** the window.

2 Start **Windows Media Player**. **Maximize** the window. Click the **Play tab**, clear the **list pane**, and then from your **Music** library, drag **ElkBellow** and **WolfHowl** into the **list pane**. From your **Videos** library, drag **Flight into Grand Canyon** into the **list pane**. Save the playlist as **Lastname_Firstname_4F_Media**

3 Create a **Full-screen snip** and save it as **Lastname_Firstname_4F_Media_Snip** Submit this file as directed by your instructor. Close all open windows. Delete the **Pr04D Audio** and **Pr04D Video** folders from their respective libraries.

End **You have completed Project 4F**

Outcomes-Based Assessments

Rubric

The following outcomes-based assessments are *open-ended assessments*. That is, there is no specific correct result; your result will depend on your approach to the information provided. Make *Professional Quality* your goal. Use the following scoring rubric to guide you in *how* to approach the problem, and then to evaluate *how well* your approach solves the problem.

The criteria—Software Mastery, Content, Format and Layout, and Process—represent the knowledge and skills you have gained that you can apply to solving the problem. The levels of performance—Professional Quality, Approaching Professional Quality, or Needs Quality Improvements—help you and your instructor evaluate your result.

	Your completed project is of Professional Quality if you:	Your completed project is of Approaching Professional Quality if you:	Your completed project Needs Quality Improvements if you:
1-Software Mastery	Choose and apply the most appropriate skills, tools, and features and identify efficient methods to solve the problem.	Choose and apply some appropriate skills, tools, and features, but not in the most efficient manner.	Choose inappropriate skills, tools, or features, or are inefficient in solving the problem.
2-Content	Construct a solution that is clear and well organized, contains content that is accurate, appropriate to the audience and purpose, and is complete. Provide a solution that contains no errors of spelling, grammar, or style.	Construct a solution in which some components are unclear, poorly organized, inconsistent, or incomplete. Misjudge the needs of the audience. Have some errors in spelling, grammar, or style, but the errors do not detract from comprehension.	Construct a solution that is unclear, incomplete, or poorly organized, contains some inaccurate or inappropriate content, and contains many errors of spelling, grammar, or style. Do not solve the problem.
3-Format and Layout	Format and arrange all elements to communicate information and ideas, clarify function, illustrate relationships, and indicate relative importance.	Apply appropriate format and layout features to some elements, but not others. Overuse features, causing minor distraction.	Apply format and layout that does not communicate information or ideas clearly. Do not use format and layout features to clarify function, illustrate relationships, or indicate relative importance. Use available features excessively, causing distraction.
4-Process	Use an organized approach that integrates planning, development, self-assessment, revision, and reflection.	Demonstrate an organized approach in some areas, but not others; or, use an insufficient process of organization throughout.	Do not use an organized approach to solve the problem.

Apply a combination of the 4A and 4B skills.

Problem Solving | Project 4G Help Desk

Project Files

For Project 4G, you will need the following file:

win04_4G_Help_Desk

You will save your file as

Lastname_Firstname_4G_Help_Desk

From the student files that accompany this textbook, open the **Chapter_Files** folder, and then in the **Chapter_04** folder, locate and open the Word document **win04_4G_Help_Desk**. Save the document in your chapter folder as **Lastname_Firstname_4G_Help_Desk**

The following e-mail question has arrived at the Help Desk from an employee at the Bell Orchid Hotel's corporate office. In the Word document, construct a response based on your knowledge of Windows 7. Although an e-mail response is not as formal as a letter, you should still use good grammar, good sentence structure, professional language, and a polite tone. Save your document and submit the response as directed by your instructor.

To: Help Desk

My supervisor sent me some DVDs that contain video training. Will these play on Windows Media Player? If so, how do I start the player and view the video?

End **You have completed Project 4G**

Outcomes-Based Assessments

Apply a combination of the 4A and 4B skills.

Problem Solving | Project 4H Help Desk

Project Files

For Project 4H, you will need the following file:

win04_4H_Help_Desk

You will save your file as

Lastname_Firstname_4H_Help_Desk

From the student files that accompany this textbook, open the **Chapter_Files** folder, and then in the **Chapter_04** folder, locate and open **win04_4H_Help_Desk**. Save the document in your chapter folder as **Lastname_Firstname_4H_Help_Desk**

The following e-mail question has arrived at the Help Desk from an employee at the Bell Orchid Hotel's corporate office. In the Word document, construct a response based on your knowledge of Windows 7. Although an e-mail response is not as formal as a letter, you should still use good grammar, good sentence structure, professional language, and a polite tone. Save your document and submit the response as directed by your instructor.

To: Help Desk

I am working on a project where I am researching three specific government Web sites and then storing all of my notes in several documents that I have created. Is there any way that I could make it easier to access these three Web sites and three documents without opening a lot of windows every time I need to start and stop work on this project?

End **You have completed Project 4H**

Apply a combination of the 4A and 4B skills.

Problem Solving | Project 4I Help Desk

Project Files

For Project 4I, you will need the following file:

win04_4I_Help_Desk

You will save your document as

Lastname_Firstname_4I_Help_Desk

From the student files that accompany this textbook, open the **Chapter_Files** folder, and then in the **Chapter_04** folder, locate and open **win04_4I_Help_Desk**. Save the document in your chapter folder as **Lastname_Firstname_4I_Help_Desk**

The following e-mail question has arrived at the Help Desk from an employee at the Bell Orchid Hotel's corporate office. In the Word document, construct a response based on your knowledge of Windows 7. Although an e-mail response is not as formal as a letter, you should still use good grammar, good sentence structure, professional language, and a polite tone. Save your document and submit the response as directed by your instructor.

To: Help Desk

I need to make my computer easier to see. Can you tell me how to find out about the ways I can do that?

End **You have completed Project 4I**

Exploring the World Wide Web with Internet Explorer 8

OUTCOMES

At the end of this chapter you will be able to:

OBJECTIVES

Mastering these objectives will enable you to:

PROJECT 5A

Browse the Web efficiently, print and save Web information, and manage your browsing history and add-ons.

1. Use Tabbed Browsing (p. 289)
2. Organize Favorites (p. 302)
3. Manage Browsing History and Browse with InPrivate (p. 308)
4. Print, Zoom, and Change the Text Size of Web Pages (p. 311)
5. Save Web Page Information (p. 319)
6. Manage Add-ons (p. 321)

PROJECT 5B

Use Web Slices, Accelerators, and search and download from the Web safely.

7. Search the Internet (p. 325)
8. Subscribe to and View an RSS Feed (p. 328)
9. Use Web Slices, Accelerators, and Suggested Sites (p. 332)
10. Block Pop-up Windows and Use the Information Bar (p. 339)
11. Protect Against Malware (p. 341)
12. Protect Your Data (p. 343)

Charles Zachritz/Shutterstock

In This Chapter

In this chapter, you will browse the Web using Internet Explorer 8. Browsing the Web is one of the most common activities of computer users. You will use tabbed browsing, in which you can open multiple Web sites in one window. You will also use Web Slices and Accelerators to speed your Web browsing.

Internet Explorer 8 includes features to make printing and saving Web pages easy. You can also save and print pictures from a Web site. You will discover how to locate, subscribe to, and view RSS feeds. Internet Explorer 8 provides for inline toolbar searching, which allows you to conduct a search without actually navigating to the Web site of the search provider. You will practice conducting searches from multiple search providers from the Internet Explorer Search box.

The projects in this chapter relate to the **Bell Orchid Hotels**, headquartered in Boston, and which own and operate resorts and business-oriented hotels. Resort properties are located in popular destinations, including Honolulu, Orlando, San Diego, and Santa Barbara. The resorts offer deluxe accommodations and a wide array of dining options. Other Bell Orchid hotels are located in major business centers and offer the latest technology in their meeting facilities. The company plans to open new properties and update existing properties over the next ten years.

Project 5A Browsing the Web with Internet Explorer 8

Project Activities

In Activities 5.1 through 5.10, you will work with Barbara Hewitt and Steven Ramos, employees in the Information Technology department at the headquarters office of Bell Orchid Hotels, as they explore how to browse and navigate the World Wide Web by using Internet Explorer 8. Bell Orchid Hotels is investigating a new hotel opportunity in Miami, Florida, which will be geared to both business travelers and family vacations. Barbara and Steven have the assignment to conduct research on the Web for this new hotel. Your completed screens will look similar to Figure 5.1.

Project Files

For Project 5A, you will need the following files:

New Snip files

You will save your files as:

Lastname_Firstname_5A_Florida_Snip
Lastname_Firstname_5A_Favorites_Snip
Lastname_Firstname_5A_Print_Snip
Lastname_Firstname_5A_Picture_Snip

Project Results

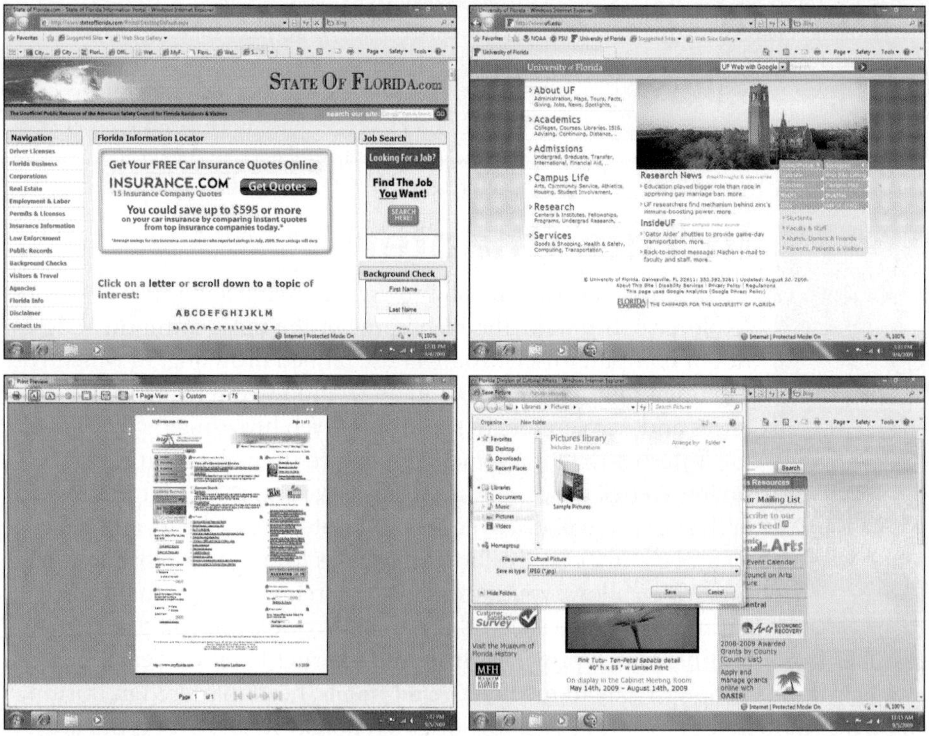

Figure 5.1
Project 5A Browsing the Web with Internet Explorer 8

Objective 1 | Use Tabbed Browsing

A ***Web browser*** is a software program that you use to display Web pages and navigate the Internet. ***Internet Explorer 8*** is the Web browser software developed by Microsoft Corporation and that is included with Windows 7. ***Browsing*** is the term used to describe the process of using your computer to view Web pages. ***Surfing*** refers to the process of navigating the Internet either for a particular item or for anything that is of interest, and quickly moving from one item to another.

Browsing the Web is one of the most common activities performed by individuals who use computers. Common tasks that you perform on the Internet might include looking at your favorite news sites, managing your finances with your bank, conducting research, shopping, sending e-mail, using social media sites such as Facebook or Twitter, or reading or writing entries in a ***blog***. A blog—short for ***Web log***—is an online journal or column used to publish personal or company information in an informal manner. For example, the developers of Microsoft Word maintain a blog of information about using Word at *http://blogs.msdn.com/microsoft_office_word*.

Activity 5.01 | Using Tabbed Browsing

Tabbed browsing is a feature in Internet Explorer that enables you to open multiple Web sites in a single browser window. You open each new Web page in a new tab, and then switch among your open Web pages by clicking the tab that displays in the upper portion of the screen. The advantage to using tabbed browsing is that you have fewer items open on the taskbar.

In this activity, you will work with Barbara and Steven, who are conducting research on the new hotel in Miami.

> **Another Way**
>
> On the Start menu, in the Search box, type Internet Explorer, and then click the program name.

1. On the taskbar, click the **Internet Explorer** button. If a Welcome screen displays, in the lower right, click **Ask me later.**

   The ***home page*** that is set on your computer displays. On your computer, *home page* refers to whatever Web page you have selected—or is set by default—to display on your computer when you start Internet Explorer. When visiting a Web site, *home page* refers to the starting point for the remainder of the pages on that site.

   For example, your computer manufacturer may have set its company site as the default home page. At your college, the home page of your college's Web site might be the home page on the computer at which you are working.

> **More Knowledge | Consider Downloading These Additional Windows 7 Programs**
>
> Some programs that were included in Windows Vista and Windows XP are no longer included in Windows 7. Instead, you can decide which programs you need and download them for free by using ***Windows Live Essentials***. The new free programs include: Windows Live Mail (replaces Windows Mail and Outlook Express), Windows Live Messenger, Windows Live Photo Gallery, Windows Live Movie Maker, and Windows Live Family Safety. You can also download for free Office Outlook Connector, Office Live Add-in, and Microsoft Silverlight. To get information about and download any of these free programs, go to www.download.live.com.

2 At the top of your screen, click in the **address bar** to select (highlight) the current Web address, and then compare your screen with Figure 5.2.

The ***address bar*** is the area at the top of the Internet Explorer window that displays, and where you can type, a ***URL—Uniform Resource Locator***—which is an address that uniquely identifies a location on the Internet.

A URL is usually preceded by *http://* and can contain additional details, such as the name of a page of hypertext, which often has the extension *.html* or *.htm*.

Figure 5.2

URL in address bar highlighted (your selected URL may differ)

Address bar

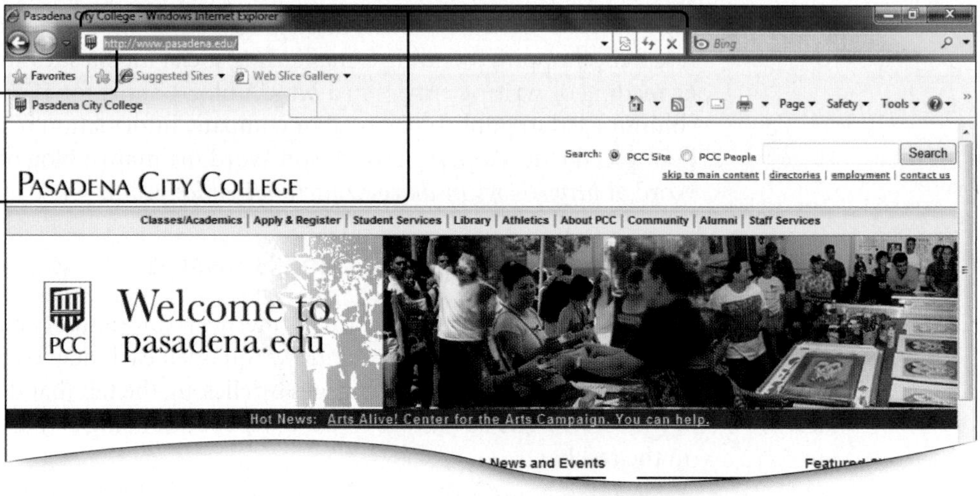

> **Another Way**
>
> Instead of pressing Enter, you can click the small blue arrow at the end of the address bar.

3 In the **address bar**, with the current URL selected, type **www.usa.gov** and then press Enter. Notice the URL in the **address bar**, and then compare your screen with Figure 5.3.

The Web site for the United States Government displays. By typing in the address bar, the new URL opens and the original URL—whatever your home page site was—closes.

A URL contains the ***protocol prefix***—in this instance ***http***—which stands for ***HyperText Transfer Protocol***. HTTP represents the set of communication rules used by your computer to connect to servers on the Web. Internet Explorer defaults to the *http* prefix, so it is not necessary to type it, even though it is part of the URL for this site.

The protocol prefix is followed by a colon and the separators //.

A URL also contains the ***domain name***—in this instance *www.usa.gov*. A domain name is an organization's unique name on the Internet, and consists of a chosen name combined with a ***top level domain*** such as *.com* or *.org* or *.gov*.

Figure 5.3

Address bar indicates URL for United States Government

Tab for *USA.gov* Web site

Alert! | Web Sites Update Content Frequently

As you progress through the projects in this chapter, the pictures of various Web sites in this textbook may not match your screens exactly, because Web site administrators frequently update content. This will not affect your ability to complete the projects successfully.

4 Take a moment to study the table in Figure 5.4 to become familiar with top level domains.

There are two types of top level domains—the generic top level domains, such as *.com*, *.org*, and so on, and the ***country codes*** such as *.ca* for Canada, *.cn* for China, and *.uk* for United Kingdom.

Common Domain Name Extensions and Organization Types

Domain Name Extension	Organization Type
.com	Commercial businesses and companies
.net	Internet service providers and other communications-oriented organizations
.org	Usually nonprofit organizations
.edu	U. S. educational only
.gov	U. S. government only
.info	Information services
.mobi	Mobile devices
.name	Individuals and families
.biz	Usually small businesses

Figure 5.4

5 Click in the **address bar** to select the URL text, and then type **miamibeachfl.gov** and press Enter.

The acronym *www*, which stands for *World Wide Web*, is used for uniformity on the Web. You can usually omit typing *www* and its following dot, because most Web servers are configured to handle a URL with or without it. If a Web page does not display without typing *www*, retype the URL and include *www*.

6 To the immediate right of the **Forward** button, locate and click the **Recent Pages** button. Compare your screen with Figure 5.5.

The ***Recent Pages*** button displays a list of recently accessed locations, and the current location is indicated by a check mark. By clicking an item on this list, you can jump to a recently accessed location quickly. The list is limited to the current session; thus, only locations you have accessed since starting Internet Explorer display on the list.

Figure 5.5

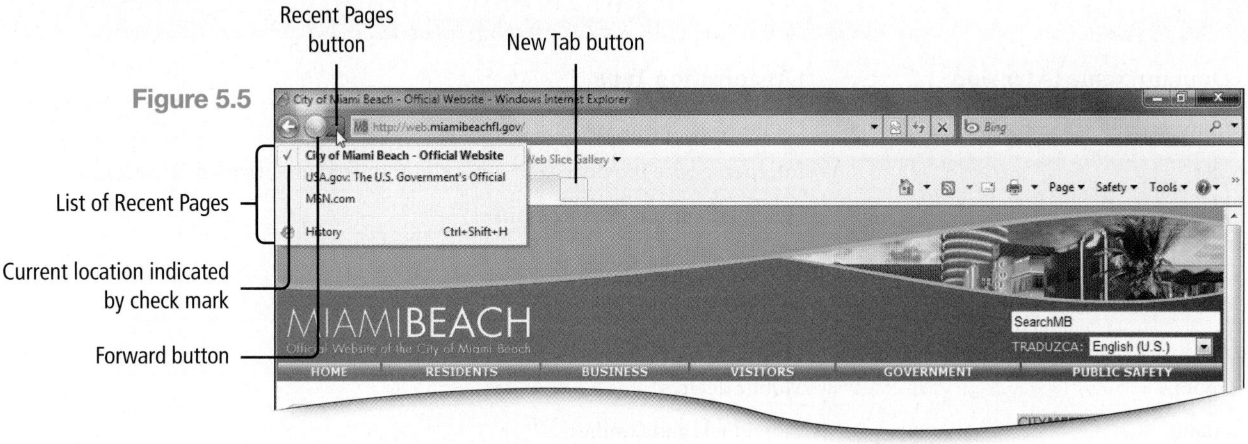

7 Click the **Recent Pages** button again to close the list, and then locate and point to the **New Tab** button, which is to the immediate right of the **City of Miami Beach tab**. Click the **New Tab** button one time. Compare your screen with Figure 5.6, and then take a moment to study the parts of the Internet Explorer window in the table in Figure 5.7.

The screen for a new tab displays, and in the address bar, *about:Tabs* is selected. This *What do you want to do next?* page will display a list of sites that you have opened and then closed during this session, which is useful if you have closed a browser window by mistake and want to go back to it.

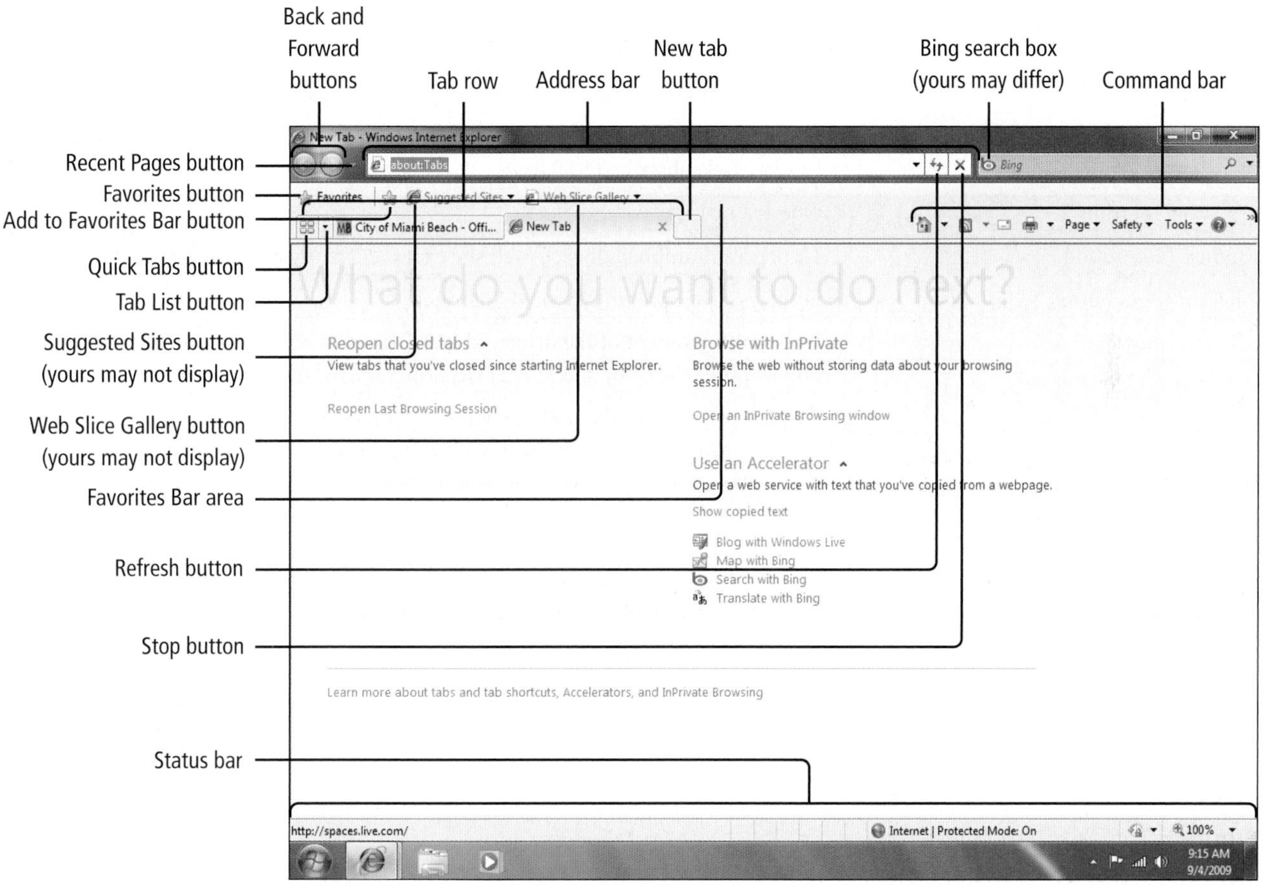

Figure 5.6

Parts of the Internet Explorer Window

Window Element	Function
Add to Favorites Bar button	Places the active URL on the Favorites Bar.
Address bar	Displays the URL of the currently active Web page.
Back and Forward buttons	Display Web pages you have previously visited.
Bing search box	Provides an area in which you type a search term to conduct an Internet search; Bing is the default search engine but you can select a different one.
Command bar	Contains, by default, the buttons to view your Home page; view your Feeds; view mail; print Web pages; manipulate Web pages, for example by saving; select safety settings; and to display a list of Tools.
Favorites Bar	Displays links to favorite Web sites that you have placed there.
Favorites button	Opens the Favorites Center pane, which is an area to manage your Favorites, browser history, and subscribed RSS feeds.
New Tab button	Opens a new tab.
Quick Tabs button	Displays a thumbnail of each Web site that is currently open on a single tab.
Recent Pages button	Displays a list of recently visited Web sites.
Refresh button	Updates the content of the displayed Web page; for example, to update temperatures on a weather site or update stock prices on a financial site.
Status bar	Displays, on the left, the URL for a link to which your mouse is pointing; on the right, displays information about the download process of a Web site and also icons to change your security settings and Zoom level.
Stop button	Stops the download of a Web page that you requested.
Suggested Sites button	Helps you discover Web sites that are similar to the sites you visit.
Tab List button	Lists the names of all Web sites currently open on a tab.
Tab row	Displays a tab for each open Web page.
Web Slice Gallery button	Enables you to subscribe to Web Slices—a specific portion of a Web page that you can subscribe to, and which enables you to see updated content, for example weather or traffic.

Figure 5.7

8 With the text in the **address bar** selected, type **miamigov.com/cms** and then press Enter to display the Web site for the **City of Miami**. Click the **New Tab** button, type **doh.state.fl.us** and then press Enter. Compare your screen with Figure 5.8.

The Web site for the Florida Department of Health opens in the new tab.

Figure 5.8

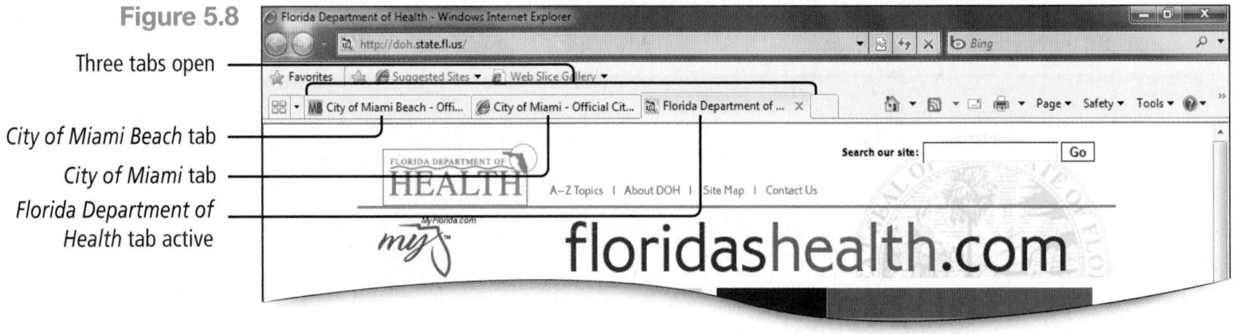

9 On the **tab row**, click the first open tab—the **City of Miami Beach tab**.

The Web site for Miami Beach redisplays. Recall that by opening multiple sites on tabs, you can switch between Web sites easily by clicking a tab.

10 On the taskbar, *point to* the **Internet Explorer** icon to display a thumbnail for each open tab.

Here you can see the Web sites that you have open in Internet Explorer, and can navigate to a site by clicking its thumbnail.

11 At the end of the **tab row**, click the **New Tab** button, type **hsmv.state.fl.us** and then press Enter to display the site for the **Florida Department of Highway Safety and Motor Vehicles**. Open another **New Tab**, type **leg.state.fl.us** and then press Enter to display the site for the **Florida Legislature**. Compare your screen with Figure 5.9.

Depending on the size of your screen and its resolution, the tabs might display differently than shown in Figure 5.9, but you can see that five Web pages are open.

Figure 5.9

Five tabs display (the width of your tabs may vary)

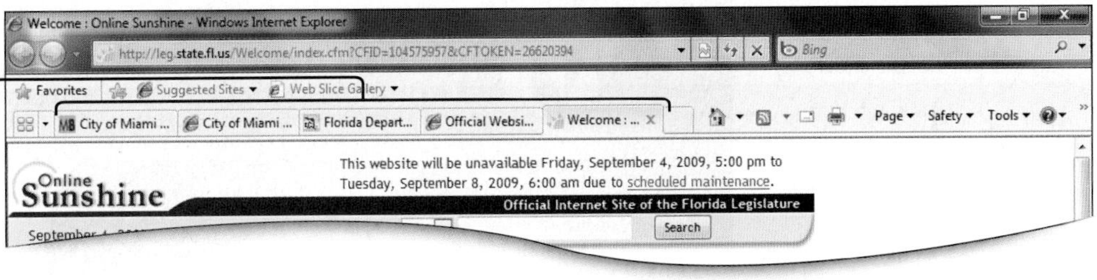

12 Click the **New Tab** button, and then type **myflorida.com** and press Enter. Click the **New Tab** button, and then type **visitflorida.com** and press Enter.

Seven Web sites are open and seven tabs display in your tab row. As you open more tabs, the width of each tab decreases slightly and you can no longer read all the text on the tab.

13 By clicking the **New Tab** button for each, open the following five sites, waiting a moment for each site to display completely. Then, compare your screen with Figure 5.10.

dep.state.fl.us

stateofflorida.com

floridastateparks.org

florida.edu

mdc.edu

Twelve Web sites are open, however on some screens, Internet Explorer will display only nine or ten tabs in the tab row, plus the New Tab button. On larger screens, you might be able to display more tabs.

Figure 5.10

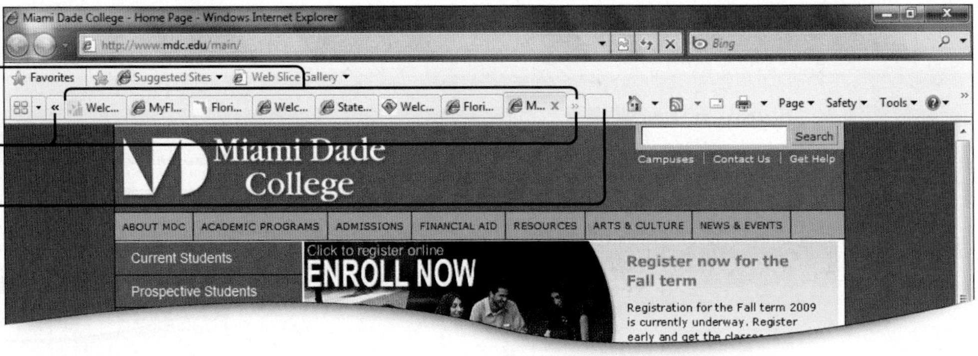

> **More Knowledge | Using the Address Bar Efficiently**
>
> The address bar, based on the first few characters that you type, will search across your History, Favorites, and RSS Feeds, displaying matches from the address or any part of the URL. When you see a match, click it to avoid retyping the entire URL of a site you have previously visited.

14 On the **tab row**, to the *left* of the first visible tab, click the « button, and then compare your screen with Figure 5.11.

When you have more sites open than Internet Explorer can display on the tab row, the small tabs with double chevrons indicate that more tabs are available. When the double chevrons are black, this indicates that additional tabs are open to the left (<<) or to the right (>>). If the double chevrons are dimmed, no additional tabs are open in the direction of the chevrons.

Figure 5.11

> **Alert! | Does your screen differ?**
>
> Your array of tabs may differ due to larger or smaller screen sizes or differing screen resolutions. If your screens do not match exactly, examine the figures shown.

Activity 5.02 | Using the Tab List, Quick Tabs, and Shortcuts to Navigate Among Open Tabs

When you have multiple Web pages open at once, each one is displayed on a separate tab. When many Web pages are open and the width of each tab is decreased, it may become difficult to determine which tab represents a specific site. In this activity, you will practice various ways to navigate the open tabs to find the one you want easily.

1 On the left end of the **tab row**, click the **Tab List** button, and then compare your screen with Figure 5.12.

The Tab List displays. When multiple tabs are open, the Web site name on each tab is truncated—cut short. By clicking the Tab List button, you can see a list of all open Web sites, in the order they were opened, and you can see the complete name of each Web site that is open on a tab.

Additionally, the highlighted section indicates tabs that are visible on the tab row; tabs outside of the highlighted area, for example at the bottom in Figure 5.12, are open, but their tabs are not in view on the tab row.

From this list, you can click a site to move to another tab, regardless of whether the tab is visible on the tab row.

Figure 5.12

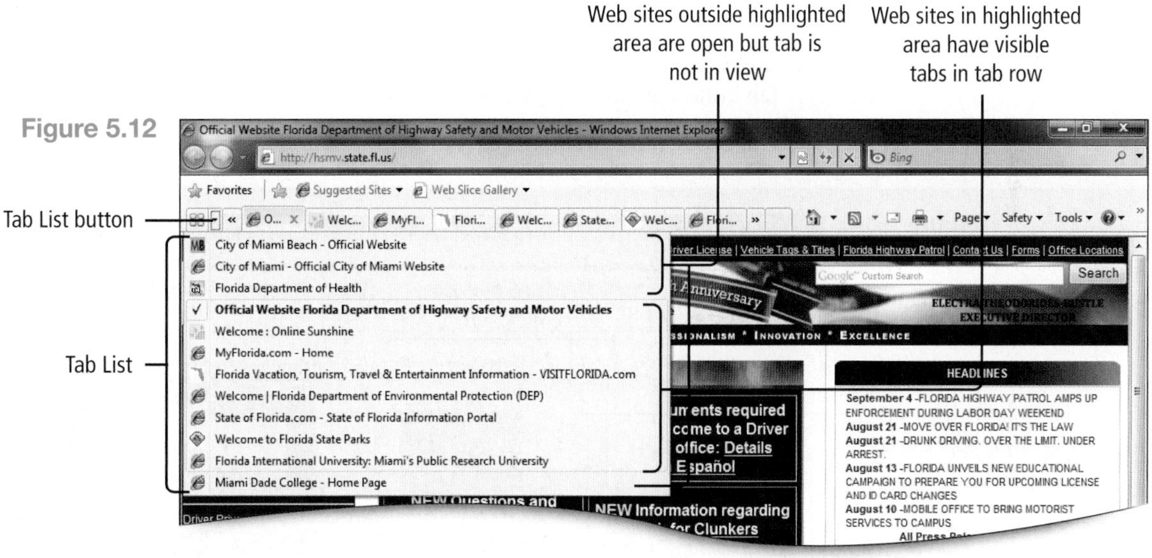

2 On the displayed **Tab List** menu, at the top, click **City of Miami Beach**. Notice that to the immediate left of the **Miami Beach tab**, *no* small tab with double chevrons displays, because all tabs to the left are in view. Point to the **City of Miami Beach tab**, and then notice that a ScreenTip displays the site name and the site's URL. Notice also that because this is the active tab, the **Close Tab** button [×] displays, as shown in Figure 5.13.

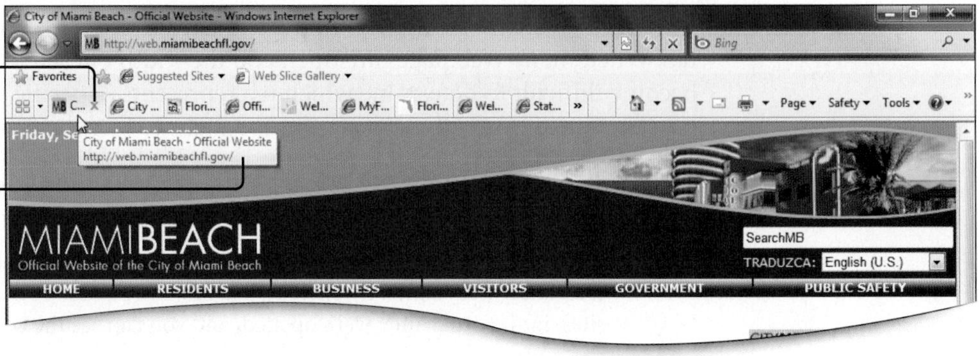
Close Tab button displays in active tab
ScreenTip displays site name and URL

Figure 5.13

Another Way

Hold down Ctrl, and then press W to close the active tab.

3 On the **City of Miami Beach tab**, click the **Close Tab** button [×] to close the **City of Miami Beach** Web site and to make the next tab in the row the active tab.

Another Way

Press Ctrl + Q.

4 On the left end of the **tab row**, click the **Quick Tabs** button [Quick Tabs], and then compare your screen with Figure 5.14.

When you have multiple Web pages open and the tab names are truncated, you can use the ***Quick Tabs*** display. The Quick Tabs feature provides a thumbnail view of all open tabs. From this view, you can click any thumbnail to open a Web page or click the Close Tab button to close a Web page.

The Quick Tabs button displays only when you have more than one Web page open.

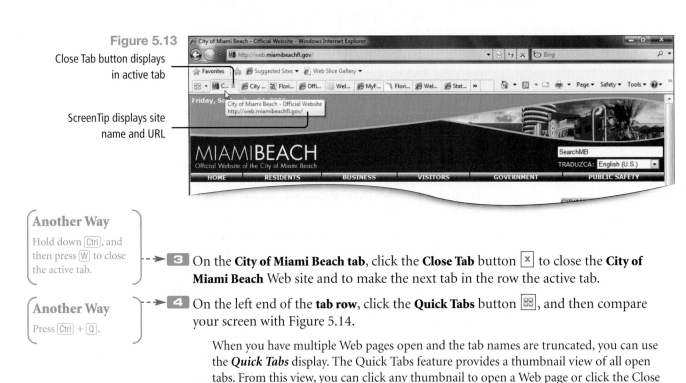

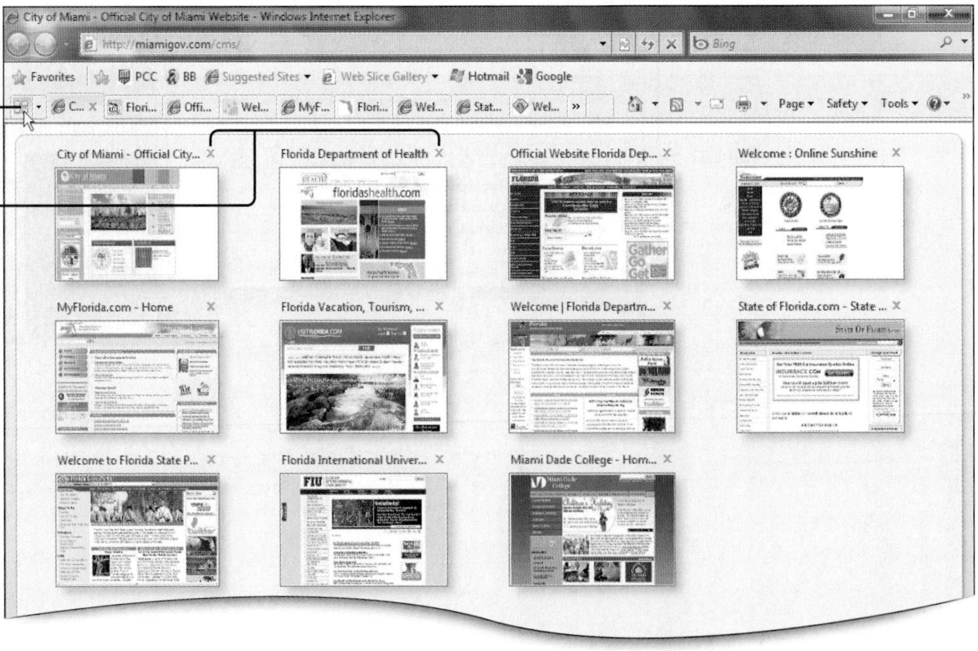
Quick Tabs button in tab row
Tab Close buttons display for each site (your sites may vary in appearance)

Figure 5.14

5 In the **Quick Tabs** display, click the thumbnail for **State of Florida.com** to display its site.

In this manner, you can display any open site from the Quick Tabs display.

6 **Start** the **Snipping Tool** program, click the **New arrow**, and then click **Full-screen Snip**. In the **Snipping Tool** mark-up window, click the **Save Snip** button.

7 In the **Save As** dialog box, in the **navigation pane**, scroll down as necessary, and then under **Computer**, click your USB flash drive so that it displays in the **address bar**. On the toolbar, click the **New folder** button, type **Windows 7 Chapter 5** and press Enter.

8 In the **file list**, double-click your **Windows 7 Chapter 5** folder to open it. Click in the **File name** box, and then replace the selected text by typing **Lastname_Firstname_5A_Florida_Snip** Be sure the file type is **JPEG file**, and then press Enter. **Close** the **Snipping Tool** mark-up window. Hold this file until you finish Project 5A, and then submit this file as directed by your instructor.

> **More Knowledge | The Display of Quick Tabs Scales to the Number of Open Tabs**
>
> The Quick Tabs display scales to the number of tabs that you have open. For example, if you have nine tabs open, Quick Tabs shows thumbnail images of all nine tabs. If you have more than 20 tabs open, you will see smaller thumbnail images of each tab, but you can still see all the tabs in a single view.

9 Click the **Quick Tabs** button again. In the **Quick Tabs** display, point to the **Close Tab** button for the **State of Florida.com** site as shown in Figure 5.15.

Figure 5.15

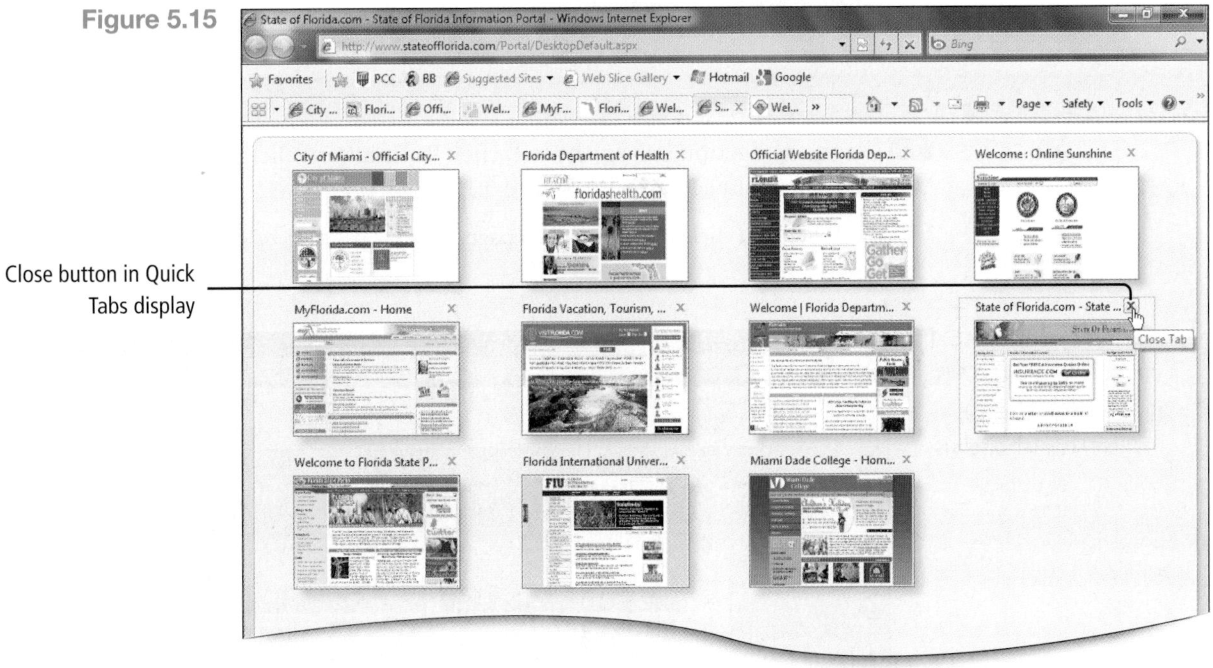

10 Click the **Close Tab** button [×] to close the Web page, and notice that in the display, the thumbnails rearrange to fill the blank space. *Except* for the **City of Miami** site (do not close it), use the same technique to close all the other sites. Then click the thumbnail image for the **City of Miami** to display the site. Compare your screen with Figure 5.16.

Although the content of this Web page may differ from what you currently have displayed, you can see that this Web page contains various links—other pages in this Web site that you can display. Groups of links are sometimes referred to as a ***navigation bar***.

Figure 5.16

Navigation bar with links (yours may differ)

Navigation bar with links (yours may differ)

Link to City Officials (yours may differ)

11 On the navigation bar on the left, click **Business**; or, click any link on the page. Compare your screen with Figure 5.17.

When you click a link on a Web page, the new page opens on the same tab.

Figure 5.17

Back button active

Link opens on *same* tab—only one tab displays

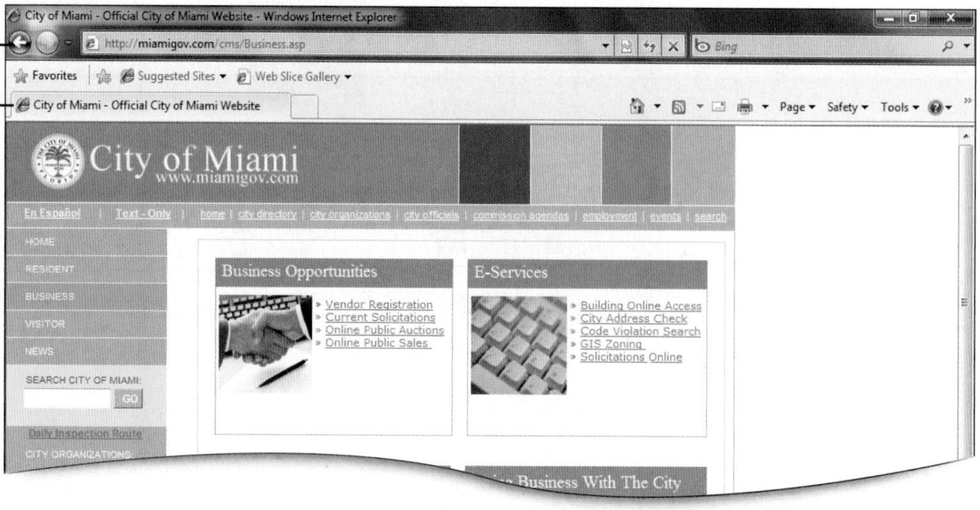

12 In the upper left corner, click the **Back** button one time to return to the previous page. Then, click the **Forward** button to redisplay the page regarding Business information in the City of Miami.

In this manner, you can click the Back and Forward buttons as necessary to redisplay pages you have visited.

> **Another Way**
> Point to a link on the page and right-click, and then click Open in New Tab.

13 Hold down Ctrl, and then in the navigation bar in the upper portion of the page, click **city directory**. Notice that a new tab opens for the **City Directory** page but the page itself does not display. Notice also that the two tabs display in the same color.

In this manner, you can open links in separate tabs without actually displaying them. When you are finished viewing the active page, you can investigate the other links you opened. Additionally, the tabs are colored to match so that you know they are related.

14 In the same navigation bar in the upper portion of the page, hold down both Ctrl and Shift, point to **employment**, and then click. Release the keys.

The link opens in a new tab, and the color coding continues to indicate that the tabs originated from the same site.

Use this technique to open a link in a new tab and simultaneously display the link.

> **Another Way**
> Double-click an empty space in the tab row to open a new tab.

15 Hold down Ctrl and press T to open a new tab. Type **sunbiz.org** and press Enter. In the **tab row**, point to the **City Directory tab**. If you have a mouse wheel, also referred to as the *middle mouse button*, click it and notice that the tab is closed. Otherwise, point to the tab, right-click, and click Close Tab.

16 Point to the middle tab—for the city's **Employee Relations Department**, right-click, and then click **Close Tab**.

Use either of these techniques to close a tab without first making it the active tab. This is useful when you have some tabs open that you no longer need and want to close them quickly.

17 Press Ctrl + T to open a new tab, and then compare your screen with Figure 5.18.

After you have opened and closed sites, you can view a list of all the sites you have visited in this session by opening a new tab. Then, if you want to do so, you can click a site name to open it on this tab.

Figure 5.18

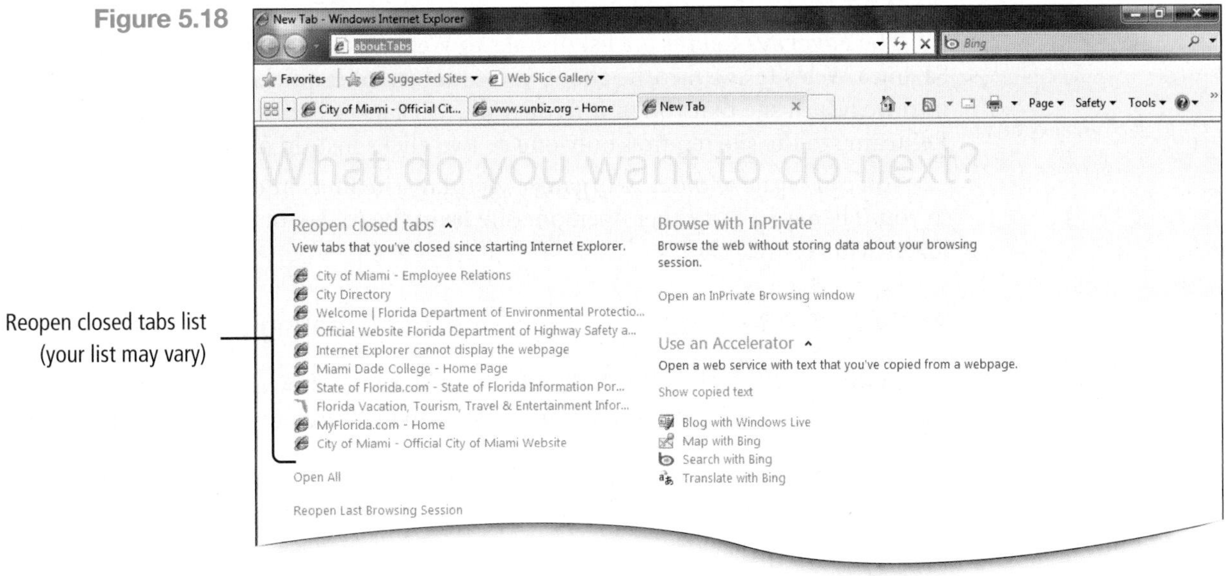

18 In the upper right corner of the Internet Explorer window, click the **Close** button.

When you close Internet Explorer, you are prompted to close all the tabs, or you can close only the current tab.

19 In the displayed **Internet Explorer** dialog box, click **Close all tabs**.

20 Take a moment to examine some additional shortcuts that you can use when navigating in Internet Explorer as shown in the table in Figure 5.19.

Keyboard and Mouse Shortcuts When Working with Tabs in Internet Explorer	
To do this:	**Press or do this:**
Open links in a new tab in the background	Ctrl + click; or point to the link, right-click, and click Open In New Tab.
Open links in a new tab in the foreground	Ctrl + Shift + click using the left or middle mouse button.
Open a new tab in the foreground	Ctrl + T
Switch between tabs	Ctrl + Tab or Ctrl + Shift + Tab (right to left and left to right).
Close current tab (or current window when there are no open tabs)	Ctrl + W
Switch to a specific tab number	Ctrl + *n* (where *n* is a number between 1 and 8).
Switch to the last tab	Ctrl + 9.
Open Quick Tabs (thumbnail view)	Ctrl + Q.
Open a link in a tab with a wheel mouse	Click the link with the mouse wheel.
Close a tab with a wheel mouse	Click the tab with the mouse wheel.
Reorder tabs in the tab row	Point to the tab you want to move, and then drag it to the desired position.

Figure 5.19

Objective 2 | Organize Favorites

The ***Favorites Center*** is a list of links to Web sites that is saved in your Web browser. Saving a Web site as a favorite allows you to return to it quickly. For example, if you have a favorite health site that you visit frequently, you can save that site's address as a Favorite. Returning to the site requires only one or two clicks instead of typing a complete URL.

You can create a folder to organize your favorite links into groups that are meaningful to you. Then, you can either open one site from the folder, or open all the sites in the folder with a single click.

Activity 5.03 | Organizing Favorites and Creating a Favorites Folder

In this activity, you will help Barbara and Steven organize a number of sites that they believe will be useful to those who are conducting research for the new hotel in Miami.

1 **Close** any open windows and display your Windows 7 desktop. On the taskbar, click the **Internet Explorer** button, click in the **address bar**, and then type **mdc.edu** and press Enter.

2 Click the **New Tab** button, type **florida.edu** and then press Enter.

Barbara and Steven know that one thing managers will be looking for are institutions of higher learning where employees can gain additional knowledge and credentials in management, computer science, and tourism management.

3 In the upper left corner, click the **Favorites** button, and then at the top of the pane, to the right of *Add to Favorites*, click the **arrow**. On the displayed list, click **Add Current Tabs to Favorites.**

4 In the **Add Tabs to Favorites** dialog box, in the **Folder Name** box, type **Colleges and Universities** If necessary, click the Create in arrow and click Favorites. Compare your screen with Figure 5.20.

Figure 5.20

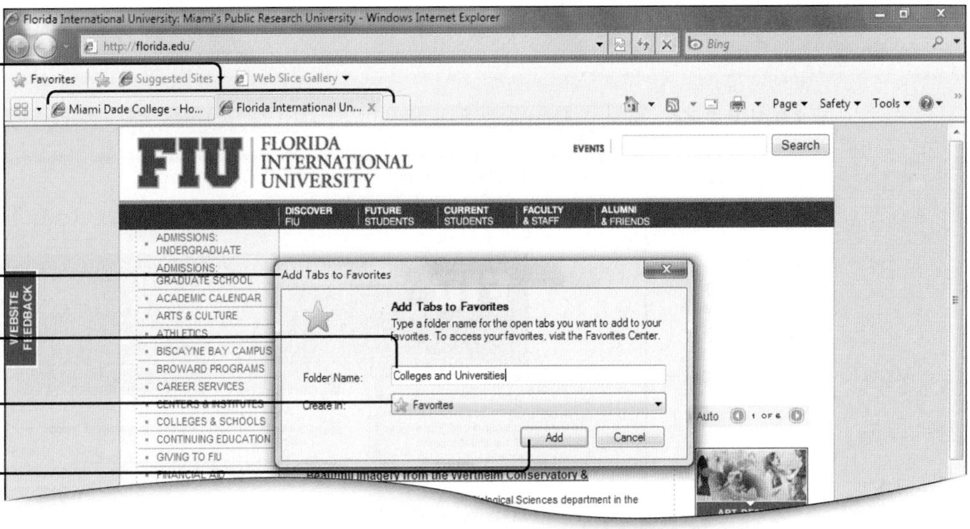

5 In the dialog box, click the **Add** button. **Close** Internet Explorer and all tabs.

6 Open **Internet Explorer** again, and then in the upper left corner, click the **Favorites** button. If necessary, at the top of the displayed list, click the Favorites tab. Scroll down as necessary, click **Colleges and Universities** to expand the list, and then point to the arrow to the right of **Colleges and Universities** to display the ScreenTip. Compare your screen with Figure 5.21.

Figure 5.21

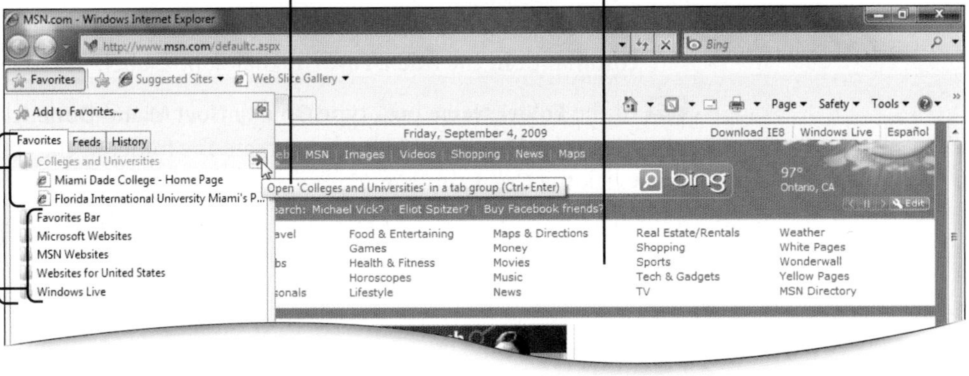

7 To the right of **Colleges and Universities**, click the arrow to open the entire group of sites on individual tabs; notice that because they are in a group, the tabs are colored to match. Point to the tab for your home page, right-click, and then click **Close Tab** so that only the two Florida college tabs display.

From the Favorites List, you can also click one of the links individually to open just one of the links.

8 Display the tab for **Florida International University**, and then on the navigation bar on the left of this site, click **Colleges & Schools**. Locate and click the link for the **College of Business Administration**.

9 Click the **Favorites** button, click **Add to Favorites**, and then in the **Add a Favorite** dialog box, click the **Create in arrow**. Compare your screen with Figure 5.22.

Figure 5.22

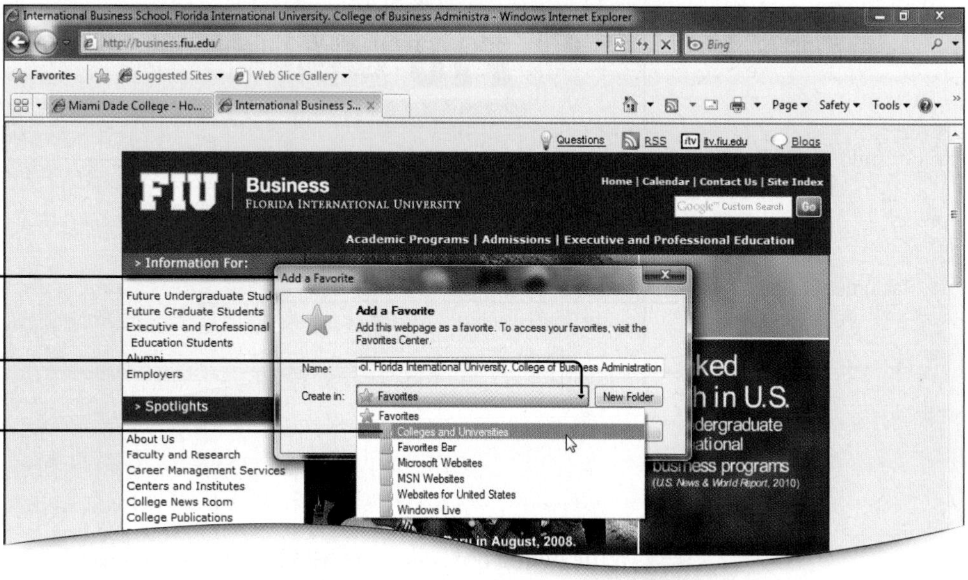

10 From the displayed list, click the **Colleges and Universities** folder, and then click the **Add** button.

The link to the College of Business Administration at Florida International University is added to the folder *Colleges and Universities*.

11 Open a **New Tab** [ ], type **miamidade.gov** and then press Enter.

12 Hold down Ctrl and press D—this is a keyboard shortcut for the Add to Favorites command. In the **Add a Favorite** dialog box, click the **New Folder** button.

13 In the **Folder Name** box, type **County Govt Miami-Dade** Click the **Create in arrow**, and then click **Favorites** so that you create the folder at the same level as other folders. Click the **Create** button.

14 In the displayed **Add a Favorite** dialog box, select the text in the **Name** box, and then replace it by typing **Miami-Dade County** Compare your screen with Figure 5.23.

You need not accept the default name of a Web site stored in your Favorites list. Change the name as necessary so that you can easily identify the site.

Figure 5.23

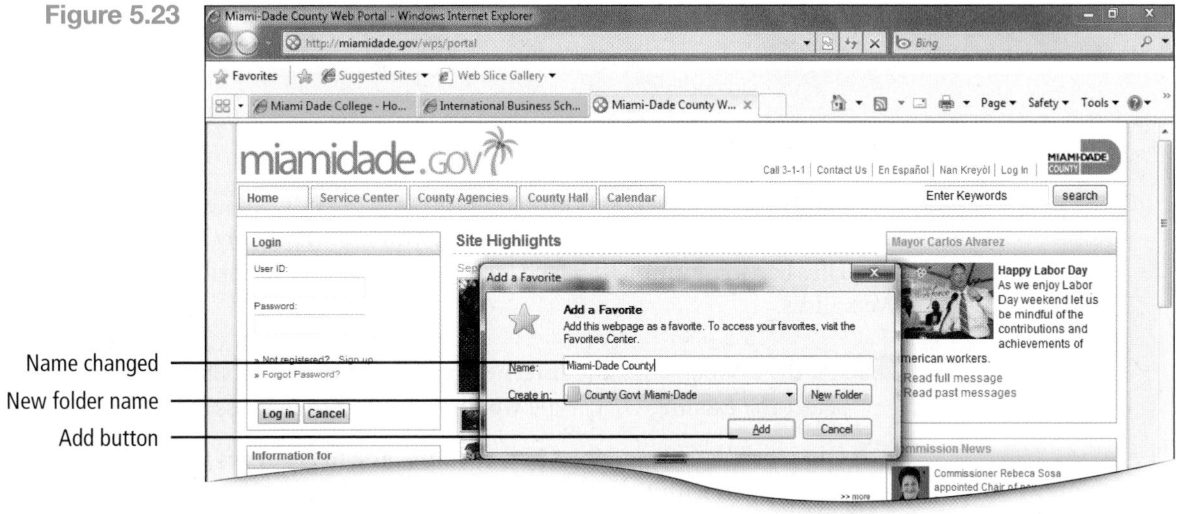

15 In the **Add a Favorite** dialog box, click the **Add** button.

In this manner, you can create folders for your favorite sites at the time you save the site as a Favorite. Be sure to notice where the folder is being stored, and place it either at the Favorites level or within other folders if you want to do so.

16 In the upper left corner, click the **Favorites** button, to the right of *Add to Favorites* click the ▾ **arrow**, click **Organize Favorites**, and then from this dialog box, create a **New Folder** named **Florida Tourism** Press Enter, and then in the lower right corner of the dialog box, click the **Close** button.

17 Open a **New Tab**, type **visitflorida.com** and then press Enter. Click the **Favorites** button, click **Add to Favorites**, in the displayed dialog box, click the **Create in arrow**, click the **Florida Tourism** folder, and then **Add** this site.

18 Hold down Alt and press Z to display the **Add to Favorites** menu. Click **Organize Favorites**, click the **County Govt Miami-Dade** folder to select it, and then in the lower portion of the dialog box, click **Rename**. Type **Florida Government** and then press Enter.

19 Point to **Colleges and Universities** and click one time to expand the list. Click **Colleges and Universities** again to collapse the list. Point to **Florida Tourism**, and then right-click.

From the displayed shortcut menu, you can see that you can take many additional actions on the list of folders such as sorting the list of folders by name, creating a new folder, and deleting a folder.

20 Click **Colleges and Universities** to expand the list. Then point to **Florida International University** and right-click.

From the displayed menu, you can perform similar commands related to a specific site in the list.

21 **Close** ☒ the **Organize Favorites** dialog box; **Close** ☒ Internet Explorer.

> **More Knowledge** | Copying Favorites from One Computer to Another and Printing Favorites
>
> You can save your Favorites from one computer and then import that list to another computer. To do so, open Windows Help and Support, type export Favorites, and follow the instructions for exporting, importing, and printing favorites.

Activity 5.04 | Using the Favorites Bar

The *Favorites bar* is a toolbar that displays directly below the address bar and to which you can add or drag Web addresses you use frequently. You can also use the Favorites bar to monitor RSS feeds to which you have subscribed and to store your Web Slices.

1 On the taskbar, click the **Internet Explorer** button 🌐. Click in the **address bar** to select the existing URL, type **weather.gov** and then press Enter.

2 Directly below the **address bar**, click the **Add to Favorites Bar** 👜 button. Compare your screen with Figure 5.24.

URL typed in address bar

Figure 5.24

Add to Favorites Bar button

NOAA's site displays on Favorites bar

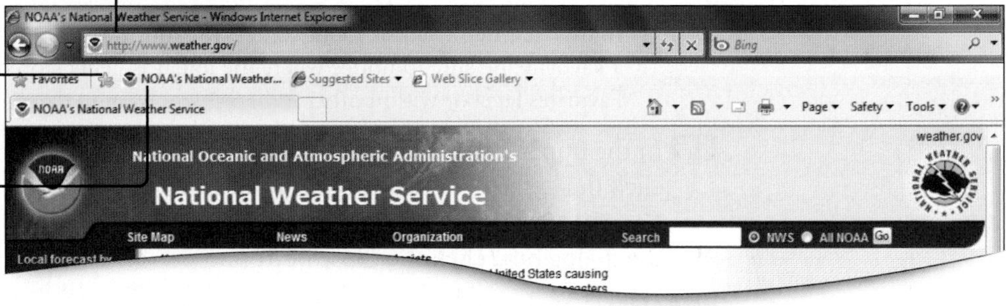

3 Click in the **address bar**, type **fsu.edu** and press Enter. At the left end of the **address bar**, point to the **Florida State University logo**, hold down the left mouse button, and then drag the logo onto the **Favorites bar** until a black line displays to the right of the NOAA's site, as shown in Figure 5.25. Then release the mouse button.

Figure 5.25

Logo being dragged

Vertical line

ScreenTip

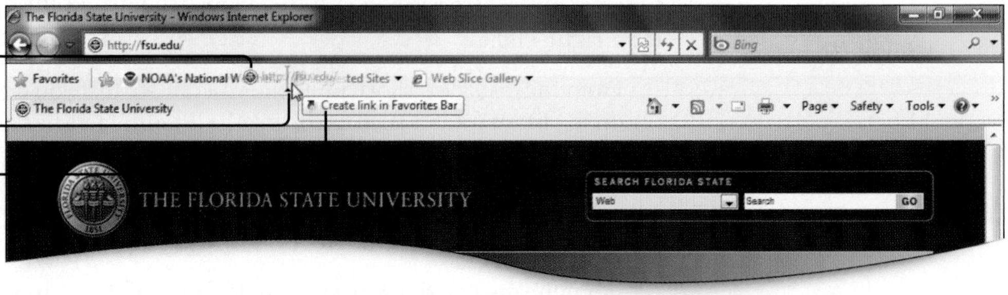

4 On the **Favorites bar**, point to the **NOAA's** site, right-click, and then click **Rename**. In the **Rename** box, type **NOAA** and then click **OK**. Using the same technique, rename *The Florida State University* link **FSU** Compare your screen with Figure 5.26.

You can change and shorten the names on your Favorites bar to make additional space. When you have more Favorites than the bar can accommodate, double chevrons will display at the right, which when clicked will display a continuation of the list.

Figure 5.26

5 Click in the **address bar**, type **ufl.edu** and press Enter, and then drag its logo to the **Favorites bar** to the right of FSU.

6 **Start** the **Snipping Tool** program, click the **New arrow**, and then click **Full-screen Snip**. In the **Snipping Tool** mark-up window, click the **Save Snip** button.

7 In the **Save As** dialog box, in the **navigation pane**, scroll down as necessary, and then under **Computer**, click your USB flash drive so that it displays in the **address bar**. Navigate to your **Windows 7 Chapter 5** folder, and then as the file name, type **Lastname_Firstname_5A_Favorites_Snip** Be sure the file type is **JPEG file**, and then press Enter. **Close** the **Snipping Tool** mark-up window. Hold this file until you finish Project 5A, and then submit this file as directed by your instructor.

8 Point to the **University of Florida** link on the **Favorites bar**, right-click, click **Delete**, and then click **Yes**. By using the same technique, delete the links for **FSU** and **NOAA**.

9 **Close** Internet Explorer.

On your own computer, place links to the sites you use most frequently on the Favorites bar, and for other favorite sites, add them to the Favorites Center.

More Knowledge | Additional Tools to Manage Your Favorites

There are additional free tools available to manage your favorites. These tools are sometimes referred to as ***bookmark managers***. Windows Live Favorites (*http://favorites.live.com*) is a free web-based service from Microsoft. The Favorites you place on this list are available from any online connection—not just from your own computer. Another service is *delicious* (delicious.com) where you can maintain a collection of Web site addresses and publish it. You can also download a toolbar button as an add-on for Internet Explorer, so it is easy and quick to add a site to your collection.

Objective 3 | Manage Browsing History and Browse with InPrivate

As you browse the Web, Internet Explorer stores information about the Web sites you visit. It also stores information that you are frequently asked to provide. For example, if you type your name and address into a Web site, Internet Explorer stores that information. All of this information is referred to as your ***browsing history***.

Usually it is useful to have this information stored on your computer, because it speeds your Web browsing and might automatically provide information so that you do not have to type it over and over.

Internet Explorer stores the following types of information:

- ***Temporary Internet files***, which are copies of Web pages, images, and media that you have downloaded from the Web. Storing this information makes viewing faster the next time you visit a site that you have visited before.
- ***Cookies***, which is the term used to refer to small text files that Web sites put on your computer to store information about you and your preferences, for example login information.
- A history of Web sites that you have visited.
- Information that you have entered into Web sites or the address bar, including your name and address if you have entered it into a site, and the URLs that you have visited before.
- Saved Web passwords.

Activity 5.05 | Viewing and Deleting Browsing History

You might want to delete your browsing history to make more space on your own computer. If you are using a public computer, such as in your college classroom or lab, you will want to delete your browsing history so that you do not leave any of your personal information stored there.

1 On the taskbar, click the **Internet Explorer** button. Click the **Favorites** button, and then at the top of the pane click the **History tab**. Under **History**, click the **arrow**, and then if necessary, click **View By Date**. Display the list again, click **Today**, and then compare your screen with Figure 5.27.

Here you can view a list of the sites you visited today.

Figure 5.27

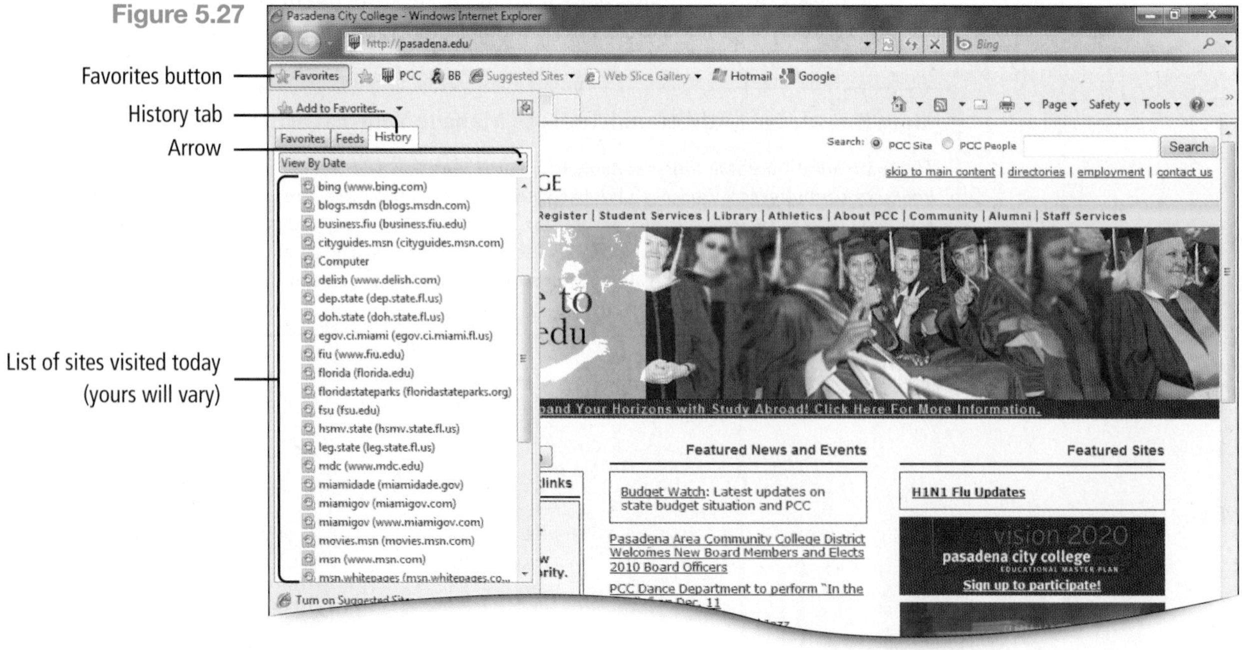

2 At the top of the pane, to the right of *View By Date*, click the **arrow**. On the displayed list, click **Search History**, and then in the displayed **Search for** box, type **Miami** Click the **Search Now** button, and then notice that a list of sites that you have visited related to *Miami* displays.

3 To the right of *Search History*, click the **arrow** again, and then click **View By Order Visited Today**.

4 In the upper right portion of your screen, on the **Command bar**, click the **Safety** button, and then click **Delete Browsing History**. Compare your screen with Figure 5.28.

Here you can delete all of your web browsing history, or individually select one or more categories of files to delete.

Figure 5.28

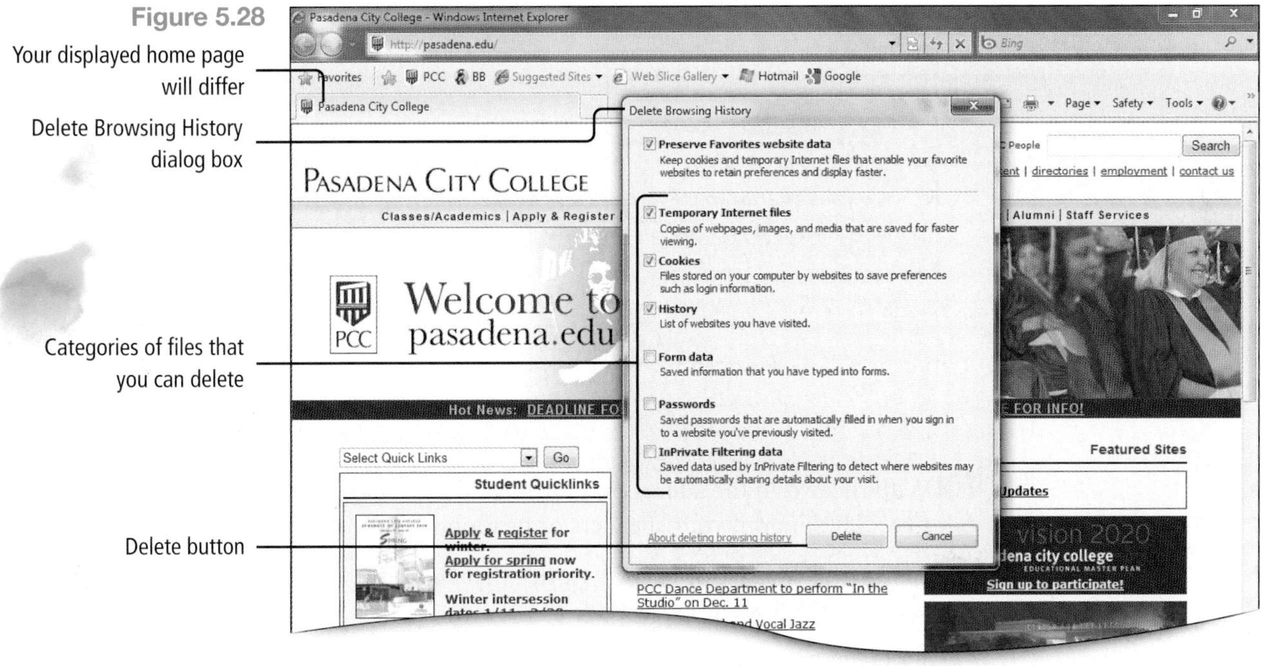

5 Unless you are working on your own computer and you do not want to delete any files, click the **Delete** button, and then wait a few moments for the deletion to complete.

Deleting all browsing history does not delete your list of Favorites or feeds to which you have subscribed. This action deletes only temporary files, your browsing history, cookies, and saved form information passwords—if their checkboxes are selected.

If you perform this action on your own computer, it might take a few seconds longer to display sites again the first time you access them. After that, the system will rebuild your browsing history as you browse the Web.

6 **Close** Internet Explorer.

More Knowledge | Close Internet Explorer After Deleting Browser History

You should close Internet Explorer after deleting your browser history to clear cookies that are still in memory from your current browsing session. This is especially important when using a public computer such as in your college computer lab.

Activity 5.06 | Using InPrivate Browsing

Use ***InPrivate Browsing*** to browse the Web without storing data about your browsing session. This feature is useful because it prevents anyone else who might be using your computer from seeing what sites you visited.

1 On the taskbar, click the **Internet Explorer** button. Click the **New Tab** button. On the right, click **Browse with InPrivate**. Compare your screen with Figure 5.29.

The InPrivate indicator displays on the address bar and the tab indicates *InPrivate*.

Figure 5.29

Address bar indicates *InPrivate*

InPrivate tab

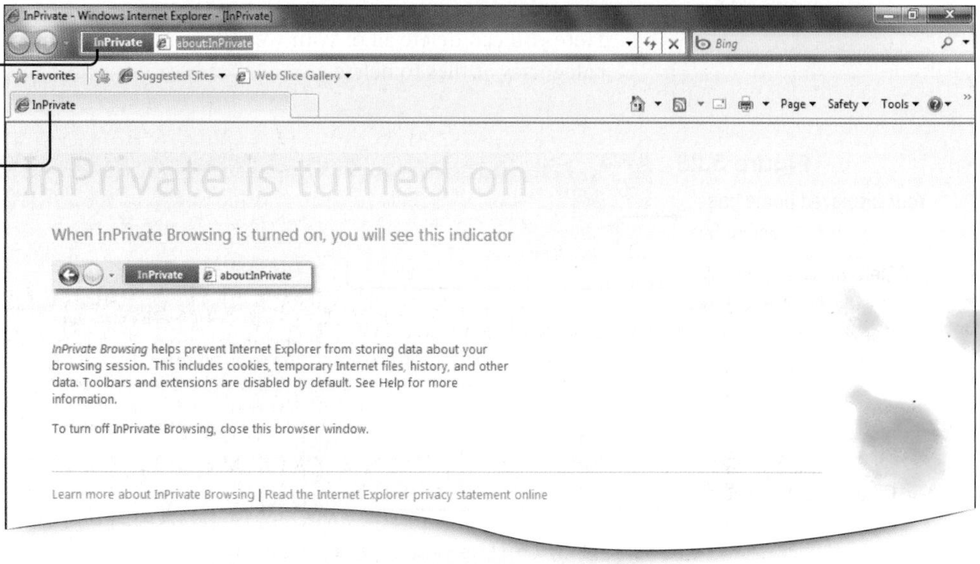

2 With the text in the **address bar** selected, type **gatorzone.com** and press Enter. (This site may play sound if your speakers or headphones are enabled.)

3 Click the **New Tab** button; notice that **InPrivate Browsing** is still in effect. Type **fsu.edu/athletics** and press Enter.

In the current Internet Explorer window, you can open as many tabs as you want, and they will be protected by InPrivate Browsing.

4 Click the **Favorites** button, and then click the **History tab**. Click the **arrow**, click **View By Order Visited Today**. Notice that the two sites you accessed while using InPrivate Browsing do *not* display on the list.

While using InPrivate Browsing, Internet Explorer stores some information. For example, cookies are kept in memory so pages work properly, but are cleared when you close the browser window. Temporary Internet files are also stored so pages work properly, but are deleted when you close the browser window. Web page history, form data, and passwords are not stored at all.

5 **Close** Internet Explorer.

Cookies are cleared and temporary Internet files are discarded.

Objective 4 | Print, Zoom, and Change the Text Size of Web Pages

By default, Internet Explorer 8 will shrink a Web page's text just enough to ensure that the entire page prints properly. The Page Zoom feature enables you to increase or decrease the page size for easier viewing. You can also adjust the size of displayed text.

Activity 5.07 | Printing Web Pages

Internet Explorer 8 provides useful options for formatting and then printing a Web page. In the following activity, you will work with Barbara and Steven to print a Web page.

1. **Close** any open windows. On the taskbar, click the **Internet Explorer** button, click in the **address bar**, type **myflorida.com** and then press Enter.

   The home page that serves as the official ***portal*** for the State of Florida displays. A portal is a Web site that displays news, content, and links that are of interest to a specific audience; for example, individuals who need information about Florida.

2. On the **Command bar**, locate and click the **Print button arrow** to display a menu. Compare your screen with Figure 5.30.

Figure 5.30

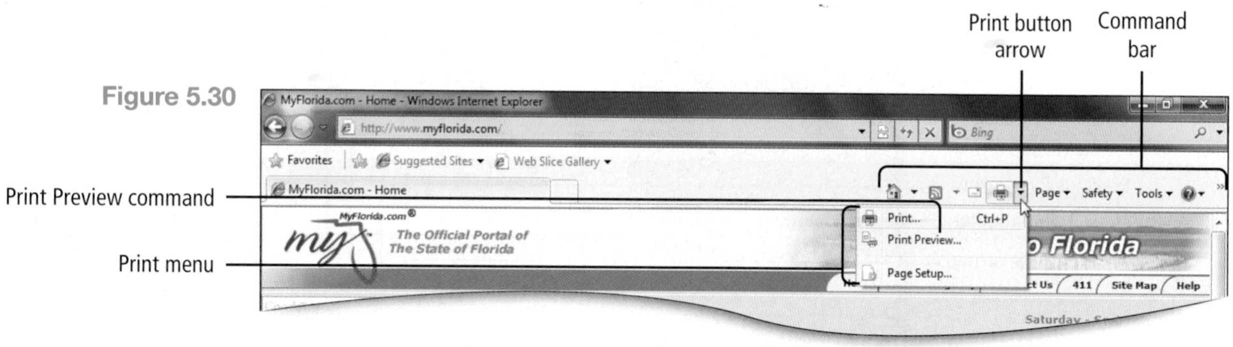

3 On the menu, click **Print Preview**. Compare your screen with Figure 5.31, and then take a moment to study the parts of the Print Preview window described in the table in Figure 5.32.

Recall that Internet Explorer will shrink the page as necessary to fit horizontally on the selected paper size. You can also drag the margins by using the adjust margin buttons on this Print Preview screen.

Figure 5.31

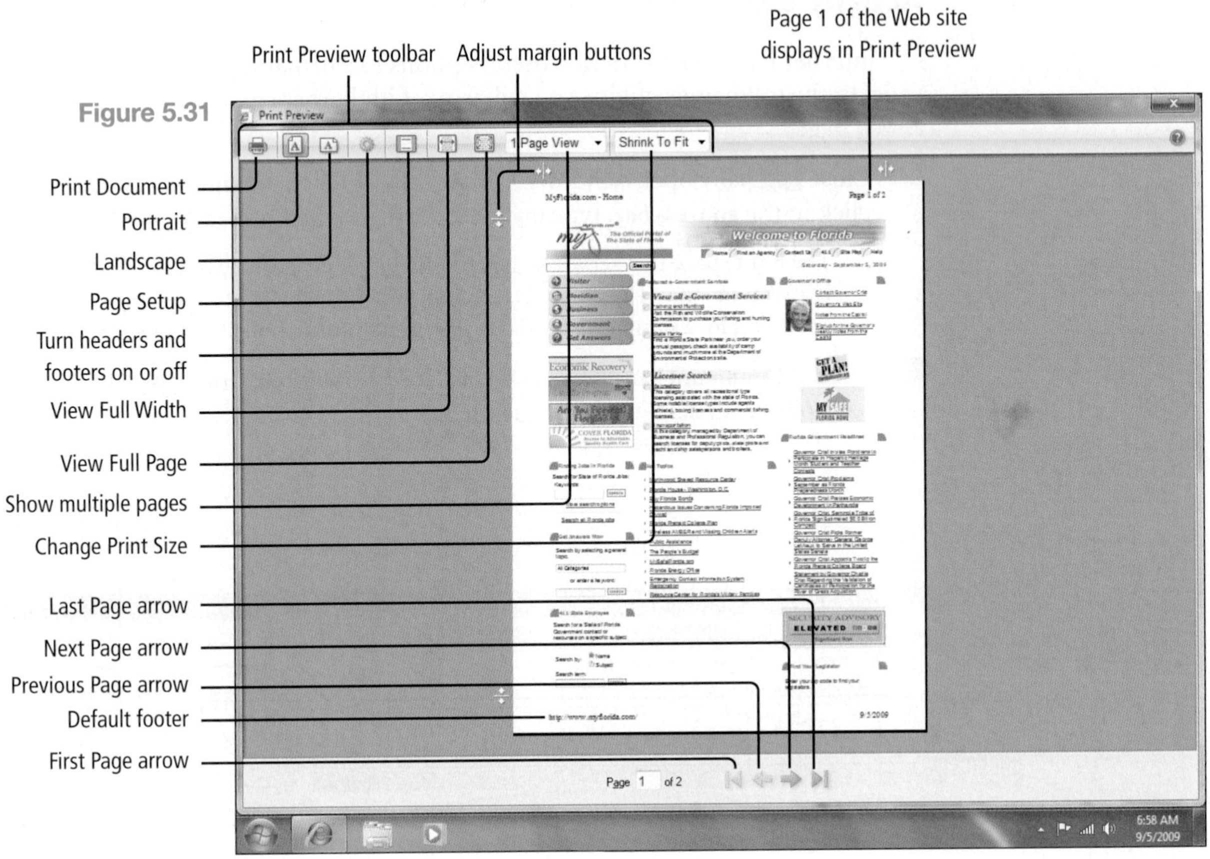

Parts of the Print Preview Window in Internet Explorer 8	
Adjust margin buttons	Adjusts the left, right, top, and bottom margins by dragging.
Change Print Size	Stretches or shrinks the page size to fill the printed page.
First Page arrow	Displays the first page of a multiple-page preview screen.
Landscape	Prints the page in landscape orientation, in which the paper is wider than it is tall.
Last Page arrow	Displays the last page of a multiple-page preview screen.
Next Page arrow	Displays the next page of a multiple-page preview screen.
Page indicator	Indicates the page displayed and the total number of pages.
Page Setup	Opens the Page Setup dialog box, in which you can change paper size, orientation, margins, and header and footer options.
Portrait	Prints the page in portrait orientation, in which the paper is taller than it is wide.
Previous Page arrow	Displays the previous page of a multiple-page preview screen.
Print Document	Opens the Print dialog box, enabling you to print the page using the current settings.
Show multiple pages	Displays multiple pages on the preview screen.
Turn headers or footers on or off	Turns the display of headers and footers off or on in the manner of a toggle button.
View Full Page	Zooms the Web page to show the full Web page in the preview screen.
View Full Width	Zooms the Web page to the width of the preview screen.

Figure 5.32

4 On the **Print Preview** toolbar, click the **Show multiple pages arrow** [▾], and then click **2 Page View.**

This Web page, as currently formatted, will print on two pages.

Another Way

Experiment with percentages on the list, or by typing in the Custom box, to shrink the page to print the way you want it to-on one or more pages.

5 On the toolbar, to the right of *Shrink To Fit*, click the **Change Print Size button arrow** [▾], and then from the displayed list, click **Custom.** In the **% box,** type **75** and press Enter. Compare your screen with Figure 5.33.

Figure 5.33

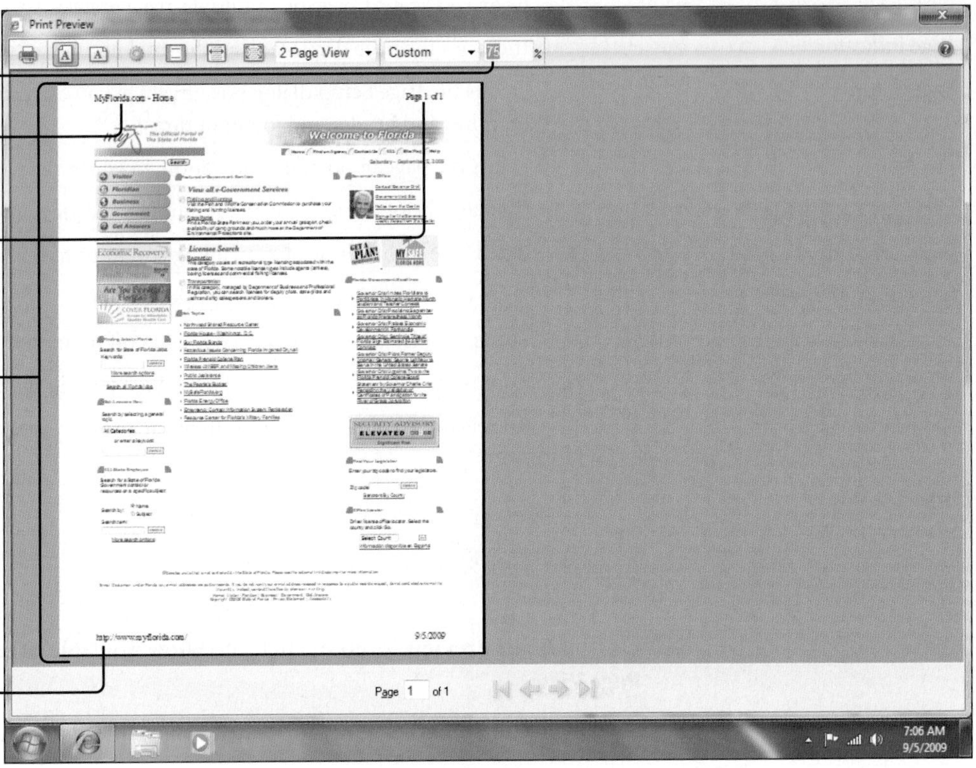

6 On the toolbar, to the right of *2 Page View*, click the **Show multiple pages button arrow** [▾], and then click **1 Page View** to return to that view and center the page on the Preview screen.

7 On the toolbar, click the **Page Setup** button. Compare your screen with Figure 5.34.

Here you can change or add to the headers and footers on a printed Web page.

By default there are two headers, one left aligned and one right aligned, which will display the page title and the URL. Similarly, there are two footers, one left aligned and one right aligned, which will display the page number with total pages and the date in short format.

The default setting for the centered header and footer is *Empty*. You can change any of the headers and footers by clicking the arrow and selecting an item or by selecting Custom and creating a new entry. You can also change the font of the headers and footers.

Figure 5.34

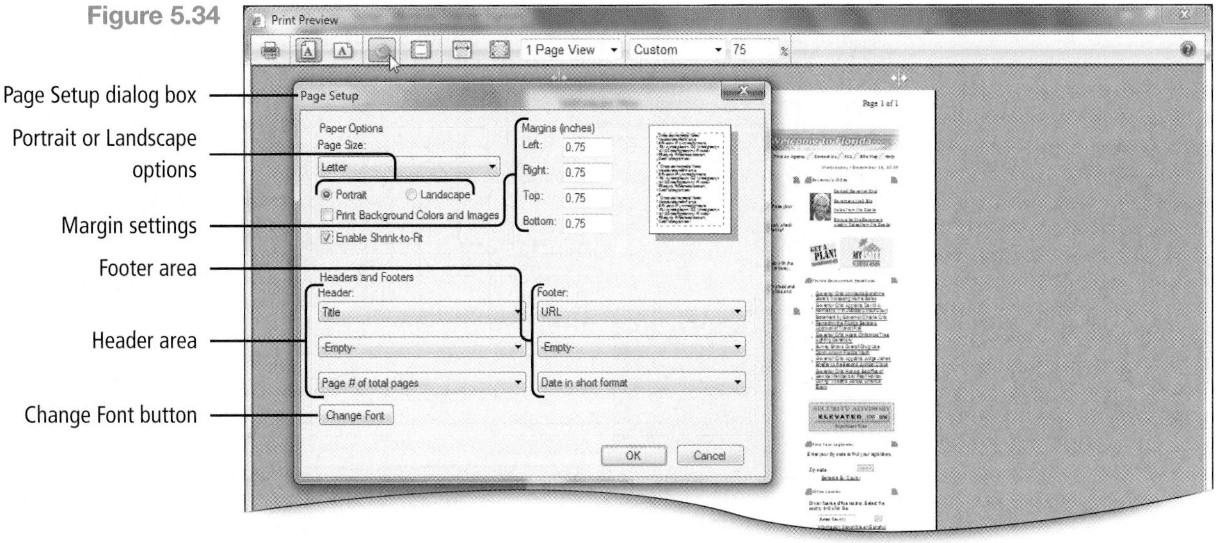

8 Under **Footer,** click the second arrow, and then point to **Custom,** as shown in Figure 5.35.

Here you can enter a centered footer.

Figure 5.35

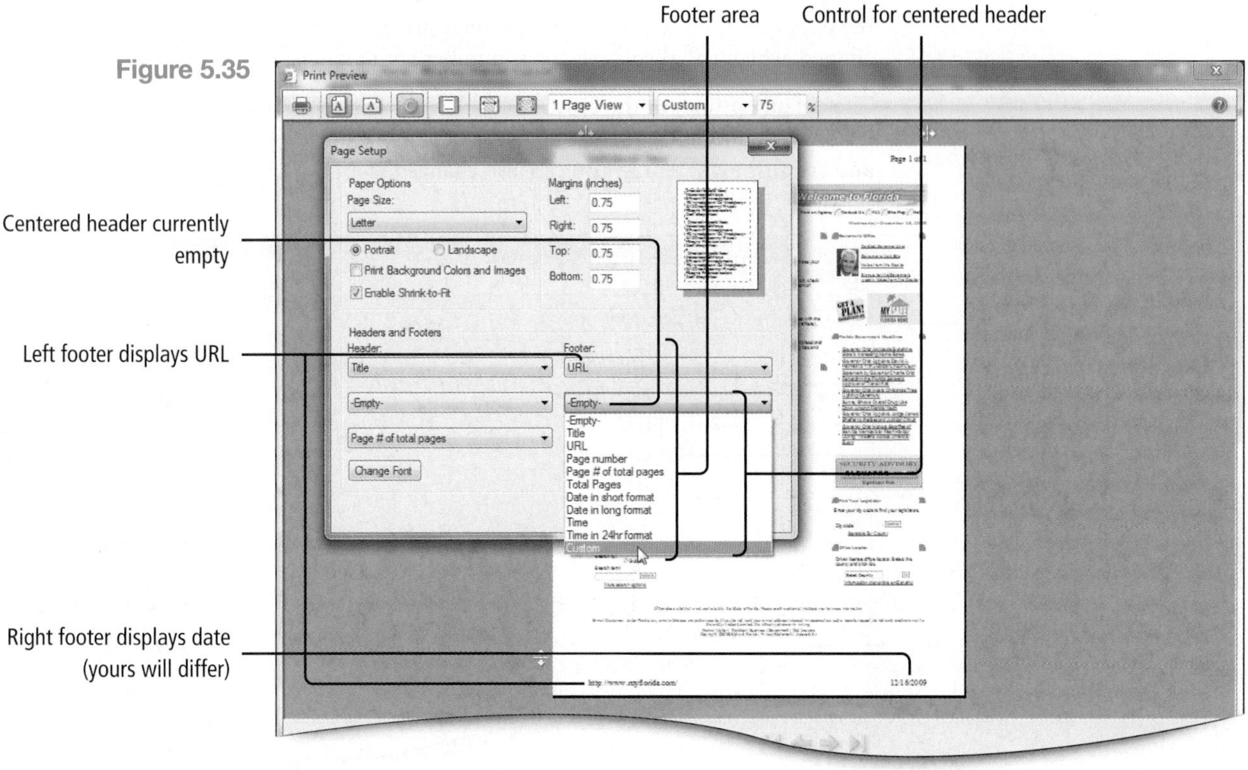

9 Click **Custom.** In the Custom dialog box, using your own name, type **Firstname Lastname** Compare your screen with Figure 5.36.

Figure 5.36

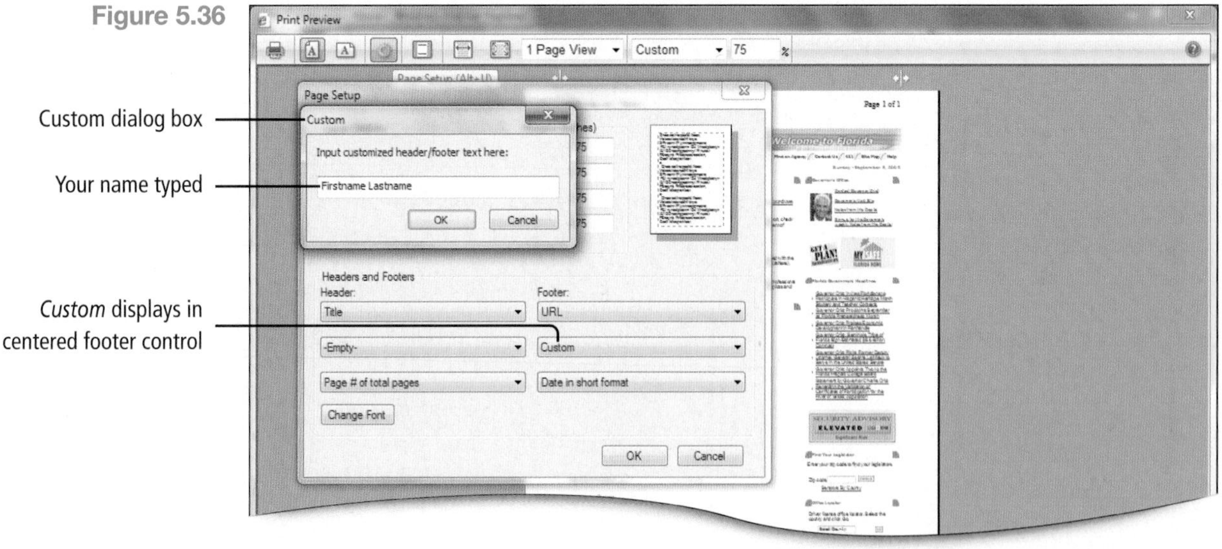

10 In the **Custom** dialog box, click **OK**. In the **Page Setup** dialog box, click **OK.**

In the Print Preview screen, your name displays as a centered heading.

11 **Start** the **Snipping Tool** program, click the **New arrow**, and then click **Full-screen Snip.** In the **Snipping Tool** mark-up window, click the **Save Snip** button.

12 In the **Save As** dialog box, in the navigation pane, scroll down as necessary, and then under Computer, click your USB flash drive so that it displays in the address bar. Navigate to your **Windows 7 Chapter 5** folder, and then as the file name, type **Lastname_Firstname_5A_Print_Snip** Be sure the file type is **JPEG** file, and then press Enter. **Close** the **Snipping Tool** mark-up window. Hold this file until you finish Project 5A, and then submit this file as directed by your instructor.

13 **Close** the **Print Preview** screen, and then **Close** Internet Explorer.

> **More Knowledge | Printing Specific Parts of a Web Page**
>
> To print only a specific part of a Web page, use your mouse to select the content that you want to print. Then, click the Print button arrow, click Print, and then in the Print dialog box, click the Selection option button. Click Print.

Activity 5.08 | Zooming and Changing the Text Size of Webpages

1 **Close** any open windows. On the taskbar, click the **Internet Explorer button**, click in the **address bar,** type **miamigov.com** and press Enter. On the **Command bar,** click the **Page** button, point to *Zoom,* and then click **200%.**

The view of the page is increased to 200%. Increasing the Zoom level increases the size of everything on the page, including graphics and controls.

2 Using the technique you just practiced, change the Zoom level to 50%.

3 Hold down Ctrl and then turn your mouse wheel backward and forward to increase and decrease the zoom.

This is a useful technique if you want to briefly magnify some text that is difficult to read or to examine a photo closely.

4 In the lower right corner of your screen, point to the **Change zoom level button**, and then click as many times as necessary to return the zoom level to 100%.

5 Open a **New Tab**, type **myflorida.com** and then press Enter. On the **Command bar,** click the **Page** button, and then point to **Text Size**.

The default text size is Medium, but if you would like to see more text on the screen you can set a smaller text size. If you have difficulty reading Web pages on your screen, you can set a larger text size.

Changing the text size affects only the text—graphics and controls continue to display in their original size.

6 On the displayed submenu, click **Largest,** and notice that the text on your screen is enlarged. Compare your screen with Figure 5.37.

Figure 5.37

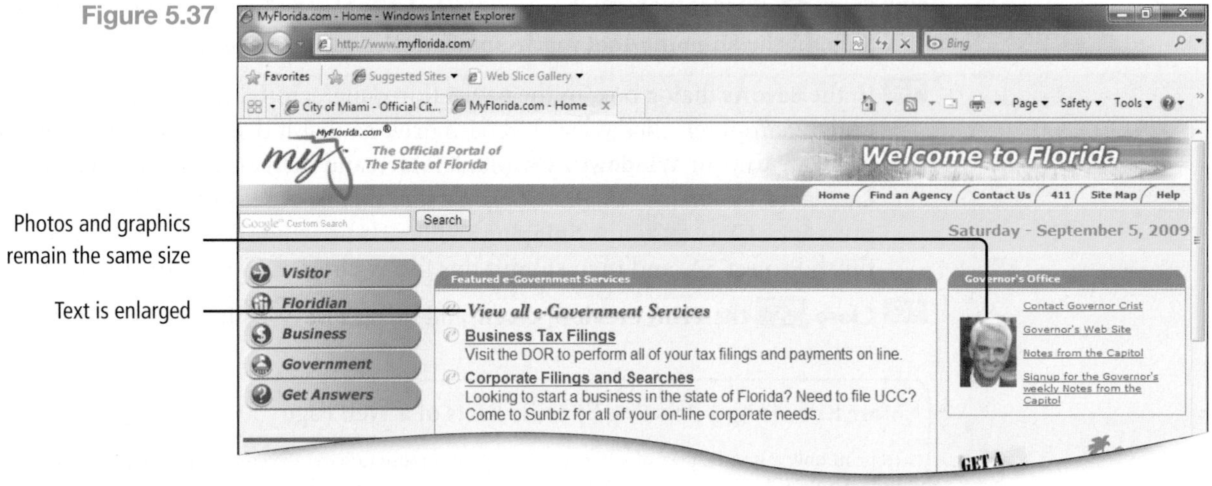

7 Using the technique you just practiced, return the **Text Size** to **Medium**.

Note | Text Size is Set at Page Creation

The text size of some Web pages is set by the person who created the page.

The creator of the Web page may set a specific text size that you cannot change with the Text Size command. If you want to do so, you can override this setting as follows: click the Tools button on the Command bar, click Internet Options, on the General tab, click the Accessibility button, and then select the Ignore font sizes specified on Web pages check box.

8 **Close** [X] Internet Explorer.

More Knowledge | **Using Full Screen Mode**

You can view a Web page in Full Screen mode, which will hide the title bar, the address bar, the Favorites Bar, the tab row, and the Command bar—unless you point to them. Full Screen mode will give you another inch or so of vertical screen space. To view Full Screen mode, press F11; or, from the Tools menu, click Full Screen. Press F11 again to return to normal view.

Objective 5 | Save Web Page Information

You can save an entire Web page, an image on a Web page, or selected text from a Web page. Doing so is a good way to capture information to which you want to refer later without accessing the Internet.

Activity 5.09 | Saving Web Page Information

1 **Close** any open windows. On the taskbar, click the **Internet Explorer** button, click in the **address bar**, type **florida-arts.org** and then press Enter. Compare your screen with Figure 5.38. If you cannot locate this page, navigate to any page that has a picture or graphic.

Because the content of Web pages changes frequently, the content and images on the displayed page will likely differ from Figure 5.38.

Figure 5.38

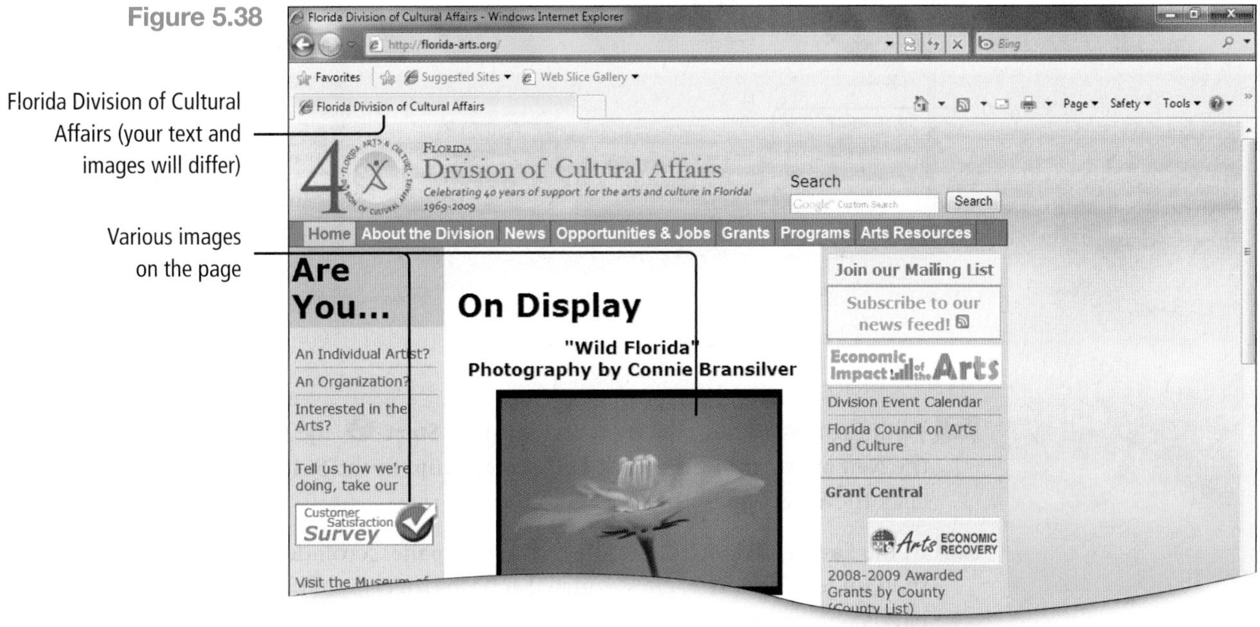

> **Alert! | The Content of Web Pages is Protected by Copyright Laws**
>
> Nearly everything you find on the Web is protected by copyright law, which protects authors of original works, including text, art, photographs, and music. If you want to use text or images that you find online, you will need to get permission. One of the exceptions to this law is the use of small amounts of information for educational purposes, which falls under Fair Use guidelines.
>
> Copyright laws in the United States are open to different interpretations, and copyright laws can be very different in other countries. As a general rule, if you want to use someone else's material, always get permission first.

2 Point to any picture or image on the page (scroll down if necessary to find a picture, or navigate to some other page with a picture), right-click, and then from the displayed menu, click **Save Picture As**. If necessary, navigate to the **Pictures** library in your personal folder, and then in the **File name** box, type **Cultural_Picture** Compare your screen with Figure 5.39.

You can save a picture displayed on a Web page in this manner.

Figure 5.39

Save Picture dialog box

Pictures library active

File name typed

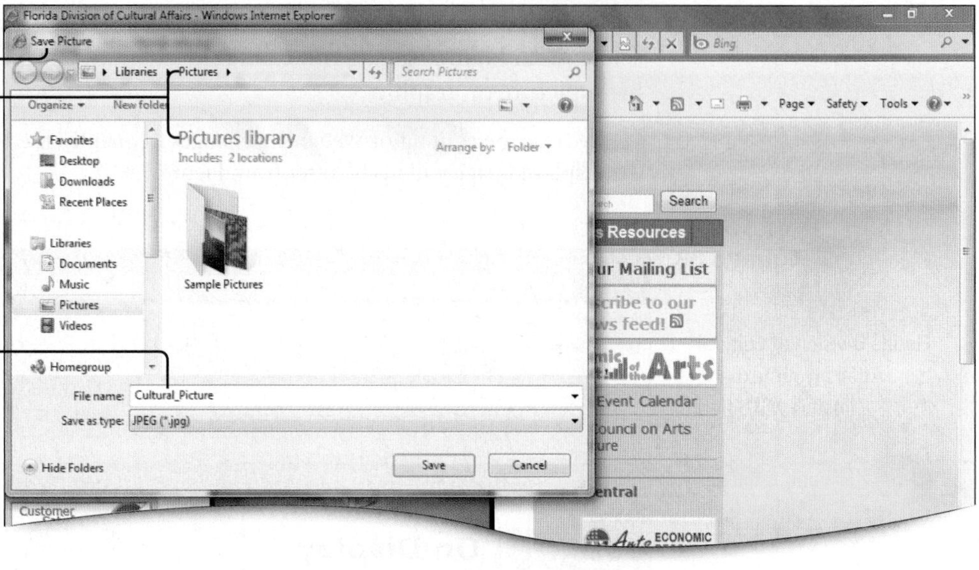

3 With the **Save Picture** dialog box displayed, **Start** the **Snipping Tool** program, click the **New arrow**, and then click **Full-screen Snip**. In the **Snipping Tool** mark-up window, click the **Save Snip** button.

4 In the **Save As** dialog box, in the **navigation pane**, scroll down as necessary, and then under **Computer**, click your USB flash drive so that it displays in the **address bar**. Navigate to your **Windows 7 Chapter 5** folder, and then as the file name, type **Lastname_Firstname_5A_Picture_Snip** Be sure the file type is **JPEG** file, and then press Enter. **Close** the **Snipping Tool** mark-up window. Hold this file until you finish Project 5A, and then submit this file as directed by your instructor.

5 In the **Save Picture** dialog box, click **Cancel**.

You can use this technique to save images on Web pages.

> **Note | Printing a Picture from a Web Page**
>
> To print a picture from a Web page, point to the image and right-click. From the displayed menu, click Print Picture, and then in the Print dialog box, click Print.

6 On the **Command bar**, click the **Page** button, and then click **Save As**. At the bottom of the displayed **Save Webpage** dialog box, click the **Save as type arrow**, and then compare your screen with Figure 5.40.

To save all files associated with the page, including graphics, frames, and style sheets in their original format, you can use the file format *Webpage, complete (*.htm;*.html)*.

To save all information as a single file, you can use the file format *Web Archive, single file (*.mht)*.

To save just the current HTML page, without graphics, sounds, or other files, you can use the file format *Webpage, HTML only (*.htm;*.html)*. To save just the text from the current Web page, you can use the file format *Text File (*.txt)*.

Figure 5.40

Save Webpage dialog box

Save as type arrow

File types

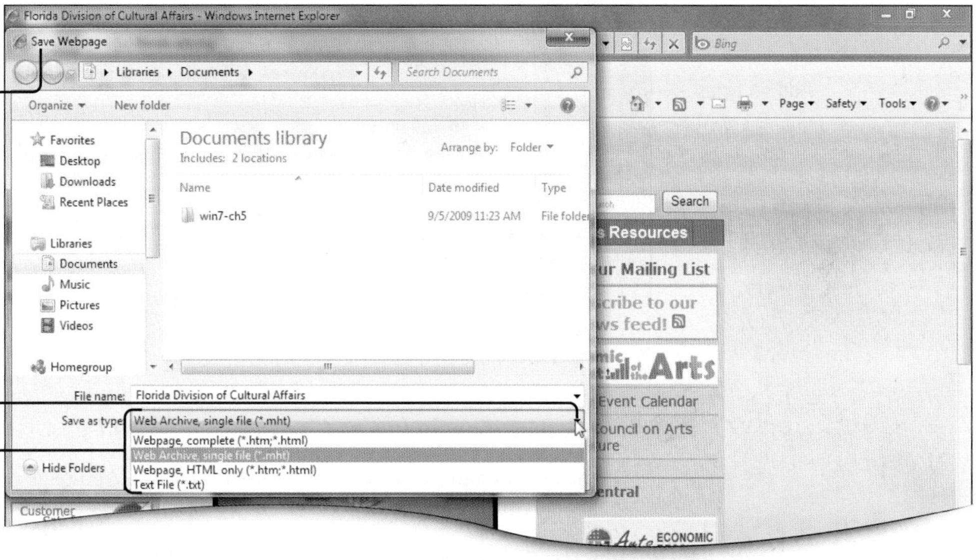

7 **Close** the **Save Webpage** dialog box without saving, and then **Close** Internet Explorer.

> **More Knowledge | E-mailing a Web Page**
>
> You can e-mail a Web page in two ways. From the Page button menu, click Send Page by E-mail; or, click Send Link by E-mail. Your default e-mail program will display. The first option inserts the entire page in the text of the e-mail. The second option inserts only the URL in the text of the e-mail message.
>
> To set a program to use for e-mail within Internet Explorer, on the Command bar, click the Tools button, click Internet Options, click the Programs tab, and then under Internet programs, click the Set programs button.

Objective 6 | Manage Add-ons

An ***add-on*** is a program that adds features to a Web browser such as Internet Explorer. Examples of add-ons include additional toolbars, animated mouse pointers, and interactive Web content. Most add-ons come from the Internet and most require that you give permission to install them on your computer. It is possible that an add-on is installed without your knowledge, for example as part of another program. Some add-ons are installed with Microsoft Windows 7.

Activity 5.10 | Managing Add-ons

1 **Close** [icon] any open windows. On the taskbar, click the **Internet Explorer** button [icon], click in the **address bar**, type **florida.edu** and press Enter. On the **Command bar**, click the **Tools** button, and then click **Manage Add-ons**. Compare your screen with Figure 5.41.

Figure 5.41

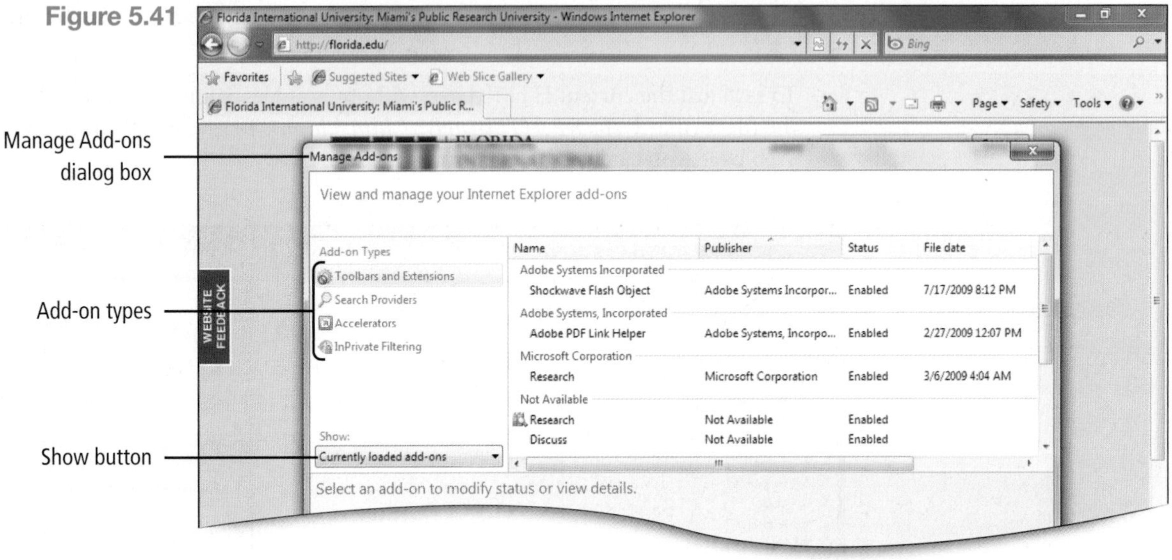

2 Be sure that **Show** indicates *Currently loaded add-ons.*

The add-ons that are necessary for the current Web page or a recently viewed Web page display on this list.

3 Click the **Show arrow**, and then click **All add-ons**.

A complete list of the add-ons that reside on your computer displays. If for any reason you need to do so, from this list you can either disable a selected add-on by selecting the add-on, and then clicking the Disable button that will display in the lower right corner of the dialog box. Or, you can delete a selected add-on by clicking the Delete button.

4 Click the **Show arrow,** and then click **Run without permission.**

A list of add-ons that are pre-approved by Microsoft, by your computer manufacturer, or by a service provider displays. All pre-approved add-ons are checked and most are digitally signed.

A ***digital signature*** is an electronic security mark that can be added to files. It enables you to verify the publisher of a file and helps verify that the file has not changed since it was digitally signed. If *(Not verified)* displays in the Publisher column, the add-on itself is not digitally signed.

5 Click the **Show arrow** again, and then click **Downloaded controls**.

A list of 32-bit ***ActiveX*** controls displays. ActiveX is a technology for creating interactive Web content such as animation sequences, credit card transactions, or spreadsheet calculations. An ***ActiveX control*** is a type of add-on.

Upon displaying some Web pages, you might see an ***Information bar*** (usually a yellow bar) display below the address bar. An information bar commonly displays information about downloads, blocked pop-up windows, and installing ActiveX controls.

Use caution when asked to download an ActiveX control. Such controls can enhance your Web browsing, but could also be a security risk. Be sure you trust the site that is asking you to install the control.

6 In the lower left corner of the **Manage Add-ons** dialog box, click **Find more toolbars and extensions**.

The Microsoft site for Internet Explorer Add-ons displays.

7 Take a moment to examine this page.

You can see that there are many interesting and useful add-ons that you can add to Internet Explorer.

8 **Close** [X] all open windows, and then **Close** [X] Internet Explorer. Submit the four snip files from this project to your instructor as directed.

End You have completed Project 5A

Project 5B Searching with Search Tools and Using the Web Safely

Project Activities

In Activities 5.11 through 5.17 you will train with Steven Ramos and Barbara Hewitt, employees in the Information Technology Department at the Bell Orchid Hotel, so that you will be able to search the Web from the Internet Explorer window and maintain the safety and security of data and computer users. Your completed screens will look similar to Figure 5.42.

Project Files

For Project 5B, you will need the following files:

New Snip files

Your will save your files as:

Lastname_Firstname_5B_Searches_Snip
Lastname_Firstname_5B_RSS_Snip
Lastname_Firstname_5B_Slice_Snip
Lastname_Firstname_5B_Accelerator_Snip

Project Results

Figure 5.42
Project 5B Searching with Search Tools and Using the Web Safely

Objective 7 | Search the Internet

The Internet can connect you to a vast amount of information, but first you have to find the information that you need. From within Internet Explorer, there are two ways in which you can search for information on the Internet without navigating to a specific Web site. The easiest method is to type a ***search term*** in the Search box in the upper right corner of the Internet Explorer screen. A search term is a word or phrase that describes the topic about which you want to find information. You can also type a search term directly in the address bar.

Activity 5.11 | Searching the Internet

A ***search provider*** is a Web site that provides search capabilities on the Web. The default search provider in Internet Explorer is Microsoft's Bing; however, you can change the default and easily switch among providers.

1. On the taskbar, click the **Internet Explorer** button. If a Welcome screen displays, close it. In the upper right corner, locate the **Search** box, and then at the right end of the box, click the **Search arrow ▼**. Compare your screen with Figure 5.43.

Figure 5.43

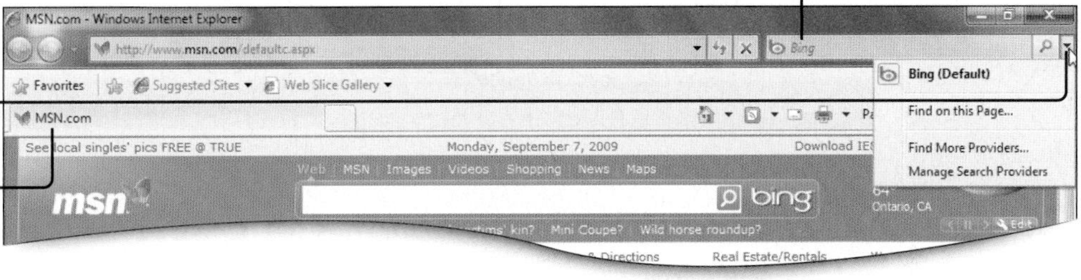

> **Note | If Bing is not your default**
>
> If Bing is not the default, set it as the default for this project as follows: On the displayed menu, click Find More Providers, and then click Bing Search. Click Add to Internet Explorer, and then click Add. Then, click the search arrow, click Manage Search Providers, click Bing, and then in the lower right corner, click Set as default. Click the Close button.

2. With **Bing** set as your default search provider, click in a blank area of the screen to close the Search menu. Then hold down Ctrl and press E to place the insertion point in the **Search** box; or, just click in the Search box.

3. Type the following, including the quotation marks: **"florida tourism"** and then press Enter. In the list of results, notice that your exact term *florida tourism* displays in bold.

   Bing displays the search results, and on the right, displays ***sponsored links***—paid advertisements shown as a links, typically for products and services related to your search term. Sponsored links are the way that search sites like Bing, Google, and others earn revenue. On the left, related searches are suggested.

   Use quotation marks to search for specific phrases. Surrounding terms with quotation marks limits the search results to only those Web pages that contain the exact phrase that you typed. Without the quotation marks, the search results will include any page that contains the terms that you typed, regardless of the order of the words.

4 In the **Search** box, click the **Search arrow** ▼, and then on the displayed list, click **Find More Providers**. Compare your screen with Figure 5.44.

Figure 5.44

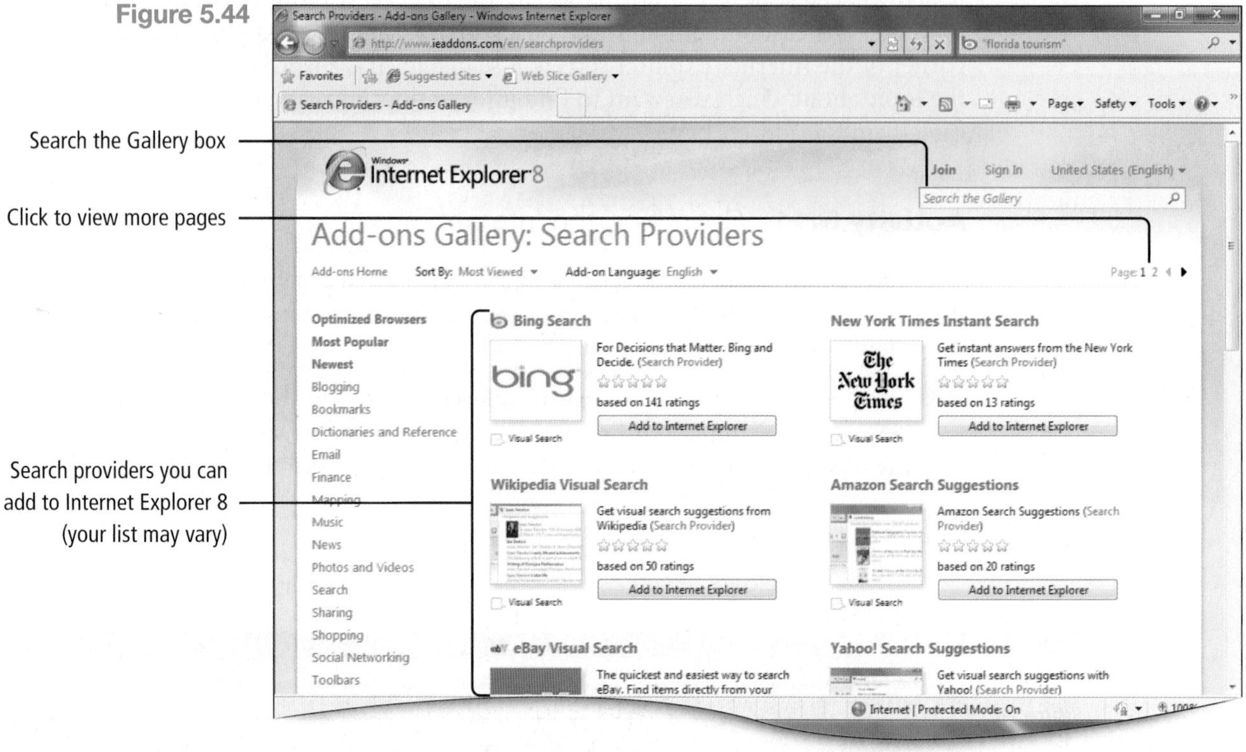

5 In the upper right corner, click in the **Search the Gallery** box, type **ask.com** and then press Enter. When the **Ask.com** logo displays, click the **Add to Internet Explorer** button. Then click **Add**. If the provider is already installed, click OK or Cancel.

6 In the upper right corner, in the **Search** box, click the **Search arrow** ▼, and then compare your screen with Figure 5.45.

Figure 5.45

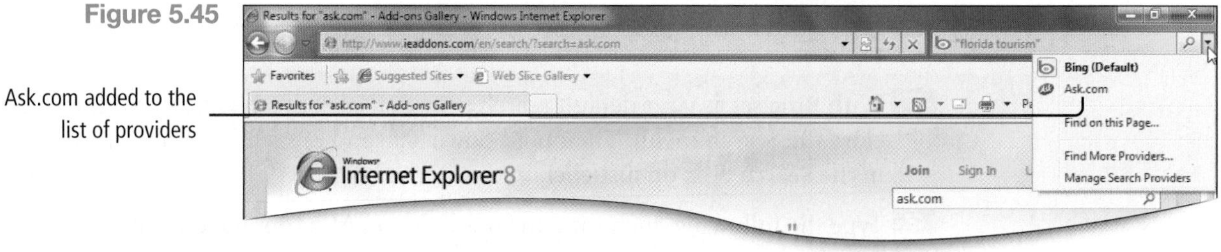

7 On the displayed list, click **Ask.com**, and notice that the same search is conducted in the Ask.com site. Compare your screen with Figure 5.46.

Internet Explorer conducts your search for *florida tourism* in the Ask.com search engine. If you do not find what you are looking for with a particular search provider, you can search using a different provider.

Figure 5.46

Search conducted using the term "*florida tourism*"

Results from Ask.com search provider

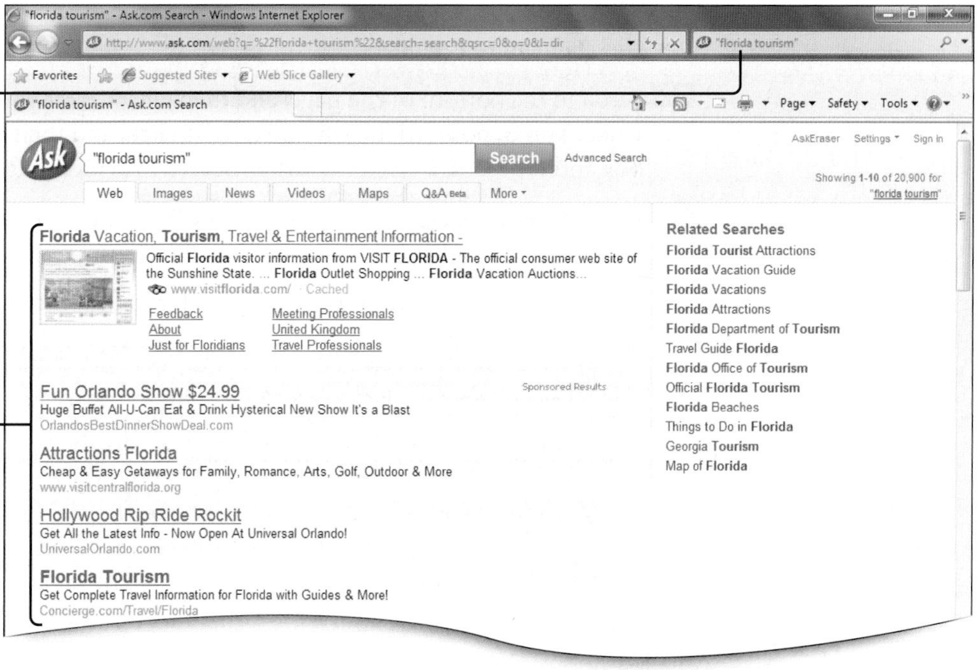

8 Using the same technique, add the **Google** provider (you may have to go to the second page of listings; use *Google Search Suggestions*). Click the **Search arrow ▼**, and then click **Google**.

Results for "florida tourism" from your Google search display.

9 In the **Search** box, click the **Search arrow ▼**, and then on the displayed list, click **Bing** to redisplay those results. Press Ctrl + E to select the text in the search box. Type the following but do *not* press Enter: **"Miami Hotels"** Hold down Alt and press Enter.

The search results display in a new tab. Use this technique to keep the results of various searches displayed.

10 **Start** the **Snipping Tool** program and create a **Full-screen** snip. **Save** the snip in your **Window 7 Chapter 5** folder as a **JPEG** file with the name **Lastname_Firstname_5B_Searches_Snip** **Close** the **Snipping Tool** mark-up window. Hold this file until you complete Project 5B, and then submit it as directed by your instructor.

11 Open a **New Tab**, in the **address bar** type **Florida Keys** and then press Enter.

When you type a search term directly in the address bar, Internet Explorer tries to find a URL that matches; if it cannot do so, the default search provider conducts the search.

12 Open a **New Tab** and then in the **address bar** type **Find Miami Chamber of Commerce** and press Enter.

In the Internet Explorer address bar, you can type *Find* or *Go* or ? followed by a keyword, a Web site name, or a phrase, and then press Enter. To display the results in a new tab, press Alt + Enter after typing the phrase.

13 Open a **New Tab** [New Tab button] and then type **cnet.com** and press Enter. Wait for any ads to complete, and then in the displayed Web site, locate the **Search** box in the upper portion of the screen. Click in the **Search** box, and in all uppercase letters type **TEST** and press Enter.

14 Click in the **address bar** to select the entire URL, point to the selected URL and right-click, and then click **Copy**. In the Internet Explorer **Search** box, click the **Search arrow** ▼, and then
click **Find More Providers**.

15 Scroll to the bottom of the page, and then click **Create your own Search Provider**. Under **Step 3**, point to the **URL** box, right-click, and then click **Paste**. Click in the **Name** box and type **CNET** Click the **Install Search Provider** button, and then click **Add**.

16 In the **Search** box, click the **Search arrow** ▼, and then on the displayed list, notice that **CNET** has been added as a search provider. Compare your screen with Figure 5.47.

Use the CNET search provider to search for computer related information.

Figure 5.47

CNET displays as a provider

Create your own Search Provider site

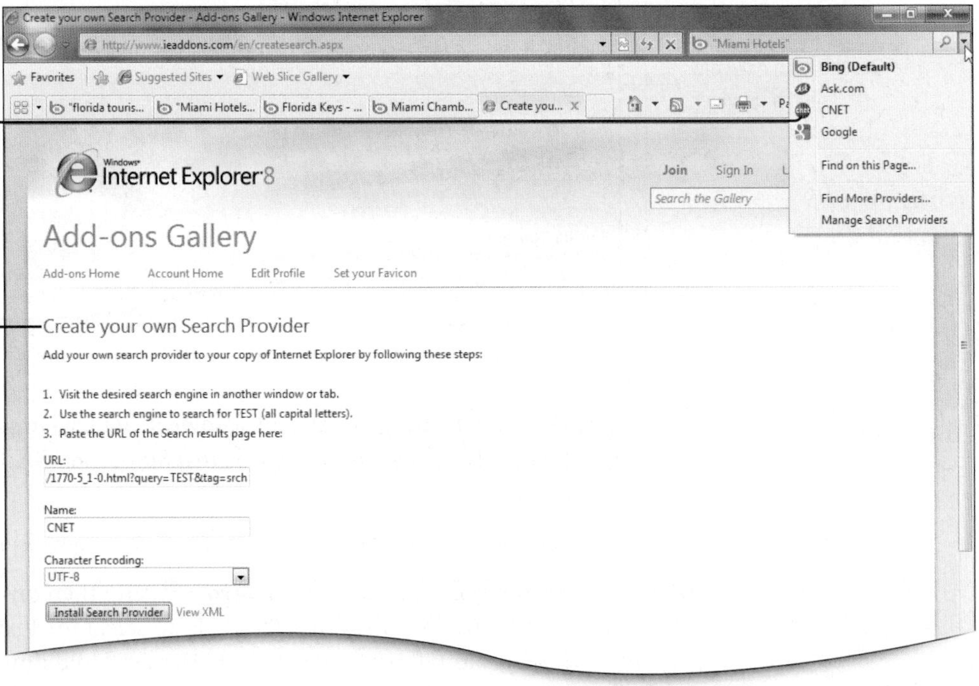

17 **Close** [Close button] Internet Explorer.

Objective 8 | Subscribe to and View an RSS Feed

RSS is an acronym for *Really Simple Syndication*, which is a syndication format popular for aggregating—gathering together—updates to blogs and news sites.

An ***RSS feed***—also known as an ***XML feed***, ***syndicated content***, or a ***Web feed***—contains frequently updated content published by a Web site. The feed consists of a list of new articles from a specific site, each with a headline, summary information, usually a date and time stamp, and a link to the full article for each item.

The advantage of an RSS feed is that you can view new information from your favorite Web sites instead of navigating to the site and scanning it for any new information. You do not have to constantly check a news site, for example, to see if anything new has been posted.

For example, if you regularly visit several sites daily—such as a national news site, a site related to your job, and a site with financial or stock market information—you can subscribe to an RSS feed for those sites and the new articles will be delivered to you as they become available.

Getting started with RSS involves two steps:

- Get an ***RSS viewer***: An RSS viewer, also referred to as a ***feed reader***, is a program that displays RSS feeds to which you have subscribed. There are a number of RSS viewers available, including the one that comes with Internet Explorer.
- Subscribe to feeds: Most Web sites let you know that you can syndicate their content by displaying an orange button. Clicking the button adds the feed to your feed reader list.

Activity 5.12 | Subscribing to and Viewing an RSS Feed

To subscribe to an RSS feed, click the orange RSS icon on any Web page, or look for an orange button that indicates *XML*.

1 **Close** any open windows. On the taskbar, click the **Internet Explorer** button, click in the **address bar**, type **usa.gov** and then press Enter. On the **Command bar**, locate the **Feeds** button, and notice that it is orange.

Internet Explorer detects the presence of a Web feed on a page that you are viewing by displaying this button in orange—or in orange with a small starburst—instead of in its default gray color. In that manner, you can know immediately if feeds are available from the displayed Web page.

2 On the **Command bar**, click the **Feeds button arrow**, and then from the displayed list, click **USA.gov Updates: News and Features**. Compare your screen with Figure 5.48.

Figure 5.48

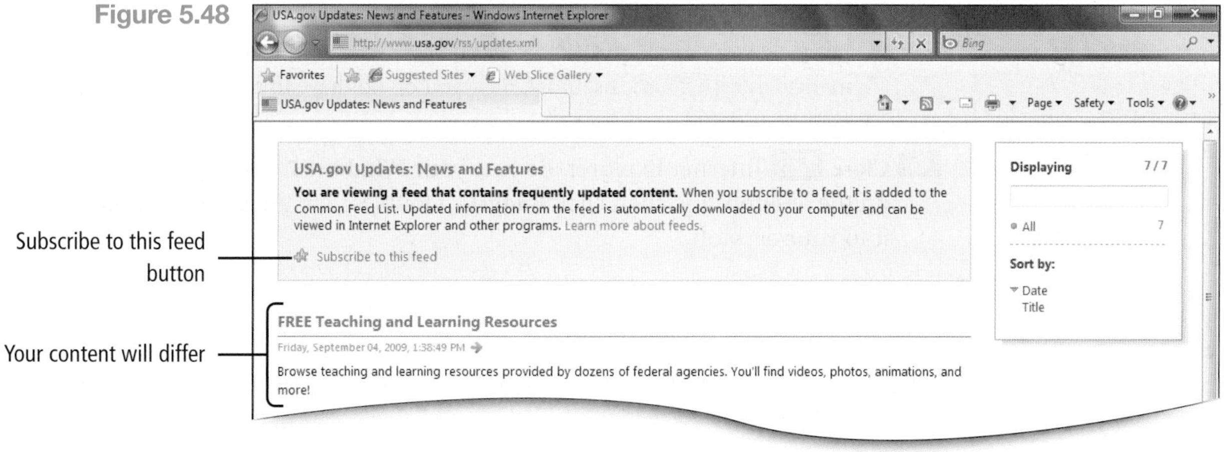

3 In the upper left portion of the screen, click **Subscribe to this feed**.

An Internet Explorer dialog box displays, indicating that if you subscribe, the feed will be added to your Favorites Center and kept up to date. The feed will be created in the Feeds folder.

Here, using the same techniques you use when saving a new Favorite, you can give the feed a more descriptive name, and, optionally file it in a subfolder of the Feeds folder or create a new folder.

4 In the dialog box, click the **Subscribe** button, and notice that in the upper portion of the screen, the message *You've successfully subscribed to this feed!* displays. Just below that message, click **View my feeds**. In the displayed list in the **Favorites Center**, point to the new feed name to display its ScreenTip, and then compare your screen with Figure 5.49.

When you subscribe to the feed, Internet Explorer automatically checks the Web site and downloads new content so you can see what is new since you last visited the feed.

When a new post appears, the link for that site displays in bold and clicking it shows the unread material in your browser window.

Figure 5.49

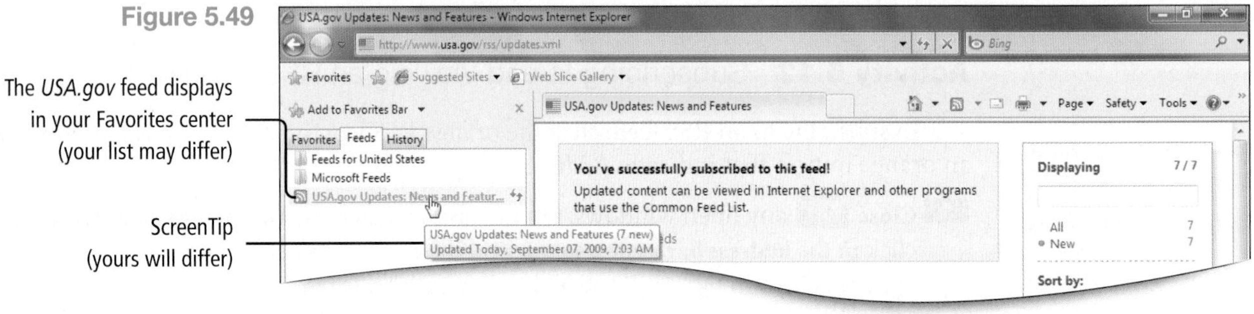

5 In the upper right corner of the **Favorites Center** pane, click the **Close** button [x].

All feeds that you open from within the Favorites Center of Internet Explorer will display in this uniform manner.

On the right, you can click various options for displaying and sorting the articles. You can also open the link to the Feed Properties dialog box, where you can adjust how often the feed is updated and the number of updates to display.

Use the *Mark feed as read* link so that if you return to this page, no current entries will be marked as new. This is useful because you do not have to remember if you have already seen an article.

6 **Close** [X] Internet Explorer. Be sure your **Windows 7** desktop displays. Right-click on the desktop, and then click **Gadgets**. Double-click the **Feed Headlines** gadget to add it to your desktop.

Alert! | Does your screen differ?

If you are unable to display the *Feed Headlines* gadget, skip the remainder of this activity; or, just read the steps and examine the figures.

7 Wait a few moments for the gadget to load. Then, on the desktop, point to the **Feed Headlines** gadget, right-click, and click **Options**. In the displayed **Feed Headlines** dialog box, click the **Display this feed arrow**, and then compare your screen with Figure 5.50.

The feeds to which you subscribed in Internet Explorer display on the list—others might also display.

Figure 5.50

Feed Headlines dialog box

List of available feeds (yours may vary)

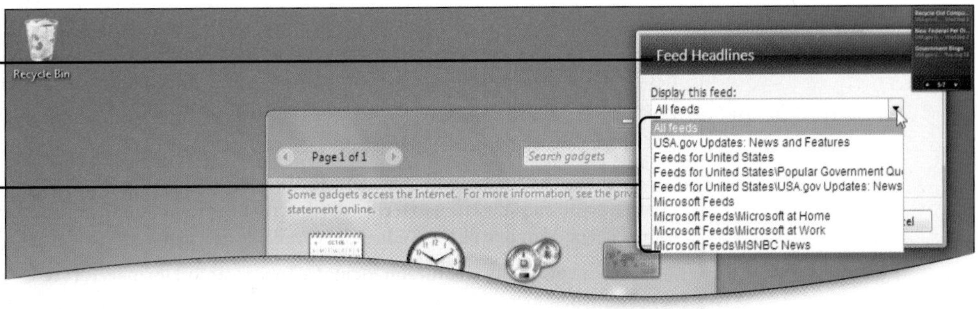

8 From the displayed list, click **USA.gov Updates: News and Features**, and then click **OK**. Notice that only headlines from this feed display. Click any headline, and then compare your screen with Figure 5.51.

To view a summary of an interesting headline, you can click any headline, as shown in Figure 5.51. In this manner, you can use a gadget to view feeds from a single source quickly. To view the entire article, click the headline in the title bar above the summary to open the Web page that contains the entire article, or click *Read online*.

Figure 5.51

Title bar, when clicked, will display webpage for entire article

Summary of article

Article headline

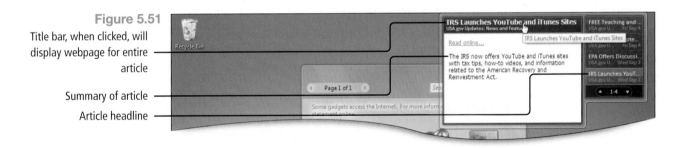

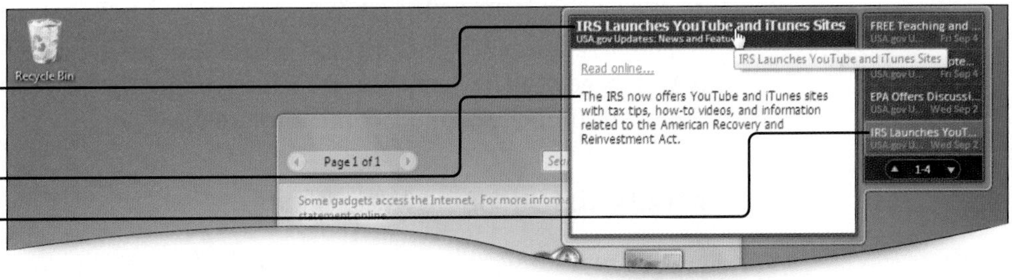

9 Click on the desktop to cancel the headline display.

10 **Start** the **Snipping Tool** program and create a **Full-screen** snip. **Save** the snip in your **Windows 7 Chapter 5** folder as a **JPEG** file with the name **Lastname_Firstname_5B_RSS_Snip Close** the **Snipping Tool** mark-up window. Hold this file until you complete Project 5B, and then submit it as directed by your instructor.

11 Point to the gadget on your desktop and right-click. Click **Close gadget** to delete it from your desktop. **Close** the Gadgets window.

12 On the taskbar, click the **Internet Explorer** button. In the upper left corner, click the **Favorites** button, and then if necessary, click the **Feeds tab**.

13 Point to the **USA.gov Updates** feed and right-click. Click **Delete**, and then click **Yes**.

14 **Close** [X] Internet Explorer.

> **More Knowledge | What else should I know about RSS Feeds?**
>
> **Feeds are different than a Web site:** A feed can have the same content as a Web page, but the feed is usually formatted differently—in the form of headline topics. Additionally, when you subscribe to a feed, Internet Explorer automatically checks the Web site and downloads new content so you can see what is new since you last visited the feed.
>
> The downside of seeing a feed instead of the actual Web site is that you do not get to benefit from the design of the Web page itself, where the format of the information or the photos and graphics could add to or possibly change your interpretation of the information.
>
> **Feeds are usually free:** It is usually free to subscribe to a feed.
>
> **Other programs can display your feeds:** Internet Explorer provides the Common Feed List to other programs, so you can subscribe to feeds with Internet Explorer and then read them in other programs such as your e-mail client or in one of the feed readers available as a gadget.
>
> **Feeds come in two common formats:** Two common formats for feeds are RSS and Atom. Feed formats are constantly being updated with new versions, and Internet Explorer supports most RSS and Atom versions. All feed formats are based on XML (Extensible Markup Language), which is a text-based computer language used to describe and distribute structured data and documents.

Objective 9 | Use Web Slices, Accelerators, and Suggested Sites

An RSS feed enables you to get frequently changing content automatically by subscribing to the feed. A technology that is similar to, and based on, RSS technology, is a ***Web Slice***. A Web Slice is a specific *portion*—a slice—of a Web page to which you can subscribe, and which enables you to see when updated content, such as the current temperature, is available from a site.

The ***Accelerators*** feature displays a blue Accelerator icon when you select text from any Web page, which when clicked enables you to accomplish tasks such as finding a map, defining a word, or e-mailing content to others.

Activity 5.13 | Using Web Slices

After you subscribe to a Web Slice, it displays as a link on the Favorites bar. When the Web Slice is updated, the link displays in bold, at which time you can click the link to see the updated content.

> **Another Way**
>
> If displayed on your Favorites bar, click Web Slices or Get more Add-ons; or, display the Manage Add-ons dialog box, and click Find more toolbars and extensions.

A Web slice is useful for things that you like to check frequently throughout the day without actually navigating to a specific site. Popular Web Slices include those for weather, traffic, and sports scores.

1 **Close** any open windows. On the taskbar, click the **Internet Explorer** button, click in the **address bar**, type **ieaddons.com** and then press Enter. Scroll to the bottom of the page, and locate **Web Slices**, as shown in Figure 5.52.

Figure 5.52

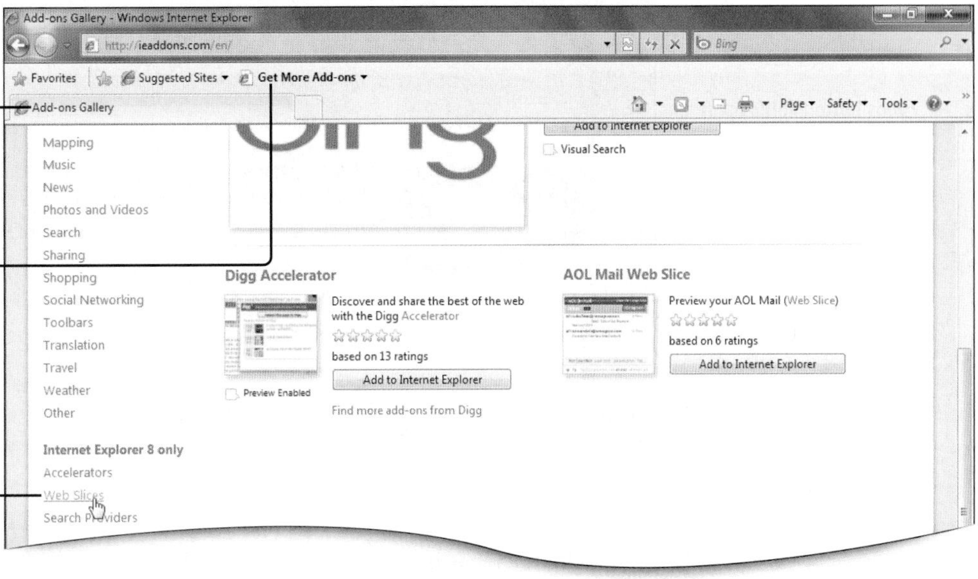

2 Click the **Web Slices** link to display the **Web Slices Add-ons Gallery**. Notice that on the left, there are many categories to choose from when looking for a Web Slice. Compare your screen with Figure 5.53.

Figure 5.53

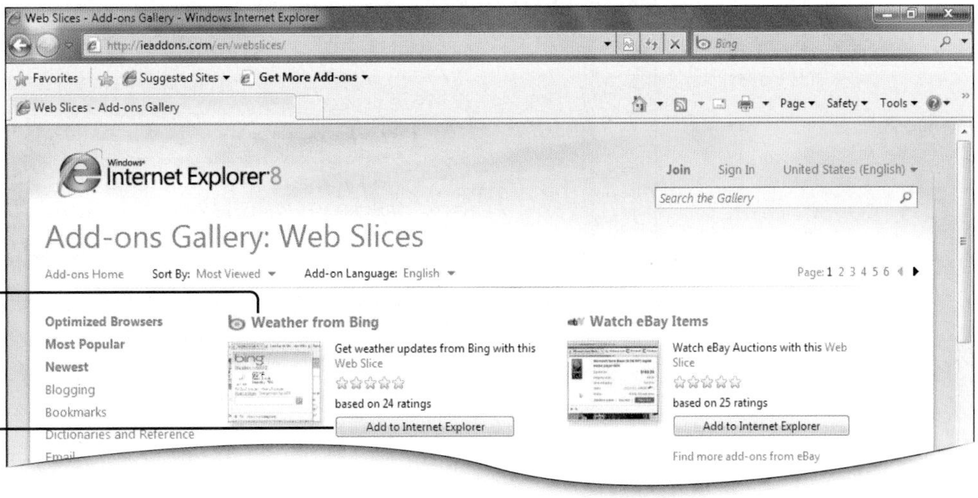

3 Under **Weather from Bing**, click the **Add to Internet Explorer** button. If you do not see this link, scroll to view the bottom of the page, and then on the left, click Weather.

4 In the new window, *point* to the text *change location*, notice the green button on the **Command bar** and on the page, and then compare your screen with Figure 5.54.

On pages where a Web Slice is available, the Feeds button on the Command bar will light up in green, and a related button on the page will also light up in green.

Figure 5.54

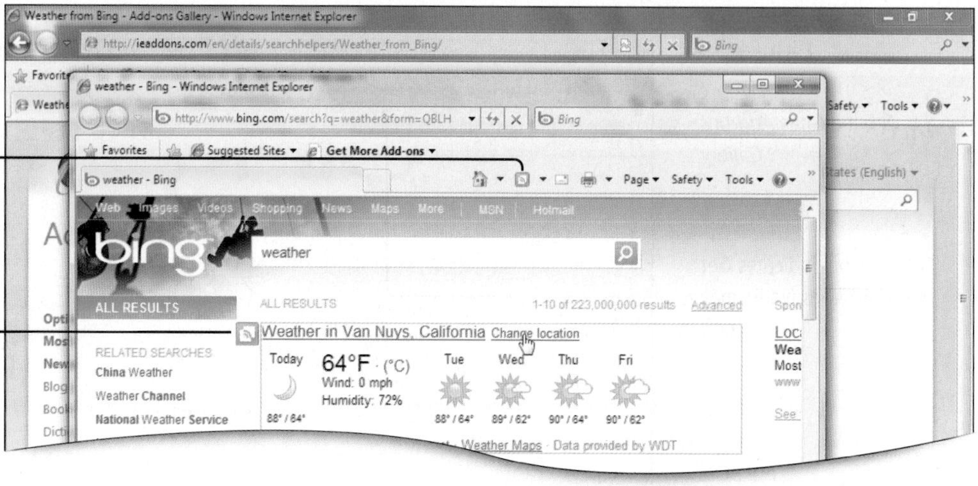

5 Click **change location**. In the **Current location** box, delete the existing text, and then type **Miami, Florida** Compare your screen with Figure 5.55.

Figure 5.55

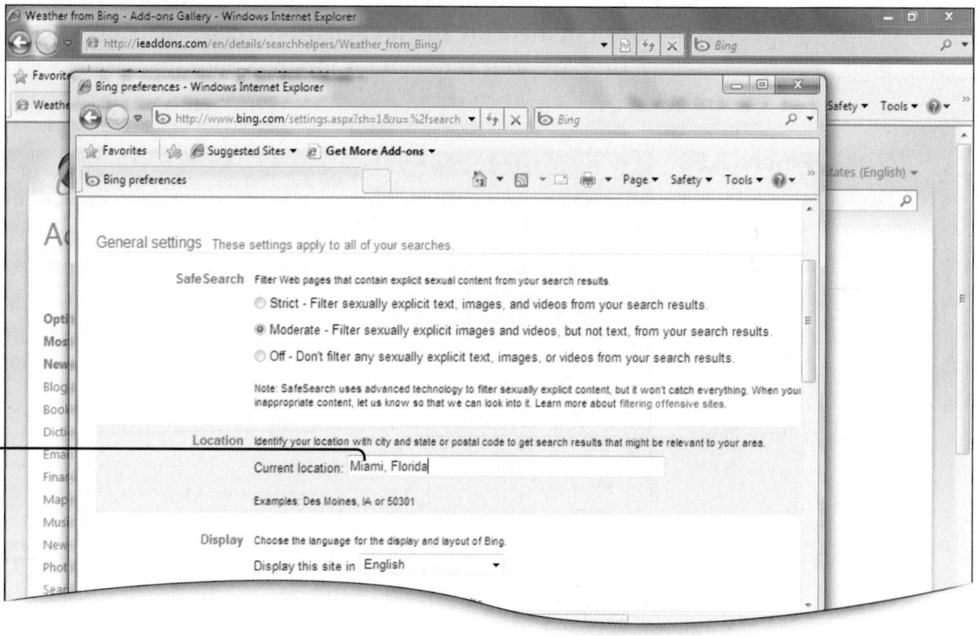

6 Press Enter to change the location to **Miami**. On the **Command bar**, point to the green **Web Slice** button and click one time. Compare your screen with Figure 5.56.

Figure 5.56

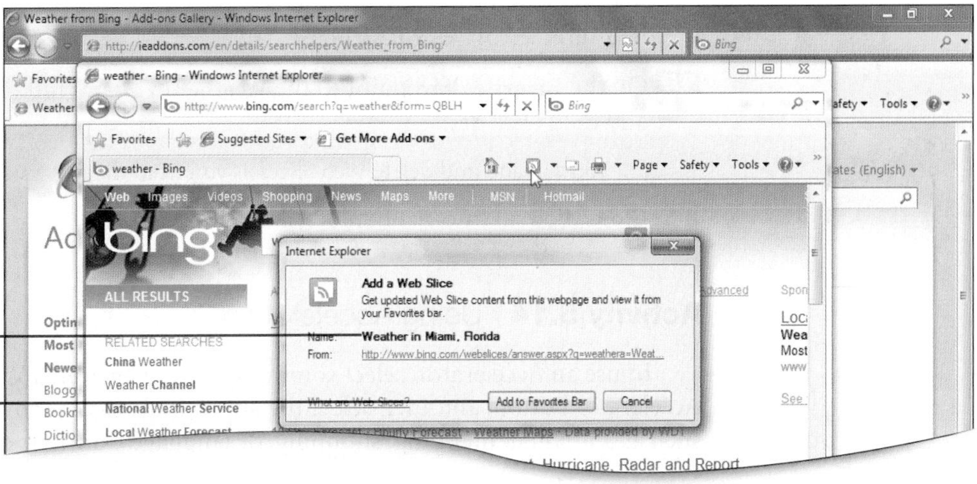

Weather in Miami, Florida indicated

Add to Favorites Bar button

7 Click the **Add to Favorites Bar** button. If necessary, **Maximize** your window.

The Web Slice displays on your Favorites bar.

8 Click in the **address bar**, type **myflorida.com** and then press Enter

9 On the **Favorites bar**, click the **Weather in Miami** link, and then compare your screen with Figure 5.57.

When you click on a Web slice, you do not navigate to a new page; rather a small *slice* of another Web page displays in a small window that you can quickly close. Or, you can click any link in the small window to navigate to the actual site.

Figure 5.57

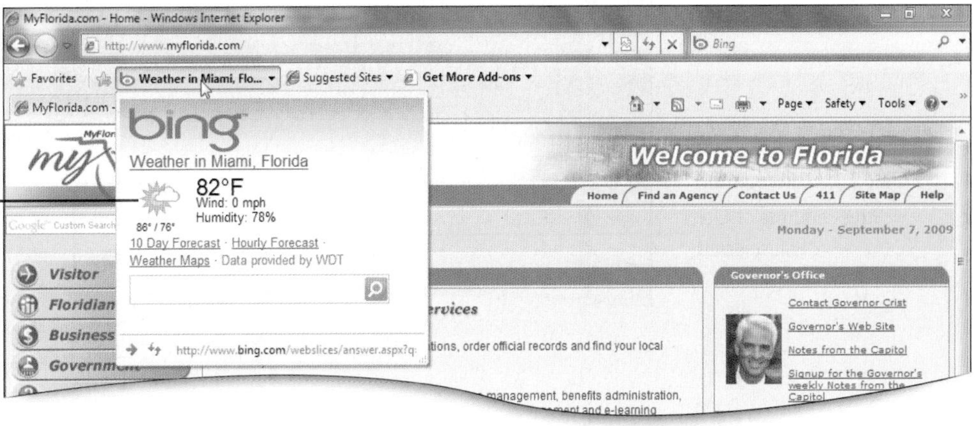

Current weather conditions in Miami display

10 Click in a blank area of the screen to close the small window.

The next time the weather conditions change, the link will display in bold, and you can view the updated information.

11 **Start** the **Snipping Tool** program and create a **Full-screen** snip. **Save** the snip in your **Windows 7 Chapter 5** folder as a **JPEG** file with the name **Lastname_Firstname_5B_Slice_Snip** **Close** the **Snipping Tool** mark-up window. Hold this file until you complete Project 5B, and then submit it as directed by your instructor.

12 On the **Favorites bar**, point to the **Weather in Miami** link, right-click, click **Delete**, and then click **Yes**.

You can add and delete Web Slices as you need them.

13 **Close** all Internet Explorer windows.

Activity 5.14 | Using Accelerators

To use an Accelerator, select some appropriate text on a Web page, click the blue Accelerator button, and then select the appropriate service to do what you want to do, such as searching, mapping, shopping, or language translation.

1 **Close** any open windows. On the taskbar, click the **Internet Explorer** button , click in the **address bar**, type **miamigov.com** and then press Enter.

2 In the site's navigation bar, click **city directory**.

The directory opens in a new window.

3 Hold down the left mouse button, and then drag to select the **street address** of **City Hall**, as shown in Figure 5.58. Notice that a **blue Accelerator button** displays.

Figure 5.58

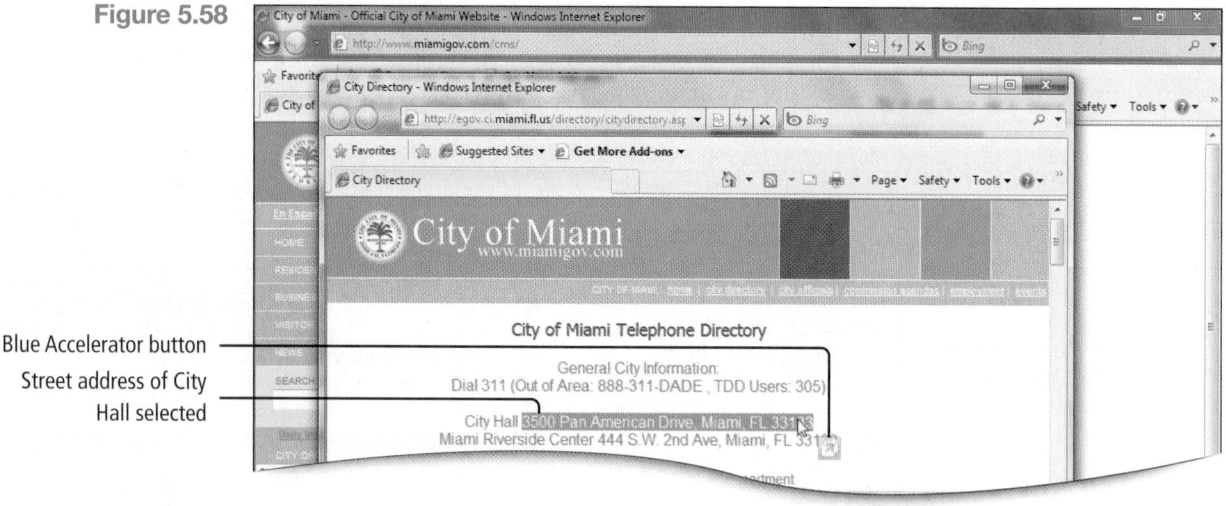

4 Click the **blue Accelerator** button to display a shortcut menu, and then click **Map with Bing**. **Maximize** the window.

A map of the street address displays. In the Bing mapping application, you can click various views of the address you selected, for example Bird's eye displays an overhead picture of the address.

5 As shown in Figure 5.59, point to **Aerial**.

Figure 5.59

Views that you can select

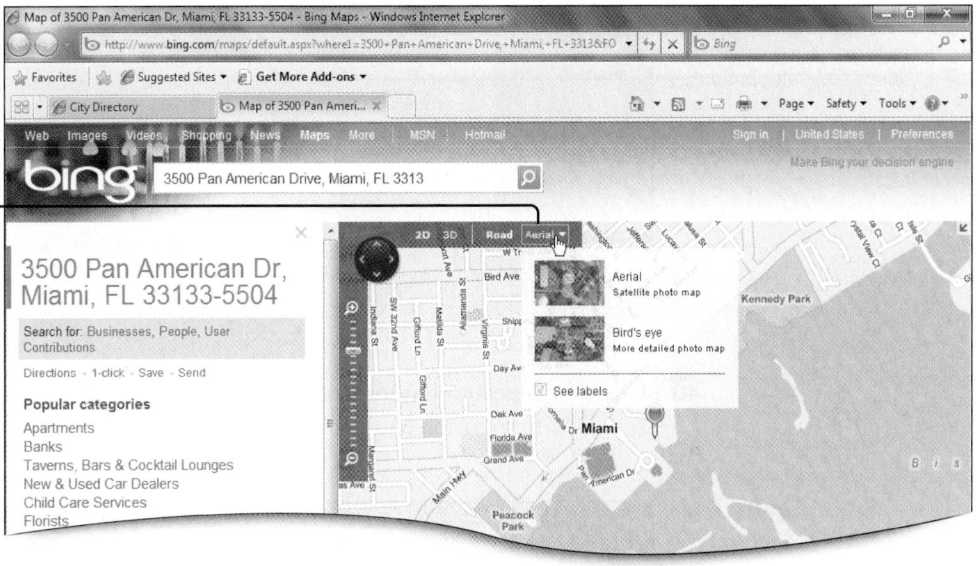

6 On the displayed list, click **Bird's eye**.

7 **Start** the **Snipping Tool** program and create a **Full-screen** snip. **Save** the snip in your **Windows 7 Chapter 5** folder as a **JPEG** file with the name **Lastname_Firstname_5B_Accelerator_Snip** **Close** the **Snipping Tool** mark-up window. Hold this file until you complete Project 5B, and then submit it as directed by your instructor.

8 Open a **New Tab**, in the **address bar** type **ieaddons.com** and press Enter. Scroll to the bottom of the page, on the left click **Accelerators**, and then in the upper right corner, click in the **Search the Gallery** box. Type **define** and press Enter.

9 Under **Define with Bing**, click **Add to Internet Explorer**, and then click **Add**.

10 Click in the **address bar**, type **miamigov.com** and then press Enter. In the site's navigation bar, click **City Organizations**. Under the heading **City Marinas**, in the first sentence, point to the word *marinas* and double-click to select the word and display the blue Accelerator button. Compare your screen with Figure 5.60.

Figure 5.60

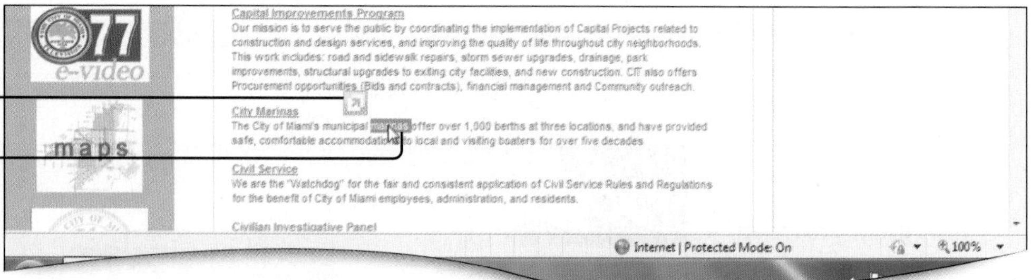

11 Click the **blue Accelerator** button, point to **All Accelerators**, and then compare your screen with Figure 5.61.

Figure 5.61

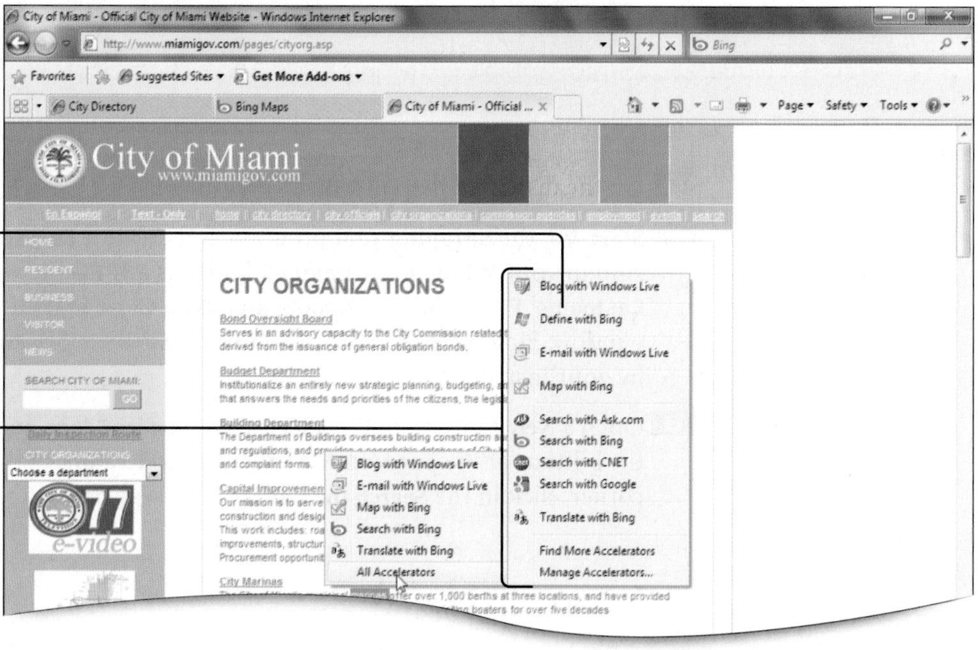

12 Click **Define with Bing**, and then compare your screen with Figure 5.62.

You can see that there are many ways to use Accelerators.

Figure 5.62

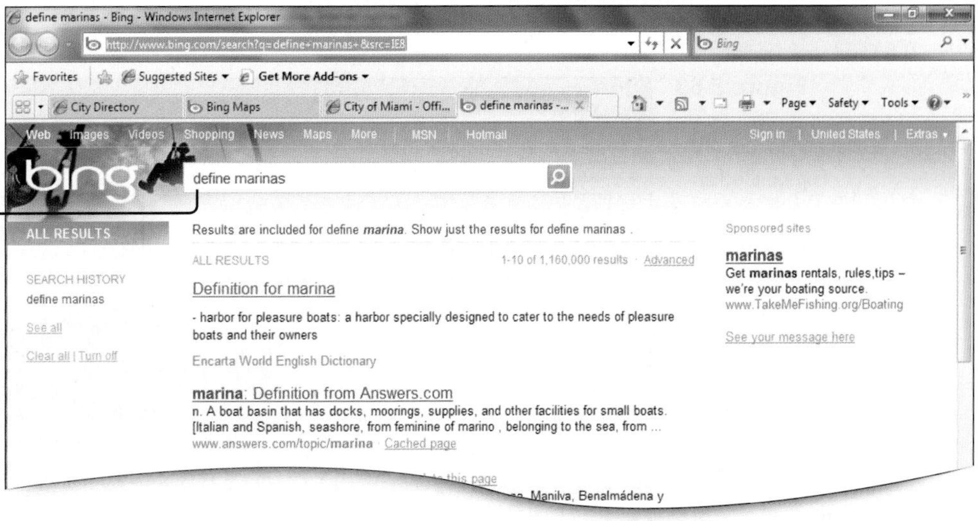

13 **Close** all Internet Explorer windows.

> **More Knowledge | Using the Suggested Sites Feature**
>
> ***Suggested Sites*** is an optional online service that suggests other Web sites in which you might be interested based on the Web sites you visit most. First, you must activate the feature by clicking it on the Favorites bar, and then clicking Turn on Suggested Sites. Or, from the Tools menu, click Suggested Sites. Once activated, your Web browsing history is sent to Microsoft. Then, as you browse the Web, you can click the Suggested Sites link to see a list of related sites. For example, after browsing the Web in Project 5A, the feature might suggest additional sites related to Miami and Florida. If you do not plan to use this feature, you can right-click the link on the Favorites bar and delete it. You can also turn it off at any time, and even if activated, it does not record any information when InPrivate Browsing is turned on.

Objective 10 | Block Pop-up Windows and Use the Information Bar

A ***pop-up*** is a small Web browser window that displays on top of the Web site you are viewing; pop-ups are usually created by advertisers. ***Pop-up Blocker*** is a feature in Internet Explorer that enables you to limit or block most pop-ups. The Information bar displays information about downloads, blocked pop-up windows, and other activities.

Activity 5.15 | Using the Internet Explorer 8 Pop-up Blocker and Information Bar

Pop-up Blocker is enabled by default. To turn it off or change the settings, display the Tools menu as shown in Figure 5.63.

Figure 5.63

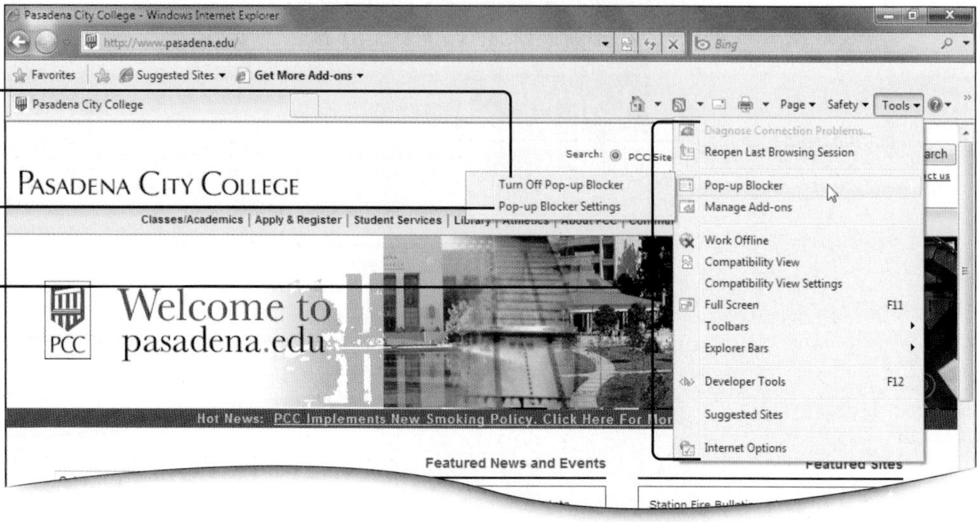

By displaying the Pop-up Blocker Settings dialog box, you can *allow* pop-ups from specific Web sites as shown in Figure 5.64. You can also select the Blocking level and decide whether to play a sound or show the Information bar when a pop-up is blocked. These default settings are appropriate for most computer users. Some sites request that you allow pop-ups from their site, and if you trust the site, it is safe to do so. For example, the learning management system known as *Blackboard*, which is used by many colleges and universities, requests that you allow pop-ups from its site.

Because the Information bar displays on a site when a pop-up is blocked, you always have the choice of viewing the pop-up message if you want to do so. Click the Information bar and then click Show Blocked Pop-up. From the Information bar, you can also click to temporarily accept pop-ups from a specific site.

Figure 5.64

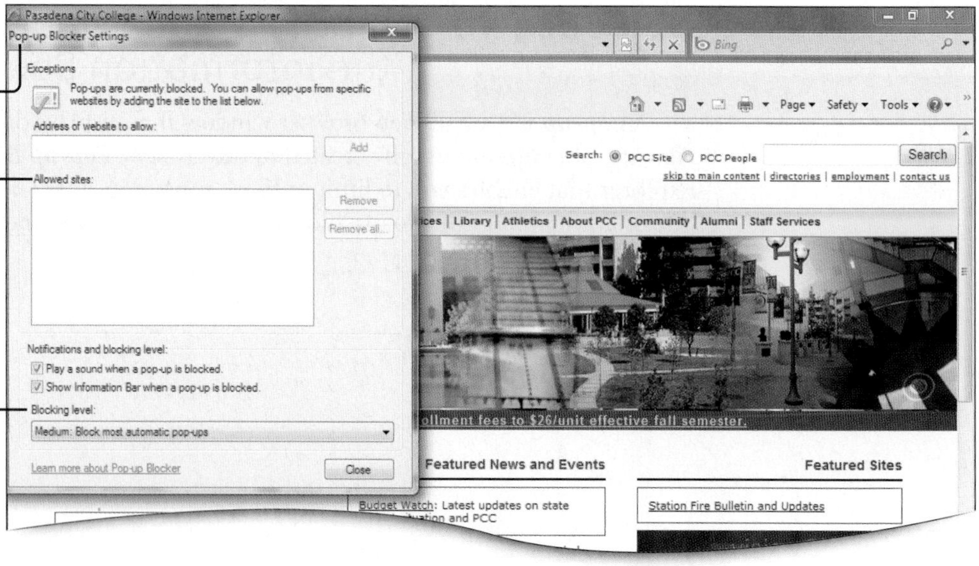

The Information bar will display at the top of the screen if:

- A site tries to install an ActiveX control, install an updated ActiveX control, install an add-on program, run an ActiveX control in an unsafe manner, or run active content.
- A site tries to download a file to your computer.
- Your security settings are below the recommended levels.
- You started Internet Explorer with add-ons disabled.

One advantage of the Information bar is that you are not required to attend to it. For example, if you display a site by mistakenly typing an incorrect URL, you can ignore the Information bar. If you want to proceed with using a feature of the displayed site, click the message and then take appropriate action. For a complete list of messages that you might see in the Information bar, display the Windows Help and Support window, and search for *information bar*.

To check how well you can identify pop-up blocking functions, take a moment to answer the following questions:

1. By default, Pop-up Blocker is ____________.
2. You always have the choice of ____________ a pop-up message if you want to do so.
3. One common reason that the Information bar will display is if a Web site tries to install, update, or run in an unsafe manner any type of ____________ control.
4. The Information bar commonly displays if a site tries to ____________ a file to your computer.
5. One advantage of the Information bar is that you are not ____________ to do anything with it.

Objective 11 | Protect Against Malware

Internet Explorer will warn you when Web pages try to install software by displaying the Information bar. There are additional ways in which Internet Explorer provides safety features to protect your computer against malware.

Activity 5.16 | Protecting Against Malware

Internet Explorer's ***protected mode*** makes it more difficult for malicious software to be installed on your computer by preventing a downloaded program from making any direct changes to the system. It also allows you to install *wanted* ActiveX controls or add-ons when you are logged on as an administrator. Protected mode is on by default and you will see it indicated in the status bar. One way that protected mode helps protect your computer from malicious downloads is by restricting where files can be saved without your consent.

Windows Defender is a spyware scanning and removal tool included with Windows 7. By default, Windows Defender, when enabled, scans your computer for spyware automatically daily at 2:00 a.m. During the scan, Windows Defender takes automatic action on various items, depending on your preferences. If any spyware is found, you are prompted with options to deal with each threat by selecting Ignore, Quarantine, Remove, or Always Allow. Windows Defender constantly updates it definitions so that it can find new spyware threats that emerge on the Internet.

The first step in using Windows Defender is to make sure it is enabled on your computer. To do so, open the Control Panel, type defender in the Search box, and then click Windows Defender. To enable or change the settings of Windows Defender, click the Tools button as shown in Figure 5.65.

Figure 5.65

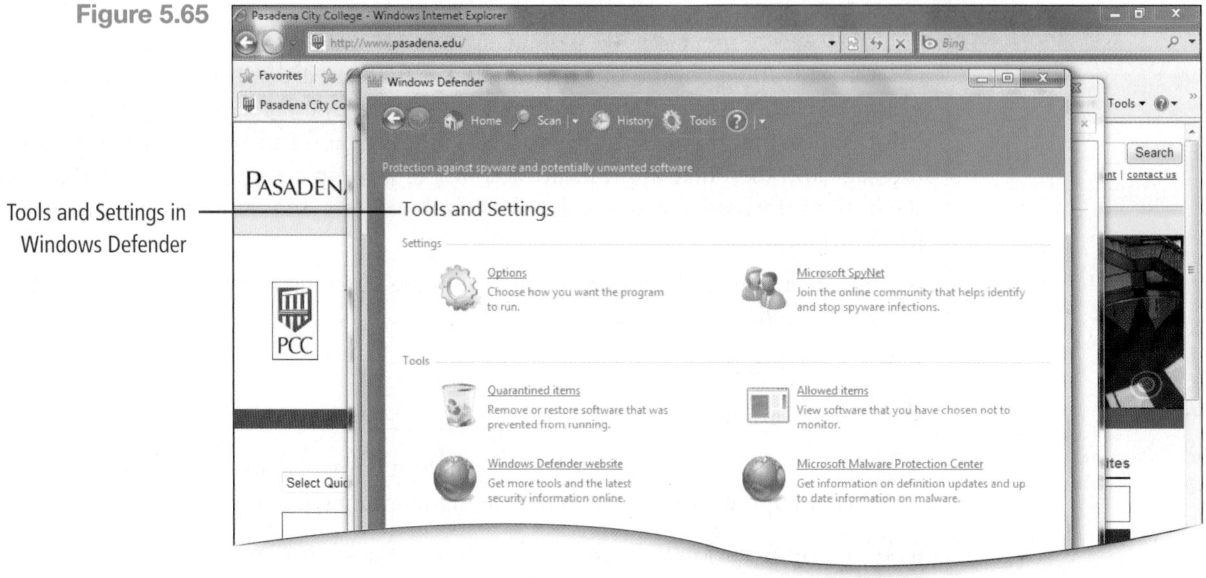

To check how well you understand protecting against malware, take a moment to answer the following questions:

1. Protected mode makes it difficult for malicious software to be installed on your computer by preventing a downloaded program from making direct ____________ to the system.
2. Protected mode is on by default and is indicated on the ____________.
3. Protected mode restricts where a downloaded file can be stored without your ____________.
4. When enabled, Windows Defender scans your computer for spyware daily at ____________.
5. Windows Defender constantly updates its ____________ so that it can find new spyware threats that emerge on the Internet.

Objective 12 | Protect Your Data

Windows 7 provides a variety of ways to protect your personal data and your electronic transactions.

Activity 5.17 | Protecting Your Data

A ***certificate*** is a digital document that verifies the identity of a person or indicates the security of a Web site. Certificates are issued by trusted companies known as ***Certification Authorities***. Certificates make secure transactions on the Internet possible. When you visit a secure Web site in Internet Explorer, a padlock icon will display in the address bar indicating that a digital certificate identifies the site. As shown in Figure 5.66, you can click the padlock icon to display information about the certificate.

Figure 5.66

Padlock icon in address bar

Information about the certificate

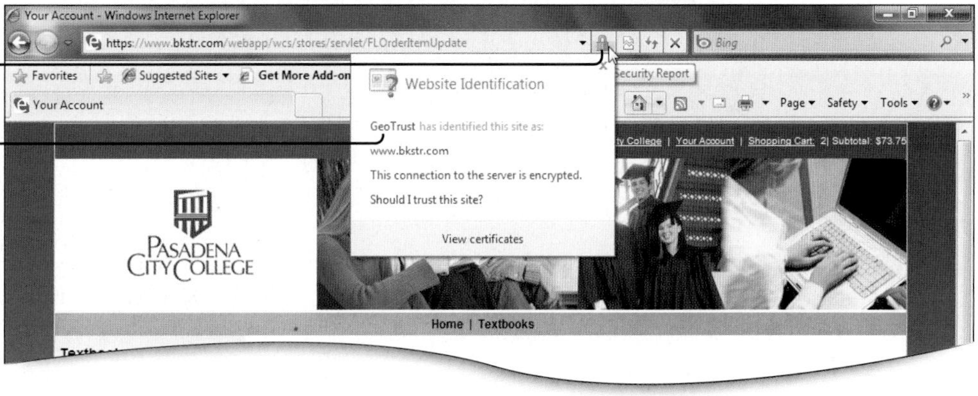

You can see specific information about the issuer of the certificate by clicking *View certificates*. You will commonly see such certificate information on any site where financial transactions are involved.

Phishing is a technique used to trick computer users into revealing personal or financial information through an e-mail message or a Web site. The message or site appears to come from a trusted source but actually directs recipients to provide information to a fraudulent Web site.

SmartScreen Filter is a feature in Internet Explorer that helps detect phishing Web sites and Web sites that distribute malware. SmartScreen Filter runs in the background and protects you by comparing the addresses of Web sites you visit against a list of sites reported to Microsoft as legitimate. This list is stored on your computer. It also analyzes the sites you visit to see if they have characteristics common to a phishing site.

To manually check a Web site that you find suspicious, navigate to the site you want to check, on the Command bar, click Safety, point to SmartScreen Filter, click Check This Website, and then click OK. If a Web site is flagged as suspicious, you should not submit any personal or financial information to it unless you are certain that the site is trustworthy. Suspicious sites are flagged by Internet Explorer by displaying the address bar in yellow along with a message. For more information about how Internet Explorer handles phishing, in the Windows Help and Support window, search for phishing and click SmartScreen Filter: frequently asked questions.

To check how well you understand data protection, take a moment to answer the following questions:

1. A certificate can verify the ____________ of a Web site.
2. Certificates make ____________ transactions on the Web possible.
3. When you visit a secure Web site, the address bar displays a ____________ icon.
4. A technique to trick computer users into revealing personal information is ____________.
5. If the SmartScreen Filter in Internet Explorer suspects a Web site of having phishing characteristics, it will display a message and display the address bar in ____________.

End **You have completed Project 5B**

Content-Based Assessments

Summary

In this chapter, you used tabbed browsing to open multiple Web sites in a single browser window. You created and organized Favorites. When you use public computers, it is a good idea to delete your browsing history, which you practiced in this chapter. You also practiced printing and saving information on a Web page.

In this chapter, you practiced locating, subscribing to, and viewing RSS feeds. You also practiced how to use Web Slices and Accelerators. There are many excellent search providers that you can use to search the Web, and in this chapter, you used several providers to search.

Key Terms

- **Accelerators** 332
- **ActiveX** 323
- **ActiveX control** 323
- **Add-on** 321
- **Address bar** 290
- **Blog** 289
- **Bookmark managers** 307
- **Browsing history** 308
- **Browsing** 289
- **Certificate** 343
- **Certification Authorities** 343
- **Cookies** 308
- **Country codes** 291
- **Digital signature** 322
- **Domain name** 290
- **Favorites bar** 306
- **Favorites Center** 302
- **Feed reader** 329
- **Home page** 289
- **http** 290
- **HyperText Transfer Protocol** 290
- **Information bar** 323
- **InPrivate Browsing** 310
- **Internet Explorer 8** 289
- **Phishing** 343
- **Pop-up** 339
- **Pop-up Blocker** 339
- **Portal** 311
- **Protected mode** 341
- **Protocol prefix** 290
- **Quick Tabs** 298
- **Recent Pages** 292
- **RSS feed** 328
- **RSS viewer** 329
- **RSS** 328
- **Search provider** 325
- **Search term** 325
- **SmartScreen Filter** 343
- **Sponsored links** 325
- **Suggested Sites** 339
- **Surfing** 289
- **Syndicated content** 328
- **Tab row** 294
- **Tabbed browsing** 289
- **Temporary Internet files** 308
- **Top level domain** 290
- **Uniform Resource Locator** 290
- **URL** 290
- **Web browser** 289
- **Web feed** 328
- **Web log** 289
- **Web Slice** 332
- **Windows Defender** 341
- **XML feed** 328

Matching

Match each term in the second column with its correct definition in the first column. Write the letter of the term on the blank line in front of the correct definition.

_____ 1. Any software program with which you display Web pages and navigate the Internet.

_____ 2. The Web browser software developed by Microsoft Corporation that is included with Windows 7.

_____ 3. The term used to describe the process of using your computer to view Web pages.

_____ 4. A feature in Internet Explorer that enables you to open multiple Web sites in a single browser window.

_____ 5. The area across the upper portion of the Internet Explorer window in which a tab for each open Web site displays.

A Accelerators
B Browsing
C Cookies
D Favorites bar
E Favorites Center
F InPrivate Browsing
G Internet Explorer 8
H Pop-up
I Quick Tabs
J RSS feed

____	6.	The feature in Internet Explorer that displays, on a single tab, a thumbnail of each Web site that is currently open.
____	7.	A list of links to Web sites that is saved in your Web browser.
____	8.	A toolbar in Internet Explorer 8 that displays directly below the address bar and to which you can add or drag Web addresses you use frequently.
____	9.	Small text files that Web sites put on your computer to store information about you and your preferences, for example logon information.
____	10.	A feature in Internet Explorer 8 with which you can browse the Web without storing data about your browsing session.
____	11.	A word or phrase that describes the topic about which you want to find information.
____	12.	Frequently updated content published by a Web site and delivered to a feed reader.
____	13.	A specific *portion*—a slice—of a Web page to which you can subscribe, and which enables you to see when updated content, such as the current temperature, is available from a site.
____	14.	An Internet Explorer feature that displays a blue button when you select text from any Web page, from which you can accomplish tasks such as finding a map or defining a word.
____	15.	A small Web browser window that displays on top of the Web site you are viewing, and which is usually created by advertisers.

K Search term
L Tab row
M Tabbed browsing
N Web browser
O Web Slice

Multiple Choice

Circle the correct answer.

1. An online journal or column used to publish personal or company information is a:
   A. web feed **B.** blog **C.** search provider
2. The ending letters of a URL such as *.com*, *.org*, and so on is the:
   A. locator **B.** country code **C.** top level domain
3. A Web site that displays news, content, and links that are of interest to a specific audience is a:
   A. portal **B.** URL **C.** feed
4. Frequently updated content published by a Web site and delivered to a feed reader is:
   A. an RSS feed **B.** a blog **C.** a cookie
5. Programs that add features to a Web browser such as Internet Explorer are:
   A. bookmark managers **B.** temporary Internet files **C.** add-ons
6. A Web site that provides search capabilities on the Web is called a:
   A. sponsored link **B.** search provider **C.** domain
7. An example of an Accelerator is a:
   A. domain name **B.** digital signature **C.** mapping site
8. A feature in Internet Explorer that makes it difficult for malicious software to be installed on your computer is:
   A. protected mode **B.** syndicated content **C.** ActiveX
9. A spyware scanning and removal tool included with Windows 7 is:
   A. Windows Blocker **B.** Windows Defender **C.** Windows Security
10. A technique used to trick computer users into revealing personal information is:
    A. hacking **B.** spying **C.** phishing

Content-Based Assessments

Apply 5A skills from these Objectives:

1. Use Tabbed Browsing
2. Organize Favorites
3. Manage Browsing History and Browse with InPrivate
4. Print, Zoom, and Change the Text Size of Web Pages
5. Save Web Page Information
6. Manage Add-ons

Skills Review | Project 5C Browsing the Web with Internet Explorer 8

Project Files

For Project 5C, you will need the following files:

Student Resource CD or USB flash drive containing the student data files
win05_5C_Answer_Sheet (Word document)

You will save your document as:

Lastname_Firstname_5C_Answer_Sheet

Project Results

1 **Close** all open windows. On the taskbar, click the **Windows Explorer** button. In the **navigation pane**, click the drive that contains the student files for this textbook, and then navigate to **Chapter_Files** ▶ **Chapter_05**. Double-click the Word file **win05_5C_Answer_Sheet** to open Word and display the document. Press F12 to display the **Save As** dialog box in Word, navigate to your **Windows 7 Chapter 5** folder, and then using your own name, save the document as **Lastname_Firstname_5C_Answer_Sheet** If necessary, click OK if a message regarding formats displays.

On the taskbar, click the **Word** button to minimize the window and leave your Word document accessible from the taskbar. **Close** the **Chapter_05** folder window. As you complete each step in this project, click the Word button on the taskbar to open the document, type your one-letter answer in the appropriate cell of the Word table, and then on the taskbar, click the button again to minimize the window for the next step.

Open Internet Explorer. Click in the **address bar** and navigate to **doh.state.fl.us** Open a **New Tab**, and then go to the site **miamigov.com** On a **New Tab**, go to the site **hsmv.state.fl.us** On the **tab row**, click the **Quick Tabs** button. What is your result?

A. Thumbnails for each open site display.
B. A list of recently visited Web sites displays.
C. The tabs in the tab row are rearranged in alphabetical order.

2 On the **tab row**, click the **Tab List** button. How many sites display on the list?

A. one
B. two
C. three

3 On a **New Tab**, go to the site **florida.edu** and then click the **Favorites** button. Click **Add to Favorites**. What is your result?

A. The Favorites Center pane displays on the left side of the screen.
B. The Create Favorites Folder dialog box displays.
C. The Add a Favorite dialog box displays.

4 Click **Cancel**. On the displayed home page for **Florida International University**, on the **navigation bar**, point to the link for **Athletics** and right-click. From the displayed shortcut menu, which of the following actions are possible?

A. You can open the Athletics link in a new tab.
B. You can send the Athletics link to your Documents folder.
C. You can create a tab group.

(Project 5C Browsing the Web with Internet Explorer 8 continues on the next page)

Skills Review | Project 5C Browsing the Web with Internet Explorer 8 (continued)

5 Click in a blank area of the screen to close the shortcut menu. Click the **Favorites** button to open the **Favorites Center** pane. Across the top, which tabs display?

A. Favorites, Tab Groups, Feeds

B. Favorites, Feeds, History

C. Favorites, History, Recent Pages

6 Click the **History tab**, and then click the **arrow**. Which of the following is *not* a viewing arrangement?

A. By Date

B. By Favorites

C. By Most Visited

7 Click in a blank area of the screen to close the **Favorites Center** pane. On the **Command bar**, click the **Safety** button, and then click **Delete Browsing History**. According to this information, cookies consist of:

A. Saved information that you have typed into forms.

B. Buttons added to the tab row.

C. Files stored on your computer by Web sites to save preferences.

8 **Close** the **Delete Browsing History** dialog box. Click the **Tools** button, and then click **Manage Add-ons**. At the bottom of the screen, click **Find more toolbars and extensions**. What is your result?

A. A list of add-ons stored on your computer displays.

B. A list of recently used add-ons displays.

C. The Microsoft site for finding and installing new add-ons displays.

9 **Close** the **Add-ons** site and the **Manage Add-ons** dialog box. Click the **New Tab**, and then click **Browse with InPrivate**. What is your result?

A. The Delete Browsing History dialog box displays.

B. InPrivate displays in the address bar.

C. Both A and B.

10 **Close** the **InPrivate** window. With the **FIU** site displayed, click the **Print button arrow**, and then click **Print Preview**. Click the **Page Setup** button to display the **Page Setup** dialog box. From this dialog box, which of the following can be changed?

A. Left and right margins

B. Headers and footers

C. Both A and B

Be sure you have typed all of your answers in your Word document. **Save** and **Close** your Word document, and submit as directed by your instructor. **Close** [X] all open windows.

End **You have completed Project 5C**

Content-Based Assessments

Apply **5B** skills from these Objectives:

- 7 Search the Internet
- 8 Subscribe to and View an RSS Feed
- 9 Use Web Slices, Accelerators, and Suggested Sites
- 10 Block Pop-up Windows and Use the Information Bar
- 11 Protect Against Malware
- 12 Protect Your Data

Skills Review | Project 5D Searching with Search Tools and Using the Web Safely

Project Files

For Project 5D, you will need the following files:

Student Resource CD or USB flash drive containing the student data files
win05_5D_Answer_Sheet (Word document)

You will save your document as:

Lastname_Firstname_5D_Answer_Sheet

Project Results

1 **Close** all open windows. On the taskbar, click the **Windows Explorer** button. In the **navigation pane**, click the drive that contains the student files for this textbook, and then navigate to **Chapter_Files ▶ Chapter_05**. Double-click the Word file **win05_5D_Answer_Sheet** to open Word and display the document. Press F12 to display the **Save As** dialog box in Word, navigate to your **Windows 7 Chapter 5** folder, and then using your own name, save the document as **Lastname_Firstname_5D_Answer_Sheet** If necessary, click OK if a message regarding formats displays.

On the taskbar, click the **Word** button to minimize the window and leave your Word document accessible from the taskbar. **Close** the **Chapter_05** folder window. As you complete each step in this project, click the Word button on the taskbar to open the document, type your one-letter answer in the appropriate cell of the Word table, and then on the taskbar, click the button again to minimize the window for the next step.

Close Internet Explorer if it is open, and then **Start** Internet Explorer again. In the **Search** box, click the **Search arrow ▼**, and then click **Manage Search Providers**. If necessary, set **Bing** as the default and close the Manage Add-ons dialog box. What is your result?

- **A.** *Bing* displays in the Search box.
- **B.** *Default Search* displays in the Search box.
- **C.** *Start your search here* displays in the Search box.

2 In the **Search** box, click the **Search arrow ▼**, and then click **Find More Providers**. What is your result?

- **A.** A list of recently used search providers displays.
- **B.** The Microsoft site for adding search providers to Internet Explorer 8 displays.
- **C.** Bing conducts an Internet search for search providers.

3 Locate the **New York Times Instant Search**, point to the logo that indicates *The New York Times*, right-click, and then click **Save Picture As**. What is your result?

- **A.** An error message indicates that you cannot save this as a picture.
- **B.** The logo displays in Windows Photo Viewer.
- **C.** The Save Picture dialog box displays.

4 Click **Cancel** to close the dialog box. In the categories of possible add-ons, click **Dictionaries and Reference**. Which of the following is true?

- **A.** Google Define is *not* among the available dictionaries.
- **B.** There are at least two Wikipedia sites that you can add.
- **C.** Both A. and B. are true.

(Project 5D Searching with Search Tools and Using the Web Safely continues on the next page)

Skills Review | Project 5D Searching with Search Tools and Using the Web Safely (continued)

5 Click in the **address bar**, type **noaa.gov** and then press Enter. On this page, what signifies that an RSS Feed is available from this site?

A. The Feeds button lights up in green.

B. The Feeds button lights up in orange.

C. The Feeds button blinks on and off.

6 **On the Command bar**, click the **Feeds** button. What is your result?

A. The Feed Headlines gadget displays.

B. The NOAA News Releases displays as a feed to which you can subscribe.

C. The Feeds tab of the Favorites Center displays.

7 On the **Command bar**, click the **Tools** button, point to **Pop-up Blocker**, and then click **Pop-up Blocker Settings**. What does the **Medium blocking level** do with pop-ups?

A. Allows pop-ups from secure sites

B. Blocks most automatic pop-ups

C. Blocks all pop-ups

8 What notifications are available to notify you when a pop-up has been blocked?

A. Play a sound

B. Display the Information bar

C. Both A and B

9 **Close** the **Pop-up Blocker Settings** dialog box. From the **Start menu**, click **Help and Support**, and then in the **Search Help** box type **information bar** and press Enter. In the displayed list, click **Internet Explorer Information bar: frequently asked questions**. Under what circumstances might the Information bar display on your computer?

A. If a Web site tries to open in a new window

B. If a Web site tries to install an ActiveX control

C. If a Web site tries to install an RSS feed

10 At the top of the **Windows Help and Support** window, delete the text *information bar*, type **protected mode** and press Enter. Which of the following is *not* true about protected mode?

A. Protected mode is turned on by default.

B. Protected mode allows you to install wanted ActiveX controls or add-ons when you are logged on as an administrator.

C. Protected mode prevents you from entering credit card information into a Web site.

Be sure you have typed all of your answers in your Word document. **Save** and **Close** your Word document, and submit as directed by your instructor. **Close** all open windows.

End **You have completed Project 5D**

Apply 5A skills from these Objectives:

1 Use Tabbed Browsing
2 Organize Favorites
3 Manage Browsing History and Browse with InPrivate
4 Print, Zoom, and Change the Text Size of Web Pages
5 Save Web Page Information
6 Manage Add-ons

Mastering Windows 7 | Project 5E Browsing the Web with Internet Explorer 8

In the following Mastering Windows 7 project, you will open related sites on separate tabs. You will capture and save a screen that will look similar to Figure 5.67.

Project Files

For Project 5E, you will need the following file:

New Snip file

You will save your document as:

Lastname_Firstname_5E_Sites_Snip

Project Results

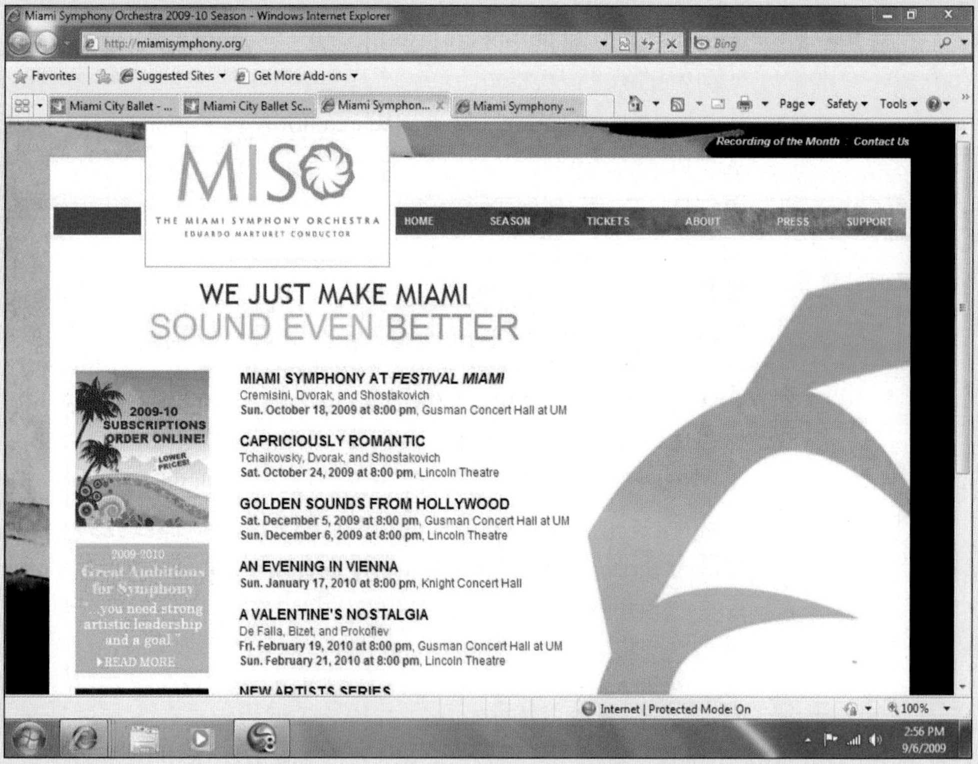

Figure 5.67

(Project 5E Browsing the Web with Internet Explorer 8 continues on the next page)

Mastering Windows 7 | Project 5E Browsing the Web with Internet Explorer 8 (continued)

1 Open Internet Explorer and be sure only the tab for your home page displays. Click in the **address bar**, type **miamicityballet.org** and press Enter. Hold down Ctrl, and then in the navigation bar in this site, click **MCB School** so that a new tab is created for the link and the two tabs are color coded.

2 On a **New Tab**, go to the site **miamisymphony.org** Hold down Ctrl, and then in the navigation bar of this site, click **Season** so that a new tab is created for the link and the two tabs are color coded.

3 Create a **Full-screen Snip**, and then **Save** the snip in your **Windows 7 Chapter 5** folder as a **JPEG** file with the name **Lastname_Firstname_5E_Sites_Snip** Submit this file as directed by your instructor.

4 **Close** all open windows and **Close** Internet Explorer.

End **You have completed Project 5E**

Apply **5B** skills from these Objectives:

- 7 Search the Internet
- 8 Subscribe to and View an RSS Feed
- 9 Use Web Slices and Accelerators, and Suggested Sites
- 10 Block Pop-up Windows and Use the Information Bar
- 11 Protect Against Malware
- 12 Protect Your Data

Mastering Windows 7 | Project 5F Searching with Search Tools and Using the Web Safely

In the following Mastering Windows 7 project, you will use an Accelerator. You will capture and save a screen that will look similar to Figure 5.68.

Project Files

For Project 5F, you will need the following file:

New Snip file

You will save your document as:

Lastname_Firstname_5F_Aerial_Snip

Project Results

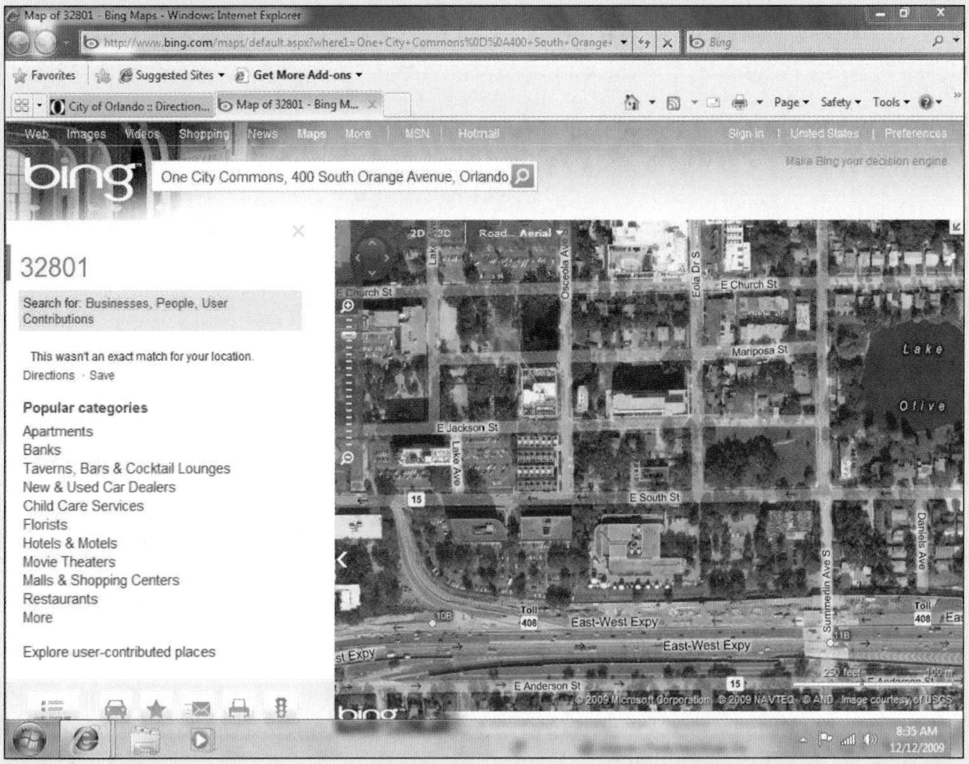

Figure 5.68

(Project 5F Searching with Search Tools and Using the Web Safely continues on the next page)

Mastering Windows 7 | Project 5F Searching with Search Tools and Using the Web Safely (continued)

1 Open Internet Explorer. In the **address bar**, type **cityoforlando.net** and press Enter. On the site's **Information Center** navigation bar, click **City Hall Hours & Directions**.

2 Select the City Hall address (include the city, state, and ZIP code), click the **Accelerator** button, and then click **Map with Bing**.

3 Set the view to **Aerial** and then **Satellite photo map**. Create a **Full-screen Snip** and **Save** it as **Lastname_Firstname_5F_Aerial_Snip** Submit this file as directed by your instructor.

4 **Close** all open windows and **Close** Internet Explorer.

End **You have completed Project 5F**

Outcomes-Based Assessments

Rubric

The following outcomes-based assessments are open-ended assessments. That is, there is no specific correct result; your result will depend on your approach to the information provided. Make Professional Quality your goal. Use the following scoring rubric to guide you in how to approach the problem and then to evaluate how well your approach solves the problem.

The *criteria*—Software Mastery, Content, Format and Layout, and Process—represent the knowledge and skills you have gained that you can apply to solving the problem. The *levels of performance*—Professional Quality, Approaching Professional Quality, or Needs Quality Improvements—help you and your instructor evaluate your result.

	Your completed project is of Professional Quality if you:	Your completed project is of Approaching Professional Quality if you:	Your completed project Needs Quality Improvements if you:
1-Software Mastery	Choose and apply the most appropriate skills, tools, and features and identify efficient methods to solve the problem.	Choose and apply some appropriate skills, tools, and features, but not in the most efficient manner.	Choose inappropriate skills, tools, or features, or are inefficient in solving the problem.
2-Content	Construct a solution that is clear and well organized, contains content that is accurate, appropriate to the audience and purpose, and is complete. Provide a solution that contains no errors of spelling, grammar, or style.	Construct a solution in which some components are unclear, poorly organized, inconsistent, or incomplete. Misjudge the needs of the audience. Have some errors in spelling, grammar, or style, but the errors do not detract from comprehension.	Construct a solution that is unclear, incomplete, or poorly organized, or that contains some inaccurate or inappropriate content, and contains many errors of spelling, grammar, or style. Do not solve the problem.
3-Format and Layout	Format and arrange all elements to communicate information and ideas, clarify function, illustrate relationships, and indicate relative importance.	Apply appropriate format and layout features to some elements, but not others. Overuse features, causing minor distraction.	Apply format and layout that does not communicate information or ideas clearly. Do not use format and layout features to clarify function, illustrate relationships, or indicate relative importance. Use available features excessively, causing distraction.
4-Process	Use an organized approach that integrates planning, development, self-assessment, revision, and reflection.	Demonstrate an organized approach in some areas, but not others; or, use an insufficient process of organization throughout.	Do not use an organized approach to solve the problem.

Apply a combination of the 5A and 5B skills.

Problem Solving | Project 5G Help Desk

Project Files

For Project 5G, you will need the following file:

win05_5G_Help_Desk

You will save your document as:

Lastname_Firstname_5G_Help_Desk

From the student files that accompany this textbook, open the **Chapter_Files** folder, and then in the **Chapter_05** folder, locate and open the Word document **win05_5G_Help_Desk**. Save the document in your chapter folder as **Lastname_Firstname_5G_Help_Desk**

The following e-mail question has arrived at the Help Desk from an employee at the Bell Orchid Hotel's corporate office. In the Word document, construct a response based on your knowledge of Windows 7. Although an e-mail response is not as formal as a letter, you should still use good grammar, good sentence structure, professional language, and a polite tone. Save your document and submit the response as directed by your instructor.

To: Help Desk

I have asked my research assistant to conduct some Internet research about what hotels around the country are doing in regard to designing innovative restaurants. Is there a way he could organize the sites he wants me to review by geographic location and by type of restaurant?

End You have completed Project 5G

Apply a combination of the 5A and 5B skills.

Problem Solving | Project 5H Help Desk

Project Files

For Project 5H, you will need the following file:

win05_5H_Help_Desk

You will save your document as:

Lastname_Firstname_5H_Help_Desk

From the student files that accompany this textbook, open the **Chapter_Files** folder, and then in the **Chapter_05** folder, locate and open **win05_5H_Help_Desk**. Save the document in your chapter folder as **Lastname_Firstname_5H_Help_Desk**

The following e-mail question has arrived at the Help Desk from an employee at the Bell Orchid Hotel's corporate office. In the Word document, construct a response based on your knowledge of Windows 7. Although an e-mail response is not as formal as a letter, you should still use good grammar, good sentence structure, professional language, and a polite tone. Save your document and submit the response as directed by your instructor.

To: Help Desk

Guests who use the computers in our hotel Business Centers have inquired about how they can prevent others from seeing the sites they visited and potentially seeing personal information. What instructions could we post at each of these computers to advise guests how to remove any such information from these public computers?

End **You have completed Project 5H**

Apply a combination of the 5A and 5B skills.

Problem Solving | Project 5I Help Desk

Project Files

For Project 5I, you will need the following file:

win05_5I_Help_Desk

You will save your document as:

Lastname_Firstname_5I_Help_Desk

From the student files that accompany this textbook, open the **Chapter_Files** folder, and then in the **Chapter_05** folder, locate and open the Word document **win05_5I_Help_Desk**. Save the document in your chapter folder as **Lastname_Firstname_5I_Help_Desk**

The following e-mail question has arrived at the Help Desk from an employee at the Bell Orchid Hotel's corporate office. In the Word document, construct a response based on your knowledge of Windows 7. Although an e-mail response is not as formal as a letter, you should still use good grammar, good sentence structure, professional language, and a polite tone. Save your document and submit the response as directed by your instructor.

To: Help Desk

Guests commonly stop by the Front Desk at our hotels and inquire about what the weather will be like in the next few days. Is there a way we could have something on all of the Front Desk computers that would provide the Desk Clerks with constantly updated weather information?

End You have completed Project 5I

Using Windows Live Essentials and Windows Media Center

OUTCOMES

At the end of this chapter you will be able to:

OBJECTIVES

Mastering these objectives will enable you to:

PROJECT 6A

Use the programs in Windows Live Essentials to organize, tag, edit, and crop photos; edit movies; and create a movie DVD.

1. Download Windows Live Essentials Photo Gallery and Movie Maker (p. 363)
2. Locate, View, and Share Photos Using Windows Live Photo Gallery (p. 366)
3. Add, Tag, Rate, and Edit Photos Using Windows Live Photo Gallery (p. 373)
4. Use Windows Live Movie Maker to Create a Movie Using Photos (p. 389)
5. Create a Movie Using Video Clips (p. 395)

PROJECT 6B

Use Windows Media Center to watch slideshows, movies, and television on your computer.

6. Navigate and Configure Windows Media Center (p. 402)
7. Use Windows Media Center to Play Media from Your Computer (p. 406)
8. Use Windows Media Center to View Sports, Internet TV, and Live TV (p. 411)

Stephen VanHorn/Shutterstock

In This Chapter

Windows Live Essentials is a set of free programs available from the Microsoft Web site with which you can organize and edit photos, edit and publish videos, stay in touch with your friends, create an e-mail account, and customize your Web browser.

Windows Media Center performs many of the same tasks that you can perform with Windows Media Player, but also gives you the ability to use your computer as a remote media player—you can play DVDs, watch television, or play music using a keyboard and mouse or a remote control device.

The projects in this chapter relate to the **Bell Orchid Hotels**, headquartered in Boston, and which own and operate resorts and business-oriented hotels. Resort properties are located in popular destinations, including Honolulu, Orlando, San Diego, and Santa Barbara. The resorts offer deluxe accommodations and a wide array of dining options. Other Bell Orchid hotels are located in major business centers and offer the latest technology in their meeting facilities. The company plans to open new properties and update existing properties over the next ten years.

Project 6A Using Windows Live Photo Gallery and Windows Live Movie Maker

Project Activities

In Activities 6.01 through 6.19, you will work with Steven Ramos and Barbara Hewitt, both of whom work for the Information Technology Department at the Boston headquarters office of the Bell Orchid Hotels, to select the photos and videos to be used in a new online ad campaign about attractions near recently opened hotels. You will capture screens that look similar to Figure 6.1.

Project Files

For Project 6A, you will need the following files:

Student Resource CD (or a USB flash drive containing these files)
New Snip files

You will save your files as:

Lastname_Firstname_6A_Imported_Folders_Snip
Lastname_Firstname_6A_Tags&Ratings_Snip
Lastname_Firstname_6A_Brochure_Tags_Snip
Lastname_Firstname_6A_Slide_Show.wlmp
Lastname_Firstname_6A_Slide_Show.wmv
Lastname_Firstname_6A_Movie.wlmp
Lastname_Firstname_6A_Movie.wmv

Project Results

Figure 6.1
Project 6A Using Windows Live Photo Gallery and Windows Live Movie Maker

Objective 1 | Download Windows Live Essentials Photo Gallery and Movie Maker

Windows Live Essentials is a set of free programs available on the Microsoft Web site, including programs that enable you to organize and edit photos, edit and publish videos, stay in touch with your friends, create an e-mail account, and customize your Web browser. You can download all of the programs at one time, or download the programs one at a time as you need them.

> **Another Way**
> Open your Web browser, search for *Windows Live Essentials*, and then click the Microsoft Windows Live Essentials link.

Activity 6.01 | Downloading Photo Gallery and Movie Maker

1 From the **Start** menu, click **All Programs**, click the **Accessories** folder, and then click **Getting Started**. Compare your screen with Figure 6.2.

Figure 6.2

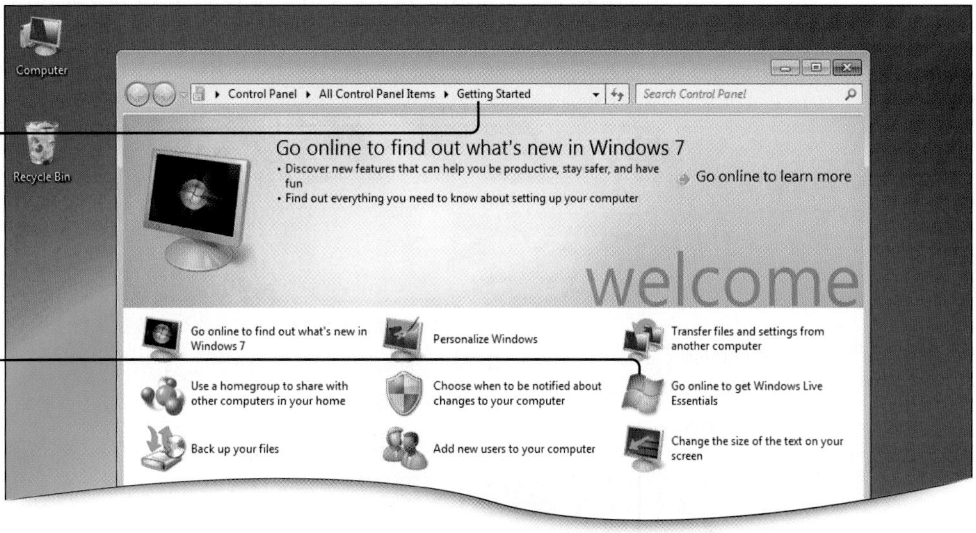

2 In the **Getting Started** window, double-click **Go online to get Windows Live Essentials**. Scroll down to view the list of available programs, and then compare your screen with Figure 6.3.

The Windows Live Essentials home page displays. This page is updated regularly, so your screen may differ from what is shown in Figure 6.3.

Figure 6.3

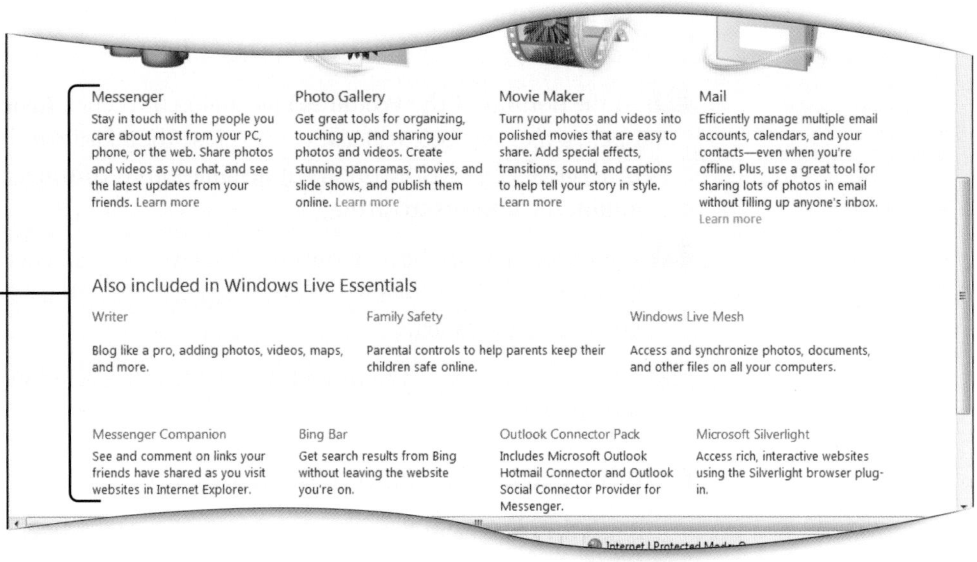

3 Scroll to the top of the window, and then click the **Download now** button. In the **File Download** dialog box, click **Run**. If a User Account Control dialog box displays, click Yes. Wait a moment, and then locate the **Windows Live Essentials** dialog box, which might display as a lighted Windows logo icon on your taskbar. If necessary, click the taskbar icon, and then under **What do you want to install?**, click **Choose the programs you want to install**.

If there are no Windows Live Essentials programs on your computer, an Installer will be downloaded. This may take a few minutes, and then the Windows Live dialog box displays with all of the Windows Live programs selected.

4 Click to *clear* (remove the check mark) all of the check boxes except **Photo Gallery and Movie Maker**—both of which will be used in this chapter—and then compare your screen with Figure 6.4. If you are interested in downloading any of the other programs, leave the check boxes to the left of the program name selected.

Figure 6.4

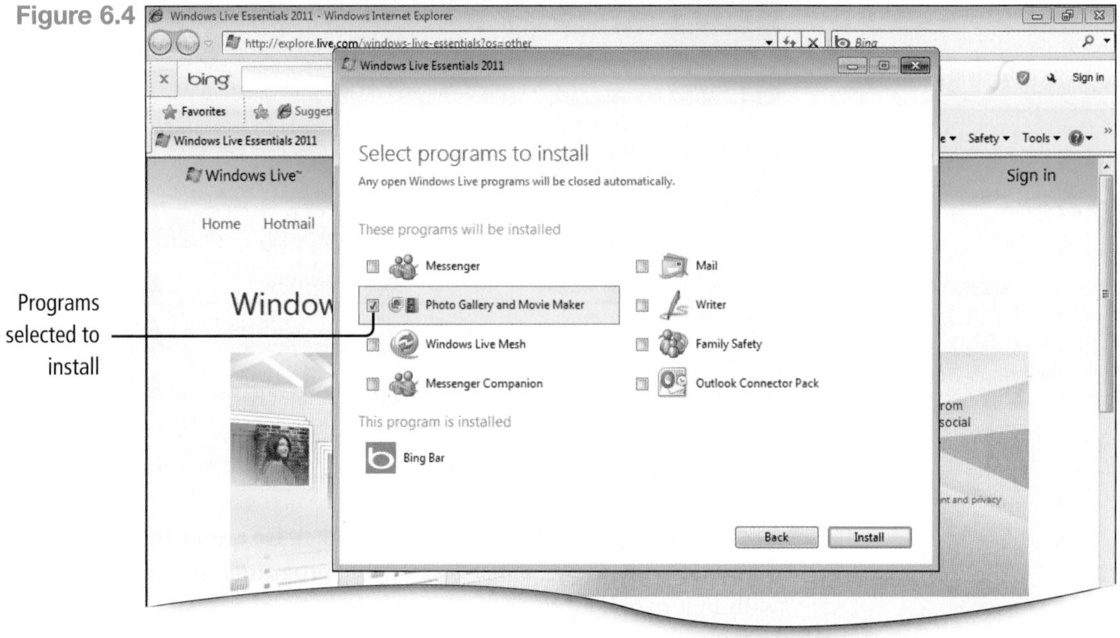

> **Alert! | Are One or Both of the Programs Already Installed on Your Computer?**
>
> If the computer at which you are working already has these programs installed, you can cancel the installation.

5 At the bottom of the **Windows Live** dialog box, click **Install**. If other programs are open, a message box will ask you to close them; follow the instructions to close the programs. Wait for the program installation to complete and then for a screen with additional options to display.

6 If a screen with additional options displays, clear all check boxes, and then click **Continue**. If your browser window opens, close it. If asked to restart your computer, go ahead and restart.

7 If you already have a Windows Live ID, **Close** the Windows Live dialog box and go to **Activity 6.3**.

Activity 6.02 | Creating a Windows Live ID

To get the most from the programs in Windows Live Essentials, you will need a Windows Live ID. If you use Hotmail, Messenger, or Xbox Live, you already have a Windows Live ID.

1. In the upper right corner of the **Windows Live** dialog box, click **Sign in**, and then click **Sign Up**.

2. If you want to use a current e-mail account, click **Continue**. Otherwise, click the **No, sign me up for a free MSN Hotmail e-mail address** check box, and then click **Continue**.

3. If necessary, click the Sign up now button, click in the address box, and then type the name you want to use as your Windows Live ID, for example Firstname_Lastname using the underscore instead of spaces. In the second box, click the arrow, and then click **live.com**.

   The live.com designation is considered to be more current than the hotmail.com designation, although you can use either. The system will check the availability of your selected address. If the name that you typed is not available, experiment with variations using your middle initial, last name first, inserting an underscore, and so on, until you have a logical address that includes your name.

> **Note | Be sure you have an e-mail address that you can use for professional messages.**
>
> If you have not already done so, now is a good time to create an e-mail address that you can use professionally, for example, when contacting potential employers. If you have an e-mail address with a cute or descriptive name, for example, doglover@yahoo.com, reserve it for use with your friends and family. For resumes and professional communications, always use an e-mail address that includes some logical arrangement of your name.

4. When you have found an appropriate Live ID name, fill out the remaining items on the page, and then compare your screen with Figure 6.5. Notice that the Live wizard rates the strength of your password.

Figure 6.5

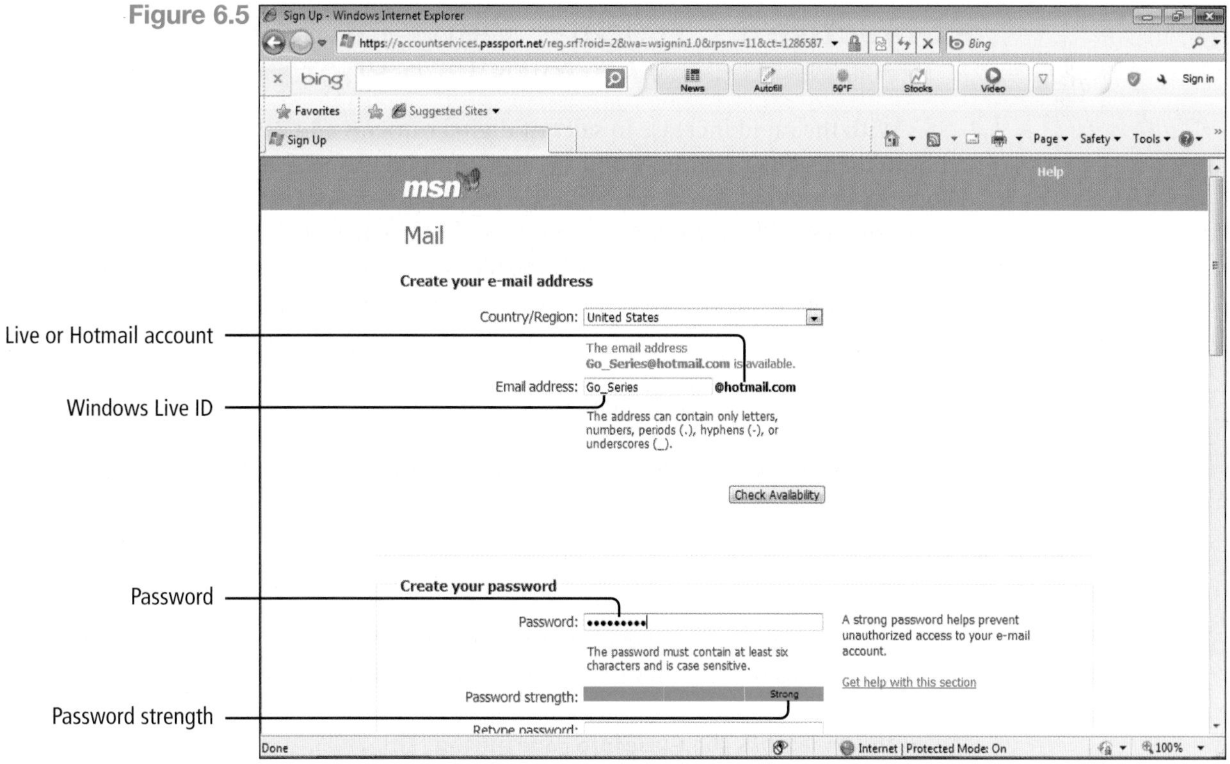

5 After you complete the form, in the **Enter the characters you see** box, type the characters, and then click **I accept**.

> You are automatically signed in to Windows Live, your user name displays in the upper right corner of the window, and a link is provided to the Windows Live home page.

6 Click the **http://home.live.com** link, and then take a moment to examine your Windows Live home page. Compare your screen with Figure 6.6.

> You can use your Windows Live home page to access your e-mail, chat with friends, link to several Microsoft Web pages, and share documents with others.

Figure 6.6

Windows Live home page

The name you created displays here, with the underscore replaced with a space

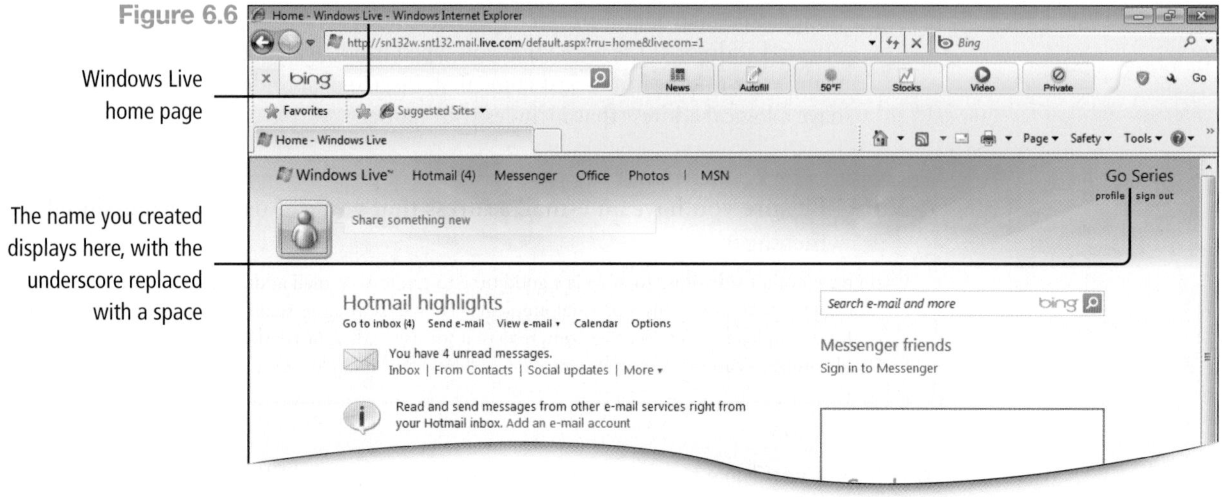

7 Close [×] your browser window.

Objective 2 | Locate, View, and Share Photos Using Windows Live Photo Gallery

With the rapid increase in sales of digital cameras and cell phones with cameras, photo management is important to most computer users. Most digital camera users take lots of photos, and with a large number of photos, file organization can be a challenge. *Windows Live Photo Gallery* is a photo and video organizer with which you can view, manage, and edit digital pictures. It enables you to locate photos—including photos you have stored outside the Pictures folder—and view detailed information about every photo. You can also acquire photos directly from a digital camera.

Activity 6.03 | Adding Photos to Windows Live Photo Gallery

When you open Photo Gallery for the first time, all of the pictures in your Pictures library display—pictures from both the My Pictures folder and the Public folder. All of the videos in your Videos library also display. *Photos* are images with continuous color. If you have photos in other locations, you can add them to Photo Gallery.

1 From the **Start** menu ⊕, click **All Programs**, and then from the list of programs, click **Windows Live Photo Gallery**. If necessary, sign in, and then **Maximize** [□] the window. If a pane displays on the right side of the screen, in the upper right corner of the pane, click the **Close info pane** button [×].

> If you installed Photo Gallery and Movie Maker on the All Programs menu, both programs display with light orange shading, indicating that they are newly installed and have not yet been used.

2 If you are running Photo Gallery for the first time, a dialog box will display, asking if you want to open different file types using Photo Gallery. Click **No** to close the dialog box unless you plan to use Photo Gallery as your primary photo management program.

This dialog box will continue to display each time you open Photo Gallery until you either click *Yes* or select the *Don't show me this again for these file types check box.*

3 Compare your screen with Figure 6.7, and then take a moment to examine the most common graphic file types as described in the table in Figure 6.8.

The navigation pane on the left side of the window enables you to view your photos by folder location. The number of items in the gallery displays at the bottom of the screen.

The Ribbon at the top of the screen displays commands that enable you to work with your photos. The navigation bar at the bottom of the screen enables you to delete or rotate pictures, run a slide show, or change the size of the displayed thumbnails.

> **Alert! | Does Your Screen Differ?**
>
> Figure 6.7 shows the Photo Gallery window with only the default pictures that come with Windows 7. If your computer has additional pictures stored, your screen will differ.

Figure 6.7

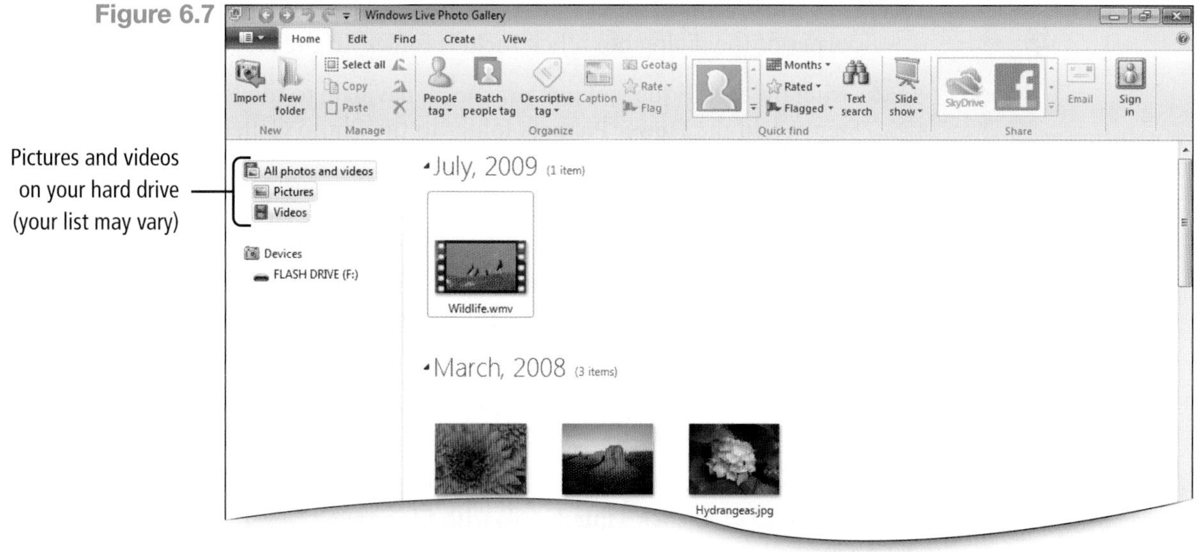

Photo and Graphic Image Formats

Extension	Format
.bmp	A ***bitmap*** image can display millions of colors and can be used to share images with others who may be using different graphic programs. Tags cannot be added to bitmap files.
.gif	The ***Graphic Interchange Format*** was the original Web graphic file format. It can display only a limited number of colors, and is best used for black and white line drawings, clip art, and pictures with large blocks of solid colors. This format is not supported by Photo Gallery.
.jpg, .jpeg	The Joint Photographic Experts Group format is used for photos and other continuous tone images on the Web. Most digital cameras save pictures in JPEG format, and these images are used extensively on the Web.
.png	The ***Portable Network Graphics*** format is a recent format that combines the features of GIFs and JPEGs on the Web.
.tif, .tiff	The Tagged Image File Format is used primarily for traditional print graphics. It can be opened and manipulated by many programs, but is not used for Web pages.

Figure 6.8

4 In the **navigation pane**, if necessary expand ▷ the **Pictures** folder, and then check to see if the **Cactus Pictures** folder or the **Flower Pictures** folder displays. If these two folders display from a previous student working at the computer at which you are seated, click the folder to select it, point to the selected folder, right-click to display a shortcut menu, click Remove from the gallery, and then click Yes.

Removing folders from the Photo Gallery does not remove the folders or files from the computer.

5 With Photo Gallery open, from the taskbar, open **Windows Explorer**. If necessary, *delete* the Bell_Orchid folder from your Documents folder—for this project, you will need a new copy of the files. Insert the Student Resource CD or other device that contains the student files that accompany this textbook. By using the **Send to** command that you have practiced, copy the **Bell_Orchid** folder to your **Documents** folder. **Close** Windows Explorer.

6 In the upper left corner of your screen, to the left of the **Home tab**, click the *blue* **File tab**, and then click **Include folder**. In the **Pictures Library Locations** dialog box, click **Add**. In the **Include Folder in Pictures** dialog box, navigate to **Documents ▶ Bell_Orchid ▶ San_Diego ▶ Sales_Marketing ▶ Media ▶ Photos**.

7 Click the **Cactus Pictures** folder one time to select it, and then in the lower right corner of the dialog box, click **Include folder**. In the displayed dialog box, click **Add**.

8 Using the technique you just practiced, navigate to the Photos folder as you did in Step 6, add the **Flower Pictures** folder to the Photo Gallery, and then in the **Pictures Library Locations** dialog box, click **OK**.

9 On the Ribbon, click the **View tab**, and then in the **Arrange list group**, click **Folder**. At the top of the **navigation pane**, click **All photos and videos**, and then if necessary, scroll down to see the Cactus Pictures and Flower Pictures you just added. At the bottom of your screen, on the right side of the **navigation bar**, click the **View details** button to display information about each picture.

Use the View details button to display basic information about the photos, including the file name, the date the picture was taken, the file type, and the file size.

10 Point to a blank area in the gallery, right-click to display a shortcut menu, point to **View**, and then click **Thumbnails with file name**.

11 On the Ribbon, click the **View tab**. In the **Arrange list group**, click the **Name** button, and then compare your screen with Figure 6.9. Notice that the pictures are sorted by name—most of the pictures still use the name assigned by the camera that took the picture.

Figure 6.9

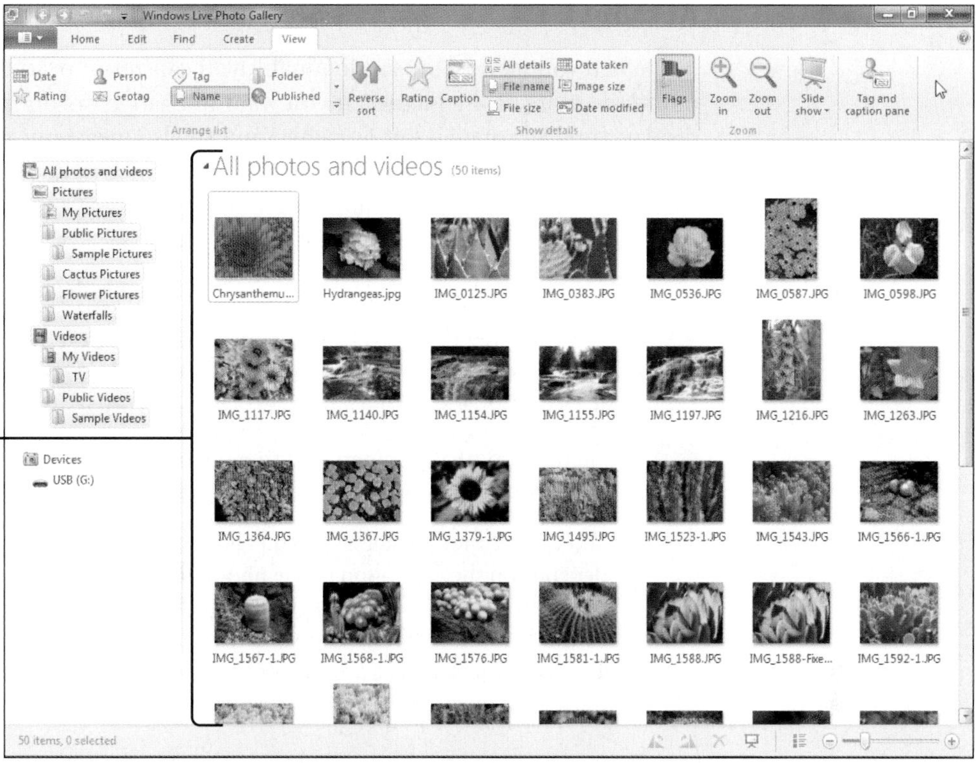

Thumbnails of all photos and videos (yours may vary)

12 On the **View tab**, in the **Arrange list group**, click **Folder**, and then scroll as necessary to display the **Cactus Pictures** at the top of your screen. **Start** the **Snipping Tool** program, click the **New arrow**, and then click **Full-screen Snip**. In the **Snipping Tool** mark-up window, click the **Save Snip** button.

13 In the **Save As** dialog box, in the **navigation pane**, scroll down as necessary, and then under **Computer** click your USB flash drive so that it displays in the **address bar**. On the toolbar, click the **New folder** button, type **Windows 7 Chapter 6** and then press Enter.

14 In the **file list**, double-click your **Windows 7 Chapter 6** folder to open it. Click in the **File name** box, and then replace the selected text by typing, using your own name, **Lastname_Firstname_6A_Imported_Folders_Snip** Be sure the file type is **JPEG file**, and then press Enter. **Close** the **Snipping Tool** mark-up window. Hold this file until you finish Project 6A, and then submit this file as directed by your instructor.

More Knowledge | Deleting Photos and Folders from Windows Live Photo Gallery

To simultaneously delete a photo from both your computer and from Photo Gallery, select the photo, and then in the navigation bar, click the Delete button. If you select multiple photos, you can delete them all at the same time. *Remember to use caution when deleting photos with this method; this method not only removes the photos from Photo Gallery, but also deletes the photos from your computer.*

To remove a folder from the Photo Gallery only—but keep the folder stored on your computer—in the navigation pane, select the folder, right-click the folder, and then click Remove from the gallery. This removes the folder *only* from Photo Gallery; it does not delete the folder of photos from your computer. The folder remains in its original storage location.

Activity 6.04 | Viewing Photos Individually and as a Slideshow

When you view photos individually, you can zoom in to display more detail, or zoom out to see more of the picture. If you want to change the orientation of the photo's display, you can rotate it left or right. You can also view your photos as a slideshow.

1 At the top of the **navigation pane**, under **All photos and videos**, click the **Cactus Pictures** folder to display only those pictures.

This action displays only the photos in the Cactus Pictures folder.

> **Another Way**
>
> Point to the picture, right-click, and then click Preview Photo.

2 Locate and then double-click the photo **IMG_1581-1.JPG** to open the photo in the **Preview Picture** window. If a pane displays on the right side of the window, at the top of the pane, click the Close button to maximize your view of the picture.

3 At the bottom of the screen, in the **navigation bar**, move the **slider** to the right to zoom in about a third of the way, as shown in Figure 6.10.

You can see more detail when you zoom in. The quality of the picture when you zoom in depends on the resolution of the photo. ***Resolution***—the amount of fine detail that is visible in an image when it is printed or displayed on a computer monitor—is determined by the number of ***pixels***. A pixel is the smallest element used to form the composition of an image. The larger the number of pixels, the higher the resolution of the photo, and the more you can zoom in without losing picture quality.

Figure 6.10

> **Another Way**
>
> On the View tab, in the Zoom group, click the Fit to window button.

4 At the bottom of the screen, on the **navigation bar**, click the **Fit to window** button to return the picture to the original size.

5 On the Ribbon, on the right end of the **Edit tab**, click the **Close file** button.

6 In the **navigation pane**, under **All photos and videos**, click the **Flower Pictures** folder, and then double-click the photo **IMG_1216.JPG**.

This picture was saved sideways, which happens when the picture is taken with the camera held vertically.

7 At the bottom of the screen, on the **navigation bar**, click the **Rotate left** button to change the photo to its proper orientation. Compare your screen with Figure 6.11.

Figure 6.11

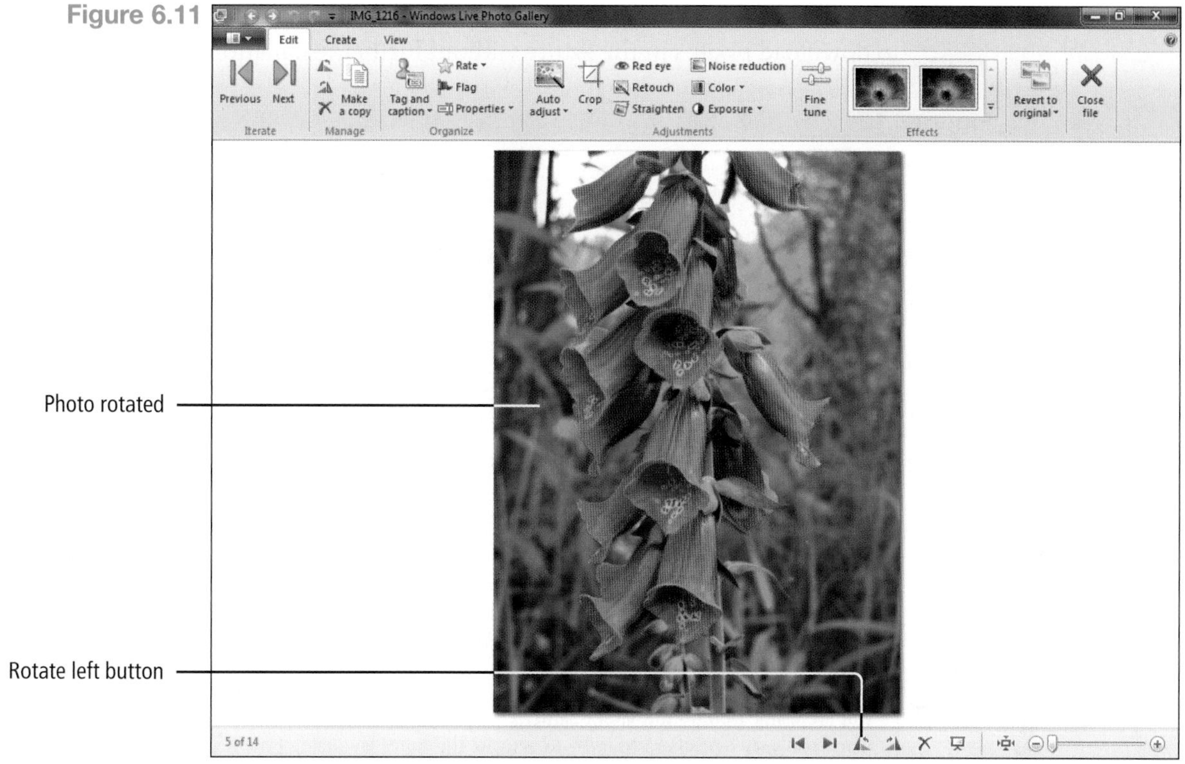

8 On the right end of the **Edit tab**, click the **Close file** button. Click the first photo in the gallery, and then, on the **navigation bar**, click the **Slide show** button.

A full-screen slideshow begins, displaying the photos beginning with the selected photo. For a short time, a Windows Live menu displays at the top of the screen, a Pause button displays near the bottom of the screen, and Previous and Next buttons display on the sides of the screen. If you do not move the mouse, the menu and button will close. To activate the menu and buttons again, move the mouse.

9 While the slide show is running, move the mouse to the top of the screen to display the **Windows Live** menu, and then click **Change theme**. Try several of the available themes. Be sure you end with the **Fade** theme selected.

10 When you are finished, press Esc to end the slide show.

> **Another Way**
> On the Windows Live menu, click *Back to Photo Gallery*.

Activity 6.05 | Downloading Photos Directly from a Digital Camera

Most digital cameras come with software that enables you to download photos directly from the camera to your computer. However, you can download the photos *without* installing the camera's accompanying software by using one of two methods—connect the camera directly to the computer, or use a card reader. A ***card reader***—also referred to as a ***memory card reader*** or ***flash memory reader***—is a device that reads and writes data to various types of flash memory cards such as the card you use in your digital camera. A card reader might be built into your computer or you can plug one into a USB port.

When downloading pictures directly from a digital camera, turn the camera off, plug the USB cable into your camera, and then plug the cable into a USB port on your computer.

With the camera plugged into your computer, turn the camera on. Wait for the AutoPlay dialog box to display, as shown in Figure 6.12. If this is the first time the camera has been attached to your computer, you will see a message indicating that a new device has been found, and then another message indicating that the device has been installed. Close the message boxes when you are through reading them. Installing the device on your computer is accomplished the first time you connect it; your computer will be ready to download photos in the future without further installations.

Figure 6.12

Example of a camera plugged into USB port

Methods available for importing photos from camera

Alert! | Did the AutoPlay Dialog Box Display?

Your computer's response to turning on an attached camera varies by both camera brand and camera type. If you are using a point-and-shoot camera, you may have to set the camera to *Playback* or *Preview* mode—the name will vary by camera brand—to activate the AutoPlay dialog box. If camera software has been installed, special download software might run automatically, or the camera software might display in the AutoPlay dialog box.

As shown in the AutoPlay dialog box, you will usually be presented with several different ways to download the photos. With your knowledge of Windows 7, you will find the Windows Explorer option useful, because you can use the skills you have practiced to create a new folder for the files, and then copy the photos to the new folder.

When you have finished copying your photos, turn the camera off. On the right side of the taskbar, in the Notification Area, right-click the Safely Remove Hardware button, select the camera from the displayed list, and then click Stop—this procedure is not necessary with some camera brands. You can now safely unplug your camera from the USB port.

To check how well you can identify techniques to download photos directly from a camera, take a moment to answer the following questions:

1. When downloading photos directly from a camera, before you plug the camera into the computer, be sure the camera is turned __________.
2. To download pictures from your camera directly to your computer, plug the camera into a __________ port on your computer.
3. A card reader is a peripheral device that reads and writes data to various types of __________ memory cards.

4 For some types of cameras, you will need to set the camera to *Preview* or *Playback* mode to activate the __________ dialog box.

5 When you have finished downloading photos, click the *Safely Remove Hardware* button located in the __________ __________.

Objective 3 | Add, Tag, Rate, and Edit Photos Using Windows Live Photo Gallery

Recall that Windows 7 supports the addition of metadata—information about a file, such as a tag, a title, a rating, the file name, and the file size—to many file types. Tags, comments, ratings, captions, and other types of information can help you organize your files, and can speed up file searches.

Photos taken with a digital camera or scanned into a computer using a scanner are not always exactly the way you want them. Photo Gallery enables you to perform basic photo editing tasks such as adjusting the contrast, exposure, and color of a photo, or reducing the size of a photo. To perform more advanced edits, Photo Gallery enables you to send the photo to another photo editing program.

Activity 6.06 | Viewing Detailed Camera Information and Adding Tags

When you take a picture, most digital cameras store the file in JPEG format. JPEG files have the capability of storing a large amount of relevant information with the picture, including focal length, shutter speed, whether or not a flash attachment was used, and many other tags that are of interest to photographers. Additional tags can be added to individual photos, or to groups of photos.

1 With **Photo Gallery** still active, be sure the contents of the **Flower Pictures** folder display. On the **View tab**, in the **Arrange list group**, click the **Folder** button.

2 At the bottom of the screen, in the **navigation bar**, move the **slider** as necessary to display six pictures across.

3 Right-click the photo **IMG_05481.JPG**, and then from the shortcut menu, click **Properties**. If necessary, click the Details tab.

4 Scroll down to locate the **Image** section, and then locate the **Dimensions** tag. Notice that the dimensions of this photo are **1024 × 683**, which is a fairly low resolution. Compare your screen with Figure 6.13.

The physical dimensions of the photo display at the top of the Image section, and the camera information displays in the Camera section. This information is helpful to photographers, and indicates how detailed the *tags*—one of several properties you can associate with a file—for each photo can be. Programs that use this feature define their own tags, and you can use the tags to search for photos that meet criteria that you specify.

Figure 6.13

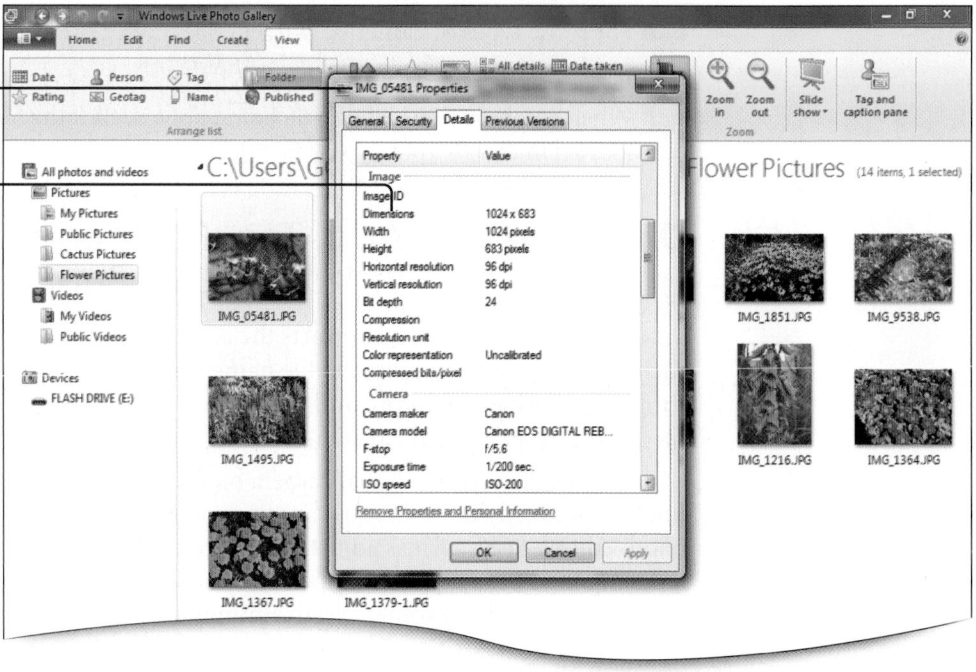

5 In the **Properties** dialog box, click **Cancel**. Right-click the photo **IMG_9538.JPG**, and then on the shortcut menu, click **Properties**. If necessary, click the Details tab, and then scroll as necessary to display the **Image** and **Camera** information.

Many of the tags differ from the previous photo—particularly the file size information. This photo is 3456 × 2304 pixels, which is a much higher resolution than the previous photo.

6 In the **Properties** dialog box, click **Cancel**. In an open area below the picture thumbnails, right-click to display a shortcut menu, and then point to **View**. Compare your screen with Figure 6.14.

You can use this menu to view the thumbnails with file names, the date the picture was taken, your ratings, or in the same view you get when you click the *View details* button in the navigation bar. This shortcut menu gives you more display options than the buttons on the View tab.

Figure 6.14

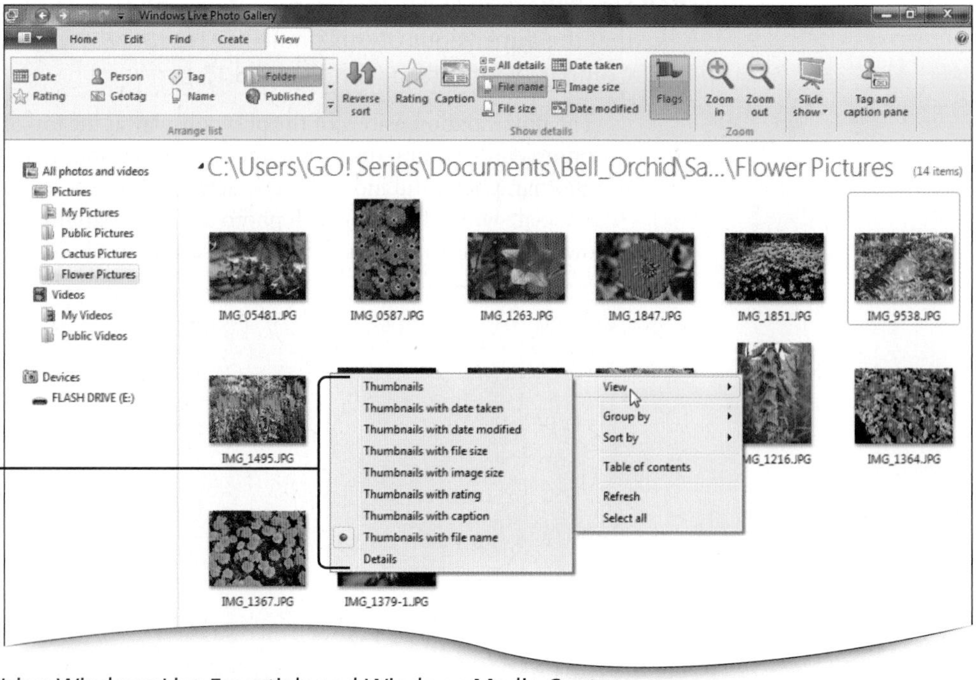

7 On the shortcut menu, click **Thumbnails with file size**, and notice the variations in file sizes.

Most digital cameras enable you to change the resolution of the pictures at any time, but even the size of photographs taken at the same resolution will vary depending on how much detail is in the photo.

8 In the **Show details group**, click the **File name** button so that the file names display below each picture. In the **navigation pane**, click the **Cactus Pictures** folder. Move the **slider** to display the cactus pictures in two rows of seven pictures each.

> **Another Way**
>
> Click to select any photo, and then press Ctrl + A.

9 At the top of the **gallery**, in the path name, point to the text *Cactus Pictures*. Notice the ScreenTip that indicates *Select all items in this group*. Click the text *Cactus Pictures* to select all of the photos in the folder.

10 On the right end of the **View tab**, click the **Tag and caption pane** button to display the **info pane** on the right side of the screen. In the **info pane**, under **Descriptive tags**, click **Add descriptive tags**. With the insertion point blinking in the box, type **Cactus** and then compare your screen with Figure 6.15.

Any tag or tags that you type when multiple files are selected will be applied to each file. The display of the pictures changes to accommodate the info pane.

Figure 6.15

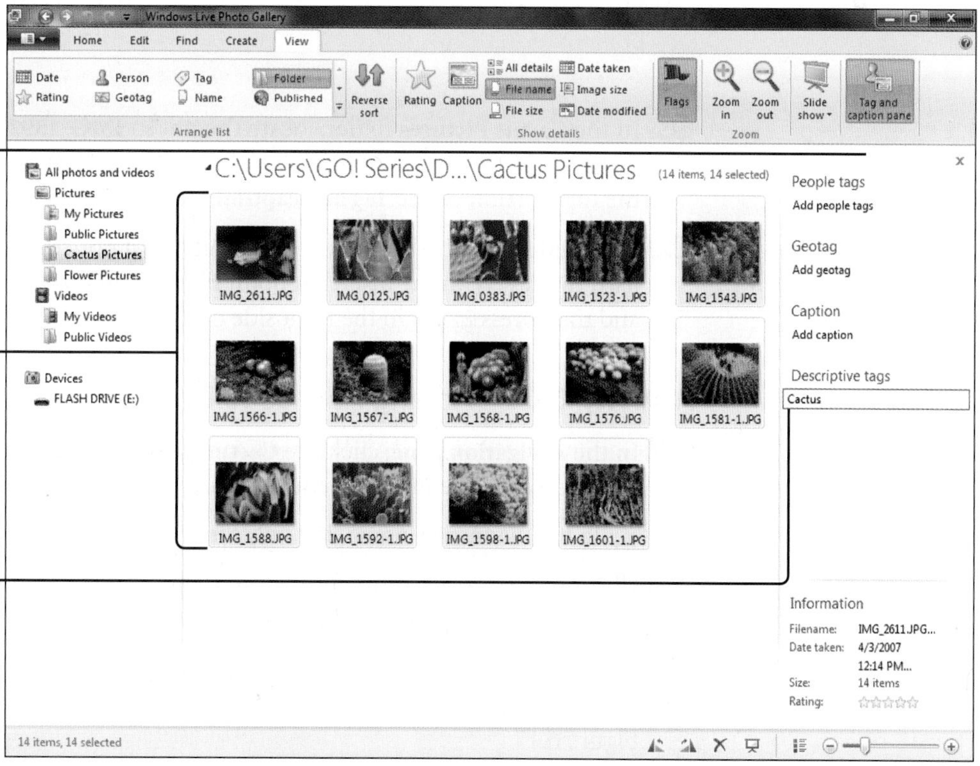

11 Display the **Flower Pictures** folder, and then by using the technique you just practiced, add the tag **Flowers** to all of the photos in the **Flower Pictures** folder.

12 Display the **Cactus Pictures** folder, select the photo **IMG_1568-1**, hold down Ctrl, and then select the photo **IMG_1581-1**. With the two photos selected, in the **info pane**, click **Add descriptive tags**, type **Golden Barrel** and then press Enter. Compare your screen with Figure 6.16.

Figure 6.16

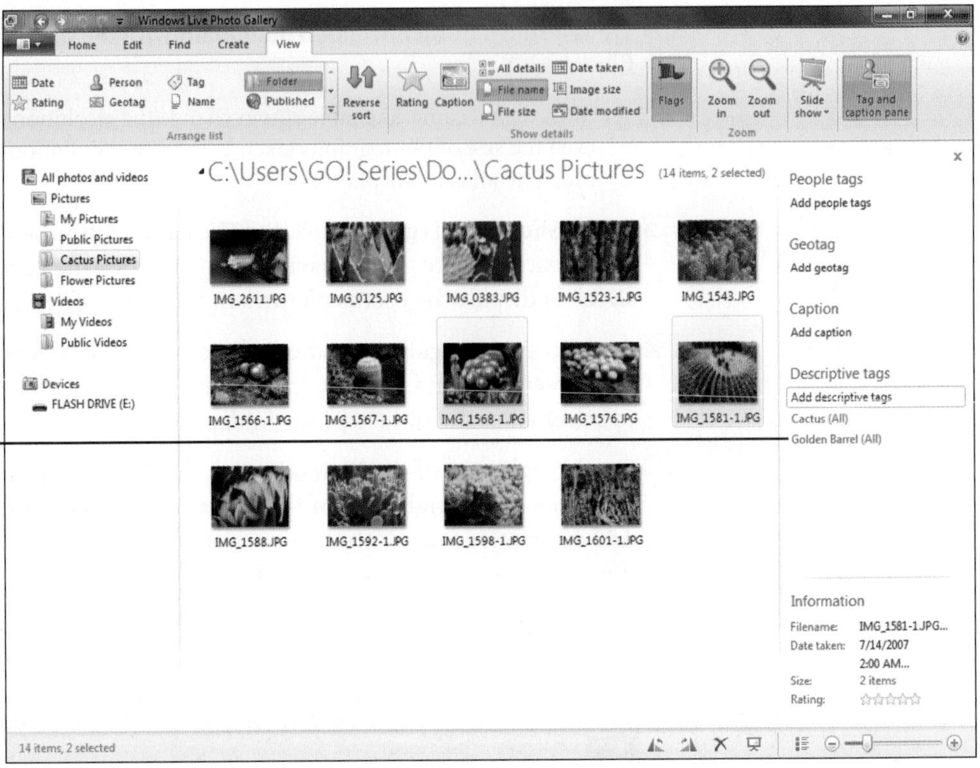

New tag added to selected photos

13 In the **Cactus Pictures** folder, locate the photo **IMG_1592-1**, and then double-click it to display it in the **Preview Picture** window. On the **Edit tab**, in the **Organize group**, click the top portion of the **Tag and caption** button to display the info pane.

14 In the **info pane**, click **Add descriptive tags**, and notice that the other tags that you have used display. With the insertion point blinking in the box, type **Spineless Prickly Pear** and then press Enter. On the right side of the **Edit tab**, click the **Close file** button.

Activity 6.07 | Adding Ratings to Photos

1 In the **navigation pane**, click the **Cactus Pictures** folder to select it, hold down Ctrl, and then click the **Flower Pictures** folder to select it and display the photos.

In this manner, you can select only those folders you want to display.

Another Way

Hold down Ctrl and click the path name above each group of photos.

2 Click to select any picture, hold down Ctrl, and then press A to select all of the displayed pictures in both folders.

3 On the right side of your screen, in the **info pane**, under **Information**, locate the row of stars, and then click the third star in the row. Compare your screen with Figure 6.17.

A three-star rating is added to *all* 28 selected files. To rate a single photo, select only that photo.

Figure 6.17

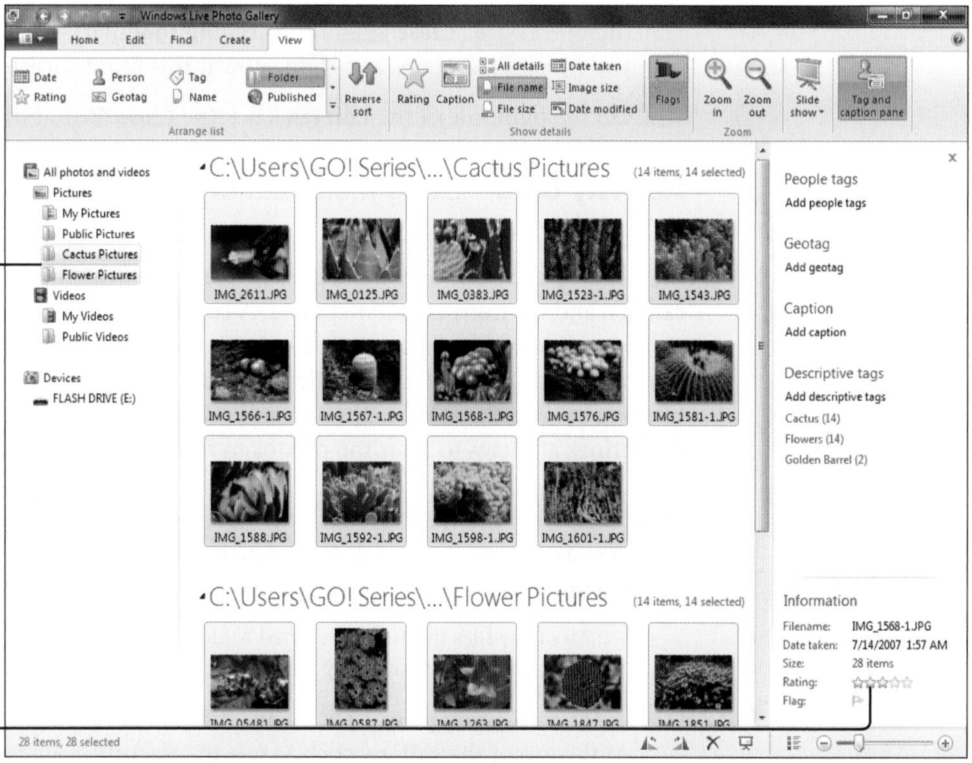

4 In the group of **Cactus Pictures**, click the photo **IMG_1523-1.JPG**, and then change the rating to **5 stars**. Change the rating of the photo **IMG_1568-1.JPG** to **5 stars**.

5 Change the rating of the following pictures as indicated:

Folder	File Name	New Rating
Cactus Pictures	IMG_0383.JPG	4 stars
Cactus Pictures	IMG_1567-1.JPG	5 stars
Cactus Pictures	IMG_1581-1.JPG	4 stars
Cactus Pictures	IMG_1592-1.JPG	4 stars
Cactus Pictures	IMG_1598-1.JPG	5 stars
Flower Pictures	IMG_0598.JPG	5 stars
Flower Pictures	IMG_1367.JPG	4 stars
Flower Pictures	IMG_1847.JPG	4 stars
Flower Pictures	IMG_05481.JPG	5 stars

6 In the **Cactus Pictures**, double-click the photo **IMG_1568-1.JPG** to display it in the **Preview Picture** window. If the info pane does not display, on the View tab, click the *Tag and caption pane* button. In the **info pane**, notice that the picture now has two tags—*Cactus* and *Golden Barrel*—and a rating of five stars.

7 **Start** the **Snipping Tool** program, click the **New arrow**, and then click **Full-screen Snip**. In the **Snipping Tool** mark-up window, click the **Save Snip** button.

8 In the **Save As** dialog box, in the **navigation pane**, scroll down as necessary, and then under **Computer**, click your USB flash drive so that it displays in the address bar. Navigate to your **Windows 7 Chapter 6** folder, and then as the file name, type **Lastname_Firstname_6A_Tags&Ratings_Snip** Be sure the file type is **JPEG file**, and then press Enter. **Close** the **Snipping Tool** mark-up window. Hold this file until you finish Project 6A, and then submit this file as directed by your instructor.

9. On the right side of the **Edit tab**, click the **Close file** button.

Activity 6.08 | Using Metadata to Filter Photos

Recall that metadata is data that describes other data. It is information about a file that is not part of the actual purpose or content of the file. In Photo Gallery, the tags, ratings, and captions are all metadata. A ***caption*** is text that accompanies images or videos, either as a supplemental description or a transcript of spoken words. An image does not require metadata, but adding metadata to some or all of your images and then filtering by metadata makes finding and managing your photos an easier task. You can use the ratings and tags to filter the photos to find exactly what you need.

1. Be sure the photos from both the **Cactus Pictures** folder and the **Flower Pictures** folder display. In an open area between pictures, right-click. On the shortcut menu, point to **Group by**, and then click **Rating**.

   All of the files in the two selected folders are grouped by rating, with 5-star ratings displayed first, followed by the 4-star ratings, and so on.

2. In the **navigation pane**, click **Cactus Pictures** to display only the photos in that folder. At the top of the **gallery**, click **5 stars** to select the four 5-star cactus photos. In the **info pane** on the right, under **Descriptive tags**, click **Add descriptive tags**, type **Brochure** and then press Enter. Compare your screen with Figure 6.18.

   The photos with a *Cactus* tag display by Rating. The four 5-star photos that have been selected for the brochure have an additional tag—*Brochure*. All of the tags associated with any of the four selected photos display in the info pane.

Figure 6.18

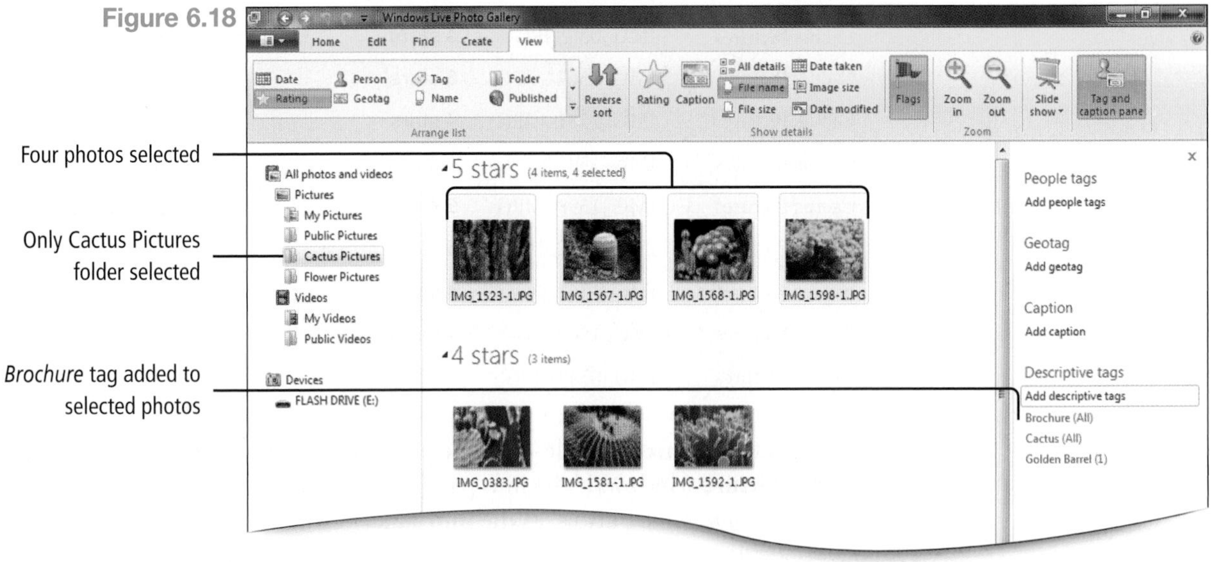

3. Scroll down as necessary to view the photos in the **3 stars** group. Select the photo **IMG_1588.JPG** file. In the **info pane**, click **Add descriptive tags**, and then on the displayed list of existing tags, click **Brochure**.

4. In the **navigation pane**, click **All photos and videos**. On the Ribbon, click the **Find tab**, click the **Tags** button, and then under **Most used tags**, click **Flowers**. Notice that active photos that have the tag *Flowers* display and that the Ratings grouping is still applied.

5 In the **5 stars** group, hold down Ctrl and select the photos **IMG_05481.JPG** and **IMG_0598.JPG**, and then add the **Brochure** tag. In the **3 stars** group, select the photos **IMG_0536.JPG** and **IMG_9538.JPG**, and then add the **Brochure** tag.

6 In the **navigation pane**, click **All photos and videos**. On the **Find tab**, click the **Tags** button, and then under **Most used tags**, click **Brochure**.

The nine photos that will be considered for the new brochure display. By filtering on metadata, you can find the photos you want without creating folders and moving photos.

7 **Start** the **Snipping Tool** program, click the **New arrow**, and then click **Full-screen Snip**. In the **Snipping Tool** mark-up window, click the **Save Snip** button.

8 In the **Save As** dialog box, in the **navigation pane**, scroll down as necessary, and then under **Computer**, click your USB flash drive so that it displays in the address bar. Navigate to your **Windows 7 Chapter 6** folder, and then as the file name, type **Lastname_Firstname_6A_Brochure_Tags_Snip** Be sure the file type is **JPEG file**, and then press Enter. **Close** the **Snipping Tool** mark-up window. Hold this file until you finish Project 6A, and then submit this file as directed by your instructor.

9 In the **navigation pane**, click **All photos and videos**. Right-click an open area between picture thumbnails. On the shortcut menu, point to **Group by**, and then click **Folder**.

All filters are removed, and all the images on the computer at which you are working redisplay grouped by folder.

Activity 6.09 | Using Auto Adjust to Modify a Photo

Taking a picture with inaccurate exposure might produce photos that are too bright or too dark. Both of these problems can be dramatically improved by correcting the brightness and contrast. ***Auto adjust*** is the automatic correction tool in Photo Gallery with which you can adjust the exposure of a photo.

1 In the **navigation pane**, click **Cactus Pictures**, hold down Ctrl, and then click **Flower Pictures**. On the **Find tab**, click the **Tags** button, and then under **Most used tags**, click **Brochure**. **Close** the **info pane**.

The nine pictures with the Brochure tag display.

2 In the **Flower Pictures** folder group, double-click the photo **IMG_0536.JPG**.

3 Examine the background, particularly the leaves in the lower left part of the photo, and then on the **Edit tab**, in the **Adjustments group**, click the upper portion of the **Auto adjust** button. Notice that more background detail displays, and that the picture is rotated slightly.

4 Near the right side of the **Edit tab**, click the upper portion of the **Revert to original** button. Examine the color of the flower, and then click the **Auto adjust** button again. Notice that the color of the flower is much lighter, and looks somewhat washed out. Compare your screen with Figure 6.19.

This picture will not have the quality needed for the brochure.

Figure 6.19

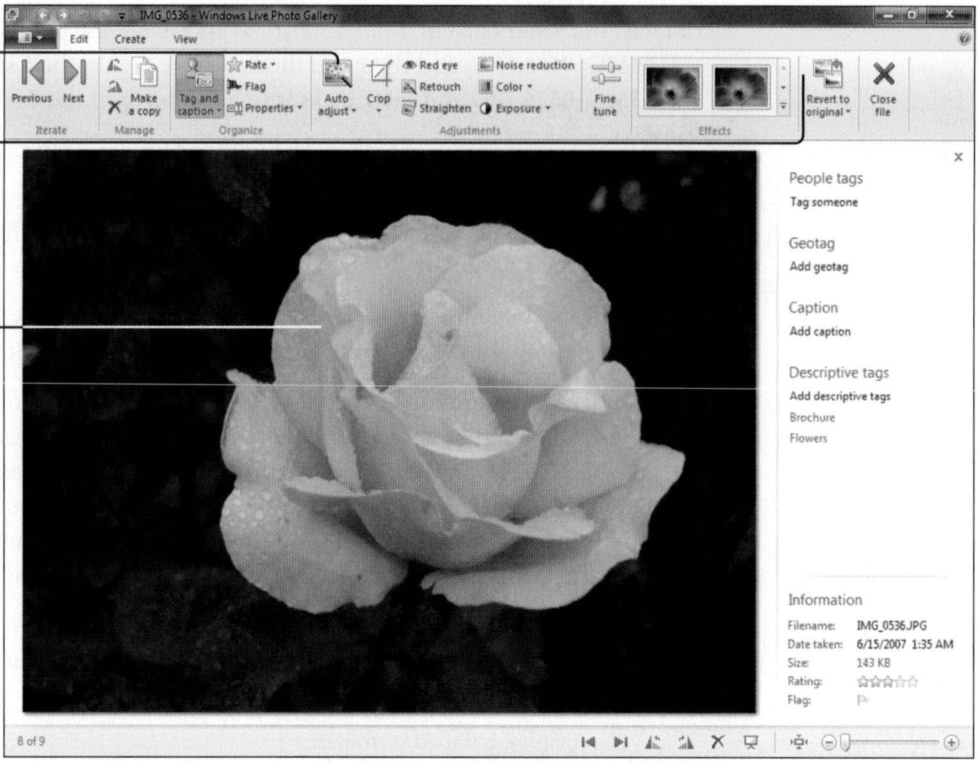

5. Near the right side of the **Edit tab**, click the **Revert to original** button.

6. If the info pane does not display, on the Edit tab, in the Organize group, click the Tag and caption button. In the **info pane**, right-click the **Brochure** tag, and then click **Remove tag**.

   Because this photo will no longer be considered for the brochure, the Brochure tag is removed.

7. On the right side of the **Edit tab**, click the **Close file** button. Notice that this photo continues to display in the *Brochure* tag group.

   To refresh the list, you must leave the group and then redisplay the group.

8. Click the **Find tab**, and then click the **Tags** button. Under **Most used tags**, click the **Brochure** tag again. Notice that the photo of the yellow rose no longer displays.

Activity 6.10 | Adjusting Exposure and Color

1. With the eight photos tagged *Brochure* displayed, double-click the picture **IMG_9538.JPG**. If necessary, Close the *info pane*.

2. On the **Edit tab**, in the **Adjustments group**, click the **Exposure button arrow**.

   The ***exposure***—brightness—of this photograph requires adjustment. You can adjust exposure in three ways. Adjusting the brightness makes all of the pixels in the photo brighter or darker. Adjusting the shadow changes the brightness of the darker parts of the pictures, and adjusting the highlights changes the brightness of the lighter areas of the picture.

3. In the **Choose exposure adjustment** gallery, point to several of the thumbnails and observe the effect on the picture.

   The brightness, shadow, and highlight settings change, and the ScreenTips show what settings are changed for each thumbnail.

4 In the first row, point to the third thumbnail—**Low brightness, high shadows, original highlights.** Compare your screen with Figure 6.20.

Figure 6.20

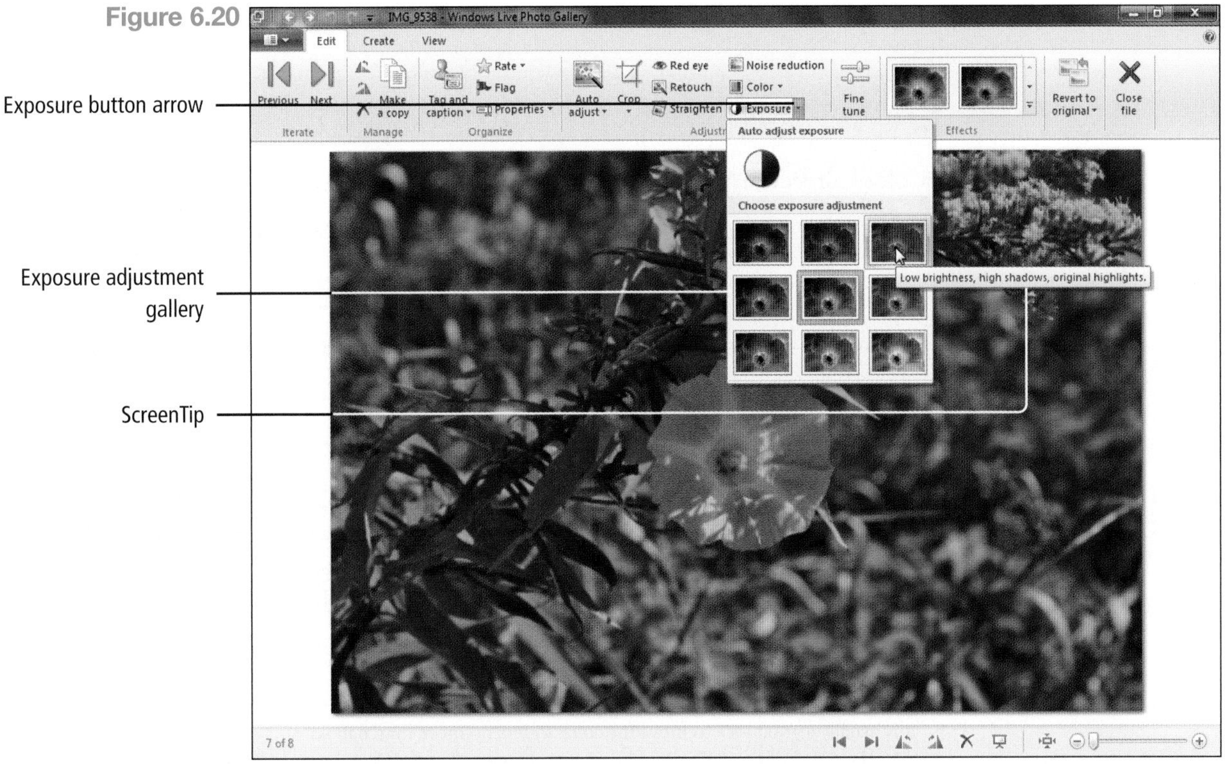

5 Click the thumbnail to apply this brightness setting. On the **Edit tab**, in the **Manage group**, click the **Make a copy** button.

6 In the **Make a copy** dialog box, in the **File name** box, name the file **IMG_9538-Fixed** and then click **Save**. When a message box displays, read the message, and then click **OK**. Near the right side of the **Edit tab**, click the **Revert to original** button, click **Revert** in the message box, and then click the **Close file** button.

Both the original photo and the edited photo display in the Brochures tag group.

Note | Save the Photo in Its Original Condition

It is always a good idea to either make a backup copy of your original file before editing, or save the edited file with a new name and undo the fixes to the original file. By doing so, you preserve the original in case you need it again.

7 Double-click the picture **IMG_1588.JPG**. On the **Edit tab**, in the **Adjustments group**, click the **Color button arrow**. Point to several of the thumbnails to see the preset color modifications that are available.

The color of the photo appears very washed out—a common occurrence when pictures of plants are taken in harsh sunlight. None of the preset adjustments change the color sufficiently.

8 Click the **Color button arrow** again to close the gallery. On the **Edit tab**, in the **Adjustments group**, click the **Fine tune** button. In the **Edit Pane**, click **Adjust color**, and then take a moment to examine the effects of the three color corrections as described in the table in Figure 6.21.

Effects of Color Correction

Color Correction	Effect
Color temperature	Makes the photo appear cooler (more blue/green) or warmer (more earth tones).
Tint	Changes the level of green or red in the photo.
Saturation	Changes the photo's color intensity. Moving the slider all the way to the left changes the photo to black and white.

Figure 6.21

9 Using Figure 6.22 as your guide, move the **Color temperature** slider to the right to make the color a little warmer. Move the **Tint** slider to the left to bring out the green in the photo. Move the **Saturation** slider to the right to increase the color intensity.

Note | Adjusting Color Effectively

It is usually a good idea to move the color sliders no more than half way between the existing slider location and the other edge of the slider. Making larger changes can give photos an artificial look when they are printed.

Figure 6.22

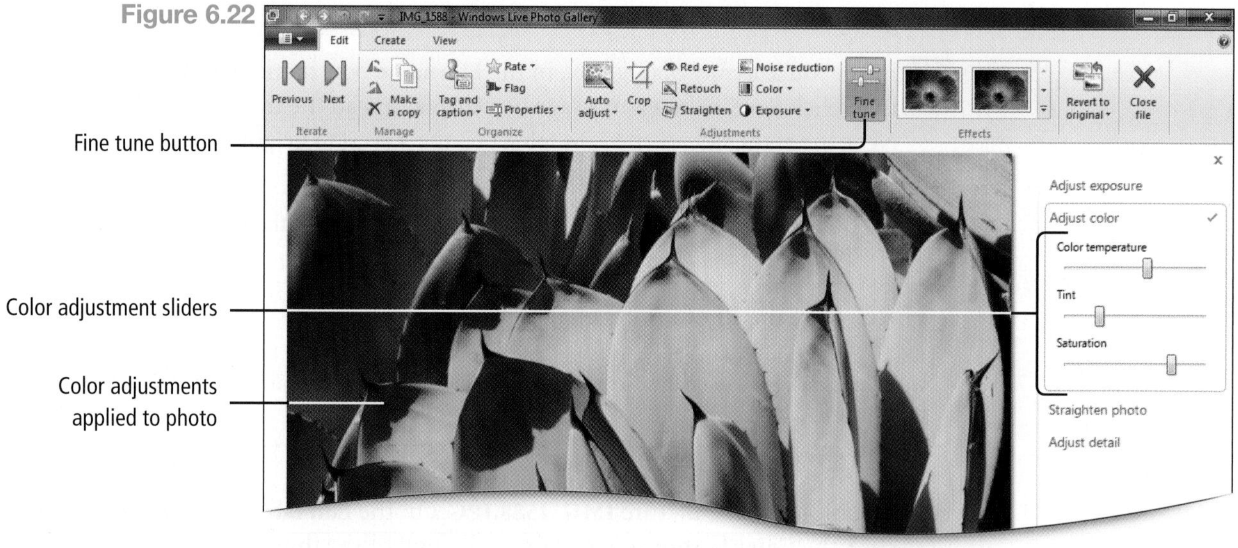

10 On the **Edit tab**, in the **Manage group**, click the **Make a copy** button. Change the file name to **IMG_1588-Fixed** and then click **Save**. In the message box, click **OK**.

11 Near the right side of the **Edit tab**, click the **Revert to original** button, click **Revert** in the message box, and then click the **Close file** button. Notice that both the original and edited files display, and notice that the difference in the attractiveness of the two photos is evident when comparing the two thumbnail images.

Activity 6.11 | Cropping a Picture

Sometimes you want only part of a photo to display instead of the entire photo. You can ***crop***—remove unwanted parts of the photo—by using the Crop photo tool.

1. With Photo Gallery still displaying the photos with a *Brochure* tag, double-click the photo **IMG_1598-1.JPG**. If necessary, Close [x] the Edit Pane.
2. On the **Edit tab**, in the **Adjustments group**, click the **Crop** button. On the displayed photo, notice that a suggested crop size is outlined.
3. In the **Adjustments group**, click the **Crop button arrow**, and then click **Rotate frame**. On the displayed photo, notice that the crop frame has a vertical orientation and that sizing handles display around the suggested crop size box. Compare your screen with Figure 6.23.

Figure 6.23

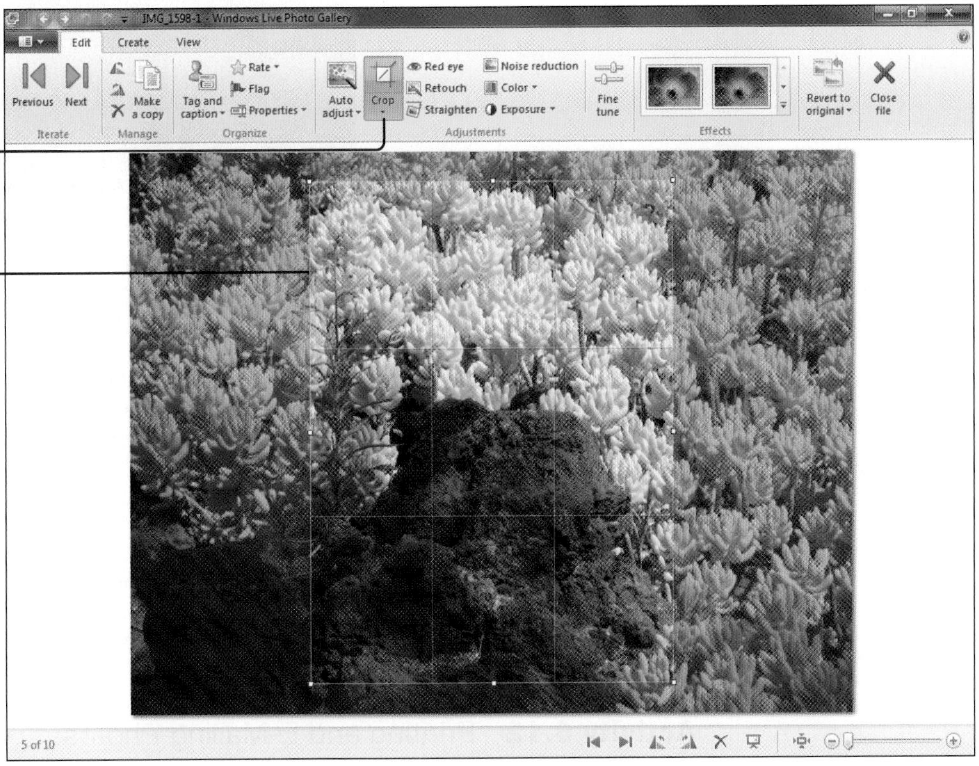

Crop button

Crop frame with vertical orientation

4. In the **Adjustments group**, click the **Crop button arrow**, and then click **Apply crop**.

   The area outside the suggested crop size is eliminated.

5. In the **Adjustments group**, click the **Crop** button again. Drag the lower right sizing handle up and to the left about one inch. Click the **Crop button arrow**, and then click **Apply crop**. Compare your screen with Figure 6.24.

Figure 6.24

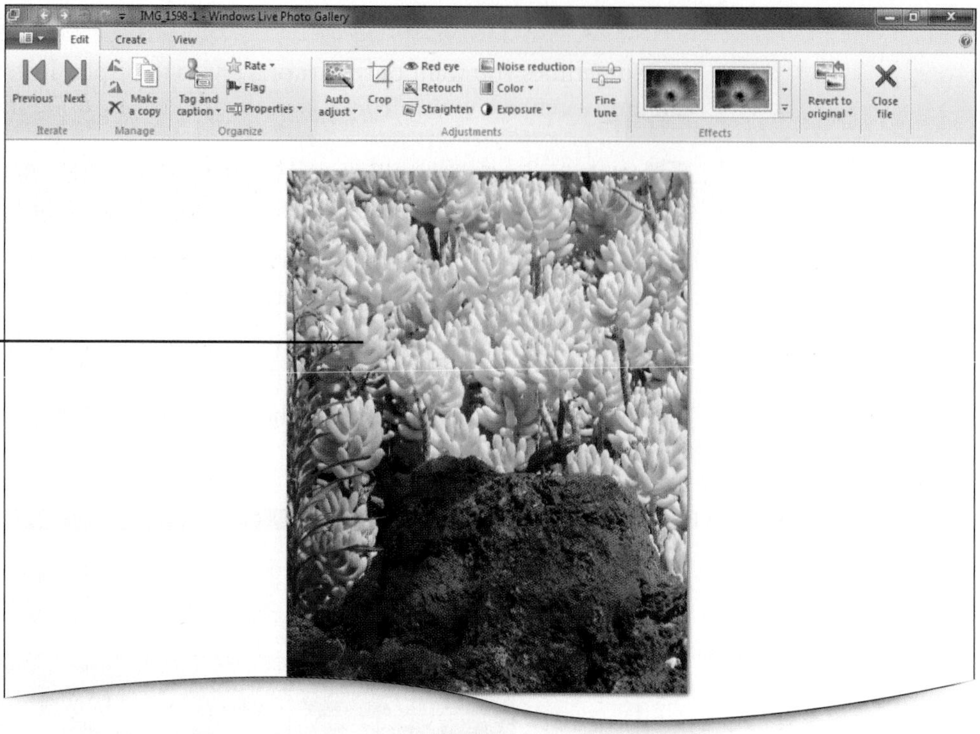

Cropping applied to photo

6 On the **Edit tab**, in the **Manage group**, click the **Make a copy** button. Change the file name to **IMG_1598-1-Cropped** and then click **Save**. In the message box, click **OK**.

7 Near the right side of the **Edit tab**, click the **Revert to original** button, click **Revert** in the message box, and then click the **Close file** button. Notice that the original and cropped files both display.

> **More Knowledge | Cropping a Photo**
>
> The amount that you can crop a photo depends on the resolution of the photo. If you crop a high-resolution photo down to 25 percent of the original area, the results when the photo is printed will usually be satisfactory. If you start with a low-resolution photo, the same crop will probably result in a fuzzy image with jagged lines.

Activity 6.12 | Printing and E-Mailing Photos

After you have organized, rated, and edited your photos, you might want to share them with others. You can print photos, or send photos as attachments to e-mail messages.

1 With Photo Gallery still displaying the photos with the *Brochure* tag, click the picture **IMG_1523-1.JPG**.

2 On the Ribbon, click the *blue* **File tab**, point to **Print**, and then click **Print**.

The Print Pictures dialog box displays. Here you can select the printer, paper type, paper size, print quality, and number of copies.

3 In the **Print Pictures** dialog box, under **Printer**, click the **arrow**, and then select the color printer connected to your computer. If you do not have a color printer, print on your default printer.

Most color printers will print photos. If you have a black and white printer, the preview will display in black and white, and you will not be able to print the photo in color.

4 In your printer paper tray, remove any paper, and then add 4 x 6-inch photo paper.

> **Note** | Printing Photos
>
> You can print photos on regular paper, but the quality will be very poor. To print a good photo, you will need photo paper. The most common photo size is 4 inches x 6 inches, but several other sizes are available. If you use a different size, be sure to set that size in the *Paper size* box. Refer to your printer manual for more information.

5 Click the **Paper size arrow**, and then click **4" × 6" 10 × 15 cm**—or whichever size paper you placed in your printer.

6 Examine the photo paper package and determine the paper type. Click the **Paper type arrow**, and then click the appropriate paper type. Compare your screen with Figure 6.25. Notice at the bottom of the dialog box that you can choose to print multiple copies of the selected photo.

Figure 6.25

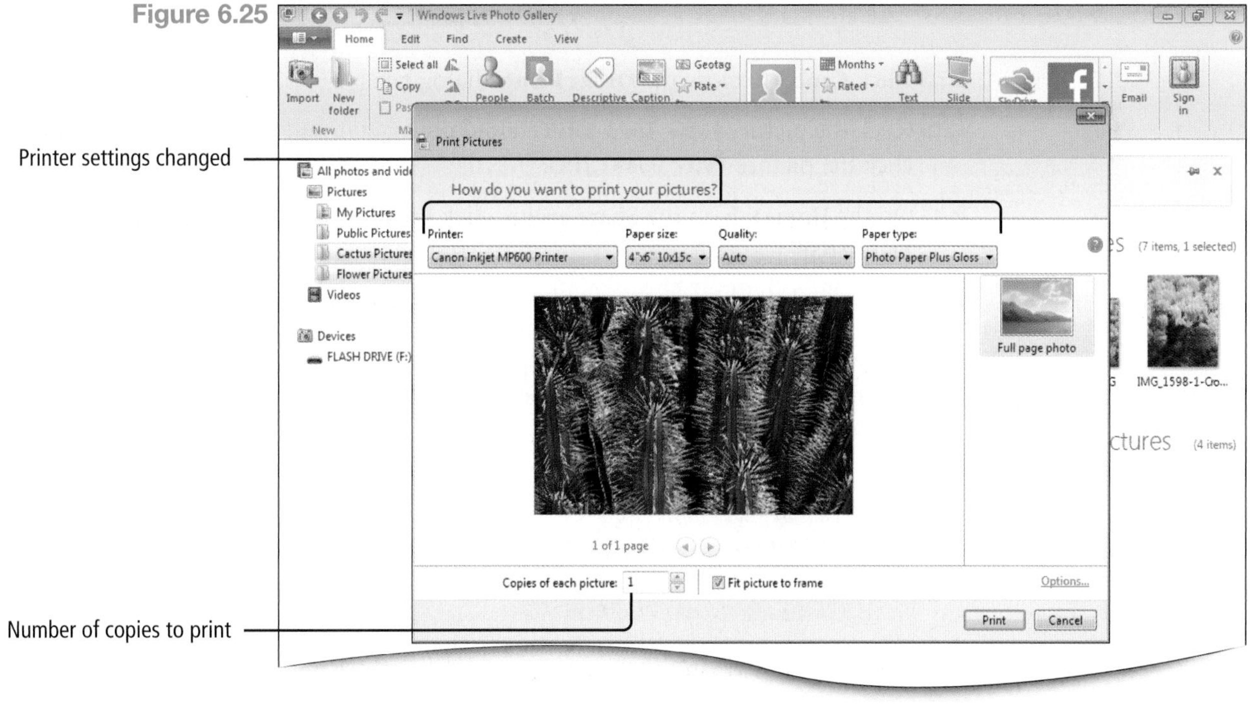

7 If you do not wish to print, click **Cancel**. Or, at the bottom of the **Print Pictures** dialog box, click **Print**.

Printing photos normally takes longer than printing a page of text. Depending on your printer, this may take up to several minutes.

8 Click the **File tab**, point to **Print**, and then click **Order prints**. Compare your screen with Figure 6.26.

If you do not have a photo printer available, you can send your files to an online service. The Order Prints dialog box displays a list of online print developers. The first time this option is selected, it takes a few moments to populate the list. At this point, you can select one of the companies and then follow the instructions for uploading your files.

Figure 6.26

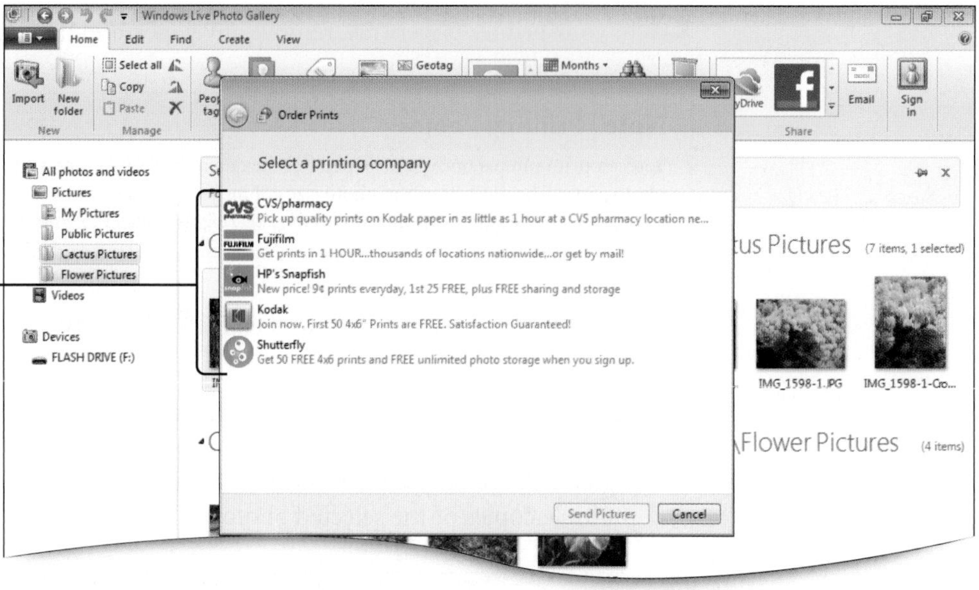

9 Click **Cancel** to close the **Order Prints** dialog box.

10 Click the picture **IMG_1523-1.JPG**. Hold down Ctrl, and then under **Flower Pictures**, click the picture **IMG_05481.JPG**.

11 On the **Home tab**, in the **Share group**, click **Email**, and then compare your screen with Figure 6.27.

In this dialog box, you can send the photos at full resolution, or you can ***compress*** the photos. To compress means to reduce the size of a file so that it takes up less storage space and is easier to send in an e-mail, particularly if you are sending the photo to someone with a slow Internet connection or to someone whose e-mail provider does not support large attachments.

Figure 6.27

12 In the **Preparing files** dialog box, click the **Photo size arrow**, click **Original size**, and then click **Attach**. If you have an e-mail client active on the computer at which you are working, it will display similar to Figure 6.28.

You can change the Subject line, and select and change all of the text in the message.

Figure 6.28

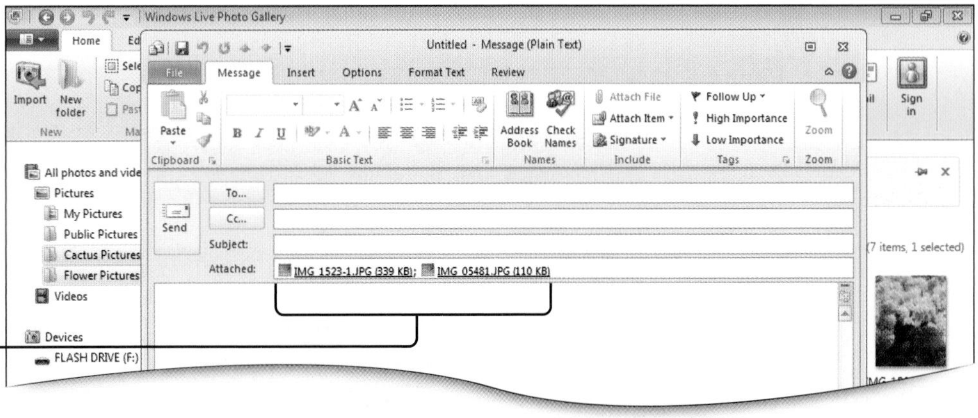

Attached photos

Alert! | If an E-mail Message Does Not Display

If you are working on a computer in a lab and do not have an e-mail account set up on your computer, you will not be able to send the e-mail. Close any messages and read the remaining step.

13 In the **To** line, type your own e-mail address, and then click **Send** to send the e-mail message and the attached photos. Check your e-mail account to be sure the message and attachments arrived.

Note | Uploading Photos to Facebook or Your SkyDrive

Through Windows Live, you can connect and upload photos in Photo Gallery to your Facebook account or to your Windows Live SkyDrive.

Activity 6.13 | Burning Photos to a CD

Burning a CD or DVD is another way to distribute your photos. It also enables you to back up your photos if your computer is damaged or ceases to function properly.

Alert! | This activity is optional.

If you do not have a blank CD, read through the steps to become familiar with the process of burning photos to a CD.

1 Place a new blank CD in your **CD/DVD drive**. If the **AutoPlay** dialog box displays, **Close** it.

2 Be sure Photo Gallery still displays the photos with a *Brochure* tag. Press Ctrl + A to select all of the photos.

3 On the Ribbon, click the **File tab**, point to **Burn**, and then click **Burn a CD**—if you are using a blank DVD, click *Burn a DVD*. If a message displays from the taskbar telling you that you have files waiting to be burned, close the message box.

4 In the displayed **Burn a Disc** dialog box, in the **Disc title** box, type **Brochure Photos** and then click the **With a CD/DVD player** option button. Compare your screen with Figure 6.29.

The *With a CD/DVD player* option creates a final disk that can be read on most computers. The *Like a USB flash drive* option enables you to add or remove photos to the CD. The *Disc title* can contain up to 16 characters.

Figure 6.29

Name of disc

Option to burn CD or DVD

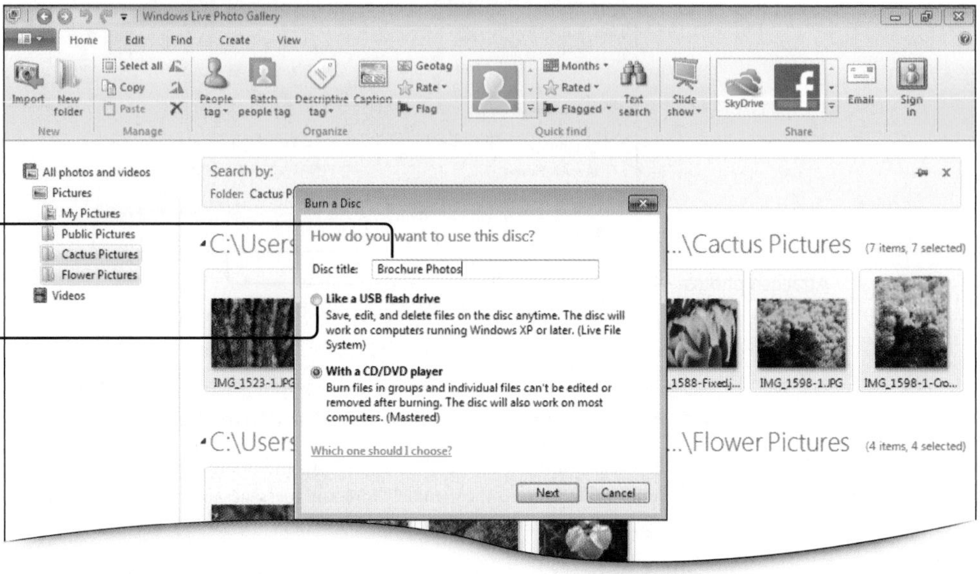

5 Near the bottom of the **Burn a Disc** dialog box, click **Next**.

A message displays from the Notification area indicating that you have files waiting to be burned to a CD.

> **Alert! | Does your disc burn automatically?**
>
> Depending on how your computer is set up, the disc-burning process might begin at this point. If so, skip to Step 8.

6 In **Windows Explorer**, locate the drive that contains the blank CD. Right-click the CD, and then compare your screen with Figure 6.30.

Figure 6.30

Burn to disc command

Files to be burned on CD or DVD

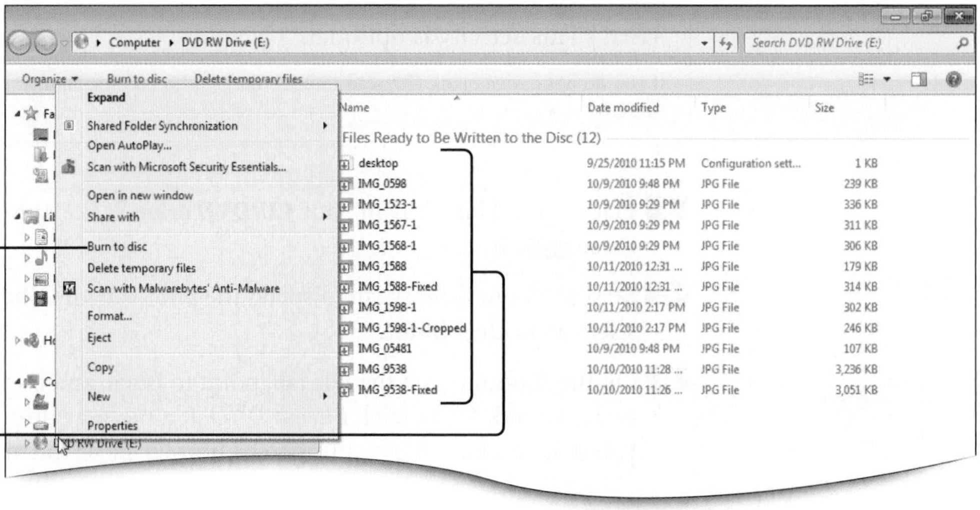

7 From the menu, click **Burn to disc**, and then in the displayed **Burn to Disc** dialog box, click **Next**. Wait for the program to write the files to the disc.

8 When the disc is completed, click **Cancel**. Open the **Computer** window, and then navigate to the CD to be sure the files were recorded.

9 Leave Photo Gallery open, but **Close** all other open windows.

Objective 4 | Use Windows Live Movie Maker to Create a Movie Using Photos

Windows Live Movie Maker is a Windows Live Essentials program with which you can combine audio, video, and still images to create a file that can be saved as a movie. This process is referred to as ***digital video editing***, and the resulting file that you create is a ***project***—a file that keeps track of the pictures, videos, and other files you have imported. After your editing is complete, you save your movie as a ***movie file***. The movie file is saved with the file extension ***.wmv***.

Movie Maker is closely integrated with Photo Gallery. By adding your movie files to Photo Gallery, you can select the photos or video clips you want to include in the movie, and then export the files directly to Movie Maker.

Activity 6.14 | Creating a Movie Project Using Windows Live Movie Maker

AutoMovie themes enable you to make a polished movie in a few seconds—you add your pictures/movies, select a theme, and you are done. This is a good way to create a movie quickly, and then edit the movie later. Depending on the theme you choose, the AutoMovie feature adds a title and credits, special effects, and—if you wish—music.

1 Be sure the Photo Gallery program is still open. In the **navigation pane**, under **All photos and videos**, click the **Flower Pictures** folder. On the **View tab**, in the **Arrange list group**, click the **Name** button to arrange the photos in ascending order by file name.

2 Press Ctrl + A to select all of the pictures in the folder. With all the pictures selected, hold down Ctrl and click **IMG_9538.JPG**, **IMG_1495.jpg**, and **IMG_0536.JPG** to deselect those three images from the selected group. Notice that 12 of the 15 items are selected, as shown in Figure 6.31.

Figure 6.31

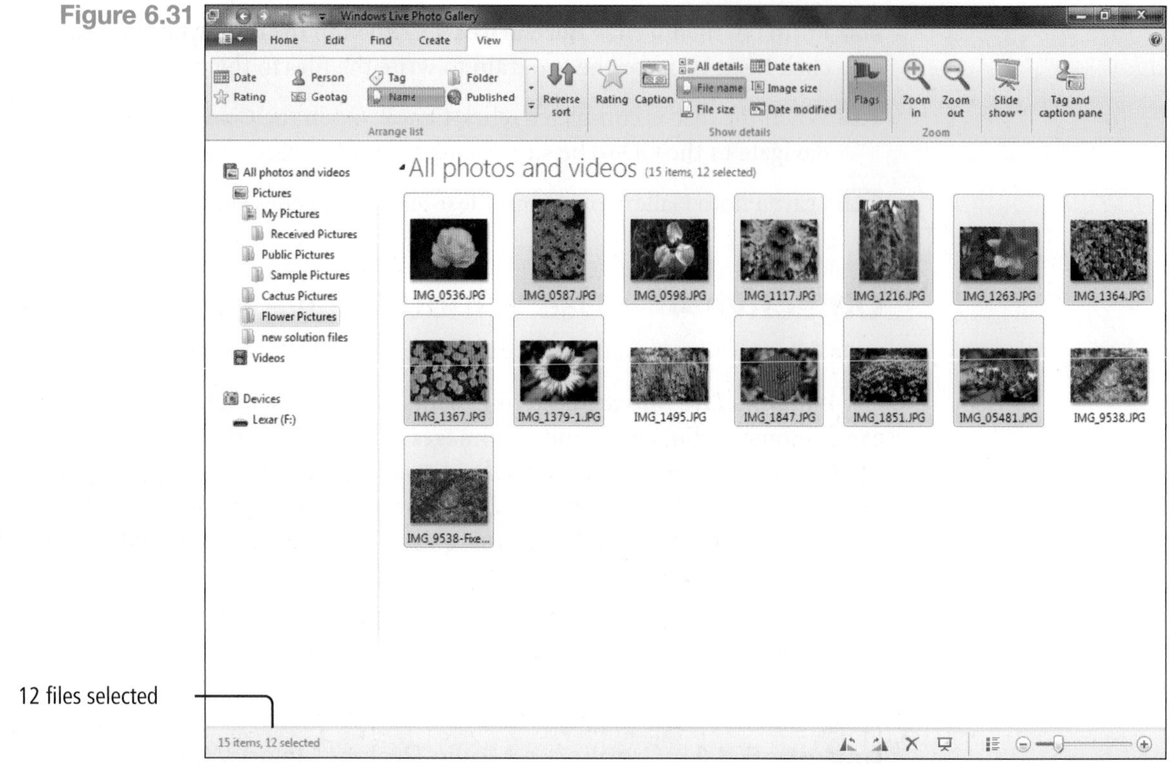

3 Click the **Create tab**, and then in the **Share group**, click the **Movie** button. Examine the layout of the Movie Maker window, as shown in Figure 6.32, and then take a moment to study the descriptions of the Movie Maker screen in the table in Figure 6.33.

Figure 6.32

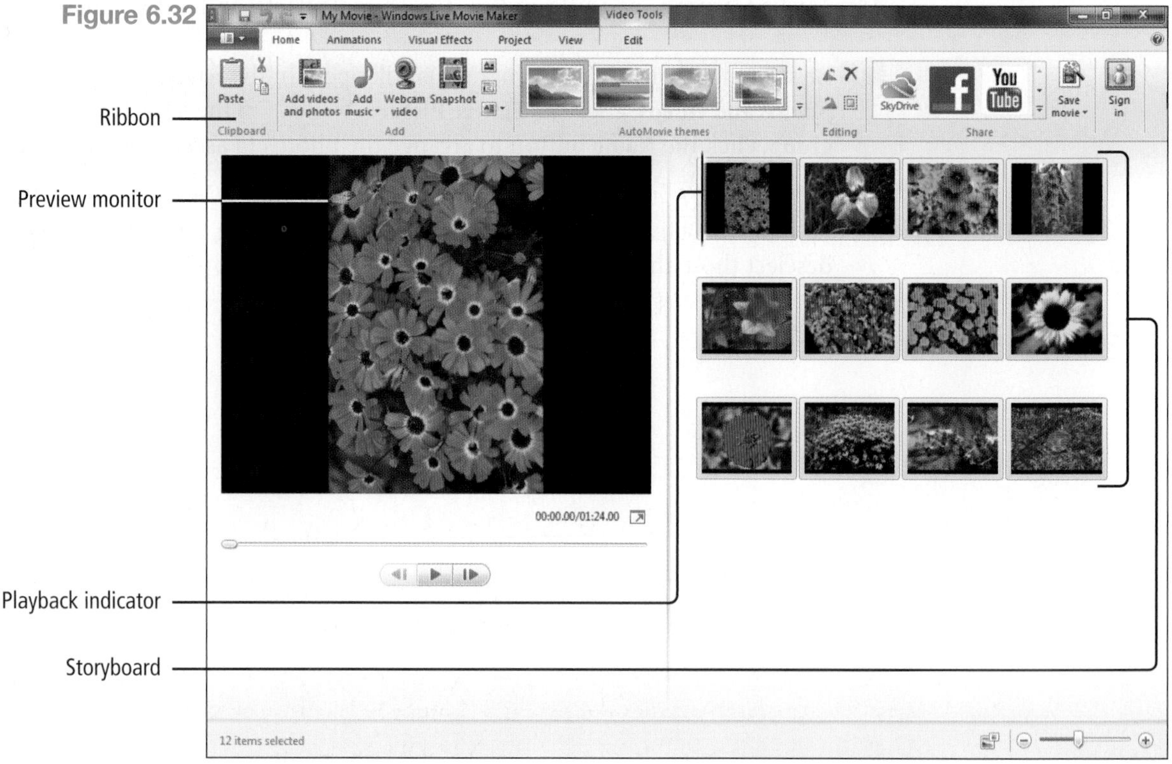

Windows Live Movie Maker Screen Elements

Screen Element	Description
Ribbon	Provides access to all of the Movie Maker commands. On the left side of the Ribbon, the ***Movie Maker tab*** enables you to save your project, save or publish your movie, or set program options. This is similar to the File tab in Microsoft Office 2010.
Preview monitor	Previews the movie, displaying transitions and effects, and plays sounds associated with the movie.
Storyboard	Provides a view that shows a simple sequence of files, clips, transitions, sounds, and special effects that make up a project. The panels show the elements of a movie in the order in which they will be shown, and include transition and effect indicators. You can rearrange elements in the storyboard.
Playback indicator	Shows, by placing a line in the storyboard, the current location in the presentation. If you click the Play button, the movie starts at the playback indicator location.

Figure 6.33

4 On the **Home tab**, in the **AutoMovie themes group**, point to several of the slides and watch the movies displayed in the Preview monitor. When you are finished, click the **Fade** theme.

5 When a message box displays asking if you want to add music, click **Yes**.

6 In the **Add Music** dialog box, if necessary, expand ▷ the **Music** library, expand ▷ the **Public Music** folder, and then click the **Sample Music** folder. In the sample files included with Windows 7, click **Maid with the Flaxen Hair**, and then click **Open**. Locate the slide that displays the caption *2005–2007*, and if necessary, drag the caption box under this first slide. Compare your screen with Figure 6.34.

The green bar that displays above the items in the storyboard indicates that the music will play throughout the movie. Transition and pan-and-zoom indicators display on each slide. A ***transition*** is the manner in which the movie moves from one clip to another. A ***pan-and-zoom*** effect moves the picture horizontally or vertically, or zooms in or out of the picture.

Figure 6.34

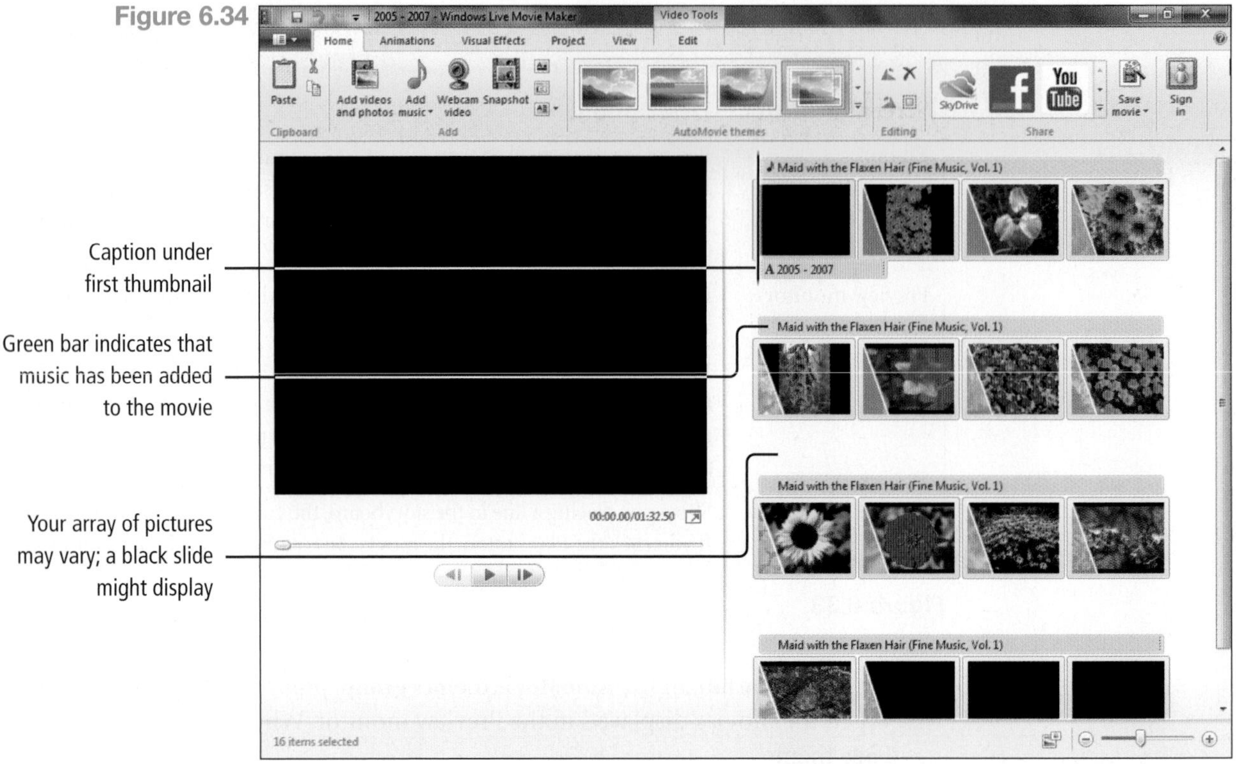

7 Turn on your computer speakers or put on headphones. Below the **Preview monitor**, click the **Play** button. Watch the entire movie, and notice that the movie has a title screen, music, transitions, effects, and three credit screens at the end.

> **Alert! | Do you hear sound from your speakers?**
>
> The video clip you just played has music that accompanies the video. If you cannot hear the sound, be sure you have speakers plugged into your computer and turned on or headphones plugged in and turned on. If you still cannot hear the audio, open Control Panel, click Hardware and Sound, and then under Sound, click Adjust system volume. Adjust the sound bars for your Speakers and your Windows Sounds.

8 On the left side of the Ribbon, click the blue **Movie Maker tab**, and then click **Save project**. Navigate to your **Windows 7 Chapter 6** folder, save the project as **Lastname_Firstname_6A_Slide_Show** and then click **Save**.

Activity 6.15 | Editing a Movie in Movie Maker

You can edit and format the text in the title, add and delete pictures, drag pictures to new locations, and edit the list of ***credits***—the list of people who worked on the movie that displays at the end of the movie.

1 Scroll to view the top of the *storyboard*. Click the first slide, which displays the default title caption. Then, click inside the Preview monitor window. Notice that the default title displays.

2 Select the existing title text, and then type **My Flower Garden** Drag the left middle sizing handle to the left edge of the Preview monitor, and then drag the right middle sizing handle to the right edge of the Preview monitor.

3 Select the text *My Flower Garden*, and then on the Ribbon, on the **Format tab**, in the **Font group**, click the **Font size arrow**, and then click **48**. Compare your screen with Figure 6.35.

Figure 6.35

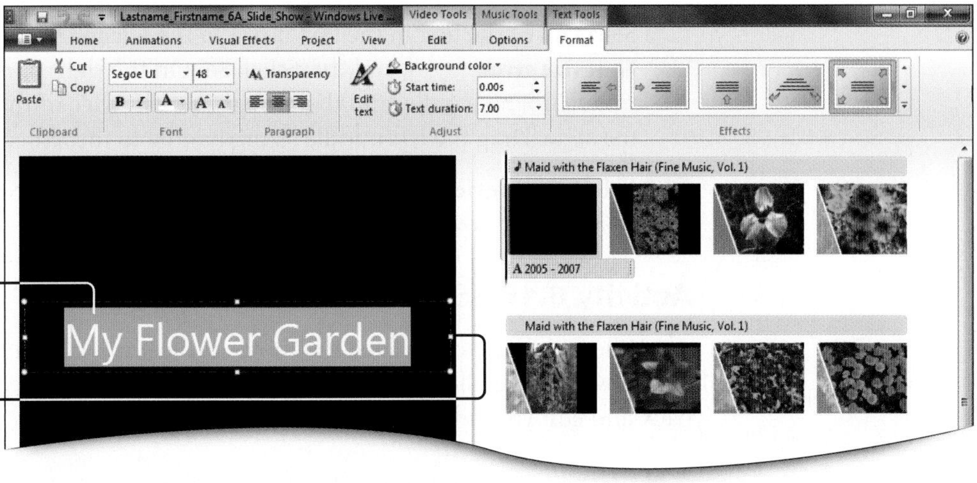

4 Below the **Preview monitor**, click the **Play** button. Watch the title screen, and then click the **Pause** button.

5 Press Ctrl + A to select all of the pictures. On the **Edit tab**, in the **Adjust group**, click the **Duration arrow**, and then click **5.00** to change the duration of each slide to five seconds.

6 In the **storyboard**, click anywhere in the third slide to place the insertion point in that slide.

7 Click the **Home tab**, and then in the **Add group**, click the **Add videos and photos** button. Navigate to the **Flower Pictures** folder, click **IMG_0536**, and then click **Open**. Notice that the new picture—the rose—is added to the **storyboard** to the *right* of the selected slide.

8 Drag the inserted rose picture just to the right of the title—first—slide, and then compare your screen with Figure 6.36.

Figure 6.36

9 Scroll down to view the last two slides in the **storyboard**—with the captions *STARRING* and *FILMED ON LOCATION*—right-click each and then click **Remove**. Be sure the last slide is selected, click in the **Preview monitor**, select the text *[Enter your name here]*, and then type your Firstname and Lastname.

10 Select all of the text in the text box. On the **Format tab**, in the **Font group**, click the **Font size arrow**, and then click **36**. On the right border of the text box, click the middle sizing handle, and then drag the right edge of the text box to the right edge of the slide. Drag the left middle sizing handle to the left edge of the screen.

11 Below the **Preview monitor**, click the **Play** button. Notice that when the last slide finishes, the movie ends. **Save** your project.

Activity 6.16 | Saving a Movie to the Computer

When you have completed the movie project to your satisfaction, you can save the file as a movie. Saving the file as a movie does not alter the project file, so you can always go back and edit your movie by opening the project again.

1 Scroll up as necessary to view the **storyboard**, click the first thumbnail which is the title slide, and then below the **Preview monitor**, click the **Play** button and view the entire movie to be sure the movie is set up the way you want it.

2 When the movie has completed playing, on the left side of the Ribbon, click the blue **Movie Maker tab**. Point to **Save movie**, and then click **Recommended for this project**.

You can also select one of the higher resolution formats if you have a high resolution monitor or want to show the movie on a television, or you can save the movie in a much lower resolution format for use with a mobile device.

3 Navigate to your **Windows 7 Chapter 6** folder. Accept the default movie name—*Lastname_Firstname_6A_Slide_Show*—and then click **Save**. Saving the movie may take several minutes, but a progress bar indicates how much of the movie has been saved. Compare your screen with Figure 6.37.

Figure 6.37

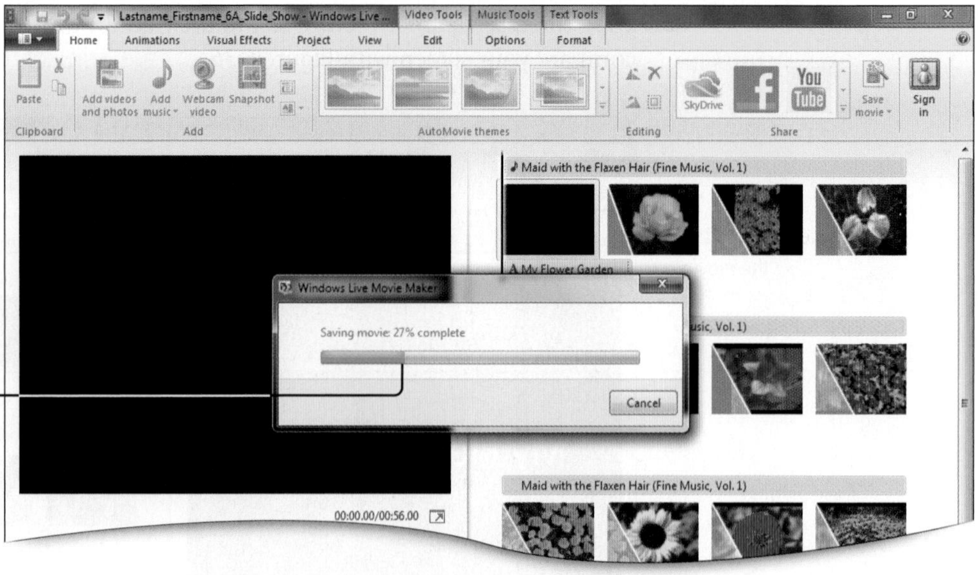

4 When the movie is saved, a message box displays. In the message box, click **Play** to play the movie. **Maximize** the movie window and watch the movie. If the Windows Media Player dialog box displays, click Recommended settings, and then click Finish, and then in the taskbar, click the Windows Media Player button.

5 **Close** the movie screen and **Movie Maker**, saving your changes if prompted, but leave **Photo Gallery** open for the next activity.

Objective 5 | Create a Movie Using Video Clips

A ***video clip*** is a short video presentation. If you have a digital camcorder, a digital camera, or even a smartphone that is capable of recording video, you can view the video clips that they record on your computer.

Video clips consist of a series of frames. A ***frame*** is a single image in a series of consecutive images. ***Frame rate*** is the number of frames displayed per second. Higher frame rates generally produce smoother movement in the video. The frame rate of the video clips that you will use in this chapter is approximately 30 ***fps***—frames per second.

Activity 6.17 | Adding Video Clips to Windows Live Movie Maker

1 If necessary, open Photo Gallery, and then in the Photo Gallery **navigation pane**, be sure the **Cactus Pictures** folder and the **Flower Pictures** folder display.

2 On the left side of the Ribbon, click the *blue* **File tab**, and then click **Include folder**. In the **Pictures Library Locations** dialog box, click **Add**. In the **Include Folder in Pictures** dialog box, navigate to **Documents ▶ Bell_Orchid ▶ San_Diego ▶ Sales_Marketing ▶ Media ▶ Videos**. In the **Videos** folder, click the **Waterfalls** folder, and then click **Include folder**. Click **OK** to close the **Pictures Library Locations** dialog box.

The Waterfalls folder contains four pictures and three video clips.

3 Press Ctrl + A to select all of the items in the **Waterfalls** folder. Click the **Create tab**, and then in the **Share group**, click **Movie**.

4 On the **Home tab**, in the **Add group**, click the **Add title** button. Select the title text, type the title **Lake Superior Shore** and then press Enter. Type the subtitle **A Hiker's Paradise** Select all of the title text, and then change the **Font size** to **28**. Compare your screen with Figure 6.38.

Figure 6.38

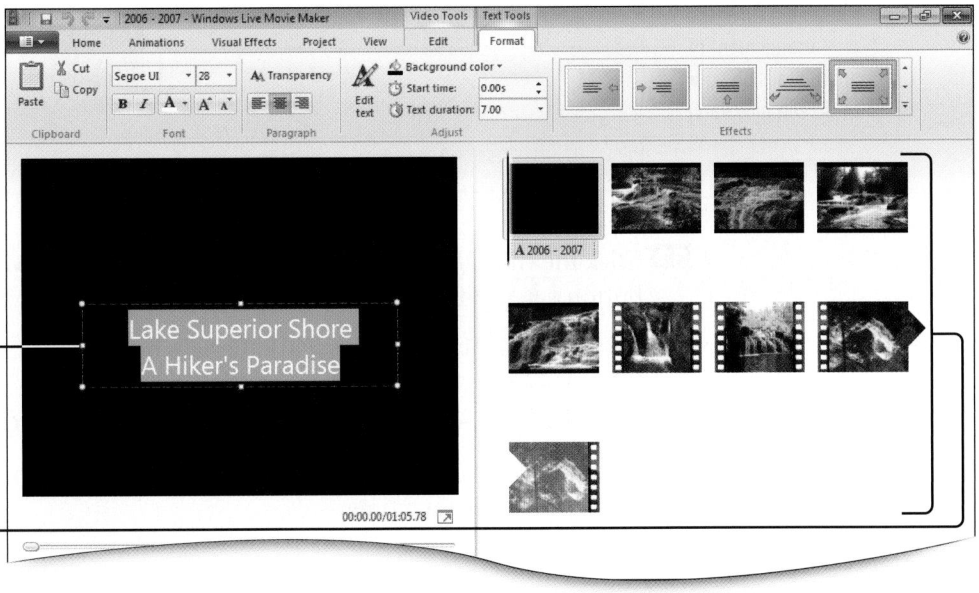

5 In the **storyboard**, notice that some thumbnails display dotted bars on the edges; these are video clips. Click the first video clip. Below the **Preview monitor**, click the **Play** button [▶], and watch the video clips play.

6 On the left side of the Ribbon, click the blue **Movie Maker tab**, and then click **Save project**. Navigate to your **Windows 7 Chapter 6** folder, and save the project as **Lastname_Firstname_6A_Movie** and then click **Save**.

7 In the **storyboard**, locate and then click the first video clip. On the **Home tab**, in the **Add group**, click the **Add title** button. Replace the existing text with **Trickle...**

8 Use the same procedure to add the title **Tumult...** to the second video clip—the clip with pale green trees in the center. Add the title **Torrent...** to the third video clip.

9 On the **Home tab**, in the **Add group**, click the **Add credits** button. In the text box, drag the left middle sizing handle to the left border of the slide, and then drag the right middle sizing handle to the right border of the slide.

10 Replace *[Enter name here]* with **Film by:** press Spacebar, and then type your **Firstname** and **Lastname** Press Enter. Type **Producer: F. B. Lewis** and then press Enter. Type **Videographer: M. J. Lewis** and then compare your screen with 6.39.

Figure 6.39

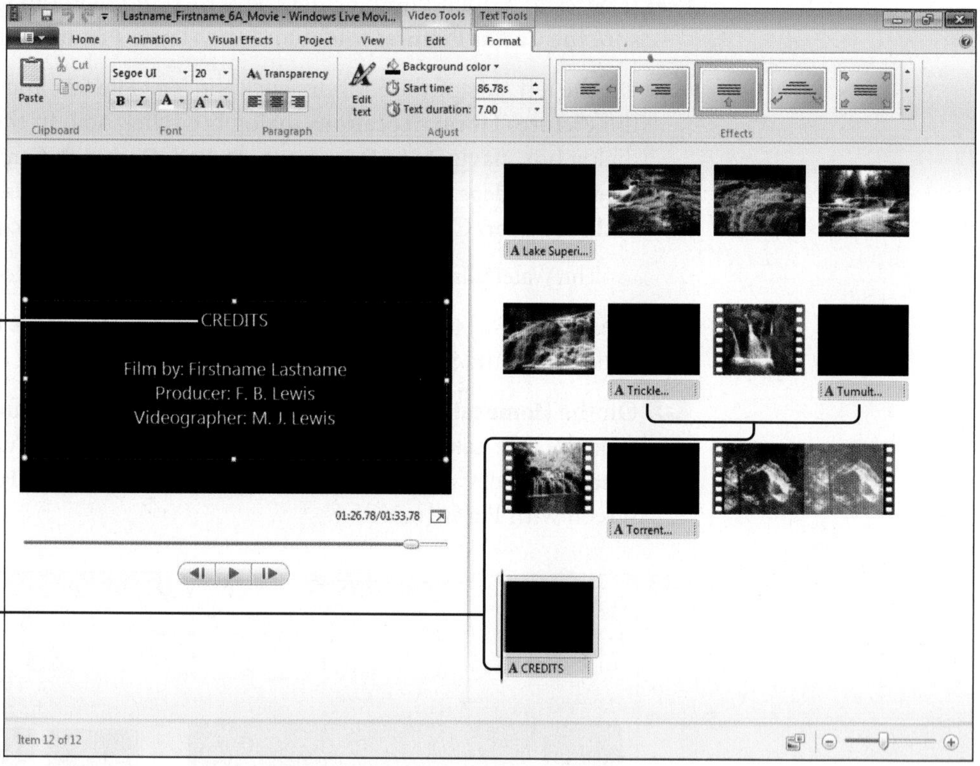

11 Click the *CREDITS* thumbnail, and then below the **Preview monitor**, click the **Play** button [▶]. Notice that the credits scroll up in the preview.

12 On the Quick Access Toolbar, click the **Save** button.

Activity 6.18 | Adding Transitions and Editing Video Clips

You can set the starting point or the end point of a video clip, and you can apply transitions to one clip at a time.

1 With the **Movies** project still open, in the **storyboard**, click near the left side of the last of the three video clips—the clip just to the left of the *CREDITS* slide.

Depending on your screen resolution, the third clip may display on two lines.

2 Drag the playback indicator to a point about three-quarters of the way through the clip, as shown in Figure 6.40.

Figure 6.40

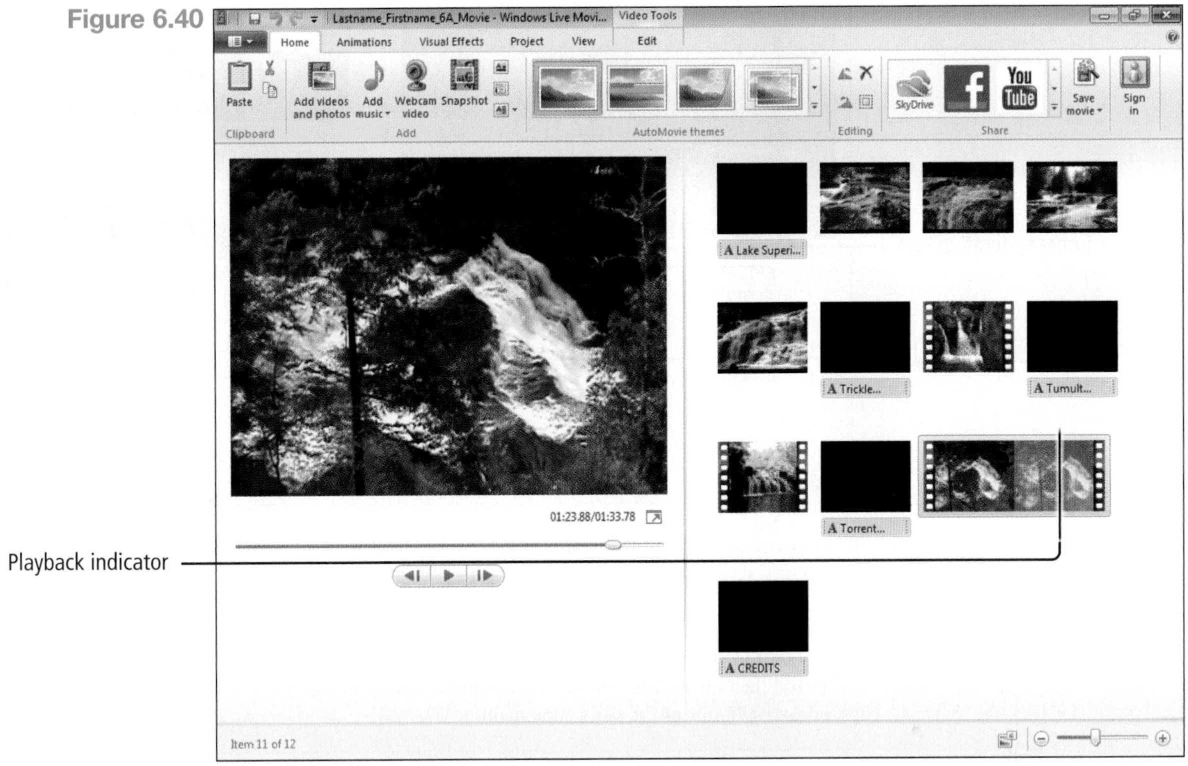

3 Click the **Edit tab**, and then in the **Editing group**, click the **Set end point** button to shorten the third video clip.

4 Click near the left edge of the second video clip. On the **Edit tab**, in the **Editing group**, click the **Trim tool** button. Notice that the play bar below the Preview monitor displays a Trimmed duration bar at either end.

5 Move the pointer over either of the **Trimmed duration** bars, and notice that in the ScreenTip, the length of the video clip is shown as nearly ten seconds.

6 Drag the *left* **Trimmed duration** bar to the right approximately 1-inch, and drag the right **Trimmed duration** bar to the left approximately 1-inch. Use the ScreenTip to adjust the bars until the duration of the clip is approximately 00:07—seven seconds—as shown in Figure 6.41.

Figure 6.41

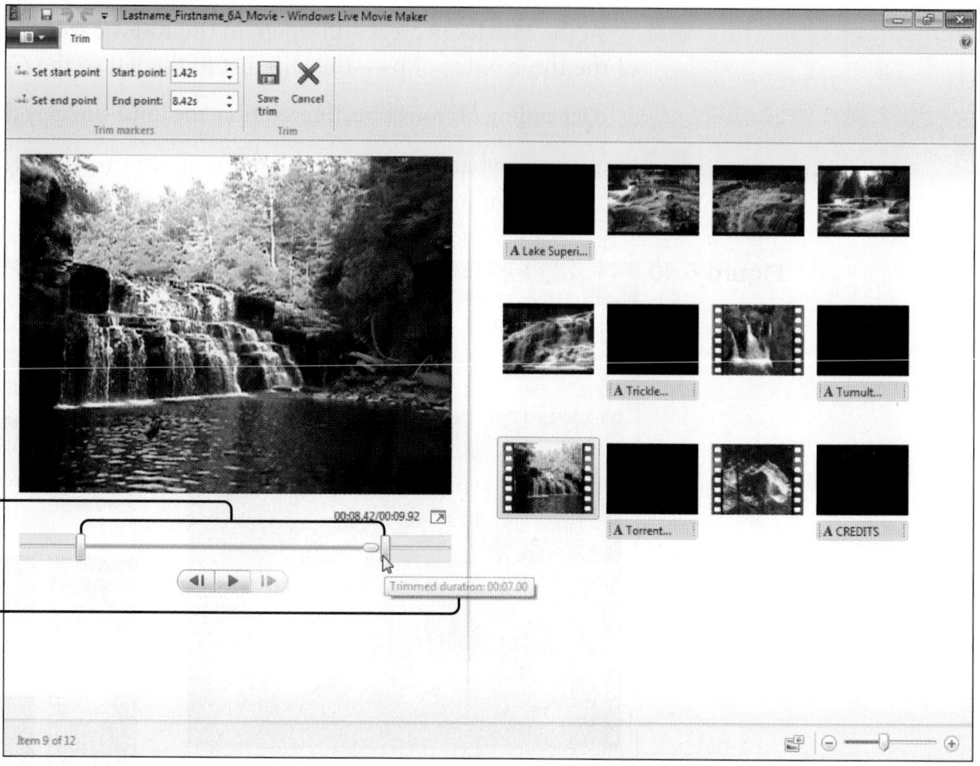

More Knowledge | Splitting Video Clips

If you want to split a video clip into two or three pieces, you can use the Split button located to the left of the Trim tool button. To split a video clip into two pieces, position the Playback indicator where you want to split the clip, and then on the Edit tab, click the Split button. You can then trim the ends of one or both of the new clips, or even split one of the news clips again.

7 On the **Trim tab**, in the **Trim group**, click the **Save trim** button.

8 Click one of the video clips, hold down Ctrl, and then click the other two video clips.

9 With all three video clips selected, click the **Animations tab.** In the **Transitions group**, click the **Diagonal down-right** button—the button with a diagonal line running from the lower left corner to the upper right corner. If necessary, use the button ScreenTips to help find the correct button.

10 Point to each of the still pictures—those without dotted bars—right-click, and then click **Remove** to remove each of the pictures and leave only the video clips.

11 If necessary, drag the *CREDITS* text below the last slide, and then drag any other text boxes as necessary—a little overlap between titles will not cause any problems. Compare your screen with Figure 6.42.

Figure 6.42

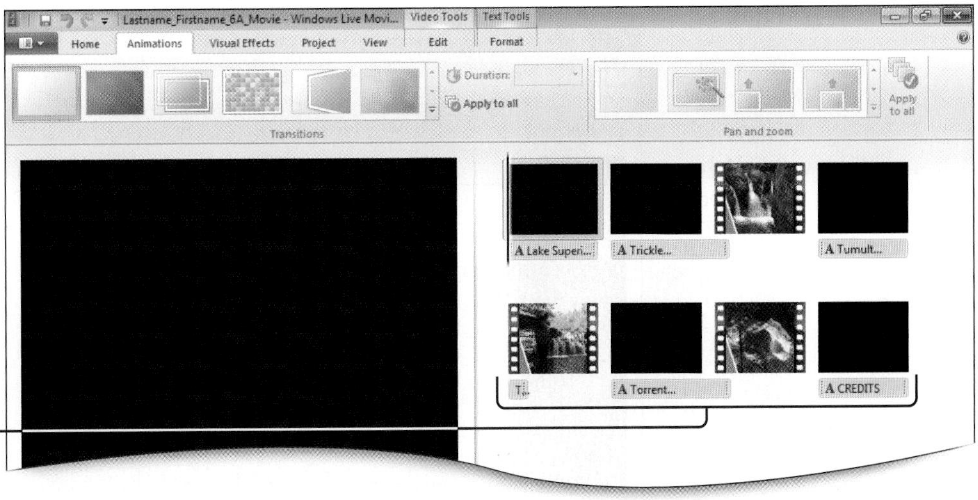

Title text markers adjusted; drag thumbnails as necessary to match this figure

12 In the **storyboard**, click the first slide, which is the title slide, and then below the Preview monitor, click the **Play** button to preview your movie.

13 After the movie completes, on the Quick Access Toolbar, click the **Save** button.

Activity 6.19 | Creating a Movie DVD

When you complete your movie, you must convert it into a format that can be read by Windows Media Player and the dozens of other video players that people have installed on their computers. The project that you created can be read only by Movie Maker. When you save the project as a movie, it combines all of the elements that you have gathered in your storyboard and creates a single movie file. The format used for these movies is Windows Media Video, which uses a *.wmv* extension.

If you prefer to watch your movie on a television, you can create a DVD by using the ***Windows DVD Maker*** feature that comes with most versions of Windows 7. Windows DVD Maker creates DVDs that can play back on a DVD player.

> **Alert! | This activity is optional.**
>
> If you do not have a blank DVD, read through the steps to become familiar with the process of burning a movie to a DVD.

1 Place a blank DVD in your DVD drive, and if the AutoPlay dialog box displays, Close it.

2 With your movie project still open, click the **Movie Maker tab**, point to **Save movie**, and then click **Burn a DVD**.

3 In the **Save Movie** dialog box, accept the default name for the movie, and then click **Save**.

The save process saves the project as a movie; however, the project file remains unchanged, and can be edited later if necessary. The save process could take several minutes.

4 The **Windows DVD Maker** program opens, as shown in Figure 6.43.

Figure 6.43

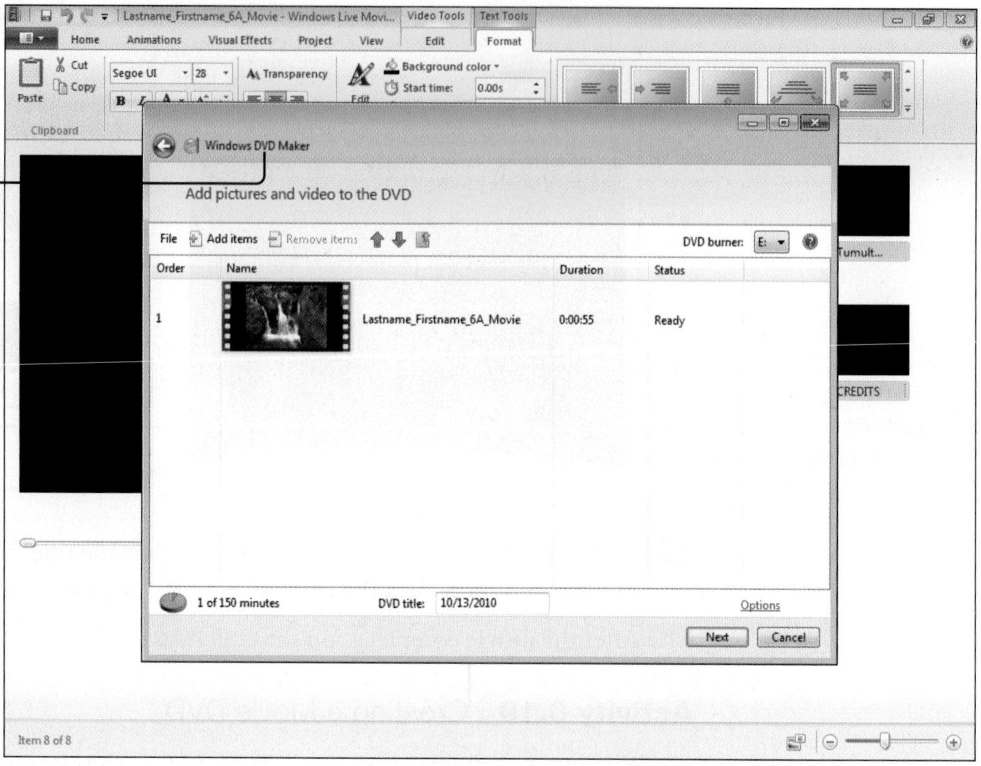

Windows DVD Maker dialog box

5 At the bottom of the **Windows DVD Maker** dialog box, click **Next**.

6 In the final **Windows DVD Maker** dialog box, click **Burn**—a process which could take several minutes.

7 When a message box displays asking if you want to burn another DVD, click the **Close** button.

8 **Close** all windows and submit your files as directed.

You should have five total files—three snip files (6A_Imported_Folders_Snip, 6A_Tags&Ratings_Snip, and 6A_Brochure_Tags_Snip) and two movie project files (6A_Slide_Show.wlmp and 6A_Movie.wlmp). Typically the movie files themselves are fairly large; it will be easier to upload the project file (.wlmp) to your instructor.

End **You have completed Project 6A**

Project 6B Using Windows Media Center

Project Activities

In Activities 6.20 through 6.27, you will use Windows Media Center to look at pictures, play a video, play music, listen to radio, set up television on your computer, and play games. You will capture screens that look similar to Figure 6.44.

Project Files

For Project 6B, you will need the following files:

New Snip files
A music CD of your choice
A DVD movie or music video of your choice

You will save your files as:

Lastname_Firstname_6B_Configure_Snip
Lastname_Firstname_6B_Music_Snip
Lastname_Firstname_6B_Pictures_Snip
Lastname_Firstname_6B_Sports_Snip

Project Results

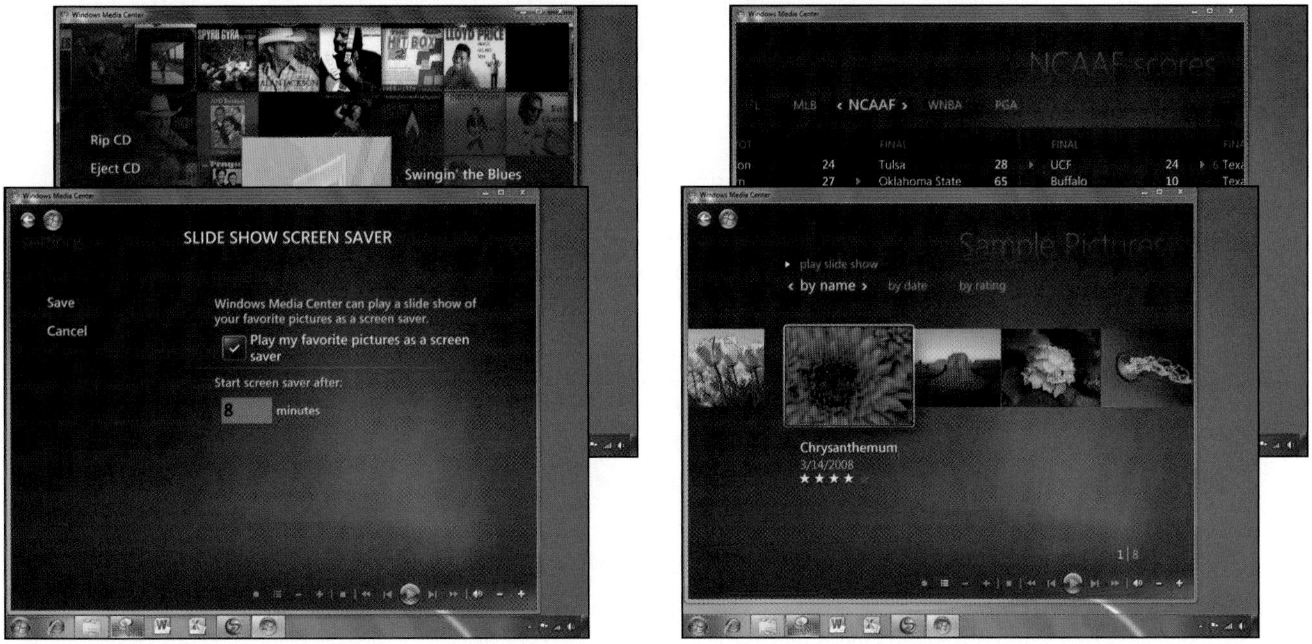

Figure 6.44
Project 6B Using Windows Media Center

Objective 6 | Navigate and Configure Windows Media Center

Windows Media Center is a feature of Windows 7—except in the Starter edition—that enables you to use your computer as your home entertainment hub. When you think of the term *media center*, you probably think about something in a living room or family room with a widescreen high-definition TV and a sophisticated sound system. But a media center can also be in a smaller room, such as your home office or bedroom, where you can use your computer and a remote control to view movies and play music.

Because you can connect your computer to a high-definition TV and use a Windows Media Center remote to control the action from your couch or favorite chair, the Windows Media Center feature is sometimes referred to as the ***10-foot interface***. In other words, you can control Windows Media Center by sitting ten feet away from it in the same manner you sit away from your TV. Alternatively, you can use Windows Media Center on a standard computer monitor with a keyboard and mouse. This is referred to as the ***2-foot interface*** because you can view and listen to entertainment by sitting the normal distance from your computer, which is commonly two feet. Regardless of whether you connect to a TV or just use your computer's monitor, you can use Windows Media Center for various types of entertainment such as:

- Watching Internet TV and live TV
- Viewing slide shows of your own photos
- Playing songs in your music library or any of your CDs or DVDs

If you have ever used the remote control device on your television or DVD player, you will be familiar with the way Windows Media Center works. You can use the Windows Media Center menu to view media, or to configure the settings for your music, television, radio, pictures, and videos.

Activity 6.20 | Navigating Windows Media Center

Windows Media Center can be used from the keyboard, but it can also be controlled using a remote control device if your computer has one. In this activity, use your mouse and keyboard.

1 From the **Start** menu, click **All Programs**, and then click **Windows Media Center**. If an initial *Welcome to Windows Media Center* screen displays, click **Continue**, and then click the large arrow above *Express* to add the contents of the media folders to the Media Library by using **Express setup**.

> **Alert! | Does Setting Up Windows Media Center Take a While?**
>
> If you have a lot of media on your computer, it will take several minutes for Media Center to finish the setup process. There will be no indication that the setup is complete.

2 If Media Center displays with the screen maximized, point to the upper right corner of the screen to display the buttons, and then click the **Restore Down** button. Then, drag the corners of the window to fill most—*but not all of*—your screen, so that the **Start** button and the **Windows taskbar** are still visible, as shown in Figure 6.45.

Normally when you run Media Center, you will use it with the screen maximized. Because you cannot use the Snipping Tool with a maximized screen, for this project you will use a window to display Media Center so you can capture screens to submit to your instructor. The shape of the window on your screen may vary.

3 Click in an empty area of the Media Center window, and then press ↑ and ↓ several times to scroll through the Media Center main menu. If you have a wheel on your mouse, roll the wheel to scroll through the main menu. Using either technique, display **Tasks**, compare your screen with Figure 6.45, and then take a moment to study the Windows Media Center categories described in the table in Figure 6.46.

The main screen consists of two intersecting menus. As you scroll upward or downward you see the categories of media described in Figure 6.46. Within a category, you can scroll horizontally through various subcategories.

Figure 6.45

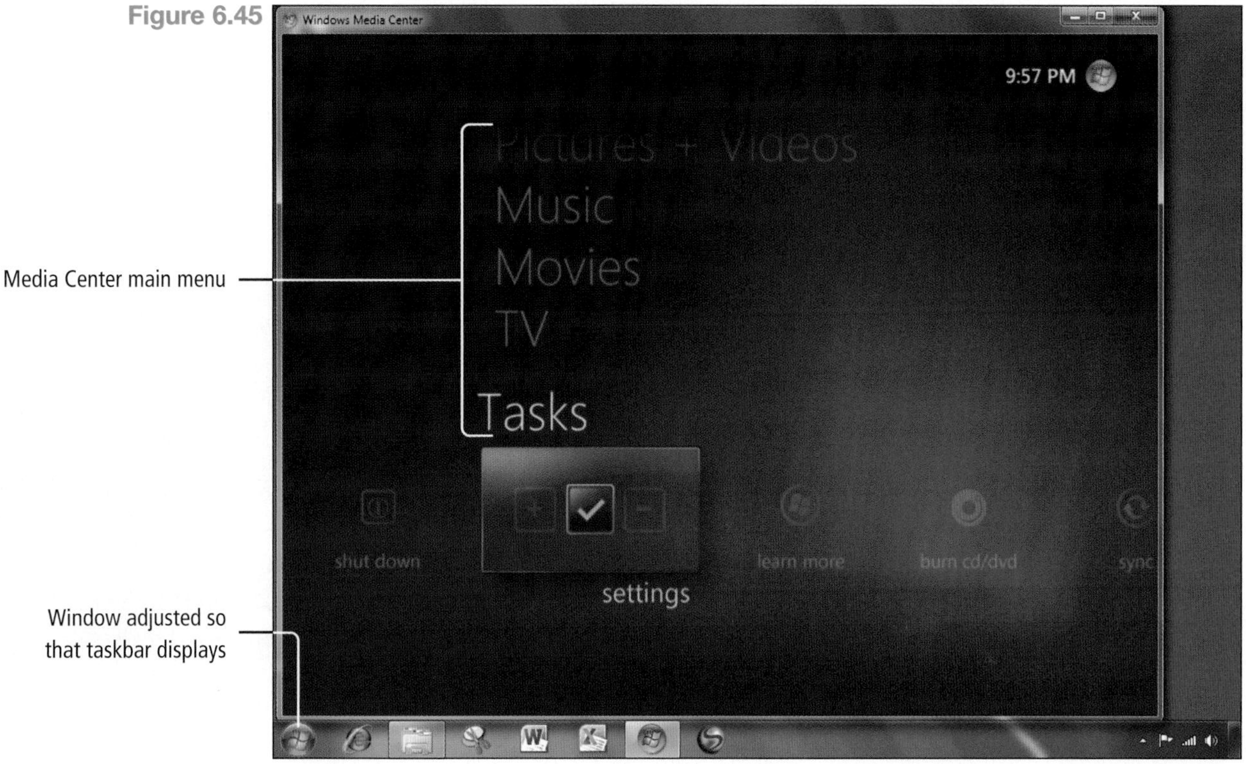

Windows Media Center Categories

Category	Description
Extras	Includes several games and a CD/DVD burning program.
Pictures + Videos	Enables you to access your pictures, add pictures to the Media Library, and play slideshows and videos.
Music	Provides access to the music in your Media Library and online radio, and enables you to play both.
Movies	Enables you to watch streaming movies, access your own movie library, and play a DVD.
TV	Enables you to set up your television connection, watch Internet TV or recorded television programs, or watch live television.
Sports	Provides access to sports information on the Internet.
Tasks	Provides access to Media Center settings; also enables you to sync a portable device, burn CDs or DVDs, or to add an extender—a device other than a PC that will play media files such as an Xbox 360.

Figure 6.46

4 With the **Tasks** category selected in the vertical menu, press → several times to scroll through the **Tasks** commands. Then press ← to scroll back until the **settings** command is selected.

The Media Center screens are designed to be viewed at the distance of a TV screen—the 10-foot interface—and with the types of controls you would find on a TV remote control.

> **Note | Windows Media Center Uses the Same Windows 7 Hardware and Software as Windows Media Player**
>
> Because Media Center uses the same Windows 7 systems that Media Player uses, you will find that your media can be used in either system. For example, your Music Library is shared, so a CD that you rip in Media Player will also display in Media Center.

5 With the **settings** command selected, press Enter. Scroll down to **Music**, press Enter, and then compare your screen with Figure 6.47.

Figure 6.47

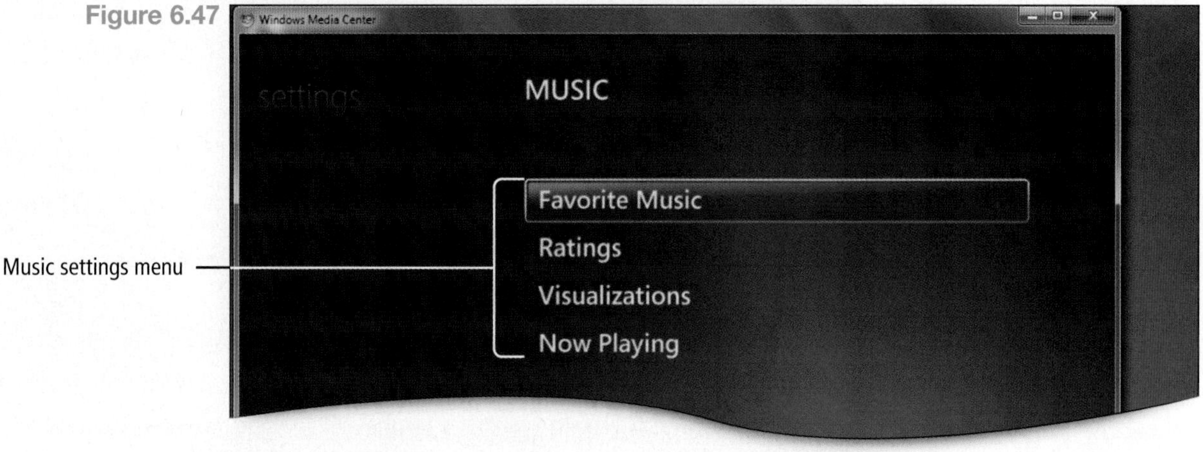

6 Point to the upper left corner of the Windows Media Center window to display the **Back** button.

7 Click the **Back** button two times to return to the Media Center main menu.

> **Alert! | Does a new screen saver display after ten minutes of inactivity?**
>
> If you open Media Center and do not do anything in the program for ten minutes, a slide show using the photos in your pictures library will begin automatically. This is the default screen saver in Media Center. To turn the slide show off, press Esc.

Activity 6.21 | Configuring Windows Media Center

Although many Media Center categories can be used without any additional setup, you will probably want to change the setup of some categories as you become more familiar with the system.

1 With Media Center still displayed, be sure the **Tasks** category is active. With the **settings** command selected, press Enter to display the settings options, and then compare your screen with Figure 6.48.

Figure 6.48

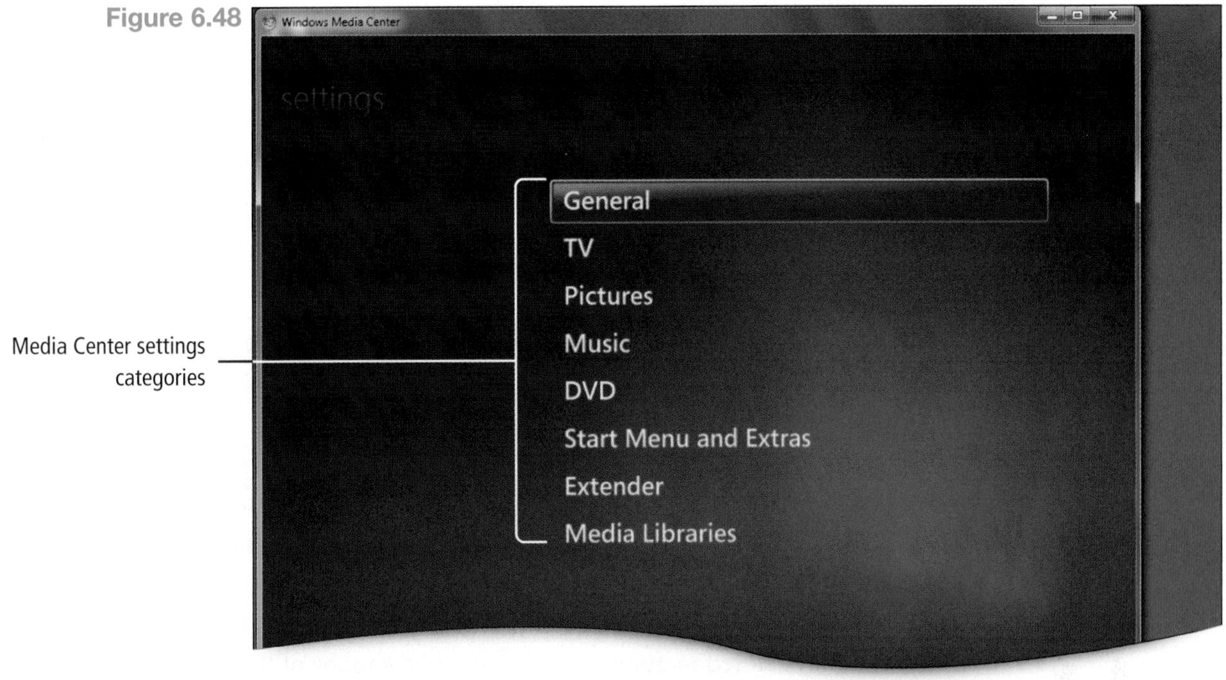

2 With the **General** category selected, press Enter, and then examine the General setup options.

Here you have options for various settings, each of which you can modify as you become more familiar with the system. You can also set Parental Controls such as TV and movie blocking.

3 Point to the upper left corner of the **Media Center** window to display the buttons, and then click the **Back** button.

4 Press ↓ to select the **Pictures** setting, and then press Enter. Press ↓ to select **Slide Show Screen Saver**, and then press Enter.

You can use a slide show of your photographs as a screen saver.

5 Be sure the check box to the left of *Play my favorite pictures as a screen saver* is selected. Click in the *Start screen saver after* box, type **8** and then click outside the box. Compare your screen with Figure 6.49.

Figure 6.49

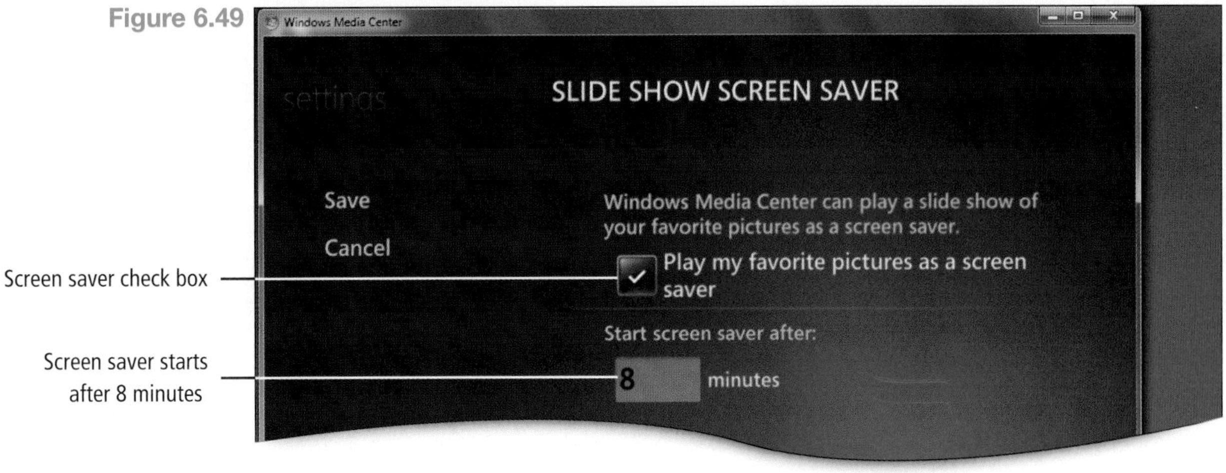

6 **Start** the **Snipping Tool** program, click the **New arrow**, and then click **Full-screen Snip.** In the **Snipping Tool** mark-up window, click the **Save Snip** button.

7 In the **Save As** dialog box, in the **navigation pane**, scroll down as necessary, and then under **Computer**, click your USB flash drive so that it displays in the address bar. Navigate to your **Windows 7 Chapter 6** folder, and then as the file name, type **Lastname_Firstname_6B_Configure_Snip** Be sure the file type is **JPEG file**, and then press Enter. **Close** the **Snipping Tool** mark-up window. Hold this file until you finish Project 6B, and then submit this file as directed by your instructor.

8 Point to the upper left corner of the window to display the buttons, and then click the **Back** button as necessary to return to the Media Center main menu. If prompted to save changes, click No.

Objective 7 | Use Windows Media Center to Play Media from Your Computer

You can use Windows Media Center to play CDs or DVDs from your computer's disk drives. You can play music or videos that you have ripped to the computer, or run a slideshow of stored pictures. You can also access many of the games that come with Windows 7, including such popular games as Chess, Solitaire, Hearts, and several others.

Activity 6.22 | Playing Games Using Media Center

Another Way

Click the Start button, point to All Programs to display a list of programs, and then click the Games folder. Click the game of your choice. The look and feel of the games are slightly different when played this way.

1 With Media Center still displayed, press ↑ or ↓ until the **Extras** category displays.

2 Press ← or → as necessary to display the **extras library**, and then press Enter. Point to the **Chess Titans** game, and notice that the name of the game displays below the game icons.

The games that display by default were installed on your computer when Windows 7 was installed.

3 Point to the **Chess Titans** game, and then click to start the game. If necessary, decide what level you want to play, and then click *Beginner*, *Intermediate*, or *Advanced*. Click **New Game Against Computer**.

4 In the lower portion of your screen, click on the piece you want to move, and then click on the square you want to move it to. After the computer responds to your move, compare your screen with Figure 6.50.

Figure 6.50

Game options

5 If you want to do so, try the game, and then when you are through, click **Exit Game**. In the **Exit Game** dialog box, click **Don't Save** to leave the game without saving it to your computer.

6 Point to the upper left corner of the window to display the buttons, and then click the **Back** button to return to the Media Center main menu.

Activity 6.23 | Playing Music Using Media Center

In this activity, you will play a CD from your CD drive.

> **Alert! | This activity is optional.**
>
> If you do not have a music CD available, you can read through this activity.

1 Place a music CD of your choice in your computer's CD/DVD drive. If the AutoPlay window or the Windows Media Player window displays, close it.

2 With Media Center still displayed, press ↓ until the **Music** category displays. Then, press → and ← to see the Music commands. Display **music library**, and then press Enter. If the Library Setup message displays, click No. Compare your screen with Figure 6.51.

Your CDs may be sorted by year, album, genre, songs, playlists, composers, or other CD details. When CD cover art is unavailable, the name of the CD displays on a yellow background.

Figure 6.51

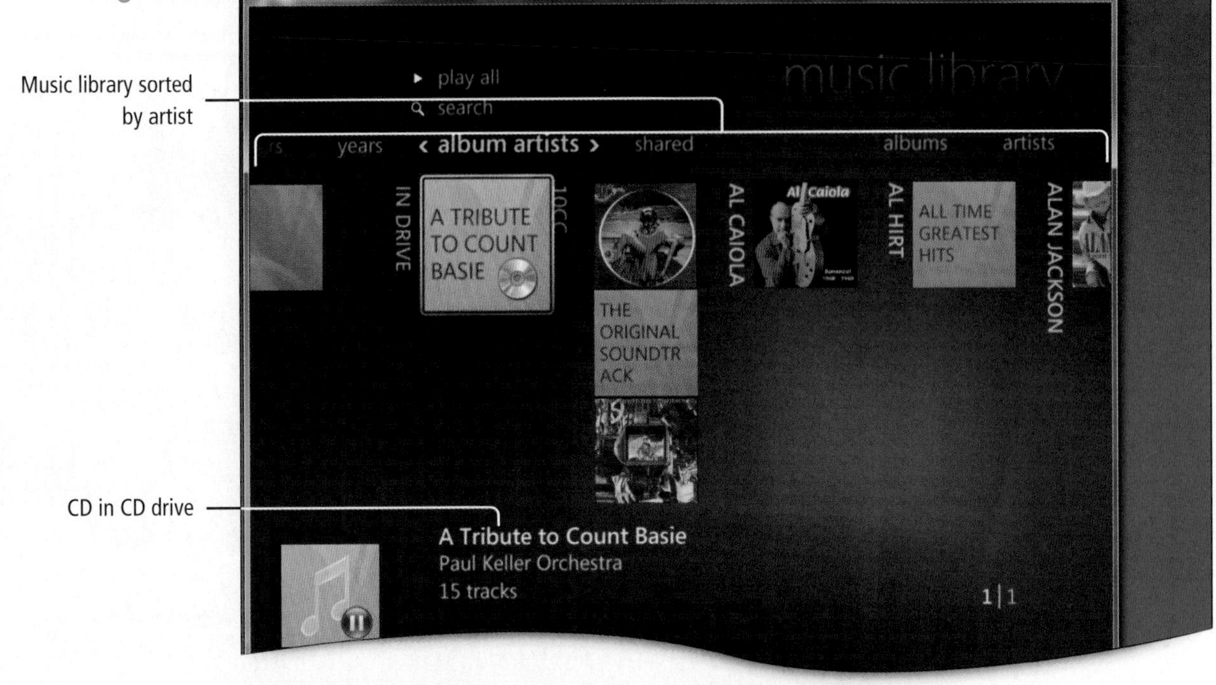

3 Press ↑ one time to move to the sort menu that displays across the upper portion of the screen, and then press → or ← to view the available sort categories. When **years** is active, press Enter.

Recall that the terms *CD* and *Album* are interchangeable.

4 Use the same technique to change the sort arrangement to **albums**.

5 Point to the icon for the CD in your CD/DVD drive, and then click one time. Compare your screen with Figure 6.52.

Figure 6.52

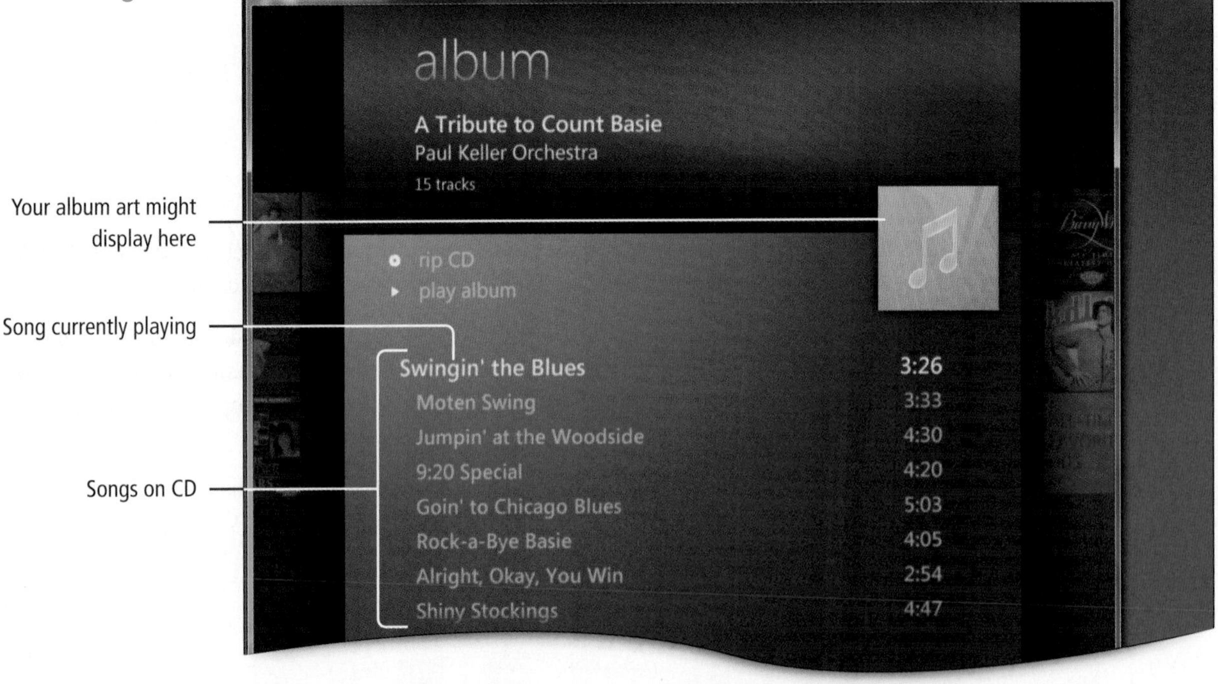

6 Near the top of the Media Center window, click the **play album** button. Listen to the music for a few moments, until the details of the track display on the screen.

7 **Start** the **Snipping Tool** program, click the **New arrow**, and then click **Full-screen Snip**. In the **Snipping Tool** mark-up window, click the **Save Snip** button.

8 In the **Save As** dialog box, in the **navigation pane**, scroll down as necessary, and then under **Computer**, click your USB flash drive so that it displays in the address bar. Navigate to your **Windows 7 Chapter 6** folder, and then as the file name, type **Lastname_Firstname_6B_Music_Snip** Be sure the file type is **JPEG file**, and then press Enter. **Close** the **Snipping Tool** mark-up window. Hold this file until you finish Project 6B, and then submit this file as directed by your instructor.

9 Move your mouse pointer slightly in any direction, and then notice that this action displays a navigation bar in the lower right corner of the window.

The navigation bar enables you to pause the CD, or to move to the next track or to the previous track.

10 In the **navigation bar**, click the **Stop** button.

11 Point to the upper left corner of the window to display the buttons, and then click the **Back** button as necessary until the Media Center main menu displays.

> **More Knowledge | Playing CDs That You Have Ripped or Playlists That You Have Saved**
>
> In Chapter 4, you ripped a CD and created and saved a playlist. To play the CD you ripped, sort on *albums*, locate and select the CD title, and then click the *play album* button. To play your playlist, sort on *playlists*, select the playlist you saved, and then click the *play* button.

Activity 6.24 | Playing a DVD Using Media Center

> **Alert! | This activity is optional.**
>
> If you do not have a movie or music video DVD available, you can read through this activity.

1 Place a movie or music video DVD into your computer's CD/DVD player. If the AutoPlay window or the Windows Media Player window displays, Close it.

2 With Media Center still displayed, press ↓ to scroll through the Media Center main menu until the **Movies** category is selected. Press → to select **play dvd**, and then press Enter.

After some introductory material, the movie's menu screen displays. From this screen, you can play the movie, select a language, view special features, or choose a scene in the movie as your starting point.

> **Alert! | DVD Enhancements**
>
> Some commercial DVDs have enhancements. If you see a message box prompting you for what you want to play, press Enter to play the DVD without the enhancements, or click the Play Enhancements button to see extra features.

3 Click **Play Movie** or whatever command is necessary to begin the movie. Watch the movie for a moment.

4 Move your mouse slightly to display the **navigation bar** in the lower right corner of the screen, and then click the **Stop** button to stop the movie.

5 Point to the upper left corner of the window to display the buttons, and then click the **Back** button to display the Media Center main menu.

Activity 6.25 | Viewing a Picture Slideshow Using Media Center

Using Media Center, you can view the pictures on your computer as a slideshow. For this activity, you will use the sample pictures that were added when Windows 7 was installed.

1 With Media Center still displayed, press ↓ to scroll through the Media Center main menu until the **Pictures + Videos** category displays. Press → and ← to see the picture and video options.

2 Display the **picture library**. If a message prompts you to add pictures, click Cancel. Scroll left or right to display the **Sample Pictures** folder—or one of the other picture folders you have on your computer.

3 With the pictures in the **Sample Pictures** picture folder displayed—or some other folder of your choice—press Enter. Notice that individual pictures in that folder display, as shown in Figure 6.53.

Figure 6.53

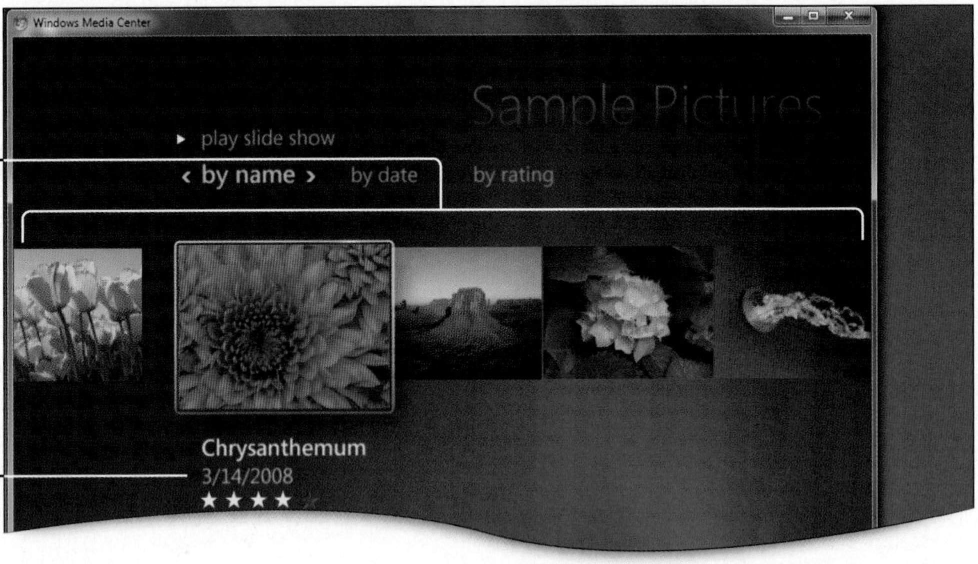

Pictures in Sample Pictures folder (your pictures may vary)

Selected picture name, date, and rating

4 **Start** the **Snipping Tool** program, click the **New arrow**, and then click **Full-screen Snip**. In the **Snipping Tool** mark-up window, click the **Save Snip** button.

5 In the **Save As** dialog box, in the **navigation pane**, scroll down as necessary, and then under **Computer**, click your USB flash drive so that it displays in the address bar. Navigate to your **Windows 7 Chapter 6** folder, and then as the file name, type **Lastname_Firstname_6B_Pictures_Snip** Be sure the file type is **JPEG file**, and then press Enter. **Close** the **Snipping Tool** mark-up window. Hold this file until you finish Project 6B, and then submit this file as directed by your instructor.

6 Click one of the pictures, and notice that the selected picture fills the Media Center window.

7 Point to the upper left corner of your screen, click the **Back** button, and then with the same folder selected, above the pictures click **play slide show**. Watch the slide show for a moment.

8 Move your mouse slightly to display the **navigation bar** in the lower right, and then click the **Stop** button. Point to the upper left corner of your screen, and then click the **Back** button as necessary until the Media Center main menu displays.

Objective 8 | Use Windows Media Center to View Sports, Internet TV, and Live TV

Windows Media Center enables you to locate and view many types of online media. You can watch current newscasts, check sports scores, or view in-depth news stories and documentaries. You can watch live television on your computer, or watch Internet television.

Activity 6.26 | Setting Up and Using the Internet in Media Center

You can set up your computer to receive live television. For this activity, you will need to have a high-speed Internet connection.

1 With Media Center still displayed, press ↓ as necessary to select **Tasks**.

2 Select **settings**, and then press Enter. With **General** selected, press Enter. Click **Windows Media Center Setup**. Be sure **Set Up Internet Connection** is selected, and then compare your screen with Figure 6.54.

Here you set up your Internet connection, television signal, speakers, and monitor or television.

Figure 6.54

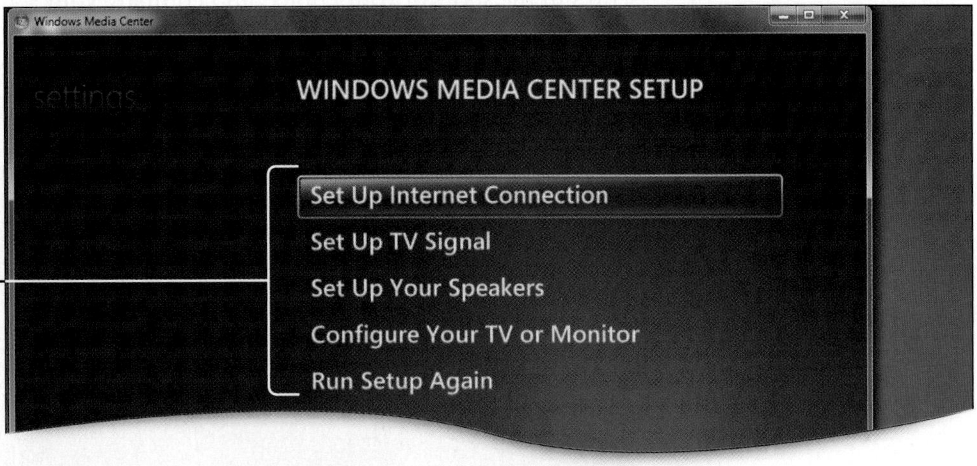

3 Press Enter. Read the first **Internet Connection** screen, and then click **Next** to begin configuring your Internet.

The first step is to confirm that you have a high-speed Internet connection, and that the connection is always on.

4 Click the **Yes** option button, and then click **Next**. When asked to test your Internet connection, click the **Test** button.

Alert! | **No Internet Connection?**

If you see a message stating that no Internet connection could be found, check your cable connection, open a browser to be sure the connection is working, and then try again.

5 Click **Next** to complete the setup, and then compare your screen with Figure 6.55.

Figure 6.55

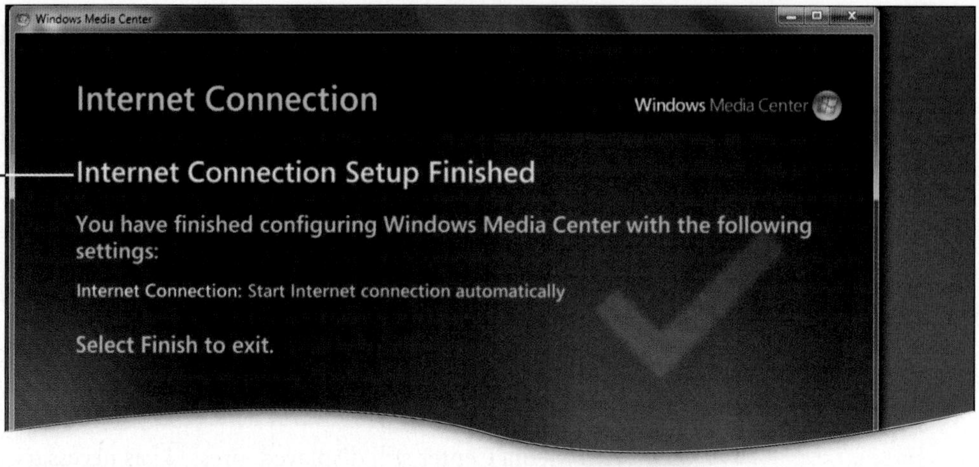

6 At the bottom of the **Internet Connection** screen, click the **Finish** button. Click the **Back** button as necessary to return to the Media Center main menu.

7 Scroll up, select **Sports**, scroll to **scores**, and then press Enter—you may have to close and then reopen Media Center before Sports will display. Notice that by connecting to the Internet, you have added features to Media Center. Scroll through current scores in the sport of your choice, and compare your screen with Figure 6.56.

Figure 6.56

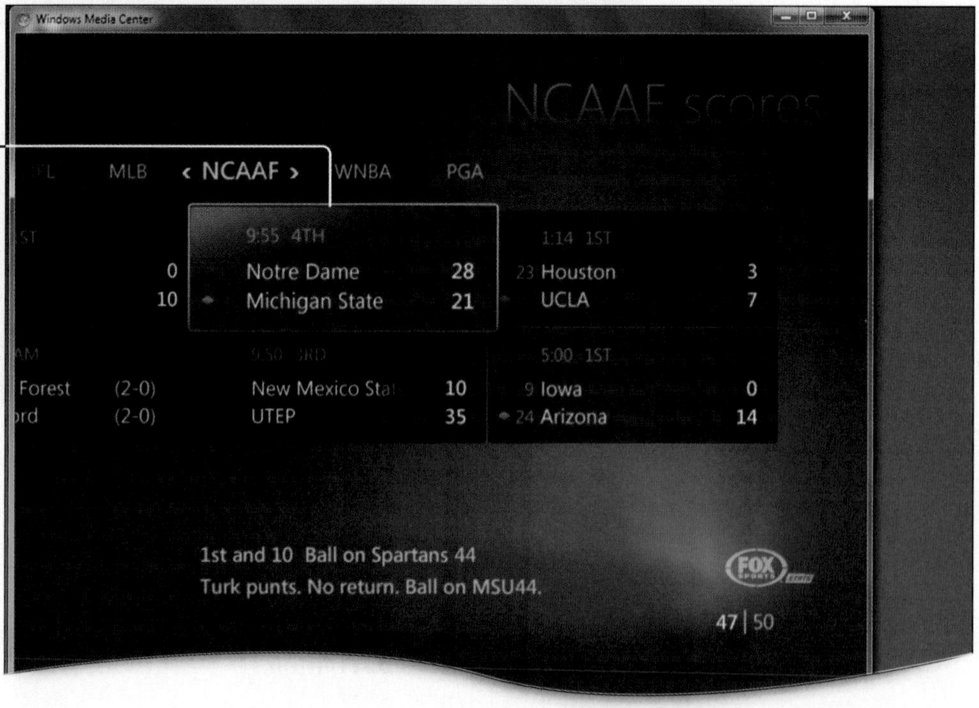

8 **Start** the **Snipping Tool** program, click the **New arrow**, and then click **Full-screen Snip**. In the **Snipping Tool** mark-up window, click the **Save Snip** button.

9 In the **Save As** dialog box, in the **navigation pane**, scroll down as necessary, and then under **Computer**, click your USB flash drive so that it displays in the address bar. Navigate to your **Windows 7 Chapter 6** folder, and then as the file name, type **Lastname_Firstname_6B_Sports_Snip** Be sure the file type is **JPEG file**, and then press Enter. **Close** the **Snipping Tool** mark-up window. Hold this file until you finish Project 6B, and then submit this file as directed by your instructor.

10 When you are finished, click the **Back** button as necessary to return to the Media Center main menu.

11 Scroll to select **TV**, click **guide**, select **internet tv**, and then press Enter. If necessary, accept the terms and install. Locate an Internet TV program and display the opening screen for that program.

12 If you want to do so, play a show. When you are finished, click the **Back** button as necessary to return to the Media Center main menu.

Activity 6.27 | Setting Up Television in Media Center

You can set up your computer to receive live television. For this activity, you will need to have a cable connection available and a tuner installed in your computer.

> **Alert! | This activity is optional.**
>
> If you have no tuner installed, just read through the steps and examine the figures. For detailed information about connecting a TV signal to your computer, go to Windows Help and Support and search for *TV signal*.

1 With Media Center still displayed, press ↓ as necessary to select **TV**.

2 Press → as necessary to select **live tv setup**, and then press Enter.

The TV Setup window displays, which begins the process of configuring your computer to receive television broadcasts.

3 Under *Is this the correct region*, check to be sure the correct region is selected, and then click the *Yes, use this region to configure TV service* option button. Compare your screen with Figure 6.57.

The first step is to confirm your region. The default region is the United States.

Figure 6.57

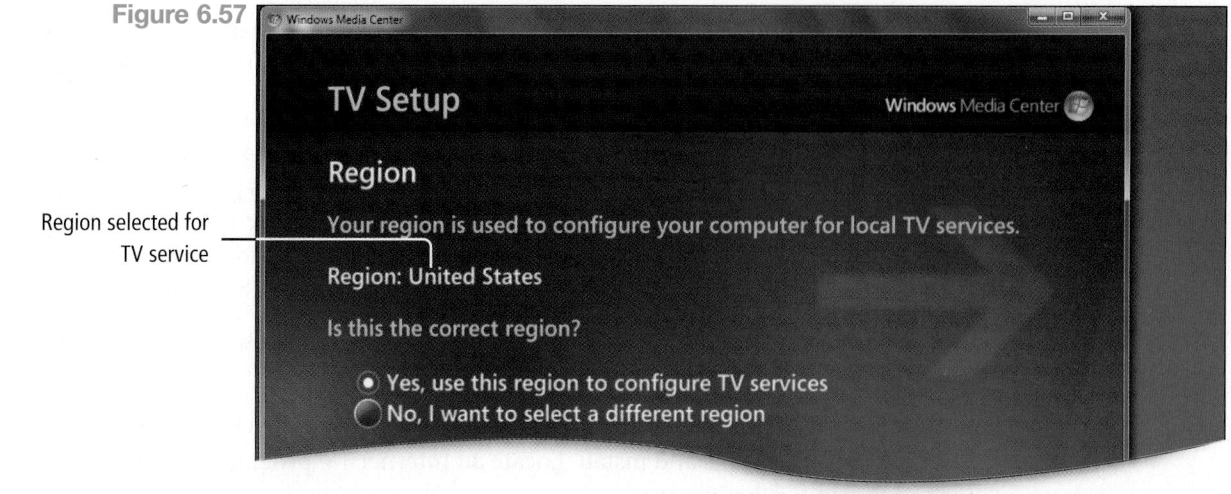

4 Click **Next**, type your ZIP code, and then click **Next**.

5 Read the *Program Guide Terms of Service*, click the **I agree** option button, and then click **Next** to download up-to-date television setup options.

Setting up your default configuration may take a few moments.

6 If the signal detection is unsuccessful, click the **Let me configure my TV signal manually** option button, and then answer the questions about your system and system provider.

7 **Confirm** the setup when it is completed, and then compare your screen with Figure 6.58.

Media Center will download the local TV Program Guide, and perform a channel scan to determine what channels are available. This may take several minutes.

Figure 6.58

Note | **If You Use the Guide**

If you choose to use the Guide to provide television program listings, some information will be sent to Microsoft. This information is anonymous, and is used to improve the quality and accuracy of the Guide service.

8 Click the **Back** button as necessary to return to the Media Center main menu. In the **TV** category, scroll to select **live tv**, and then press Enter. Follow the instructions to test your television signal.

9 When you are finished, click the **Stop** button , and then **Close** Media Center.

End You have completed Project 6B

Content-Based Assessments

Summary

Windows Live Photo Gallery enables you to import pictures, organize them, and add associated information, such as tags, keywords, ratings, and captions. You can edit photos and share photos by sending them as e-mail attachments or by burning them to a CD.

Windows Live Movie Maker enables you to work with video clips to create movies. After you have completed your movie, you can publish it to your computer or burn it to a DVD.

Windows Media Center turns your computer into an all-in-one entertainment device. By connecting your PC to a TV, you can use a remote control to listen to your music, view and record live TV, and view your movies and photos. Windows Media Center is optimized for widescreen and HD displays.

Key Terms

- **10-foot interface** 402
- **2-foot interface** 402
- **Auto adjust** 379
- **AutoMovie theme** 389
- **Bitmap** 367
- **.bmp** 367
- **Caption** 378
- **Card reader** 371
- **Color Temperature** 382
- **Compress** 386
- **Credits** 392
- **Crop** 383
- **Digital video editing** 389
- **Exposure** 380
- **Flash memory reader** 371
- **fps** 395
- **Frame** 395
- **Frame rate** 395
- **.gif** 367
- **Graphic Interchange Format** 367
- **Memory card reader** 371
- **Movie file** 389
- **Movie Maker tab** 391
- **Pan-and-zoom** 391
- **Photos** 366
- **Pixel** 370
- **Playback Indicator** 391
- **.png** 367
- **Portable Network Graphics** 367
- **Project (Windows Live Movie Maker)** 389
- **Resolution** 370
- **Saturation** 382
- **Storyboard** 391
- **Tint** 382
- **Transition** 391
- **Video clip** 395
- **Windows DVD Maker** 399
- **Windows Live Essentials** 363
- **Windows Media Center** 402
- **Windows Live Movie Maker** 389
- **Windows Live Photo Gallery** 366
- **.wmv** 389

Matching

Match each term in the second column with its correct definition in the first column by writing the letter of the term on the blank line in front of the correct definition.

____ 1. A collection of free programs downloadable from Microsoft that includes programs that enable you to organize and edit photos, edit and publish videos, stay in touch with your friends, create an e-mail account, and customize your Web browser.

____ 2. A photo and video organizer in Windows 7 with which you can view, manage, and edit digital pictures.

____ 3. The amount of fine detail that is visible in an image when it is printed or displayed on a computer monitor.

____ 4. The smallest element used to form the composition of an image.

____ 5. Text that accompanies images or videos, either as a supplemental description or a transcript of spoken words.

____ 6. The brightness and contrast of a photo.

A Caption
B Color temperature
C Crop
D Digital video editing
E Exposure
F Movie file
G Pixel
H Project
I Resolution
J Saturation
K Tint
L Windows Live Essentials

____ 7. A photo effect that makes a photo appear cooler (more blue) or warmer (more earth tones).

____ 8. A photo effect that changes the level of green or red in a photo.

____ 9. A photo effect that changes a photo's color intensity.

____ 10. To remove unwanted parts of the photo.

____ 11. A program with which you can combine audio, video, and still images to create a file that can be converted into a movie.

____ 12. The process of combining audio, video, and still images to create a file that can be converted into a movie.

____ 13. A file that keeps track of the pictures, videos, and other files you have imported, and how those files have been arranged.

____ 14. The file created by Windows Live Movie Maker when you publish a completed project.

____ 15. The file extension for a Windows Media Video file.

M Windows Live Movie Maker

N Windows Live Photo Gallery

O .wmv

Multiple Choice

Circle the correct answer.

1. The Movie Maker feature with which you can create a polished movie in a few seconds by adding your content and then selecting a theme is:
   A. storyboard **B.** pan-and-zoom **C.** AutoMovie

2. In Movie Maker, the line in the storyboard that shows the current location is the:
   A. frame **B.** playback indicator **C.** auto adjust

3. In Movie Maker, the view that shows a simple sequence of files, clips, transitions, and effects is the:
   A. storyboard **B.** frame **C.** caption

4. The manner in which a movie moves from one clip to another is:
   A. pan-and-zoom **B.** a transition **C.** exposure

5. A list at the end of a movie to identify people who worked on the movie or sources of information is the:
   A. bitmap **B.** storyboard **C.** credits

6. In Movie Maker, a short video presentation is referred to as a:
   A. frame **B.** video clip **C.** pixel

7. A feature with which you can create DVDs is:
   A. Windows Media Center **B.** Windows Live Essentials **C.** Windows DVD Maker

8. A feature with which you can use your computer as your home entertainment center is:
   A. Windows Media Center **B.** Windows Live Essentials **C.** Windows Live Movie Maker

9. The term that refers to the ability to control Windows Media Center by sitting 10 feet away from the screen is:
   A. frame rate **B.** 10-foot interface **C.** saturation

10. To view live television on your computer using Windows Media Center, your PC must have a:
    A. 2-foot interface **B.** card reader **C.** tuner

Content-Based Assessments

Apply 6A skills from these Objectives:

1. Download Windows Live Essentials Photo Gallery and Movie Maker
2. Locate, View, and Share Photos Using Windows Live Photo Gallery
3. Add, Tag, Rate, and Edit Photos Using Windows Live Photo Gallery
4. Use Windows Live Movie Maker to Create a Movie Using Photos
5. Create a Movie Using Video Clips

Skills Review | Project 6C Using Windows Live Photo Gallery

Project Files

For Project 6C, you will need the following files:

Student Resource CD (or a USB flash drive containing these files)
win06_6C_Answer_Sheet (Word document)

You will save your snip file as:

Lastname_Firstname_6C_Answer_Sheet

Project Results

1 **Close** [X] all open windows. On the taskbar, click the **Windows Explorer** button. In the **navigation pane**, click the drive that contains the student files for this textbook, and then navigate to **Chapter_Files ▶ Chapter_06**. Double-click the Word file **win06_6C_Answer_Sheet** to open Word and display the document. Press F12 to display the **Save As** dialog box in Word, navigate to your **Windows 7 Chapter 6** folder, and then using your own name, save the document as **Lastname_Firstname_6C_Answer_Sheet** If necessary, click OK if a message regarding formats displays.

On the taskbar, click the **Word** button to minimize the window and leave your Word document accessible from the taskbar. Close Windows Explorer. As you complete each step in this project, click the Word button on the taskbar to open the document, type your one-letter answer in the appropriate cell of the Word table, and then on the taskbar, click the button again to minimize the window for the next step.

Be sure that the **Cactus Pictures** folder and the **Flower Pictures** folder display in the navigation pane. Then, hold down Ctrl and click the **Cactus Pictures** folder name and the **Flower Pictures** folder name. As a result of this action, which of the following statements is true?

A. A tag named *Folders* is added to all of the photos.
B. All the pictures from the two selected folders display.
C. Both A. and B.

2 In the **navigation pane** click **Cactus Pictures** to display only the cactus photos. Right-click in a blank area under the photos, point to **View**, and then if necessary, click **Thumbnails with file name** to make it the active view. From the same menu, point to **Sort by**, and then if necessary, sort the photos by **File name** in **Ascending** order. How many photos are in this folder?

A. 15
B. 16
C. 17

3 Double-click the photo **IMG_1567-1**. The result of this action is:

A. The Add Tags box opens in the Info Pane.
B. The photo displays in the Preview Picture window.
C. The photo is moved to the first item in the list.

4 Which of the following steps could you take to rate this photograph?

A. Both B. and C.
B. On the Edit tab, in the Organize group, click the Rate button.
C. On the View tab, click the Tag and caption pane to display the Info Pane if it is not already displayed, and then click one of the stars displayed below the file size.

(Project 6C Using Windows Live Photo Gallery continues on the next page)

Skills Review | Project 6C Using Windows Live Photo Gallery (continued)

5 On the **Edit tab**, in the **Iterate group**, click the **Next** button *three* times to display **IMG_1581-1** in the Preview Picture window. On the **Edit tab**, in the **Adjustments group**, click the top portion of the **Auto adjust** button. What is the result of this action?

A. The picture becomes lighter and whiter.

B. The picture becomes smaller in size.

C. The Preview Picture window closes.

6 On the **Edit tab**, in the **Iterate group**, click the **Previous** button one time; if a message displays, click **OK**, and then view the picture of the group of small white cacti. To create a picture that shows only the lower portion of the picture without the cacti, what command in the **Adjustments group** could you use?

A. Crop

B. Red eye

C. Straighten

7 At the right end of the Ribbon, click **Close file** to close the **Preview Picture** window. On the **Home tab**, in the **Share group**, click the upper portion of the **Slide show** button. When the slide show begins, point to the upper portion of the screen to display a black bar with commands, click **Change theme**, and then click **Sepia**. What is the result of this action?

A. The photos display in brighter colors.

B. The photos display like faded old photos without color.

C. The photos display borders.

8 Using the same technique, change the theme to **Cinematic**. Press Esc to return to the gallery. On the **Create tab**, in the **Share group**, click **Order prints**. What is the result of this action?

A. A list of companies that can accept your electronic photos and create prints displays.

B. The Print dialog box displays.

C. A list of photo paper sizes displays.

9 Click **Cancel**. In the navigation pane, click the **Flower Pictures** folder. Press Ctrl + A to select all 15 files, and then on the **Create tab**, in the **Share group**, click **Movie**. According to the **Preview monitor**, how long is the movie you have created?

A. 01:45.00 (1 minute and 45 seconds)

B. 15.00 seconds

C. 30 seconds

10 Be sure that the **playback indicator** is to the left of the first image—if necessary click the first image to place it here. On the **Home tab**, in the **Add group**, click the **Add title** button. As the title text type **Colorful Flowers** and then play the entire movie. The length of your movie is now:

A. Shorter than it was before

B. Longer than it was before

C. The movie length did not change

Close the movie window and do not save the changes. Be sure you have typed all of your answers in your Word document. **Save** and close your Word document, and submit it as directed by your instructor. **Close** all open windows.

End You have completed Project 6C

Content-Based Assessments

Apply **6B** skills from these Objectives:

- **6** Navigate and Configure Windows Media Center
- **7** Use Windows Media Center to Play Media from Your Computer
- **8** Use Windows Media Center to View Sports, Internet TV, and Live TV

Skills Review | Project 6D Using Windows Media Center

Project Files

For Project 6D, you will need the following files:

Student Resource CD (or a USB flash drive containing these files)
win06_6D_Answer_Sheet (Word document)

You will save your snip files as:

Lastname_Firstname_6D_Answer_Sheet

Project Results

1 **Close** all open windows. On the taskbar, click the **Windows Explorer** button. In the **navigation pane**, click the drive that contains the student files for this textbook, and then navigate to **Chapter_Files ▶ Chapter_06**. Double-click the Word file **win06_6D_Answer_Sheet** to open Word and display the document. Press F12 to display the **Save As** dialog box in Word, navigate to your **Windows 7 Chapter 6** folder, and then using your own name, save the document as **Lastname_Firstname_6D_Answer_Sheet** If necessary, click OK if a message regarding formats displays.

On the taskbar, click the **Word** button to minimize the window and leave your Word document accessible from the taskbar. Close Windows Explorer. As you complete each step in this project, click the Word button on the taskbar to open the document, type your one-letter answer in the appropriate cell of the Word table, and then on the taskbar, click the button again to minimize the window for the next step.

Start Windows Media Center and examine the screen. If Media Center displays using the full screen, click the Restore Down button and increase the size of the window to just inside the borders of the screen. What happens when you point to the upper left corner of the window?

A. The Back button and the Windows Media Center logo display.

B. The Internet Explorer icon displays.

C. A TV icon displays.

2 On a keyboard, which keys are used to move vertically to display the categories within the main Media Center menu?

A. ↑ and ↓

B. ← and →

C. Home or End

3 On a keyboard, which keys are used to move horizontally through the commands within a category?

A. ↑ and ↓

B. ← and →

C. Home or End

4 To change the Media Center settings, navigate to which main menu category?

A. Extras

B. Tasks

C. Pictures + Video

(Project 6D Using Windows Media Center continues on the next page)

Skills Review | Project 6D Using Windows Media Center (continued)

5 Go to **Tasks** and display the **settings** menu. On the **settings** menu, which option includes the **Parental Controls**?

A. Media Libraries

B. Extender

C. General

6 On the **settings** menu, click **Pictures**, and then click **Favorite Pictures**. Which of the following is *not* an option?

A. Use all pictures

B. Use pictures added in the last 3 months

C. Use pictures over 1 year old

7 Point to the upper left corner of the window, and then click the **Back** button as necessary to return to the main menu. Display the **Extras** category, and then display the **Extras Library**. What is the name of the game that displays a picture of a spider on a playing card?

A. Spider man

B. Spider Solitaire

C. Bug Game

8 Point to the upper left corner of the window, and then click the **Back** button as necessary to return to the main menu. Display the **Music** category, display the music library, and then display **artists**. Point to any artist's name. Which of the following best describes what displays at the bottom of the screen when you point to an artist name?

A. The artist's picture displays.

B. The number of tracks and the total time of the tracks displays.

C. The artist's most recently played song displays.

9 Point to the upper left corner of the window, and then click the **Back** button as necessary to return to the main menu. Display the **TV** category and then select **guide**. What is your result?

A. Categories such as *News*, *Comedy*, and *Drama* display.

B. Thumbnail images of shows in each category display.

C. Both A. and B.

10 Point to the upper left corner of the window, and then click the **Back** button as necessary to return to the main menu. From which category on the main menu can you burn a CD or a DVD?

A. Music

B. Tasks

C. Pictures + Videos

Be sure you have typed all of your answers in your Word document. **Save** and close your Word document, and submit it as directed by your instructor. **Close** all open windows.

End **You have completed Project 6D**

Apply 6A skills from these Objectives:

1. Download Windows Live Essentials Photo Gallery and Movie Maker
2. Locate, View, and Share Photos Using Windows Live Photo Gallery
3. Add, Tag, Rate, and Edit Photos Using Windows Live Photo Gallery
4. Use Windows Live Movie Maker to Create a Movie Using Photos
5. Create a Movie Using Video Clips

Mastering Windows 7 | Project 6E Using Windows Live Photo Gallery

In the following Mastering Windows 7 project, you will view a slideshow, edit the contrast and brightness of a picture, and then crop the picture. You will capture and save a screen that will look similar to Figure 6.59.

Project Files

For Project 6E, you will need the following files:

Student Resource CD (or a USB flash drive containing these files)
New Snip file

You will save your file as:

Lastname_Firstname_6E_Cropped_Photo_Snip

Project Results

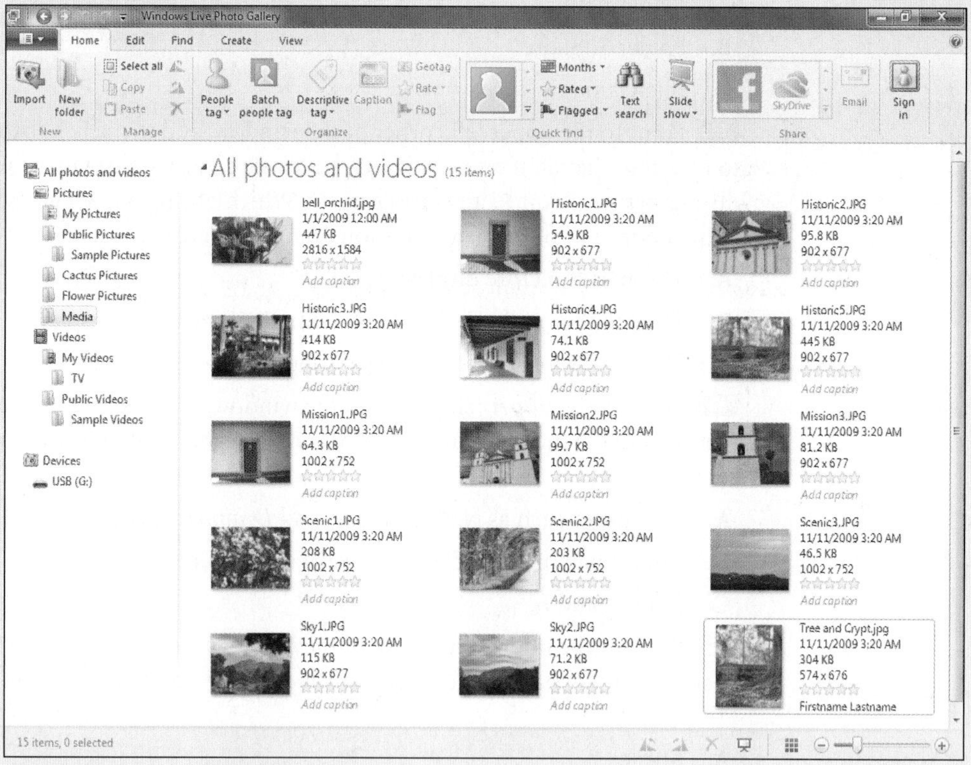

Figure 6.59

(Project 6E Using Windows Live Photo Gallery continues on the next page)

Mastering Windows 7 | Project 6E Using Windows Live Photo Gallery (continued)

1 From Windows Explorer, navigate to your **Student Resource CD**. Add the **Media** folder to the Photo Gallery, which can be found at **Documents ▶ Bell_Orchid ▶ Santa_Barbara ▶ Sales_Marketing**. If necessary, open the folder to display the 14 photos in the gallery window. Be sure the **View** is set to **Thumbnails with file name**. Play a slideshow of the 14 photos in the gallery. Press Esc to end the slideshow.

2 On the **View tab**, in the **Show details group**, click **All details**. At the bottom of the screen, on the **navigation bar**, move the slider so that the thumbnails display with no more than three pictures in a row.

3 Double-click **Historic5.jpg** to display it in the **Preview Picture** window. On the **Edit tab**, in the **Adjustments group**, click the **Fine tune** button. In the **Edit Pane** on the right, click **Adjust exposure**, and then increase the **Brightness** slightly and decrease the **Contrast** slightly. Adjust the color by increasing both the **Color temperature** and the **Saturation** slightly.

4 In the **Adjustments group**, click **Crop**, and then drag the corners of the crop area as necessary so that only the large tree and the crypt on the right are included, along with the entire top and bottom of the picture. In the **Manage group**, click **Make a copy**. As the **File name**, type **Tree and Crypt** and then click **Save**. If a message displays, click **OK**. **Close** the **Edit Pane**, and then at the right end of the **Edit tab**, click **Close file** to redisplay the gallery. The original picture is cropped, and a copy of the original is saved with the name *Tree and Crypt*.

5 In the details displayed to the right of the cropped picture named *Tree and Crypt*, click **Add caption**, type your first name and last name, and then press Enter. Create a **Full-screen Snip**, and then **Save** the snip in your chapter folder as **Lastname_Firstname_6E_Cropped_Photo_Snip** Submit this file as directed by your instructor. **Close** all windows.

End **You have completed Project 6E**

Apply **6B** skills from these Objectives:

- **6** Navigate and Configure Windows Media Center
- **7** Use Windows Media Center to Play Media from Your Computer
- **8** Use Windows Media Center to View Sports, Internet TV, and Live TV

Mastering Windows 7 | Project 6F Using Windows Media Center

In the following Mastering Windows 7 project, you will configure Media Center. You will capture and save a screen that will look similar to Figure 6.60.

Project Files

For Project 6F, you will need the following file:

New Snip file

You will save your file as:

Lastname_Firstname_6F_Optimization_Snip

Project Results

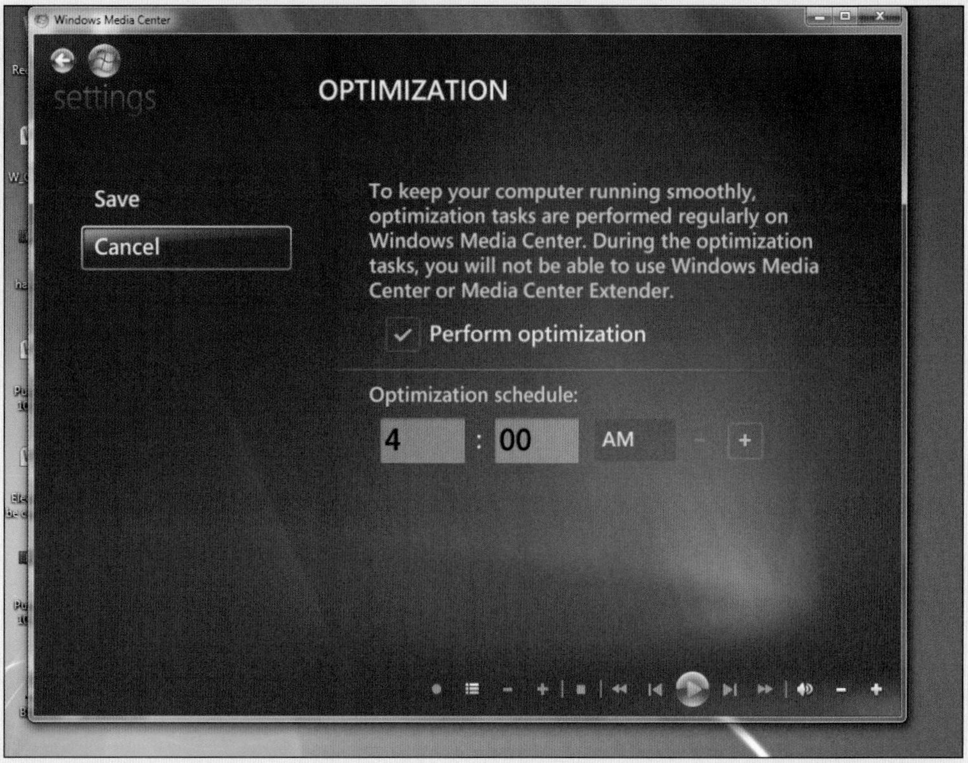

Figure 6.60

(Project 6F Using Windows Media Center continues on the next page)

Mastering Windows 7 | Project 6F Using Windows Media Center (continued)

1 **Start** Windows Media Center. Be sure the window is not maximized, but occupies the majority of your screen in a window.

2 From the **Tasks** category, click **Settings**, click the **General** command, and then open the **Optimization** window. Click the **Perform optimization** check box.

3 Create a **Full-screen Snip**, save it as **Lastname_Firstname_6F_Optimization_Snip** and then submit this file as directed by your instructor.

4 If you want to have your Media Center optimized on a regular basis, set a time and click Save; otherwise, click Cancel. Return to the Media Center main menu. **Close** Media Center and any other open windows.

End **You have completed Project 6F**

Outcomes-Based Assessments

Rubric

The following outcomes-based assessments are *open-ended assessments*. That is, there is no specific correct result; your result will depend on your approach to the information provided. Make *Professional Quality* your goal. Use the following scoring rubric to guide you in *how* to approach the problem, and then to evaluate *how well* your approach solves the problem.

The *criteria*—Software Mastery, Content, Format and Layout, and Process—represent the knowledge and skills you have gained that you can apply to solving the problem. The *levels of performance*—Professional Quality, Approaching Professional Quality, or Needs Quality Improvements—help you and your instructor evaluate your result.

	Your completed project is of Professional Quality if you:	**Your completed project is Approaching Professional Quality if you:**	**Your completed project Needs Quality Improvements if you:**
1-Software Mastery	Choose and apply the most appropriate skills, tools, and features and identify efficient methods to solve the problem.	Choose and apply some appropriate skills, tools, and features, but not in the most efficient manner.	Choose inappropriate skills, tools, or features, or are inefficient in solving the problem.
2-Content	Construct a solution that is clear and well organized, contains content that is accurate, appropriate to the audience and purpose, and is complete. Provide a solution that contains no errors in spelling, grammar, or style.	Construct a solution in which some components are unclear, poorly organized, inconsistent, or incomplete. Misjudge the needs of the audience. Have some errors in spelling, grammar, or style, but the errors do not detract from comprehension.	Construct a solution that is unclear, incomplete, or poorly organized; contains some inaccurate or inappropriate content; and contains many errors in spelling, grammar, or style. Do not solve the problem.
3-Format and Layout	Format and arrange all elements to communicate information and ideas, clarify function, illustrate relationships, and indicate relative importance.	Apply appropriate format and layout features to some elements, but not others. Overuse features, causing minor distraction.	Apply format and layout that does not communicate information or ideas clearly. Do not use format and layout features to clarify function, illustrate relationships, or indicate relative importance. Use available features excessively, causing distraction.
4-Process	Use an organized approach that integrates planning, development, self-assessment, revision, and reflection.	Demonstrate an organized approach in some areas, but not others; or, use an insufficient process of organization throughout.	Do not use an organized approach to solve the problem.

Outcomes-Based Assessments

Apply a combination of the 6A and 6B skills.

Problem Solving | Project 6G—Help Desk

In this project, you will construct a solution by applying any combination of the skills you practiced from the Objectives in Projects 6A and 6B.

Project Files

For Project 6G, you will need the following file:

win06_6G_Help_Desk

You will save your document as:

Lastname_Firstname_6G_Help_Desk

From the student files that accompany this textbook, open the **Chapter_Files** folder, and then in **Chapter_06** folder, locate and open the Word document **win06_6G_Help_Desk**. Save the document in your chapter folder as **Lastname_Firstname_6G_Help_Desk**

The following e-mail question has arrived at the Help Desk from an employee at the Bell Orchid Hotel's corporate office. In the Word form, construct a response based on your knowledge of Windows 7. Although an e-mail response is not as formal as a letter, you should still use good grammar, good sentence structure, professional language, and a polite tone. Save your document and submit the response as directed by your instructor.

To: Help Desk

I take a large number of pictures and distribute them widely to coworkers in all of our hotels. I use Windows Live Photo Gallery to edit and organize my photographs, but they are very large and take a long time to send. In fact, if I combine two or three photos, some e-mail accounts will reject the attachment because it is too large. I know there is no way to compress photo files in Windows Live Photo Gallery. Is there a way to go directly from Windows Live Photo Gallery to another program to compress files?

End **You have completed Project 6G**

Apply a combination of the 6A and 6B skills.

Problem Solving | Project 6H—Help Desk

In this project, you will construct a solution by applying any combination of the skills you practiced from the Objectives in Projects 6A and 6B.

Project Files

For Project 6H, you will need the following file:
win06_6H_Help_Desk

You will save your document as:
Lastname_Firstname_6H_Help_Desk

From the student files that accompany this textbook, open the **Chapter_Files** folder, and then in **Chapter_06** folder, locate and open the Word document **win06_6H_Help_Desk**. Save the document in your chapter folder as **Lastname_Firstname_6H_Help_Desk**

The following e-mail question has arrived at the Help Desk from an employee at the Bell Orchid Hotel's corporate office. In the Word form, construct a response based on your knowledge of Windows 7. Although an e-mail response is not as formal as a letter, you should still use good grammar, good sentence structure, professional language, and a polite tone. Save your document and submit the response as directed by your instructor.

To: Help Desk

I am working on a new Web site for the corporate office. I have several people who want to send me photographs to include in the site, and I would like to organize them in Windows Live Photo Gallery. What file formats are compatible with Windows Live Photo Gallery?

End You have completed Project 6H

Outcomes-Based Assessments

Apply a combination of the 6A and 6B skills.

Problem Solving | Project 6I—Help Desk

In this project, you will construct a solution by applying any combination of the skills you practiced from the Objectives in Projects 6A and 6B.

Project Files

For Project 6I, you will need the following file:

win06_6I_Help_Desk

You will save your document as:

Lastname_Firstname_6I_Help_Desk

From the student files that accompany this textbook, open the **Chapter_Files** folder, and then in **Chapter_06** folder, locate and open the Word document **win06_6I_Help_Desk**. Save the document in your chapter folder as **Lastname_Firstname_6I_Help_Desk**

The following e-mail question has arrived at the Help Desk from an employee at the Bell Orchid Hotel's corporate office. In the Word form, construct a response based on your knowledge of Windows 7. Although an e-mail response is not as formal as a letter, you should still use good grammar, good sentence structure, professional language, and a polite tone. Save your document and submit the response as directed by your instructor.

To: Help Desk

I am the Front Desk manager at the Miami hotel. We just installed a new computer in the Business Center for our guests to use. The computer includes a large flat-screen monitor. The box indicates that the computer is capable of playing live television. What program should I use to set up television reception, and what do I need to do to get started? I think guests in the Business Center might value this feature.

End **You have completed Project 6I**

Backing Up Your Computer and Setting Up a Home Network

OUTCOMES

At the end of this chapter you will be able to:

OBJECTIVES

Mastering these objectives will enable you to:

PROJECT 7A

Back up and restore your computer; restore earlier versions of files.

1. Back Up and Restore Files and Folders (p. 433)
2. Back Up and Restore Your Entire Computer (p. 438)
3. Configure System Restore and Recover Using Restore Points (p. 440)

PROJECT 7B

Install and secure a wired or wireless network and troubleshoot network problems.

4. Use the Network and Sharing Center to Set Up a Home Network (p. 445)
5. Secure and Troubleshoot a Home Network (p. 455)
6. Use Homegroup to Share Files and Printers on a Home Network (p. 461)

Tatiana Popova/Shutterstock

In This Chapter

It is always a good idea to protect against any loss of data by making a backup copy of all of your data. Additionally, there is always a chance that your computer could be damaged physically resulting in a catastrophic hardware failure. In this chapter, you will make backup copies of your data and restore your data so that you will be prepared in the event something causes the loss of your important files.

Connecting computers to a network enables each computer to share files and peripheral devices such as printers and scanners. You can use a network to control another computer in a remote location using your own computer's monitor, keyboard, and mouse. Networks are also used to collaborate with others in an organization.

The projects in this chapter relate to the **Bell Orchid Hotels**, headquartered in Boston, and which own and operate resorts and business-oriented hotels. Resort properties are located in popular destinations, including Honolulu, Orlando, San Diego, and Santa Barbara. The resorts offer deluxe accommodations and a wide array of dining options. Other Bell Orchid hotels are located in major business centers and offer the latest technology in their meeting facilities. The company plans to open new properties and update existing properties over the next ten years.

Project 7A Backing Up and Restoring Your Computer

Project Activities

In Activities 7.01 through 7.05, you will train with Steven Ramos and Barbara Hewitt, employees in the Information Technology Department at the Bell Orchid Hotels, so that you will be able to back up and restore your computer system and restore previous versions of documents. You will capture a screen that looks similar to Figure 7.1.

Project Files

For Project 7A, you will need the following files:

Student Data CD or a flash drive containing the student data files
New Snip file

You will save your file as:

Lastname_Firstname_7A_Alaska_Snip

Project Results

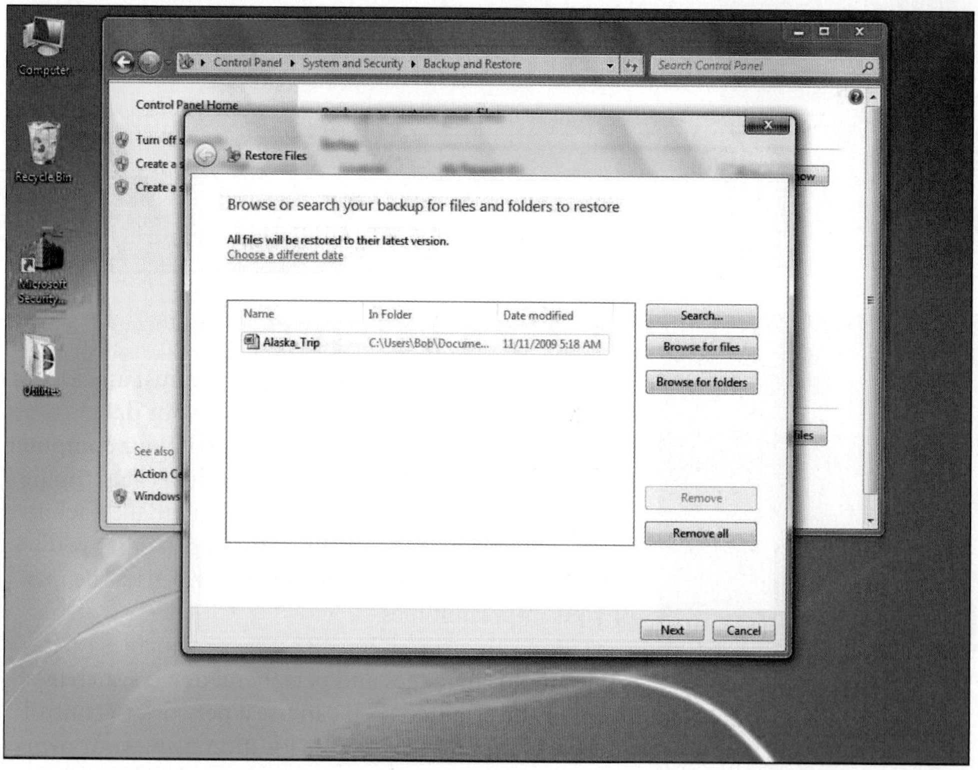

Figure 7.1
Project 7A Backing Up and Restoring Your Computer

Objective 1 | Back Up and Restore Files and Folders

Backing up is the process of creating a copy of your files somewhere other than on your computer—for example on a CD, a DVD, an ***external hard drive***, or by using an ***online backup service***. An external hard drive, also known as a ***portable hard drive***, is a disk drive that plugs into an external port on your computer, typically into a USB port. An online backup service—also referred to as a ***remote backup service*** or a ***managed backup service***—is a service that provides a system for backing up your computer files over the Internet on a scheduled basis and then storing the data securely on their computers. Two popular companies that provide this type of service are Carbonite and Mozy.

Back up your files so that you can restore them in the event of a virus attack on your computer, a hard disk drive failure, theft of your laptop computer, or a disaster such as a fire or flood. In the event of a fire, flood, or some other disaster in which you also lose your physical backups, you will be glad that you invested in an online backup service.

If you work in an organization, there is likely an automatic backup system in place, although it is always a good idea to confirm this with someone in your organization's Information Technology department. On your own computer, you will want to back up regularly to preserve your documents, photos, music, and all of the important information you have.

Alert! | Do You Have an External Hard Drive or a Writable CD or DVD Drive in the Computer at Which You Are Working?

For this activity, you will need an external hard drive. Alternatively, you will need a writable CD or DVD drive in your computer and a blank CD or DVD. You will also need to be logged on as the administrator. If you do not have this equipment, just read through this activity, or complete it when you have the appropriate equipment.

Activity 7.01 | Backing Up Files and Folders

Previously you practiced copying files and folders to a CD using the process known as *burning* a CD. When you burn a copy of a file or folder to a CD or DVD, or when you copy a file or folder to an external hard drive, each time you want to do a backup, you must manually select each file and folder that you want to back up. This can be time consuming.

The ***Set up backup wizard*** is a feature in Windows 7 that walks you step by step through the process of backing up your data. When you use the *Set up backup* wizard, Windows 7 keeps track of which files and folders are new or modified since the last backup. Then, when you make a new backup, you can back up all of the data on your computer, or only the files that have changed since the last time you made a backup.

It is good practice to establish a routine for backing up the files you create. Normally you do not need to back up program files or system files, because they rarely change and you can reinstall them from the original installation CDs.

For your files and folders, you can back up manually, or you can choose to have Windows 7 do it automatically according to a schedule that you establish.

In this activity, you will back up a document to a storage device.

Alert! | Is Automatic Backup Already Set Up on Your Computer?

If the computer you are using is already set up for automatic backups, and you know that the Bell_Orchid folder has been backed up, skip to Activity 7.02.

1 Be sure the **Bell_Orchid** folder has been copied to your **My Documents** folder. If necessary, copy the folder by using the technique that you practiced.

2 Plug in an external hard drive—if you have many documents, this is your best choice—or insert a blank CD or DVD. **Close** the AutoPlay dialog box. From the **Start** menu, display the **Control Panel**, and then under **System and Security**, click **Back up your computer**. Compare your screen with Figure 7.2.

> **Alert! | Is a CD or DVD Large Enough to Hold Your Data?**
>
> If you have a large number of documents, the backup could stop if the CD or DVD cannot hold your entire Documents library. If this happens, click More information, cancel the backup, and start it again by using an external hard drive.

If you plan to set up a regular schedule of backups, an external hard drive is the best device to use, especially if you have a lot of music files, videos, or pictures that you want to back up.

> **Alert! | Does a Date and Time for Last Backup or Next Backup Display in the Upper Portion of the Screen?**
>
> If a date and time for *Last backup* or *Next backup* display, a backup has already been set up on your computer. To complete this activity, under *Backup*, click the *Back up now* button. Follow the onscreen instructions, and when you are finished, close the Control Panel and move to Activity 7.02.

Figure 7.2

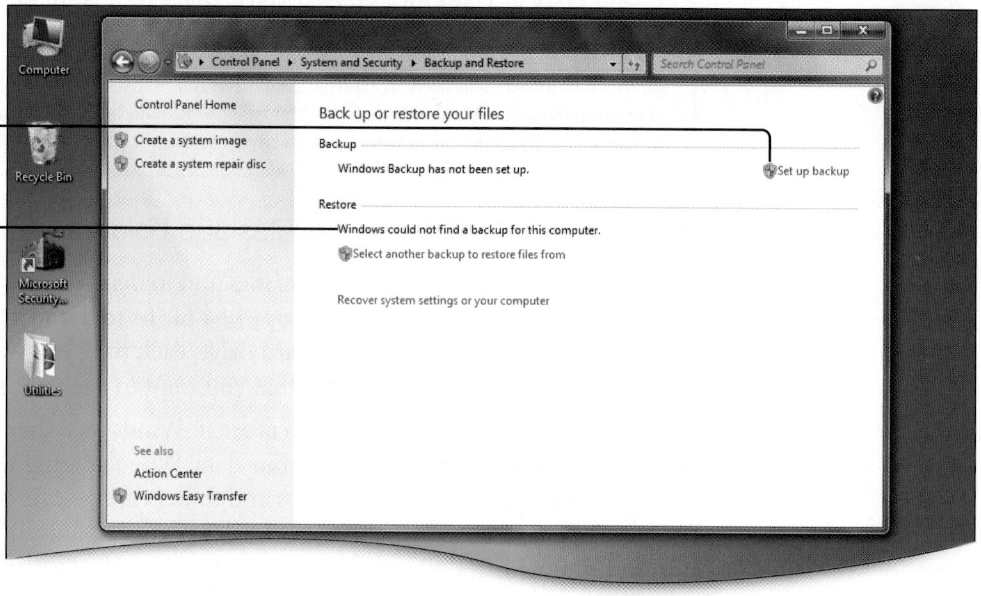

3 Under **Backup**, click **Set up backup**. Wait a few moments while the *Set up backup* wizard searches your system for an appropriate backup device—an alternative hard disk drive in your computer, an external hard drive, or a CD/DVD writer. Compare your screen with Figure 7.3.

The Windows recommendation is to save the backup on a drive other than the drive that contains the system files.

> **Alert! | Does Your Screen Differ?**
>
> If your computer has more than one hard disk drive, both drives will display, and the drive that does *not* contain the system files will be listed.

Figure 7.3

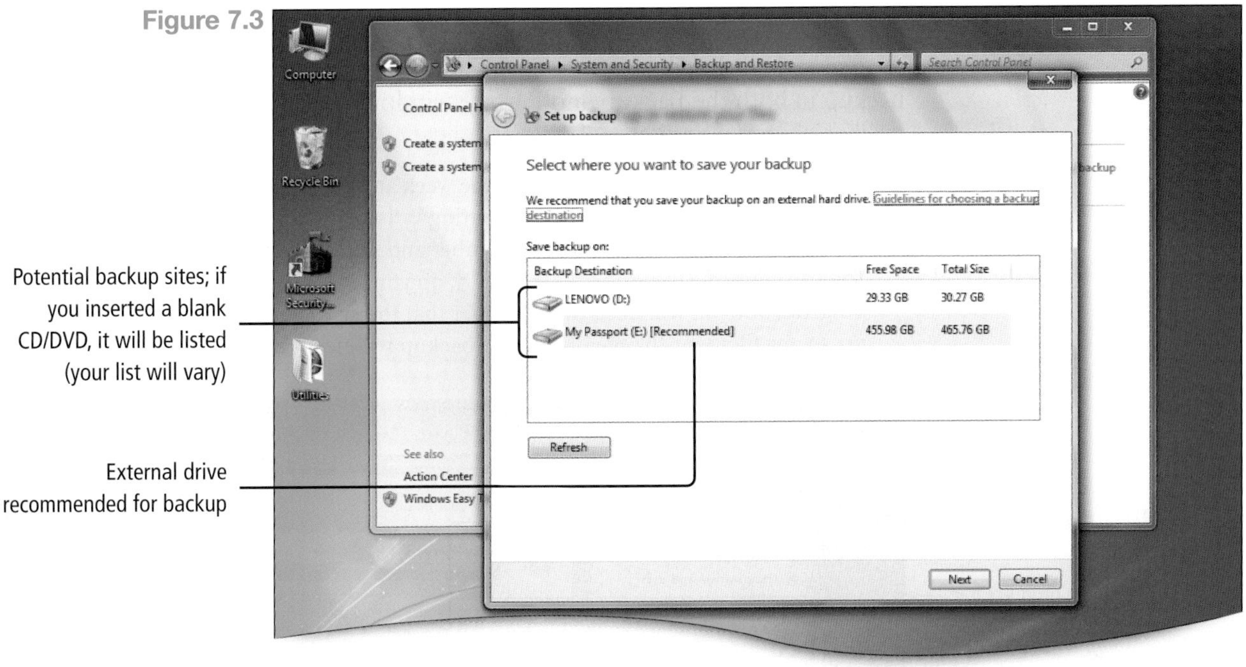

4 Under **Save backup on**, select your external hard drive or DVD/CD drive, and then click **Next**.

5 Under **What do you want to back up**, select the **Let me choose** option button, and then click **Next**. If necessary, clear—deselect—the *Include a system image of drives* check box.

6 Under **Data Files**, expand ▷ the **Libraries**, and then clear all check boxes *except* **Documents Library**. Compare your screen with Figure 7.4.

In this activity, you will back up only documents.

Figure 7.4

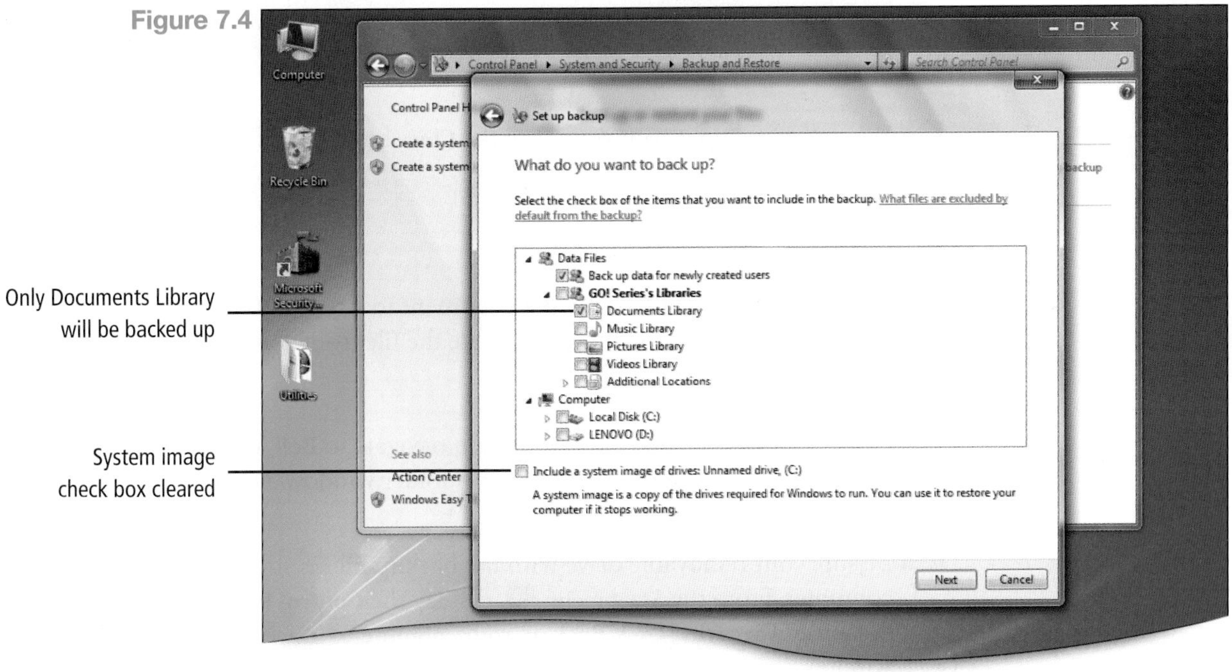

7 Click **Next**. Take a moment to review your backup settings, and then click the **Save settings and run backup** button. Notice that a progress bar indicates the status of the backup in both the Backup and Restore window and on the Control Panel icon in the taskbar, as shown in Figure 7.5.

Here you can also change the day of the week and the time of day of your automatic file backups. In this activity, the default setting is used. This process will take several minutes; the length of time depends on the number and size of the files in the Documents Library. You can continue to perform other work on your computer while the backup is in progress, but you will need to remember that the last saved version of each file is backed up, so any files you change during the backup will need to be backed up the next time.

Figure 7.5

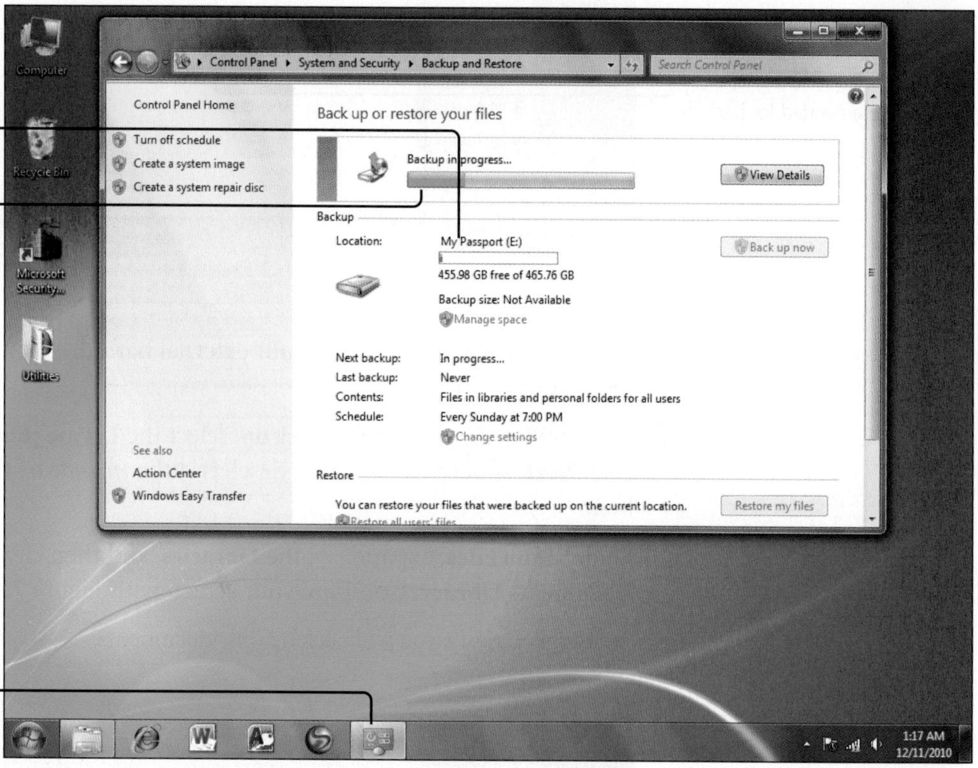

8 When the backup is complete, click the **Close** button to close the Control Panel window.

Activity 7.02 | Restoring a File

In this activity, you will back up a document to a removable storage device, set a schedule for future backups, and then delete the file from your system and restore it from the backup.

1 Open your **Documents** folder, and then navigate to **Bell_Orchid ▶ Corporate ▶ Information_Technology** to display this folder window. Delete the file **Alaska_Trip**. **Close** the folder window.

2 Be sure your removable drive with the backup files is still plugged into your computer. From the **Start** menu, display the **Control Panel**, and then under **System and Security**, click **Back up your computer**. Notice that the Backup and Restore window displays the size and date of the previous backup, and the date and time of the next scheduled backup, similar to Figure 7.6.

Figure 7.6

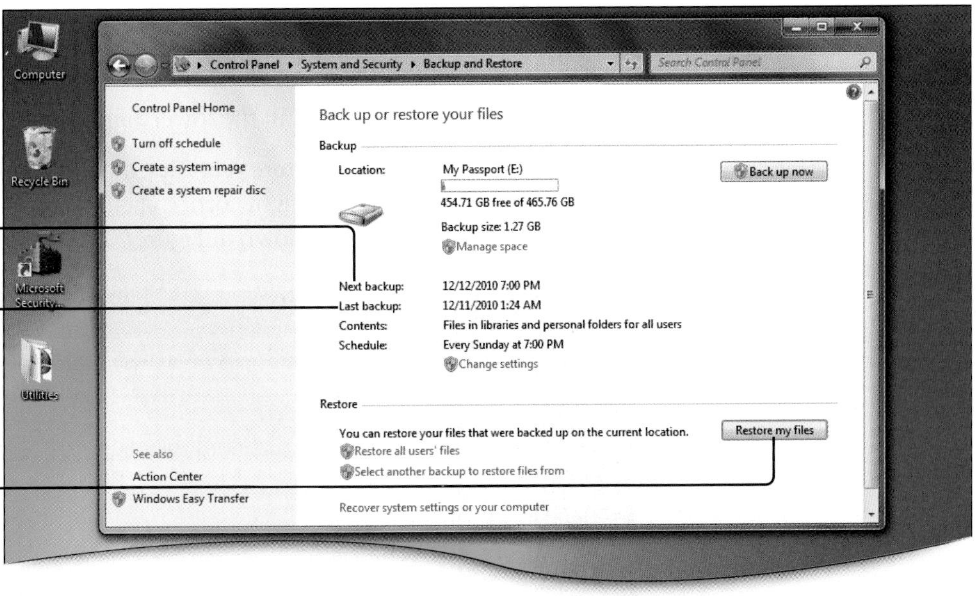

3 To restore the file from your backup, in the lower portion of the **Backup and Restore** window, under **Restore**, click the **Restore my files** button—it may take a few seconds for the screen to display.

4 In the **Restore Files** dialog box, click the **Browse for files** button. In the **Browse the backup for files** dialog box, in the **file list**, double-click the most recent backup. Navigate to **Bell_Orchid ▶ Corporate ▶ Information_Technology**. Click the **Alaska_Trip** document, and then at the bottom of the dialog box, click the **Add files** button. Notice that the file displays in the **Restore Files** dialog box, as shown in Figure 7.7.

Figure 7.7

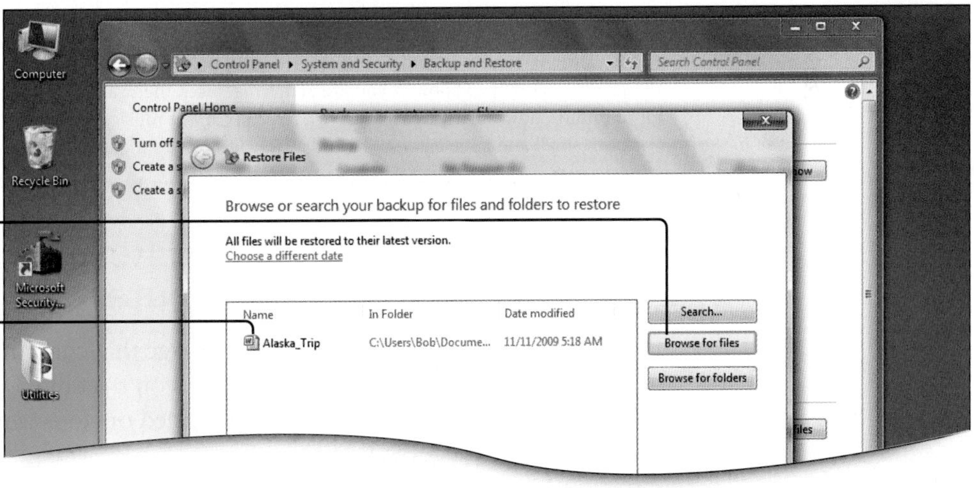

5 **Start** the **Snipping Tool** program, click the **New arrow**, and then click **Full-screen Snip**. In the **Snipping Tool** mark-up window, click the **Save Snip** button.

6 In the **Save As** dialog box, in the **navigation pane**, scroll down as necessary, and then under **Computer** click your USB flash drive so that it displays in the **address bar**. On the toolbar, click the **New Folder** button, type **Windows 7 Chapter 7** and then press Enter.

7 In the **file list**, double-click your **Windows 7 Chapter 7** folder to open it. Click in the **File name** box, and then replace the selected text by typing, using your own name, **Lastname_Firstname_7A_Alaska_Snip** Be sure the file type is **JPEG**, and then press Enter. **Close** the **Snipping Tool** mark-up window. Hold this file until you finish Project 7A, and then submit this file as directed by your instructor.

8. In the **Restore Files** dialog box, in the lower right corner, click **Next**.

9. Under **Where do you want to restore your files**, be sure that **In the original location** is selected, and then in the lower right corner, click **Restore**. When the message *Your files have been restored* displays, as shown in Figure 7.8, in the lower right corner, click **Finish**.

Figure 7.8

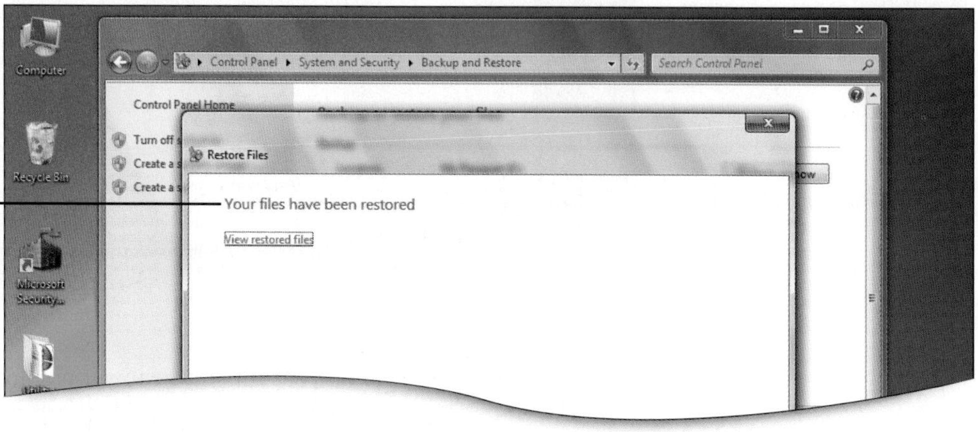

10. **Close** all open windows. Open your **Documents** folder, and then navigate to **Bell_Orchid ▶ Corporate ▶ Information_Technology** to display this folder window. Notice that the **Alaska_Trip** file is restored to your folder. **Close** all open windows.

> **More Knowledge | Choosing an External Hard Drive**
>
> External hard drives come in two basic shapes and many sizes. The most compact hard drives are about the size of a deck of playing cards, and can be carried in a pocket. The drives with the largest capacities tend to be about the size of a hardcover book. If you are an average user, the smaller drives are probably sufficient. If you take a lot of photos, download videos, or have a large library of music, you might want to use a higher-capacity drive. For both small and large external hard drives, *www.westerndigital.com* is a good source of information.

Objective 2 | Back Up and Restore Your Entire Computer

A Windows ***system image*** is a backup image that contains copies of your programs, system settings, and files. The image is created on a set of CDs, DVDs, or on an external hard disk, and then if your computer is damaged or stops working, you can use this image to restore the contents of your computer.

If you must use a system image to restore your computer, it is a *complete* restoration of all programs, system settings, and files. Thus, you must keep in mind that:

- *You cannot selectively restore only programs or only system settings.* The *files* that will be restored are those that were on your computer at the time the image was created. Since that time, certainly you will have updated many files and created many new files.
- *The programs that will be restored are those that were on your computer at the time the image was created.* If you have installed new programs or updates to existing programs, they will not be restored. You will have to update or reinstall those programs.

Thus, the importance of making frequent backups of files and folders that contain your *data* is evident. After a complete restoration of your computer, you would then restore your latest backup of files and folders to get your most up-to-date data.

Activity 7.03 | Backing Up and Restoring Your Entire Computer

This type of backup can only be made on a CD, a DVD, or an external hard drive. If you try to use CDs or DVDs, you will probably need quite a few of them. A large external hard drive is probably a better choice for this type of backup.

You create the image from the Backup and Restore window, as shown in Figure 7.9. On the left side of the screen, click the *Create a system image*, and then follow the steps in the wizard. The steps include choosing a destination drive and selecting which—if any—drives other than the system drive should be backed up. Creating a system image of this type is commonly a lengthy process. Be sure your system is exactly the way you want it before you start the image. For example, install any new programs, install updates to any existing programs, delete old shortcuts and create new ones, and so on. When the backup is complete, you will be asked if you want to create a bootable system CD—it is always a good idea to have a boot disc available.

Figure 7.9

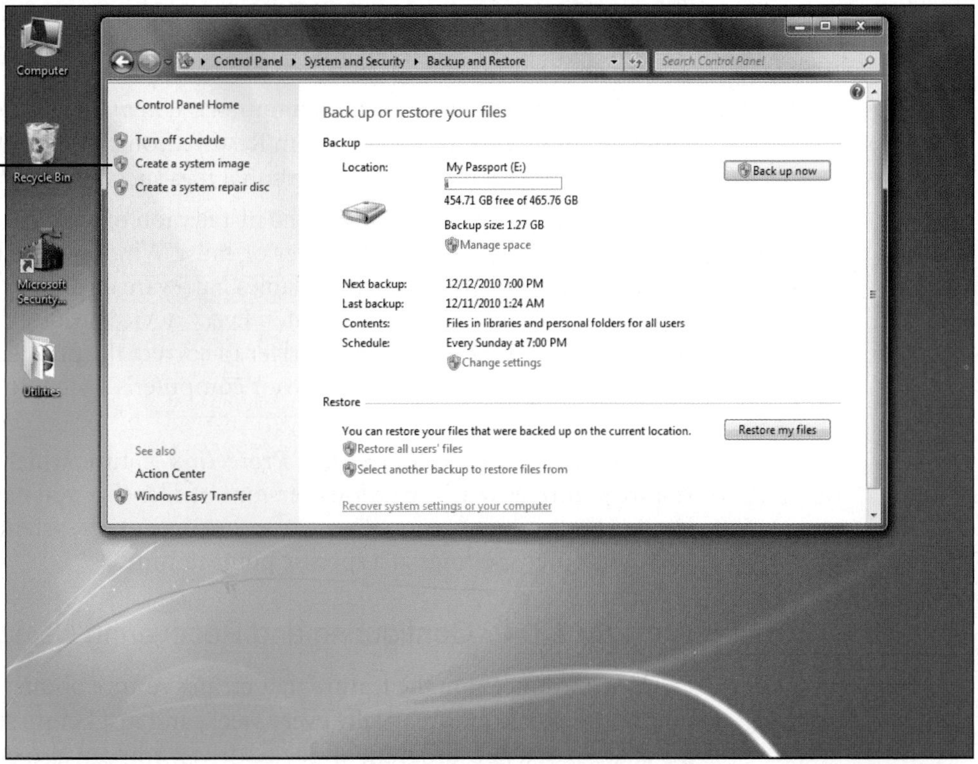

The process for restoring your entire computer varies depending on whether or not you have a Windows 7 installation disc—one may have come with your computer, but that is not always the case. If you have the disc, the process includes inserting the disc, restarting the computer, and then following the prompts after clicking *Repair your computer*. If you do not have the Windows 7 installation disc, the process includes restarting the computer, pressing F8 to display the *Advanced Boot Options* menu, and then following the prompts after clicking *Repair your computer*.

To check your comprehension of backing up and restoring your entire computer, take a moment to answer the following questions:

1. A ______________ ______________ is used to restore your computer and contains copies of your programs, system settings, and files.
2. A key thing to know about a system image backup is that if you use it to restore your computer, it is a ______________ restoration of the programs, system settings, and files that were in place at the time of the backup—you cannot restore only programs or settings selectively.
3. A system image backup can be made on a CD, DVD, or an ______________ ______________ ______________.
4. Before creating an image with Windows Complete PC, you should install any new programs and install ______________ to any existing programs.
5. The process for restoring your entire computer varies depending on whether or not you have a ______________ ______________ ______________ ______________.

Objective 3 | Configure System Restore and Recover Using Restore Points

System Restore restores your computer's *system* files—*not* your data files—to an earlier point in time. By using System Restore, you can undo system changes to your computer without affecting your personal files such as e-mail, documents, and photos.

For example, in rare instances the installation of a program or a ***driver*** can cause an unexpected change to your computer or cause Windows 7 to behave in an unpredictable manner. A driver is software that enables hardware or devices such as a printer, mouse, or keyboard to work with your computer. Every device needs a driver for it to work. Usually you can uninstall the program or driver to correct the problem, but if uninstalling fails to solve the problem, you can restore your computer's system to an earlier date when everything worked correctly.

System Restore uses the ***System Protection*** feature, which regularly creates and saves ***restore points***, as well as previous versions of files that you have modified. A restore point is a representation of a stored state of your computer's system files—like a snapshot of your computer's settings at a specific point in time.

Activity 7.04 | Configuring and Recovering Using Restore Points

System Protection, the feature that creates restore points, is on by default. Restore points are created automatically every week, and just before significant events, such as the installation of a new program or device driver. You can also create a restore point manually at any time.

You can control how System Restore works from the System Protection tab of the System Properties dialog box. To view this dialog box, display the Control Panel, click System and Security, click System, and then on the left side of the System window, click *System protection*. In the System Properties dialog box, you can click the System Restore button to start the restore wizard, as shown in Figure 7.10. You can change the System Restore settings, but the default settings are probably the best for your computer and it is not recommended that you make any changes to these settings.

Figure 7.10

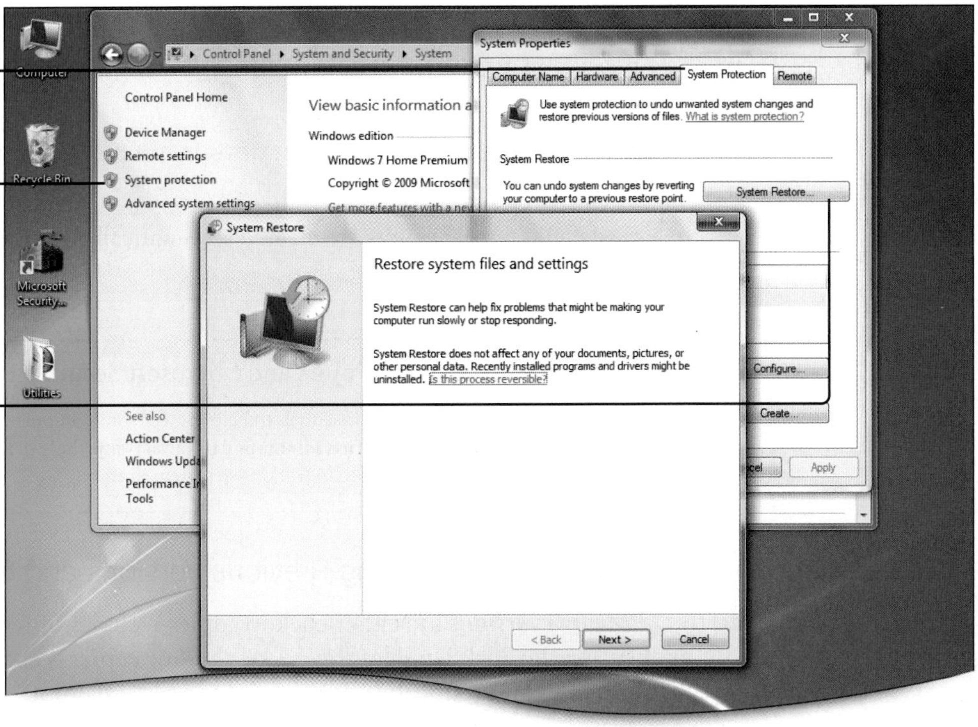

To recover from a system problem by using a restore point, complete the System Restore wizard. Display all available restore points, and then select the restore point you want to use, as shown in Figure 7.11. Restore points that you created manually will be identified with the word *Manual*. Do not interrupt the process after it has started.

Figure 7.11

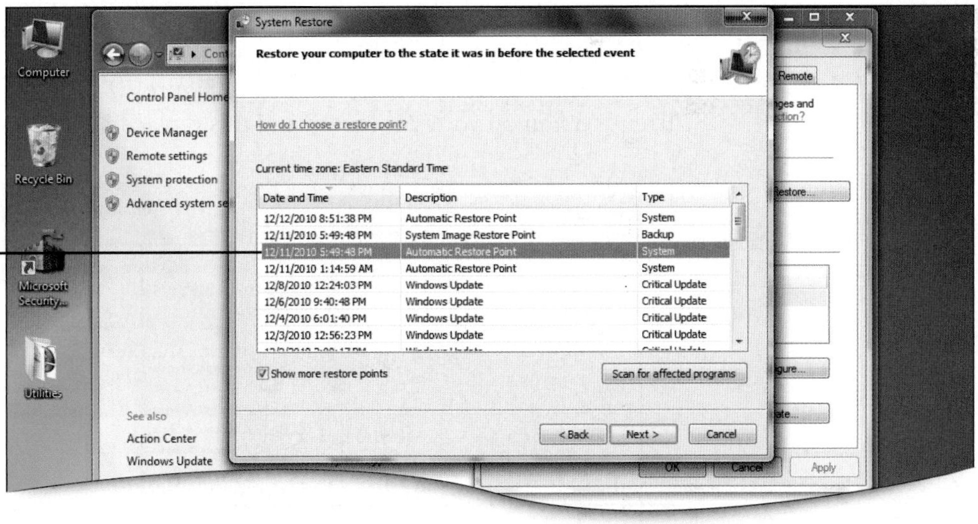

To check your comprehension of System Restore, take a moment to answer the following questions:

1 System Restore restores your computer's system files to an ______________ point in time.

2 System Restore enables you to ______________ system changes to your computer without affecting your personal files such as e-mail, documents, and photos.

3 An example of a problem that System Restore can solve is when your computer behaves in an unpredictable manner following the installation of a ______________ or a ______________.

4 A restore point is like a snapshot of your computer's settings at a specific point in ______________.

5 By default, restore points are created automatically on your computer every ______________.

> **More Knowledge | Restore Points and Microsoft Security Essentials**
>
> If you are using Microsoft Security Essentials to help protect your computer, as long as there is an Internet connection, the program will update virus definitions daily. Every time these definitions are updated, a restore point is created, giving you daily—rather than weekly—restore points.

Activity 7.05 | Restoring Previous Versions and Shadow Copies

Previous versions are either backup copies—copies of files and folders that you back up by using the Back Up Files wizard, or ***shadow copies***—change logs of files and folders that Windows automatically saves as part of a restore point.

If you make a change to a file or folder, and then wish you had not made that change, you can open the shadow copy and save it as a new file. In a similar manner, you can open versions of files that have been saved during a backup. To view shadow copies and backup versions, right-click the file or folder, click Properties, and then click the Previous Versions tab. Here you will see a list of available previous versions of the file or folder. The list will include files saved on a backup as well as shadow copies—assuming both types are available.

To restore from one of the listed previous versions, click the version in the list and then click the Restore button, as shown in Figure 7.12. The file or folder will replace the current version on your computer, and this replacement cannot be undone.

Figure 7.12

Previous Versions tab

Previous version of document

Type of file to be restored

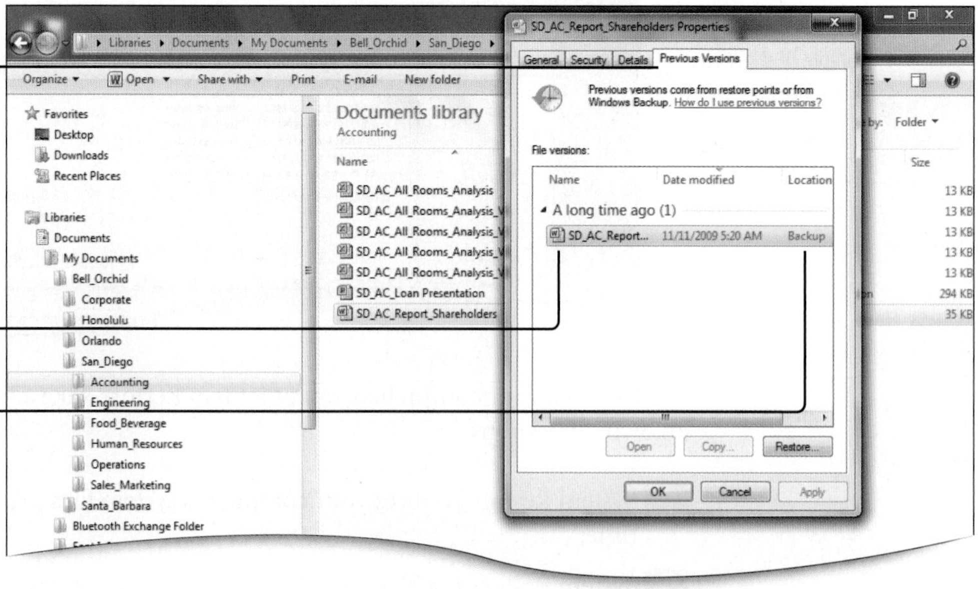

Shadow copies are automatically saved as part of a restore point as long as System Protection is enabled. To check this setting, open the Control Panel, click System and Security, click System, and then in the left pane, click *System protection*. Click Continue, and then under *Automatic restore points*, be sure the check box to the left of the disk where you want System Protection is selected.

To check your comprehension of restoring previous versions and shadow copies, take a moment to answer the following questions:

1. Previous versions are either _______________ copies or _______________ copies of files and folders.
2. A _______________ copy is a change log of a file or folder saved automatically when a restore point is created.
3. To view a shadow copy or backup version of a file, display the _______________ dialog box for that file.
4. When you restore a file, this replacement _______________be undone.
5. Shadow copies are automatically saved as long as _______________ _______________ is enabled.

End You have completed Project 7A

Project 7B Setting Up and Securing a Home Network

Project Activities

In Activities 7.06 through 7.14, you will participate in training along with Barbara Hewitt and Steven Ramos, both of whom work for the Information Technology Department at the headquarters office of the Bell Orchid Hotels. After completing this part of the training, you will be able to set up and secure a home or small office network, share files and printers over a network, control a computer using Remote Desktop Connection, and troubleshoot network problems. You will capture screens that look similar to Figure 7.13.

Project Files

For Project 7B, you will need the following files:

New Snip files

You will save your files as:

Lastname_Firstname_7B_WCN_Snip
Lastname_Firstname_7B_Firewall_Snip

Project Results

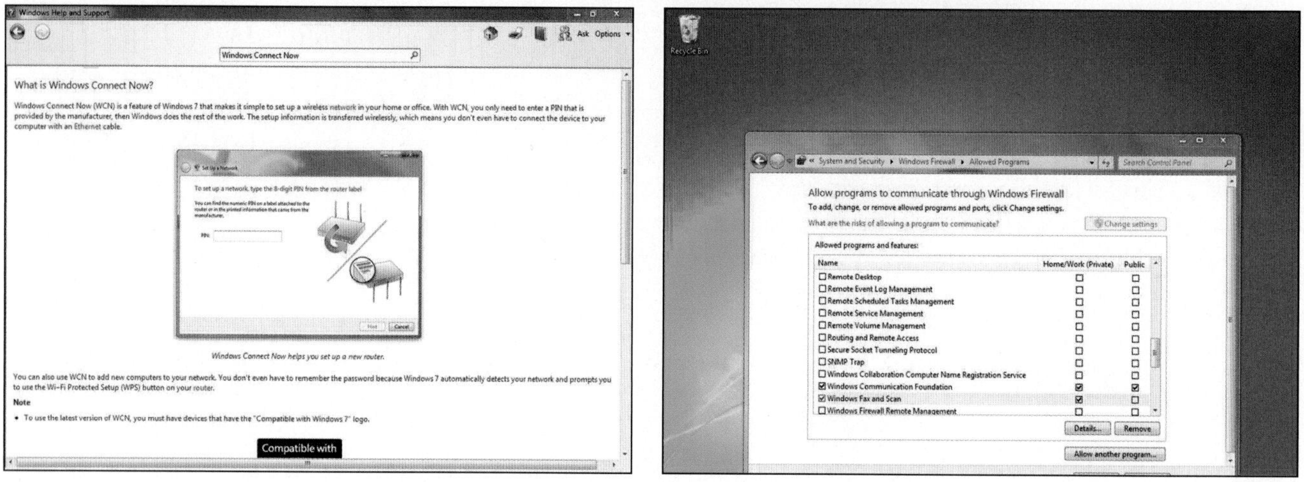

Figure 7.13
Project 7B Setting Up and Securing a Home Network

Objective 4 | Use the Network and Sharing Center to Set Up a Home Network

If you have two or more computers in one location, such as in your home or office, you will probably want to connect them to a network so that you can share an Internet connection, share files, and share resources such as a printer. A network is a group of computers or other devices, such as printers and scanners, that communicates either wirelessly or by using a physical connection, such as a cable or phone line. A network of this type that is within a relatively limited area—for example, in a home or in a building—is also referred to as a ***LAN*** (***local area network***).

Two common network arrangements are the client/server network and the peer-to-peer network. Larger organizations—ones with more than ten computers, for example—commonly use a ***client/server network***. In this arrangement, account logon information and files are stored on a ***server***. A server is a computer that provides shared resources, such as files or printers, to network users. A computer connecting to, or requesting the services of, the server is called a ***client***. In this arrangement, you can log on to any computer connected to the network, and then your personal settings and files are retrieved from the server by the client computer to which you are currently logged on.

Homes and smaller businesses typically use a ***peer-to-peer network***. In a peer-to-peer network, computers connect directly to each other over a private network *without* the need for a server. Your account logon information and personal files are stored on your own networked computer.

For computers that are all running Windows 7, installing a *wired* network typically requires only plugging in the network cables between each computer and a central connection. Windows 7 then detects the network and configures it for you.

For computers that are all running Windows 7 in a *wireless* environment, a wizard walks you step by step through the process.

If you have computers that are running a mix of Windows 7 and Windows XP, the process is still straightforward.

> **More Knowledge | Windows 7 User Accounts in a Network**
>
> If individuals using a network have user accounts in Windows 7, they can log on only to the computer or computers on which they have an established user account. A user account in Windows 7 controls users on an individual computer, *not* on a network. However, your networking software might also provide for some types of user accounts to access the network.

Activity 7.06 | Identifying Network Needs and Solutions

First you must decide whether to use a ***wired network*** or a ***wireless network*** to connect your computers and devices to your network. In a wired network, each computer and device communicates with the network by using wires—either existing phone wires or cables that you put in place. In a wireless network, each device communicates with the network by using radio signals.

If you can run wires to each computer on your network, consider using a wired network. Wired network hardware is less expensive, and wired networks are fast, reliable, and easy to secure. For example, with a wired network, someone must enter your house or building to connect to your network.

If it is not convenient or practical to run wires between computers in different rooms in your home or small office, use a wireless network. Wireless technology is convenient and relatively inexpensive. Because radio signals usually go outside of your building where others can try to connect to your network, be sure to take the necessary steps to secure your wireless network.

> **More Knowledge | Using Your Building's Wires to Connect Computers on a Network**
>
> Two types of wired networks allow you to use your building's existing phone lines or power lines. In this manner, a wired network can be built without having to run new wires. A ***phone line network***—also called an ***HPNA (HOME Phoneline Networking Alliance) network***—connects network computers using a building's existing phone lines. With a phone line network, each computer connects to a phone jack. The phone jack is specially wired so that the network will not conflict with incoming and outgoing phone calls.

A ***power line network*** communicates using a building's existing electrical wires. In a power line network, special equipment connects each device to the building's electrical wall plugs. Instead of drawing electrical power, the connection uses the building's power lines to transmit signals for the network.

To check how well you understand identifying network needs and solutions, take a moment to answer the following questions:

1. One reason why you might want to connect your home or office computers to a network is to share a connection to the __________.
2. Larger organizations commonly use the __________ network arrangement.
3. In a peer-to-peer network, computers connect directly to each other without the need for a __________.
4. A wireless network is useful when it is not practical to install __________ between rooms.
5. Because the signals from a wireless network can go outside of your building, which might permit others to connect to your network, you must take the necessary steps to __________ a wireless network.

Activity 7.07 | Installing a Wired Network in Your Home

A wired network must have a central connection to manage ***network traffic***. Network traffic refers to the signals sent through a network so that devices on the network can communicate with one another. For typical wired networks in a home or small office, each computer or device connects to a ***router***. A router, which can be wired or wireless, is a device that sends—*routes*—information between two networks, for example, between a home network and the Internet. Routers find the quickest path for sending information, making network connections fast.

Each device that connects to a wired network must have an adapter, which is referred to as a ***network interface card*** or ***NIC*** (pronounced *nick*). A network adapter enables your computer to connect to and communicate with a network. A wire runs from the NIC to a ***switch*** or router, and the connection is usually based on the ***Ethernet*** hardware requirement. Ethernet is a networking standard that uses cables to provide network access; Ethernet is the most widely installed technology for connecting computers. A switch is a device that connects two or more computers to a network.

Ethernet networks send signals using three speeds as summarized in the table in Figure 7.14. Network adapters, routers, and cables must support the network speed that you want to achieve. For example, most home networks use Fast Ethernet. Both the router and network adapter must support Fast Ethernet to have the network send signals at 100 ***Mbps***—megabits per second. Network hardware that supports Gigabit Ethernet is not as common as, and is more expensive than, Fast Ethernet hardware.

Ethernet Speeds	
Megabits per second (Mbps)	**Ethernet Type**
10	Ethernet
100	Fast Ethernet
1000	Gigabit Ethernet

Figure 7.14

Most computers include an Ethernet network adapter with a port into which you can plug an ***RJ-45 connector***. An RJ-45 port looks similar to a phone jack, but it is wider and contains eight wires, as shown in Figure 7.15. On a desktop computer, the port is usually on the back of the computer. On a notebook computer, the RJ-45 port is usually on the back or side of the computer. Ethernet cables have an RJ-45 connector on each end, and are used to connect each computer's network adapter to the router or switch. Ethernet cable is also referred to as ***Cat5*** (for Fast Ethernet) and ***Cat6*** (for Gigabit Ethernet).

Figure 7.15

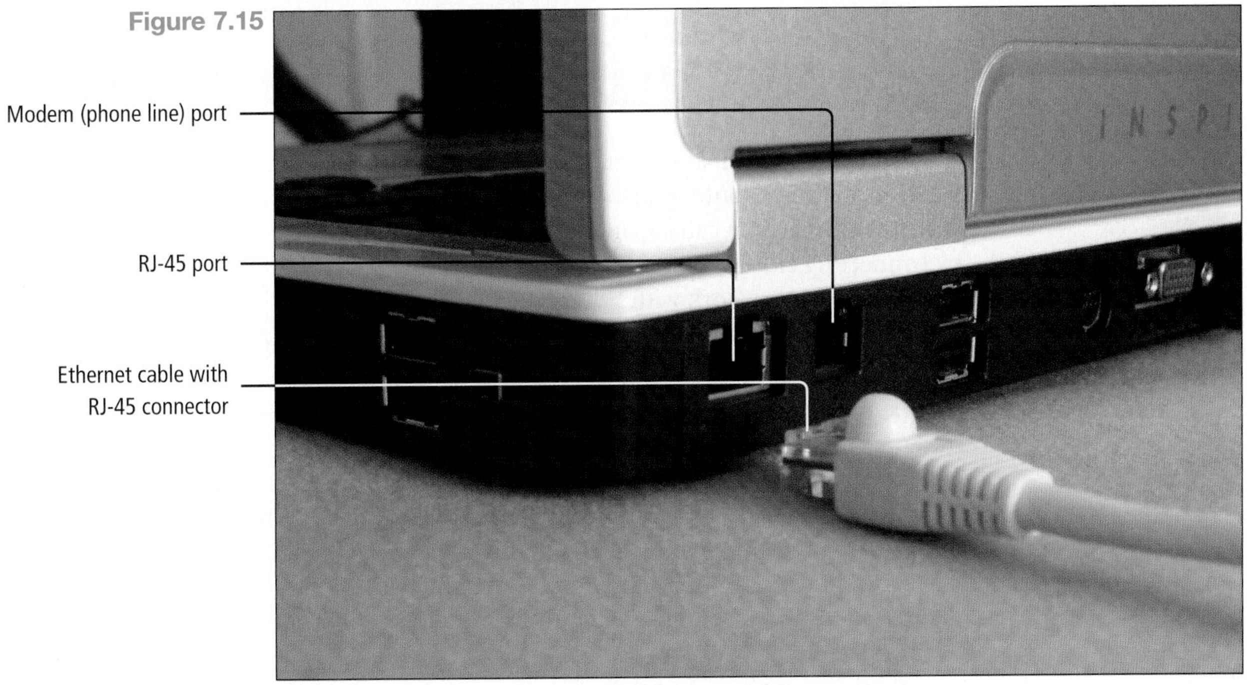

To connect your wired network hardware, turn off all devices. If necessary, install a network interface card in any computer that does not have one by following the direction supplied by the NIC's manufacturer. Connect each computer's network adapter to the router with a network cable. Turn on your router. When you restart your computers, Windows 7 will recognize your new network and take the steps necessary to make the network function. Always check the directions included with your router before turning on the computers. Your router manufacturer might provide installation software or ask you to perform certain steps to configure your router.

After detecting a new network, Windows 7 displays the Set Network Location dialog box, similar to Figure 7.16. Here you select *Home*, *Work*, or *Public network*. Windows 7 sets a network security level appropriate for the location that you select. For example, the security level for Public location is very high because more threats exist when using a network in a public location than at work or at home.

Figure 7.16

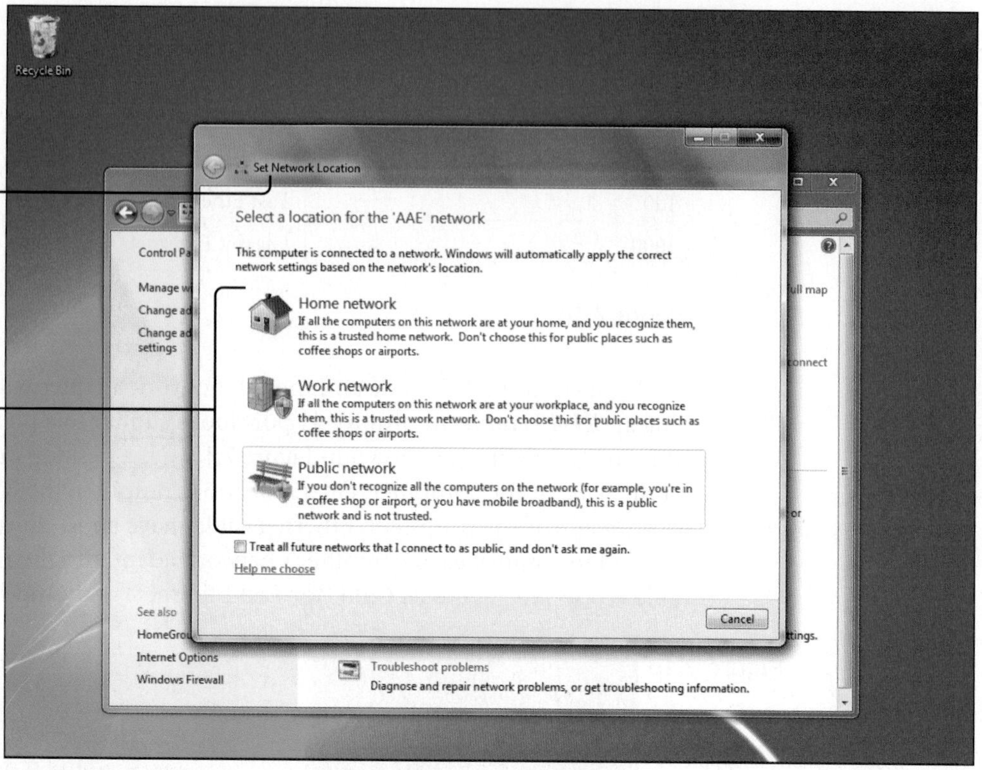

Set Network Location box

Three network types from which you can select

Routers are useful as central connections because they act as a switch for your network, and they route information between two networks such as your home network and the Internet. You can expand the number of computers that connect to your network by connecting either a ***hub*** or a switch to your router. A hub is a device used to connect computers on a network with Ethernet cables.

Both hubs and switches are devices that connect two or more computers to an Ethernet network. When a single computer sends information—for example, a print request to a printer connected to the network—a hub sends the print information to all the computers connected to the hub. Because the print data is not meant for them, these computers must ignore the data. A switch, however, would send the print information only to the printer. In this way, a switch speeds the transfer rate of information, and is less prone to communication errors than a hub. With a switch connected to your router, you can connect computers and devices to either the router or the switch as shown in Figure 7.17. By connecting a switch to the router, you increase the number of devices that can connect to the network.

Figure 7.17

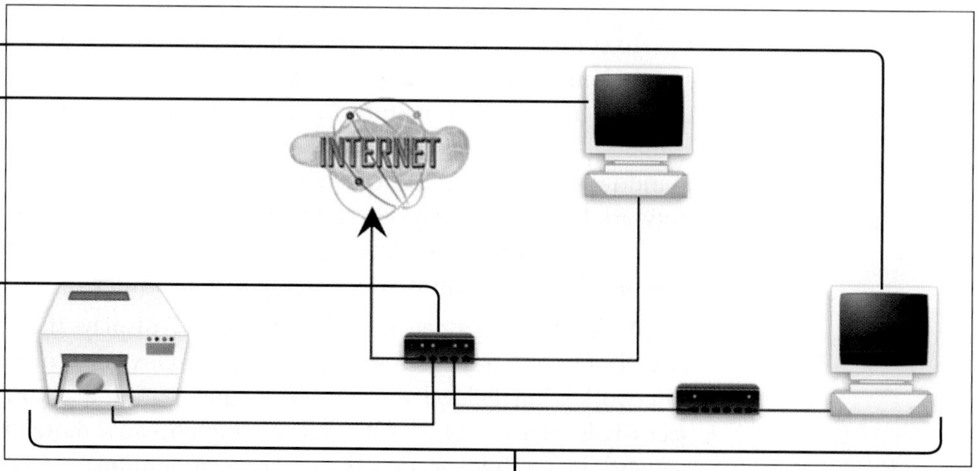

Computer connected to switch

Computer connected to router

Router

Switch connected to router

Your network

To check how well you understand installing a wired network, take a moment to answer the following questions:

1. Routers find the __________ path for sending information, which makes network connections fast.
2. The most widely installed technology for connecting computers is __________.
3. Most computers include an Ethernet __________ into which you can plug an RJ-45 connector.
4. After Windows 7 detects a new network, it displays the __________ __________ __________ dialog box.
5. You can increase the number of computers that connect to your network by connecting either a __________ or a __________ to your router.

Activity 7.08 | Using Windows Connect Now to Install a Wireless Network in Your Home

In a wireless network, radio waves are used to send and receive signals between devices. With a wireless network, a ***wireless access point*** serves as the central connection that manages network traffic. A wireless access point is a device that connects wireless computers and other wireless devices to a wired network, for example, the Internet.

For most home and small businesses, a ***wireless router*** serves as the wireless access point. A wireless router has all the features of a wired router, but it can also communicate using radio waves. Wireless routers include RJ-45 ports so that nearby computers or devices can connect using Ethernet network cables.

For a computer or device to communicate using radio waves, it must have a wireless network adapter. Most notebook computers have a built-in wireless network adapter; most desktop computers do *not* come with a wireless network adapter. To add a wireless adapter, install a wireless network interface card inside of the computer, or attach a USB wireless adapter device into an open USB port by following the directions provided by the manufacturer.

Wireless networks adhere to a group of standards for wireless networks referred to as ***802.11***—also known as ***Wi-Fi***. Wi-Fi stands for *wireless fidelity*, and refers to the Wi-Fi Alliance organization, which certifies that wireless products conform to the standard. You might see products labeled *802.11a*, *802.11b*, *802.11g*, and *802.11n*, all of which refer to different standards in the 802.11 group. Just be sure that any wireless network adapters you purchase support the same 802.11 standard used by your wireless router. The supported standards will be listed on the adapter's packaging. If you use a popular device, for example, the Cisco Valet shown in Figure 7.18, the setup is easy and straightforward by following the device's setup instructions.

Figure 7.18

The Cisco Valet for a home wireless network

Windows 7 uses the *Set up a wireless router or access point* wizard to walk you through the steps of setting up your wireless router. During that process, you will need to name your wireless network and assign a password that will be required to connect to the network. ***Windows Connect Now*** is a feature of Windows 7 that makes it simple to set up a wireless network in your home or office, and enables wireless routers to be configured using a USB device.

During the setup process, you will name your network—this is referred to as ***SSID***, or ***Service Set Identifier***, which is a group of up to 32 characters that uniquely identify your wireless network. The SSID functions as the name of a wireless network. When your neighbors or building tenants have their own wireless networks, you might see them listed as networks available to your computer. For this reason, your network name should make it easy for you to identify.

You will also use a ***passphrase***—a string of characters used to control access to a network or program. When others attempt to connect to your wireless network, they will be required to enter the passphrase. For this reason, the characters in your passphrase should be very difficult for unauthorized individuals to guess; this will reduce the likelihood that someone unauthorized can connect to your network. Use a strong passphrase—at least sixteen characters including numbers and both uppercase and lowercase letters.

1 **Close** any open programs and windows. From the **Start** menu, click **Help and Support**, and then in the **Search Help** box, type **Windows Connect Now** and then press Enter. Click **What is Windows Connect Now?**, and then **Maximize** the window. Compare your screen with Figure 7.19.

Wireless routers are easy to configure by using the information here.

Figure 7.19

Information about *Windows Connect Now*

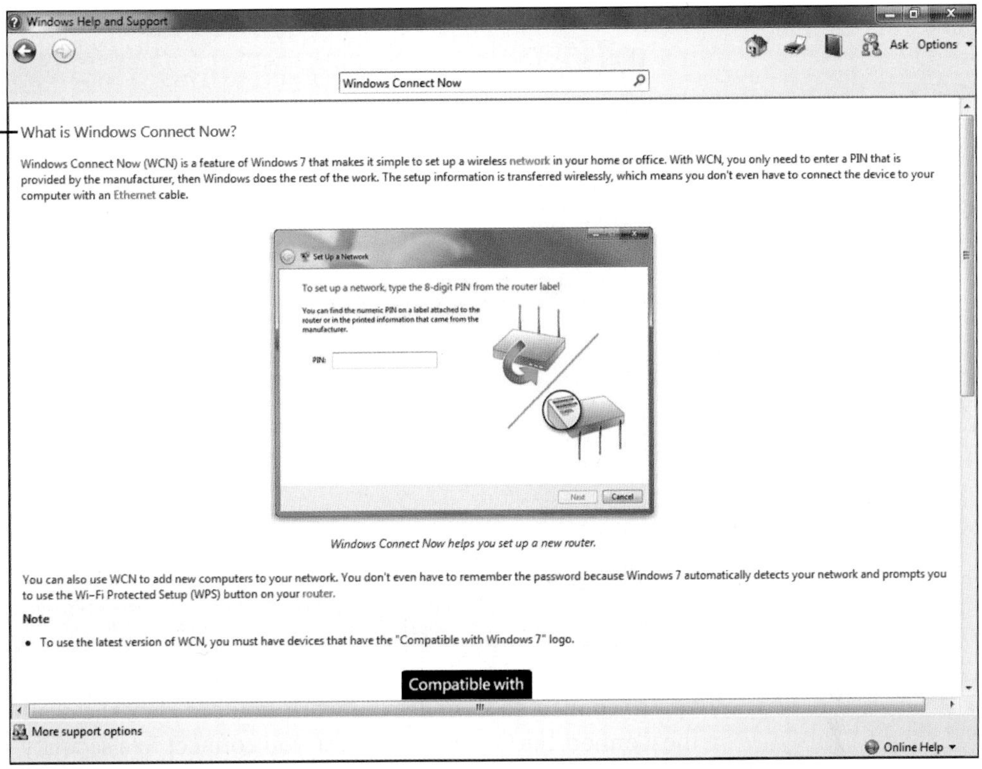

2 **Start** the **Snipping Tool** program, click the **New arrow**, and then click **Full-screen Snip**. In the **Snipping Tool** mark-up window, click the **Save Snip** button.

3 In the **Save As** dialog box, in the **navigation pane**, scroll down as necessary, and then under **Computer**, click your USB flash drive so that it displays in the address bar. Navigate to your **Windows 7 Chapter 7** folder, and then as the file name, type **Lastname_Firstname_7B_WCN_Snip** Be sure the file type is **JPEG file**, and then press Enter. **Close** the **Snipping Tool** mark-up window. Hold this file until you finish Project 7B.

4 **Close** the Help and Support Window.

Activity 7.09 | Connecting to a Wireless Network and Managing Wireless Network Connections

Before you use a wireless network, you must initiate the connection from your computer. If you want to connect to a wireless network, from the Control Panel, click Network and Internet. Under Network and Sharing Center, click Connect to a network to display the *Connect to a network* dialog box. A list of all available wireless networks displays as shown in Figure 7.20. In Figure 7.20, two wireless networks are available. Each is listed by its network name, and the green bars indicate the strength of each network's signal. Signal strength is adversely affected by distance, the presence of concrete or brick walls, and the presence of reflective surfaces such as glass and mirrors.

The ScreenTip of the second network shown in Figure 7.20 indicates this is an ***unsecured network***. Unsecured networks are wireless networks that do not require a passphrase to connect to them. A ***security-enabled network*** requires a passphrase to connect to that network. You might also see a network that displays as *Unnamed Network*. An ***unnamed network***, also known as a ***hidden network***, hides its network name. To increase security, some networks do not display a name. For example, to log on to a hidden network, you must enter both the network name, or SSID, *and* the passphrase.

Figure 7.20

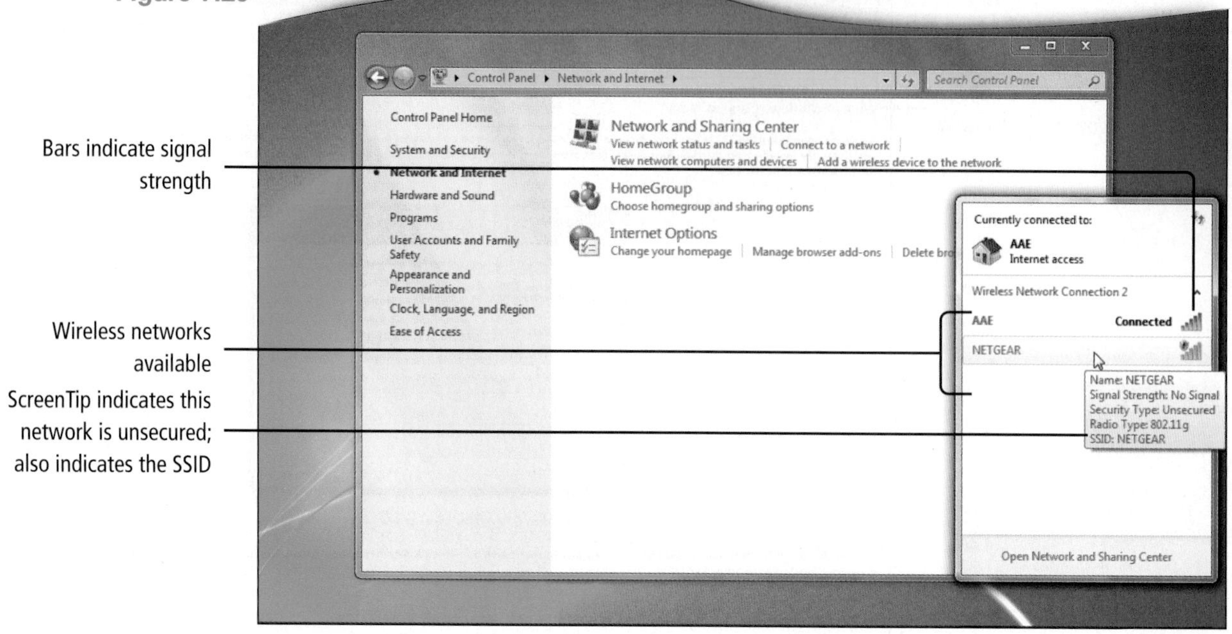

To connect to a wireless network, you can click the desired network, and then click the Connect button. The first time you connect to a security-enabled network, you are prompted for the passphrase.

To disconnect from a wireless network, on the right end of the taskbar, click the Network icon to display the list of networks, right-click the network to which you are connected, and then click Disconnect, as shown in Figure 7.21.

Figure 7.21

The Manage Wireless Networks window, as shown in Figure 7.22, displays a list of all saved wireless network connections—even when those networks are out of range. Use the Manage Wireless Networks window when you need to change how you connect to a wireless network, or when you manage several wireless networks. For example, you might connect to one wireless network at home, another at your college, and to yet another at your workplace. To open the Manage Wireless Networks window, open the Control Panel, click Network and Internet, click Network and Sharing Center, and then on the left, click Manage wireless networks.

Figure 7.22

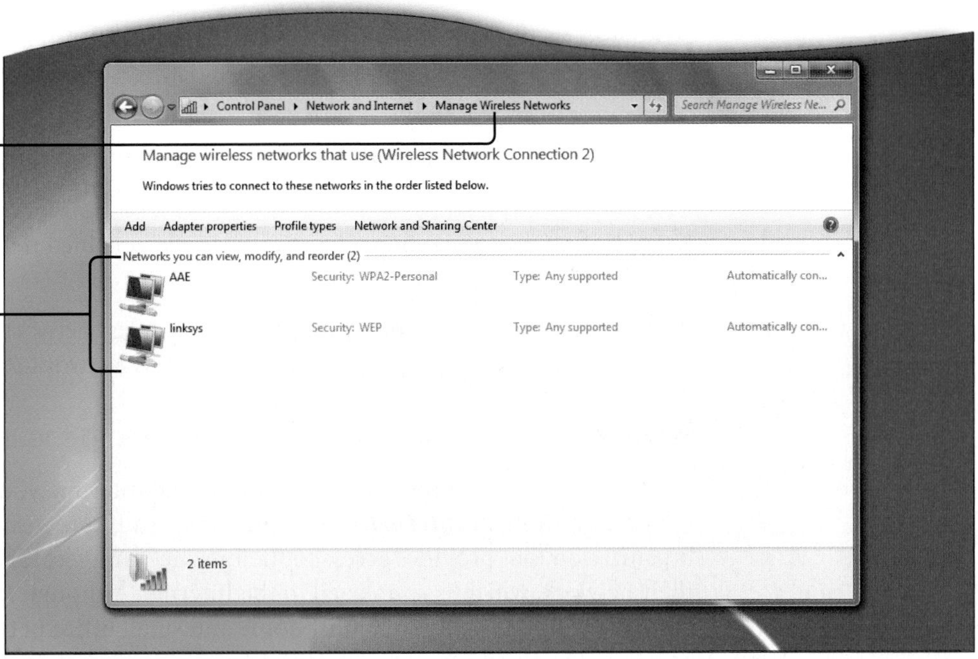

In the Manage Wireless Networks window, you can change a stored connection's options. For example, you may want to stop Windows 7 from connecting to a wireless network automatically. To do so, right-click the network name, and then click Properties. Use the Connection tab of the Wireless Network Properties dialog box, as shown in Figure 7.23, to make any necessary changes.

Figure 7.23

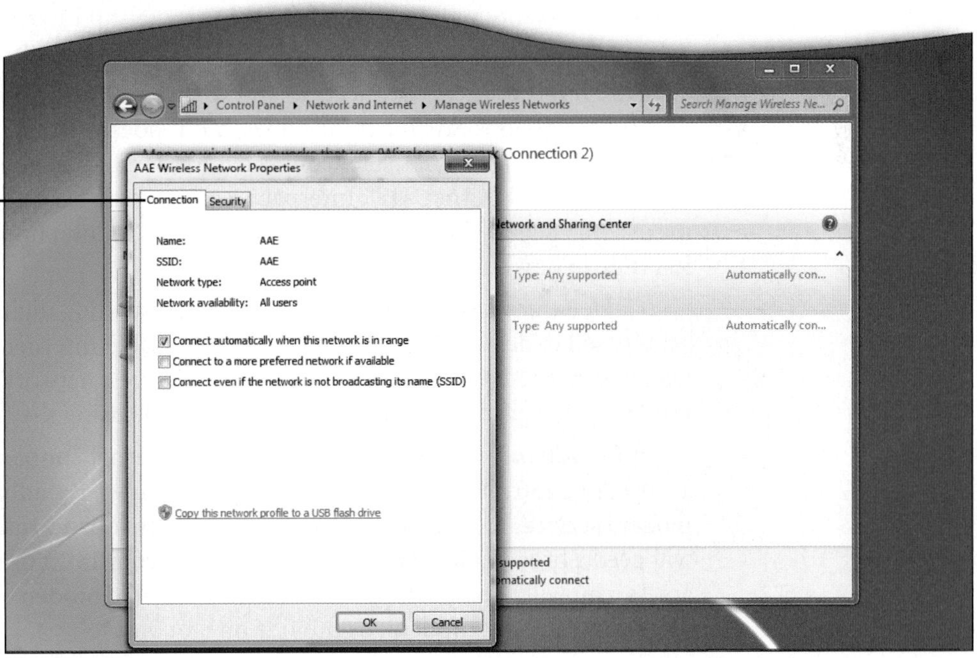

To check how well you understand connecting to a wireless network, take a moment to answer the following questions:

1 Before you can use a wireless network, you must initiate the __________ from the computer to the network.

2 Distance, the presence of concrete or brick walls, and the presence of reflective surfaces such as glass and mirrors could adversely affect wireless network __________ strength.

3 To log on to a hidden network, you must enter both the __________ and the __________.

4 The first time that you connect to a security-enabled network, you are prompted for the __________.

5 To stop Windows 7 from connecting to a wireless network automatically, change the setting on the __________ tab of the Wireless Network Properties dialog box.

Activity 7.10 | Connecting Your Network to the Internet

Before you can connect your network to the Internet, you must have an Internet connection from an ***Internet service provider***. An Internet service provider, or ***ISP***, is an organization that provides access to the Internet for a fee. ISPs enable you to connect to their network, which is connected to the Internet. Although ISPs offer several methods for connecting to their network, most home and small office networks connect by one of four access methods: dial-up, DSL, cable, or fiber.

Dial-up Internet access uses a regular phone line, or landline, to connect to an Internet service provider. To connect to the Internet using dial-up, a computer's phone ***modem*** dials the phone number of the ISP, and then uses the established phone connection to send and receive signals. A modem is a device that enables computer information to be transmitted and received over a telephone line by translating the signals used by two different network types. In this case, the modem translates the signals your computer uses into a form that can be sent to another phone modem. While a dial-up Internet connection is connected to the ISP, the phone line cannot be used to make or receive other phone calls.

DSL Internet access connects to an ISP by sending digital signals over local telephone networks. DSL uses existing phone lines, but it does not initiate an actual phone call. With DSL, your network always stays connected to the ISP, and you can still make phone calls when using the Internet. DSL Internet access is much faster than dial-up access. This means Web pages will display faster, and files—Windows updates, for example—will take less time to download.

Cable Internet access connects to an ISP by sending digital signals over the coaxial cables used to deliver cable television services. Cable Internet access is usually faster than DSL Internet access. With cable Internet access, your network is always connected to the ISP, and you can still receive cable television while using the Internet.

A ***broadband connection*** is a high-speed Internet connection that typically operates at speeds of 256 kilobytes per second (***kbps***) or faster. Broadband includes DSL and cable modem service. To connect your network to a broadband Internet service provider, you will need a broadband modem that works with your ISP. For most broadband Internet access, you will need either a DSL modem or a cable modem. Your ISP will either help you select the right modem, or provide one for you.

When you connect a router to a broadband modem, each computer connected to the router will be able to access the Internet, as shown in Figure 7.24. Most broadband routers have a port labeled ***WAN***—Wide Area Network—which is a network that connects geographically separated locations by using telecommunications services. Use this port to connect to the broadband modem. Some manufacturers combine a modem and router into one unit, eliminating the need for such a connection. To connect your router and broadband modem, follow the directions given to you by your ISP and modem manufacturer.

Figure 7.24

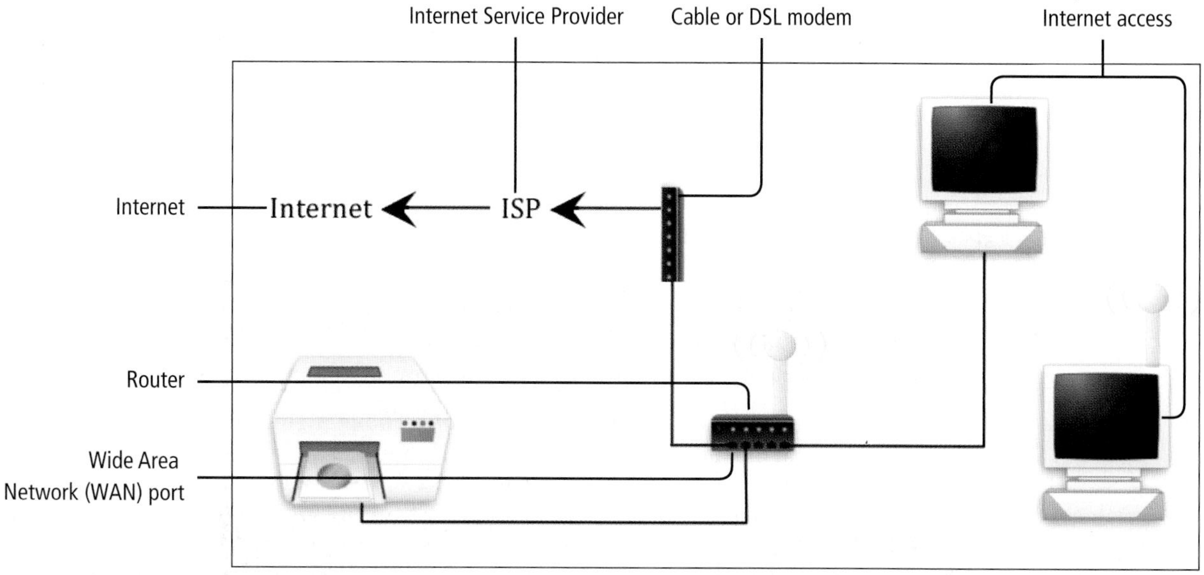

To check how well you understand connecting your local area network to the Internet, take a moment to answer the following questions:

1. Before you can connect your network to the Internet, you must have an Internet connection from an Internet __________ __________.
2. Four common Internet connection methods are dial-up, DSL, __________, or fiber.
3. __________ Internet access uses existing phone lines, but it does not place an actual phone call.
4. Typically, __________ Internet access is faster than __________ Internet access, which is faster than dial-up Internet Access.
5. Most broadband routers have a port labeled __________ that can be used to connect to a broadband modem by using a network cable.

Objective 5 | Secure and Troubleshoot a Home Network

When you connect your local area network to the Internet, the computers on your network become part of a much larger community—a community with both good and bad members. The bad members of the Internet community are those who would like to install malware, search your computer for personal data, or take control of your computer. There are several steps that you can take to protect your computers from these outside threats.

Activity 7.11 | Protecting Your Computer Using Windows Firewall

To protect an Internet-connected computer from malware, the computer should have a ***firewall***. A firewall is software or hardware that can help protect a computer from hackers, or prevent malicious software from gaining access to a computer through a network or over the Internet. It also helps prevent a computer from sending malicious software to other computers. ***Hacker*** is a term used to describe a person who uses computer expertise to gain access to computer systems without permission. Windows 7 installs Windows Firewall and enables it by default. Several other publishers offer their own firewall software.

There are several legitimate programs that need to receive data from the Internet, and a firewall must know when to allow them to do so. For example, Windows Live Messenger needs to receive data from the Internet as you send and receive instant messages. Windows Live Messenger is added to the Windows Firewall ***exception*** list when it is installed. An exception is a program that will not be blocked by the firewall.

Sometimes the Windows Firewall exceptions need to be edited manually. For example, a program may not work correctly until it is added to the exception list, or you may have a program that you want to block. In this activity, you will check your firewall's status, and then practice adding a program to the exceptions list.

1 **Close** any open programs and windows. Display the **Control Panel**, click **System and Security**, and then click **Windows Firewall**. Compare your screen with Figure 7.25.

Here, you can disable all ***incoming connections***. An incoming connection is traffic sent from the Internet to your computer. If you suspect that your computer is currently threatened, you can block all outside access. This action would also prevent you from receiving mail and prevent Internet Explorer from displaying Web pages.

Figure 7.25

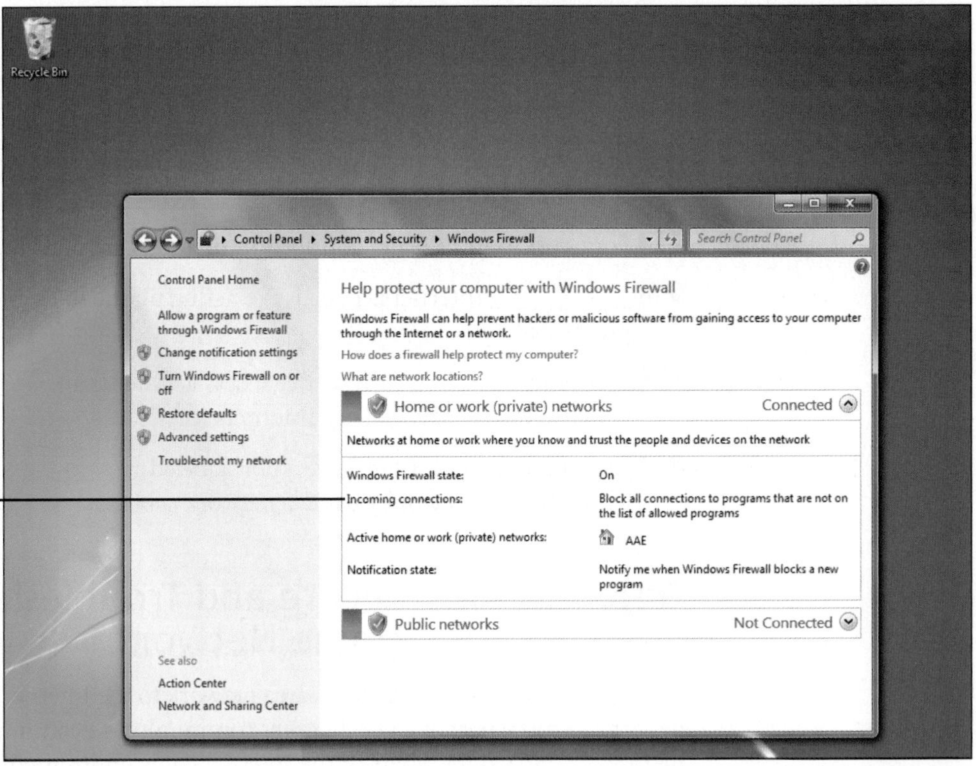

Incoming connections

2 On the left, click **Allow a program or feature through Windows Firewall**, and then compare your screen with Figure 7.26.

Figure 7.26

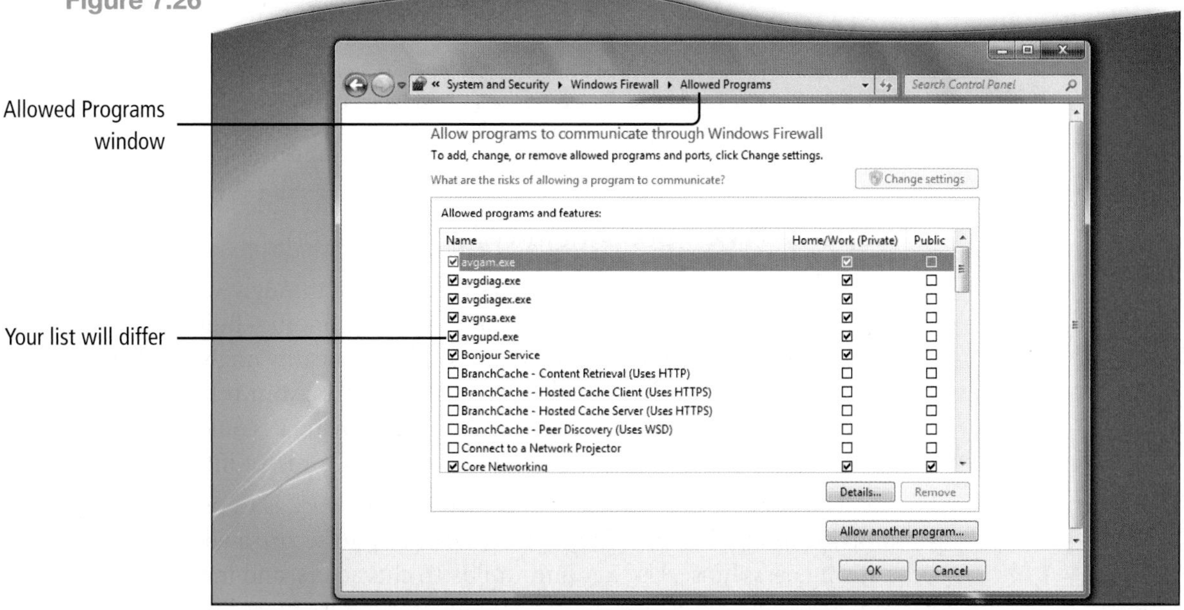

3 Click the **Change settings** button, and then click the **Allow another program** button. In the **Add a Program** dialog box, scroll down if necessary, click **Windows Fax and Scan**, and then click **Add**. In the **Allowed Programs** window, scroll down to display the **Windows Fax and Scan** program.

4 **Start** the **Snipping Tool** program, click the **New arrow**, and then click **Full-screen Snip**. In the **Snipping Tool** mark-up window, click the **Save Snip** button.

5 Navigate to your **Windows 7 Chapter 7** folder, click in the **File name** box, and then using your own name, name the file **Lastname_Firstname_7B_Firewall_Snip** Press Enter. Hold this file until you finish Project 7B.

6 **Close** the **Snipping Tool** mark-up window. In the displayed window, click **Windows Fax and Scan**, and then click the **Remove** button. In the message box, click **Yes** to restore your computer to its original setting; you are not deleting the program.

7 **Close** all open windows.

More Knowledge | Using a Firewall to Monitor Outbound Traffic

Adding programs to the list of Windows Firewall exceptions affects ***inbound traffic***—data that is sent to your computer from other computers on the Internet. By default, Windows Firewall allows all programs to send ***outbound traffic*** to the Internet. Outbound traffic is data sent from your computer to another computer on the Internet. Programs use outbound connections to allow you to communicate over the Internet, register a program, or check for updates. Malware programs also use outbound connections for malicious purposes, such as sending personal information to other computers or using your computer to attack other computers on the Internet. For this reason, computer security experts recommend that your firewall block all outbound traffic except for those programs that you specifically allow.

The Windows Firewall with Advanced Security dialog box is used to configure Windows Firewall to monitor outbound traffic. You can open the dialog box from the Administrative Tools window. Recall that the Administrative Tools window is opened from the System and Security control panel. Here you can set Windows Firewall to monitor outbound traffic, and then add programs to the exceptions lists as needed. For example, when you first enable the feature to block outbound traffic, Internet Explorer will not work correctly until the Internet Explorer program is added to the outbound exceptions list.

Several software publishers offer firewall software. When you install a different firewall, Windows Firewall is disabled, and the new firewall takes its place. These firewalls notify you when a program is blocked and, with a single click, you can allow the program through the firewall, either one time or permanently. In this way, the exceptions lists for inbound and outbound traffic are managed.

More Knowledge | Other Ways to Secure Your Network

You cannot rely on a firewall to completely protect your network from outside threats. There are several other actions that you should take. Be sure to change your router's password. Malicious individuals know the default passwords assigned to routers, and can use them to change your router's security settings. You should also turn on automatic Windows updates, and install programs that block or remove malware from your computer.

Activity 7.12 | Securing a Wireless Network

Wireless networks use radio waves that can pass through walls, and thus your network's signal can go beyond the boundaries of your home or office building. Without proper security, unauthorized individuals with computers nearby might be able to access the information stored on your network computers or use your Internet connection to access the Internet. When connected, these unauthorized individuals could access your public folders, log on to computers or devices that have weak passwords, or intercept network traffic.

The main objective of securing a wireless network is to prevent unauthorized individuals from connecting to it. The first step to secure a wireless network is to use a strong passphrase. Use a minimum of 16 characters, and include numbers and both uppercase and lowercase letters. A strong passphrase makes it difficult for unauthorized individuals to guess the passphrase of your wireless network.

To secure your wireless network, a strong ***encryption*** method to scramble network traffic is also recommended. Encryption is a way to enhance the security of a message or file by scrambling the contents so that it can be read only by someone who has the appropriate key to unscramble it. Your wireless router supports various encryption methods. A knowledgeable individual can quickly decrypt wireless networks encrypted using WEP—Wired Equivalent Privacy. For this reason, if your router and network interface card support WPA—Wi-Fi Protected Access—or WPA2, use one of these encryption methods instead of WEP.

Wireless router manufacturers assign a default network name—SSID—to all of their wireless routers. The default SSID usually displays the make and model of the wireless router. With this knowledge, an unauthorized individual could know your router's default settings, including the address of the configuration pages and the default administrator logon. For this reason, you should always change the SSID of your wireless network and change the default password for your wireless router's administrator account.

You can also increase security by configuring your wireless router to stop broadcasting its SSID. Recall that a wireless network that does not broadcast its SSID displays as an unknown network. When attempting to log on to an unknown network, a malicious person would need to know both the network name and your password.

To check how well you understand securing a wireless network, take a moment to answer the following questions:

1. The goal of securing your wireless network is to prevent unauthorized individuals from __________ to your network.
2. To make it difficult for unauthorized individuals to connect to your wireless network, you should set a strong __________.
3. You should encrypt your wireless network using either the __________ or __________—but not the WEP—encryption method.
4. To secure a wireless network, you should change your router's default network name and change the default __________ for your wireless router's administrator account.
5. For additional security, you can hide your network name by stopping the broadcast of its __________.

Activity 7.13 | Troubleshooting Network Problems

Networks are systems that involve multiple components—such as operating systems, network adapters, routers, modems, and Internet service providers. If one component stops working correctly, you may experience problems with your network. If you encounter a problem with your network, Windows 7 provides several tools to help you fix it.

The Network and Sharing Center window provides tools to help you troubleshoot network problems. When you ***troubleshoot***, you analyze the problem, determine possible causes, and implement solutions. The Network and Sharing Center, as shown in Figure 7.27, is used to manage your network. Here you will find links to tasks, a map of your existing network, the name of your network, and the status of your sharing and discovery settings. ***Network discovery*** is a network setting that controls how you see other computers on your network, and whether other computers on your network can see your computer.

Figure 7.27

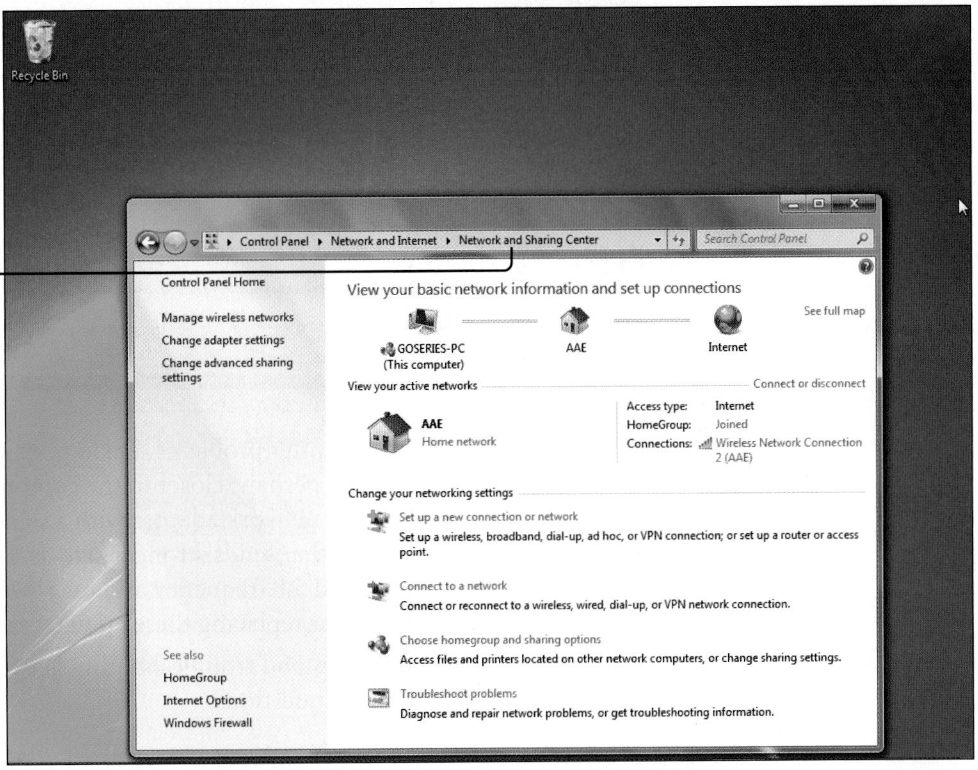

The network map that displays in the Network and Sharing Center window is interactive. For example, clicking the icon for your computer displays the Computer folder window, and clicking the Internet icon starts Internet Explorer. If a connection is not working, it might be indicated on this map.

Clicking *See full map* displays your local area network in greater detail as shown in Figure 7.28. Clicking or pointing to each item displays more information about the item. Routers function as both a switch and a ***gateway***. A gateway connects two different networks such as your local area network and the Internet.

Figure 7.28

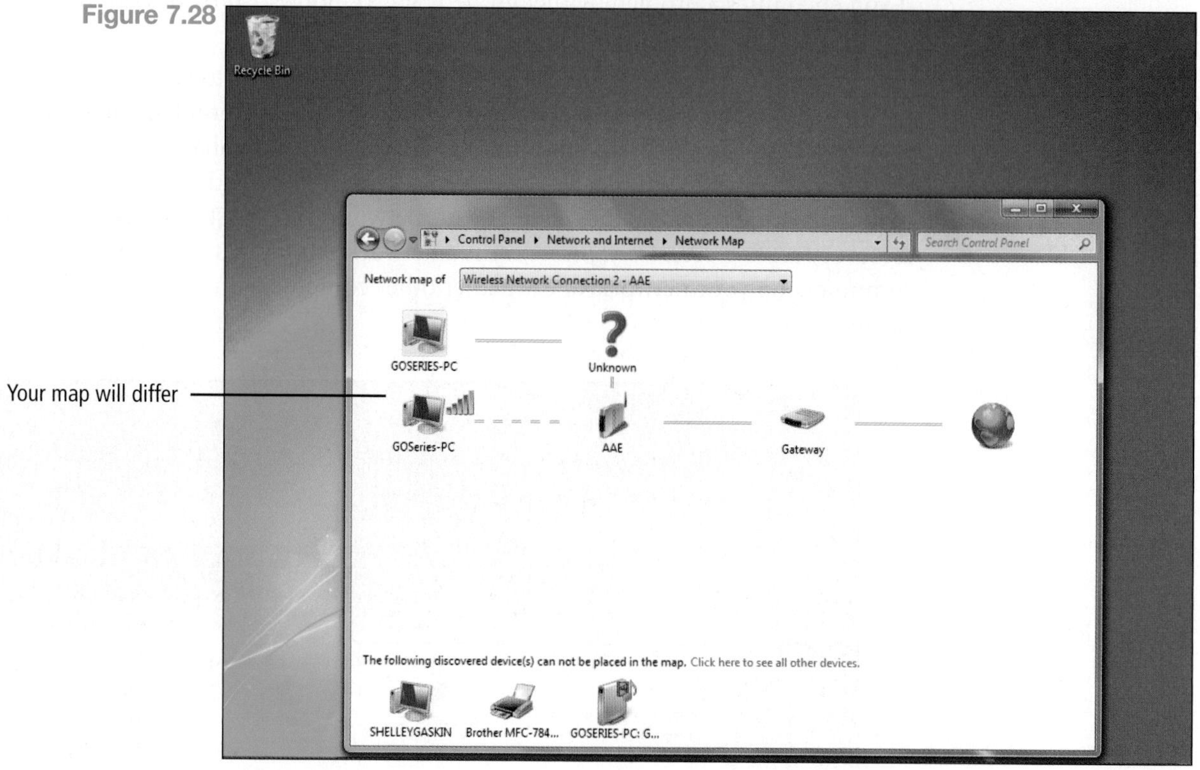

Wireless networks may encounter problems due to poor signal strength. Try moving the router to a different location, perhaps closer to the computer that is having difficulty connecting. Consider installing a network adapter with a signal booster and remote antenna, or use a wireless router that sends stronger signals. Be aware that cordless phones that operate at the 2.4 and 5.8 frequency and microwave ovens may interfere with wireless networks. Moving or replacing these appliances may solve this problem.

To check how well you understand troubleshooting network problems, take a moment to answer the following questions:

1. When you __________, you analyze a problem, determine possible causes, and implement solutions.
2. A network setting that controls how you see other computers on your network, and whether other computers on your network can see your computer, is __________ __________.
3. A __________ connects two different networks such as your local area network and the Internet.
4. Wireless networks may encounter problems due to poor __________ strength.
5. Sometimes __________ a router to a different location will improve its signal strength.

Objective 6 | Use Homegroup to Share Files and Printers on a Home Network

One advantage of a network is the sharing of resources. A ***shared resource*** is a device connected to or a file saved on one computer that can be accessed from another computer over a network. Sharing files over the network simplifies moving files between computers, and enables two or more individuals to work on the same project without having to synchronize two separate files. A network also enables you to share devices such as a printer. Using a shared printer eliminates the cost and space requirements required for each computer to have its own printer.

Activity 7.14 | Using Homegroup to Share Files and Printers on a Home Network

The easiest way to share printers and files—documents, music, photos, videos—with others on your home network is to create or join a ***homegroup***. A homegroup is a group of computers that share files and printers. To be part of a homegroup, each computer on the network must be running Windows 7. If you are installing Windows 7, joining a homegroup is part of the setup process. Homegroup sharing does not work with domain networks found in businesses; rather, it is a feature specifically designed for home networks.

To join a computer to the homegroup, on the Control Panel click Network and Internet, and then click HomeGroup. All the user accounts on the computer become members of the homegroup.

Until other computers join your homegroup, you cannot access their shared files and resources. Here you can check the password and choose what you want to share. In Figure 7.29, a computer is shown as belonging to a homegroup, but nothing has been shared.

Figure 7.29

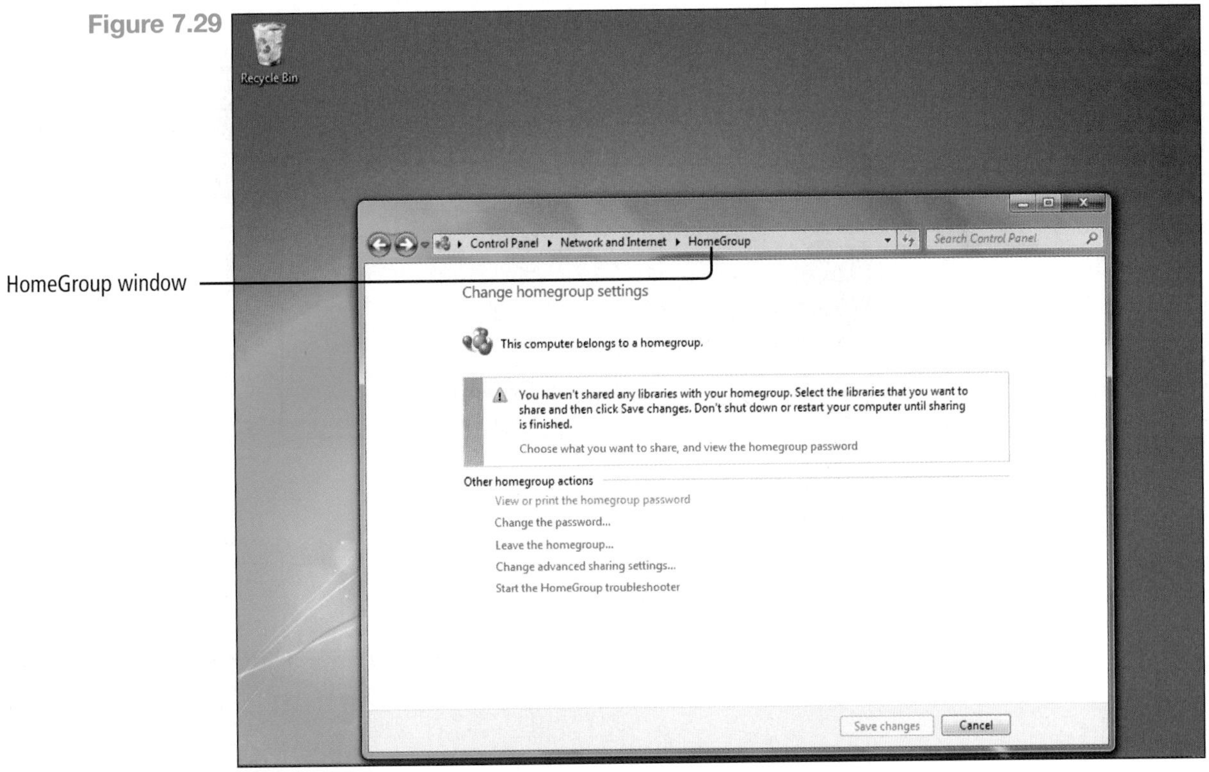

To share, click Choose what you want to share, as shown in Figure 7.30.

Figure 7.30

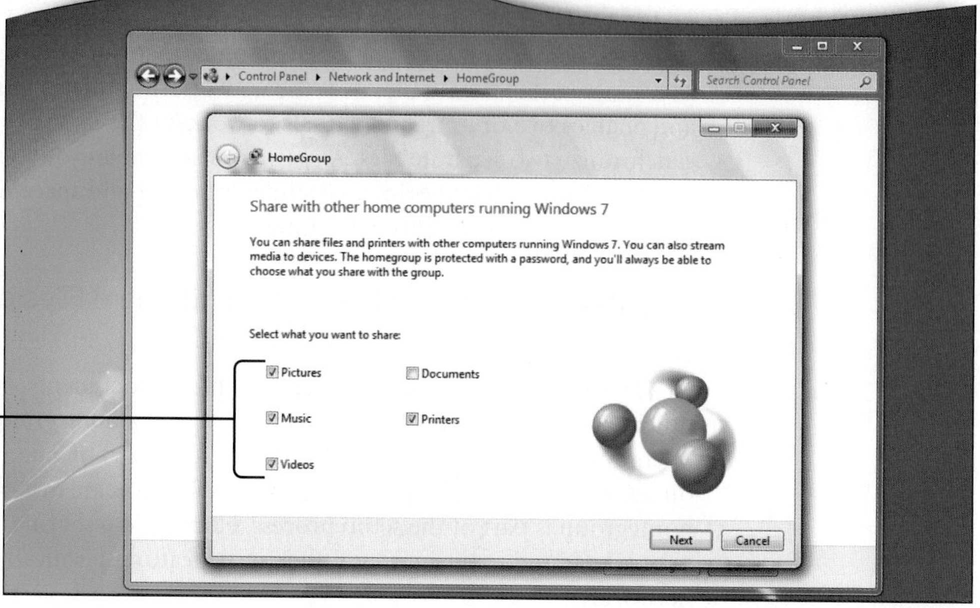

Check boxes enable you to select what you want to share

To connect to a homegroup printer, from the Start button, click Devices and Printers. If you see the printer there, you are done and the printer is ready to use. If the printer is not listed, but you see a message indicating *Windows found a homegroup printer*, click the message to install the printer. For a printer that is not listed, you can manually connect the printer. Search Help and Support for *Manually connect to a homegroup printer*.

To share a specific folder, in Windows Explorer, right-click the folder, and then point to Share with, as shown in Figure 7.31.

Figure 7.31

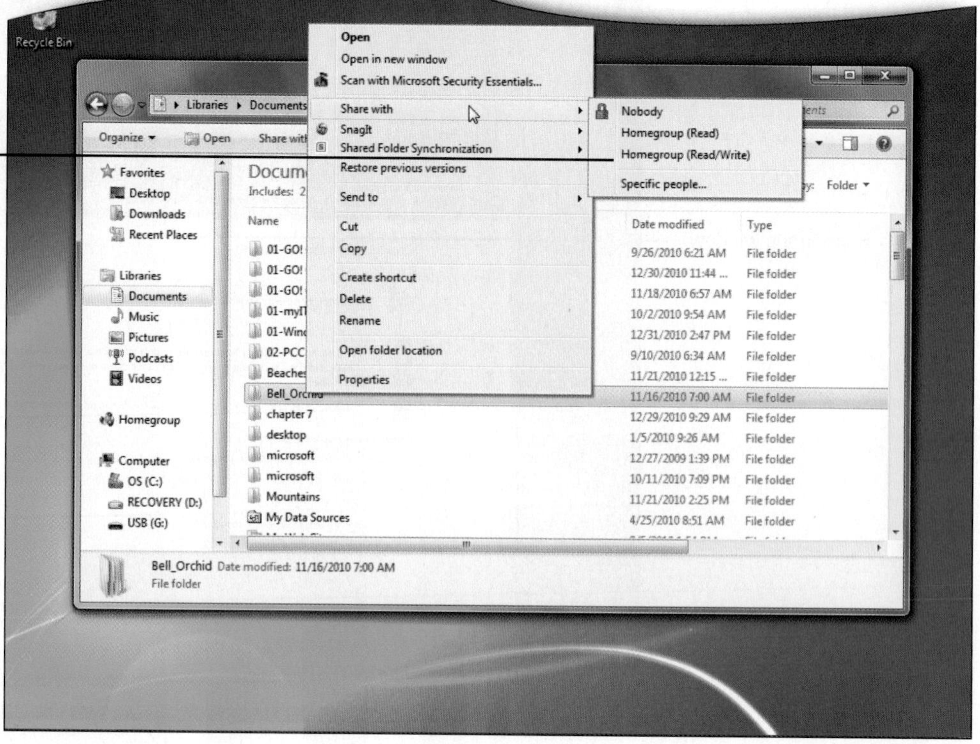

Share with menu

To check how well you understand a Windows 7 homegroup, take a moment to answer the following questions:

1. One advantage of a network is the sharing of __________.
2. Sharing files over a network simplifies moving files between computers, and enables two or more individuals to work on the same project without having to __________ two separate files.
3. To be part of a homegroup, a computer on the network must be running __________ __________.
4. When installing Windows 7 on a computer, joining a homegroup is part of the __________ process.
5. Using a shared printer eliminates the cost and __________ requirements required for each computer to have its own printer.

End You have completed Project 7B

Content-Based Assessments

Summary

You never want to experience a permanent loss of your data or spend tedious hours reinstalling programs and reconfiguring your favorite system settings. In this chapter, you explored various ways to back up and restore your data and system settings so that you will never experience a permanent loss of your data or spend needless time reinstalling programs.

In this chapter, you explored how to install and configure a home network. You saw how most home networks are built using one of two technologies—wired or wireless. Attention was given to installing and securing such a network with extra attention given to securing a wireless network. This chapter also discussed connecting a network to the Internet and troubleshooting network problems. You examined how to connect your home computers by using the HomeGroup feature in Windows 7.

Key Terms

Matching

Match each term in the second column with its correct definition in the first column by writing the letter of the term on the blank line in front of the correct definition.

A Backing up
B Client
C Client/server network
D Driver
E Ethernet
F Local area network

_____ 1. The process of creating a copy of your files somewhere other than on your computer—for example, on a CD, a DVD, or on an external hard drive.

_____ 2. A service that provides a system for backing up your computer files over the Internet on a scheduled basis and then storing the data securely on their computers.

_____ 3. Another name for an external hard drive.

_____ 4. A feature in Windows 7 that creates a backup image containing copies of your programs, system settings, and files.

____ 5. Special software that enables programs to communicate with computer hardware devices, for example, with a graphics card.

____ 6. A representation of a stored state of your computer's system files—like a snapshot of your computer's settings at a specific point in time.

____ 7. A feature in Windows 7 that restores your computer's system files—*not* your data files—to an earlier point in time.

____ 8. A network that is within a relatively limited area; for example, in a home or in a building.

____ 9. A network in which account logon information and files are stored on a server computer, and a computer connecting to, or requesting the services of, the server is referred to as the client.

____ 10. A computer that provides shared resources, such as files or printers, to network users.

____ 11. A computer connecting to, or requesting the services of, the server.

____ 12. A network in which computers connect directly to each other over a private network without the need for a server—the network type commonly used in a home or small office.

____ 13. A device that sends—*routes*—information between two networks; for example, between a home network and the Internet.

____ 14. A networking standard that uses cables to provide network access, and is the most widely installed technology for connecting computers.

____ 15. A type of network connector that holds up to eight wires, and is commonly used to connect a computer to a wired network.

G Online backup service
H Peer-to-peer network
I Portable hard drive
J Restore point
K RJ-45 connector
L Router
M Server
N System image
O System restore

Multiple Choice

Circle the correct answer.

1. A computer hardware component with which your computer connects to and communicates with a network is a:
A. NIC B. Network Interface Card C. Both A. and B.

2. The term for a group of standards for wireless networks that refer to various rates of data transfer speed is:
A. Cat5 B. Cat6 C. 802.11

3. A network arrangement in which each computer and device communicates with the network by using radio signals is a:
A. wired network B. peer-to-peer network C. wireless network

4. A network arrangement that uses a building's existing phone lines is a:
A. hard-wired network B. phone line network C. Ethernet network

5. A network that connects geographically separated locations by using telecommunication services is a:
A. WAN B. LAN C. SPAN

6. A group of up to 32 characters that uniquely identifies a wireless network is a:
A. passphrase B. Service Set Identifier C. HPNA network

7. A Windows 7 feature that makes it easy to set up a wireless network is referred to as:
A. Windows Connect Now B. Wi-Fi C. Network Discovery

8. A high-speed Internet connection typically operating at speeds of 256 kbps or faster is a:
A. broadband connection B. LAN connection C. dial-up connection

9. Software or hardware that checks information coming from the Internet and then either blocks it or allows it to pass through is a:
A. hacker B. firewall C. gateway

10. A wireless network that does not require a passphrase is said to be:
A. encrypted B. unnamed C. unsecured

Apply 7A skills from these Objectives:

1. Back Up and Restore Files and Folders
2. Back Up and Restore Your Entire Computer
3. Configure System Restore and Recover Using Restore Points

Skills Review | Project 7C Backing Up and Restoring Your Computer

Project Files

For Project 7C, you will need the following files:

Student Resource CD (or a USB flash drive containing these files)
Win07_7C_Answer_Sheet (Word document)

You will save your file as:

Lastname_Firstname_7C_Answer_Sheet

Project Results

1 **Close** [X] all open windows. On the taskbar, click the **Windows Explorer** button. In the **navigation pane**, click the drive that contains the student files for this textbook, and then navigate to **01_student_data_files ▶ Chapter_Files ▶ Chapter_07**. Double-click the Word file **win07_7C_Answer_Sheet** to open Word and display the document. Press F12 to display the **Save As** dialog box in Word, navigate to your **Windows 7 Chapter 7** folder, and then using your own name, save the document as **Lastname_Firstname_7C_Answer_Sheet** If necessary, click OK if a message regarding formats displays.

For this project, *refer to both the displayed screens and your textbook*. Insert a blank DVD or connect an external hard drive to activate backup settings.

From the **Control Panel**, display the **Backup and Restore** window. From this window, you can:

A. Back up files in libraries.
B. Restore backed up files.
C. Both A. and B.

2 From the **Backup and Restore** window, you can:

A. Change the settings for the backup schedule.
B. Recover system settings on your computer.
C. Both A. and B.

3 Backing up is the process of creating a copy of your files:

A. On a DVD
B. On an external hard drive
C. Somewhere other than on your computer

4 To start the **Set up backup wizard** from the **Backup and Restore** window, you should:

A. Click the Restore files button.
B. Click the Set up backup (or Back up now) button.
C. Click Windows Easy Transfer.

5 Regarding the program files on your computer:

A. You should back them up every day.
B. Normally you need not back up program or system files.
C. You should back them up once a month.

(Project 7C Backing Up and Restoring Your Computer continues on the next page)

Skills Review | Project 7C Backing Up and Restoring Your Computer (continued)

6 When you back up, you can:

A. Back up all of the data (non-system files) on your computer.

B. Back up only the files that have changed since the last backup.

C. Both A. and B.

7 In the **Backup and Restore** window, under **Back up or restore your files**, if a date and time display, you know that:

A. A backup has already been completed on your computer.

B. No backup is necessary.

C. You cannot back up at this time.

8 **Close** the **Backup and Restore** window. In **Windows Help and Support**, search for **back up my computer** and then click **Back up your files**. According to this information, after you create your *first* backup, Windows Backup will:

A. Add new or changed information to your subsequent backups.

B. Erase your subsequent backups.

C. Move your subsequent backups to another location.

9 In **Windows Help and Support**, search for **system restore** and then click **What is System Restore?** According to this information, which of the following is true?

A. System Restore helps you restore your computer's system files to an earlier point in time.

B. System Restore can undo system changes to your computer without disturbing your personal files.

C. Both A. and B.

10 Click the link **Create a restore point**. According to the displayed information, which of the following is true?

A. Restore points are automatically created by System Restore daily.

B. System image backups stored on hard disks can be used for System Restore.

C. During a system restore, your data files are deleted.

Be sure you have typed all of your answers in your Word document. **Save** and close your Word document, and submit it as directed by your instructor. **Close** all open windows.

End **You have completed Project 7C**

Content-Based Assessments

Apply **7B** skills from these Objectives:

- **4** Use the Network and Sharing Center to Set Up a Home Network
- **5** Secure and Troubleshoot a Home Network
- **6** Use Homegroup to Share Files and Printers on a Home Network

Skills Review | Project 7D Setting Up and Securing a Home Network

Project Files

For Project 7D, you will need the following files:

Student Resource CD (or a USB flash drive containing these files)
Win07_7D_Answer_Sheet (Word document)

You will save your file as:

Lastname_Firstname_7D_Answer_Sheet

Project Results

1 **Close** all open windows. On the taskbar, click the **Windows Explorer** button. In the **navigation pane**, click the drive that contains the student files for this textbook, and then navigate to **01_student_data_files ▶ Chapter_Files ▶ Chapter_07**. Double-click the Word file **win07_7D_Answer_Sheet** to open Word and display the document. Press F12 to display the **Save As** dialog box in Word, navigate to your **Windows 7 Chapter 7** folder, and then using your own name, save the document as **Lastname_Firstname_7D_Answer_Sheet** If necessary, click OK if a message regarding formats displays.

Display the **Control Panel**, click **Network and Internet**, and then click **Network and Sharing Center**. Click **Set up a new connection or network**. In the **Choose a connection option** screen, which of the following is *not* a connection option?

A. Connect to the Internet
B. Set up a new network
C. Connect to an Internet Service Provider

2 Display **Windows Help and Support**, search for **set up a network**, and then click **What you need to set up a home network**. Which type of network technology is *not* indicated as a common network technology?

A. Wireless
B. Ethernet
C. VPN

3 Under **Network technologies**, click **Wireless** to expand the information. According to this information, which of the following is *not* an advantage of a wireless network?

A. Easier to move computers around
B. Easier to install
C. Faster than other networks

4 Under **Network technologies**, click **Ethernet** to expand the information. Which of the following is an advantage of an Ethernet network?

A. Cables are easy to install
B. Inexpensive and fast
C. Easy to use when computers are in different rooms

(Project 7D Setting Up and Securing a Home Network continues on the next page)

Skills Review | Project 7D Setting Up and Securing a Home Network (continued)

5 In the upper left corner of the **Windows Help and Support** window, click the **Back** button, and then click **Install a printer on a home network**. How many basic ways are there to make a printer available to the computers on your home network?

A. One
B. Two
C. Three

6 Connecting a printer to one computer and then setting Windows 7 to share the computer is referred to as a:

A. Shared printer
B. Managed printer
C. USB printer

7 A disadvantage of sharing a printer in the traditional manner is:

A. Not all USB printers can be shared
B. The host computer must always be powered up
C. Both A. and B.

8 A big advantage of a network printer, which connects directly to a computer network as a stand-alone device, is:

A. It is always available
B. It is faster than a shared printer
C. Both A. and B.

9 In the upper left corner of the **Windows Help and Support** window, click the **Back** button, and then click **Setting up a wireless network**. According to this information, which of the following will assist in getting the strongest signal for your wireless router?

A. Positioning the wireless router away from walls and large metal objects
B. Positioning the wireless router on the floor
C. Positioning the wireless router in a closet

10 To secure your home network, you should:

A. Change the default user name and password
B. Lock the router in a file cabinet
C. Both A. and B.

Be sure you have typed all of your answers in your Word document. **Save** and close your Word document, and submit it as directed by your instructor. **Close** all open windows.

End You have completed Project 7D

Content-Based Assessments

Apply 7A skills from these Objectives:

1. Back Up and Restore Files and Folders
2. Back Up and Restore Your Entire Computer
3. Configure System Restore and Recover Using Restore Points

Mastering Windows 7 | Project 7E Backing Up and Restoring Your Computer

In the following Mastering Windows 7 project, you will locate where to back up your files. You will capture and save a screen that looks similar to Figure 7.32.

Project Files

For Project 7E, you will need the following file:

New Snip file

You will save your file as:

Lastname_Firstname_7E_Change_Snip

Project Results

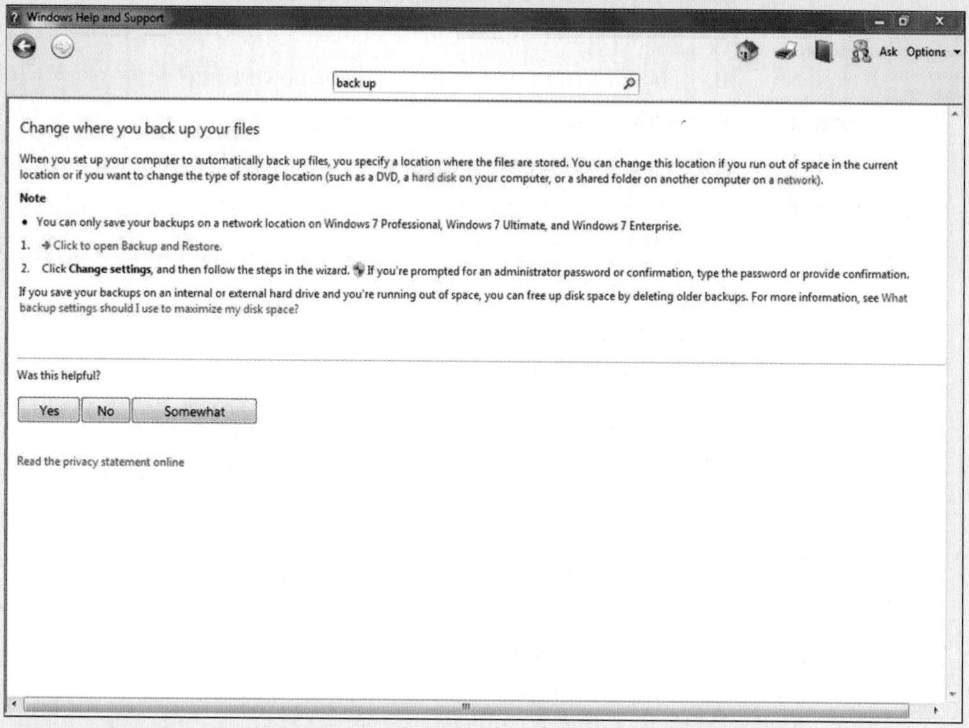

Figure 7.32

(Project 7E Backing Up and Restoring Your Computer continues on the next page)

Mastering Windows 7 | Project 7E Backing Up and Restoring Your Computer (continued)

1 Display the **Windows Help and Support** window, search for **back up** and then click **Change where you back up your files**.

2 Maximize the window. Create a **Full-screen snip**, and save it as **Firstname_Lastname_7E_Change_Snip** Submit this file as directed by your instructor, and then close all open windows.

End You have completed Project 7E

Apply 7B skills from these Objectives:

- 4 Use the Network and Sharing Center to Set Up a Home Network
- 5 Secure and Troubleshoot a Home Network
- 6 Use Homegroup to Share Files and Printers on a Home Network

Mastering Windows 7 | Project 7F Displaying the Network and Sharing Center

In the following Mastering Windows 7 project, you will display the Network and Sharing Center. You will capture and save a screen that looks similar to Figure 7.33.

Project Files

For Project 7F, you will need the following file:

New Snip file

You will save your file as:

Lastname_Firstname_7F_Map_Snip

Project Results

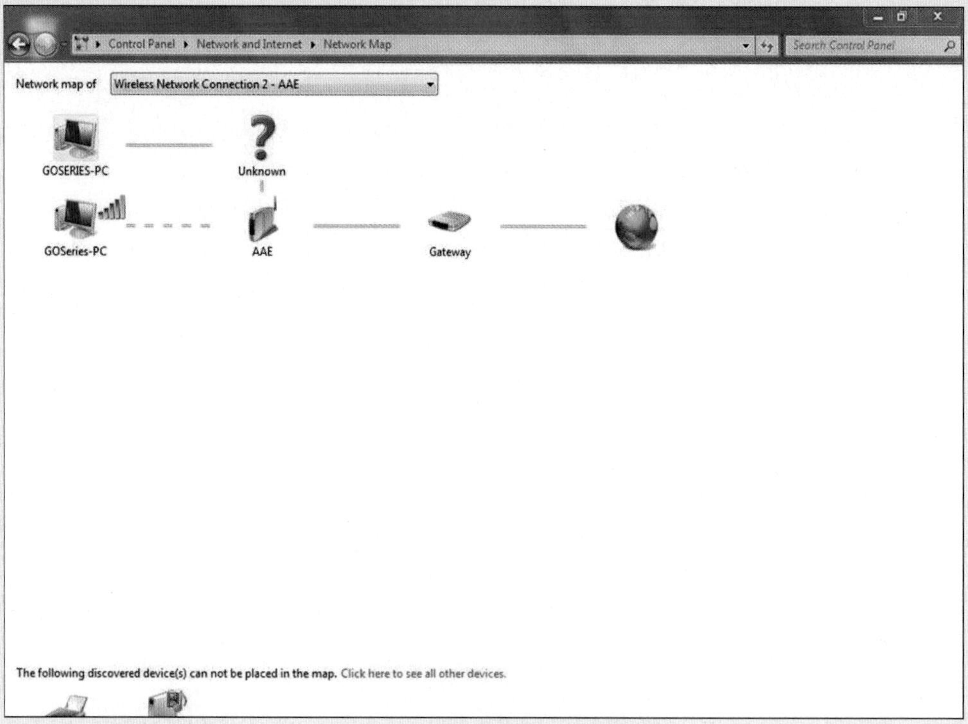

Figure 7.33

(Project 7F Displaying the Network and Sharing Center continues on the next page)

Mastering Windows 7 | Project 7F Displaying the Network and Sharing Center (continued)

1 Display the **Network and Sharing Center**, and then click **See full map**.

2 Maximize the window. Create a **Full-screen snip**, and save it as **Firstname_Lastname_7F_Map_Snip** Submit this file as directed by your instructor, and then close all open windows.

End **You have completed Project 7F**

Outcomes-Based Assessments

Rubric

The following outcomes-based assessments are *open-ended assessments*. That is, there is no specific correct result; your result will depend on your approach to the information provided. Make *Professional Quality* your goal. Use the following scoring rubric to guide you in *how* to approach the problem, and then to evaluate *how well* your approach solves the problem.

The *criteria*—Software Mastery, Content, Format and Layout, and Process—represent the knowledge and skills you have gained that you can apply to solving the problem. The *levels of performance*—Professional Quality, Approaching Professional Quality, or Needs Quality Improvements—help you and your instructor evaluate your result.

	Your completed project is of Professional Quality if you:	Your completed project is Approaching Professional Quality if you:	Your completed project Needs Quality Improvements if you:
1-Software Mastery	Choose and apply the most appropriate skills, tools, and features and identify efficient methods to solve the problem.	Choose and apply some appropriate skills, tools, and features, but not in the most efficient manner.	Choose inappropriate skills, tools, or features, or are inefficient in solving the problem.
2-Content	Construct a solution that is clear and well organized, contains content that is accurate, appropriate to the audience and purpose, and is complete. Provide a solution that contains no errors in spelling, grammar, or style.	Construct a solution in which some components are unclear, poorly organized, inconsistent, or incomplete. Misjudge the needs of the audience. Have some errors in spelling, grammar, or style, but the errors do not detract from comprehension.	Construct a solution that is unclear, incomplete, or poorly organized; contains some inaccurate or inappropriate content; and contains many errors in spelling, grammar, or style. Do not solve the problem.
3-Format and Layout	Format and arrange all elements to communicate information and ideas, clarify function, illustrate relationships, and indicate relative importance.	Apply appropriate format and layout features to some elements, but not others. Overuse features, causing minor distraction.	Apply format and layout that does not communicate information or ideas clearly. Do not use format and layout features to clarify function, illustrate relationships, or indicate relative importance. Use available features excessively, causing distraction.
4-Process	Use an organized approach that integrates planning, development, self-assessment, revision, and reflection.	Demonstrate an organized approach in some areas, but not others; or, use an insufficient process of organization throughout.	Do not use an organized approach to solve the problem.

Apply a combination of the 7A and 7B skills.

Problem Solving | Project 7G Help Desk

In this project, you will construct a solution by applying any combination of the skills you practiced from the Objectives in Projects 7A and 7B.

Project Files

For Project 7G, you will need the following file:

win07_7G_Help_Desk

You will save your document as:

Lastname_Firstname_7G_Help_Desk

From the student files that accompany this textbook, open the **Chapter_Files** folder, and then in **Chapter_07** folder, locate and open the Word document **win07_7G_Help_Desk**. Save the document in your chapter folder as **Lastname_Firstname_7G_Help_Desk**

The following e-mail question has arrived at the Help Desk from an employee at the Bell Orchid Hotel's corporate office. In the Word form, construct a response based on your knowledge of Windows 7. Although an e-mail response is not as formal as a letter, you should still use good grammar, good sentence structure, professional language, and a polite tone. Save your document and submit the response as directed by your instructor.

To: Help Desk

When I am traveling on business, I create a lot of files on the hard disk drive of my laptop computer. Sometimes I am out of the office for over a week. Should I back up the files on my laptop, and if so, how can I do that?

End **You have completed Project 7G**

Outcomes-Based Assessments

Apply a combination of the 7A and 7B skills.

Problem Solving | Project 7H Help Desk

In this project, you will construct a solution by applying any combination of the skills you practiced from the Objectives in Projects 7A and 7B.

Project Files

For Project 7H, you will need the following file:

win07_7H_Help_Desk

You will save your document as:

Lastname_Firstname_7H_Help_Desk

From the student files that accompany this textbook, open the **Chapter_Files** folder, and then in **Chapter_07** folder, locate and open the Word document **win07_7H_Help_Desk**. Save the document in your chapter folder as **Lastname_Firstname_7H_Help_Desk**

The following e-mail question has arrived at the Help Desk from an employee at the Bell Orchid Hotel's corporate office. In the Word form, construct a response based on your knowledge of Windows 7. Although an e-mail response is not as formal as a letter, you should still use good grammar, good sentence structure, professional language, and a polite tone. Save your document and submit the response as directed by your instructor.

To: Help Desk

One of our offices needs to set up a local network, but we cannot decide if we should use a wired or wireless network. What are the advantages and disadvantages of each type of network?

End **You have completed Project 7H**

Apply a combination of the 7A and 7B skills.

Problem Solving | Project 7I Help Desk

In this project, you will construct a solution by applying any combination of the skills you practiced from the Objectives in Projects 7A and 7B.

Project Files

For Project 7I, you will need the following file:

win07_7I_Help_Desk

You will save your document as:

Lastname_Firstname_7I_Help_Desk

From the student files that accompany this textbook, open the **Chapter_Files** folder, and then in **Chapter_07** folder, locate and open the Word document **win07_7I_Help_Desk**. Save the document in your chapter folder as **Lastname_Firstname_7I_Help_Desk**

The following e-mail question has arrived at the Help Desk from an employee at the Bell Orchid Hotel's corporate office. In the Word form, construct a response based on your knowledge of Windows 7. Although an e-mail response is not as formal as a letter, you should still use good grammar, good sentence structure, professional language, and a polite tone. Save your document and submit the response as directed by your instructor.

To: Help Desk

In the Business Center of our hotel, we have three computers and one printer. How can we set up the printer so that guests can print from each of the three computers?

End You have completed Project 7I

Maintaining Your Computer and Optimizing Its Performance

OUTCOMES

At the end of this chapter you will be able to:

OBJECTIVES

Mastering these objectives will enable you to:

PROJECT 8A

Maintain your computer's hard disk drive, keep your Windows 7 software secure and up to date, and automate hard disk drive maintenance tasks.

1. Maintain Your Computer's Hard Disk Drive (p. 481)
2. View Windows Update Settings (p. 491)
3. Schedule Maintenance Tasks by Using Task Scheduler (p. 495)

PROJECT 8B

Locate system information, install and remove programs, and optimize system performance.

4. Locate System Information (p. 505)
5. Install and Uninstall Programs (p. 511)
6. Optimize Computer Performance (p. 515)

beltsazar/Shutterstock

In This Chapter

Microsoft Windows 7 is the operating system software that manages your computer's hardware, software, and data files. All of these components work together as a single system, and Windows 7 includes the tools you need to maintain that system. It is good practice to perform some maintenance tasks periodically; some maintenance tasks are configured to run automatically.

Windows 7 also includes tools for measuring a computer's performance. By examining this performance information, you can make adjustments to optimize the performance level of your computer.

In this chapter, you will use programs that maintain your computer's disks, schedule maintenance tasks to run automatically, and optimize your computer's performance.

The projects in this chapter relate to the **Bell Orchid Hotels**, headquartered in Boston, and which own and operate resorts and business-oriented hotels. Resort properties are located in popular destinations, including Honolulu, Orlando, San Diego, and Santa Barbara. The resorts offer deluxe accommodations and a wide array of dining options. Other Bell Orchid hotels are located in major business centers and offer the latest technology in their meeting facilities. The company plans to open new properties and update existing properties over the next ten years.

Project 8A Maintaining a Computer

Project Activities

In Activities 8.01 through 8.06, you will participate in training along with Steven Ramos and Barbara Hewitt, both of whom work for the Information Technology Department at the headquarters office of the Bell Orchid Hotels. After completing this part of the training, you will be able to delete unneeded files, consolidate the files on your hard disk drive, repair errors on disks, check your Windows 7 Update settings, and schedule tasks to run automatically. You will capture screens that look similar to Figure 8.1.

Project Files

For Project 8A, you will need the following files:

New Snip files

You will save your files as:

Lastname_Firstname_8A_Cleanup_Snip
Lastname_Firstname_8A_Check_Disk_Snip
Lastname_Firstname_8A_Update_Snip
Lastname_Firstname_8A_Task_1_Snip
Lastname_Firstname_8A_Task_2_Snip

Project Results

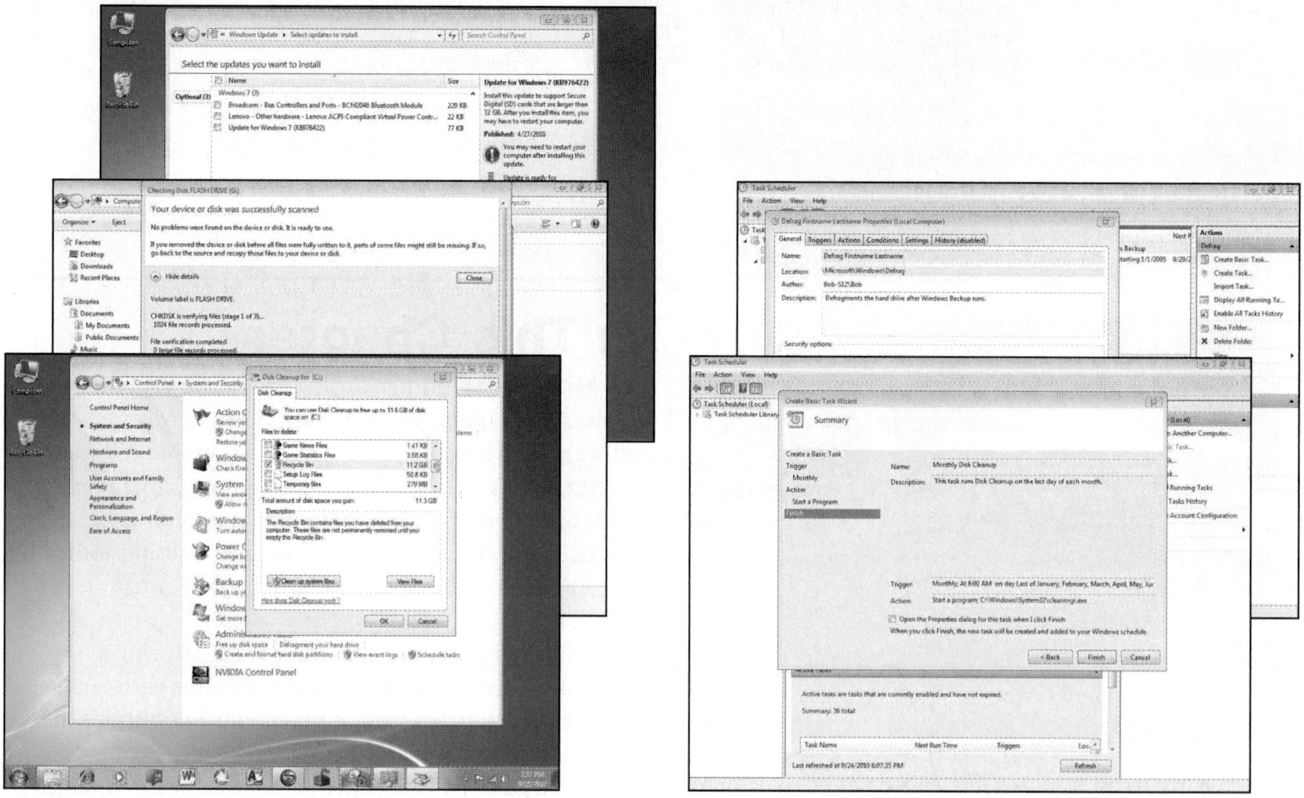

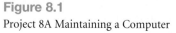

Figure 8.1
Project 8A Maintaining a Computer

Objective 1 | Maintain Your Computer's Hard Disk Drive

Your computer has at least one hard disk drive—some computers have two or more hard disk drives. Your computer's primary hard disk drive stores your data and programs, including the operating system program, Windows 7. Because almost everything you do on your computer begins in some way with the hard disk drive—for example, starting programs or locating your data files—it is good practice to regularly perform some simple tasks that will keep your hard disk drive in good working condition.

Windows 7 provides tools to assist you in performing the tasks that will maintain your hard disk drive. If your hard disk drive encounters a problem or fails completely, you will need to rely on the backups of your files that you have made, from which you can retrieve your data.

Activity 8.01 | Using Disk Cleanup

Eventually your hard disk drive will become full, especially if you install large programs or store a large number of pictures, songs, or videos on your computer—in general, files that contain sound or images are larger than files that contain only words or numbers. Although you have practiced techniques to organize your data efficiently, in the day-to-day use of your computer you will probably generate many files that, after a while, you no longer need. Additionally, Windows 7 and Internet browsing create files on your computer that take up space.

When a hard disk drive becomes low on ***free disk space***, Windows 7 will operate slowly or display messages indicating that additional free disk space is needed. Windows 7 requires some free disk space to operate properly and perform its own system functions.

The easiest way to increase the amount of free disk space is to use ***Disk Cleanup***. Disk Cleanup is a program within Windows 7 that scans your hard disk drive and removes temporary files, empties the Recycle Bin, and removes a variety of system files and other items that you may no longer need.

In this activity, you will practice using Disk Cleanup to delete unneeded files. Rely on Disk Cleanup for a simple and useful way to delete unnecessary files and to increase the amount of free disk space on your hard disk drive.

> **Alert! | Do You Have an Administrator Account?**
>
> Learning to customize and control your computer by using Windows 7 as an administrator is the best way to learn Windows 7, because many features are available only to an individual who has an administrator account. For the instruction in this chapter, it is assumed that you are logging on with an administrator account.

1. Insert your USB flash drive, and wait a moment for your computer to recognize the removable media. If necessary, **Close** the **AutoPlay** dialog box.

   You will use your USB flash drive toward the end of this project to record your progress.

2. Display the **Start** menu, open the **Control Panel**, and then click **System and Security**. Near the bottom of the window, under **Administrative Tools**, click **Free up disk space**.

> **Another Way**
>
> From the Start menu, point to All Programs, and then click Accessories. Under Accessories, click System Tools, and then click Disk Cleanup.

3 In the **Disk Cleanup: Drive Selection** dialog box, under **Drives**, click the **arrow**, select the drive you want to clean up—typically drive C:—and then click **OK**.

Disk Cleanup displays a green progress bar while it scans for files that *could* be deleted—no files are actually deleted during this scan process—and calculates an estimate of how much free disk space you would gain by deleting the suggested files.

4 Wait a few moments for the scan to complete, and then in the displayed **Disk Cleanup for (C:)** dialog box, under **Files to delete**, if necessary, point to and then click the words *Downloaded Program Files* to select this category of files so that you can view its description in the lower portion of the dialog box. Compare your screen with Figure 8.2.

This dialog box lists several categories from which you can choose to delete files. In the column of check boxes on the left, certain file groups are already selected, which indicates that Windows 7 recommends these files for deletion. In the right column, the amount of potential free disk space displays.

Figure 8.2

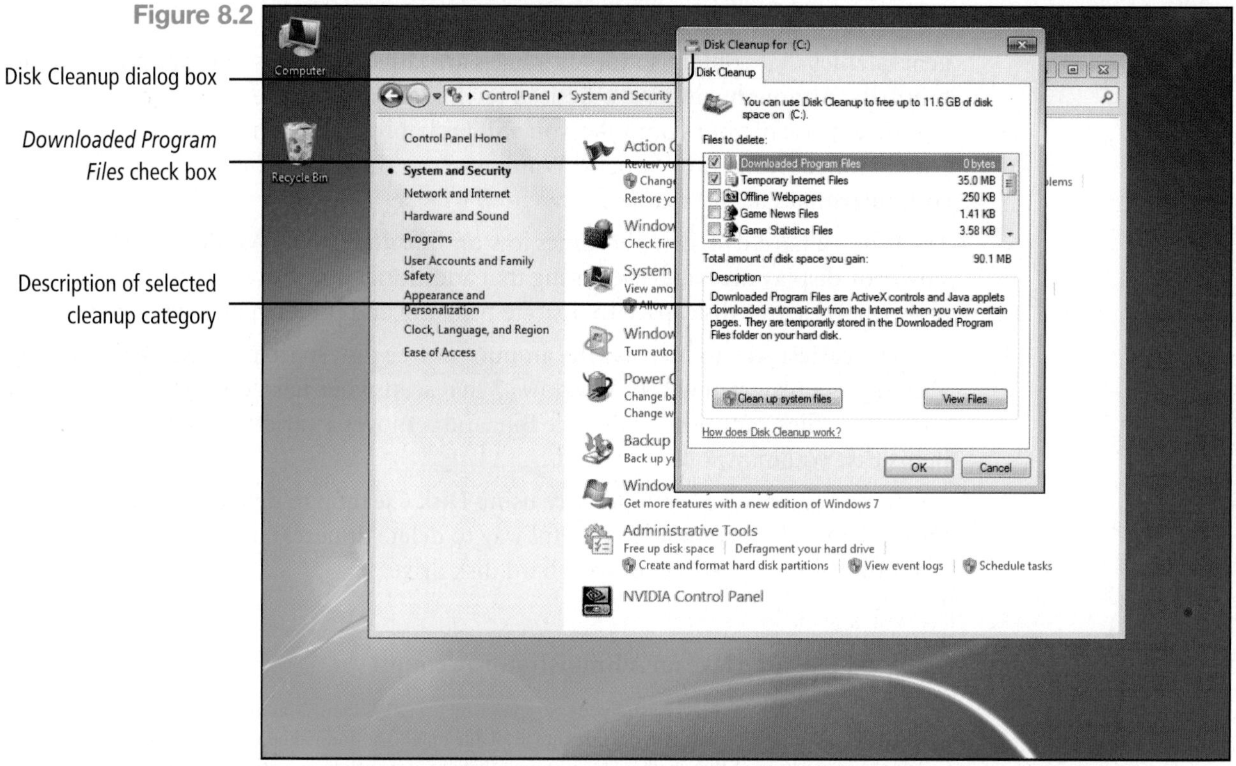

5 Take a moment to click each category of file, read its **Description**, and then study the table in Figure 8.3.

File Categories that the Disk Cleanup Program Can Delete (Your list may vary)

Category	Description and Notes
Downloaded Program Files	Special programs used by Internet Explorer and downloaded when you visit Web pages; does *not* include new programs that you purposely download from the Internet. Note: Do *not* delete the files in this category because generally they contain useful programs that help other programs run on your computer. For example, the learning management system used by your college might download small programs here.
Temporary Internet Files	Files stored by Internet Explorer when you are browsing the Internet. Note: Deleting these files may cause a temporary increase in the time it takes to display your frequently viewed Web sites; however, you should delete the files in this category because it includes many files from sites you may never visit again.
Offline Webpages	Web pages that have been stored on your computer so you can browse them even if you do not have an Internet connection. Note: Unless you have saved Web pages to be accessed when an Internet connection is not available, you will probably want to delete these files.
Game News Files *and/or* Game Statistics Files	Files that contain information about games that you play. Note: You may have one, both, or neither of these categories. The files are usually very small, and it is seldom necessary to delete them.
Recycle Bin	Files that you have deleted from your hard disk drive but that still remain in the Recycle Bin. Note: It is good practice to empty your Recycle Bin periodically, but if you forget to do so, Disk Cleanup will do it for you. Recall that emptying the Recycle Bin permanently deletes the files that have been moved there. If you have a large number of files in your Recycle Bin, deleting them could free up a significant amount of hard disk space on your computer.
Setup Log Files	Files that track the process of installing Windows 7. Note: These files can be safely deleted after you are satisfied with your Windows 7 installation; deleting these files may not free up a significant amount of disk space.
Temporary files	Files that are created by some programs, and that are older than one week. For example, programs that install software often create temporary files that are not deleted when the installation is complete. Note: Selecting this check box will delete temporary files that are older than one week. You might want to delete temporary files manually so that you can delete *all* temporary files—including those that are less than one week old.
Thumbnails	Copies of your picture, video, and document thumbnails—for example, the Word and Excel file icons—stored so they can be quickly displayed when you need them. Note: If these files, which are stored in a small database, are deleted, they will be re-created the next time the folder is opened in a view that displays thumbnails.
Files discarded by Windows upgrade	Files created if you upgraded to a higher version of Windows 7. Note: If you have upgraded Windows 7, for example from Home Premium to Ultimate, a significant amount of space can be freed by deleting these files; select this option when you are satisfied that your new version is working properly.
Per user archived Windows Error Report *and* System archived Windows Error Report	Files that Windows 7 uses to check for problems and suggest solutions. For example, the Performance and Reliability Monitor uses these files to create a reliability report. Note: Delete these files only if you are confident that your computer will continue to run error free and that you will not need to run problem-solving programs that depend on these files.

Figure 8.3

6 If necessary, scroll up to view the top of the list, and then click to *clear* the **Downloaded Program Files** check box.

Recall that *Downloaded Program Files* refers to programs downloaded and used by Internet Explorer that are generally useful. If the computer at which you are working is used by an organization, deleting these files could disable important features.

7 In the list, scroll down, click the words *Recycle Bin*, and then in the lower right corner of the dialog box, click the **View Files** button. If necessary, change the view to **Details**. Compare your screen with Figure 8.4.

The *Recycle Bin* folder window displays—the same folder window that you used to permanently delete files in previous projects. Recall that when an item is placed in the Recycle Bin, it is not deleted from the hard disk drive until the Recycle Bin is emptied.

Figure 8.4

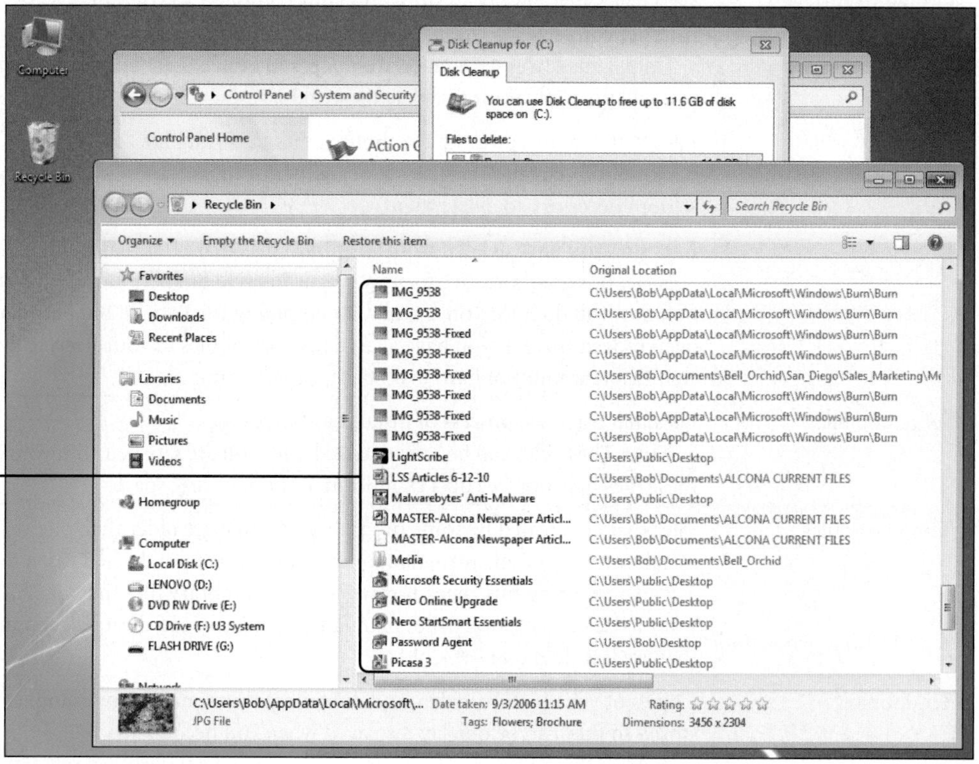

8 **Close** the **Recycle Bin** folder window. Select the **Recycle Bin** check box.

When *Recycle Bin* is checked, Disk Cleanup will permanently remove all the items in the Recycle Bin. Recall that after the Recycle Bin is emptied, files moved there cannot be recovered.

9 **Start** the **Snipping Tool** program, click the **New arrow**, and then click **Full-screen Snip**. In the **Snipping Tool** mark-up window, click the **Save Snip** button.

10 In the **Save As** dialog box, in the **navigation pane**, scroll down as necessary, and then under **Computer** click your USB flash drive so that it displays in the **address bar**. On the toolbar, click the **New folder** button, type **Windows 7 Chapter 8** and press Enter.

11 In the **file list**, double-click your **Windows 7 Chapter 8** folder to open it. Click in the **File name** box, and then replace the selected text by typing **Lastname_Firstname_8A_Cleanup_Snip** Be sure the file type is **JPEG file**, and then press Enter. **Close** the **Snipping Tool** mark-up window. Hold this file until you finish Project 8A, and then submit this file as directed by your instructor.

12 If you are working on your own computer and would like to delete the selected file types, click **OK**; otherwise click **Cancel** to close the dialog box without making any changes. **Close** [X] the **System and Security** window.

> **More Knowledge | The Low Disk Space Warning**
>
> If a message displays on your computer indicating *low disk space*, click the warning to display the Disk Cleanup program. Disk Cleanup should be the first step in creating more available space on your computer.

Activity 8.02 | Using Disk Defragmenter

A hard disk drive formatted for the Windows 7 operating system contains blocks of space in which data and program files are stored. By remembering where specific information is stored on the hard disk drive, Windows finds and displays your data and your programs when you need them.

The method used to store files on a disk drive is called a ***file system***. Windows 7 typically uses a file system called ***NTFS—New Technology File System***. USB flash drives typically use another type of file system called ***FAT—File Allocation Table***. Both of these file systems divide the disk into ***sectors***, and the sectors are then grouped together to form ***clusters***. A sector is a block of space on the drive and a cluster is the smallest area in which data can be written on a disk using NTFS or FAT.

On most drives formatted for the Windows 7 operating system, a cluster holds only 4 KB. ***KB*** is the abbreviation for ***kilobyte***. According to the International System of Standards, a single kilobyte stores approximately 1,000 ***bytes***. A byte typically stores a single character, such as a digit or letter, and is commonly used to measure storage sizes on computers. File size, disk capacity, and computer memory are all measured using some multiple of bytes, such as the kilobyte, as shown in the table in Figure 8.5. Files larger than 4 KB are stored in multiple clusters—for example, a 5 MB music file would require at least 1,250 clusters of storage space.

Common Storage Sizes Measured in Bytes (1 byte = A single character such as a letter, number, space, or punctuation mark)

Name	Abbreviation	Number of Bytes (Based on the International System of Standards)	Approximate Capacity
Kilobyte	KB	1,000 bytes	One page of text
Megabyte	MB	1 million bytes (1,000 KB)	100 pages of text One digital photo One minute of MP3 music
Gigabyte	GB	1 billion bytes (1,000 MB)	100,000 pages of text 1,000 digital photos 18 hours of MP3 music
Terabyte	TB	1 trillion bytes (1,000 GB)	100,000,000 pages of text 1,000,000 digital photos 17,520 hours (two years) of MP3 music

Figure 8.5

As you delete files and move files, gaps of unused space are created. Files, when saved, are split apart to fill those unused spaces. The pieces of a file that has been split apart are called ***fragments***. A ***fragmented file*** is a file that has been split apart and whose fragments (clusters) are stored in separate blocks of the hard disk drive.

Windows 7 keeps track of all this, and you need not be concerned with where data is stored. Sometimes however, if many files are split apart, your computer may perform more slowly because it takes more time for Windows 7 to gather all the fragments together and then display the file. The more files that are fragmented, the more computer performance slows.

Disk defragmentation, commonly referred to as ***defragging***, is a process to consolidate fragmented files on your hard disk drive into contiguous blocks—blocks that are next to each other. The process rearranges the data on your hard disk by reorganizing each fragmented file into a single location and rearranging the unused spaces into one large block. In Windows 7, the Disk Defragmenter program runs automatically on a schedule, so you do not have to remember to run it. However, you can still run it manually, use it to defrag another drive, or change its schedule.

To begin a manual defrag, display the Computer window, right-click your hard disk drive, and then click Properties. In the Properties dialog box, display the General tab. A graphic representation of the amount of free space on this device displays, as shown in Figure 8.6.

Figure 8.6

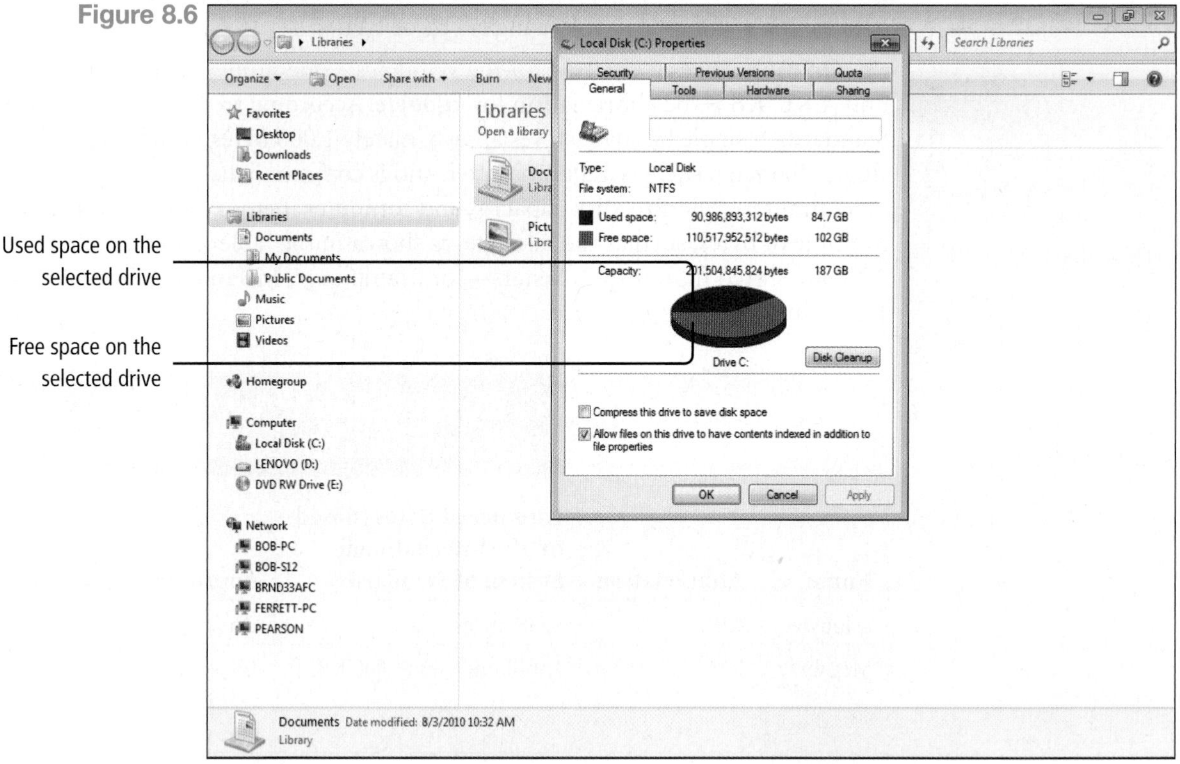

To start the disk defragmentation process, in the Properties dialog box, click the Tools tab. Under Defragmentation, you can click the *Defragment now* button, as shown in Figure 8.7. This may display a User Account Control box requiring your permission to begin the process.

Figure 8.7

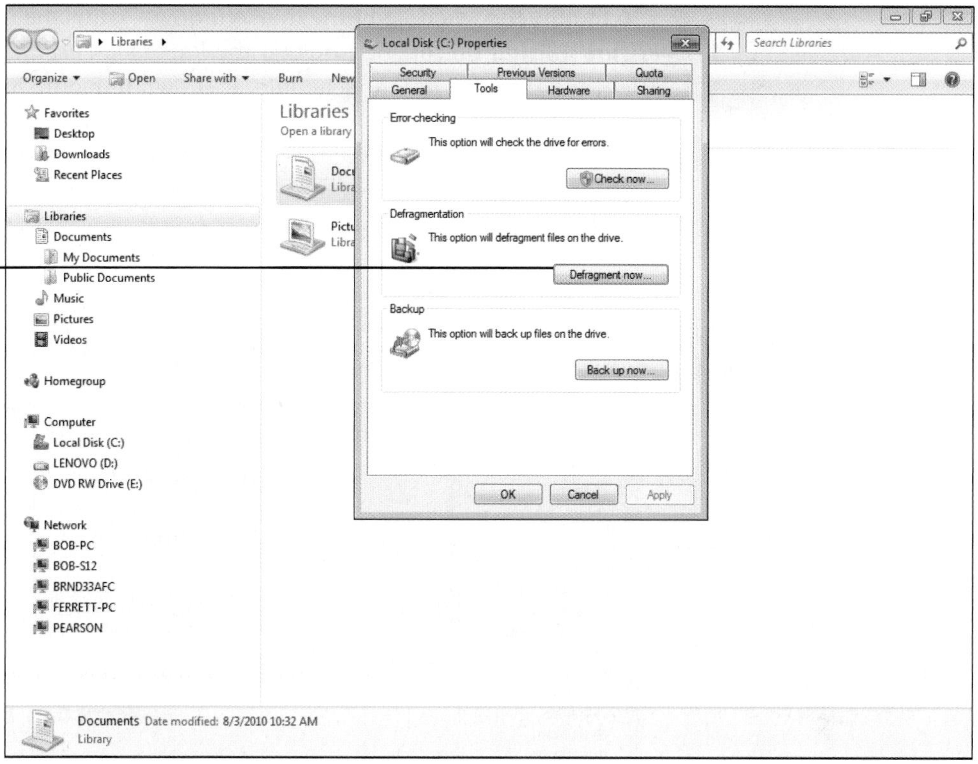

Then, as shown in Figure 8.8, the Disk Defragmenter dialog box displays. By default, Disk Defragmenter is enabled and automatically runs on a weekly schedule. Here you can modify the schedule for defragmenting if you want to do so. The scheduled time assigned by Windows 7 is a time when you are not likely using your computer.

Figure 8.8

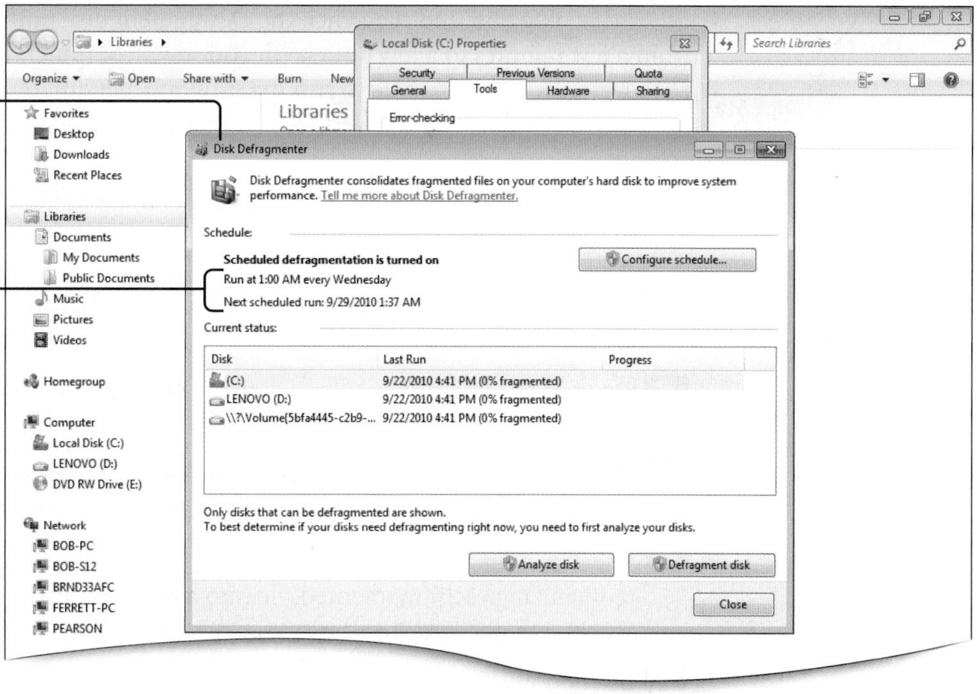

The defragmenting process on a large hard disk drive might take several hours. If you want to defrag at a time other than the scheduled time, you can do so here by clicking the *Defragment disk* button, which will begin the process immediately.

To modify the scheduled time that Windows 7 runs the Disk Defragmenter, click the *Configure schedule* button, be sure that the *Run on a schedule (recommended)* check box is selected, and then modify the schedule, as shown in Figure 8.9.

Figure 8.9

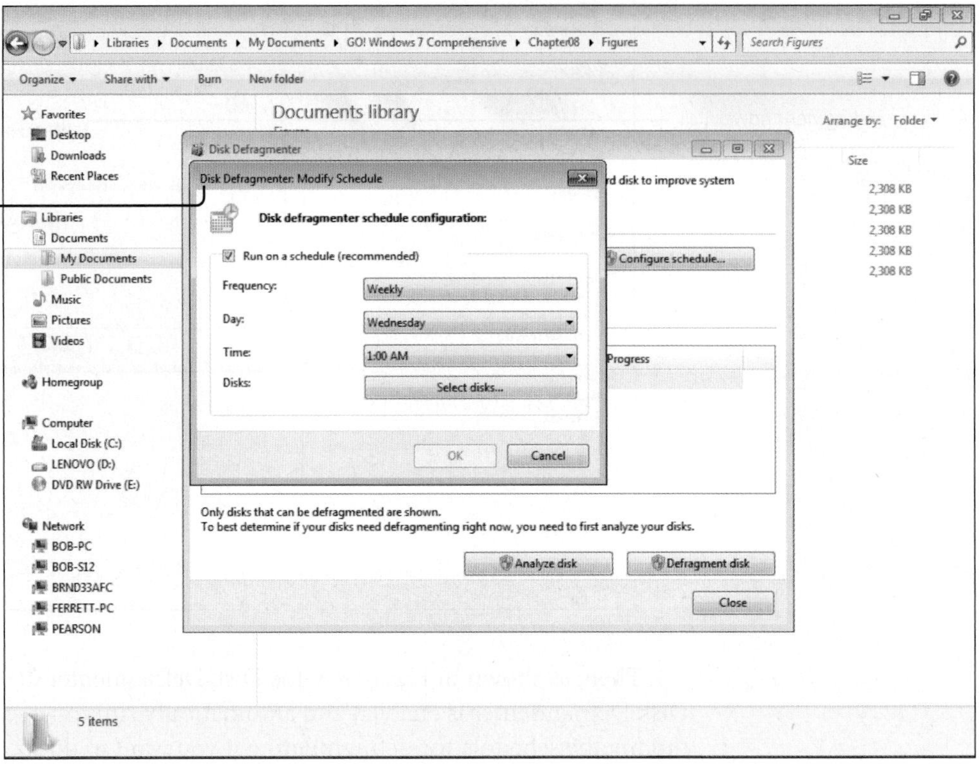

Modify Schedule dialog box

To run the Disk Defragmenter manually, close the *Disk Defragmenter: Modify Schedule* dialog box, and then click the Defragment disk button. The process may take from a few minutes to a few hours. On your own computer, you may want to modify the Disk Defragmenter schedule to run the program at a different time. If you have more than one hard disk drive, you can defragment that drive using the techniques described in this activity.

To check your understanding of the disk defragmentation process, take a moment to answer the following questions:

1. As you delete and move files on your hard disk drive, __________ of unused space are created.
2. On your hard disk drive, files, when saved, might be split apart to fill __________ spaces.
3. If many files are split apart, your computer may perform more __________ because it takes more time to gather fragments and display a file.
4. The disk defragmentation process __________ the data on your hard disk by reorganizing each fragmented file into a single location and rearranging the unused spaces into one large block.
5. In Windows 7, the Disk Defragmenter program runs __________ on a schedule; however, you can still run the program manually if you want to do so.

Activity 8.03 | Detecting and Repairing Errors on Disks

Hard disk drives contain magnetic spinning platters, which Windows 7 has mapped and divided into sectors. Windows 7 saves your data to, and reads your data and programs from, clusters of the hard disk drive.

At any time, a sector can fail—become damaged and unable to store data—and is referred to as a ***bad sector***. NTFS, the file system commonly used by Windows 7, keeps track of bad sectors, attempts to move any data in a bad sector to a new sector, and then marks the sectors as unusable.

USB flash drives have ***firmware*** that prevents storing data in any bad areas of the drive. Firmware is a computer program embedded by a manufacturer into a hardware device.

The Check Disk program scans disks for bad sectors and other errors and attempts to repair them. If a computer is not shut down properly, Check Disk will usually run automatically the next time the computer is started. Check Disk can also be run manually on a removable drive. In this activity, you will practice running Check Disk manually.

1. **Close** any open windows. Be sure that your USB flash drive is inserted in the computer. From the **Start** menu, click **Computer**. On the toolbar, click the **View button arrow**, and then set the view to **Tiles**.

2. In the **file list**, point to your **USB flash drive**, and then right-click. From the shortcut menu, click **Properties**.

> **More Knowledge | Checking Your Hard Disk Drive**
>
> If your computer is not performing properly, or if a file will no longer open, you may want to use the Check Disk program to scan your hard disk drive. When scanning the hard disk drive that stores the Windows 7 operating system, the scan takes up to several hours. Additionally, the scan cannot run while Windows 7 itself is running; thus, the scan must be scheduled to run the next time Windows 7 is started.
>
> To schedule a Check Disk scan on your hard disk drive, from the Computer window, display the Properties dialog box for the hard disk drive, click the *Tools tab,* and then click *Check now.* Under *Check disk options,* select both check boxes—*Automatically fix file system errors* and *Scan for and attempt recovery of bad sectors.* When you click Check Disk's Start button, a message displays asking if you want to run Check Disk the next time you start your computer. To run Check Disk, click the *Schedule disk check* button, and then restart your computer.
>
> Upon restart, a black screen displays with white text informing you that a disk check has been scheduled. You can cancel the scan at this point by pressing any key within ten seconds of this screen appearing. Because this screen has none of the graphical user interface objects found in Windows 7, the mouse is disabled. Only the keyboard can be used to enter commands.
>
> During this process, the Check Disk program uses another name—***CHKDSK***. CHKDSK scans the disk in five stages and commonly takes more than an hour to run. After CHKDSK has started, it can be stopped only by turning off the computer by using the power switch.

3. In the **Properties** dialog box, click the **Tools tab**. Under **Error-checking**, click the **Check now** button. If necessary, in the User Account Control dialog box, click Continue, and then compare your screen with Figure 8.10.

   The Check Disk dialog box displays, and the name of the drive that will be checked displays in the title bar.

   If selected, *Automatically fix file system errors* checks for errors in the data that Windows 7 uses to find files on the disk and attempts to repair that information.

   If selected, *Scan for and attempt recovery of bad sectors* scans for and attempts to recover any readable information from bad sectors and relocate that data into good sectors. If no option is checked, Check Disk creates a report, but makes no changes to the drive.

Figure 8.10

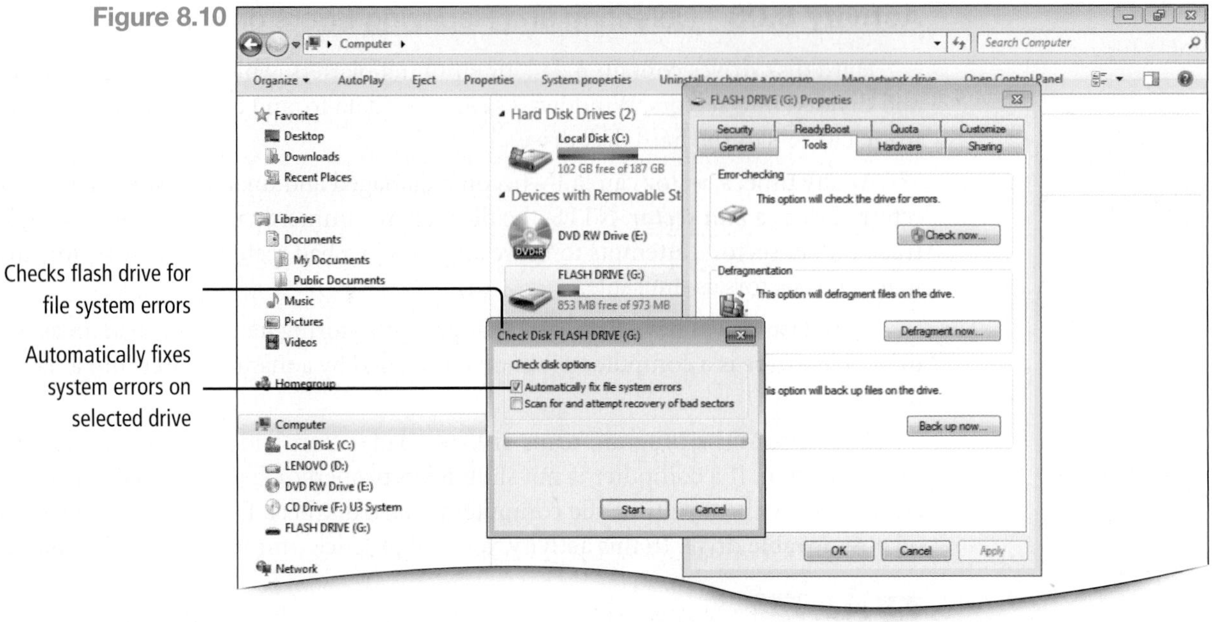

4 If necessary, select the **Automatically fix file system errors** check box, and *clear* the **Scan for and attempt recovery of bad sectors** check box. Click **Start**.

On a USB flash drive, the check for file system errors will probably complete in a minute or less. On a USB flash drive, Check Disk will skip the scan for bad sectors, so there is no need to select that check box for this activity.

5 When the scan is complete, in the lower left corner of the **Checking Disk** dialog box, click the **See details arrow**, and then compare your screen with Figure 8.11.

The Checking Disk dialog box displays the results of the scan. If this is the first scan of your USB flash drive, Check Disk likely fixed some errors. The number of items in your report may vary.

Figure 8.11

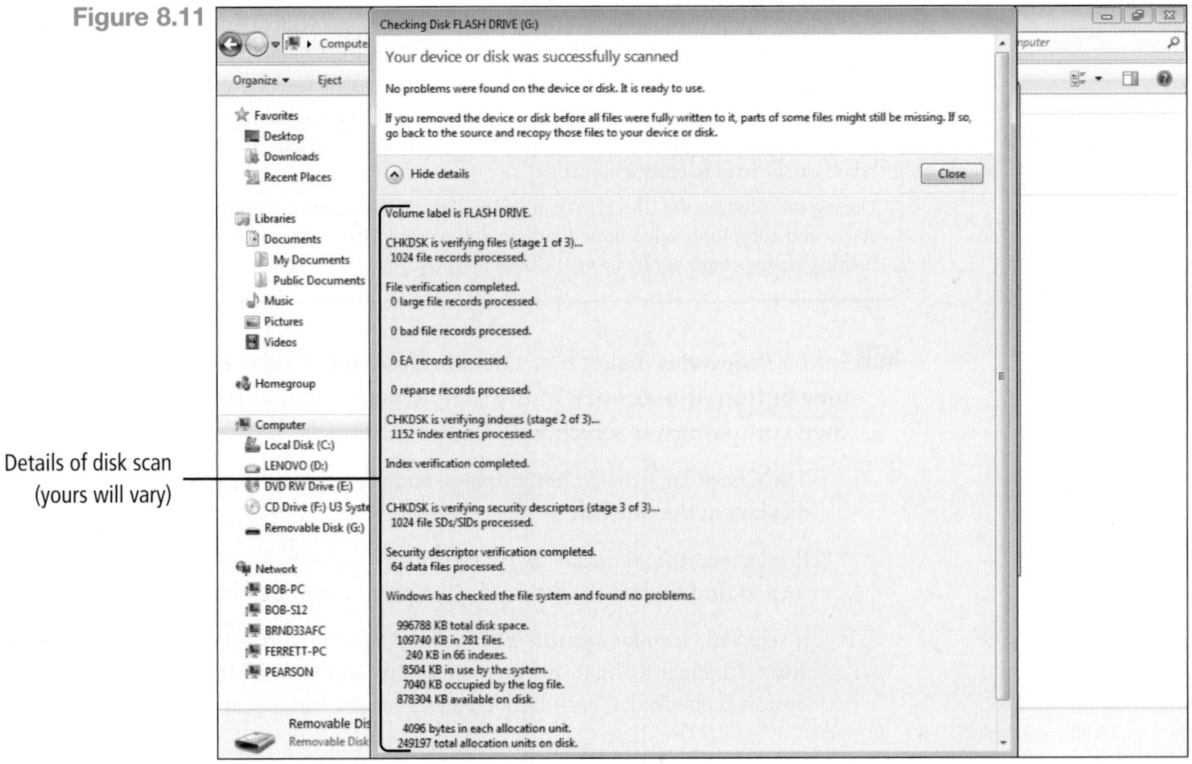

6 **Start** the **Snipping Tool** program, click the **New arrow**, and then click **Full-screen Snip**. In the **Snipping Tool** mark-up window, click the **Save Snip** button.

7 In the **Save As** dialog box, in the **navigation pane**, scroll down as necessary, and then under **Computer**, click your USB flash drive so that it displays in the address bar. Navigate to your **Windows 7 Chapter 8** folder, and then as the file name, type **Lastname_Firstname_8A_Check_Disk_Snip** Be sure the file type is **JPEG**, and then press Enter. **Close** the **Snipping Tool** mark-up window. Hold this file until you finish Project 8A, and then submit this file as directed by your instructor.

If errors were found on your USB flash drive, you may want to scan the disk one more time. Fixing errors often enables Disk Check to find additional errors when it scans a second time.

8 In the **Checking Disk** dialog box, click the **Close** button. **Close** all open windows.

More Knowledge | Dealing with Corrupted Files

A ***corrupted file*** is a file that no longer works properly because it has been accidentally altered by a hardware or software failure. If a file is corrupted, you will not be able to open the file properly. In a corrupted file, the bits are rearranged and the result is that either the file is unreadable to your computer hardware, or it is readable but cannot be deciphered by the program in which it was created. You will not be able to open a corrupted file.

Recall that a file must be opened in the program in which it was created, or a similar program that is compatible. Thus, just because a file will not open does not mean it is corrupted. It means only that your computer may not have, or cannot determine, which program to use to open the file. In such an instance, display the file in a folder window, select the file, on the toolbar, click the Open arrow, click Choose default program, and then use one of the suggested methods to find a suitable program to open the file.

It is very rare for a file to become corrupted. The most common reason for a corrupted file is that something went wrong while the file was being saved; for example, during the save operation, the program experienced a problem or the computer lost power.

Occasionally a corrupted file can be repaired by using a program that can repair such files. If you determine that a file is corrupted, the file should be deleted or replaced. Most corrupted files cannot be repaired.

When a sector fails, the file using that sector will probably fail to open. Recall that a file system is the method used to store files on a disk drive and that the file system divides hard drive disks into blocks called sectors. Running Check Disk may fix this problem by moving the data to good sectors.

Recall that files are stored in clusters, which are groups of sectors. Recall also that the clusters used to store a single file could be scattered in separate locations throughout the drive. Both the FAT and NTFS file systems store data about each file in tables. The most important of these tables tracks which clusters are used to store each file. If a cluster contains a bad sector, the file system table will mark that cluster as bad so that it will no longer be used. If a file system table contains errors, the file system may no longer know which clusters are used to store a file. Running Check Disk with the *Automatically fix the file system errors* option selected repairs most errors in file system tables.

Fortunately, the NTFS file system used by Windows 7 has many safeguards in place that prevent file corruption. When a corrupt file cannot be repaired or recovered, you must rely on your backup system. In many organizations, data is backed up every day. If a file does become corrupted and goes unnoticed, the corrupted version will be copied to the backup file. For this reason, organizations store backup sets from multiple days. Using these backup sets, the last known good version of the file can be found and restored.

Objective 2 | View Windows Update Settings

Microsoft continually improves Windows 7 and then offers those improvements to you—for free—in the form of an ***update***. An update is an addition to Windows 7 that helps prevent or fix problems or that improves the performance of your computer. Windows 7 updates are assigned one of three priorities: *important*, *recommended*, and *optional*.

Important updates usually improve security, recommended updates often improve the way Windows 7 performs, and optional updates typically install new features or programs.

Windows Update is the program that checks for updates, downloads them, and then installs them on your computer. In addition to Windows 7 updates, Windows Update also checks for and installs updates to Microsoft Office.

Activity 8.04 | Viewing Windows Update Settings

For best performance, be sure that your Windows Update is configured correctly. On your own computer, you will likely want to have Windows Update check for updates regularly, and then automatically download and install *important* and *recommended* updates. With this configuration, however, you might miss *optional* updates that are available. In this activity, you will check the Windows Update settings on your computer and then view the optional updates.

> **Alert! | Are You Connected to the Internet?**
>
> Windows Update requires an open connection to the Internet. If you use a dial-up connection on your computer, you will be asked to connect to the Internet during this activity.

1. Be sure that your USB flash drive or other removable media is inserted in the computer. Display the **Start** menu, and then click **Control Panel.**

2. In the **Control Panel**, click **System and Security**, and then under **Action Center**, click **Review your computer's status and resolve issues**. Click **Security**, and then compare your screen with Figure 8.12.

   The Security settings for several essential system security features display, including: *Network firewall*, *Windows Update*, *Virus protection*, *Spyware and unwanted software protection*, and several other security settings. The status of most of these settings should all be *On* or *OK*.

Figure 8.12

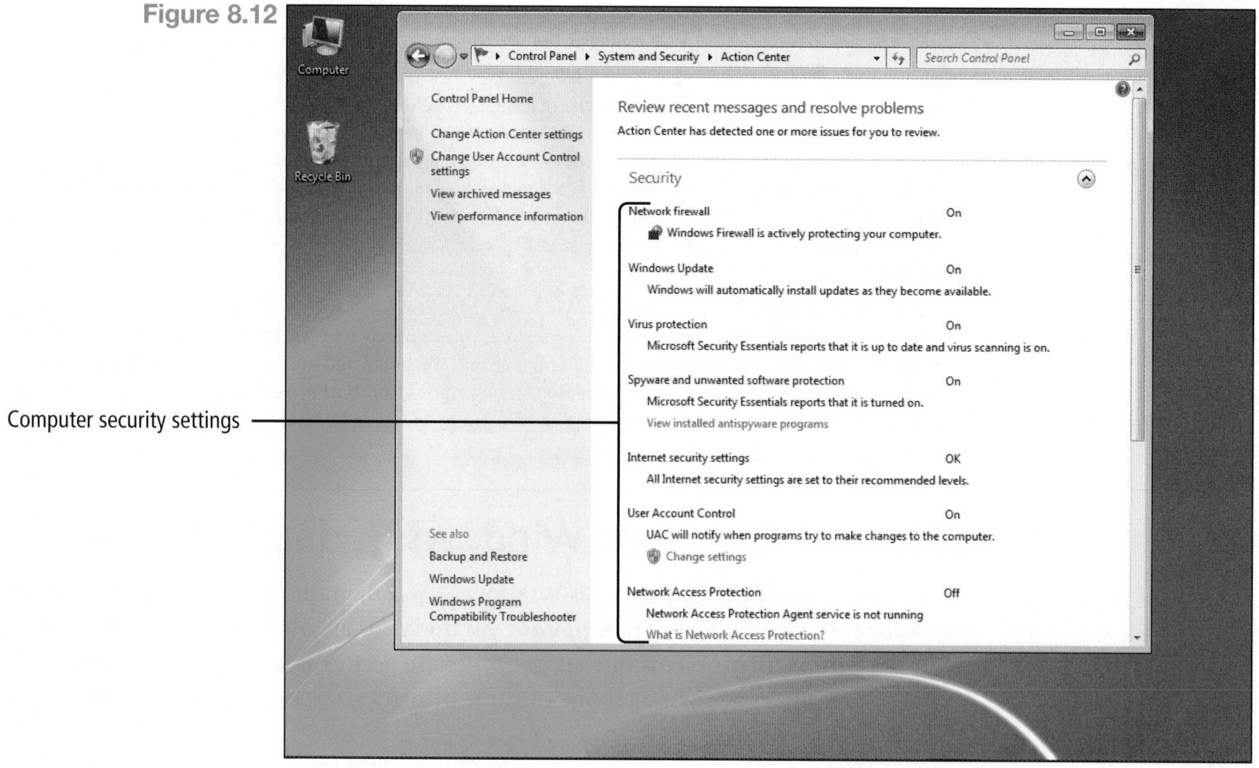

3 Near the bottom of the left pane, click **Windows Update**, and then compare your screen with Figure 8.13.

The left pane of the Windows Update window provides links to related tasks. In the larger pane on the right, a message informs you if your computer is up to date. The number of optional Windows updates displays, and extra updates may be listed for your specific version of Windows 7.

Optional updates may give you extra features, but installing them will not increase the security of your computer—security updates are always in the *important* category and should be installed automatically. At the bottom of the window, information about the most recent Windows Update displays, along with a link to *View update history*.

Figure 8.13

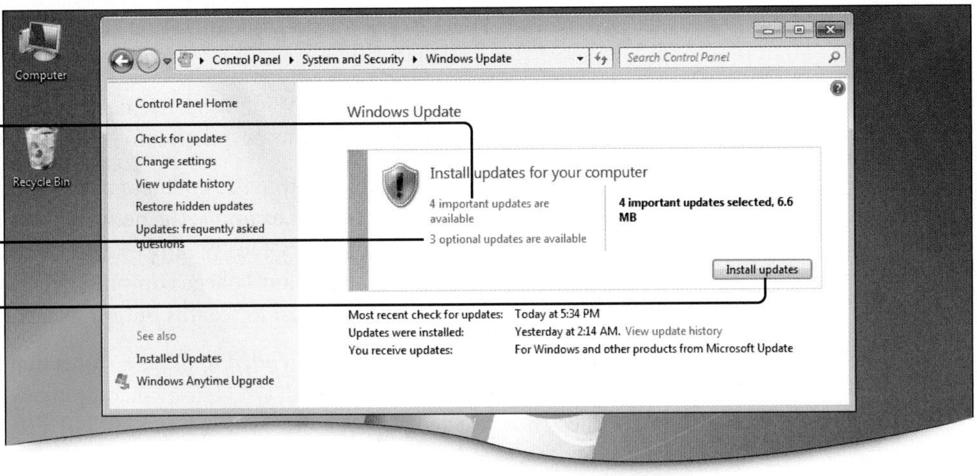

4 In the left pane, click **View update history**. In the **Date Installed** column, notice that you can sort the list of updates in ascending or descending order by date. Compare your screen with Figure 8.14.

Although your list of updates will differ from those shown in Figure 8.14, you can see that updates have been downloaded and installed on your computer. For each update, the Status, Importance, and Date Installed are included.

Figure 8.14

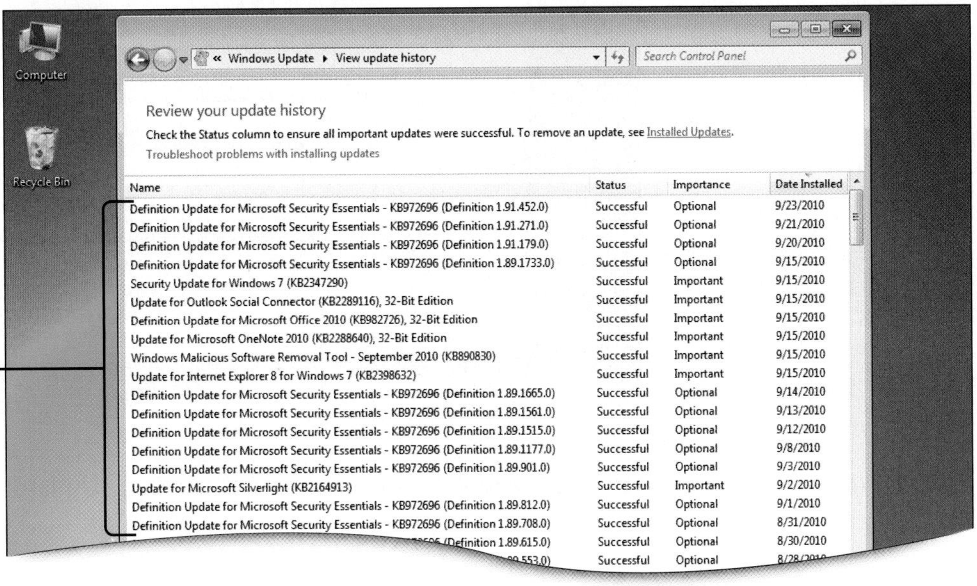

5 In the lower right corner, click **OK** to close the **View update history** window. In the left pane, click **Change settings.** Compare your screen with Figure 8.15.

On your own computer, you should be sure that the *Install updates automatically (recommended)* option is selected. With this option selected, you can be sure that important and recommended updates will be downloaded and installed on your computer.

To the right of *Install new updates*, the *Every day* option should be selected. The longer that a computer goes without an important update, the more vulnerable it is to security problems. If the computer is turned off when the Windows Update is set to run, then Windows Update will run the next time the computer is turned on.

Three other *Important updates* options are available. The second option automatically downloads, but does not install, updates. After the download, Windows 7 requests your permission to install the update.

If you select the third option, Windows 7 notifies you when an important update is available and then requests your permission to download and install it.

The fourth option disables automatic updates entirely. Professional administrators of large computer networks—for example, the network of computers at your college—might choose this option because they receive notices directly from Microsoft about important updates via e-mail. Because many college computer labs are maintained by professional administrators, it is not unusual to see this option selected.

The check box under ***Recommended updates*** ensures that updates flagged as *recommended* are also included. On your own computer, you will probably want this check box selected. The last three check boxes should also be selected.

Figure 8.15

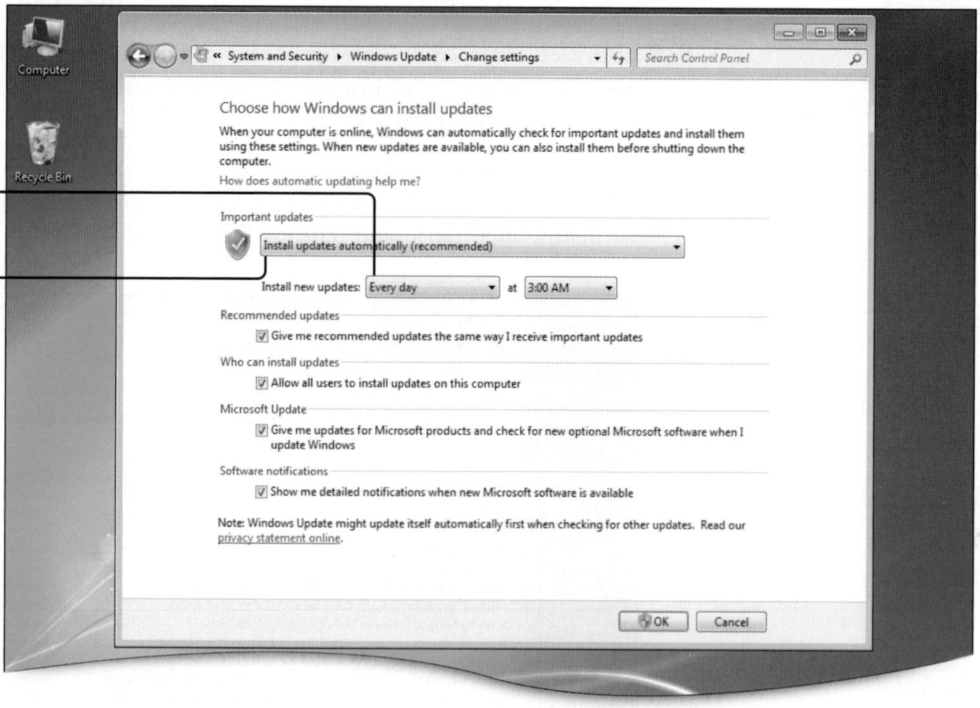

Note | All Users of Your Computer Get the Same Updates

Updates to Windows 7 are provided to all the user accounts of a computer.

6 In the lower right corner, click **Cancel** so that no changes are made. In the **Windows Update** window, click the **optional updates** link. Compare your screen with Figure 8.16.

Several optional updates and programs display. Windows Update does not notify users that these optional updates and programs are available. You might want to periodically open Windows Update and view the optional updates. To install a desired feature, select the appropriate check box, and then click OK.

Figure 8.16

Description of selected update

List of optional updates (yours will vary)

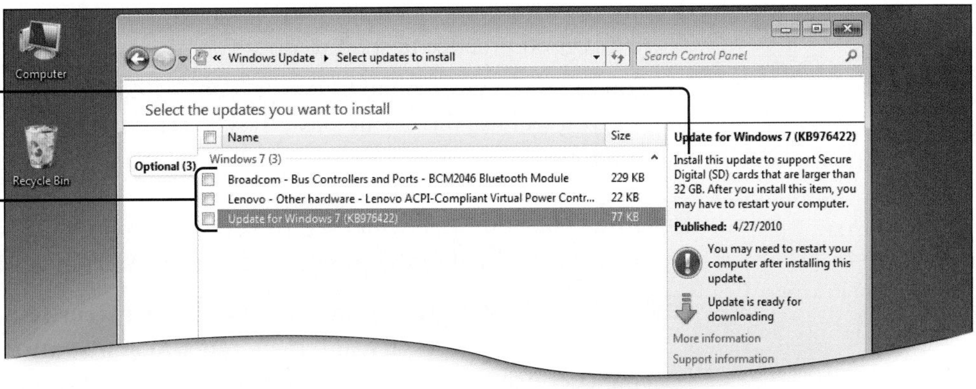

7 Click one of the updates listed, and then read the displayed description.

This feature helps you decide if you would like to download and install an update.

8 **Start** the **Snipping Tool** program, click the **New arrow**, and then click **Full-screen Snip**. In the **Snipping Tool** mark-up window, click the **Save Snip** button.

9 In the **Save As** dialog box, in the **navigation pane**, scroll down as necessary, and then under **Computer**, click your USB flash drive so that it displays in the address bar. Navigate to your **Windows 7 Chapter 8** folder, and then as the file name, type **Lastname_Firstname_8A_Update_Snip** Be sure the file type is **JPEG file**, and then press Enter. **Close** the **Snipping Tool** mark-up window. Hold this file until you finish Project 8A, and then submit this file as directed by your instructor. **Close** any open windows.

More Knowledge | Updating Other Programs

Many non-Microsoft programs on your computer also have an update feature. The companies that create software often add features or fix known problems. Sometimes, these updates fix security problems that have been discovered since you purchased the software.

Each program has its own update method. Some programs automatically check for updates when the computer is connected to the Internet. Others have a menu command that, when clicked, checks for updates. Some software companies place their updates on their Web site for you to download and install.

One important program that should be updated every day is your computer's virus or malware checking program. As you progress in your study of Windows 7, you will practice techniques to update virus checking programs and other security programs.

Objective 3 | Schedule Maintenance Tasks by Using Task Scheduler

Task Scheduler is a program with which you can schedule regular hard disk maintenance tasks. Any repetitive task that should be performed on your hard disk drive, and which you might forget to perform, can be scheduled by using Task Scheduler.

Task Scheduler also benefits those who administer large computer networks, such as the computer labs at your college. For example, a professional administrator could schedule maintenance tasks, such as defragmenting the hard disk or backing up the computer, when the computer is not in use by any students.

Activity 8.05 | Scheduling Disk Cleanup with Task Scheduler

Recall that Disk Cleanup removes unneeded files and increases the amount of free disk space on your computer's hard disk drive. Unlike Disk Defragmenter, which, by default, is set to run periodically, Disk Cleanup is *not*, by default, set to run periodically. Thus, it is good practice to set it to do so.

You can set Disk Cleanup to run at regular intervals by using Task Scheduler. In this activity, you will use the Create Basic Task Wizard to schedule Disk Cleanup to run automatically.

1. **Close** any open windows. Be sure that your USB flash drive or other removable media is inserted in the computer. From the **Start** menu, click **Control Panel.**

2. In the **Control Panel** window, click **System and Security**. Scroll down to the bottom of the window as necessary, and then under **Administrative Tools**, click **Schedule tasks.** If the User Account Control dialog box displays, click Continue. Compare your screen with Figure 8.17.

   The Task Scheduler window displays and is divided into three panes. In the left pane, you can expand a view of currently defined tasks using the same expand and collapse techniques that you use in a folder window.

   In the center, in the Task Scheduler Summary pane, you can scroll to view detailed information about what tasks are active, the status of tasks, and an overview of the Task Scheduler itself. If you scroll down to view Active Tasks, the number of active tasks displays. Most of these tasks were created by Windows 7. On the right, the Actions pane displays a list of actions that you can perform, such as creating a new task to schedule.

Figure 8.17

Task Scheduler Summary dialog box

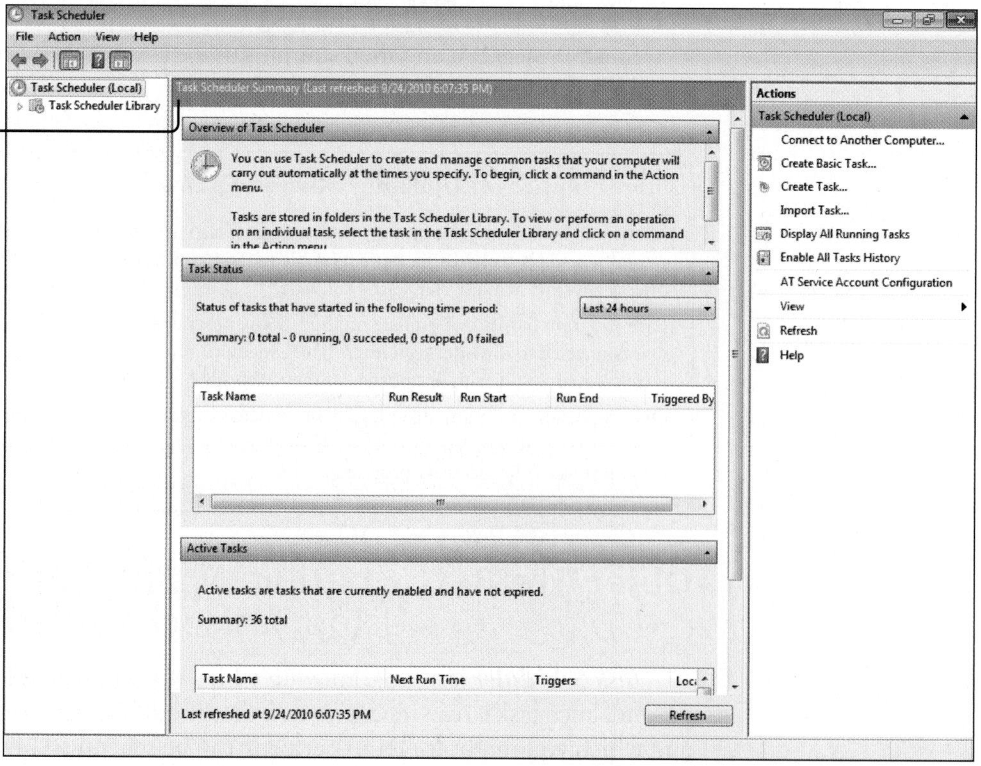

3 In the **Actions** pane, click **Create Basic Task** to start the Create Basic Task Wizard.

Recall that a wizard walks you step by step through a process.

4 In the **Create Basic Task Wizard** dialog box, in the **Name** box, type **Monthly Disk Cleanup** Click in the **Description** box, and then type **This task runs Disk Cleanup on the last day of each month.**

5 Click **Next**. Under **When do you want the task to start?**, click the **Monthly** option button, and then click **Next**. Compare your screen with Figure 8.18.

The Monthly screen displays and indicates the settings for the selected ***trigger***. A trigger is an action that causes a procedure to be carried out automatically in response to a specific event. For example, a trigger might be a date and time that is reached, starting up or shutting down the computer, or logging on to Windows 7.

In this instance, the trigger event will be when the computer's internal calendar sees the date and time that you will set. In the Start box, the current date and time display. No months or days have been selected yet.

Figure 8.18

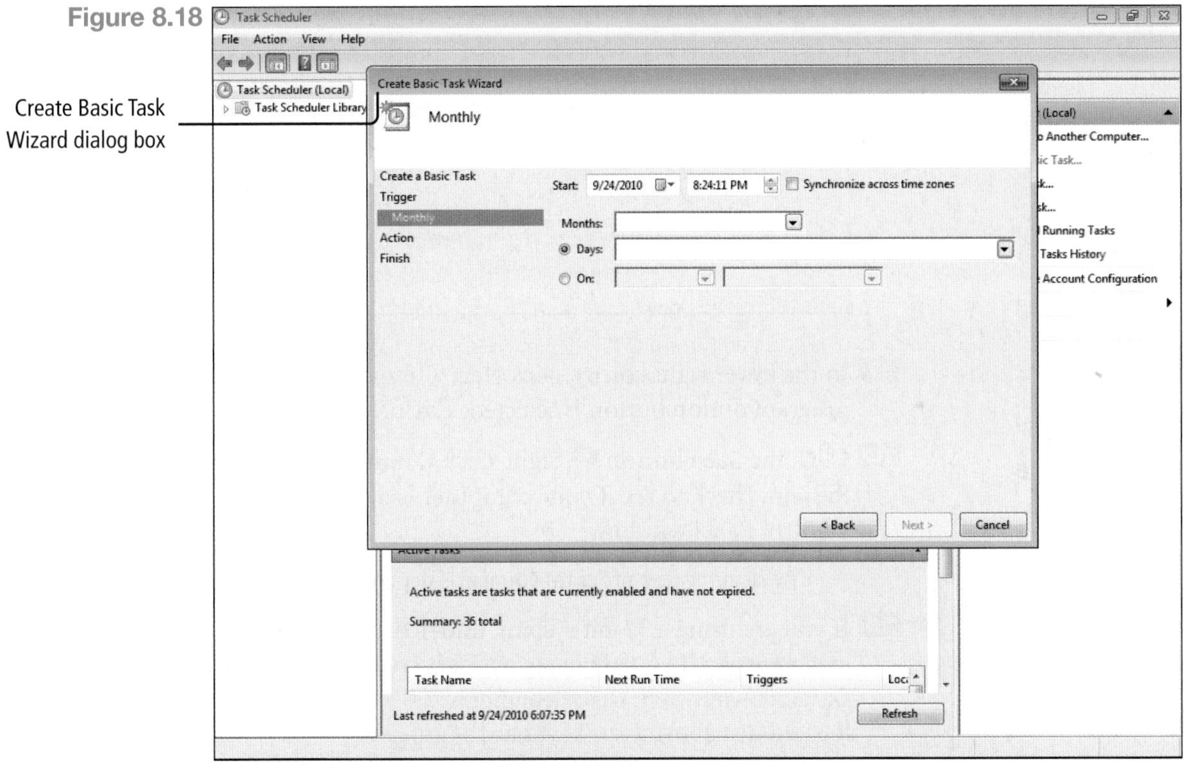

6 In the **Start** box, click the **arrow** to display the current month's calendar, and then click the last day of the current month.

7 In the **time of day** spin box, point to and then click the **hour number**. Then, click the **spin box arrows** as necessary to set the hour to **8**. Click the **minutes number**, and then type **00** Use either technique to set the seconds to **00** and the 12-hour period to **AM**

Recall that when Disk Cleanup runs, it displays a dialog box in which you check various options. For this reason, you may want to set Disk Cleanup to run at a time when you are likely to be at your computer.

8 Click the **Months arrow**, and then select the **<Select all months>** check box. Click a blank area in the wizard to close the **Months** menu. Click the **Days arrow**, select the **Last** check box, and then click a blank area in the wizard. Compare your screen with Figure 8.19.

Figure 8.19

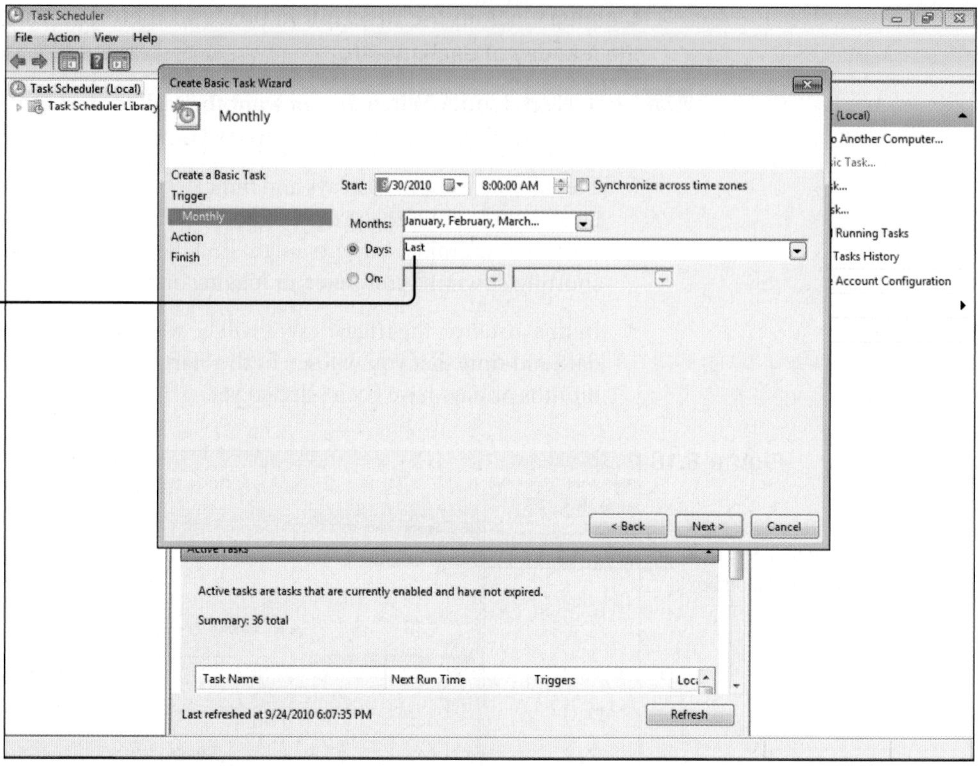

Task scheduled for the last day of each month

9 In the lower right corner, click **Next**. On the **Action** screen, be sure that the **Start a program** option button is selected. Click **Next**.

10 Click the **Start** button, right-click **Computer**, and then click **Properties**. Under **System**, check to see if your computer is a 32-bit or a 64-bit system. **Close** the Control Panel window.

The *cleanmgr.exe* program you use is dependent on the type of hardware you are using.

> **Another Way**
>
> Click the Browse button and use the Open dialog box to navigate to cleanmgr.exe as shown in the path.

11 If you are using a 32-bit system, under **Program/script**, type **C:\Windows\System32\cleanmgr.exe** If you are using a 64-bit system, under **Program/script**, type **C:\Windows\SysWOW64\cleanmgr.exe** Be sure to use the backslash key \, located just above your keyboard's Enter key.

Recall that *C:\Windows\System32\cleanmgr.exe* is a path to a file. The file is in the System32 folder, which is located in the Windows folder on the C drive. This path uses backslashes.

12 Click **Next**, and then compare your screen with Figure 8.20.

The Summary screen displays all of the settings for the Disk Cleanup task. If your settings are different, use the Back button and adjust your settings.

Figure 8.20

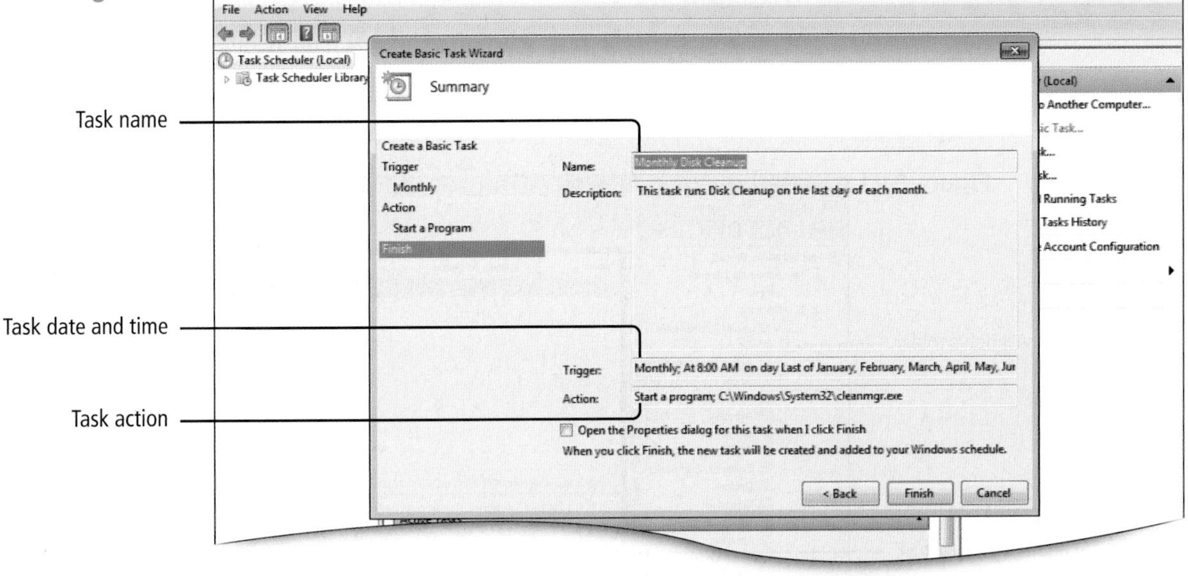

13 **Start** the **Snipping Tool** program, click the **New arrow**, and then click **Full-screen Snip**. In the **Snipping Tool** mark-up window, click the **Save Snip** button.

14 In the **Save As** dialog box, in the **navigation pane**, scroll down as necessary, and then under **Computer**, click your USB flash drive so that it displays in the address bar. Navigate to your **Windows 7 Chapter 8** folder, and then as the file name, type **Lastname_Firstname_8A_Task_1_Snip** Be sure the file type is **JPEG**, and then press Enter. **Close** the **Snipping Tool** mark-up window. Hold this file until you finish Project 8A, and then submit this file as directed by your instructor.

15 If you are working on your own computer and want to use this schedule for Disk Cleanup, click **Finish**; otherwise, click **Cancel. Close** all open windows.

Activity 8.06 | Using Advanced Task Scheduler Features

Task Scheduler has many options that affect when and how a scheduled task will run. Tasks can be set to run in response to many different events or set to run only when certain conditions are present. For example, it is good practice to run Disk Defragmenter after the Windows Backup process completes backing up files. If any data is lost during the defragmentation process, it can be restored using an up-to-date backup.

In this activity, you will create a new task that automatically runs Disk Defragmenter whenever the Windows Backup utility finishes backing up files.

1 Be sure that your USB flash drive is inserted in the computer. Display the **Start** menu, and then type **task** to search for and display the **Task Scheduler** program name. Under **Programs**, click **Task Scheduler**.

2. If the User Account Control dialog box displays, click Continue. On the left, under **Task Scheduler (Local)**, expand ▷ **Task Scheduler Library**, expand ▷ **Microsoft**, and then expand ▷ **Windows**.

3. Click the **Defrag** folder. In the center pane, under **Name**, click **ScheduledDefrag**. **Maximize** the window, and then compare your screen with Figure 8.21.

   At the bottom of the Task Scheduler Summary, the details of the ScheduledDefrag task display. This task is created by Windows 7 and runs each week. On the right, the Actions pane lists the available actions for the selected task.

Figure 8.21

Windows folder

Scheduled Defrag task

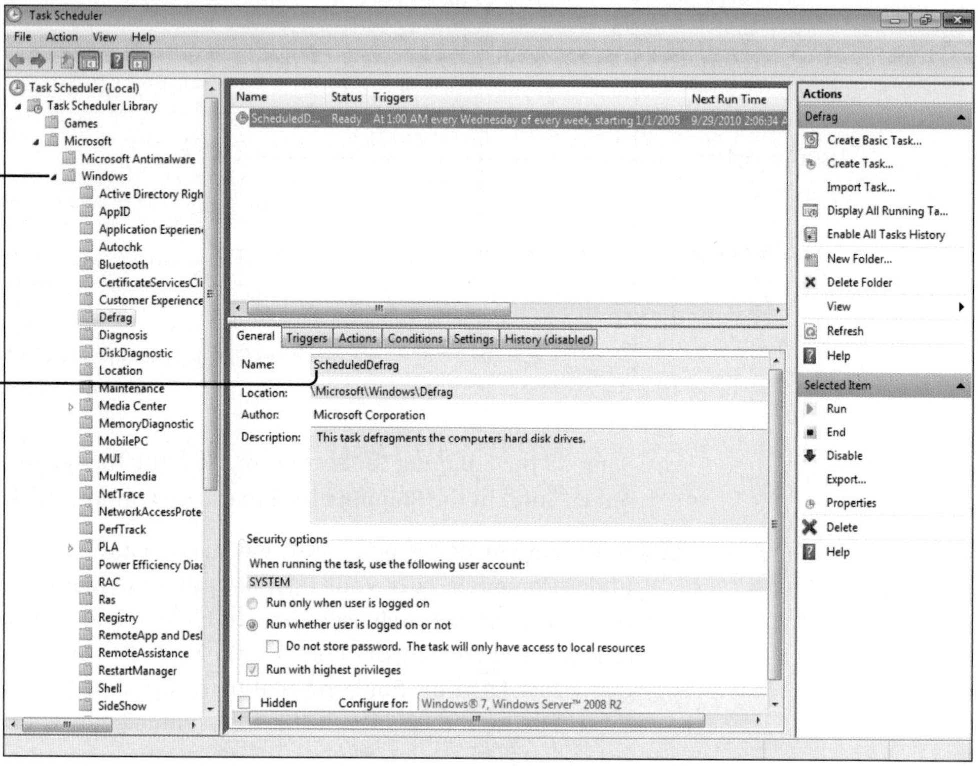

4. In the **Actions** pane, click **Create Task**. In the **Create Task** dialog box, in the **Name** box, using your own first and last name, type **Defrag Firstname Lastname**

5. Click in the **Description** box and type **Defragments the hard drive after Windows Backup runs.**

6. Under **Security options**, click the **Run whether user is logged on or not** option button, and then select the **Run with highest privileges** check box.

   These two settings enable Disk Defragmenter to run without requiring you to be logged on to the computer. The User Account Control dialog box will not display, and thus the task can complete without any action on your part.

7 Near the bottom of the **Create Task** dialog box, in the **Configure for** box, be sure **Windows 7, Windows Server 2008 R2** is selected—if it is not, click the arrow and select it. Compare your screen with Figure 8.22.

Figure 8.22

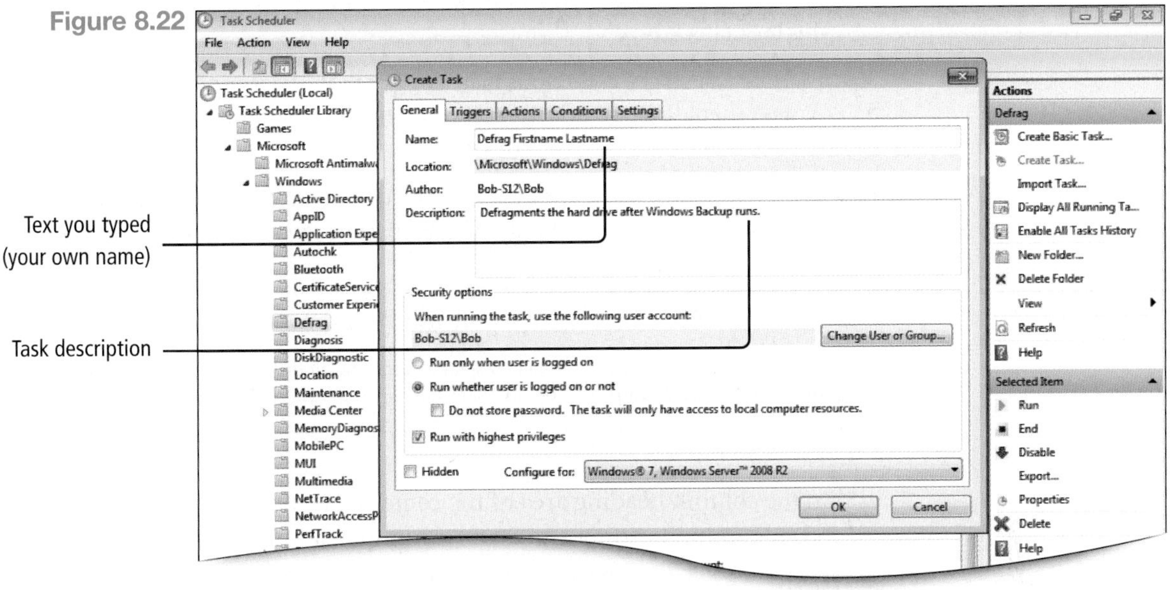

8 Click the **Triggers tab**, and then in the lower left corner, click the **New** button. In the displayed **New Trigger** dialog box, click the **Begin the task arrow**, and then click **On an event**.

9 Under **Settings**, click the **Log arrow**, and then click **Application**. Click the **Source arrow**, scroll to the bottom of the displayed list, and then click **Windows Backup**. Compare your screen with Figure 8.23.

Figure 8.23

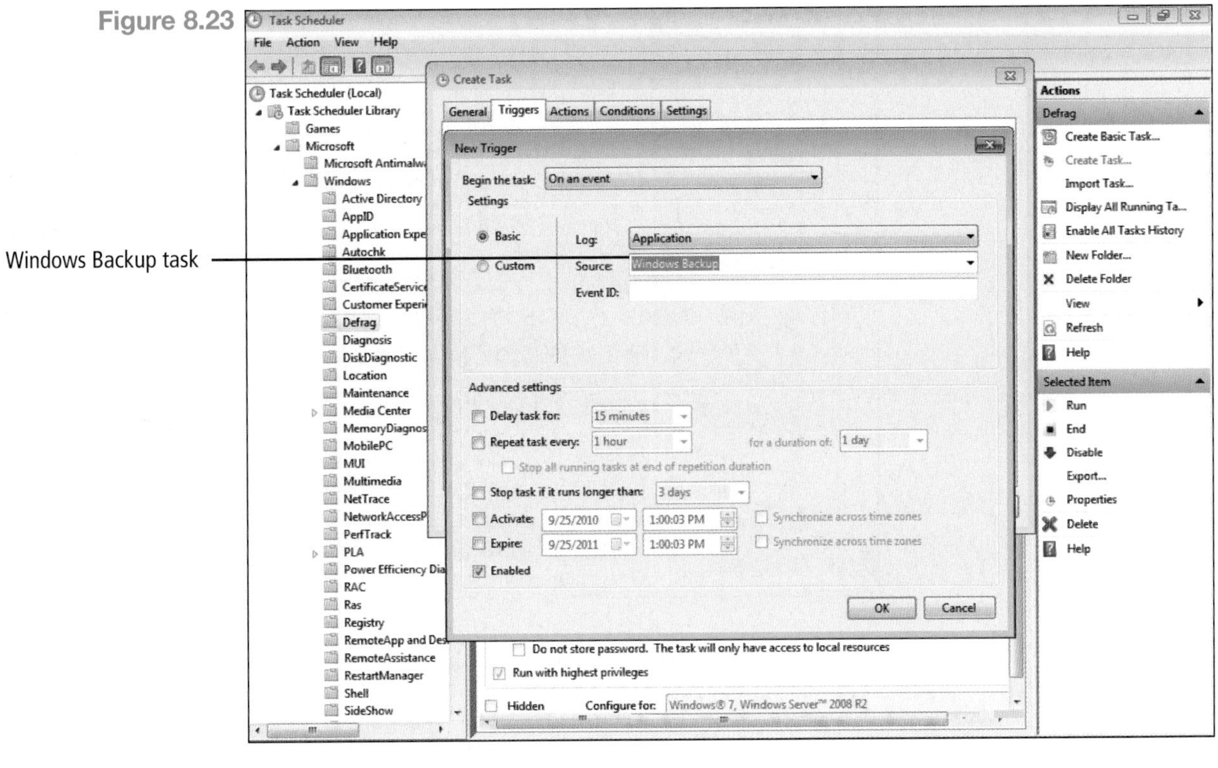

10 At the bottom of the **New Trigger** dialog box, click **OK**. Click the **Actions tab**, and then click the **New** button. Click in the **Program/script** box and type **C:\Windows\System32\Defrag.exe**

11 Click **OK**. Click the **Conditions tab**. Under **Power**, select the **Wake the computer to run this task** check box.

Here you set the conditions that, along with the triggering event, determine whether the task should run. By selecting this option, if your computer is in Sleep mode when the triggering event occurs, your computer will wake and run the scheduled task.

12 Click **OK** to create the new task. In the displayed **Task Scheduler** window, type the password that you use to log on to your Windows 7 account, and then click **OK**.

> **Alert! | Has a Password Been Set on Your Windows 7 Account?**
>
> If no password is set, an error message displays. Click OK, and then complete your snip named **Lastname_Firstname_8A_Task_2_Snip** at this point. Skip the remainder of this activity.

13 In the column heading area of the center pane, point to the separator between the **Name** column heading and **Status** column heading to display the [+] pointer. Double-click to resize the **Name** column. Compare your screen with Figure 8.24.

Task Scheduler asks for your user name and password so that it can store them for later use. When the task runs, Windows 7 will use this user name and password to give Disk Defragmenter permission to run.

Figure 8.24

Scheduled tasks

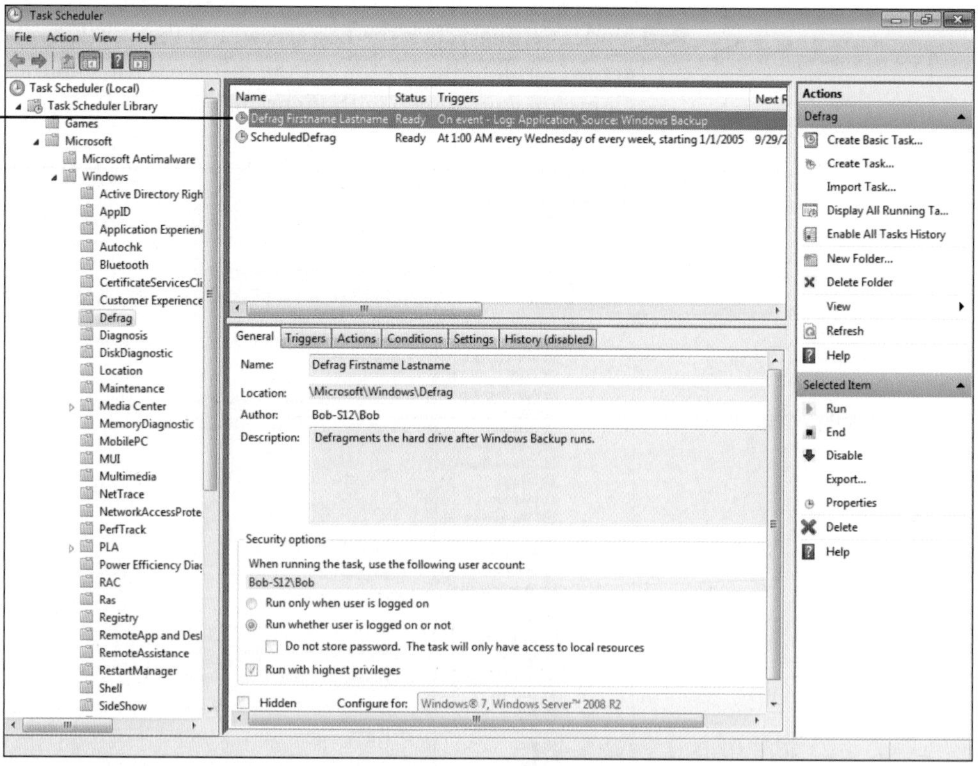

14 In the **Task Scheduler Summary** pane, click **Defrag Firstname Lastname**—the Defrag task with your own name. In the **Actions** pane, click **Properties**.

If necessary, you can edit existing tasks in the Properties dialog box.

15 **Start** the **Snipping Tool** program, click the **New arrow**, and then click **Full-screen Snip**. In the **Snipping Tool** mark-up window, click the **Save Snip** button.

16 In the **Save As** dialog box, in the **navigation pane**, scroll down as necessary, and then under **Computer**, click your USB flash drive so that it displays in the address bar. Navigate to your **Windows 7 Chapter 8** folder, and then as the file name, type **Lastname_Firstname_8A_Task_2_Snip** Be sure the file type is **JPEG**, and then press Enter. **Close** the **Snipping Tool** mark-up window. Hold this file until you finish Project 8A, and then submit this file as directed by your instructor.

17 If you are working on your own computer and want to use this schedule for defragmentation, click **OK**; otherwise, click **Cancel**. **Close** all open windows.

18 As directed by your instructor, submit the five snips that are the results of this project.

More Knowledge | Scheduling Automatic Tasks

Windows 7 schedules Windows Backup and Disk Defragmenter to run every week. Using the techniques in this chapter, you can modify when these tasks run. For example, you may want to change Windows Backup to run every day instead of weekly. If you turn your computer off at night, you should change the times for these tasks so that they run when your computer is turned on. Disk Cleanup is not scheduled by default, so consider creating a task to run this program automatically.

End You have completed Project 8A

Project 8B Optimizing Computer Performance

Project Activities

In Activities 8.07 through 8.12, you will train with Steven Ramos and Barbara Hewitt, employees in the Information Technology Department at the corporate office of the Bell Orchid Hotels, so that you will be able to measure computer performance and then change settings to optimize performance. You will capture screens that look similar to Figure 8.25.

Project Files

For Project 8B, you will need the following files:

New Snip files

Your will save your files as:

Lastname_Firstname_8B_Windows_Index_Snip
Lastname_Firstname_8B_Info_Snip
Lastname_Firstname_8B_Startup_Snip
Lastname_Firstname_8B_Effects_Snip

Project Results

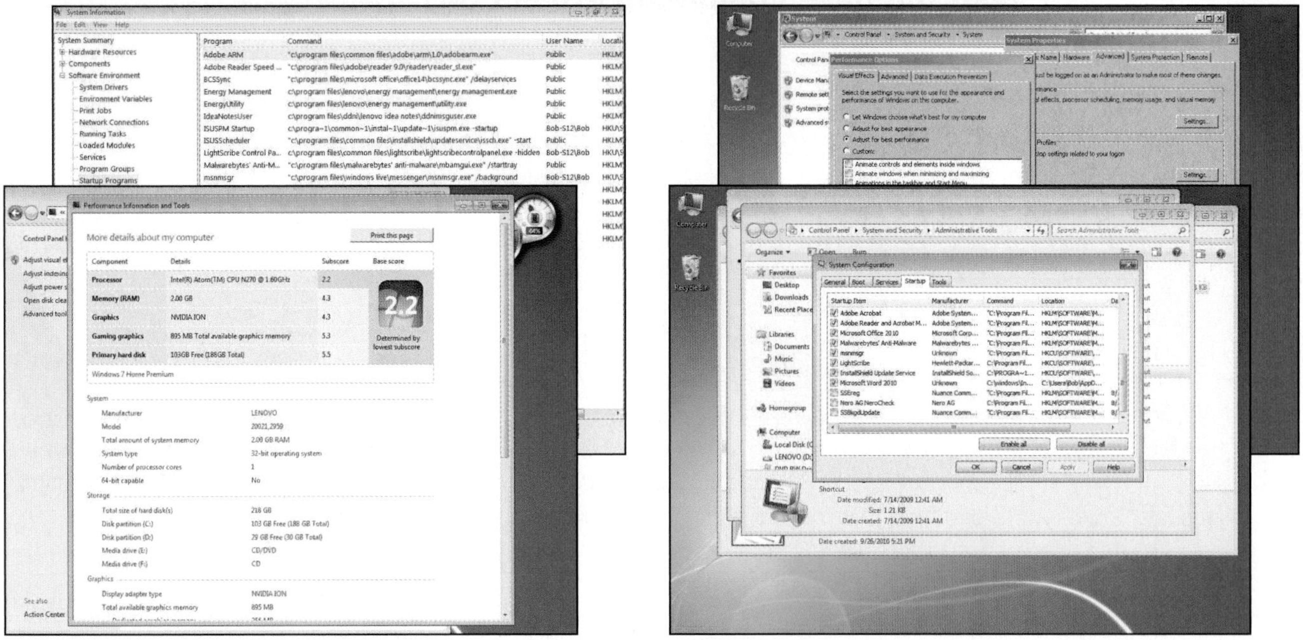

Figure 8.25
Project 8B Optimizing Computer Performance

Objective 4 | Locate System Information

Your computer consists of hardware and software that together form a system. Windows 7 includes tools to inform you about how your system is performing. Some tools are basic, for example, a simple meter gadget that displays on your desktop. Other tools are highly detailed. Regardless of the tool, you can use system information to identify strengths and weaknesses in your computer's performance, and then make informed decisions about actions you can take to optimize that performance.

Activity 8.07 | Viewing Basic Computer Information

The first step to optimize your computer's performance is to view basic computer information. The ***central processing unit***, also referred to as the ***CPU***, is the main integrated circuit chip in your computer. The CPU processes your data and your program instructions, so it is useful to examine how your computer's CPU is being used by Windows 7 and other programs.

The ***CPU Meter*** is a Windows gadget that displays how hard your computer is working. Windows 7 has another tool—***System***—that displays basic information about your computer by measuring several performance ***benchmarks***. A benchmark is a standardized test that measures computer system performance. The process of running benchmark tests is called ***benchmarking***. In this activity, you will use the CPU Meter and System to view basic information about your computer.

1. **Close** all open windows. Insert your USB flash drive, and if necessary, Close the AutoPlay dialog box. Be sure that your Windows desktop displays.

2. Right-click anywhere on the desktop, and then on the shortcut menu, click **Gadgets**. Double-click **CPU Meter**, and then **Close** the **Gadget** dialog box. Point to the **CPU Meter**, and then click the **Larger size** button.

3. In the **CPU Meter** gadget, point to the larger of the two **CPU Meter** dials to display its ScreenTip—*CPU usage*—and then point to the smaller dial to display its ScreenTip—*Random access memory (RAM)*. Compare your screen with Figure 8.26.

   The larger meter displays a percentage of the total CPU processing capability that is currently in use. The higher the percentage in use, the harder your CPU is working. When the computer is idle, this should be a very low number.

   The CPU Meter's smaller dial displays the amount of ***random access memory***—also referred to as ***RAM***—currently being used. RAM is temporary storage used by the computer to store data and instructions. When Windows 7 boots, it reads data and instructions from the hard disk drive and stores many of these instructions in RAM. The Windows 7 operating system typically uses a relatively large percentage of a computer's RAM.

Figure 8.26

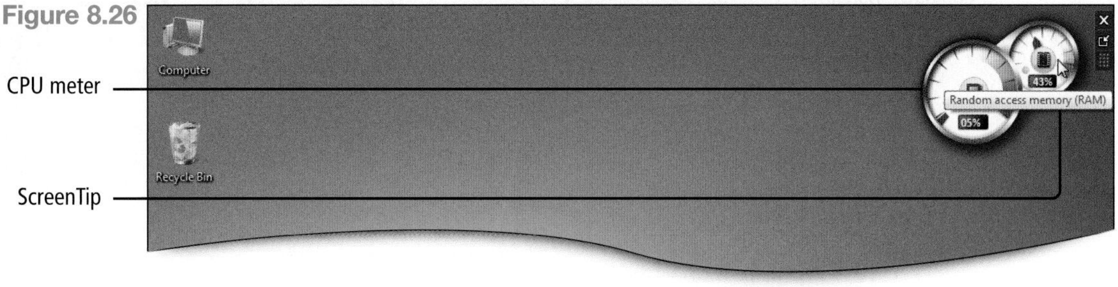

4. Start **Microsoft Word 2010**. Then, start **Microsoft Excel 2010**, and then start **Microsoft PowerPoint 2010** so that all three programs are open.

5. For each application window, **Minimize** the window. Notice the values in the **CPU meter**.

6 While watching the **CPU Meter**, in the taskbar, right-click **Word**, and then click **Close window**. While observing the values in the **CPU Meter**, **Close** the **Excel** program, and then **Close** the **PowerPoint** program.

You can see that closing a program temporarily increases CPU usage and that running several programs at one time requires more computer resources, especially more RAM.

> **Another Way**
>
> From the Start menu, right-click Computer, and then click Properties.

7 From the **Start** menu, click **Control Panel**. In the **Control Panel**, click **System and Security**, and then click **System**.

8 Move or enlarge the **System** window so that it displays from the top to the bottom of the screen and does not block your view of the **CPU Meter**. Compare your system information with the information displayed in Figure 8.27.

To the right of *Processor*, information about your computer's CPU chip displays. CPU chip manufacturers determine what information displays. In addition to the model name, manufacturers typically list the CPU chip ***architecture***. Architecture refers to the data-handling capacity of a microprocessor—CPU chips receive and send data in groups, and chip architecture refers to the size of these data groups.

For most desktop computers, the CPU chip's architecture is either 32-bit or 64-bit. Most 64-bit CPU chips require less time to complete tasks than 32-bit CPU chips—at least for software written to take advantage of this architecture. Some processors are listed as ***dual core***—two separate CPU units that share processing tasks.

Clock rate, measured in megahertz (MHz) or gigahertz (GHz), is the rate of speed at which the CPU performs. Generally, the larger the number, the faster and more powerful the processor. In Figure 8.27, the *System type* information indicates that a 32-bit version of Windows 7 is currently installed. Windows 7 is designed to support both 32-bit and 64-bit CPU architectures.

System includes other important information such as the computer name and Windows activation status.

Figure 8.27

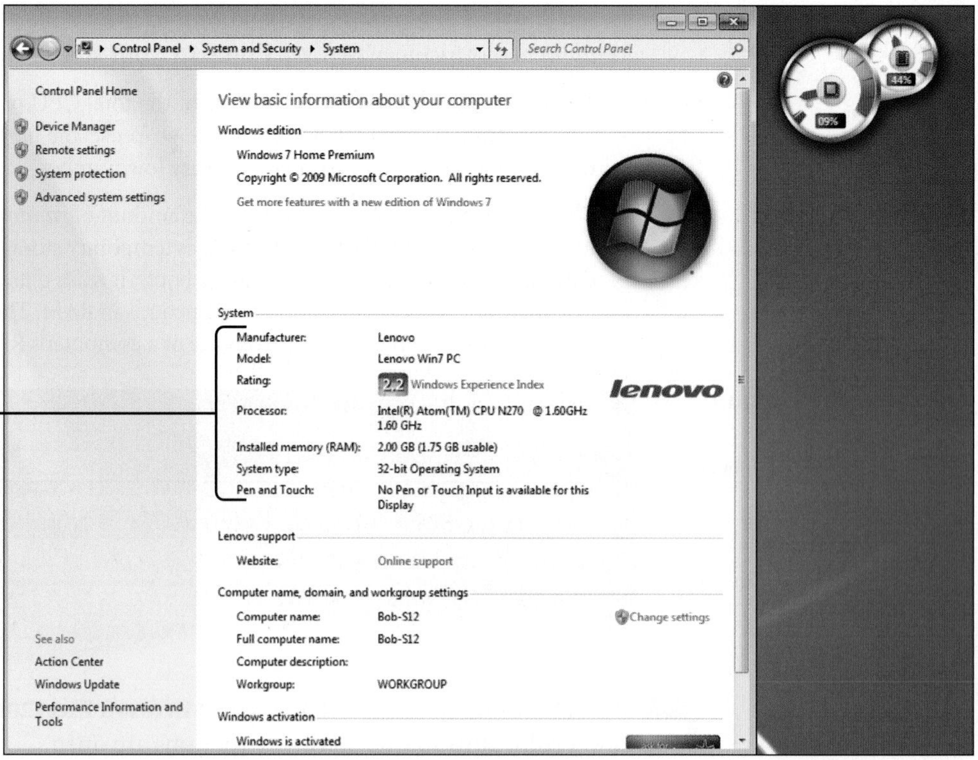

Computer system information (yours will vary)

9 Under **System**, click **Windows Experience Index**, and then compare your screen with Figure 8.28.

The ***Windows Experience Index*** tests five components that affect computer performance and rates each one on a scale from 1 to 7.9, with 7.9 as the highest rating.

A slow computer component is referred to as a ***bottleneck***. A bottleneck restricts the flow of data and slows the performance of the entire computer. For this reason, the Windows Experience Index base score is the lowest subscore.

For the computer shown in Figure 8.28, the strongest component is the hard disk drive. The weakest component is the processor—which is common in laptop computers.

Figure 8.28

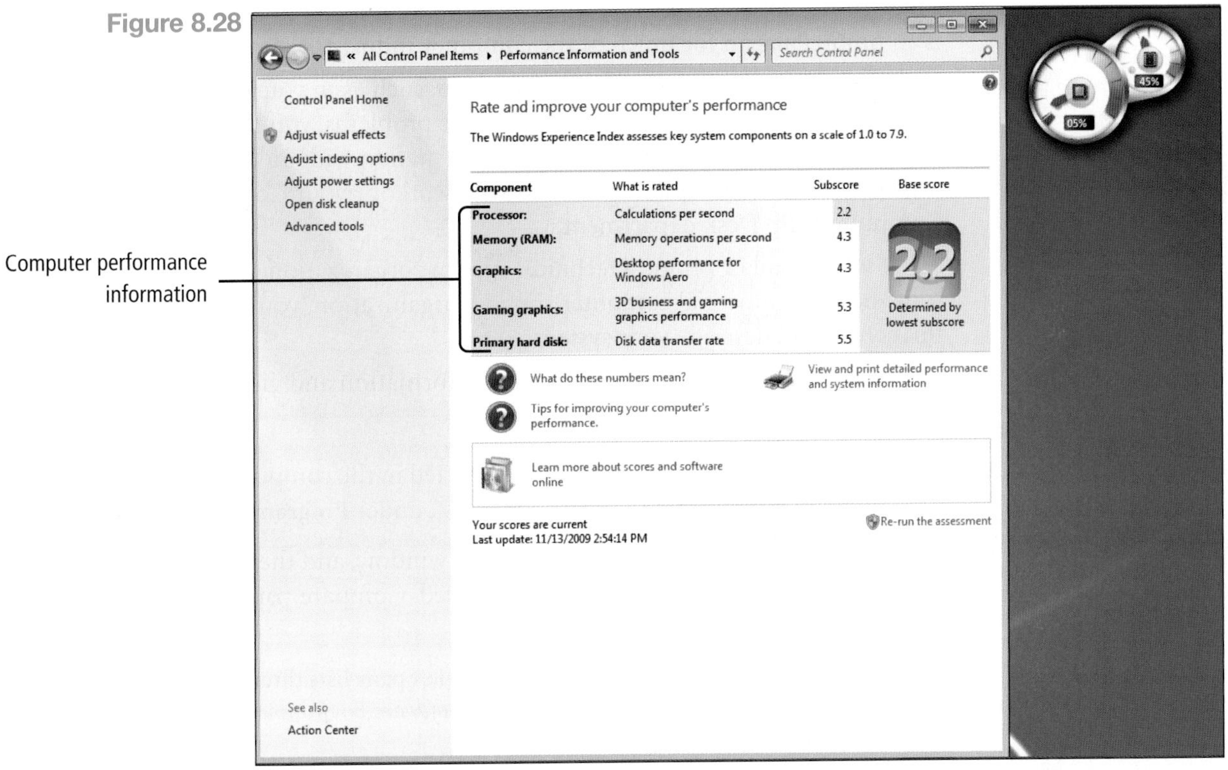

10 Under the computer performance information, click the link **View and print detailed performance and system information**.

This report combines the system information and Windows Experience Index into a single report that you can print.

11 **Start** the **Snipping Tool** program, click the **New arrow**, and then click **Full-screen Snip**. In the **Snipping Tool** mark-up window, click the **Save Snip** button.

12 In the **Save As** dialog box, in the **navigation pane**, scroll down as necessary, and then under **Computer**, click your USB flash drive so that it displays in the address bar. Navigate to your **Windows 7 Chapter 8** folder, and then as the file name, type **Lastname_Firstname_8B_Windows_Index_Snip** Be sure the file type is **JPEG**, and then press Enter. **Close** the **Snipping Tool** mark-up window. Hold this file until you finish Project 8B, and then submit this file as directed by your instructor.

13 **Close** all open windows. On the desktop, right-click the **CPU Meter** gadget, and then click **Close gadget**.

If you think that your computer is running too slowly, you can use the Windows Experience Index to help you decide what type of upgrade would help the most. If you are working on your own computer, you may want to continue displaying the CPU Meter gadget.

Activity 8.08 | Viewing System Information

System Information displays details about your computer's hardware configuration, computer components, and operating system software from within a single dialog box. The information displayed in System Information is typically viewed by ***IT professionals***. An IT professional is someone who works in the Information Technology field—the term is an umbrella term for much of the computer industry.

If you use a computer in an organization, such as in your college labs or your place of employment, and that computer experiences problems, you might need to locate and share the information found in System Information with an IT professional in your organization; for example, individuals who work for your Computer Technical Support or Computer Help Desk department.

If you e-mail or phone a technical support organization, for example Microsoft or some other commercial computer support organization, you might be asked to display this screen and describe your system.

In this activity, you will open System Information and view information about your computer system.

> **Another Way**
>
> From the Start menu, point to All Programs, click the Accessories folder, click the System Tools folder, and then click System Information.

1 Be sure that your USB flash drive is inserted in the computer. Click the **Start** button, and then type **system** In the displayed list, under **Programs**, click **System Information**.

2 **Maximize** the **System Information** window, and then take a moment to examine the *System Summary* information displayed. Compare your screen with Figure 8.29; your system information will differ.

In the System Information window, the left pane lists three expandable categories—*Hardware Resources*, *Components*, and *Software Environment*. The right pane displays detailed information.

When *System Summary* is highlighted in the left pane, the right pane displays general information about the computer hardware, BIOS, and Windows 7 operating system. Recall that the BIOS (Basic Input/Output System) is *not* a part of Windows 7; rather, it is used to direct the computer startup procedure. IT professionals often want to know which BIOS version is installed on a computer if you are experiencing problems.

In the lower portion of the window, a search pane displays.

Figure 8.29

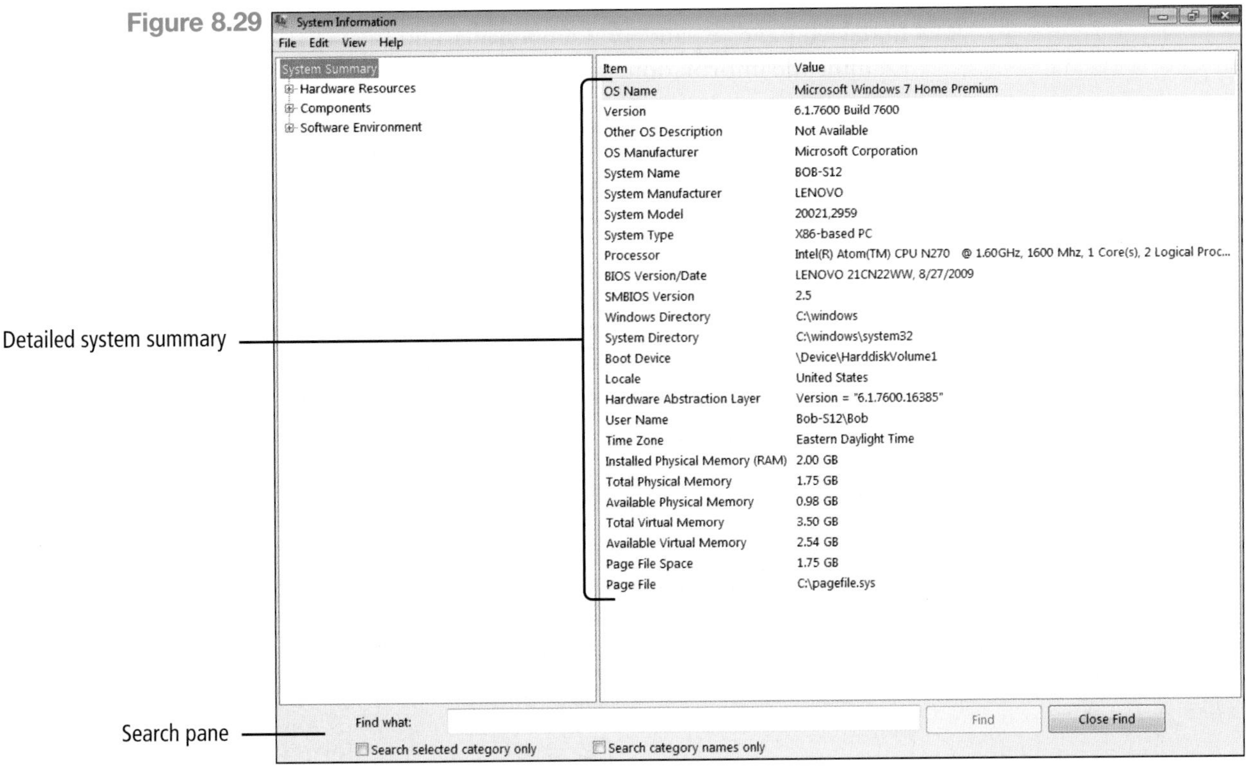

3 In the left pane, expand ⊞ **Hardware Resources**, and then in the displayed list, click **Memory**. Compare your screen with the computer information shown in Figure 8.30.

The Hardware Resources category displays advanced details about your computer's hardware. Your IT staff might ask you to check the status of these resources, and from this window, you can verify the status as *OK* or not *OK*. For example, a technician assisting you might ask you to report which Device does *not* display as *OK*.

Figure 8.30

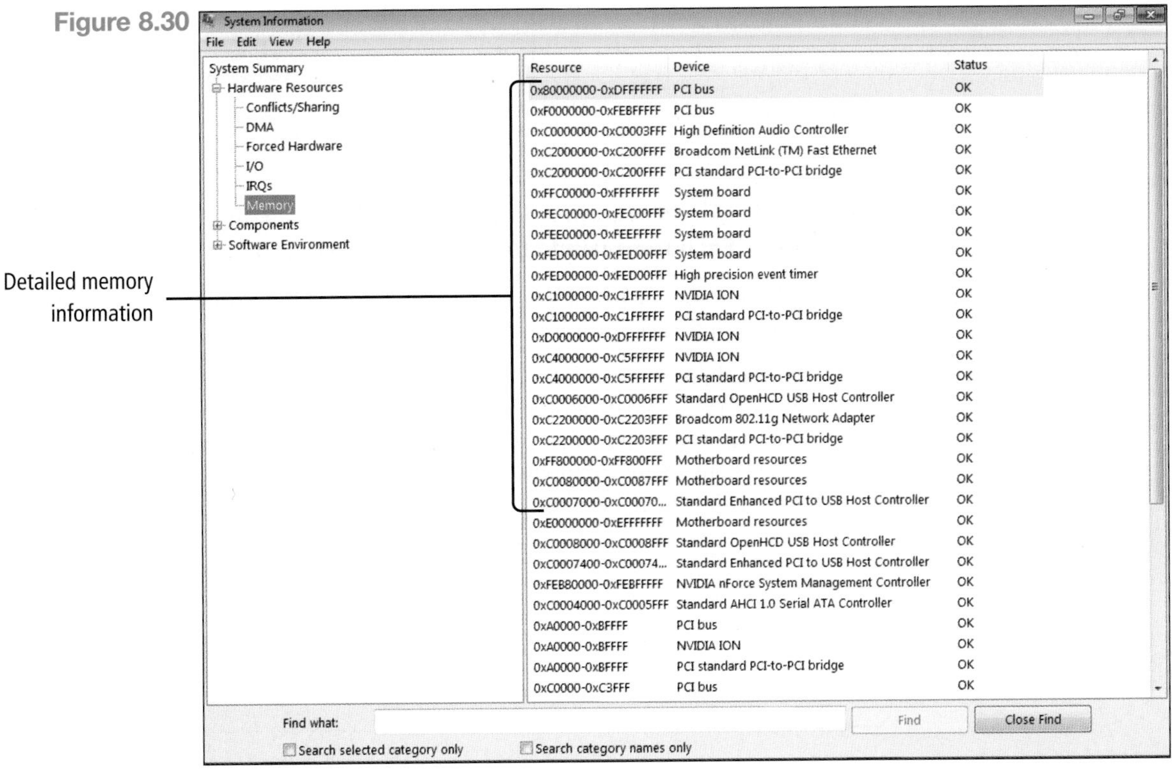

4 In the left pane, expand ⊞ **Components**, and then click **Display**. Take a moment to examine the information, and then compare it with the information shown in Figure 8.31.

The Components list displays information about disk drives, sound devices, modems, and other components installed on your computer.

Under Display, information about your display adapter is indicated. Recall that a ***display adapter*** is more commonly referred to as a ***graphics card***. A graphics card is a separate integrated circuit board with its own processor and memory dedicated to processing graphics. The description includes information about the driver used by the graphics card. A ***driver*** is special software that enables programs to communicate with computer hardware devices, for example, with a graphics card.

You need not be concerned with how driver software works, but knowing where to find the specifics about the driver will enable others to help you—your IT staff members, technical support staff, and so on.

In Figure 8.31, the System Information indicates that the display adapter has 256 MB of RAM. This information is helpful if you are considering upgrading your video card.

Figure 8.31

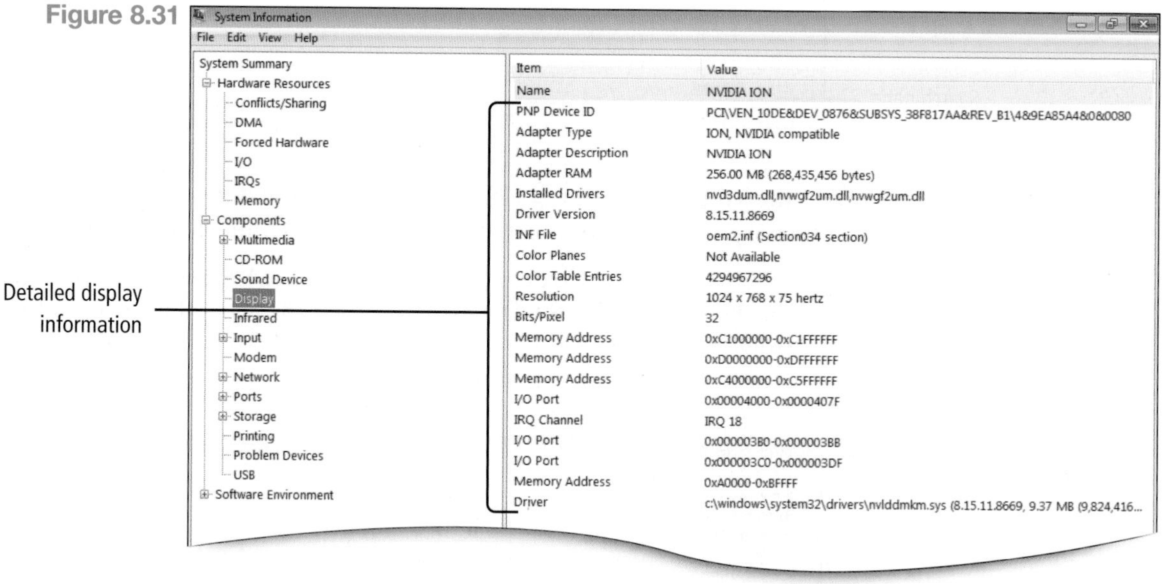

5 Collapse ⊟ the **Hardware Resources** and **Components** categories. Expand ⊞ **Software Environment**, and then click **Startup Programs**.

The Software Environment list displays information about various background operations that support the software on your computer.

In the right pane, numerous programs may be listed. A ***startup program*** is a program that starts automatically whenever your computer is started. For example, if MSN Instant Messenger displays when you start your computer, then the msnmsgr program will be listed here. Many startup programs run without your knowledge unless you know where to look for them; here you can get a complete list of such programs.

> **Note | Find a Specific Detail in System Information**
>
> To find a specific detail in System Information, type the information you are looking for in the *Find what* box at the bottom of this window. For example, to find your computer's sound card driver, type *sound* in the Find what box and click Find. The appropriate screen will display.

6 In the right pane, in the column heading area, point to the separator between the **Command** column heading and the **User Name** column heading to display the [+] pointer. Double-click to resize the **Command** column, and then compare your screen with Figure 8.32. If necessary, use the scroll box at the bottom of the window to scroll to the right to view the **Command** column and the **User Name** column.

The *Command* column displays the path to each startup program on the list. The *User Name* column lists the user account name with which the startup program is associated. Notice that many of the users are Public. The Public user is created by Windows 7. During the software installation process, you can often choose whether or not to make a program available to all users. Software assigned to the Public user is available to all users of the computer. Software assigned to an individual user is available only to that user.

Figure 8.32

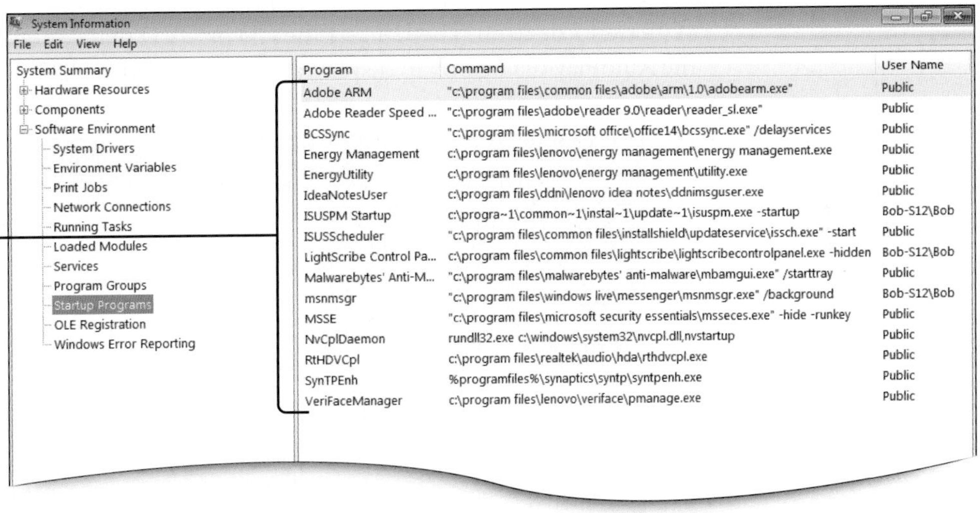

System startup programs

7 **Start** the **Snipping Tool** program, click the **New arrow**, and then click **Full-screen Snip**. In the **Snipping Tool** mark-up window, click the **Save Snip** button.

8 In the **Save As** dialog box, in the **navigation pane**, scroll down as necessary, and then under **Computer**, click your USB flash drive so that it displays in the address bar. Navigate to your **Windows 7 Chapter 8** folder, and then as the file name, type **Lastname_Firstname_8B_Info_Snip** Be sure the file type is **JPEG**, and then press Enter. **Close** the **Snipping Tool** mark-up window. Hold this file until you finish Project 8B, and then submit this file as directed by your instructor.

9 When you are done exploring **System Information**, **Close** all open windows.

Knowing how to open and explore System Information is useful if you need to share information about your computer with an IT professional or want to learn more about your computer.

Objective 5 | Install and Uninstall Programs

Recall that a program is a set of instructions that a computer uses to accomplish a task, such as word processing, accounting, or data management. Several programs are included with Windows 7, including Internet Explorer, Windows Media Player, and in some versions, several games. Some programs might be installed by your computer's manufacturer. Finally, there are the programs that you purchase and install yourself.

When purchasing software for your computer, determine that the software will work with your version of Windows 7, that you have the necessary amount of RAM, and in the case of game programs, that you have the appropriate video card. You can easily check your computer's capabilities by using System Information.

It is good practice to uninstall programs that you do not want or no longer use. Uninstalling unused programs frees up disk space.

Activity 8.09 | Installing and Uninstalling Programs

How you install a program depends on where the installation files for the program are located. Typically, programs are installed from a CD or DVD, from the Internet, or from a network. In this activity, Barbara and Steven will install Microsoft OneNote—an information manager that you can use to collect and share many kinds of information—that was not installed when the IT department installed Microsoft Office. They have the CD that contains the program.

When installing a program, you should first close any open programs and display the Windows 7 desktop. Then, insert the CD or DVD that contains the software and wait for the AutoPlay dialog box to display, as shown in Figure 8.33.

Figure 8.33

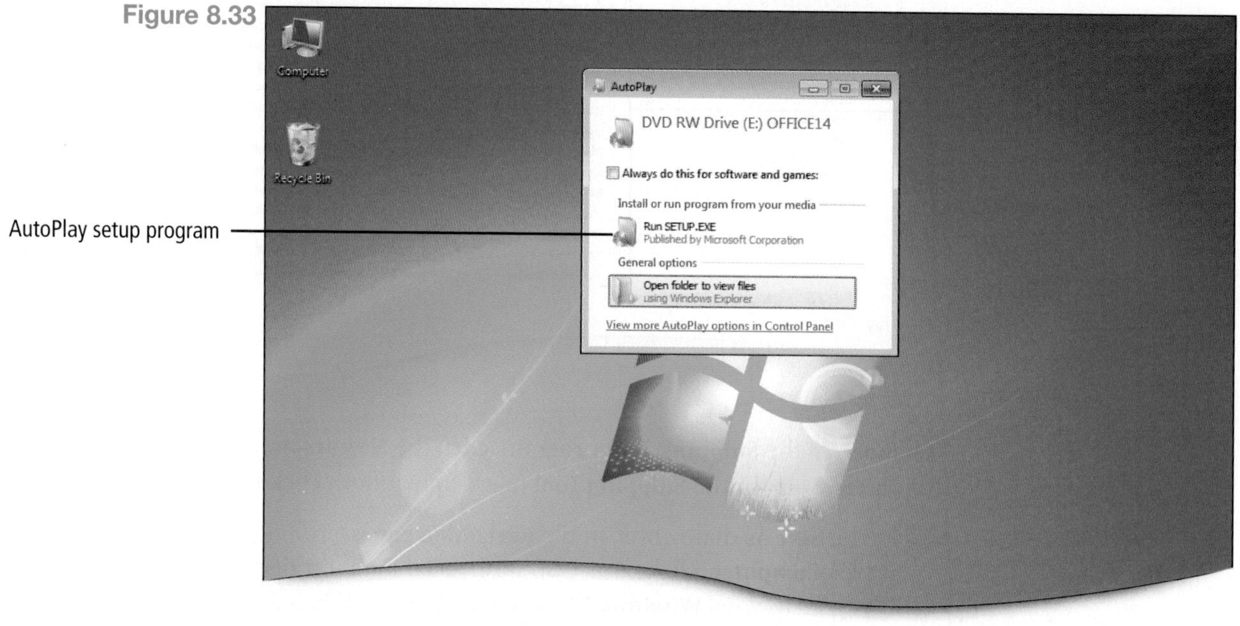

Most software programs contain a ***setup program***, also called an ***install program***, which is a program that prepares a software package such as Microsoft OneNote to run on a computer. The setup program is an ***executable file***, which you can identify by the file extension ***.exe***. An executable file is any file that starts a program. Typically, the setup.exe program creates a folder with a default name on your hard disk drive and copies the files from the CD or DVD to that folder. The process typically includes an uninstall option so that later you can uninstall the program if you want to do so. The install program might also add or update extensions to Windows 7.

After clicking *Run SETUP.EXE* in the AutoPlay dialog box, the Windows 7 User Account Control will display asking your permission to continue with the software installation. Most software companies will ask you to type a product key or serial number for the software as shown in Figure 8.34. This number is usually located on the outside or inside of the CD case or in the user guide for the software.

Figure 8.34

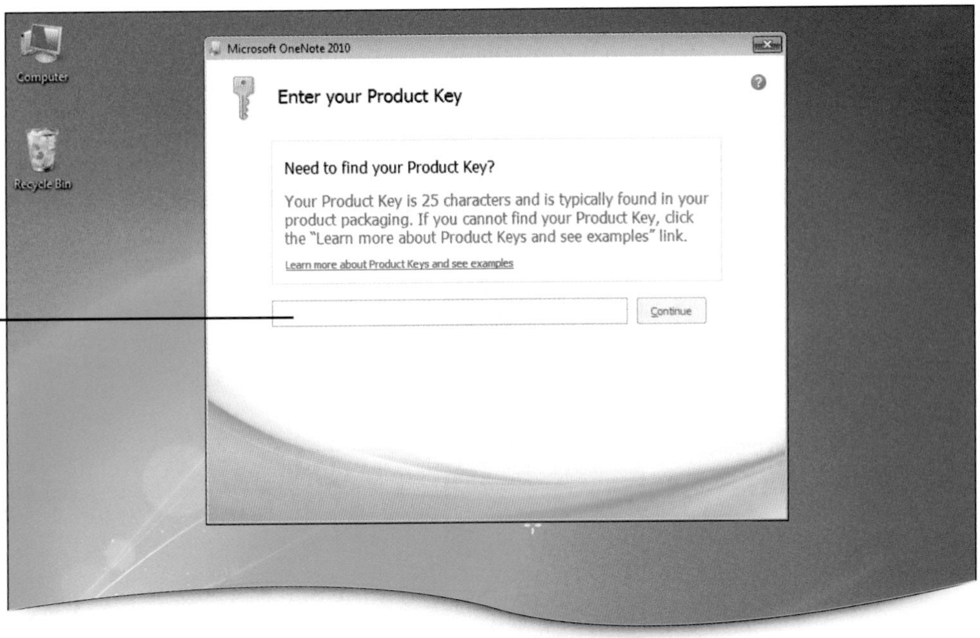

Enter product key here

After you enter an appropriate product key or serial number, a license agreement typically displays, as shown in Figure 8.35. To continue with the installation, you must accept the terms of the agreement.

Figure 8.35

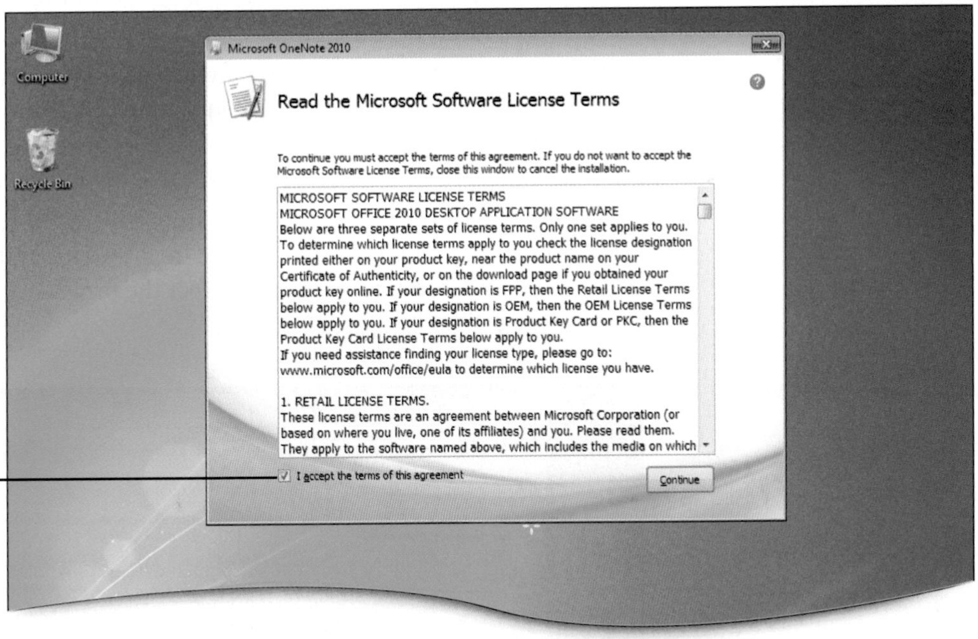

Accept software license terms here

Note | Installer Programs Vary

Software programs are packaged with their own setup programs and will vary in how they look.

After accepting the terms, click Install Now, or whatever appropriate message displays, to begin the installation. As the installation progresses, a green progress bar might display, as shown in Figure 8.36, and you might also be asked to make other decisions regarding how the software is installed.

Figure 8.36

Installation progress

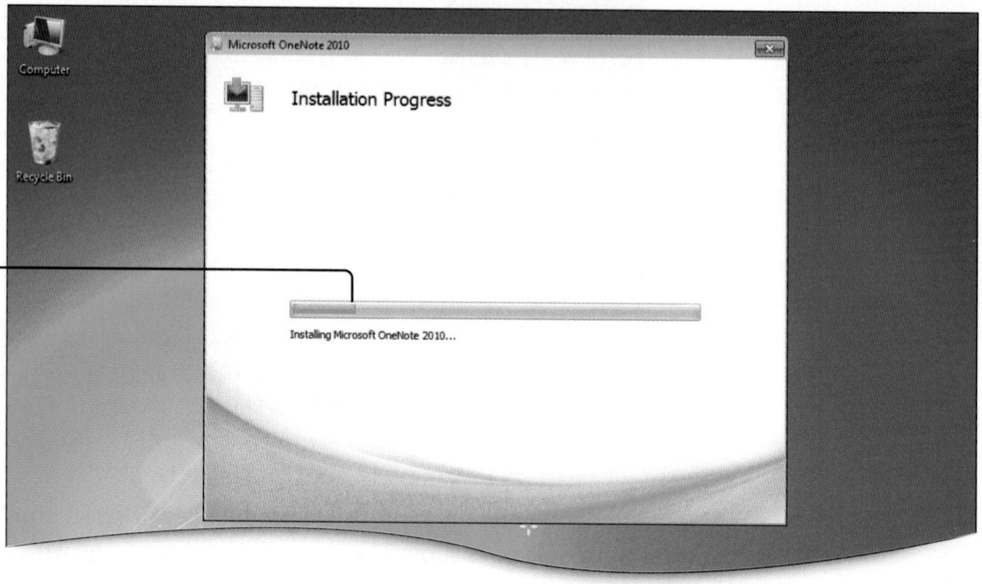

When the installation is complete, a message indicating that the installation was successful usually displays.

After a new program is installed, the first time you display the Start menu, the All Programs button will be highlighted. If you click All Programs, the new program will also be highlighted.

You can uninstall a program from your computer if you no longer use it or if you want to free up space on your hard disk. To uninstall, display the Control Panel, and then under Programs, click *Uninstall a program*. The Programs and Features window displays. In the Name column, scroll to locate and select the program you want to uninstall, as shown in Figure 8.37.

Figure 8.37

Uninstall selected program here

Installed programs

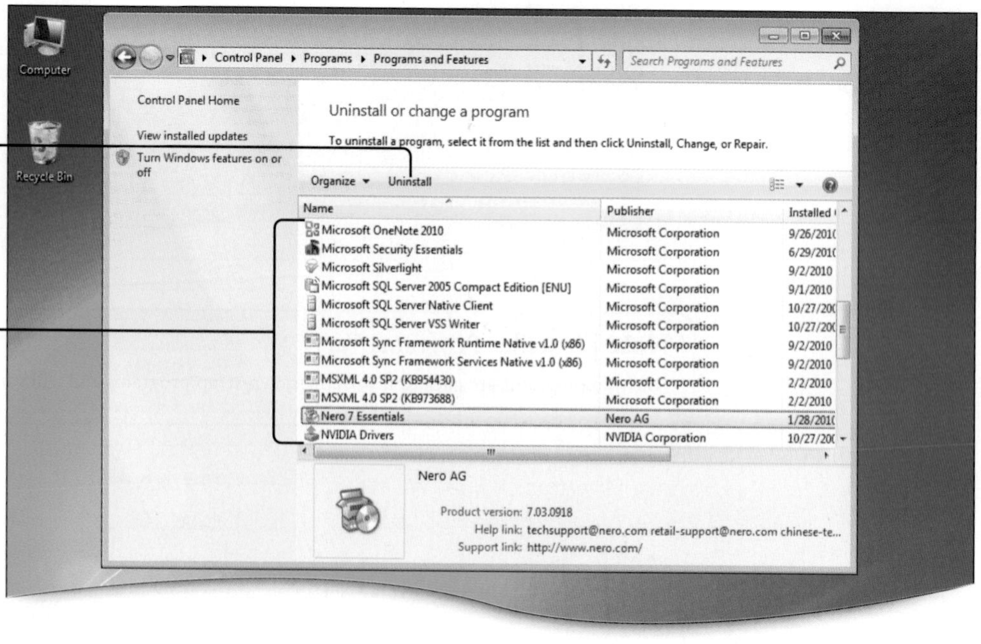

With the program selected, click the Uninstall button, and then in the User Account Control dialog box, click Continue. In most instances, Windows 7 will confirm your request.

The uninstall process begins, and a progress bar may display. Always use this Uninstall process to uninstall a program. Do not attempt to remove a program by deleting its folder from the hard disk drive, because you will not remove all the pieces of the program that are stored in other locations, for example in the ***registry***. The registry is a repository for information about your computer's configuration.

> **More Knowledge | Change or Repair a Program**
>
> Some programs—such as Microsoft Office—include the option to change or repair the program in addition to uninstalling it. To change a program, click Change or Repair. You can also use Change or Repair to remove components of some software suites—such as Microsoft Office—or to install programs that were not installed during a custom installation.

To check how well you can identify techniques to install and uninstall programs, take a moment to answer the following questions:

1. When installing a program, you should first close any ______________ programs and display the Windows 7 desktop.
2. Typically, the setup program of a software package creates a ______________ with the default name on your hard disk drive.
3. Most software that you install will require you to enter a Product Key or ______________ ______________ before the installation can begin.
4. After a new program is installed, the first time you display the Start menu, the ______________ ______________ button will be highlighted.
5. Uninstall a program from your computer if you no longer use it or if you want to ______________ ______________ space on your hard disk drive.

Objective 6 | Optimize Computer Performance

Windows 7 has several tools to boost computer performance that do *not* require you to install new hardware such as a new video card or more computer memory (RAM). The actual computer performance you will require is determined by the types of tasks that you need to accomplish. For example, browsing the Internet and creating documents in Microsoft Word do not require a high level of computer performance, whereas playing sophisticated computer games or creating video or audio files do require a high level of performance. Windows 7 enables you to optimize your computer for the types of tasks that you need to accomplish.

Activity 8.10 | Managing Startup Programs

Recall that startup programs are programs that automatically run when Windows 7 is started. Removing unneeded startup programs frees up your computer's resources for other tasks. Some startup programs are needed by Windows 7 to keep the computer running correctly. You can also add your own programs to the startup list. Unfortunately, some malware programs might also add themselves to the startup list. Windows 7 provides a dialog box to manage startup programs. In this activity, you will add a startup program, and then remove it from the Startup folder.

1 Be sure that your USB flash drive is inserted in the computer. Display the **Start** menu, and then point to **All Programs**. In the displayed list of programs, scroll as necessary to locate the **Microsoft Office** folder, and then click the **Microsoft Office** folder.

2 Point to **Microsoft Word 2010** and right-click. From the displayed shortcut menu, point to **Send to**, and then click **Desktop (create shortcut)**.

3 In the list of programs, scroll toward the bottom of the list, and then point to the **Startup** folder and right-click. From the shortcut menu, click **Open**.

4 If the window is maximized, click the Restore Down button, and then drag the window so that the **Microsoft Word 2010** shortcut is visible.

5 On the desktop, point to the **Microsoft Word 2010** shortcut, and then drag the icon into the **file list** of the **Startup** folder. Set the view to **Details**, and then compare your screen with Figure 8.38.

When shortcuts are placed in the Startup folder, the shortcut's target object will open whenever Windows 7 is started. In addition to programs, shortcuts to files and folders can be placed in the Startup folder. The result of this action will be that Microsoft Word 2010 will automatically start the next time the computer is restarted.

Figure 8.38

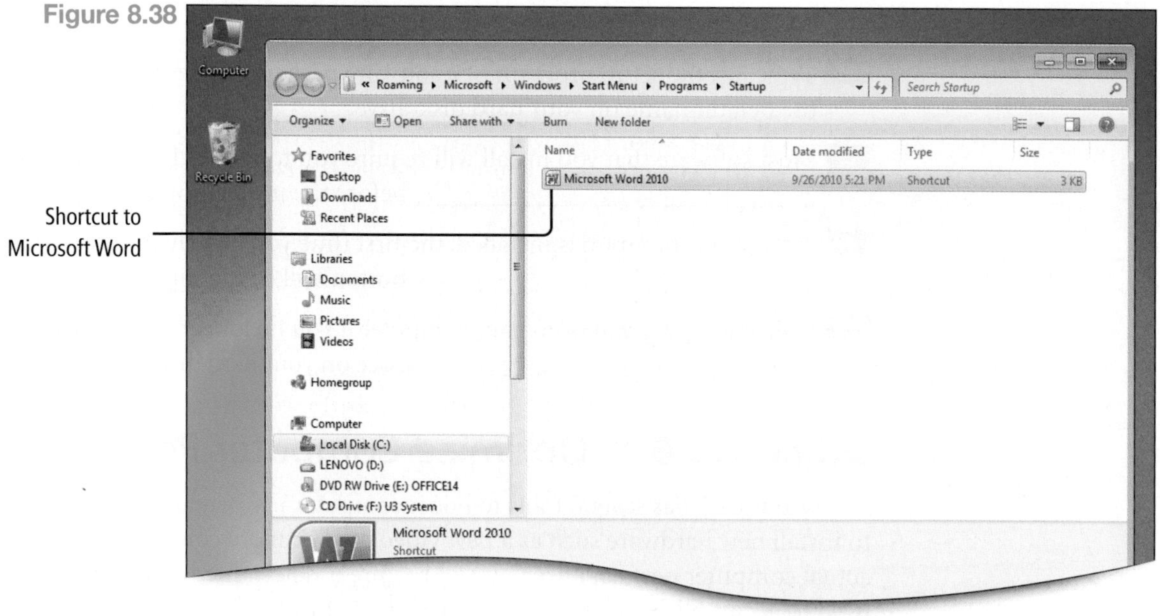

6 Leave the **Startup** folder window open. Click the **Start** button, and then click **Control Panel**. Click **System and Security**, scroll to the bottom of the displayed window if necessary, and then click **Administrative Tools**.

7 In the **Administrative Tools** file list, in the **Name** column, double-click **System Configuration**. If the User Account Control dialog box displays, click Continue.

8 In the **System Configuration** dialog box, click the **Startup tab**. Widen the column heading **Startup Item**, and then scroll as necessary until you see *Microsoft Word 2010* on the list. Compare your screen with Figure 8.39.

Some programs display in the Startup tab of the System Configuration dialog box, but not in the Startup folder. These programs are typically your ***virus checker***—software that scans your computer for viruses and other malware—and programs needed by Windows 7.

To temporarily disable a program from automatically starting up, clear its check box. If the program is already running, this action will not close it.

Figure 8.39

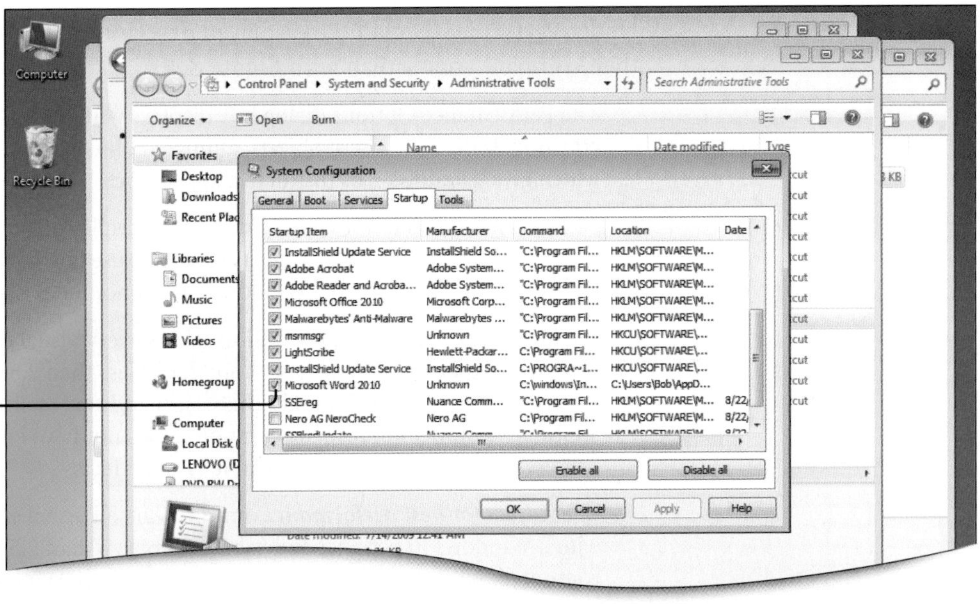

Microsoft Word is a startup program

9 **Start** the **Snipping Tool** program, click the **New arrow**, and then click **Full-screen Snip**. In the **Snipping Tool** mark-up window, click the **Save Snip** button.

10 In the **Save As** dialog box, in the **navigation pane**, scroll down as necessary, and then under **Computer**, click your USB flash drive so that it displays in the address bar. Navigate to your **Windows 7 Chapter 8** folder, and then as the file name, type **Lastname_Firstname_8B_Startup_Snip** Be sure the file type is **JPEG**, and then press Enter. **Close** the **Snipping Tool** mark-up window. Hold this file until you finish Project 8B, and then submit this file as directed by your instructor.

11 Switch to the **Startup** folder window. Point to the **Microsoft Word 2010** shortcut, right-click, click **Delete**, read the message, and then click **Yes. Close** all open windows.

Because the shortcut to *Microsoft Office Word 2010* is no longer in the Startup folder, *Microsoft Word 2010* will be removed from the startup programs listed in the System Configuration dialog box the next time the computer is started.

On your own computer, you may want to place shortcuts to the programs you use every day in the Startup folder.

Activity 8.11 | Changing Performance Options

The Performance Options dialog box provides access to several settings that optimize system performance. These settings enable you to disable and enable certain Windows 7 features that affect computer performance. The most significant feature enables you to choose which visual effects should be incorporated into the look and feel of Windows 7. For computers with lower graphics capabilities, altering the visual effects can dramatically improve overall computer performance. In this activity, you will open the Performance Options dialog box, make several changes, and view the results of those changes.

1 Be sure that your USB flash drive is inserted in the computer. Click the **Start** button, and then click **Control Panel**.

2 Click **System and Security**, click **System**, and then in the left pane, click **Advanced system settings**. In the **System Properties** dialog box, click the **Advanced tab**.

3 Under **Performance**, read the displayed description. Click the **Settings** button, and then compare your screen with Figure 8.40.

The Performance Options dialog box displays with the Visual Effects tab active. ***Visual effects*** include transparent objects, animated objects, and shadows under objects, all of which give Windows 7 its distinctive appearance.

Here you have options for which visual effects display on your computer. The first option lets Windows 7 decide what visual effects should be used by the operating system. To make this decision, Windows 7 uses the Windows Experience Index benchmarks that you have viewed.

The *Adjust for best appearance* option selects every visual effect. If a computer has a Windows Experience Index base score that is less than 2.5, this option could adversely affect computer performance. In this case, windows, menus, and dialog boxes would appear very slowly because the computer does not have enough resources to quickly process and display all of the available visual effects.

The ***Adjust for best performance*** option clears all visual effects check boxes. Computers with a Windows Experience Index base score less than 2.5 will perform faster because the computer will not need to process the visual effects. Windows, menus, and dialog boxes will display and respond to changes much more quickly.

Figure 8.40

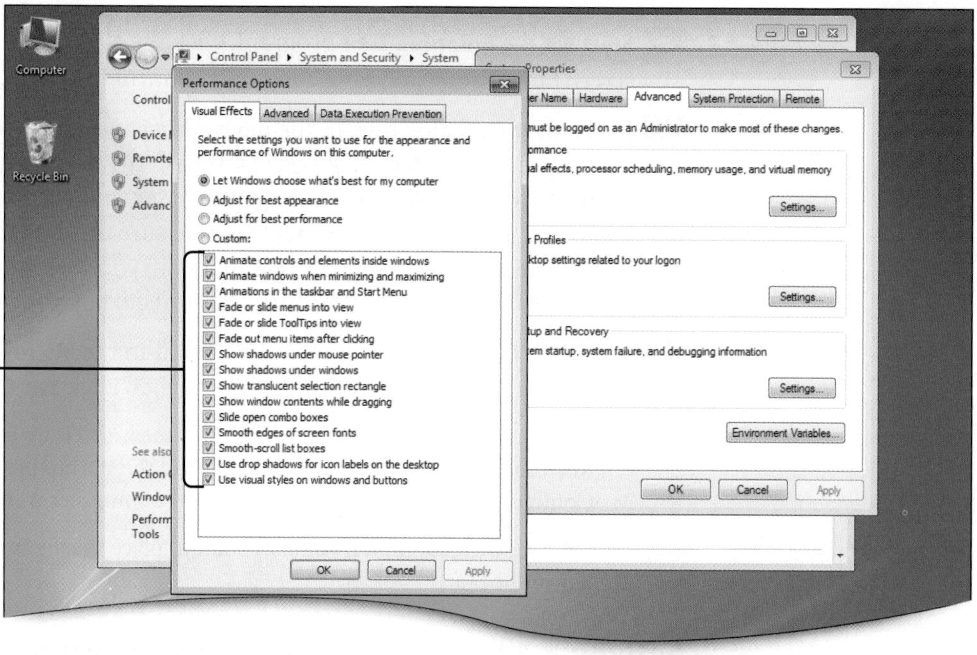

Default visual effects

4 In the **Performance Options** dialog box, click the **Advanced tab**, and then compare your screen with Figure 8.41.

Processor scheduling refers to the manner in which the CPU prioritizes its tasks. Most desktop computers are used to run programs, for which the *Programs* option is usually best. Some computers are used only to provide network services or act as a Web server, for which the *Background services* option would be the best performance choice.

Virtual memory is a technique that uses a small part of the hard disk drive as if it were random access memory (RAM). This enables a computer to run programs that require more memory than the computer actually has available.

Virtual memory enables the computer to perform more complex tasks without having to add more RAM. Because virtual memory uses the hard disk drive to store data instead of using RAM, computer performance slows somewhat when it is used. Most often, the setting provided by Windows 7 will achieve the best performance. Increasing the amount of RAM decreases the amount of Virtual Memory used by Windows 7, and in this manner improves computer performance.

Figure 8.41

Performance options Advanced tab

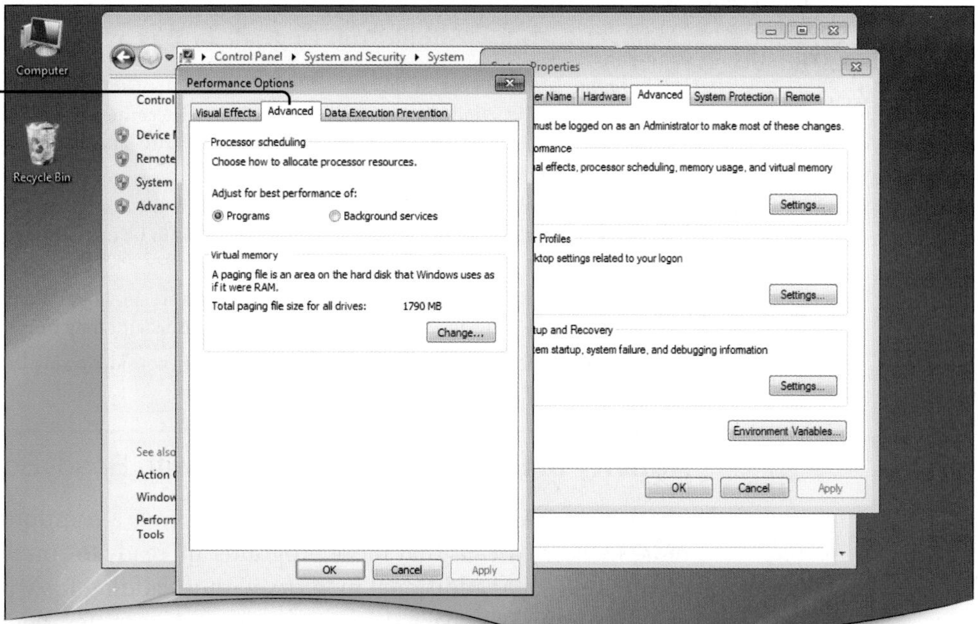

5 In the **Performance Options** dialog box, click the **Data Execution Prevention tab**.

Data Execution Prevention—also referred to as *DEP*—is a security feature that can help prevent damage to your computer from viruses and other malware by monitoring your programs to make sure they are using memory safely. When DEP monitors all programs, security increases, but performance degrades. To learn more about this feature, click the link *How does it work?*

6 In the **Performance Options** dialog box, click the **Visual Effects tab**.

7 Click the **Adjust for best performance** option button, click the **Apply** button, and then wait a few moments for the changes to take place—your screen might go dark for a few seconds. Notice that the look and feel of the open windows and the Task Bar have changed.

These visual effects mimic older versions of Windows. Although the *Adjust for best performance* option does not display the typical Windows 7 visual effects, choosing this option could significantly improve computer performance.

8 **Start** the **Snipping Tool** program, click the **New arrow**, and then click **Full-screen Snip**. In the **Snipping Tool** mark-up window, click the **Save Snip** button.

9 In the **Save As** dialog box, in the **navigation pane**, scroll down as necessary, and then under **Computer**, click your USB flash drive so that it displays in the address bar. Navigate to your **Windows 7 Chapter 8** folder, and then as the file name, type **Lastname_Firstname_8B_Effects_Snip** Be sure the file type is **JPEG**, and then press Enter. **Close** the **Snipping Tool** mark-up window. Hold this file until you finish Project 8B, and then submit this file as directed by your instructor.

10 Click the **Let Windows choose what's best for my computer** option button, or click the option that was selected when you first opened **Performance Options**. Click **OK** two times, and then **Close** all open windows.

On your own computer, you may want to change your Performance Options to improve the performance of your computer. For times when you need faster performance, the visual effects can be quickly disabled and then enabled again later.

More Knowledge | Should You Upgrade or Buy a New Computer?

Upgrading is the process of buying new hardware components or software programs to increase computer performance. The Windows Experience Index helps determine which hardware components would increase performance the most. Buying a dedicated graphics card and increasing RAM are relatively inexpensive; both provide noticeable improvements.

Unless your hard disk drive is failing, the performance boost from replacing it will be less noticeable. Replacing the CPU is usually not helpful at all. If your CPU needs to be upgraded, you should probably consider buying a new computer.

Some individuals buy newer versions of their software in hopes that the new versions will run faster. Unfortunately, when a new version of software is published, it rarely runs faster than the earlier version.

Before buying new hardware or an entire new computer, consider trying the techniques presented in this chapter to see if they increase performance.

Activity 8.12 | Increasing Memory with ReadyBoost

Adding RAM is often the best way to improve a computer's performance, because more memory means that more programs are ready to run without accessing the hard disk drive. To add additional memory without adding RAM, use ***ReadyBoost***, which enables certain USB flash drives to be used as computer memory. Because USB flash drives manipulate electrons to store data, they can read and write data significantly faster than a hard disk drive, which relies on magnetic patterns to store data.

To take advantage of this speed, ReadyBoost stores data that would otherwise be stored on the hard disk drive or in RAM. Increasing your computer's memory capability boosts computer performance, especially for computers whose Windows Experience Index indicates a low memory score. In this activity, Barbara and Steven will use ReadyBoost to increase computer memory.

The ReadyBoost settings are accessed in the ReadyBoost tab of the Properties dialog box. To open a USB flash drive's Properties dialog box, in the Computer folder window, right-click the desired USB flash drive, and then click Properties. The ReadyBoost tab can also be opened by clicking *Speed up my system* in the AutoPlay dialog box.

When a USB flash drive is inserted, Windows 7 tests to see if ReadyBoost can use the particular USB flash drive. One of the options in the AutoPlay dialog box is *Speed up my system*, as shown in Figure 8.42.

Figure 8.42

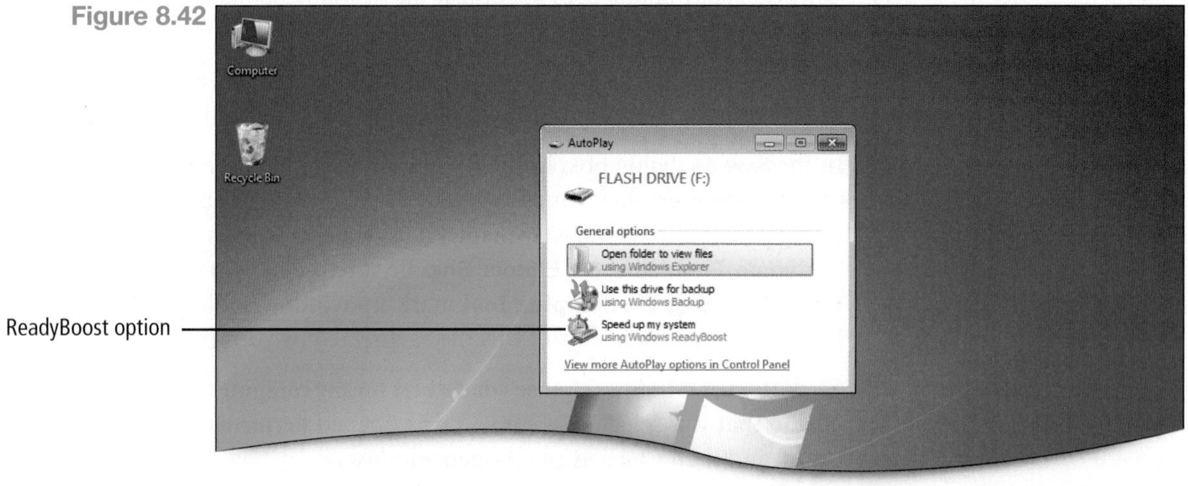

When you click the *Speed up my system* option, the FLASH DRIVE Properties dialog box displays. In Figure 8.43, the ReadyBoost tab displays a message that FLASH DRIVE (F:) *cannot* be used for ReadyBoost. During the ReadyBoost test, data is written to the USB flash drive and then read. To pass the test, this read/write cycle must be completed within a specific amount of time.

Figure 8.43

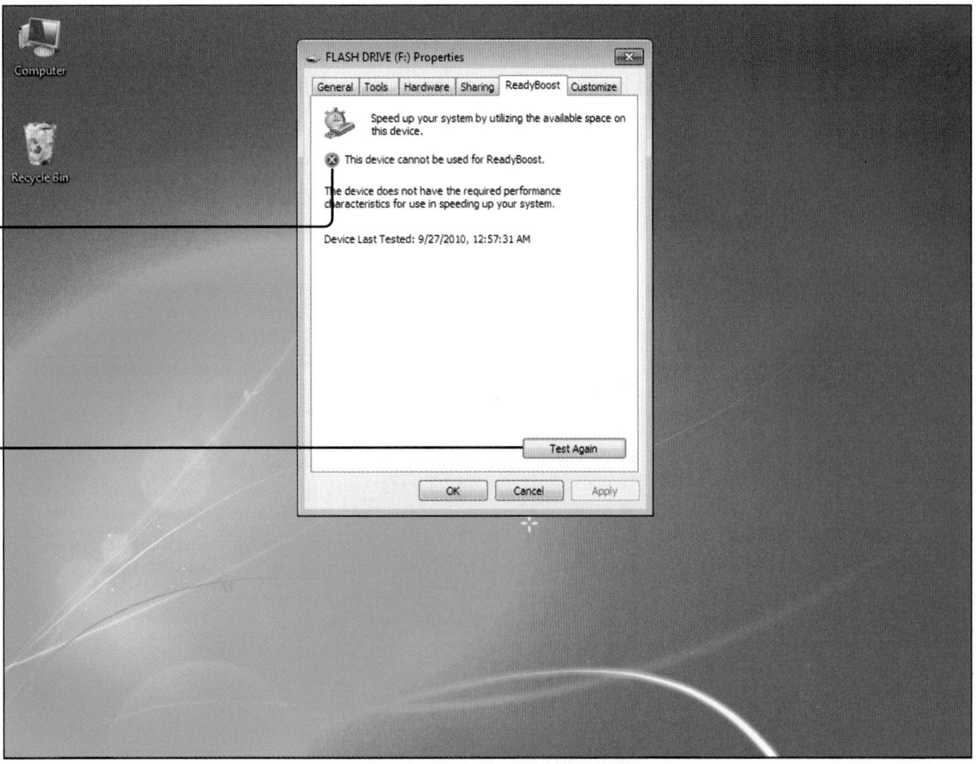

Many times, the initial test when you first plug in the flash drive indicates that the drive is unusable for ReadyBoost, even though the device is actually capable of being used. To test the flash drive again, click the *Test Again* button. Figure 8.44 displays the ReadyBoost tab for the FLASH DRIVE (F:) drive, which *can* be used for ReadyBoost.

Figure 8.44

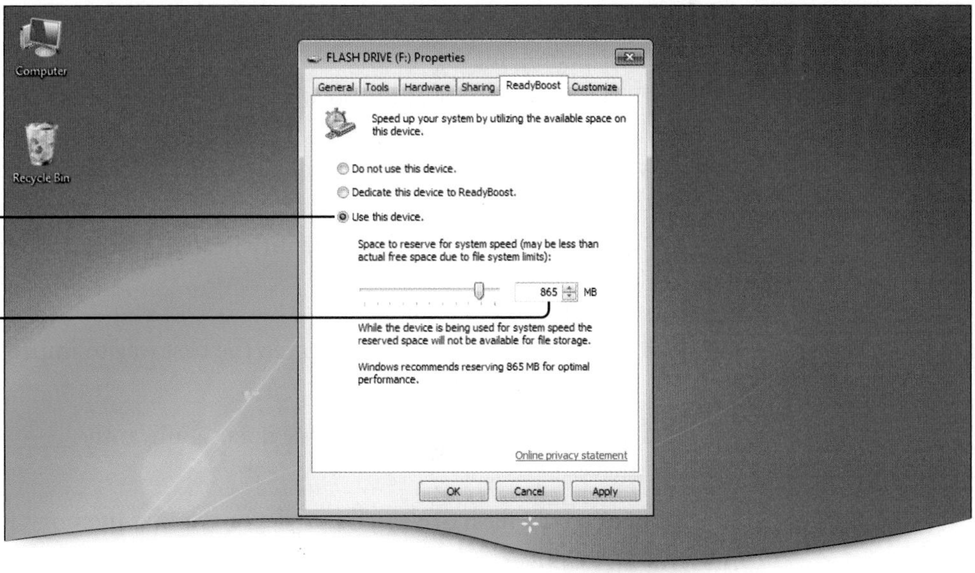

When a USB flash drive passes the ReadyBoost test, you will see a screen similar to Figure 8.45. The default option is *Do not use this device*. With this option, the USB flash drive will not be used for ReadyBoost, and will operate normally. By selecting the *Use this device* option, the USB flash drive will be used to expand computer memory by the amount displayed in the spin box. The slider enables you to change the amount of flash drive space dedicated to computer memory. When ReadyBoost is enabled, any files already stored on the USB flash drive will remain and will not be harmed in any way.

To start using ReadyBoost, click the *Use this device* option button, and then click *OK* or *Apply*. Figure 8.45 shows the General tab for the FLASH DRIVE (F:) while it is being used by ReadyBoost. ReadyBoost is using 865 MB of the USB flash drive. About 100 MB of free space remains to save files. When the entire free space on the disk is used for ReadyBoost, then you will not be able to save any additional files to the USB flash drive. When ReadyBoost is disabled, the space that was formerly used by ReadyBoost returns as free space. ReadyBoost should be disabled before the drive is removed from the computer.

Figure 8.45

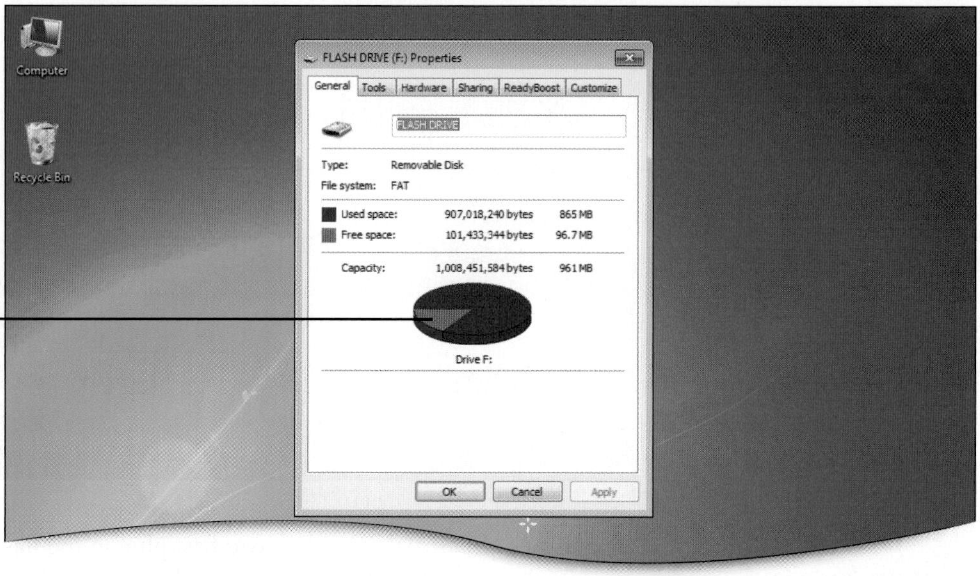

Free space left on flash drive after ReadyBoost is applied

ReadyBoost works with most USB flash drives and two types of flash memory cards: CompactFlash and SD (Secure Digital) cards. Memory cards use flash technology and are typically used to store picture files in digital cameras. On your own Windows 7 computer, if you have a compatible USB flash device, you can improve performance by using it to increase your computer's memory.

ReadyBoost has several security features. First, ReadyBoost encrypts data written to the USB flash drive. ***Encryption*** is the process of encoding the data so that others cannot view it. ReadyBoost also keeps a backup of the data it writes to the USB flash device on the hard disk drive.

To check how well you can identify ReadyBoost functions, take a moment to answer the following questions:

1. Adding ______________ is often the best way to improve your computer's performance.
2. USB flash drives read and write data significantly ______________ than a hard disk drive.
3. For a USB flash drive to be used as computer memory, it must first pass the ReadyBoost ______________.
4. ReadyBoost works with two types of flash memory cards: ______________ and ______________ cards.
5. When ReadyBoost is disabled, the space that was formerly used by ReadyBoost returns as ______________ ______________.

More Knowledge | Safely Removing a USB Flash Drive from Your Computer

Before removing a USB flash drive from your computer, be sure that its light is *not* flashing. The flashing light indicates that one or more operations are still in progress. Removing the device while the light is flashing could result in one or more corrupted files.

If you see the Safely Remove Hardware icon in the notification area, you can use this to ensure that devices have finished all operations in progress and are ready to remove. Click the icon and you will see a list of devices; click the device you want to remove to confirm whether or not it has any operations in progress.

End You have completed Project 8B

Content-Based Assessments

Summary

Windows 7 provides tools to help keep your computer system in good working condition. Periodic maintenance improves the speed and reliability of your computer system. For example, removing unneeded files and uninstalling unused programs reduces demand on computer resources, and periodically defragmenting disks and running Disk Check helps keep your hard disk drives in good working condition.

Key Terms

Matching

Match each term in the second column with its correct definition in the first column by writing the letter of the term on the blank line in front of the correct definition.

____ 1. A Windows 7 program that scans your hard disk drive and then removes temporary files, empties the Recycle Bin, and removes a variety of system files and other items that you no longer need.

____ 2. The manner in which files are stored on a disk drive.

____ 3. The file system typically used by Windows 7.

____ 4. The smallest area in which data can be written on a disk using the file systems NTFS or FAT.

____ 5. A file that has been split apart and whose fragments are stored in separate blocks of the hard disk drive.

A Architecture
B Bad sector
C Benchmarks
D Cluster
E Disk Cleanup
F Disk defragmentation
G File system
H Firmware
I Fragmented file

____ 6. The process of consolidating fragmented files on your hard disk drive into continuous files.

____ 7. A sector of a disk drive that has experienced a failure.

____ 8. A computer program embedded by a manufacturer into a hardware device.

____ 9. An addition to Windows 7 that helps prevent or fix problems or that improves how your computer performs.

____ 10. The program that checks for updates, downloads them, and then installs them on your computer.

____ 11. A program with which you can schedule regular hard disk drive maintenance tasks.

____ 12. An action that causes a procedure to be carried out automatically in response to a specific event.

____ 13. Standardized tests that measure computer system performance.

____ 14. The data-handling capacity of a microprocessor in terms of the size of the data groups in which a CPU receives and sends data.

____ 15. A feature in Windows 7 that displays details about your computer's hardware configuration, computer components, and operating system software from within a single dialog box.

J New Technology File System (NTFS)
K System Information
L Task Scheduler
M Trigger
N Update
O Windows Update

Multiple Choice

Circle the correct answer.

1. One billion bytes is referred to as a:
A. gigabyte **B.** megabyte **C.** terabyte

2. One million bytes is referred to as a:
A. gigabyte **B.** megabyte **C.** terabyte

3. One trillion bytes is referred to as a:
A. gigabyte **B.** megabyte **C.** terabyte

4. A program that starts automatically whenever your computer is started is a:
A. setup program **B.** startup program **C.** install program

5. A program that prepares a software package to run on a computer is a:
A. setup program **B.** startup program **C.** driver

6. Software that enables programs to communicate with computer hardware devices, such as a graphics card, is a:
A. driver **B.** startup program **C.** install program

7. A file that starts a program and is identified by the file extension *.exe* is:
A. a startup file **B.** a setup file **C.** an executable file

8. The repository for information about your computer's configuration is the:
A. file system **B.** CPU **C.** registry

9. A Windows 7 feature that enables certain USB flash drives to be used as computer memory is:
A. virtual memory **B.** ReadyBoost **C.** defragging

10. The process of encoding data so that others cannot view it is:
A. defragging **B.** upgrading **C.** encryption

Apply 8A skills from these Objectives:

1 Maintain Your Computer's Hard Disk Drive

2 View Windows Update Settings

3 Schedule Maintenance Tasks by Using Task Scheduler

Skills Review | Project 8C Maintaining a Computer

Project Files

For Project 8C, you will need the following files:

Student Resource CD (or a USB flash drive containing these files)
win08_8C_Answer_Sheet (Word document)

You will save your file as:

Lastname_Firstname_8C_Answer_Sheet

Project Results

1 **Close** all open windows. On the taskbar, click the **Windows Explorer** button. In the **navigation pane**, click the drive that contains the student files for this textbook, and then navigate to **Chapter_Files ▶ Chapter_08**. Double-click the Word file **win08_8C_Answer_Sheet** to open Word and display the document. Press F12 to display the **Save As** dialog box in Word, navigate to your **Windows 7 Chapter 8** folder, and then using your own name, save the document as **Lastname_Firstname_8C_Answer_Sheet** If necessary, click OK if a message regarding formats displays.

On the taskbar, click the **Word** button to minimize the window and leave your Word document accessible from the taskbar. As you complete each step in this project, click the Word button on the taskbar to open the document, type your one-letter answer in the appropriate cell of the Word table, and then on the taskbar, click the button again to minimize the window for the next step.

Click the **Start** button, display **All Programs**, and then click **Accessories**. Under **Accessories**, click **System Tools**, and then click **Disk Cleanup**. Be sure that the **C:** drive is selected, and then click **OK**. After the calculation is complete, view the **Description** for **Downloaded Program Files**. What type of program files are downloaded automatically from the Internet when you view certain pages?

A. ActiveX controls

B. Java applets

C. Both ActiveX controls and Java applets

2 In the **Disk Cleanup** dialog box, click on the words *Recycle Bin*, and then click the **View Files** button. What is your result?

A. The Recycle Bin folder window displays.

B. The Recycle Bin folder window displays and all the files are selected.

C. The Recycle Bin folder window displays options for deleting files you no longer want.

3 **Close** the **Recycle Bin** folder window, and then click **Cancel**. Open the **Computer** window. Right-click your **USB flash drive**, and then click **Properties**. Click the **Tools tab**, and then click the **Defragment now** button. Click **Configure schedule**. If necessary, select the **Run on a schedule (recommended)** check box. Click the **Frequency arrow**. What time periods display?

A. Daily and Weekly

B. Weekly and Monthly

C. Daily, Weekly, and Monthly

(Project 8C Maintaining a Computer continues on the next page)

Skills Review | Project 8C Maintaining a Computer (continued)

4 Click the **Frequency arrow** again to close the list, and then click **Cancel**. **Close** the **Disk Defragmenter** dialog box. In the **Properties** dialog box, click the **Check now** button. In the **Check Disk** dialog box, which option is already selected when you open it?

A. Automatically fix the file system errors.

B. Scan for and attempt recovery of bad sectors.

C. Both Automatically fix the file system errors and Scan for and attempt recovery of bad sectors are checked.

5 Click **Cancel** two times and then **Close** the **Computer** window. Click the **Start** button, and then click **Control Panel**. Click **System and Security**, and then under **Windows Update**, click **Check for updates**. In the left pane, click **View update history**. Which of the following is true?

A. The updates are listed by date with the oldest updates listed first.

B. The updates are listed by date with the newest updates listed first.

C. The updates are listed by name in alphabetical order.

6 In the lower right corner of the **View update history** window, click **OK**. Click the link for **optional updates** that are available, and then click the name (do not select the check box) of one of the available updates. Your result is:

A. The update was downloaded.

B. The update was downloaded and installed.

C. A description of the update displays.

7 Click **Cancel**. In the **Windows Update address bar**, click **Control Panel**. Click **System and Security**, scroll down if necessary to locate **Administrative Tools**, and then click **Schedule tasks**. Under **Overview of Task Scheduler**, read the displayed information. According to this information, where are tasks stored?

A. In the Tasks folder located in the path C:\Users\Tasks

B. In the Documents folder

C. In folders in the Task Scheduler Library

8 In the **Actions** pane on the right, click **Create Basic Task**. On the **Create a Basic Task** screen of the **Create Basic Task Wizard**, which two boxes have settings that can be filled in?

A. Name and Description

B. Trigger and Action

C. User name and Password

9 Click **Cancel**. In the **Actions** pane, click **Create Task**. Click the **Triggers tab**, and then click the **New** button. Click the **Begin the task arrow**. Which of the following is *not* an available trigger from which to begin the task?

A. At startup

B. On workstation lock

C. On restart

(Project 8C Maintaining a Computer continues on the next page)

Skills Review | Project 8C Maintaining a Computer (continued)

10 Click the **Begin the task arrow** to close the list, click **Cancel**, click the **Actions tab**, and then click the **New** button. Click the **Action arrow**. Which of the following is *not* an action that a task can perform?

A. Start a program

B. Turn off the computer's monitor

C. Send an e-mail

Click the **Action arrow** to close the list. Click **Cancel** two times, and then **Close** all open windows. Be sure you have typed all of your answers in your Word document. **Save** and **Close** your Word document; submit it as directed by your instructor.

End **You have completed Project 8C**

Content-Based Assessments

Apply 8B skills from these Objectives:

- 4 Locate System Information
- 5 Install and Uninstall Programs
- 6 Optimize Computer Performance

Skills Review | Project 8D Optimizing Computer Performance

Project Files

For Project 8D, you will need the following files:

Student Resource CD (or a USB flash drive containing these files)
win08_8D_Answer_Sheet (Word document)

You will save your file as:

Lastname_Firstname_8D_Answer_Sheet

Project Results

1 **Close** all open windows. On the taskbar, click the **Windows Explorer** button. In the **navigation pane**, click the drive that contains the student files for this textbook, and then navigate to **Chapter_Files ▶ Chapter_08**. Double-click the Word file **win08_8D_Answer_Sheet** to open Word and display the document. Press F12 to display the **Save As** dialog box in Word, navigate to your **Windows 7 Chapter 8** folder, and then using your own name, save the document as **Lastname_Firstname_8D_Answer_Sheet** If necessary, click OK if a message regarding formats displays.

On the taskbar, click the **Word** button to minimize the window and leave your Word document accessible from the taskbar. As you complete each step in this project, click the Word button on the taskbar to open the document, type your one-letter answer in the appropriate cell of the Word table, and then on the taskbar, click the button again to minimize the window for the next step.

Display the **Start** menu, click **Control Panel**, click **System and Security**, and then under **System**, click **Check the Windows Experience Index**. Click **View and print detailed performance and system information**. In the displayed report, under **Graphics**, which term is used to indicate the *graphics card*?

A. Display adapter type
B. Graphics accelerator
C. Video card

2 **Close** the report window, and then click **What do these numbers mean?** In the displayed **Windows Help and Support** window, scroll to the bottom and expand **About your computer's base score**. What is the minimum base score needed to run all of the new features of Windows 7?

A. 2.0 or 3.0
B. 3.0 or 4.0
C. 4.0 or 5.0

3 **Close** all open windows. Click **Start**, type **system** and then at the top of the **Start** menu, under **Programs**, click **System Information**. Expand **Hardware Resources**, and then click **DMA**. What is the DMA device?

A. Digital media accelerator
B. Digital management assistant
C. Direct memory access controller

(Project 8D Optimizing Computer Performance continues on the next page)

Skills Review | Project 8D Optimizing Computer Performance (continued)

4 Expand **Components**, and then expand **Ports**. What two ports are listed under the **Ports** subcategory?

A. PS/2 and keyboard

B. Serial and Parallel

C. USB and FireWire

5 **Close** the **System Information** window. Open the **Control Panel**, and then under **Programs** click **Uninstall a program**. In the left pane, click **View installed updates**. Scroll as necessary to locate **Microsoft Windows** in the list. What company is listed as the **Publisher** for these updates?

A. Microsoft Corporation

B. Windows 7

C. Microsoft Windows

6 In the left pane, click **Turn Windows features on or off**. Point to the words *Internet Information Services* and read the displayed ScreenTip. What does the Internet Information Services feature do?

A. Speeds up Web searches

B. Provides support for Web and FTP servers

C. Installs an online library of e-books

7 Click **Cancel**, and then return to the **Control Panel**. Click **System and Security**, scroll down as necessary, and then click **Administrative Tools**. In the **Name** column, double-click **System Configuration**. In the **System Configuration** dialog box, click the **General tab**. Which of the following is *not* a startup selection?

A. Normal startup

B. Diagnostic startup

C. Manual startup

8 Click **Cancel** and then **Close** all open windows. **Start** the **Control Panel**, click **System and Security**, and then click **System**. At the bottom of the left pane, click **Performance Information and Tools**, and then in the displayed **Performance Information and Tools** window, in the left pane, click **Adjust visual effects**. Click the **Adjust for best performance** option button. How would you describe the list of visual effects?

A. All of the visual effects are selected.

B. Some of the visual effects are selected.

C. None of the visual effects are selected.

9 Click **Let Windows choose what's best for my computer**, and then click the **Data Execution Prevention tab**. Click the **How does it work?** link and then in the **Windows Help and Support** window, read the information. Based on this information, what does DEP do?

A. Closes programs and notifies you if a program tries to run instructions from the portion of memory used for data.

B. Provides a list of hackers.

C. Prevents the entry of data into malicious programs.

(Project 8D Optimizing Computer Performance continues on the next page)

Skills Review | Project 8D Optimizing Computer Performance (continued)

10 **Close** the **Windows Help and Support** window, and then **Close** all open windows. Click **Start**, and then click **Computer**. Right-click your USB flash drive, and then click **Properties**. What is the **File system** for your USB flash drive?

A. EXT3

B. FAT

C. XFS

Close all open windows. Be sure you have typed all of your answers in your Word document. **Save** and **Close** your Word document; submit it as directed by your instructor.

End **You have completed Project 8D**

Content-Based Assessments

Apply 8A skills from these Objectives:

1. Maintain Your Computer's Hard Disk Drive
2. View Windows Update Settings
3. Schedule Maintenance Tasks by Using Task Scheduler

Mastering Windows 7 | Project 8E System Maintenance

In the following Mastering Windows 7 project, you will run Disk Cleanup, run Check Disk, view installed updates, and create a task using Task Scheduler. Your captured screens will look similar to Figure 8.46.

Project Files

For Project 8E, you will need the following files:

New Snip files

You will save your files as:

Lastname_Firstname_8E_Cleanup_Snip
Lastname_Firstname_8E_Checking_Snip
Lastname_Firstname_8E_Updates_Snip
Lastname_Firstname_8E_Task_Snip

Project Results

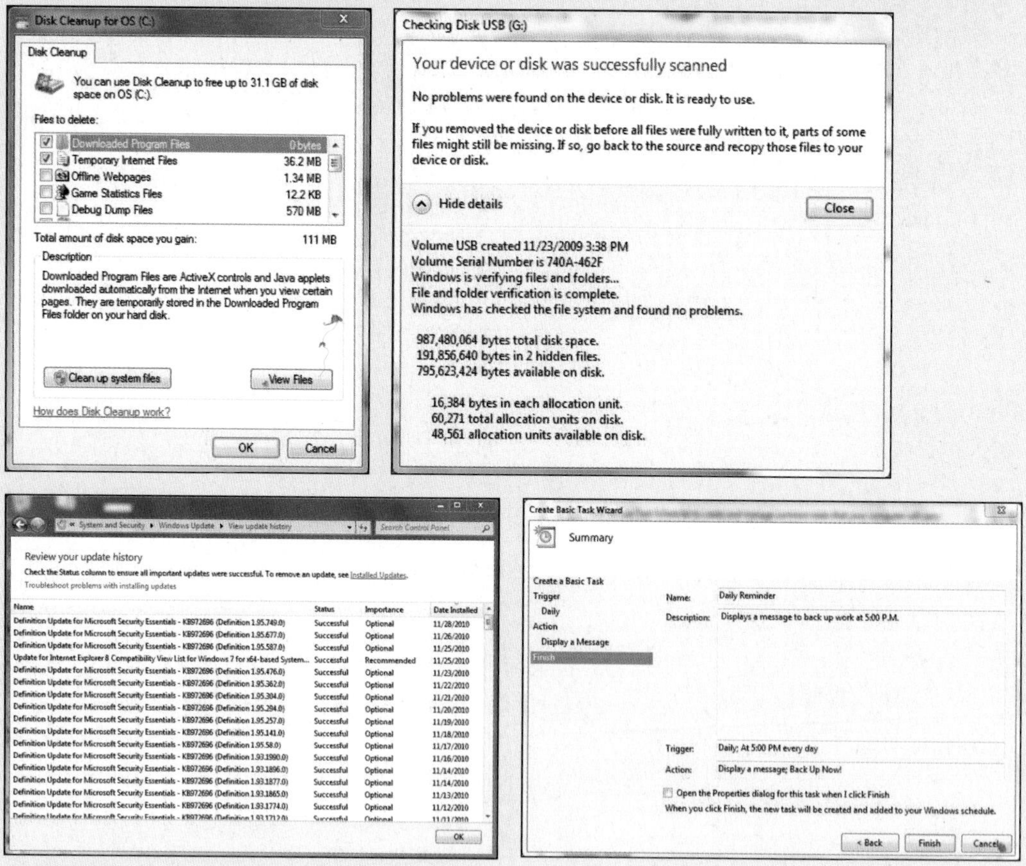

Figure 8.46

(Project 8E System Maintenance continues on the next page)

Mastering Windows 7 | Project 8E System Maintenance (continued)

1 Insert your USB flash drive. Start **Disk Cleanup**, and then scan your hard disk drive. Create a **Window Snip** for the **Disk Cleanup** suggestions, click in the window to display the Snipping Tool markup window, and then **Save** the snip as **Lastname_Firstname_8E_Cleanup_Snip** Hold this file until you finish Project 8E. In the **Disk Cleanup** window, click **Cancel** to close without deleting any files.

2 Display the **Computer** window, right-click your USB flash drive, click **Properties**, click the **Tools tab**, and then under **Error-checking**, click **Check now**. When the scan is complete, click **See details.** Create a **Window Snip** for the **Checking Disk** window, and then **Save** the snip as **Lastname_Firstname_8E_Checking_Snip** Hold this file until you finish Project 8E.

3 **Close** all open windows and dialog boxes. Display the **Control Panel**, click **System and Security**, and then under **Action Center**, click **Review your computer's status and resolve issues.** In the lower left, click **Windows Update**. Display your computer's update history. Create a **Window Snip** for the **View update history** window and **Save** it as **Lastname_Firstname_8E_Updates_Snip** Hold this file until you finish this project.

4 **Close** all open windows, and then open the **Task Scheduler**. Start the **Create Basic Task Wizard**. In the **Name** box, type **Daily Reminder** and in the description box, type **Displays a message to back up work at 5:00 P.M.** Click **Next**, and then in the **Create Basic Task Wizard**, set the **Trigger** to **Daily**. In the next screen, set the **Start time** to **5:00:00 PM**

5 In the next screen of the **Create Basic Task Wizard**, set the **Action** to **Display a message**, and then click **Next**. In the **Title** box, type: **Back Up Now!** and then in the **Message** box, type **Remember to back up your work before you leave.**

6 In the **Create Basic Task Wizard**, click **Next.** Create a **Window snip** for the **Create Basic Task Wizard Summary** window and **Save** it as **Lastname_Firstname_8E_Task_Snip** In the lower right corner, click **Cancel**, and then **Close** all open windows. Submit the four snip files that are the results of this project to your instructor as directed.

End **You have completed Project 8E**

Content-Based Assessments

Apply 8B skills from these Objectives:

- **4** Locate System Information
- **5** Install and Uninstall Programs
- **6** Optimize Computer Performance

Mastering Windows 7 | Project 8F Performance Settings

In the following Mastering Windows 7 project, you will manage startup programs, view systems information, view Windows Features, and change performance options. Your captured screens will look similar to Figure 8.47.

Project Files

For Project 8F, you will need the following files:

New Snip files

You will save your files as:

Lastname_Firstname_8F_Startup_Snip
Lastname_Firstname_8F_Features_Snip
Lastname_Firstname_8F_Effects_Snip

Project Results

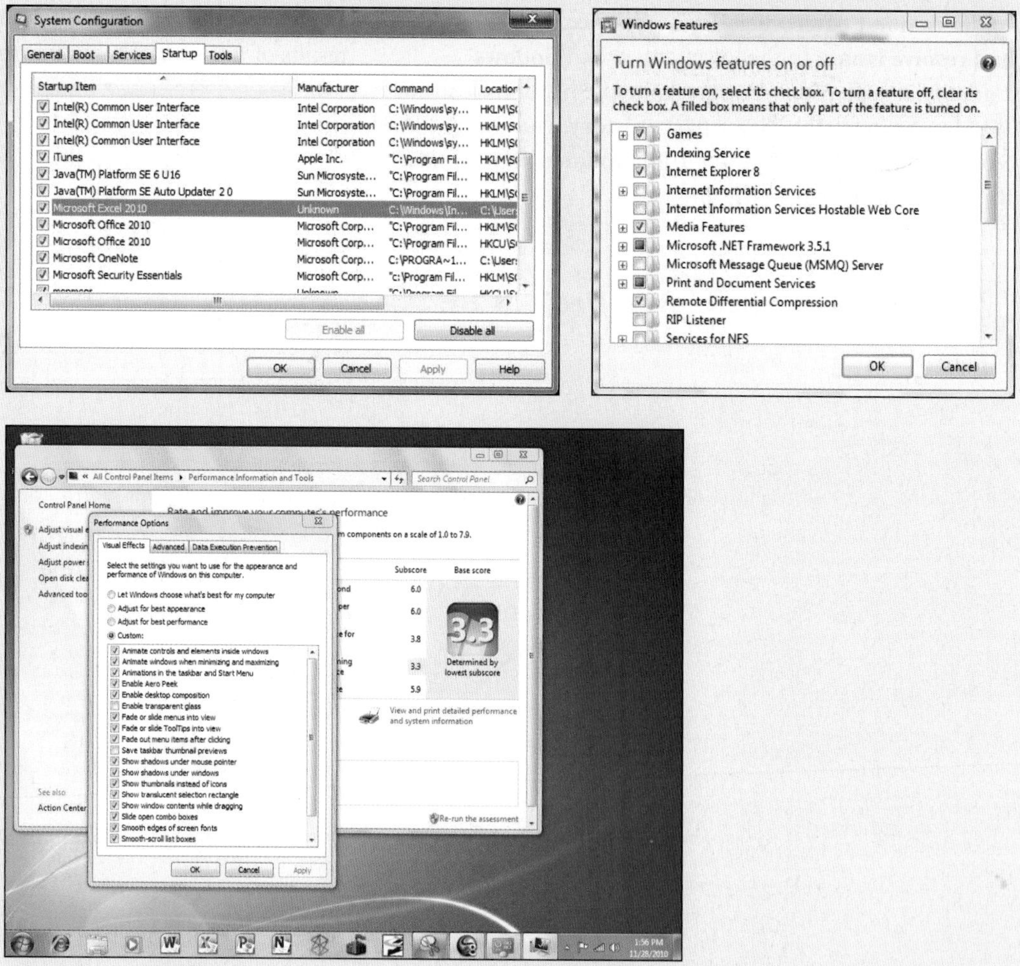

Figure 8.47

(Project 8F Performance Settings continues on the next page)

Mastering Windows 7 | Project 8F Performance Settings (continued)

1 On your desktop, create a shortcut to Microsoft Excel. From the **Start** menu, display the **Startup** folder window, and then drag the shortcut into the **Startup** folder.

2 By using the **Start** menu search feature, open the **System Configuration** dialog box. Display the **Startup tab**. Click the **Startup Item** column title to sort it alphabetically, and then widen the column and scroll as necessary to display the entire *Microsoft Office Excel 2010* text. Click the text to select it. Create a **Window Snip** for the **System Configuration** window, click in the window to capture the snip, and then save it as **Lastname_Firstname_8F_Startup_Snip** Hold this file until you finish Project 8F.

3 **Close** the **System Configuration** dialog box, and then in the **Startup** folder window, delete the **Microsoft Office Excel 2010** shortcut. **Close** the **Startup** folder window. Open the **Control Panel**, and then under **Programs**, click **Uninstall a program**.

4 On the left, click **Turn Windows features on or off**. Create a **Window Snip** for the **Windows Features** dialog box, click in the window to capture the snip, and then **Save** it as **Lastname_Firstname_8F_Features_Snip** Hold this file until you finish the project.

5 **Close** the **Windows Features** window, and then return to the **Control Panel**. Open the **System and Security** window, open the **System** window, and then at the bottom of the left pane, click **Performance Information and Tools**. In the left pane, click **Adjust visual effects**.

6 Click the **Custom** option button, and then clear the **Enable transparent glass** check box. Apply your changes, and then create a **Full-screen snip**. **Save** the snip as **Lastname_Firstname_8F_Effects_Snip** In the **Performance Options** dialog box, return the **Visual Effects** back to their original setting. **Apply** your changes, click **OK**, and then **Close** all open windows. Submit the three snip files that are the results of this project as directed by your instructor.

End **You have completed Project 8F**

Outcomes-Based Assessments

Rubric

The following outcomes-based assessments are *open-ended assessments*. That is, there is no specific correct result; your result will depend on your approach to the information provided. Make *Professional Quality* your goal. Use the following scoring rubric to guide you in *how* to approach the problem, and then to evaluate *how well* your approach solves the problem.

The *criteria*—Software Mastery, Content, Format and Layout, and Process—represent the knowledge and skills you have gained that you can apply to solving the problem. The *levels of performance*—Professional Quality, Approaching Professional Quality, or Needs Quality Improvements—help you and your instructor evaluate your result.

	Your completed project is of Professional Quality if you:	**Your completed project is Approaching Professional Quality if you:**	**Your completed project Needs Quality Improvements if you:**
1-Software Mastery	Choose and apply the most appropriate skills, tools, and features and identify efficient methods to solve the problem.	Choose and apply some appropriate skills, tools, and features, but not in the most efficient manner.	Choose inappropriate skills, tools, or features, or are inefficient in solving the problem.
2-Content	Construct a solution that is clear and well organized, contains content that is accurate, appropriate to the audience and purpose, and is complete. Provide a solution that contains no errors in spelling, grammar, or style.	Construct a solution in which some components are unclear, poorly organized, inconsistent, or incomplete. Misjudge the needs of the audience. Have some errors in spelling, grammar, or style, but the errors do not detract from comprehension.	Construct a solution that is unclear, incomplete, or poorly organized; contains some inaccurate or inappropriate content; and contains many errors in spelling, grammar, or style. Do not solve the problem.
3-Format and Layout	Format and arrange all elements to communicate information and ideas, clarify function, illustrate relationships, and indicate relative importance.	Apply appropriate format and layout features to some elements, but not others. Overuse features, causing minor distraction.	Apply format and layout that does not communicate information or ideas clearly. Do not use format and layout features to clarify function, illustrate relationships, or indicate relative importance. Use available features excessively, causing distraction.
4-Process	Use an organized approach that integrates planning, development, self-assessment, revision, and reflection.	Demonstrate an organized approach in some areas, but not others; or, use an insufficient process of organization throughout.	Do not use an organized approach to solve the problem.

Apply a combination of the 8A and 8B skills.

Problem Solving | Project 8G Help Desk

In this project, you will construct a solution by applying any combination of the skills you practiced from the Objectives in Projects 8A and 8B.

Project Files

For Project 8G, you will need the following file:

win08G_Help_Desk

You will save your document as:

Lastname_Firstname_8G_Help_Desk

From the student files that accompany this textbook, open the **Chapter_Files** folder, and then in **Chapter_08** folder, locate and open the Word document **win08_8G_Help_Desk**. Save the document in your chapter folder as **Lastname_Firstname_8G_Help_Desk**

The following e-mail question has arrived at the Help Desk from an employee at the Bell Orchid Hotel's corporate office. In the Word form, construct a response based on your knowledge of Windows 7. Although an e-mail response is not as formal as a letter, you should still use good grammar, good sentence structure, professional language, and a polite tone. Save your document and submit the response as directed by your instructor.

To: Help Desk

My computer has several files that are critical to the success of our company. These files are automatically backed up every day. Besides these daily updates, what other maintenance tasks would you suggest I run to keep my computer in good working condition? How do I find these maintenance tasks and how often do you suggest I perform them?

End You have completed Project 8G

Apply a combination of the 8A and 8B skills.

Problem Solving | Project 8H Help Desk

In this project, you will construct a solution by applying any combination of the skills you practiced from the Objectives in Projects 8A and 8B.

Project Files

For Project 8H, you will need the following file:

win08H_Help_Desk

You will save your document as:

Lastname_Firstname_8H_Help_Desk

From the student files that accompany this textbook, open the **Chapter_Files** folder, and then in **Chapter_08** folder, locate and open the Word document **win08_8H_Help_Desk**. Save the document in your chapter folder as **Lastname_Firstname_8H_Help_Desk**

The following e-mail question has arrived at the Help Desk from an employee at the Bell Orchid Hotel's corporate office. In the Word form, construct a response based on your knowledge of Windows 7. Although an e-mail response is not as formal as a letter, you should still use good grammar, good sentence structure, professional language, and a polite tone. Save your document and submit the response as directed by your instructor.

To: Help Desk

In my previous request to the Help Desk, I asked for a new computer because Windows 7 is slowing down when I run several programs at once. You then asked me for my computer's Windows Experience Index subscores. What are the Windows Experience subscores, how do I find them, and what do they mean when I do find them?

End You have completed Project 8H

Apply a combination of the 8A and 8B skills.

Problem Solving | Project 8I Help Desk

In this project, you will construct a solution by applying any combination of the skills you practiced from the Objectives in Projects 8A and 8B.

Project Files

For Project 8I, you will need the following file:

win08_8I_Help_Desk

You will save your document as:

Lastname_Firstname_8I_Help_Desk

From the student files that accompany this textbook, open the **Chapter_Files** folder, and then in **Chapter_08** folder, locate and open the Word document **win08_8I_Help_Desk**. Save the document in your chapter folder as **Lastname_Firstname_8I_Help_Desk**

The following e-mail question has arrived at the Help Desk from an employee at the Bell Orchid Hotel's corporate office. In the Word form, construct a response based on your knowledge of Windows 7. Although an e-mail response is not as formal as a letter, you should still use good grammar, good sentence structure, professional language, and a polite tone. Save your document and submit the response as directed by your instructor.

To: Help Desk

As you requested, I have reported my Windows Experience subscores in a separate e-mail. According to my score, I need more RAM on my computer. I understand that flash memory can be used as RAM on Windows 7. What do I need to do in order to use my USB flash drive to increase computer memory?

End **You have completed Project 8I**

Monitoring and Tracking System Performance

OUTCOMES

At the end of this chapter you will be able to:

OBJECTIVES

Mastering these objectives will enable you to:

PROJECT 9A

Use Task Manager to manage applications and processes, view services, and monitor system performance.

1. Manage Applications by Using Task Manager (p.543)
2. Manage Processes by Using Task Manager (p.548)
3. View Services by Using Task Manager (p.555)
4. Track Performance by Using Task Manager (p.558)

PROJECT 9B

Track performance with Performance and Reliability Monitors, view disks with Disk Management, and manage services by using the Services window.

5. Track Performance by Using the Performance and Reliability Monitors (p.565)
6. View Disks by Using Disk Management (p.574)
7. Manage Services by Using the Services Window (p.579)

Tatiana Popova/Shutterstock

In This Chapter

Nearly everyone experiences times when his or her computer seems to slow down or stops responding completely. When this happens frequently, you may need to find out what could be causing the slowdown. Task Manager and the Performance and Reliability Monitors track various system resources as you work on your computer. These tools display information that helps you discover the cause of performance slowdowns. After the problem is located, you—or a computer technician—will be able to find solutions to have your computer performing well again. In this chapter, you will use Task Manager, Performance Monitor, and Reliability Monitor to monitor and track your computer's performance.

The projects in this chapter relate to the **Bell Orchid Hotels**, headquartered in Boston, and which own and operate resorts and business-oriented hotels. Resort properties are located in popular destinations, including Honolulu, Orlando, San Diego, and Santa Barbara. The resorts offer deluxe accommodations and a wide array of dining options. Other Bell Orchid hotels are located in major business centers and offer the latest technology in their meeting facilities. The company plans to open new properties and update existing properties over the next ten years.

Project 9A Using Task Manager

Project Activities

In Activities 9.01 through 9.06, you will participate in training along with Steven Ramos and Barbara Hewitt, both of whom work for the Information Technology Department at the headquarters office of the Bell Orchid Hotels. After completing this part of the training, you will be able to stop unresponsive applications, find out which background processes and services consume the most computer resources, and create charts displaying computer performance over time. You will capture screens that look similar to Figure 9.1.

Project Files

For Project 9A, you will need the following files:

Student Resource CD or a USB flash drive containing the student data files
New Snip files

You will save your files as:

Lastname_Firstname_9A_Processes_Snip
Lastname_Firstname_9A_Services_Snip
Lastname_Firstname_9A_Performance_Snip
Lastname_Firstname_9A_Networking_Snip

Project Results

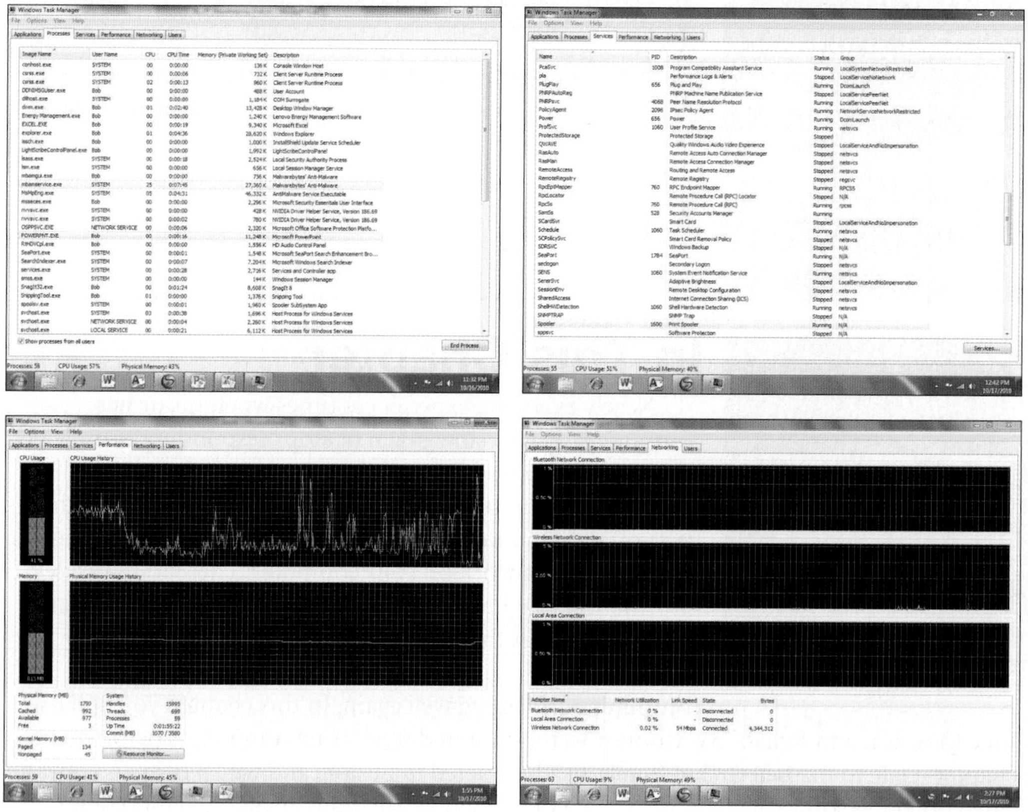

Figure 9.1
Project 9A Using Task Manager

Objective 1 | Manage Applications by Using Task Manager

Task Manager is a Windows 7 tool that shows you the programs, processes, and services that are currently running on your computer. A ***process*** is a file that is part of a running program and performs a specific task such as starting the program. For example, a file with a file name extension of *.exe* is a process file that your computer uses to start a program or to start other services. ***Services*** are computer programs or processes that run in the background and provide support to other programs.

There are two reasons that you will want to use Task Manager:

- To monitor your computer's performance.
- To close a program that is not responding—referred to as a ***nonresponsive program***.

A nonresponsive program is a program that is open but has stopped responding to your commands, which means it has stopped communicating with Windows 7. In this nonresponsive state, the program cannot respond to your actions or update any of its windows; nor can the program be closed by using any of the program's commands.

Activity 9.01 | Managing Applications by Using Task Manager

Task Manager displays a list of currently running programs—also called *applications*—and indicates the status of each one. When a program you are using enters a nonresponsive state and you are unable to close it, display the Task Manager tool, from which you can close a nonresponsive program.

A program may become nonresponsive when it performs a task that has no way of ending, or when the program cannot access the correct instructions that it had stored in memory. Closing a nonresponsive program stops all tasks that the program is performing and removes the program's instructions from computer memory. Thus, closing a nonresponsive program and then reopening it frequently corrects the problem.

In this activity, you will open several programs, use Task Manager to view each open program's status, and then close one of the applications from within Task Manager.

> **Note | It Is Assumed That You Have an Administrator Account**
>
> Learning to customize and control your computer by using Windows 7 as an administrator is the best way to learn Windows 7, because many features are available only to an individual who has an administrator account. For the majority of the instruction in this chapter, it is assumed that you are logging on with an administrator account.

1. Insert the Student Resource CD in the appropriate drive, and if necessary, Close the AutoPlay dialog box.
2. Insert your USB flash drive, and if necessary, Close the AutoPlay dialog box.
3. On the taskbar, click the **Windows Explorer** button. In the **navigation pane**, under **Computer**, click your **CD/DVD Drive** to display its contents in the **file list**. In the **address bar**, navigate to **01_student_data_files** ▶ **Bell_Orchid** ▶ **San_Diego** to display its contents in the **file list**.
4. In the **file list**, right-click the **Operations** folder, point to **Send to**, and then in the displayed list, click the name and drive letter of your USB flash drive.

5 In the **navigation pane**, scroll down as necessary and click your USB flash drive to display its contents in the **file list**. Then, double-click the **Operations** folder to display its contents in the file list. If necessary, set the view to **Details**, and then compare your screen with Figure 9.2.

In the file list, three files display: a PowerPoint presentation, an Excel worksheet, and a Word document.

Figure 9.2

Path to Operations folder

Three files in Operations folder

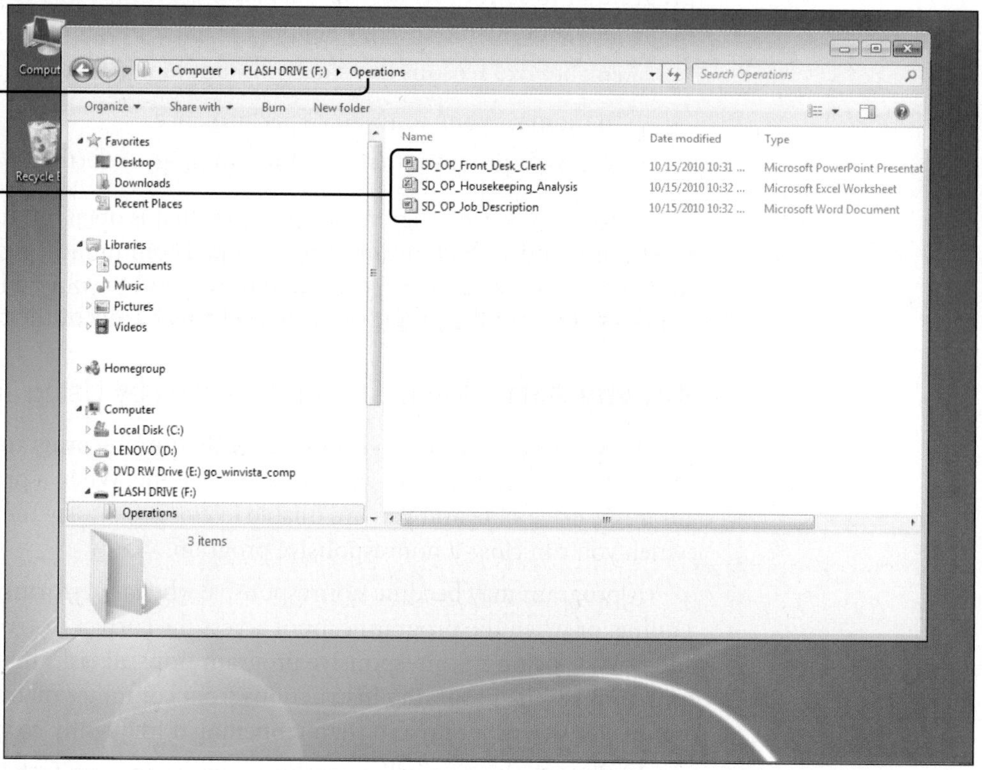

6 In the **file list**, double-click the file **SD_OP_Front_Desk_Clerk** to start PowerPoint and open the presentation. On the taskbar, click the **Operations** folder button to switch to this window, and then double-click to open the Excel file **SD_OP_Housekeeping_Analysis**.

7 From the taskbar, display the **Operations** folder window again, and then double-click the Word file **SD_OP_Job_Description**.

8 On the taskbar, right-click in an empty area to display the shortcut menu, as shown in Figure 9.3.

Figure 9.3

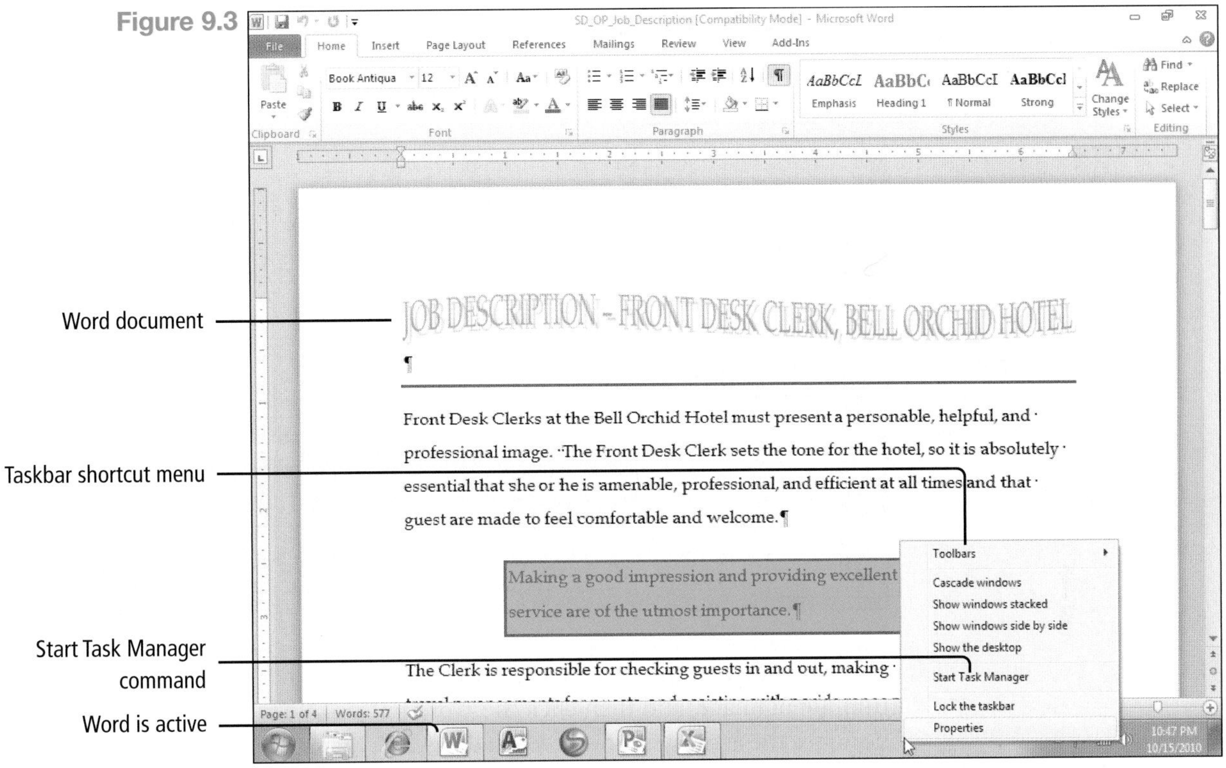

> **Another Way**
>
> Hold down both Ctrl and Shift on your keyboard and press Esc. Or, in the Start menu Search box, type *task manager* and press Enter.

9 On the shortcut menu, click **Start Task Manager**. In the **Windows Task Manager** dialog box, click the **Applications tab**. Be sure the **Task** column is sorted in alphabetical order—the pale arrow in the column heading area points upward. If necessary, click the Task column heading to sort in ascending order. Compare your screen with Figure 9.4.

The Applications tab of the Windows Task Manager dialog box lists all programs that are currently open and display active buttons on the taskbar. The Task column displays the title from each application's title bar. The arrow at the upper edge of the Task column heading indicates that the column can be sorted.

The Status column lists each application's current status as *Running*. A program that is not responding properly will indicate a status of *Not Responding*.

Sometimes an application's status will indicate *Not Responding* while it performs a complex task, and then its status returns to *Running* when the task is completed. If an application's status remains as *Not Responding* after several minutes, the program may no longer be operating properly and it may need to be closed.

At the bottom of the Windows Task Manager dialog box, Windows 7 displays performance information indicating the number of active processes, the percentage of CPU usage, and the percentage of physical memory (RAM) in use; this information displays regardless of which tab in the dialog box is active.

Figure 9.4

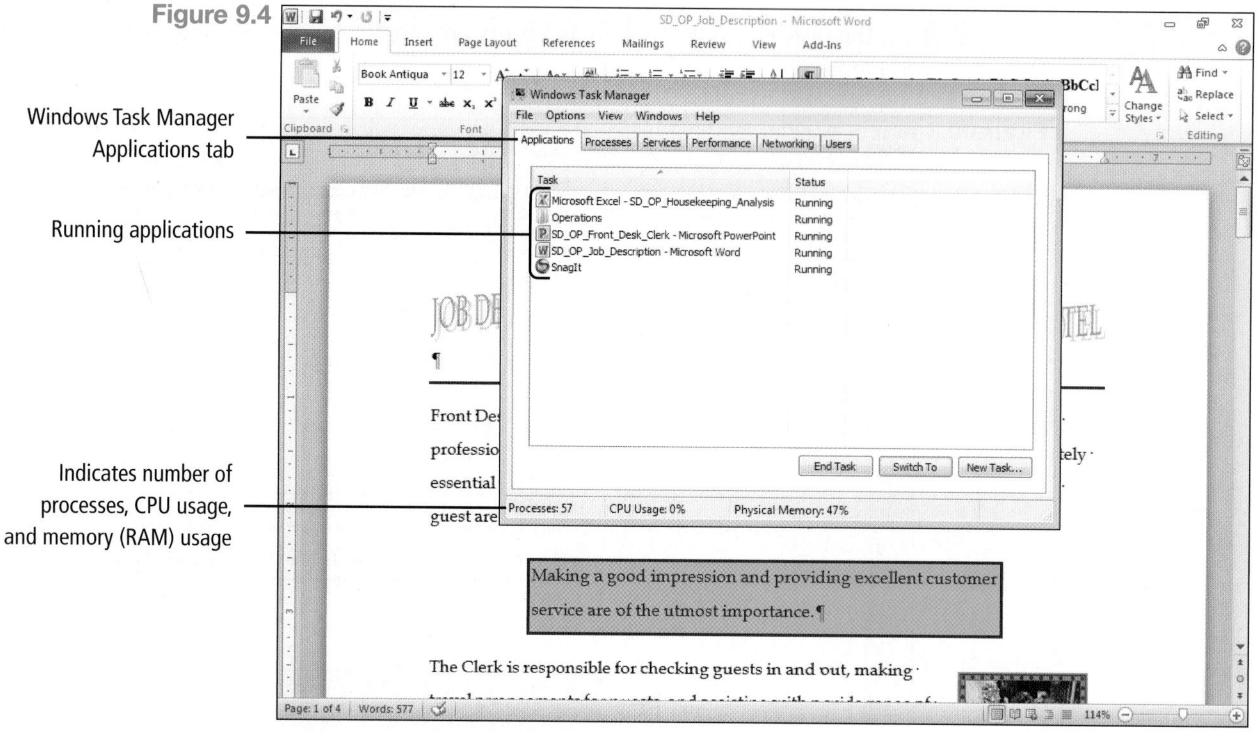

10 On the taskbar, point to the **Word** button to display the *SD_OP_Job_Description* thumbnail image, and then click the **Word** button. Notice that although the Word file becomes the active window, the **Windows Task Manager** dialog box remains open, but behind the active window.

> **Alert! | Does Your Task Manager Window Display in Front of the Word Window?**
>
> If your Task Manager window displays in front of the Word window, from the Options menu, click *Always on top* to remove the check mark.

11 In the Word window, scroll down slightly so that you can view the picture of the buffet table. Click to select the picture, and then press Del.

By deleting the picture, you have made a change to this document.

12 On the taskbar, click the **Windows Task Manager** button to redisplay the dialog box. In the **Task** column, click **SD_OP_Job_Description.** In the lower portion of the **Windows Task Manager** dialog box, click the **End Task** button. Wait a few seconds for the **End Program** dialog box to display, and then compare your screen with Figure 9.5.

The *End Program* dialog box indicates that Windows Task Manager will not close Microsoft Word because Microsoft Word is waiting for a response from you.

When you close an application from Windows Task Manager, Windows 7 attempts to work with the program so that you will have a chance to save changes. For example, in the Word document, you made a change to the document by deleting the picture. When Task Manager attempted to close the Word program, the Word program responded by opening a dialog box that asks if you want to save changes.

Typically, you use Task Manager to close nonresponsive programs. For nonresponsive programs, Windows 7 attempts to work with the program, but if a program does not respond, you will not be given the opportunity to save any changes.

In the *End Program* dialog box, clicking the *End Now* button will immediately close Word without enabling you to save any changes. Clicking the *Cancel* button returns you to the application, where the dialog box that prompts you to save changes is waiting for your response.

Figure 9.5

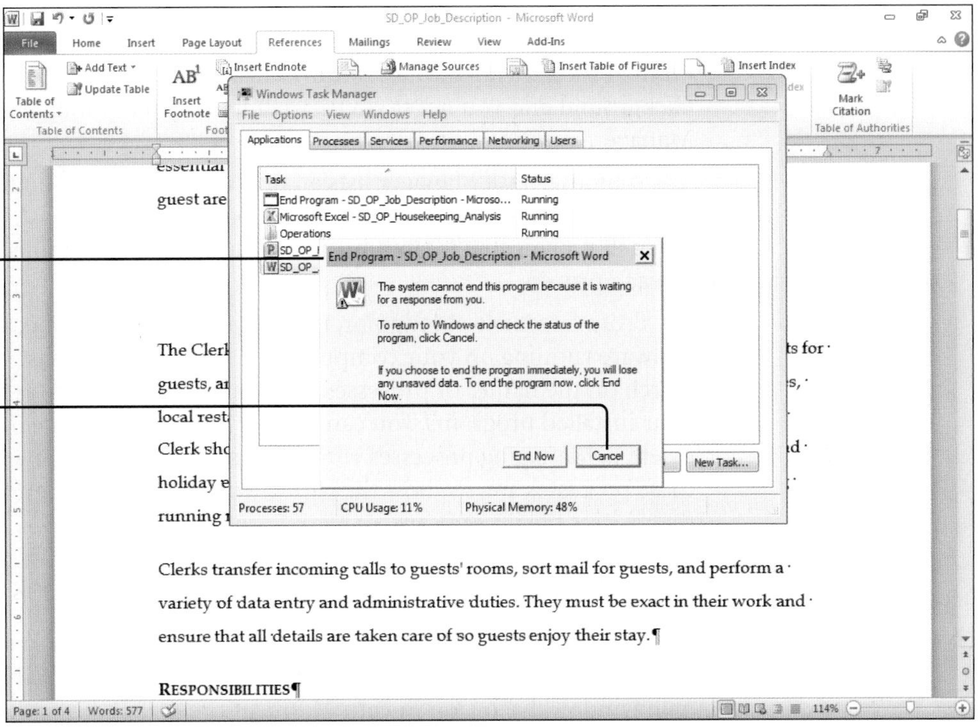

13 In the **End Program** dialog box, click **Cancel**. Minimize the **Windows Task Manager** dialog box, read the Microsoft Word message, and then click **Save** to save the changes you made to the document. On the taskbar, click the **Windows Task Manager** button.

The Microsoft Word program closes and no longer displays on the list of running applications. Because the program is no longer open, its button is no longer active on the taskbar.

> **Note | Use This Technique Only If Your Program Is Not Responding**
>
> In your everyday computing, use the previous steps *only* if Word—or whatever program you are using—stops responding. For responsive programs, you should use that program's menus or buttons to save the changes, to close the file, or to exit the application.

14 Leave the **Operations** folder, the **Excel** file, the **PowerPoint** file, and **Windows Task Manager** open for the next activity.

> **More Knowledge | Allow a Program Some Time to Respond Before Ending It**
>
> Recall that a program can seem nonresponsive if it is performing a complex task or is competing with other programs or system tasks for the computer's resources. Before ending the program in the Task Manager, give the program a little time to complete the task. If the task is one that normally completes in a few seconds, wait a minute or so. If the task is a large one, for example searching a large database, and you can hear disk activity or see the disk activity light flickering, consider waiting several minutes before ending the program.
>
> Using Task Manager to end a program might be faster than waiting, but recall that any unsaved changes will be lost.

Objective 2 | Manage Processes by Using Task Manager

The programs that you run on your computer have one or more processes associated with them. Recall that a process is a part of a running program that performs a specific task such as starting the program. For example, if you open Microsoft Word, the *WINWORD.EXE* process runs until you close the program. Likewise, Internet Explorer runs a process named *iexplore.exe*.

Every program on the Applications tab will have at least one corresponding process on the Processes tab of the Windows Task Manager dialog box. Most processes run in the background and you never see them unless you view them with a tool like Windows Task Manager.

Windows Task Manager lists all of the processes running on your computer and provides many arrangements by which you can view the list. By viewing the list, you can see each process that is running and the amount of computer resources that are consumed by each process.

From a security standpoint, this list of processes is especially valuable, because most malware running on your computer will show up in this list. By performing an Internet search on the names of processes that you cannot identify as being associated with one of your installed programs, you can usually identify the name of a malware program and delete it. Managing processes with Windows Task Manager enables you to find out what these processes are, see how they affect your computer's performance, and end or delete the process file if necessary.

Activity 9.02 | Viewing Processes by Using Task Manager

Many processes are running on your computer; there are always many more processes running than applications. Some processes, for example WINWORD.EXE, display in their own window. Each icon in your Notification Area indicates a running process that may or may not have a window currently opened. Many other processes perform entirely in the background, and you will never see them directly. In this activity, you will use Windows Task Manager to view the processes running on your computer.

1. Be sure that the following windows are open and display on the taskbar: the **Operations** folder on your USB flash drive, the PowerPoint file **SD_OP_Front_Desk_Clerk**, the Excel file **SD_OP_Housekeeping_Analysis**, and **Windows Task Manager**.

   Recall that you can point to the buttons on the taskbar to verify the content of each open window—both a thumbnail and a ScreenTip containing the name of the file will display.

2. On the taskbar, click the **Windows Task Manager** button as necessary to display the dialog box. In the **Windows Task Manager** dialog box, locate the menu bar above the tabs, and then display the **View** menu. Click **Refresh Now**, and then compare your screen with Figure 9.6.

   The Refresh Now command updates the status of each displayed application, and updates the performance statistics located at the bottom of the Windows Task Manager Window. Three applications are running.

Figure 9.6

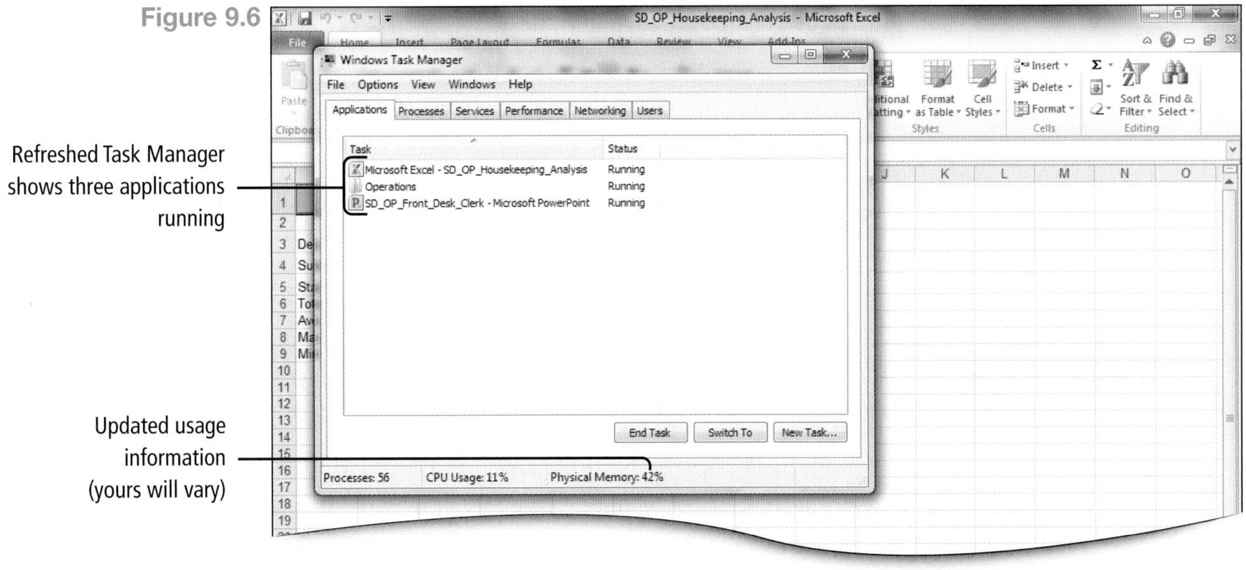

3 In the **Task** column, right-click **Microsoft Excel – SD_OP_Housekeeping_Analysis**, and then on the shortcut menu, click **Go To Process**. **Maximize** the window. Notice that the EXCEL.EXE process is highlighted on the **Processes tab**.

4 In each column heading, point to the right separator line to display the pointer, and then drag to the right to resize each column to view its longest entry—the longest entry might be the column heading itself. Compare your screen with Figure 9.7.

The Processes tab is selected. The User Name column displays the name of the user who initiated the task. Notice that almost every user name is the one that you used to log on to Windows 7. Most of the processes listed here were started when you logged on. The remaining processes are those that you started during this project, such as EXCEL.EXE, which is highlighted.

The *Image Name* column displays the process name. The *Description* column helps you to identify the displayed processes. For example, the process named *dwm.exe* is described as *Desktop Window Manager*. It is here that you might want to search the Internet for a process name (Image Name) that you cannot identify as being associated with one of your installed programs or with the Windows 7 operating system.

Figure 9.7

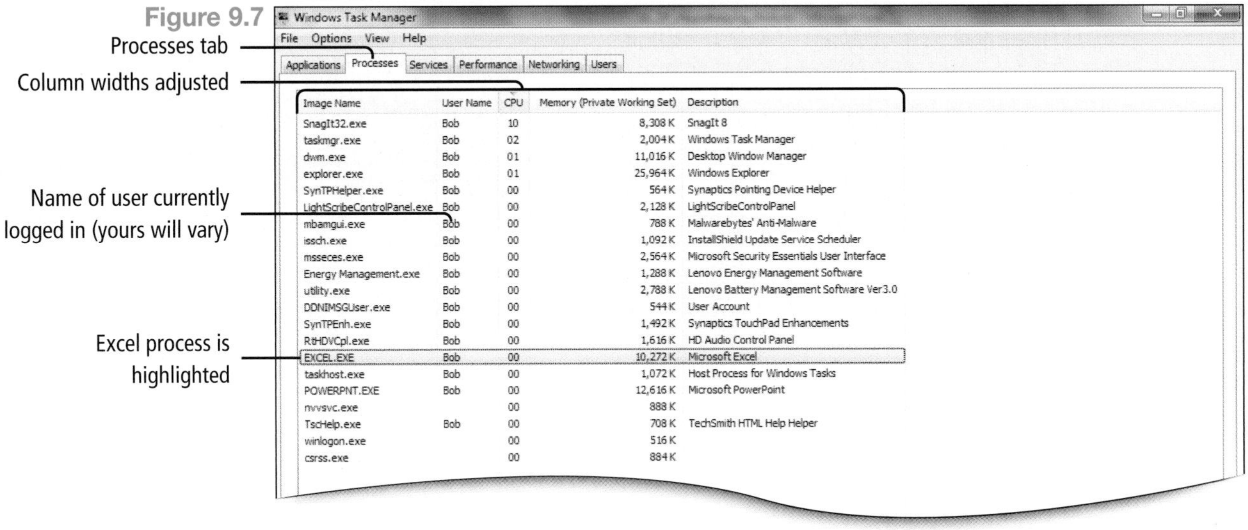

5 In the lower left corner, click the **Show processes from all users** button, and then **Maximize** [button] the window.

The processes that were started by the Windows 7 operating system during its boot process are added to the list of displayed processes.

6 Click the **User Name** column heading to sort the list in ascending order. In the column heading area, point to the separator to the right of the **User Name** column heading to display the [+] pointer. Double-click to resize the **User Name** column.

The User Name column displays processes that, among others, are run by the Windows 7 operating system. The User Name for many of these processes is LOCAL SERVICE, NETWORK SERVICE, and SYSTEM. The wait time that you experience when booting your computer is caused by the time it takes for these processes to start.

7 Click the **CPU** column heading as necessary to sort the column in *descending* order.

Sorting by the CPU column is a quick way to determine which processes are demanding the most from your computer's central processing unit.

8 In the **Image Name** column, notice that the first process is *System Idle Process*. If necessary, widen the Image Name column, and then compare your screen with Figure 9.8.

The System Idle Process indicates the amount of CPU capability that is *not* being used. This number changes constantly as the CPU works with the various processes listed in the Windows Task Manager. The Task Manager program itself is running through the *taskmgr.exe* process and is listed high on the list.

You can see that the CPU percentage for *taskmgr.exe* changes as Windows Task Manager monitors your computer. With this knowledge, you can determine how much of your CPU capability would become available if you closed the Windows Task Manager dialog box.

Figure 9.8

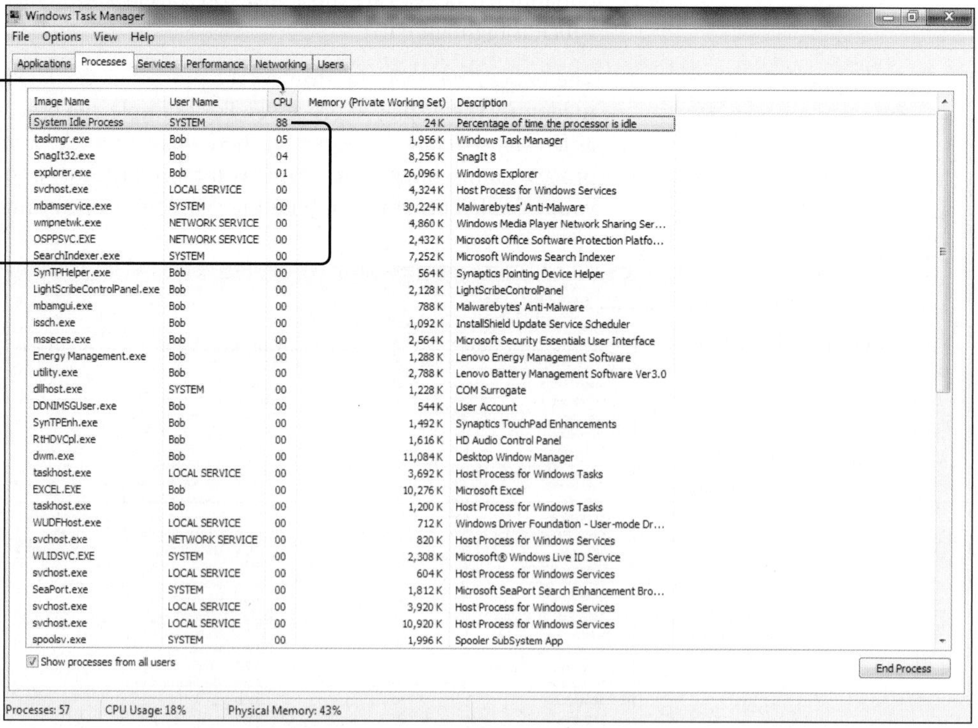

CPU column sorted in descending order

System Idle Process shows CPU resources *not* being used

9 Click the **Memory (Private Working Set)** column heading as necessary to sort the column in *descending* order, and then compare your screen with Figure 9.9.

The list of processes is sorted in descending order by the Memory (Private Working Set) column. *Private Working Set* refers to the amount of memory that must be *reserved* by each process, which is not necessarily the amount of memory currently being *used* by that process. Programs reserve blocks of memory to prevent other programs from using memory that it may need as you work. This prevents the program from performing too slowly.

Ordering your processes by the Memory (Private Working Set) column provides an assessment of which processes consume the largest portion of your system memory. For example, in Figure 9.9, notice that the two processes run by Excel and PowerPoint do not consume as much memory as several of the processes used by the System. If your system was running low on memory, closing Excel and PowerPoint would not free up a significant amount of memory. This indicates that another solution, such as adding more system memory, may be needed.

Figure 9.9

Amount of memory *reserved* for each process

Private Working Set for Excel

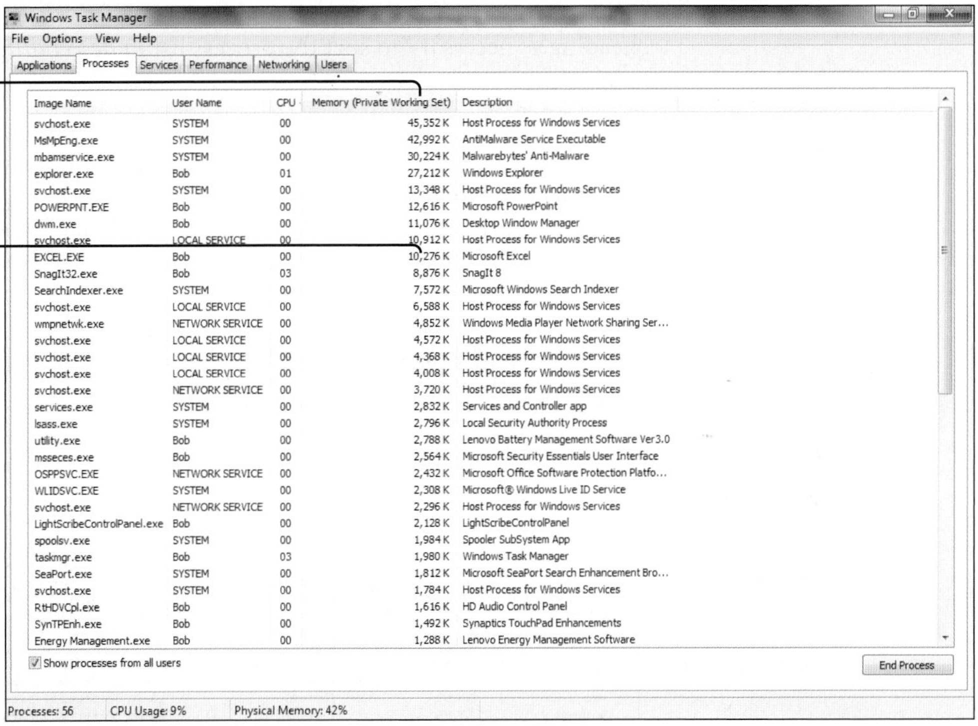

10 Display the **View** menu, and then click **Select Columns**. Compare your screen with Figure 9.10.

The Select Process Page Columns dialog box displays. Here you can select numerous additional columns to add to the Processes tab to find out more about how each process is affecting your computer.

For example, if your hard disk drive seems to be working actively without stopping—you can hear constant hard disk activity—displaying the I/O Reads and I/O Writes in this dialog box can assist in determining which program might be responsible for such activity.

Adding the Threads column also provides useful information. A process often divides itself into one or more tasks that are processed simultaneously—each task is called a ***thread***. The higher the thread count, the more resources the CPU must devote to managing these threads. The thread count is another way to measure how much of available CPU resources a process uses.

Figure 9.10

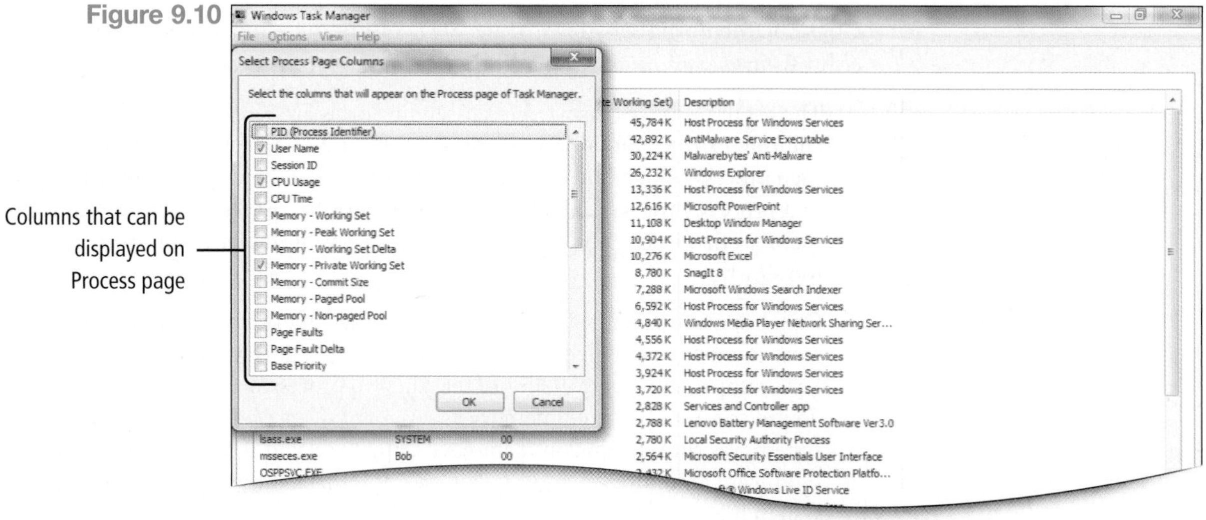

11 Select the **CPU Time** check box, and then click **OK**. Click the **CPU Time** column heading as necessary to sort the process list in *descending* order. Compare your screen with Figure 9.11.

CPU Time measures the actual time that a processor spends working on a task. The CPU Time column displays the elapsed time that the CPU has worked with each process since you opened the Task Manager. In the example shown in Figure 9.11, the Picasa3 program, *Picasa3.exe*, has used the CPU for a greater amount of time than all of the other processes. Knowing which processes have the highest CPU times is another way to determine which processes consume the most CPU resources.

Figure 9.11

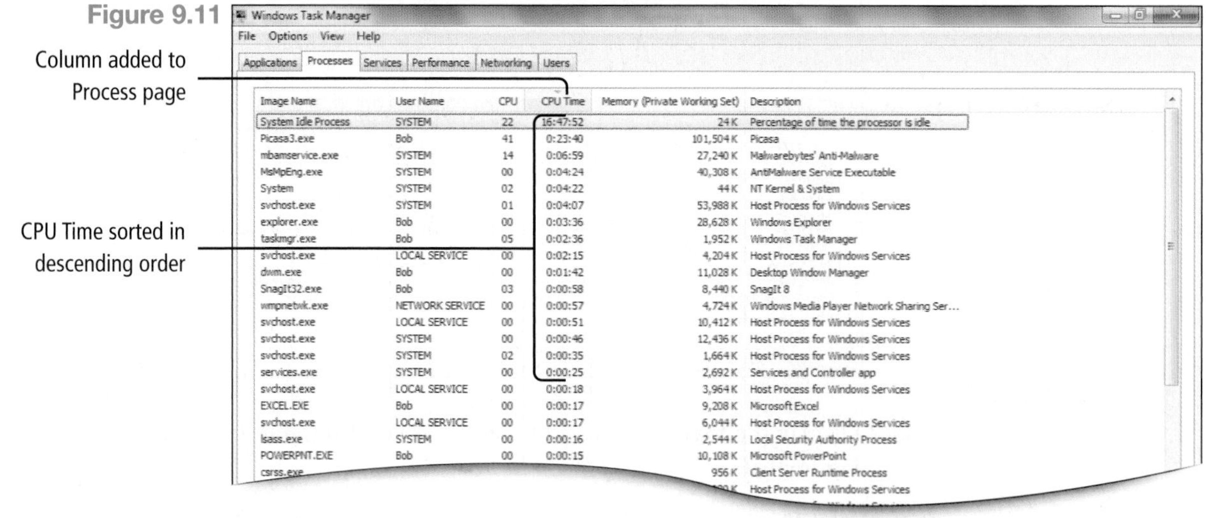

12 Leave all of the programs and windows open for the next activity.

More Knowledge | Using Task Manager as a CPU Monitor

Task Manager can be used to monitor CPU usage while you perform your normal computer tasks. To do so, minimize the Windows Task Manager dialog box. Right-click anywhere in the Notification Area, click *Customize notification options*, click the Windows Task Manager arrow, and the click *Show icon and notifications*. The Task Manager icon displays in your Notification Area, and the icon acts as a meter to indicate the level of CPU usage.

Activity 9.03 | Managing Processes by Using Task Manager

Windows Task Manager also enables you to change settings and properties that change how your computer works with a process. For example, if you give a PowerPoint presentation with many complex animations, you can use Windows Task Manager to dedicate more of the processor time to the POWERPNT.EXE process. This helps your animations run more smoothly during your presentation.

Windows Task Manager is often used to end processes that do not display a window or an icon in the Notification Area. For example, you may be instructed by a computer technician or the Web site of your virus checking program to stop a malware process by using Task Manager. In this activity, you will view methods for changing process settings, and then practice ending a process with Windows Task Manager.

1 Be sure that your USB flash drive is inserted in the computer and that the following windows are open and display on the taskbar: the **Operations** folder on your USB flash drive, the PowerPoint file **SD_OP_Front_Desk_Clerk**, the Excel file **SD_OP_Housekeeping_Analysis**, and **Windows Task Manager**. Be sure that **Windows Task Manager** is the active window and that the **Processes** tab displays.

2 Click the **Image Name** column heading as necessary to sort the column in *ascending* alphabetical order. In the **Image Name** column, point to **EXCEL.EXE**, and then right-click. On the shortcut menu, click **Open File Location**. Compare your screen with Figure 9.12.

The Office14 folder window displays and the EXCEL application is selected. In this instance, the path is *C: > Program Files > Microsoft Office > Office14*. Most software programs installed on your computer are stored in a folder in the Program Files folder. *Office14* is Microsoft's internal name for Microsoft Office 2010. Sometimes a computer technician will ask you to locate a program file so that you change, add, or delete a file in that program's folder.

You can use Windows Task Manager to find the exact location of process files stored on your hard disk drive. If the process is malware, you may need to know the location of the process file in order to delete it. A computer technician would inform you when this is necessary to solve a problem that you have reported.

Figure 9.12

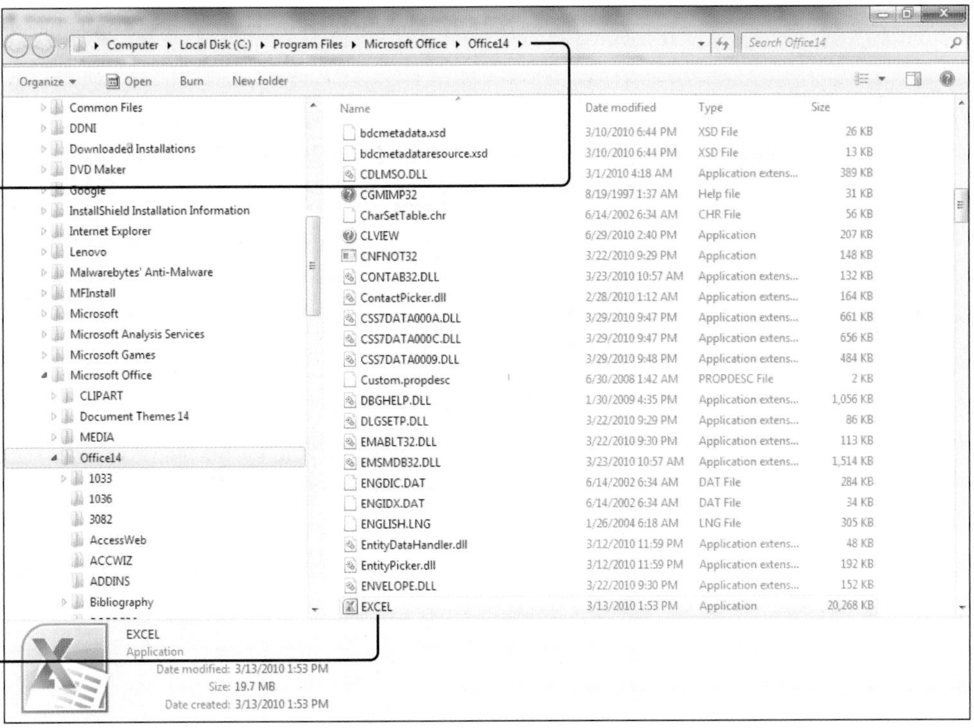

Path to Excel program

Excel program file

3 **Close** the **Office14** folder window, and then if necessary, on the taskbar click Windows Task Manager. In the **Image Name** column, right-click **POWERPNT.EXE**. On the shortcut menu, point to **Set Priority**, and then compare your screen with Figure 9.13.

Each process running on your computer can be assigned a different priority level. When two processes send tasks to the CPU at the same time, the CPU works with the one that has higher priority first. In this example, processes with a lower priority than PowerPoint would have to wait for the CPU to finish tasks sent to it by PowerPoint. This setting dedicates more CPU resources to your PowerPoint program.

Figure 9.13

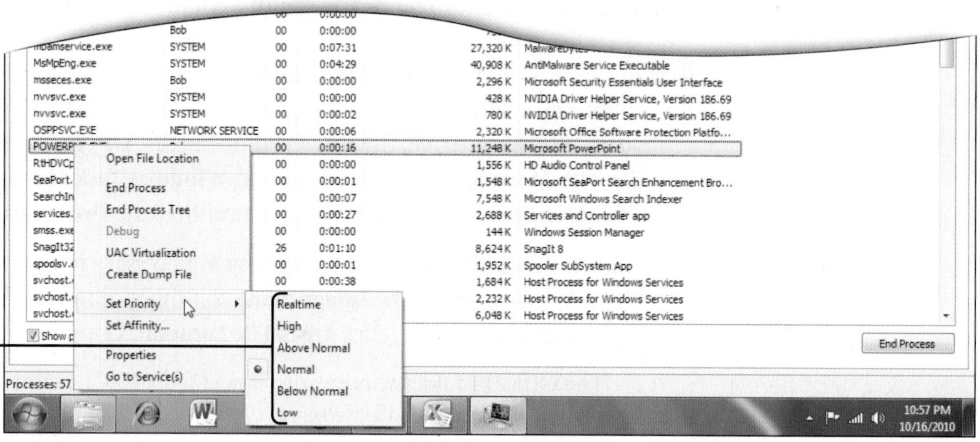

Program priority levels

4 Press Esc two times to close the shortcut menu without making any changes. Right-click **POWERPNT.EXE**. On the shortcut menu, click **End Process**. Read the displayed message, and then compare your screen with Figure 9.14.

Windows Task Manager asks for confirmation that you want to end the process. Ending a process from the Processes tab closes the associated application immediately, and you will not be given a chance to save any changes that you have made to an open file.

If, for example, you were instructed to end a malware process, you would click the End Process button. Sometimes a malware process must be stopped so that the malware program can be entirely removed from your computer.

Figure 9.14

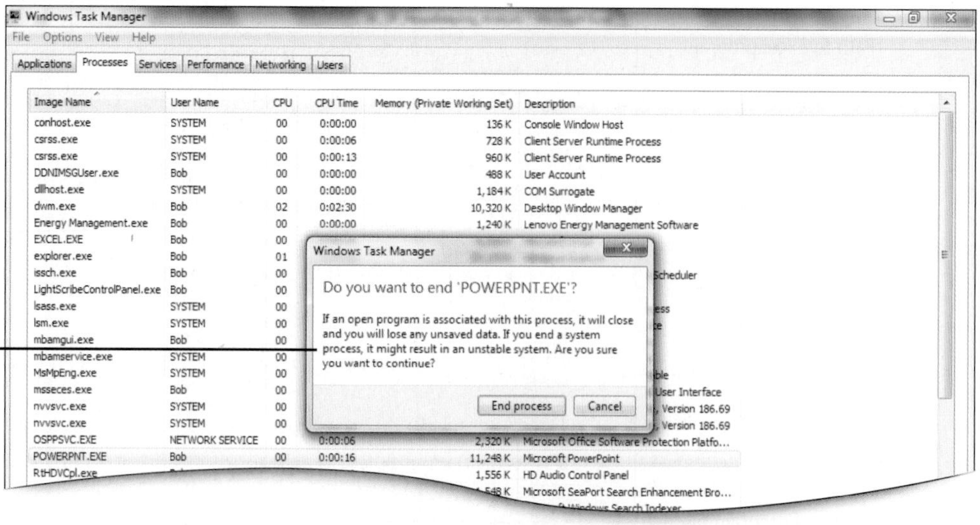

Ending a process could mean loss of data

5 In the **Windows Task Manager** message, click the **Cancel** button.

6 **Start** the **Snipping Tool** program, click the **New arrow**, and then click **Full-screen Snip**. In the **Snipping Tool** mark-up window, click the **Save Snip** button.

7 In the **Save As** dialog box, in the **navigation pane**, scroll down as necessary, and then under **Computer**, click your USB flash drive so that it displays in the **address bar**. On the toolbar, click the **New Folder** button, type **Windows 7 Chapter 9** and then press Enter.

8 In the **file list**, double-click your **Windows 7 Chapter 9** folder to open it. Click in the **File name** box, and then replace the selected text by typing **Lastname_Firstname_9A_Processes_Snip** Be sure the file type is **JPEG**, and then press Enter. **Close** the **Snipping Tool** mark-up window. Hold this file until you finish Project 9A, and then submit this file as directed by your instructor.

9 From the **View** menu of the **Windows Task Manager**, click **Select Columns**. Clear the **CPU Time** check box, and then click **OK**.

10 **Close** **Windows Task Manager**, and then **Close** the **Excel** window and the **PowerPoint** window.

11 In the **Operations** folder window, in the **navigation pane**, locate your USB flash drive, and then delete the **Operations** folder. **Close** any open windows.

More Knowledge | Using Task Manager to Manage Malware

If you are unsure about the Image Name of a process listed on the Processes tab, go to www.processlibrary.com, where you can search processes by name and determine whether a process might be a virus or some other malware. You can also go to any search engine—such as www.bing.com or www.google.com—and type the image name.

To close a process that you believe to be malware, click the process name, and then click End Process. When the Windows Task Manager window displays, click End Process to end the process. This will not remove the process file from your computer, so consult with a computer technician or other resource to find out how to remove the malware from your computer. Because malware developers try to use names that are similar to legitimate processes, use caution before ending the process.

Objective 3 | View Services by Using Task Manager

Recall that a service is a computer program or process that runs in the background and that provides support to other programs. Many services operate at a low level; that is, the service interacts directly with a hardware device, and thus needs to run even when no account holder is logged on. Most of the services that are essential to running your computer are set to start automatically when you start your computer and stop when you shut down your computer.

On rare occasions, you might need to stop a service if directed to do so by a computer technician or other IT professional. For example, if too many print requests have caused your printer to become nonresponsive, one remedy might be to stop and then restart a service named *Spooler*.

Activity 9.04 | Viewing Services by Using Task Manager

In this activity, you will use Windows Task Manager to display your system's services, sort the list of services, and view the process that is using a specific service.

1 Be sure that your USB flash drive or other removable media is inserted in the computer. Right-click in the taskbar, and then from the menu, click **Start Task Manager**.

2 In the **Windows Task Manager** window, click the **Services tab**. **Maximize** the window, and then adjust the width of each column so that you have a clear view of each column's content. Compare your screen with Figure 9.15.

The Status column displays either *Running* or *Stopped*. Most of the running services were started during the boot process or when you logged on to your computer. Other services are started and stopped by processes as they are needed.

Figure 9.15

Services tab selected

Column widths adjusted

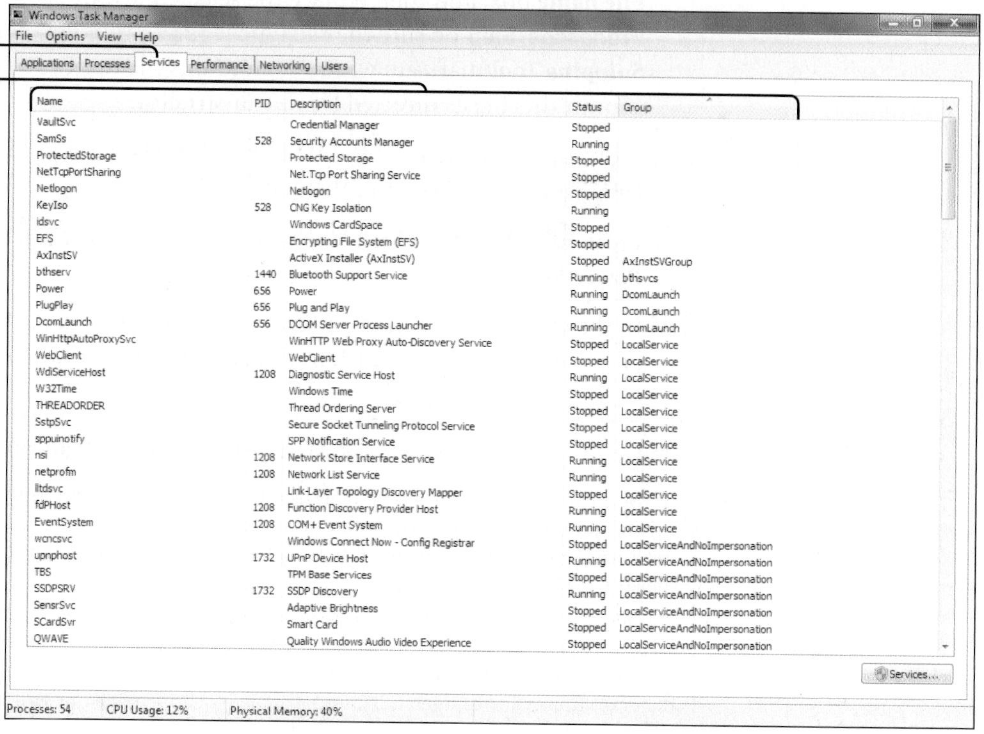

3 Click the **PID** column heading as necessary to sort the column in *descending* order. If necessary, scroll to the top of the list, and then compare your screen with Figure 9.16.

In Figure 9.16, three services are used by the process with ***PID 4068***—yours may vary. A PID, or ***Process Identifier***, is a unique number assigned to each process while it runs. A single process may use several services. For example, a single instance of the *svchost.exe* process uses separate services for the Task Scheduler, Windows Update, and Desktop Themes, to name just a few of the many services it uses. This enables each service to focus on small, specific tasks.

Figure 9.16

Process Identifier (PID) column sorted in descending order

Multiple services used by a single process (yours will vary)

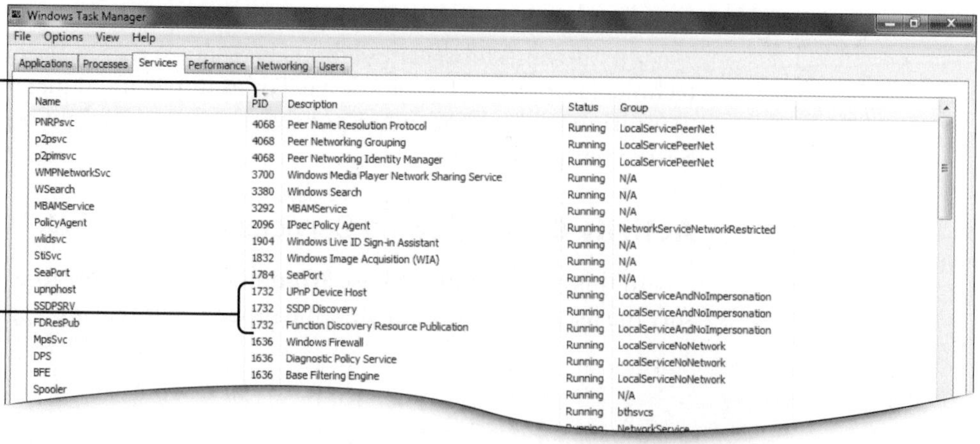

4 Click the **Name** column heading as necessary to sort the column in alphabetical order. Click the **Processes tab**, and then in the lower left corner, click the **Show processes from all users** button. **Maximize** [button] the **Windows Task Manager** window.

5 In the **Image Name** column, scroll down to locate and right-click **spoolsv.exe**, and then on the shortcut menu, click **Go to Service(s)**. Compare your screen with Figure 9.17.

Windows Task Manager displays the Services tab with *Spooler* selected. The *spoolsv.exe* process uses the *Spooler* service, which manages printing tasks. When you experience printing problems, such as not being able to add a printer or your printer stops printing, stopping and restarting this service often fixes the problem.

Figure 9.17

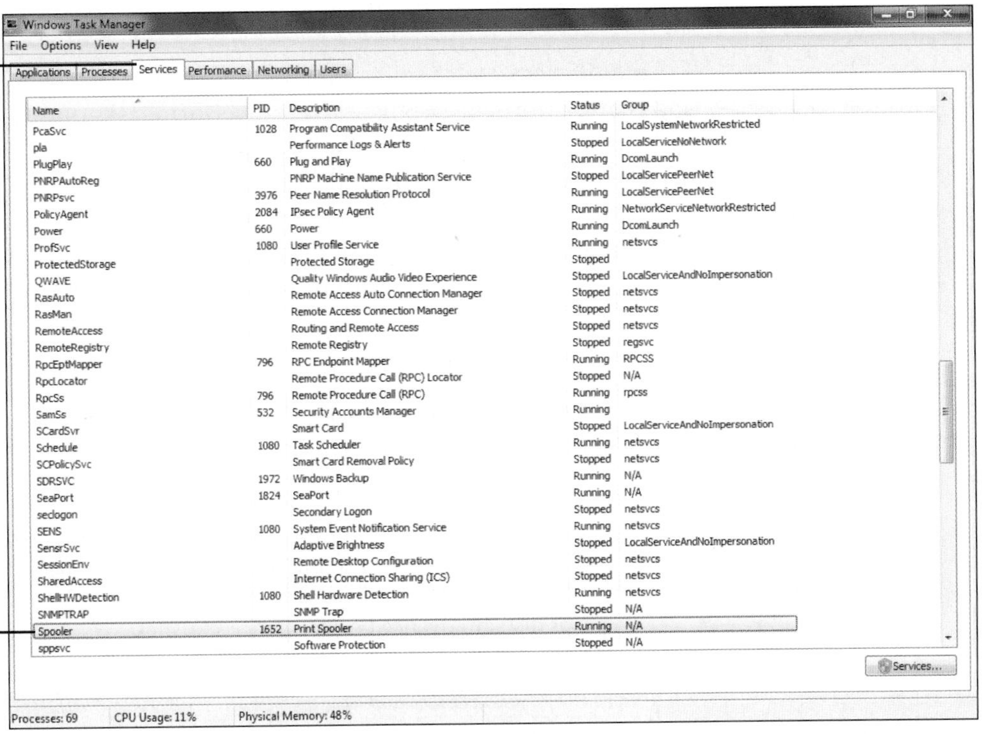

6 **Start** [Start button] the **Snipping Tool** program, click the **New arrow**, and then click **Full-screen Snip**. In the **Snipping Tool** mark-up window, click the **Save Snip** button [button].

7 In the **Save As** dialog box, in the **navigation pane**, scroll down as necessary, and then under **Computer**, click your USB flash drive so that it displays in the address bar. Navigate to your **Windows 7 Chapter 9** folder, and then as the file name, type **Lastname_Firstname_9A_Services_Snip** Be sure the file type is **JPEG**, and then press Enter. **Close** [button] the **Snipping Tool** mark-up window. Hold this file until you finish Project 9A.

8 **Close** [button] the **Windows Task Manager** window, and then **Close** [button] any open windows.

> **More Knowledge | Stopping Services**
>
> To stop a service, right-click the service, and then click *Stop Service*. To start a service, right-click, and then click *Start Service*. Unless you are working with an IT professional or you are familiar with the purpose for a service, you should not stop or start services.

Objective 4 | Track Performance by Using Task Manager

Recall that computer performance is often measured by CPU usage and RAM usage. The Performance tab in Windows Task Manager provides several graphs that chart these two important indicators. Such charts provide a view of your computer's CPU usage and RAM usage over a period of time. If your computer is connected to a network, the Networking tab displays a chart for network usage. Recall that a network is a group of computers or hardware such as printers that communicate with each other to share information and resources.

Activity 9.05 | Tracking Performance by Using Task Manager

In this activity, you will use the Windows Task Manager Performance tab to capture and chart performance statistics as you perform tasks on your computer. After completing each task, you will return to Windows Task Manager and observe the changes that occurred while you performed the task.

1 Be sure that your USB flash drive or other removable media is inserted in the computer. Display the **Start menu**, type **taskmgr** and then press Enter.

If you know an application's process name, you can locate and start the application by typing its process name into the Start menu Search box and pressing Enter.

2 In the **Windows Task Manager**, click the **Performance tab**, and then **Maximize** the window. Compare your screen with Figure 9.18.

The Performance tab displays several panes. The *CPU Usage* and *Memory* panes provide a graphical representation of the performance statistics that are displayed in the lower left corner of Windows Task Manager. The *CPU Usage History* and *Physical Memory Usage History* panes chart performance statistics over time at one-second intervals. The lower panes display advanced performance statistics.

Figure 9.18

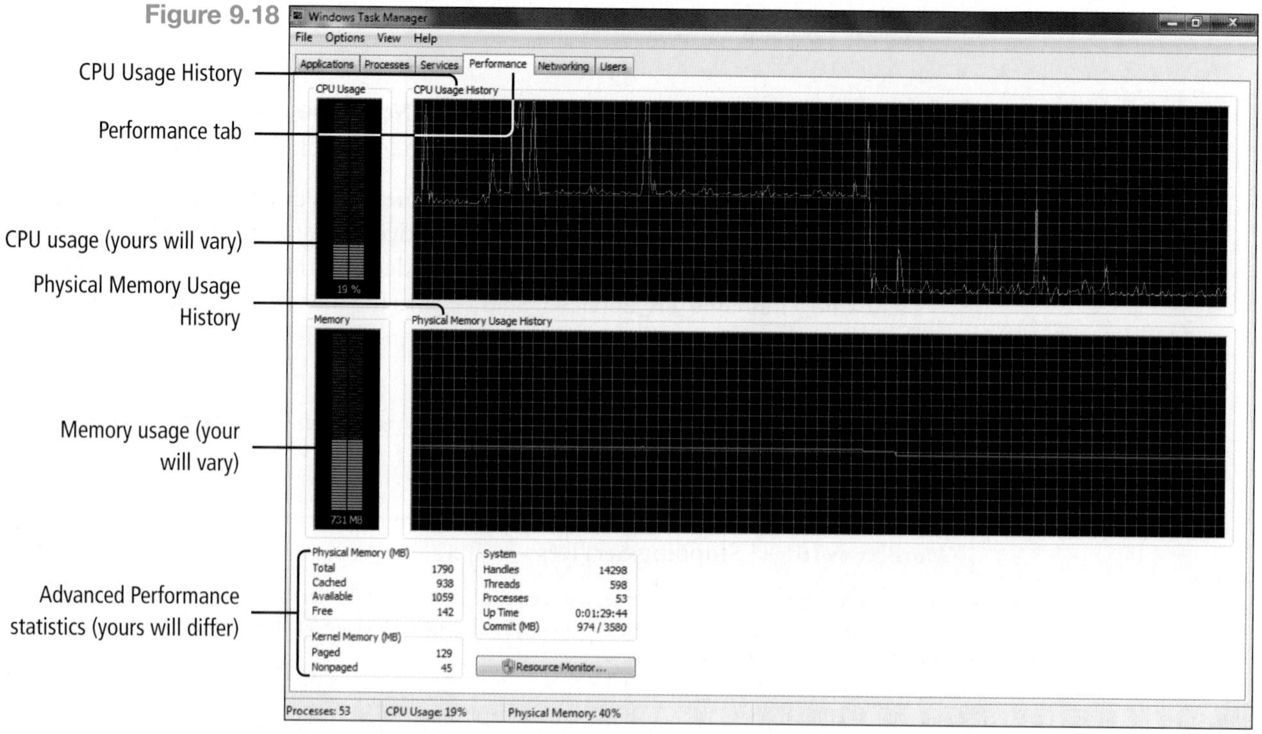

> **Alert! | Does Your Screen Display Two CPU Usage History Charts?**
>
> If your computer has two or more CPU chips, Windows Task Manager displays a chart for each CPU. To see CPU usage for all processors combined into one chart, from the View menu, point to CPU History, and then click One Graph, All CPUs.

3 If necessary, from the Options menu, clear the check mark from Always On Top. **Minimize** ☐ the **Windows Task Manager** window, and then from the **Start menu** ⊕, click **Computer**.

4 In the **navigation pane**, right-click your **(C:) drive**, and then click **Properties**. In the **Properties** dialog box, click the **Tools tab**, and then click **Defragment now**. If necessary, in the User Account Control dialog box, click Continue.

> You will use Task Manager to track your computer's performance while the Disk Defragmenter runs.

5 In the **Disk Defragmenter** window, click the **Defragment disk** button. On the taskbar, click the **Windows Task Manager** button, and then compare your screen with Figure 9.19.

> As Disk Defragmenter works, CPU activity increases. In the CPU Usage History pane, this activity first displays on the right, and moves to the left with each passing second.

Figure 9.19

CPU activity increases when program is running —

Disk Defragmenter program running —

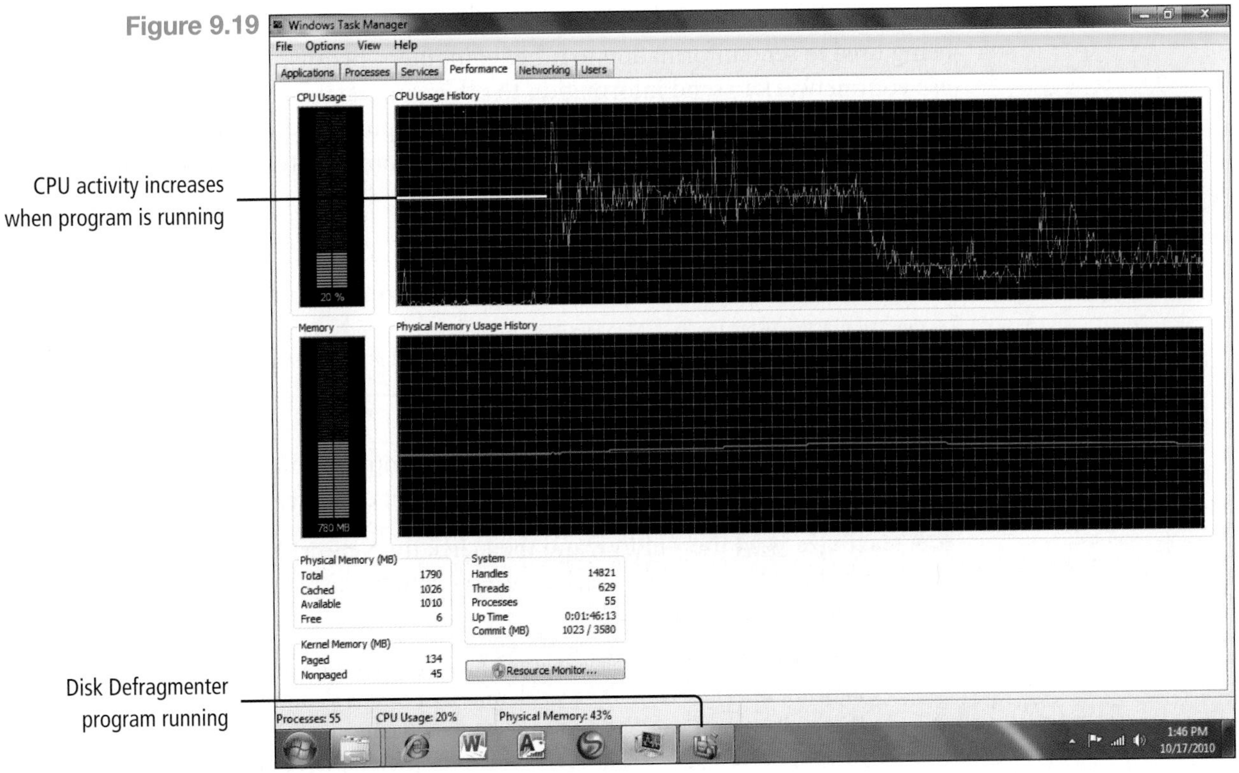

6 From the **View** menu, point to **Update Speed**, and then click **Low**. Notice that the **History** charts now update every few seconds instead of each second.

7 On the taskbar, click the **Disk Defragmenter** button, and then click the **Stop operation** button. **Close** ☒ the **Disk Defragmenter** window and the **Properties** window.

8 **Start** ⊕ **Microsoft Word**, and then **Start** ⊕ **Microsoft Excel**. On the taskbar, click the **Windows Task Manager** button.

9 **Start** the **Snipping Tool** program, click the **New arrow**, and then click **Full-screen Snip**. In the **Snipping Tool** mark-up window, click the **Save Snip** button.

10 In the **Save As** dialog box, in the **navigation pane**, scroll down as necessary, and then under **Computer**, click your USB flash drive so that it displays in the address bar. Navigate to your **Windows 7 Chapter 9** folder, and then as the file name, type **Lastname_Firstname_9A_Performance_Snip** Be sure the file type is **JPEG**, and then press Enter. **Close** the **Snipping Tool** mark-up window. Hold this file until you finish Project 9A, and then submit this file as directed by your instructor.

11 In the **Windows Task Manager**, from the **View** menu, point to **Update Speed**, and then click **Normal** to return to the default setting.

12 **Close** **Windows Task Manager**, and then **Close** all open windows.

On your own computer, if you are concerned that certain programs or tasks consume too many of your computer's resources, start Windows Task Manager, perform the techniques that you have practiced, and then view the resulting performance graphs available in the Performance tab of Windows Task Manager.

Activity 9.06 | Tracking Network Performance by Using Task Manager

The Networking tab in Windows Task Manager tracks the resources used by your computer to communicate with your local network. The Networking tab has many options to alter views and to customize the types of network data that you want to track. For example, you can determine how much of your computer's network capability is being used to send information to other computers. Because spyware programs often use your network to send information to other computers, you can use this method to determine when data is being sent from your computer. In this activity, you will use Task Manager to track your network activity as you communicate with other computers on the Internet.

> **Note | You Will Need a Computer Connected to the Internet for This Activity**
> You will practice using the Task Manager Networking tab by using your computer's network to communicate with other computers on the Internet. You must be connected to the Internet to complete this activity.

1 Be sure that your USB flash drive or other removable media is inserted in the computer. Right-click on the taskbar, and then click **Start Task Manager**.

2 **Maximize** the window, and then click the **Networking tab**. In the lower pane, resize the columns so that each column's content displays fully, and then compare your screen with Figure 9.20.

The Networking tab displays a graph and statistics showing the performance of your ***network interface card***. A network interface card is a computer hardware component that enables your computer to connect to and communicate with a network. A network interface card is also called a ***NIC*** or a ***network adapter***. In Figure 9.20, the chart reveals that there has been very little recent network activity.

Figure 9.20

Networking tab

Column widths adjusted

Network connections

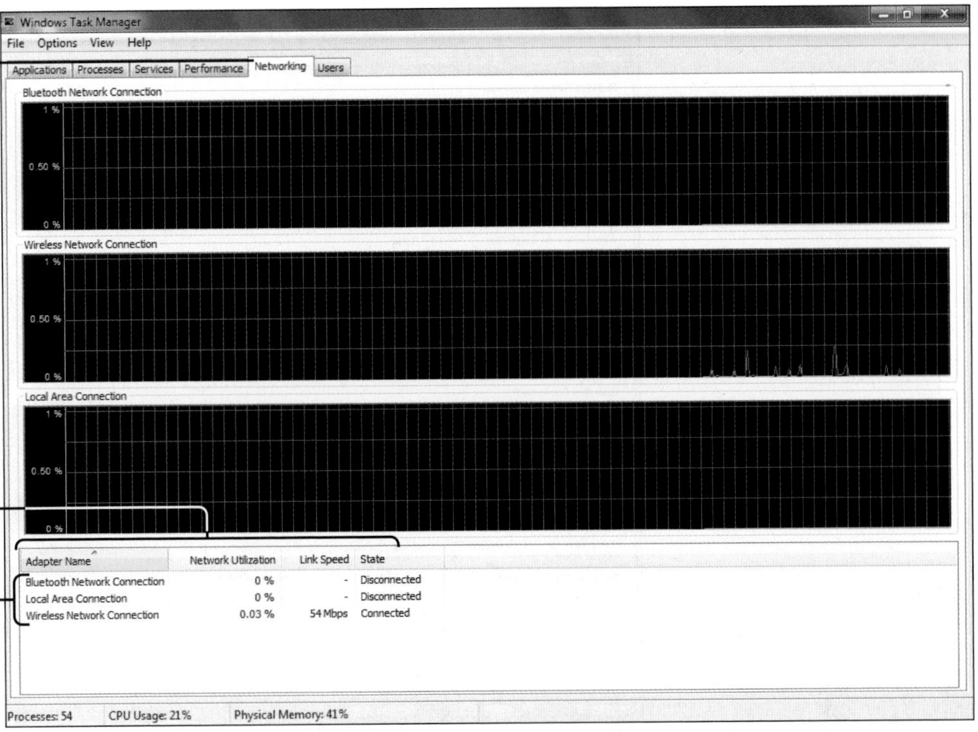

3. **Minimize** the **Windows Task Manager** dialog box. **Start** Internet Explorer, and then open the United States Department of Health & Human Services home page at **http://www.hhs.gov**

4. In this site's navigation bar, click the **About Us** tab. If that hyperlink no longer exists, click any other link.

5. From the **Start** menu, point to **All Programs**, and then click **Windows Update**. On the left side of the **Windows Update** window, click **Check for updates**.

   You will track your network usage while Windows Update checks with the Windows Update server to see if there are any new updates for your computer.

6. Wait for Windows Update to finish checking, and then on the taskbar, click the **Windows Task Manager** button. From the **View** menu, point to **Update Speed**, and then click **Paused**.

   Pausing stops Task Manager from monitoring your network performance. This will enable you to complete the following steps without losing the data that you just collected.

7. From the **View** menu, click **Select Columns**. Select the **Bytes** check box, and then click **OK**. In the lower portion of the screen, increase the width of the **Bytes** column to display the entire number, and then compare your screen with Figure 9.21.

   The spikes—sharp increases depicted by taller lines on the chart—reflect network use at the point that you opened the two Web pages and while Windows 7 checked for updates. The *Bytes* column displays the total number of bytes sent through your network interface card since you opened Windows Task Manager. Data sent through networks is often measured in bytes.

   The larger spike in Figure 9.21 indicates that checking for Windows updates demanded more networking resources than opening the two Web pages—your results may vary. This information is useful when your network activities slow down and you need to see how well your network interface card is performing.

Figure 9.21

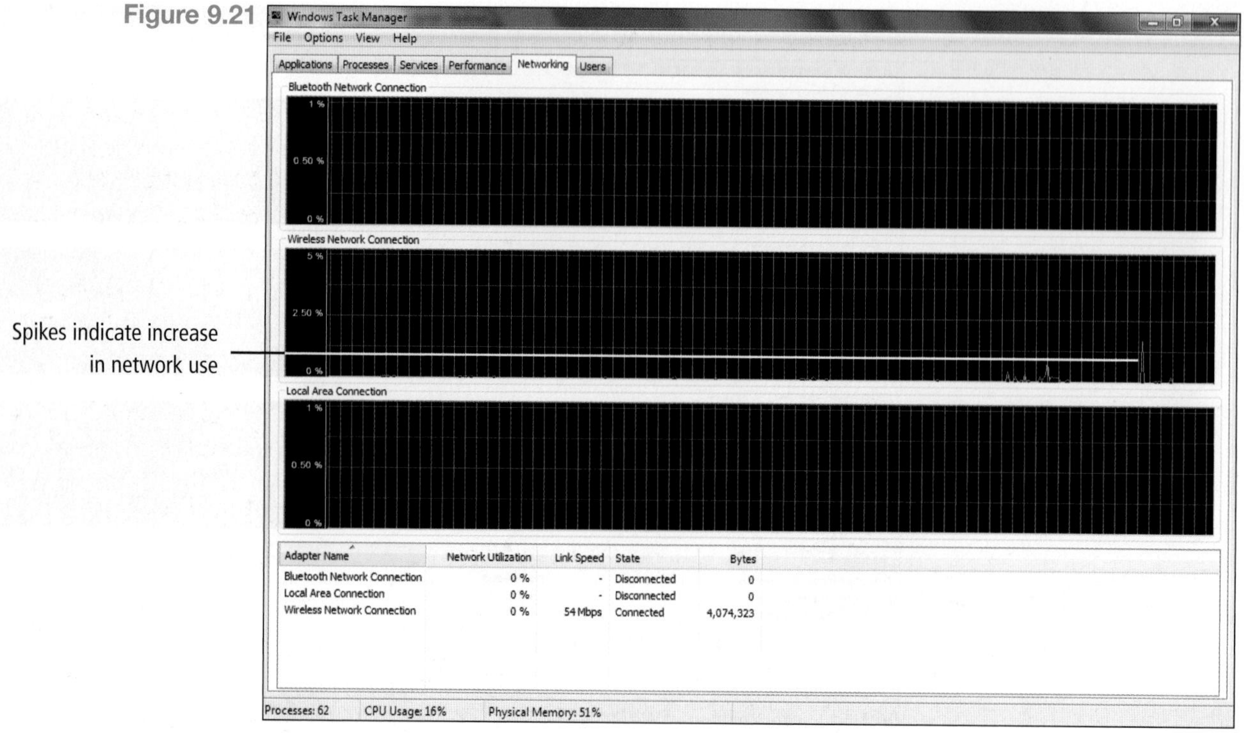

8 From the **View** menu, point to **Network Adapter History**, and then click to check **Bytes Received**. From the **View** menu, point to **Network Adapter History**, and then click **Bytes Total** to deselect this feature. From the **View** menu, click **Refresh Now**. Compare your screen with Figure 9.22.

The color of the chart line changes from green to yellow, indicating the performance of your network adapter to receive data. In this example, the two larger spikes indicate the moments that your computer was downloading the two Web pages from the United States Department of Health & Human Services Web server. The smaller spike indicates the data received from the Windows Update server.

Figure 9.22

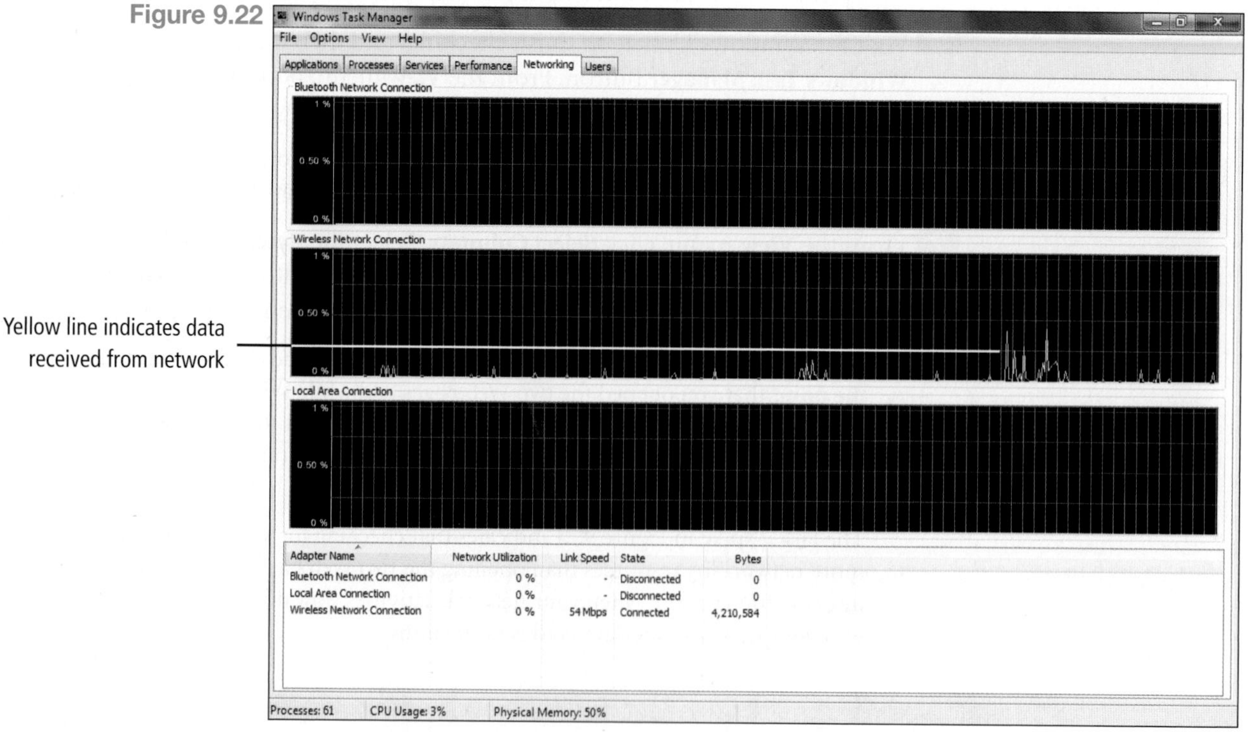

9 From the **View** menu, point to **Network Adapter History**, and then click to select **Bytes Sent**.

The red line indicates the amount of data that your computer *sent to* other computers on the Internet. This view can be used if you want to know when your computer is sending data to other computers on the Internet. For example, if you suspect that malware is using your computer to send messages to other computers, you can use the Bytes Sent graph to view when your computer is sending data to other computers.

10 If necessary, display the Options menu, and then deselect Always On Top. **Start** the **Snipping Tool** program, click the **New arrow**, and then click **Full-screen Snip**. In the **Snipping Tool** mark-up window, click the **Save Snip** button.

11 In the **Save As** dialog box, in the **navigation pane**, scroll down as necessary, and then under **Computer**, click your USB flash drive so that it displays in the address bar. Navigate to your **Windows 7 Chapter 9** folder, and then as the file name, type **Lastname_Firstname_9A_Networking_Snip** Be sure the file type is **JPEG**, and then press Enter. **Close** the **Snipping Tool** mark-up window.

12 In **Windows Task Manager**, from the **View** menu, point to **Update Speed**, and then click to check **Normal** to return to the default setting.

13 From the **View** menu, point to **Network Adapter History**, and then click **Bytes Sent** to deselect the feature and return to the default setting. From the **View** menu, point to **Network Adapter History**, and then click **Bytes Received** to deselect the feature and return to the default setting. From the **View** menu, point to **Network Adapter History**, and then click to check **Bytes Total** to enable the feature, which is the default setting.

14 From the **View** menu, click **Select Columns**, and then clear the **Bytes** check box. Click **OK**. **Close** all open windows.

15 Submit the four snip files that are the results of this project to your instructor as directed.

By customizing the graph or customizing the column, almost any network activity can be monitored and measured.

End You have completed Project 9A

Project 9B Tracking System Performance

Project Activities

In Activities 9.07 through 9.12, you will train with Steven Ramos and Barbara Hewitt, employees in the Information Technology Department at the corporate office of the Bell Orchid Hotels. After completing this part of the training, you will be able to track and report computer performance using the Performance monitor and the Reliability monitor, view disks with Disk Management, and manage services using the Services window. You will capture screens that look similar to Figure 9.23.

Project Files

For Project 9B, you will need the following files:

New Snip files

Your will save your files as:

Lastname_Firstname_9B_Network_Snip
Lastname_Firstname_9B_Performance_Snip
Lastname_Firstname_9B_Report_Snip
Lastname_Firstname_9B_Disks_Snip
Lastname_Firstname_9B_Services_Snip

Project Results

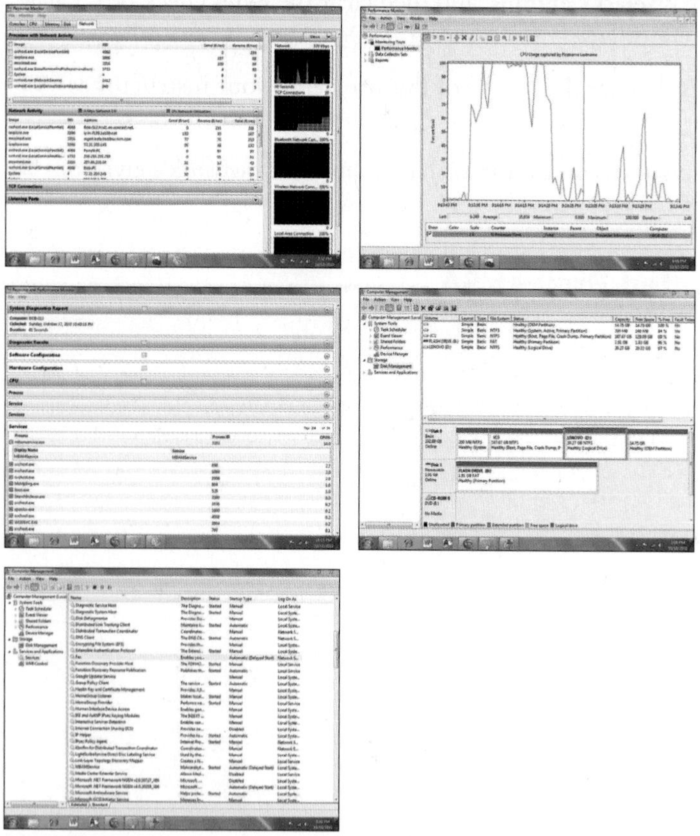

Figure 9.23
Project 9B Tracking System Performance

Objective 5 | Track Performance by Using the Performance and Reliability Monitors

The Performance and Reliability Monitors are Windows 7 tools that combine system information, performance tests, and data collected over time to monitor computer performance.

Each tool contains ***real time*** graphs and detailed descriptions. Real time is the actual time during which something takes place. Each component can be saved as an HTML Web page so that you can save your performance data for later reference or share the information with others—a computer service technician for example. You can also customize the Performance Monitor to monitor various system-related data.

Activity 9.07 | Tracking Performance by Using Resource Overview

The ***Resource Monitor*** area of the Performance Monitor provides both instantaneous and recent-history (45 seconds) readouts of your computer's four key performance measurements—CPU usage, hard disk drive usage, network usage, and memory usage.

This tool is similar to the Task Manager, but Resource Overview has more graphs of computer resources. This visual representation makes it faster to get an overall view of your computer's performance. One advantage is that the monitor lists each process only when it is using a computer resource.

If your computer is having performance problems, use the Resource Overview for a fast and informative view to see which area is slowing performance. In this activity, you will use the Resource Overview to track your computer's performance as you complete other tasks on your computer.

1. Be sure that your USB flash drive is inserted in the computer. **Start** the **Control Panel**. Click **System and Security**, and then click **System**. At the bottom left pane of the **System** window, click **Performance Information and Tools**.

Another Way

Display the Start menu, and then in the Search box, type *perfmon* and press Enter.

2. In the left pane, click **Advanced tools**, and then click **Open Performance Monitor**. If necessary, in the User Account Control dialog box, click Continue.

3. **Maximize** the **Performance Monitor** window. Under **Overview of Performance Monitor**, click **Open Resource Monitor**. **Maximize** the **Resource Monitor** window. If the CPU information does not display, click the **CPU arrow** to display its summary information, and then compare your screen with Figure 9.24.

   The Resource Monitor window opens. The Resource Overview pane displays real time graphs for four key performance areas: CPU usage, hard disk drive usage, network usage, and memory usage. To the left of the four graphs, summary information for each resource that is being monitored is accessible.

Figure 9.24

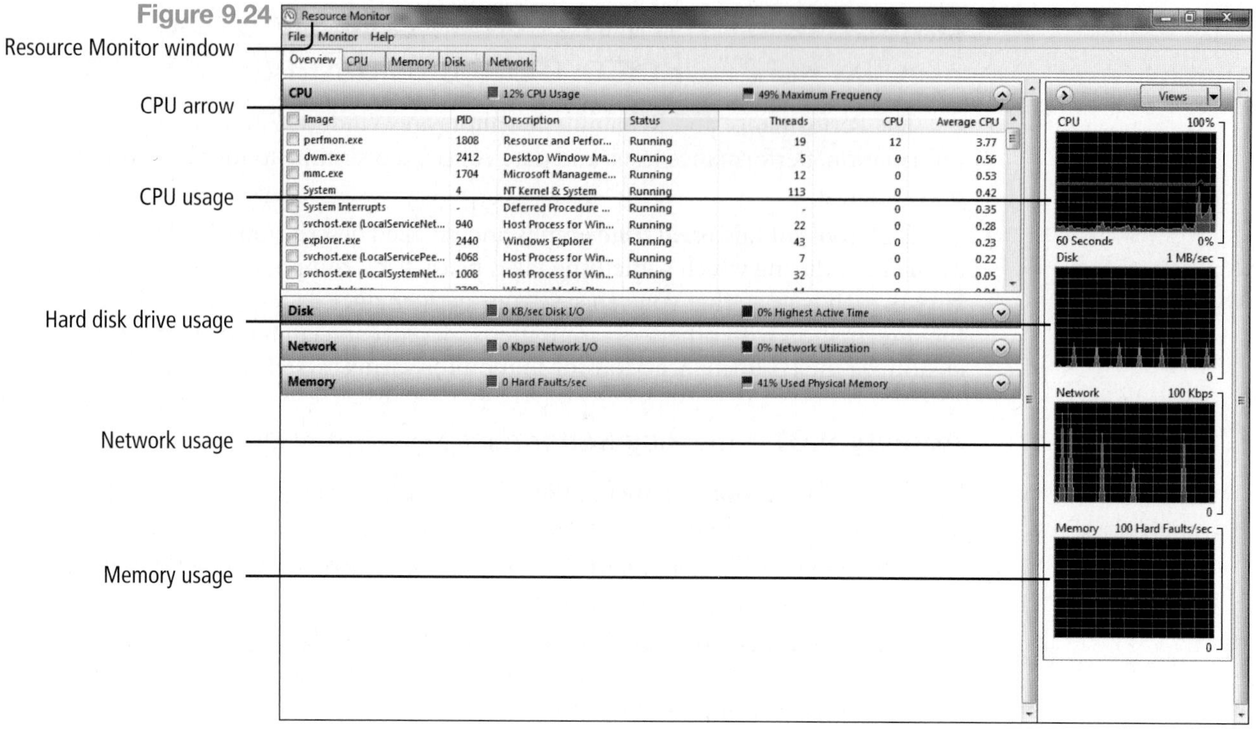

4 Click the **CPU tab** to display the CPU resources that are currently running. Compare your screen with Figure 9.25.

In the summary information for the CPU, only those processes that are currently using the CPU resources display. Because processes consume computer resources for only brief periods of time, the list changes frequently. In the CPU resources list, the columns can be resized and sorted, and like Windows Task Manager, columns can be added or removed from the summary text area.

The CPU graphs and summary information report your processor's activity. Your processor could reach 100% usage, but it will typically have considerable idle time.

Figure 9.25

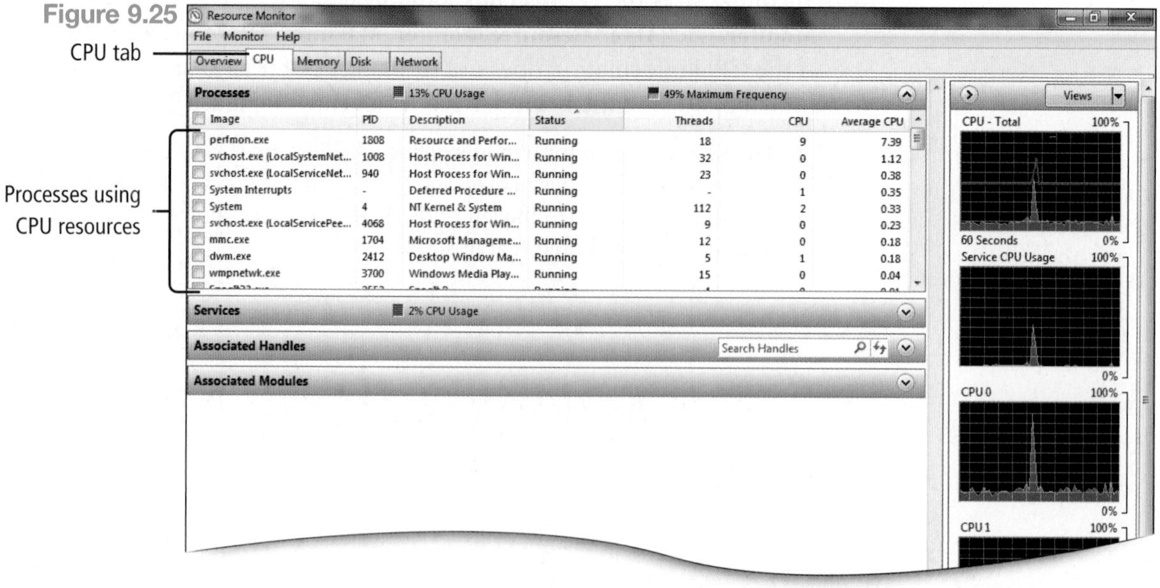

5 **Start** Microsoft Word, and then immediately after the Word screen displays, on the taskbar switch to the **Resource Monitor** window. Quickly look at the **CPU** summary information to locate **WINWORD.EXE** on the list, and then compare your screen with Figure 9.26.

While it is loading, the WINWORD.EXE process uses considerable CPU resources, and then ceases to use these resources. Recall that WINWORD.EXE is the process used by Microsoft Word. Because you are not currently working in the Word window, the WINWORD.EXE process may stop displaying on the CPU lists.

Figure 9.26

CPU resource usage at 100%

Microsoft Word uses considerable CPU resources while loading

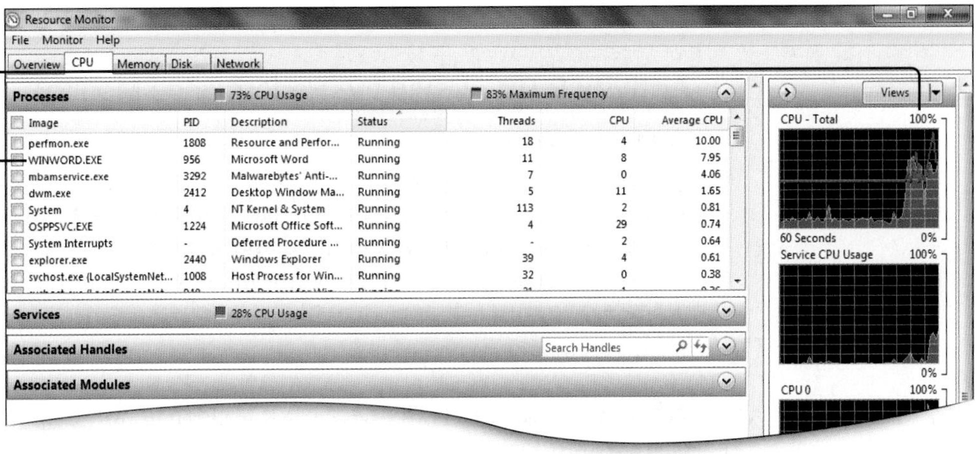

6 Near the top of the **Resource Monitor**, click the **Network tab**. Click the **Network Activity arrow** to display the current network activity.

The network summary information displays network activity including Internet traffic.

7 **Start** Internet Explorer, and then navigate to the site **www.usa.gov** While the Web page is loading, switch to the **Resource Monitor** window, and then compare your screen with Figure 9.27.

While the page loads, the *iexplore.exe* process uses network resources. Recall that this is the process used by Internet Explorer. The Network summary text shows the IP addresses of the Web servers being used and the speed, in bytes per second, that the page is loading.

Figure 9.27

Internet Explorer causes increased Network resource usage

Network Activity arrow

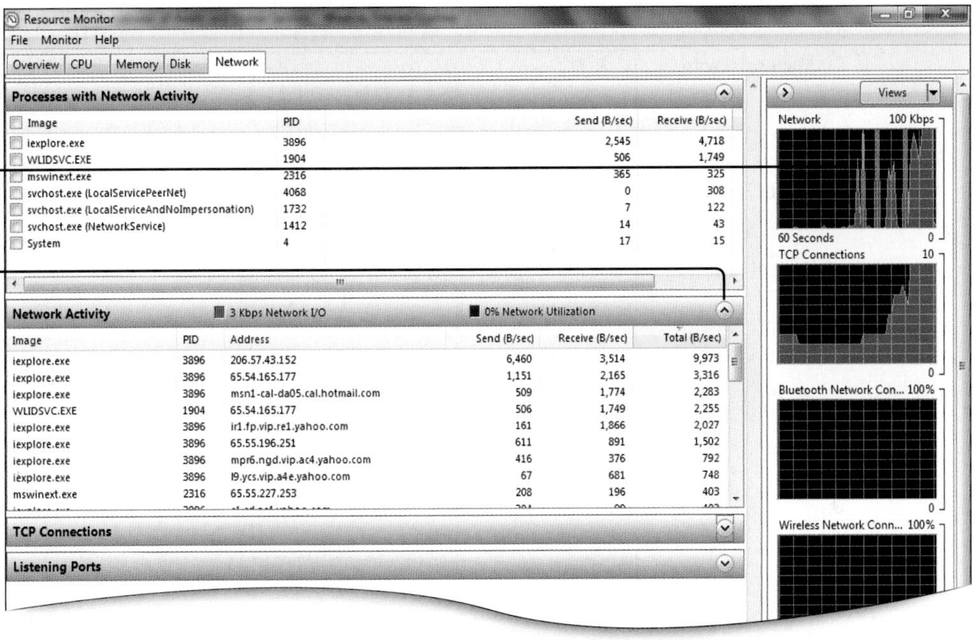

8 **Start** the **Snipping Tool** program, click the **New arrow**, and then click **Full-screen Snip**. In the **Snipping Tool** mark-up window, click the **Save Snip** button.

9 In the **Save As** dialog box, in the **navigation pane**, scroll down as necessary, and then under **Computer**, click your USB flash drive so that it displays in the address bar. Navigate to your **Windows 7 Chapter 9** folder, and then as the file name, type **Lastname_Firstname_9B_Network_Snip** Be sure the file type is **JPEG**, and then press Enter. **Close** the **Snipping Tool** mark-up window. Hold this file until you finish Project 9B.

10 **Close** the **Resource Monitor** window, **Close** Word, and **Close** Internet Explorer. Leave the **Performance Monitor** window open for the next activity.

Activity 9.08 | Using the Performance Monitor

Performance Monitor is an area of the Performance Monitor tool that focuses on computer performance. Performance Monitor creates charts with more detail than the charts you have viewed in Task Manager and the Resource Overview. Performance Monitor charts can also be modified and saved as image files, so that you can store them for later reference or share them with others—for example, with a computer support technician. In this activity, you will use the Performance Monitor to chart CPU usage while you open two programs.

1 Be sure that your USB flash drive is inserted in the computer. In the left pane, if necessary, expand **Monitoring Tools**, and then click **Performance Monitor**. **Start** Internet Explorer, and then **Start** Microsoft Word.

2 In the taskbar, click the **Performance Monitor** button. On the **Performance Monitor** toolbar directly above the graph, click the **Freeze Display** button. Compare your screen with Figure 9.28.

With the Performance Monitor paused, you will be able to work with the chart without it collecting more CPU usage data. The Performance Monitor displays a graph that shows CPU usage while you opened Internet Explorer and Microsoft Word.

Figure 9.28

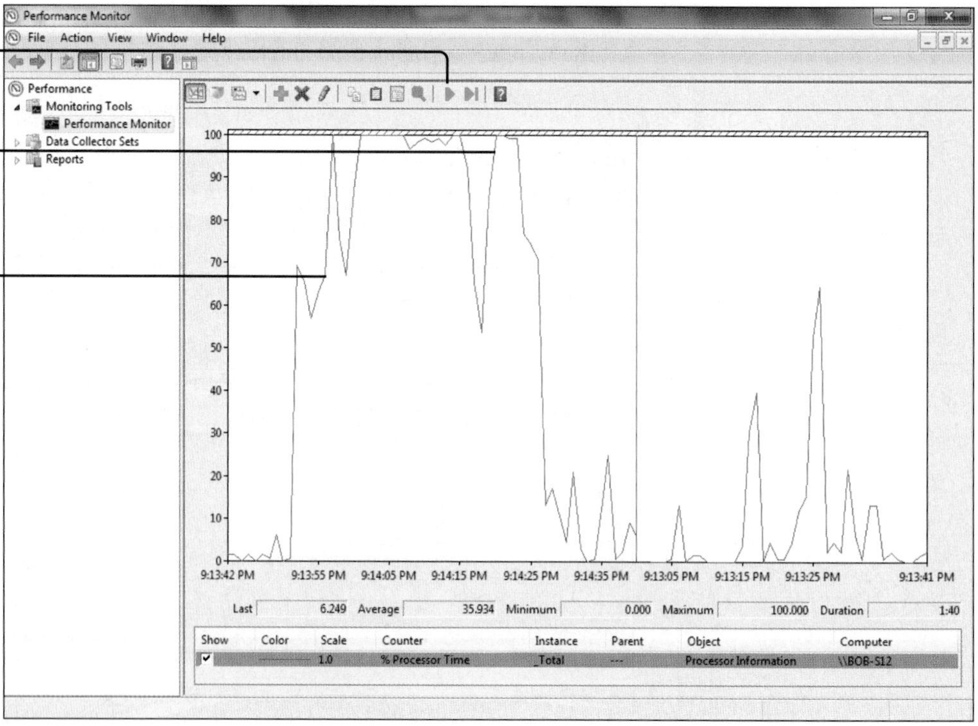

3 Display the **Action** menu, and then click **Properties**. In the **Performance Monitor Properties** dialog box, click the **Graph tab**.

4 On the **Graph tab**, click in the **Title** box, and then, using your own first and last name, type **CPU Usage captured by Firstname Lastname**

5 Click in the **Vertical axis** box, and then type **Percent Used** Click **OK**, and then compare your screen with Figure 9.29.

The chart displays a title that includes your name, and the vertical axis label describes what the chart is measuring.

Figure 9.29

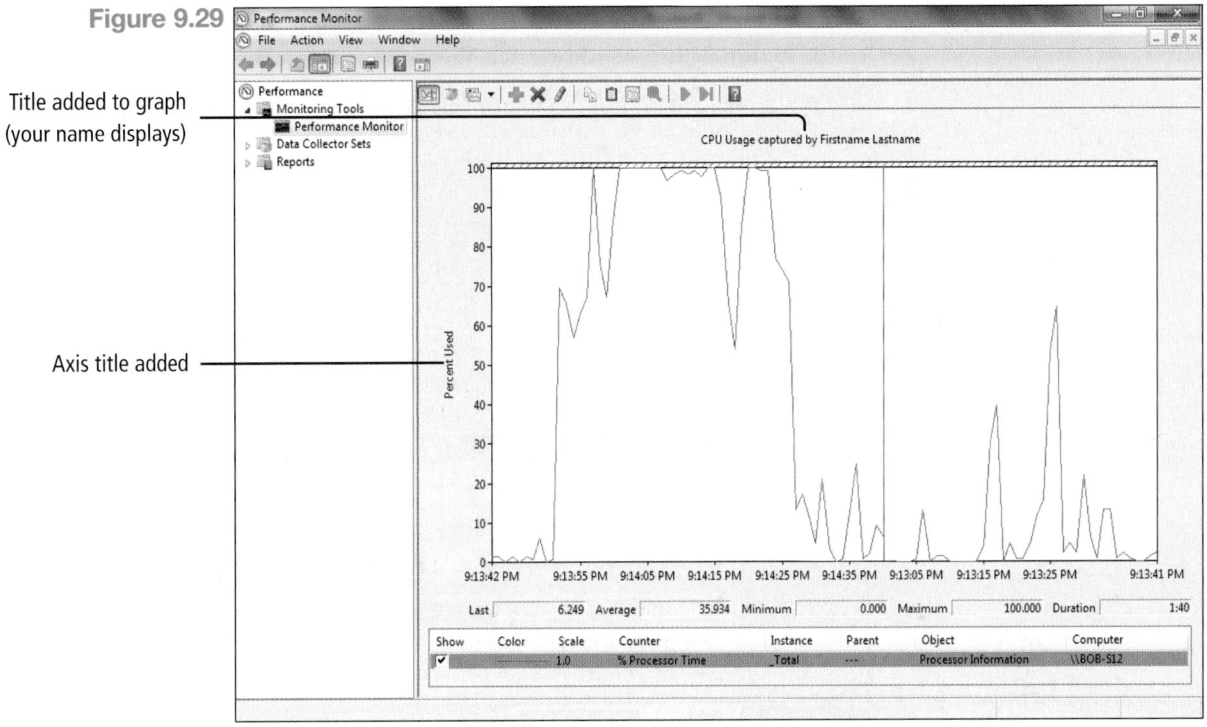

6 **Start** the **Snipping Tool** program, click the **New arrow**, and then click **Full-screen Snip**. In the **Snipping Tool** mark-up window, click the **Save Snip** button.

7 In the **Save As** dialog box, in the **navigation pane**, scroll down as necessary, and then under **Computer**, click your USB flash drive so that it displays in the address bar. Navigate to your **Windows 7 Chapter 9** folder, and then as the file name, type **Lastname_Firstname_9B_Performance_Snip** Be sure the file type is **JPEG**, and then press Enter. **Close** the **Snipping Tool** mark-up window. Hold this file until you finish Project 9B.

8 **Close** Internet Explorer and Word, and **Close** **Performance Monitor**.

Activity 9.09 | Creating a System Diagnostics Report

The ***System Diagnostics Report*** is a pre-built report that contains an easy to understand summary of your computer's overall performance. Additionally, the report provides detailed information areas that you can expand or collapse for easy viewing. You can save this report as an HTML Web page, which makes the report easy to share with others.

In this activity, you will create a System Diagnostics Report and view different areas of the report.

1. Be sure that your USB flash drive is inserted in the computer. **Start** the **Control Panel**. Under **System and Security**, click **Review your computer's status.** In the left pane of the **Action Center** window, click **View performance information.**

2. In the **Performance and Information Tools** window, in the left pane, click **Advanced tools**.

3. In the lower portion of the **Advanced Tools** window, click **Generate a system health report**. If necessary, in the User Account Control dialog box, click Continue, and then compare your screen with Figure 9.30.

   The Performance Monitor opens. Under Report Status, the message indicates that the Performance Monitor will monitor your computer for 60 seconds. The data collected during this period will be used to build the report.

Figure 9.30

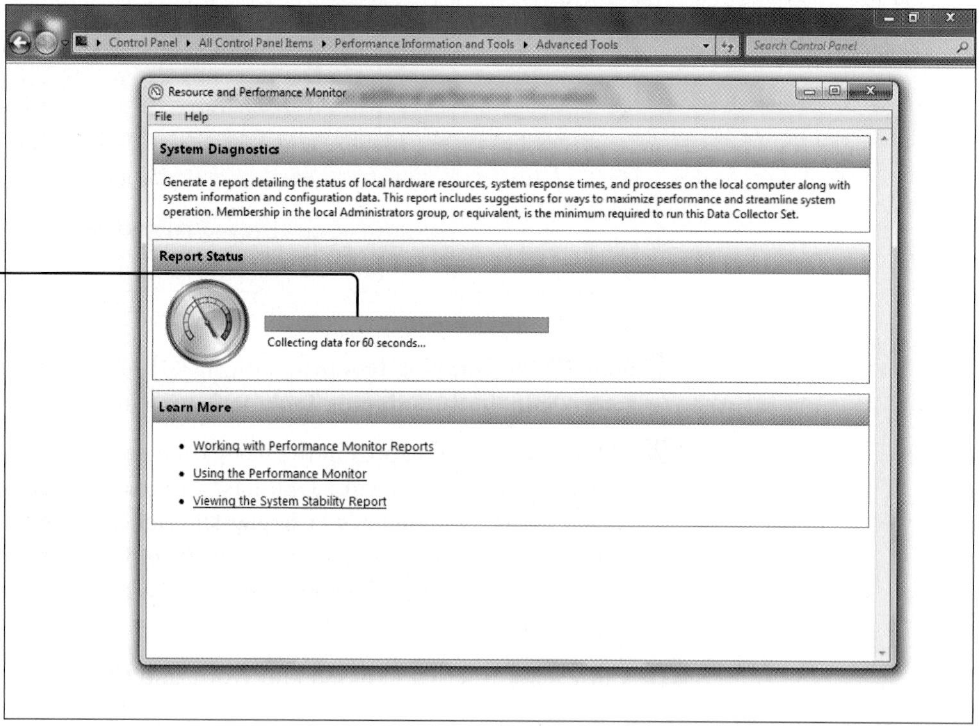

4. While the Performance Monitor monitors your computer, **Start** Internet Explorer and navigate to **http://www.ed.gov** Wait for the page to load, and then **Close** Internet Explorer.

   As you performed this step, the Performance Monitor collected performance data for your CPU, Network, Disk, and Memory.

5 **Maximize** [Maximize button] the **Resource and Performance Monitor** window, and then wait for the data collection to complete. After collecting data, the Performance Monitor takes several seconds to generate the **System Diagnostics Report**. When the report displays, compare your screen with Figure 9.31.

In Figure 9.31, under *Diagnostic Results*, the *Warnings* value displays a problem—the system cannot find an anti-virus program on the computer. Under *Basic System Checks*, five tests display as *Passed*.

Under *Performance*, the *Resource Overview* section interprets the data and displays a green circle if the component is healthy, yellow if the component came close to being overused, and red if the component has been overused.

Figure 9.31

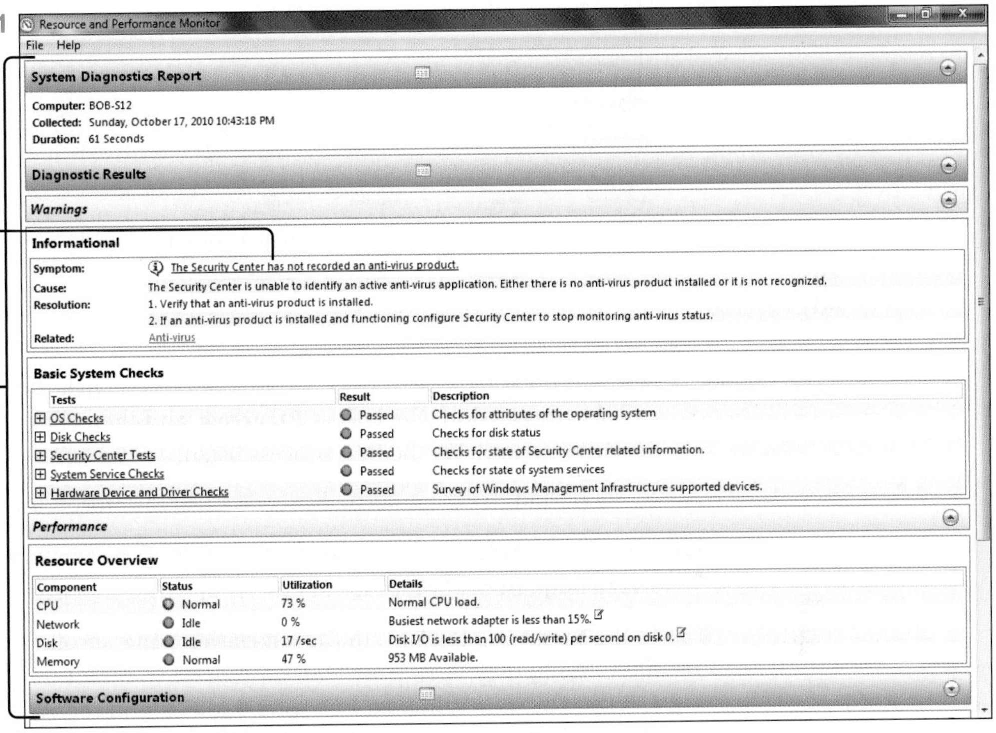

System warning (yours may vary)

System Diagnostics report

6 Under **Basic System Checks**, expand [expand button] the **Hardware Device and Driver Checks**, and then scroll through the list. Compare your screen with Figure 9.32.

The Performance Monitor tests all of the computer's essential hardware. You can see that even the computer's cooling system is checked. In Figure 9.32, the cooling system was not tested because this particular computer model could not perform the test. Cooling information is important because a computer that overheats due to inadequate cooling will not perform reliably.

Figure 9.32

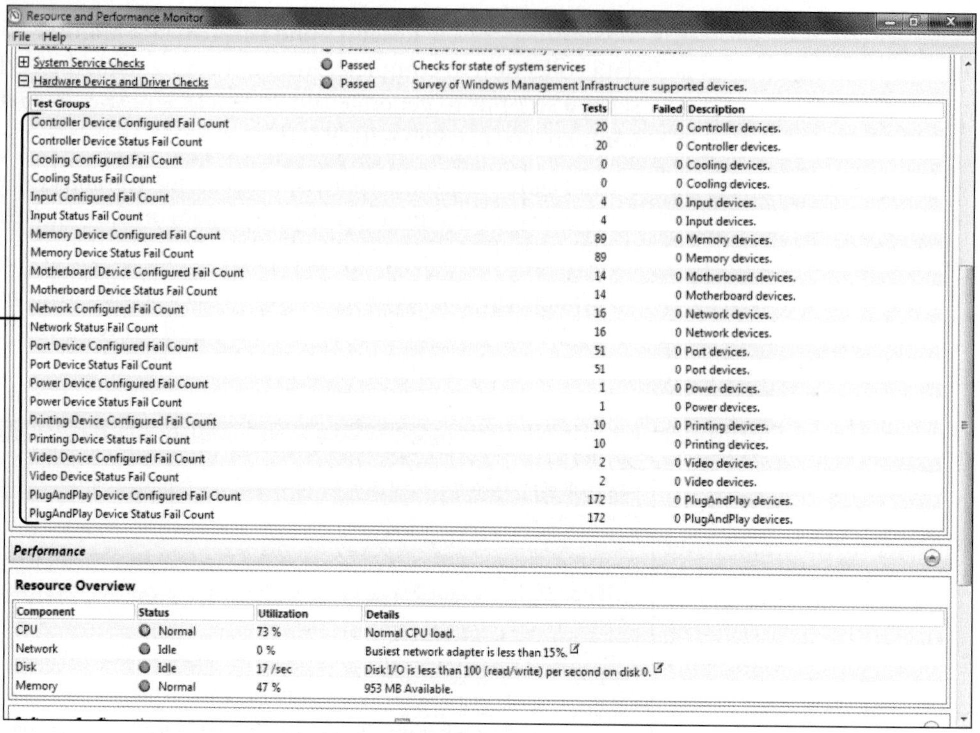

7 Scroll to the top of the report window, and then click the **Diagnostic Results arrow** to collapse the section. Click the **CPU arrow**, and then click the **Services arrow**. Under **Services**, expand ⊞ the first process listed.

By expanding each process, the services that the process uses display.

8 **Start** the **Snipping Tool** program, click the **New arrow**, and then click **Full-screen Snip**. In the **Snipping Tool** mark-up window, click the **Save Snip** button.

9 In the **Save As** dialog box, in the **navigation pane**, scroll down as necessary, and then under **Computer**, click your USB flash drive so that it displays in the address bar. Navigate to your **Windows 7 Chapter 9** folder, and then as the file name, type **Lastname_Firstname_9B_Report_Snip** Be sure the file type is **JPEG**, and then press Enter. **Close** the **Snipping Tool** mark-up window. Hold this file until you finish Project 9B.

10 **Close** all open windows.

> **Note | Saving Your System Diagnostics Report as a Web Page**
>
> You can save your System Diagnostics Report as a Web page. From the File menu, click Save As, click the Browse Folders button if necessary, and then navigate to the storage location of your choice. The file will be saved as an HTML document. The System Diagnostics Report Web page can be viewed on any computer with Windows 7. On your own computer, you may want to create a System Diagnostics Report every quarter, and save it as a Web page. Your report collection will provide an accessible and thorough history of your computer system's performance.

Activity 9.10 | Using the Reliability Monitor

The ***Reliability Monitor*** provides data about a computer's overall ***reliability***. Reliability refers to the likelihood that your computer will work as intended. The Reliability Monitor tracks events that affect system reliability over the lifetime of the system. Such events include improper shutdowns and nonresponsive applications and positive events, such as the installation of important updates by the Windows Update feature.

To view the Reliability Monitor, you can open the Control Panel, and then under System and Security, click *Review your computer's status*. Click Maintenance, and then under *Check for solutions to problem reports*, click *View reliability history*. The Reliability Monitor displays, similar to the screen shown in Figure 9.33. For each day the system was running, the System Stability Chart charts a data point, which is then charted as a blue line—in Figure 9.33, there is one event that lowers system reliability. The ***System Stability Index*** is a number between 1 and 10, and is determined by how many system errors have occurred up to that day. Ten indicates the highest reliability. The line chart indicates when significant events occurred that affected system reliability.

Figure 9.33

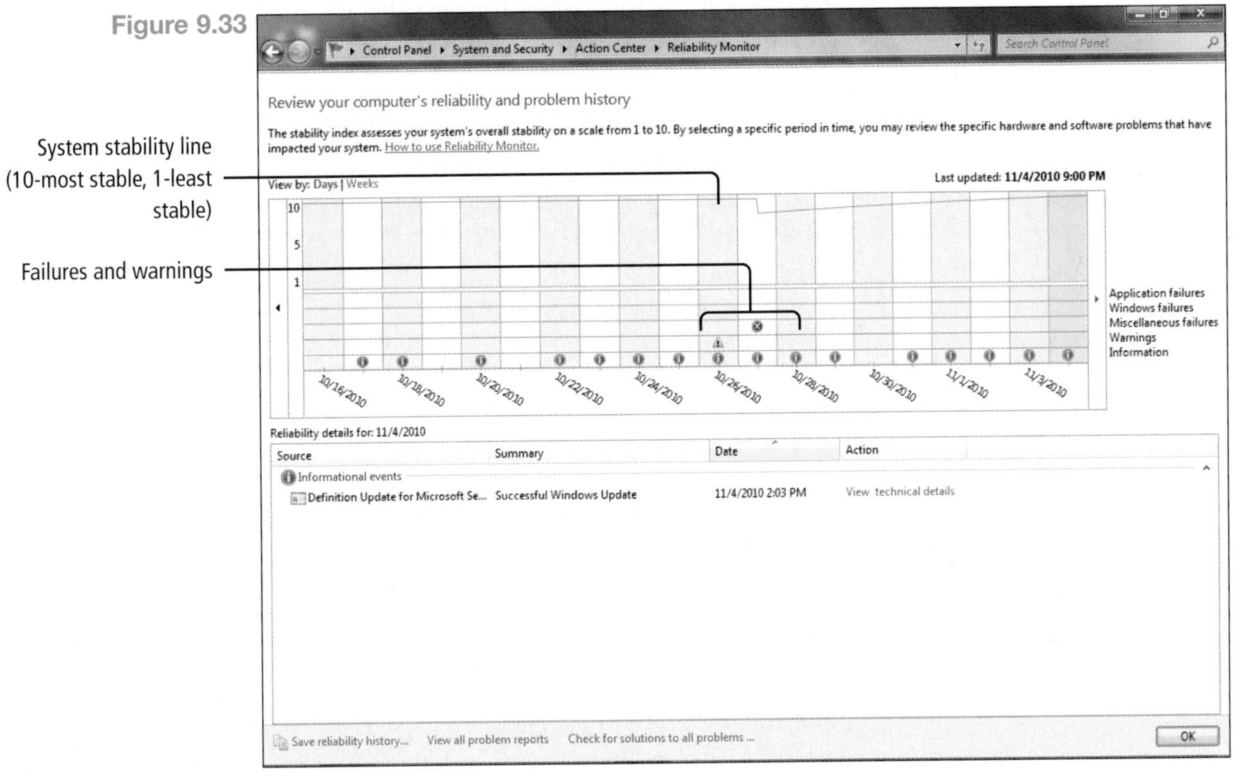

To see information about a specific date, either click that day in the System Stability Chart, or use the date selector in the upper right corner. Below the chart, *Reliability details* indicate problems or positive system occurrences. To see more information about the events that may have contributed to system instability, expand the report areas that correspond to that day's icons in the System Stability Chart. The System Stability Report organizes the information into five categories—Application failures, Windows failures, Miscellaneous failures, Warnings, and Information.

In Figure 9.33, the date 11/4/2010 has been selected and the Warnings and Informational events are displayed in the bottom half of the screen. On that day, Microsoft Security Essentials virus definition updates were installed, and are listed as an Informational event. The line on the chart indicates that these occurrences did not affect system reliability.

To check your comprehension of the Reliability Monitor, take a moment to answer the following questions:

1. The Reliability Monitor tracks events that affect system reliability over the __________ of the system.
2. The System Stability Index rates system stability by assigning a number between __________ and __________ with __________ being the most reliable.
3. Below the line chart, __________ __________ indicate that significant events occurred.
4. The System Stability Report organizes the information into __________ categories.
5. If virus definitions are successfully installed, that information would be found in the System Stability Report's __________ area.

Objective 6 | View Disks by Using Disk Management

Your hard disk drive defines your computing life, because in most situations everything is stored there—your programs, your data, your photos and video, and your music. Managing a hard disk is different from managing the programs and data that are stored there. Managing a hard disk involves formatting the disk so it can store information and partitioning the disk so that separate volumes can be assigned to distinct uses.

A ***partition*** is part of a hard disk that functions like a separate disk. A ***volume*** is a storage area on a hard disk that is formatted with a file system; a volume is assigned a drive letter.

Disk Management is the Windows 7 tool with which you can view the arrangement of disk drives on your computer, and also perform partitioning and formatting tasks if you must do so. You will not work with the hard disk drives of your computer very often—if ever—because hard disk drives normally need to be prepared only one time, and that is usually done by the computer manufacturer.

Disk Management displays every drive attached to your computer and provides information about how that drive is configured. Disk Management enables you to configure drives, or areas of drives, even when those drives do not display in the Computer folder window. Disk Management provides advanced features with which the functionality of your computer's hard disk drives can be customized.

> **Alert! | Should You Attempt to Format a Hard Disk Drive?**
>
> Unless you are a computer expert, do not attempt to format a hard disk drive without reliable assistance from an IT professional. Formatting a drive erases all of its programs and data, including the Windows 7 operating system.

Activity 9.11 | Viewing Disks by Using Disk Management

You have viewed information about your disks using Windows Explorer and the Properties dialog box. In this activity, you will view information about the disks attached to your computer using the Disk Management window. Then you will use Disk Management to change the drive letter assigned to your USB flash drive or other removable media.

1 Be sure that your USB flash drive is inserted in the computer. **Start** the **Control Panel**, and then click **System and Security**. In the **System and Security** window, click **Administrative Tools**. Compare your screen with Figure 9.34.

The Administrative Tools window contains shortcuts to common tools used to administer Windows 7. In this project, you will use the *Computer Management* and *Services* tools.

Figure 9.34

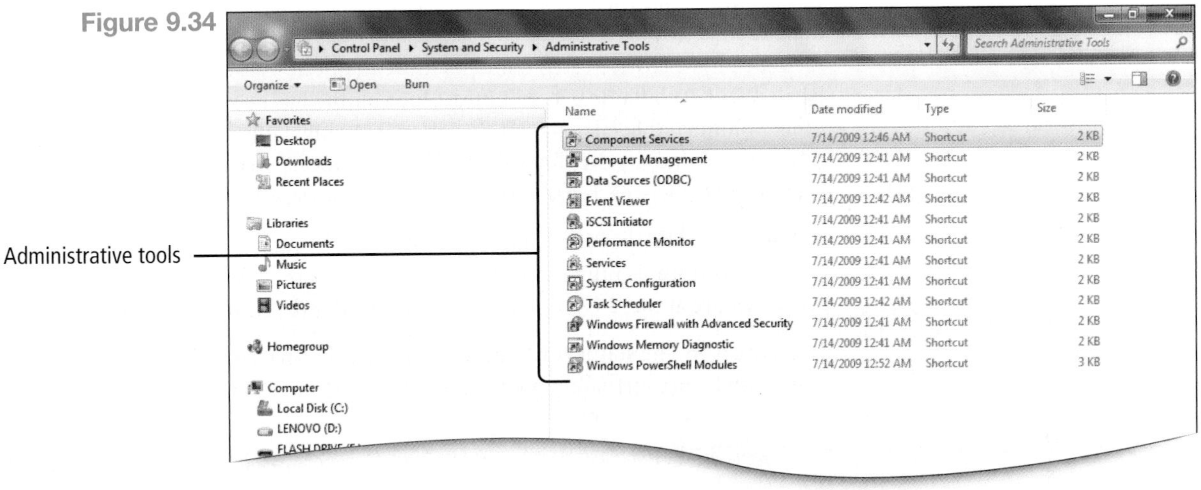

2 In the **Administrative Tools** file list, double-click **Computer Management.** If the User Account Control dialog box displays, click Continue.

3 In the **Computer Management** window, on the toolbar, click the **Show/Hide Action Pane** button, which is the last button on the toolbar, to close the Actions pane that displays on the right. Compare your screen with Figure 9.35.

Computer Management is a collection of tools with which you can perform tasks such as monitoring system events, configuring hard disks, and managing system performance all from one screen. Each tool is available individually, but Computer Management adds convenience by providing a single location to perform common administrative tasks.

Figure 9.35

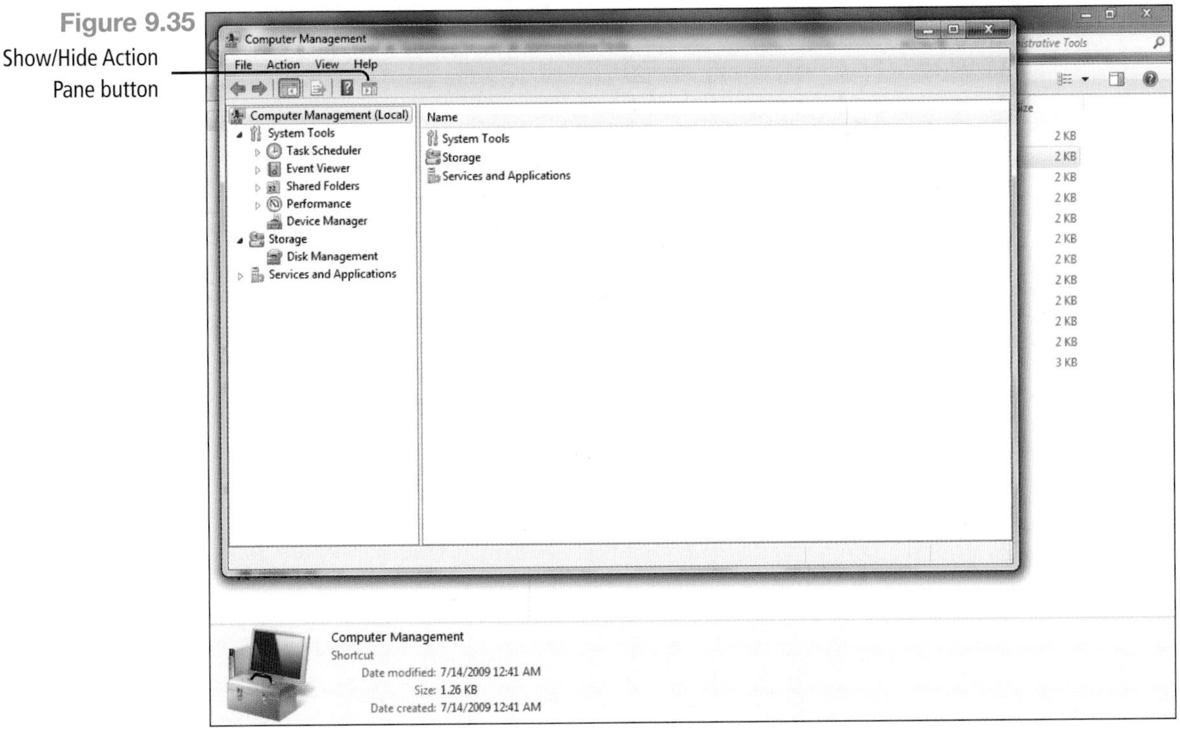

4 **Maximize** the **Computer Management** window. In the left pane, under **Storage**, click **Disk Management**. Wait a few moments for the **Disk Management** pane to collect information about your computer, and then compare your screen with Figure 9.36.

In the upper pane, a list of volumes displays. Recall that a volume is a disk or part of a disk that is assigned a drive letter; it displays as a separate device in Windows Explorer.

In the lower pane, each attached ***physical drive*** is described in its own row. A physical drive is an actual drive such as a hard disk drive, a USB flash drive, or a CD/DVD drive. A single physical drive often contains more than one volume. In Figure 9.36, the hard disk labeled *Disk 0* contains two volumes. One volume has been assigned the letter *C* and the other volume has been assigned the letter *D*. A single physical drive can be assigned multiple volumes by dividing the disk into partitions. Recall that a partition is a separate storage area where each partition operates as if it were a separate disk drive.

In Figure 9.36, the partition named LENOVO (D:) can store about 30 GB of data, while the (C:) partition is unnamed and can store about 187 GB of data. The FLASH DRIVE (F:) can store about 2 GB of data, and the CD-ROM (E:) drive is empty.

In Figure 9.36, the status for Volume (C:) indicates that this partition is used to boot the system and store virtual memory files (Page File).

Figure 9.36

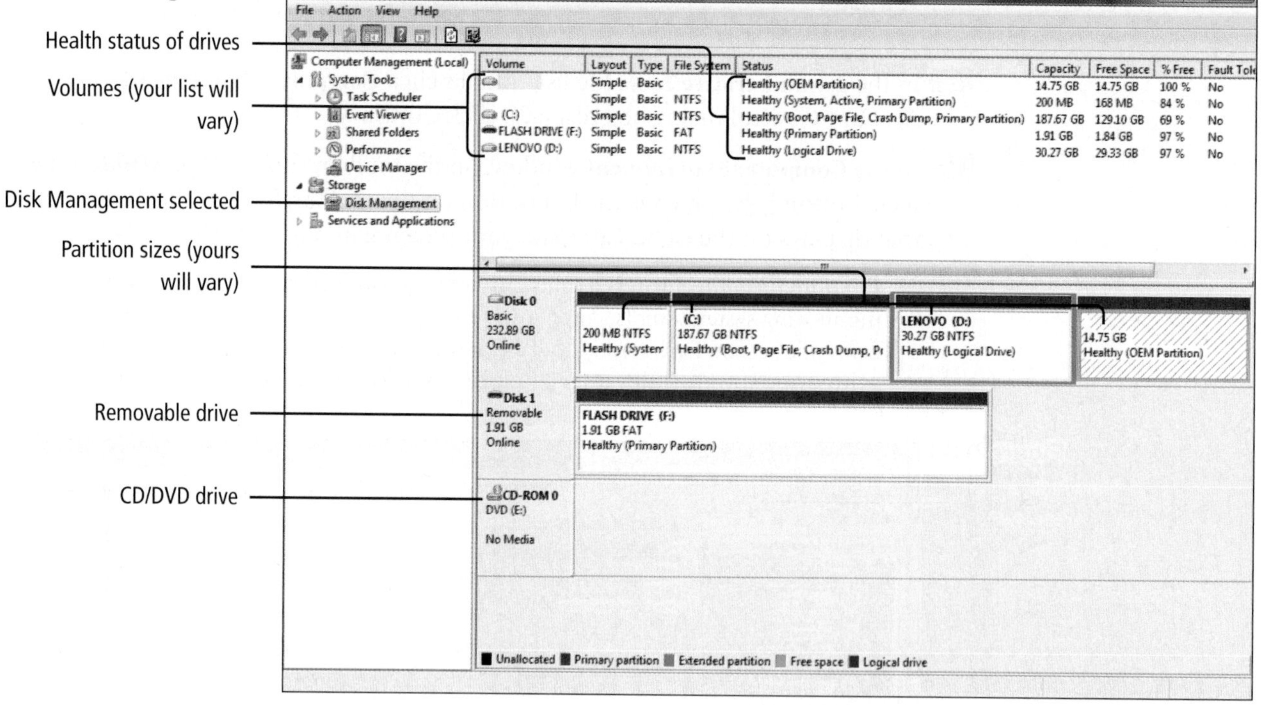

5 In the lower pane, in the row for your USB flash drive, note the letter that is assigned to the volume on your USB flash drive. You will need to remember this letter later in the activity. If you have more than one volume, remember the letter assigned to its first volume.

6 In the lower pane, in the row for your USB drive, right-click the volume but do *not* click any of the displayed commands. Compare your screen with Figure 9.37.

All of the available commands for an object display in the shortcut menu. The ***Format*** command prepares the disk to store data. *Formatting the disk will erase the contents of the disk; any data stored there will be lost.*

Partitions are deleted using the *Delete Volume* command. These commands should be used with extreme caution. Disk Management uses ***destructive partitioning***, which erases data when partitions are deleted.

The ***Extend Volume*** and ***Shrink Volume*** commands are used to resize partitions, which can be done without losing data. For example, a large partition that does not contain a large amount of data can be made smaller using the Shrink Volume command. In the new space created, a new partition can be added. These two commands do not use destructive partitioning. When Disk Management determines that a partition cannot be resized without losing data, the commands become unavailable.

Figure 9.37

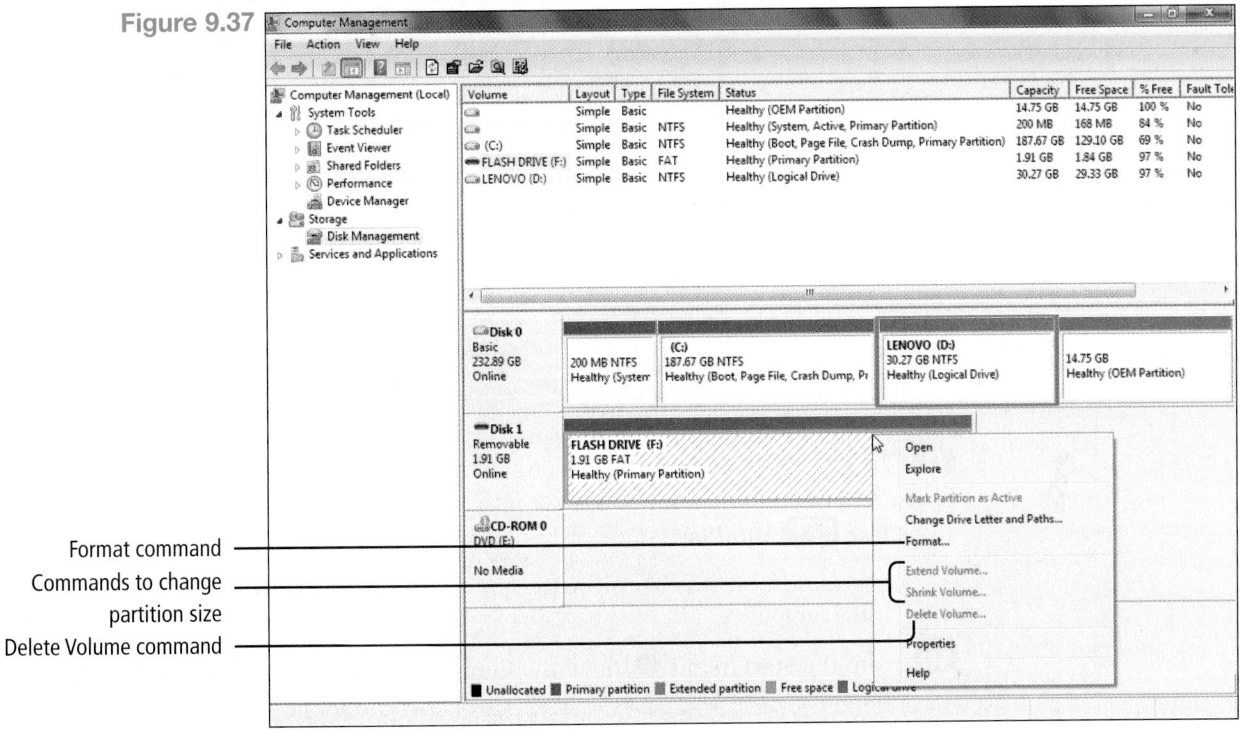

7 From the shortcut menu, click **Change Drive Letter and Paths**.

8 In the **Change Drive Letter and Paths** dialog box, click the **Change** button. Click the **Assign the following drive letter arrow**, and then compare your screen with Figure 9.38.

A list of available drive letters displays. Letters A and B have been traditionally reserved for floppy disks. If your computer does not have a floppy disk drive, both of these letters will be available.

Figure 9.38

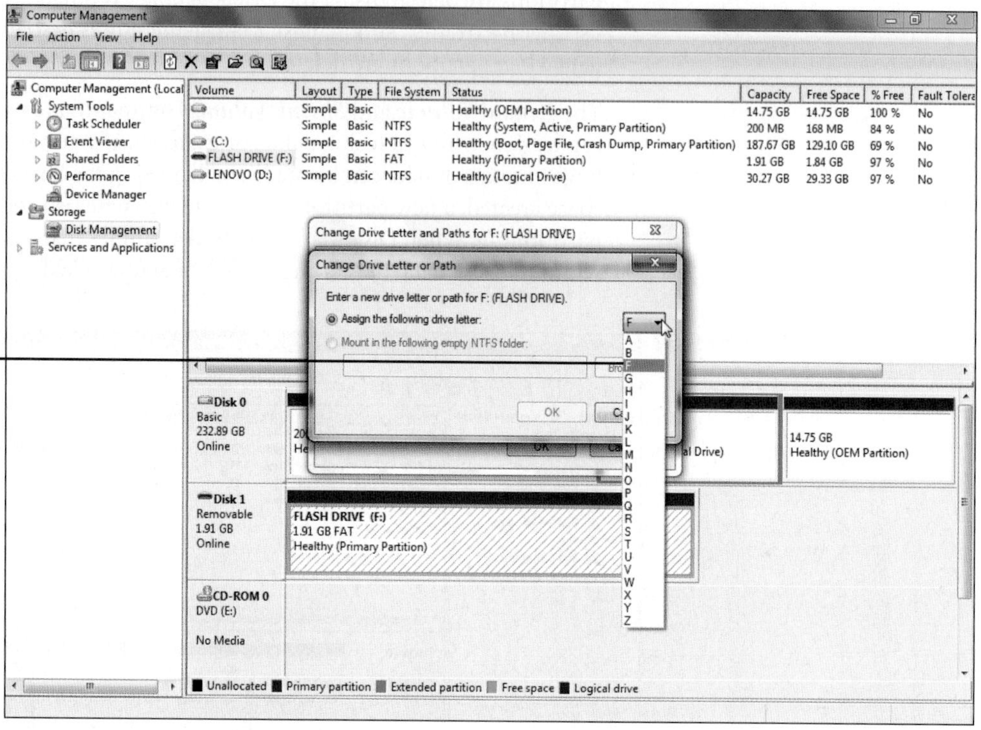

Current drive letter of flash drive (yours may vary)

9 Click **B**, and then click **OK**. Read the displayed message, and then click **Yes**. Wait a few moments, and then if necessary, on the taskbar, click the **AutoPlay** button, and then **Close** **AutoPlay**.

Because the drive was assigned a new letter, the drive behaves as if it was just inserted into the computer.

10 From the **Start** menu, open the **Computer** window. In the **navigation pane**, under **Computer**, notice that your USB flash drive is now listed as Drive B.

For removable drives, drive letters are assigned to the removable drive itself, not the USB port into which it was inserted. The assigned letter is stored on the computer's hard disk, not on the USB drive itself. For example, if you insert the USB into one of your other computer's USB ports, it will still be assigned the letter B. When you insert the same USB drive into another computer, however, the drive will be whatever letter the computer assigns to it.

11 **Close** the **Computer** window. In the **Computer Management** window, be sure that your USB flash drive displays in the lower pane.

12 **Start** the **Snipping Tool** program, click the **New arrow**, and then click **Full-screen Snip**. In the **Snipping Tool** mark-up window, click the **Save Snip** button.

13 In the **Save As** dialog box, in the **navigation pane**, scroll down as necessary, and then under **Computer**, click your USB flash drive so that it displays in the address bar. Navigate to your **Windows 7 Chapter 9** folder, and then as the file name, type **Lastname_Firstname_9B_Disks_Snip** Be sure the file type is **JPEG**, and then press Enter. **Close** the **Snipping Tool** mark-up window. Hold this file until you finish Project 9B.

14 In the lower pane of the **Computer Management** window, right-click your USB flash drive volume. From the shortcut menu, click **Change Drive Letter and Paths**. Click the **Change** button, click the **Assign the following drive letter arrow**, and then click the letter that was originally assigned to your USB drive. If you forgot your original letter, assign the first available letter after *B*. Click **OK**, and then click **Yes**.

15 If necessary, on the taskbar, click the **AutoPlay** button, and then **Close** [X] AutoPlay. **Close** [X] all open windows.

On your own computer, you might use Disk Management in the future. You could assign your removable USB flash drive a new letter to make it easier to find in Windows Explorer. If you install a second hard disk drive, you can use Disk Management to format the drive, divide the drive into partitions, and then assign volume letters to each partition.

Objective 7 | Manage Services by Using the Services Window

Recall that services are low level programs that typically run in the background waiting to be called on by processes. The Services window is a Windows 7 tool that lists all services and provides a way to change their settings. Disabling unnecessary services increases computer performance. For example, if you never use your computer as a fax machine, you could disable the Fax service. Boot time can be shortened by setting a service to start after Windows 7 finishes the boot process. If you seldom use your computer as a fax as soon as you turn on your computer, you could set the Fax service to start after Windows 7 boots. Some problems, such as printing problems, can be solved by restarting a service. You can make all of these changes in the Services window.

Activity 9.12 | Managing Services by Using the Services Window

In the Services window, you can view and manage services. In earlier activities you viewed services by using Task Manager. In this activity, you will use the Services window to change two services—Print Spooler and Fax.

1 Be sure that your USB flash drive is inserted in the computer. Display **Control Panel**, click **System and Security**, scroll to the bottom, and then click **Administrative Tools**. In the **file list**, double-click **Computer Management**. If necessary, in the User Account Control dialog box, click Continue.

2 **Maximize** [□] the **Computer Management** window. In the left pane, expand [▷] **Services and Applications**, and then click **Services** to display the **Services** pane. On the toolbar, click the **Show/Hide Action Pane** button [▥], so that the Action pane does not display.

3 Point to the column separator between the **Name** column and the **Description** column, and then double-click to widen the column. In the lower portion of the window, be sure that the **Extended tab** is selected. In the **Name** column, click **Application Experience**, and then compare your screen with Figure 9.39.

The Services toolbar displays four buttons that control a service: the Start Service (or Resume Service) button, the Stop Service button, the Pause Service button, and the Restart Service button.

When the Extended tab is selected, a column displays to the left of the Name column, which includes a *Description* of the service and a link to *Start*, *Stop*, and/or *Restart* the selected service—the links vary depending on the current status of the service.

Figure 9.39

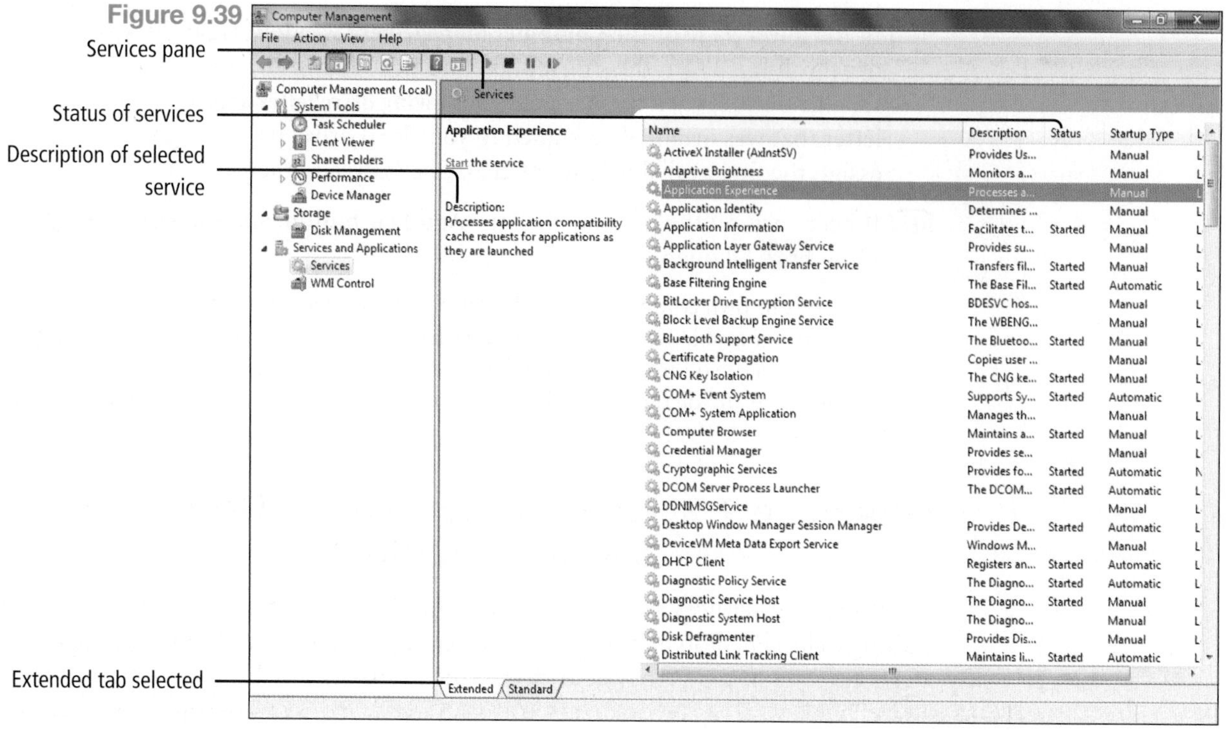

> **Another Way**
>
> On the toolbar, click the Restart Service button. If a message displays, click Yes.

4 Scroll down the list of services, and then locate and click **Print Spooler**. In the column to the left of the **Name** column, click **Restart**.

The Service Control message briefly displays as the Print Spooler service is stopped and then restarted. Recall that the Print Spooler handles print requests so that you can continue using your computer for other tasks while your document is printing. When printing problems occur, restarting the print spooler service often solves the problem.

5 Scroll as necessary in the list of services, and then right-click **Fax**. From the shortcut menu, click **Properties**. On the **General tab**, click the **Startup type arrow**, and then compare your screen with Figure 9.40.

The Fax service enables you to send and receive faxes on your computer. Services can be assigned one of four service startup types. By default, the *Fax* service is assigned the *Manual* startup type, which means the service is started by the logged on user or by a program only when it is needed.

A service assigned the *Automatic* startup type means the service will start during the Windows 7 boot process. A service assigned the *Automatic (Delayed Start)* startup type will wait for Windows 7 to boot before it is started. With fewer services to start, Windows 7 will boot faster and you can start working sooner. The delayed services will start while you work on other tasks.

A service set to the *Disabled* startup type cannot be started until its startup type is changed to one of the other types. Disabling unused services improves performance. However, you should always be aware of what a service does before you disable it.

Figure 9.40

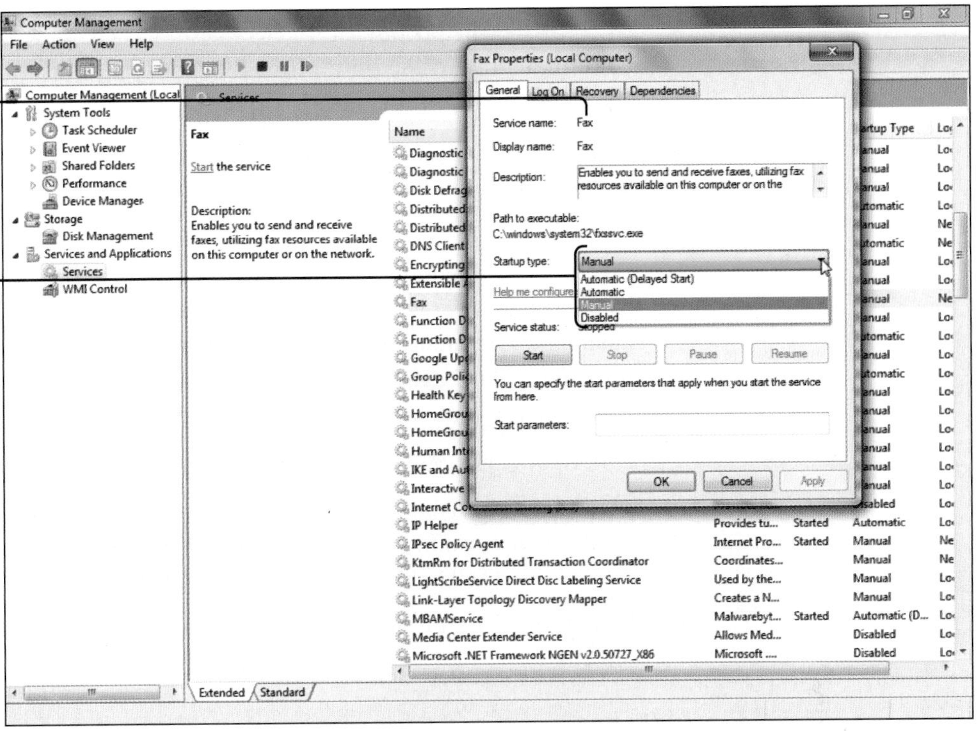

6 Click **Automatic (Delayed Start)**, and then click **Apply**.

Changing a service from *Manual* to *Automatic (Delayed Start)* makes the service always available, but does not increase the time needed for Windows 7 to boot. The Fax service will wait until after Windows finishes its boot process before it is started.

7 Click the **Dependencies tab**, and then compare your screen with Figure 9.41.

Before disabling or delaying when a service is started, it is good practice to check that no other services depend on that service.

Figure 9.41

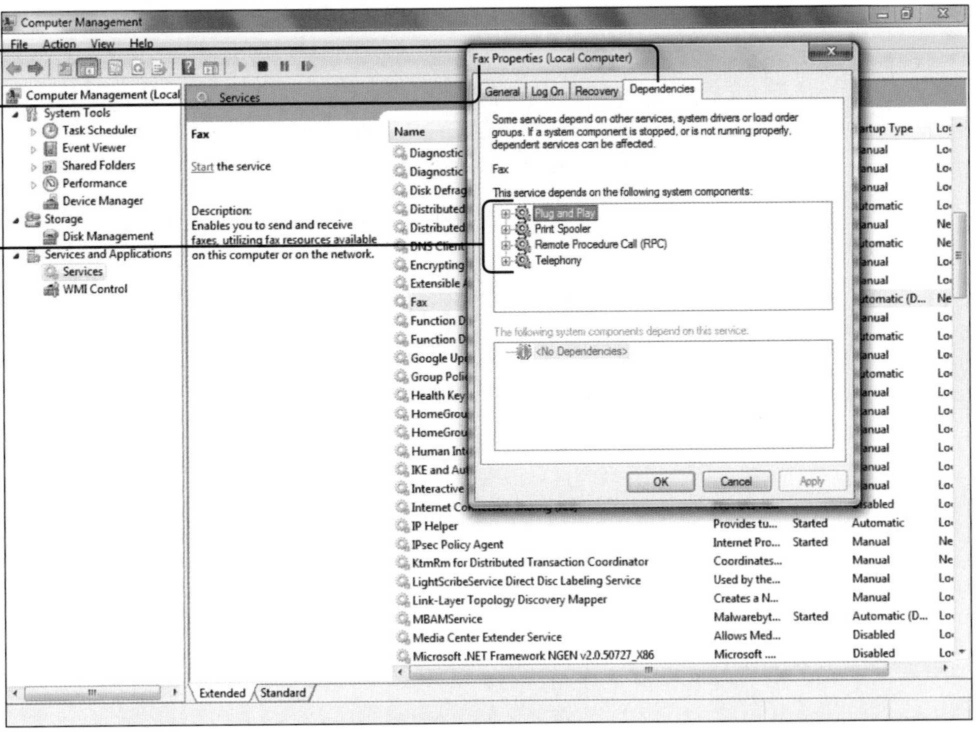

8. Click **OK**. At the bottom of the **Services** pane, click the **Standard tab**. Point to the column divider to the right of the **Startup Type** column, and then double-click so that all of the column information displays.

9. **Start** the **Snipping Tool** program, click the **New arrow**, and then click **Full-screen Snip**. In the **Snipping Tool** mark-up window, click the **Save Snip** button.

10. In the **Save As** dialog box, in the **navigation pane**, scroll down as necessary, and then under **Computer**, click your USB flash drive so that it displays in the address bar. Navigate to your **Windows 7 Chapter 9** folder, and then as the file name, type **Lastname_Firstname_9B_Services_Snip** Be sure the file type is **JPEG file**, and then press Enter. **Close** the **Snipping Tool** mark-up window.

11. Right-click **Fax**, and then from the shortcut menu, click **Properties**. Click the **Startup type arrow**, click **Manual**, and then click **OK**. **Close** all open windows.

    On your own computer, you may want to use the Services window to view and manage the services running on your computer. Generally, the settings used by Windows 7 are ideal, so consult with an IT professional before making any changes.

12. Submit the five snip files that are the results of this project to your instructor as directed.

End **You have completed Project 9B**

Content-Based Assessments

Summary

Monitoring and tracking your computer system's performance enables you to determine whether your computer is running reliably and efficiently. In this chapter, you viewed your computer's performance information using several different methods. You used Task Manager to view and manage applications, processes, and services. Task Manager also provided real time data for several key performance areas. You used several features of the Performance and Resource Monitors to track real time performance and to track system reliability over time. You also used Disk Management to view your computer's disks and the Services window to stop and restart a service.

Key Terms

Computer Management 575
CPU Time 552
Destructive partitioning 577
Disk Management 574
Extend Volume 577
Format 577
Network adapter 560
Network interface card 560
NIC 560
Nonresponsive program 543
Partition 574
Performance Monitor 568
Physical drive 576
PID 556
Process 543
Process Identifier 556
Real time 565
Reliability 572
Reliability Monitor 572
Resource Monitor 565
Service 543
Shrink Volume 577
System Diagnostics Report 570
System Stability Index 573
Task Manager 543
Thread 551
Volume 574

Matching

Match each term in the second column with its correct definition in the first column by writing the letter of the term on the blank line in front of the correct definition.

____ 1. A Windows 7 tool that shows you the application programs, processes, and services that are currently running on your computer.

____ 2. A file that is part of a running program and performs a specific task such as starting the program.

____ 3. A program that is open but has stopped responding to your commands, which means it has stopped communicating with Windows 7.

____ 4. The time a processor spends working on a task.

____ 5. A shortened term for *process identifier*.

____ 6. A computer program or process that runs in the background and provides support to other programs.

____ 7. The actual time during which something takes place.

____ 8. A component of the Reliability and Performance Monitor tool that provides detailed data and charts.

A CPU Time
B Disk Management
C Nonresponsive program
D Partition
E Performance Monitor
F PID
G Process
H Real time
I Reliability
J Reliability Monitor
K Service
L System Diagnostics Report
M System Stability Index
N Task Manager
O Volume

____ 9. A component of the Reliability and Performance tool that provides data about a computer's overall reliability.

____ 10. The likelihood that your computer will as work as intended.

____ 11. A number between 1 and 10 determined by how many system errors occurred on a specific day.

____ 12. A pre-built report that contains an easy to understand summary of your computer's overall performance.

____ 13. A part of a hard disk that functions like a separate disk.

____ 14. A storage area on a hard disk that is formatted with a file system.

____ 15. The Windows 7 tool with which you can view the arrangement of hard disk drives on your computer, and also perform partitioning and formatting tasks if you must do so.

Multiple Choice

Circle the correct answer.

1. A task created when a process divides itself into tasks that are processed simultaneously is:
   A. a thread **B.** an index **C.** a service
2. A hardware component that connects your computer to a network is a:
   A. network adapter **B.** PID **C.** network monitor
3. The tool that provides both instantaneous and recent history readouts of your computer's four key performance measurements is the:
   A. Resource Monitor **B.** Performance Monitor **C.** Reliability Monitor
4. A tool that provides data about a computer's overall reliability is the:
   A. Resource Monitor **B.** Performance Monitor **C.** Reliability Monitor
5. A collection of tools with which you can perform tasks such as monitoring system events is:
   A. Disk Management **B.** Computer Management **C.** Task Manager
6. A drive such as a hard disk drive, a USB flash drive, or a CD/DVD drive is a:
   A. backup drive **B.** virtual drive **C.** physical drive
7. The command that prepares the disk to store data is:
   A. start process **B.** format **C.** prepare
8. The process that erases data when partitions are deleted is:
   A. destructive partitioning **B.** formatting **C.** indexing
9. The command to enlarge the size of a partition and in which no data is lost is:
   A. Format Volume **B.** Extend Volume **C.** Shrink Volume
10. The command to reduce the size of a partition and in which no data is lost:
    A. Format Volume **B.** Extend Volume **C.** Shrink Volume

Apply 9A skills from these Objectives:

1. Manage Applications by Using Task Manager
2. Manage Processes by Using Task Manager
3. View Services by Using Task Manager
4. Track Performance by Using Task Manager

Skills Review | Project 9C Using Task Manager

Project Files

For Project 9C, you will need the following files:

Student Resource CD (or a USB flash drive containing these files)
win09_9C_Answer_Sheet (Word document)

You will save your file as:

Lastname_Firstname_9C_Answer_Sheet

Project Results

1 **Close** [X] all open windows. On the taskbar, click the **Windows Explorer** button. In the **navigation pane**, click the drive that contains the student files for this textbook, and then navigate to **Chapter_Files ▶ Chapter_09**. Double-click the Word file **win09_9C_Answer_Sheet** to open Word and display the document. Press F12 to display the **Save As** dialog box in Word, navigate to your **Windows 7 Chapter 9** folder, and then using your own name, save the document as **Lastname_Firstname_9C_Answer_Sheet** If necessary, click OK if a message regarding formats displays.

On the taskbar, click the **Word** button to minimize the window and leave your Word document accessible from the taskbar. As you complete each step in this project, click the Word button on the taskbar to open the document, type your one-letter answer in the appropriate cell of the Word table, and then on the taskbar, click the button again to minimize the window for the next step.

On the taskbar, right-click, and then click **Start Task Manager**. Do *not* maximize the window. Which of the following is *not* a tab in the **Windows Task Manager** dialog box?

A. Performance

B. Services

C. Startup

2 Click the **Applications tab** and the **Processes tab** as necessary, and then indicate which statement is true.

A. There are fewer applications running than processes.

B. The number of applications running is equal to the number of processes running.

C. There are more applications running than processes.

3 Click **Start**, and then click **All Programs**. Locate and then click **Windows Live Photo Gallery**. If a message displays, click No. In the **Windows Task Manager Applications tab**, point to **Windows Live Photo Gallery**, and then right-click. On the displayed shortcut menu, click **Go To Process**. What process is selected?

A. Windows Photo Gallery

B. Windows Live PhotoGallery.exe

C. WLXPhotoGallery.exe

4 On the **Processes tab**, scroll over as necessary, and then read the description for the *explorer.exe* process. According to the description, what other name does this process have?

A. Desktop Explorer

B. Internet Explorer

C. Windows Explorer

(Project 9C Using Task Manager continues on the next page)

Skills Review | Project 9C Using Task Manager (continued)

5 Point to **dwm.exe**, and then right-click. On the displayed shortcut menu, point to **Set Priority**. Which of the following is *not* one of the priority levels listed?

A. Average
B. High
C. Realtime

6 From the **View** menu, click **Select Columns**. In the displayed **Select Process Page Columns** dialog box, scroll to the bottom of the list. Which of the following is *not* an available column?

A. Command Line
B. Data Execution Prevention
C. Related Service(s)

7 Click **Cancel**, and then click the **Show processes from all users** button. Click the **Services tab**. Point to **Appinfo**, and then right-click. On the displayed shortcut menu, click **Go to Process**. In the **Processes tab**, what service selected?

A. Appinfo.exe
B. dwm.exe
C. svchost.exe

8 Click the **Performance tab**. From the **View** menu, point to **Update Speed**. Which of the following is *not* a selection?

A. Paused
B. Stopped
C. Low

9 Click the **Networking tab**. From the **View** menu, point to **Network Adapter History**. According to the submenu, what data will display as a yellow line?

A. Bytes Sent
B. Bytes Received
C. Bytes Total

10 Click the **Applications tab**. Click **Windows Live Photo Gallery**, and then click the **End Task** button. What is your result?

A. Windows Photo Gallery closes and is no longer listed in the Task column.
B. A message displays indicating that the application cannot be closed.
C. A message displays asking if you would like to save changes.

Close Windows Task Manager. Be sure you have typed all of your answers in your Word document. **Save** and **Close** your Word document, and submit as directed by your instructor.

End **You have completed Project 9C**

Content-Based Assessments

Apply 9B skills from these Objectives:

5 Track Performance by Using the Performance and Reliability Monitors
6 View Disks by Using Disk Management
7 Manage Services by Using the Services Window

Skills Review | Project 9D Optimizing Computer Performance

Project Files

For Project 9D, you will need the following files:

Student Resource CD (or a USB flash drive containing these files)
win09_9D_Answer_Sheet (Word document)

You will save your file as:

Lastname_Firstname_9D_Answer_Sheet

Project Results

1 **Close** all open windows. On the taskbar, click the **Windows Explorer** button. In the **navigation pane**, click the drive that contains the student files for this textbook, and then navigate to **Chapter_Files ▶ Chapter_09**. Double-click the Word file **win09_9D_Answer_Sheet** to open Word and display the document. Press F12 to display the **Save As** dialog box in Word, navigate to your **Windows 7 Chapter 9** folder, and then using your own name, save the document as **Lastname_Firstname_9D_Answer_Sheet** If necessary, click OK if a message regarding formats displays.

On the taskbar, click the **Word** button to minimize the window and leave your Word document accessible from the taskbar. As you complete each step in this project, click the Word button on the taskbar to open the document, type your one-letter answer in the appropriate cell of the Word table, and then on the taskbar, click the button again to minimize the window for the next step.

Start the **Control Panel**. Click **System and Security**, and then click **System**. On the left, click **Performance Information and Tools**. On the left, click **Advanced tools**, and then click **Open Performance Monitor**. On the right, click the blue link **Open Resource Monitor**, and then **Maximize** the window. Click the **Overview tab**. On the right, which resource area does *not* have its own graph?

A. CPU

B. Disk

C. Printer

2 If necessary, click the **CPU arrow** to expand the **CPU** section. In the **CPU** section, which of the following is *not* a displayed column?

A. PID

B. Services

C. Threads

3 **Close** the **Resource Monitor** window to redisplay the **Performance Monitor**. In the left pane, if necessary expand the **Monitoring Tools**, and then click **Performance Monitor**. From the **Action** menu, click **Properties**. In the displayed **Performance Monitor Properties** dialog box, be sure the **General tab** is selected. Under **Graph elements**, how often is the graph sampled?

A. Every second

B. Every two seconds

C. Every five seconds

(Project 9D Optimizing Computer Performance continues on the next page)

Skills Review | Project 9D Optimizing Computer Performance (continued)

4 Click **Cancel** to close the **Performance Monitor Properties** dialog box. From the **Action** menu, click **Properties**. In the **Performance Monitor Properties** dialog box, click the **Graph tab**. Under **View**, click the **arrow**, and then click **Report**. Click **OK**. What performance statistic is given in the report?

A. % Processor Time

B. RAM usage

C. Disk usage

5 From the **Action menu**, click **Properties**, and then click the **Graph tab**. Click the **View arrow**, and then click **Line**. Under **Show**, select the **Horizontal grid** check box, and then click **OK**. Which statement best describes the result of this action?

A. Green usage bars display.

B. A pie chart displays.

C. A line chart displays and measures data from left to right.

6 **Close** the **Performance Monitor** and the **Advanced Tools** window. Open **Control Panel**, and then under **System and Security**, click **Review your computer's status and resolve issues**. Expand the **Maintenance** section, and then click **View reliability history**. Click on any of the blue circles that represent an Information event. Which of the following describes the result?

A. In the lower portion of the screen, reliability details for the selected date display.

B. Information about the day represented by the data point displays in a ScreenTip.

C. All of the data points display in red.

7 On the right side of the window, which of the following is *not* listed as a possible failure type?

A. Application failures

B. Startup failures

C. Windows failures

8 In the **address bar**, click **Action Center**, and then in the left pane, click **View performance information**. On the left, click **Advanced tools**, and then scroll to the bottom of the window and click **Generate a system health report**. Wait 60 seconds for the report to display. Click the **Diagnostic Results arrow** to collapse the section, and then click the **Memory arrow** to expand the section. What subsection is *not* listed in the **Memory** section?

A. Counters

B. Process

C. Virtual Memory

(Project 9D Optimizing Computer Performance continues on the next page)

Skills Review | Project 9D Optimizing Computer Performance (continued)

9 **Close** the **Resource and Performance Monitor** window, and then **Close** the **Advanced Tools** window. **Start** the **Control Panel**, click **System and Security**, and then click **Administrative Tools**. In the **Name** column of the **Administrative Tools** window, double-click **Computer Management**. In the left pane, under **Storage**, click **Disk Management**, and then wait for the information to display. In the lower pane, what is the disk number assigned to the volume that indicates *System* and *Boot* in parentheses?

A. Disk 0

B. Disk 1

C. Disk 2

10 In the left pane, expand **Services and Applications**, and then click **Services**. In the **Services** pane, if necessary, increase the width of the **Name** column, and at the bottom of the screen, display the **Extended tab**. In the **Name** column, click **Background Intelligent Transfer Service**. Which statement best describes the purpose of this service?

A. Enhances artificial intelligence capabilities for computer games.

B. Transfers files in the background using idle network bandwidth.

C. Transfers CPU performance data to Internet Explorer.

Be sure you have typed all of your answers in your Word document. **Save** and **Close** your Word document; submit it as directed by your instructor. **Close** all open windows.

End You have completed Project 9D

Apply 9A skills from these Objectives:

1. Manage Applications by Using Task Manager
2. Manage Processes by Using Task Manager
3. View Services by Using Task Manager
4. Track Performance by Using Task Manager

Mastering Windows 7 | Project 9E Use Task Manager

In the following Mastering Windows 7 project, you will use Task Manager to view computer performance and manage applications and processes. Your captured screens will look similar to Figure 9.42.

Project Files

For Project 9E, you will need the following files:

New Snip files

You will save your files as:

Lastname_Firstname_9E_Networking_Snip
Lastname_Firstname_9E_Performance_Snip
Lastname_Firstname_9E_Processes_Snip

Project Results

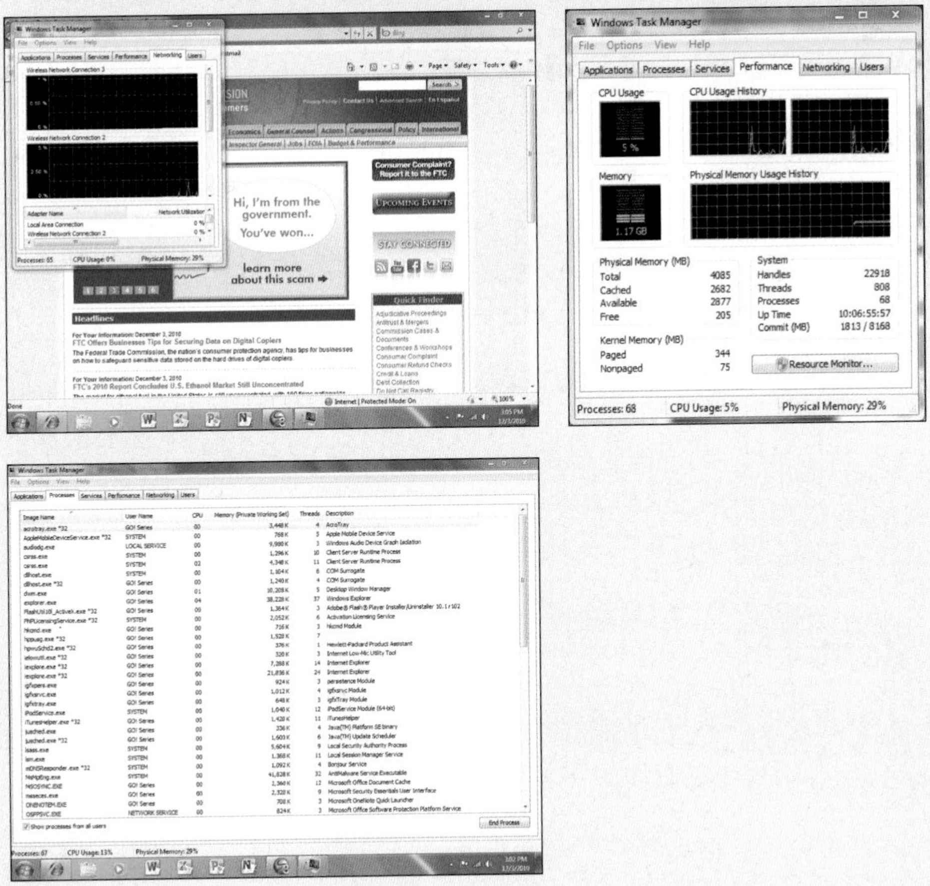

Figure 9.42

(Project 9E Use Task Manager continues on the next page)

Mastering Windows 7 | Project 9E Use Task Manager (continued)

1 Insert your USB flash drive, and then open **Task Manager**. Do *not* maximize the window. Click the **Networking tab**. **Minimize** the **Windows Task Manager** window. **Start** Internet Explorer, and navigate to **www.ftc.gov**

2 Switch to **Windows Task Manager**. Wait five seconds, display the **View** menu, point to **Update Speed**, and then click **Paused**.

3 Create a **Full-screen Snip**, and then in the **Snipping Tool** mark-up window, **Save** the snip as **Lastname_Firstname_9E_Networking_Snip**

4 Close the **Snipping Tool** mark-up window. In the **Windows Task Manager** window, display the **View** menu, point to **Update Speed**, and then click **Normal**. Click the **Performance tab**. Create a **Window Snip**, click in the **Windows Task Manager** window, and then **Save** the snip as **Lastname_Firstname_9E_Performance_Snip**

5 **Close** the **Snipping Tool** mark-up window. In the **Windows Task Manager** window, click the **Processes tab**, and then display the processes from all users. Add the **Threads** column to the **Processes tab**. **Maximize** the window so that you can view the **Threads** column. Create a **Full-screen Snip**, and then **Save** the snip as **Lastname_Firstname_9E_Processes_Snip**

6 **Close** the **Snipping Tool** mark-up window. Remove the **Threads** column from the **Processes tab**. Click the **Applications tab**, and then from this tab, click **Internet Explorer** and end the task. **Close** the **Windows Task Manager** window. Submit the three files that are the results of this project to your instructor as directed.

End **You have completed Project 9E**

Apply 9B skills from these Objectives:

- **5** Track Performance by Using the Performance and Reliability Monitors
- **6** View Disks by Using Disk Management
- **7** Manage Services by Using the Services Window

Mastering Windows 7 | Project 9F System Maintenance

In the following Mastering Windows 7 project, you will view disks using Disk Management, display information about system services using the System window, and track performance using the Reliability and Performance Monitor. Your captured screens will look similar to Figure 9.43.

Project Files

For Project 9F, you will need the following files:

New Snip files

You will save your files as:

Lastname_Firstname_9F_Services_Snip
Lastname_Firstname_9F_Reliability_Snip
Lastname_Firstname_9F_Report_Snip

Project Results

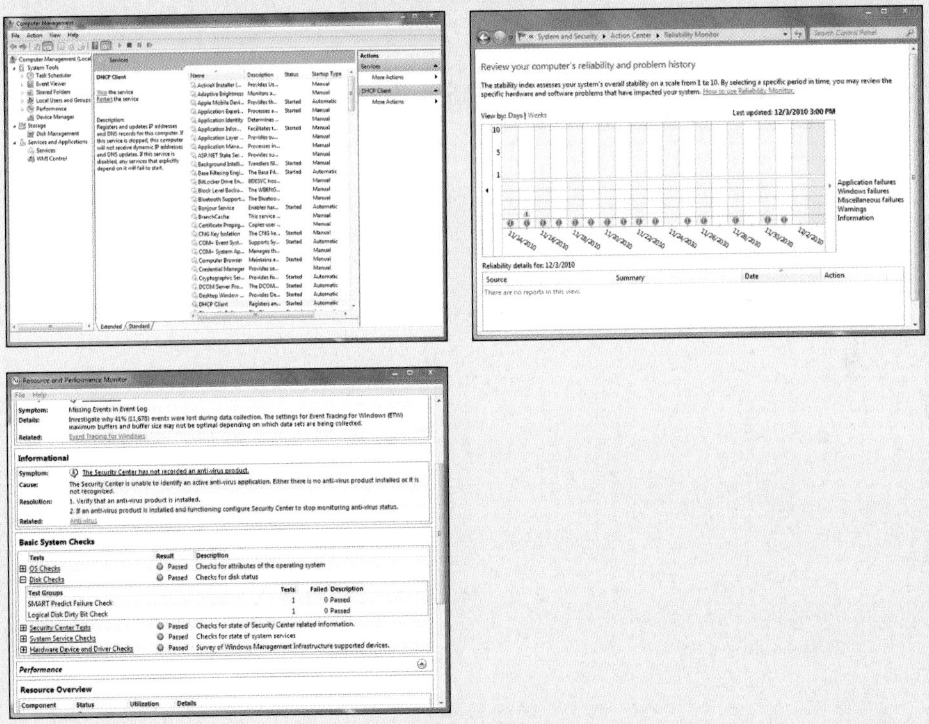

Figure 9.43

(Project 9F System Maintenance continues on the next page)

Mastering Windows 7 | Project 9F System Maintenance (continued)

1 From the **Control Panel**, open **System and Security**, if necessary, scroll to the bottom, and then open **Administrative Tools**. Open **Computer Management**.

2 In the left pane, expand **Services and Applications**, and then click **Services**. Be sure that the **Extended tab** is active, and then in the **Name** column, click the **DHCP Client** service. With the **Services** pane displayed, create a **Window Snip** of the **Computer Management** window, click in the window to create the snip, and then **Save** it as **Lastname_Firstname_9F_Services_Snip** **Close** the **Snipping Tool** mark-up window.

3 **Close** the **Computer Management** window, and then **Close** the **Administrative Tools** window. In the **System and Security** window, click **Action Center**, expand **Maintenance**, and then click **View reliability history**. Create a **Window Snip** of the **Reliability Monitor** window, and then **Save** it as **Lastname_Firstname_9F_Reliability_Snip**

4 **Close** the **Snipping Tool** mark-up window. In the **address bar**, click **Action Center**, and then in the left pane, click **View performance information**. On the left, click **Advanced tools**, and then scroll to the bottom of the window and click **Generate a system health report**. Wait 60 seconds for the report to display.

5 After the **System Diagnostics Report** displays, under **Basic System Checks**, expand **Disk Checks**. With the test groups displayed under **Disk Checks**, create a **Window Snip** for the **Resource and Performance Monitor** window, and then **Save** it as **Lastname_Firstname_9F_Report_Snip** **Close** all open windows, and then submit the three files that are the results of the project to your instructor as directed.

End **You have completed Project 9F**

Rubric

The following outcomes-based assessments are *open-ended assessments*. That is, there is no specific correct result; your result will depend on your approach to the information provided. Make *Professional Quality* your goal. Use the following scoring rubric to guide you in *how* to approach the problem, and then to evaluate *how well* your approach solves the problem.

The *criteria*—Software Mastery, Content, Format and Layout, and Process—represent the knowledge and skills you have gained that you can apply to solving the problem. The *levels of performance*—Professional Quality, Approaching Professional Quality, or Needs Quality Improvements—help you and your instructor evaluate your result.

	Your completed project is of Professional Quality if you:	**Your completed project is Approaching Professional Quality if you:**	**Your completed project Needs Quality Improvements if you:**
1-Software Mastery	Choose and apply the most appropriate skills, tools, and features and identify efficient methods to solve the problem.	Choose and apply some appropriate skills, tools, and features, but not in the most efficient manner.	Choose inappropriate skills, tools, or features, or are inefficient in solving the problem.
2-Content	Construct a solution that is clear and well organized, contains content that is accurate, appropriate to the audience and purpose, and is complete. Provide a solution that contains no errors in spelling, grammar, or style.	Construct a solution in which some components are unclear, poorly organized, inconsistent, or incomplete. Misjudge the needs of the audience. Have some errors in spelling, grammar, or style, but the errors do not detract from comprehension.	Construct a solution that is unclear, incomplete, or poorly organized; contains some inaccurate or inappropriate content; and contains many errors in spelling, grammar, or style. Do not solve the problem.
3-Format and Layout	Format and arrange all elements to communicate information and ideas, clarify function, illustrate relationships, and indicate relative importance.	Apply appropriate format and layout features to some elements, but not others. Overuse features, causing minor distraction.	Apply format and layout that does not communicate information or ideas clearly. Do not use format and layout features to clarify function, illustrate relationships, or indicate relative importance. Use available features excessively, causing distraction.
4-Process	Use an organized approach that integrates planning, development, self-assessment, revision, and reflection.	Demonstrate an organized approach in some areas, but not others; or, use an insufficient process of organization throughout.	Do not use an organized approach to solve the problem.

Outcomes-Based Assessments

Apply a combination of the 9A and 9B skills.

Problem Solving | Project 9G Help Desk

In this project, you will construct a solution by applying any combination of the skills you practiced from the Objectives in Projects 9A and 9B.

Project Files

For Project 9G, you will need the following file:

win09_9G_Help_Desk

You will save your document as:

Lastname_Firstname_9G_Help_Desk

From the student files that accompany this textbook, open the **Chapter_Files** folder, and then in **Chapter_09** folder, locate and open the Word document **win09_9G_Help_Desk**. Save the document in your chapter folder as **Lastname_Firstname_9G_Help_Desk**

The following e-mail question has arrived at the Help Desk from an employee at the Bell Orchid Hotel's corporate office. In the Word form, construct a response based on your knowledge of Windows 7. Although an e-mail response is not as formal as a letter, you should still use good grammar, good sentence structure, professional language, and a polite tone. Save your document and submit the response as directed by your instructor.

To: Help Desk

I have discovered that a program can be started by typing its process name in the Search box in the Start menu. I would like to use this method to start my favorite programs. How can I find out the process names used by my favorite applications?

End **You have completed Project 9G**

Apply a combination of the 9A and 9B skills.

Problem Solving | Project 9H Help Desk

In this project, you will construct a solution by applying any combination of the skills you practiced from the Objectives in Projects 9A and 9B.

Project Files

For Project 9H, you will need the following file:

win09_9H_Help_Desk

You will save your document as:

Lastname_Firstname_9H_Help_Desk

From the student files that accompany this textbook, open the **Chapter_Files** folder, and then in **Chapter_09** folder, locate and open the Word document **win09_9H_Help_Desk**. Save the document in your chapter folder as **Lastname_Firstname_9H_Help_Desk**

The following e-mail question has arrived at the Help Desk from an employee at the Bell Orchid Hotel's corporate office. In the Word form, construct a response based on your knowledge of Windows 7. Although an e-mail response is not as formal as a letter, you should still use good grammar, good sentence structure, professional language, and a polite tone. Save your document and submit the response as directed by your instructor.

To: Help Desk

My computer has two hard disk drives. The second hard disk drive has four partitions. In the Computer window, these four partitions are assigned the drive letters *F*, *G*, *H*, and *I*. In the Computer window, there is no drive assigned the letter *E*. I would like to change the letter currently assigned to drive *H* so that it appears as drive *E*. How can I do this?

End You have completed Project 9H

Outcomes-Based Assessments

Apply a combination of the 9A and 9B skills.

Problem Solving | Project 9I Help Desk

In this project, you will construct a solution by applying any combination of the skills you practiced from the Objectives in Projects 9A and 9B.

Project Files

For Project 9I, you will need the following file:

Win09_9I_Help_Desk

You will save your document as:

Lastname_Firstname_9I_Help_Desk

From the student files that accompany this textbook, open the **Chapter_Files** folder, and then in **Chapter_09** folder, locate and open the Word document **win09_9I_Help_Desk**. Save the document in your chapter folder as **Lastname_Firstname_9I_Help_Desk**

The following e-mail question has arrived at the Help Desk from an employee at the Bell Orchid Hotel's corporate office. In the Word form, construct a response based on your knowledge of Windows 7. Although an e-mail response is not as formal as a letter, you should still use good grammar, good sentence structure, professional language, and a polite tone. Save your document and submit the response as directed by your instructor.

To: Help Desk

My computer has been crashing at least once a day for the past two weeks. I understand that in Windows 7 I can see a report that documents computer crashes and other failures. What is this report and what steps do I need to take to create it? Finally, how can I save this report so that I can send it to you?

End You have completed Project 9I

Controlling Computer Security and Troubleshooting Your Computer

OUTCOMES

At the end of this chapter you will be able to:

OBJECTIVES

Mastering these objectives will enable you to:

PROJECT 10A

Protect your computer from malware, increase Internet Explorer security, apply Parental Controls, and encrypt files.

1. Protect Your Computer from Viruses and Spyware (p. 601)
2. Secure Internet Explorer (p. 610)
3. Set Parental Controls (p. 619)
4. Encrypt Files with Encryption File System (p. 622)

PROJECT 10B

Analyze computer problems and find solutions, manage computer hardware devices, and remove malware from your computer.

5. Troubleshoot Computer Problems (p. 627)
6. Find and Use Help from Others (p. 630)
7. Manage Hardware Devices (p. 635)
8. Remove Malware from Your Computer (p. 642)

William Berry/Shutterstock

In This Chapter

When you secure your computer, you safeguard its programs and data so that it performs as intended. To control computer security, you should use software that guards against malware. If you are a parent, you can control how your child uses the computer and the Internet. Windows 7 also has tools to encrypt files that contain sensitive data.

When your computer experiences a problem, Windows 7 can help you find a solution. Windows 7 has several tools that install hardware, analyze problems, and find solutions. For example, when you connect a new printer or scanner, Windows 7 typically sets up the device to work with your computer. Other programs look for problems and offer solutions.

The projects in this chapter relate to the **Bell Orchid Hotels**, headquartered in Boston, and which own and operate resorts and business-oriented hotels. Resort properties are located in popular destinations, including Honolulu, Orlando, San Diego, and Santa Barbara. The resorts offer deluxe accommodations and a wide array of dining options. Other Bell Orchid hotels are located in major business centers and offer the latest technology in their meeting facilities. The company plans to open new properties and update existing properties over the next ten years.

Project 10A Controlling Computer Security

Project Activities

In Activities 10.01 through 10.08, you will participate in training along with Barbara Hewitt and Steven Ramos, both of whom work for the Information Technology Department at the headquarters office of the Bell Orchid Hotels. After completing this part of the training, you will be able to secure Internet Explorer, set parental controls, protect your computer from malware, and protect files from unauthorized access. You will capture screens that look similar to Figure 10.1.

Project Files

For Project 10A, you will need the following files:

Student Resource CD or a USB flash drive containing the student data files
New Snip files

You will save your files as:

Lastname_Firstname_10A_Scan_Snip
Lastname_Firstname_10A_Trusted_Sites_Snip
Lastname_Firstname_10A_Cookies_Snip
Lastname_Firstname_10A_Popups_Snip
Lastname_Firstname_10A_Parental_Snip
Lastname_Firstname_10A_Encryption_Snip

Project Results

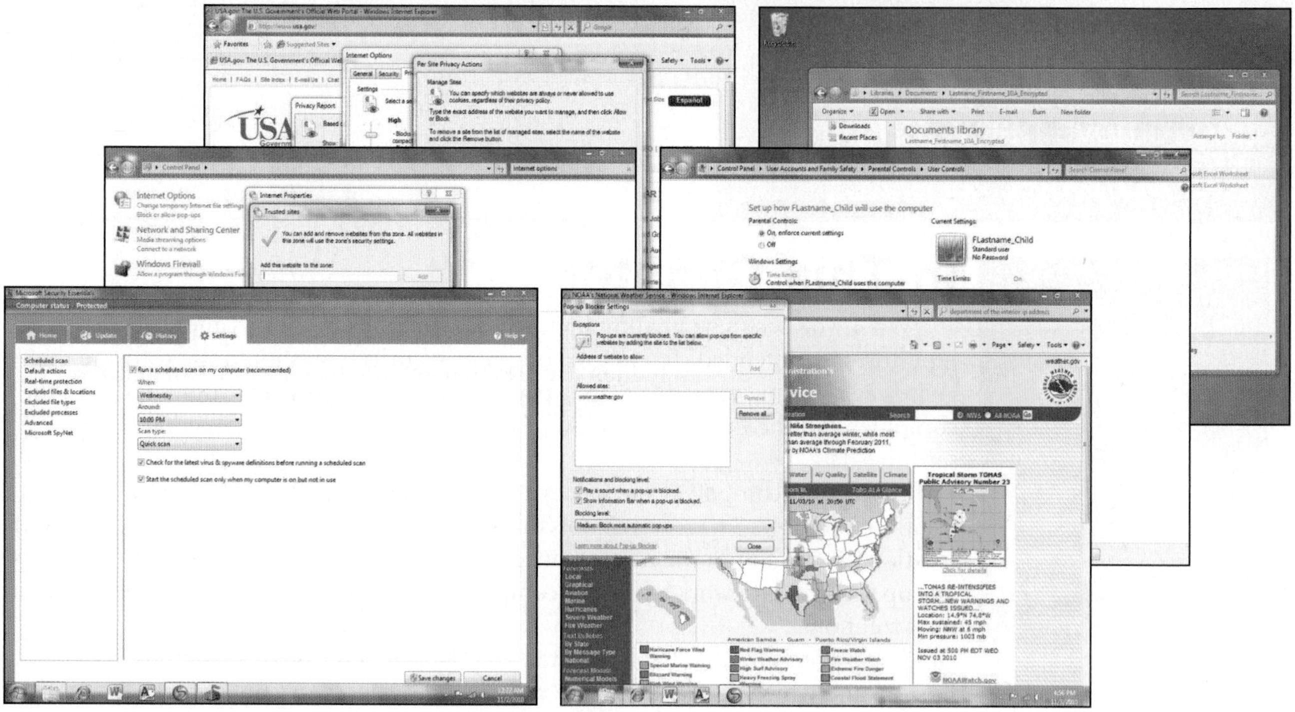

Figure 10.1
Project 10A Controlling Computer Security

Objective 1 | Protect Your Computer from Viruses and Spyware

Recall that ***malware***—a shortened term for *malicious software*—is a computer program that intentionally harms your computer. If a malware program installs itself and then runs on your computer, your computer is said to be ***infected***. Anti-malware programs protect your computer from a malware infection.

Anti-malware programs specialize in protecting your computer from either ***viruses*** or ***spyware***. A virus is a type of malware designed specifically to replicate itself by spreading its infection from computer to computer; a virus can damage the operating system, software, or data. Spyware is a type of malware that collects personal information, displays advertisements, or changes your browser settings. Spyware can infect your computer without your knowledge when you download a program or install a program from a CD or other removable media. Spyware is most commonly installed through free software, such as file sharing software, screen savers, or search toolbars.

To protect your computer from both types of malware, you may need to use more than one anti-malware program and follow safe practices to keep malware from infecting your computer.

Activity 10.01 | Protecting Your Computer from Viruses

A virus can delete files on your hard drive, format your hard drive, or take control of your computer so that it can attack other computers. A virus can look for sensitive information on your hard drive such as your list of e-mail addresses and credit card information. Some viruses have the capability to shut down or change your computer's security programs so that they no longer protect your computer. In this unprotected state, viruses can easily spread throughout many locations on your hard drive, or leave your computer vulnerable to an attack from another computer.

Viruses are commonly classified by the methods they use to infect other computers. A traditional virus infects your computer when you open a file on your computer. This type of virus is commonly hidden in files attached to e-mail messages or in files downloaded from Web sites. A ***worm*** is a self-replicating program—similar to a virus—that spreads on its own to every computer on a network. You do not have to open a file to spread this type of malware. After one computer on the network is infected, a worm spreads extremely fast, often before its presence is discovered.

A ***Trojan horse*** is a malicious software program that hides inside legitimate programs, such as a game or media player or screen saver. For example, a free game may work as you intended, but the software has hidden features that are initiated later. A Trojan horse might place code into the operating system, which enables a hacker to take control of your computer.

With the exception of worms, viruses infect the computer only after you take some action to allow it to do so, such as viewing an e-mail file attachment. Virus authors make it difficult for you to know that such an action may be dangerous. For example, Trojan horse authors persuade individuals to download and install their malware by offering free or inexpensive software. Others send you e-mail attachments in hopes that you will open the attachment, and by doing so, install the virus. Determined virus authors have discovered ways to install a virus on your computer when you view a Web site designed to spread the virus. A Web site that spreads a virus is referred to as a ***poisoned Web site***.

Viruses take advantage of ***security holes***—vulnerabilities in an operating system or program that allow malware to infect a computer without your knowledge. As security holes are discovered, programmers work to write a ***patch***—a small repair to an operating system or program that closes a security hole. To receive the latest Windows 7 patches, be sure that Windows Update installs new updates every day. Many of these updates repair newly discovered security holes.

Be wary of all file attachments, even when they are from people that you know. Do not open any attachment that has the *.exe* file extension unless you are absolutely certain it is safe. Recall that files with this extension can install programs on your computer. Potentially dangerous files can be identified by their file extensions and are summarized in the table in Figure 10.2.

Potentially Dangerous File Types

File Extension	File Type
.exe	Program
.com	MS-DOS program
.pif	Shortcut to MS-DOS program
.bat	Batch file
.scr	Screen saver file

Figure 10.2

You should also install an ***antivirus program***—also referred to as a ***virus checker***. An antivirus program scans your computer for known viruses trying to get into your e-mail, operating system, or files, and attempts to disable and remove them from your computer. You should not install more than one antivirus program. Because of the way these programs work, installing more than one antivirus program could cause your computer to slow down or stop.

The companies that provide antivirus programs hire experts to look for new viruses. When a new virus is discovered, they write a new ***virus definition***. A virus definition is the information needed by the antivirus program to find and remove a virus. New virus definitions are written every day, and you should configure your antivirus program to download these new definitions daily. You should also configure your antivirus program to scan your computer daily or weekly. During the scan, the antivirus program looks at every file on your computer, and then compares your files with your virus definition files. If a match is found, the antivirus program will attempt to disable the virus.

Windows Update and an antivirus program cannot protect your computer completely. For example, a ***zero-day exploit*** is an attack that takes place shortly after a security hole is publicized for which no downloadable patch is yet available. Attackers take advantage of the small amount of time between an announcement of a security hole and the publication of a patch to fix it. Additionally, there is a lag between the time a virus is discovered and the time you scan your computer using its new definition file. For these reasons, you should be aware when the risk of a virus is present and take steps to prevent it from infecting your computer.

Be wary of files from peer-to-peer file sharing sites. ***Peer-to-peer file sharing sites*** let you share files such as music, videos, and software with others using the Internet. Virus authors often place infected files at these sites in hopes that you will download and thus install their virus.

Periodically check your computer's overall security settings. From the Control Panel, click System and Security, click Action Center, and then click the Security arrow. As shown in Figure 10.3, your firewall, virus protection, spyware protection, and automatic updating should be turned on. Internet security settings should be set to recommended levels, and User Account Control should be *On*.

Figure 10.3

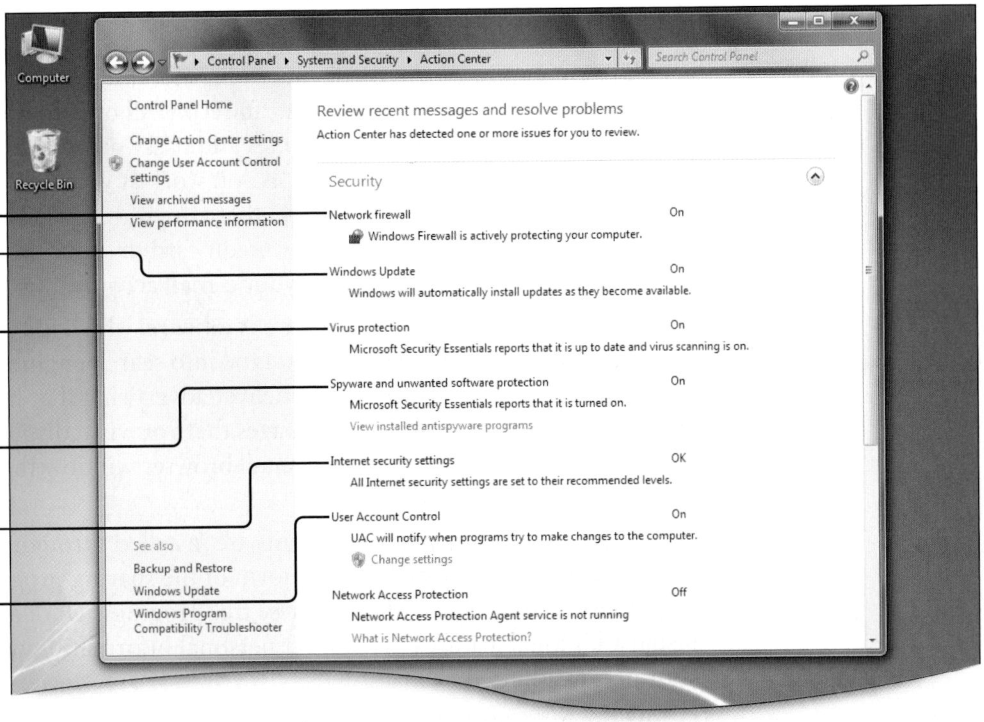

You can check to see what programs are installed by clicking *View installed antispyware programs*. An antispyware program called ***Windows Defender*** is included with all versions of Windows 7. Windows Defender alerts you when spyware attempts to install itself or run on your computer, alerts you when programs attempt to change important Windows settings, and scans your hard drive for spyware. If you are using ***Microsoft Security Essentials***—also referred to as ***MSE***—Windows Defender is built into the program, along with other Windows 7 antivirus and malware protection. Microsoft Security Essentials is a free downloadable program from Microsoft that guards against viruses, spyware, Trojans, ***rootkits***, and other malicious software. A rootkit is malware that enables continued administrator-level access to a computer and is typically hidden from the administrator and the operating system. MSE is always kept up to date, and some security professionals are comfortable recommending it as the only security software necessary on a personal PC. Always investigate the quality free security software available—such as MSE—before paying for such software.

To check how well you understand protecting your computer from viruses, take a moment to answer the following questions:

1. Viruses are commonly classified by the method they use to __________ other computers.
2. One type of malware is an e-mail __________ that, when opened, installs a virus.
3. To receive the latest Windows 7 security patches, be sure that __________ __________ regularly checks for and installs new updates.
4. You should configure your antivirus program to download new virus definitions every __________.
5. In a zero-day exploit, attackers take advantage of the time between the announcement of a security hole and the publication of a downloadable __________ to fix it.

Activity 10.02 | Protecting Your Computer from Spyware

Spyware programs can track your computer usage patterns in a variety of ways. A ***keystroke logger*** is a program that can record all of your keystrokes and then send your typed data—including user names and passwords—to someone else. Another type of spyware can capture your screens as you work at your computer and send the image files to someone else. The private data that a spyware program can capture enables unauthorized individuals to use your credit card to shop online, log on to your online bank accounts, or send spam using your e-mail account.

Another common type of spyware is ***adware***, which is a program that tracks the Web sites you visit and the terms you type into search engines. Adware programs then capture and use this information to deliver advertising that matches your interests. These customized ads appear on the Web pages that you visit, display as pop-ups, or are sent to your e-mail account. A pop-up is a small browser window that appears in addition to the Web page that you are viewing.

Recall that most spyware programs are installed through free software that you download and install, usually in the form of file sharing programs, browser toolbars, screen savers, and games. Most of these free programs work as intended, but they often install additional features that collect personal information without properly obtaining your permission to do so.

Before most programs are installed, the computer owner must agree with the program's terms of use and privacy policy. When a computer owner installs a desired program—a browser toolbar, for example—that contains a spyware component, the terms of use and privacy policy describe the personal information that it will collect, how the spyware will be installed, and how it may affect the computer. Because most people do not read these policies, and those who do find them difficult to understand, the computer owner often clicks to agree to the terms. The desired program is installed—along with its spyware features. The computer owner has unknowingly given the malware his or her permission to perform the various tasks described in the terms of use and privacy policy.

Included in many spyware terms of use policies is a clause that permits additional spyware to be installed without further permission from the computer owner. Marketing companies pay the original spyware company to install spyware programs for them. In this way, the number of spyware programs running on a single computer might increase. A computer that has been infected for several months may have so many spyware programs running that there are not enough computer resources to run other programs efficiently. When this happens, computer performance slows dramatically.

Because spyware's purpose is different than a virus, you need both an antivirus program and an ***antispyware program***. An antispyware program—also referred to as a ***spyware checker***—scans your computer for spyware and attempts to remove or disable it. Microsoft's free Microsoft Security Essentials includes a component that intercepts spyware before you install it. The program also scans your hard drive for spyware. Antispyware programs maintain a list of known spyware programs, and use this list to determine if you have spyware on your computer.

Installing additional antispyware programs can provide extra security, but check to be sure the programs are compatible. One antispyware program can detect spyware that another such program may miss. Just like antivirus programs, you should update their definitions and use them to perform scans at least once a week. Anti-malware programs such as Microsoft Security Essentials alert you when your spyware and other malware definitions are out of date, and when you have not performed a recent scan, as shown in Figure 10.4.

Figure 10.4

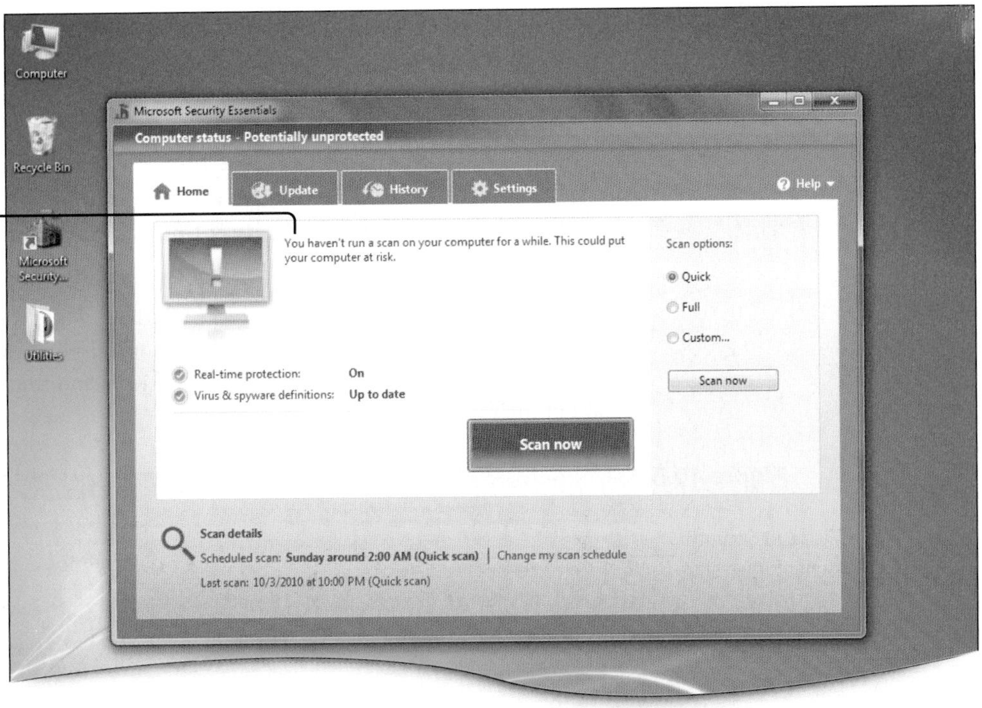

Security software alerts you that a scan is needed

You cannot rely solely on spyware checkers to prevent spyware. Before installing any free program from the Internet, ask this question: *Why is the program offered for free and are the creator's intentions good or bad*? Conduct an Internet search using the software name or publisher's name, and include the search term *spyware*. Use the search results to find out what other people's experiences have been with the program. If you decide to install the program, be sure to look through its terms of use and privacy policy. Look for what types of information will be collected, how it is collected, and whether or not additional programs can be installed without your consent. The best way to avoid malware is to exercise common sense when using the Internet.

To check how well you understand protecting your computer from spyware, take a moment to answer the following questions:

1. Adware programs track your browsing habits to deliver __________ that matches your interests.
2. Most spyware programs are installed through __________ software that you download and install.
3. Because spyware's purpose differs from that of a virus, you need an __________ program to check for viruses and an __________ program to check for spyware.
4. In the same manner as antivirus programs, you should update the __________ of your antispyware programs frequently.
5. If you decide to install a free program from the Internet, be sure to read through its terms of use and __________ policy.

Activity 10.03 | Installing and Configuring Microsoft Security Essentials to Protect Your Computer from Malware

Microsoft Security Essentials protects your computer from spyware, adware, rootkits, Trojans, and viruses. It is a free program, and after it is installed, it runs by default on all Windows 7 computers. Microsoft Security Essentials scans your computer to see if spyware or other malware has been installed. It can detect known spyware before it is installed and block it. It also prevents certain Web sites from performing dangerous actions from within Internet Explorer, such as running an executable file. In this activity, you will install Microsoft Security Essentials to protect your computer from malware.

1 Insert your USB flash drive, and close the AutoPlay dialog box if necessary. Open Internet Explorer, and then go to **www.microsoft.com** On the navigation bar at the top of the window, point to **Security & Updates**, and then click **Microsoft Security Essentials**. Scroll down to see a description of the program, and then compare your screen with Figure 10.5.

On the Microsoft Security Essentials page, you can read a product description, watch a video that shows you how to install the program, and find links to more information about malware.

Figure 10.5

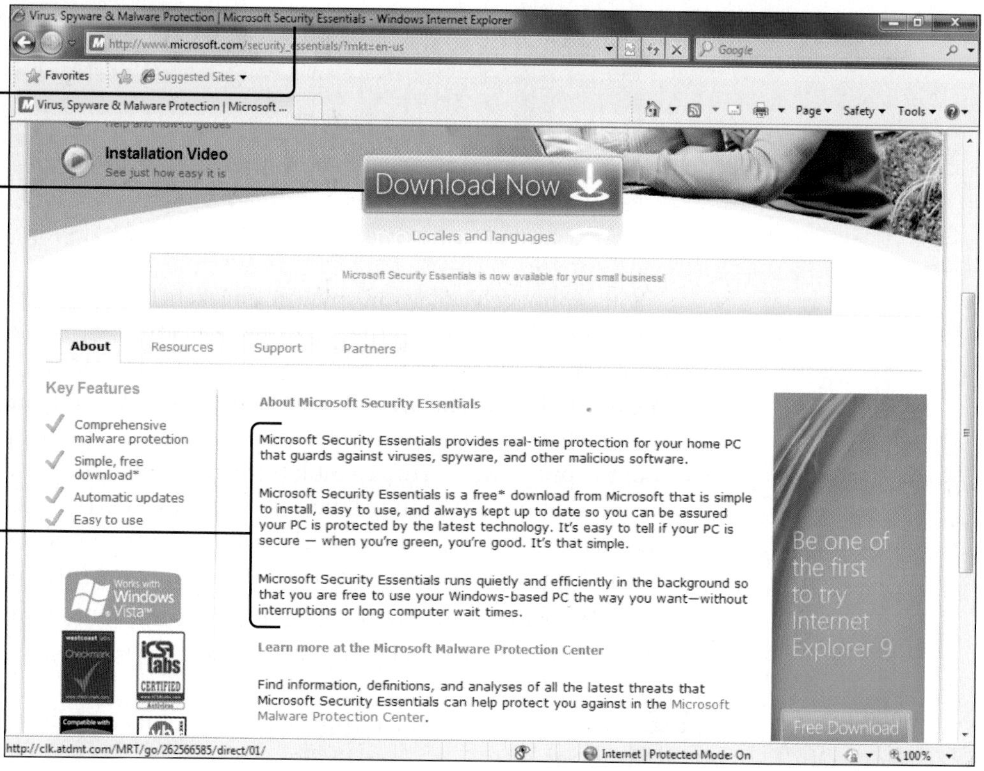

Alert! | Do You Already Have an Antivirus Program Installed?

To complete this activity, you will either install Microsoft Security Essentials, or if you already have Microsoft Security Essentials installed, you will refer to it. If you have another antivirus software program installed, do not attempt to install Microsoft Security Essentials—just read through the information. Running multiple antivirus programs can cause your computer to slow down, and may cause other problems. If you have other antivirus programs installed, you might consider uninstalling them and using Microsoft Security Essentials exclusively.

2 If you already have Microsoft Security Essentials installed, close your Web browser, **Start** Microsoft Security Essentials, and then move to Step 7. Otherwise, in the Microsoft Security Essentials window, click **Download Now**. In the **File Download** dialog box, click **Run**. If the User Account Control dialog box displays, click Yes to continue the installation.

3 When the Microsoft Security Essentials installation wizard displays, compare your screen with Figure 10.6, and then click **Next**.

Figure 10.6

Microsoft Security Essentials Installation Wizard

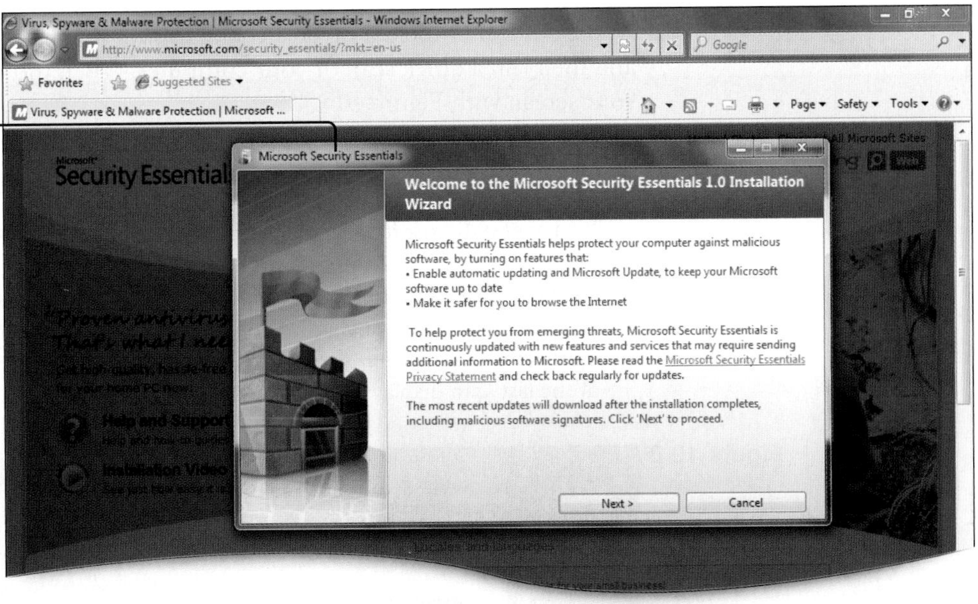

4 When the Microsoft Security Essentials License Agreement displays, click **I accept**, and then when the **Ready to install Microsoft Security Essentials** screen displays, click **Install**.

When the installation is complete, a dialog box displays, asking if you want to scan your computer.

5 Be sure the *Scan my computer* check box is selected, as shown in Figure 10.7.

Figure 10.7

Microsoft Security Essentials successfully installed

Scan my computer check box selected

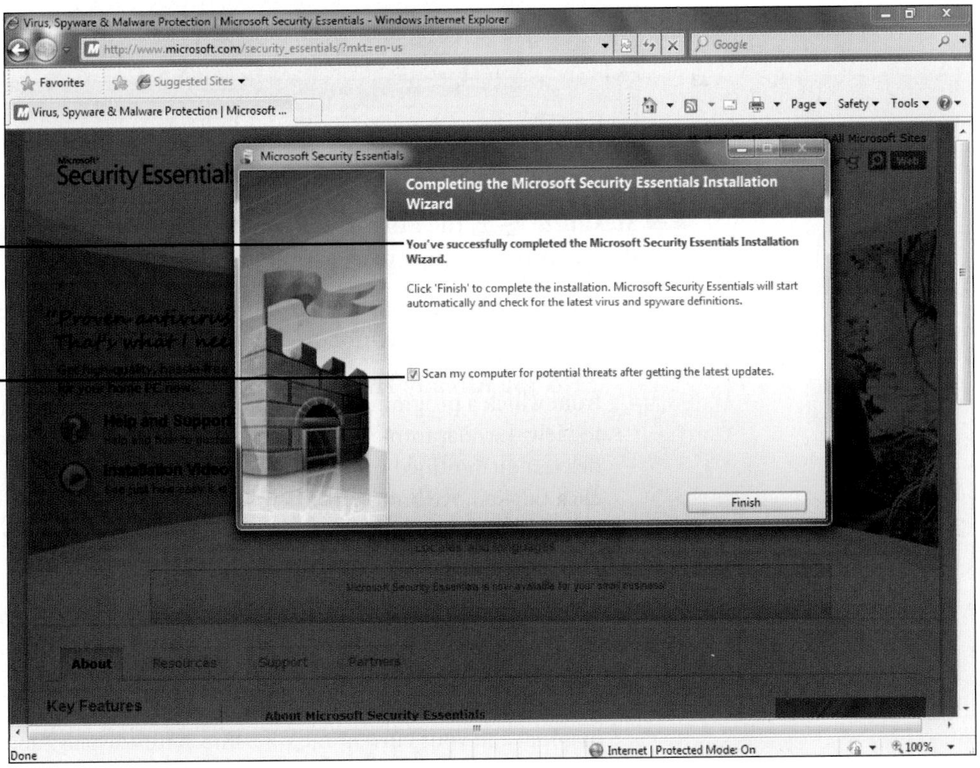

6 At the bottom of the dialog box, click **Finish**, which will update the virus definitions, and then run a quick scan of your computer. When the scan is complete, compare your screen with Figure 10.8.

The scan may take several minutes. If no malware is detected, Microsoft Security Essentials displays a message with a white check mark on a green background.

By default, Microsoft Security Essentials downloads updated definitions and performs a quick scan of your computer every day. The default settings will probably provide adequate protection for your computer. A ***quick scan*** checks the areas on your hard drive where malware programs are most likely to reside. A ***full scan*** checks every file on your hard drive(s). A ***custom scan*** searches only those drives or folders that you select. The date of the last scan displays at the bottom of the dialog box.

Figure 10.8

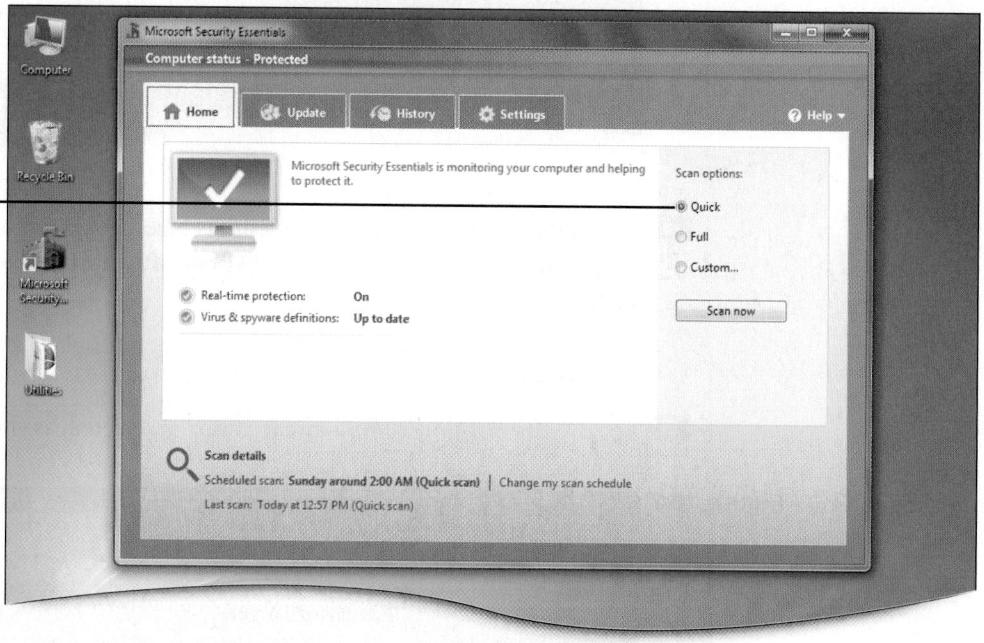

7 **Maximize** the **Microsoft Security Essentials** window, click the **History tab**, and then compare your screen with Figure 10.9.

If malware is detected, Microsoft Security Essentials provides options to quarantine or remove it. When Microsoft Security Essentials deletes a program, it places a copy in a ***quarantine area***. A quarantine area is another designated location on your computer from which a program cannot run. Placing the program in the quarantine area allows you to view the quarantined programs before they are permanently deleted. To permanently delete a quarantined program, select the check box to the left of the deleted item, and then click the Remove button. If Microsoft Security Essentials quarantined the program by mistake, you can select the item, and then click the Restore button. The program will be moved from the quarantine area.

The decisions that you make on this screen are sent to ***Microsoft SpyNet***, which is an online community that collects information about the decisions you and others make regarding spyware identified by Microsoft Security Essentials. Sharing such information helps to keep your malware definitions up to date. Membership in Microsoft SpyNet is optional and your current membership status displays above the list of quarantined items.

Figure 10.9

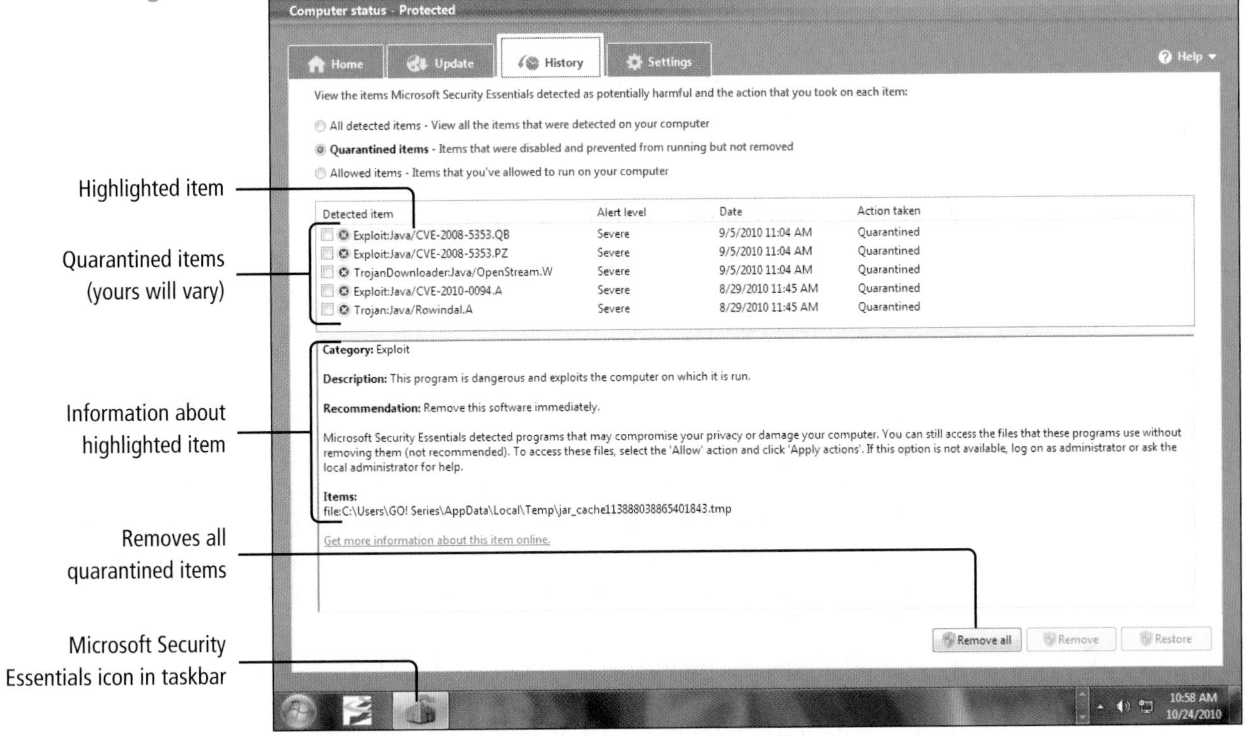

8 In the **Microsoft Security Essentials** dialog box, click the **Settings tab**. On the left side, be sure *Scheduled scan* is selected. If necessary, select the *Run a scheduled scan on my computer* check box.

9 Under **When**, click the **arrow**, and then click **Wednesday**. Under **Around**, click the **arrow**, and then click **10:00 PM**.

10 **Start** the **Snipping Tool** program, click the **New arrow**, and then click **Full-screen Snip**. In the **Snipping Tool** mark-up window, click the **Save Snip** button.

11 In the **Save As** dialog box, in the **navigation pane**, scroll down as necessary, and then under **Computer** click your USB flash drive so that it displays in the **address bar**. On the toolbar, click the **New folder** button, type **Windows 7 Chapter 10** and press Enter.

12 In the **file list**, double-click your **Windows 7 Chapter 10** folder to open it. Click in the **File name** box, and then replace the selected text by typing **Lastname_Firstname_10A_Scan_Snip** Be sure the file type is **JPEG file**, and then press Enter. **Close** the **Snipping Tool** mark-up window. Hold this file until you finish Project 10A.

13 Change the day and time of the scheduled scan to run at an appropriate time for you, and then click **Save changes**.

14 **Close** **Microsoft Security Essentials**, and then **Close** any other open windows.

More Knowledge | Using Other Programs to Protect Against Malware

Consider adding one or two antispyware programs in addition to Microsoft Security Essentials. Beware of spyware checkers found by searching on the Internet. Many of these do not remove spyware and are themselves spyware! Consult a reputable review of programs, such as reviews found on www.cnet.com or www.bestcovery.com or consider one of the following:

- Ad-Aware, http://www.lavasoft.com
- Bit Defender, http://www.bitdefender.com
- Malwarebytes Anti-Malware, http://www.malwarebytes.org
- Spybot Search & Destroy, http://www.safer-networking.org
- Trend Micro HijackThis, http://www.trendmicro.com

Objective 2 | Secure Internet Explorer

Web sites deliver content that enables Web pages to be interactive, entertaining, and useful. Features embedded in the Internet Explorer Web browser take advantage of this type of ***Web content***. Web content is anything that you download and use on a Web page, such as an HTML code file, pictures, small programs, and animations. Unfortunately, malware authors use certain types of Web content to install harmful programs on computers, collect private information, or place pop-up windows on your screen. Internet Explorer has several features to protect your computer from harmful Web content. Internet Explorer's security and privacy features can be set to a level of protection that best meets your needs.

Activity 10.04 | Setting Security Levels in Internet Explorer

Recall that programs downloaded from a Web page may actually be malware. Another type of potentially dangerous Web content is a ***script***. A script is a program that runs in the browser to add interactive content to the Web page. For example, a script may display a clock showing your local time or it may inform you when you forget to fill out a box on a form. Some scripts are designed to install malware without your knowledge when you are viewing a poisoned Web page containing the script.

Another type of potentially dangerous Web content is an ActiveX control. Recall that an ActiveX control is a type of add-on that uses ActiveX technology. An ActiveX control allows another program to run from within Internet Explorer. For example, when you use Internet Explorer to check for Windows updates, the Windows Update Web site uses an ActiveX control to complete the update process using Internet Explorer. A poisoned Web page may use an ActiveX control to install malware or take control of your computer.

In this activity, you will practice setting a high level of security for Internet Explorer to protect your computer from potentially harmful Web content.

Another Way

Display the Control Panel, click Network and Internet, and then click Internet Options.

1. **Start** the **Control Panel**. With the insertion point blinking in the search box, type **internet options** Then, click **Internet Options** to display the **Internet Properties** dialog box. Click the **Security tab**, and then compare your screen with Figure 10.10.

   Internet Explorer divides Web content into four zones so that you can set a different level of security for each zone. You control the security level given to a Web site by placing it in one of these zones. Any Web site not assigned to a zone is a member of the Internet zone.

   By default, the Internet zone has Protected Mode enabled. Recall that Protected Mode is a feature in Internet Explorer that makes it more difficult for malicious software to be installed on your computer by preventing a downloaded program from making any direct changes to the system.

   Protected Mode protects you from ***drive-by downloads***. A drive-by download is a program installed from a poisoned Web site—without your knowledge—caused by just visiting the site; you do not have to click on any particular link to cause the download. Drive-by downloads are a common method used to install malware on computers. When Protected Mode is enabled, Internet Explorer displays a message when any program is about to be installed while you are browsing. The installation will continue only if you give it permission. In this way, you are made aware when a drive-by download attempts to install a program on your computer.

Figure 10.10

Internet Properties dialog box

Search box

Protected Mode active by default

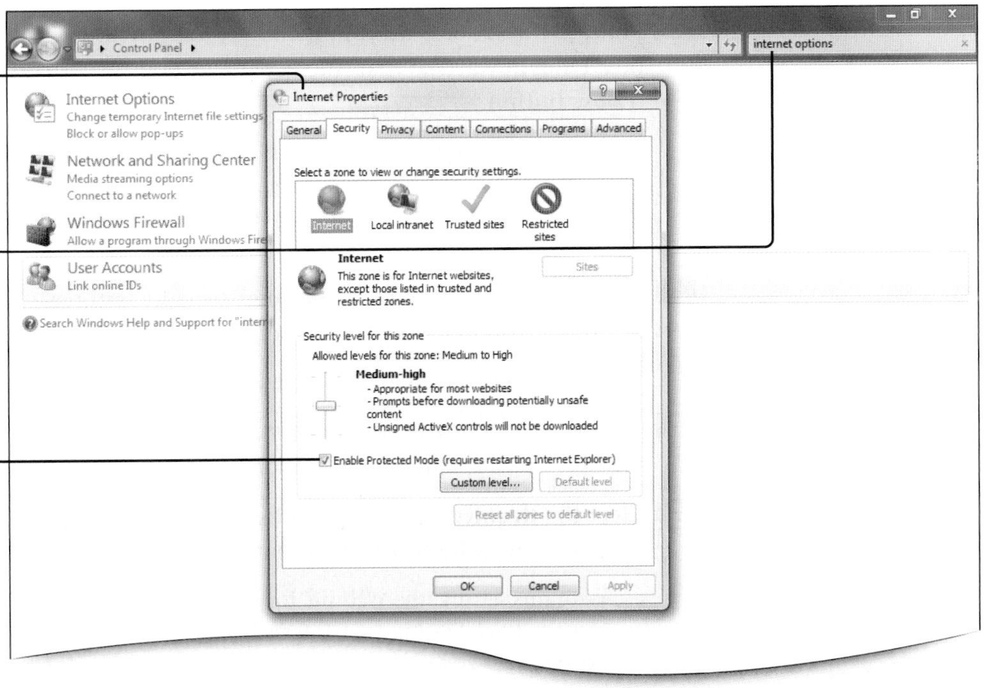

2 Take a moment to study the table in Figure 10.11 to determine how to protect your computer from harmful Web content.

To protect your computer from harmful Web content, Internet Explorer enables you to assign one of up to five preset security levels for each zone.

Internet Explorer Security Levels	
Low	Files are downloaded without prompts. Scripts and ActiveX controls are run without prompts. This level is available only in the *Local intranet* and *Trusted sites* zones and is appropriate only for sites that you trust absolutely.
Medium-low	Files can be downloaded and scripts can be run. All but ***unsigned ActiveX controls*** are run without prompts. An unsigned ActiveX control is one whose source cannot be verified. This level is available only in the *Local intranet* and *Trusted sites* zones and is appropriate for the *Local* ***intranet*** zone. An intranet is a Web site that serves computers on your local area network, and is not available to the general Internet user.
Medium	Files can be downloaded. This level prompts you before running potentially unsafe scripts and ActiveX controls. This level is the default level for the Trusted sites zone.
Medium-high	Files can be downloaded, but display a prompt before you are able to do so. This level is the same as the Medium level, but it classifies a wider range of scripts and ActiveX controls as unsafe. This level is the default level for the Internet zone.
High	No files can be downloaded. This level disables all file downloads, scripts, and ActiveX controls. This is the only setting available for the Restricted sites zone.

Figure 10.11

3 Point to the slider button in the lower left portion of the **Internet Properties** dialog box. Drag upward so that the security level displays as **High**, and then release the left mouse button.

In this manner, the security level for the Internet zone is changed. All Web sites in the Internet zone will be assigned the High security level. With this high security level, some Web sites will not work correctly. For this reason, sites that you trust should be added to the Trusted sites zone.

4 Under **Select a zone to view or change security settings**, click **Trusted sites**. Use the technique you just practiced to set the security level to **Medium-low**.

All Web sites added to the Trusted sites zone will be given the Medium-low security level.

5 Click the **Sites** button. With your insertion point blinking in the **Add this website to the zone** box, type **update.microsoft.com**

6 Clear the **Require server verification (https:) for all sites in this zone** check box, and then click the **Add** button. Compare your screen with Figure 10.12.

With this setting, the Web site for Windows Update will be assigned the Medium-low security level. Setting your Internet zone to High and then adding sites you trust to the Trusted sites zone is a very high level of security for Internet Explorer. All Web sites will be assigned the high level of security except for those you specifically add to the Trusted sites zone.

Figure 10.12

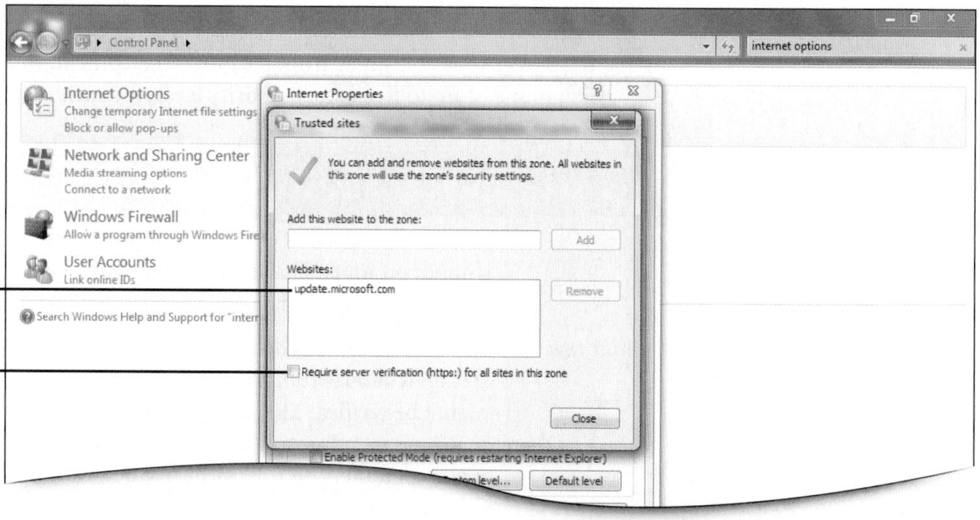

7 **Start** the **Snipping Tool** program, click the **New arrow**, and then click **Full-screen Snip**. In the **Snipping Tool** mark-up window, click the **Save Snip** button.

8 In the **Save As** dialog box, in the **navigation pane**, scroll down as necessary, and then under **Computer**, click your USB flash drive so that it displays in the address bar. Navigate to your **Windows 7 Chapter 10** folder, and then as the file name, type **Lastname_Firstname_10A_Trusted_Sites_Snip** Be sure the file type is **JPEG file**, and then press Enter. **Close** the **Snipping Tool** mark-up window. Hold this file until you finish Project 10A.

9 In the **Trusted sites** dialog box, click **update.microsoft.com**, click the **Remove** button, and then click the **Close** button.

10 In the **Internet Properties** dialog box, click the **Reset all zones to default level** button.

This technique changes the security levels for each zone back to their original levels, but it does not remove any sites that you may have added to each zone.

11 **Close** the **Internet Properties** dialog box, and then **Close** the **Control Panel** window.

> More Knowledge | **Maintaining the Restricted Sites Web Content Zone**
>
> Recall that the Restricted sites zone is assigned the highest security level. To add a site to the Restricted sites zone, you must add one site at a time using the same technique used to add a site to the Trusted sites zone. Managing a list of restricted sites in this manner would be very time consuming. There are programs that can add sites to the Restricted sites zone for you. For example, the program IE-SPYAD will add a list of dangerous Web sites to your Restricted sites zone for you. IE-SPYAD can be downloaded from *www.spywarewarrior.com*.

Activity 10.05 | Managing Privacy with Internet Explorer

Internet Explorer privacy settings control how Web sites collect information when you browse the Internet. Web sites place small text files called cookies on your computer's hard drive. Recall that a cookie is a small text file that Web sites put on your computer to store information about you and your preferences, such as login information. When you shop online, for example, the items placed in your shopping cart are usually stored in a cookie until you start the checkout process.

Cookies can also track which pages you visit at a site, and how long you spend viewing each page. This information helps Web site designers improve their sites. In these ways, cookies are very useful.

Cookies can also be used to collect personal information without your knowledge. This is done by using a ***third-party cookie***, which is a cookie created by a Web site other than the Web site you are currently viewing. Marketing companies pay Web sites to let them write cookies. The marketing company pays hundreds of Web sites in this manner. This enables the marketing company to use a single, third-party cookie to track your surfing habits across many different Web sites. Most marketing companies use the information stored in third-party cookies to provide banner ads that match your interests as indicated by your surfing habits. Other marketing companies create a profile about you and your surfing habits to target marketing efforts and to sell to other marketing companies.

Using Internet Explorer privacy tools, you can set a privacy level that determines what types of cookies are accepted by Internet Explorer. Many individuals find that all cookies are an invasion of their personal privacy, and they set a privacy level that blocks them. Others allow all cookies except for third-party cookies. Others prefer to accept all cookies. You can also use Internet Explorer to view a Web site's Privacy Summary. Based on the Privacy Summary, you can choose to enable or disable that site from writing cookies. In this activity, you will view a Privacy Summary, and then practice changing Internet Explorer's privacy protection settings.

1 **Start** **Internet Explorer**, and then navigate to **http://www.usa.gov** If necessary, Maximize the Internet Explorer window.

> **Another Way**
>
> In any Internet Explorer window, on the Command bar, click Tools, click Internet Options, and then display the Privacy tab.

2 In the upper right corner of the **Internet Explorer** window, on the **Command bar**, click the **Safety** button. On the displayed **Safety** menu, click **Webpage Privacy Policy**.

3 Scroll through the list and notice that most of the Web content on this page comes from the *www.usa.gov* Web server.

A second Web server, such as a marketing company's server, must be used to write third-party cookies. If only one Web server is listed, third-party cookies would not be possible. When other Web sites are listed, be sure that they are sites that you trust to store information about you.

4 Under **Websites with content on the current page**, in the **Site** column, click **http://www.usa.gov/**, and then click the **Summary** button. Scroll through the displayed **Privacy Summary** for this Web page, and then compare your screen with Figure 10.13.

The Privacy Policy dialog box displays the site's ***Privacy Summary*** and displays options for allowing cookies. A Privacy Summary is a special Web page that summarizes a Web site's privacy policy in a simple, easy to understand format. Privacy Summaries enable you to make an informed decision as to whether you want to accept cookies from a Web site.

Web sites are not required to provide a Privacy Summary. When no Privacy Summary is available, you must view the site's official privacy policy. A link to a site's privacy policy is commonly provided at the bottom of a Web site's home page.

Figure 10.13

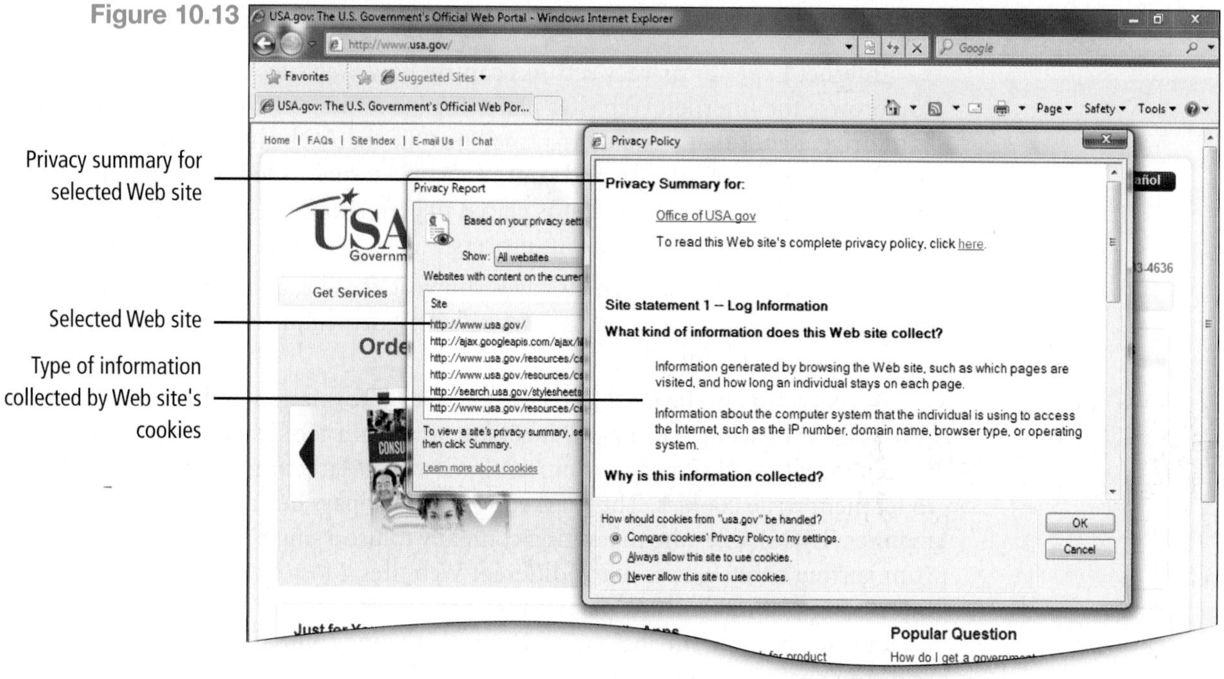

5 Under **How should cookies from "usa.gov" be handled?**, click the **Always allow this site to use cookies** option button, and then click **OK**.

The www.usa.gov Web site will always be able to store cookies on your hard drive.

6 In the **Privacy Report** dialog box, click the **Settings** button.

The Internet Options dialog box displays with the Privacy tab active. Here you can change your overall privacy level and add sites to your *allow* list. The default privacy setting is *Medium*, which blocks cookies that collect information that could be used to contact you.

7 Point to the slider button, and drag up until the privacy level indicates **High**.

This level blocks all cookies except for the sites that you add to your list of allowed sites.

8 Click the **Sites** button, and then compare your screen with Figure 10.14.

The Per Site Privacy Actions dialog box lists all of the sites that are allowed to write cookies and all sites that are explicitly blocked from writing cookies. The *usa.gov* site was added to your list of managed Web sites as an allowed site. Because your privacy setting is currently set to High, the only Web site that can place cookies on your computer is *www.usa.gov*. All other Web sites are blocked until you add them to your allow list. Allowing sites to write cookies only when they are listed in your allowed sites list is a very high level of privacy.

Figure 10.14

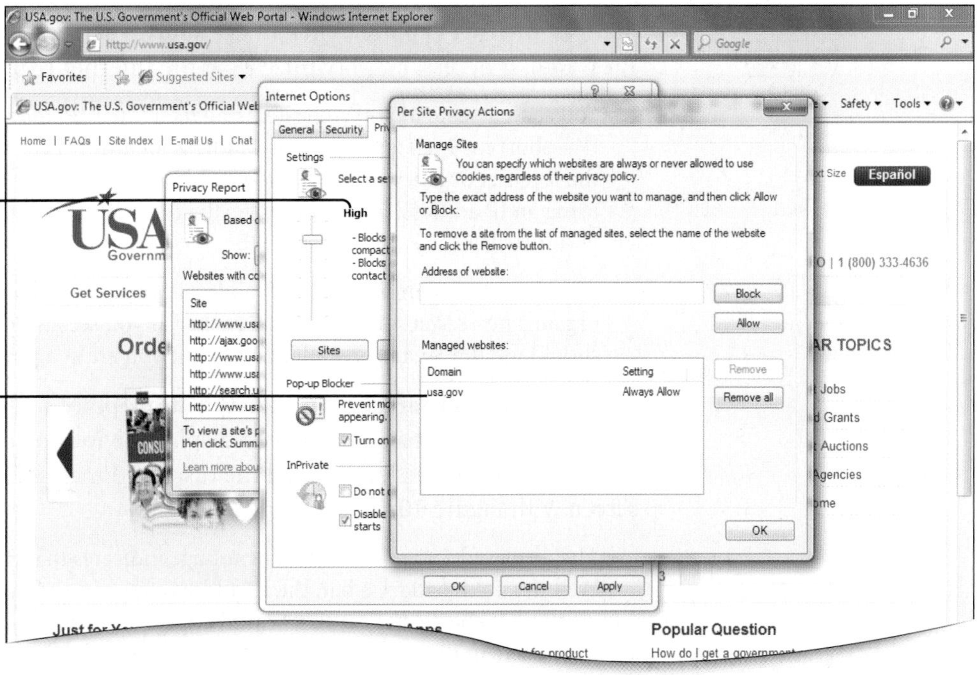

9 **Start** the **Snipping Tool** program, click the **New arrow**, and then click **Full-screen Snip**. In the **Snipping Tool** mark-up window, click the **Save Snip** button.

10 In the **Save As** dialog box, in the **navigation pane**, scroll down as necessary, and then under **Computer**, click your USB flash drive so that it displays in the address bar. Navigate to your **Windows 7 Chapter 10** folder, and then as the file name, type **Lastname_Firstname_10A_Cookies_Snip** Be sure the file type is **JPEG file**, and then press Enter. **Close** the **Snipping Tool** mark-up window. Hold this file until you finish Project 10A.

11 Under **Managed websites**, click **usa.gov**, click the **Remove** button, and then click **OK**.

12 In the **Internet Options** dialog box, click the **Default** button to return to the default privacy setting.

13 **Close** the **Internet Options** dialog box, and then **Close** all open dialog boxes and windows.

Activity 10.06 | Using Pop-up Blockers and SmartScreen Filters to Protect Your System

Recall that a pop-up is a small Web browser window that displays in addition to the Web page you are viewing, and which is often created by an advertiser. Internet Explorer can filter these pop-ups according to your preferences. Recall that a phishing Web site poses as a legitimate Web site to acquire sensitive personal information. A phishing site often hides the Web site's domain name, and displays pictures from the legitimate organization's Web site. Internet Explorer has tools to help you determine if you are at a phishing Web site. In this activity, you will practice using Internet Explorer's SmartScreen filter to determine if a Web site is a phishing site, and then practice setting Internet Explorer's Pop-up Blocker settings.

1 **Start** **Internet Explorer**, click in the **address bar**, and then type **140.90.113.200** Press Enter. If necessary, Maximize the Internet Explorer window.

You can navigate to any Web site using its unique ***IP address*** instead of its URL. An IP—short for Internet Protocol—address identifies a computer that is connected to the Internet or a network. On the World Wide Web, each URL is assigned to a server using an IP address. In this instance, the IP address of the Web server with the URL *www.weather.gov* is 140.90.113.200.

Phishing sites often display an IP address because they cannot display the URL of the real organization's Web site in the address bar. If you see an IP address instead of a URL, you should use the SmartScreen Filter to see if you are at a phishing site.

2 On the **Command bar**, click the **Safety** button, point to **SmartScreen Filter**, and then click **Check This Website**. If a screen displays giving you a link to the *Internet Explorer privacy statement*, click OK. Read the displayed message, and then compare your screen with Figure 10.15.

The displayed SmartScreen Filter message indicates that the site is not a reported phishing Web site. In the address bar, the IP address displays instead of the site's URL. If this was a phishing Web site, the content would appear similar but you would actually be viewing a page from an illegitimate Web server.

Figure 10.15

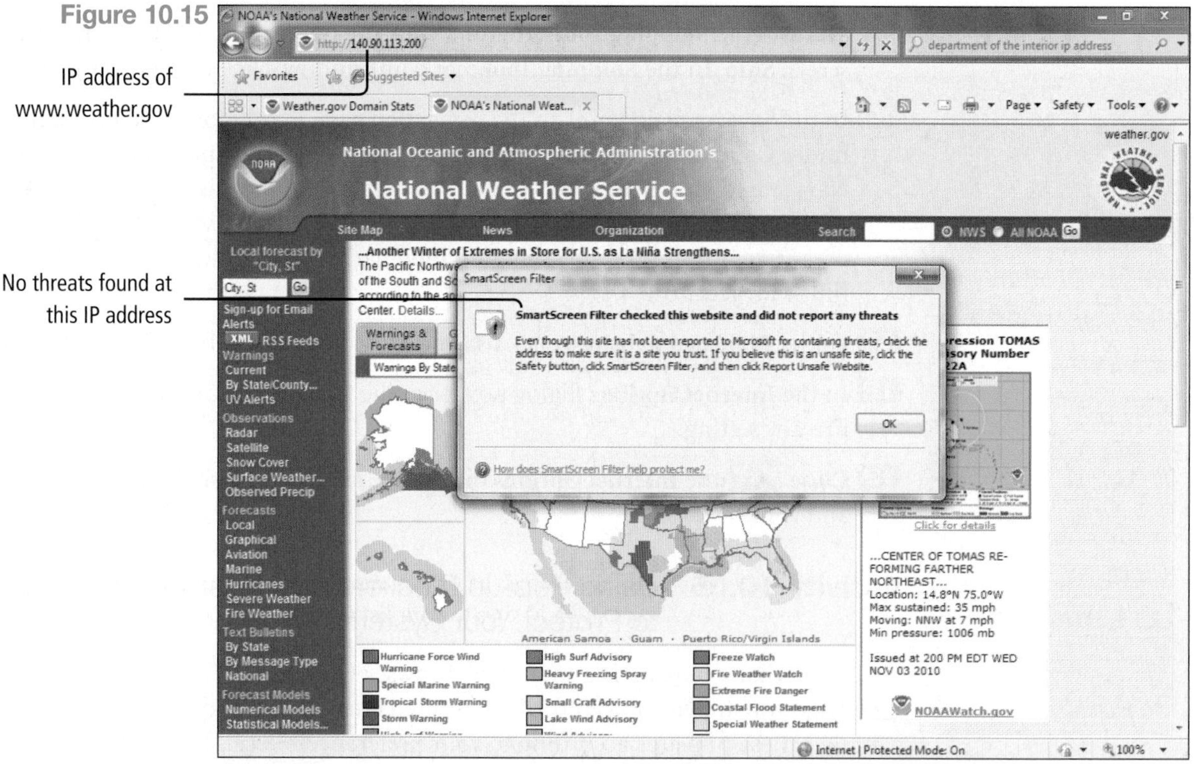

3 Click **OK** to close the message. On the **Command bar**, click the **Safety** button, point to **SmartScreen Filter**, and then click **Report Unsafe Website**. **Maximize** the Feedback window, and then compare your screen with Figure 10.16.

This feature enables you to report suspected phishing Web sites. The site IP address displays near the top of the window. To complete the report, you have to answer a few questions. Recall that this site is *not* an actual phishing Web site.

Figure 10.16

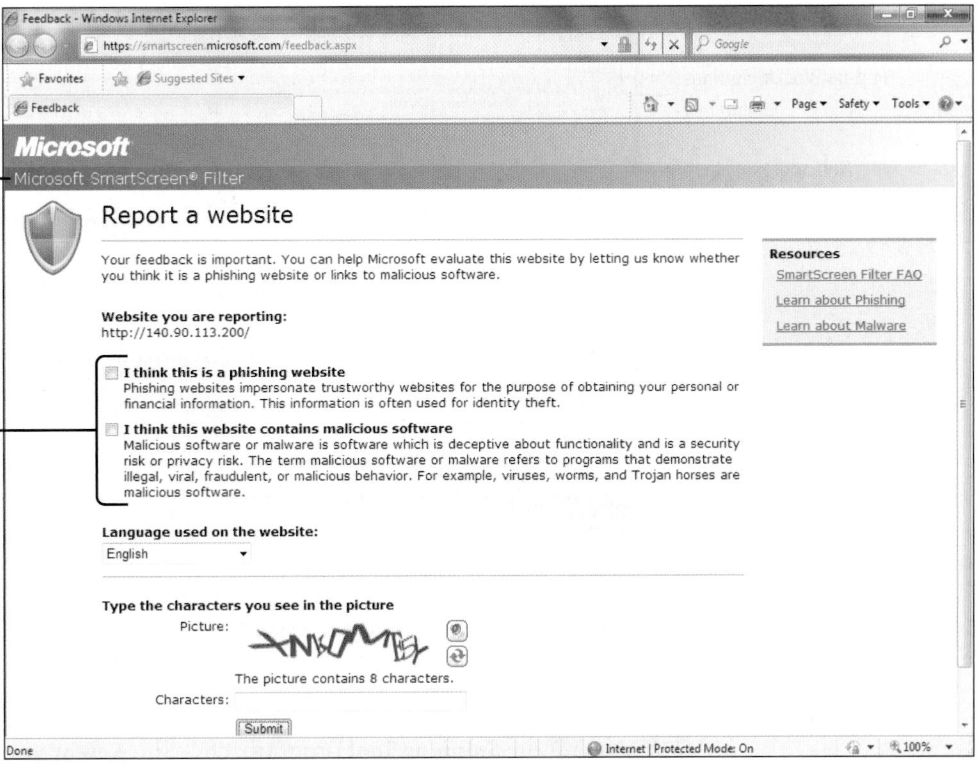

Microsoft SmartScreen Filter window

Enables you to report suspicious Web sites

4 **Close** the **Feedback** window without submitting this site. Click in the **address bar**, type **www.weather.gov** and then press Enter.

The same page displays, but now the address bar displays the Web site's URL. The *.gov* portion of the URL confirms that this page is coming from a government Web server.

5 On the **Command bar**, click the **Tools** button, point to **Pop-up Blocker**, and then observe the status of Internet Explorer's **Pop-up Blocker**. If *Turn On Pop-up Blocker* displays, click it to turn on the Pop-up Blocker.

Another Way

Display the Internet Options dialog box, click the Privacy tab, click the Settings button, and then under Pop-up Blocker, click Settings.

6 On the **Command bar**, click the **Tools** button, point to **Pop-up Blocker**, and then click **Pop-up Blocker Settings**.

7 At the bottom of the **Pop-up Blocker Settings** dialog box, click the **Blocking level arrow**, and then compare your screen with Figure 10.17.

The Pop-up Blocker Settings dialog box enables you to change your overall pop-up blocker filter level and add sites to your list of allowed sites. Other options enable you to change how you are notified when a pop-up is blocked.

The highest level blocks all pop-ups, even when the pop-up is needed to make the site run correctly. The medium level prevents most advertising pop-ups, and the low level allows pop-ups from all sites that Internet Explorer identifies as safe Web sites.

Figure 10.17

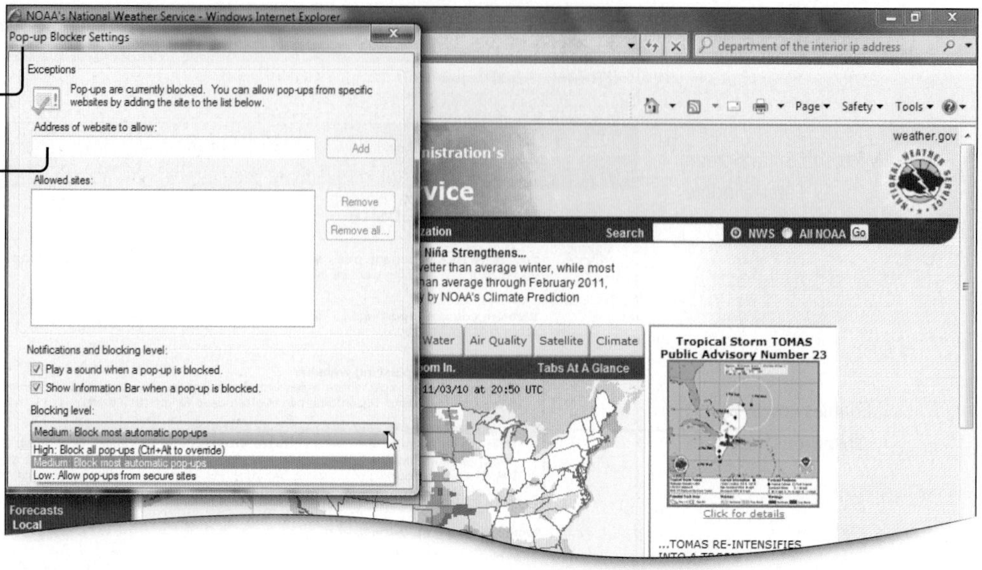

8 Click in the **Address of website to allow** box, and then type **www.weather.gov** Notice that Internet Explorer's AutoComplete feature displays the domain name as you type. Click the **Add** button.

9 **Start** the **Snipping Tool** program, click the **New arrow**, and then click **Full-screen Snip**. In the **Snipping Tool** mark-up window, click the **Save Snip** button.

10 In the **Save As** dialog box, in the **navigation pane**, scroll down as necessary, and then under **Computer**, click your USB flash drive so that it displays in the address bar. Navigate to your **Windows 7 Chapter 10** folder, and then as the file name, type **Lastname_Firstname_10A_Popups_Snip** Be sure the file type is **JPEG file**, and then press Enter. **Close** the **Snipping Tool** mark-up window. Hold this file until you finish Project 10A.

11 In the **Pop-up Blocker Settings** dialog box, under **Allowed sites**, click **www.weather.gov**, and then click the **Remove** button.

12 **Close** the **Pop-up Blocker Settings** dialog box, and then **Close** **Internet Explorer**.

As you gain experience with Windows 7, you can use these techniques to check if a site is a phishing Web site or to change how Internet Explorer handles pop-ups.

More Knowledge | Using Secure http to Send Private Information to a Web Server

Secure http, also known as ***https***, is a protocol that encrypts the data sent between you and a Web server. Recall that to encrypt a file is to scramble the file so that others cannot view its data. Recall also that malicious individuals can intercept data sent over the Internet. When data that is encrypted by https is transmitted, malicious individuals are unable to decipher the data.

Whenever you are filling out sensitive information on a Web page, you should be sure that secure http will be used to send your data to the server. For example, secure http should be used during the checkout process when shopping online. You can tell that secure http is being used because *https* displays before the URL in the browser's address bar instead of *http*. In the right edge of the address bar, a locked padlock also indicates when secure http will be used to encrypt the data.

Objective 3 | Set Parental Controls

Computers and the Internet have become a part of everyday life for many children. Parents are aware that unsupervised computer use may not always be in the child's best interests. To help parents protect children from the potential dangers of computer use, Windows 7 provides the Parental Controls control panel.

Activity 10.07 | Setting Parental Controls

Parental Controls help parents manage how their children use the computer. For example, parents can block Web sites, set times when a child can log on to the computer, or control which games and applications a child can open. Parental Controls also provide an activity report, which details a child's computer use, including a list of Web sites visited, what files were downloaded, and what times a child was logged on to the computer. In this activity, you will practice using Parental Controls by creating a new user account and then setting parental controls for that account.

> **Alert! | Are Parental Controls Unavailable?**
>
> The Parental Controls feature is not available in the Business and Enterprise Editions of Windows 7.

1 **Start** the **Control Panel**. Under **User Accounts and Family Safety**, click **Set up parental controls for any user**. If necessary, in the User Account Control dialog box, click Yes.

> **Another Way**
>
> From Control Panel, click User Accounts and Family Safety, and then click Parental Controls.

2 At the bottom of the **Parental Controls** window, click **Create a new user account**. In the **New account name** box, type the initial of your first name, your own last name, and then an underscore followed by the text *Child*—for example, **FLastname_Child** Click the **Create account** button.

Windows 7 enables you to set parental controls for standard user accounts only, because an account with administrator privileges can disable parental controls.

3 Under **Users**, click the new account. Under **Parental Controls**, click the **On, enforce current settings** option button, and then compare your screen with Figure 10.18.

The parental controls for the child's account are enabled and the Windows Settings area is enabled. Under Current Settings, all areas are set to Off.

> **Alert! | Do You Have Windows Live Installed?**
>
> If you have Windows Live installed, a *Sign in to Windows Live Family Safety* dialog box displays when you click the new user name. Click Cancel, and then under *Additional controls*, in the *Select a Provider* box, select (None). Click the new user name again.

Figure 10.18

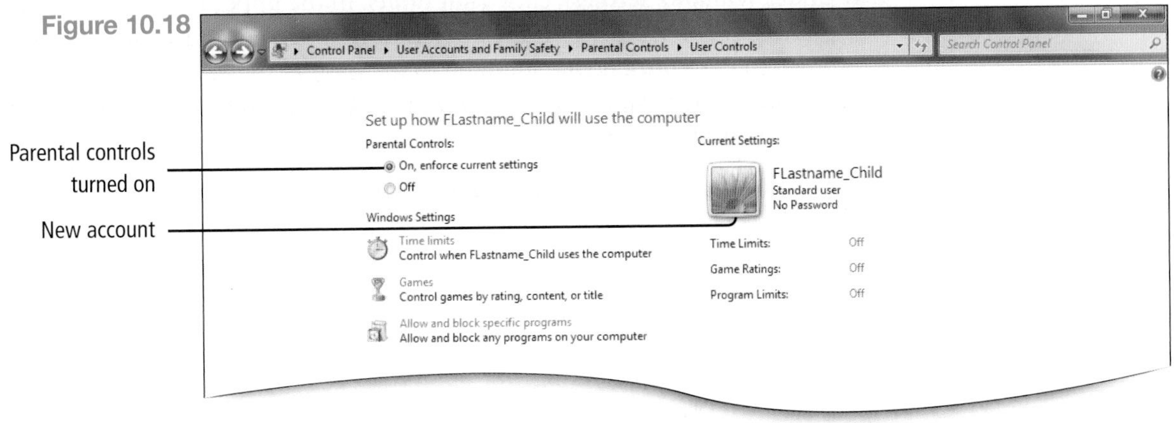

4 Under **Windows Settings**, click **Allow and block specific programs**. Under **Which programs can FLastname_Child use?**, click the **FLastname_Child can only use the programs I allow** option button. When the program has finished cataloging the programs on your computer, if necessary scroll to the bottom of the window, click the **Check All** button, scroll down to display the programs in *C:\Program Files\Microsoft Office\Office 14*, and then compare your screen with Figure 10.19.

The program may take several minutes to catalog all of the programs on your computer. After the programs are displayed, you can check the ones you want your child to use, or check all of the programs, and then clear the check boxes for those programs you do not want him or her to use.

Figure 10.19

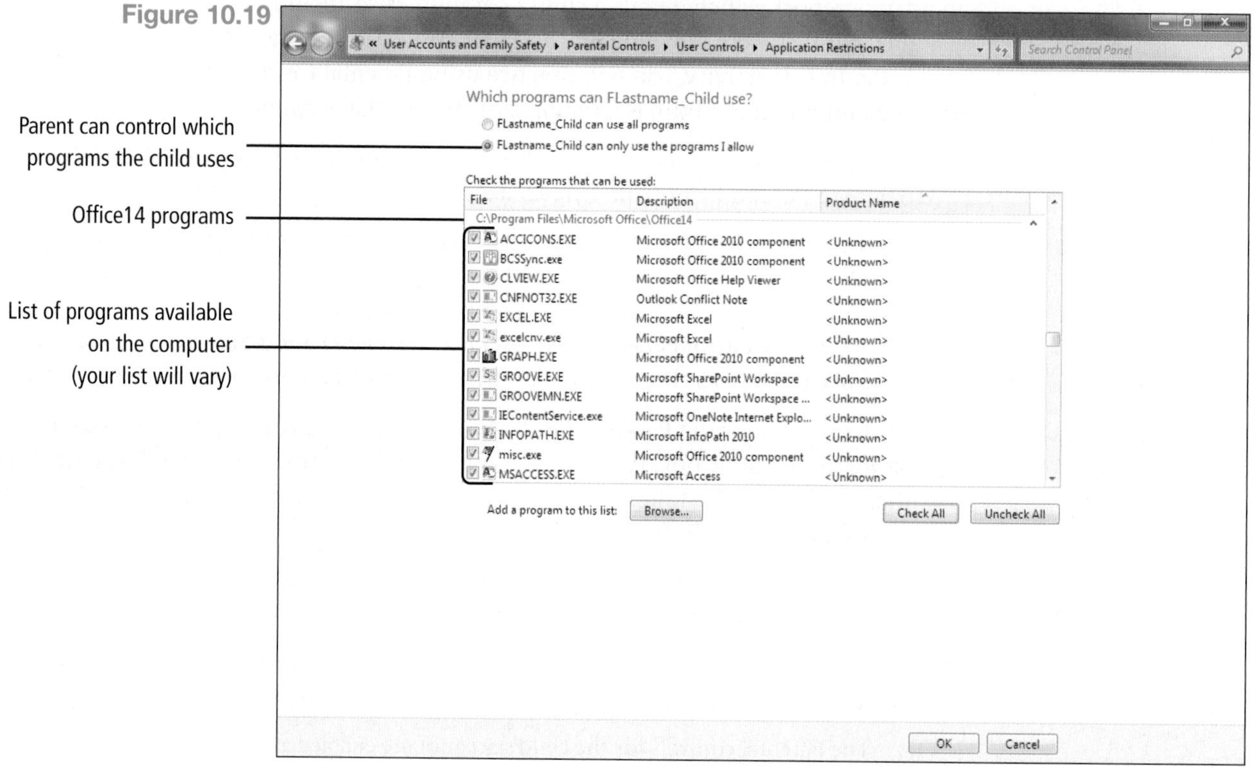

5 Under **Check the programs that can be used**, scroll down to locate **OUTLOOK.EXE**, and then clear the check box to the left of that program. Click **OK** to close the Application Restrictions window. Notice that under Current Settings, *Program Limits* are now *On*.

The child is now restricted from using Outlook. In the same manner, you can allow or block any programs you want.

6 Under **Windows Settings**, click **Time limits**. In the upper left corner of the time grid, point to the first block—at the intersection of **Sunday** and **12 Midnight (AM)**. Drag down to the **Saturday row** and then to the right to the **8 AM** grid line and release the button. Use the same technique to restrict **10** PM to **12** PM. Compare your screen with Figure 10.20.

With the current setting, the child will not be able to log on to the computer between 10:00 p.m. and 8:00 a.m. In this manner, a parent can control *when* a child uses the computer.

Figure 10.20

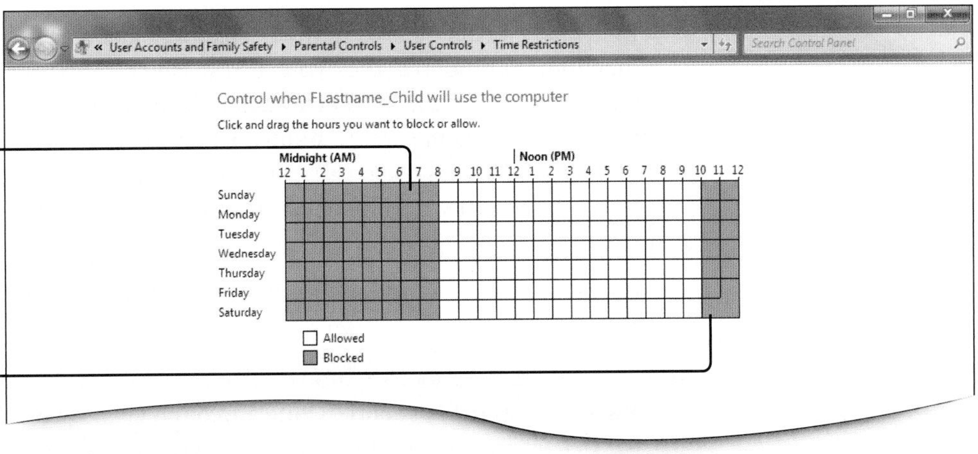

Computer blocked from Midnight to 8 AM

Computer blocked from 10 PM to Midnight

7 Click **OK** to set the time restrictions.

8 Under **Windows Settings**, click **Games**. Under **Block**, click **Set game ratings**. Under **If a game has no rating**, click the **Block games with no rating** option button. Under **Which ratings are ok for FLastname_Child to play?**, click the **EVERYONE** option button, and then compare your screen with Figure 10.21.

Windows 7 uses the Entertainment Software Rating Board (ESRB) categories to filter games. Choosing the *Everyone* rating allows the child to play games with an *Everyone* rating and all categories above that rating—in this case, *Everyone* or *Early Childhood*.

Figure 10.21

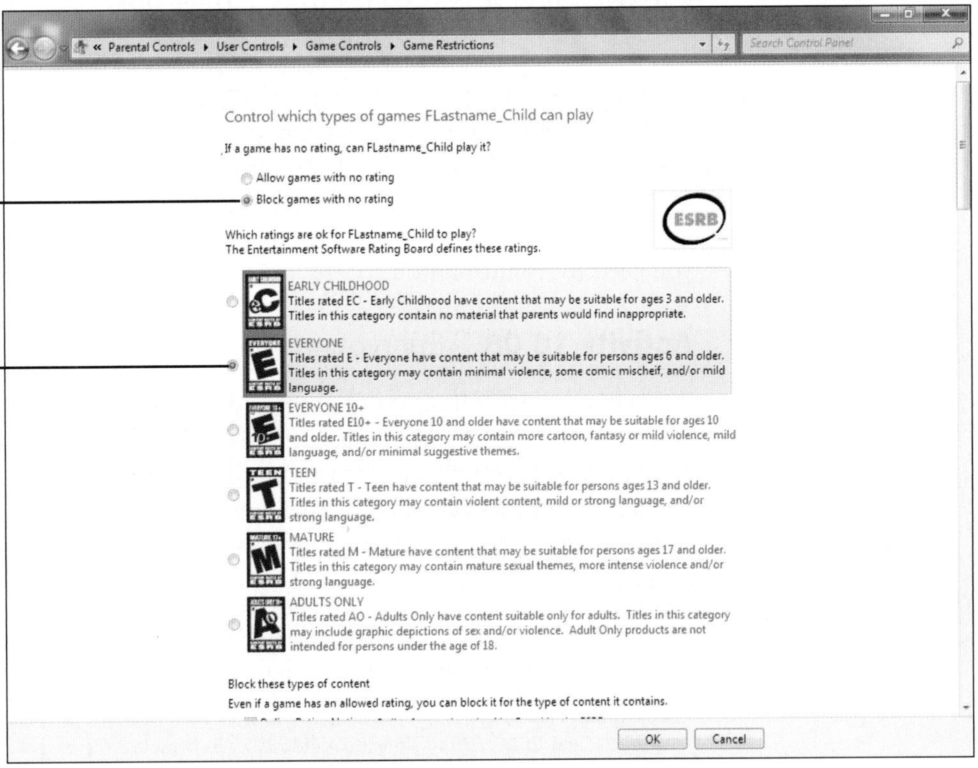

Block games with no rating option button

Everyone option button

9 Click **OK** to restrict the game ratings. Read the information on the *Control which types of games* window, and then click **OK** to return to the *User Controls* window.

10 **Start** the **Snipping Tool** program, click the **New arrow**, and then click **Full-screen Snip**. In the **Snipping Tool** mark-up window, click the **Save Snip** button.

11 In the **Save As** dialog box, in the **navigation pane**, scroll down as necessary, and then under **Computer**, click your USB flash drive so that it displays in the address bar. Navigate to your **Windows 7 Chapter 10** folder, and then as the file name, type **Lastname_Firstname_10A_Parental_Snip** Be sure the file type is **JPEG file**, and then press Enter. **Close** the **Snipping Tool** mark-up window. Hold this file until you finish Project 10A, and then submit this file as directed by your instructor.

12 In the **User Controls** window, click **OK**. In the **Control Panel**, display the **User Accounts and Family Safety** window, and then under **User Accounts**, click **Add or remove user accounts**.

13 In the **Manage Accounts** window, click the **Child** user account that you created. Under **Make changes to FLastname_Child's account**, click **Delete the account**, and then click the **Delete Files** button. In the next displayed window, click the **Delete Account** button.

14 **Close** the **Control Panel** window.

> **More Knowledge | Set Parental Controls in Internet Explorer**
>
> Parental Controls can also be used to allow or block a child's use of the Internet if Internet Explorer is used as the Web browser. On the Command bar, click Tools, and then click Internet Options. Display the Content tab, and then click the Parental Controls button. Select the user account, and then set the rules for the child using that account. You can even create a report that tracks Web use from that account.

Objective 4 | Encrypt Files with Encryption File System

To prevent the theft of the data contained on computer hard drives, businesses and individuals can encrypt files that contain sensitive data. Windows 7 Business, Enterprise, and Ultimate editions provide ***Encryption File System***. Encryption File System, or ***EFS***, is a Windows 7 feature that enables you to store information on your hard disk drive in an encrypted format. Encryption is the strongest protection that Windows 7 provides to help you keep your information secure.

Activity 10.08 | Encrypting Files with Encryption File System

Without encryption, anyone with a Windows administrative account could open and view your files. If your computer was stolen, its hard drive could be placed in another computer, and the administrator of that computer would be able to open and view any file that was not encrypted. Files that you encrypt with EFS can be opened only when you are logged on to your own Windows 7 account. In this activity, you will encrypt files using EFS.

> **Alert! | Is File Encryption Unavailable?**
>
> Encryption File System is not available in the Home Editions of Windows 7, but is available in the Business, Ultimate, and Enterprise versions of Windows 7. To complete this activity, you will need to have access to a computer that uses one of these three versions of Windows 7. If you cannot complete the steps, read through them to understand how EFS operates.

1 Insert the Student Resource CD in the appropriate drive, and if necessary, Close the AutoPlay dialog box. On your Student Resource CD, navigate to **01_student_data_files ▶ Bell_Orchid ▶ Corporate ▶ Human_Resources** to display its contents in the file list.

2 Point to the Excel file **CO_HR_Salary_Analysis**. Right-click, and then in the displayed shortcut menu, click **Copy**. In the **navigation pane**, under **Libraries**, expand ▷ **Documents**, and then click **My Documents**. In your Documents library, create a new folder and name it **Lastname_Firstname_10A_Encrypted**

3 Double-click the folder you just created to open it. In the **file list**, right-click a blank area, and then in the displayed shortcut menu, click **Paste**.

4 From your Student Resource CD, navigate to **01_student_data_files** ▶ **Bell_Orchid** ▶ **Honolulu** ▶ **Human_Resources** to display its contents in the file list. In the **file list**, point to the Excel file **HO_HR_Salary_Analysis**, right-click, and then click **Copy**.

5 Navigate to your **Documents** ▶ **Lastname_Firstname_10A_Encrypted** folder. In the **file list**, right-click a blank area, and then click **Paste**.

With these two files copied to the Documents folder on your hard disk drive, you can use EFS to encrypt them. EFS works only on hard disk drives that use the NTFS file system. EFS cannot encrypt files on a USB flash drive, CD, or DVD.

6 Right-click in a blank area of the file list, and then on the shortcut menu, click **Properties**. On the **General tab**, under **Attributes**, click the **Advanced** button.

7 In the **Advanced Attributes** dialog box, select the **Encrypt contents to secure data** check box, and then compare your screen with Figure 10.22.

Figure 10.22

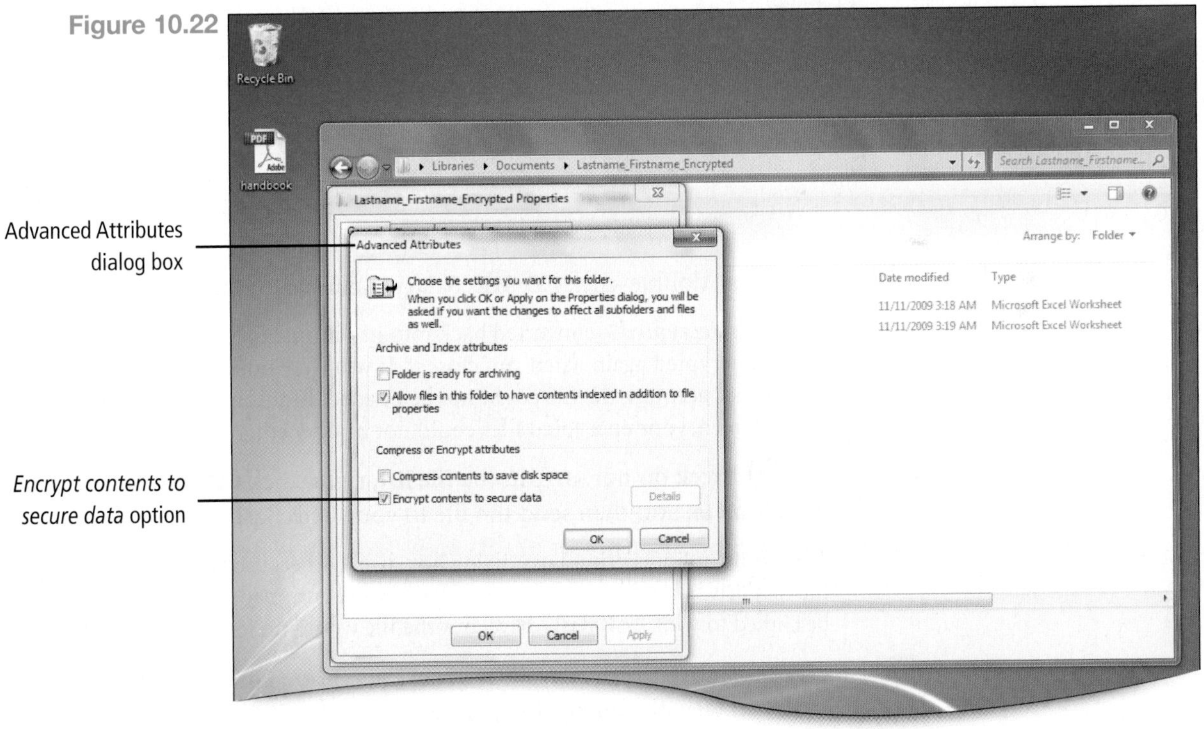

8 Click **OK** two times. In the displayed **Confirm Attribute Changes** dialog box, be sure the **Apply changes to this folder, subfolders and files** option button is selected, and then click **OK**.

9 If necessary, in the **navigation pane**, click the **Lastname_Firstname_10A_Encrypted** folder to display its contents in the **file list**, and then compare your screen with Figure 10.23. If necessary, close the folder and then reopen it to display the file names in green.

In this activity, you will not create this backup. This backup is used to recover encrypted files if for any reason you can no longer log on to your Windows 7 account. The regular Windows Backup program does not back up this file, so it should be done the first time EFS is applied.

In the file list, the file names display in green; this indicates that they are encrypted. When you encrypt a folder, any file that is in the folder or added to the folder later will also be encrypted. In this manner, a single folder can be used to manage your encrypted files.

Figure 10.23

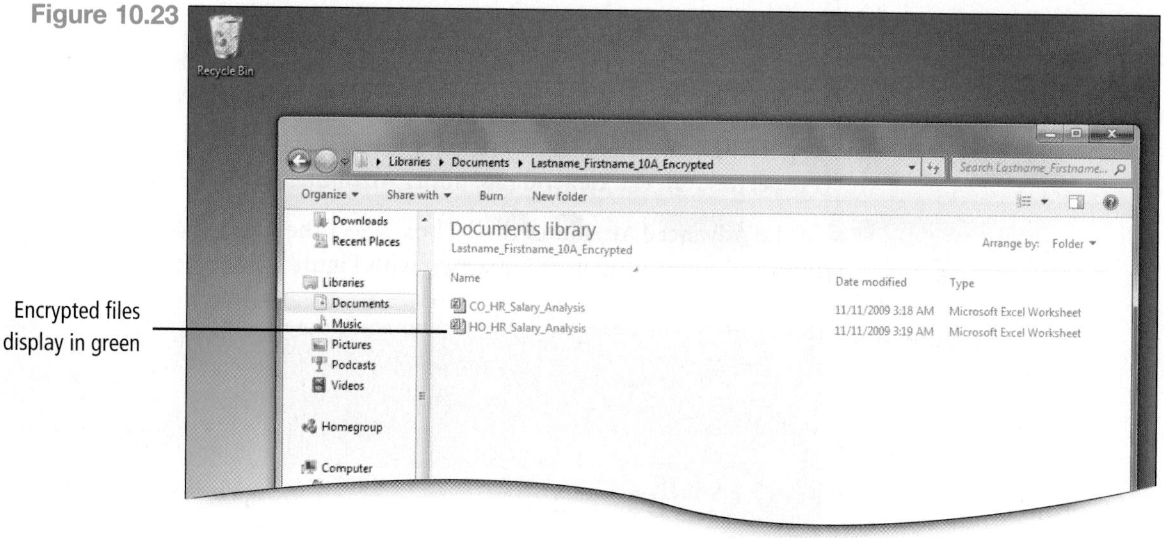

10 In the **file list**, double-click **CO_HR_Salary_Analysis** to start Excel and open the file.

The file is ***decrypted***—converted back into its original form—when you open it, and it will be encrypted again when you close it. If you were not logged on to your current Windows 7 account, the file could not be opened. In this manner, if your computer is lost or stolen, your encrypted files could not be opened.

11 **Close** Excel; do not save. In the **file list**, right-click **CO_HR_Salary_Analysis**, point to **Send to**, and then send the file to your USB flash drive.

The Confirm Encryption Loss dialog box displays because you are attempting to copy the file to a drive that does not support EFS. If you continued with this action, the file would be copied to your USB flash drive, but the file would no longer be encrypted.

12 If necessary, move the displayed **Confirm Encryption Loss** dialog box to the right so that you can view the **navigation pane** and the two files in the **file list**. **Start** the **Snipping Tool** program, click the **New arrow**, and then click **Full-screen Snip**. In the **Snipping Tool** mark-up window, click the **Save Snip** button.

13 In the **Save As** dialog box, in the **navigation pane**, scroll down as necessary, and then under **Computer**, click your USB flash drive so that it displays in the address bar. Navigate to your **Windows 7 Chapter 10** folder, and then as the file name, type **Lastname_Firstname_10A_Encryption_Snip** Be sure the file type is **JPEG file**, and then press Enter. **Close** the **Snipping Tool** mark-up window. Submit the six files that are the results of this project as directed by your instructor.

14 In the displayed **Confirm Encryption Loss** dialog box, click **No. Close** the folder window.

If you have sensitive data on your own computer, consider encrypting the files using EFS. Remember to use a strong password for your Windows 7 logon so that others cannot access your encrypted folders and files.

More Knowledge | Encrypting an Entire Drive by Using BitLocker Drive Encryption

Encryption File System can encrypt specific files and folders. ***BitLocker Drive Encryption*** is a security feature that encrypts all the data stored on a ***volume***. A volume consists of one or more partitions on one or more hard disk drives. BitLocker Drive Encryption is included with the Ultimate and Enterprise editions of Windows 7. To start BitLocker, open it from the Security control panel and turn the feature on. The BitLocker Drive Encryption wizard helps you set up BitLocker Drive Encryption to work with your computer.

End **You have completed Project 10A**

Project 10B Troubleshooting Your Computer

Project Activities

In Activities 10.09 through 10.18, you will train with Steven Ramos and Barbara Hewitt, employees in the Information Technology Department at the corporate office of the Bell Orchid Hotels. After completing this part of the training, you will be able to troubleshoot and solve common computer problems, manage hardware devices, and remove malware from your computer. You will capture screens that look similar to Figure 10.24.

Project Files

For Project 10B, you will need the following files:

New Snip files

Your will save your files as:

Lastname_Firstname_10B_Events_Snip
Lastname_Firstname_10B_Answers_Snip
Lastname_Firstname_10B_AutoPlay_Snip
Lastname_Firstname_10B_Registry_Snip
Lastname_Firstname_10B_Add-ons_Snip

Project Results

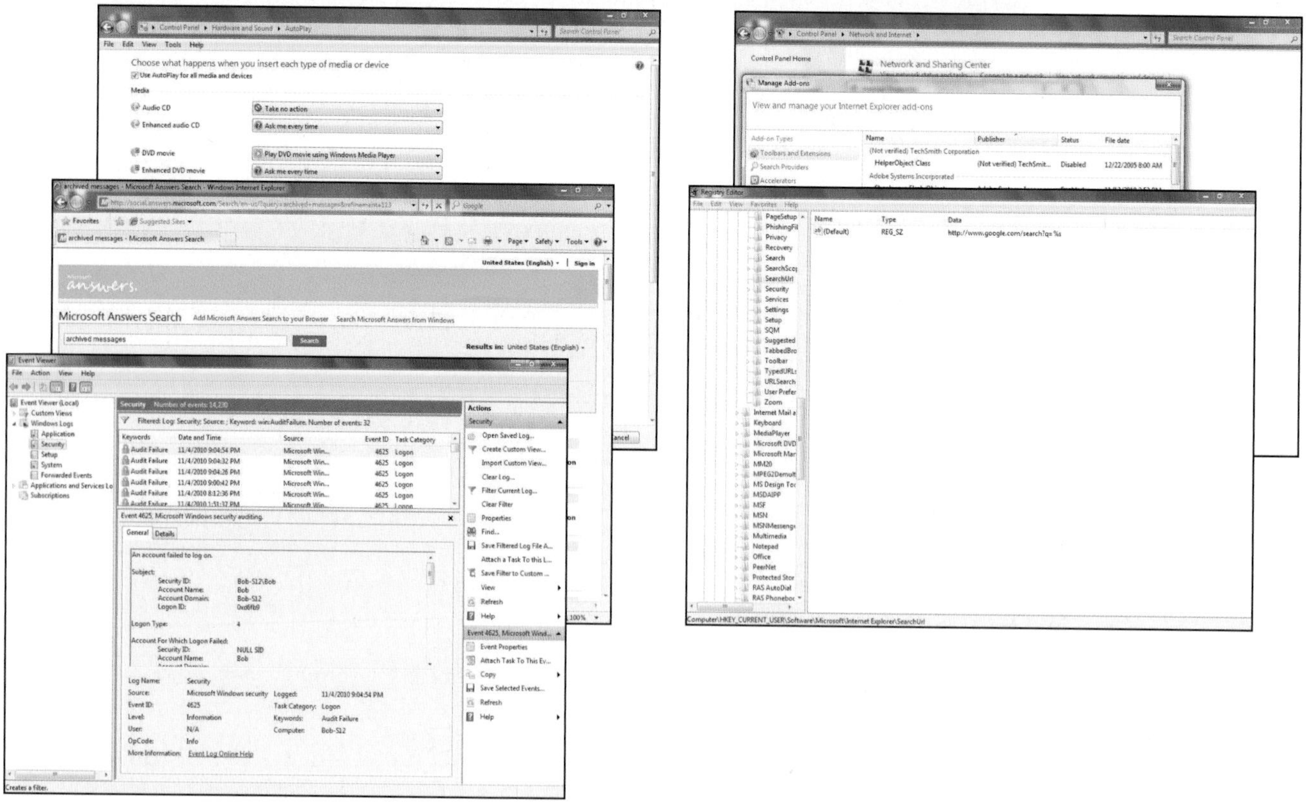

Figure 10.24
Project 10B Troubleshooting Your Computer

Objective 5 | Troubleshoot Computer Problems

Recall that when you troubleshoot a computer, you analyze the problem, determine possible causes, and implement solutions. One method Windows 7 uses to help you troubleshoot problems is to record the events that affect your system—recall that you can view identified problems by clicking the Action Center button in the notification area of the taskbar. The most significant of these events are reported to Microsoft to see if a solution exists. If your computer is experiencing problems, such as poor performance or an unresponsive application, Windows 7 has tools to view the events that affect your system so that you can determine a cause and apply a solution.

Activity 10.09 | Analyzing Problems with Event Viewer

Event Viewer is a Windows 7 tool that displays detailed information about significant events on your computer. The record of events that have happened on your computer is the ***event log***, which records important activities on your computer such as when software is installed, when an individual logs on to the computer, or when a program stops responding. Viewing event logs can help you or a computer technician identify problems.

Every time an individual logs on to Windows 7, the event is recorded in an event log. You can view this log to determine if someone has been attempting to log on to your account. In this activity, you will practice using Event Viewer by attempting to log on with the wrong password three times, and then viewing the failed logon attempts in Event Viewer.

1 If necessary, log off the computer at which you are seated. In the displayed logon screen, click or type your regular Windows 7 account name. In the **Password** box, type an *incorrect* password, and then press Enter.

A message indicates that the user name or password is incorrect; this failed log on attempt was recorded in an event log.

> **Alert! | Do You Need to Add a Password?**
>
> If your Windows 7 user account does not require a password, log on correctly, and then open the Control Panel. Under *User Accounts and Family Safety*, click *Add or remove user accounts*. In the Manage Accounts window, click your account name, and then click Create a password. In the Create Password screen, enter a password in both boxes, and then click the Create password button. Close the Control Panel, and then log off. When you are done with this activity, return to the Manage Accounts window, click your account name, and click Remove password.

2 In the screen that informs you that the user name or password is incorrect, click **OK**. In the **Password** box, type an *incorrect* password, and then press Enter. Click **OK**, log on with an *incorrect* password for a third time, and then click **OK**.

All three failed logon attempts are recorded in an event log.

3 Log on to the computer at which you are working using the correct Windows 7 account name and password.

4 Display the **Control Panel**, click **System and Security**, and then under **Administrative Tools**, click **View event logs**.

> **Another Way**
>
> In the Start menu Search box, type Event Viewer, and in the displayed results, click Event Viewer.

5 If necessary, in the User Account Control dialog box, click Yes. If necessary, Maximize your window, and then compare your screen with Figure 10.25.

The Event Viewer window displays and is divided into three panes. The left pane enables you to navigate event logs, the middle pane displays information about the event logs, and on the right, the Actions pane lists the actions that you can perform for the selected item. Currently, the Event Viewer Overview and Summary displays with events categorized into five event types.

Figure 10.25

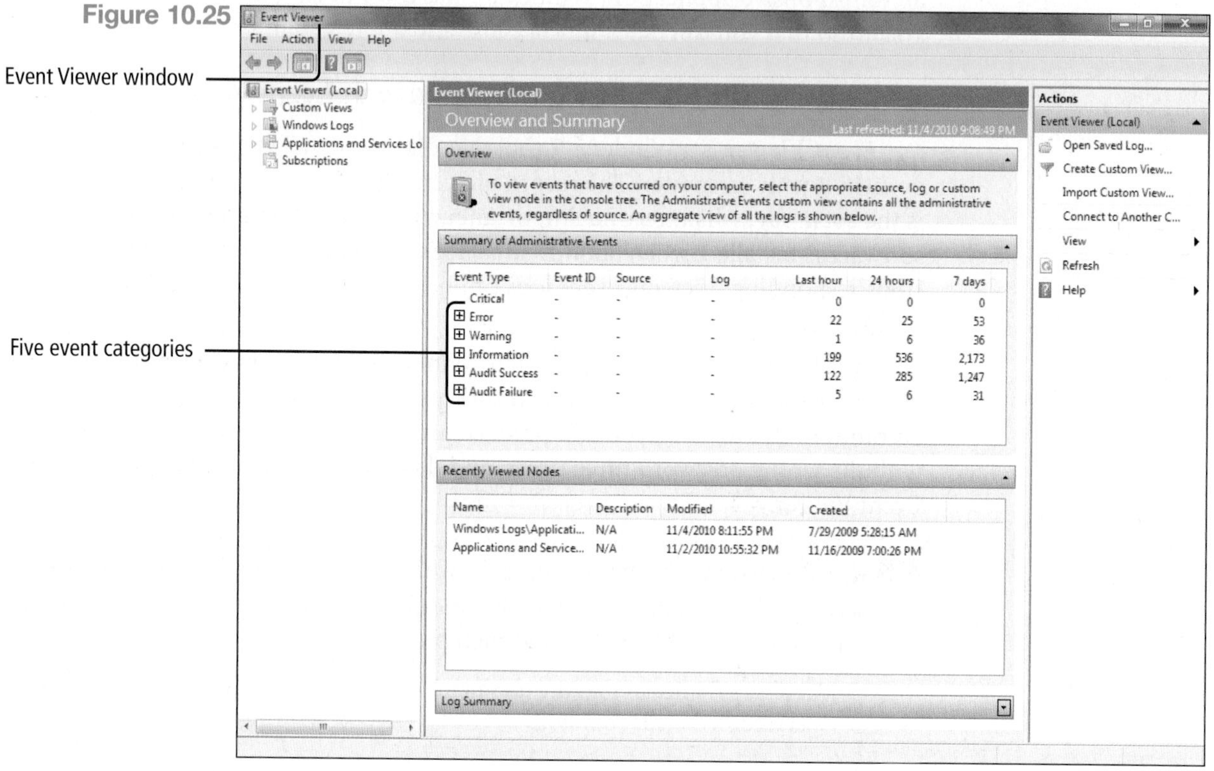

6 Take a moment to study the types of events that are summarized by Event Viewer as shown in the table in Figure 10.26.

Event Types in Event Viewer

Event Type	Description
Error	An event that could cause the loss of data or computer functionality, such as an application not responding or a network interface card that quits working.
Warning	An event with moderate consequences, such as a failed print job, a scheduled task that did not run, or a USB flash drive that was removed improperly from the computer.
Information	An event without serious consequences, such as opening the Windows Security Center or Windows Update while updates are downloading.
Audit Success	A successful event related to a Windows 7 user account, such as a log on or a change in user account settings.
Audit Failure	A failed event related to a Windows 7 user account, such as a failed logon attempt.

Figure 10.26

7 Under **Summary of Administrative Events**, expand ⊞ **Error**. Under **Error**, double-click the first error listed.

Under *Summary page events*, several errors might be listed. The General tab displays information about the selected event. In this manner, you can find out more about an event.

8 In the left pane of the **Event Viewer** window, expand ▷ **Windows Logs**, and then click **Security**.

The security log tracks when you log on and log off, with the most recent events listed first.

9 On the right, in the **Actions pane**, click **Filter Current Log**. In the **Filter Current Log** dialog box, click the **Keywords** arrow, and then click **Audit Failure**. Press (Enter), click **OK**, and then compare your screen with Figure 10.27.

The Security events display, and the funnel icon indicates that the list is filtered. The three failed logon attempts that you made display first.

Failed logons are common, but ten or more failed logon attempts within a short amount of time indicate that someone may have been attempting to log on by guessing your password. In this type of computer attack, it is not uncommon to see fifty or more failed logon attempts.

Figure 10.27

Security log ——

Audit failures ——

Description of log on failure ——

Funnel icon ——

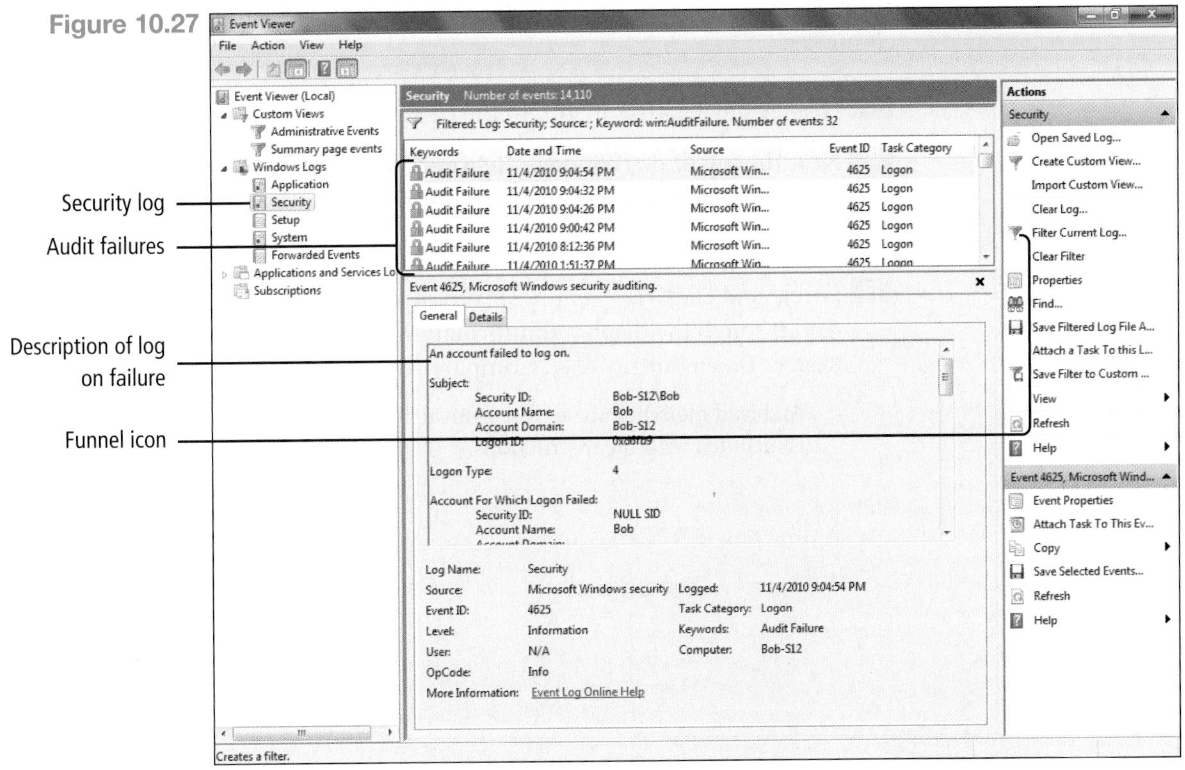

10 Start 🔵 the **Snipping Tool** program, click the **New arrow**, and then click **Full-screen Snip**. In the **Snipping Tool** mark-up window, click the **Save Snip** button 🖫.

11 In the **Save As** dialog box, in the **navigation pane**, scroll down as necessary, and then under **Computer**, click your USB flash drive so that it displays in the address bar. Navigate to your **Windows 7 Chapter 10** folder, and then as the file name, type **Lastname_Firstname_10B_Events_Snip** Be sure the file type is **JPEG file**, and then press (Enter). **Close** ❌ the **Snipping Tool** mark-up window. Hold this file until you finish Project 10B, and then submit this file as directed by your instructor.

12 **Close** [X] the **Event Viewer**, and then **Close** [X] any other open windows.

If you suspect someone has been trying to use your Windows 7 user account, you can view the Security log to look at logon times and failures. If you are experiencing other problems, a computer technician may direct you to other event logs in Event Viewer.

Objective 6 | Find and Use Help from Others

There may be times when you cannot solve a problem by yourself, and you need help from others. For example, you may have a USB flash drive that stops working, or an Internet connection that is too slow. Windows Help and Support provides help for such problems. Windows Help and Support also connects you to online resources where you can ask others for help. Here you will usually find individuals who have experienced the same problem, and experts willing to share a solution.

Activity 10.10 | Using Windows Help and Support

The Windows Help and Support window provides information and step-by-step directions for performing maintenance tasks and solving problems. Windows Help and Support is different from the Windows Help system found within applications. For example, when you need help using Microsoft Word, the Help system found in that program focuses on that program. In this activity, you will practice using Help and Support by finding out how to view archived messages sent to Microsoft from your computer.

1 Display the **Start** menu. In the right pane, click **Help and Support**.

2 Near the top of the **Windows Help and Support** dialog box, in the **Search Help** box, type **archived messages** and then press Enter.

Several topics are displayed that relate to archived messages.

3 Locate and click *How do I use archived messages to solve computer problems?*, and then read through the displayed information. If the window is maximized, click the **Restore Down** button. Compare your screen with Figure 10.28.

Archived messages are accessed through the Action Center, and a link to the Action Center is included with the instructions.

Figure 10.28

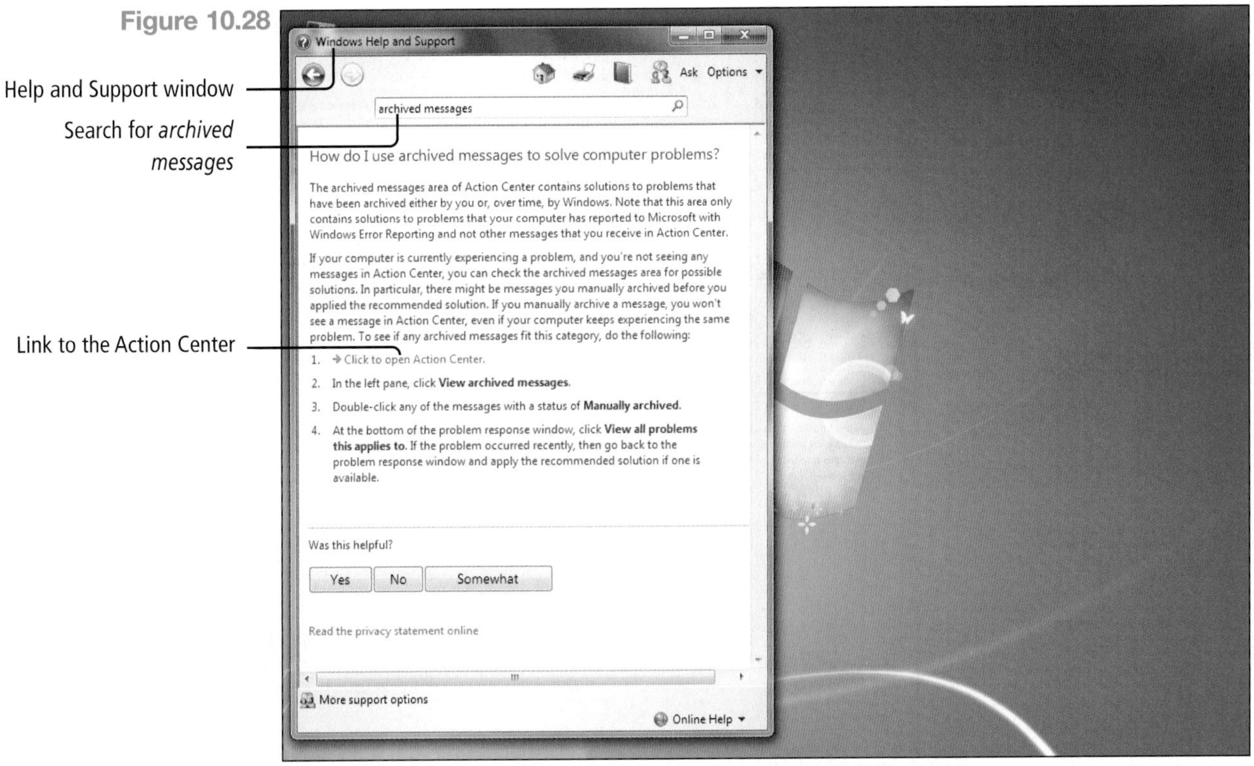

4 In the **Windows Help and Support** window, click the text *Click to open Action Center.* On the left side of the **Action Center** window, click **View archived messages**. Compare your screen with Figure 10.29.

After a few seconds, a list of recently solved problems displays. Your list will vary, and may even be empty.

Figure 10.29

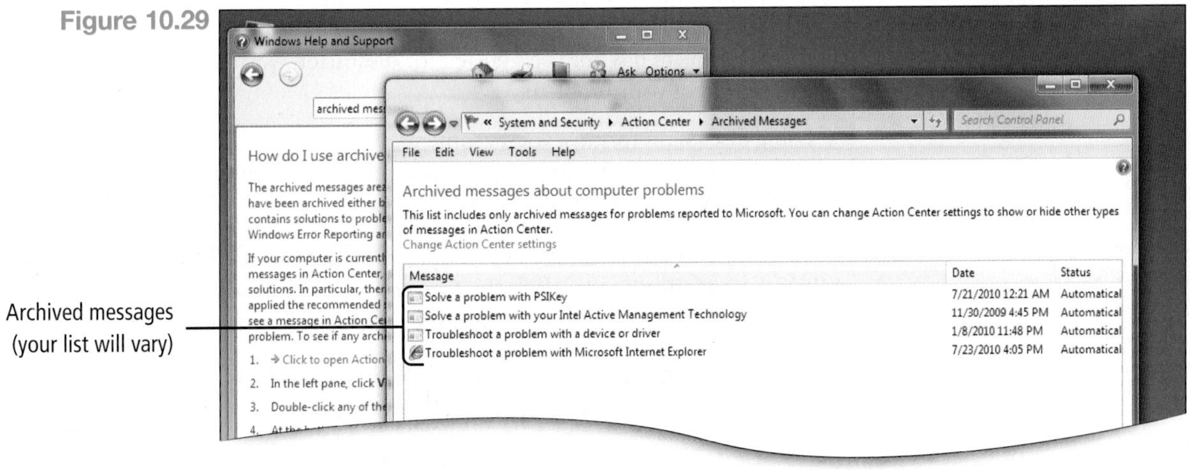

5 Double-click one of the messages, and then compare your screen with Figure 10.30.

A detailed description of the selected problem displays, and possible solutions to the problem are provided. If this particular problem has happened on more than one occasion—the problem is listed once for each time it occurs—it is a good idea to use these steps to try to solve the problem.

Figure 10.30

Archived message
sent to Microsoft

Description of the problem

Links to possible solutions
to the problem

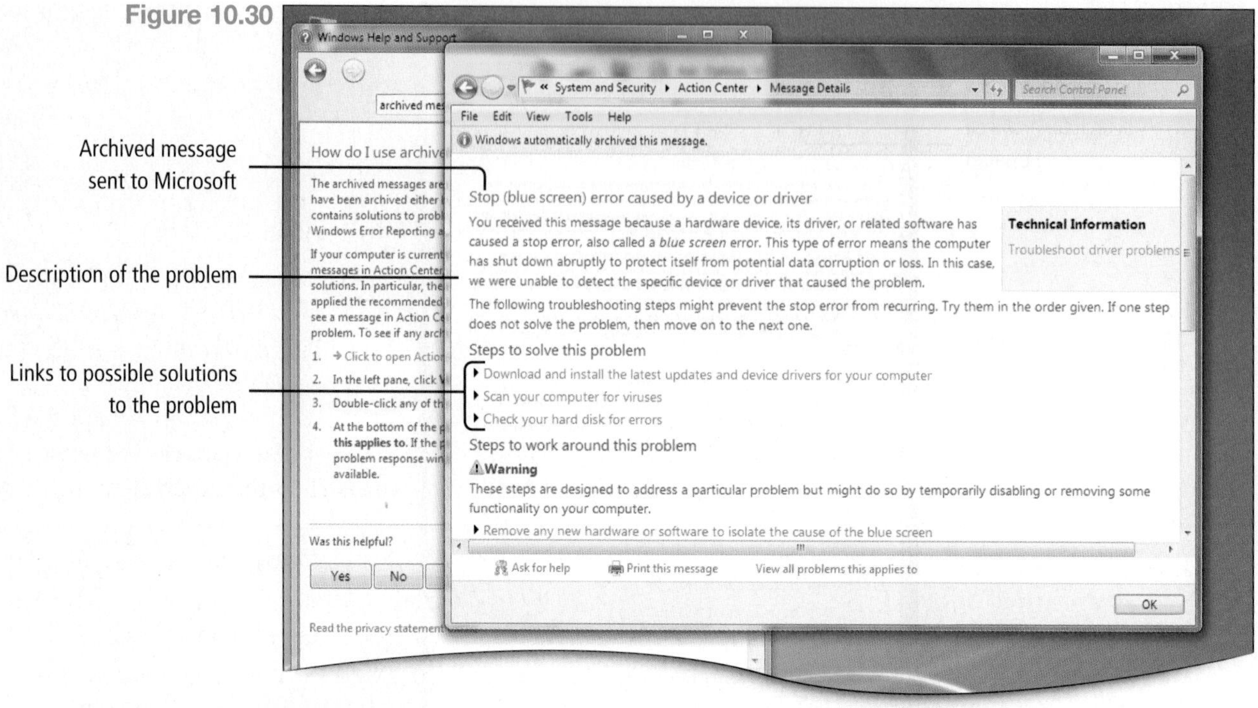

6 **Close** [×] the **Message Center** window. At the top of the **Windows Help and Support** window, click the **Ask** button to display more Help options.

7 Under **Ask a person for help**, click the text *Microsoft Answers* to access the Microsoft Answers site.

> Microsoft Answers provides links to **discussion forums**, which are places on the Web where groups of individuals with common interests or information can share their knowledge. Individuals submit questions for discussion and others can respond. A list of discussion topics are referred to as **threads**. Individual messages regarding the thread are called **posts**. Here you can expand a thread to view the solutions posted for a question. If your problem has not been posted for discussion, you can create a new thread with a description of your problem.
>
> Using discussion forums, you become part of a larger community seeking to solve common problems. In this way, discussion forums often provide solutions that cannot be found in Windows Help and Support.

8 If necessary, **Maximize** [□] the window. In the **Search Windows Forums** box, type **archived messages** again, click the **Search** button, and notice that the topics are much different than those found in Windows Help and Support.

9 **Start** 🌐 the **Snipping Tool** program, click the **New arrow**, and then click **Full-screen Snip**. In the **Snipping Tool** mark-up window, click the **Save Snip** button [💾].

10 In the **Save As** dialog box, in the **navigation pane**, scroll down as necessary, and then under **Computer**, click your USB flash drive so that it displays in the address bar. Navigate to your **Windows 7 Chapter 10** folder, and then as the file name, type **Lastname_Firstname_10B_Answers_Snip** Be sure the file type is **JPEG**, and then press [Enter]. **Close** [×] the **Snipping Tool** mark-up window. Hold this file until you finish Project 10B.

11 **Close** [×] **Internet Explorer**, and then **Close** [×] all open windows.

> **More Knowledge | Searching for Help on the Internet**
>
> You can also use your preferred search engine to search for answers to computer problems. Your results will likely display links to many helpful articles and discussion forums. Hard-to-find solutions can often be located by using this method.

Activity 10.11 | Using Windows Remote Assistance

Windows Remote Assistance is a tool that enables two computers to establish a direct connection so that an expert can provide help. When two computers are connected using Windows Remote Assistance, the desktop of the computer needing help, called the ***Remote Assistance novice***, displays on the screen of the person providing the help, called the ***Remote Assistance expert***. Windows Remote Assistance connects two computers over the Internet, or within a local area network. The expert can watch as the novice demonstrates his or her problem, and the novice can watch as the expert demonstrates a solution.

Remote Assistance is similar to Remote Desktop Connection, but with Remote Assistance, both the novice and expert can control the same computer at the same time. With Remote Desktop Connection, only one user can be logged in at a time.

Before you can use Remote Assistance, you may need to enable it. To do so, display the Control Panel, click *System and Security*, and then click *System* to display the System properties window. On the left, you can click *Remote settings*, and then be sure the *Allow Remote Assistance connections to this computer* check box is selected, as shown in Figure 10.31.

Figure 10.31

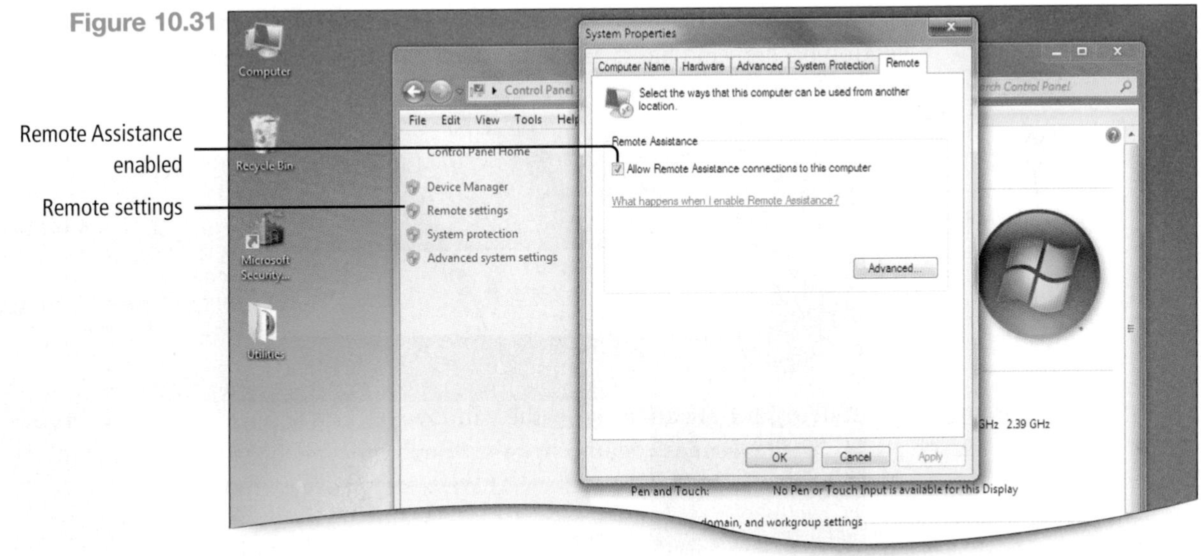

To start a Remote Assistance session, you must invite the other person to participate. To create an invitation, in the Start menu search box, type *remote assistance*, and then click *Windows Remote Assistance*. In the Windows Remote Assistance window, click *Invite someone you trust to help you* if you want to be the novice. If you want to be the expert, click *Help someone who has invited you*. Windows Remote Assistance helps you create an invitation, as shown in Figure 10.32. Here you can save the invitation as a file, use e-mail to send an invitation, or use *Easy Connect*, which is a password-created link between two computers. Easy Connect requires that a number of settings be the same on both computers, and that only one network be available on each end of the connection.

Figure 10.32

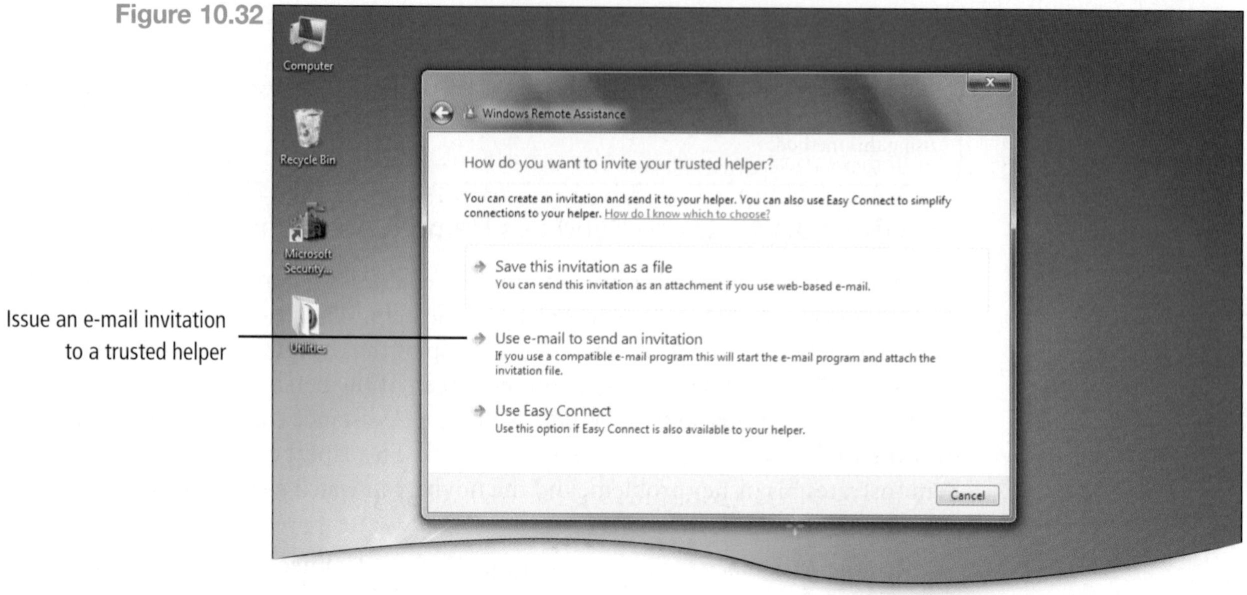

As part of the process to create an invitation file, you will be given a new password for the session. The password prevents someone you did not invite from connecting to your computer. After creating the invitation file, you must send the password to the expert. This can be done as an e-mail attachment or by using Windows Live Messenger.

When an expert opens an invitation file on his or her computer, he or she must enter the session password. After the expert is connected, the Windows Remote Assistance window displays on your screen as shown in Figure 10.33. Using this window, you can disconnect, pause the session, or open a chat window. Notice that in Figure 10.33, the Desktop background has changed to black. Not all backgrounds are supported during a Remote Assistance session.

Figure 10.33

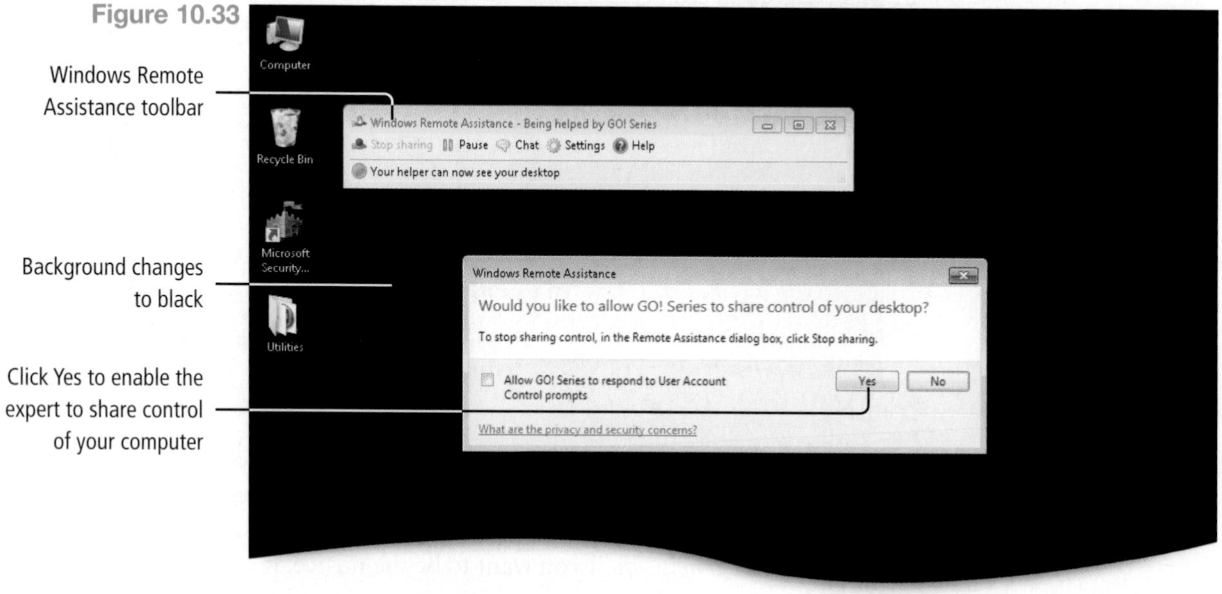

During the session, your desktop displays on the expert's screen. In this way, the expert can watch every action you perform on your computer. In Figure 10.33, the expert has asked to share control of your computer. After you grant the expert shared control, the mouse and keyboard from *both* the expert and novice computers can control the novice computer. In this way, the novice can demonstrate problems and the expert can demonstrate solutions. When the *Allow expert to respond to User Account Control prompts* check box is cleared, the expert must wait for you to click Continue in any User Account Control dialog boxes that display. This feature prevents the expert from making any changes to your system that you do not approve.

Remote Assistance should be used with caution. You are allowing an individual to view your computer and perhaps share control of your computer. It is important to be sure that you know and trust the expert. If you are unsure about the identity of an expert, use the telephone to exchange the password for the Remote Assistance session.

To check how well you understand using Windows Remote Assistance, take a moment to answer the following questions:

1. To start a Remote Assistance session, you must __________ the other person to participate.
2. As part of the process to create an invitation file, you will be given a new __________ for the session.
3. During the session, the novice's desktop displays on the __________ screen.
4. After you grant the expert __________ control, the mouse and keyboard from *both* the expert and novice computers can control the novice's computer.
5. If you are unsure about the identity of an expert, use the __________ to exchange the password for the Remote Assistance session.

Objective 7 | Manage Hardware Devices

Windows 7 controls the communication between your computer and its hardware devices. Many devices—a USB flash drive, a camera, or a printer for example—install a driver and communicate with Windows 7 as soon as you attach them to your computer. Other devices, such as older hardware, need a special driver installed or settings adjusted before they can work properly. Occasionally, a device that has been working properly stops working.

Activity 10.12 | Installing a Plug and Play Device

Most of the devices that you connect to your computer are ***plug and play***, which means that Windows 7 is able to recognize the device as soon as you connect it to your computer, and then automatically install the appropriate drivers and configure the device. Plug and play devices, also known as ***PnP*** devices, commonly include keyboards, mouse pointing devices, USB flash drives, and most newer printers, scanners, and cameras.

When you connect a plug and play device, Windows 7 looks for the correct driver. Recall that a driver is a program that enables Windows 7 to communicate with a device. Windows 7 stores, but does not use, driver files for many of the different devices provided by various manufacturers. Windows 7 installs and uses only the drivers that are needed for your computer's hardware devices. When you first connect a plug and play device to your computer, Windows 7 searches your hard drive for the correct driver and if one is found, it is installed. When more than one driver is found, you will be asked to identify the best choice. For most devices, the correct driver usually installs automatically, and a message displays from the notification area, as shown in Figure 10.34.

Figure 10.34

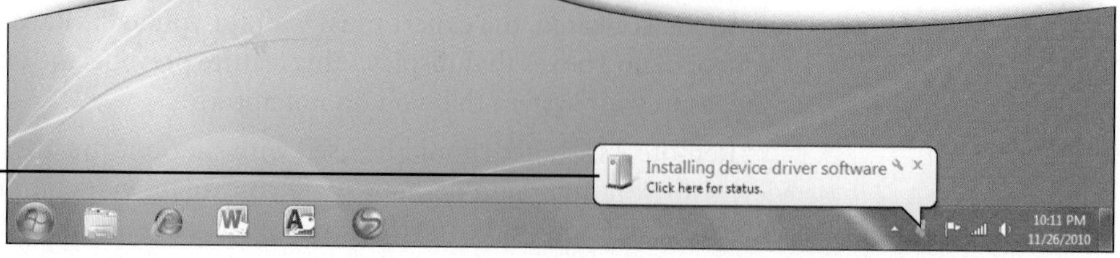

Message indicates device driver has been found

When the device driver is installed, and the device is configured and ready to use, another message displays, letting you know that the device is ready to use. If Windows 7 needs to install multiple drivers, or has to search for the correct drivers online, a different dialog box displays, as shown in Figure 10.35. When large device driver files have to be downloaded and installed, this procedure can take several minutes to complete.

Figure 10.35

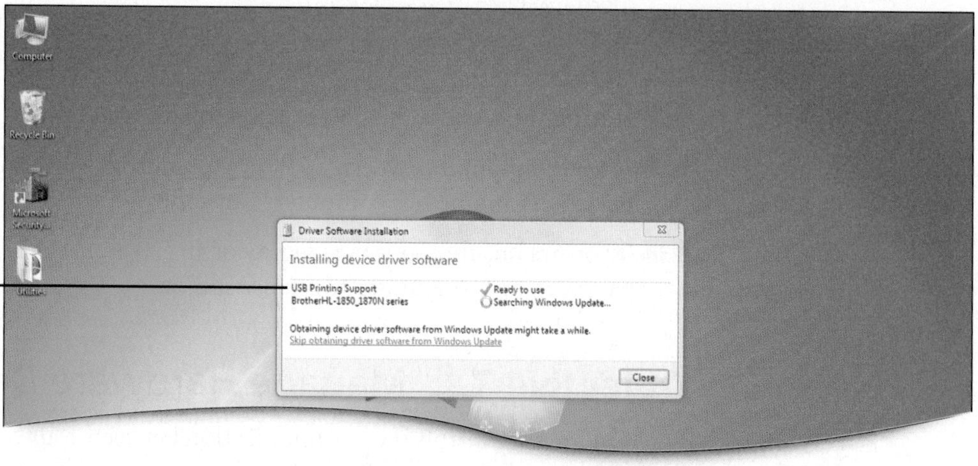

Windows installed one driver, is searching for a second driver

Windows 7 cannot store drivers for every possible hardware device. On rare occasions, if the device being installed is old or requires drivers and other files found online or on a CD included with the device, Windows 7 may not recognize the device being installed. If no driver is found, the *Found New Hardware* wizard displays, giving you options for locating the correct driver. In some instances you must retrieve the driver from the packaged CD that came with the device. In other instances, you must download the driver from the manufacturer's Web site. If this happens, the wizard walks you through the installation of the files necessary to run the new device.

To check how well you understand installing a plug and play device, take a moment to answer the following questions:

1. Plug and play devices, also known as __________ devices, include keyboards, mouse pointing devices, and USB flash drives.
2. Windows 7 installs __________ for plug and play devices the first time the device is connected.
3. When a plug and play device is used for the first time, and is recognized by Windows 7, a message displays from the __________ __________ that lets you know the device is being installed.
4. When you connect a plug and play device that is not recognized by Windows 7, the __________ __________ __________ wizard walks you through the process of finding and installing the correct drivers.
5. If no driver is found, you must use the driver supplied with the device, or download the driver from the device __________ Web site.

Activity 10.13 | Configuring Devices Using the Control Panel

Many of the hardware devices that connect to your computer can be configured by using the Control Panel. For example, from the Control Panel, you can change your keyboard settings or configure the sound quality of your speakers. In this activity, you will practice using the Control Panel to configure hardware devices by changing settings for your mouse and by changing the AutoPlay settings for your CD/DVD ROM.

1 **Start** the **Control Panel**, and then click **Hardware and Sound**. Under **Devices and Printer**, click **Mouse**. Compare your screen with Figure 10.36.

In the displayed Hardware and Sound window, you can configure many of the hardware devices connected to your computer.

For example, if you are having difficulty with double-clicking, on the Buttons tab of the Mouse Properties dialog box, you can change the double-click speed for your mouse. Setting a slower speed increases the amount of time that you have between clicks.

Figure 10.36

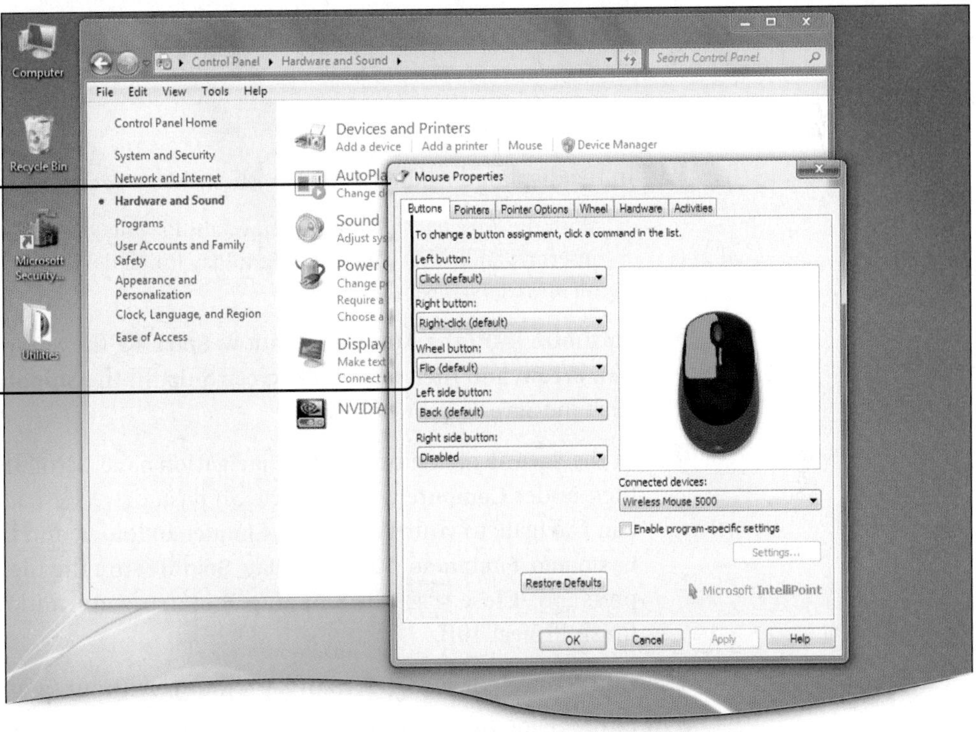

2 Click the **Pointer Options tab**. Under **Visibility**, select the **Display pointer trails** check box, and then select the **Show location of pointer when I press the CTRL key** check box.

3 Move the mouse on your screen and notice the mouse trails effect. Then press and release Ctrl and notice how the pointer location is circled.

4 Click **OK** to save changes and close the **Mouse Properties** dialog box. In the **Hardware and Sound** window, click **AutoPlay**. Under **Media**, to the right of **Audio CD**, click the **arrow**, and then compare your screen with Figure 10.37.

In the AutoPlay window, you can configure the AutoPlay behavior of many of your devices. For example, if the *Play audio CD using Windows Media Player* option is selected, when you insert an audio CD into your CD/DVD drive, Windows Media Player will immediately start playing the CD without displaying the AutoPlay dialog box.

Figure 10.37

AutoPlay window

Audio CD options

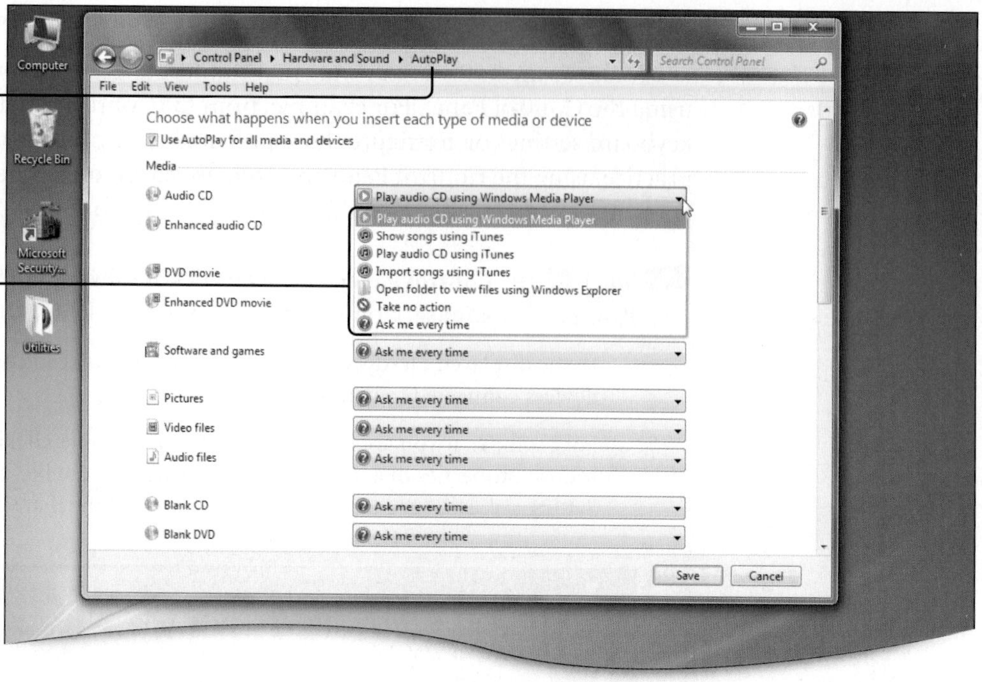

5 In the displayed **Audio CD** menu, click **Take no action.**

With the *Take no action* option, the AutoPlay dialog box will stop displaying whenever you insert an audio CD. To disable AutoPlay for all devices, you can clear the *Use AutoPlay for all media and devices* check box.

6 **Maximize** the **AutoPlay** window. **Start** the **Snipping Tool** program, click the **New arrow**, and then click **Full-screen Snip**. In the **Snipping Tool** mark-up window, click the **Save Snip** button.

7 In the **Save As** dialog box, in the **navigation pane**, scroll down as necessary, and then under **Computer**, click your USB flash drive so that it displays in the address bar. Navigate to your **Windows 7 Chapter 10** folder, and then as the file name, type **Lastname_Firstname_10B_AutoPlay_Snip** Be sure the file type is **JPEG**, and then press Enter. **Close** the **Snipping Tool** mark-up window. Hold this file until you finish Project 10B.

8 Click **Cancel** to close the **AutoPlay** window without saving any changes.

9 In the **Hardware and Sound** window, click **Mouse**, and then click the **Pointer Options tab**. Under **Visibility** clear the **Display pointer trails** and **Show location of pointer when I press the CTRL key** check boxes. Click **OK** to close the **Mouse Properties** dialog box.

10 **Close** the **Hardware and Sound** window.

> **More Knowledge | Setting Up Multiple Monitors**
>
> If your computer has multiple video outputs, you can configure Windows 7 to display your desktop on more than one monitor. Check your computer or consult the manual for your video card to see if you have more than one video port to which a monitor can be attached. To display your desktop on more than one monitor, shut down your computer, attach the second monitor, and then start Windows 7. Windows 7 will detect both monitors, and determine what to display on the second monitor. The *Extended* option displays your desktop across two monitors so that you can place windows on either screen or stretch one window across both monitors. To change this setting later, open the Display Settings dialog box from the Control Panel.

Activity 10.14 | Adding a Local Printer

A ***local printer*** is a printer connected directly to a USB port, serial port, or parallel port on your computer. The serial and parallel ports, if any, are located on the back of most computers; these two ports were used to connect printers before computers had USB ports. Some printers still support parallel ports, but most local printers connect using a USB port.

> **Note | Consult Your Printer's Manual**
>
> Before you connect your printer to the computer, consult the manual that came with your printer. Your printer may come with a CD that will install the drivers and other software for your printer—often before the printer is first connected to the computer. Check the printer's manual to see if the CD has the software required for Windows 7. If not, check the manufacturer's Web site for directions for adding the printer to a computer with the Windows 7 operating system.

When you need to add a local printer to your computer, you should use the Add Printer wizard—particularly if the printer does not install immediately using plug and play. The Add Printer wizard provides options for installing the correct driver. When you plug your printer into a USB port, Windows 7 will attempt to install a driver for the printer. If this happens, and the printer does not appear to be installing correctly, cancel this process so that you can install the correct driver using the Add Printer wizard.

To add a printer, open the Control Panel, and then click Hardware and Sound. Under *Devices and Printers*, click *Add a printer*. Click *Add a local printer*. The first screen of the displayed *Add Printer* wizard prompts you to choose a port for the new printer. The common port names begin with LPT, COM, or USB, as shown in Figure 10.38. Use an LPT port to connect a parallel printer, use a COM port to connect a serial printer, and use a USB port to connect a USB printer. The manual that comes with your printer will indicate which port to use.

Figure 10.38

Add Printer dialog box

Available printer ports

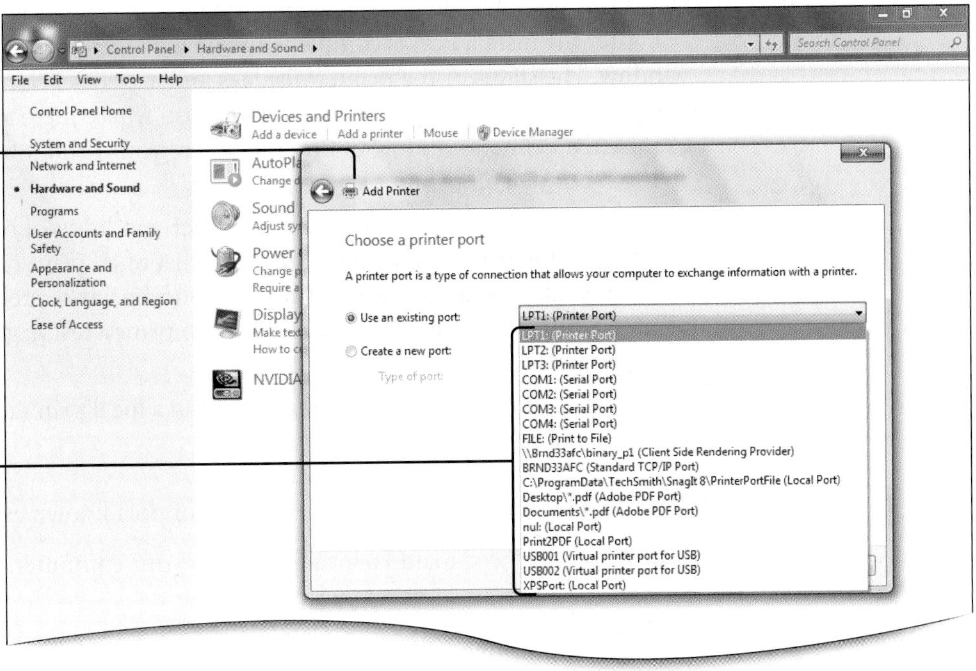

The next screen in the Add Printer wizard prompts you to select the printer manufacturer and model so that it can install the correct driver, as shown in Figure 10.39. If your printer model is not listed, the Add Printer wizard provides two other options. Click the *Windows Update* button to search the Windows Update database to determine if a driver is available. If you have downloaded a driver from the printer manufacturer's Web site, click the *Have Disk* button to use that driver.

Figure 10.39

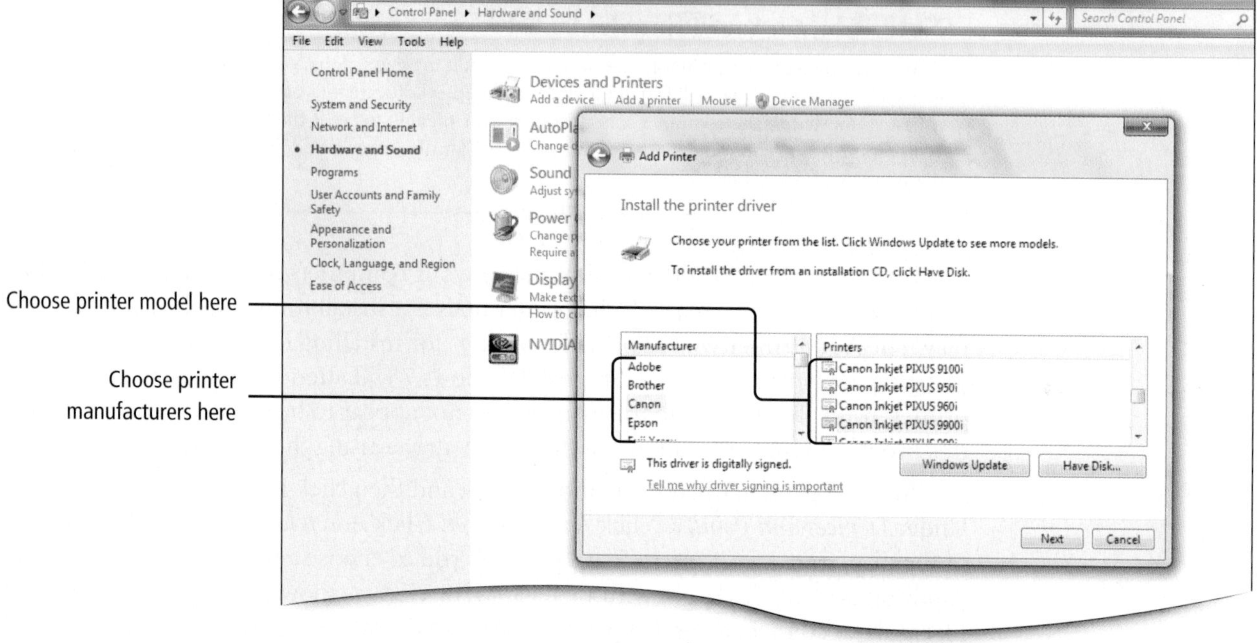

The next screen of the Add Printer wizard prompts you to assign a name for the printer and gives you the option to make the printer the ***default printer***. A default printer receives all print commands unless you specify otherwise when initiating the print command.

After the installation is complete, the new printer displays in the Printers folder window. The status of the printer displays and a green check mark indicates that it is the default printer. If you are working in a location where there are multiple printers, you can use the Printers window to find out where your print jobs will be sent, and you can change your default printer if necessary.

To manage a printer, in the Printers folder window, double-click the printer's icon. By opening the printer in its own window, a list of all print requests currently printing displays. Here you can pause printing and cancel print requests. You can also display the printer's Properties dialog box where you can print a test page or set advanced options for your printer.

To check how well you understand adding a local printer to your computer, take a moment to answer the following questions:

1. Most local printers connect to the type of port known as __________.
2. When you need to add a local printer to your computer, you should use the __________ __________ wizard.
3. The Add Printer wizard searches your hard drive for the correct __________.
4. A green check mark on a printer's icon indicates that this printer is the __________ printer.
5. To manage a printer, in the __________ folder window, double-click the printer's icon.

Activity 10.15 | Managing Drivers Using Device Manager

The Device Manager provides access to all your computer hardware devices. Use Device Manager to view information about each device, identify problems, and change settings when necessary. For example, if you have a device that stops working, you can use Device Manager to test the device or change the driver used by that device.

To open Device Manager, display the Control Panel, and then click Hardware and Sound. Under Devices and Printers, click Device Manager. The Device Manager window lists every hardware device used by your computer. In Figure 10.40, the *Network adaptors* area is expanded and the computer's network devices are listed.

Figure 10.40

Device Manager window

Hardware devices on your computer

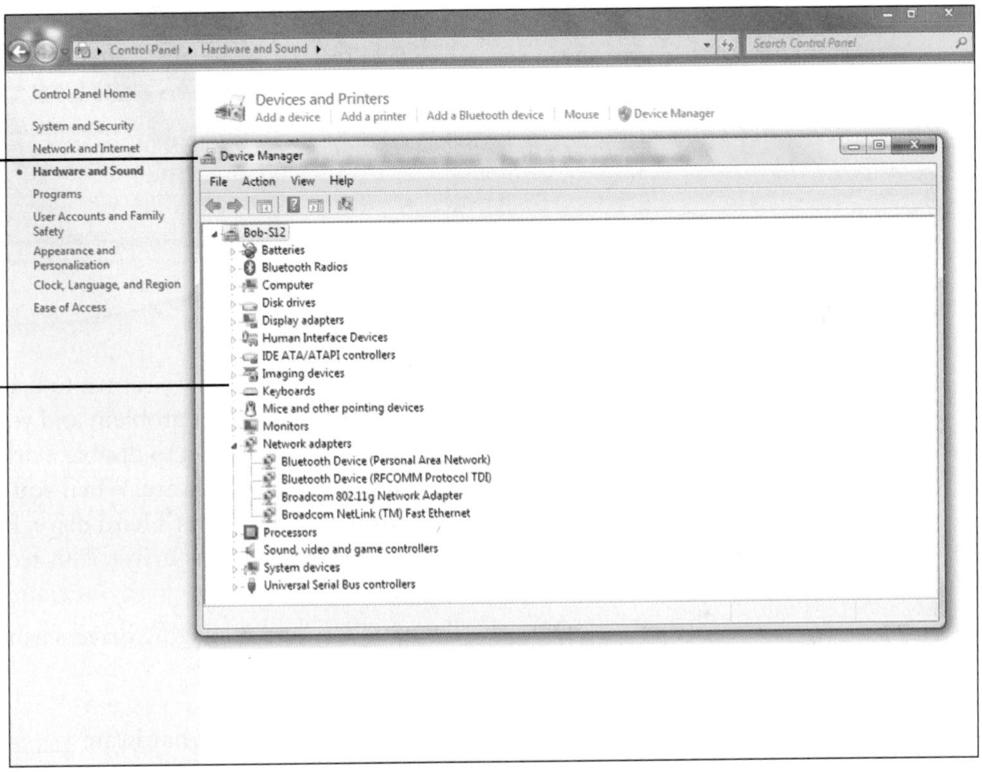

Double-clicking a device opens the Properties dialog box for that device. In Figure 10.41, the Driver tab for the *Display adaptors* displays. Here you can find out which version of the driver is installed. You may need to share this information when seeking help from a computer technician or discussion forum. If you have a new version of the driver on a CD or have downloaded one from the Internet, it can be installed by clicking the Update Driver button.

Figure 10.41

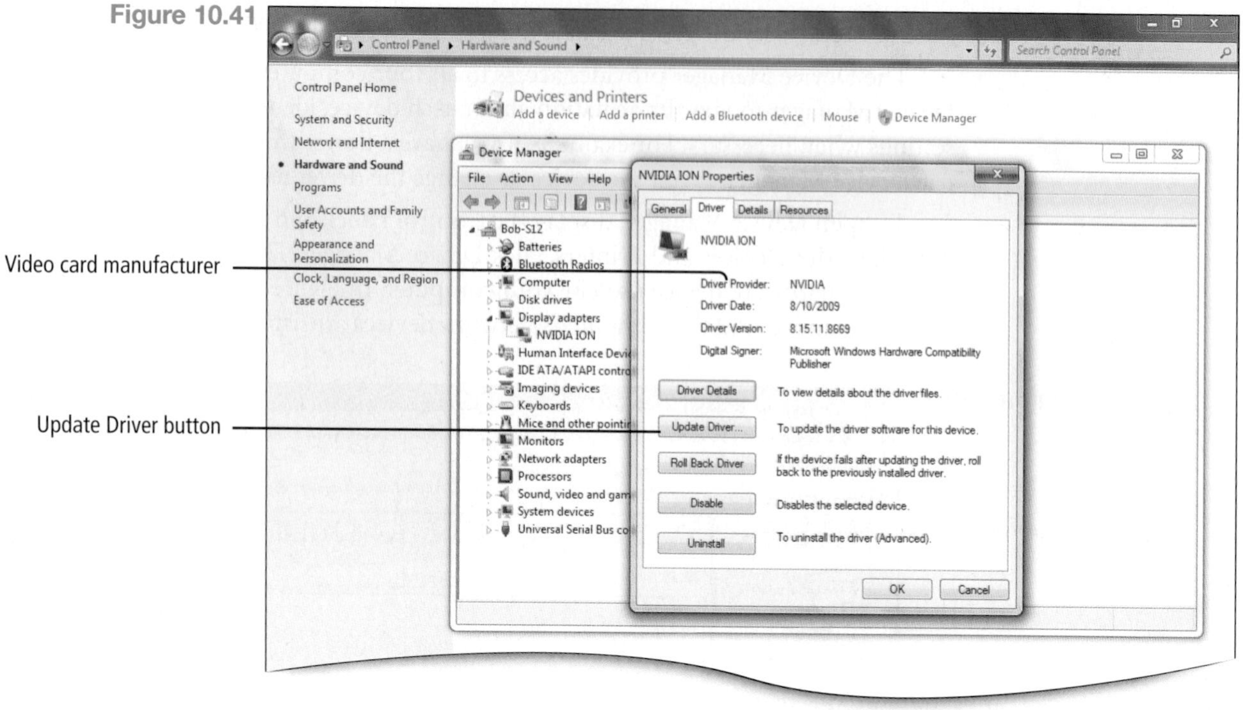

The Roll Back Driver button enables you to return to using an older driver. In certain situations, a new version of a driver creates a problem and you need to roll back to an older version. The Driver tab also enables you to disable a driver. This action is useful if your hardware is conflicting with other hardware. When you click the Uninstall button, the driver is not removed from your computer's hard drive. Instead, the next time you start your computer, Windows 7 reinstalls the driver. This technique is useful when you want to force Windows 7 to reinstall a driver.

To check how well you understand managing drivers using Device Manager, take a moment to answer the following questions:

1. The Device Manager window lists every hardware __________ used by your computer.
2. In __________ __________, double-clicking the device name will open the device's Properties dialog box.
3. If you have a new version of a driver, it can be installed by clicking the __________ Driver button in the device's Properties dialog box.
4. If you would like to use an older version of a driver, in the device's Properties dialog box, click the __________ __________ Driver button.
5. When you want to force Windows 7 to reinstall a driver, in the device's Properties dialog box, click the __________ driver button.

Objective 8 | Remove Malware from Your Computer

If your computer becomes infected with malware, you must take numerous steps to completely remove its effects from your computer. First, you must remove the malware program(s) from your computer after your antivirus program or antispyware program discovers and isolates the infection. After removing the malware, you will probably need to restore several system settings. The amount of time it takes to completely remove malware depends on the type of malware and how long it has been active on your computer.

Activity 10.16 | Removing Malware from Your Computer

Malware authors constantly find new ways to infect computers and they use many techniques to make it difficult for you to completely remove the malware from an infected computer. One way of removing malware is to reformat your hard drive, although this is an extreme measure. Recall that when you format a hard drive, you lose all of its data and all of the installed software. Fortunately, there are other techniques you can use before resorting to a reformat operation.

Try to detect the presence of malware as early as possible. Run regular scans using both an antivirus program and at least one antispyware program. Be aware of the following indications that malware may have infected your computer:

- Your computer suddenly performs slowly.
- You experience pop-up ads when you are not browsing the Internet.
- Your home page or default search page changes.
- When you navigate by typing an address, you are taken to a different Web site.
- There are new icons in your Notification Area for programs that you have not installed.
- There are processes running in Task Manager that do not appear to be system processes or programs that you are running.
- Others tell you that the e-mails you send them are being blocked.
- You become a victim of identity theft.

After you have detected malware and have identified it by name, try to remove it by scanning your computer with your antivirus and antispyware programs. If this fails, search the Internet for information on removing the malware. Many Web sites provide detailed, step-by-step instructions for removing a specific malware program. The table in Figure 10.42 summarizes Web sites that can help you identify and remove malware from your computer.

Web Sites with Help for Identifying and Removing Malware

Sponsor	URL
CA Spyware Encyclopedia	www3.ca.com/securityadvisor
Microsoft Security Essentials	http://www.microsoft.com/security_essentials
Microsoft Security	www.microsoft.com/security
PC Magazine Security Watch	blogs.pcmag.com/securitywatch
ZDNet (Security tab)	www.zdnet.com

Figure 10.42

There are many techniques that you may need to use to remove malware. If you are not comfortable performing any of these techniques yourself, you should ask a computer technician to perform them for you. Try using Windows 7 Programs and Features to uninstall the program or program. Some malware can be completely removed from your computer using this technique.

If your anti-malware program can identify but not isolate malware, use Task Manager to end all processes that the malware is currently running. Unplug your computer from your network, and then scan your computer. Sometimes malware processes must be ended before a malware checker can isolate them. Unplugging your network cable prevents secondary programs that may have skipped detection from downloading the malware and re-installing it.

If you are using Microsoft Security Essentials and want to check the names of malware files that have been removed and those that have not been removed, run the program, and then click the History tab, as shown in Figure 10.43. If any of the items have not been removed, you can use the name in the *Detected item* column to search for a solution on the Internet.

Figure 10.43

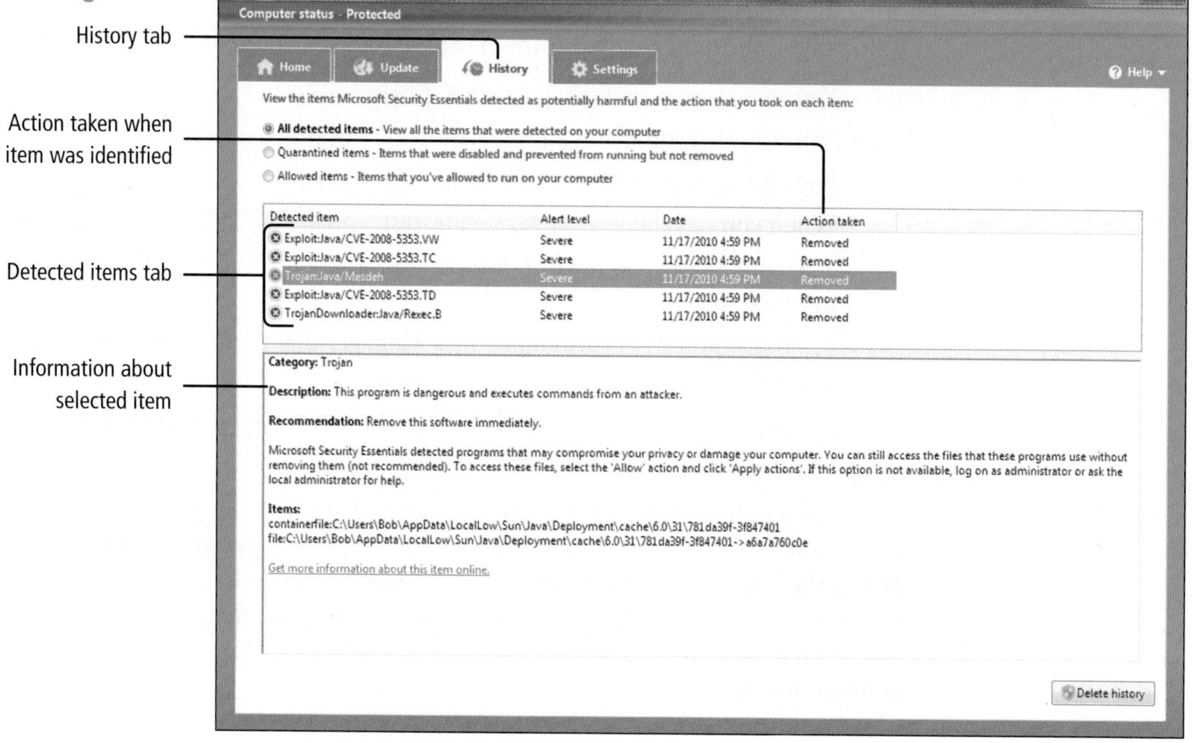

If your anti-malware program cannot isolate the malware, start your computer in ***Safe Mode*** and scan your computer. Safe Mode is a startup option where only the most basic operating system processes are started. Many malware programs will not start in this mode. To start your computer in Safe Mode, press and hold F8 after turning on your computer.

If the malware has disabled your malware checking programs from working properly, you will need to scan your computer using uninfected copies. Using a computer that is not infected, install malware checkers or a ***removal tool*** on a USB drive or CD ROM. A removal tool is a program that uninstalls a specific malware program. For example, *csShredder.exe* removes *CoolWebSearch*, which is very difficult to remove completely using other methods. Use the uninfected programs stored on the USB flash drive or CD ROM to remove the malware.

If all of the previous attempts fail, locate a ***bootable CD ROM***. A bootable CD ROM, or *boot disk*, contains its own operating system. When you start your computer with a bootable CD ROM in the CD/DVD drive, the computer uses the operating system on the boot disk instead of the infected operating system on your hard drive. Sometimes, you can successfully remove the malware using the programs on the CD ROM. Useful bootable CD ROM disks include *Knoppix*, available from http://www.knoppix.org—you may have to click the link to change the page from German to English—and the *Ultimate Boot Disk* from http://www.ultimatebootcd.com.

If you are unable to remove the malware using any of these techniques, consider hiring a computer technician to assist you. If you are not concerned about losing files that you have recently worked with, use System Restore to pick an earlier restore point. Recall that a restore point is a representation of a stored state of your computer's system files. Pick a restore point before the malware was installed. Unfortunately, some malware programs delete all of your restore points to prevent you from using this strategy.

If you decide to format your hard drive, first back up critical files. If needed, start the computer using a bootable CD ROM so that you can back up your files. Re-install Windows 7 using the option that formats your hard drive, and then install all of your programs. Before copying backup files onto your hard drive, be sure to scan them for malware.

To check how well you understand removing viruses from your computer, take a moment to answer the following questions:

1. The most extreme measure to remove malware is to __________ your hard drive.
2. One indication that your computer might be infected with malware is if __________ ads display when you are not browsing the Internet.
3. To start your computer in Safe Mode, press the __________ key after turning on your computer.
4. A removal tool is a program that __________ a specific malware program.
5. One technique to remove malware is to use System Restore to roll your computer back to an earlier __________ __________.

Activity 10.17 | Viewing the Windows Registry

The ***Windows Registry*** is a central repository that stores the settings used by Windows 7 and the applications on your computer. Normally, only a computer technician will need to view your Windows Registry, but sometimes you may need to work with the Windows Registry yourself.

Malware programs often leave settings in the registry that must be changed. Anti-malware software cannot always delete or alter these registry values. For this reason, you may be instructed by a technician or an anti-malware software Web site to change these values yourself. In this activity, you will practice using the Windows Registry by displaying a value that is often altered by browser hijackers.

> **Another Way**
> Click the Start button, and then type *regedit* in the Search box.

1. Hold down [Windows] and press R. In the displayed **Run** dialog box, type **regedit** and then press Enter. In the displayed **User Account Control** dialog box, click **Yes**.

   Any program can be started by typing its process name in the Run dialog box.

2. **Maximize** [Maximize button] the **Registry Editor** window. In the pane on the left, expand [▷] **HKEY_CURRENT_USER**, and then expand [▷] **Software**. Compare your screen with Figure 10.44.

   The ***Registry Editor*** is a tool to view and edit the Windows Registry files that are stored in various locations on your computer. The five major areas of the Windows Registry are called ***hives***. Each hive is divided into ***keys***, which are represented as folders within each hive.

   In the Software key, keys for several programs display, including programs that may have been completely uninstalled from the computer. For example, in Figure 10.44, the Dragon Systems program has been uninstalled using *Uninstall or change a program* in the Control Panel. The settings are left in the Registry so that if you re-install the program, your original settings are preserved. In this same manner, malware can leave settings in the Windows Registry.

Figure 10.44

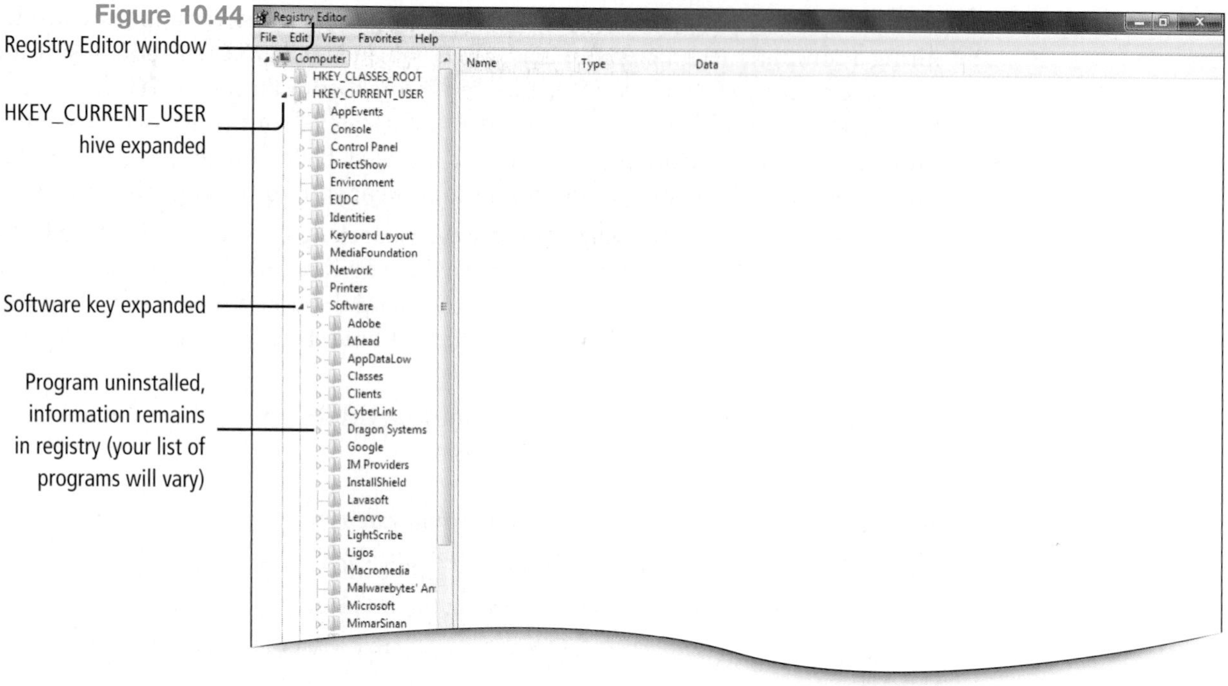

3 Under **Software**, scroll down and expand ▷ the **Microsoft** key. Scroll down and expand ▷ the **Internet Explorer** key. Under the **Internet Explorer** key, scroll down and click the **SearchUrl** key. Compare your screen with Figure 10.45.

The values for the **SearchUrl** key display. This value is often changed by browser hijackers. In Figure 10.45, the URL for the default search engine has been set to the Google search engine. If necessary, these values can be edited or deleted.

Figure 10.45

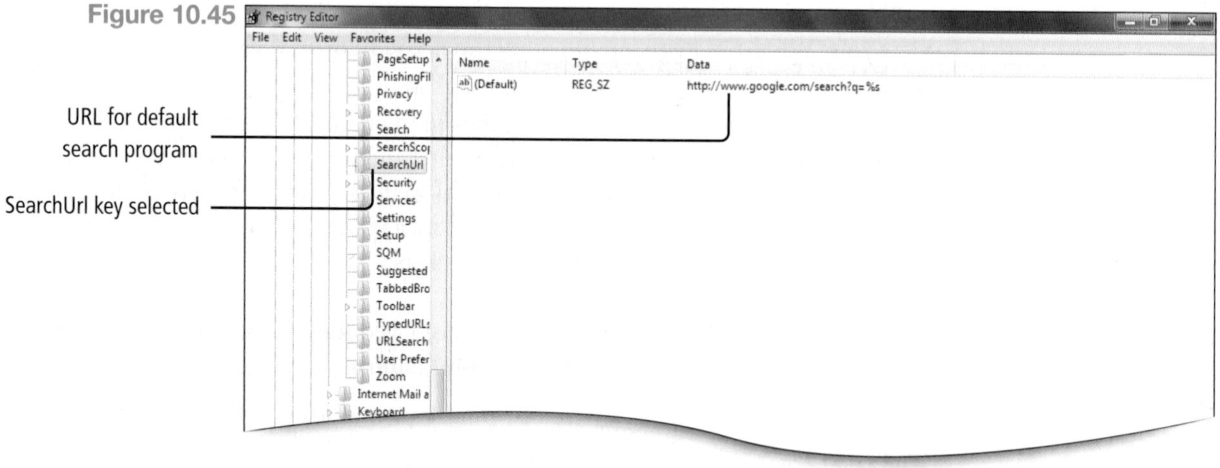

4 **Start** the **Snipping Tool** program, click the **New arrow**, and then click **Full-screen Snip**. In the **Snipping Tool** mark-up window, click the **Save Snip** button.

5 In the **Save As** dialog box, in the **navigation pane**, scroll down as necessary, and then under **Computer**, click your USB flash drive so that it displays in the address bar. Navigate to your **Windows 7 Chapter 10** folder, and then as the file name, type **Lastname_Firstname_10B_Registry_Snip** Be sure the file type is **JPEG**, and then press Enter. **Close** the **Snipping Tool** mark-up window. Hold this file until you finish Project 10B.

6 In the left pane, collapse Internet Explorer, scroll up, and then collapse the **Microsoft** key. Collapse the **Software** key, and then collapse the **HKEY_CURRENT_USER** hive. **Close** the **Registry Editor** window.

> **More Knowledge | Seek Guidance and Create a Restore Point Before Making Changes Using Registry Editor**
>
> When the Windows Registry has improper or missing values, your computer may not work correctly, or it may not work at all. For this reason, you should use the Registry Editor only if you have the knowledge necessary to do so or have guidance from a computer professional.
>
> Because editing the Windows Registry has the potential to worsen the problem you are trying to solve, you should create a Restore Point before you open Registry Editor. When you create a Restore Point, a backup of the Windows Registry is saved as part of the Restore Point. If necessary, you can use this Restore Point to return the computer to its original state.

Activity 10.18 | Restoring Internet Explorer

If you have discovered and removed malware from your computer, there are several settings in Internet Explorer that should be checked and files that should be removed. In this activity, you will practice restoring Internet Explorer files and settings to ensure that your computer is no longer open to attack from malware.

1 Display the **Control Panel**, click **Network and Internet**, and then click **Internet Options**. Compare your screen with Figure 10.46.

In the General tab of the Internet Properties dialog box, you can reset many items that may have been changed by a malware program. For example, some malware programs can make changes to your home page. Here you can change the Home page back to your preferred page.

Figure 10.46

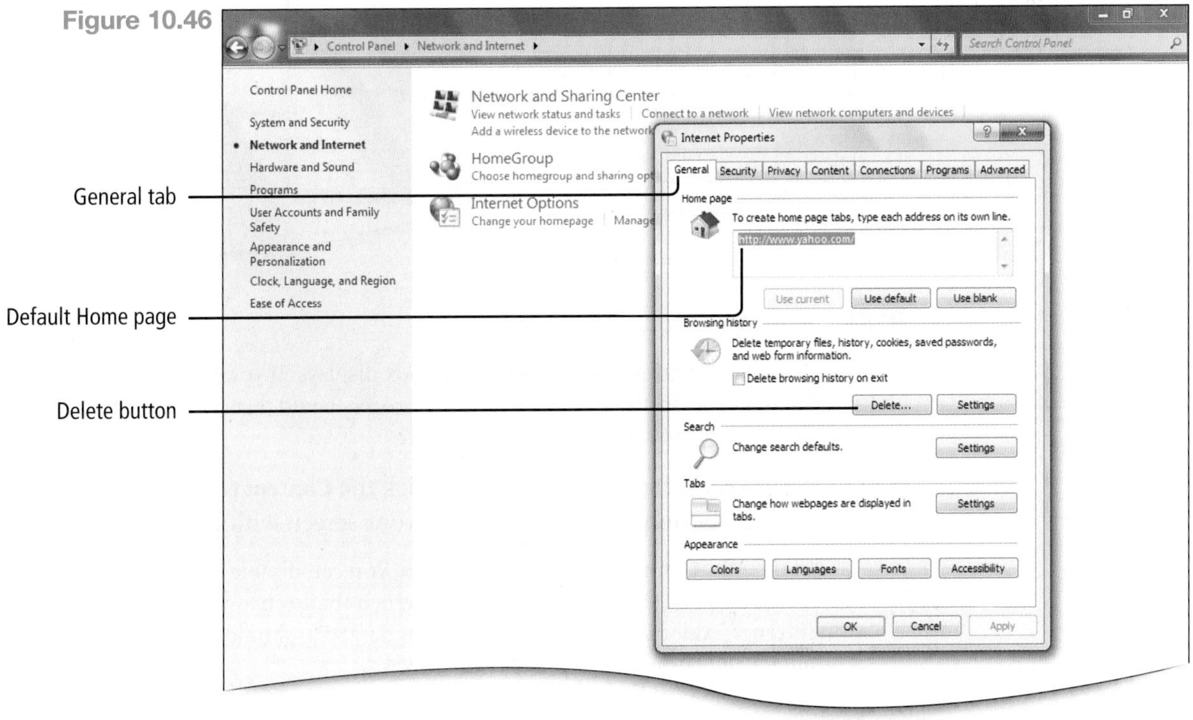

2 Under **Browsing history**, click the **Delete** button and compare your screen with Figure 10.47.

The Delete Browsing History dialog box allows you to delete many of the files and data saved by Internet Explorer. Temporary Internet Files are files downloaded with a Web page, such as the images that display on the page. When you return to a Web site, pages with images stored in the Temporary Internet Files display faster because they do not need to be downloaded from the Web server. If you have visited an infected Web site, you will want to delete all temporary Internet files.

Recall that Web sites may store information about you in cookies. If your computer has been infected by malware, you can delete all of the cookies on your computer.

When you fill out online forms, AutoComplete often tries to complete fields for you. AutoComplete stores commonly typed data such as your e-mail address, credit card numbers, and passwords. If you are concerned that malware has been accessing this AutoComplete data, you should clear the form data and password files.

Figure 10.47

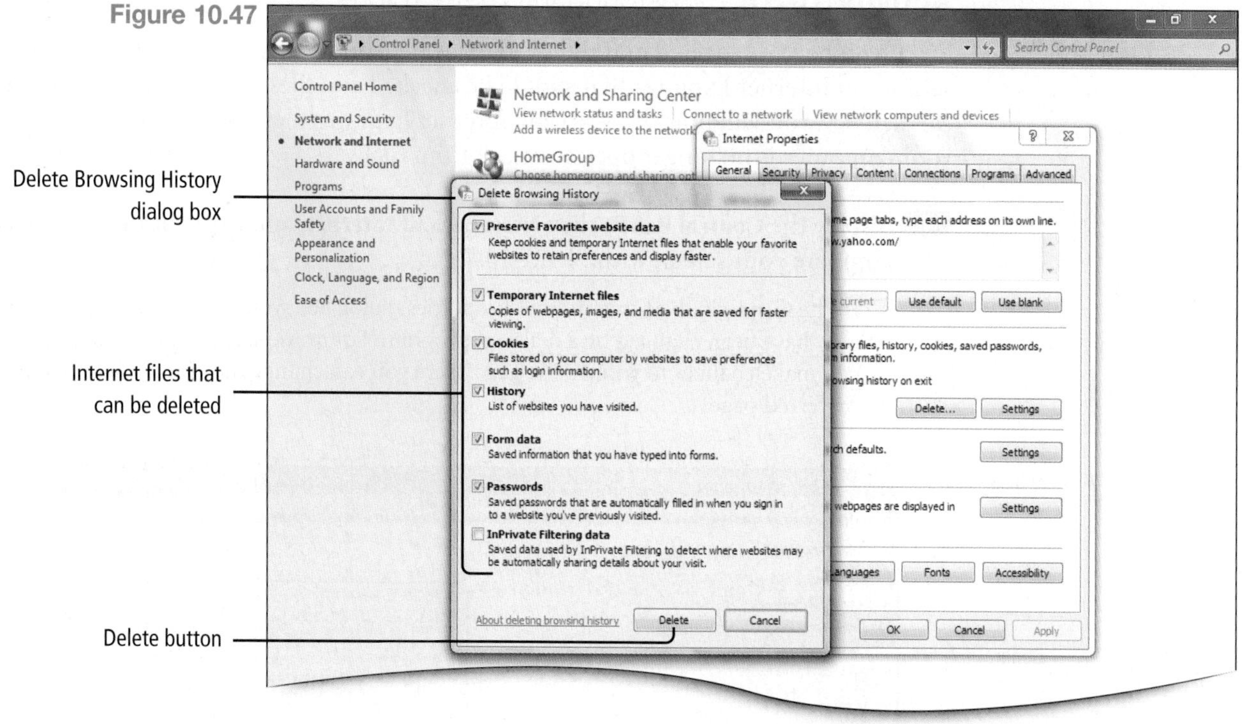

3 Click the **Delete** button.

The Delete Browsing History message box displays. If you have not deleted your browsing history or temporary files recently, the process could take a few moments. When the dialog box closes, the process is complete.

4 In the **Internet Properties** dialog box, click the **Content tab**. Under **AutoComplete**, click the **Settings** button, and then compare your screen with Figure 10.48.

In the AutoComplete Settings dialog box, you can disable any or all of Internet Explorer's AutoComplete features. If you are concerned that someone will find a way to access Internet Explorer's password list or form data, you should clear the *Forms* and *User names and passwords on forms* check boxes.

Figure 10.48

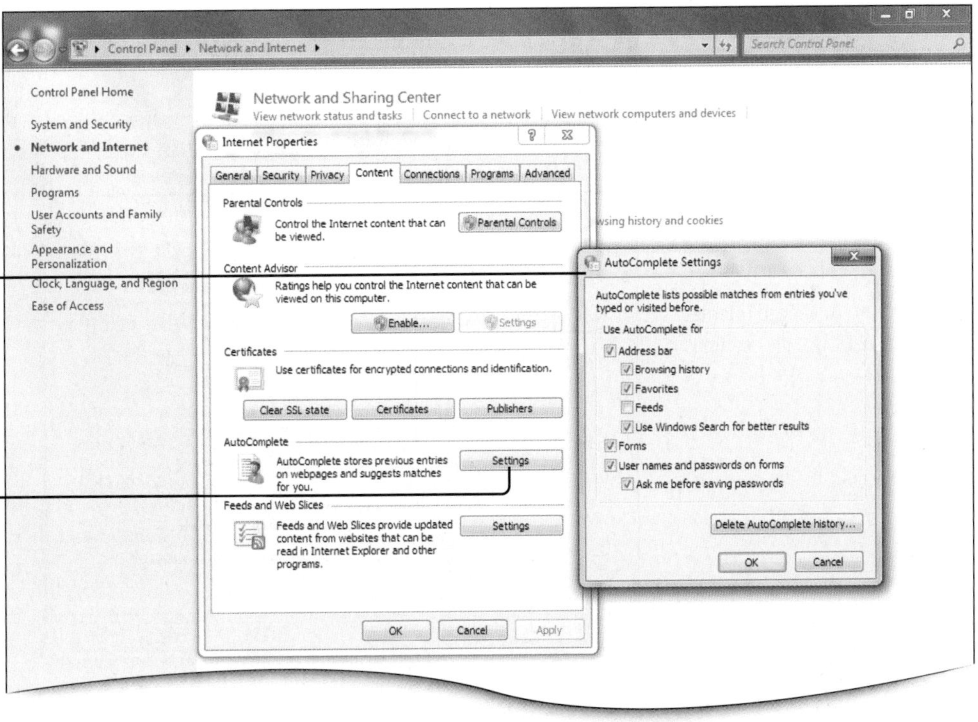

5 Click the **Cancel** button. In the **Internet Properties** dialog box, click the **Programs tab**. Under **Manage add-ons**, click the **Manage add-ons** button. If necessary, click the **Show arrow**, and then click **All add-ons.**

This screen displays the most likely location for drive-by add-ons that have been downloaded to your computer without your knowledge. Here they can be disabled or deleted.

6 **Start** the **Snipping Tool** program, click the **New arrow**, and then click **Full-screen Snip**. In the **Snipping Tool** mark-up window, click the **Save Snip** button.

7 In the **Save As** dialog box, in the **navigation pane**, scroll down as necessary, and then under **Computer**, click your USB flash drive so that it displays in the address bar. Navigate to your **Windows 7 Chapter 10** folder, and then as the file name, type **Lastname_Firstname_10B_Add-ons_Snip** Be sure the file type is **JPEG**, and then press Enter. **Close** the **Snipping Tool** mark-up window. Hold this file until you finish Project 10B.

8 In the **Manage Add-ons** dialog box, click the **Close** button. In the **Internet Properties** dialog box, click the **Advanced tab**, and then compare your screen with Figure 10.49.

In the Advanced tab of the Internet Properties dialog box, you can customize your Internet Explorer settings. One type of malware, a ***browser hijacker***, can change your home page, add shortcuts to your Favorites menu, or lower your security settings by downloading a JavaScript or ActiveX module.

If all of the techniques practiced in this activity fail to restore Internet Explorer, you can click the Reset button. This setting returns Internet Explorer to a state similar to when it was installed on your computer.

Figure 10.49

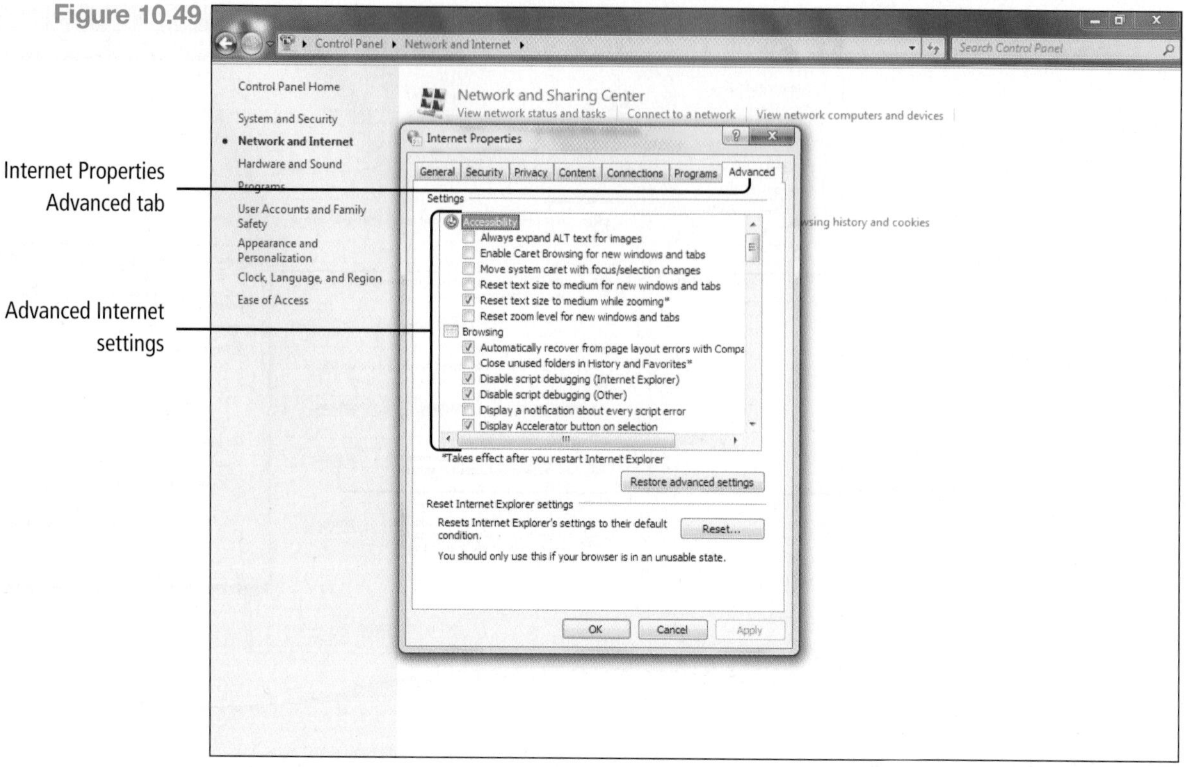

9 **Close** [X] the **Internet Properties** dialog box, and then **Close** [X] all open dialog boxes and windows. As directed by your instructor, submit the five files that are the results of this project.

End **You have completed Project 10B**

Content-Based Assessments

Summary

By using Microsoft Security Essentials and other software, you can reduce the risks of infecting your computer with a virus or spyware. If you are concerned about your computer's security and your personal privacy when you use the Internet, you can increase the security and privacy levels in Internet Explorer. In this chapter, you practiced protecting children using Parental Controls, and you practiced protecting data by encrypting files using the Encryption File System.

Windows 7 provides several tools to help solve problems. In this chapter, you practiced viewing events in Event Viewer. Using Help and Support and Windows Remote Assistance also provides solutions for your computer problems. When hardware does not perform as expected, you can use the Control Panel or Device Manager to make adjustments or fix problems with drivers. Finally, you practiced techniques for removing malware and its residual effects from your computer.

Key Terms

Adware 604
Antispyware program 604
Antivirus program 602
BitLocker Drive Encryption 625
Bootable CD ROM 644
Browser hijacker 649
Custom scan 608
Decrypted 624
Default printer 640
Discussion forum 632
Drive-by downloads 610
EFS 622
Encryption File System 622
Event log 627
Event Viewer 627
Full scan 608
Hives 645
https 618
Infection 601
Intranet 611
IP Address 616
Key 645
Keystroke logger 604
Local printer 639
Malware 601
Microsoft Security Essentials 603
Microsoft SpyNet 608
MSE 603
Patch 601
Peer-to-peer file sharing sites 602
Plug and play 635
PnP 635
Poisoned Web site 601
Posts 632
Privacy Summary 614
Quarantine area 608
Quick scan 608
Registry Editor 645
Remote Assistance expert 633
Remote Assistance novice 633
Removal tool 644
Rootkit 603
Safe Mode 644
Script 610
Secure http 618
Security holes 601
Spyware 601
Spyware checker 604
Third-party cookie 613
Threads 632
Trojan horse 601
Unsigned ActiveX control 611
Virus 601
Virus checker 602
Virus definition 602
Volume 625
Web content 610
Windows Defender 603
Windows Registry 645
Windows Remote Assistance 633
Worm 601
Zero-day exploit 602

Matching

Match each term in the second column with its correct definition in the first column by writing the letter of the term on the blank line in front of the correct definition.

____ 1. The term used to describe the condition of your computer if a malware program installs and runs itself.

____ 2. A type of malware designed specifically to replicate itself by spreading its infection from computer to computer, and which can damage hardware, software, or data.

____ 3. A type of malware that collects personal information, displays advertisements, or changes your browser settings.

____ 4. A self-replicating program—similar to a virus—that spreads on its own to every computer on a network.

A Adware
B Antivirus program
C Infected
D Keystroke logger
E Microsoft SpyNet
F Patch
G Plug and play
H Quarantine area
I Security holes

_____ 5. A malicious software program that hides inside legitimate programs, such as a game, media player, or screen saver.

_____ 6. Vulnerabilities in an operating system or program that allow malware to infect a computer without your knowledge.

_____ 7. A small repair to an operating system or program that closes a security hole.

_____ 8. A program that scans your computer for known viruses trying to get into your e-mail, operating system, or files, and which then attempts to disable and remove them from your computer.

_____ 9. A computer attack that takes place immediately after a known security hole—for which no patch is yet available—is publicized.

_____ 10. A program that records all of your keystrokes and then sends your typed data—including user names and passwords—to someone else.

_____ 11. A program that tracks the Web sites you visit and the terms you type into search engines, and then captures and uses this information to display advertising that matches your interests.

_____ 12. A program within Windows 7 that intercepts spyware before it installs itself on your computer and also scans your hard drive for spyware.

_____ 13. A designated location on your computer from which a program cannot run.

_____ 14. An online community sponsored by Microsoft that collects information about the decisions you and others make regarding spyware identified by Windows Defender.

_____ 15. The capability of Windows 7 to recognize a device as soon as you connect it to your computer, and then automatically install the appropriate drivers and configure the device.

J Spyware
K Trojan horse
L Virus
M Windows Defender
N Worm
O Zero-day exploit

Multiple Choice

Circle the correct answer.

1. A free downloadable program from Microsoft that protects your computer from spyware, adware, and viruses is:
A. Windows Remote Assistance **B.** Microsoft Security Essentials **C.** Microsoft SpyNet

2. A type of malware that enables continued administrator-level access and is typically hidden from both the administrator and the operating system is a:
A. rootkit **B.** drive-by download **C.** third-party cookie

3. The information needed by an antivirus program to find and remove a virus is the:
A. custom scan **B.** spyware checker **C.** virus definition

4. A scan of your computer that checks every file on your hard drive is a:
A. custom scan **B.** full scan **C.** quick scan

5. A program that runs in the browser to add interactive content to a Web page is a:
A. script **B.** post **C.** patch

6. A security feature that encrypts all the data stored on a volume is:
A. BitLocker Drive Encryption **B.** https **C.** EFS

7. In a discussion forum, a list of topics is referred to as:
A. hives **B.** posts **C.** threads

8. A storage area on a hard disk that is formatted with a file system is a:
A. PnP **B.** volume **C.** cookie

9. A program that uninstalls a specific malware program is a:
A. Remote Assistance expert **B.** removal tool **C.** peer-to-peer file sharing site

10. A division of hives in the Windows Registry represented by a folder is a:
A. key **B.** log **C.** partition

Content-Based Assessments

Apply **10A** skills from these Objectives:

1. Protect Your Computer from Viruses and Spyware
2. Secure Internet Explorer
3. Set Parental Controls
4. Encrypt Files with Encryption File System

Skills Review | Project 10C Control Computer Security

Project Files

For Project 10C, you will need the following files:

Student Resource CD (or a USB flash drive containing these files)
win10_10C_Answer_Sheet (Word document)

You will save your file as:

Lastname_Firstname_10C_Answer_Sheet

Project Results

1 **Close** [X] all open windows. On the taskbar, click the **Windows Explorer** button. In the **navigation pane**, click the drive that contains the student files for this textbook, and then navigate to **01_student_data_files ▶ Chapter_Files ▶ Chapter_10**. Double-click the Word file **win10_10C_Answer_Sheet** to open Word and display the document. Press F12 to display the **Save As** dialog box in Word, navigate to your **Windows 7 Chapter 10** folder, and then using your own name, save the document as **Lastname_Firstname_10C_Answer_Sheet** If necessary, click OK if a message regarding formats displays.

On the taskbar, click the **Word** button to minimize the window and leave your Word document accessible from the taskbar. As you complete each step in this project, click the Word button on the taskbar to open the document, type your one-letter answer in the appropriate cell of the Word table, and then on the taskbar, click the button again to minimize the window for the next step.

Close [X] Windows Explorer. Display the **Control Panel**, click **System and Security**, click **Action Center**, and then click the **Security arrow** to expand the area. Which item is *not* listed under **Security**?

a. Internet security settings
b. User Account Control
c. Windows Defender settings

2 At the bottom of the list, click the link labeled *How do I know what security settings are right for my computer?* and then under **Windows Defender**, click the link labeled *Using Windows Defender*. According to this information, spyware can:

a. Be installed on your computer from removable media
b. Be programmed to run at unexpected times
c. Both A. and B.

3 According to this information, Windows Defender keeps spyware from infecting your computer by offering:

a. Real-time protection with displayed alerts
b. E-mail notifications of spyware attempts
c. Both A. and B.

(Project 10C Control Computer Security continues on the next page)

Skills Review | Project 10C Control Computer Security (continued)

4 According to this information, definitions are:

a. Types of spyware
b. Types of software
c. Files that contain information about potential software threats

5 Click the link labeled *Understanding Windows Defender alert levels*. According to this information, an alert level of Low means that:

a. Programs are collecting personal information without your consent.
b. Programs are changing your computer's settings.
c. Programs are collecting information within the licensing terms to which you agreed when you installed the program.

6 **Close** the **Windows Help and Support** window, and then **Close** the **Action Center** window. Redisplay the **Control Panel**, click **Network and Internet**, and then click **Internet Options**. Click the **Security tab**. With **Internet** selected as the zone, move the slider to view the available security levels. Which security level is not available in the *Internet zone*?

a. High
b. Medium-low
c. Medium

7 Return the **Internet** zone security level to **Medium-high**—or to its original level—and then click the **Privacy tab**. Which privacy setting *cannot* be changed on the *Privacy* tab?

a. InPrivate
b. Phishing Filter
c. Pop-up Blocker

8 **Close** the **Internet Properties** dialog box, and then in the **Network and Internet** window, on the left, click **User Accounts and Family Safety**. Click **Parental Controls**, and then click **Create a new user account**. As the new account name, type **myChild** and then click the **Create account** button. Click the new account name to display the **User Controls**. Which of the following is a setting that *can* be controlled from this window?

a. Gambling
b. Games
c. Chat rooms

9 Under **Parental Controls**, click the **On, enforce current settings** options button. Under **Windows Settings**, click **Games**, and then click **Set game ratings**. Which rating applies to titles that contain *no* material that parents would find inappropriate?

a. Early Childhood
b. Everyone
c. Everyone 10+

10 Click **Cancel**, and then click **OK** two times. In the left pane of the **Parental Controls** window, under **See also**, click **User Accounts**. Click **Manage another account**, click the **myChild** account, and then click **Delete the account**. Click the **Delete Files** button, and then click the **Delete Account** button. **Close** the **Manage Accounts** window. Display the **Documents**

(Project 10C Control Computer Security continues on the next page) window. In the **file list**, right-click a blank area, point to **New**, click **Text Document**, and then press Enter. Right-click **New Text Document**, and then click **Properties**. To the right of **Attributes**, click the **Advanced** button. Select the **Encrypt contents to secure data** check box, and then click **OK** two times. Which of the following is *not* a choice in the **Encryption Warning** dialog box?

a. Encrypt the file and its parent folder

b. Encrypt the file only

c. Encrypt the folder only

Click **Cancel**. In the **file list**, delete **New Text Document**, and then **Close** the **Documents** window. Be sure you have typed all of your answers in your Word document. Save and close your Word document, and submit as directed by your instructor.

End You have completed Project 10C

Apply **10B** skills from these Objectives:

- 5 Troubleshoot Computer Problems
- 6 Find and Use Help from Others
- 7 Manage Hardware Devices
- 8 Remove Malware from Your Computer

Skills Review | Project 10D Troubleshoot Your Computer

Project Files

For Project 10D, you will need the following files:

Student Resource CD (or a USB flash drive containing these files)
win10_10D_Answer_Sheet (Word document)

You will save your file as:

Lastname_Firstname_10D_Answer_Sheet

Project Results

1 **Close** all open windows. On the taskbar, click the **Windows Explorer** button. In the **navigation pane**, click the drive that contains the student files for this textbook, and then navigate to **01_student_data_files ▶ Chapter_Files ▶ Chapter_10**. Double-click the Word file **win10_10D_Answer_Sheet** to open Word and display the document. Press F12 to display the **Save As** dialog box in Word, navigate to your **Windows 7 Chapter 10** folder, and then using your own name, save the document as **Lastname_Firstname_10D_Answer_Sheet** If necessary, click OK if a message regarding formats displays.

On the taskbar, click the **Word** button to minimize the window and leave your Word document accessible from the taskbar. As you complete each step in this project, click the Word button on the taskbar to open the document, type your one-letter answer in the appropriate cell of the Word table, and then on the taskbar, click the button again to minimize the window for the next step.

Close Windows Explorer. Display the **Control Panel**, click **System and Security**, and then under **Administrative Tools**, click **View event logs**. What is the purpose of the Event Viewer?

- **a.** To schedule maintenance events on your computer
- **b.** To view events that have occurred on your computer
- **c.** Both A. and B.

2 **Maximize** the **Event Viewer** window on your screen. Which of the following is *not* an event type?

- **a.** Error
- **b.** Logon Success
- **c.** Warning

3 **Close** the **Event Viewer** window and the **System and Security** window. Click **Start**, and then click **Help and Support**. Click **Learn about Windows Basics**, and then under **Learn about your computer**, click **Parts of a computer**. Under **In this article**, click **Printer**. Which of the following is *not* a type of printer discussed in the article?

- **a.** Dot matrix
- **b.** Inkjet
- **c.** Laser

(Project 10D Troubleshoot Your Computer continues on the next page)

Skills Review | Project 10D Troubleshoot Your Computer (continued)

4 At the top of the **Windows Help and Support** window, click the **Help and Support home** button. Under **Not sure where to start?**, click **Browse Help topics**, click **Security and privacy**, and then click **Understanding security and safe computing**. In this information, click the green word *viruses* to display its definition. Which of the following statements best matches the definition of a virus as shown in this article?

a. A virus is a malicious program that controls your Web browser.

b. A virus is a malicious program that collects your personal information without properly obtaining permission.

c. A virus is a malicious program designed to replicate itself.

5 Click the **Help and Support home** button. In the **Search Help** box, type **registry** and then press Enter. Click **What is Registry Editor?**. Click the green word *registry* to display its definition. Which of the following statements best matches the definition for this term?

a. The registry is a repository of information about the computer's configuration.

b. The registry is a file of registered computer programs.

c. The registry is a database of Windows updates made to the computer.

6 At the end of the article, click the link labeled *Back up the registry*. In the first step, click the link labeled *Click to open Registry Editor*. In the **User Account Control** dialog box, click **Yes**. On the left, expand ▶ **HKEY_ CURRENT_USER**, expand ▶ **Software**, expand ▶ **Microsoft**, expand ▶ **Internet Explorer** and then click **Document Windows**. Which of the following is not a listed name?

a. Height

b. Minimized

c. Width

7 In the pane on the left, collapse **Internet Explorer**, collapse **Microsoft**, collapse **Software**, and then collapse **HKEY_CURRENT_USER**. **Close** the **Registry Editor** window. In the displayed **Windows Help and Support** window, click the **Help and Support home** button, click **Browse Help topics**, click **Hardware, devices, and drivers**, click **Drivers**, and then click **Tips for fixing common driver problems**. Expand **I just installed a new hardware device, and it's not working properly**. Which of the following is typically the cause of this problem?

a. A noncompatible or missing driver

b. An out-of-date network adapter driver

c. An out-of-date version of Internet Explorer

8 Click the green word *USB port*. Which bests describes this definition?

a. A USB port is a device.

b. A USB port is a connection point on a computer or device.

c. A USB port is a driver.

9 **Close** the **Windows Help and Support Window**. Display the **Control Panel**, in the **Search Control Panel** box type **keyboard** and press Enter. Click **Keyboard** to display the **Keyboard Properties** dialog box. On the **Speed tab**, which of the following is *not* a Character repeat setting?

a. Repeat delay

b. Repeat rate

c. Repeat speed

(Project 10D Troubleshoot Your Computer continues on the next page)

Skills Review | Project 10D Troubleshoot Your Computer (continued)

10 **Close** all open windows. Open **Internet Explorer**, on the **Command bar**, click the **Tools** button, and then click **Internet Options**. On the **General tab**, under **Browsing history**, click the **Delete** button. In the displayed **Delete Browsing History** dialog box, which of the following can be deleted?

a. Add-ons

b. Favorites

c. Passwords

Click **Cancel** to close the **Delete Browsing History** dialog box. Be sure you have typed all of your answers in your Word document. Save and close your Word document; submit it as directed by your instructor. **Close** all open windows.

End You have completed Project 10D

Apply 10A skills from these Objectives:

1. Protect Your Computer from Viruses and Spyware
2. Secure Internet Explorer
3. Set Parental Controls
4. Encrypt Files with Encryption File System

Mastering Windows 7 | Project 10E Control Computer Security

In the following Mastering Windows 7 project, you will change Internet privacy and security settings, set parental controls, and create an encrypted folder. You will capture screens that look similar to Figure 10.50.

Project Files

For Project 10E, you will need the following files:

New Snip files

You will save your file as:

Lastname_Firstname_10E_Security_Snip
Lastname_Firstname_10E_Privacy_Snip
Lastname_Firstname_10E_Parental_Controls_Snip
Lastname_Firstname_10E_Encrypted_Snip

Project Results

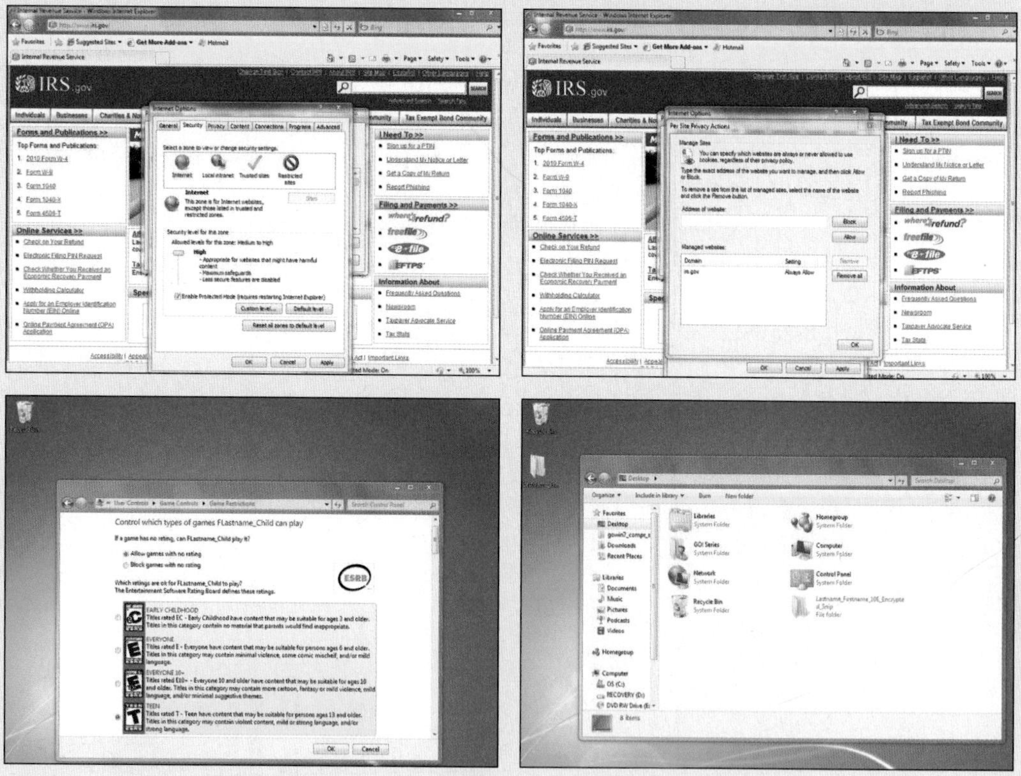

Figure 10.50

(Project 10E Control Computer Security continues on the next page)

Mastering Windows 7 | Project 10E Control Computer Security (continued)

1 **StartInternet Explorer** and navigate to **http://www.irs.gov** On the **Command bar**, click the **Safety** button, click **Webpage Privacy Policy**, in the **Privacy Report** dialog box, click the site's name at the top of the list, and then view the site's **Summary**. In the **Privacy Policy** dialog box, always allow this site to use cookies. Click **OK**.

2 In the **Privacy Report** dialog box, click **Settings** to display the **Internet Options** dialog box. On the **Security tab**, for the **Internet** zone, change the security level to **High**. Create a **Full-screen Snip**, and then save it as **Lastname_Firstname_10E_Security_Snip**

3 In the **Internet Options** dialog box, display the **Privacy tab**, and then click the **Sites** button. Create a **Full-screen Snip**, and then save it as **Lastname_Firstname_10E_Privacy_Snip**

4 Remove **irs.gov** from the list of managed websites, and then **Close** the **Per Site Privacy Actions** dialog box. Click the **Security tab**, and then click the **Reset all zones to default level** button. **Close** the dialog boxes and Internet Explorer.

5 From the **Control Panel**, display the **Parental Controls** window, and then, using your own first initial and last name, create a new user account named **FLastname_Child** For the new account you just created, set **Parental Controls** to **On**. Set the **Games rating** to **TEEN**. Create a **Full-screen Snip**, and then save it as **Lastname_Firstname_10E_Parental_Controls_Snip**

6 Delete the **FLastname_Child** user account that you created earlier along with its associated files. Open Windows Explorer, and then in the **navigation pane**, scroll up if necessary, and then click **Desktop**. Create a new folder, and then name it **Lastname_Firstname_10E_Encrypted_Snip**

7 Encrypt the new folder, and then click in a blank area to deselect. Create a **Full-screen Snip**, and then save it as **Lastname_Firstname_10E_Encrypted_Snip**

8 Delete the **10E_Encrypted_Snip_Firstname_Lastname** folder, and then **Close** the **Desktop** window. Submit the four snip files that are the results of this project to your instructor as directed.

End **You have completed Project 10E**

Content-Based Assessments

Apply 10B skills from these Objectives:

5 Troubleshoot Computer Problems
6 Find and Use Help from Others
7 Manage Hardware Devices
8 Remove Malware from Your Computer

Mastering Windows 7 | Project 10F Troubleshoot Your Computer

In the following Mastering Windows 7 project, you will find information in Help and Support, and view information on Device Manager. You will also use Registry Viewer to view the Control Panel's settings for your mouse device, and then view the add-ons that have been used by Internet Explorer. You will capture screens that look similar to Figure 10.51.

Project Files

For Project 10F, you will need the following files:

New Snip files

You will save your files as:

Lastname_Firstname_10F_Help_Snip
Lastname_Firstname_10F_Device_Snip
Lastname_Firstname_10F_Registry_Snip
Lastname_Firstname_10F_Add-ons_Snip

Project Results

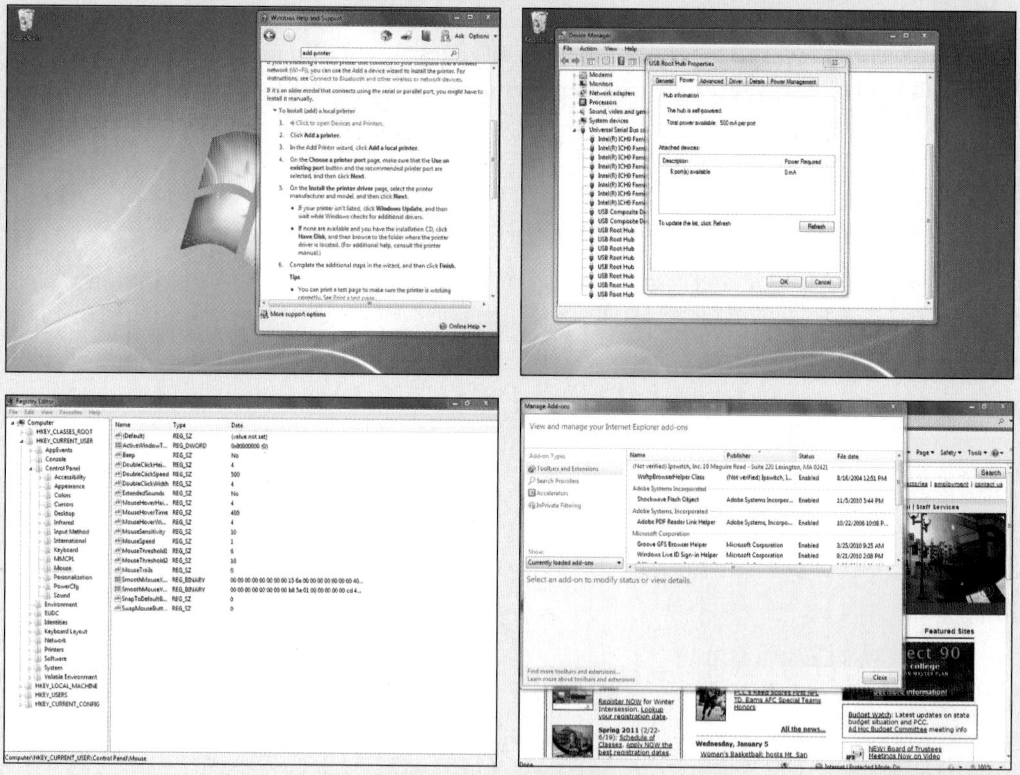

Figure 10.51

(Project 10F Troubleshoot Your Computer continues on the next page)

Mastering Windows 7 | Project 10F Troubleshoot Your Computer (continued)

1 From the **Start** menu, open **Help and Support**, and then search for the phrase **add printer** Follow the link to **Install a printer**. Expand **To install (add) a local printer**. Create a **Full-screen Snip**, and then save it as **Lastname_ Firstname_10F_Help_Snip Close** all open windows.

2 Click **Start**, in the **Search** box type **device manager** and then open the **Device Manager**. Expand **Universal Serial Bus controllers**. Point to the first displayed **USB Root Hub**, right-click, click **Properties**, and then click the **Power tab**. Create a **Full-screen Snip**, and then save it as **Lastname_Firstname_10F_Device_Snip. Close** all open windows.

3 Click **Start**, in the **Search** box type **regedit** and then open the **regedit**; if necessary, click Yes. Expand the **HKEY_CURRENT_USER** hive, expand **Control Panel**, and then in the displayed list, click **Mouse**. Create a **Full-screen Snip**, and then save it as **Lastname_Firstname_10F_Registry_Snip**

4 Collapse **Control Panel**, collapse the **HKEY_CURRENT_USER** hive, and then **Close** the **Registry Editor** window.

5 Start **Internet Explorer**, on the **Command bar** click **Tools**, and then open the **Internet Options** dialog box. On the **Programs tab**, display the add-ons that have been used by Internet Explorer. Create a **Full-screen Snip**, and then save it as **Lastname_Firstname_10F_Add-ons_Snip** **Close** all open windows, and then submit the four files that are the results of this project to your instructor as directed.

End **You have completed Project 10F**

Outcomes-Based Assessments

Rubric

The following outcomes-based assessments are *open-ended assessments*. That is, there is no specific correct result; your result will depend on your approach to the information provided. Make *Professional Quality* your goal. Use the following scoring rubric to guide you in *how* to approach the problem, and then to evaluate *how well* your approach solves the problem.

The *criteria*—Software Mastery, Content, Format and Layout, and Process—represent the knowledge and skills you have gained that you can apply to solving the problem. The *levels of performance*—Professional Quality, Approaching Professional Quality, or Needs Quality Improvements—help you and your instructor evaluate your result.

	Your completed project is of Professional Quality if you:	**Your completed project is Approaching Professional Quality if you:**	**Your completed project Needs Quality Improvements if you:**
1-Software Mastery	Choose and apply the most appropriate skills, tools, and features and identify efficient methods to solve the problem.	Choose and apply some appropriate skills, tools, and features, but not in the most efficient manner.	Choose inappropriate skills, tools, or features, or are inefficient in solving the problem.
2-Content	Construct a solution that is clear and well organized, contains content that is accurate, appropriate to the audience and purpose, and is complete. Provide a solution that contains no errors in spelling, grammar, or style.	Construct a solution in which some components are unclear, poorly organized, inconsistent, or incomplete. Misjudge the needs of the audience. Have some errors in spelling, grammar, or style, but the errors do not detract from comprehension.	Construct a solution that is unclear, incomplete, or poorly organized; contains some inaccurate or inappropriate content; and contains many errors in spelling, grammar, or style. Do not solve the problem.
3-Format and Layout	Format and arrange all elements to communicate information and ideas, clarify function, illustrate relationships, and indicate relative importance.	Apply appropriate format and layout features to some elements, but not others. Overuse features, causing minor distraction.	Apply format and layout that does not communicate information or ideas clearly. Do not use format and layout features to clarify function, illustrate relationships, or indicate relative importance. Use available features excessively, causing distraction.
4-Process	Use an organized approach that integrates planning, development, self-assessment, revision, and reflection.	Demonstrate an organized approach in some areas, but not others; or, use an insufficient process of organization throughout.	Do not use an organized approach to solve the problem.

Apply a combination of the 10A and 10B skills.

Problem Solving | Project 10G Help Desk

In this project, you will construct a solution by applying any combination of the skills you practiced from the Objectives in Projects 10A and 10B.

Project Files

For Project 10G, you will need the following file:

win10_10G_Help_Desk

You will save your document as:

Lastname_Firstname_10G_Help_Desk

From the student files that accompany this textbook, open the **Chapter_Files** folder, and then in **Chapter_10** folder, locate and open the Word document **win10_10G_Help_Desk**. Save the document in your chapter folder as **Lastname_Firstname_10G_Help_Desk**

The following e-mail question has arrived at the Help Desk from an employee at the Bell Orchid Hotel's corporate office. In the Word form, construct a response based on your knowledge of Windows 7. Although an e-mail response is not as formal as a letter, you should still use good grammar, good sentence structure, professional language, and a polite tone. Save your document and submit the response as directed by your instructor.

To: Help Desk

I am concerned about protecting my privacy as I browse the Internet. I would like to prevent all but a few sites from writing cookies on my computer. What steps do I need to take to block all cookies except for the four sites that I want to allow?

End **You have completed Project 10G**

Outcomes-Based Assessments

Apply a combination of the **10A** and **10B** skills.

Problem Solving | Project **10H** Help Desk

In this project, you will construct a solution by applying any combination of the skills you practiced from the Objectives in Projects 10A and 10B.

Project Files

For Project 10H, you will need the following file:

win10_10H_Help_Desk

You will save your document as:

Lastname_Firstname_10H_Help_Desk

From the student files that accompany this textbook, open the **Chapter_Files** folder, and then in **Chapter_10** folder, locate and open the Word document **win10_10H_Help_Desk**. Save the document in your chapter folder as **Lastname_Firstname_10H_Help_Desk**

The following e-mail question has arrived at the Help Desk from an employee at the Bell Orchid Hotel's corporate office. In the Word form, construct a response based on your knowledge of Windows 7. Although an e-mail response is not as formal as a letter, you should still use good grammar, good sentence structure, professional language, and a polite tone. Save your document and submit the response as directed by your instructor.

To: Help Desk

I am having a problem on my computer that is hard to describe using e-mail. I would like to show you the problem using Remote Assistance. What do I need to do to start a Remote Assistance session with you?

End You have completed Project 10H

Apply a combination of the 10A and 10B skills.

Problem Solving | Project 10I Help Desk

In this project, you will construct a solution by applying any combination of the skills you practiced from the Objectives in Projects 10A and 10B.

Project Files

For Project 10I, you will need the following file:

win10_10I_Help_Desk

You will save your document as:

Lastname_Firstname_10I_Help_Desk

From the student files that accompany this textbook, open the **Chapter_Files** folder, and then in **Chapter_10** folder, locate and open the Word document **win10_10I_Help_Desk**. Save the document in your chapter folder as **Lastname_Firstname_10I_Help_Desk**

The following e-mail question has arrived at the Help Desk from an employee at the Bell Orchid Hotel's corporate office. In the Word form, construct a response based on your knowledge of Windows 7. Although an e-mail response is not as formal as a letter, you should still use good grammar, good sentence structure, professional language, and a polite tone. Save your document and submit the response as directed by your instructor.

To: Help Desk

My computer is infected with spyware named *Adware.Websearch*. I have scanned my computer, but the program keeps reappearing. Is there anything that I can do so that I can completely remove this program? Also, what can I do to prevent this from happening again?

End You have completed Project 10I

Glossary

2-foot interface The term that refers to the normal distance that you sit from your computer, which is commonly two feet.

802.11 The term for a group of standards for wireless networks that refer to various rates of data transfer speed.

10-foot interface The term that refers to the ability to control Windows Media Center by sitting 10 feet away from it in the same manner as you sit away from your TV.

Accelerator An Internet Explorer feature that displays a blue Accelerator icon when you select text from any Web page, and which when clicked enables you to accomplish tasks such as finding a map, defining a word, or e-mailing content to others.

Action Center A central place to view alerts and take actions, for example to view and install updates and view important messages about security and maintenance settings on your computer.

ActiveX A technology for creating interactive Web content such as animation sequences, credit card transactions, or spreadsheet calculations.

ActiveX control A type of add-on that uses ActiveX technology.

Add-on A program that adds features to a Web browser such as Internet Explorer.

Address bar (Windows Explorer) Displays your current location in the folder structure as a series of links separated by arrows.

Address bar (Internet Explorer) The area at the top of the Internet Explorer window that displays, and where you can type, a URL.

Adjust for best performance A setting that does not display the typical Windows 7 visual effects.

Administrator account A user account that lets you make changes that will affect other users of the computer; the most powerful of the three types of accounts, because it permits the most control over the computer.

Adware A program that tracks the Web sites you visit and the terms you type into search engines, and then captures and uses this information to display advertising that matches your interests.

Aero The term that refers to the desktop experience that features a translucent glass design for windows, attractive graphics, taskbar previews of open windows, and the Aero features such as Snap and Aero Peek.

Aero Flip 3D A feature that arranges your open windows in a three-dimensional stack that you can flip through quickly without having to click buttons on the taskbar.

Aero Peek A technology that assists you when you have multiple windows open by allowing you to *peek* at either the desktop that is behind open windows or at a window that is hidden from view by other windows; then, you can move the mouse back into the taskbar to close the peek.

Aero Shake A feature in which you can shake an active window by moving the mouse vigorously back and forth on the title bar to have all other open windows minimize; you can then restore all the windows by shaking the open window again.

All Programs An area on the Start menu that displays all the programs on your computer system that are available to you; some groups of programs display in a folder.

AND filter When used in a search, finds files that contain both search terms even if those terms are not next to each other.

Antispyware program A program that scans your computer for spyware and attempts to remove or disable it.

Antivirus program A program that scans your computer for known viruses trying to get into your e-mail, operating system, or files, and then attempts to disable and remove them from your computer.

Application Another term for a program.

Architecture The data-handling capacity of a microprocessor in terms of the size of the data groups in which a CPU receives and sends data.

Arrange by In a folder window, a feature that enables you to arrange the items by Author, Date modified, Tag, Type, or Name; the default arrangement is Folder.

Auto adjust The automatic correction tool in Windows Photo Gallery with which you can adjust the exposure of a photo.

AutoMovie theme A Movie Maker feature that enables you to create a polished movie in a few seconds by adding your pictures and movies and then selecting a theme; AutoMovie adds a title, credits, and special effects.

AutoPlay A Windows 7 feature that lets you choose which program to use to start different kinds of media, such as music CDs, or CDs and DVDs containing photos; it displays when you plug in or insert media or storage devices.

Backing up The process of creating a copy of your files somewhere other than on your computer—for example, on a CD, a DVD, or an external hard drive.

Bad sector A sector of a disk drive that has experienced a failure.

Base locations Locations that you frequently need to access to manage your computer including Libraries, Homegroup if you have one, your personal folder, Computer, Network, Control Panel, and Recycle Bin.

Benchmarking The process of running benchmark tests.

Benchmarks Standardized tests that measure computer system performance.

Bing An Internet search engine by Microsoft.

BIOS (Basic Input/Output System) A program installed by a computer's manufacturer that runs at startup, checks the hardware devices, and then loads the operating system.

Bit rate The number of bits transferred per unit of time, typically expressed in bits per second.

BitLocker Drive Encryption A security feature that encrypts all the data stored on a volume.

Bitmap An image format that can display millions of colors and can be used to share images with others who may be using different graphic programs.

Blog An online journal or column used to publish personal or company information in an informal manner.

.bmp The file extension for a bitmap image.

Bookmark managers Free Web tools available to manage your favorites.

Boolean operators The terms AND, OR, and NOT that govern the logical functions and express a condition that is either true or false.

Bootable CD ROM A CD that contains its own operating system and from which you can boot your computer.

Booting the computer The process of turning on a computer when the computer has been completely shut down and during which the BIOS program will run.

Bottleneck A slow computer component that restricts the flow of data and slows the performance of the entire computer.

Broadband connection Any high-speed Internet connection that typically operates at speeds of 256 kilobytes per second (kbps) or faster.

Browser hijacker A type of malware that can change your home page, add shortcuts to your Favorites menu, or lower your security settings by downloading a JavaScript or an ActiveX module.

Browsing (Windows Explorer) A term used to describe the process of navigating within Windows 7 to look for a specific program, file, e-mail, Control Panel feature, or Internet favorite.

Browsing (Internet Explorer) The term used to describe the process of using your computer to view Web pages.

Browsing history The information stored by Internet Explorer about the sites you have visited and the information you have typed into a site.

Burning a disc The process of writing files on a CD or DVD.

Byte A storage unit that typically stores a single character such as a number or letter, and is commonly used to measure storage size on computers.

Cable Internet access An Internet connection that connects to an Internet Service Provider by sending digital signals over the coaxial cables used to deliver cable television services.

Caption Text that accompanies images or videos, either as a supplemental description or a transcript of spoken words.

Card reader A device that reads and writes data to various types of flash memory cards such as the card you use in your digital camera; can be built into your computer or can be plugged into a USB port on your computer.

Cascade An arrangement of open windows on your screen that display in a single stack fanned out so that each title bar is visible.

Case sensitive A requirement, especially for computer passwords, in which capitalization must match each time the characters are typed.

Cat5 The Ethernet cable that supports Fast Ethernet.

Cat6 The Ethernet cable that supports Gigabit Ethernet.

Central processing unit The main circuit chip in a computer that processes the data and program instructions.

Certificate A digital document that verifies the identity of a person or indicates the security of a Web site.

Certification Authorities Companies, for example Verisign, that issue digital certificates.

CHKDSK Another name for the Check Disk program.

Check box feature A folder option which, when applied, displays a check box to the left of folders and files.

Click The action of pressing the left mouse button.

Client A computer connecting to, or requesting the services of, the server.

Client/server network A network in which account logon information and files are stored on a server computer, and a computer connecting to—or requesting the services of—the server is referred to as the client.

Clipboard A temporary storage area for information that you have copied or moved from one place and plan to use somewhere else.

Clock rate The rate of speed at which a CPU performs; measured in megahertz (MHz) or gigahertz (GHz).

Cluster The smallest area in which data can be written on a disk using the file NTFS or FAT systems.

Color temperature A photo effect that makes a photo appear cooler (more blue) or warmer (more earth tones).

Common dialog boxes The dialog boxes, such as Save and Save As, provided by the Windows programming interface that enable programs to have a consistent appearance and behavior.

Common folders and features The right side of the Start menu that provides quick access to the folders and features you use most often.

Compress To reduce the size of a file; compressed files take up less storage space and can be transferred to other computers, for example in an e-mail message, more quickly than uncompressed files.

Computer A command on the Start menu that displays a window from which you can you can access disk drives, cameras, printers, scanners and other hardware connected to your computer.

Computer Management A collection of tools with which you can perform tasks such as monitoring system events, configuring hard disk drives, and managing system performance—all from one screen.

Content view A folder window view in which the files display a vertical list that includes the program icon, the date the file was last modified, the file size, and other properties such as author names or tags.

Control Panel A window from which you can customize the appearance and functionality of your computer, add or remove programs, set up network connections, and manage user accounts.

Cookies Small text files that Web sites put on your computer to store information about you and your preferences, for example logon information.

Corrupted file A file that no longer works properly because it has been accidentally altered by a hardware or software failure.

Country codes Top level domains for countries, for example *.ca* for Canada.

CPU The acronym for *central processing unit.*

CPU Meter A Windows gadget that displays how CPU and RAM usage work on your computer.

CPU Time The time a processor spends working on a task.

Credits In Movie Maker, a list at the end of the movie to identify the people who worked on the movie or sources of information in the movie.

Criteria Text that specifies the conditions that identify the specific files you are looking for in a search.

Crop Remove unwanted parts of a photo.

Custom scan A scan of your computer that searches only those drives or folders that you select.

Custom search A search feature in which you can define a specific scope—range of locations—for your search.

Data All the files—documents, spreadsheets, pictures, songs, and so on—that you create and store during the day-to-day use of your computer.

Data Execution Prevention A security feature that can help prevent damage to your computer from viruses and other malware by monitoring your programs to make sure they are using memory safely.

Data management The process of managing your files and folders in an organized manner so that you can find information when you need it.

Decrypted The term used to describe a file that has been converted back to its original, unencrypted form.

Default printer The printer that receives all print commands unless you specify otherwise.

Defragging Another term for *disk defragmentation.*

Deselect To cancel the selection of one or more selected items.

Desktop Serves as a surface for your work, like the top of an actual desk, and is the main screen area that you see after you turn on your computer; here you can arrange icons on the desktop—such as shortcuts to programs, files, folders, and various types of documents—in the same manner you would arrange physical objects on top of a desk.

Desktop background Displays the colors and graphics of your desktop; you can change the desktop background to look the way you want it.

Desktop gadget Another term for a gadget.

Destructive partitioning The process that erases data when partitions are deleted.

Details pane Displays the most common properties associated with the selected file.

Details view A file list view that displays a list of files or folders and their most common properties.

Dial-up Internet access Internet access that uses a regular phone line, or landline, to connect to an Internet service provider.

Digital signature An electronic security mark that can be added to files.

Digital video editing The process of combining audio, video, and still images to create a file that can be converted into a movie.

Directory A file folder on a disk in which you store files; also called a *path*.

Discussion forum A place on the Web where a group of individuals with common interests or information can share their knowledge.

Disk Cleanup A Windows 7 program that scans your hard disk drive and then removes temporary files, empties the Recycle Bin, and removes a variety of system files and other items that you no longer need.

Disk defragmentation The process of consolidating fragmented files on your hard disk drive into continuous files.

Disk Management The Windows 7 tool with which you can view the arrangement of hard disk drives on your computer, and also perform partitioning and formatting tasks if you must do so.

Display adapter Another name for a graphics card.

Domain name An organization's unique name on the Internet, which consists of a chosen name combined with a top level domain such as *.com* or *.org* or *.gov*.

Double-click The action of pressing the left mouse button twice in rapid succession while holding the mouse still.

Drag The action of moving something from one location on the screen to another while holding down the left mouse button; the action of dragging includes releasing the mouse button at the desired time or location.

Drilling down The process of navigating downward through multiple levels of your folder structure to find what you are looking for.

Drive An area of storage that is formatted with a file system compatible with your operating system and is identified by a drive letter.

Drive-by downloads A program installed from a poisoned Web site—without your knowledge—caused by just visiting the site.

Driver Special software that enables programs to communicate with computer hardware devices, for example, with a graphics card.

DSL Internet access An Internet connection that connects to an ISP by sending digital signals over local telephone networks; uses existing phone lines, but it does not initiate an actual phone call.

Dual core A CPU chip with two separate CPU units that share processing tasks.

Ease of Access Center A centralized location for accessibility settings and programs that can make your computer easier and more comfortable for you to use.

EFS An acronym for *Encryption File System*.

Encryption A technique to enhance the security of a message or file by scrambling the contents so that it can be read only by someone who has the appropriate key to unscramble it; the process of encoding data so that others cannot view it.

Encryption File System A Windows 7 feature that enables you to store information on your hard disk drive in an encrypted format.

Ethernet A networking standard that uses cables to provide network access, and is the most widely installed technology for connecting computers.

Event log A record of events that have happened on your computer.

Event Viewer A Windows 7 tool that displays detailed information about significant events on your computer.

Exception A program that will not be blocked by the firewall.

.exe The file extension that identifies an executable file.

Executable file Any file that starts a program and which is identified by the file extension *.exe*.

Exposure The brightness and contrast of a photo.

Extend Volume A command used to enlarge the size of a partition and in which no data is lost.

External hard drive A disk drive that plugs into an external port on your computer, for example, into a USB port.

Extract The action of decompressing—pulling out—files from a compressed form.

FAT The acronym for *File Allocation Table*.

Favorites bar A toolbar in Internet Explorer that displays directly below the address bar and to which you can add or drag web addresses you use frequently.

Favorites Center A list of links to Web sites that is saved in your Web browser.

Federated Search A technology that enables you to search a remote server or Web service from Windows Explorer using the same techniques that you use to search for files that are stored on your own computer.

Feed reader Another name for an RSS viewer.

Feeds Frequently updated content published by a Web site.

File A collection of information that is stored on a computer under a single name, for example, a text document, a picture, or a program.

File association The association between a file and the program that created the file.

File list Displays the contents of the current folder or library. If you type text into the Search box, only the folders and files that match your search will display here—including files in subfolders.

File name extension A set of characters at the end of a file name that helps Windows 7 understand what kind of information is in a file and what program should open it.

File properties Information about a file such as its author, the date the file was last changed, and any descriptive tags.

File system The manner in which files are stored on a disk drive.

Filtered A display of files that is limited based on specified criteria.

Firewall Software or hardware that can help protect a computer from hackers, or prevent malicious software from gaining access to a computer through a network or over the Internet.

Firmware A computer program embedded by a manufacturer into a hardware device.

Flash memory reader Another name used to refer to a card reader.

Folder A container in which you store files.

Folder structure The hierarchy of folders in Windows 7.

Folder window A window that displays the contents of the current folder, library, or device, and contains helpful parts so that you can navigate within the organizing structure of Windows.

Format The command that prepares the disk to store data.

fps An acronym for *frames per second*, which is a measurement of frame rate in a video.

Fragmented file A file that has been split apart and whose fragments are stored in separate blocks of the hard disk drive.

Fragments The pieces of a file that has been split apart.

Frame A single image in a series of consecutive images.

Frame rate In a video, the number of frames displayed per second.

Free disk space The amount of space on a disk drive that is unused.

Free-form snip When using Snipping Tool, the type of snip that lets you draw an irregular line, such as a circle, around an area of the screen.

Full scan A scan of your computer that checks every file on your hard drive.

Full-screen snip When using Snipping Tool, the type of snip that captures the entire screen.

Full-Screen Window Preview In the Aero Peek technology, the ability to *peek* at a window that is hidden from view by other windows.

Gadget A mini-program that offers information and provides easy access to tools that you use frequently.

Gateway A hub or a switch that connects two different networks such as your local area network and the Internet.

Getting Started In Windows 7, a task-centered grouping of links to tools that can help you get started with and add new features to your computer.

.gif The file extension for an image in the Graphic Interchange Format.

Gigabyte One billion bytes.

Graphic equalizer In Windows Media Player, the controls that enable you to adjust the bass and treble that you hear.

Graphic Interchange Format The original Web graphic file format; it can display only a limited number of colors, and is best used for black-and-white line drawings, clip art, and pictures with large blocks of solid colors.

Graphical user interface The system by which you interact with your computer and which uses graphics such as an image of a file folder or wastebasket that you click to activate the item represented.

Graphics card A separate circuit board with its own processor and memory dedicated to processing graphics.

Guest account A user account for users who do not have a permanent account on the computer; it permits only temporary access to the computer.

GUI The acronym for *graphical user interface*, pronounced *GOO-ee*.

Hacker A person who uses computer expertise to gain access to computer systems without permission.

Hard disk drive The primary storage device located inside your computer and where most of your files and programs are typically stored; usually labeled as drive C.

Hidden network A network that hides its network name or SSID.

Hierarchy An arrangement where items are ranked and where each level is lower in rank than the item above it.

Hives The term used to describe the five major areas of the Windows Registry.

Home page On your own computer, the Web page you have selected—or that is set by default—to display on your computer when you start Internet Explorer; when visiting a Web site, the starting point for the remainder of the pages on that site.

Homegroup A group of computers that share files and printers.

HPNA network Another name for a phone line network; HPNA stands for *home phone line network adapter*.

http The protocol prefix for HyperText Transfer Protocol.

https Another term for *secure http*.

Hub A device used to connect computers on a network with cables; it sends information received from one computer to all other computers on the network.

HyperText Transfer Protocol The set of communication rules used by your computer to connect to servers on the Web.

Icons Small images that represent commands, files, or other windows.

Inbound traffic Data that is sent *to* your computer from other computers on the Internet.

Incoming connections Traffic sent from the Internet to your computer.

Index A collection of detailed information about the files on your computer that Windows 7 maintains for the purpose conducting fast searches; when you begin a search,Windows 7 searches this summary information rather than searching file by file on your hard disk drive.

Indexed Locations All of the folders in your personal folder (Documents, Pictures, and so on) and offline files, if any, that Windows 7 includes in a search.

Infection The term used to describe the condition of your computer if a malware program installs and runs itself.

Information bar A bar at the top of an Internet Explorer screen that displays information about downloads, blocked pop-up windows, and installing ActiveX controls.

InPrivate Browsing A feature in Internet Explorer with which you can browse the Web without storing data about your browsing session; useful when using a public computer.

Insertion point A blinking vertical line that indicates where text or graphics will be inserted.

Install program Another name for a *setup program*.

Internet Explorer The Web browser software developed by Microsoft Corporation that is included with Windows 7.

Internet service provider An organization that provides access to the Internet for a fee.

Intranet A Web site that serves computers on your local area network and is not available to the general Internet user.

IP Address A unique address that identifies a computer that is connected to the Internet or a network.

IT professionals Individuals who work in the Information Technology field—the term is an umbrella term for the entire computer industry.

ISP Acronym for *Internet service provider*.

JPEG The acronym for *Joint Photographic Experts Group* that is a common file type used by digital cameras and computers to store digital pictures—a popular file type because it can store a high-quality picture in a relatively small file.

Jump List A list that displays when you right-click a button on the taskbar, and which displays locations (in the upper portion) and tasks (in the lower portion) from a program's taskbar button; functions as a mini Start menu for a program.

KB The abbreviation for *kilobyte*.

kbps Kilobytes per second.

Key A division of a hive in the Windows Registry and which is represented by a folder.

Keystroke logger A program that records all of your keystrokes and then sends your typed data—including user names and passwords—to someone else.

Kilobyte One thousand bytes.

LAN Acronym for *local area network*.

Library A collection of items, such as files and folders, assembled from various locations.

Library pane Enables you to customize the library or arrange files by different file properties and any descriptive tags you might have added to the file. This pane displays only when you are in a library, such as the Documents library.

Live File System A file storage system with which you can create CDs and DVDs; discs formatted with Live File System enable you to copy files to the disc at any time, instead of copying (burning) them all at once.

Local area network A network that is in a relatively limited area; for example, in a home or in a building.

Local printer A printer connected directly to a USB port, serial port, or parallel port on your computer.

Location Any disk drive, folder, or other place in which you can store files and folders.

Location icon A button on the address bar that depicts the location—library, disk drive, folder, and so on—you are accessing.

Lock A process that sets your computer so that your password is required to log back on to your desktop; others can log on to their own desktops while your desktop is locked.

Log off A process that exits the active user account from Windows, and then displays the Welcome screen ready for another user to log on.

Magnifier A screen enlarger that magnifies a portion of the screen in a separate window; helpful for computer users with low vision and for those who require occasional screen magnification for such tasks as editing art.

Malware A shortened version of the words *malicious software* referring to any software that intentionally does harm to computers.

Managed backup service Another name for an online backup service.

Mastered A file system with which you can create CDs and DVDs; discs created using the Mastered format are more likely to be compatible with older computers, but an additional step is required to burn the collection of files to the disc.

Mbps Megabits per second.

Megabyte One million bytes.

Memory card reader Another name used to refer to a card reader.

Menu A list of commands within a category.

Menu bar A group of menus at the top of a program window.

Metadata The data that describes other data; for example, the collective group of a file's properties, such as its title, subject, author, and file size.

Microsoft Security Essentials A free program from Microsoft that protects your computer from spyware, adware, and viruses; also referred to as *MSE*.

Microsoft SpyNet An online community sponsored by Microsoft that collects information about the decisions you and others make regarding spyware identified by Windows Defender or Windows Security Essentials.

Mouse pointer Any symbol that displays on your screen in response to moving your mouse.

Movie file The file created by Windows Movie Maker when you publish a completed project.

Movie Maker tab The tab on the left side of the Movie Maker Ribbon that enables you to save your project, save or publish your movie, or set program options.

Modem A device that enables computer information to be transmitted and received over a telephone line by translating the signals used by two different network types.

MSE An acronym for *Microsoft Security Essentials.*

Naming convention A plan that provides a consistent pattern for naming files and folders on your computer.

Natural language A search feature than enables you to perform searches with simple language without entering colons or Boolean operators.

Navigate To explore within the folder structure of Windows Vista for the purpose of finding files and folders.

Navigation The actions you perform to display a window to locate a command or display the folder window for a folder whose contents you want to view.

Navigation pane The area on the left side of a folder window; it displays favorites, libraries, and an expandable list of drives and folders.

Network A group of computers or other devices, such as printers and scanners, that communicate either wirelessly or by using a physical connection.

Network adapter Another name for a *network interface card.*

Network discovery A network setting that controls how you see other computers on your network and whether other computers on your network can see your computer.

Network interface card A computer hardware component that enables your computer to connect to and communicate with a network.

Network notification icon In the notification area, an icon that displays the status of your network.

Network traffic Signals sent through a network so that devices on the network can communicate with one another.

New Technology File System The file system typically used by Windows 7.

NIC The acronym for *network interface card.*

Nonresponsive program A program that is open but has stopped responding to your commands, which means it has stopped communicating with Windows 7.

NOT filter When used in a search, finds files that contain the first word but that do not contain the second word.

Notification A small pop-up window providing information about status, progress, and the detection of new devices.

Notification area Displays notification icons and the system clock; sometimes referred to as the *system tray.*

Now Playing mode A simplified Player view that enables you to play music in the background while you are performing other tasks.

NTFS The acronym for *New Technology File System.*

Offline files Files from a network that have been copied to your hard disk drive for easy access when you are not connected to the network.

Online backup service A service that provides a system for backing up your computer files over the Internet on a scheduled basis and then storing the data securely on their computers.

Operating system A computer program that manages all the other programs on your computer, stores files in an organized manner, and coordinates the use of computer hardware such as the keyboard and mouse.

OR filter When used in a search, finds files that contain either search term.

Outbound traffic Data that is sent *from* your computer to another computer on the Internet.

Paint A program that comes with Windows 7 with which you can create and edit drawings and display and edit stored photos.

Pan-and-zoom A movie effect that moves the picture horizontally or vertically, or zooms in or out of the picture.

Partial matching A technique employed by the Windows 7 search feature that matches your search criteria to part of a word or phrase rather than to whole words.

Partition A part of a hard disk that functions like a separate disk.

Passphrase A string of characters used to control access to a network or program.

Patch A small repair to an operating system or program that closes a security hole.

Path A sequence of folders (directories) that leads to a specific file or folder.

Peer-to-peer file sharing sites Web sites that let you share files such as music, videos, and software with others over the Internet.

Peer-to-peer network A network in which computers connect directly to each other over a private network without the need for a server—the network type commonly used in a home or small office.

Performance Monitor A component of the Reliability and Performance Monitor tool that provides detailed data and charts.

Personal folder A folder created for each user account, labeled with the account holder's name, and which contains the subfolders *Documents*, *Pictures*, *Music*, among others; always located at the top of the Start menu.

Phishing A technique used to trick computer users into revealing personal or financial information through an e-mail message or a Web site.

Phone line network A network arrangement in which each computer and device connects using a building's existing phone lines.

Photos Images with continuous color.

Physical drive A drive such as a hard disk drive, a USB flash drive, or a CD/DVD drive.

PID An acronym for *process identifier*.

Pinned Placing programs on the Start menu in a manner that remains until you remove it.

Pixel The smallest element used to form the composition of an image.

Playback controls area The area in Windows Media Player that enables you to play, pause, stop, rewind, or fast forward multimedia files; also enables you to control the order in which objects play, and to control the volume.

Playback Indicator A line in the storyboard that shows the current location in the presentation. If you click the Play button, the movie starts at the playback indicator location.

Player Library mode A comprehensive Player view in which you have control over the numerous features of the Player.

Playlist A list of digital media items that you create and save.

Plug and play The capability of Windows 7 to recognize a device as soon as you connect it to your computer, and then automatically install the appropriate drivers and configure the device.

.png The file extension for an image in the Portable Network Graphics format.

PnP A shortened version of the term *plug and play*.

Point The action of moving the mouse pointer over something on the screen.

Pointer Any symbol that displays on your screen in response to moving your mouse and with which you can select objects and commands.

Pointing device A mouse, touchpad, or other device that controls the pointer position on the screen.

Poisoned Web site A Web site that spreads a virus.

Pop-up A small Web browser window that displays on top of the Web site you are viewing, and which are usually created by advertisers.

Pop-up Blocker A feature in Internet Explorer that enables you to block most pop-ups.

Portable device Any mobile electronic device that can exchange files or other data with a computer or device; for example, a smartphone or a portable music player.

Portable hard drive Another name for an external hard drive.

Portable Network Graphics An image format that is recent format that combines the features of GIFs and JPEGs on the Web.

Portal A Web site that displays news, content, and links that are of interest to a specific audience.

Posts In a discussion forum, messages regarding a thread.

Power line network A network arrangement in which the devices communicate using a building's existing electrical wires.

Preview Desktop In the Aero Peek technology, the ability to *peek* at the desktop that is behind open windows.

Preview pane An additional pane on the right side of the file list to display a preview of a file (not a folder) that you select in the file list.

Previous versions Backup copies—copies of files and folders that you back up by using the Back Up Files wizard—or shadow copies—copies of files and folders that Windows automatically saves as part of a restore point.

Privacy Summary A special Web page that summarizes a Web site's privacy policy in a simple, easy to understand format.

Process A file that is part of a running program and which performs a specific task such as starting the program.

Process Identifier A unique number assigned to each process while it runs.

Problem Steps Recorder A Windows 7 feature that captures the steps you perform on your computer, including a text description of where you clicked and a picture of the screen during each click.

Program A set of instructions that a computer uses to accomplish a task, such as word processing, accounting, or data management; also referred to as an *application*.

Programs list The left side of the Start menu that displays recently used programs on the bottom, programs that you have pinned to the Start menu at the top, and a button to display all the programs on your computer.

Progress bar In a dialog box or taskbar button, a bar that indicates visually the progress of a task such as a download or file transfer.

Properties Descriptive pieces of information about a folder or file such as the name, the date modified, the author, the type, and the size.

Project (Windows Live Movie Maker) A file that keeps track of the pictures, videos, music, and other files you have imported into Movie Maker, and how those files have been arranged.

Protected mode A feature in Internet Explorer that makes it more difficult for malicious software to be installed on your computer by preventing a downloaded program from making any direct changes to the system.

Protocol prefix The letters that represent a set of communication rules used by a computer to connect to another computer.

Quarantine area A designated location on your computer from which a program cannot run.

Quick scan A scan of your computer that checks the areas on your hard drive where malware programs are most likely to reside.

Quick Tabs The feature in Internet Explorer that displays, on a single tab, a thumbnail of each Web site that is currently open.

Quotes filter When used in a search, finds files that contain the exact phrase placed within the quotes.

RAM The acronym for *random access memory*.

Random access memory Temporary storage used by a computer to store data and instructions.

ReadyBoost A Windows 7 feature that enables certain USB flash drives to be used as computer memory.

Real time The actual time during which something takes place.

Really Simple Syndication A syndication format popular for aggregating updates to blogs and news sites.

Recent Pages A button on the address bar that displays a list of recently accessed locations; the current location is indicated by a check mark.

Recommended updates A setting on your computer that ensures that updates flagged as *recommended* are included in any Windows Updates.

Rectangular snip When using Snipping Tool, the type of snip that lets you draw a precise box by dragging the mouse pointer around an area of the screen to form a rectangle.

Recycle Bin A folder that stores anything that you delete from your computer, and from which anything stored there can be retrieved until the contents are permanently deleted by activating the Empty Recycle Bin command.

Registry A repository for information about your computer's configuration.

Registry Editor A tool used to view and edit the Windows Registry files that are stored in various locations on your computer.

Reliability The likelihood that your computer will as work as intended.

Reliability Monitor A tool that provides data about a computer's overall reliability.

Remote Assistance expert In a Windows Remote Assistance connection, the person providing help.

Remote Assistance novice In a Windows Remote Assistance connection, the person whose desktop is displayed and who needs help.

Remote backup service Another name for an online backup service.

Removable storage device A portable device on which you can store files, such as a USB flash drive, a flash memory card, or an external hard drive, commonly used to transfer information from one computer to another.

Removal tool A program that uninstalls a specific malware program.

Resolution The amount of fine detail that is visible in an image when it is printed or displayed on a computer monitor.

Resource Monitor A tool that provides both instantaneous and recent history readouts of your computer's four key performance measurements.

Resources A term used to refer collectively to the parts of your computer such as the central processing unit (CPU), memory, and any attached devices such as printers or scanners.

Restart A process that turns your computer off and then on again during which time the system cache is cleared; useful if your computer is operating slowly or having technical problems, or after installing new software or software updates.

Restore point A representation of a stored state of your computer's system files—like a snapshot of your computer's settings at a specific point in time.

Right-click The action of clicking the right mouse button.

Rip The process of copying digital media content from an audio CD.

RJ-45 connector A type of network connector that holds up to eight wires, and is commonly used to connect a computer to a wired network.

Rootkit Malware that enables malicious administrator-level access, and is typically hidden from the administrator and the operating system.

Router A device that sends—*routes*—information between two networks; for example, between a home network and the Internet.

RSS An acronym for *Really Simple Syndication*, which is a syndication format popular for aggregating—gathering together—updates to blogs and news sites.

RSS feed Frequently updated content published by a Web site and delivered to a feed reader.

RSS viewer A program that displays RSS feeds to which you have subscribed.

Safe Mode A startup option where only the most basic operating system processes are started.

Saturation A photo effect that changes a photo's color intensity.

Screen capture An image file that contains the contents of a computer screen.

Screen saver A moving picture or pattern that displays on your screen after a specified period of inactivity—that is, when the mouse or keyboard has not been used.

Screenshot The term used for an image of the contents of a computer screen.

ScreenTip Useful information that displays in a small box on the screen when you perform various mouse actions, such as pointing to screen elements.

Script A program that runs in the browser to add interactive content to the Web page.

Scroll arrow Arrows at the top and bottom, or left and right, of a scroll bar that when clicked, move the window in small increments.

Scroll bar A bar that displays on the bottom or right side of a window when the contents of a window are not completely visible; used to move the window up, down, left, or right to bring the contents into view.

Scroll box The box in a vertical or horizontal scroll bar that you drag to reposition the document on the screen.

Search box A box found on the Start menu and in windows that display libraries, folders, and files that provides a way to find specific files and folders by typing search terms.

Search folder The Windows 7 folder in which you conduct searches in the entire set of indexed locations.

Search provider A Web site that provides search capabilities on the Web.

Search term A word or phrase that describes the topic about which you want to find information.

Sector A block of space on a drive.

Secure http A protocol that encrypts the data sent between you and a Web server.

Security holes Vulnerabilities in an operating system or program that allow malware to infect a computer without your knowledge.

Security-enabled network A wireless network that requires a passphrase to connect to it.

Select To specify, by highlighting, a block of data or text on the screen with the intent of performing some action on the selection.

Server A computer that provides shared resources, such as files or printers, to network users.

Service A computer program or process that runs in the background and that provides support to other programs.

Service Set Identifier A group of up to 32 characters that uniquely identifies your wireless network and functions as the name of a wireless network.

Set up backup wizard A command in the Windows 7 Backup and Restore Center that walks you step by step through the process of backing up your data.

Setup program A program that prepares a software package to run on a computer.

Shadow copies Change logs of files and folders that Windows automatically saves as part of a restore point.

Shared resource A device connected to or a file saved on one computer that can be accessed from another computer over a network.

SharePoint A Microsoft technology that enables employees in an organization to access information across organizational and geographic boundaries.

Shift Click A technique in which the SHIFT key is held down to select all the items in a consecutive group; you need only click the first item, hold down SHIFT, and then click the last item in the group.

Shortcuts Desktop icons that link to any item accessible on your computer or on a network, such as a program, file, folder, disk drive, printer, or another computer.

Show desktop button Displays the desktop by making any open windows transparent (when pointed to) or minimized (when clicked).

Shrink Volume A command used to reduce the size of a partition and in which no data is lost.

Shut down Turning off your computer in a manner that closes all open programs and files, closes your network connections, stops the hard disk, and discontinues the use of electrical power.

Shut down button On the Start menu, a button that displays a menu for switching users, logging off, restarting, or shutting down.

Side by side An arrangement of open windows on your screen that displays side by side.

Skin A user interface that displays an alternative appearance and customized functionality for software such as Windows Media Player.

Skin mode An operational state of Windows Media Player in which its user interface is displayed as a skin.

Sleep Turning off your computer in a manner that automatically saves your work, stops the fan, and uses a small amount of electrical power to maintain your work in memory; the next time you turn the computer on, you need only to enter your password (if required) and your screen will display exactly like it did when you turned off.

SmartScreen Filter A feature in Internet Explorer that helps detect phishing Web sites and Web sites that distribute malware.

Snap A Windows 7 feature that automatically resizes windows when you move—*snap*—them to the edge of the screen.

Snip The image captured using Snipping Tool.

Snipping Tool A program included with Windows 7 with which you can capture an image of all or part of a computer screen, and then annotate, save, copy, or share the image via e-mail.

Speakers icon Displays the status of your speakers (if any).

Split button A button that has two parts—a button and an arrow; clicking the main part of the button performs a command and clicking the arrow opens a menu with choices.

Sponsored links Paid advertisements shown as a links, typically for products and services related to your search term; sponsored links are the way that search sites like Bing, Google, and others earn revenue.

Spyware Software that sends information about your Web surfing habits to a Web site without your knowledge.

Spyware checker Another term for an antispyware program.

SSID An acronym for *Service Set Identifier*.

Stack An arrangement of open windows on your screen that display each window across the width of the screen in a vertical stack.

Standard user account A user account that lets you use most of the capabilities of the computer, but requires permission from an administrator to make changes that affect other users or the security of the computer.

Start button Displays the Start menu—a list of choices that provides access to your computer's programs, folders, and settings.

Start menu A list of choices that provides access to your computer's programs, folders, and settings when you press the Start button.

Startup program A program that starts automatically whenever your computer is started.

Status area Another term for the notification area.

Storyboard In Windows Movie Maker, the view that shows a simple sequence of files, clips, transitions, and effects that make up a project.

Subfolder A folder within a folder.

Suggested Sites In Internet Explorer, an optional online service that suggests other Web sites in which you might be interested based on the Web sites you visit most.

Surfing The process of navigating the Internet either for a particular item or for anything that is of interest, and quickly moving from one item to another.

Switch A device that connects two or more computers.

Sync The process of maintaining digital media files on your portable device based on specific rules.

Syndicated content Another name for an RSS feed.

System A tool in Windows 7 that displays basic information about the computer by measuring five performance benchmarks.

System cache An area of the computer's memory where Windows 7 stores information it needs to access quickly.

System Diagnostics Report A pre-built report that contains an easy to understand summary of your computer's overall performance.

System image A feature in Windows 7 that creates a backup image containing copies of your programs, system settings, and files.

System Information A feature in Windows 7 that displays details about your computer's hardware configuration, computer components, and operating system software from within a single dialog box.

System Protection A feature in Windows 7 that regularly creates and saves restore points—a snapshot of your computer's settings at a specific point in time—as well as previous versions of files you have modified.

System Restore A feature in Windows 7 that restores your computer's system files—*not* your data files—to an earlier point in time.

System Stability Index A number between 1 and 10 determined by how many system errors have occurred up to a designated day.

System tray Another name for the notification area on the taskbar.

Tab row The area across the upper portion of the Internet Explorer screen in which a tab for each open Web site displays.

Tabbed browsing A feature in Internet Explorer that enables you to open multiple Web sites in a single browser window.

Tag A custom file property that you create to help find and organize your files.

Task Manager A Windows 7 tool that shows you the application programs, processes, and services that are currently running on your computer.

Task Scheduler A program with which you can schedule regular hard disk drive maintenance tasks.

Taskbar The area of the desktop that contains the Start button, optional program buttons, and buttons for all open programs; by default, it is located at the bottom of the desktop, but you can move it.

Temporary Internet files Copies of Web pages, images, and media that you have downloaded from the Web, which makes viewing faster the next time you visit a site that you have visited before.

Terabyte One trillion bytes.

Theme A combination of pictures, colors, and sounds on your computer; includes a desktop background, a screen saver, a window border color, and a sound scheme.

Third-party cookie A Web cookie created by a Web site other than the Web site you are currently viewing.

Thread A task that is created when a process divides itself into one or more tasks that are processed simultaneously.

Threads A list of discussion topics in a discussion forum.

Thumbnail A reduced image of a graphic.

TIFF The acronym for *Tagged Image File Format* that is a file type used when a very high level of visual quality is needed, for example if the file will be used to print 8-by-10-inch enlargements.

Tint A photo effect that changes the level of green or red in a photo.

Title bar The bar across the top of the window that displays the program name.

Toolbar A row, column, or block of buttons or icons, usually displayed across the top of a window, which contains commands for tasks you can perform with a single click.

Top level domain The ending letters of a URL such as *.com*, *.org*, and so on.

Transition The manner in which a movie in Windows Movie Maker moves from one clip to another.

Trigger An action that causes a procedure to be carried out automatically in response to a specific event.

Trojan horse A malicious software program that hides inside legitimate programs, such as a game, media player, or screen saver.

Troubleshoot The process of analyzing a problem, determining its possible causes, and implementing solutions.

Uniform Resource Locator An address that uniquely identifies a location on the Internet.

Unnamed network Also known as a hidden network, a network that hides its network name or SSID.

Unsecured network A wireless network that does not require a passphrase to connect to it.

Unsigned ActiveX control An ActiveX control whose source cannot be verified.

Update An addition to Windows 7 that helps prevent or fix problems or that improves how your computer performs.

Upgrading The process of buying new hardware components or software programs to increase computer performance.

URL The acronym for *Uniform Resource Locator.*

User account A collection of information that tells Windows 7 what files and folders the account holder can access, what changes the account holder can make to the computer system, and what the account holder's personal preferences are.

Video clip A short video presentation.

Virtual folder A folder that does not represent a physical location but rather contains the results of a search.

Virtual memory A technique that uses a small part of the hard disk drive as if it were random access memory (RAM) to allow a computer to run a program that needs more memory than the computer actually has.

Virus A type of malware designed specifically to replicate itself by spreading its infection from computer to computer, and can damage hardware, software, or data.

Virus checker Software that scans your computer for viruses and other malware.

Virus definition The information needed by an antivirus program to find and remove a virus.

Visual effects In Windows 7, the transparent objects, animated objects, and shadows under objects that give Windows 7 its distinctive appearance.

Visualizations In Windows Media Player and Media Center, splashes of color and geometric shapes that change along with the rhythm and intensity of the music.

Volume A storage area on a hard disk that is formatted with a file system.

Wallpaper Another term for the desktop background.

WAN Acronym for *wide area network*, which is a network that connects geographically separated locations by using telecommunications services.

Web browser A software program with which you display Web pages and navigate the Internet.

Web content Anything that you download and use on a Web page, such as HTML code, pictures, small programs, and animations.

Web feed Another name for an RSS feed.

Web log The term from which *blog* is derived; an online journal or column used to publish personal or company information in an informal manner.

Web Slice A specific *portion*—a slice—of a Web page to which you can subscribe, and which enables you to see when updated content, such as the current temperature, is available from a site.

Wi-Fi The term that stands for *wireless fidelity*; refers to the Wi-Fi Alliance organization that certifies that wireless products conform to standards.

Window A rectangular area on your screen that displays programs and content, and that can be moved, resized, minimized, or closed; the content of every window is different, but all windows display on the desktop.

Window snip When using Snipping Tool, the type of snip that captures the entire displayed window.

Windows Connect Now A feature of Windows 7 that makes it simple to set up a wireless network in your home or office and enables wireless routers to be configured using a USB drive.

Windows Defender A spyware scanning and removal tool—or antispyware program—included with Windows 7.

Windows DVD Maker A feature that comes with Windows 7 with which you can create DVDs that can play back on a DVD player.

Windows Experience Index A test of five components that affect computer performance and which then rates each one on a scale from 1 to 7.9, with 7.9 as the highest rating.

Windows Explorer The program in Windows 7 that displays the contents of libraries, folders, and files on your computer, and that also enables you to perform tasks related to your files and folders such as copying, moving, and renaming. Windows Explorer is at work anytime you are viewing the contents of a library, a folder, or a file.

Windows Help and Support The built-in help system for Windows 7.

Windows Live Essentials A collection of free programs available on the Microsoft Web site, including programs that enable you to organize and edit photos, edit and publish videos, stay in touch with your friends, create an e-mail account, and customize your Web browser.

Windows Live Movie Maker A program provided with Windows 7 in which you combine audio, video, and still images to create a file that can be converted into a movie.

Windows Live Photo Gallery A photo and video organizer in Windows 7 with which you can view, manage, and edit digital pictures.

Windows Media Center A feature of Windows Home Premium and Ultimate editions that enables you to use your computer as your home entertainment center.

Windows Media Player A feature in Windows 7 that provides an easy-to-use way for you to play digital media files, organize your digital media collection, burn CDs of your favorite music, rip music from CDs, sync digital media files to a portable device, and shop for digital media content from online stores.

Windows Registry A central repository that stores the settings used by Windows 7 and the applications on your computer.

Windows Remote Assistance A tool that enables two computers to establish a direct connection so that an expert can provide help.

Windows 7 An operating system developed by Microsoft Corporation.

Windows Update The program that checks for updates, downloads them, and then installs them on your computer.

Wired network A network arrangement in which each computer and device communicates with the network by using wires—either existing phone wires or cables that you put in place.

Wireless access point A device that connects wireless computers and other wireless devices to a wired network; for example, the Internet.

Wireless network A network arrangement in which each computer and device communicates with the network by using radio signals.

Wireless router A device that has all the features of a wired router, but can also communicate using radio waves.

.wmv The file extension for a Windows Media Video file.

Word wheel A lookup method in which each new character that you type into the search box further refines the search.

Worm A self-replicating program—similar to a virus—that spreads on its own to every computer on a network.

Writable disc A CD or DVD disc onto which files can be copied.

XML feed Another name for an RSS feed.

Zero-day exploit A computer attack that takes place immediately after a known security hole, for which no patch is yet available, is publicized.

Index

A

B

E

M

O

P

Q

R

S

T

X

Z